The Blackwell Encyclopedia of Sociology

P9-CNB-968

D0004913

Volume IV

F–HE

Edited by

George Ritzer

Blackwell
Publishing

© 2007 by Blackwell Publishing Ltd

BLACKWELL PUBLISHING
350 Main Street, Malden, MA 02148-5020, USA
9600 Garsington Road, Oxford OX4 2DQ, UK
550 Swanston Street, Carlton, Victoria 3053, Australia

First published 2007 by Blackwell Publishing Ltd

1   2007

Library of Congress Cataloging-in-Publication Data

Blackwell encyclopedia of sociology, the / edited by George Ritzer.
   p. cm.
Includes bibliographical references and index.
ISBN 1-4051-2433-4 (hardback : alk. paper) 1. Sociology—Encyclopedias. I. Ritzer, George.

HM425.B53 2007
301.03—dc22

                                                2006004167

ISBN-13: 978-1-4051-2433-1 (hardback : alk. paper)

A catalogue record for this title is available from the British Library.

Set in 9.5/11pt Ehrhardt
by Spi Publisher Services, Pondicherry, India
Printed in Singapore
by COS Printers Pte Ltd

The publisher's policy is to use permanent paper from mills that operate a sustainable forestry policy, and which has been manufactured from pulp processed using acid-free and elementary chlorine-free practices. Furthermore, the publisher ensures that the text paper and cover board used have met acceptable environmental accreditation standards.

For further information on
Blackwell Publishing, visit our website:
www.blackwellpublishing.com

Contents

facework

J. I. (Hans) Bakker

The concept of "facework" (or face-work) was articulated by Erving Goffman in 1955 in his book *Interaction Ritual*. He provides a "subject–object" model of human symbolic interaction in which individuals interact with other individuals in terms of subjective perceptions. Whatever is "universal" about human beings, it is not – according to Goffman – something automatic. Instead, it is a matter of self-regulation and the ritual recreation of "face."

He defines the term "face" as "the positive social value a person effectively claims for himself." If a person makes "a good showing," then the image of him or her is perceived by that social actor as approved by members of the reference group. If there is a mismatch between expectations and events, there is likely to be a negative emotional reaction. When a person presents a certain face, then we say she "has" that face. In conventionalized encounters there is little choice about which face to "be in" or "maintain." A person can be said to be "in wrong face" or "out of face" when she cannot integrate the situation or deal with it in expected ways. When one is out of face there may be a sense of shame, while being "in face" tends to be associated with pride.

An interaction involves people trying to follow expected patterns. Expected signs such as glances and gestures are either given or withheld (Collins 1988: 16). Greetings and farewells are ritualized ceremonies which compensate for previous or future separations. The tendency, according to Goffman, is for all actors to support one another's face, an idea similar to the "etcetera principle" in ethnomethodology.

Moreover, human encounters help one to construct a sense of one's own face, or "self-image." People tend to try to protect their own inner idea of themselves even when, like the proverbial schoolboy, they may rebel in open or hidden ways. The ritual code requires that self-regulating members of an interaction express a "face" and help preserve the "faces" of other participants. If a ritual order is going to be sustained, then a great deal of facework has to be done in the course of any social activity in order for the group to maintain equilibrium. There is an element of "make-believe" (Winkin 1999: 33). Thomas (1923: 1–69) stresses that "recognition" from others is one of the key "wishes" and that it is related to the "definition of the situation."

These ideas can in principle be applied to any symbolic interaction at any level of social organization, from dyads and small groups to neighborhoods and communities, although Goffman tends to stress examples from small groups. (In other works he often makes more macro statements.) In complex formal organizations such as the military or industry there is also a process of "saving face." The unwritten rules are followed by most social actors most of the time. One not only tries to "save" one's own face, one also tries to arrange things so that others will not lose face. (The Chinese saying is "to give face.") The visual imagery of the concept of "face" is very concrete and Goffman claims it is manifest in a person's whole bodily demeanor, not just the expression on one's face.

The idea of facework is heuristic but can be criticized empirically and epistemologically. At the empirical ("ontological") level, one limitation of Goffman's approach is that he does not give adequate recognition to the possibility that one's "voice" (Walker 1999: 279–82) may be silenced and that this "loss of face" is not just determined by a ritual process that occurs *within* the smaller collectivity. Especially in larger groups – such as complex formal organizations or national-level institutions – there may be utilitarian, goal-rational exchange principles at work as well as the internal social constructions that Goffman is more directly concerned with. Epistemologically, the idea of facework tends to reinforce a Cartesian split between the "inner self" of the subject and the "objective" status of the "other" in the environment. The stereotypical version of the ethnographer is that of a bit of a loner, a lone "subject," a utilitarian rational actor and streetwise researcher who is not easily duped (Winkin 1999: 35). An example would be Nels Anderson (1923), author of one of the first Chicago School ethnographic studies. His work was done before the modern concept of "participant observation" emerged (Platt 1996: 117–22). But that highly "individualistic" epistemological stance may reduce awareness of the embeddedness of all social relations and the importance of "the field," or what Goffman himself refers to as "syntactical relations" (Goffman 1967 [1955]: 2). A more Peircian pragmatist epistemology, by stressing the way in which all subject–object relations are mediated by "signs," might have made it possible for Goffman to more easily generalize his conclusions about the construction of face to all "syntactical" forms of symbolic interaction in general, providing a way for him to more easily connect his earlier work on explicit interactionist events of the 1950s with his later, more implicit and "structurationalist" analysis of "frames." The key linking concept might be "frame attunement" as a ritual and system requirement (Collins 1988: 31).

SEE ALSO: Ethnomethodology; Generalized Other; Goffman, Erving; Labeling Theory; Looking-Glass Self; Phenomenology; Role; Role-Taking; Self; Symbolic Interaction

REFERENCES AND SUGGESTED READINGS

Anderson, N. (1923) *The Hobo*. University of Chicago Press, Chicago.
Collins, R. (1988) Theoretical Continuities in Goffman's Work. In: Drew, P. & Wootton, A. (Eds.), *Erving Goffman: Exploring the Interaction Order*. Northeastern University Press, Boston, pp. 41–63.
Goffman, E. (1967 [1955]) *Interaction Ritual*. Anchor, Garden City, NY.
Platt, J. (1996) *A History of Sociological Research Methods in America: 1920–1960*. Cambridge University Press, Cambridge.
Thomas, W. I. (1923) *The Unadjusted Girl*. Supplement to the *Journal of the American Institute of Criminal Law and Criminology, Criminal Science Monograph* No. 4. Little, Brown, Boston.
Walker, R. (1999) Finding a Silent Voice for the Researcher: Using Photographs in Evaluation and Research. In: Bryman, A. & Burgess, R. G. (Eds.), *Qualitative Research*, Vol. 2. Sage, London, pp. 279–301.
Winkin, Y. (1999) Erving Goffman: What is a Life/ The Uneasy Making of an Intellectual Biography. In: Smith, G. (Ed.), *Goffman and Social Organization: Studies in a Sociological Legacy*. Routledge, London, pp. 19–41.

fact, theory, and hypothesis: including the history of the scientific fact

Stephen Turner

The terms theory, fact, and hypothesis are sometimes treated as though they had clear meanings and clear relations with one another, but their histories and uses are more complex and diverse than might be expected. The usual sense of these words places them in a relationship of increasing uncertainty. A fact is usually thought of as a described state of affairs in which the descriptions are true or highly supported. A highly corroborated or supported hypothesis is also a fact; a less well corroborated one is still a hypothesis. A hypothesis which is not supported by or corroborated by other evidence would not be a fact, but could become a fact if it came to be corroborated to a high degree of certainty by other evidence. Similarly, a theory, which is a logically connected set of hypotheses, could come to be a fact if the hypotheses in the theory were to be highly corroborated by the evidence.

THE CONCEPTUAL CHARACTER OF "FACTS"

Even with this simple picture of the relationship between these terms, one can see a number of potential difficulties and raise a number of difficult questions. Begin with the notion of corroboration. If a fact is a highly corroborated hypothesis, this would seem to mean that there is a level that is prior to facts which supplies the evidence that goes into corroboration. If the corroborating evidence consists of other facts, one would want to know how these facts were corroborated. So it is more common to talk about some more fundamental level of evidence, such as data. "Data" literally means "given." But the idea that there is something in the world that is simply given, and true or valid as such, has its own difficulties.

However, when we collect data we have already described them or have a conceptual category for them. Since the "data" are already in a predefined category, we are not dealing directly with the world but with an already categorized world. This idea of fact as already conceptual had a long history in writing about science and is particularly associated with the nineteenth-century philosopher William Whewell. Whewell said the following: "*Fact* and *Theory* correspond to Sense on the one hand, and to Ideas on the other, so far as we are *conscious* of our Ideas; but all facts involve ideas *unconsciously*; and thus the distinction of Facts and Theories is not tenable, as that of Sense and Ideas is" (Whewell 1984: 249). And this raises the questions of where the categories themselves come from and what their status is. In 1932, L. J. Henderson wrote an article which was cited by the sociologist Talcott Parsons (Parsons 1968: 41) which defined a scientific fact as an "empirically verifiable statement about phenomena in terms of a conceptual scheme" (Henderson 1932). What this implied, especially for Parsons, was that to be a fact it was necessary to be a part of or to depend on a conceptual scheme. And conceptual schemes were not givens but were, like theories, invented for the purpose of enabling us to make statements such as the statements in theories.

The question of where categories come from and how something becomes a fact has been a major concern of sociologists of scientific knowledge. An important book by Ludwig Fleck (1979), a physician-scientist, provided the basic framework for this study. Fleck argued that to be accepted as a fact required something social, which he called a "thought collective," in terms of which a concept is transformed from idea into accepted truth. The emphasis was on the social phenomenon of acceptance, something which, Fleck showed, did not merely result from the accumulation of evidence, but rather from the activity of a community of persons, with a common thought-style, exchanging ideas. This implied that "discovery" was never an individual act, but rather collective; and that conceptual content was part of the collective thought of the community, which developed in the course of exchange. Only retrospectively, once the discovery had been fit into the collective thought of the community, could the significance of discoveries be fully understood.

INDUCTIVISM VS. HYPOTHETICO-DEDUCTIVISM

The methodological understanding of science that fits best the insight that facts are already conceptual is hypothetico-deductivism, which contrasts to a different view of methodology called inductivism. Inductivism was the traditional understanding that science consists of generalizations which can be built up on the basis of the collection of information or data which can then be arranged into generalizations. The problem with inductivism is that there is no logical way to get from a collection of finite singular pieces of information to a generalization which goes beyond the particulars that have been collected. Hypothetico-deductivism deals with this limitation by turning the problem upside down by beginning with hypotheses that are generalizations and asking whether the observable particulars are consistent with (because they are implied by) the generalization. The hypothesis "all crows are black" has the potential to be contradicted every time we see a crow. Thus, each particular crow can be used as a test of the hypothesis and the more stringently we test the hypothesis, the more secure we are in our belief that the hypothesis is true.

Hypothetico-deductivism has an advantage over inductivism as a method in that hypothetico-deductivism can be used to corroborate theories where the concepts in the theories are not themselves directly observable. The wave hypothesis in physics is a traditional example of this. The hypothesis logically implied generalizations for which observations could be collected. Because the theory correctly predicted these and other facts that could be observed, the claims about what could not be observed were themselves corroborated. This is an especially important possibility in sociology because many of the concepts in sociology do not directly apply to observable facts in the world, but instead to grounding concepts such as "society," or "role," or "attitude." These concepts can be understood as having observable manifestations, but are not limited to or equivalent to observable manifestations.

In physics the term observation and the notion of the logical relations between claims in a theory had a more straightforward meaning. The logical relations were mathematical. The way in which an implication was derived from a theory was by deriving it mathematically through a proof. The theories of sociology, in contrast, rarely if ever have this structure, although in many cases theories are presented with verbal formulations which have "logical connections" in a looser sense, namely that the claims in the theory provide a good reason, in context, for expectations that can be tested or applied to cases. Sociological theories thus resemble physical theories in the hypothetico-deductive sense in some ways, but differ in others. A "theory" may be a part of a theoretical structure, such as a system of conceptual categories which enable description. But it may instead be a description of unobservable forces or unobservable mechanisms, such as the mechanism that reinforces social hierarchy by selectively excluding members of the lower classes from the paths which lead to positions of wealth and power.

SENSE-MAKING IN THEORIES

The major difference between sociological and physical theory is that the concepts in sociology are typically sense-making: they serve to enable a fact described in its terms to be more fully intelligible. Making a fact more intelligible will usually make its consequences more predictable. If I even do something as simple as characterizing an action as a product of the agent's beliefs and positive attitudes towards some outcome specified by the agent's beliefs, I have improved the prediction over alternative descriptions or over chance. This is not the same thing as a prediction in physics, but it is predictive nevertheless.

If the sociologist can add to this simple situation of explaining in terms of beliefs and attitudes by characterizing the set of beliefs that support the particular belief that relates directly to the action, for example by understanding a religiously motivated action in terms of a typology of religious belief, and if the sociologist can explain how those beliefs come to be distributed in particular groups, she will have something that begins to look like a theory that explains those actions sociologically, that is to say at some level beyond the level of the individual. Similarly, for characterizations about such things as role, for example. If an individual's behavior can be characterized in terms of the roles which they are fulfilling, this explanation can be extended by accounting for the process of socialization into the role in question and the ways in which role behavior is enforced as normative, or enacted and supported by the expectations of other agents.

These descriptions of mechanisms are more general claims than the explanation of the individual's action; they are "social" in the sense that they serve to organize the behavior of individuals in relation to a limited category of individuals. The characterizations are sense-making in that they explicate the beliefs and expectations of the people involved, and predictive in the sense that they improve our own expectations about what people will actually do and what role-conduct is likely to persist or appear in different social settings. Similarly, a good categorization scheme using intelligibility enhancing concepts (e.g., Weber's categories of legitimate authority) will enable the sociologist equipped with it to improve expectations as well as achieve understanding.

Sociologists have traditionally differed with respect to the emphasis they place on different aspects of these kinds of loose theories.

Parsons, for example, was particularly concerned with the elaboration of conceptual distinctions which could be used to organize comprehensively the concepts of sociology and relate them to one another and to the concepts of other disciplines. Parsons placed little emphasis on making individual actions or beliefs intelligible and little emphasis on prediction; although he envisioned future possibilities of prediction he also believed that many of the central variables of sociology were unquantifiable and that this was an inherent limitation on sociological theories approximating physics.

DIVERSITY IN THEORY IN SOCIOLOGY

Some sociologists have tried strictly to adhere to the idea of deductive theorizing as modeled on physics. Typically, these sociologists have attempted to devise experimental settings in which limited variables or sets of variables can be measured in relation to other variables in such ways that predictions can be made and confirmed. This strategy has the potential of illuminating basic concepts which can then be applied to social life outside the laboratory as fundamental theories which approximate the more complex realities of actual social life. One problem with this strategy is that there are often alternative theories which are equally effective or ineffective as means of making sense of and predicting in the more complex actual settings of the real world.

Some theories, generally called interpretive theories, are focused primarily on intelligibility itself. For these theorists, providing a more fully realized and rich interpretation of the actions, attitudes, and beliefs of individuals is the appropriate and most productive strategy for dealing with a world of agents, that is to say a world of individuals who are themselves interpreters of one another and who act in terms of these interpretations.

Other theories, such as rational choice theory, borrow the theoretical structure of decision theory, game theory, or economics to provide a particular kind of intelligibility to actions of individuals who are treated in abstraction from considerations about the specific actual beliefs and attitudes of the individuals, and the explanations are evaluated in terms of their ability to predict the choices of these individuals. In one sense this represents the highest level of intelligibility, namely rational choice. In another sense it is removed from the subjective experience and ongoing interpretive activities of individual agents and thus serves as a poor guide to these aspects of experience.

SEE ALSO: Chance and Probability; Experimental Methods; Laboratory Studies and the World of the Scientific Lab; Metatheory; Science, Social Construction of; Scientific Models and Simulations; Theory Construction; Theory and Methods

REFERENCES AND SUGGESTED READINGS

Fleck, L. (1979 [1935]) *Genesis and Development of a Scientific Fact.* University of Chicago Press, Chicago.

Henderson, L. J. (1932) An Approximate Definition of Fact. *University of California Studies in Philosophy* 14: 179–99.

Parsons, T. (1968 [1937]) *The Structure of Social Action*, Vol. 1. Free Press, New York.

Whewell, W. (1984) *Selected Writings on the History of Science.* Ed. Y. Elkana. University of Chicago Press, Chicago.

factor analysis

Bruce Thompson

Factor analysis is a statistical method for empirically identifying the structure underlying measured or factored entities (e.g., variables). The three purposes for which factor analysis can be used are (1) empirically creating a theory of structure (e.g., Cattell's Structure of Intellect model), (2) evaluating whether factored entities (e.g., variables) cluster in a theoretically expected way (e.g., construct validity evaluation), and (3) estimating latent variables scores (i.e., factor scores) that are then used in subsequent statistical analyses (e.g., MANOVA, descriptive discriminant analysis) in place of the measured factored entities (e.g., variables).

In common analytic practice, the factored entities are usually (1) variables, although (2) people and (3) occasions of measurement also can be factored (Thompson 2000). Factor analysis statistical software does not know if it is factoring variables, people, or time, and from a statistical point of view, the mathematics of factor analysis can sensibly be invoked for any of these possibilities.

The data matrix for the analysis is created such that the entities to be factored (e.g., variables) constitute the columns of the matrix. The rows constitute the dimension over which patterns of association (e.g., correlation, covariance) among the factored entities are estimated. The factors are then estimated based on these association statistics.

Cattell (1966) identified six possible two-mode combinations of factored entities and raw data matrix row replicates of the association patterns: (1) *R*-technique factor analysis, which factors variables with people defining the rows of the raw data matrix, with measurement at a single time; (2) *Q*-technique factor analysis, which factors people with variables defining the rows of the raw data matrix, with measurement at a single time; (3) *O*-technique factor analysis, which factors occasions with variables defining the rows of the raw data matrix, with measurement of a single person (or use of a single group mean or median for each unique combination of occasions and variables); (4) *P*-technique factor analysis, which factors variables with occasions defining the rows of the raw data matrix, with measurement of a single person (or use of a single group mean or median for each unique combination of occasions and variables); (5) *T*-technique factor analysis, which factors occasions with participants defining the rows of the raw data matrix, with measurement using a single variable (or use of a single group mean or median for each unique combination of occasions and participants); and (6) *S*-technique factor analysis, which factors participants with occasions defining the rows of the raw data matrix, with measurement using a single variable (or use of a single group mean or median for each unique combination of occasions and participants).

Although factor analysis is relatively old, the required mathematics are so complex that the methods were not widely used until the advent of modern computers and statistical software. There are two major classes of factor analytic methods (Thompson 2004). First, exploratory factor analysis (EFA) can be used when the researcher has no theory about structure, or does not wish expected structure to be invoked as part of the analytic calculations. EFA dates back to the first decade of the 1900s, when Spearman (1904) conceptualized the method to address questions such as the nature of IQ. Second, confirmatory factor analysis (CFA) requires that the researcher has a theory of factor structure, and this theory must be declared as part of the analysis, and is used in the analysis to limit which parameters are and are not estimated. CFA originated in the 1960s and 1970s, largely in the work of Jöreskog (1969).

Factor analysis can be used to address three primary research questions. These three issues involve (1) the number of factors, (2) which factored entities (e.g., variables, people) are most associated with a given factor, and (3) how correlated the factors are with each other.

In EFA, either four or five decisions must be made, in turn. First, which matrix of association statistics to analyze (e.g., a Pearson r matrix, a covariance matrix) must be decided. Second, how many factors to extract must be decided. There are numerous ways to inform this EFA decision, including use of Guttman's suggestion to extract all factors with eigenvalues greater than 1.0 (sometimes erroneously called the "Kaiser > 1" rule), Cattell's scree plot (based on a plot of eigenvalues), and more sophisticated methods, such as parallel analysis or the bootstrap (see Thompson 2004). Third, a statistical method for computing the factor pattern coefficients, which are weights algebraically equivalent to beta weights in regression, or standardized function coefficients in descriptive discriminant analysis or in canonical correlation analysis, must be decided. Common factor extraction methods include principal components analysis and principal axis methods. Fourth, a factor rotation method must be selected, if more than one factor is extracted. Rotation is necessary to ensure the interpretability of the factors. Two classes of rotation methods are orthogonal rotation, in which the uncorrelated initial factors are rotated such that they remain perfectly uncorrelated, and oblique rotation, in which the uncorrelated initial factors are rotated such that they become correlated. The most commonly used orthogonal and oblique rotation methods are varimax and promax, respectively.

Orthogonal rotation is more parsimonious, and consequently varimax rotation tends to yield results that (1) fit sample data less well than oblique methods (because there is less opportunity to capitalize on sampling error), but (2) replicate better in future samples (for the same reason). Thompson (2004) estimated that varimax rotation works well in roughly 85 percent of applied EFA research situations.

Fifth, if factors scores are to be used in a subsequent analysis (e.g., MANOVA), a factor score computation method must be selected. However, if principal components has been selected as the analytic method, the various factor score algorithms all yield identical factor scores. Another benefit of principal components analysis is that only with this method do the correlations of the factors with each other and of the factor scores with each other exactly match.

Commonly used statistical packages have as the default choices factor extraction from the Pearson *r* matrix, principal components extraction, and varimax rotation. Most applied researchers rely on these defaults, and thus the preponderance of published EFA research invokes these choices. However, these choices do often work quite well for many data sets.

In CFA, most of the same analytic decisions must be made. However, in CFA factors are never rotated. Instead, a "simple," interpretable factor structure is realized in CFA by fixing certain factor pattern coefficients to be zero, and freeing other factor pattern coefficients to be estimated. Researchers make these decisions to free and fix parameter estimates such that the nature of the factors is interpretable.

SEE ALSO: General Linear Model; Replicability Analyses; Statistical Significance Testing; Structural Equation Modeling

REFERENCES AND SUGGESTED READINGS

Cattell, R. B. (1966) The Data Box: Its Ordering of Total Resources in Terms of Possible Relational Systems. In: Cattell, R. B. (Ed.), *Handbook of Multivariate Experimental Psychology*. Rand McNally, Chicago, pp. 67–128.

Graham, J. M., Guthrie, A. C., & Thompson, B. (2003) Consequences of Not Interpreting Structure Coefficients in Published CFA Research: A Reminder. *Structural Equation Modeling* 10: 142–53.

Jöreskog, K. G. (1969) A General Approach to Confirmatory Maximum Likelihood Factor Analysis. *Psychometrika* 34: 183–202.

Spearman, C. (1904) "General Intelligence," Objectively Determined and Measured. *American Journal of Psychology* 15: 201–93.

Thompson, B. (2000) Q-Technique Factor Analysis: One Variation on the Two-Mode Factor Analysis of Variables. In: Grimm, L. & Yarnold, P. (Eds.), *Reading and Understanding More Multivariate Statistics*. American Psychological Association, Washington, DC, pp.207–26.

Thompson, B. (2004) *Exploratory and Confirmatory Factor Analysis: Understanding Concepts and Applications*. American Psychological Association, Washington, DC.

Fajnzylber, Fernando (1940–91)

Norma Rondero López

The vastness of Fernando Fajnzylber's work clearly places him among the most important Latin American thinkers. Rather than highlighting the many documents he wrote or the many projects he participated in, it is indispensable to note that what is outstanding in Fajnzylber's work is not only its importance as a critical vision of the development conditions in Latin America, but also the influence his ideas had on the development of policy strategies for the region.

Born into a family of Jewish immigrants in Santiago de Chile in 1940, Fernando Fajnzylber studied economic sciences in Chile. His work is without doubt a detailed analysis of the economic conditions in developing countries in Latin America. It is nevertheless important to acknowledge his influence on the development of sociology in Latin America in the 1970s and 1980s thanks to his contributions toward an explanation of the social and political problems in Latin America that showed the conditions of inequity of the poorest populations in the region based on the economic formulae Fajnzylber developed to reach economic growth.

Fajnzylber's work was mainly based on case studies and comparative studies between countries or sectors and/or productive branches. Fajnzylber's research was typically based on empirical work, the generation of studies that could provide "first-hand" information, which allowed him to master a method of carrying out research on industrial organizations based on recognizing the non-linear causal relationships between growth, international competitiveness, technical progress, and equity.

Fajnzylber's most important work started with the publication in 1970 of *Sistema industrial y exportación de manufacturas: análisis de la experiencia brasileña*, an analysis of the Brazilian industrial system and the export of manufactured goods. He studies the role transnational corporations play in industrial development and the potential of industrial spaces considered "sectors that carry technical progress" to expand competitively and the capacity to develop the productive apparatus.

During the early 1970s, Fajnzylber's work focused on the analysis of international industrial organizations. These studies led Fajnzylber to lay down one of the primary lines of his research: the growth problems in the manufacturing sector. This created the foundation for concepts that would emerge in his later work. Among the most important of these concepts is the notion of "sectors that carry technical progress." He would later analyze them as "endogenous nuclei of growth" because of the role they played in industrial development. These sectors are typically spaces with a high technological content that articulated with a broader productive apparatus to allow substantial advances in crucial productive sectors and branches.

In this sense, Fajnzylber's first works, which include the research he carried out on Mexican industry, "Las empresas transnacionales y el sistema industrial de México" ("Transnational Firms and the Mexican Industrial System") (1975), configured the core issue Fajnzylber never abandoned: the macroeconomic determination of competitiveness. In these first studies,

Fajnzylber emphasized the structural analysis of export-oriented industries, the development of export strategies for the countries in the region, and, to a lesser extent, the analysis of business strategies related to international markets.

The competitiveness axis stands out due to the notion of the prevailing need for national industries to link up with areas of production that are better positioned in the international markets. This issue was based on notions that took into account the importance of advanced technologies of certain productive areas, the incorporation of diversified structures, and, in general, the strategies set forth by leading firms that could be incorporated by industrial branch or sector, considered nuclei of competitive development.

As can be seen in this first stage of Fajnzylber's work, the core problem is located in the organizational analysis of certain industrial branches (export-oriented goods and manufactured goods). Although this stage of Fajnzylber's work is haunted by topics associated with the development of industrial leaderships and nuclei of technological development, Fajnzylber's thinking and analytical elaborations had not yet reached their greatest complexity.

In the 1980s, exiled in Mexico, Fajnzylber participated directly in the United Nations Industrial Development Organization (UNIDO), focusing on the analysis of technological modernization and the export possibilities of Latin American industry. With works like *La industrialización trunca de América Latina* (*The Truncated Industrialization of Latin America*) (1983), Fajnzylber was developing a system of associated ideas with a greater emphasis on recognizing technological lags and the lack of an industry of capital goods as elements that explain the region's development problem more firmly. This axis of his work thus incorporated more complex concerns: the capital goods industry in itself is not enough for economic development. It is here that Fajnzylber developed more specifically the theme of the endogenous nuclei of growth, since it is their articulation with the whole of the productive apparatus that enables the branches in which it is possible to compete internationally to become more dynamic.

This brought an understanding of the actual export possibilities of the Latin American industry. It should be noted that the kind of studies set forth in this stage see Latin America as a whole, acknowledging differences between the countries that have relatively stronger economies, such as Mexico and Brazil, which Fajnzylber considered to be economies that had important lessons to teach regarding exports. Diagnostics and projections in specific industrial sectors allowed Fajnzylber to set forth specific strategies that would serve as points of reference for the generation of concrete industrial policy and actions of the regional institutions for development.

Later on, in the second half of the 1980s, Fajnzylber went back to Chile where he joined the Economic Commission for Latin America and the Caribbean (ECLAC) as director of the Department of Industrial Development. By 1987, a new stage was initiated in the analysis of themes associated with development. This stage was opened with the publication in 1987 of "La industrialización de América Latina: de la 'caja negra' al 'casillero vacío'" ("Industrialization in Latin America: From the 'Black Box' to the 'Empty Locker'"). In this work, again based on empirical comparisons, Fajnzylber analyzes technological development in a more refined way: this is theme of the "black box" for Latin America, which, as Fajnzylber shows, constitutes the shadow of Latin American industrial development. In addition, he delved more deeply into issues that he had already set forth, such as productive dynamism and competitiveness.

From this point, technical progress will constitute an important aspect of Fajnzylber's reflections and contributions to the formulation of development strategies. It is therefore important to record that it is now that one of Fajnzylber's most polemical themes emerged: the differences between the more traditional structuralist perspectives of ECLAC members and Fajnzylber's so called "neo-structuralist" vision. In his perspective, Fajnzylber uses the same diagnosis as the original structuralist perspective, but recognizes that in the 1980s the conditions in Latin America, given the economic crisis it was going through, were substantially modified. This recognition is in fact his core innovation. He therefore set forth new development options for the Latin American countries. These options were contrary to previous formulae of "inward growth" and suggested promoting new pathways to development within the framework of international markets as well as industrial strategies that would place productive sectors in a more competitive position vis-à-vis international markets.

Fajnzylber developed in greater detail the aforementioned ideas, such as creative integration into the international economy based on strengthening the endogenous nuclei of growth. This integration aimed to incorporate not only the more developed industries with foreign markets but also all those agents involved in the implementation of more general industrial and economic policies. In other words, it did not exclude the state as an important agent. Had he excluded the state, he would have left the possibility of promoting development exclusively in the hands of market conditions. Above all, he gave transnational corporations an important role to play, which generated intense polemics especially in comparison to ECLAC's traditional structuralism.

Fajnzylber's core idea of "empty lockers" refers to the incapacity of the countries in the region to relate sustained growth with equity. It refers to a more specific development of the problems related to social inequality, social opportunities, and even some ideas associated with social mobility. All the works Fajnzylber headed as coordinator of the ECLAC work teams addressed these issues.

With this step, we find one of the most interesting lines in Fajnzylber's research profile: it is here that his work is enriched through its adoption of a more sociological perspective. The studies of problems of economic development, competitiveness, industrial strategies, and the promotion of endogenous nuclei of development are now accompanied by studies on inequality and equity as crucial problems to be faced in order to achieve sustained growth, based on an evaluation of the real conditions of the third world economies focusing on social equity.

In these studies, equity is embedded in a context that includes other countries beyond the Latin American region. These studies aim to approach the issue of globalizing trends and the changes experienced in national policies on technological development. These globalizing tendencies are related not only to the opening of markets but also to the crisis of the Taylorist–Fordist model of production, until then followed by the countries of developed capitalism in the western world. Fajnzylber therefore turned his eyes to the East Asian countries, in comparison to which the Latin American countries lack technological development, the "black box" and the "empty locker" of distributional equity.

From this perspective, the themes of Fajnzylber's later works diversified, constructing a more complex vision. Fajnzylber later looked into themes such as the structures and working conditions of labor that lead to low productivity in the region and associated this problem with the social conditions that can have an adverse impact on competitiveness.

The inclusion of these social issues strongly reinforces the arguments of the analysis and proposals on structural strengthening and competitiveness. Fajnzylber thus comes up with another crucial concept, for the understanding of his position of "authentic competitiveness" incorporates equity as a fundamental factor because of its direct relation to technical progress and therefore to competitiveness and growth.

The analysis linked to this new concept is directly associated with the public policy-making processes. The core recommendations incorporated equity not only in areas such as labor but also in impulse reforms within national institutions, as the concept of equity that is set forth not only refers to addressing and integrating the sectors of the poor, but is also a concept that aims to articulate society as a whole: from the poor to the entrepreneurs.

This point leads to a fair understanding of the complexity of Fajnzylber's thought around the more global idea of regional growth. It implies understanding the role played by both national and transnational firms especially in the space of the endogenous nuclei of development, these nuclei's drive toward technological progress, and the recognition of the global conditions of competitiveness and national institutional conditions. All these spaces are composed of public and private actors who could influence the development and implementation of national policies. In this sense, Fajnzylber clarifies that it is not a question of transferring formulae from other countries, but

of recognizing and seeing to the specific local and national contexts.

This is why institutional reforms that promote equity are gaining increasing importance. They set out by considering inequalities not only or even primarily as an economic problem, but as a challenge to be faced by the various political, economic, and social actors. It is no longer a question of seeing to the poor sectors through a welfare state, as ECLAC's past perspective foresaw. It is now a question of integrating all the social sectors in a structural transformation.

The most refined development of these ideas was materialized in an ECLAC document, *Transformación productiva con equidad* (*Productive Transformation with Equity*), published in 1990. Although this document is signed by ECLAC as a product of institutional authorship, it was the product of the hard work of a team headed by Fajnzylber, recognizing the so-called "renovation of ECLAC thought." In this document, we can find once again the construction of more complex versions of the concepts originally incorporated in earlier works. It refers to authentic competitiveness, but with a systemic character. The specific proposals for institutional reforms are precisely systemic. It is now a question of reaching a transformation that goes beyond partial agreements between unconnected levels that take decisions around sectoral public policies.

This transformation should be sought not only in the economic sector but also in the political realm. This is clearly expressed in the emphasis placed on the theme of democracy, which is understood as an indispensable, but not sufficient, condition in the search for equity since it broadens the possibilities of participation of sectors that have so far been excluded. It is thus a transformation that is based on the possibility of having a "framework of social and political coexistence."

According to this work, institutional change, indicated in the political system, should include broad sectors and institutions. Education is one of the most important sectors that will gain significance with the ideas associated with the development of necessary and indispensable human resources to promote productive and technological development.

Bringing in the educational issue offers a very interesting shift in what we have recognized as one of Fajnzylber's most important sociological contributions. *Transformación productiva con equidad* introduces the possibility of exploring the analysis and search for strategies to deal with the relationship between technological development and the productive system, on the one hand, and education, training, science, and technology, on the other. This relationship is based on ideas that became part of the education policies in the late 1980s and early 1990s and which are guided by the notion of a "society of knowledge," based on the consideration that access to knowledge – i.e., educational equity – is the essential foundation for the development of both individuals and nations.

The emphasis on education is also placed on the process of institutional transformation. This is the reason why, beyond the reforms to economic and political spaces, educational institutions at all levels must also be reformed. In this sense, it is indispensable to talk about another of ECLAC's works that delves more deeply into the need to face a series of conditions of educational equity and the development possibilities of the productive system: *Educación y conocimiento: eje de la transformación productiva con equidad* (*Education and Knowledge: An Axis of Productive Transformation with Equity*). This work was published in 1992, after Fernando Fajnzylber's death, but the research and the work behind this publication were still carried out by Fajnzylber. An introductory note in the document mentions Fajnzylber's guidance.

Fajnzylber's influence can still be appreciated in this document, which sustains the arguments set forth in their initial stage in ECLAC's previous works: the need for institutional reforms, the systemic character of growth and competitiveness, as well as the need to train and develop human resources not only to face the technological changes coming from other countries, but also to participate in the technological drive of the Latin American countries.

The role sustainability plays in economic development is just as important as the role of education. Fajnzylber's thinking always included the ecological dimension, particularly in *Transformación productiva con equidad*, and in ECLAC's *El desarrollo sustentable: transformación productiva, equidad y medio ambiente* (*Sustainable Development: Productive Transformation, Equity, and the Environment*), published in 1991. The ecological dimension was also considered a basic condition linked to economic development and was set forth as a "condition that enables competitive patterns to be sustainable."

In retrospect, these latter ECLAC publications can be considered Fajnzylber's first steps in a new line of work that was even more complex than the initial publications. Unfortunately, this new line of work only remained as a proposal since Fajnzylber's early death interrupted what promised to be the consolidation of this "new ECLAC perspective."

Those who study ECLAC and Fajnzylber's work have recognized that his ideas, concepts, and analysis were constructed while foreseeing the changes he was studying. The apparent simplicity of Fajnzylber's developed, detailed, and deep research work, mostly based on comparative experiences, allowed him to present his ideas in an accessible and understandable way.

Over 20 years of uninterrupted production (publications, courses, conferences, and documents) distinguished Fernando Fajnzylber. His work never ceased to reflect his commitment to Latin American development. Fajnzylber's work is not only an exemplary analysis of Latin American economic conditions, but also managed to be transferred into direct action in developing and implementing public policies for the productive sector that faced economic growth and social justice at the same time. While Fajnzylber had an undeniable influence on economics, his contribution to sociology was equally important.

SEE ALSO: Culture, Economy and; Democracy; Development: Political Economy; Education and Economy

REFERENCES AND SUGGESTED READINGS

Bielchovsky, R. (1988) Evolución de las ideas de la CEPAL. *Revista de la CEPAL, 50 aniversario.*
Buitelaar, R., Guerguil, M., Macario, C., & Pérez, W. (1992) Una obsesión por el crecimiento y la justicia

social: el legado de Fernando Fajnzylber. *Pensamiento Iberoamericano* (21): 263–76.

CEPAL (1990) *Transformación productiva con equidad.* United Nations, Santiago de Chile.

CEPAL (1991) *El desarrollo sustentable: transformación productiva, equidad y medio ambiente.* United Nations, Santiago de Chile.

CEPAL (1992) *Educación y conocimiento: eje de la transformación productiva con equidad.* CEPAL/UNESCO, Santiago de Chile.

Claudio, M. & Messner, D. (2004) *Fernando Fajnzylber (1940–1991): Desarrollo tecnológico, competitividad y equidad.* Institut für Entwicklung und Frieden (INEF), Duisburg University.

Fajnzylber, F. (1970) *Sistema industrial y exportación de manufacturas: análisis de la experiencia brasileña.* CEPAL, Rio de Janeiro.

Fajnzylber, F. (1975a) Las empresas transnacionales y el sistema industrial de México. *El Trimestre Económico* 42(168): 903–31, Mexico City.

Fajnzylber, F. (1975b) Oligopolio, empresas transnacionales y estilos de desarrollo. *El Trimestre Económico* 43(171): 625–56, Mexico City.

Fajnzylber, F. (1976) Empresas transnacionales y el "Collective Self-Reliance." *El Trimestre Económico* 43(172): 879–921, Mexico City.

Fajnzylber, F. (1979) Sobre la reestructuración del capitalismo y sus repercusiones en América Latina. *El Trimestre Económico* 46(184): 889–914, Mexico City.

Fajnzylber, F. (1980) *Industrialización e internacionalización en América Latina*, 2 vols. Fondo de Cultura Económica, Mexico City.

Fajnzylber, F. (1983a) *La industrialización trunca de América Latina.* CET, Mexico City.

Fajnzylber, F. (1983b) Intervención, autodeterminación e industrialización en América Latina. *El Trimestre Económico* 50(197): 307–28, Mexico City.

Fajnzylber, F. (1984) Especificidades del desarrollo industrial latinoamericano. *Revista de la Cámara de Comercio de Bogotá* 17(60): 143–5, Bogota.

Fajnzylber, F. (1987) La industrialización de América Latina: de la "caja negra" al "casillero vacío." *Revista Internacional de Ciencias Sociales* 118: 495–501, Paris.

Fajnzylber, F. (1988) *Crecimiento y equidad en América Latina.* CEPAL, División Agrícola Conjunta CEPAL/FAO.

Fajnzylber, F. (1989) *América Latina ante los nuevos desafíos del mundo en transición.* Comisión Sudamericana de Paz, Buenos Aires.

Fajnzylber, F. (1990a) El medio ambiente en la actual estrategia de crecimiento económico. *Ambiente y Desarrollo* 6(2): 7–9, Santiago de Chile.

Fajnzylber, F. (1990b) Reflexiones sobre la propuesta "Transformación productiva con equidad." *Informe Industrial* 13(123): 4–6, Buenos Aires.

Fajnzylber, F. (1991) Inserción internacional e innovación institucional. *Revista de la CEPAL* (45): 149–78, Santiago de Chile.

Ocampo, J. A. (1999) Más allá del consenso de Washington: una vision desde la CEPAL. *Revista de la CEPAL* 60.

Rosenthal, P. (1992) In Memory of Fernando Fajnzylber. *CEPAL Review* 46.

Faletto, Enzo (1935–2003)

Ricardo Gamboa Ramírez

Enzo Doménico Faletto Verné was born in Chile in 1935 and died in Santiago de Chile on July 22, 2003. He studied history in the Faculty of Philosophy and Education at the University of Chile and received an MA in sociology at the Latin American Faculty of Social Studies (FLACSO). Faletto must be considered as a representative of social sciences and humanities in Latin America, two disciplines which achieved the peak of their development in the early 1970s.

Faletto's social and humanist vocation can be appreciated in the various disciplines treated in his books and articles, as well as in the lectures he gave while a teacher at the Sociology Department of the University of Chile and at FLACSO. From 1967 to 1973 he taught classes to students of sociology and journalism at the University of Chile. In addition, Faletto was a researcher at the Latin American Institute for Economic and Social Planning (ILPES), and after 1973 he worked as an expert in the Social Development Division of the United Nations Economic Commission for Latin America and the Caribbean (ECLAC). He also worked in several foreign universities, including the University of Rosario in Argentina, which awarded him an honorary doctorate.

Faletto combined his academic career with political activity in the heart of the Socialist Party of Chile, where he was part of a group known as the "Swiss" faction which included Ricardo Lagos, president of Chile (2002–6), among its members. Two important aspects of Faletto's political career should be highlighted.

The first is that, despite the intellectual and friendship bonds he enjoyed for most of his life with Fernando Henrique Cardoso and Ricardo Lagos, presidents of Brazil and Chile at the end of the twentieth century and beginning of the twenty-first, Faletto refused to be present when they assumed their respective terms of office. After Lagos had won the elections in 2000, Faletto even warned him that he would not see him again until the end of his term in 2006. This attitude reveals how Faletto, a convinced social democrat, understood the kind of relationship that an intellectual should have with the highest political circles.

The second aspect is that after the coup d'état which overthrew president Salvador Allende on September 11, 1973, Faletto decided to remain in Chile instead of living in exile. Even though this decision led to many problems on account of the military junta's censure, it also offered Faletto the opportunity of holding a point of view on the Chilean reality during the hard years of the military dictatorship different from that of his exiled colleagues.

Nevertheless, the circumstances imposed by the repression made him abandon the university to "take labor refuge" in the heart of ECLAC and FLACSO, until finally in 1990 he was reinstated to his academic work at the house of Andrés Bello, where he was the head of the Seminar of Social History of Latin America until his death.

As with his vast written work, the name of the seminar was only a pretext to develop an analysis of the reality of Latin America, where economy, sociology, politics, and history merged in a multidisciplinary exercise that gave rise to works that constitute real milestones of social knowledge. Before the avalanche of the so-called unique thought characteristic of neoliberalism, these works deserve to be rescued in a double sense: as a sample of the history of social thought in Latin America, and as an example of a methodological and epistemological approach that nowadays should be incorporated into the knowledge of disciplines such as sociology and particularly economy, which has strayed so far in recent years from its social and humanist origins.

HISTORICAL CONTEXT OF ENZO FALETTO'S WORK

Throughout his academic career, Faletto published a wide range of books and articles in specialized journals. To gain an idea of the extent of his written work, it should be mentioned that in January 2005 the dean's office of the University of Chile announced the creation of the Enzo Faletto Seminar. During this ceremony Carlos Ruiz, a disciple, colleague, and friend of Faletto, mentioned that work had just begun on compiling the scattered writings of this prominent scientist, and so far there were already 80 titles.

Faletto published articles in specialized journals, the most relevant ones since 1990. Without doubt, the circumstances associated with the fall of the Soviet bloc, as well as the predominance of social, political, and economic individualism imposed by neoliberal policies, motivated his work on topics such as the role of the state in contemporary capitalist societies, particularly in Latin America; modernity and the role of social classes in today's world; the relation between democracy and political culture; and the theory of dependency and its role in the neoliberal project at the end of the twentieth century.

Of all the books by Faletto, undoubtedly the most powerful is that co-written with Fernando Henrique Cardoso, *Dependencia y desarrollo en América Latina* (*Dependency and Development in Latin America*), first published in 1969. Because of its number of printings (30 until 2002), this is one of the most important social science publications throughout the world; it has also been translated into other languages, including English and Portuguese. The importance of this work lies in the fact that it was the first attempt to systematize an interpretive model of the economic development of Latin America, having as the focal point of its line of argument the dependency relation between developed countries and the periphery, from the first world expansion of capitalism in the sixteenth century to the internationalization of capital in the second half of the twentieth.

Nevertheless, as with other intellectual undertakings, this book is not a product of chance. It was written by professors Faletto and Cardoso at the peak of a process in which the relationship between academia and politics, between the theoretical and the ideological, would define many of the characteristics of political culture in Latin America after 1950.

The background of 15 years' work by ECLAC interpreting Latin America's economic development, taking as its starting point the relationship between center and periphery, was one of the primary influences in Faletto and Cardoso's work. ECLAC was created in 1948 by the Economic and Social Council of the United Nations. This international organization was headed for almost 15 years after its foundation by the Argentinean economist Raúl Prebisch.

The Latin American and Caribbean Demographic Center (CELADE) as well as ILPES were created inside ECLAC. In 1964, the second event influencing the intellectual trajectory of Cardoso and Faletto's work occurred. Following the 1964 coup d'état in Brazil, a group of Brazilian intellectuals and scholars sought refuge in Chile where they could continue developing their academic and political reflection. At this time important figures in the academic world could be found at ILPES, such as Ruy Mauro Marini, Theotonio Dos Santos, Fernando Henrique Cardoso, American professor André Gunder Frank, and the still young Enzo Faletto. The discussions inside ILPES daily recreated many of the topics of interest defined by ECLAC, which considered that an essential element of Latin America's backwardness was the unequal relations in terms of technology, productivity, and commercial exchange established between central and peripheral countries.

There are three overarching topics. The first two relate to the industrialization of Latin America and to the state's role in developing that process as a way of analyzing the unequal conditions imposed by the core–periphery relation. The third consists in a thorough understanding of the economic problems faced by Latin American countries as a result of structural conditions historically confronted by those nations, and not only of monetary phenomena such as price rises and inflation.

Another important factor in Faletto and Cardoso's work was the publication in 1960 of Washington Whitman Rostow's *Stages of Economic Development*. In this work, Rostow argues that the underdeveloped nations must repeat the economic growth styles of developed countries, particularly in their definitions of economic policies, in order to move beyond the stage of underdevelopment. This apparently simple formula met with immediate criticism from Latin American social scientists, especially in relation to its ahistorical, indeed anti-historical, nature, since it left aside an element that would afterwards be taken up again by Faletto and Cardoso: the historical nature of dependency relationships between center and periphery.

Rostow's position in relation to the economic takeoff was influenced by the German historicist stream of thought at the end of the nineteenth century, but above all by the quantitative historical studies on the economic variables associated with growth promoted mainly by the American economist Simon Kuznets. The transposition of economic growth behavior from the central countries to the underdeveloped nations faced immediate theoretical rejection from the different streams that merged in ECLAC and in the Chilean ILPES.

This theoretical rejection emerged from a cultural tradition in Latin America that stressed the importance of understanding the historical process of the development of nations and states, as well as the inequality of prevailing conditions in the region. This tradition began in the nineteenth century in the context of the struggles for independence and in the political processes that gave rise to the formation of Latin American states.

The Cold War and its particular features in the area provide an additional element in the context in which Faletto and Cardoso wrote the book. The victory of the Cuban Revolution in 1959, and its early definition as a socialist revolution, cleared the way for the possibility of economic development different from the capitalist system. This essentially ideological discussion prevailed among Latin American social scientists beginning in the 1960s. Moreover, the determined political attitude and affiliation of many of these intellectuals made it inevitable that their theoretical developments would be accompanied by an essentially anti-capitalist definition.

DEPENDENCY AND DEVELOPMENT IN LATIN AMERICA

Most Latin American experts agree on characterizing the work of Faletto and Cardoso as part of the structuralist stream that finds in dependency the key to explaining the roots of Latin America's underdevelopment. Structuralism attributes the main causes of economic backwardness to the deformations and imbalances in the economic structures of Latin American countries.

In Faletto and Cardoso's book, the imbalances in the economic structure are determined by the dependency relations established between peripheral and central countries, dependency relations that have their own historical features depending on the kind of integration within the global market that developed after the colonial pact was broken off. The characterization of the different historical stages of integration within the global market is one of the book's major contributions. The first stage is outward development, the second is the transition to capitalism, the third is the consolidation of the inner market and the beginning of the industrialization process, and the final stage relates to the internationalization of Latin American economies. In this historical model, Faletto and Cardoso distinguish between consolidated national economies and enclaved economies. However, this structuralist vision surpasses the economic sphere. As Faletto repeatedly stressed, his intention was to give a sociological dimension to economic backwardness and to dependency.

One of the main contributions of Enzo Faletto's work can be found in the definition of the sociological dimension of dependency and economic backwardness, which is still useful for the analysis of contemporary societies in the early twenty-first century. For Cardoso and Faletto, the problem of backwardness in Latin American countries cannot be considered only from the point of view of economic variables, least of all by comparing them to how they behave in developed countries. Comparison makes no sense unless the following elements are considered:

- The special features of historical processes that led to the formation of national economies.

- The role of the state in the formation of the economic structures of individual countries.
- The formation of the different social classes, particularly the entrepreneurs and the oligarchy, as well as the working class.
- The way in which these social classes are linked with the oligarchies of the central nations.
- The way in which the national economies integrate into the international market.

In this respect, an essential element emerges for an understanding of the neoliberal order in recent years. From the publication of *Dependency and Development in Latin America* and in later articles and essays, Faletto defines Latin American national economies as capitalist economies integrated into the world market, particularly since the internationalization of capital that took place after 1950.

This definition is neither obvious nor pointless. Since so-called globalization turned out to be a kind of leitmotif of social analysis after 1990, there was a tendency to define Latin American societies as isolated from the tendencies of the market that supposedly encouraged capitalist development after the Bretton Woods Agreements in 1944. The contributions of Faletto demonstrate that there is nothing more distant from reality; the presence of capitalism and integration within the global market has been constant in the history of Latin America.

The consequence of the loss of sociological perspective, in the sense that Faletto understood it, was the emphasis on market forces as the means by which the nations of Latin America would gain access to economic development. This led to the idea that it was sufficient to imitate the so-called emergent market economies, like those in Southeast Asia, in order to achieve high standards of economic growth and welfare. The revision of economic takeoff theory, now based on the impulse of market forces and of so-called economic miracles, suffers from the same flaws as its distant and forgotten predecessor devised by Rostow: its clearly unhistorical element, which in itself makes it necessary to return to theoretical aspects developed by Latin American social scientists, of whom Enzo Doménico Faletto Verné was one of the main exponents.

false consciousness

SEE ALSO: Dependency and World-Systems
Theories; Development: Political Economy;
Economy (Sociological Approach); Neoliberal-
ism; Organizations; Structuralism

REFERENCES AND SUGGESTED
READINGS

Baño, R. & Faletto, E. (1994) *Institucionalidad política
y proceso social: el debate sobre presidencialismo o
parlamentarismo*. Research Program, CLAD,
Caracas.
Cardoso, F. H. & Faletto, E. (1965) Estancamiento y
desarrollo económico en América Latina: Condi-
ciones sociales y políticas (consideraciones para un
programa de estudio). Manuscript.
Cardoso, F. H. & Faletto, E. (1969) *Dependencia y
desarrollo en América Latina. Ensayo de interpreta-
ción sociológica*. Siglo XXI, Mexico City.
Faletto, E. (1987) *Las bases sociales de los partidos
comunista y socialista*. Documentos de Trabajo,
FLACSO, Santiago.
Faletto, E. (1994) *El desarrollo latinoamericano. Sus
características*. Colección de Viva la Ciudadanía.
Módulos de la Escuela de Liderazgo Democrático,
Corporación SOS, Bogotá.
Faletto, E. & Baño, R. (1993) *Propuesta para la con-
strucción de un sistema de indicadores sociales en
función del desarrollo productivo y la equidad*. INE-
UNICEF, Santiago de Chile.
Faletto, E. & Kirkwood, J. (1977) *El liberalismo*. El
Cid Editor, Madrid.
Faletto, E., Ruiz, E., & Zemelman, H. (1972) *Génesis
Histórica del Proceso Político Chileno*. Editorial
Quimantú, Santiago de Chile.

false consciousness

Brian Starks and Azamat Junisbai

False consciousness is a Marxist theoretical
concept referring to the circumstance, or
state-of-being, in which workers hold views
that are contrary to workers' objective class
interests. This subjective consciousness does
not arise organically from among workers, but
is imposed (or foisted) upon them by the dominant ideology of the capitalist class. False
consciousness and class consciousness are intimately linked. Whereas class consciousness

denotes workers' awareness of their historical
position and enables the transformation of
society, false consciousness denotes workers'
failure to recognize their position and bring
about the transformation of society. Because
of its elitist and arguably negative view of
workers (as dupes), the concept of false consciousness often offends modern democratic
sensibilities. Not only that, but with its apparent reference to objective truth, false consciousness in an era of postmodernism smacks of
intellectual arrogance. Perhaps for these reasons, the concept has fallen into disuse among
sociologists.

It appears that the term was first coined by
Friedrich Engels; there is no evidence that Karl
Marx himself ever used this in his writing
(Eagleton 1991). The term's initial appearance
in print was in a letter written by Engels to
Franz Mehring in 1893:

Ideology is a process accomplished by the so-
called thinker consciously, it is true, but with a
false consciousness. The real motive forces
impelling him remain unknown to him; otherwise it simply would not be an ideological
process. (Tucker 1978: 766)

The concept, as developed in Engels's letter
and in later writings, is rooted in the earlier
writings of Marx and Engels in *The German
Ideology*. While theorists have debated whether
Marx himself would have accepted the precise
term *false consciousness*, the concept is closely
tied to Marx's notion of a "dominant ideology"
and is useful for understanding Marx's theory
of historical change. As with many sociological
ideas, the meaning of false consciousness has
varied and changed over time as new theorists
have drawn upon it and as these new formulations have been challenged and contested (see
Eyerman 1981; Eagleton 1991).

Engels, for example, tended to equate false
consciousness with ideology and applied the
concept primarily to intellectuals and capitalists, whom Marx and he had always criticized
for producing a distorted picture of reality.
Somewhat idealistically, Marx and Engels
tended to credit the working class with freedom
from illusions due to its subordinate position in
capitalist society. Aware that not all of the
working class fit this description, however, they
reasoned that the working class was composed

of not just the proletariat but also the lumpen-proletariat, or rabble who failed to act as revolutionaries. Later Marxists, such as Antonio Gramsci and Georg Lukács, expanded upon these ideas in their elaborations on false consciousness.

For Gramsci, the concepts of dominant ideology and false consciousness are distinct. False consciousness refers to flawed perception on the part of workers, whereas the dominant ideology is understood as a system of ideas and propositions espoused by owners to support the status quo. In an effort to understand the power of capitalist ideology over the working class, Gramsci examined the effect of culture and especially religion (part of Marx's superstructure) on the ideas and consciousness of the working class. Gramsci argued that hegemonic rule, in which a majority of the population supports or accepts the status quo, requires that owners manufacture consent and this is made possible by false consciousness on the part of the oppressed. Gramsci believed that movements for progressive social change must reeducate the masses to liberate them from false consciousness. Workers' support for gradual political and economic reforms rather than revolutionary action is a sign of their false consciousness or failure to recognize the true origins and proper means to end class-based oppression. Thus, genuine reeducation would occur only with the illumination of Marxist ideology, which offers an explanation of exploitation and poverty to workers. For Gramsci, false consciousness is a problem of working-class (mis)perception that can be countered only by a competing ideology (i.e., Marxism).

Whereas Gramsci emphasized the need for Marxist ideology to combat capitalist hegemony, Georg Lukács argued that false consciousness is not purposefully manufactured by the bourgeois intellectuals to subjugate the proletariat; rather, it is an outcome of living and working in a capitalist society permeated by exchange relations and commodity fetishism (in which people commodify and objectify not only things but themselves). Consequently, capitalist societies create a veil of mystification that precludes a true understanding of the social order. Functioning in a world of commodity relationships, in which markets appear to determine outcomes and in which the value of something is understood as its price in exchange rather than the labor contained within it, inevitably produces false consciousness. To the extent that commodity fetishism dominates, false consciousness becomes the normal way of perceiving and acting within capitalist society, thereby concealing the true nature of capitalism from all involved. While this mystification is beneficial to the bourgeoisie, the working class suffers from it. For Lukács, not surprisingly, only the working class is structurally capable of achieving a total/real understanding of itself and of capitalism as a social system, and eventually transforming it into a more rational system. This is because of its location at the center of the main capitalist contradiction and irrationality – the workplace where surplus value is extracted.

Lukács's approach to false consciousness served as a point of departure for members of the Frankfurt School (Max Horkheimer, Theodor Adorno, Herbert Marcuse, Erich Fromm, etc.). These scholars sought to understand the striking absence of working-class opposition to the rise of fascism in Germany in the 1930s. They argued that a full explanation of working-class acceptance of Nazi authoritarianism must examine workers' activities outside of the labor process and must take into account their unconscious or "irrational" impulses and emotions. For example, Fromm added an affective psychological dimension to the study of false consciousness and attempted to synthesize Marxist and Freudian theory. Consequently, he argued that working-class experience in a capitalist society produces not only a false perception of one's economic interest but also a false sense of self/identity. Thus, false consciousness has an emotional as well as cognitive dimension and is not easily demystified or transcended by a mere rational ideology such as Marxism. As the Frankfurt School broadened the definition of false consciousness to include self and identity, it became increasingly difficult to speak of "objective" class interests and discussions of false consciousness became embroiled in philosophical debates regarding the nature of "true experience."

While the term false consciousness has been variously used by a number of European scholars, sociologists in the US have rarely used it. A modern-day application of the concept of false consciousness, however, can be found in some explanations of American exceptionalism. The absence of a well-developed working-class party in the US has lent itself to many different hypotheses and explanations over the years. Whereas some sociologists and historians have sought to explain the lack of a working-class labor party by reference to the US's higher standard of living, increased capitalist organization and resistance, and/or absence of an aristocracy, others have argued that it is the widespread ideology of the American Dream that has hampered the development of working-class consciousness.

In this latter view, the American Dream of "rags to riches" and "opportunity for all" is the dominant ideology in America. It serves to legitimize inequalities within the US by providing workers with "false promises." When workers believe promises that they will be able to get rich in the future, they accept their disadvantaged positions in the present (Robinson & Bell 1978). As Aronowitz (1973) recounted, the labor movement in the US emerged largely as a trade union movement seeking a place at the table rather than to revolutionize the means of production itself. This is due, in no small part, to the fact that workers are focused on moving up economically rather than in transforming the capitalist system itself. In accepting this system, however, Americans often end up blaming themselves, rather than the economic system, for their own lack of success (Sennett & Cobb 1972).

While belief in the American Dream can thus be understood as a form of false consciousness, the term false consciousness is almost never used by these researchers. The conspicuous absence of this term may simply reflect a diminished Marxist influence on sociologists in the US. More likely however, its absence from modern American sociology underscores most sociologists' attempts to grant authenticity to workers' own views, even if these views sometimes have negative repercussions for workers themselves. Much to the chagrin of committed Marxists, in the current age of identity politics, the prospects for this term in US sociology appear bleak.

SEE ALSO: Adorno, Theodor W.; Class Consciousness; Engels, Friedrich; Fromm, Erich; Gramsci, Antonio; Horkheimer, Max; Ideological Hegemony; Lukács, Georg; Marcuse, Herbert; Marx, Karl

REFERENCES AND SUGGESTED READINGS

Aronowitz, S. (1973) *False Promises: The Shaping of American Working-Class Consciousness*. McGraw-Hill, New York.
Eagleton, T. (1991) *Ideology*. Verso, New York.
Eyerman, R. (1981) *False Consciousness and Ideology in Marxist Theory*. Humanities Press, Atlantic Highlands, NJ.
Gramsci, A. (1971) *Selections From the Prison Notebooks of Antonio Gramsci*. International Publishers, New York.
Lukács, G. (1972) *History and Class Consciousness*. MIT Press, Cambridge, MA.
Robinson, R. V. & Bell, W. (1978) Equality, Success, and Social Justice in England and the United States. *American Sociological Review* 43 (April): 125–43.
Sennett, R. & Cobb, J. (1972) *The Hidden Injuries of Class*. Vintage Books, New York.
Tucker, R. (Ed.) (1978) *The Marx–Engels Reader*. Norton, New York.

falsification

Andrew Tudor

The concept of falsification is indelibly marked by the methodological doctrine of falsificationism, associated above all with the work of Karl Popper. He first developed the elements of his position in the early 1920s as part of a project to establish a logically defensible criterion of scientificity, culminating in the publication of *Logik der Forschung* (later translated as *The Logic of Scientific Discovery*) in 1934. Falsifiability emerged as the basis of his solution to the so-called "problem of demarcation." Much elaborated over subsequent years, his analysis of falsification became the foundation for the Popperian school in the philosophy and history of science and the central feature in their influential account of scientific growth. However, in the 1960s and 1970s, dissatisfaction with this analysis, not least among some of Popper's own followers, gave rise to variously radical revisions of the basic falsificationist position. Today, both the Popperian doctrine and the concept of falsification should be understood as component elements in a more diverse, though perhaps less rigorous, conceptualization of theory testing in science.

Falsificationism was inextricably bound up with the problem of demarcation: the perceived need to distinguish science from a variety of other intellectual activities, not least what Popper called "pseudo-science" – a category within which he included the theories of Freud and Marx. His argument begins with the recognition that the traditional view of science as based on systematic, inductive generalization is logically indefensible. Echoing Hume, Popper suggests that there is no reason why we should expect that further instances of a phenomenon will resemble those that we have already experienced: famously, however many white swans we may observe will not justify the conclusion that all swans are white. There may be a black swan just around the corner.

What, then, does distinguish the statements of empirical science? By the logic of the modus tollens it is permissible to argue from the truth of a singular statement (this swan is black) to the falsity of a universal one (all swans are white). So, although we cannot confirm a general statement without fear of subsequent contradiction, we can falsify it. This, then, is the criterion of demarcation: "it must be possible for an empirical scientific system to be refuted by experience" (Popper 1968: 41). In principle, scientific conjectures must always be open to refutation.

Taken as an isolated logical point about the relation between hypothesis and evidence, this view attained widespread legitimacy in the social sciences and elsewhere in the mid-twentieth century. Indeed, as late as 1993 the US Supreme Court elaborated its Daubert criteria for scientific expert witness testimony in unashamedly falsificationist terms. However, interpreted thus, falsificationism is little more than a dogmatic application of the Popperian view. Even "naïve falsificationism" – the term Lakatos (1970) uses to describe Popper's initial formulation – is not as reductively simplistic as this. Falsifiability-in-principle, after all, is a general criterion of scientificity, not a specific methodological instruction. Furthermore, when

a statement is actually falsified, it is the whole system from which it is derived that is rendered suspect, and quite what aspect of that system is taken to be problematic remains a matter for scientists' practical decision-making. As Duhem and, later and more forcefully, Quine suggested, there is no simple thread of falsification relating the world of observables to that of theory. And as sociology of science studies of scientific controversies suggest, the reasons for actually rejecting a hypothesis or theory are many and varied.

Nevertheless, there always remains an element in the falsificationist doctrine which understands the growth of scientific knowledge in terms of the successive improvement of theories in consequence of attempts at falsification: "severe tests," as Popper describes them in his discussion of corroboration. It is this core belief that scientific progress is fostered by critical-rational method which was increasingly to founder on the rocks of historical evidence. Scientists, it was observed by historians and sociologists of science, did not behave as the falsificationist model proposed. To such observations Popper was inclined to reply, well they should, a reflection of his perception of philosophy of science as an essentially normative endeavor. But that commitment was increasingly at odds with the more relativistic tenor of the times, and criticism of falsificationism became more vocal even from within the Popperian camp.

The most interesting of the critical revisions, and certainly the one most focused upon issues of falsification, was that advanced by Imre Lakatos (1970). He suggested that Popper's position had been misrepresented as a somewhat naïve and dogmatic account of falsification. While in some respects the Popperian model was dogmatic, there was also an implicit, more "sophisticated" Popper who was aware of the limitations that needed to be placed upon the initial, naïve model. Thus, although Popper does not fully incorporate the insights of other more conventionalist and historically aware accounts of science, his views do not exclude that possibility. So in proposing his "methodology of research programmes," Lakatos sets out to modify falsificationism accordingly. In effect, he replaces the core supposition, that specific theories must be falsifiable, with a more pluralist account which emphasizes (in) consistency among theories. "It is not that we propose a theory and Nature may shout NO," he writes; "rather we propose a maze of theories, and Nature may shout INCONSISTENT" (Lakatos 1970: 130).

Nonetheless, Lakatos remains committed to the characteristically Popperian view that, although much of scientific inquiry is a matter of convention, science is at heart a critical-rational enterprise. He wants to "save science from fallibilism." Extensive historical and sociological study of science and scientists in the later twentieth century has made that an increasingly difficult position to defend, with the result that falsificationism is no longer central to academic debate. However, the issues of method raised under its flag remain vital to any full understanding of the processes whereby we seek to confront our statements about the world with what Quine once called "the tribunal of sense experience."

SEE ALSO: Controversy Studies; Fact, Theory, and Hypothesis: Including the History of the Scientific Fact; Induction and Observation in Science; Kuhn, Thomas and Scientific Paradigms; Positivism; Realism and Relativism: Truth and Objectivity

REFERENCES AND SUGGESTED READINGS

Collins, H. M. (1985) *Changing Order: Replication and Induction in Scientific Practice.* Sage, London.
Duhem, P. (1954) *The Aim and Structure of Physical Theory.* Princeton University Press, Princeton.
Harding, S. G. (Ed.) (1976) *Can Theories Be Refuted?* Reidel, Dordrecht, Boston, and London.
Lakatos, I. (1970) *Falsification and the Methodology of Research Programmes.* In: Lakatos, I. & Musgrave, A. (Eds.), *Criticism and the Growth of Knowledge.* Cambridge University Press, Cambridge.
Popper, K. (1968) *The Logic of Scientific Discovery.* Hutchinson, London.
Popper, K. (1974) *Conjectures and Refutations.* Routledge & Kegan Paul, London.
Quine, W. V. O. (1963) *Two Dogmas of Empiricism.* In: Quine, W. V. O., *From a Logical Point of View.* Harper & Row, New York.
Radnitzky, G. & Andersson, G. (Eds.) (1978) *Progress and Rationality in Science.* Reidel, Dordrecht, Boston, and London.

families and childhood disabilities

Valerie Leiter

Families of children with disabilities experience challenges that other families do not face. They may experience stigma as a result of having a child with a disability and may perform health care and advocacy work for their children beyond that performed by other families. The extent of these additional concerns varies tremendously across families, depending upon the nature and severity of the children's disabilities and the social context in which the meaning of the children's disabilities is interpreted and acted upon. At the individual level, some children may have disabilities that affect their functioning slightly, while others may have disabilities that affect their functioning severely, across multiple areas, including physical, cognitive, emotional, and behavioral functioning. At a broader social level, some children with disabilities live in families and communities that attempt to eliminate social barriers that could result from disability, while others live in social contexts that do not strive to promote children's full participation.

While it is important to acknowledge these ways in which children with disabilities and their families are "exceptional," it is equally important to acknowledge that families of children with disabilities are in many ways just like other families. Over the past four decades, parents of children with disabilities in the US, UK, and Canada have sought recognition for the caring labor that they perform, and some have fought against the ways that some professionals, researchers, and public programs have treated them as pathological and in need of intervention.

Disability is often stigmatized in the way that Erving Goffman described in his 1963 book, *Stigma: Notes on the Management of Spoiled Identity*, and families may face what Goffman called "courtesy stigma" when individuals stigmatize the entire family because of the child's disability. In its most severe form, this stigmatization of families may be found in Bruno Bettelheim's 1967 book, *The Empty Fortress*.

There, Bettelheim presented his "refrigerator mother" theory of autism, which blamed mothers for their children's autism. Less severe forms of courtesy stigma may also be found in social science research and in service systems that focus only or primarily upon families' needs and weaknesses, ignoring their knowledge and strengths. Recent social research and public policy provide a more balanced view of families of children with disabilities, and of the children themselves, acknowledging that they face added concerns and stresses as a result of disability, but also documenting the capabilities, expertise, and strengths that children and families may bring to these challenges.

These changes in policy and professional attitudes regarding families of children with disabilities are the result of parental activism over the last 40 years. Children with disabilities and their families were largely invisible in public policy until the 1960s and 1970s, when the parents organized on behalf of their children, transforming the nature and location of therapeutic care and education for children with disabilities. Until the 1960s in the US and the 1970s in the UK, parents had to choose between keeping their children at home and not receiving any public services, or placing their children in residential institutions, called "schools" in the US and "long-stay hospitals" in the UK (Read 2000; Leiter 2004).

In the UK, the thalidomide disaster and problems regarding vaccine damage created public concern regarding children with disabilities (Read 2000). Parents' organizing began a little earlier in the US, in the 1960s and 1970s, when parents borrowed tactics from the Civil Rights Movement to fight for community-based services that would allow them to keep their children at home. Most of those battles centered on public education, resulting in the US Congress passing the Education of All Handicapped Act in 1975, which is now called the Individuals with Disabilities Education Act (IDEA). Then in the 1980s, parents collaborated with professionals who provided services to children with disabilities and lobbied the US Congress to extend public services to children with disabilities from birth. This parent–professional collaboration resulted in the creation of additional community-based public services, in substantial changes in the way that public programs describe families, and in additional legal rights for parents. There is now considerably more emphasis upon families' strengths, knowledge, and capabilities in programs that serve children with disabilities. Parents also have more rights to participate in making decisions about their children's health care and education. Parents' uptake of those rights varies tremendously, and parents with higher levels of education are more likely to advocate for their children within service systems. While parental rights have been an important tool for families when advocating for their children within public programs, this rights-based approach to social change has put the burden of creating change upon parents rather than upon the professionals within public programs who wield decision-making authority.

In addition to advocacy work, families may also provide substantial health and therapeutic care to children with disabilities (Read 2000). Although fathers may perform some carework, most carework is performed by mothers, due to traditional gender roles that emphasize mothers' provision of care to children and fathers' economic support of the household. There is an important distinction here between the carework that mothers *typically* provide, such as taking care of children when they have colds, etc., and the *additional, atypical* carework that mothers provide that is associated with their children's disabilities. Both the extent and scope of carework are greater within families of children with disabilities. Within a sample of mothers of children with special health care needs, Leiter et al. (2004) found that almost one-fifth of the mothers performed 20 hours or more of carework per week, doing therapies, dressing changes, care of feeding or breathing equipment, and so on. Mothers' provision of carework to their children with disabilities can also have other ripple effects within the family. For example, mothers may cut down their working hours or stop working altogether, and families may have less income as a result.

Much of the current knowledge regarding families of children with disabilities focuses upon the early parts of a family's life course, when the child is still a minor, with few exceptions (such as Krauss & Seltzer 1997). Far less is known about families of children with disabilities later in life, providing a rich area for future sociological research.

SEE ALSO: Childcare; Childhood; Disability as a Social Problem; Social Problems, Politics of; Social Services

REFERENCES AND SUGGESTED READINGS

Featherstone, H. (1980) *A Difference in the Family: Life with a Disabled Child.* Basic Books, New York.

Krauss, M. W. & Seltzer, M. M. (1997) Life Course Perspectives in Mental Retardation Research: The Case of Family Caregiving. In: Burack, J. A., Hodapp, R. M., & Zigler, E. (Eds.), *Handbook on Mental Retardation and Development.* Cambridge University Press, New York.

Leiter, V. (2004) Parental Activism, Professional Dominance, and Early Childhood Disability. *Disability Studies Quarterly* 24. Online. www.dsq-sds.org.

Leiter, V., Krauss, M. W., Anderson, B., & Wells, N. (2004) The Consequences of Caring: Maternal Impacts of Having a Child with Special Needs. *Journal of Family Issues* 25: 379–403.

Panich, M. (2003) Mothers of Intention: Women, Disability, and Activism. In: Stienstra, D. & Wight-Felske, A. (Eds.), *Making Equality: History of Advocacy and Persons with Disabilities in Canada.* Captus Press, Concord, Ontario.

Read, J. (2000) *Disability, the Family and Society: Listening to Mothers.* Open University Press, Philadelphia.

Robinson, C. & Stalker, K. (1998) *Growing Up with Disability.* Jessica Kingsley, New York.

family and community

Betty Hilliard

From the earliest days of sociology, family and community have been central concerns of the discipline. The dense interpenetration of these two dimensions of life was associated in particular with simple societies. This is especially evident in the work of early social thinkers such as the German Ferdinand Tönnies and the Frenchman Frederick Le Play.

The development of more complex societies brought with it the emergence of specialized institutions catering to discrete aspects of social life which previously were catered to within the family and local community (e.g., economic, educational, and religious activities). With the development of these more complex societies the nature of social relationships also changed. It was thought that both family and community, if not actually in decline, were certainly less pivotal than before in the life of society. This was the theme of much work in English-language sociology in the middle decades of the twentieth century. Aspects of it may even be traced in the writings of the highly influential American sociologist Talcott Parsons in his discussions of societal differentiation, the narrowing of the functions of the family, and the sometimes misrepresented concept of the "isolated" nuclear family.

In subsequent decades of the twentieth century the study of family and community became less fashionable in sociology, as an overview of many textbooks of the time will testify. It seemed that in modern society community extended beyond the locality and the family, and their interrelationship no longer seemed unproblematic. In practice, empirical research continued to attest to the persistence of both family and community, and in more recent times the centrality of the family, the significance of community, and the continued importance of the relationship between them have been reasserted (Crow & Maclean 2004).

MEANING OF FAMILY AND COMMUNITY

The definition of these concepts is contested. In empirical terms what constitutes a family has varied throughout history and between cultures. For present purposes the discussion of family and community refers only to these phenomena in western societies. In sociology the debate around a standard definition of family dates from the late 1960s. A functionalist definition of the family as an adaptive system which takes responsibility for a particular range of tasks had been dominant, particularly in the middle decades of the twentieth century. These tasks may include the reproduction, socialization, and maintenance (emotional as well as physical) of members, as well as the exercise of social control and the transmission of culture. However, it is widely recognized that the existence of different family forms across time and cultures makes it very difficult to formulate a definition of family which is both comprehensive and concise.

As a result, many writers now prefer to speak of "families" (Allan & Crow 2001), "family life" (Cheal 2002), or "family practices" (Morgan 1996) rather than deal in such a contested term as "the family." Recent practice in many western welfare systems has expanded the concept of family units to nonmarital cohabiting couples and in some countries to same-sex marriage and partnerships. There is an ideological complexion to much of the debate on what should or should not be regarded as a family. The empirical reality is of course that "family" is not a static construction, but a dynamic phenomenon which is negotiated and renegotiated in relationships, always within the context of a social structure which itself is subject to change. Also, a family exists as part of a network of kin relationships, the salience of which may vary significantly even within a culture, and certainly across cultures.

Similarly, the concept of community refers to a dynamic phenomenon which does not readily lend itself to narrow definition (Crow & Allan 1994). Over 50 years ago Hillery (1955) identified over 90 definitions of community even then. Tönnies's (1963: 65) idea of community as a group of people "essentially united in spite of all separating factors" is still relevant. The concept is essentially associated with a body of people who, although unrelated in a family sense, are conscious of having some things in common which contribute to a sense of shared interests, shared identity, and feelings of solidarity, whether weak or strong. In societies where mobility is limited, people share a common life, and there is much neighborly contact, the resultant interaction builds up a sense of solidarity and "we-ness" associated with a locality, or in the case of nomads, a tribe. Even in neighborhood communities, however, relations of solidarity are not simply between neighbors as a category, but between particular neighbors who have developed sufficiently close relationships. In more recent times the concept of community has been expanded to include groupings beyond the local. Giddens (1990: 21)

asserts that social relations have suffered a "disembedding," meaning "the 'lifting out' of social relations from local contexts." Even as Giddens made this claim, however, there was ample evidence to suggest that in fact locality still persisted as a vibrant dimension of community life in many settings.

INTERWEAVING OF FAMILY AND COMMUNITY IN SOCIAL RESEARCH

As in the theoretical discussions of the nineteenth century, in the middle decades of the twentieth century sociological research reflected a close relationship between the concepts of family and community. Community studies were especially popular at this time, with the emergence of several classic works such as those of the Chicago School in America, Gans's Boston study published as *The Urban Villagers* in 1962, the 1950s Bethnal Green studies in Britain, and the 1930s County Clare study by Arensberg and Kimball in Ireland. Many of these community studies were closely interwoven with accounts of family life. Indeed, some of them may not have been so successful were it not for the involvement of the researcher with families in the community, as was the case with Whyte's association with the Martini family in his study of *Street Corner Society* (1943). This interpenetration of family and community is further borne out in Frankenberg's (1966) overview of community research in Britain.

Similarly, much family research was inextricably linked to community, as for instance the seminal study of *Family and Kinship in East London* (1957) by Young and Willmott. What is evident from much of this work is the identification of family and community with a spatial location; the social linkages are primarily those of family, kin, and neighbors, who were often also friends.

It would not be fair to say that these social linkages did not extend into other domains; frequently, the world of work is a central feature of family and community study. However, there was a particular emphasis on the identification of family and community with a spatial location, and the spatial reconfigurations of modern society impacted on this. The mobility and dispersion which became a more common feature of family life in the 1960s fed into concerns regarding the "eclipse of community," arising from the growth of the suburbs and the establishment of dormitory towns and commuter belts. Indeed, with such change, it has been suggested that family and kinship relations came to be perceived as "the chief, if not the sole, carrier of the idea of community or of a sense of locality" (Morgan 1996: 5). There is a great deal of evidence that family and kin continue to be highly significant in modern society, fulfilling many community-like functions; however, family and community are not interchangeable terms.

Besides significant spatial reconfigurations in modern society, a number of developments in sociology from the 1960s on contributed to what was sometimes perceived as a separation of the two areas of family and community as interrelated foci of sociological research. Penetrating critiques of the sociology of the family, from feminist sources in particular, opened up the family unit to considerable scrutiny and to a recognition of the individual interests, economic dimensions, and power relations within the group.

The subsequent concern with relations *within* the family contributed to moving the focus away from community dimensions of family life. This has been further exacerbated by the emphasis in more recent work on the individual rather than the group, as portrayed in the work of Giddens (1991), Beck (1992), and Beck and Beck-Gernsheim (2002) on individualization. These writers point out that modern society presents us with a myriad of choices not available to earlier generations, which necessitate a degree of personal reflexivity more conducive to individual action than to a collective orientation. Beck (1992) alerts us to the expanded possibilities for individual choice regarding participation in community, and others have identified communities which need roots in neither family nor locality (Willmott 1986). Families, however, continue to be studied in context and that context includes the local spatial setting.

FAMILY AND COMMUNITY IN SIMPLE SOCIETIES

The portrayals of family and community in earlier societies, and particularly in relatively

simple peasant societies, indicate that these dimensions of life, if not exactly coterminous, were at least closely interwoven. For example, Tönnies conceptualized simpler societies as those characterized by close, intimate, holistic bonds of a primary nature, with the dominant social relationships being those of kinship, neighborliness, cooperation, and fellowship (*Gemeinschaft*), and more developed societies as characterized by rational calculation and segmented, specialized, secondary-type association or relationships (*Gesellschaft*). These two terms have been commonly translated in the sociological literature as community and society, respectively. An example of the portrayal of a *gemeinschaft*-type society is to be found in the classic work by the Harvard anthropologists Arensberg and Kimball (2001), *Family and Community in Ireland*. This book, based on ethnographic research in the 1930s, paints a picture of rural life characterized by familism, where family ties are the main organizing and structuring principle in the community, both as a social and an economic system. Economic life in particular revolved around the cooperative interpenetration of family and community. The *meitheal* was a common feature of life in this peasant society; this was a cooperative work group where neighbors worked alongside each other to complete various farm tasks which necessitated help beyond that of the immediate family, such as saving the hay in season. Such cooperative practices brought about an identification of the family with the wider community. This identification of course comes also from many other shared experiences, including local schooling, shared social activity, and participation in group religious practices, identified by Durkheim as a particularly powerful form of community cohesion.

One of the features of community-type societies is an orientation towards the collectivity, as distinct from a focus on the individual. Family members put the collective interests of the group before their own individual needs; this is especially the case as depicted by Arensberg and Kimball (2001) in relationship to landownership and inheritance. (Their portrayal of such issues as non-conflictual has been robustly critiqued: see Gibbon 1973.) Le Play saw this collective orientation as revolving around family enterprises, which acted as a sort of magnet keeping the larger family grouping together in a specific location as a form of community.

Tönnies's ideas were developed, not only theoretically (e.g., by Parsons in his discussion of the pattern variables), but also in the empirical research of the Chicago School, of which Redfield was an exemplary member. While Tönnies recognized that kin networks were not incompatible with urban life, Redfield hypothesized from his comparative research on families and communities in Mexico that the embeddedness of an individual in his family and neighborhood group was a feature of non-city life. In his view, as peasant societies come into contact with urban culture they tend to change in the direction of *Gemeinschaft*-type society. Redfield contrasted "folk" with "urban" societies and associated the latter witha weakening of the cohesive nature of community.

For Le Play and others, the advent of the industrial revolution, and with it the growth of cities, changed the close identification of family and community described above. In his view the movement of individuals off the land to seek paid employment in centers of industrialization led to individualism, self-interest, and a rootlessness which threatened the family. It gave rise to smaller family forms of the type now called nuclear, which lacked the strong structural ties of local community and pre-industrial kinship systems; for this reason he identified the new type of family as "unstable" as compared to what he believed to be the "traditional" stem family (*la famille souche*).

He was not alone in seeing industrialization as a threat to group cohesion. Tönnies and others believed that the modernization which accompanied it was eroding the old ways of life and with them the interpenetration of family and community.

INDUSTRIALIZATION AS A THREAT TO FAMILY AND COMMUNITY

The identification by Le Play and others of nineteenth-century industrialization with an unraveling of ties between family, the wider kin group, and the community became a dominant theme in twentieth-century sociology.

A rapidly changing division of labor was seen as leading to the disruption of social solidarity. The demise of the so-called "traditional" family was linked to the theme of the eclipse of community. In revisiting the research interests of Arensberg and Kimball 30 years later, for example, Brody (1973) represented the changed roles of family members in the community as coinciding with the overthrow of the traditional family.

The mainstream perception of the role of industrialization in the unraveling of the ties between family and community, with the decline of both, has been widely challenged. Many argue that the most significant change factors for social relations occurred much earlier, with Stone (1977) claiming that significant changes in the nature of family relations can be dated to the mid-seventeenth century with the development of affective individualism. Others pointed out that despite theoretical claims concerning the collapse of community, empirical research indicated that community was indeed alive and well. Not only that, it would seem that the concepts of community and family are still perceived as interconnected; Dempsey's (1990) concept of community as "one big happy family" is strongly evocative of Tönnies's perception of communities as large families. To evaluate the extent to which industrialization, along with its attendant features of urbanization and mobility, has indeed caused an unraveling of the interpenetration of family and community, it is necessary to consider these themes in modern sociology.

Family and community exist within the context of society, and the changes in developed western society cannot but be reflected in its members, however they are grouped. Thus the phenomena of globalization and of individualism, so central to discussions of modernity and postmodernity, are also central to discussions of family and community in developed western societies. The development of the concepts of choice, reflexivity, individualization, and globalization in late twentieth-century sociology contributed to a rethinking of the bases of social cohesion in groupings such as family and community. For example, Beck (1992) suggests that there is now a much greater element of individual choice regarding participation in community. Giddens (1991) emphasizes the centrality of reflexivity in the project of the self as an aspect of contemporary life, with its attendant obsessive anxiety and lack of focus on the collective. This theme of individualization was further developed by Beck and Beck-Gernsheim (2002). All of this suggests a movement away from the ascribed nature of group membership associated with family and community.

Nonetheless, as Bauman (1988: 53) asserts, "the need for freedom and the need for social interaction – inseparable, though often at odds with one another – seem to be a permanent feature of the human condition." This, in his view, gives rise to the "dream of community," a fantasy embraced to alleviate the twin fears of loneliness and lack of freedom. Community is in a sense an aspiration. It is one, however, which has tended to enjoy widespread and continuing support, despite exaggerated rumors of its demise. Even very recent work on community attests to positive associations with the concept, despite attention to its potentially negative dimensions.

In the late twentieth century new conceptions of community emerged. Cohen (1985) made a distinction between community as structure and community as symbol. Willmott (1986) distinguished three bases for community; these were locality ("place community"), communities of interest (e.g., occupational groupings), and communities of attachment (e.g., ethnic communities, or groups of people identified as sharing a disability such as deafness). Although it is impossible to draw firm boundaries around these different conceptions, it would seem that the first one, place community, is most likely to be involved with family. Occupational groupings, for example, are less likely to involve all members of a family, although there are many exceptions to this, as in the case of large-scale local employment, local family businesses, or among clergy families. Some have written of "personal communities" beyond the confines of locality, encompassing friends and colleagues as well as kin. Others draw on the concept of "imagined communities," which involve a sense of identification with a notional grouping which does not necessarily involve direct contact (e.g., the idea of nationhood). Recently, too, the idea of Internet communities has also been receiving attention. Clearly, concepts of community in modern and postmodern times emphasize that community does not *necessarily* imply propinquity, although it is a relevant dimension of some kinds of community.

In traditional community studies, however, where there was an interpenetration of family and community, the type of community in question was overwhelmingly that which was associated with a geographical locality. The locality was frequently used as the title of the published study, albeit disguised. Examples of this are *Greenwich Village* by Ware (1935), *Middletown in Transition* by Lynd and Lynd (1937), Littlejohn's (1954) *Westrigg*, Mogey's (1956) work in Oxford and Williams's (1956) in Gosworth, Durant's (1959) *Watling*, Stacey's (1960) work in Banbury, *Yankee City* by Lloyd Warner (1965), Brody's (1973) *Inniskillane*, and Dempsey's *Smalltown* (1990). It has also been noted that the interpenetration of family and community continues to be an important aspect of life in more recent times in places where there is little geographic mobility. It can be argued, then, that while the interpenetration of family and community can be seen to survive in such studies, it is bound up with geographic locality and the significance of shared place for the establishment of personal relationships. However, geographic locality is not an essential feature of the many new conceptualizations of community identified earlier. Further, even in small, relatively static communities, the amount of face-to-face interaction may be lessened with the advent of high levels of car ownership and usage.

A relevant feature of the relationship between family and twentieth-century concepts of community is the privatization of the domestic sphere. This is hypothesized as coinciding with the separation of paid and unpaid work, most especially perhaps in the middle decades of the twentieth century, and suggests the physical restriction of family life to a limited area. Once communities extending beyond the boundaries of geographic locality became common, and family life became more privatized, the interpenetration of family and community could no longer be taken for granted. Perhaps because of this, family and kin often came to be thought of as a community in itself. Crow and Maclean (2004) draw attention to studies showing the enduring nature of kin support even in the face of geographical mobility.

As the aspiration to some form of community has persisted, so has the aspiration to family. Despite the enduring claims of family crisis – which indeed stretch back into at least the nineteenth century – and individual negative experiences, people still look to this human grouping with hope and longing. Both small-scale locally specific and large-scale international empirical research attest to its continued importance for ordinary individuals in everyday life. There is also strong evidence for the persistence of intergenerational bonds. In that family continues in general to embody such attributes as supportiveness, solidarity, and identity, it is sometimes represented as a form of community in itself.

However, an essential aspect of community is that it exists on a more inclusive level than that of family. Even in the geographically local community there are networks of friends and neighbors as well as kin. In other forms of community family may not be of more than tangential significance. Community as it is commonly understood in both a traditional and a contemporary sense is greater than individual families and households. It has essential elements of linkage between individuals and the larger social structure which are on a scale different from the linkages offered by family and kin. In that sense it is always different from, even if sometimes interwoven with, family.

It must also be borne in mind that great variations exist in the relations between individual family members and the family's networks. Such relations are often highly gendered. In Arensberg and Kimball's (2001) study, for example, while the men went out "visiting" (*ag bothántaiocht*), women, once married, were largely confined to the home place. In other studies of traditional industries like mining, men are often portrayed as socializing with workmates while their wives were, again, far more home- and kin-centered. Women have often been seen as central to community life, especially in urban working-class settings. In some welfare provision there may even appear to be a confusion of "community" with "women"; there has been much comment on how the state has embraced a version of "community care," which in practice has meant imposing heavy responsibilities for care on the family, and usually on women in the family. In another vein, Bott in her classic study *Family and Social Network* showed that spouses' linkage with their wider networks varied with the nature of the conjugal role relationship. Other structural factors are also of significance for variations in the family – community relationship, including age, class, ethnicity, and differential power. The significance of *local* community networks is often a feature of an individual's stage in the life course. A potential local network is likely to be much more salient for families with young children than for young single employed persons.

A particularly important development is the now widespread engagement of mothers in the paid labor force. This has prompted a rethinking of gender roles. Much of the putative change is in attitude rather than in behavior, but one outcome has been the emergence of a new concern with work–family balance. This in turn has led to a new interest in the related areas of community, work, and family. Indications of this focus are seen in the establishment of the journal *Community, Work, and Family* in 1998. While the orientation may be changing, there can be no doubt that the themes of family and community will continue to exercise the sociological community on into the twenty-first century. While there is change, there is also continuity, and above all there is diversity in the relations between the two phenomena.

CONCLUSION

Having considered some of the issues relating to the interrelationship of community and family, it is clear that these two aspects of society continue to be of major concern to sociologists. Both are understood differently today, however, than they were by the social theorists of the nineteenth century. Various concepts of community have developed which no longer assume that family is a central component. The emergence of communities of interest and of attachment suggest that the interpenetration of family and community associated with simpler societies is no longer an *indispensable* feature of community. Globalization contributes to the development of occupational communities not rooted in family or kinship networks (although in the case of employment by transnational corporations in less developed societies these links may endure). However, family and community continue to be closely interwoven in settings characterized by limited geographical or social mobility. Even where there are high levels of such mobility in modern western societies, shared place remains an important basis for the establishment of personal relationships, and technological advances in transport and communication facilitate the maintenance of such relationships. While the relationship between the concepts of family and community has changed, and the dense interpenetration of these phenomena has become attenuated, it is by no means defunct. Notwithstanding the reality of expanded choice and its attendant anxieties in modern society, both family and community have remained central values in western cultures, albeit with more developed conceptualizations of each. These are, after all, the contexts within which most people spend the major part of their lives.

SEE ALSO: Community; Community and Economy; Family Diversity; Family Migration; Family Structure; Immigrant Families; Retirement Communities; Secondary Groups; Social Worlds; Urban Community Studies; Urbanization

REFERENCES AND SUGGESTED READINGS

Allan, G. & Crow, G. (2001) *Families, Households and Society*. Palgrave, Basingstoke.

Arensberg, C. & Kimball, S. (2001 [1940]) *Family and Community in Ireland*. CLASP Press, Ennis.

Bauman, Z. (1988) *Freedom*. Open University Press, Milton Keynes.

Beck, U. (1992) *Risk Society*. Sage, London.

Beck, U. & Beck-Gernsheim, E. (2002) *Individualization*. Sage, London.

Brody, H. (1973) *Inishkillane: Change and Decline in the West of Ireland*. Allen Lane, London.

Cheal, D. (2002) *Sociology of Family Life*. Palgrave, Basingstoke.

Cohen, A. (1985) *The Symbolic Construction of Community*. Routledge, London.

Crow, G. & Allan, G. (1994) *Community Life*. Harvester Wheatsheaf, Hemel Hempstead.

Crow, G. & Maclean, C. (2004) Families and Local Communities. In: Scott, J., Treas, J., & Richards, M. (Eds.), *The Blackwell Companion to the Sociology of Families*. Blackwell, Oxford, pp. 69–83.

Dempsey, K. (1990) *Smalltown: A Study of Social Inequality, Cohesion and Belonging*. Oxford University Press, Oxford.

Frankenberg, R. (1966) *Communities in Britain*. Penguin, London.

Gibbon, P. (1973) Arensberg and Kimball Revisited. *Economy and Society* 2: 479–98.

Giddens, A. (1990) *The Consequences of Modernity*. Polity Press, Cambridge.

Giddens, A. (1991) *Modernity and Self-Identity*. Stanford University Press, Stanford.

Hillery, G. (1955) Definitions of Community: Areas of Agreement. *Rural Sociology* 20: 72–84.

Morgan, D. H. J. (1996) *Family Connections*. Polity Press, Cambridge.

Stone, L. (1977) *Family, Sex and Marriage in England 1500–1800*. Weidenfeld & Nicolson, London.

Tönnies, F. (1963 [1887]) *Community and Society*. Harper & Row, New York.

Willmott, P. (1986) *Social Networks, Informal Care and Public Policy*. Policy Studies Institute, London.

family conflict

Jean Kellerhals

Although present since the nineteenth century, particularly in Marxist thinking (more specifically in Engels's work), interest in family conflict within the sociology of the family only really developed as a theme during the 1960s and 1970s.

In the 1950s the dominant functionalist perspective tended to analyze the family in terms of internal equilibrium and its complementarity to the global society. Parsons's point of view (notably, Parsons & Bales 1955) is that the values of competition, achievement, and rationality in relation to the workings of the economic, educational, and political systems find a necessary counterweight in the family. This privileges affective expression, emphasizing "being" over "having," and the totality of the person over his or her division into functions. In addition, the division of work between the man and the woman ensures good management of the expressive group dimension (by the woman) and the instrumental group dimension (by the man), and assures adequate socialization of the children. Through this process of socialization on the one hand, and the stabilization of the adult personality on the other, the family was seen to provide society with motivated and well-oriented "normal" people, and at the same time procure the resources and abilities necessary for the family to function.

Important socio-demographic changes started intervening in the western world during the 1960s, including rapid growth in divorce rates, falls in marriage, significant declines in fecundity, increases in cohabitation, and higher levels of employment of married women (Roussel 1985). Somewhat paradoxically, research attention was drawn at this time to concerns about overloading the family system; the reproduction of the inequalities in marriage and the family; the effect of cultural tensions on domestic intimacy; and the lack of resources available to some families.

As much in conservative theories as in radical ones, conflict has consequently been viewed as an intrinsic component of family dynamics, with its nature and causes being investigated along with its management.

MODELS OF FAMILY CONFLICT

In examining the nature of family conflict, we need to be clear about some commonsense assumptions. First, separation and divorce are not valid indicators of family conflict overall: a frequent observation is that many marriages are very stable, although unhappy or conflicting. Second, family conflict is not limited to open fights: quite often, tensions in the couple or the family remain silent; quite often also, they are not perceived as such by the entire family. And third, reciprocated differences of opinion or taste do not necessarily entail family conflict. More constructively, family conflict can be understood as relational tensions – overt or latent – arising out of the difficulty the family group has in defining its objectives, in finding the resources and the organizational structure suitable for reaching its goals, or in safeguarding

sufficiently its members' individual interests. In broad terms, five distinct models for explaining the reasons for such family conflict have been produced.

"Deficit" Model

This model highlights the role of socialization, arguing that inadequacies in people's socialization experiences contribute to family conflict. For example, those who marry at a young age tend to be relatively immature psychologically and socially. This is liable to compromise how well they adapt to marriage and family life, a factor linked to high rates of separation and divorce. Similarly, growing up in a disunited or conflictual family not only increases the probability of maladjustment but is also likely to limit opportunities for learning suitable modes of relating. Poverty and economic insecurity of the family during one's childhood are seen as undermining processes of childhood socialization and increasing the risk of conjugal conflict in adulthood. Low levels of educational achievement are also seen as compromising the development of aptitudes for negotiation and communication, both of which are judged as essential for success in contemporary marriage. Above all, the deficit model stresses the lack of resources available in particular families (Cherlin 1999: 365–422). In these, the gap between the family's objectives and the means at its disposal becomes too great, resulting in high levels of frustration (Webster et al. 1995). From the same point of view, such families may also be deprived of support because they lack the social integration and/or links with kin which can help prevent conflict (Shelton 1987).

"Overload" Model

This model takes a more historical perspective and stresses the extent to which the progressive weakening of public participation has led to individuals placing too great an emphasis on the private sphere of home, family, and children (Ariès 1978). Under these conditions, the individual is led to expect the family to compensate for the failings of the wider society by meeting all his or her needs. Some, such as

Sennett (1974), see this as the product of the disappearance of the "public man." Others, like Donzelot (1977), see it as the consequence of specific family policies designed to undermine class consciousness and solidarity. Either way, the family as a refuge is transformed into the family as a ghetto. The growth of family conflict as expressed through increasing levels of divorce is thus interpreted, by Berger and Kellner (1964) for instance, not as a loss of family functions, but as the expression of this excessive investment in these very important expectations of family and conjugal life (Roussel 1985).

"Cultural Tensions" Model

In this model the emphasis is placed on the gap that exists between the commitments required by and implicated in family life and the importance attached to the individual in contemporary culture. For authors such as Bellah et al. (1986), the individual today is seen above all as having a moral responsibility to search for personal identity and authenticity of the self. That is, they have a "duty" of "self-discovery" and "self-fulfillment." This endless quest for the self translates into a weakening of family commitments and responsibilities. It is this same critique of the growth of individualism within contemporary social life that makes Popenoe (1988) state that the family is functioning increasingly less effectively as a mediator between the individual and society.

"Conflict of Interest" Model

In this model the drive for equality in contemporary family relationships is seen as in opposition to broader structural inequalities affecting both employment and the domestic sphere. More specifically, the growth of dual-career families has not translated into conjugal equality, as most wives continue to carry a far greater responsibility than their husbands for domestic labor and household management. Moreover, in spite of increasing educational achievements, women are generally the ones who adapt their employment commitments to family needs, thereby often compromising their promotion prospects. In contrast, husbands are more often able to use the family resources as a springboard for their occupational mobility. Of course, this tension between equality and inequality frequently leads to feelings of injustice which are sometimes expressed in divorce, sometimes in psychological distress, and sometimes in violence towards the children. However, as equity theory would suggest, feelings of injustice are not directly proportional to the degree of inequality: different cognitive processes often lead to both the husband and wife tolerating this for the sake of higher interests judged to be more important. From this point of view, the concept of power acquires great importance. The first empirical studies on this theme notably showed that decision-making powers in the family are strongly correlated with the gap in the respective socioeconomic resources of the spouses (Blood & Wolfe 1960). Moreover, later studies drawing on resource theory also show that family negotiation depends heavily on the resources available to each spouse outside the nuclear family. While these gender divisions may benefit the family collectively, they also increase the social distance between the husband and wife.

"Anomie" Model

This model focuses on the degree to which contemporary couples are required to negotiate the organization of their relationship individually because traditional models of marriage are no longer considered appropriate or legitimate. Among other things, this involves defining family priorities; organizing the division of work inside and outside the home; defining the areas of intimacy and privacy; agreeing on the sharing of material resources; and defining the extent and intensity of contacts with the world outside. Yet these constructions are often rendered conflictual by (1) subjective uncertainty toward the duration of the union; (2) incompatibilities between individualist aspirations and fusional models of conjugal relationships; and (3) tension between the equalitarian aspirations and the unequal status of the husband and wife. This situation can generate very high levels of stress, particularly when children are young (Kellerhals et al. 2004).

MANAGEMENT OF CONFLICT

Various sociologists have been concerned with investigating ways in which family conflict can be resolved. Many recognize that ideologies of love often result in the husband and wife feeling guilty about any conflicts they have, with the result that any potentially positive consequences of these conflicts tend to be masked. Not only can this compound the conflict, but it may also lead to a more serious crisis (Eshleman 1997; Olson & DeFrain 1997).

Different approaches have been developed to facilitate conflict resolution. Some, such as Kilmann and Thomas (1975), focus on the degree of aggression and cooperation within the relationship, and on this basis define different strategies for conflict resolution – collaborative, competitive, compromise, avoidance, accommodating. Other approaches oppose "task-oriented" strategies with "relation-oriented" strategies (Kellerhals et al. 2004), with conflict resolution being dependent on the equilibrium established between these two. A synthesis of studies on this theme lead Olson and DeFrain (1997) to identify six basic steps in conflict resolution: (1) clarifying the issue; (2) finding out what each person wants; (3) identifying various alternatives; (4) deciding how to negotiate; (5) solidifying the agreements; and (6) reviewing and renegotiating. Other approaches suggest that there are three principal dimensions to the resolution process: the degree of activity (decision-taking, investment of ad hoc resources, evaluation of the effects); cognitive elaboration (definition of the stressor, communicating its purpose, gathering pertinent information); and the extent of relational concern (attention given to cohesion, to mutual support, and to relational re-equilibrium) (Widmer et al. 2003). These authors show that a propensity to over-invest in one of the terms (action, cognition, or relation) is a frequent reaction to the anxiety engendered by the conflict. Equilibrium between the three dimensions can be expected more commonly in families with good levels of cohesion and flexibility.

SEE ALSO: Divisions of Household Labor; Domestic Violence; Engels, Friedrich; Family Poverty; Family Therapy; Inequalities in Marriage; Marital Power/Resource Theory; Marital Quality; Socialization

REFERENCES AND SUGGESTED READINGS

Ariès, P. (1978) La Famille et la ville. *Esprit* 1: 3–12.

Bellah, R., Madsen, R., Sullivan, W., Swidler, A., & Tipton, S. (1986) *Habits of the Heart*. Harper & Row, New York.

Berger, P. & Kellner, H. (1964) Marriage and the Construction of Reality. *Diogenes* 45: 1–25.

Blood, R. & Wolfe, D. (1960) *Husbands and Wives: The Dynamics of Married Living*. Free Press, New York.

Cherlin, A. (1999) *Public and Private Families*. McGraw Hill, Boston.

Donzelot, J. (1977) *La Polices des familles*. Minuit, Paris.

Eshleman, J. (1997) *The Family*. Allyn & Bacon, Boston.

Kellerhals, J., Widmer, E., & Levy, R. (2004) *Mesure et demesure du couple*. Payot, Paris.

Kilmann, R. & Thomas, K. (1975) Interpersonal Conflict: Handling Behaviour as Reflections of Jungian Personality Dimensions. *Psychological Reports* 7: 971–80.

Olson, D. & DeFrain, J. (1997) *Marriage and the Family: Diversity and Strengths*. Mayfield Publishing, Mountain View, CA.

Parsons, T. & Bales, R. (1955) *Family, Socialization and Interaction Process*. Free Press, New York.

Popenoe, D. (1988) *Disturbing the Nest*. Aldine de Gruyter, New York.

Roussel, L. (1985) *La Famille incertaine*. Odile Jacob, Paris.

Sennett, R. (1974) *Les Tyrannies de l'intimité*. Seuil, Paris.

Shelton, B. A. (1987) Variations in Divorce Rates by Community Size: A Test of the Social Integration Explanation. *Journal of Marriage and the Family* 49: 827–32.

Webster, P., Orbuch, T., & House, J. (1995) Effects of Childhood Family Background on Adult Marital Quality and Perceived Stability. *American Journal of Sociology* 1001: 404–32.

Widmer, E., Kellerhals, J., & Levy, R. (2003) *Couples contemporains: cohésion, régulation et conflit*. Seismo, Zurich.

family demography

Lynne M. Casper

Family demography is a subfield of demography and is the study of the changing nature of intergenerational and gender ties that bind individuals into households and family units. The core of family demography uses basic demographic information collected about household members, including the numbers of members, their relationships to each other, and each person's sex, age, and marital status, to describe the composition of families and households. *Composition* describes the *structure* of families and households: the set of statuses and associated roles that are important for the functioning of society. American families and households have diverse and complex structures. For example, households can contain married couples, cohabiting couples, single mothers, children, grandparents, other relatives (e.g., brothers, sisters, or in-laws), roommates, or simply one person living alone. Family composition is the result of demographic *processes* or family related events such as marriage, divorce, and fertility or childbearing. Changes in the timing, number, and sequences of these events transform family and household composition. Family demographers aggregate the composition and processes of individual families into larger units (e.g., nations, states, counties, neighborhoods) to examine family change in societies and other units. They aggregate them separately by other social and economic groups (e.g., racial and ethnic groups, poor families, immigrants) and by countries to examine family variation. Thus, family demographers study family change and variation to understand both individual and societal behavior.

Several theoretical strands are influential in interpreting family change and variation in family demographic research. They include (second) demographic transition theory, the life course perspective, household and family decision-making theories, biodemographic interactions, and the focus on culture and context.

The bedrock of demographic data analysis on family change is descriptive cross-sectional and trend analysis of family structures and processes, most often with census or survey data, although increasingly qualitative methods are also used. The field of demography has its own toolkit full of measures and methods that are suited to studying family change. Measures of age and age-related processes are fundamental. Change is understood as reflecting age, period, or cohort processes or effects; explanations of change emphasize the aging of

the population (or life course change of individuals), broad, sweeping societal or time period effects, and/or the replacement of older cohorts by successively younger ones with different life experiences. An indispensable measure in family demography is the rate: the number of people experiencing the event out of the population "at risk" of experiencing that event. Another important tool for examining family change is decomposition, in which family change is empirically separated into two components: the proportion of change attributable to shifts in population composition versus that part that is due to change in the likelihood that some family event occurs. However, family demography has increasingly moved toward explaining family change and variation. In the last three decades, a number of panel surveys and various labor force and educational cohort studies have been developed. These studies include many more "explanatory" variables and provide prospective sequencing data that are better suited to inferring causality.

COMMON DEFINITIONS

The core of family demography continues to be based on concepts developed by the US Census Bureau. A household, as defined by the US Census Bureau, consists of one or more people who occupy a house, apartment, or other residential unit (but not "group quarters" such as dormitories). One of the people who owns or rents the residence is designated the *householder*. The householder is said to *maintain* the household. For the purposes of examining family and household composition using census data, two types of households have been defined: family and non-family. A *family household* has at least two members related by blood, marriage, or adoption, one of whom is the householder. *Families* consist of all related people in a family household. Families can be maintained by married couples with or without children or by a man or woman with children and no spouse in the home. A *non-family household* can either be a person living alone or a householder living only with non-relatives. Family units within family or non-family households that do not include the householder are *subfamilies*. Subfamilies include either a married couple, with or without children, or a parent–child pair. A *related subfamily* is related to the householder, whereas an *unrelated subfamily* is not. *Family groups* are family households plus all related and unrelated subfamilies. For example, a family household that is maintained by a grandmother and contains her daughter and her daughter's daughter has two family groups. *Children* include sons and daughters by birth, stepchildren, and adopted children of the householder regardless of the child's age or marital status. *Own children* are a subset of *children* and identify the householder or family reference person as a parent in the household, family, or subgroup – they are usually defined as never-married children under the age of 18.

FAMILY AND HOUSEHOLD COMPOSITION AND LIVING ARRANGEMENTS

Changes in the number and types of households depend on population growth, shifts in the age composition of the population, and decisions individuals make about their living arrangements. Demographic trends in marriage, cohabitation, divorce, fertility, and mortality also influence family and household composition. Economic shifts and improvements in the health of the elderly over time can also have an impact.

In the US, families have traditionally accounted for a large majority of all households – as recently as 1940, nine out of ten households were family households. This proportion decreased steadily to 81 percent in 1970 and by 2003 family households made up only 68 percent of all households, with the remaining 32 percent accounted for by non-family living arrangements. Part of the increase in non-family households was due to the growth in one-person households – people living alone. The proportion of households containing one person increased from 17 percent in 1970 to 26 percent in 2003.

The increase in non-family households resulted from many social, economic, and demographic shifts. A postponement of marriage took place after 1960 leading to a substantial increase in the percentage of young, never-married adults and to greater diversity and fluidity in living arrangements in young adulthood. In 1970, 6 percent of women and 9 percent of men aged 30–34 had never married. By 2003, these figures increased to 23 percent and 33 percent, respectively. The delay of marriage means that young adults in 2003 were less likely to be living with their spouses and more likely to be living alone, in a parent's home, or with roommates, than they were in the past. Thirty-one percent of men aged 18–24 lived with their spouses in 1970, for example, while only 9 percent lived with a spouse in 2003. A similar drop occurred for women: from 45 percent in 1970 to 16 percent in 2003. As a declining share of young adults chose married life, a greater share lived on their own, with roommates, or cohabited with an unmarried partner. In 1970, 15 percent of women and 13 percent of men were living in these arrangements compared with 38 percent and 37 percent, respectively, in 2003.

The delay in marriage coincided with an increase in cohabitation and these trends also decreased the proportion of married-couple families and increased the proportion of non-family households. Unmarried-couple (cohabiting) households have grown dramatically since 1970 and in 2003 numbered 4.6 million, or over 4 percent of households. Cohabitation historically has been most likely to occur before a first marriage, but, more recently, cohabitation has been replacing remarriage after divorce occurs. Researchers have offered several explanations for the rapid increase in cohabitation, including increased uncertainty about the stability of marriage, the erosion of norms against cohabitation and sexual relations outside of marriage, the wider availability of reliable birth control, and increased individualism and secularization. Some have argued that cohabitation allows a couple to experience the benefits of an intimate relationship without committing to marriage. If a cohabiting relationship isn't successful, one can simply move out; if a marriage is not successful, one suffers through a sometimes lengthy and messy divorce.

Significant improvements in the health and economic well-being of the elderly over the period have increased the life expectancy and the quality of life of both men and women. This means that elderly men and women are increasingly able to maintain their own homes.

Not only has this augmented the number of households, but also the fact that women continue to outlive men by a significant number of years has led to a greater number and proportion of one-person non-family households. The proportion of women 65 years and over who live alone grew from 34 percent in 1970 to 40 percent in 2003.

Households and families have become smaller over time, with the most profound changes occurring at the extremes – the largest and smallest households. Between 1970 and 2003 the share of households with five or more people decreased from 21 percent to 10 percent. During the same period, the share of households with only one or two people increased from 46 percent to 60 percent. Another measure of household size is the average number of members in the household. Between 1970 and 2003 the average number of people per household declined from 3.1 to 2.6.

Changes in fertility, marriage, divorce, and mortality all contributed to the shrinkage of American families and households. Between 1970 and 2003, births to married women declined sharply while births to unmarried women increased. These two trends decreased the proportion of two-parent families and increased the proportion of one-parent families, which also tend to have fewer children. The cumulative effect of these trends was to shrink family and household size. Increases in divorce also reduced the size of households and families; divorce generally separates one household into two smaller households. Meanwhile, the proportion of divorced people increased about fourfold from 2 percent to 8 percent for men and from 3 percent to 11 percent for women from 1970 to 2003.

The delay in marriage and improvements in the mortality and health of the elderly increased one-person households, thereby decreasing the average family and household size.

Other aspects of the composition of families changed as well. The number of families maintained by people with no spouse at home increased rapidly from 1970 to 2003. Single-mother families grew by 147 percent from 5.5 million in 1970 to 13.6 million in 2003. Single-father families grew even more over the same period, tripling from 1.2 million to 4.7 million. By contrast, married-couple families grew from 44.1 million to 50.7 million over the same period – only a 15 percent increase. These differential increases shifted the composition of family households from married-couple to single-mother and single-father families. In 1970, married couples maintained 89 percent of family households, but by 2003 this proportion had declined to 72 percent.

Several demographic trends have affected the shift from two-parent to one-parent families. A larger proportion of births occurred to unmarried women in 1990 compared with 1970, increasing the proportion of never-married parents. The delay of marriage also augmented the risk of a nonmarital birth, because adults were single for more years. In addition, the growth in divorce among couples with children increased the proportion of unmarried parents.

Most of the decline in family households reflects the decrease in the share of married-couple households with children. In 2003, 48 percent of families contained own children compared with 56 percent in 1970. These changes reflect several demographic trends, including the delay of childbearing, the decline in the number of children people have, the delay of marriage, and the aging of the population. Due to the trend toward delayed marriage and childbearing, younger families were more likely to be childless in 2003 than in 1970. For example, in 1970, 94 percent of women aged 30–34 had been married at least once; of them, only 12 percent were childless. In 2002–3, only 77 percent of women aged 30–34 had ever been married; of them, 19 percent were childless. Thus, fewer women in these prime childbearing ages had ever been married in 1990 and nearly twice as many of them were childless (reflecting primarily a delay in childbearing, but also a delay in marriage).

Change in family and household structure began slowly in the 1960s, just as society was embarking on some of the most radical social changes in US history, and the leading edge of the huge baby boom generation was reaching adulthood. The steepest decline in the share of family households was in the 1970s when the first baby boomers entered their twenties. By the 1980s, change was still occurring, but at a much less rapid pace. By the mid-1990s, household composition reached relative equilibrium, where it has been since.

FAMILY CHANGE IN OTHER INDUSTRIALIZED COUNTRIES

The changes in family that occurred in the US have also occurred throughout most industrialized countries, for many of the same reasons. In most European countries marriage rates have been declining since the late 1960s and early 1970s. Since the 1980s, marriage rates have continued to decline, but at a slower pace. Europeans are also postponing marriage. For example, the median age at first marriage in Sweden was 25 in 1975, but increased to 29 by 1995. The increase was even greater in Denmark: from 23 in 1975 to 29 in 1995. Although women tend to marry earlier in most other Northern and Central European countries, the average age of marriage increased from 1975 to 1995 and now stands at 26 or above in these countries.

As in the US, a rise in cohabitation has contributed to the decline and postponement of marriage. In the 1960s in Sweden and Denmark, cohabitation as a prelude to or an alternative to marriage began to rise. By the 1970s, this type of cohabitation began to rise in other countries. Postmarital cohabitation has also increased.

Women in other industrialized countries are postponing births and having more nonmarital births. For example, in most European countries, the age-specific fertility rates declined for women under 25 and rose substantially for women aged 30 and over in the 1980s. Nonmarital births in Scandinavia grew about 20 percent between 1975 to 1988. In Northern Europe, Australia, and New Zealand the growth rate was not as large – in the single digits for all countries except for the United Kingdom (16 percent) and France (18 percent).

SOCIAL DEMOGRAPHY OF THE FAMILY

Early family demographic studies documented change and variation in fertility, marriage, households and families, and living arrangements, with each of these areas typically studied in isolation. Growing diversity in the timing, number, and sequencing of family events led researchers in the US and other industrialized countries to study the interaction of these events (e.g., nonmarital childbearing) and to incorporate other events (e.g., cohabitation) into family demography to provide a more accurate accounting of family change and variation. Family demography has also expanded to examine the causes and consequences of family change and variation, including the social and economic context in which it occurs. This change has led many demographers who study the family to refer to the field as *social* demography of the family. It has also increased the number of disciplines that have adopted the demographic perspective. Historically, the majority of family demographers had training in sociology and a substantial minority had training in economics. More researchers in the fields of anthropology, child development, family studies, genetics, geography, medicine, psychology, and public health have come to employ the concepts and tools of family demography.

Several key changes in the family occurring in developed countries in the second half of the twentieth century have expanded the borders of family demography beyond the traditional measures of family composition, processes, and living arrangements. Historically, family demography only included the study of marriage, remarriage, and divorce. However, changing union (marriage and cohabitation) formation and dissolution, low fertility, increases in nonmarital fertility and a growing diversity of family structures, changing intergenerational relations, and increases in women's paid work have made it necessary for family demographers to study a broad set of processes to adequately characterize and explain family change and variation and to explore the consequences of these changes.

The rise of cohabitation and the delay and decline in marriage have prompted family demographers to examine cohabitation. Cohabitation, marriage, divorce, and childbearing are entwined in complicated ways. Cohabitation increasingly precedes marriage, is often an alternative to remarriage after separation and divorce, and, in several European countries, has become a long-term substitute for marriage.Intimate Union Formation and Dissolution Tracking and explaining the increase in cohabiting couples, both heterosexual and same-sex, and examining the consequences of cohabitation for adults and children require not only a better understanding of cohabitation, but also a better understanding of marriage; the meaning, value, and nature of both of these relationships are poorly understood in contemporary developed economies.

A second area of family change of increasing interest is explaining low fertility in industrialized economies. Fertility is a core focus of family demography, but until relatively recently most research focused on high fertility in developing regions of the world. The rapid decline in fertility in all parts of the developing world has shifted attention away from high fertility and toward the very low fertility levels of Southern and Eastern Europe and Japan. Most of these countries have fertility levels far below the 2.1 children per woman needed to replace the population. Explanations for these low levels of fertility include changing normative, social, and economic contexts, particularly women's changing work and family roles.

Third, recent increases in childrearing within cohabiting and other nonmarital unions have also heightened the awareness that trends in childbearing and childrearing cannot be studied independently of union (marriage and cohabitation) formation and dissolution. Whereas timing of entry into marriage, parenthood, and, to a much lesser extent, cohabitation can be distinguished empirically, conceptually and analytically they are intertwined. In the US, where fertility levels remain close to replacement (around two births per woman, on average), the questions of greatest interest are about two distinct fertility behaviors that characterize US fertility trends. On the one hand, both marriage and children are being postponed to older ages among the better educated segments of the population. On the other hand, there seems to be increased willingness to disassociate childbearing from marriage altogether, particularly among less educated, minority groups – to have children relatively early, outside of marriage, and to raise them in environments that will not include two co-residential biological parents. Policymakers and researchers seek to better understand the underlying causes of these different behaviors. They are also interested in the consequences for children and men and women of the separation of marriage and

childbearing, on the one hand, and the postponement of both, on the other, and how the consequences vary for different groups within the population.

Fourth, the intergenerational family is changing in form – from a *pyramid* structure with few living grandparents and many children and grandchildren to the *beanpole family* with more grandparents than parents and, increasingly, more parents than children. Demographically, these changes occur when mortality is low, life expectancy is high, and fertility is relatively low, as in most industrialized countries. Changes in marriage, divorce, and childbearing complicate the intergenerational picture, as financial and care obligations are no longer necessarily dependent on biological or marital ties. In groups where marriage is increasingly fragile, intergenerational ties may supersede nuclear ties in the rearing of children. Researchers are interested in the economic and social consequences of these changes.

Fifth, the steady increase in women's labor force participation in the US and most other industrialized countries, especially among married women, in the second half of the twentieth century, and the accompanying decline in the one-wage-earner, two-parent family, provides a greatly altered context for understanding and interpreting family demographic trends. The interrelationship between increased female employment and changes in union formation, fertility, cross-generation caregiving and the gender division of labor in non-market spheres is receiving increased attention in the family demographic literature of both developed and developing economies.

SEE ALSO: Demographic Transition Theory; Family Theory; Fertility: Low; Fertility: Transitions and Measures; Households; Intimate Union Formation and Dissolution; Life Course and Family; Marriage; Second Demographic Transition

REFERENCES AND SUGGESTED READINGS

Bachrach, C. & and McNicoll, G. (2003) Causal Analysis in the Population Sciences: Introduction. *Population and Development Review* 29: 442–7.

Bengtson, V. L. (2001) Beyond the Nuclear Family: The Increasing Importance of Multigenerational Bonds. *Journal of Marriage and Family* 63: 1–16.

Bianchi, S. M. & Casper, L. M. (2004) Explanations of Family Change: A Family Demographic Perspective. In: Bengtson, V., Acock, A., Allen, K., Dilworth-Anderson, P., & Klein, D. (Eds.), *Sourcebook of Family Theory and Methods*. Thousand Oaks, CA: Sage.

Casper, L. M. & Bianchi, S. M. (2002) *Change and Continuity in the American Family*. Sage, Thousand Oaks, CA.

Casper, L. M. & O'Connell, M. (2000) Family and Household Composition of the Population. In: Anderson, M. J. (Ed.), *Encyclopedia of the US Census*. CQ Press, Washington, DC.

Daly, M. & Wilson, M. I. (2000) The Evolutionary Psychology of Marriage and Divorce. In: Waite, L. J. et al. (Eds.), *The Ties That Bind*. Aldine de Gruyter, New York, pp. 91–110.

Goldscheider, F. K. (1995) Interpolating Demography with Families and Households. *Demography* 32 (August): 471–80.

Lesthaeghe, R. (1995) The Second Demographic Transition in Western Countries: An Interpretation. In: Mason, K. O. & Jensen, A.-M. (Eds.), *Gender and Family Change in Industrialized Countries*. Clarendon Press, Oxford, pp. 17–62.

Lundberg, S. & Pollak, R. A. (1996) Bargaining and Distribution in Marriage. *Journal of Economic Perspectives* 10 (Fall): 139–58.

Seltzer, J. A., Bachrach, C. A., & Bianchi, S. M. et al. (2005) Designing New Models for Explaining Family Change and Variation: Challenges for Family Demographers. *Journal of Marriage and the Family*.

Waite, L. J., Bachrach, C. A., Hindin, M., Thomson, E., & Thornton, A. (Eds.) (2000) *The Ties That Bind: Perspective on Marriage and Cohabitation*. Aldine de Gruyter, New York.

Willis, R. J. (1987) What Have We Learned from the Economics of the Family? *American Economic Review* 77: 68–71.

family diversity

Brad van Eeden-Moorefield and David H. Demo

Family living arrangements in the US and throughout much of the world are considerably more diverse, pluralistic, and fluid than they were just a few decades ago. We have witnessed profound demographic changes, including longer life expectancy, postponed marriage and childbearing, dramatic increases in both childbearing and childrearing outside of marriage, and substantial growth of singlehood, cohabitation, divorce, and remarriage (Teachman et al. 2000). As a result, there has been a sharp increase in the visibility of diverse family forms such as single-parent (mostly single-mother) families, stepfamilies, households headed by gays and lesbians, and families living in poverty (Rank 2000). These changes have stirred considerable debate surrounding the definition of family. For example, do two cohabiting adults and their dependent children constitute a family? Are they still a family without the presence of children in the household? What if the two adults are gay or lesbian?

Beginning in the middle of the twentieth century, a strong value was attached to a "benchmark" family type in the United States, or what is commonly termed the "traditional" nuclear family. Following World War II, rapid social changes including men returning to the labor force, a post-war economic boom, an increasing standard of living, increases in marriage and birth rates, and a decline in the divorce rate supported a set of values and beliefs that privileged the two biological parent, male breadwinner, female homemaker family. Although families of the 1950s often are viewed with nostalgia, evidence shows that many traditional families were characterized by severe inequities, male dominance, men's overinvolvement in work and underinvolvement in family activities, wife abuse, and alcoholism (Coontz 1992). Since then, changing historical contexts and powerful social movements (e.g., civil rights, women's rights, gay and lesbian liberation, and men's movements) have been associated with the establishment of a wide variety of family forms, making the diversity of families more visible and normative, and spurring debates over the future of marriage and whether there is one best type of family.

There are many issues and complexities inherent in studying and defining families. Our purpose here is to provide an overview of family diversity by (1) defining the study of family diversity and its historical context; (2) defining family; (3) discussing the major structural dimensions of diversity (e.g., ethnicity, socioeconomic status, sexual orientation); and

(4) illustrating the diversity characterizing family processes.

DEFINING FAMILY DIVERSITY AS A FIELD OF STUDY

Historically, the term family diversity referred to variations from a traditional family. This implied that there was one best type of family, and that all other family types were dysfunctional and deviant. In a more contemporary view, family diversity refers to a broad range of characteristics or dimensions on which families vary, along with a recognition that there are a multitude of different family types that function effectively. Family diversity thus refers to variations along structural or demographic dimensions (e.g., race/ethnicity, socioeconomic status), as well as in family processes (e.g., communication and parenting behaviors).

We caution readers to be particularly mindful of comparisons in which one family is upheld as a "better" family than that to which it is compared. In this, we do not take a purely relativistic view by assuming that all families function effectively, nor do we believe there is one best type of family. Our view is that families are diverse and there are many ways that families can function effectively regardless of family type. As stated earlier, historical accounts of family diversity were concerned with pathological views that perpetuated marginalization of many family types. However, social movements and demographic changes have increased the visibility of diverse families, thus facilitating a shift away from pathological views to a recognition of family strengths and resilience (Walsh 1998). Thus, the study of family diversity is embedded within historical and social contexts, as is the intensifying debate over how to define family.

DEFINING FAMILY

Families are characterized by a rich variety of compositions that mix gender, ethnicity, sexuality, and marital history. Families also vary widely in their dynamics, or how family members interact with and relate to one another. As a result, family researchers have invested considerable energy in designing and conducting studies that examine the flexibility and creativity with which individuals create and sustain a sense of family. To be sure, there are myriad ways that individuals experience and define family. However, there is a need to define family in a way that is useful, meaningful, and inclusive, yet not devoid of theoretical or empirical meaning. It also is important to recognize the difficulty in establishing an appropriate and inclusive definition of family that is flexible over time, i.e., a definition that reflects historical, demographic, social, and family change. No definition of family applies universally across cultures and historical periods (Coontz 2000).

The US Census Bureau defines a family as two or more individuals related by birth, marriage, or adoption. While practical, this definition excludes many groups who consider themselves to be families, such as couples who cohabit (with or without children), foster parents residing with their children, and gay and lesbian couples. Further complicating this debate and its implications for families is the disparity in family policies and laws across local, state, and federal levels. For example, the state of Massachusetts now recognizes same-sex marriages, but such marriages are not recognized by other states or by federal law. A second example is a woman who adopts a child and lives with her lesbian partner. According to the US Census Bureau definition, the lesbian partner is considered a member of the household, but not a member of the family.

For our purposes, family is defined more broadly and involves consideration of both family structure and family process. Structurally, a family is defined as two or more persons related by birth, marriage, adoption, or choice (Allen et al. 2000). Adding the element of choice recognizes that individuals have human agency, or the ability to choose those whom they consider family, such as individuals who might be close friends. An inclusive definition of family also recognizes that family members do not need to be physically present or live in the same household. To illustrate, non-residential fathers are family members even though they typically live apart from their children much of the year. Similarly, individuals may consider a deceased parent or other relative to be part of their family.

Typically, families also provide emotional and financial support, recreational opportunities, nurturance, discipline, and affection (Allen et al. 2000). As such, family also needs to be defined by process. Again, we do not take a purely relativistic view and assume all families function adequately, but we do believe that we need to be explicit about the definitions we use. Taken together, incorporating choice and process allows for a broader, more inclusive, and more meaningful definition of family.

DIMENSIONS OF FAMILY DIVERSITY

Race/Ethnicity

In the early twenty-first century, racial/ethnic families represent a growing proportion of society, including substantial numbers of interracial couples and transnational families. Understanding the diversity of intersecting cultures and the influence of diversity on society and family life is important, particularly when developing public policy. Given that the proportion of Hispanic families is growing faster than any other family groups, we are witnessing an increased research emphasis on Hispanic family life, including examination of the effects of immigration and acculturation (see Zinn & Wells 2000). According to the most recent Current Population Survey (Fields 2004), 71 percent of all family groups in the US are white, with 12 percent black, 4 percent Asian, and 13 percent Hispanic. (It is worth noting that many of those categorized as Hispanic may have reported as being both white and Hispanic.)

Socioeconomic Status

Socioeconomic status (SES) is defined in terms of a family's combined index of income, education, occupational prestige, and the number of related adults and dependent children in the household (Rank 2000). Research consistently shows that economic hardship and stress adversely affect individual and family well-being (White & Rogers 2000). Unemployment, underemployment, and low family income are associated with poor mental and physical

health, lower marital quality, diminished parenting effectiveness, and child maladjustment (Fox & Bartholomae 2000). Currently in the US, 12.4 percent of the total population lives below the poverty level, and 10.8 percent of all people living in families and 16.1 percent of families with children under age 18 live below the poverty level. A disproportionate number of black (24.9 percent) and Hispanic (22.6 percent) families live in poverty compared with white (9.1 percent) and Asian (12.8 percent) families. Interestingly, 15.8 percent of single fathers live below the poverty level compared to 32.2 percent of single mothers. As troubling as these statistics are, they do not include millions of children and adults in the US who live in severe economic hardship but have family income that falls just above the official poverty threshold (Rank 2000).

Gender

Gender refers to social meanings regarding masculinity and femininity that are produced through social processes and interactions (West & Zimmerman 1987), whereas sex refers to biological distinctions between a man and a woman. Each individual, whether male or female, is the product of complex configurations of both masculine and feminine characteristics that influence daily interactions (Thompson & Walker 1995). As a dimension of family diversity, gender is an ever-present and powerful force in family relationships. For example, one family might divide labor on the basis of traditional gender beliefs and values such that the woman "stays home" to care for children and the man is the sole or primary earner. In this instance, gender is related to power in families because the man makes all or most of the family's income and controls the family's financial decision-making. With each choice families make, such as how mothers and fathers parent, how they divide household labor, and how they provide care for aging parents, they are doing gender (West & Zimmerman 1987). Patterns unfold with enormous implications for family life and future generations because families exert a primary influence on gender socialization. Gender is thus a critical axis of both social stratification and family diversity.

Sexual Orientation

One of the influential social movements of the twentieth century was the gay and lesbian liberation movement, which continues to draw attention to issues of civil and family rights. Sexual orientation refers to an individual's beliefs, attractions, and behaviors toward members of the opposite and same sex. From a family diversity perspective, families do not have a sexual orientation, but are comprised of individuals with varying sexual orientations. Consider, for example, a family in which one parent identifies as heterosexual, the other as gay, an aunt as bisexual, and a child as transsexual. These variations are of increasing importance as more families are faced with how to accept, or whether to accept, a family member whose sexual orientation differs. Due to the difficulties involved in collecting sensitive information regarding sexual orientation, available statistical evidence regarding the prevalence and types of gay and lesbian-headed households is likely to be conservative. Using data from the 2000 Census, Gates and Ost (2004) suggested that approximately 5 percent of the US population over age 18 are gay or lesbian. Of those who were identified as gay or lesbian and in couple relationships, 27.5 percent had children present in the household. Other estimates suggest anywhere between 9 and 11 million children are being reared by a gay or lesbian parent (Patterson 2000). Studies of sexual orientation often compare the adjustment of children who live with gay or lesbian parents with that of children who live with heterosexual parents (Patterson 2000). This area of research is of great concern given current policy debates concerning same-sex marriage, adoption, and foster care. Collectively, research in this area suggests no negative differences in child outcomes based on parental sexual orientation (Patterson 2000). Studies also suggest that relationship quality and relationship outcomes are similar for families of gays and lesbians compared with families of heterosexuals (Kurdek 2004). Unfortunately, we know little about the important topics of bisexuality, transgenderism, transexualism, and family life.

Family Structure

Recent demographic changes, notably including high rates of non-marital childbearing, divorce, and remarriage, have changed the face of American families. Less than half of American children now live in traditional nuclear families, defined as families consisting of two biological parents married to each other, full siblings only, and no other household members (Brandon & Bumpass 2001). Variations in family structure and the consequences for individual well-being have been widely studied. Most of the research has focused on the impact of different family forms (e.g., first-married families, divorced families, and remarried families) on children's development and well-being. In general, when compared with children in first-married families, children in single-parent families and remarried families are slightly disadvantaged on measures of academic performance, psychological adjustment, conduct, social competence, and physical health (Amato 2000; Demo et al. 2004). However, for most children the effects of family disruption are temporary. Studies suggest that 80 percent of children who have experienced parental divorce function within normal ranges of adjustment within one to two years of the divorce (Barber & Demo 2006). Similarly, divorced adults report more negative life events, more difficulties in parenting, and lower psychological well-being during the separation process, but most are resilient and function normally within a couple of years post-divorce. Although family composition and family transitions are important to understand, the evidence suggests that family processes exert stronger effects on the well-being of family members.

Family Process

Family process refers to the interpersonal dynamics (e.g., support, communication, decision-making, conflict resolution, violence) between family members (e.g., parent–child, husband–wife, partner interactions). Given societal concerns related to couples who divorce or dissolve their relationships, examination of family process is especially important and has the potential to provide valuable insight. For example, once a conflict between partners starts, the discussion that follows and the rate at which the conflict escalates is related to the prediction of divorce/dissolution. Gottman et al. (2003) examined communication among heterosexual, gay, and lesbian couples and found that gay and lesbian couples used humor more effectively during initial stages of conflict discussions, leading to lower escalation rates compared to heterosexual couples. Attending to the diversity of family process provides a better understanding of family dynamics and has potential to guide prevention and intervention efforts for practitioners.

CONCLUSION

Contemporary families are remarkably diverse both in structure and process, and the social and demographic changes propelling family diversity are likely to accelerate (Stacey 2000). Unfortunately, much of the extant research relies on samples of predominantly white, middle-class, heterosexual families and their children, limiting our ability to generalize to increasingly pluralistic family forms. Students, scholars, practitioners, and policymakers need to be more inclusive and explicit with their definitions of families and attend more fully to the rich, fluid, and multidimensional diversity of family experiences.

SEE ALSO: Class, Status, and Power; Cohabitation; Divorce; Family Conflict; Family Structure; Family Structure and Child Outcomes; Gender Ideology and Gender Role Ideology; Inequality/Stratification, Gender; Lesbian and Gay Families; Lone-Parent Families; Stepfamilies; Stratification, Race/Ethnicity and

REFERENCES AND SUGGESTED READINGS

Allen, K. R., Fine, M. A., & Demo, D. H. (2000) An Overview of Family Diversity: Controversies, Questions, and Values. In: Demo, D. H., Allen, K. R., & Fine, M. A. (Eds.), *Handbook of Family Diversity*. Oxford University Press, New York, pp. 1–14.

Amato, P. R. (2000) The Consequences of Divorce for Adults and Children. *Journal of Marriage and the Family* 62: 1269–87.

Barber, B. & Demo, D. H. (2006) The Kids are Alright (At Least, Most of Them): Links between Divorce and Dissolution and Child Well-Being. In: Fine, M. A. & Harvey, J. (Eds.), *Handbook of Divorce and Relationship Dissolution*. Erlbaum, Mahwah, NJ.

Brandon, P. D. & Bumpass, L. L. (2001) Children's Living Arrangements, Coresidence of Unmarried Fathers, and Welfare Receipt. *Journal of Family Issues* 22: 3–26.

Coontz, S. (1992) *The Way We Never Were: American Families and the Nostalgia Trap*. Basic Books, New York.

Coontz, S. (2000) Historical Perspectives on Family Diversity. In: Demo, D. H., Allen, K. R., & Fine, M. A. (Eds.), *Handbook of Family Diversity*. Oxford University Press, New York, pp. 15–31.

Demo, D. H., Aquilino, W. S., & Fine, M. A. (2004) Family Composition and Family Transitions. In: Bengtson, V. L., Acock, A. C., Allen, K. R., Dilworth-Anderson, P., & Klein, D. M. (Eds.), *Sourcebook of Family Theory and Research*. Sage, Thousand Oaks, CA, pp. 119–34.

Fields, J. (2004) America's Families and Living Arrangements: 2003. *Current Populations Reports, P20–553*. US Census Bureau, Washington, DC.

Fox, J. J. & Bartholomae, S. (2000) Economic Stress and Families. In: McKenry, P. C. & Price, S. J. (Eds.), *Families and Change*. Sage, Thousand Oaks, CA, pp. 250–78.

Gates, G. & Ost, J. (2004) *The Gay and Lesbian Atlas*. Urban Institute Press, Washington, DC.

Gottman, J., Levenson, R., Swanson, C., Swanson, K., Tyson, R., & Yoshimoto, D. (2003) Observing Gay, Lesbian, and Heterosexual Couples' Relationships: Mathematical Modeling of Conflict Interaction. *Journal of Homosexuality* 45: 65–92.

Kurdek, L. A. (2004) Are Gay and Lesbian Cohabiting Couples Really Different from Heterosexual Married Couples? *Journal of Marriage and Family* 66: 880–900.

Patterson, C. J. (2000) Family Relationships of Lesbians and Gay Men. *Journal of Marriage and the Family* 62: 1052–69.

Rank, M. (2000) Poverty and Economic Hardship in Families. In: Demo, D. H., Allen, K. R., & Fine, M. A. (Eds.), *Handbook of Family Diversity*. Oxford University Press, New York, pp. 293–315.

Stacey, J. (2000) The Handbook's Tail: Toward Revels or a Requiem for Family Diversity? In: Demo, D. H., Allen, K. R., & Fine, M. A. (Eds.),

Handbook of Family Diversity. Oxford University Press, New York, pp. 424–39.

Teachman, J., Tedrow, L. M., & Crowder, K. D. (2000) The Changing Demography of America's Families. *Journal of Marriage and Family* 62: 1234–46.

Thompson, L. & Walker, A. (1995) The Place of Gender in Family Studies. *Journal of Marriage and the Family* 57: 847–66.

Walsh, F. (1998) *Strengthening Family Resilience.* Guilford Press, New York.

West, C. & Zimmerman, D. H. (1987) Doing Gender. *Gender and Society* 1: 124–51.

White, L. & Rogers, S. (2000) Economic Circumstances and Family Outcomes: A Review of the 1990s. *Journal of Marriage and Family* 62: 1035–52.

Zinn, M. & Wells, B. (2000) Diversity within Latino Families: New Lessons for Family Social Science. In: Demo, D. H., Allen, K. R., & Fine, M. A. (Eds.), *Handbook of Family Diversity.* Oxford University Press, New York, pp. 252–73.

family, history of

Mark Hutter

European societies during the nineteenth century underwent massive changes. The old social order anchored in kinship, the village, the community, religion, and old regimes was attacked and fell to the twin forces of industrialism and revolutionary democracy. The sweeping changes had particular effect on the family. There was a dramatic increase in such conditions as poverty, child labor, desertions, prostitution, illegitimacy, and the abuse of women and children. These conditions were particularly evident in the newly emerging industrial cities. The vivid writings of a novelist such as Charles Dickens in *Oliver Twist* and *Hard Times* provide startling portraits of a harsh new way of life.

The industrial revolution dramatically changed the nature of economic and social life. The factory system developed, and, with its development, there was a transformation from home industries in rural areas to factories in towns and cities of Europe and America. Rural people were lured by the novelty of city life and the prospects of greater economic opportunity. The domestic economy of the pre-industrial family disappeared. The rural and village-based family system no longer served as a productive unit. The domestic economy had enabled the family to combine economic activities with the supervision and training of its children; the development of the factory system led to a major change in the division of labor in family roles.

Patriarchal authority was weakened with urbanization. Previously, in rural and village families, fathers reigned supreme; they were knowledgeable in economic skills and were able to train their children. The great diversity of city life rendered this socialization function relatively useless. The rapid change in industrial technology and the innumerable forms of work necessitated a more formal institutional setting – the school – to help raise the children. Partially, in response to the changing family situation, the British passed legislation to aid children. Separated from parental supervision, working children were highly exploited. Laws came into existence to regulate the amount of time children were allowed to work and their working conditions. The law also required that children attend school. These legal changes reflected the change in the family situation in the urban setting; families were no longer available or able to watch constantly over their children.

The separation of work from the home had important implications for family members. Increasingly, the man became the sole provider for the family and the women and children developed a life comprised solely of concerns centered on the family, the home, and the school. Their contacts with the outside world diminished and they were removed from community involvements. The family's withdrawal from the community was tinged by its hostile attitude toward the surrounding city. The city was depicted as a sprawling and planless development bereft of meaningful community and neighborhood relationships. The tremendous movement of a large population into the industrial centers provided little opportunity for the family to form deep or lasting ties with neighbors. Instead, the family viewed neighbors with suspicion and weariness. Exaggerated beliefs developed on the prevalence of urban poverty, crime, and disorganization.

This entry deals with the different approaches taken by social scientists in their analysis of the family in the wake of the industrial revolution. Throughout the nineteenth and early twentieth centuries they voiced concern about the excesses of industrial urban society and the calamitous changes in the family system. Social Darwinists and Marxists tried to make sense of these changes through utilization of evolutionary theories. Radicals, conservatives, and social reformers called for fundamental changes in the society and in the family and its new way of life. However, by the mid-twentieth century, the dominant perspective in sociology, structural functionalism, proclaimed that the family was alive, well, and functioning in modern industrial society.

EVOLUTIONARY THEORIES

Sociological interest in the study of thex history of the family was very strong in the mid-nineteenth century in Western Europe. Prior to the nineteenth century, western thought generally held to a biblical belief in the origins of the family stemming from God's creation of the world, including Adam and Eve. Although there was recognition of relatively minor familial changes over time, the biblical family form and its underlying patriarchal ideological precepts were seen as continuing intact into the nineteenth century. Western thought clung to uniformity throughout the world in terms of family structures, processes, and underlying familial beliefs and values. These governed the behavior of men, women, and children in families. The belief in universal family uniformity led to ramifications on the nature and place of the human species and affected the traditional institutions of the church, the state, and the family. Coinciding with the doctrine of evolutionism was the development of individualism and democracy.

There are a number of important factors to help account for the historical study of the family. First, the fabric of Western European and American society was undergoing major changes. Societies were rapidly industrializing and urbanizing. The old social-class systems were being reworked and a new class structure was developing. Family relationships were also undergoing radical changes. The individual's rights, duties, and obligations to the family and, in turn, to the larger community were being questioned and challenged. Second, western colonial expansionism and imperialism were developed fully. Unknown and hitherto unsuspected cultural systems with strange and diverse ways of life were discovered and analyzed. Family systems were found to have differences almost beyond imagination. Third, an intellectual revolution was occurring. The controversy surrounding evolutionary theory was sweeping Western Europe and America. Developing out of this social and intellectual ferment was the application of evolutionary thought to the analysis and understanding of the social origins of the human species. This discussion is concerned with the resultant theories of social change and their applicability to the study of the history of the family and to family change.

The theory of evolutionary change developed by Charles Darwin in his *Origin of the Species* in 1859 was the culmination of an intellectual revolution begun much earlier that promoted the idea of progressive development. Progressive development believed that the human species evolved from stages of savagery to civilization. As the theory of evolution became the dominant form in explaining biological principles, social scientists of the nineteenth century developed the belief that there was a link between biological and cultural evolution. The basic argument was that since biological evolution proceeded by a series of stages (from the simple to the complex), the same process would hold for cultures. Thus, the Social Darwinists shared in the basic assumption of unilinear evolution (the idea that all civilizations pass through the same stages of development in the same order). They then sought to apply the ideas of progressive development to social forms and institutions – a primary concern being the development of explanatory schema on the evolution of marriage and family systems.

Social Darwinism was associated with, among others, Herbert Spencer (*The Principles of Sociology*, 1897), J. J. Bachofen (*Das Mutterecht* [The Mother Right], 1861/1948), Henry Sumner Maine (*Ancient Law*, 1861/1960), and Lewis Henry Morgan (*Ancient Society*, 1877/

1963). Social Darwinists seemingly dealt with such non-immediate concerns as the origins and historical development of the family, yet their theories had social and political implications. Social Darwinism provided "scientific" legitimation for western colonization and exploitation of "primitive" peoples through the erroneous belief that western culture represented "civilization" and non-western cultures (particularly among nonliterate, low-technology societies) represented a primeval state of savagery or barbarity. And through its advocacy of evolutionary progress, Social Darwinism provided laissez-faire guidelines that supported neglect of the poorer classes of American and Western European societies.

The Social Darwinists differed concerning specific lines of development. Some argued that there was a historical stage of matriarchy in which women ruled the society, whereas most others argued that a matriarchal stage of social evolution never existed. This controversy had implications for the roles of men and women in nineteenth-century family systems. The prevalent view was for a patriarchal evolutionary theory of male supremacy and dominance over females. Thus, Social Darwinists gave implicit support to the Victorian notions of male supremacy and female dependency.

In summary, the evolutionary theory of the Social Darwinists ostensibly dealt with such non-immediate concerns as the origins and historical development of the family, but underlying their theorizing were implications for the roles of men and women in contemporary nineteenth-century family systems. Indeed, their twentieth-century evolutionary theory counterparts continued to put forth these same arguments over a century later. The initiative for this rebirth of interest in the evolutionary reconstruction of family forms has been the development of arguments and counter-arguments stemming from the concern of the women's movement with the origins of patriarchy and male sexual dominance.

An important rebuttal to Social Darwinism that in part developed out of evolutionary theory was made by the nineteenth-century founders of communist thought, Marx and Engels. They made gender role relationships a central and dominating concern of evolutionary theory. Engels (1972) used it to address his primary concern: the social condition of the poor and working classes and the exploitation of men, women, and children. Concern for gender role egalitarianism, as opposed to patriarchy and male sexual dominance, achieved their fullest evolutionary theory expression in this work. Engles's evolutionary theory saw economic factors as the primary determinants of social change and linked particular technological forms with particular family forms. Echoing Lewis Henry Morgan, Engels depicted a stage of savagery as one with no economic inequalities and no private ownership of property. The family form was group marriage based on matriarchy. During the stage of barbarism, men gained economic control over the means of production. In civilization, the last stage, women became subjugated to the male-dominated economic system and monogamy. This stage, in Engels's view, rather than representing the apex of marital and familial forms, represented the victory of private property over common ownership and group marriage. Engels speculated that the coming of socialist revolution would usher in a new evolutionary stage marked by gender equality and by common ownership of property. Engels's main achievement was in defining the family as an economic unit. This has become a major focus in much of the subsequent historical research on the family and is of great theoretical importance in the sociology of the family. But, insofar as Engels's Marxist view constituted a branch of evolutionary thought, it was subject to many of the same objections raised against other evolutionary theories.

By the end of the nineteenth century the popularity of Social Darwinism was rapidly declining. Contributing to this decline were the methodological weaknesses of the approach (data obtained by untrained, impressionistic, and biased travelers and missionaries) and a growing rejection of both its explicit value assumptions on the superiority of western family forms and its belief in unilinear evolutionary development of the family. This belief was replaced by multilinear evolutionary theory that recognizes that there are many evolutionary tracks that societies can follow. It rejects the unilinear evolutionary view that all cultures advance toward a model represented by western culture as ultimately ethnocentric and often racist.

Social Darwinism also made the fatal error of equating contemporary nonliterate cultures with the hypothetical primeval savage society. It failed to understand that *all* contemporary peoples have had a prolonged and evolved past. The failure of many of them to have a written record of the past led the Social Darwinists to assume erroneously that they had none. Further, they did not understand that many nonliterate societies deemphasize changes in the past to stress their continuity with it. This is especially true in cultures that glorify traditions and reify their sameness with their ancestors. Social Darwinists made ethnocentric and subjective pronouncements. They viewed their own society's art, religion, morals, and values according to their notions of what was good and correct, explaining such "barbaric" practices as polygamy and sexual promiscuity based on their own national and individual norms. They biased their analysis with their own moral feelings on such customs and practices.

Another factor in the decline of evolutionary theory was that it was involved with an irrelevant set of questions. For instance, what difference does it make which society represents the apex of civilization and which the nadir if it does not aid in understanding contemporary marriage and family systems? This is especially the case in a world undergoing revolutionary changes and one in which formally isolated cultures are becoming more and more involved with western civilization as a result of colonization. Social scientists felt that attempts to theorize about the historical evolutionary process were not as important as examining the influences which cultures had on each other. Societies did not evolve in isolation, but continually interacted and influenced each other. One final factor in the decline of evolutionary theory was the shift in focus of the sociology of the family. This shift was in part precipitated by the sweeping changes in American and European societies during the nineteenth century. Social scientists were appalled by the excesses of industrial urban society and the calamitous changes in the family system. The precipitating factor seen in this change in the family were the sweeping changes in American and European societies during the nineteenth century brought about by the industrial revolution.

SOCIAL POLICY AND REFORM

Toward the end of the nineteenth century and through the early twentieth century social scientists concerned about the abuses arising from rapid urbanization and industrialization began to see the decline in the importance of kinship and community participation and the changes in the makeup of the nuclear family as more important areas of investigation than the study of the evolutionary transformations of the family. Their research and theories focused on the causal connections relating family change to the larger industrial and urban developments occurring in the last two centuries. Much attention was given to theoretical analyses of the effects these changes had on the individual, on women, men, and children, on the family, on kinship structures, and on the larger community and the society.

Sociology in the US shifted its emphasis away from the study of social evolution to the study of social problems and the advocacy of social reform. The paramount concern was the study of the family in the context of the abuses of rapid industrialization and urbanization. The emphasis switched from the development of theories of family systems to the more urgent concerns of individual families and their members. Illegitimacy, prostitution, child abuse, and other resultant abuses were seen as arising from non-governmental supervision of industrial and urban institutions. This underlying assumption about the causes of social problems was held by the social reform movement's major advocate, the Chicago School of Sociology, which was composed of such important sociologists as Robert E. Park, Ernest W. Burgess, Louis Wirth, E. Franklin Frazier, W. I. Thomas, and Florian Znaniecki. They contributed much to the development of family sociology and urban sociology. The Chicago School developed a distinct contrast between urban and rural life. They saw traditional patterns of life being broken down by debilitating urban forces, resulting in social disorganization within the family. An underlying theme was the loss of family functions as a result of urbanization and industrialization.

In traditional societies, the family (following the argument of Chicago School sociologists William Ogburn and Ernest Burgess) performed economic, educational, recreational, religious, and protective functions. In modern society most of these functions have been taken over as a consequence of the increased participation of government, economic enterprises, and education. The cornerstone of family life was its companionship and emotional functions. This shift in family functions led to Burgess's famous classification of family types as moving from "institution to companionship." According to Burgess, the institutional family is sustained by external community pressures and involvements; the companionate family, on the other hand, is sustained by the emotional attachments among its members.

Beginning in the late 1930s and accelerating after World War II, many of the views of the Chicago School either merged with or influenced newer perspectives. By the 1950s the dominant school was structural functionalism, under the intellectual leadership of Talcott Parsons, who was one of the most predominant and influential sociologists of the twentieth century. According to Parsons (1943), the isolation of the nuclear family "is the most distinctive feature of the American kinship system and underlies most of its peculiar functional and dynamic problems." The typical American household consisted of a husband, wife, and children economically independent of their extended family and frequently located at considerable geographical distance from it. Parsons viewed American society as having been greatly changed by industrialization and urbanization. In particular, he believed it had become highly "differentiated," with the family system's previous educational, religious, political, and economic functions being taken over by other institutions in the society. By differentiation, Parsons meant that functions performed earlier by one institution in the society are now distributed among several institutions. Thus, schools, churches, peer groups, political parties, voluntary associations, and occupational groups have assumed functions once reserved for the family. Rather than viewing industrialization and urbanization negatively, Parsons saw the family as becoming a more specialized group. It concentrates its functions on the socialization of children and providing emotional support and affection for family members.

Parsons further suggested that the isolated nuclear family may be ideally suited to meet the demands of occupational and geographical mobility inherent in industrial urban society. Unencumbered by obligatory extended kinship bonds, the nuclear family is best able to move where the jobs are and better able to take advantage of occupational opportunities. In contrast, the traditional extended-family system of extensive, obligatory economic and residential rights and duties is seen to be dysfunctional for industrial society.

Arguing against the social disorganization thesis on the breakdown of the contemporary family, Parsons (1955) found support for the importance of the nuclear family in the high rates of marriage and remarriage after divorce, the increase in the birthrate after World War II, and the increase in the building of single-family homes (particularly in suburbia) during this period. All these trends provided evidence of the continuing visibility, *not* social disorganization, of the family and of the *increased* vitality of the nuclear family bond. Thus, a specialized family system functionally meets the affectional and personality needs of its members. Further, it may be admirably fitted to a family system that is a relatively isolated and self-sustaining economic unit of mother, father, and children, living without other relatives in the home and without close obligations and ties to relatives who live nearby.

In summary, Parsons emphasized the importance of the nuclear family – in the absence of extended kinship ties – in that it meets two major societal needs: the socialization of children and the satisfaction of the affectional and emotional demands of husbands, wives, and their children. Further, the isolated nuclear family, which is not handicapped by conflicting obligations to extended relatives, can best take advantage of occupational opportunities and is best able to cope with the demands of modern industrial urban life.

MODERNIZATION THEORY

Modernization theory combines conceptual orientations from both Social Darwinism and structural functionalism to elaborate the theoretical relationship between societal development and family change. The concept of modernization, derived from structural functionalism, and the theories stemming from it have been the dominating perspective in the analysis of global social change and the family since the last quarter of the twentieth century. Modernization is usually used as a term in reference to processes of change in societies that are characterized by advanced industrial technology. Science and technology are seen to guide societies from traditional, preindustrial social institutions to complex, internally differentiated ones.

Modernization is often linked with a wide range of changes in the political, economic, social, and individual spheres. For example, there is a movement from tribal or village authority to political parties and civil service bureaucracies; from illiteracy to education that would increase economically productive skills; from traditionalistic religions to secularized belief systems; and from ascriptive hierarchical systems to greater social and geographical mobility resulting in a more achievement-based stratification system. Likewise the extended family kinship ties are seen to lose their pervasiveness and nuclear families gain in importance.

Modernization theory, while it recognized to some extent that cultural values of non-western societies might have an impact on the pace of industrialization, argued that they would not affect its inevitability. Diffusion theory and the convergence hypothesis, offshoots of modernization theory, predicted that cultural differences would diminish as less developed countries industrialized and urbanized. The held belief was that as societies modernized, they would come to resemble one another more and more over time. These societies would lose their cultural uniqueness as they began to act and think more like one another and more like the more developed countries. Accompanying modernization would be a shift to "modern" attitudes and beliefs and a change in the family and kinship system. The family change would see the diminishing control and power of extended kinship systems and emergence of affectional ties and obligations with the nuclear family.

The classic statement of modernization theory, centering on the family and change, is William J. Goode's *World Revolution and Family Patterns* (1963). This work has had a profound impact on the comparative study of social change and the family. Goode's major contribution is the comprehensive and systematic gathering and analyses of cross-cultural and historical data to attack the notion that industrial and economic development was the principal reason that the family is changing. Goode concluded that changes in industrialization and the family are parallel processes, both being influenced by changing social and personal ideologies – the ideologies of economic progress, the conjugal family, and egalitarianism. Finally, Goode proposes that in the "world revolution" toward industrialization and urbanization there is a convergence of diverse types of extended family forms to some type of conjugal family system.

DEPENDENCY THEORIES

Dependency theories take strong exception to these predictions articulated by modernization theory's hypotheses. Further, and more importantly, proponents of dependency theories have changed the focus of the analysis of the impact of industrialization and globalized economy. Rather than focus on whether or not there is a convergence to western models of modernity and family structure, they have focused on the impact of the globalization of the economy on the poor, not only in third world societies but in industrial ones as well. Dependency theories are of particular relevance in their analysis of global inequality on those who are most economically vulnerable: women, children, elderly people, and families living in poverty.

Women are particularly impacted by global poverty. Modernization theory often does not examine the experiences or structural location of women in their own right as societies undergo change. The belief that women's status improves with economic development does not fully realize that widespread structures of patriarchy often keep women in subordinate positions. Patriarchy is the ideology of masculine supremacy that emphasizes the dominance of males over females in virtually all spheres of life, including politics, economics, education, religion, and the family. Its worldwide pervasiveness is particularly acute in the third world, where women have relatively little political power. Economically, when women's work is not solely relegated to the household they are often found in lower-echelon jobs where they work longer hours for less pay than men. Land, the principal source of wealth in most third world countries, continues to be controlled by men. Education is often seen as a male prerogative, and lacking education they have fewer economic options. Women's role in religion often is of secondary or of little religious importance. Modernization, rather than significantly increasing women's independence, often results in and perpetuates their dependency and subordination.

GLOBALIZATION THEORY

Globalization theory has become another perspective in examining family change. Here the emphasis is on an examination of the transnational processes that have an impact on families. Rather than focusing solely on families in the modernized countries or on families in third world societies, of paramount importance are relationships that exist and are experienced by individuals who have family members living in both rich and poor countries. For example, one concern is the impact of globalization on generational relationships among family members, particularly as a consequence of differential socialization experiences in different cultural settings. Also of much interest (Ehrenreich & Hochschild 2002) is the broadscale transfer of domestic service associated with female migration of women whose traditional roles result in their employment as child and elderly caretakers or as domestics in affluent countries while their families in their home countries suffer the absence of their services. The problems associated with international sex tourism are also of great concern. Another area of interest is the involvement of men who have migrated from poorer countries to wealthier ones primarily for economic motives. Not only do they maintain their contacts with their families in their home countries through financial support, but they develop trader communities that are transnational and which link them to their families and to economic networks (Stoller 2001).

Essentially, in evaluating contemporary perspectives on family change, we become cognizant of a twentieth/twenty-first century replay of the ideological positions and arguments put forth by the Social Darwinists in the nineteenth century and underlining moral valuations inherent in these orientations. Modernization theory, through its utilization of structural functionalism, can be seen as the twentieth-century counterpart of Social Darwinism. Likewise, developmental theory can be seen as a twentieth-century counterpart that shares many of the assumptions put forth by nineteenth-century radicals such as Marx and Engels.

SEE ALSO: Chicago School; Family and Community; Family, Sociology of; Family Theory; Modernization; Parsons, Talcott; Social Darwinism

REFERENCES AND SUGGESTED READING

Boserup, E. (1971) *Women's Role in Economic Development*. George Allen & Unwin, London.

Cheal, D. (1991) *Family and the State of Theory*. University of Toronto Press, Toronto.

Coleman, M. & Ganong, L. H. (2004) *Handbook of Contemporary Families*. Sage, Thousand Oaks, CA.

Coontz, S. (1992) *The Way We Never Were*. Basic Books, New York.

Ehrenreich, B. & Hochschild, A. R. (Eds.) (2002) *Global Woman: Nannies, Maids, and Sex Workers in the New Economy*. Metropolitan Books, New York.

Engels, F. (1972 [1884]) *The Origins of the Family, Private Property, and the State*. Pathfinder Press, New York.

Giddens, A. (200) *Runaway World: How Globalization is Reshaping Our Lives*. Routledge, New York.

Glenn, E., Chang, G., & Forcey, L. (Eds.) (1994) *Mothering: Ideology, Experience and Agency*. Routledge, New York.

Goode, W. J. (1963) *World Revolution and Family Patterns*. Free Press, Glencoe, IL.

Hareven, T. (2000) *Families, History and Social Change*. Westview Press, Boulder.

Ingoldsby, B. B. & Smith, S. (1995) *Families in Multicultural Perspective*. Guilford Press, New York.

Lasch, C. (1977) *Haven in a Heartless World*. Basic Books, New York.

O'Kelly, C. & Carney, L. (1986) *Women and Men in Society: Cross Cultural Perspectives on Gender Stratification*. Wadsworth, Belmont, CA.

Parsons, T. (1943) The Kinship System of the Contemporary United States. *American Anthropologist* 45: 22–38.

Parsons, T. (1955) The American Family: Its Relation to Personality and to the Social Structure. In: Parsons, T. & Bales, R. F. (Eds.), *Family, Socialization and Interaction Process*. Free Press, New York, pp. 3–33.

Stoller, P. (2001) *Money Has No Smell: The Africanization of New York City*. University of Chicago Press, Chicago.

Trost, J. & Adams, B. (Eds.) (2005) *Handbook of World Families*. Sage, Thousand Oaks, CA.

family, men's involvement in

Sandra L. Hofferth

Father involvement refers to involvement by fathers in the daily responsibilities of parenthood. According to data from the early 1990s, only 12.6 percent of men 45 to 64 years of age report never having had children (Bachu 1996). Thus, although not all men are fathers, most eventually father a child and have, therefore, the opportunity to act as a father to their own children. Men without their own biological children have the opportunity to be a father to their partners' children through marriage or cohabitation. Sixty-four percent of children live with their biological or adoptive mother and father, 6.7 percent live with a biological parent and a stepparent, 21 percent live with a single mother, another 2 percent live with their single mother and the mother's cohabiting partner, 2.5 percent live with their single biological father, and 4 percent do not live with a parent (Hofferth et al. 2002).

SOCIAL AND DEMOGRAPHIC CHANGES AFFECTING FATHERS AND FATHERING

Adjustments in the roles of fathers and mothers have resulted from social changes over the past decades. Such changes include women's increased labor force participation, the absence of many men from families, the increased involvement of other types of fathers in children's lives, and increased cultural diversity in the US (Cabrera et al. 2000). A concern about the well-being of children raised in low-income families is linked to these same changes. Although many of the same concerns are recognized in developed countries across the globe, this discussion is limited to the US context.

In the recent past much of the focus on fathers was occasioned by their absence. The focus on father absence sprang from large increases in divorce and separation beginning in the 1970s that resulted in fathers substantially reducing their financial and other commitments to family and children. Early research focused upon the effects of the absence of the father on the financial condition of the family. Since the mid-1990s, research has focused on the involvement of non-residential fathers with children, not just on the father's financial contribution. Research from the Fragile Families and Child Wellbeing study suggests that unmarried fathers are more involved with their families than popularly believed. At birth 82 percent were romantically involved with the baby's mother and 44 percent were living together (Fragile Families and Child Wellbeing 2000).

The other major change is the increased labor force participation of married mothers. Women have always worked; however, the increase in employment of married mothers with young children in the 1970s and 1980s, and in the 1990s of single mothers, was remarkably rapid. Maternal labor force participation, which has increased maternal financial support for the family and removed financial support as fathers' primary responsibility, has led to the focus on paternal responsibility for non-financial involvement and care of children.

CONCEPTUAL FRAMEWORK

The most frequently used framework conceptualizes father involvement as having three major components: (1) the time fathers are engaged with or accessible to children overall or in specific activities; (2) the responsibility they take for them; and (3) the quality or nature of the relationship (Lamb 2004).

Research has found that fathers in intact families spend about 1 hour and 13 minutes on a weekday and about 3.3 hours on a weekend day with children under age 13 (Yeung et al. 2001). Because both parents' time with children may vary, relative levels of involvement may provide a better sense of father involvement. Based upon data from the 1980s and 1990s, fathers' time engaged in activities with their children is about two-fifths of mothers' time. Fathers are accessible to their children about two-thirds as often as mothers. These figures are higher than in the 1970s and early 1980s. A recent study from the mid-1990s shows that fathers' time engaged with children on a weekday is about two-thirds of mothers' time, and on a weekend day almost 90 percent of mothers' time, additional evidence for increased father involvement. In these more recent data, the ratio of fathers' to mothers' time accessible to their children is about the same as that of engaged time. As children get older and the absolute amount of parental time declines, fathers' time rises as a proportion of mothers' time with children.

Of course, the increasing ratio of fathers' to mothers' time since the 1970s could be due to either a decline in mothers' or an increase in fathers' time. However, one comparison between 1965 and 1997 suggests that mothers' time with children has remained fairly constant, and, hence, the rise in the ratio of fathers' to mothers' time with children is not due to a decline in mothers' time, at least in two-parent families. Other research also suggests that fathers' time with children has risen in two-parent families where the average amount of time children spent with fathers rose about 3 hours per week between 1981 and 1997 and time with mothers rose as well. The time children spent with fathers did not rise significantly over all families because of the offsetting increased number of single-parent families and because non-residential fathers are less involved with their children (Sandberg & Hofferth 2001).

Although the overall amount of time may be important to child development, developmental psychologists are concerned about the nature of those activities. As has been found in several studies, play and companionship account for the largest fraction of time children spend with their fathers. About 39 percent of children's engaged time with fathers is spent in play and companionship on a weekday or weekend day. Learning, household work, and social activities comprise a relatively small fraction of children's time with their fathers, about 31 percent. The time children spend in learning and educational activities with their fathers is quite small, averaging only 3 to 5 percent of engaged time.

A second important category is personal care received by the child from the father, about 25 percent of the father's engaged time on a weekend day and 35 percent on a weekday. Childcare by fathers when mothers are working is an important aspect of caregiving. In the US a substantial minority of dual-earner parents keep their use of non-parental care to a minimum by adjusting their work schedules so that a parent can care for their children when needed. About one-third of working parents in two-parent families with a preschool child work different schedules and can share childcare responsibilities. The proportion of fathers who care for children during the hours when mothers work rises to three-quarters as the number of non-overlapping hours increases. Other evidence that fathers' time in childcare is responsive to available time is that, during the 1991 recession in which more men were presumably out of work or working fewer hours, the proportion of men who provided childcare as primary or secondary provider while their wives were working rose by one-third. It declined again following the end of the recessionary period.

Much of what parents do for children demands time indirectly, through management of their lives and activities – the extent of responsibility fathers take is a key variable across families. Fathers can participate in a wide variety of managerial and supervisory activities, including selecting doctors and childcare programs, managing appointments, arranging transportation, coordinating with schools, and monitoring children's activities (Cabrera et al. 2000). Although fathers take less responsibility than mothers, and few fathers take sole responsibility for any parenting tasks, fathers are likely to share direct care, to transport children to activities, and to participate in choosing activities and selecting a childcare program, preschool, or school (Hofferth et al. 2002). They are less likely to be involved in purchasing clothing, and in selecting and making appointments for doctor visits.

An additional aspect of fathering considered here is the quality of the father–child relationship. Most developmental psychologists argue that the quality of parenting and of the parent–child relationship is crucial to developing competent children. A combination of responsiveness with control has been shown by research to be linked to optimal child development. Fathers who were affectionate, sensitive, spent time with their child, and had more positive attitudes had securely attached infants at 9 months. Positive father involvement has also been linked to greater social skills, cognitive ability, school performance, self-esteem, and social confidence in children (Lamb 2004).

WHAT FACTORS MOTIVATE FATHERS TO BE INVOLVED WITH THEIR CHILDREN?

Family structural variables are expected to be associated with paternal involvement because they may influence fathers' motivation to participate. Particularly important are the relationships of the male to the child (biological/other) and to the mother (married/cohabiting). From the point of view of evolutionary psychology, genetic benefits arise from fathering and investing in one's own natural offspring. Such "parenting investment" increases the reproductive fitness of the next generation. Stepfathers gain little genetic benefit by investing in the care of stepchildren, and such investment detracts from time they might otherwise spend ensuring their own biological progeny. However, many examples of caring behavior by stepparents exist, suggesting that paternal investment is not restricted only to biological offspring. One of the mechanisms behind such investment is "relationship investment." By investing in their spouse's children from a prior union, remarried men increase the prospect of further childbearing as well as continuation of supportive exchanges with their partner. Thus investment in one's partner's children may have payoffs. However, there is also less normative support for involvement by stepfathers than biological

fathers, consistent with findings that stepfathers are behaviorally less involved (Hofferth & Anderson 2003). It is likely that cohabiting (especially non-biological cohabiting) fathers also receive less normative support for being involved. In addition, both stepfathers and cohabiting fathers may receive less support than married biological fathers for involvement from the child's mother.

Fathers are likely to differ on a variety of social and demographic factors that could also be linked to father involvement. For example, fathers' motivation for involvement with older children may be greater because interaction with them is more gratifying. On the other hand, adolescent children may become less interested and motivated to spend time with their father. Cultural variation also exists. Recent research found African American and Hispanic fathers taking more responsibility for managerial tasks than white fathers, even after adjusting for differences in socioeconomic and demographic characteristics (Hofferth 2003). African American fathers have been found to be less warm and more controlling than white fathers and Hispanic fathers equally warm but less controlling than white fathers. Better-educated fathers may have more positive fathering attitudes and more equitable gender role attitudes, which may relate to greater engagement with children. Their expectations may also be higher. On the other hand, fathers with longer work hours will be constrained from spending more time with children. Fathers' income could be positively or negatively related to engagement with children, depending upon whether the level of income is a function more of education or of work hours.

CURRENT RESEARCH ON FATHER INVOLVEMENT

Much of the current research focuses on effects of father involvement on child development (Lamb 2004). One of the major issues in examining outcomes of father involvement is to identify unique effects of fathers separate from mothers. There are three basic ways it is thought that fathers affect their children's development. The first is by direct interaction and involvement with the child, including teaching, helping, playing, etc. A second is by taking responsibility for aspects of the child's life, such as making appointments, talking with teachers, arranging care, and monitoring the child's activities. The third is through interaction with the mother, including supporting the mother in childrearing, both emotionally and financially. All avenues are likely to be important, but only the first has been widely researched.

Research has failed to find a strong association between amount of time spent doing things with children and their well-being and development. Rather, research tends to find significant links between the warmth of the father and mother and child development. It has been extremely difficult to show links between specific parenting behaviors, such as helping with homework, and child achievement. Parental involvement in children's schooling, for example, has been found to be associated with greater school achievement. Thus it is likely that the quality and type of parenting matters more to child development than the total amount of father involvement. It is possible, of course, that the types of involvement measures used to date are not specific enough to capture these linkages.

There is substantial support for the hypothesis that a positive relationship between mother and father is good for children. Parents who have a good relationship feel better about themselves, are better parents, and their children are better adjusted, whereas conflict leads to maladjustment.

Most of the above research has been conducted on residential parents. Increasing research on amount and quality of involvement has focused on non-residential fathers (Hofferth et al. 2002). Research has found greater frequency of contact with the non-resident father to be associated with better child outcomes (Amato & Gilbreth 1999).

METHODOLOGICAL ISSUES IN STUDYING MEN AS FATHERS

Fathers are difficult to study. A report that summarized some of the methodological issues in studying fathers was produced in the 1990s by the Forum on Child and Family Statistics

(Federal Interagency Forum on Child and Family Statistics 1998). Obtaining the cooperation of fathers in order to obtain the best information about their involvement is not the easiest task. To begin with, men are undercounted in surveys. Many men are loosely connected to households and are simply not included in our enumeration of households. Low-income fathers, in particular, may be living in several places, on the street, or be in jail or in the military. Even if they are identified, men's fertility is usually underestimated. Fathers are accessed mainly through the mothers of their children. Married fathers can be located; however, fathers are much less likely to agree to participate than mothers. They work full-time more often, are at home less frequently, and are less likely to agree to be interviewed. Thus much of the information on fathers that is used today is reported by the mother. That is unlikely to provide the best information about father involvement as it may depend upon the mother's attitude toward the father. This has always been a problem for non-residential fathers, because many mothers do not want to provide access to these fathers or do not know their whereabouts. The Child Development Supplement to the Panel Study of Income Dynamics (PSID-CDS) was able to interview only about 25 percent of the non-residential fathers of the children in the study. Most of the contact problem was due to failure to obtain contact information from the mother. Mothers refused in one-third of the cases and one-third could not be located. Upon contacting the father, cooperation was reasonably high, about 64 percent. In the Early Head Start Study, 60 percent of mothers gave information that could be used to identify the father of the child, and of these 60 percent participated.

Interviewing residential fathers is also problematic. Obtaining an interview with a second family member is expensive and time-consuming because it takes additional contact and interview time. The use of a self-administered questionnaire in the PSID-CDS resulted in a response rate of only about 60 percent of fathers.

An alternative way to obtain information about fathers is by starting with the man as the study respondent and following him as he becomes an adult. The problem here is in obtaining accurate reports of having fathered a child. Men who were without a high school degree, who were black, who fathered a child at a young age, and who did not consistently live with the child from birth were less likely to be verifiable as children's fathers in the National Longitudinal Survey of Youth 79 (NLSY79). Besides reports that may not be accurate, male fertility reports are often missing. In the Survey of Income and Program Participation (SIPP), 8 percent of men did not report on the number of children ever born (Bachu 1996). An alternative strategy that has worked well is to start with the birth of a baby and get the couple at this "magic moment." In the Study of Fragile Families and Child Wellbeing, which took this approach in studying unmarried couples, response rates for mothers were 87 percent and for fathers were 75 percent (Fragile Families and Child Wellbeing 2000).

FUTURE DIRECTIONS

The research on fathers' involvement in the family increasingly focuses on two areas: (1) examining the relationship between father involvement and child development in special types of families, such as minority families, low-income and "fragile" families, and stepfamilies; and (2) conducting qualitative interviews with fathers to examine such topics as the meaning of fatherhood in men's lives and how men become fathers to children they did not sire. These qualitative studies should be helpful in designing a new generation of studies that examines the process of becoming a father and how becoming a father links to men's later involvement with children.

SEE ALSO: Childhood; Family Structure and Child Outcomes; Fatherhood; Fertility: Nonmarital; Life Course and Family; Life Course Perspective; Marriage; Parental Involvement in Education; Stepfamilies; Stepfathering

REFERENCES AND SUGGESTED READINGS

Amato, P. R. & Gilbreth, J. G. (1999) Nonresident Fathers and Children's Well-Being: A Meta-Analysis. *Journal of Marriage and the Family* 61 (August): 557–73.

Bachu, A. (1996) *Fertility of American Men* (Population Division Working Paper No. 14). US Bureau of the Census, Washington, DC.

Cabrera, N., Tamis-LeMonda, N., Bradley, B., Hofferth, S., & Lamb, M. (2000) Fatherhood in the 21st Century. *Child Development* 71: 127–36.

Federal Interagency Forum on Child and Family Statistics (1998) *Nurturing Fatherhood: Improving Data and Research on Male Fertility, Family Formation, and Fatherhood.* Forum on Child and Family Statistics, Washington, DC.

Fragile Families and Child Wellbeing (2000) *Dispelling Myths about Unmarried Fathers* (Fragile Families Research Brief No. 1). Bendheim-Thomas Center for Research on Child Wellbeing, Princeton.

Hofferth, S. L. (2003) Race/Ethnic Differences in Father Involvement in Two-Parent Families: Culture, Context, or Economy. *Journal of Family Issues* 24(2): 185–216.

Hofferth, S. L. & Anderson, K. (2003) Are All Dads Equal? Biology vs. Marriage as Basis for Paternal Investment. *Journal of Marriage and Family.*

Hofferth, S., Pleck, J., Stueve, J., Bianchi, S., & Sayer, L. (2002) The Demography of Fathers: What Fathers Do. In: Tamis-LeMonda, C. & Cabrera, N. (Eds.), *Handbook of Father Involvement.* Lawrence Erlbaum, Mahwah, NJ.

Lamb, M. E. (Ed.) (2004) *The Role of the Father in Child Development*, 4th edn. Wiley, New York.

Sandberg, J. F. & Hofferth, S. L. (2001) Changes in Parental Time with Children. *Demography* 38: 423–36.

Yeung, W. J., Sandberg, J., Davis-Kean, P. E., & Hofferth, S. L. (2001) Children's Time with Fathers in Intact Families. *Journal of Marriage and the Family* 63(1): 136–54.

family migration

Darren P. Smith

Since the late 1970s the topic of family migration has increasingly been examined by sociologists, geographers, economists, and demographers. Studies of family migration have clearly become a wide-ranging, interdisciplinary endeavor, with discussions cross-cutting the social sciences. Although family migration occurs at many geographic scales, from the neighborhood to the global, academic discourses within the developed world have tended to focus on the movement of family units over long distances at a subnational level. Kofman (2004) and Smith and Bailey (2006) argue, for example, that the "family" has been lost from accounts of population movements between European states, or across wider international boundaries, respectively. In addition, there is limited interchange between accounts of family movements within the developed and developing world, with the latter often being absorbed within wider development studies.

North American and European studies of family migration have generally focused on the *outcomes* of family migration (Halfacree 1995). More specifically, there has been an emphasis on pinning down the *socioeconomic* effects, which are often measured by the post-migration employment or occupational status of family migrants. There has been less concern with the non-economic outcomes of family migration (e.g., quality of life, caring, family forming, marriage). At the same time, there have been limited empirical explorations of *how* and *why* family migration unfolds, or the subjective dimensions which underpin the decision to move the family unit.

This longstanding perspective is tied to an epistemological and methodological engagement, with many scholars of family migration drawing upon the tenets of positivism. As a result, researchers of family migration have tended to adopt quantitative research methods, particularly statistical modeling, and utilize large-scale aggregated data sets to test hypotheses about the general patterns and trends of family migration (Smith 2004). Indeed, during the 1970s and 1980s there were a number of defining hallmarks associated with studies of family migration. First, one of the major conventions was to view labor motivations as the primary stimulus of family migration. To investigate this dimension hypotheses were often constructed from the theoretical models of neoclassical economics, and the a priori behavior of economic rational actors (see Bailey & Boyle 2004). Second, there was an underlying assumption that family migration is triggered when the movement of the family unit yields an increase in total family income, irrespective of the impacts on the employment earnings or career aspirations of individuals

within the family. Third, family migration was often viewed as being induced by the male partner, in order to enhance his career development. This normalization of family life and behavior is clearly influenced by the taken-for-granted model of the traditional "male breadwinner/ female homemaker" couple. Many early studies therefore asserted that the employment aspirations of female partners are often "sacrificed" (i.e., unemployment or economic inactivity) or "satisficed" (i.e., part-time employment) following the movement of the family. Such a disenfranchisement of female partners within the labor market is borne out by the widely used terms "female tied migrant" and the "trailing spouse." Importantly, since the early 1990s this treatment of family migration has been widely critiqued, and theorizations and conceptualizations of family migration have shifted in three important, and interconnected, directions.

First, within quantitative studies of family migration there has been a more critical thinking to the ways in which family migrants are conceptualized and categorized. Traditionally, and tied to the limitations of data sets, analyses of family migration were predominantly based on aggregations of family migrants, with family migrants generally treated as "homogeneous lumps." With this in mind, some recent studies have constructed more nuanced categorizations of family migrants, which are more sensitive to intra-familial differences and diversity. One example is Boyle et al.'s (2002) use of microdata from the 1990 US and 1991 UK Census to reconstruct family units by linking together male and female partners. This technique allows an examination of the relational characteristics between migrant partners, and a consideration of the effects of different family and household arrangements and relations. In addition, early studies of family migration tended to focus on wholly-moving family units (i.e., male and female partners moving together), which implicitly treats family migration as a simplistic "neat" event.

Understandings of the links between family migration and processes of family and household formation were therefore, until recently, extremely limited (Smith 2004). This point is integral to Smith and Bailey's (2006) manipulation of UK Census microdata to explore how migrant families use different strategies which involves partners joining or moving together, and how these different strategies influence the post-migration labor-market status of both partners. Moreover, the above studies clearly adhere to Halfacree's (2001) call for scholars to be more reflexive when establishing taxonomic classifications of family migrants.

Second, ideas from social theory are now more fully embraced by scholars of family migration. One fruitful development has been a more critical perspective of the gendered dimensions of family migration, linked to critiques of the substantive relevance of human-capital hypotheses to explain tied migration. A pioneering work here is Halfacree's (1995) commentary of how and why female tied migrants are, in part, reproduced through the "structuration of patriarchy." This structurationist reading of family migration explicitly draws upon the writings of Anthony Giddens and Sylvia Walby, and demonstrates how theorizations of family migration can be usefully informed by wider social theories. In a similar vein, other recent studies have provided insights of the ways in which diverse familial arrangements and relations mediate family migration. Important accounts include Cooke's (2001) investigation of the effects of the onset of parenting and childrearing, and the presence and different numbers of dependent children; Bailey et al.'s (2004) assessment of how childcare and the care of elderly family members allow and constrain family migration; and Bonney et al.'s (1999) examination of the implications of marriage events and the rise of cohabitation on family migration. All of these studies incorporate a deeper-level analysis of the impacts of gendered power relations, and gender role ideology and task allocation on family migration decision-making and behavior.

A third development, and linked to the above, has been the implementation of post-positivist, inductive approaches within studies of family migration. Recent theory-building endeavors have involved the use of in-depth, qualitative research methods and the gathering of rich qualitative data to tease out the decision-making processes and behavior of family migrants. In the British context, for example, Hardill et al. (1997) and Green (1997) utilize biographical methods to explore the complex intra-familial negotiations, compromises, and tradeoffs which take place between male and female partners within dual-career couples. These studies draw attention to the importance of non-economic and cultural concerns (e.g., locational and residential preferences) within family migration decision-making processes, particularly quality-of-life aspirations, and stress that family migration is not always motivated by labor-related issues. In doing so, recent qualitative studies also reveal that family migration is not a straightforward, neat event. Rather, family migration is identified as a complex and experiential process, which involves many compromises, stresses, and anxieties for family members. One particular benefit of such qualitative research is that it is possible to more accurately assess changes in the pre- and post-migration status of family migrants, therefore providing a precise understanding of the effects of family migration when compared to quantitative studies using cross-sectional data sets (e.g., US and UK Censuses).

The above three interconnected developments have undoubtedly enabled scholars to capture the diversity of the processes and effects of family migration. However, one general commonality between recent findings is that family migration often has a negative impact on women's labor-market status. On the whole, the female tied migrant thesis is reaffirmed by recent studies; although it is important to note that many of the interpretations are based on short-term measures (i.e., within one year of move) of post-migration labor-market participation. Indeed, in a cross-national study of the effects of subnational family migration on the labor-market status of female partners in the US and UK, Boyle et al. (2002) reveal that the socioeconomic effects are remarkably similar for women in both contexts, despite major institutional and ideological differences. Likewise, studies in the Netherlands and Sweden point to family migration having a negative effect on women's labor-market status. It would appear, therefore, that despite rising levels of female employment in Europe and North America, family migration continues to be detrimental to women's labor-market participation.

Nevertheless, some recent studies disrupt the tied migrant thesis, and have demonstrated that geographical contingencies (e.g., labor-market opportunities, childcare support, public transportation) have a major impact on post-migration labor-market status of male and female partners. For example, Cooke and Bailey (1996) show that long-distance migration can have a positive effect on female labor-market status in some contexts within the US. It is contended that this positive effect is tied to family migrants moving into economic growth areas. Importantly, this interpretation overlaps with other migration studies which have examined links between rising female occupational status and movement into specific locations, such as Fielding's (1992) conceptualization of London and the southeast of England as an "escalator" region. In essence, these studies beg questions of the wider geographic pertinence of the tied migrant thesis.

Overall, the shifting treatment of family migration since the early 1990s has stimulated a vibrant interdisciplinary research agenda, with scholars now posing a broader range of research questions to investigate the diversity of family migration. This includes a richer appreciation of the influence of sociospatial contingencies on processes and outcomes of family migration. Tied to this is a growing interest with the ways in which family formations, ethnicity, race, age, life course, sexuality, class, and culture cross-cut with different expressions of family migration. Another useful entry point for future research is the inclusion of other types of family structure, such as lone parent, single-adult, multi-person, and same-sex couples within analyses of family migration, and the need to transcend the considerable focus on heterosexual nuclear families.

SEE ALSO: Immigrant Families; Migration: International; Migration and the Labor Force

REFERENCES AND SUGGESTED READINGS

Bailey, A. J. & Boyle, P. J. (2004) Untying and Retying Family Migration in the New Europe. *Journal of Ethnic and Migration Studies* 30: 229–41.

Bailey, A. J., Blake, M., & Cooke, T. J. (2004) Migration, Care, and Linked Lives of Dual-Earner Households. *Environment and Planning A* 36: 1617–32.

Bonney, N., McCleary, A., & Forster, E. (1999) Migration, Marriage and the Life Course: Commitment and Residential Mobility. In: Boyle, P. J. & Halfacree, K. H. (Eds.), *Migration and Gender in the Developed World*. Routledge, London, pp. 136–50.

Boyle, P. J., Cooke, T., Halfacree, K. H., & Smith, D. P. (2002) A Cross-National Study of the Effects of Family Migration and Women's Labour Market Status: Some Difficulties with Integrating Microdata from Two Censuses. *Journal of the Royal Statistical Society A* 165: 465–80.

Cooke, T. J. (2001) "Trailing Wife" or "Trailing Mother"? The Effect of Parental Status on the Relationship Between Family Migration and the Labor-Market Participation of Married Women. *Environment and Planning A* 33: 419–30.

Cooke, T. J. & Bailey, A. J. (1996) Family Migration and the Employment of Married Women and Men. *Economic Geography* 72: 38–48.

Fielding, A. J. (1992) Migration and Social Mobility: Southeast England as an "Escalator" Region. *Regional Studies* 26: 1–15.

Green, A. E. (1997) A Question of Compromise? Case Study Evidence on the Location and Mobility Strategies of Dual Career Households. *Regional Studies* 31: 641–57.

Halfacree, K. H. (1995) Household Migration and the Structuration of Patriarchy: Evidence from the USA. *Progress in Human Geography* 19: 159–82.

Halfacree, K. H. (2001) Constructing the Object: Taxonomic Practices, "Counterurbanization" and Positioning Marginal Rural Settlement. *International Journal of Population Geography* 7: 395–411.

Hardill, I., Green, A. E., Dudleston, A. C., & Owen, D. W. (1997) Who Decides What? Decision Making in Dual Career Households. *Work, Employment and Society* 22: 313–26.

Kofman, E. (2004) Family-Related Migration: A Critical Review of European Studies. *Journal of Ethnic and Migration Studies* 30: 243–62.

Smith, D. P. (2004) An "Untied" Research Agenda for Family Migration: Loosening the "Shackles" of the Past. *Journal of Ethnic and Migration Studies* 30: 263–82.

Smith, D. P. & Bailey, A. J. (2006) International "Family" Migration and Differential Labour Market Participation: Is There a "Gender Gap" in Great Britain? *Environment and Planning A*.

family planning, abortion, and reproductive health

Ann E. Biddlecom

Many societies have made the transition from high mortality and large family sizes to settings where most children survive, small families are desired, and most people control their fertility. In the early 1960s, the average woman could expect to have almost five children over her life, but now she can expect to have fewer than three children. The conscious use of contraception and abortion to control fertility thus assumes paramount importance in explaining basic aspects of contemporary human society. However, substantial differences exist in fertility and contraceptive levels and access to services between developed and developing regions of the world. For example, while in more developed regions women now have fewer than two children on average and nearly 7 in 10 women in marital or consensual unions use contraceptives (mainly sterilization, the pill, or the male condom), women in Africa have about five children on average and fewer than 3 in 10 women in marital or consensual unions use contraceptives (mainly the pill, injectables, and implants) (United Nations 2004). Other factors such as social structure, culture, gender relations, and economic opportunities also contribute to these regional differences.

The area of sexual and reproductive health is broad and encompasses *sexual behavior* (as it relates to marriage, pregnancy, and fertility; adolescents' sexual activity; and risky sexual behaviors that can lead to unintended pregnancy, sexually transmitted infections (STIs) and the human immunodeficiency virus (HIV)); *STIs and other reproductive tract infections* (the prevention, diagnosis, and treatment of these infections); *contraceptive use* (measuring the demand for and effective use of contraceptive methods, reasons for non-use, and method choice and discontinuation); *abortion* (levels of and access to abortion, unsafe abortion and its consequences, and post-abortion care); *reproductive morbidities* (e.g., infertility and reproductive cancers, obstetric fistula, and consequences of female genital cutting); *contraceptive and abortion technology* (the feasibility, acceptability, and demand for new methods such as medical abortion, female condoms, microbicides, and various male contraceptive methods); *family planning-related information and education* (including sex education in schools and condom promotion); and *reproductive health care* (e.g., financing, access to, and quality of reproductive health care and its effects on reproductive outcomes). Studies tend to have close ties to health policies and programs and focus on levels, determinants, and consequences of family planning, abortion, and sexual and reproductive health-related problems. Sources of evidence have changed immensely over time, moving from a heavy reliance on indirect estimates based on census data to population-based surveys (from the 1970s onward) and clinic-based studies to the use of qualitative evidence (from the 1990s onward), mainly from focus group discussions, in-depth interviews, and ethnographies.

Research and public policy emphases up until the early 1990s were grounded in arguments for reducing population growth, and the areas of abortion and reproductive health were not very visible. The 1994 International Conference on Population and Development (ICPD) in Cairo, Egypt, and its final document, the Program of Action, shifted the focus from overpopulation concerns and demographic targets to an emphasis on reproductive rights. An example of this shift is reflected in the increasing use of the concept of "unmet need for family planning," which includes both contraceptive behavior and fertility preferences and reflects the situation of individuals who want to avoid or delay a birth but who are not using any method of contraception, as a justification for and indicator of family planning program efforts and needs (Casterline & Sinding 2000). Understanding why people are in this apparently paradoxical situation and how best to meet their contraceptive needs adheres to the overall approach of satisfying individual reproductive choice rather than meeting national targets. Recent studies point to lack of knowledge about contraceptive methods, social opposition to contraceptive use, and concerns about health side-effects as important reasons for why women and men do not use contraceptives though they want to delay or avoid pregnancy (Casterline & Sinding 2000).

The ICPD conference also expanded sexual and reproductive health to encompass a broad set of issues beyond family planning, such as women's rights to control their sexuality. Subsequent policymaking, advocacy, and scholarship turned to gender inequities that affect key determinants of sexual and reproductive health. The often unstated assumption that women hold full decision-making power over their health has been supplanted by research on the influence of spouses, parents, and peers, gender-based power and violence in sexual relationships, women's status and access to resources, and neighborhood and community-level characteristics. For example, while a community-based family planning program in Ghana led to increased contraceptive use, there were related strains in gender relations in the communities and fears among women of beatings by their husbands if they used contraceptives (Bawah et al. 1999). There is also increased attention to how voluntary sexual intercourse is, especially for young women, and the implications of these findings for women's rights as well as sexual and reproductive health. Several studies in developed and developing countries show evidence that women who experience sexual or physical abuse (in childhood or in relationships as adults) are also more likely to experience STIs, pelvic inflammatory disease, and unwanted fertility (Jejeebhoy & Koenig 2003).

Broadening the interpretation of reproductive health to include more than family planning has been supported by the dramatic spread of HIV/AIDS since the 1980s. The epidemic has spurred research on male condom use for HIV and STI prevention, including investigations of the barriers to consistent and correct use of condoms and women's difficulties in negotiating condom use, and has legitimated the study of sexual behavior as it relates to sexual and reproductive health. Issues that continue to plague researchers and program planners alike include the difficulty of increasing condom use (especially within marriage), how protection from disease is reconciled with planning births, and how the nature of reproductive decision-making has changed in the context of HIV/AIDS, especially for people who are HIV-positive.

Historically, women's experiences dominated research studies and data on family planning, abortion, and reproductive health, since women were deemed more accurate reporters of reproductive events and perceived as the people "at risk." Many data collection efforts in the 1960s were limited to married women and then expanded in the 1970s, and later in some regions, to include unmarried women. Evidence on men's sexual and reproductive health is mainly from the 1990s and 2000s. A recent worldwide study documented that men are involved in family planning decisions – many have discussed family planning with their partners and used methods to space or limit births – and many men who have an STI say they have informed their partners of the infection or have sought treatment (Alan Guttmacher Institute 2003). Nevertheless, established family planning and reproductive health care services are much better developed for women in most countries (though there are still subgroups of women who are underserved) than for men.

Recent research incorporates men's views and experiences by studying couples and their reproductive behaviors. Studies of couples reflect the broader social context in which decisions like contraceptive use are made, and evidence shows that partners have significant influence over one another's contraceptive behavior via their individual fertility preferences and approval of and communication about family planning. Couple studies have tended to focus on contraceptive use (including condom use for preventing STIs), and much less on abortion or other sexual and reproductive health outcomes. One methodological challenge which arises is when partners have different reports of the same behavior. For example, men have been shown to report much higher levels of condom use than do women, both in the aggregate and within couples.

Abortion remains one of the more difficult topics to study despite its widespread practice – estimates suggest that about one-quarter of pregnancies worldwide end in abortion – because of the moral arguments surrounding abortion, the criminalization of the practice in many countries, and the clandestine nature of abortion for many women and abortion providers. Measuring the extent of abortion and abortion-related complications, particularly in countries where abortion is illegal and records are not maintained at health facilities, is critical to understanding the magnitude of the public health impact of abortion. Methods to measure the prevalence of abortion include records from registration systems (based on reports from hospitals, clinics, and private doctors), surveys of abortion providers, and surveys of women in the community. Other techniques, such as third-party reports, where women report on abortions they know other women in the community or in their social networks have had, have also been used. Most evidence is on the level of abortion and much less on reasons why women obtain abortions and the social, health, and economic consequences of unsafe abortion. Monitoring changes in public opinion toward abortion, especially the conditions under which it should be legal, is also important given links between popular acceptance of abortion and the politics of its legal status. Yet even abortion attitudes are difficult to measure; for example, more people in the United States agree that abortion should be legal for any reason when a survey question specifies a first trimester pregnancy than when no pregnancy gestation is stated (Bumpass 1999).

With the continued decline of fertility worldwide, persistent inequities in sexual and reproductive health (including access to services), and the spread of HIV/AIDS, questions about the ways that women and men – as individuals and as partners in sexual relationships – can better achieve their childbearing desires and protect their sexual and reproductive health become increasingly important to address. Future directions for social research will include a focus on the contextual factors that shape individuals' use of contraception, abortion, and reproductive health services; the continued inclusion of men in analyses of sexual and reproductive health; understanding the barriers to effective contraceptive use; ways to increase the dual use of contraceptive methods for pregnancy and STI prevention; the conditions under which risky or coercive sex occurs; greater attention to sexual and reproductive decision-making; and new techniques to improve reporting of sexual behavior and abortion.

SEE ALSO: Abortion as a Social Problem; Fertility: Adolescent; Fertility: Nonmarital; Fertility and Public Policy; HIV/AIDS and Population; Infant, Child, and Maternal Health and Mortality; Infertility; New Reproductive Technologies

REFERENCES AND SUGGESTED READINGS

Alan Guttmacher, Institute (2003) *In Their Own Right: Addressing the Sexual and Reproductive Health Needs of Men Worldwide*. Alan Guttmacher Institute, New York.

Bawah, A. A., Akweongo, P., Simmons, R., & Phillips, J. F. (1999) The Impact of Family Planning on Gender Relations in Northern Ghana. *Studies in Family Planning* 30(1): 54–66.

Blanc, A. K. (2001) The Effect of Power in Sexual Relationships on Sexual and Reproductive Health: An Examination of the Evidence. *Studies in Family Planning* 32(3): 189–213.

Bumpass, L. (1999) The Measurement of Public Opinion on Abortion: The Effects of Survey Design. *Family Planning Perspectives* 29(4): 177–80.

Casterline, J. B. & Sinding, S. W. (2000) Unmet Need for Family Planning in Developing Countries and Implications for Population Policy. *Population and Development Review* 26(4): 691–723.

Hatcher, R. A., Trussell, J., Stewart, F., Cates, Jr., W., Stewart, G. K., Guest, F., & Kowal, D. (1998) *Contraceptive Technology*, 17th revised edition. Ardent Media Inc., New York.

Jejeebhoy, S. & Koenig, M. (2003) The Social Context of Gynaecological Morbidity: Correlates, Consequences and Health Seeking Behaviour. In: Jejeebhoy, S., Koenig, M., & Elias, C. (Eds.), *Reproductive Tract Infections and Other Gynaecological Disorders*. Cambridge University Press, Cambridge, pp. 30–81.

Sen, G., Germain, A., & Chen, L. C. (Eds.) (1994) *Population Policies Reconsidered: Health, Empowerment, and Rights*. Harvard University Press, Cambridge, MA.

Singh, S., Henshaw, S. K., & Berentsen, K. (2003) Abortion: A Worldwide Overview. In: Basu, A. M. (Ed.), *The Sociocultural and Political Aspects of Abortion: Global Perspectives*. Praeger, Westport, CT, pp. 15–48.

Tsui, A. O., Wasserheit, J. N., & Haaga, J. G. (Eds.) (1997) *Reproductive Health in Developing Countries: Expanding Dimensions, Building Solutions*. National Academy Press, Washington, DC.

United, Nations (2004) *World Contraceptive Use 2003*. United Nations, New York.

United, Nations (2005) *World Population Prospects: The 2004 Revision*. United Nations, New York.

Van de Walle, E. & Renne, E. P. (Eds.) (2001) *Regulating Menstruation: Beliefs, Practices, Interpretations*. University of Chicago Press, Chicago.

family poverty

Mark R. Rank

Family poverty generally refers to households lacking a minimum amount of income. However, specific definitions and measurements of poverty vary widely across countries. In the US, family poverty is officially measured in terms of whether various sized households fall below specific annual income levels. In Europe, poverty is frequently defined as residing in a household that falls below one half of the national median income. In developing countries the standard is often that of living in a family earning less than a dollar a day. The underlying concept behind all of these approaches is that there is a basic minimum amount of income necessary in order for families to carry on their day-to-day activities adequately. Families that fail to acquire such income are considered poor.

The social scientific study of family poverty dates back to the turn of the twentieth century with Seebohm Rowntree's study of 11,560 working-class families in the English city of York. Rowntree's research indicated that working-class families were more likely to experience poverty at certain stages in the family life cycle during which they were particularly economically vulnerable (e.g., the period of starting a new family and during retirement). Since that time, social scientists have been interested in family poverty for at least three major reasons. First, there has been a longstanding concern regarding the role that families play in the intergenerational transmission of poverty. Second, there is considerable interest in the importance of family structure as a causal factor leading to poverty, and in particular, understanding the relationship between single-parent families and the risk of poverty. A third line of research has examined the detrimental effects that poverty exerts upon family functioning and development. In each case, much of the social scientific research on poverty has taken place in the developed world, particularly within the US.

Early work addressing family poverty frequently assumed that poverty was chronic and handed down from generation to generation. One longstanding argument to explain this pattern was that it resulted from the larger economic reproduction of social class. Families with few resources are unable to provide their offspring with the types of advantages necessary for getting ahead economically, resulting in a perpetuation of poverty from one generation to the next. Recent economic and sociological work in this area has shown a strong correlation between parents' and children's socioeconomic status.

An important variation of this perspective was the culture of poverty framework derived from the ethnographic work of Oscar Lewis in the 1950s and 1960s. Lewis studied lower-class Mexican and Puerto Rican families residing in slum communities in both New York and Puerto Rico. He argued that chronic high unemployment and underemployment, coupled with little opportunity for upward mobility, led to what he called a culture of poverty. Such a culture was most likely to arise in economically depressed and isolated areas such as urban inner cities or remote rural areas. The culture provided families with a means for coping with their poverty. Traits include a present-time orientation, strong networks of kinship ties, and an unwillingness to delay gratification. These traits were then passed on from parents to children, contributing to an intergenerational transmission of poverty. Lewis wrote: "it is both an adaptation and a reaction of the poor to their marginal position in a class-stratified, highly individuated capitalistic society . . . Once the culture of poverty has come into existence it tends to perpetuate itself" (Lewis 1966: 22). While such a culture allows families to better cope with their environment, it also makes it more difficult for them and their children to break out of poverty.

Although Lewis stressed that only approximately 20 percent of US poor families fell into such a culture of poverty, those who utilized this perspective during the 1960s and 1970s often linked the majority of families in poverty with a culture of poverty. In particular, it was closely associated with poverty among African American families. The culture of poverty perspective also exerted a significant effect on the social policy of the US in the 1960s. Policy initiatives and programs arising out of the War on Poverty such as the Moynihan report, Head Start, and community action were all influenced by this perspective. In addition, popular books such as Michael Harrington's *The Other America* (1962) were strongly influenced by the culture of poverty framework.

With the advent of several large, longitudinal data sets such as the Panel Study of Income Dynamics (PSID) and the National Longitudinal Survey of Youth (NLSY) in the late 1960s and 1970s, the assumption that family poverty was chronic, longlasting, and intergenerational could be empirically examined. Of particular significance was the 1984 book by Greg Duncan entitled *Years of Poverty, Years of Plenty*. Using 10 years of the PSID data, Duncan demonstrated that family poverty was to a large extent episodic rather than chronic. The typical pattern was that households were impoverished for one or two years and then managed to get above the poverty line, perhaps experiencing an additional spell of poverty at some later point in their lives. This and other longitudinal work showed a much more fluid and dynamic picture of family poverty than had frequently been assumed. Duncan and others also demonstrated that one of the critical factors leading households into poverty was family dissolution and the formation of single-parent (generally female-headed) families.

The rise of female-headed families with children during the last third of the twentieth century (fueled by the high rate of divorce and an increasing number of out-of-wedlock births) became a major area of research among US sociologists and social scientists studying the patterns and causes of poverty. The popularity of the term *the feminization of poverty*, coined by Diana Pierce, illustrated the emphasis in the 1980s and 1990s of looking at gender and family structure as important factors leading to poverty. A large volume of research demonstrated that female-headed families with children were at a significant risk of encountering poverty and economic destitution. Various

studies showed that following a divorce, the standard of living for women and their children declined sharply. Many women worked at lower-paying jobs and lacked child-support payments. The result was that female-headed families with children had a substantially higher rate of poverty than other types of families, and experienced poverty for longer periods of time.

Of particular importance to the area of single-parent families and poverty has been the work of William Julius Wilson. In both of his two major books, *The Truly Disadvantaged* (1987) and *When Work Disappears* (1996), Wilson focused on the deteriorating conditions of inner city minority families in Chicago. Somewhat along the lines of Oscar Lewis, he argued that declining economic opportunities in central cities have led to the breakdown of the family and to the rise of poverty. In particular, Wilson notes there has been a decreasing number of employable men in central cities, resulting in greater numbers of female-headed families with children. Such families, in turn, are at a heightened risk of long-term poverty.

These and other research findings spotlighting the significance of family structure have led to an academic and political debate regarding the importance of encouraging marriage as a strategy for alleviating family poverty. Recent welfare reform legislation in the US has placed a strong emphasis on policies and programs to encourage marriage and to discourage out-of-wedlock births. Others have argued that a more reasonable and effective policy approach is to provide the supports necessary for all families and children to succeed, not just those in married-couple families.

A third research emphasis within the area of family poverty has been to examine the independent effect that poverty has upon family development and functioning. This body of research has shown that poverty influences family functioning in a variety of ways. Poverty exerts a profound influence upon the health and development of family members. Poverty is associated with a host of health risks, including elevated rates of heart disease, diabetes, hypertension, cancer, infant mortality, malnutrition, mental illness, and a variety of other diseases. The result is that family members living in poverty have significantly higher mortality rates and shorter life expectancies than the non-poor. Furthermore, poor infants and young children are likely to have far lower levels of physical and mental growth (as measured in a variety of ways) than their non-poor counterparts. Both the duration and the depth of poverty intensify these negative outcomes. The result is that poverty can have longlasting physical and mental consequences as children become adults.

Research has also demonstrated that poverty affects family structure and functioning. First, the likelihood of marriage is substantially reduced among the poverty stricken. Second, women at lower income and educational levels tend to have children at earlier ages and are more likely to bear children out of wedlock. Third, several ethnographic studies have indicated that the poor are more likely to use a larger network of kinship than the non-poor to exchange resources and services. Fourth, poverty and lower income are associated with greater levels of marital stress, dissatisfaction, and dissolution. Fifth, higher levels of domestic violence tend to be found within poverty-stricken households. In each of these cases, the economic stress caused by poverty is hypothesized as an important factor behind these associations.

In addition to the direct effects on the family, researchers have also examined the effect that high rates of neighborhood poverty have on the viability of the community, which in turn influences the viability of the family. Major research areas include the relationships between neighborhood poverty and elevated rates of crime, neighborhood poverty and declining social capital, and neighborhood poverty and the increasing risk of environmental pollution and hazards. Each of these in turn have been shown to have a detrimental effect on the health and functioning of low-income families residing in impoverished neighborhoods.

Finally, recent work has examined the wider effects of family poverty upon society at large. Mark Robert Rank's book *One Nation, Underprivileged* (2004) illustrates the connections between family poverty and a host of societal problems and issues. This body of work has also documented the widespread risk of family poverty and economic vulnerability for the population as a whole. Between the ages of

20 and 75, approximately three-quarters of Americans will reside in a household that experiences poverty or near poverty for at least one year. Research in European countries has also begun to demonstrate the prevalent nature of families experiencing poverty at some point during the life course.

SEE ALSO: Children and Divorce; Culture of Poverty; Family Structure and Poverty; Feminization of Poverty; Lone-Parent Families; Poverty; Welfare Dependency and Welfare Underuse

REFERENCES AND SUGGESTED READINGS

Danziger, S. H. & Haveman, R. H. (2001) *Understanding Poverty*. Russell Sage Foundation, New York.

Duncan, G. J. (1984) *Years of Poverty, Years of Plenty: The Changing Economic Fortunes of American Workers and Families*. Institute for Social Research, Ann Arbor.

Harrington, M. (1962) *The Other America: Poverty in the United States*. Macmillan, New York.

Leisering, L. & Leibfried, L. (1999) *Time and Poverty in Western Welfare States: United Germany in Perspective*. Cambridge University Press, Cambridge.

Lewis, O. (1966) The Culture of Poverty. *Scientific American* 215: 19–25.

McLanahan, S. & Sandefur, G. (1994) *Growing Up with a Single Parent: What Hurts, What Helps*. Harvard University Press, Cambridge, MA.

Rank, M. R. (2004) *One Nation, Underprivileged: Why American Poverty Affects Us All*. Oxford University Press, New York.

Rowntree, B. S. (1901) *Poverty: A Study of Town Life*. Macmillan, London.

Wilson, W. J. (1987) *The Truly Disadvantaged: The Inner City, the Underclass, and Public Policy*. University of Chicago Press, Chicago.

Wilson, W. J. (1996) *When Work Disappears: The World of the New Urban Poor*. Knopf, New York.

family, sociology of

Joel Powell and Karen Branden

Sociology of family is the area devoted to the study of family as an institution central to social life. The basic assumptions of the area include the universality of family, the inevitable variation of family forms, and the necessity of family for integrating individuals into social worlds. Family sociology is generally concerned with the formation, maintenance, growth, and dissolution of kinship ties and is commonly expressed in research on courtship and marriage, childrearing, marital adjustment, and divorce. These areas of research expanded in the twentieth century to encompass an endless diversity of topics related to gender, sexuality, intimacy, affection, and anything that can be considered to be family-related.

A recognizable, modern sociology of family emerged from several different family studies efforts of the nineteenth century. Early anthropologists speculated that family was a necessary step from savagery to civilization in human evolution. Concentrating on marital regulation of sexual encounters, and debating matriarchy versus patriarchy as the first enduring family forms, these explanations framed family studies in terms of kinship and defined comprehensive categories of family relations. In consideration of endogamy, exogamy, polygamy, polyandry, and monogamy, these efforts also fostered discussion of the best or most evolved family forms, with most commentators settling on patriarchy and monogamy as the high points of family evolution.

Nineteenth-century sociologists such as Herbert Spencer and William Sumner adopted evolutionary views of family and made use of anthropological terms, but discussions of best family types gave way to considering the customs, conventions, and traditions of family life. The evolutionary view of family pushed sociology toward the pragmatic vision of the family as adaptable to surrounding social conditions. And sociology's emphases on populations, societies, and the institutions embedded within them allowed the observation that American and European families were rapidly changing in response to the challenges of modern society.

Another important development in early family sociology resulted from the growing distinction of sociology from religion, charity, and activism. Commentaries of the middle and late nineteenth century warned urgently of the social problems of divorce and abandonment – citing individualism, easy morals, and lax divorce laws for a breakdown of family. Family

advocates saw such decline as a sure cause of more social calamities and sought reliable social data and solutions. While sociologists of the day were concerned with social pathologies, they were also working to establish sociology as an objective, scientific discipline. Scientific work on family issues specifically had already been completed. Shortly after the US Census Bureau published a report on marriage and divorce statistics in 1889, Walter Willcox completed *The Divorce Problem: A Study in Statistics* (1891). This study presented the family as a strong, flexible institution, and linked divorce to social conditions. Casting family change as a dependent variable and subjecting divorce to demographic analysis were two strong indicators of an emerging science of family that would be relatively independent from moral concerns. This type of analysis also satisfied scientific urges to predict and explain.

Interest in the properties of family as an institution, and the incidental necessity of describing family for other sociological work, contributed to the development of scientific, sociological approaches as well. This was shown in the breadth and scope of Thomas and Znanieki's *The Polish Peasant in Europe and America* (1929). The family as a socializing agency, the pressures of urbanization and industrialization on family, the effects of immigration, and the problems of migration from rural to urban life were all addressed in *The Polish Peasant*. Thomas and Znaniecki cast the Polish immigrant family as an object for neutral sociological analysis and examined the effects of rapid change and disorganization on the integrity of the family. In these ways the family was revealed as an institution situated in society and subject to social influences.

During the first two decades of the twentieth century, sociological study was seldom devoted exclusively to family. The family as a topic in its own right was still most often the province of social workers concerned with social problems and therapeutic issues. Still, these interests overlapped with sociological concerns about social pathologies and helped to maintain general, academic interest in a scientific sociology of family. In the 1920s the landmark accomplishments for sociology of family included the first American Sociological Association sessions on family and the development of a section on family in the journal *Social Forces*. At the University of Chicago, Ernest Burgess elaborated the properties of family as a collection of interacting individuals, and encouraged a commitment to prediction and explanation in all of sociology including the area of family. This further distinguished sociological family research from the concerns of activists and social workers, and by the end of the decade a fully formed, scientific sociology of family was visible in textbooks, classrooms, and scholarly journals.

During the institution-building phase (Maines 2001) of sociology up to World War II, sociology was empirical, quantitative, and theoretical. Family sociology was compatible with abiding, understandable variables in sociology such as race, class, and religion, and topics associated with family sociology multiplied rapidly in the 1930s, 1940s, and 1950s. Sociological research on family investigated rural, urban, and black families, explored the impact of the Depression, observed the migration of families from the country to the city, and described the characteristics of single-parent families. Much of this work presented families in structure and process (as in the roles of grandparents and the process of grandparenting), types of families (like military families), internal dynamics such as decision-making or emotional conflict, or basic life processes such as housing and employment. Many more topics were developing, of course, and research continued on the topics that had come to represent family sociology – courtship, marriage, socialization, and divorce. Family sociology grew to be among the largest specialty areas of the discipline during the middle decades of the twentieth century. It was a robust and diverse area. Family sociology also became historical in its orientation to changes, trends, and patterns over time. For example, researchers noted a constant increase in the percentage of marriages ending in divorce and linked the increases to changes in economy, law, and the changing roles of women who were entering the workforce in increasing numbers. Family sociology was comparative within and between cultures. It compared families by race, geography, income, and occupation in the United States, and as the sociological community became more global, American sociologists conducted more international family comparisons and American journals published significant international work. As was much of American sociology at mid-century, family was relentlessly empirical, demographic, and quantitative. The known and understood areas of family such as marriage, fertility, and divorce were particularly amenable to statistical analysis.

Although the popularity of family sociology was represented in a large body of empirical research, the theoretical contributions of family sociologists were relatively narrow. The commitment to an explanatory and predictive family sociology first expressed by Burgess came to be represented by a sociology of straightforward, testable propositions and quantitative descriptions of phenomena. For example, family sociologists might be interested in measuring the effects of divorce on the school performance of children, determining the influence of birth order on personality, or collecting the personal traits of the ideal mate. Family theory aimed at phenomena no more general than family roles, organization, life cycles, and the like. While theoretical work tended to be topic specific, and did not offer refinements to established sociological perspectives, it was also evident that family sociology was relatively free of the intellectual directives of major schools. Attempts to show how family sociology should be framed by theory were rare; so much so that a 1979 collection by Burr and his associates is still considered particularly noteworthy. Family sociology rather kept pace with advances in descriptive and inferential statistics. Researchers produced thousands of journal articles from the 1950s through the 1980s that were increasingly data-driven and quantitative. Half of all articles in the *Journal of Marriage and Family* were empirical by the end of the 1970s. By the end of the 1980s, 90 percent of *Journal of Marriage and the Family* articles were empirical (Adams 1988).

Because research and commentary in family sociology are guided more often by topical interests than by gaps in theory, family has been one of the most fluid and open areas of sociology. The open quality of family sociology has widened the array of staple topics to include cohabitation, childlessness, and extramarital sex, to name only a few, and family is clearly among the most responsive specialties to popular and political issues. In the 1980s this was already apparent in the frequency of research enterprises related to policy. Responding to conservative shifts in fiscal politics, family sociologists in the US conducted extensive research on the impact of changes in welfare, Medicaid and Medicare, and Aid to Families with Dependent Children (AFDC). Family planning, contraception, and abortion policies also received attention during the 1980s in a time of a perceived reactionary cultural climate. This attention has persisted as private sector funding sources reevaluate their support for family planning agencies, state legislatures tighten abortion restrictions, and contraceptive technologies advance. Real and proposed changes in social security in the late twentieth century have pushed policy research on aging families. Government and business practices associated with a globalizing economy have been scrutinized in recent years. In these and other areas, family sociologists have explored reciprocal effects of family and family policy, considering how changes in family behavior have influenced policies, and how policy changes have affected different types of families.

The large balance of sociological research on family is still as insulated as most professional intellectual activity, and concentrates on issues primarily of interest to scholars. But the policy and issue discussions of the 1980s reflected deeper cultural and political divides that did become important to public presentations of contemporary family sociology. In the most accessible venues of classrooms, texts, trade books, periodicals, and weblogs, family sociologists have slipped into debunking roles in responding to popular social criticism or common myths and misunderstandings. Typically this involves minor factual correctives that address sensational but accepted media narratives – there is not an epidemic of teen pregnancy (rates continue to decrease), there is no precipitous decline in US households with children, but slow changes related to delayed marriage, low unemployment, and an aging population. More often family sociologists address diffuse, popular anxiety about the family in "decline," in "crisis," or the "breakdown" of the family. The common view of divorce rates as an indicator of family decline

can be addressed by historical analysis of changing divorce laws, the relative marital satisfaction of modern couples, the desire for marriage expressed by the overwhelming majority of young people, the blending of families after divorce, or the abiding interest in their children shared by divorced parents. Common concerns about the negative effects on children and marriage of two-career families are countered by an examination of the benefits – more income, less stress, healthier and happier women, and men more engaged with their children. What is brought to the public from family sociology is the established and unified view that the family is a tough, flexible institution that is constantly in transition, and that decline and crisis are critical evaluations rather than scientific conclusions.

In recent years family sociologists seem especially sensitive to national discussions of family issues. Family research and commentary often amplify political rhetoric, and scientific findings are obscured by political debate. Moreover, well-funded moral entrepreneurs (Becker 1973) have adopted nomenclatures and trappings that ape the process of peer-reviewed science. Clinicians and academics from a variety of disciplines founded the Council on Contemporary Families in 1996 specifically to bring accurate information about family research to the public. The foundational assumption of the Council is that shifts in family life are best met with investigations of underlying causes rather than moralizing discourse. Though a decidedly progressive organization, its stance against the framework of families-in-decline because of selfishness and immorality is within the mainstream of sociological thought.

If family sociology were more visible to the lay public, its basic assumptions would be recognized as politically liberal and culturally progressive. This is nowhere more apparent than in the passionate inclusiveness of sociological definitions of family. Having established the perspective that family is plastic and resilient, rather than fixed and vulnerable, sociology necessarily accounts for families in all of their emergent forms. This standpoint was manageable for a twentieth-century sociology that had variations of the two-parent household as its units of analysis. Now, along with single-parent families, extended families, stepfamilies, and blended families, contemporary family sociology accounts for gay and lesbian families. That gay and lesbian relationships are accorded the family label attests to the non-judgmental attitude popularly associated with liberal thinking. Invocations of family in political debate reveal the deep understanding that most people belong to families and hold cherished values associated with family life. And family sociologists commonly observe that everyone who has been in a family is somewhat expert in family sociology. However, in its refusal to find an ideal family form and the causes of family decline, family sociology departs from this commonsense expertise. This is the scientific quality of family sociology. It will remain topical, comparative, and empirical, but the politics and rhetoric of family will increasingly frame its issues.

SEE ALSO: Divorce; Family Demography; Family Diversity; Family, History of; Family Structure; Family Theory; Kinship; Lesbian and Gay Families; Marriage; Socialization

REFERENCES AND SUGGESTED READINGS

Adams, B. N. (1988) Fifty Years of Family Research: What Does It Mean? *Journal of Marriage and the Family* 50: 5–17.

Becker, H. S. (1973) *Outsiders: Studies in the Sociology of Deviance*, 2nd edn. Free Press, New York.

Berardo, F. M. (1990) Trends and Directions in Family Research in the 1980s. *Journal of Marriage and the Family* 52: 809–17.

Burgess, E. W. (1926) The Family as a Unity of Interacting Personalities. *Family* 7: 3–9.

Burr, W. R., Hill, R., Nye, F. I., & Reiss, I. L. (Eds.) (1979) *Contemporary Theories About the Family: General Theories/Theoretical Orientations*. Free Press, New York.

Busch, R. C. (1990) *Family Systems: Comparative Study of the Family*. Peter Lang, New York.

Cherlin, A. (2005) *Public and Private Families*, 4th edn. McGraw-Hill, Boston.

Coontz, S. (1992) *The Way We Never Were: American Families and the Nostalgia Trap*. Basic Books, New York.

Howard, R. L. (1981) *A Social History of American Family Sociology, 1865–1940*. Greenwood Press, Westport, CT.

Maines, D. R. (2001) *The Faultline of Consciousness: A View of Interactionism in Sociology*. Aldine de Gruyter, New York.

Scott, J., Treas, J., & Richards, M. (Eds.) (2004) *The Blackwell Companion to the Sociology of Families*. Blackwell, Malden, MA.

Shannon, C. L. (1989) *The Politics of the Family: From Homo Sapiens to Homo Economicus*. Peter Lang, New York.

Stacey, J. (1997) *In the Name of the Family: Rethinking Family Values in the Postmodern Age*. Beacon Press, Boston.

Willcox, W. F. (1891) *The Divorce Problem: A Study in Statistics*. Columbia University Studies in History, Economics, and Public Law, Vol. 1. Columbia University Press, New York.

family structure

Graham Allan

Within any society there are more or less common ways of "doing" family relationships. That is, there are ways of organizing family relationships which are broadly accepted as appropriate and given legitimacy in that society. This does not mean that all family relationships are similar or that all follow the same societally imposed "rules." There are always variations, exceptions, and alternative practices. Moreover, the more complex and diverse the society, the more variation there will be in the family practices given legitimacy by different social groupings within it. Indeed, one aspect of different family systems is the social tolerance given to divergent patterns of family relationships. Nonetheless, it is useful, at least heuristically, to ask questions about the dominant family structures existing in different societies, in part to facilitate comparison and understand the variations that arise. The types of questions posed by sociologists concerned with family structures involve such issues as the distribution of power and authority within families; the patterns of solidarity and obligation that arise between different family members; and the differential access to resources that different family members have. A key prior question concerns the boundaries of family membership and belonging: Who is considered "family," when, and for what purposes?

In examining family structure it is important to distinguish "family" from "household," though the two are frequently elided, a tendency which itself is indicative of contemporary understandings of family structure. Household structure refers to the demography of households, domestic living arrangements, and domestic economies. Family structure, on the other hand, is concerned with the organization of kin relationships, though part of this also concerns how domestic life is framed and the different roles and responsibilities that different family members have within this. Indeed, historically, many of the key debates in the early years of family sociology were integrally concerned with the types of household structure that predominated in different societies. In particular, debates about the transformations that industrial capitalism generated in family structures often reflected the changed household composition found in developing industrial urban areas, legitimately so as these demographic changes reflected different familial obligations and solidarities. Nonetheless, analytically it is important to recognize that family structure reflects more than just household structure.

This becomes of consequence in examining some of the key theoretical developments in family sociology in the mid-part of the twentieth century. In these, the dominant model of change, expressed with greater or lesser subtlety, was one that highlighted the movement from an "extended family" system to a "nuclear family" – one of parents and dependent children. The most compelling and sophisticated account of this shift was produced by Parsons (1943), who argued the "structural isolation" of the nuclear (or in Parsons's terms, "conjugal") family was a dominant aspect of mid-twentieth century American kinship. Parsons's starting point was that industrialization involved increased functional specialization. The family as a social institution was affected by this as much as any other institution. It too became more specialized, with its prime roles becoming the socialization of the young and the stabilization of adult personalities. The family structure that Parsons saw as most compatible with this was a nuclear family structure in which husbands and wives also had differentiated roles – employment for husbands and domestic responsibilities for wives. Parsons's argument was that within this family structure,

each individual's primary kinship responsibility was to the other members of his or her nuclear family. An advantage of this family structure for industrialized societies was that it facilitated geographical mobility, seen as essential for meeting the dynamic workforce requirements of a developed economy.

Parsons did not argue that other kinship responsibilities were of no consequence. Rather, he claimed these were secondary to the responsibilities individuals had to nuclear family members (Harris 1983). Nonetheless, other writers took issue with Parsons's work, arguing that kin outside the nuclear family remained significant in people's lives, especially parents, siblings, and (adult) children. This is undoubtedly so. Many studies in different developed societies have shown that kin outside the household are routinely drawn on to provide support, assistance, and companionship. At this level, it is evident that nuclear families are not *socially* isolated from other kin. However, this does not of itself contradict the argument that nuclear families are *structurally* isolated within economically developed societies. As noted, structural isolation refers to primacy of obligation rather than level of social contact, though clearly the two are not entirely discrete.

Other tendencies within contemporary family patterns also indicate the structural priority given to nuclear families. In particular, the increased emphasis placed on "the couple" reflects the centrality of nuclear families over wider kinship ties. The trend towards higher rates of marriage, and more youthful marriage, across much of the twentieth century is one indication of this, as is the growth in the number and variety of different experts and guides offering advice on how couples should best maintain and organize their relationships. At a cultural level, this clearly reflects the continuing shift from marriage as an institution to marriage as a relationship. Similarly, the emphasis placed on the rights and needs of children, the increased responsibilities of care, and the growth of child- and adolescent-centered markets highlights the level of priority given to dependent children within contemporary family systems. While recognizing the emotional and practical significance of some kin relationships outside the household, it is evident that in terms of structural properties, the conjugal family continues to be prioritized.

However, recognizing this does not imply that family structure has been unaltered since the mid-twentieth century when Parsons was writing. It very clearly has, throughout the developed world. Two aspects of this are particularly significant. First, the family structure characteristic of the mid-twentieth century involved a very marked division of labor between spouses. Each spouse had their own sphere of responsibility and obligation: employment for husbands, childcare and domestic servicing for wives. While this gendered division of labor is still evident, it is not now as powerful as it previously was. Wives usually continue to carry primary responsibility for domestic organization and care within the family, but changes in employment patterns as well as the cultural impact of second wave feminism have reduced the level of their financial and social dependence on husbands. In this regard, while the distribution of responsibilities and obligations within families remains gendered, there is now somewhat less rigidity about this than there was throughout most of the twentieth century.

And just as there is now greater flexibility in the division of familial responsibilities, so too there is greater acceptance of diversity in other family practices. Patterns that were previously understood to be in some sense problematic, if not pathological, are now accepted as legitimate alternative family forms. The most obvious example here is lone-parent families, which have increased dramatically since the early 1970s, but other examples include stepfamilies, cohabitation, and gay partnerships. Moreover, life course trajectories are now far more diverse than they were. With new forms of partnership, increasing levels of separation and divorce, and what can be termed "serial commitment" (i.e., committed relationships which may or may not involve marriage), the patterning of people's family lives over time has become increasingly variable. Indeed, there is now greater cultural uncertainty about who counts as "family." Think here of stepparents who may be household members but not necessarily regarded by stepchildren as family members; cohabiting heterosexual and gay partners where the commitment is comparatively recent; or even non-custodial fathers where there has been no

relationship. In addition, with globalization, in most developed societies there is now also increased ethnic variation, which frequently entails diverse beliefs about the legitimacy of different family practices.

This greater diversity within the familial relationships people construct is a key characteristic of contemporary family structure in developed societies. It is linked to both the growth of individualization and an increasing recognition that sexual and domestic arrangements are matters of choice, and thus legitimately located within the private rather than the public sphere. However, it also makes the specification of family structure within contemporary developed societies more problematic. No single form of family organization or pattern of constructing familial relationships holds normatively or experientially in the way Parsons's nuclear family model did in the mid-twentieth century. Yet accepting this diversity as a feature of contemporary family life, it is also clear that there are continuities and consistencies patterning the ways family members usually construct and negotiate their relationships. Three warrant highlighting. First, as noted above, gender remains a primary organizational principle within most families, in part as a consequence of gendered labor market realities. Second, in the main, people prioritize their commitment to their partner and dependent children above those to other family members, though this does not imply that relationships with these latter are necessarily inconsequential. Many studies have shown the reverse is true, with ties to parents and siblings in adulthood continuing to be significant in people's lives. And third, albeit with some ethnic diversity, love as a personal and emotional commitment is generally understood as the prime basis for contemporary partnership, whether or not this involves marriage. Conversely, the evident absence of emotional commitment within a partnership is accepted legally and culturally (in most instances) as a prima facie reason for ending the partnership.

SEE ALSO: Cohabitation; Divisions of Household Labor; Divorce; Family Diversity; Family Structure and Child Outcomes; Family Structure and Poverty; Households; Inequalities in Marriage; Kinship; Lone-Parent Families; Marriage

REFERENCES AND SUGGESTED READINGS

Allan, G. & Crow, G. (2001) *Families, Households and Society*. Palgrave, Basingstoke.

Cherlin, A. (2004) The Deinstitutionalization of American Marriage. *Journal of Marriage and Family* 66: 848–61.

Duncan, S. & Edwards, R. (Eds.) (1997) *Single Mothers in an International Context*. UCL Press, London.

Finch, J. & Mason, J. (1993) *Negotiating Family Responsibilities*. Routledge, London.

Gillis, J. (1997) *A World of Their Own Making*. Oxford University Press, Oxford.

Harris, C. C. (1983) *The Family in Industrial Society*. Allen & Unwin, London.

Parsons, T. (1943) The Kinship System of the Contemporary United States. *American Anthropologist* 43: 22–38.

Weeks, J., Heaphy, B., & Donovan, C. (2001) *Same Sex Intimacies*. Routledge, London.

family structure and child outcomes

Susan M. Jekielek and Kristin A. Moore

The implications of family structure for child well-being have been a central topic of research for several decades. In its simplest form, it is the comparison between two-parent and one-parent families that is the root of concern for child well-being. Children who live with two married parents are defined in most government statistics as living in two-parent families, whereas children who live with just one biological parent due to death, divorce, or having never married have been considered to live in single-parent families. However, the issue is much more complex, and trends in family structure among American children over recent decades make it increasingly necessary to specify the biological and social relationships between children and the adults in their lives in order to understand the implications for child well-being.

The most highly researched areas of child well-being in the context of family structure include socioemotional well-being, such as aggressive behavior problems and emotional distress; academic outcomes, such as math and reading scores; economic well-being, such as family poverty; and life course and intergenerational outcomes, such as low weight at birth, educational achievement, and offspring's own marital stability and quality in adulthood.

This entry focuses primarily on family structure and child well-being in industrialized countries, and particularly in the US. The implications of family structure for children in other countries may differ to the extent that family and child policies also differ, cultural definitions of family differ, and the patterns of family structure differ, among other factors.

SOCIAL CONTEXT

Since the family is a primary setting for the care and socialization of children, it is of interest to both scholars and the general public that an increasing proportion of children have been growing up with a single parent, although this trend may be leveling off. In 1960, about 9 percent of all children lived in a single-parent family in the US; this percentage was up to 28 percent in 2003, with 68 percent living in married-parent families. Both estimates have remained within 2 percentage points in each year since 1994.

In the 1970s, divorce replaced parental death as the primary cause of single-parent families. It is estimated that about four in ten children will eventually experience their parents' divorce. However, divorce is only one factor contributing to estimates that about half of all children are expected to reside with a single parent at some point during their childhood. More recently, the increased proportion of births to unmarried women has also contributed. In 1970, 11 percent of children were born to unmarried couples. By 2002, about one in three births occurred outside of marriage. Contrary to popular perceptions, teenagers account for less than three in ten nonmarital births, with women in their twenties accounting for more than half.

Of recent interest are nonmarital births of second or higher order parity. Only about half of all nonmarital births were first births in 1998. Between 1992 and 1995, more than one in three nonmarital births to women aged 20 or older were preceded by a teenage birth. There is a growing recognition that multiple births to the same woman may not be births by the same father.

An unmarried parent is not necessarily a parent without a partner. In the early 1990s, 39 percent of all nonmarital births occurred to cohabiting couples, up from 29 percent ten years earlier. A national study places this at 51 percent, based on a survey of mothers who gave birth in large cities between 1998 and 2000. According to this survey (the Fragile Families Study), the majority of nonmarital births (82 percent) are to parents who are romantically involved at the time of birth, either in a cohabiting or a visiting relationship. All in all, about 40 percent of all children are expected to spend some portion of their childhoods living with cohabiting parents, and cohabitation has become an increasingly recognized family form.

Living in a stepfamily is also a common experience. About half of current marriages are actually a second or higher marriage for at least one of the spouses. About one in three children will spend some of their childhood living in a remarried or cohabiting stepfamily.

These social changes are also apparent in people's attitudes. Acceptance of cohabitation and nonmarital childbearing, as measured in public opinion surveys, has increased since the 1960s–1970s, although having a birth out of wedlock is still not viewed as a positive goal. This pattern is consistent with research that examines how single-parent families are depicted in popular magazines. Portrayals of single-parent families as unacceptable or negative for children have declined over time.

After decades of increase, accepting attitudes toward divorce have stabilized, although the plateau of acceptance is quite high. About four of every five young people believe that divorce is acceptable even if children are involved. At the same time, "having a good marriage and family life" was rated as extremely important to 81 percent of females and 72 percent of males who were high school seniors in 1997 and 1998.

A child's family structure is often viewed in terms of the child's connections to the parent-figures in the household. It is notable, however, that 8 percent of all children resided with a grandparent in 2002, most of whom were the heads of households.

IMPLICATIONS OF FAMILY STRUCTURE

For some, having children within marriage and preserving the sanctity of marriage are essential societal functions. Others argue for the importance of marriage based on research indicating that married adults tend to be wealthier, healthier, live longer, and have more social support than unmarried adults. Others argue that changes in family structure are inevitable and represent "new" family forms that are not necessarily inferior family forms for raising children. Still others take a policy perspective, arguing that reducing the number of single-parent families would reduce the economic burden on the taxpayer, and this is a goal of current welfare reform law. Despite this disagreement, at the heart of these concerns, and cutting across many different perspectives, is the well-being of children.

Research on family structure is consistent: the majority of children who are not raised by both biological parents manage to grow up without serious problems. Yet, on average, children in single-parent families, children who experience divorce, and children who live in stepfamilies all experience worse outcomes, on average, compared with children who are brought up with both biological parents.

There are many possible explanations for these patterns. A stressful life events perspective posits that family structure transitions cause instability in family routines and therefore are detrimental to both parental and child well-being. Indeed, multiple family transitions themselves increase a child's risk of negative outcomes. A parental absence perspective suggests that biological parents are the most likely to provide social and economic resources to their own children, and therefore the absence of a parent puts children at risk of diminished well-being. A selection perspective suggests that the characteristics that predate family transitions are actually responsible for negative effects. An economic resources perspective would posit that children are at a greater risk of living in poverty and having poor outcomes when they do not have access to two parents – in part due to the economies of scale involved in maintaining one household as compared to two.

Indeed, compared to children who live with two married parents, those whose parents divorce are more prone to academic and behavior problems, including depression, anti-social behavior, impulsive/hyperactive behavior, academic achievement, and school behavior problems. Mental health problems linked to marital disruption have also been identified among young adults. These findings are consistent across many outcomes and many studies; however, there are also many caveats.

Advances in data collection, namely longitudinal surveys that collect data on the same children over multiple time points, have shown that many of the problems that are observed in children post-divorce can actually be attributed to pre-divorce factors – this is often referred to as selection bias. For example, parents with anti-social personalities are more likely to both administer poor parenting and also divorce, and therefore the observed relationship between divorce and child well-being is due, in part, to parental characteristics. Using longitudinal, national survey data, Andrew Cherlin and colleagues (1991) demonstrated that much of the difference in well-being scores between children of divorced and intact families is apparent prior to the date of divorce.

Numerous studies indicate that parental conflict is detrimental to child well-being, and a handful of studies measuring both divorce and marital quality have shown that children from high-conflict families are better off on a number of outcomes when their parents divorce rather than remain married. However, it has been estimated that fewer divorces are preceded by high conflict than are preceded by low conflict. It is also noteworthy that the differences between children of divorced and intact couples, although arguably small at about one-fifth of a standard deviation, tend to remain significant, even after accounting for important pre-divorce factors. Further, due to the variability in the capacity of children and families to cope with divorce, this average "small" effect likely masks larger effects among certain subgroups of children.

An additional advance in research on children of divorce is the investigation of outcomes that might occur later over the life course when they are adults. For example, research has shown that children whose parents divorce are more likely to experience divorce themselves as adults, to have increased marital problems and lower socioeconomic achievement, and to report poorer subjective well-being.

Stepchildren also do not do as well, on average, as children living with both biological parents. A review of the literature suggests that, on average, stepchildren have lower grades and scores on achievement tests, and have greater internalizing and externalizing behavior problems. They fare worse in terms of dropout rates, school attendance, and high school or GED completion. Similar to explanations for the effects of divorce on children, researchers often posit that the stress of reorganizing as a stepfamily is an important reason for these differences. Children often move to new cities and possibly lower-quality schools; children in stepfamilies have likely experienced a number of other family changes; and conflict might still exist between the child's original two parents. In addition, children in stepfamilies are found to have less access to parental involvement than children living with two biological parents. Not only might a child's biological parent be distracted and focus attention on her/his new spouse, but stepparents tend to spend less time with stepchildren than biological children, and relationships with absent biological parents, namely fathers, tend to diminish with time.

Children in single-parent families are about twice as likely to have problems as children who live in intact families headed by two biological parents. Children born to unmarried mothers are more likely to be poor, to grow up in a single-parent family, and to experience multiple living arrangements during childhood. These factors, in turn, are associated with lower educational attainment and a higher risk of teen and nonmarital childbearing.

It is important to note that the implications of single-parent family structure can differ for children in other countries. For example, single parenthood has been found to be less detrimental for children's academic achievement in countries where family policies equalize resources between single- and two-parent families.

CHANGES OVER TIME AND CONTEMPORARY RESEARCH ISSUES

The study of family structure and child outcomes has paralleled the changing demographic trends in children's families. Research has shifted from a focus on the effects of divorce on children to an increasing focus on the diversity of family structures, especially those other than the biological two-parent family as a setting for bearing and raising children.

As described above, the majority of nonmarital births are to couples who are romantically involved at the time of the birth. While most unmarried couples have plans to stay together and get married around the time of the birth of their child, one year later only 9 percent were actually found to marry, while another 49 percent of parents continued to be romantically involved. In general, cohabiting relationships are more likely to break up than marriages. Parents of children in cohabiting unions typically have lower earnings, lower levels of education, higher rates of poverty, and elevated rates of incarceration, substance use, and domestic violence, compared with parents of children in married-couple families. In addition, their children may not have full legal access to paternal resources. We would expect that these characteristics would undermine child well-being compared with married-parent families. On the other hand, cohabitation might incur greater economic resources for children than single-parent families, but there is as yet little documentation of whether and how cohabitors share their resources. Overall, we know very little about actual child outcomes in relation to cohabitation, although a recent study documents significantly fewer behavior problems and greater school engagement among school-age children living with two biological married parents compared to children living with two biological cohabiting parents.

As divorce has become more common, so has the study of how custody after divorce affects children. It is not clear whether joint physical custody of children is beneficial, and frequency of father visitation is not consistently linked with better child well-being. While more work is needed, some research suggests that contact with a non-resident father is beneficial when conflict between parents is low or when the non-resident father is warm but sets limits in his parenting.

Gay marriage and family life has received much attention, but research on gay families is still in development. Census questions in 1990 and 2000 included categories that made it possible for researchers to identify same and different-sex couples in "marriage-like" relationships, but even these are not direct measures, and the census data do not include child outcome assessments. It is rare for any national data set to collect information on gay couples, let alone match it to children in the household. Nonetheless, in the 2000 Census, approximately one-third of female householders with same-sex partners were living with their own children, and about one-fifth of male householders with same-sex partners were living with their own children. Marriage between same-sex partners gained particular relevance in 2004 and attempts were made to confine marriage to heterosexual couples as a constitutional amendment. In terms of child development, rigorous research on representative samples is lacking.

METHODOLOGICAL ISSUES

There are at least three clear methodological issues in the study of how family structure affects child outcomes. First, addressing selection bias is perhaps the most critical issue. Longitudinal data are critical here.

A second critical methodological element is that when children experience one family structure outside of the traditional married two-parent family, they typically experience multiple changes. Therefore, it becomes difficult to disentangle the effects of previous family transitions, such as divorce, from the effects of current family structure, such as a stepfamily.

Third, data quality has not "caught up" with the many different types of family structures in which children live. Knowing a mother's marital status is not enough information to determine whether she is living with her child's father, or whether all children in the household share the same father. It has become increasingly critical to understand the biological connection of that child to the people in the household, as well as the marital status of that child's parents, and also the timing of parental marital/cohabiting/dating transitions. While this seems straightforward, there are very few data sets that collect such information (for an exception, see the Survey of Income and Program Participation), and it is even more of a rarity for child outcomes to be assessed in the same data source.

Further development is also necessary to accurately measure parental cohabitation. For example, couples who are living together do not necessarily identify with the terms "cohabiting" or "unmarried partner" on questionnaires.

FUTURE DIRECTIONS

The family context for childrearing in the US is changing. Significant proportions of children will spend time living in single-parent families, families headed by cohabiting biological parents, or families headed by their biological parent and a cohabiting or married stepparent, and will experience transitions in their family structure in general.

With regard to child well-being, it will be important to examine how cohabiting biological parents rear their children and how children in cohabiting families fare relative to others. A point of departure for this inquiry is to assume that cohabiting biological parents provide the same home environments for their children as married biological parents, but empirical evidence is not definitive with regard to this assumption. Empirical evidence is also lacking in regards to children whose parents may not reside together but remain romantically involved.

The past two decades of research have shown that there is diversity in how children adjust to divorce. Understanding the conditions under which children adjust poorly or successfully to divorce, and disruption in general, is an important next step. In the same vein, most research on the effects of family disruption examine potential *negative* effects. Qualitative research suggests that there also may be *positive* implications of divorce transitions. Systematically

testing this possibility could help inform the knowledge base of the conditions under which children might adjust well to family disruption.

While children in one-parent families typically have fewer economic and social resources at their disposal than do children in two-parent families, accumulating evidence warns that socioeconomic inequality for children in these two family structures is growing. This is due in part to the rise in dual-earner families. For the sake of child well-being, it will be important to monitor this trend.

Child outcomes with regard to the structure of siblings in the household are also likely to be a topic of continued research interest. Some research suggests that paternal investments in children may depend upon whether the children in his household are his own, his wife's, or a combination of both.

With federal funding targeted at experimental evaluations of interventions to improve the marital quality and stability of low-income couples, a much anticipated topic of future research is whether an intervention can improve marital stability and quality among low-income families. If such an intervention is successful at improving child well-being, this would be a significant milestone. However, low-income couples face many challenges to marital stability, such as inadequate employment and economic hardship. Further, most research showing evidence that couple interventions can affect relationship stability has been targeted towards white, middle-class samples. The same is true for the development of marital quality measures. Therefore, a great deal of research is needed to answer the question of whether an intervention can improve marital stability and quality and enhance child well-being in low-income families.

Pregnancy intentions have been monitored for decades as indicators of control over fertility and the need for reproductive health services. Moreover, the implications for children of being mistimed or unwanted has received increased attention; but more work is needed. In addition, the effect of having unintended or unwanted pregnancies on marriage and family formation more generally, as well as on marital disruption or family disruption, needs further examination with data from males as well as females. What are the implications of different levels of intendedness for each partner? How does pregnancy intendedness affect male commitment to their partner and investments in the child? Under what circumstances do unintended pregnancies undermine couple stability? Finally, there is a need for research on the implications of infertility and new fertility technologies for family formation and stability.

Long overlooked is systematic investigation of family processes and child well-being in nonwhite families. Studies in the past decade have made strides towards describing fathering and gender roles, particularly in African American and Hispanic families, and also describing how parenting is shaped by grandparents and neighborhood context. Further high-quality longitudinal studies are needed, not only for high-risk families of color, but also for families of color in general. Further highlighting the need to pay attention to race and ethnicity is the fact that immigrant children are the fastest growing segment of the child population, up by over 50 percent in the last decade.

SEE ALSO: Children and Divorce; Cohabitation; Family Demography; Family Structure and Poverty; Fertility: Nonmarital; Intimate Union Formation and Dissolution; Lesbian and Gay Families; Stepfamilies

REFERENCES AND SUGGESTED READINGS

Amato, P. R. (2000) Consequences of Divorce for Adults and Children. *Journal of Marriage and the Family* 62: 1269–87.

Cherlin, A. J., Furstenberg, Jr., F. F., Chase-Lansdale, P. L., Kiernan, K., Robins, P. K., Morrison, D. R., & Teitler, J. O. (1991) Longitudinal Studies of Effects of Divorce on Children in Great Britain and the United States. *Science* 252: 1386–9.

Coleman, M., Ganong, L., & Fine, M. (2000) Reinvestigating Remarriage: Another Decade of Progress. *Journal of Marriage and the Family* 62(4): 1288–1307.

McLanahan, S. (2004) Diverging Destinies: How Children Fare Under the Second Demographic Transition. *Demography* 41(4): 607–27.

McLanahan, S. & Sandefur, G. (1994). *Growing Up With a Single Parent: What Hurts, What Helps.* Harvard University Press, Cambridge, MA.

McLanahan, S., Garfinkel, I., Reichman, N., Teitler, J., Carlson, M., & Audigier, C. N. (2003) *The Fragile Families and Child Wellbeing Study: Baseline National Report, Revised.*

Manning, W. (2002) The Implications of Cohabitation for Children's Well-Being. In: Booth, A. & Crouter, A. C. (Eds.), *Just Living Together: Implications of Cohabitation on Families, Children and Social Policy.* Erlbaum Associates, Mahwah, NJ.

family structure and poverty

Daniel T. Lichter

Family structure and poverty are inextricably linked. Different types of families have much different risk profiles for poverty and welfare dependence. Family structure typically refers to the myriad organizational and compositional parts that make up the family. Among others, these include headship patterns (e.g., female-headed families), the marital histories of family members (e.g., single or married or cohabiting), the presence of multiple generations, family size, and the presence of co-residential children. These structural features of families (hence, family structure) reflect individual choices that are shaped by cultural values and norms, economic constraints, and demographic events, such as childbearing or death.

Data from the US Census Bureau highlight the strong statistical relationship between family structure and poverty in the United States. The poverty rate of female-headed families with children was 35.5 percent in 2003, compared with 7.0 percent among their married-couple counterparts. The Census Bureau defines poverty on the basis of absolute money income of all family members, i.e., whether annual family income falls below a specific poverty income threshold. Poverty thresholds vary by family size and other structural features of the family, such as the number of adults or children. In 2003, for example, the official poverty threshold for a three-person family of one adult and two children was $14,824. Family structure is also linked to other manifestations of low income – inadequate housing, food insecurity, lack of access to health care, and poor physical and mental health.

In most other western industrial societies, the relationship between family structure and poverty is much weaker. Lee Rainwater and Timothy Smeeding report in *Poor Kids in a Rich Country* (2003) that about 20 percent of children in the United States and Sweden live in single-mother families. Yet, data from the Luxemborg Income Study show the child poverty rate for these children is over 50 percent in the United States, compared with only 7 percent in Sweden. Moreover, the poverty rate of children living in single-mother families increases sharply as family size increases. This is much less true in other countries, where income transfers help offset the tendency for single-mother families and larger families to be less well off economically.

In the United States, the strong statistical relationship between family structure and poverty is rarely questioned. Instead, debates center on the appropriate interpretation of this relationship and on the alternative policy solutions they imply. At the heart of the debate is whether poverty is a *cause* or a *consequence* of changing family structure. This debate is not new. Indeed, the key issues were probably encapsulated first in scholarly reactions to Daniel Patrick Moynihan's controversial 1965 report entitled *The Negro Family: The Case for National Action*. An excerpt from the so-called Moynihan Report states: "The fundamental problem [of blacks] . . . is that of family structure. The evidence – not final, but powerfully persuasive – is that the Negro family in the urban ghettos is crumbling. . . . So long as this situation persists, the cycle of poverty and disadvantage will continue to repeat itself."

Moynihan's views were seemingly straightforward: (1) "crumbling" black families were typically poor families; (2) changes in black family structure contributed to growth in poverty and its many manifestations (e.g., welfare dependency, crime, alienation, unwed childbearing); and (3) changes in black family structure exacerbated black–white inequality in poverty and welfare. The policy implications followed accordingly. In Moynihan's view, a concerted national effort was needed to strengthen the family, which had created a

"tangle of pathology" in the black community. Many scholars today view Moynihan's conclusions as prescient. In 1965, the percentage of black women raising children alone exceeded in 2000 the percentage of white unmarried mothers.

At the time, however, Moynihan's critics charged him with "blaming the victim." They questioned whether changes in family structure caused poverty among blacks or instead reflected the effects of poverty. His critics argued that chronic poverty or welfare dependence undermined marriage, contributed to more marital dissolution, and led to out-of-wedlock childbearing – the underlying components of changing family structure. Some also believed that poverty and family structure simply reflect the effects of other conditions in the black community, such as low education or too few job opportunities. In other words, the relationship between family structure and poverty was spurious rather than causal.

Establishing causality is difficult in the absence of experimental data. Instead, most non-experimental studies are based on survey data that compare the economic circumstances of married and unmarried women, while controlling for other observed variables associated with both (e.g., education). The problem is that other unobserved variables may cause a spurious association between family structure and poverty. More generally, we do not know what the poverty rate would be for currently single or unmarried women if they actually married. And we do not know the poverty rate of currently married women if they divorced or became widowed. Simply, the counterfactual situation is not observed.

Much of the recent research on racial differences or trends in poverty has employed a demographic accounting framework that avoids issues of causality altogether. These descriptive studies estimate the share of racial or temporal change in poverty that is accounted for by shifts in family structure, such as the rise in single-parent families. These analyses are often based on methods of demographic standardization or shift-share analyses. Researchers ask what percentage of individuals would be poor today if (1) the distribution of family types had not changed over time or if the distribution was identical to a comparison group (e.g., whites), and (2) they experienced current family-specific poverty rates. Differences between the observed and expected poverty uncovers the effects of changing family structure. Using such an approach, Eggebeen and Lichter (1991) reported that roughly one-half of the upward rise in child poverty in the 1980s was accounted for by increases in the percentage of US children in "high-risk" families (e.g., female-headed). More recent studies have shown that changes in poverty during the 1990s were largely unrelated to changes in family structure; changes in maternal employment matter more (Iceland 2003; Lichter & Crowley 2004).

As with Moynihan's report, it remains controversial to claim that poverty differences across racial groups are due to racial differences in family structure. The debate pivots on the usual canard: are individuals (in this case blacks) to blame for making economically self-destructive decisions about unwed childbearing, marriage, and divorce? Or are larger structural forces (e.g., economic restructuring and high unemployment) responsible for high poverty rates? Eggebeen and Lichter (1991), for example, reported that about two-thirds of the black–white difference in family structure is responsible for black–white differences in child poverty. At the same time, even if blacks had the same family structure as whites, their poverty rates would remain high. Family structure is only part of the explanation, and such analyses cannot assign causality. Demographic studies typically do not address the question of why family structure changes, although a large literature suggests that economics – the availability of good jobs and good incomes – is fundamental.

These demographic approaches contrast sharply with behavioral models that emphasize individual decision-making. Such analyses typically link out-of-wedlock childbearing, divorce, or marriage changes or other factors to individual changes in poverty or economic deprivation (Bianchi 1999). Perhaps the largest body of work is on the economic consequences of divorce. These studies show that divorce is strongly associated with subsequent declines in women's economic well-being. One recent study showed that poor women were more likely than non-poor women to subsequently

divorce (Smock et al. 1999). More significantly, this study attempted to estimate the counterfactual situation. If these poor women had not divorced they would be much better off economically, but not as well off as other women who had remained married. This study illustrates the potential inferential problems – common to most previous studies – with statistical comparisons of the economic well-being of currently divorced and married women.

Studies of divorce disagree most often about the magnitude of economic declines and on the specific economic and demographic pathways that shape income trajectories. Lenore Weitzman, in *The Divorce Revolution* (1985), for example, reported a 73 percent decline in women's standard of living after divorce and a 42 percent increase in men's standard of living. Other work shows much smaller negative effects on women's economic well-being. Peterson (1996) estimates a 27 percent decline in women's standard of living after divorce and only a small increase (10 percent) in men's standard of living. Studies show that the loss of husband's income, even after several years, cannot fully offset increases in cash assistance from the government, earnings from more work, or financial assistance from friends or relatives. Moreover, the best route to economic recovery seems to be remarriage (Morrison & Ritualo 2000).

Indeed, scholars have increasingly emphasized the link between marriage and economic well-being. Transitions to marriage are associated with declines in poverty and reductions in welfare dependency (Lichter et al. 2003). The improvement reflects the addition of another potential source of family income (i.e., the spouse). Marriage also seems to make men more productive in the workplace, if measured by hours worked and earnings. The counter-argument is that marriage selects on those with the greatest earnings potential. Earnings growth is reinforced by marriage itself, which strengthens the underlying economic foundation of marriage, while reducing the likelihood of divorce and poverty. This is a mutually reinforcing process. Drawing strong causal arguments, however, is difficult. Individuals who marry or divorce may be different from single people on a number of observed and unobserved characteristics. This is the fundamental problem in drawing strong causal inferences about links between family structure and poverty.

More recently, efforts to establish causality have made use of natural experiments. In the early 1990s, Geronimus and Korenman (1992) claimed that out-of-wedlock childbearing was not responsible for the negative outcomes experienced by disadvantaged unwed mothers (e.g., low schooling, higher poverty, etc.). Despite sharing genes and family background, adolescents who became unwed mothers were no different on a variety of adult outcomes than their sisters who did not bear children. Other studies have drawn similar conclusions by comparing women who miscarried a pregnancy with those whose pregnancies ended in live births. Any differences between women who miscarry and women who become mothers arguably must be due to unwed childbearing if miscarriages are randomly drawn from the same population of unmarried women. No differences suggest that out-of-wedlock childbearing is a symptom of poverty and family disadvantage rather than a cause. Such studies have spawned many subsequent studies that have critically evaluated the putative causal effects of teenage childbearing on later life outcomes (Hoffman 1998).

Conceptual and technical debates in the scholarly community about causality have not prevented lawmakers and the public policy community from addressing the issue of changing family structure and its potential deleterious relationship with poverty. This willingness to act on behalf of American families is new. For example, the 1996 welfare reform bill, the Personal Responsibility and Work Opportunity Reconciliation Act, has "encouraging the formation and maintenance of two-parent families" as a way to increase economic self-sufficiency. States have developed and implemented experimental marriage initiatives aimed at encouraging marriage or reducing divorce. These have taken the form of public announcement campaigns about the value of marriage, counseling programs that develop conflict resolution techniques or promote relationship skills, and new efforts to change the tax code or welfare system to eliminate any economic disincentives to marriage or out-of-wedlock childbearing.

Whether such programs will work to reduce poverty and promote economic self-sufficiency is unclear a priori. This is a social experiment on an unprecedented scale in American history. As state program evaluations are completed, however, scholars will have a much stronger basis in evidence concerning whether manipulating family structure (i.e., promoting stable two-parent families) will have the intended salutary effects on poverty and welfare dependency.

SEE ALSO: Culture of Poverty; Divorce; Family Poverty; Family Structure and Child Outcomes; Feminization of Poverty; Marriage

REFERENCES AND SUGGESTED READINGS

Bianchi, S. M. (1999) Feminization and Juvenilization of Poverty: Trends, Relative Risks, and Consequences. *Annual Review of Sociology* 25: 307–33.

Eggebeen, D. J. & Lichter, D. T. (1991) Race, Family Structure, and Changing Poverty among American Children. *American Sociological Review* 56(6): 801–17.

Geronimus, A. T. & Korenman, S. (1992) The Socioeconomic Consequences of Teen Childbearing Reconsidered. *Quarterly Journal of Economics* 107(4): 1187–1214.

Hoffman, S. D. (1998) Teenage Childbearing is Not So Bad After All . . . Or is it? A Review of the New Literature. *Family Planning Perspectives* 30(5): 236.

Iceland, J. (2003) Why Poverty Remains High: The Role of Income Growth, Economic Inequality, and Changes in Family Structure, 1949–1999. *Demography* 40(3): 499–519.

Lichter, D. T. & Crowley, M. L. (2004) Welfare Reform and Childhood Poverty: Effects of Maternal Employment, Marriage, and Cohabitation. *Social Science Research* 33(3).

Lichter, D. T., Graefe, D. R., & Brown, J. B. (2003) Is Marriage a Panacea? Union Formation among Economically Disadvantaged Unwed Mothers. *Social Problems* 50(1): 60–86.

Morrison, D. R. & Ritualo, A. (2000) Routes to Children's Economic Recovery after Divorce: Are Cohabitation and Remarriage Equivalent? *American Sociological Review* 65(4): 560–80.

Peterson, R. R. (1996) A Reevaluation of the Economic Consequences of Divorce. *American Sociological Review* 61(3): 528–36.

Smock, P. J., Manning, W. D., & Gupta, S. (1999) The Effect of Marriage and Divorce on Women's Economic Well-Being. *American Sociological Review* 64(6): 794–812.

family theory

David Cheal

Family theory consists of sets of propositions that attempt to explain some aspect of family life. Theorizing involves making general statements about some phenomenon, and an important characteristic of family theory, therefore, is that it involves a degree of abstraction from reality. Theoretical statements are abstract statements employing concepts that refer to things in the real world. Theories differ in the concepts that they use, and in the statements that are made about them. There are many different theories in family theory, and the relationships between them range from complementary borrowing of ideas, through mutual indifference, to antagonism.

INTELLECTUAL AND SOCIAL CONTEXT

The history of family theory varies according to the national context of family theorists. For example, in the 1970s and early 1980s Marxism had a significant influence on family theorizing in Britain and, especially, in Canada, but it was rarely mentioned in the United States. On the other hand, British and other European theorists have not paid much attention to exchange theory, which has been popular in the United States.

Family theory has changed from a consensus on the value of nuclear family living in the period immediately after World War II to the current situation of theoretical pluralism. In the post-war period the standard theory of family life held that the nuclear family was an adaptive unit that mediates between the individual and society. An early, and very influential, version of standard sociological theory was structural functionalism. This approach held that families perform essential functions for family members and for society. Talcott Parsons, for example, argued that the nuclear family household has two main functions in modern industrial society. It socializes children and manages tensions for adults.

Influenced by the prestige of grand theory in structural functionalism, the period of the late 1960s and 1970s saw a move in family studies toward theory construction combined with theory integration. The phrase that was most often used to describe the goal of creating a unified body of family theory was theory systematization. By the early 1970s the sociology of the family had entered a phase of systematic theory building and theory unification. However, this phase did not last long.

Beginning with the impact of feminism on family studies, the sociology of the family went through a Big Bang in the mid-1970s. There was a rush of theorizing about family issues, but only a portion of this growth resulted from the application of theory construction techniques. By the mid-1970s it was clear that the move toward theoretical convergence had omitted issues and theories which did not fit the image of the family favored in standard sociological theory. New types of theory were developed that asked new kinds of questions. This was especially true of feminism.

From the 1980s onwards family studies has been characterized by the acceptance of theoretical pluralism. One way of looking at this theoretical pluralism is presented next.

MAJOR DIMENSIONS

In North America, James White and David Klein (2002) have identified seven major dimensions of family theory. These are theoretical frameworks from which specific theories are derived. The seven theoretical frameworks are: (1) the social exchange and choice framework; (2) the symbolic interaction framework; (3) the family life course development framework; (4) the systems framework; (5) the conflict framework; (6) the feminist framework; and (7) the ecological framework.

Exchange Theory

The individual is the unit of analysis in exchange theory. Individuals are seen as making rational choices about behavior based on the balance of rewards and costs that the behavior has for them. The relationship between rewards and costs defines the profit that is derived from behavior, and individuals are assumed to try to maximize their profits. Actors rationally calculate their expected profits for all possible choices in a situation and then choose the action that they calculate will bring the greatest rewards for the least costs. A theory of choice is at the heart of the exchange approach to family interaction. Behavior becomes exchange when the actions of one individual enter into the rewards and costs of another individual, and each individual modifies the behavior of the other.

Applications of exchange theory include the study of the choice of marriage partner, the quality of the marriage relationship, marriage bargaining, and separation and divorce. One of the advantages of exchange theory is that it enables the investigator to think about rewards provided within the family, and rewards provided by sources outside the family, as alternatives between which individuals choose. Marriages are seen as breaking down when one or both partners no longer find them profitable by comparison with the alternatives. The probability of divorce is thought to be a result of two comparisons that individuals make. First, individuals compare the profits they derive from their own marriage with the profits that others derive from their marriages. If the sense of relative deprivation is high then the motive to divorce is enhanced. Second, individuals compare the rewards and costs associated with the alternatives to the existing marriage, including being divorced or remarrying. Rewards might include finding a more compatible partner, and costs might include social disapproval for divorce.

Symbolic Interactionism

Symbolic interactionism rests on three simple premises. First, human beings act toward things on the basis of the meanings that things have for them. Symbolic interactionists therefore believe that to understand social behavior, the researcher must understand the meanings that actors assign to the situation and action. Second, the meanings that people assign to the objects in their environment are drawn from the social interactions in which they engage. That is to say, we do not simply form our meanings as a result of psychological elements in our personalities, but other people's actions

define the meanings for us. Third, the meanings of things are handled in, and modified through, an interpretive process. There is a process of interaction that goes on within the individual, as people engage in an internal conversation about what things mean and how they should respond.

The emphasis in symbolic interactionism is on the family as a unity of interacting personalities. Whatever unity exists in family life can only be the result of interactions between family members. One of the most basic concepts in symbolic interactionism is that of role. Roles are the rules of behavior for positions in a family, and as such they are taken into account by individual members as they construct their lines of action. Symbolic interactionists have therefore often believed that individual behavior can only be understood within the context of the family role that an individual occupies. Interactionist work on patterns of family life includes studies of the ways in which behavior is negotiated and renegotiated among family members. It is through negotiations that members adjust their individual claims to produce joint actions.

Family Life Course Development

The family life course development framework is a dynamic approach that looks at family life as a process that unfolds over time. It focuses on the systematic and patterned changes experienced by families as they move through stages and events of their family life course. This approach has gone through several phases itself. The first phase consisted of an approach that studied families as moving through deterministic, invariant stages of the family life cycle. This approach was heavily criticized. The principal difficulty has been the impossibility of fitting all of the many different living arrangements that exist into a universal set of stages. Accordingly, this approach was replaced by an emphasis on family careers. More recently, it has been followed by an approach stressing patterns of the life courses of individuals. The focus here is upon the individual life course, and on how it affects and is affected by the life courses of other individuals.

Systems Theory

A system is a set of interconnected parts that exhibits some boundary between itself and the surrounding environment. Families may be considered as systems, as they are in the systems framework. Assumptions of the systems framework include the idea that all parts of the system are interconnected; the idea that understanding is only possible by viewing the whole; and the idea that a system's behavior affects its environment, and in turn the environment affects the system. It is also commonly held that systems exhibit equilibrium, that is to say, they tend to maintain a steady state in the face of environmental changes.

Family processes are understood as the product of the entire system. Family systems theory therefore shifts the primary focus away from the individual family member toward relationships among the members of the family system. The systems approach to the family has therefore been welcomed by some scholars and practitioners as a way to understand family problems and intervene in family processes without blaming any one family member. For example, the eating disorders of bulimia and anorexia nervosa can be conceptualized as disorders involving the entire family system rather than the identified patient alone.

The concept of boundary is an essential one in systems thinking. Systems theorists have therefore been interested in the issue of boundary redefinition when spouses divorce and remarry. Boundaries are defined by rules that identify who participates in a family, and how they do so. Blended families require drawing new boundaries and establishing a consensus on those boundaries. Confusion over boundaries, in other words boundary ambiguity, is thought to create a variety of interpersonal problems. It is held that boundary confusion in remarried families leads to confusion in the rights and duties associated with different positions in the family.

Conflict Theory

Conflict theory maintains that conflict is a normal part of social life, and it therefore deserves to be a focus of explicit attention. Sources of conflict include the competition for scarce resources, and incompatible goals, such as the tension between privacy and jointness. Most conflict theorists accept the assumption that individuals act out of self-interest, and that interests are often contradictory. There are many dimensions of conflict, such as class conflict, age-based conflict, and gender conflict. Conflict can occur between groups or within groups.

The concept of power is as central to many versions of conflict theory as is the concept of conflict itself. The resources that are available within families are not only the subject of competition, they are also the means by which one individual may gain power over others. The unequal distribution of power can be seen as important in several respects. First, the distribution of legitimate power can be seen as a structural mechanism of conflict management that operates to suppress overt conflict. Second, power differentials can themselves become a source of conflict. And third, power inequalities influence the outcomes of conflict, including who wins and who loses.

Applications of conflict theory include the study of family violence. One of the major issues here is the fact that most family violence is violence against women. Because of the interest in gender divisions, there is some overlap here between conflict theory and feminist theory.

Feminist Theory

Feminist theory is concerned with the position of women in society, and specifically with the disadvantages that women face in a society that is dominated by men. It is a diverse approach, but three premises can be identified as it is applied to the study of family life. First, family life is envisaged as an arena within which individuals who pursue different economic and social interests meet and struggle. That struggle is not equal. There is thought to be an internal stratification of family life, in which men receive more benefits than do women. The allocation of tasks among family members is seen as taking the form of a gendered division of labor. Although this division of labor has the appearance of an equal exchange, feminists maintain that women contribute more than they receive in return. Second, processes of control and domination are thought to come into play whenever men and women interact. Relations between husbands and wives are identified as power relations, in which men dominate over women. Feminist theories of marriage and family therefore devote much attention to analyzing structures of patriarchy, or the oppression of women by men. Third, ideological legitimations of gender inequality are held to be responsible for the acceptance by women of their own subjection. It is claimed that there exists an ideology of familism, or familialism, that supports traditional family norms, including traditional gender norms. Feminist theory considers familism to be a restrictive ideology that is a barrier to women's liberation. For example, there is the domestic ideology which encourages girls to think that putting family responsibilities first is the normal pattern for women.

Viewed from the perspective of feminist theory, the family is a concept which has been created and distributed by those whose interests it serves (mainly men). Scholars working in the feminist tradition therefore argue that existing concepts of the family must be deconstructed, or decomposed. As a result, the social scientific concept of the family as a system is replaced by the concept of the family as an ideology. That is to say, "the family" is thought to be a set of ideas which obscures more fundamental relations, such as the sex/gender system.

One of the most obvious applications for feminist theory has been the study of the division of household labor between husbands and wives. For example, feminists have been interested in time use studies which have examined the contrasting amounts of time that men and women devote to housework.

Family Ecology

A concern with individuals and their environment is at the heart of the ecological approach. A person's behavior is seen as a function of the interaction between the person's traits and abilities and their environment. One of the most popular ways of thinking about this is to conceive of the nested ecosystems in which the individual human being develops. First, there is the microsystem of connections between persons who are present in the immediate setting directly affecting the developing person. Second, there is the mesosystem consisting of linkages between settings in which the developing person actually participates. Third, there is the exosystem that consists of linkages between settings that do not involve the developing person as an active participant, but in which events occur that affect, or are affected by, what happens in the setting. And finally, there is the macrosystem consisting of overarching patterns of ideology and organization of the social institutions common to a particular culture or subculture. Individuals develop within the family microsystem, and families are situated within society. The relations between a family and the larger society are meso-, exo-, and macrosystem issues.

An ecological approach can be taken to family decision-making. Here the family is viewed as a system interacting with its environment. The embeddedness of the family system in the larger ecosystem is emphasized, and the interchanges that take place between the various levels are described.

CURRENT EMPHASES

The main current emphasis in family theorizing does not fit into any of the theoretical frameworks identified above. Perhaps it deserves to be identified as a distinctive theoretical approach. This approach is concerned with the deinstitutionalization of family life. It is associated with the work of Ulrich Beck and Elisabeth Beck-Gernsheim as well as the work of Anthony Giddens.

Beck and Beck-Gernsheim have advanced individualization theory. This states that many of the changes occurring in families are the result of a long-term trend in modern societies to accord more autonomy to individuals. Individualization involves liberation from traditional commitments and personal emancipation. Individuals construct their own lives, and they therefore make decisions about whether and whom they shall marry, whether or not to have children, what sort of sexual preference they will have, and so on. As a result, the traditional family, which consisted of a lifelong officially legitimated community of father–mother–child, is being replaced by a diverse array of ways of living.

Giddens argues that traditional family ties have been replaced by the pure relationship as the foundation of personal life. A pure relationship is one based upon emotional communication, where the rewards derived from such communication are the main basis for the relationship to continue. It is not maintained by external forces, but it is constructed by the participants out of their own unaided efforts. Interpersonal trust is, therefore, no longer based on customary obligations between the occupants of well-defined roles. In a pure relationship trust can only be gained through the mutual disclosure of feelings and beliefs. There is therefore a great demand for intimacy in pure relationships. Intimacy is found within marriage, but it is also found outside marriage, in cohabitation for example. The focus of attention today is the relationship between a couple, not the institution of marriage.

SEE ALSO: Conflict Theory; Divisions of Household Labor; Family and Community; Family Conflict; Family Diversity; Family Structure; Gender, Work, and Family; Inequality/Stratification, Gender; Life Course and Family; Love and Commitment; Marital Power/Resource Theory; Marital Quality; Marriage; Structure and Agency; Symbolic Interaction; System Theories; Theory

REFERENCES AND SUGGESTED READINGS

Beck, U. & Beck-Gernsheim, E. (2002) *Individualization: Institutionalized Individualism and its Social and Political Consequences*. Sage, London.

Beck-Gernsheim, E. (2002) *Reinventing the Family*. Polity, Cambridge.

Bengtson, V. L., Acock, A. C., Allen, K. R., Dilworth-Anderson, P., & Klein, D. M. (Eds.) (2005) *Sourcebook of Family Theory and Research*. Sage, Thousand Oaks, CA.

Boss, P. G., Doherty, W. J., La Rossa, R., Schumm, W. R., & Steinmetz, S. K. (Eds.) (1993) *Sourcebook of Family Theories and Methods: A Contextual Approach*. Plenum, New York.

Cheal, D. (1991) *Family and the State of Theory*. University of Toronto Press, Toronto.

Giddens, A. (1992) *The Transformation of Intimacy*. Polity, Cambridge.

Giddens, A. (2000) *Runaway World*. Routledge, New York.

White, J. M. & Klein, D. M. (2002) *Family Theories*, 2nd edn. Sage, Thousand Oaks, CA.

family therapy

Leigh A. Leslie

Family therapy is a clinical approach to treating mental health and relationship problems based on the assumption that dysfunction can best be understood and treated by examining the social context in which it exists. Emerging as an identifiable "field" in the 1950s, family therapy was, and continues to be, characterized by attention to the interaction and communication patterns existing within couples and families. Several precursors set the stage for what, at the time, was thought to be a dramatic and controversial shift in clinical treatment from a focus on individuals to families.

First, the profession of social work emphasized the need to treat families as units. Recognizing that treatment of one family member would both impact and be impacted by other family members led to the practice of family casework in the early 1900s. Second, the early 1900s also saw the child guidance field begin in Europe and move to the United States. Psychiatrists working with children gradually came to acknowledge and write about the significance of the family in understanding the child. Nonetheless, this new orthopsychiatry movement continued to promote individual psychoanalytic treatment with children. Third, the 1920s and 1930s gave rise to the marriage counseling movement in the US. Made up largely of physicians, clergy, and social workers, this group began working with spouses together.

While writings and practice from the fields of social work, child guidance, and marriage counseling readied the larger mental health field for a paradigm shift, it was changes in psychiatry that are generally seen as the major impetus in the development of family therapy. Frustrated by the limited effectiveness of psychoanalysis for mental illness, particularly schizophrenia, and influenced by the writing emanating from social psychiatry, most notably the work of Harry Stack Sullivan, several individuals and teams began to study and develop new treatment modalities with families of schizophrenic patients. Although the treatment models developed throughout the late 1940s and 1950s varied on many dimensions, it was their similarities and their contrast to the prevailing psychoanalytic thought of the time that led ultimately to a unified field. The primary theme that ran throughout the models was the concept of wholeness; families were more than the sum of their members and the emergent relational and interactional components were the focus of the therapist's intervention. Common characteristics of what came to be called "family systems" models of therapy included circular causation, function of symptoms, boundaries and organization, and communication patterns.

Multidirectional/circular causation is the notion that change in any part of the family impacts all other parts and that any given behavior cannot be understood linearly by what preceded or followed it. Instead, behavior must be considered by looking more broadly at the interactional field in which it is located.

Function/purpose of symptoms refers to the assumptions that symptoms exist for reasons in families. Although the purpose a symptom served may not be obvious to family members and be counter to stated family goals, early family therapy maintained that the symptom was currently or had been functional at some point in a family's history. For example, while the young adult child who cannot successfully separate from parents and lead an independent life may seem like a problem to parents, the continuation of this behavior may serve to keep the parents united by their joint focus on a troubled child.

Boundaries and organization refer to structural characteristics of families. Organization addresses how the family has structured roles and relationships to meet its tasks or goals. Boundaries, on the other hand, address the degree of fluidity and adaptability in family organization. While boundaries need to be flexible enough to respond to changes in family needs and environmental demands, they should not be so malleable that family members and subsystems lose their sense of distinctiveness. For example, parents who allow children to become involved in their arguments, or share marital discontents with their children, would be said to have weak boundaries around the marital subsystem. Conversely, families who could not adapt and take on different tasks when a mother becomes ill, or families that could not respond effectively to age-appropriate changes in children's needs for guidance and affection, might be thought of as rigid in their boundaries and organization.

Communication patterns refer to the messages that family members send one another. The emphasis here is not simply on the words spoken but on both the multiple levels of messages sent and the metacommunications about how messages are to be interpreted in the context of this relationship. Thus, the statement, "tell me how you feel," will be interpreted and responded to very differently in a family that has low tolerance for anger and dissension than in a family that respects differences of opinion.

Throughout the 1960s and 1970s family therapy increased in prominence in the mental health field as publications and training programs proliferated. However, the late 1970s and 1980s saw several critiques of the field. The field's singular focus on the system and lack of attention to individual biology, psychology, and responsibility were criticized from two primary quarters. Families of the mentally ill challenged family therapy for blaming them for their children's illnesses by focusing on the function of a symptom in the family and using language (such as "schizophrenic family" or "alcoholic family") that held the entire system accountable for a problem. Likewise, feminist scholars criticized the circular systemic thinking and language that held both victim and abuser responsible for the violence. Additionally, feminists criticized the field for promoting traditional family structure and failing to incorporate the larger cultural system into therapists' understanding of how gender and race impact family dynamics.

Both in response to these criticisms and as part of the movement toward integration in the mental health field in general, family therapy is continuing to evolve.

The last decade has seen a refocusing on the individual within the family system, and increased attention to issues of race/ethnicity, gender, and sexual orientation in treatment. Further, the strict division between models is eroding as integrative models emerge, and non-systemic postmodernist models – such as narrative and social constructionist models – grow in prominence in the field. An additional change is the integration of family therapy with other systems of service delivery, most notably family medicine.

The primary challenge currently facing family therapy is the challenge facing all mental health fields. The increased demand by insurers for evidence-based treatment has led to an increase in research assessing the effectiveness of specific treatment protocols with specific populations.

SEE ALSO: Bateson, Gregory; Family Conflict; Family Structure; Interaction; Interpersonal Relationships

REFERENCES AND SUGGESTED READINGS

Broderick, C. B. & Schrader, S. S. (1991) The History of Professional Marriage and Family Therapy. In: Gurman, A. S. & Kniskern, D. P. (Eds.), *Handbook and Family Therapy*, Vol. 2. Brunner/Mazel, New York, pp. 3–40.
Haley, J. (1976) Development of a Theory: A History of a Research Project. In: Sluzki, C. E. & Ransom, D. C. (Eds.), *Double Bind: The Foundation of the Communicational Approach to the Family*. Grune & Stratton, New York.
Kaslow, F. W. (1980) History of Family Therapy in the United States: A Kaleidoscopic Overview. *Marriage and Family Review* 3: 77–111.
Kaslow, F. W. (2000) Continued Evolution of Family Therapy: The Last Twenty Years. *Contemporary Family Therapy* 22: 357–86.
Leslie, L. A. (1995) Family Therapy's Evolving Treatment of Gender, Ethnicity, and Sexual Orientation. *Family Relations* 41: 256–63.
Minuchin, S. (1974) *Families and Family Therapy*. Harvard University Press, Cambridge, MA.
Nichols, M. P. & Schwartz, R. C. (2004) *Family Therapy: Concepts and Methods*, 6th edn. Pearson, Boston.
Walters, M., Carter, B., Papp, P., & Silverstein, O. (1988) *The Invisible Web: Gender Patterns in Family Relationships*. Guilford Press, New York.
Watzlawick, P., Beavin, J., & Jackson, D. (1967) *Pragmatics of Human Communication*. W. W. Norton, New York.

Fanon, Frantz (1925–61)

Alan Bairner

Born in Martinique and a psychiatrist by training, Frantz Fanon's sociological legacy lies mainly in the study of "race" and, above all, in the development of postcolonial studies. Having fought for the Free French Army during World War II, Fanon studied medicine and psychiatry in Lyon. In 1952 he began to practice psychiatry in Algeria and thereafter he became associated, particularly in the minds of the political left for whom he became an iconic figure during the 1960s, with the cause of Algerian independence. In arguably his most famous work, *The Wretched of the Earth* (1961), Fanon sought to combine traditional Marxist revolutionary theory with ideas more appropriate to struggles in the developing world.

For some, he was an unattractive thinker who romanticized killing and whose rhetoric was typical of a strain of politics which glorifies violence in pursuit of an imagined future. Others, however, saw in his forensic analysis of the dehumanizing impact of the colonized condition, as evidenced in his first book, *Black Skin, White Masks* (1952), an honest and compelling justification for the use of political violence. Only through acts of violence could the subjugated individual destroy not only the colonial oppressor but also his or her former self.

It could be argued that national liberation struggles of the type for which Fanon proved to be a source of inspiration have been superseded by new challenges centered on globalization. On the other hand, there is an equally strong case for asserting that questions about "race" and about the extended repercussions of colonialism which Fanon sought to answer are as relevant today as when he was writing.

In many respects, for example, it is possible to situate the events of 9/11 or the war in Iraq as the direct consequences of the kind of trauma that Fanon explored both as a physician and as a political activist. Ironically, however, despite Fanon's undoubted contribution to postcolonial studies, his own theoretical approach, like that of C. L. R. James, owes almost everything to the western tradition of social and political thought. To that extent, therefore, while he would most certainly have understood the reasons that lie behind the violence of some Islamic fundamentalists, he would have been ill at ease with the theocratic ambitions of men such as Osama bin Laden. Regardless of the deep-seated psychological need for third world revolution, the concrete objective of revolutionary movements, as understood by Fanon, consisted of material goals, including an equitable distribution of wealth and technology. At no time did he advocate a return to precolonial conditions or, indeed, a requirement to view the world from a perspective that was wholly distanced from western Enlightenment thought.

Having resigned from his position as director of the psychiatric department at Blida-Joinville's hospital, Fanon became more directly involved in the struggle of the National Liberation Front (FLN) to free Algeria from French rule and in 1959 was seriously wounded. He served briefly as the provisional Algerian government's ambassador to Ghana. In 1960 he became seriously ill and died of leukemia in Washington, DC, on December 12, 1961. He was buried in Algeria.

Fanon's other major works were *A Dying Colonialism* (1959) and *Toward the African Revolution* (1964).

SEE ALSO: Marx, Karl; Marxism and Sociology; Methods, Postcolonial; Revolutions; Revolutions, Sociology of; Violence

REFERENCES AND SUGGESTED READINGS

Caute, D. (1970) *Frantz Fanon*. Viking, New York.
Gendzier, I. L. (1973) *Frantz Fanon: A Critical Study*. Wildwood House, London.
Gibson, N. (Ed.) (1999) *Rethinking Fanon: The Continuing Dialogue*. Humanity Books, Amherst.
Gibson, N. (2003) *Frantz Fanon: The Postcolonial Imagination*. Polity Press, Cambridge.
Gordon, L. R. (1995) *Fanon and the Crisis of European Man*. Routledge, New York.
Gordon, L. R., Denean Sharpley-Whiting, T., & White, R. T. (Eds.) (1996) *Fanon: A Critical Reader*. Blackwell, Oxford.
Macey, D. (2000) *Frantz Fanon: A Biography*. Picador, New York.

fans and fan culture

Matthew Hills

Fans have become important to work in media sociology and cultural studies for a variety of reasons: they can be taken to represent a dedicated, active audience; they are consumers who are often also (unofficial, but sometimes official) media producers (Jenkins 1992; McKee 2002); and they can be analyzed as a significant part of contemporary consumer culture. Fandom – the state of being a fan – is usually linked to popular culture rather than high culture. People who appreciate high culture, often being as passionately partisan as pop culture's "fans," are described as "connoisseurs" or "aficionados" rather than as fans (Jensen 1992). Whilst connoisseurship is typically deemed culturally legitimate, fandom has been analyzed as rather more problematic: the stereotype of "the fan" has been one of geeky, excessive, and unhealthy obsession with (supposedly) culturally trivial objects such as TV shows. Henry Jenkins has highlighted and opposed this negative fan stereotype, arguing that such portrayals of fandom should be critiqued, and that fans should instead be viewed more positively as building their own culture out of media products, and as selectively "poaching" meanings and interpretations from favored media texts. Jenkins, whose seminal work *Textual Poachers* (1992) helped to make fandom a viable object of academic study, suggests that the creativity of fans is downplayed in cultural common sense in favor of viewing fans as "cultural dupes" who are perfect consumers, always accepting what the culture industry produces for them. Against this narrative, depicted as belonging to the Frankfurt School of Marxist theorists such as Theodor Adorno as much as to forms of cultural common sense, Jenkins argues that fans discriminate keenly between and within their objects of fandom, developing an aesthetic sense of what counts as a "good" episode of television series such as *Star Trek* or *Doctor Who* (see Tulloch & Jenkins 1995).

Fans develop extensive knowledge and expertise about their shows or sports teams, also characteristically feeling a sense of ownership over "their" object of fandom. They also "tend to seek intimacy with the object of their attention – a personality, a program, a genre, a team" (Kelly 2004: 9). This "intimacy" could involve meeting a celebrity, getting a sportswoman's autograph, seeing an actor give a talk onstage at a convention, chatting with him or her in the bar afterwards, or even visiting real locations used in the filming of a TV series (see Hills 2002). Fans thus seek to break down barriers between themselves as subjects and their objects of fandom, their fan identity becoming a meaningful aspect of cultural and self-identity. Indeed, Tulloch and Jenkins (1995: 23) distinguish between "fans," who claim a cultural identity on the basis of their fandom, and "followers," who despite following pop cultural texts, pop groups, TV series, and so on more than casually, do not make such an identity claim.

As can be seen from this, fandom is generally discussed in relation to media consumption and media texts, sometimes being referred to specifically as "media fandom" (Jenkins 1992: 1), although this prefix is often assumed. Scholars have tended to isolate out and focus on specific fandoms such as fans of science fiction film and TV (Bacon-Smith 1992; Jenkins 1992); fans of soap operas (Harrington & Bielby 1995; Baym 2000); fans of the *Star Wars* films (Brooker 2002); fans of particular TV series and radio shows (Thomas 2002); and sports fans (Crawford 2004).

Fans and fan culture are, however, not quite the same thing. By using the term "fans" we can refer to individuals who have a particular liking or affection for a range of popular cultural texts, celebrities, sports (teams), or artifacts. These individuals – typically displaying an affective relationship with their fan object; that is, they are passionately interested in and committed to following their beloved pop group, sports team, or soap opera – may nevertheless *not* take part in socially organized fan activities. They may not attend fan conventions, be part of fan clubs, post to online fan message boards, or even attend live sporting events – instead perhaps supporting a baseball or football team by reading about games or watching them on television.

By contrast, collective activities such as convention-going or fan club membership are very much indicative of what is meant by "fan culture." Nicholas Abercrombie and Brian Longhurst (1998: 138) mark this distinction by contrasting "fans" with what they term "cultists": the former display their fandom privately or personally rather than communally, whilst the latter are participants in communal fan cultures and activities. However, many writers simply use the term "fans" when referring to members of a fan culture (Bacon-Smith 1992; Jenkins 1992; Hills 2002).

Here, fans are socialized within affective communities of fandom, and engage in subculturally distinctive fan practices such as writing their own fan fiction ("fanfic") based on characters and situations from official films and TV shows, producing their own fan magazines ("fanzines"), writing their own lyrics to popular songs or standards ("filking"), and engaging in costuming at fan conventions by making replicas of costumes worn onscreen by film or TV actors (Jenkins 1992; Joseph-Witham 1996; Hills 2002). "Fans" in the first, socially atomized, sense have been far less studied than "fan culture," probably in part because the latter is more sociologically and culturally visible to researchers, and because such socially organized communities and practices have provided a rich terrain for media ethnographers such as Camille Bacon-Smith (1992) and scholars such as Henry Jenkins (1992). Despite this partial focus in fan studies to date, scholars and students of media fandom should take care not to replay fan debates over "authenticity," where socially atomized fans are considered to be somehow not "true" or "authentic" fans in comparison with those organizing or attending conventions, or regularly attending live sports matches (see Crawford 2004). Furthermore, we should take care not to always explore specific fan cultures as singular objects of study: many soap fans may also be fans of particular celebrities or popular music, and many science fiction TV fans may also be fans of horror movies, and so on. Repertoires of media fandom are thus also important, as fans move between different fan objects and navigate through intertextual networks of TV shows and films (Jenkins 1992; Hills 2002, 2004).

Although it would be fair to say that there is no singular body of work that can be counted as the "sociology of media fandom," the work of French sociologist Pierre Bourdieu has nevertheless been key to studies of fan cultures. John Fiske (1992) has drawn on Bourdieu's theorization of cultural distinction to illuminate how fans, meaning participants in fan cultures, distinguish themselves from non-fan audiences. Fiske emphasizes how such fans work to accumulate "fan cultural capital" or "popular cultural capital," namely, knowledge about, and literacy in relation to, their object of fandom. In this instance, Fiske applies and develops Bourdieu's (1984) take on "cultural capital," by which is broadly meant the level of education and "training" in legitimate culture and its appreciation that a cultural agent holds. Sarah Thornton and Mark Jancovich have also applied Bourdieuian theories to fandom, with Thornton (1995: 11) coining the term "subcultural capital" to describe that form of capital which is not common across an entire culture, but is, instead, specific to a subculture or fan culture. Hills (2002: 57) has further related Bourdieuian concepts to media fandom, discussing "fan social capital" (the network of contacts that a fan has within his or her fan culture) as well as fan cultural capital. This sociological focus has led to fan cultures being thought of as hierarchical rather than romanticized as anti-capitalist, "resistant" communities magically free of power differentials and struggles over status. Many media fandoms and sports fandoms can also be analyzed as male-dominated cultural groups as well as middle-class-dominated elective affinities, meaning that Bourdieu's emphasis on structural inequality in the distribution of forms of capital, beyond economic capital (money) alone, remains important here.

Nick Couldry (2003) has suggested that Bourdieu's work is somewhat weakened by its lack of focus on the operation of the media in relation to "symbolic capital" (prestige), arguing that sociologists should consider the "media's meta-capital" (p. 672), through which "what counts as symbolic capital in particular fields" is altered (p. 668). Thus, fans who become regular sources for the media – or who run popular message boards or websites/Internet news sites – may not merely be reflecting their already acquired fan cultural capital. Rather, by virtue of their own role within mass or niche mediation, these fans, people such as cinephile Harry Knowles (founder of aintitcoolnews.com) or *Doctor Who* fan Shaun Lyon (founder of gallifreyone.com), may be accruing and exercising "media meta-capital." Such fans can even become "subcultural celebrities" in their own right (Hills 2003), being recognized and respected by many others in their subculture or fan culture, while being largely unknown outside this subculture.

Alongside the importance of Pierre Bourdieu's (1984) work on forms of capital, other key theories within recent work on fandom have been those of performance (Abercrombie & Longhurst 1998; Lancaster 2001) and performativity (Hills 2002; Thomas 2002; Crawford 2004). In particular, and drawing on Judith Butler's work, Matt Hills (2002) has suggested that fans should not be thought of either as "consummate consumers" (Kelly 2004: 7) or as "cultural dupes" in thrall to the culture industry. Rather, Hills (2002: 159) suggests that fans display "performative consumption," performing their identities as fans in ways that are simultaneously highly self-reflexive or self-aware *and* non-reflexive or self-absent, given that they cannot always account for why they became fans in the first place (Harrington & Bielby 1995). Crawford (2004: 122) applies Hills's concept to sports fans, finding it to be of use here. The notion of "performative consumption" indicates that we should not treat fandom via a sociological either/or, where fans are either agents whose fan-cultural practices can be celebrated, or they are subjects whose fan-cultural practices can be accounted for, and critiqued, as effects of structural/capitalist forces. It also suggests that depth psychology or psychoanalytic theories may be useful in exploring aspects of fan identities that operate below the level of discursive consciousness (and a number of writers have pursued post-Freudian and sociologically contextualized discussions of this: see Harrington & Bielby 1995; Hills 2002).

In short, media fandom acutely poses problems of "structure" versus "agency" that have dogged contemporary sociological debate, and although Bourdieu's work has been influential in work on fan cultures, surprisingly little attention has yet been paid to utilizing other competing theories of structuration such as those of, for example, Anthony Giddens and Margaret Archer, although J. B. Thompson and Sean McCloud have sociologically analyzed fandom as a "late modern project of the self" (McCloud 2003: 199), using the Giddens of *Modernity and Self-Identity* (1991) rather than *The Constitution of Society* (1984).

As the sociology of media fandom moves toward maturity, we might therefore expect further work on structuration theory, as well as further applications of post-Marxist work on commodification and post-Durkheimian work on ritual and the "collective effervescence" of contemporary neotribes (Hills 2002). Work to date has either tended to push toward the status of a general theory of media fandom (Hills 2002), or it has taken specific (and limited) fan cultures as objects of study (see McKee 2002). These maneuvers have left a range of comparative questions open: are all fan cultures similarly structured through issues of "fan cultural capital" and "fan social capital"? And are fan cultures in Japan, say, structurally and affectively similar to those in the US? Indeed, what of transnational fan cultures? A research agenda relating fandom to matters of globalization has yet to be fully pursued, although one major research project under way at the University of Aberystwyth, and headed up by Martin Barker, promises to deal with the transnational consumption and meanings of *The Lord of the Rings* trilogy of films. Fans and fan cultures have offered one test case for theories of audience "activity" (Fiske 1992) and "performance" (Abercrombie & Longhurst 1998), as well as allowing for the ethnographic exploration of fan communities (Bacon-Smith 1992), but the study of fandom continues to face many challenges and new opportunities.

SEE ALSO: Audiences; Bourdieu, Pierre; Consumption, Mass Consumption, and Consumer Culture; Ethnography; Popular Culture; Structure and Agency; Subculture

REFERENCES AND SUGGESTED READINGS

Abercrombie, N. & Longhurst, B. (1998) *Audiences: A Sociological Theory of Performance and Imagination*. Sage, London.

Bacon-Smith, C. (1992) *Enterprising Women: Television Fandom and the Creation of Popular Myth*. University of Pennsylvania Press, Philadelphia.

Baym, N. K. (2000) *Tune In, Log On: Soaps, Fandom, and Online Community*. Sage, London.

Bourdieu, P. (1984) *Distinction: A Social Critique of the Judgment of Taste*. Harvard University Press, Cambridge, MA.

Brooker, W. (2002) *Using the Force: Creativity, Community, and Star Wars Fans*. Continuum, New York and London.

Couldry, N. (2003) Media Meta-Capital: Extending the Range of Bourdieu's Field Theory. *Theory and Society* 32(5–6): 653–77.

Crawford, G. (2004) *Consuming Sport: Fans, Sport, and Culture*. Routledge, London and New York.

Fiske, J. (1992) The Cultural Economy of Fandom. In: Lewis, L. A. (Ed.), *The Adoring Audience: Fan Culture and Popular Media*. Routledge, London and New York, pp. 30–49.

Harrington, C. L. & Bielby, D. (1995) *Soap Fans: Pursuing Pleasure and Making Meaning in Everyday Life*. Temple University Press, Philadelphia.

Hills, M. (2002) *Fan Cultures*. Routledge, London and New York.

Hills, M. (2003) Recognition in the Eyes of the Relevant Beholder: Representing "Subcultural Celebrity" and Cult TV Fan Cultures. *Mediactive* 2: 59–73.

Hills, M. (2004) Defining Cult TV: Texts, Inter-Texts and Fan Audiences. In: Allen, R. C. & Hill, A. (Eds.), *The TV Studies Reader*. Routledge, New York and London, pp. 509–23.

Jenkins, H. (1992) *Textual Poachers: Television Fans and Participatory Culture*. Routledge, New York and London.

Jensen, J. (1992) Fandom as Pathology: The Consequences of Characterization. In: Lewis, L. A. (Ed.), *The Adoring Audience: Fan Culture and Popular Media*. Routledge, London and New York, pp. 9–29.

Joseph-Witham, H. R. (1996) *Star Trek Fans and Costume Art*. University Press of Mississippi, Jackson.

Kelly, W. W. (Ed.) (2004) *Fanning the Flames: Fans and Consumer Culture in Contemporary Japan*. SUNY Press, New York.

Lancaster, K. (2001) *Interacting with Babylon 5: Fan Performances in a Media Universe*. University of Texas Press, Austin.

McCloud, S. (2003) Popular Culture Fandoms, the Boundaries of Religious Studies, and the Project of the Self. *Culture and Religion* 4(2): 187–206.

McKee, A. (2002) Fandom. In: Miller, T. (Ed.), *Television Studies*. BFI Publishing, London, pp. 66–70.

Thomas, L. (2002) *Fans, Feminisms, and "Quality" Media*. Routledge, London and New York.

Thornton, S. (1995) *Club Cultures: Music, Media, and Subcultural Capital*. Polity, Cambridge.

Tulloch, J. & Jenkins, H. (1995) *Science Fiction Audiences: Watching Doctor Who and Star Trek*. Routledge, London and New York.

fantasy city

John Hannigan

"Fantasy City" refers to a new urban form located at the intersection of leisure, consumption, tourism, and real estate development. In *Fantasy City: Pleasure and Profit in the Postmodern Metropolis* (1998), Canadian sociologist John Hannigan points to six defining features: fantasy cities are characteristically themo-centric (scripted), aggressively branded, active day and night, modular (mixing a standard array of retail and entertainment components), solipsistic (isolated physically and economically from the neighborhoods that surround them), and postmodern (in their reliance on simulation and spectacle). This set of phenomena is empirically manifested in an infrastructure of themed restaurants, nightclubs, shopping malls, multiplex cinemas, virtual reality arcades, casino-hotels, book and record megastores, sports stadiums and arenas, and other urban entertainment destinations. While the only urban centers that currently qualify as full-scale fantasy cities are Las Vegas and Orlando, Florida, most cities today have some commercial neighborhoods and developments that display these characteristics to a greater or lesser extent. Furthermore, fantasy city development has spread aggressively beyond the borders of North America, with large-scale projects currently operating or under construction in such countries as Australia, Singapore, Malaysia, China, Saudi Arabia, and Dubai.

The contemporary trend toward saleable leisure spaces in the city has its roots in the past. During the "golden age" of popular urban entertainment (1890–1930) in North America, an extensive array of amusements emerged, from the "Trip to the Moon" ride at Coney Island to the elaborately themed vaudeville theaters and motion picture palaces of the 1920s and 1930s. Despite claims by leisure merchants of the day that they were front and center in the movement toward the democratization of leisure, most urban leisure spaces were, in fact, effectively segregated by social class, race, and gender.

The contemporary fantasy city differs from its earlier predecessor in several key aspects. First, it is more pervasive and portable, the cornerstone of urban economic development efforts in North America, Europe, Asia, and the Middle East. Second, fantasy city construction has been undertaken on an unprecedented scale, encompassing not only single venues but also entire neighborhoods and districts. Third, fantasy city development has spread beyond its traditional base in the central city to exurban malls, sports complexes, and lifestyle centers, as well as port lands and other reclaimed waterfront locations. Fourth, these new urban spaces are conceived, branded, and managed by a new set of corporate players – multinational retail, media, and entertainment conglomerates such as Disney, Nike, and Sony – in partnership with the local and regional real estate developers and construction firms that previously shaped the commercial landscapes of the city.

Fantasy cities appeal especially to tourists and suburban visitors because they satisfy a bourgeois preference for sanitized environments of "riskless risk." That is, they are the end products of a longstanding cultural contradiction between the American middle-class desire for experience and their equally strong parallel reluctance to take risks, especially those that involve face-to-face contact with the "lower orders" in big cities. In this regard, the technologies of simulation and virtual reality that characterize the theme park city at one and the same time both dazzle and reassure. Excitement is divorced from actual experience and made safe. The sanitized consumption that is characteristic of the fantasy city is realized by three central, strategic processes: theming, branding, and experiential storytelling.

Theming invites consumers to participate in structured fantasies derived from an exotic geographical locale (a tropical rainforest, a Moroccan bazaar), a distinctive historical period (pioneer days, medieval times), a popular motion picture or television show (Star Trek, the Flintstones), or a sports, music, fashion, or film celebrity (Wayne Gretsky, Dolly Parton, Cindy Crawford). As such, theming serves both to unify and market leisure sites, rendering them entertaining, easy to read visually, and controllable through a centrally directed corporate script. Theming has become pervasive, George Ritzer (1999) suggests, because it is a unique means of "re-enchanting" a world that has become excessively dull and practical. Ritzer refers to such themed venues as "cathedrals of consumption" to indicate their quasi-religious appeal for postmodern consumers in search of enchantment and identity.

Branding has three interrelated dimensions, each of which relates to the production and marketing of fantasy cities. Insofar as it invites instant consumer recognition, branding encourages "synergies" with global sports and entertainment conglomerates such as Nike, Disney, and Sony with their rosters of widely publicized and recognized celebrities. Furthermore, successful branded leisure spaces play on our desire for comfort and certainty, key attributes of postmodern theme parks. Third, branding provides a ready-made point of identification for consumers in an increasingly crowded commercial marketplace.

Finally, fantasy cities are constructed around the creation of guest-centered experiences. This is a testament to the power of narrative to imbue leisure environments, products, and services with an added dimension of interest and meaning. Urban entertainment destinations and attractions are increasingly outfitted with a "back story" that purports to link them with a historical (or mythical) repertoire of iconic events, personalities, and milestones.

Consumption in the fantasy city is further characterized by a dedifferentiation of the spheres of education, shopping, dining, and entertainment. This results in the growth of synergistic, hybridized consumer activities, as described by the terms "shopertainment, entertainment, and edutainment." This further extends the urban entertainment economy into such community institutions as museums, hospitals, churches, and schools.

Promoted by civic boosters as the panacea of urban revival, fantasy cities nevertheless bring with them a host of social, political, and economic liabilities.

As Mike Davis demonstrates in *City of Quartz* (1990), his apocalyptic vision of contemporary Los Angeles, fantasy city-style development aggressively colonizes public space, limiting access to a select leisure class. It is an environment constructed out of fear, uncertainty, and the desire for exclusion, just the opposite of the traditional city park or market. In order to guarantee a sense of security, these spaces are regulated through a battery of surveillance and control techniques. Chief among these are CCTV (closed circuit television) and privately operated BIDs (business improvement districts). The latter routinely utilize private security guards and street clean-up crews and lack any direct public accountability. This infrastructure of surveillance and control is especially evident in urban settings in which the pleasure-seeking, entertainment economy operates at night and where bars, nightclubs, and the like are suspected of fostering a higher degree of lawlessness and disorder. The current proliferation of entertainment development endangers what Sharon Zukin (1995) calls "the dream of a public culture." That is, the ideal of a diverse metropolis where residents of varied ethnic, racial, and socioeconomic backgrounds mingle freely and work together to build a civil society is undercut by the operation of prepackaged urban entertainment destinations that furnish safe, random encounters within the confines of a "tourist bubble." This contributes to the growth of what Sorkin (1992) has termed "ageographical cities," urban spaces that are stripped of any identifiable sense of place and sealed off from the surrounding environment.

Furthermore, the argument that fantasy city development functions as an economic multiplier more often than not turns out to be deeply flawed. The "urban growth machines" that control municipal business and politics justify sports and entertainment projects on the grounds that they act as catalysts, generating increased trade for the local small businesses such as bars, restaurants, and corner stores that dot local neighborhood streets. Alas, in this context the oft-cited saying that "a rising tide lifts all ships" is faulty. Rather, these are more likely to be cannibalized by entertainment megaprojects than to be catalyzed by them. In Baltimore, Maryland, after nearly a quarter century of festival marketplace development around the Inner Harbor, much of it publicly financed, prosperity has scarcely spilled over to the surrounding inner city. Visitors rarely venture far from the waterfront. This further erodes an inner-city landscape of vacant storefronts, dilapidated residential buildings, and escalating poverty. Most jobs in the tourism and entertainment industry are of dubious quality: part-time, minimum wage, few fringe benefits or career ladders (Levine 2000).

Finally, fantasy cities are problematic insofar as they exhibit marked undemocratic qualities. Poster-children for the "new entrepreneurial city," they are designed, built, and managed by "public–private partnerships" in which the latter holds the upper hand. As such, they stand apart from everyday municipal governance. Key decisions are increasingly made by public/private institutions rather than by elected representatives. Grassroots input is minimal. What has paved the way for this is the widespread deindustrialization and movement of manufacturing offshore encountered by North American urban economies in recent decades. In the face of this downward spiral, local government has embraced a promotional and marketing role, encouraging the privatization of urban development and culture.

Since the term was introduced in the late 1990s, fantasy city has proven to be a useful construct in a variety of different theoretical and empirical contexts. Bauman (2003: 25) locates its "magic blend of security and adventure – of supervision and freedom, of routine and surprise, of sameness and variety" as central to the contradictory desires and expectations of urban residents. This reflects, he says, the combination of globalizing pressures and territorially oriented identity search that shapes the structural development of the contemporary city. Atkinson and Flint (1995) link the idea with "gated communities." The key imperative

of the fantasy city for city center development, they observe, is the desire for experience without danger leading to the desire for "urbanoid spaces" (spaces that resemble "real" streets but are devoid of the diversity that they formerly supported). This provides the means for people to exercise control over where, how, and when social encounters are made. Chatterton and Hollands (2003) focus on the production, regulation, and consumption of "urban nightscapes," most notably those that provide branded, themed, and stylized experiences to young adults in search of hedonism and cool. In the brew pubs, themed "super-clubs" (combined bar, restaurant, and club) and sports bars that are proliferating in urban entertainment districts, they encountered many of the same elements of "Disneyfication" and global corporate ownership that are characteristic of the fantasy city, as described by Hannigan (1998). Hubbard (2003) situates fantasy city development in the exurban fringe of the metropolis, where urban dwellers "increasingly seek distraction in spectacular, peripheral landscapes located away from the 'inner city.'" He empirically illustrates this with survey data describing patterns of cinema-going among the population of Leeds (UK). McGuire (2003) writes that Sony's PlayStation 2 gaming environment not only exhibits all of the features that characterize the fantasy city, but also builds on its central attraction – amplifying the thrill of the spectacle without any exposure to the personal risks found that physical presence entails. As is the case with other 3D virtual communities, players are guaranteed freedom from the confines of the physical body, freedom from the constraints of geographical space, freedom from strangers, and freedom from control.

SEE ALSO: Brands and Branding; Consumption, Cathedrals of; Consumption, Landscapes of; Consumption, Spectacles of; Consumption, Tourism and; Consumption, Urban/City as Consumerspace; Shopping Malls; Urban Tourism

REFERENCES AND SUGGESTED READINGS

Atkinson, R. & Flint, J. (1995) *Fortress UK? Gated Communities, the Spatial Revolt of the Elites, and*

Time-Space Trajectories of Segregation. Department of Urban Studies, University of Glasgow.

Bauman, Z. (2003) *City of Fears, City of Hopes.* Goldsmiths College, University of London.

Chatterton, P. & Hollands, R. (2003) *Urban Nightscapes: Youth Cultures, Pleasure Spaces, and Corporate Power.* Routledge, London and New York.

Davis, M. (1990) *City of Quartz: Excavating the Future in Los Angeles.* Verso, London.

Gottdiener, M. (1997) *The Theming of America: Dreams, Visions, and Commercial Spaces.* Westview Press, Boulder, CO.

Hannigan, J. (1998) *Fantasy City: Pleasure and Profit in the Postmodern Metropolis.* Routledge, London and New York.

Hubbard, P. (2003) Fear and Loathing at the Multiplex: Everyday Anxiety in the Post-Industrial City. *Capital and Class* 80: 51–76.

Levine, M. V. (2000) A Third-World City in the First World: Social Exclusion, Racial Inequality, and Sustainable Development in Baltimore, Maryland. In: Polèse, M. & Stren, R. (Eds.), *The Social Sustainability of Cities: Diversity and the Management of Change.* University of Toronto Press, Toronto.

McGuire, M. (2003) PlayStation 2: Selling the Third Place. *eZine* 17, 8 (August): online.

Ritzer, G. (1999) *Enchanting a Disenchanted World.* Pine Forge Press, Thousand Oaks, CA.

Sorkin, M. (Ed.) (1992) *Variations on a Theme Park: The New American City and the End of Public Space.* Noonday Press, New York.

Zukin, S. (1995) *The Cultures of Cities.* Blackwell, Cambridge, MA.

fascism

Mabel Berezin

Fascism as a historical entity began in 1922 when Mussolini came to power in Italy. As a political ideology, fascism defines many of the movements that were present in post-World War I Europe from the British Union of Fascists to the Romanian Iron Guard. Fascism could have remained simply a characteristic of a group of historically specific political formations, but the term rather quickly developed a life of its own. Today, it serves as what Alexander (2003) has described as a bridging metaphor, that is, a term that one uses independently of historical or definitional context when confronted with acts of arbitrary violence or authoritarianism in political and, in some instances, social life.

The entries in the 1931 and 1968 editions of the *Encyclopedia of the Social Sciences* discuss fascism exclusively in terms of the regime in Italy. The authors make some effort to distinguish Italian Fascism from German National Socialism. The 2002 edition of the *Encyclopedia* 1990s, scholars viewed fascism as a descriptor of events in post-World War I Europe or as an ideology with only historical interest. Precise conceptualization has eluded past, as well as current, exegeses of historical fascism. Attempts to theorize fascism have mined specific historical instances for generalities and yielded catalogs of characteristics. Even a cursory reading of this scholarship suggests that it is difficult to generalize across cases and leaves the impression that Benedetto Croce was correct when he described fascism as a "parenthesis" in European history.

The historian Gilbert Allardyce (1979) wrote a frequently cited analysis that claimed to have closed the question of "generic" fascism. He asserted fascism had no meaning outside of Italy and that it was neither an ideology nor a mental category. Comparing fascism to romanticism (and curiously obtuse to fascism's other ideological kin, modernism), he stated that both terms "mean virtually nothing." Resigned to the fact that "fascism [as a political term] is probably with us for good," Allardyce asserts the proper analytic task is to "limit the damage." Allardyce argues that fascism should be considered as descriptive of a historical period within a single nation-state. The historicity of fascism renders it imprecise as an analytic frame.

The death knell of fascism has not sounded either in the real world of political practice or in the relatively cloistered world of the academy. For example, Griffin (1991: 26) begins where earlier studies left off. He argues that the term fascism has undergone an "unacceptable loss of precision" and proposes a new "ideal type" of fascism based on the following definition: "Fascism is a genus of political ideology whose mythic core in its various permutations is a palingenetic form of populist ultra-nationalism." The collapse of communism in 1989, the electoral success of European right-wing populist parties that began in the early 1990s coupled with a resurgence of neo-Nazi violence, and the more recent rise of Islamic fundamentalism have reawakened social science interest in historical fascism. Three basic approaches to fascism have emerged over the last 50 years.

Existing studies of fascism fall into two schools that may be broadly categorized as follows. The first tries to answer the "what" or definitional question. Frequently, this is articulated in a discussion of whether or not fascism is a "generic" concept or a national variation of historically specific political instances. Of those who try to define fascism, the central theme is the impossibility of definition. The second approach bypasses definition and tries to establish the characteristics of regimes and constituencies. Lipset's (1981) classic account of the class composition of fascist movements attributes fascism's success to the political disaffection of the middle classes. Linz's (1976) approach to constituency formation starts from the premise that an independent "phenomenon" of fascism existed and defines it as "hyper-nationalist, often pan-nationalist, anti-parliamentary, anti-liberal, anti-communist, populist and therefore anti-proletarian, partly anti-capitalist and anti-bourgeois." Linz emphasizes that European fascists (he uses the term for a range of cases while recognizing national differences) combined paramilitary tactics with standard electoral procedures to gain legitimate power. Fascism, for Linz, was a peculiar combination of law and violence.

Linz's definition rests on his assumption that fascism occupies a residual political field. As a "late-comer" to the political scene, fascism had to capture whatever "political space," in the form of ideological doctrine and political constituencies, was available to it. His argument is dependent upon analyzing the social bases of fascism's political competitors (Linz 1980). Linz recognizes the importance of national case studies and the characteristics that he outlines are applicable in various combinations to a broad range of fascist movements and regimes. In general, studies of institutions and constituencies display greater degrees of analytic precision than those that wrestle with definition.

A central weakness in much of the writing on fascism, past and present, has been a failure to draw a sharp distinction between fascist movements and regimes, between fascism as ideology and fascism as state, between political impulse and political institution. In general, analysts elide the question of culture and ideology or simply deal with it in a descriptive manner. The forces that enable a political movement to assume state power are different from, but not unconnected to, the forces that define a new regime. During the 1920s and 1930s virtually every country in Europe had a fascist movement, or political movements that displayed the characteristics of the fascist impulse, but relatively few of these movements progressed to political regimes, that is, took control of the state. Culture and ideology figure differently at both stages. In the movement phase, culture and ideology act as a powerful mobilizing device that frames the political beliefs of committed cadres of supporters. In the regime phase, culture and ideology serve as conversion mechanisms to ensure the consent of a broad public constituency.

Totalitarian states are not necessary outcomes and historical evidence suggests that they are as much fascist fictions as political realities. Mussolini declared that his regime was the first totalitarian state. Although recent historiography has shown that the fascist cultural project was highly fissured, the intention (if not the reality) of coherence was a goal. Arendt (1973) built terror into the definition of totalitarianism. Her quasi-psychoanalytic approach to fascism paints a portrait of mass societies, mobs, and atomized individuals responding to the congeries of a police state and evokes contemporary neo-Nazis and images of an Orwellian 1984. Terror and violence as analytic frames may capture the political realities of Stalinist Russia and Holocaust horrors, but terror did not represent the quotidian experience of Italian Fascism and distracts from historical and theoretical understanding. In contrast to Nazi Germany and Stalinist Russia, the Italian Fascist regime was relatively non-repressive.

Scholars have argued that it should be possible to establish a "fascist minimum," by which they mean a set of criteria without which fascism could not exist. Yet they have been reluctant to ascribe greater or lesser degrees of importance to the variables that they view as characteristic of fascism. For example, Italian Fascism was anti-Socialist and anti-clerical, despite its conciliation with the Catholic Church, but above all it was anti-liberal as liberalism was understood in early twentieth-century Italy.

Discussions of Marxism have confounded discussions of fascism. Positing that fascism is not Marxism, or is a form of "anti-Marxism," fails to address the salient features of both ideologies. Many Fascists – including Mussolini himself – began their political careers as socialists. What were the differences and points of confluence between Fascism and Marxism which made the transition from one to the other possible?

The beginning of an answer lies in Sternhell's (1994) analysis of fascism as an "independent cultural and political phenomenon" representing a "revision" of Marxism. According to Sternhell, fascism was a political hybrid that rejected, first, the liberal ideals of rationalism, individualism, and utilitarianism, and second, the materialistic dimensions of Marxism. From Marxism, fascism borrowed a concept of communitarianism embodied in a new form of revolutionary syndicalism; and from liberalism, it borrowed a commitment to free markets. Sternhell's contention that market economies are compatible with fascist ideology and regimes forecloses purely economic interpretations of fascism. Sternhell's analysis lends support to fascism's disavowal of liberal political culture, but it is overly dependent upon the writings of national, and sometimes obscure, avant-garde intellectuals to serve as a fulcrum for generating new theories of fascism.

Fascism refuses to go away. There are four identifiable stages in the career of fascism as a concept: first, the post-World War II period when the classic analyses were written, spanning roughly from 1950 to the early 1970s (much of these writings have been discussed above); second, the social interpretations phase; third, the cultural institutional turn; and fourth, the return to political explanations.

Social interpretations of fascism began to reemerge in the 1980s. Heirs of Lipset's mode of analysis, these studies were less deterministic and grounded in a nuanced notion of class and political action. De Grazia's (1981) study of the Fascist leisure organization the *Dopolavoro* examines how Fascism coopted the Italian working classes through the regime's colonization of its leisure time. De Grazia focuses on how workers pursued political projects that on the face of it were against their interests instead of locating the charisma of Fascism in the collective psychology of class groupings.

Social interpretations have occupied more historians of Nazi Germany than of Fascist Italy. Two central and contrasting works in this genre are Browning's (1992) history of a German police battalion in Poland and Goldhagen's (1996) study of how ordinary Germans were not only complicit but actively engaged in the murder of the Jews. Browning provides a measured analysis of how ordinary citizens became involved in the Nazi genocide. Goldhagen argues "ordinary Germans" became killers because they were inherently anti-Semitic and enjoyed hunting down their Jewish neighbors and engaging in acts of violence against them. Brustein (1996) argues membership in the Nazi Party was a rational and not an emotional decision. Career advancement demanded party membership and German citizens who wanted to feed and clothe their families fell in line.

In the mid-1990s the social approach to the study of fascism shaded into an approach that focused on political culture. Gentile (1993) studied the symbols of Italian Fascism and concluded that it was a form of political religion that sacralized politics. Another thread of the cultural analysis was the focus upon how cultural institutions intersected with political regimes. Berezin's (1997) study of public political events links the study of fascist ritual to comparative political analysis.

The millennium has seen a resurgence of interest in fascism within the social sciences. Paxton (2004) begins where earlier generations of studies left off. Paxton sets himself the task of trying to define the parameters of fascism as a political phenomenon and he astutely chooses the term "anatomy" to characterize his project. As his title *Fascists* suggests, Mann (2004) reinvigorates the class approach to fascism. Mann analyzes six cases of inter-war European fascism and identifies the presence of paramilitarism combined with the usual array of anti-statism and nationalist ideology as a distinguishing feature of fascism. Despite the vast array of new scholarship at their disposal, Mann and Paxton more or less conclude that fascism was an inter-war European phenomenon that is not likely to repeat itself in its early twentieth-century form.

Political scientist Nancy Bermeo's *Ordinary People in Extraordinary Times* (2003) is not exclusively a study of fascism and it has the advantage of including Latin America in the analysis. Bermeo views transitions to and from democracy as a series of choices that ordinary people make as they try to get on with their lives. This book taps into the attraction of individuals to political groups who offer solutions to practical problems. The attraction is based on potential efficacy rather than any prior moral assessment of ideology – whether that ideology is democratic or not. Bermeo offers a first step in demarcating the experience of the varieties of popular political choice.

A striking feature of various approaches, past and present, to fascism is lack of specificity. For example, violence is constitutive of political ideologies that are not fascist as well as those that have been labeled fascist. Berezin (1997) reviews an array of available theories. She argues that if one examines fascism in the historical moment in which it occurs, the early twentieth century, then its ideological opposite was socialism and communism. Indeed, many prominent fascists such as Mussolini himself began their careers as socialists and then became fascists. She concludes that the defining characteristic of fascism was that it was political disposition that conflated the public and private dimension of the self. The fascist self was a political self submerged in the nation. As such, fascism privileged public life over private life and demanded a perpetually mobilized citizenry. This conception of fascism has the advantage that it dehistoricizes fascism and creates an analytic frame that can be applied to other ideologies and historical instances. Examining other movements, regimes, and ideologies that demand the fusion of public and private self has the potential to lead to a more precise and conceptually refined definition of fascism.

SEE ALSO: Authoritarianism; Communism; Democracy; Ideology; Totalitarianism

REFERENCES AND SUGGESTED READINGS

Alexander, J. C. (2003) *The Meanings of Social Life.* Oxford University Press, New York.
Allardyce, G. (1979) What Fascism is Not: Thoughts on the Deflation of a Concept. *American Historical Review* 84: 388.
Arendt, H. (1973 [1951]) *The Origins of Totalitarianism.* Harcourt Brace Jovanovich, New York.
Berezin, M. (1997) *Making the Fascist Self: The Political Culture of Inter-War Italy.* Cornell University Press, Ithaca, NY.
Bermeo, N. (2003) *Ordinary People in Extraordinary Times: The Citizenry and the Breakdown of Democracy.* Princeton University Press, Princeton.
Browning, C. R. (1992) *Ordinary Men: Reserve Police Battalion 101 and the Final Solution in Poland.* Harper Collins, New York.
Brustein, W. I. (1996) *The Logic of Evil.* Yale University Press, New Haven.
De Grazia, V. (1981) *The Culture of Consent.* Cambridge University Press, New York.
Gentile, E. (1993) *Il culto del littorio.* Laterza, Rome.
Goldhagen, D. J. (1996) *Hitler's Willing Executioners.* Knopf, New York.
Griffin, R. (1991) *The Nature of Fascism.* St. Martin's Press, New York.
Linz, J. J. (1976) Some Notes Toward a Comparative Study of Fascism in Sociological Historical Perspective. In: Laqueur, W. (Ed.), *Fascism: A Reader's Guide.* University of California Press, Berkeley.
Linz, J. J. (1980) Political Space and Fascism as a Late-Comer. In: Larsen, S. U. (Ed.), *Who Were the Fascists: Social Roots of European Fascism.* Universitetsforlaget, Bergen, pp. 153–89.
Lipset, S. M. (1981) *Political Man.* Johns Hopkins University Press, Baltimore.
Mann, M. (2004) *Fascists.* Cambridge University Press, Cambridge.
Paxton, R. O. (2004) *The Anatomy of Fascism.* Knopf, New York.
Sternhell, Z. (1994) *The Birth of Fascist Ideology.* Princeton University Press, Princeton.

fatherhood

Esther Dermott

Fatherhood is a social institution and includes the rights, duties, responsibilities, and statuses associated with being a father. A useful distinction is made between the terms father, fathering, and fatherhood. The first refers to the connection made between a particular child and a particular man (whether biological or social). The second refers to behavior; the actual practices of "doing" parenting. The third refers to more general ideologies and public meanings associated with being a father.

Fatherhood research is conducted in a number of academic disciplines and commentaries on fatherhood have also become commonplace outside academia in literature and non-fiction. Within the social sciences, researchers working from a developmental perspective use quantitative techniques to explore the effect of paternal influence and father–child relationships on the well-being of children and fathers. Statistical techniques, applied to survey material, are also used to develop cause-and-effect linkages between men's structural positions and their fathering behavior. Qualitative approaches, often associated with a symbolic interactionist perspective, are adopted by scholars interested in exploring individuals' perceptions and experiences of diverse forms of fatherhood. Discourses of fatherhood are examined by poststructuralists using images of fatherhood in policy documents and the popular media. Apparent discrepancies between representations of fatherhood and fathering behavior mean that exploring the alleged gulf between the "culture" and "conduct" of fatherhood (La Rossa 1988) has become a major focus for scholarly attention.

The breadth and depth of research on fatherhood have developed exponentially since the 1970s. Debates about women's role in society that emerged at this time stimulated a complementary interest in exploring masculinity. Women's increasing participation in the labor market intensified discussion about the construction of motherhood and led to an awareness of the relative lack of comment about men's roles in the family. Thus fatherhood research gained attention to provide balance to family research that was dominated by analyses of motherhood. Justification for the significance of fatherhood as a research topic in its own right drew on psychological evidence, which emphasized the importance of fathers for the successful emotional and educational development of children (Lamb 2003).

The changing nature of fatherhood is a consistent theme in research. The stereotypical image of Victorian fatherhood as strict and detached has been frequently adopted as a basis for comparison with contemporary ideas, and the emergence of scholarship on fatherhood in the 1970s sometimes led to an impression that a fundamentally different kind of fatherhood began during this period. The absence of a "usable past" (La Rossa 1997) may explain the tendency towards making overly neat distinctions between old/traditional and new fatherhood. A simplistic historical pattern describes the father as moving from moral guardian, disciplinarian, and educator, to the single role of financial provider, to the modern version of nurturing involvement (Pleck & Pleck 1997). However, more nuanced accounts have challenged this narrative by drawing attention, for example, to the presence of emotional responses to parenthood in men's lives in earlier periods. It is now widely accepted that a linear progression does not easily fit onto historical reality or adequately indicate the complexity of fatherhood.

While there is general agreement that the meanings of fatherhood have altered, there is less consensus over the extent of change and the meaning of modern fatherhood. A key question is the degree to which being the financial provider remains a significant aspect of fatherhood. Those who claim the ideology of breadwinner/ricewinner has been replaced with the nurturing father model suggest it is the quality of the father–child relationship and childcare that is increasingly prioritized by men. Given women's higher levels of participation in the labor market throughout the life course and the rise of dual-income households, providing money to support family life can no longer be described as the preserve of the male parent. On the other hand, in two-parent households men continue to contribute a larger proportion of the family income than women and the continuing expectation that men will provide for their family is exemplified in the common legal requirement that a father continues to be financially responsible for his children after divorce or separation.

Another focus is describing the components of "new" fatherhood. One characteristic is the development of an emotional relationship between father and child, but there is an increased emphasis on "caring for" in addition to "caring about." The words "nurturing" and "involved" are frequently invoked in order to capture this aspect of modern fatherhood. Nurturing is often applied to mothers and can be conceptualized as encompassing day-to-day care within the private sphere and focused on child development. Its application to men suggests a growing similarity between the roles of mothers and fathers. Involvement is a broad term that has been the subject of further qualification. In terms of childcare, three aspects have been demarcated: engagement, accessibility, and responsibility (Lamb et al. 1987). These refer respectively to interaction with a child through care or play; availability for interaction; and taking on the planning and forward thinking around children. Some authors have commented that providing money should be recognized as a form of involvement, although this suggests that involved fatherhood is a counter to negligent or absent fatherhood rather than to "traditional" fatherhood.

There is an awareness of fatherhood in political and policy arenas, which both reflects and encourages academic discussion. Concern over deadbeat dads (US) or feckless fathers (UK) is mainly associated with the absence of financial support for families, but also the potential impact of the lack of male role models and paternal influence over children's lives. This has been characterized as the problem of "fatherless families" and has prompted right-wing authors to support a return to traditional family values and the male breadwinner model. An alternative explanation for fathers' absence from families is because they are undervalued and discriminated against in society. Many of the expanding fathers' rights groups focus on the legal position of fathers with respect to issues such as the right of fathers to insist on or veto abortions and, perhaps most notably, custody access post-divorce. Structural, especially workplace, constraints have also been noted as influential in men's frustrated attempts to be "good dads." Authors interested in this position concentrate on the extension of parental rights to fathers, such as paternity leave and access to reduced working hours. From a feminist perspective an increased role for men in relation to childcare seems essential in order to move towards gender equality, but there is skepticism over whether an extension of rights by employers and states will lead to wholesale transformation.

Recognition of the heterogeneity of fathers' social situation and relationship to their children has been an important development in fatherhood studies. Until recently, fatherhood, unlike motherhood, has not been a proven biological fact. Instead, fatherhood was confirmed indirectly through a man's relationship to the mother of a child. The significance of biological fatherhood has increased with the arrival of DNA testing and the possibility of identifying the genetic parent. Perhaps paradoxically, social fatherhood without any biological tie is also gaining more attention. Increasing divorce and remarriage rates have led to more men entering fatherhood through either formal or informal adoptive and step relationships. Variations in the experiences and ideals of fatherhood due to differences in residency, age, class, sexuality, and ethnicity are also increasingly the subject of study. Further research can be expected to explore these terrains in order to develop a fuller picture of fatherhood. The future aim will be to establish the sociology of fatherhood as a *sui generis* area of study within the social sciences, albeit one which draws strongly on interdisciplinary perspectives.

SEE ALSO: Child Custody and Child Support; Childhood; Family, Men's Involvement in; Gender, Work, and Family; Marriage, Sex, and Childbirth; Motherhood; Stepfathering

REFERENCES AND SUGGESTED READINGS

Deinhart, A. (1998) *Reshaping Fatherhood: The Social Construction of Shared Parenting*. Sage, Thousand Oaks, CA.

Hobson, B. (Ed.) (2002) *Making Men Into Fathers*. Cambridge University Press, Cambridge.

La Rossa, R. (1988) Fatherhood and Social Change. *Family Relations* 37: 451–7.

La Rossa, R. (1997) *The Modernization of Fatherhood: A Social and Political History*. University of Chicago Press, Chicago.

Lamb, M. E. (2003) *The Role of the Father in Child Development*, 4th edn. John Wiley & Sons, New York.

Lamb, M. E., Pleck, J. H., Charnov, E. L., & Levine, J. A. (1987) A Biosocial Perspective on

Paternal Behavior and Involvement. In: Lancaster, J. B., Altmann, J., Rossi, A. S., & Sherrod, L. R. (Eds.), *Parenting Across the Lifespan: Biosocial Dimensions*. Aldine de Gruyter, New York.

Lupton, D. & Barclay, L. (1997) *Constructing Fatherhood: Discourses and Experiences*. Sage, London.

Marsiglio, W., Amato, P., Day, R. D., & Lamb, M. E. (2000) Scholarship on Fatherhood in the 1990s and Beyond. *Journal of Marriage and the Family* 62: 1173–91.

Peters, E. & Day, R. D. (Eds.) (2000) *Fatherhood: Research, Interventions, and Policies*. Haworth, New York.

Pleck, E. H. & Pleck, J. H. (1997) Fatherhood Ideals in the United States: Historical Dimensions. In: Lamb, M. E. (Ed.), *The Role of the Father in Child Development*, 3rd edn. John Wiley & Sons, New York.

Van Dongen, M. C. P., Frinking, G. A. B., & Jacobs, M. J. G. (Eds.) (1995) *Changing Fatherhood: A Multidisciplinary Perspective*. Thesis Publishers, Amsterdam.

fear

Jackie Eller and Andrea Eller

How do sociologists theoretically and empirically study fear? A simple answer is that the literature can be divided into two rather broad and overlapping areas of emphasis: fear as an emotion and fear as a consequence of or motivation for social relations.

While fear has its traditional roots in psychology, the sociological study of emotions draws on a rich heritage from theorists such as Durkheim, Mead, Cooley, Freud, Homans, and Goffman. It has been over the past 30 years that the sociology of emotions has emerged, emphasizing emotion as a crucial aspect of both micro- and macrosociological examinations of social reality. Although there is general agreement among sociologists that emotions (fear included) are socially constructed and made meaningful within sociohistorical contexts, there is also some disagreement as to the importance of including certain elements such as biological and cognitive processes in the sociological examination of emotions (Barbalet 1998, 2002; Turner & Stets 2005; Turner 2006).

When sociologists examine fear as an emotion, they are in general consensus that it varies in interpretation and expression. But fear is also considered to be universal to the human experience, along with happiness, anger, and sadness. As a primary emotion, then, fear contributes to the experience of such secondary emotions as anxiety, shame, repulsion, and regret (Kemper 1987; Scheff 2000). However, as Tudor (2003: 244) notes, a sociology of fear "must examine the cultural matrix within which fear is realized and attend to the patterns of social activity routinely associated with it."

In the conceptualization of fear as a consequence of or motivation for social relations, the concern is less with the examination of the emotion per se and more with the relationship of fear to anxiety, panic, risk, victimization, and social control. Of particular interest for researchers and apparently the public in general is fear of crime and victimization, especially as it relates to children, women, the elderly, drugs, terrorism, and the media (Glassner 1999; Altheide 2002, 2004; Elchardus et al. 2005).

The study of fear as an emotion has emerged alongside the 30-year development of a sociology of emotions in general. Of particular relevance for theorizing fear is the work of Kemper (power-status model), who argues that loss of power and status leads to fear and that fear can be meaningfully conceptualized as an emotion that differentiates people. Drawing on Kemper's work, Barbalet's macrostructural theory of emotion argues not only that fear is potentially incapacitating, but also that it can motivate groups either to increase power in order to enhance interests or to work to maintain current power levels.

Although crime and concerns with security dominate the "fear of" literature, it is of significance to mention the emergence of an ever-expanding list of that which is feared, by whom, and with what consequences for social control: falling from the middle class, gaining or losing weight, growing old, "different others," impotency, disasters, and even knowledge. Most relevant is the growing body of literature that seeks to understand the relationship of fear and the media.

In addition to Turner and Stets, who work toward an integrated theory of the sociology of emotions, current and future work on fear can be separated into three main areas: a (macro) sociology of fear, fear of crime, and media consumption and the discourse/politics of fear.

Tudor frames the social construction of fear in terms of six interlocking but distinct parameters: environments, cultures, and social structures (the modes of institutional fearfulness) and bodies, personalities, and social subjects (the modes of individual fearfulness). He then argues that this model may be used to test and further develop our understanding of a "culture of fear."

Elchardus et al. argue that the empirical literature addressing the relationships between victimization and media consumption can be used to test the two most frequently appearing, although not necessarily identified, paradigms of fear: a rationalistic paradigm of fear of crime (consequence of risk and vulnerability) or a symbolic paradigm (consequence of a "collective malaise"). Ditton et al. (2004) add to this discussion by emphasizing that the weak relationships found between the counting of fear of crime and media consumption are less important than the consumers' interpretation of the relevance of media content to their lives.

Despite the many "fear of" approaches, Altheide, among others, argues that a more useful approach is to study fear as "a perspective or an orientation to the world" (2002: 178) that emerges through a mass-mediated discourse of fear – "the pervasive communication, symbolic awareness, and expectation that danger and risk are a central feature of the effective environment" (p. 41). He convincingly explains this discourse through the analysis of framing strategies, topics of fear, and the expanding list of victims and victimization. As Weigert (2003: 95) notes, fear and anxiety sow "dis-ease," the "social pathology of interaction" which threatens public order and personal identity. Altheide concludes that this discourse of fear has implications for the possible realization of a just society. Fear becomes the framework for constructing the social world but not necessarily a *safer* or more humane one.

SEE ALSO: Deviance, the Media and; Emotion: Cultural Aspects; Emotion Work; Insecurity and Fear of Crime; Moral Panics; Terrorism

REFERENCES AND SUGGESTED READINGS

Altheide, D. L. (2002) *Creating Fear: News and the Construction of Crisis.* Aldine de Gruyter, New York.

Altheide, D. L. (2004) Consuming Terrorism. *Symbolic Interaction* 27(3): 289–308.

Barbalet, J. (1998) *Emotion, Social Theory, and Social Structure: A Macrosociological Approach.* Cambridge University Press, Cambridge.

Barbalet, J. (Ed.) (2002) *Emotions and Sociology.* Blackwell, Oxford.

Ditton, J., Chadee, D., Farrall, S., Gilchrist, E., & Bannister, J. (2004) From Imitation to Intimidation: A Note on the Curious and Changing Relationship Between the Media, Crime, and Fear of Crime. *British Journal of Criminology* 44(4): 595–610.

Elchardus, M., De Groof, S., & Smits, W. (2005) Rational Fear or Collective Representation of Malaise: A Comparison of Two Paradigms Concerning Fear of Crime. *Mens & Maatschappij* 80, 1 (March): 48–68.

Glassner, B. (1999) *The Culture of Fear: Why Americans Are Afraid of the Wrong Things.* Basic Books, New York.

Kemper, T. D. (1987) How Many Emotions Are There? Wedding the Social and Autonomic Components. *American Journal of Sociology* 93: 263–89.

Scheff, T. J. (2000) Shame and the Social Bond: A Sociological Theory. *Sociological Theory* 18: 84–99.

Tudor, A. (2003) A (Macro) Sociology of Fear. *Sociological Review*: 238–56.

Turner, J. H. (2006) Sociological Theories of Human Emotions. *Annual Review of Sociology* 32.

Turner, J. H. & Stets, J. E. (2005) *The Sociology of Emotions.* Cambridge University Press, New York.

Weigert, A. J. (2003) Terrorism, Identity, and Public Order: A Perspective from Goffman. *Identity: An International Journal of Theory and Research* 3(2): 93–113.

federalism

Brian Galligan

Federalism consists of two spheres of government, national and state, operating in the one political entity according to defined arrangements for sharing powers so that neither is sovereign over the other. According to William

Riker (1964), the activities of government must be divided in such a way that each government has some activities on which it makes final decisions. Daniel Elazar (1987) summed up federalism as a system of "self-rule plus shared rule" – self-rule in regional communities and shared rule at the national level. The older notion of federalism was an association of associations, or a league or confederation of independent member states whose delegates managed central institutions. This was the institutional form of the American Articles of Confederation that provided a weak form of national government during the War of Independence. In the 1789 Constitution, as explained in the Federalist Papers, the American founders created modern federalism by strengthening the powers of national government and making its key offices directly responsible to the people. Modern federalism was a significant innovation in both institutional design and popular sovereignty: the people became dual citizens, or members of the new national union while remaining members of the smaller state unions. Federalism was also a key feature of republican government, with powers controlled and limited through being divided between governments and constitutionally specified. The federal constitution was based upon popular sovereignty, with the leading institutions either directly elected or indirectly accountable to the people.

Federalism is a popular form of government adopted by quite heterogeneous countries. A survey by Ronald Watts (1999) lists 24 countries – 23 since the collapse of Yugoslavia – that account for about 40 percent of the world's population, although the bulk of these are in India. The list includes quasi-federations and federations that retain some overriding national powers that are more typical of unitary government. Examples are India, Pakistan, and Malaysia that have central emergency powers, while South Africa retains elements of its pre-1996 unitary system. Because of their diversity in political culture and stage of development, federations are usually grouped in clusters of more similar countries by scholars. The well-established Anglo and European federations, Australia, Canada, and the United States, together with Austria, Germany, and Switzerland, are often assumed to be the core federal

systems. Other groupings in comparative studies are Latin American federations, to which Spain is now added, and less developed countries, of which Nigeria is a leading example. India tends to be studied separately because of its vast size and complexity. Federalism is also used as a paradigm for articulating federal tendencies in unitary countries, for example fiscal decentralization in China, or describing aspects of groupings of countries such as the European Union, which is more a confederation of nation-states.

Federalism's popularity is due to its flexibility as a form of government that can serve diverse and multiple purposes. It has proved resilient in the enduring older federations of Switzerland, the United States, Canada, and Australia, all of which have their origins in smaller established states coming together to form new national unions, and have prospered for more than a century. Federalism has been successfully reestablished in Germany and Austria, countries with long federal traditions, after World War II and periods of centralist rule. Federalism has become an attractive way for enabling unitary states like Belgium, Spain, and South Africa to decentralize. Federalism can be adopted primarily for any or all of a variety of purposes: to decentralize government and serve regional communities in large and diverse countries, to control government powers in order to safeguard individual rights and preserve market economies, to serve ethnically diverse societies that are regionally based, or to accommodate regions that are geographically distinct or at different stages of economic development. The United States and Australian federations have mainly decentralist and liberal purposes; Switzerland and Canada have a more fundamental ethnic purpose, as does Ethiopia, which allows a right of succession; Russia and the Latin American federations, Argentina, Brazil, Venezuela, and Mexico, have a combination of purposes including accommodating different stages of economic development among regions; while India has elements of all purposes.

While federalism is embodied in a variety of ways in federal countries, there is a set of institutions commonly identified as typical by federalism scholars. These are (1) a written constitution that specifies the division of powers between national and state governments and is hard to amend; (2) a bicameral legislature with a strong federal chamber to represent the states; (3) a supreme court to protect the constitution through exercising the power of judicial review; and (4) a system of intergovernmental institutions to facilitate collaboration in areas of shared or overlapping jurisdiction. None of these features is exclusively federal, and each one can be found in varying forms in non-federal counties. Taken together, they are considered to constitute the core federal institutions. Additional institutions that have been proposed as essential for federalism are a political party system that channels elites' behavior to support federalism; and well-established state institutions that are sufficiently robust to withstand the tendency toward centralist power. Whether federalism suits a particular country and how well it works depends as much on political culture, traditions, and politics as it does on institutional design. For example, state governance that serves ethnically distinct regions can facilitate national integration or fragmentation.

While some have advocated a coordinate model of federalism – having separate and distinct powers for each sphere of government – concurrent or shared jurisdiction is the norm. Both levels of government are usually present in most major policy areas, so that intergovernmental arrangements and management are required to keep the systems working. Federal policymaking can be "interstate," with varying degrees of competition between national and state governments, as tends to be the case in Anglo federations, or "intrastate," as in the German and Austrian cases where the states, or Länder, are incorporated into national policymaking. Federalism has been variously criticized in the past as a weak, obsolete, or obstructive form of government, but its survival and recent flourishing belie those claims. The ways in which federalism affects policy innovation and development are complex, variable over time, and contingent upon political and cultural developments. Federalism provides both multiple veto points for blocking new policies and multiple entry points and sites for innovators. Federalism seems more compatible with the paradigm shift from a world of sovereign nation-states to one of increased interstate linkages and international rule-making and standard-setting. Even so, the effects of globalization, for better or worse, will be mediated through national institutions including federalism, and depend to a considerable extent upon national attributes, including heritage, ethnocultural composition, and political economy.

SEE ALSO: Democracy; Institution; Nation-State; Organizations; Pluralism, American; Power

REFERENCES AND SUGGESTED READINGS

Elazar, D. (1987) *Exploring Federalism*. University of Alabama Press, Tuscaloosa.

Riker, W. (1964) *Federalism: Origin, Operation, Significance*. Little, Brown, Boston.

Watts, R. (1999) *Comparing Federal Systems*, 2nd edn. McGill-Queen's University Press, Montreal.

female genital mutilation

Susan Hagood Lee

Female genital mutilation (FGM) is the ancient cultural practice of removing portions of a girl's genitalia. It occurs extensively in northern Africa on girls from infancy to puberty, with significant negative medical consequences. Many Muslims believe that it is a religious duty. The procedure reduces sexual desire and the patriarchal groups which practice FGM consider it necessary to maintain a girl's good reputation for marriage. Uncircumcised girls are believed to be unclean and promiscuous. In response to political pressure from African women's organizations, 14 countries have banned the procedure. Nonetheless, it continues to be practiced and has become increasingly medicalized. Grassroots change efforts working within cultural norms have been the most successful.

The World Health Organization defined FGM in 1995 as follows: "Female genital mutilation comprises all procedures that involve partial or total removal of female external genitalia and/or injury to the female genital organs for cultural or any other non-therapeutic reasons." The practice is also known as female circumcision (FC) or female genital cutting (FGC). The term FGM is used by international agencies, led by the World Health Organization. Some see the term as culturally judgmental and prefer the terms used by practitioners, namely circumcision (English-speaking areas), excision (French-speaking areas), or cutting. In Arabic, the language of many proponents of female circumcision, the practice is known as *tahara*, cleanliness or purification.

FGM occurs in four patterns or types. In Type I, the prepuce or hood over the clitoris is removed, sometimes together with part or all of the clitoris itself. This type is known by some as Sunnah circumcision, meaning in accordance with Muslim law. In Type II, the most common form with 80 percent of cases, the clitoris is removed (clitoridectomy), together with parts or all of the labia minora. Type III excision involves removal of all external genitalia, including clitoris, labia minora, and labia majora, and stitching together of the remaining tissue with a small opening for the passage of urine and menstrual blood. This type is called infibulation, Pharaonic circumcision, or Sudanese circumcision, and comprises 15 percent of cases. Type IV refers to other sorts of female genital mutilation, such as pricking, piercing, stretching or incision of the clitoris or labia, cauterization of the clitoris, cutting of the vagina, and introduction of corrosive substances or herbs into the vagina.

The practice occurs most frequently in northern Africa. In Somalia, Egypt, and Djibouti, 97 percent to 98 percent of all adult women have been circumcised. In the Sudan, 90 percent of adult women have been circumcised. Infibulation, the most severe type of FGM, is the traditional practice in these countries, though clitoridectomy has become more common in Egypt. Female circumcision is practiced in 28 African countries in all, including the East African countries of Ethiopia and Eritrea as well as the West African nations of Mali, Sierra Leone, Gambia, Guinea, Burkina Faso, and Nigeria. The prevalence within these countries sometimes varies dramatically by ethnic group. Education and urban residence reduce the incidence of FGM somewhat. However, as many as 90 percent of Egyptian women with a secondary degree have been circumcised. Arabian countries near eastern Africa, such as Yemen, Oman, and the United Arab Emirates, also practice female circumcision. Muslim communities in other parts of the world, such as Indonesia and Malaysia, practice a less severe form of female circumcision, where a single drop of blood is drawn from the prepuce or clitoris. The practice of FGM has been carried to Europe and North America by African immigrants. It is estimated that in the US, 10,000 girls are at risk of being circumcised. Worldwide, around 140 million women or about 5 percent of the world's female population have been subjected to FGM. Two million additional girls are circumcised annually, around 6,000 girls per day.

The age at which girls undergo FGM varies according to the customs of their local village and region. The most common age is from 4 to 8 years. In some areas, infant girls are circumcised, while in other places, circumcision takes place upon the onset of menstruation or when a girl reaches the marriageable age of 14 to 16 years. In Egypt, girls are circumcised between the ages of 8 and 14 years. Typically, the procedure is performed in unsanitary conditions with ordinary cutting utensils such as razor blades, scissors, kitchen knives, or broken pieces of glass. The same cutting utensils are often used on several girls in succession without cleaning. Anesthesia is rarely used in village settings. In most areas, circumcision is carried out by older women, known in eastern Africa as *dayas*, who derive a substantial portion of their income from the ritual. In Sierra Leone, circumcisers are highly respected women viewed as priestesses by their followers. They head the traditional secret societies for excised girls in West Africa.

In a typical circumcision, according to Kathleen Kilday (1990), the girl lies down or sits on a low stool while her female relatives hold her head and arms tightly and stretch her legs apart. The women shout chants of encouragement to the girl, sometimes accompanied by loud drumming, as she struggles and cries out under the pain of cutting. After the excision, the relatives inspect the wound to verify that enough has been removed and the girl is sewn up with catgut or silk. In Somalia, thorns are used. The open wound is covered with herbs to stem the bleeding and promote healing. The girl's legs are often bound together for a period of time during recovery and urination is particularly painful. According to Nawal El Saadawi (1980), who worked as a physician in rural Egypt, girls remember their circumcision as a searing pain, "like a burning flame" (p. 34). They feel betrayed by the people they trusted the most, their mother and other female relatives. Most come to accept the cultural explanation that the procedure is necessary to be a clean and pure woman prepared for marriage. When they become mothers of girls, they perpetuate the practice. Ellen Gruenbaum (2001) notes that women interviewed about their own circumcision remembered it vividly as a pivotal event of their childhood. Some laughed off the memories of the pain while others attributed it to the inevitable fate of women. A few work for cultural change.

Health consequences of FGM vary according to the conditions under which the procedure is conducted and the extent of the excision. In the typical village setting, the immediate health consequences for all types of FGM are infection from the use of unsanitary instruments, including HIV transmission. In some cases, girls die due to shock, hemorrhage, or septicemia. With infibulation, the urethral opening may be inadvertently blocked, preventing the girl from urinating, and she must be taken to a hospital for surgical intervention. Over the long term, women who have undergone FGM are more likely than non-circumcised women to have urinary tract infections and pelvic inflammatory disease, sometimes resulting in infertility. Women who have experienced clitoridectomy and infibulation may have problematic abscesses and scarring as well as delayed menarche and difficulty reaching orgasm. Upon marriage, infibulated women must be opened for intercourse. In some areas, the husband is expected to open his wife with his penis or face dishonor. To avoid the humiliation of calling in the midwife if he is unable, a husband may cut his wife open himself with a razor or piece of glass. In other areas, the groom is expected to open his wife with a dagger on their wedding night.

Childbirth poses special risks for women with extensive excisions. Since scar tissue does not stretch, labor is more likely to be prolonged and difficult and may involve additional cutting to permit delivery. Infibulated women may endure obstructed labor, resulting in a ruptured perineum for the mother and brain damage or death for the infant. Newborns of infibulated women are more vulnerable to infection. Infibulated women are almost always reinfibulated after delivery, and each subsequent delivery becomes more difficult as the amount of scar tissue in the area increases. Concomitant with these physical consequences of FGM, women may experience psychological repercussions such as depression, anxiety, and fear of sexual intercourse.

Female circumcision is a meaningful cultural event for practitioners. Among Muslim groups, it is widely believed to be a religious duty stipulated in the Qur'an. In reality, the Qur'an does not mention circumcision at all, for either females or males. Muslim references to circumcision occur in the secondary writings called the hadith or sayings of Mohammed where, in a conversation with an exciser called Um 'Atiyyah, the Prophet confirmed that female circumcision was allowed within limits. Some Muslim commentators have challenged the validity of this hadith. Many Muslim leaders have supported the practice of female circumcision, with one imam ruling that while it is not obligatory, it is an honorable deed and recommended for Muslims. A few Muslim leaders have strongly condemned the practice and have led efforts to abolish it in places such as Senegal. They point out that the practice predates Islam and it is not observed in Saudi Arabia, the birthplace of Mohammed. Not only Muslims but also other religions engage in female circumcision in East Africa, including Protestants, Catholics, Coptic Christians, and Ethiopian Jews.

Practitioners give many non-religious reasons for FGM. Concerns about virginity and marriage are paramount. Female circumcision reduces sexual desire and increases the likelihood that the girl will remain a virgin. A girl is considered unclean and promiscuous if she is not circumcised and so is a less attractive marriage choice. Marriage is the predominant occupation for women in these traditional low-income societies. Parents who do not circumcise their daughters are seen as inexcusably neglectful of their daughter's future. Infibulation, the most severe sort of circumcision, increases a girl's marriage value since the very small opening ensures the girl's virginity. Infibulation is thought to increase male pleasure in sexual intercourse and so to contribute to a stable marriage. In the Sudan, infibulation confers higher class status on the girl and her family than more mild types of FGM. Parents consider these cultural benefits for their daughters and their families when deciding about circumcision.

FGM takes place in patriarchal cultures where women's status or even survival is dependent on pleasing men. Women take drastic steps to change their bodies in ways which improve their appeal to a male audience. Mothers arrange the circumcision of their daughters, midwives perform the operation, and female relatives serve as the cheering squad. One may compare the practice to cosmetic surgery in the West, another case where cultural notions of female beauty move women to engage in drastic medical interventions to increase their appeal to men. The significant difference is the lack of anesthesia or sanitary conditions in female genital mutilation.

FGM reveals the ancient patriarchal concern with control of female sexuality, key to maintaining the male-dominated social structure. In regions which practice FGM, female sexuality is believed to be wild, aggressive, and threatening to the social order. Without preventive restraints, girls will be promiscuous and wives will wander. The West has also resorted to genital surgery to control female sexuality. In nineteenth-century Britain and the United States, surgical removal of the clitoris was an accepted way to cure hysteria, masturbation, and other alleged female illnesses.

In colonial Africa, the British opposed the practice of FGM in their colonies, especially Sudan and Kenya, despite popular protests. Legal efforts to abolish FGM today are hampered by identification with colonialism. Some African leaders believe that to ban the practice is to undermine both African culture and Islam. They fear repercussions on other aspects of African culture, such as the West African female secret societies. Other African leaders have led the fight against FGM. The president of Burkina Faso, Thomas Sankara, strongly

opposed FGM before his assassination in 1987. Awa Thiam of Senegal was a pioneer in organizing female opposition and bringing political pressure on her country to abolish FGM. Fourteen African countries have passed laws banning FGM. The laws are not enforced, however. Low-income countries do not have effective law enforcement even in urban areas, much less in rural villages. Progressive central governments, influenced by modern ideas, may pass laws that rural areas never hear of, much less obey. Even in urban areas, the cultural forces setting the stage for FGM require more than legislation to change.

In 1984, African women's non-governmental organizations working on FGM met in Dakar, Senegal and formed the Inter-African Committee on Traditional Practices Affecting the Health of Women and Children (IAC). The Committee has affiliates in 26 African countries and coordinates abolition efforts. The IAC opposes the growing medicalization of FGM in countries such as Egypt, which passed laws to restrict the procedure to medical settings with anesthesia. In Kenya, hospitals perform FGM despite a total legal ban. Medical professionals argue that the practice is better done in a hospital than in unsanitary conditions, while women's groups lobby the government to enforce the ban.

Successful efforts to change the prevalence of FGM have featured comprehensive action by government, the medical community, communities of faith, and public education. The most effective efforts have worked within the cultural context at the grassroots level. One such approach has been to replace FGM with another initiation ritual, such as a one-week program in Kenya called "Circumcision through words." It teaches girls about self-esteem, health issues, and problem solving and culminates in a coming-of-age ceremony with certificates, gifts, and feasting. In some areas, traditional midwives are trained to become salaried community health care workers who educate villagers on the dangers of FGM as well as other women's health issues. Some efforts have looked at the need for girls' education and economic development to lessen women's dependence on men. The most successful eradication efforts have been in Senegal with the Tostan project. Organized by local women working with village religious leaders and supported by the national government, entire villages have taken a public pledge to refrain from circumcising their girls or marrying their sons to circumcised women.

SEE ALSO: Culture, Gender and; Gender, the Body and; Patriarchy; Sexual Cultures in Africa; Women, Religion and; Women's Health

REFERENCES AND SUGGESTED READINGS

Carr, D. (1997) *Female Genital Cutting: Findings from the Demographic and Health Surveys Program.* Macro International, Calverton, MD.

Denniston, G. C. & Milos, M. F. (Eds.) (1997) *Sexual Mutilations: A Human Tragedy.* Plenum, New York and London.

Dorkenoo, E. (1996) Combating Female Genital Mutilation: An Agenda for the Next Decade. *World Health Statistics Quarterly* 49(2): 142–47.

El Saadawi, N. (1980) *The Hidden Face of Eve: Women in the Arab World.* Beacon Press, Boston.

Gruenbaum, E. (2001) *The Female Circumcision Controversy: An Anthropological Perspective.* University of Pennsylvania Press, Philadelphia.

Kilday, K. (1990) Female Circumcision in Africa: Not Just a Medical Problem. *Iris* (June 30): 38.

Shell-Duncan, B. & Hernlund, Y. (2000) *Female Circumcision in Africa: Culture, Controversy, and Change.* Lynne Rienner, Colorado.

Toubia, N. & Izett, S. (1998) *Female Genital Mutilation: An Overview.* World Health Organization, Geneva.

female masculinity

Silvia Posocco

Female masculinity refers to a range of masculine-inflected identities and identifications. Debates over the status and meaning of female masculinity and the bodies and selves to whom the terms may be ascribed emerge in the context of analyses of sex, gender, and sexuality.

Research in social and cultural history has documented the lives of individual women who defied gendered conventions, adopted masculine clothing, and/or engaged in gendered nonconformist behavior in Anglo-American and European contexts from the eighteenth to the early twentieth centuries (Wheelwright 1989). The case of Colonel Victor Barker, for instance, caused notable controversy in England in the early twentieth century, as this military man was exposed to be female-bodied and deserving a perjury trial (Wheelwright 1989). Scholarly approaches to archival material have tended to challenge transhistorical claims of stable forms of female masculinity across time (Halberstam 1998; Doan 2001). Assumed relations of equivalence and translatability between and across culturally specific practices relating to female masculinity have also appeared suspect (Blackwood 1998).

Key to the development of innovative conceptual trajectories on female masculinity in interdisciplinary academic gender studies are the numerous critical readings of Radclyffe Hall's novel *The Well of Loneliness* (1928) and related analyses of its cultural, social, and historical context. In her pioneering essay on the subject, anthropologist Esther Newton (2000 [1984]) notes that Hall's novel constitutes a central reference for paradigmatic imaginings of female masculinity in the twentieth century, and the ground for the entrenchment and popularization of a relation between female masculinity and lesbianism. Newton (2000 [1984]: 177) shows how, since the obscenity trial that took place in London in 1928, the novel's protagonist Stephen Gordon has acquired "mythic" archetypal status as a "mannish lesbian," that is, "a figure who is defined as lesbian because her behavior or dress (and usually both) manifests elements designated as exclusively masculine." Further analysis reveals that the subject matter of the novel exemplifies the cultural salience of discourses of sexology in early twentieth-century England, the social significance of the medicalized category of "the invert," and the ways in which these discourses played out in the public domain (Prosser 1998; Doan 2001). A different reading is offered by de Lauretis (1994), who highlights the relevance of psychoanalysis to an understanding of the relation between masculine identification and lesbianism in *The Well of Loneliness*. It is de Lauretis's contention that the Freudian "masculinity/virility complex," with the female subject's longing for a masculine identification, should be reinterpreted and not entirely dismissed. De Lauretis (1994: 211–12) argues that Stephen Gordon's subjectivity comes into being through a fantasy of "bodily dispossession," as the melancholic subject mourns a feminine embodiment that she can desire but does not fully embody, and a masculinity that she does embody but that is never maleness. In short, an original fantasy of castration underpins Stephen Gordon's bodily dispossession, with her muscular body standing for the paternal phallus which ultimately places the female body beyond reach.

Halberstam (1998) challenges this psychoanalytic reading and instead proceeds from the premise that unhinging the relation between masculinity and men can yield important insights into the social and cultural production of masculinity. This theoretical move reveals a spectrum of female masculine-inflected subject positions, identities, and identifications that in the nineteenth century included the androgyne, the tribade, and the female husband. In mid- to late twentieth-century Anglo-American contexts, female masculinity comprises soft butch, butch, stone butch, and transbutch identities and identifications, the youthful exuberance of tomboys and the parodic performances of drag kings. Building on Rubin's (1992: 467) classic definition of butch as "a category of lesbian gender that is constituted through the deployment and manipulation of masculine gender codes and symbols," Halberstam (1998) aligns her spectrum of female masculinities, including the figure of the stone butch, firmly with lesbianism. However, in his analysis of transsexual autobiographies, Prosser (1998) contests this point and speaks of butch and stone butch identities as "propellers" toward transgender and transsexual identifications. Butch and stone butch thus become entangled in "border wars" (Hale 1998) that are as much about subjectivities as they are about the intellectual strategies at our disposal for understanding the articulation and experience of sex, gender, and sexuality.

In view of this, future research should aim to clarify the relation between female masculinity and queer theory. Whilst the emphasis on masculinity may correspond to a generalized rejection of the feminine and a specific form of misogyny associated with queer theory (Martin 1994), previous analyses should be complemented by a sustained focus on the psychic and performative processes of production of masculine-inflected identities and how these may be implicated in processes of identification and disidentification with, for instance, femme and feminine identities. Second, a response to Newton's call (2000 [1984]: 66) for analyses that address the ways in which aesthetic, social, and cultural categories may function ethnographically is long overdue. This confirms the importance of investigating social taxonomies of female virility and masculine experience, their contexts and meanings in everyday life.

SEE ALSO: Drag Queens and Drag Kings; Femininities/Masculinities; Lesbianism; Queer Theory; Transgender, Transvestism, and Transsexualism

REFERENCES AND SUGGESTED READINGS

Blackwood, E. (1998) Tombois in West Sumatra: Constructing Masculinity and Erotic Desire. *Cultural Anthropology* 13(4): 491–521.

De Lauretis, T. (1994) *The Practice of Love: Lesbian Sexuality and Perverse Desire*. Indiana University Press, Bloomington and Indianapolis.

Doan, L. (2001) *Fashioning Sapphism: The Origins of Modern English Lesbian Culture*. Columbia University Press, New York.

Halberstam, J. (1998) *Female Masculinity*. Duke University Press, Durham, NC.

Hale, J. C. (1998) Consuming the Living, Dis(re)membering the Dead in the Butch/FTM Borderlands. *GLQ: A Journal of Lesbian and Gay Studies* 4(2): 311–48.

Martin, B. (1994) Sexualities Without Genders and Other Queer Utopias. *Diacritics* 24(2–3): 104–21.

Newton, E. (2000 [1984]) *Margaret Mead Made Me Gay: Personal Essays, Public Ideas*. Duke University Press, Durham, NC.

Prosser, J. (1998) *Second Skins: The Body Narratives of Transsexuality*. Columbia University Press, New York.

Rubin, G. (1992) Of Catamites and Kings: Reflections on Butch, Gender, and Boundaries. In: Nestle, J. (Ed.), *The Persistent Desire: A Femme-Butch Reader*. Alyson, Boston.

Wheelwright, J. (1989) *Amazons and Military Maids: Women Who Cross-Dress in the Pursuit of Life, Liberty, and Happiness*. Pandora, London.

female sex work as deviance

Ronald Weitzer

Sex work (in this case, involving female workers) refers to sexual services or performances provided in return for material compensation. Examples include pornography, prostitution, stripping, and telephone sex. The most common forms of sex work involve female workers and male customers – which reflects larger, traditional gender relations between men and women. Objectification of women is taken to the extreme in sex work, where the workers are valued almost exclusively for sexual purposes. The existence of commercial sex also provides men with an avenue for reaffirming their masculinity, by satisfying their "need" for sexual stimulation and fantasy or their desire for a certain type of sex with a certain type of woman. The gendered character of the sex industry is also evident in its power structure: most managers are men who exercise control over female workers and reap much of the profit. In general, power is largely concentrated in the hands of pimps, traffickers, and those who run brothels, strip clubs, and companies that produce and distribute.

Many people view sex work as deviant behavior. The opinion polls presented in Table 1 reveal that the majority of Americans see both prostitution and pornography as immoral; three-quarters believe that we need "stricter laws" to control pornography; and a substantial number want prostitution to remain illegal, strip clubs and massage parlors closed, and pornographic magazines/videos banned.

Over the past three decades some cities and suburbs have indeed banned or restricted massage parlors, strip clubs, and X-rated video stores. During the Reagan administration the Justice Department launched a massive campaign against distributors of adult pornography, prosecuting them for obscenity in conservative areas of the country ("obscenity" is determined by local "community standards" as determined by a jury). The campaign was successful in putting a significant number of distributors out of business. Under President Clinton the Justice Department shifted its attention away from adult pornography and intensified enforcement against child pornography (Weitzer 2000: 11–12). Prostitution is illegal throughout the US, with the exception of rural counties in Nevada, where legal brothels have existed since 1971.

Americans are less tolerant of the sex industry than citizens in several other western societies. Certain types of prostitution, for example, are legal or tolerated in some European nations (e.g., the Netherlands, Germany), and opinion polls indicate that a majority of the population in Britain, Canada, France, and Portugal favor legalizing prostitution (Weitzer 2000: 166).

Some types of sex work are more heavily stigmatized than others. As Table 1 shows, stripping is less widely condemned than work

Table 1 Public opinion on sex work

	% Agreeing
Pornography leads to a "breakdown of morals"	62
Internet porn is a "major cause of the decline in moral values" in US	62
Looking at pornographic magazines is morally wrong	58
Pornography "degrades women because it portrays them as sex objects"	72
Need "stricter laws" to control pornography	77
Telephone-sex numbers should be illegal	76
Strip clubs should be illegal	46
Morally wrong for a "man to spend an evening with a prostitute"	61
Prostitution should be illegal	70
Media should publish names and photos of men convicted of soliciting prostitutes	50
Close massage parlors and porn shops that "might permit casual sex"	70

Sources: Opinion polls of Americans conducted between 1977 and 1996 (Weitzer 2000).

that involves direct sexual contact (prostitution, pornography). In general, sex workers are more stigmatized than their customers. This is because, first, the former engage in disreputable activity more regularly, whereas the customers typically participate occasionally and, second, a cultural double standard exists, whereby the sexual behavior of female sex workers is more circumscribed than the sexual behavior of their male clients. One reason for this disparity is that female sex workers break gender norms for women – by being sexually aggressive and promiscuous – whereas male customers' behavior is consistent with traditional male sexual socialization, which puts a premium on sexual titillation and valorizes sexual conquest as evidence of masculinity. Many men are willing to pay for sexual titillation in the form of pornography, exotic dancing, and Internet and telephone sex, and a minority has had contact with a prostitute. One-third of American men report that they have watched an X-rated video in the past year, 11 percent have been to a strip club in the past year, and 18 percent admit to having paid for sex at some time in their lives (Weitzer 2000: 1–2).

Because they are stigmatized, female sex workers typically attempt to deflect the stigma. They compartmentalize or separate their deviant work persona from their "real identity"; conceal their work from family and friends; describe their work in neutral or professional terms ("dancer" or "entertainer" instead of "stripper"; "actress" instead of "porn star"); and they may see themselves as performing a useful service (keeping marriages intact, engaging in sex therapy, providing emotional support to customers).

There are some major differences between street prostitution and indoor sex work (escorts, call girls, strippers, telephone sex workers, workers in brothels and massage parlors). First, street prostitutes are more heavily stigmatized than indoor workers. Some popular cultural depictions romanticize call girls while denigrating women who work the streets. Second, risk of exposure to sexually transmitted diseases varies between street and indoor workers. HIV infection rates vary markedly among street prostitutes (with the highest incidence among street workers who inject drugs or smoke crack cocaine), but HIV infection is rare among call

girls and other indoor workers. Third, indoor workers, and especially call girls and escorts, generally exercise more control over working conditions, express greater job satisfaction, and have higher self-esteem than do street workers (Weitzer 2005). Fourth, street prostitutes are much more likely to be victimized. Street workers are more vulnerable to being assaulted, robbed, and raped by customers, pimps, and other men, and some have been kidnapped and killed. Indoor workers are much less vulnerable to such victimization, as several comparative studies show (Weitzer 2005). There is one important exception: women and girls who are recruited by force or fraud and trafficked to work in indoor venues (brothels, massage parlors, etc.) in another country (Kempadoo 2005). Such individuals are victimized from the very outset, and they differ dramatically from other types of indoor workers who make a conscious choice to enter the trade and have more control over their working conditions.

In sum, workers in different sectors of the sex trade have different kinds of work experiences – that is, varying degrees of stigma, victimization, exploitation, and freedom. The type of sex work makes a significant difference, and grand generalizations about "sex work" should be avoided.

Traditionally, the authorities in the US and elsewhere paid fairly little attention to customers involved in the purchase of illegal sex services or products. Until recently the criminal justice system targeted workers almost exclusively, all but ignoring the customers of prostitutes (or "johns"). Laws in the US and other societies continue to punish patronizing less severely than prostitution, and in most jurisdictions arrests of prostitutes far exceed those of customers. Customers who are prosecuted and convicted typically receive lower fines and are less likely to receive custodial sentences than prostitutes. This, despite the fact that arrested johns are much less likely to recidivate than arrested prostitutes. Only recently have the authorities in some cities begun to arrest customers in substantial numbers, but this is exceptional. But a substantial number of Americans want customers sanctioned: in a representative poll conducted in 1995 for *Newsweek*, half the population favored a policy of displaying in the media the names and photos of men convicted of soliciting a prostitute (see also Table 1). The one area where law enforcement has intensified the most is against those who possess child pornography. This development is a fairly recent trend in the social control of persons involved in sexual exploitation of minors.

Customers have attracted far less research than sex workers, but some recent studies do focus on the clients. Many johns are middle aged, middle class, and married, but we are only beginning to understand their motivations, attitudes, and behavior patterns. A few studies suggest that customers patronize prostitutes for the following reasons: they desire certain types of sexual experiences (e.g., oral sex); they desire sex with a person with a certain image (e.g., sexy, raunchy, etc.) or with specific physical attributes (e.g., racial, transgender); they find this illicit and risky conduct thrilling; they wish to avoid the obligations or emotional attachment involved in a conventional relationship; they have difficulty finding someone for a conventional relationship (Jordan 1997; Monto 2000).

In the largest study yet conducted, 43 percent of customers reported that they "want a different kind of sex than my regular partner" provides; 47 percent said that they were "excited by the idea of approaching a prostitute"; 33 percent said they did not have the time for a conventional relationship; and 30 percent said they did not want the responsibilities of a conventional relationship (Monto 2000). Men who patronize call girls or escorts are often looking for companionship and emotional support, in addition to sex. Lever and Dolnick's (2000) comparison of call girls and street prostitutes in Los Angeles found that customers expected and received much more emotional support from the call girls, and Prince (1986) found that 89 percent of call girls in California and 74 percent of Nevada's brothel workers believed that "the average customer wants affection or love as well as sex" – the view of only one-third of streetwalkers.

Some other studies examine customers of legal sectors of the sex industry, such as men who watch pornography, who call telephone sex lines, and who visit strip clubs. Flowers (1998) found that some telephone sex callers

want to fulfill ordinary sexual scenarios while others fantasized about incest, rape, pedophilia, bestiality, and mutilation. (Some phone sex operators refuse to take part in these fantasies and even try to curb some of the more extreme interests of the caller.) Customers of strip clubs, as Frank (2002) found, seek not only sexual stimulation and fantasy, but also want the company of attractive women. They enjoy talking, flirting, and sharing details of their lives with the women, and regular customers try to become friends with the dancers. Frank's book is the only study to focus on the customers rather than the strippers.

A largely unexplored area is that of female customers of male prostitutes – a small but important fraction of the market. Some women tourists in the Caribbean and other vacation spots buy sex from young male prostitutes, whom they meet on the beaches and at clubs. Taylor's (2001) study of 75 female tourists in Jamaica and the Dominican Republic who reported that they had had sexual encounters with local men found that 60 percent of the women had paid the men with money, gifts, and/or meals. There are some basic similarities between female sex tourism and male sex tourism (e.g., economic inequality between buyer and seller), as well as some differences (e.g., female sex tourists rarely assault or rob male prostitutes).

The sex industry has grown in the past two decades and has spread into new markets. This trend began with the creation of video recorders, followed by the advent of pornography on cable television, the rise of telephone sex operations, the growth of escort agencies, and the opportunities afforded by the Internet. The Internet offers unprecedented access to every kind of pornography imaginable, and also facilitates cyber exchanges, information sharing, and subsequent face-to-face encounters between clients and strippers, escorts, and other female sex workers. Furthermore, Internet message boards and chat rooms allow customers and others to discuss personal experiences with providers and share more general opinions of the sex industry. Participants discuss where to locate certain kinds of workers or a massage parlor; what to expect in terms of prices and services; "reviews" of a specific worker's appearance and behavior; and warnings on recent law enforcement activity in a particular city. The sites also provide unique insight into customer beliefs, expectations, justifications, and behavioral norms. Review of these sites confirms that many customers are looking for more than sex; they place a premium on the provider being friendly, conversational, kissing, cuddling, and providing what they call a "girlfriend experience" with a semblance of romance and intimacy (Weitzer 2005). Many of the cyber exchanges discuss appropriate and inappropriate client behavior toward sex workers, and errant individuals are chided for violating this emergent code of ethics. This normative order is a byproduct of discourse on Internet sites, something that did not exist previously.

Despite the proliferation of commercial sex over the past two decades, sex workers and their customers continue to be seen by many Americans as involved in disreputable, deviant behavior. In other words, it would be premature to say that any part of the sex industry has become "mainstream." Both the workers and their clients remain stigmatized.

SEE ALSO: Gender, Deviance and; Pornography and Erotica; Prostitution; Sex Tourism; Sexual Deviance

REFERENCES AND SUGGESTED READINGS

Abbott, S. (2000) Motivations for Pursuing an Acting Career in Pornography. In: Weitzer, R. (Ed.), *Sex for Sale: Prostitution, Pornography, and the Sex Industry*. Routledge, New York, pp. 17–34.

Flowers, A. (1998) *The Fantasy Factory: An Insider's View of the Phone Sex Industry*. University of Pennsylvania Press, Philadelphia.

Frank, K. (2002) *G-Strings and Sympathy: Strip Club Regulars and Male Desire*. Duke University Press, Durham, NC.

Jordan, J. (1997) User Pays: Why Men Buy Sex. *Australian and New Zealand Journal of Criminology* 30: 55–71.

Kempadoo, K. (Ed.) (2005) *Trafficking and Prostitution Reconsidered: New Perspectives on Migration*. Paradigm, Boulder.

Lever, J. & Dolnick, D. (2000) Clients and Call Girls: Seeking Sex and Intimacy. In: Weitzer, R. (Ed.), *Sex for Sale: Prostitution, Pornography, and*

the Sex Industry. Routledge, New York, pp. 85–100.

Monto, M. (2000) Why Men Seek Out Prostitutes. In: Weitzer, R. (Ed.), *Sex for Sale: Prostitution, Pornography, and the Sex Industry*. Routledge, New York, pp. 67–83.

Prince, D. (1986) *A Psychological Study of Prostitutes in California and Nevada*. Doctoral dissertation, United States International University, San Diego.

Taylor, J. (2001) Dollars are a Girl's Best Friend: Female Tourists' Sexual Behavior in the Caribbean. *Sociology* 35: 749–64.

Weitzer, R. (Ed.) (2000) *Sex for Sale: Prostitution, Pornography, and the Sex Industry*. Routledge, New York.

Weitzer, R. (2005) New Directions in Research on Prostitution. *Crime, Law, and Social Change* 43: 211–35.

femininities/ masculinities

Amy Lind

Femininities and masculinities are acquired social identities: as individuals become socialized they develop a gender identity, an understanding of what it means to be a "man" or a "woman" (Laurie et al. 1999). How individuals develop an understanding of their gender identity, including whether or not they fit into these prescribed gender roles, depends upon the context within which they are socialized and how they view themselves in relation to societal gender norms. Class, racial, ethnic, and national factors play heavily into how individuals construct their gender identities and how they are perceived externally (hooks 2004). Gender identities are often naturalized; that is, they rely on a notion of biological difference, "so that 'natural' femininity [in a white, European, middle-class context] encompasses, for example, motherhood, being nurturing, a desire for pretty clothes and the exhibition of emotions" (Laurie et al. 1999: 3). "Natural" masculinity, in contrast, may encompass fatherhood, acting "tough," a desire for sports and competition, and hiding emotions (Connell

1997; Thompson 2000). In both cases, these constructions of gender identity are based on stereotypes that fall within the range of normative femininities and masculinities. Yet, as many sociologists have pointed out, not all individuals fit within these prescribed norms and as such, masculinities and femininities must be recognized as socially constituted, fluid, wide ranging, and historically and geographically differentiated (Connell 1997; Halberstam 1998; Laurie et al. 1999).

Feminist scholars have long addressed the social construction of femininities, particularly in the context of gender inequality and power (Lorber 1994). Early second wave feminist scholars such as Simone de Beauvoir (1980) argued that women's subordinated status in western societies was due to socialization rather than to any essential biological gender difference, as evidenced in her often-cited phrase, "One is not born, but rather becomes, a woman." Many feminist scholars in Anglo-Saxon and European countries have emphasized social construction over biological difference as an explanation for women's ways of being, acting, and knowing in the world and for their related gender subordination (Gilligan 1993). Some feminist scholars have addressed the social construction of femininities as a way to explain wage inequality, the global "feminization of poverty," and women's relegation to "feminine" labor markets (e.g., secretarial labor, garment industry, caring labor) and to the so-called private realm of the household and family (Folbre 2001). Because feminists were primarily concerned with the question of women's subordination, masculinities themselves were rarely analyzed except in cases where scholars sought an explanation for male aggression or power. Likewise, hegemonic femininity was emphasized over alternative femininities such that the experiences of women who did not fit into socially prescribed gender roles were either left unexamined or viewed through the normative lens of gender dualisms (Halberstam 1998).

Particularly since the 1980s, at least three areas of research on gender identity have helped shift the debate on femininities and masculinities: (1) masculinity studies, which emerged primarily in the 1980s and 1990s; (2) queer studies and lesbian, gay, bisexual, and transgender (LGBT) studies, including the pivotal research of Butler (1990); and (3) gender, race, ethnic, and postcolonial studies, a trajectory of scholarship in which researchers have long critiqued hegemonic forms of masculinity and femininity on the basis that these racialized constructions helped reinforce the criminalization and subordination of racial/ethnic minorities in industrialized societies and the colonization of both men and women in poor and/or non-western regions.

In contrast to feminist scholarship that focused primarily on women's experiences with femininity, Connell's (1987) research on "hegemonic masculinity and emphasized femininity" was among the first to systematically analyze both sets of constructions as they contribute to global gender inequality. Connell argues "hegemonic masculinity," a type of masculinity oriented toward accommodating the interests and desires of men, forms the basis of patriarchal social orders. Similarly, "emphasized femininity," a hegemonic form of femininity, is "defined around compliance with [female] subordination and is oriented to accommodating the interests and desires of men" (p. 23). Borrowing from Gramsci's analysis of class hegemony and struggle, Connell develops a framework for understanding multiple competing masculinities and femininities. He argues that hegemonic masculinity is always constructed in relation to various subordinated masculinities as well as in relation to women. Thus, for example, non-European, poor, non-white, and/or gay men tend to experience subordinated masculinities, whereas men of middle-class European, white, and/or heterosexual backgrounds tend to benefit from the privileges of hegemonic masculinity.

Especially since the 1980s, scholars of masculinity studies have produced innovative research on various aspects of men's lives and experiences. Messner (1992), for example, examines men's identifications with sports as an example of how masculinities are constructed and maintained. Messner analyzes the "male viewer" of today's most popular spectator sports in terms of the mythology and symbolism of masculine identification: common themes he encounters in his research include patriotism, militarism, violence, and meritocracy. Scholars of gay masculinities have addressed how gay men of various ethnic, racial, class, and national backgrounds have negotiated hegemonic masculinity, sometimes in contradictory ways, and constructed alternative masculinities through their everyday lives (Messner 1997).

Importantly, research on hegemonic masculinities sheds light on how and why masculinity has been largely "invisible" in the lives of men who benefit from hegemonic masculinity and in the field of women's/gender studies, which tends to focus on the experiences of women. Although there are obvious reasons why the field of women's/gender studies has focused primarily on women, since women experience gender inequalities more than men, scholars increasingly have pointed out that male socialization processes and identities, as well as masculinist institutions and theories, should be examined as a way to rethink gender inequality. As Kimmel (2002) notes: "The 'invisibility' of masculinity in discussions of [gender] has political dimensions. The processes that confer privilege on one group and not another group are often invisible to those upon whom that privilege is conferred. Thus, not having to think about race is one of the luxuries of being white, just as not having to think about gender is one of the 'patriarchal dividends' of gender inequality."

Judith Butler's research on gender performativity has opened space for discussion about the naturalized linking of gender identity, the body, and sexual desire. Butler (1990) argues feminism has made a mistake by trying to assert that "women" are a group with common characteristics and interests. Like sociobiologists, feminists who rely exclusively on a sociocultural explanation of gender identity construction also fall prey to essentialism. Many individuals, especially those who define as "queer" or as lesbian, gay, bisexual, or transgendered, do not experience gender identity, embodiment, and sexual desire through the dominant norms of gender and heterosexuality. Influenced by Foucault, Butler suggests, like Connell, that certain cultural configurations of gender have seized a hegemonic hold. She calls for subversive action in the present: "gender trouble," the mobilization, subversive confusion, and proliferation of genders, and therefore identity. This idea of identity as free-floating and not connected to an "essence" is one of the key ideas expressed in queer theory (EGS 2005).

Butler and other queer theorists have addressed how normative femininities and masculinities play a role in disciplining the lives of LGBT individuals. Halberstam's (1998) research addresses constructions of "female masculinity" and argues that scholars must separate discussions of gender identity (e.g., masculinities, femininities) from discussions of the body. Women can "act masculine" just as men can "act feminine"; how individuals identify in terms of their gender is not and should not be linked to their biological anatomies, however defined. Halberstam's own research addresses how masculine-identified women experience gender, the stratification of masculinities (e.g., "heroic" vs. alternative masculinities), and the public emergence of other genders. Other scholars have examined how medical and scientific institutions have managed normative gender (and sexual) identities through psychological protocols and surgical intervention (Fausto-Sterling 2000). This type of research points toward a broader understanding of gender that places dualistic conceptions of "masculine" vs. "feminine" and "male" vs. "female" into question.

Scholars of race, ethnic, and postcolonial studies have addressed how normative femininities and masculinities, which tend to benefit those with racial/ethnic privilege, help reinforce a racialized social order in which subordinated groups are demasculinized or feminized in ways that maintain their racial/ethnic subordination in society. One example involves the stereotyping of African American men as unruly and hypersexual. The "myth of the male rapist," as Davis (2001) has discussed, has played a highly destructive role in black men's lives and has influenced legal, political, and social actions toward them, including their disproportionate criminalization for rape, often based on fraudulent charges. Another example concerns immigrant men racialized as minorities in the US. Thai (2002) illustrates how working-class Vietnamese American men have developed innovative strategies to achieve higher status in their communities by marrying middle- to upper-class Vietnamese women and bringing them to the US. Faced with few marriage options and low-paying jobs in the US, working-class Vietnamese American men who experience a form of subordinated masculinity seek upward mobility through these transnational marriage networks.

Women of color in the US and working-class women in developing countries also face unequal access to hegemonic femininity, as defined in western terms. Hill Collins (2004) addresses how African American women have been hypersexualized in US popular culture, thereby placing them outside the realm of normative femininity according to hegemonic white, western standards. Postcolonial studies scholars have demonstrated how poor women in developing regions (particularly non-white women) have been sexualized by male tourists from industrialized countries and sometimes also by local men (Freeman 2001). More broadly, scholars of masculinities and/or femininities have pointed out how constructions of masculinities and femininities are embedded in social institutions (e.g., the state, economy, nation, educational system) and processes (e.g., social welfare policy, globalization, colonization, political campaigns, popular culture, everyday life) and shape individuals' everyday experiences and gendered self-perceptions (Connell 1987, 1997; Laurie et al. 1999; Freeman 2001; Hill Collins 2004).

Critics have defended normative femininity and masculinity on religious, moral, and/or biological grounds. Some, for example, have argued that these social norms (what Connell would call hegemonic masculinity and emphasized femininity) are "naturally" aligned with men's and women's assumed biological roles in reproduction and/or with their assumed heterosexual desire (see Lorber 1994; Messner 1997). On all sides of the ideological spectrum, individuals have participated in interesting political responses and social movements that either embrace or challenge dominant societal constructions of masculinity and femininity. Some women have joined feminist movements and challenged traditional notions of femininity; whereas other women have joined right-wing women's movements that embrace traditional gender roles and identities (e.g., Concerned Women for America). Men have formed feminist men's movements, based largely on the principles of women's feminist movements, as well as movements to embrace traditional notions of fatherhood, as in the divergent examples of the Christian-based (and largely white, middle-class) Promise Keepers and the Million Man Marches, first organized in 1995 by Nation of Islam leader Louis Farrakhan and attended by over 800,000 African American men as part of a movement to reclaim black masculinity (Messner 1997).

Future research on femininities and masculinities will likely be influenced by the recent scholarship in the fields of masculinity studies, queer theory and LGBT studies, and race, ethnic, and postcolonial studies. Although scholars vary in their disciplinary backgrounds and methodological approaches to the study of femininities and masculinities, most would agree that femininities and masculinities can be seen as sets of rules or norms that govern female and male behavior, appearance, and self-image.

SEE ALSO: Consumption, Girls' Culture and; Consumption, Masculinities and; Female Masculinity; Gender Oppression; Gendered Organizations/Institutions; Sex and Gender; Sexuality, Masculinity and

REFERENCES AND SUGGESTED READINGS

Butler, J. (1990) *Gender Trouble: Feminism and the Subversion of Identity*. Routledge, New York.

Connell, R. W. (1987) *Gender and Power: Society, the Person and Sexual Politics*. Stanford University Press, Palo Alto.

Connell, R. W. (1997) Hegemonic Masculinity and Emphasized Femininity. In: Richardson, L., Taylor, V., & Whittier, N. (Eds.), *Feminist Frontiers IV*. McGraw-Hill, New York, pp. 22–5.

Davis, A. (2001) Rape, Racism and the Myth of the Black Rapist. In: Bhavnani, K.-K. (Ed.), *Feminism and "Race."* Oxford University Press, Oxford, pp. 50–64.

de Beauvoir, S. (1980 [1952]) *The Second Sex*. Random House/Alfred Knopf, New York.

European Graduate School (EGS) (2005) Judith Butler. Online. www.egs.edu/faculty/butler.htm.

Fausto-Sterling, A. (2000) *Sexing the Body: Gender Politics and the Construction of Sexuality*. Basic Books, New York.

Folbre, N. (2001) *The Invisible Heart: Economics and Family Values*. New Press, New York.

1666 *feminism*

Freeman, C. (2001) Is Local : Global as Feminine : Masculine? Rethinking the Gender of Globalization. *Signs* 26(4): 1007–38.

Gilligan, C. (1993) *In A Different Voice: Psychological Theory and Women's Development*. Harvard University Press, Cambridge, MA.

Halberstam, J. (1998) *Female Masculinity*. Duke University Press, Durham, NC.

Hill Collins, P. (2004) *Black Sexual Politics: African Americans, Gender, and the New Racism*. Routledge, New York.

hooks, b. (2004) *We Real Cool: Black Men and Masculinity*. Routledge, New York.

Kimmel, M. (2002) Foreword. In: Cleaver, F. (Ed.), *Masculinities Matter! Men, Gender and Development*. Zed Books, London, pp. xi–xiv.

Laurie, N., Dwyer, C., Holloway, S., & Smith, F. (1999) *Geographies of New Femininities*. Longman, London.

Lorber, J. (1994) *Paradoxes of Gender*. Yale University Press, New Haven.

Messner, M. A. (1992) *Power at Play*. Beacon Press, Boston.

Messner, M. A. (1997) *Politics in Masculinities: Men in Movements*. Sage, Walnut Creek, CA.

Thai, H. C. (2002) Clashing Dreams: Highly Educated Overseas Brides and Low-Wage US Husbands. In: Ehrenreich, B. & Hochschild, A. R. (Eds.), *Global Woman: Nannies, Maids, and Sex Workers in the New Economy*. Metropolitan Books, New York, pp. 230–53.

Thompson, D. C. (2000) The Male Role Stereotype. In: Cyrus, V. (Ed.), *Experiencing Race, Class, and Gender in the United States*. Mayfield Publishing, Mountain View, CA, pp. 85–7.

feminism

Patricia Lengermann and Gillian Niebrugge

Feminism is the system of ideas and political practices based on the principle that women are human beings equal to men. Feminism may be the most wide-ranging social movement in history, effecting change in the institutions, stratificational practices, and culture of nearly all societies. Its impact on sociology is the focus here. A study of this impact shows that sociology as an intellectual discipline and as a professional organization is itself deeply gendered, located in and affected by the society it attempts to study, and that its gendered character changes only in response to changes in the gender dynamics within society – changes in part produced by the action of feminist sociologists.

As a system of ideas, feminism includes alternative discourses: liberal, cultural, materialist or socialist, radical, psychoanalytic, womanist, and postmodernist. Among these, liberal feminism and materialist feminism have been most important to sociology. Liberal feminism argues that equality with men means equal rights for women; it has focused on achieving those rights through political action, enlisting the state to prohibit practices of discrimination against women; while basically accepting the capitalist organization of society, it works for a more level playing field for women in that society. Materialist feminism attempts to incorporate Marxist or socialist ideas and focuses on social production as the key social process wherein equality must be achieved. Radical feminism has helped sociology define violence – domestic violence, spouse abuse, rape – as central to gender dynamics. Psychoanalytic feminism has effected a reworking of socialization theory. Womanist feminism challenges the concept of a unitary standpoint of "woman," making intersectionality a key idea in feminist analysis. Postmodernist feminism has, as postmodernism has done everywhere, challenged some of the basic conceptual categories of feminist analysis, such as woman and gender.

As political practice, feminism is understood as a social movement with several periods of high mobilization, called "Waves." First wave feminism is the period from about either 1792 (the date of Mary Wollstonecraft's *Vindication of the Rights of Women*) or 1848 (the date of the first Women's Rights Convention in Seneca Falls, New York) to 1920 (the date that US women got the vote). Second wave feminism is the period of activism that began in the 1960s – starting events were President Kennedy's 1961 Commission on the Status of Women headed by Esther Peterson and Betty Friedan's *The Feminine Mystique* (1963). Third wave feminism refers to the ideas and actions of women and men who will spend the majority of their lives in the twenty-first century. Between first and second wave feminism there was a period of relative quiet, a seeming hiatus (though this is debated among scholars).

The relationship between feminism and sociology has existed from the beginning of the discipline. Women have been contributors to the enterprise of sociology as creators of professional organizations, sociological theory, sociological methods, and empirical research; they have made these contributions in the discipline's founding, classic, modern, and contemporary generations – and the majority of these women have been feminists, attracted to sociology's promise that social life can be studied as a human creation, that as such it can be controlled and changed in directions that are more just. It is possible to trace four generations of feminist sociologists. First wave feminism spanned two generations of sociology: the founding (1830–80) and classic (1890–1930) generations. The primary message of first wave feminist sociologists was that women could claim a right to participate in the discipline, to do sociology – theory, method, practice. Second wave feminism began at the midpoint of modern sociology (1930–90) and continues to influence the momentum of feminist sociologists in the contemporary generation (1990–). The primary message of second wave feminist sociologists has been that women have a right to participate equally with men in the enterprise of sociology and that sociology itself is not free of the sexism that shapes the societies it studies. Despite this long continuity, the history of women's sociology has followed the rule of women's history generally – it is lost and recovered, lost again, and rediscovered generation by generation. One work of second wave feminist sociologists has been the recovery of the founding and classic generations of women in sociology. Third wave feminism will presumably pattern the dynamics of the profession in the twenty-first century – a prediction that draws its strength from the fact that women increasingly constitute the majority of students at all levels in sociology programs.

FEMINISM AND THE CONCEPTUAL PRACTICES OF SOCIOLOGY

Despite the gap in historical memory between the founding and classical generations and the modern generation of feminist sociologists, it is possible to generalize about themes that mark feminist sociology across all four generations. These themes constitute feminism's contribution to the conceptual practices of sociology. But the presence and effect of these themes in sociology turn in part on their validity as descriptors of social reality and in part on the influence of feminism as a political movement.

The major contribution of feminism to sociological practice has probably been the concept of gender, which feminism has both centralized and refined. The first attempt at identifying gender as a sociological variable was made by Gilman (1898) when she described human society as distorted by "excessive sex distinction"; by "excessive" she means any distinction between men and women beyond the biologically necessary differentiation for reproduction. But Gilman's insight, while widely hailed by women, was not followed up in sociology. The term gender was used only infrequently in sociological publications until the 1970s – and only as a synonym for sex. A sample run of a computerized database shows that between 1895 and 1969 only 69 sociology articles used the concept and in none is it a major variable or title feature; but in the decade 1970 to 1979, over 500 articles are recorded as using gender, with many featuring it in the title.

In the modern usage of gender, feminist scholars worked to distinguish it from sex and sexuality. Three main understandings of gender have emerged from the engagement of feminism and sociology: gender has been understood as a part of role performance across institutions – and most recently as an institution in its own right (Martin 2004); as a product of ongoing individual activities in which social actors consciously and unconsciously "do gender" (West & Zimmerman 1987); as a stratificational category (Acker 1973) – including the concept of "gender class" (MacKinnon 1989). Whichever of these definitions a sociologist may work out of, the key feminist achievement has been to separate gender from sex as an analytic category and to define gender as a social construction imposed on perceived biological differences. The most radical claim urged by some feminist sociologists is that "gender" can and should be dismantled, that it is a dysfunctional social structure (Lorber 1994).

Central to all these approaches to gender is the process of gender socialization: the question of how people learn to conduct themselves and to configure their identities around the socially constructed categories of masculine and feminine. Gender socialization is seen as occurring through a variety of social experiences – parent–child interaction, peer group experiences, children's play, media representations. An important addition to this analysis is R. W. Connell's discussion of "hegemonic masculinity," a cultural construct that presents the exaggerated and idealized traits of manhood as a goal for all men; as idealizations, no individual can fully realize these traits, but they serve as an instrument of social control as individuals try to do so. Hegemonic masculinity legitimizes both male dominance over women and the dominance within patriarchy by some men – the most hegemonically masculine – over other men. The cultural complement to hegemonic masculinity is emphasized femininity.

The standpoint of women is the epistemological claim made by feminist sociologists that the social world can and should be analyzed from the perspective of women and that a complete sociological knowledge requires such an analysis. From Harriet Martineau's Introduction to *Society in America* in 1836 to Charlotte Perkins Gilman's analysis of food production in *Women and Economics* (1898) to Dorothy E. Smith's landmark 1979 essay "A Sociology for Women," feminist sociology has been shaped by the assertion that women's standpoint offers an essential lens for discovering the organization of society and that the organization they discover is different from that of sociology based in male experience. The idea of a standpoint of women rests on three main claims in feminist epistemology: (1) that understanding of the world is created by embodied actors situated in groups that are variously located in social structure; (2) this understanding, therefore, is always partial and interest-based; and (3) this understanding is shaped by the individual's and the group's experience of power or disempowerment in relation to others. There can be, feminists argue, a standpoint of women because women constitute a definable group, recognizable in part by their embodiedness, who share a common interest in terms of their assignment to specific tasks in social production and a common relation to power as it is exercised in patriarchy.

The idea of the standpoint of women has been limited and refined by Donna Haraway and Patricia Hill Collins (1998) to capture the fact of what Collins has termed "intersectionality" – the lived experience in an individual biography of the daily workings of social power as multifaceted and involving besides inequalities of gender, inequalities of race, class, geosocial location, age, and sexuality. This intersection produces what Haraway calls "situated vantage points" or shifting understandings of the world arising out of the relevant structures of a particular context at a particular moment.

Feminist epistemology charts the dynamic interplay between a standpoint of women and the experiences of intersectionality and situated vantage point. But in all forms, feminist epistemology challenges the universalizing voice of traditional and androcentric social theory.

MODEL OF SOCIETY

Feminist sociology's model of society turns on a reworking of the traditional concept of social production. In this reworking feminists expand the concept of social production, critique the concept of "public and private spheres," show how gender stratification permeates all of production, and offer a distinctive model of the way in which power and production in interaction organize the social world. From the standpoint of women, social production is seen as encompassing all the activities necessary to maintain human life – paid work in the economy, unpaid work in the home, the production of material goods – but also the production of emotional goods such as security, kindness, love, acceptance, etc., of order in time and space through coordination of schedules, waiting, cleaning, replenishing; and the reproduction of the worker both biologically in birth and childrearing and daily in all the activities of maintenance, including care of the sick.

This production is gendered. A gender ideology divides it into public and private spheres, and patriarchy as an organizing principle of social production means that women of every class find themselves responsible in some way for the private sphere. From the standpoint of women these spheres overlap so that an individual's position in one sphere affects their position in the other. The public sphere is organized around the unacknowledged assumption of ongoing, uncompensated private-sphere labor by women; a woman's work in the private sphere hinders her participation in the public sphere; her gender role in the private sphere patterns expectations of her in the public sphere; where public-sphere participation for women intensifies the difficulty of private-sphere performance, public-sphere participation for men gives privileges in the private sphere; the sexual harassment of women is part of a battle between men and women over spheres and domains; for women who work as domestics, private-sphere work is their public-sphere participation; and for all women private-sphere work is undervalued by the society. Feminist studies of the gendering of work have produced a vocabulary that has entered the everyday world: "women's double day or second shift," "sexual harassment," "equal pay," "pay equity," "comparable worth," "municipal housekeeping," "the glass ceiling," "domestic violence," "his marriage and hers," "the ideal worker norm," "juggling work and family."

Perhaps the most large-scale generalization from this line of thought is Dorothy E. Smith's division of the social world into the local actualities of lived experience, where the world's production is done, and the relations of ruling, the interconnections of power which control and appropriate that production. In Smith's model all women are part of the local actualities of lived experience – as are most men; the domain of the relations of ruling is a masculine one, fulfilling what one might see as the ethic of hegemonic masculinity – control. This control is exercised through anonymous, impersonal, generalized texts – documents created by the apparatus of ruling that determine who can legitimately do what.

From the beginnings of their engagement with the discipline, feminist sociologists have been concerned with methodology, inventing many of sociology's most characteristic and innovative strategies for collecting and presenting data. They pioneered the survey, the interview, the questionnaire, personal budget keeping, participant observation, key informants, and secondary data analysis (census, legislation, memoirs and diaries, wage and cost of living records, court reports, social worker reports, tax rolls, nursery rhymes, industrial accident reports). They were equally pioneering in methods of presentation, using photographs, detailed colored maps of neighborhoods, tables, bar charts, graphs, statistical analyses, narrative accounts, and extended quotation from subjects (Reinharz 1992; Lengermann & Niebrugge-Brantley 1998).

Growing out of the lived experience of asserting the validity of women's standpoint in the world, feminist sociology has made as the cornerstone of its research ethic respect for the subject. It has argued from its beginnings (Holbrooke 1895) that the researcher is not at liberty ethically to "use" the subject as a source of information and then forget about him or her. Hallmarks of feminist research methodology are the practices of selecting research topics that may contribute to bettering the lives of women, taking the research back to the subject for comment, and active and helpful engagement in the life of the research subject as it is lived in the local actualities. Feminist method also emphasizes keeping alive the voice of the subject in the final report of the research.

FEMINISM AND THE ORGANIZATIONAL DEVELOPMENT OF SOCIOLOGY

The presence of these conceptual achievements of feminist practice in sociology rests ultimately on feminism as a political movement. Although the history of sociology is often told as a history of its great ideas transmitted from Europe to America, sociology in the US and Europe did not spring full grown as a set of ideas; its development turned equally on the establishment in the nineteenth and early twentieth centuries of organizational bases for professional practice. Of these, the academy was only one of many and in the establishment of these various bases feminists played an important but, until the 1990s, underappreciated role.

In the middle of the nineteenth century women spurred by first wave feminism were among the first adherents of the new social science movement (Bernard & Bernard 1943). The social science movement began as volunteer activity by concerned citizens who believed that scientific inquiry could be used to address the social problems produced by the expansion of capitalism and industrialism. In Britain, feminist sociologist Harriet Martineau was an early supporter of the National Association for the Promotion of Social Science established in 1856. In the US, feminist Caroline Healey Dall corresponded with the British association and was one of the founding members of the American Social Science Association (1865) (ASSA). ASSA spawned and affiliated with many progressive organizations in which feminists played significant roles, including the National Conference of Charities and Corrections (NCCC) begun in 1874 and the Association for the Advancement of Women (which had begun as the Ladies' Social Science Association in 1873). State and local chapters of ASSA provided a base in which local feminists could play an important role. As sociologists began to establish an academic presence in the latter part of the nineteenth century, sexism in the academy meant that men became the professional face of sociology in that setting; women were welcome as students but not as professors. But between 1885 and 1910 sociology was also being practiced intelligently, innovatively, and self-consciously outside the academy in the social settlements that grew up in America's major cities. For many citizens, settlement sociology was the face of the discipline and in that location women were the primary actors, particularly Jane Addams, consistently voted among the most admired Americans, in part for her sociological practice (Lengermann & Niebrugge-Brantley 1998).

In the new American Sociological Society (ASS) formed in 1905, an indirect offshoot of ASSA, women were a very small minority; in the first year, women constituted about 12 percent of the society's membership – 15 out of a membership of 116. That percentage of professional activity within the association remained fairly constant down to about 1969. Though women maintained membership, presented papers at meetings, and wrote for the society's official publication the *American Journal of Society* (and had so done since its inaugural issue in 1895), they only occasionally were elected to national offices. Between 1932 and 1969 – a hiatus in the waves of women's activism – only 7 women reached the office of vice

president. Only one woman was elected president: Dorothy Swaine Thomas in 1952. Women in unknown numbers entered the profession indirectly as faculty wives, of whom the most influential for the profession was Helen McGill Hughes, who served the *AJS* as *de facto* and then acknowledged managing editor from 1944 to 1961, establishing practices for editing manuscripts and affecting the review process itself. In the years 1949 to 1958, while women represented slightly more than half of all bachelor's degrees in sociology in the US, they constituted only about one-third of master's degrees, and only about 12 percent of all doctorates, authored only slightly more than 5 percent of journal articles in *AJS* and the *American Sociological Review*, and made up less than 10 percent of the attendance at annual meetings.

However, with the beginnings of second wave feminism, feminist sociologists began to organize – a move symbolized by Alice Rossi's 1964 declaration "An Immodest Proposal" that argued that society was free of "antifeminism" not because of an absence of sexism but because of an absence of feminist consciousness, that women had to "reassert the claim to sex equality." The reassertion of this claim within sociology had its first major impact on professional sociology at the 1969 ASA annual meeting in San Francisco, when the Women's Caucus produced a series of 10 resolutions voted on and accepted at the ASA Business Meeting, calling for equity in ASA organization, departmental hiring, training of graduate students, and in sociological curricula, for the promotion of women's history and for sociological study of sex inequality. In February 1971 some 20 members of the Women's Caucus met at Yale and formed Sociologists for Women in Society (SWS). Representative of the success of this effort is the 1973 *AJS* issue on "changing women in a changing society" in which Jessie Bernard (1973) described the four revolutions she had lived through in professional sociology, with feminism becoming the fourth.

But by the 1980s, while research on gender and women was certainly more present in journal discourse than in the past, what were considered the leading journals – *AJS*, *ASR*, and *Social Forces* – still published less on gender and women than other journals. Responding to what Stacey and Thorne (1985) called the "missing feminist revolution in sociology," the SWS in 1987 founded its own journal *Gender and Society*, which today has the largest readership of any SAGE-sponsored journal. The SWS helped establish an ASA section on Sex and Gender which was in 2005 the largest section in the ASA. Since 1970 there have been 8 women presidents of ASA and 21 women vice presidents.

The 1990s represented a high water mark of feminist activism in professional sociology: 1993 marked the beginning of a period in which women have consistently received more doctorates than men; in 1994 women constituted 75 percent of the ASA Governing Council; by 1995 women were almost 50 percent of assistant professors and were approaching 40 percent of the associate professors; in 1996 they were 40 percent of the editors of ASA-sponsored journals. Since then, there has been a leveling off of women's participation in professional policymaking in the association. While from 2001 women constituted over 50 percent of all members of the ASA, this figure reflects the growth of female student membership – and also the general decline across the social sciences of male graduate students. The 2004 Report of the ASA Committee on the Status of Women in Sociology showed that women were still underrepresented in significant ways – on editorial boards, as editors, as recipients of major awards – and that women tend to leave the ranks of assistant professors in significantly greater numbers than men. One challenge for third wave feminist sociologists is to address equity issues in a situation where, while much has been achieved, much remains to be done.

SEE ALSO: Addams, Jane; Bernard, Jessie; Black Feminist Thought; Cultural Feminism; Ecofeminism; Feminism: First, Second, and Third Waves; Feminism and Science, Feminist Epistemology; Feminist Methodology; Feminist Pedagogy; Lesbian Feminism; Liberal Feminism; Materialist Feminisms; Multiracial Feminism; Postmodern Feminism; Psychoanalytic Feminism; Radical Feminism; Socialist Feminism; Third World and Postcolonial Feminisms/Subaltern; Transnational and Global Feminisms

REFERENCES AND SUGGESTED READINGS

Acker, J. (1973) Women and Social Stratification: A Case of Intellectual Sexism. *American Journal of Sociology* 78(4): 936–45.

Bernard, J. (1973) My Four Revolutions: An Autobiographical History of the ASA. *American Journal of Sociology* 78(4): 773–91.

Bernard, L. & Bernard, J. (1943) *The Origins of American Sociology: The Social Science Movement in the United States*. Thomas Y. Crowell, New York.

Collins, P. H. (1998) *Fighting Words: Black Women and the Search for Justice*. University of Minnesota Press, Minneapolis.

Gilman, C. P. (1898) *Women and Economics*. Small & Maynard, Boston.

Hochschild, A. & Machung, A. (1989) *The Second Shift*. Basic Books, New York.

Holbrooke, A. S. (1895) Map Notes and Comments. In: *Hull-House Maps and Papers, By Residents of Hull-House*. Crowell, Boston, pp. 3–23.

Laslett, B. & Thorne, B. (1997) *Feminist Sociology: Life Histories of a Movement*. Rutgers University Press, New Brunswick, NJ.

Lengermann, P. & Niebrugge-Brantley, J. (1998) *The Women Founders: Sociology and Social Theory, 1830–1930*. McGraw-Hill, New York.

Lorber, J. (1994) *Paradoxes of Gender*. Yale University Press, New Haven.

MacKinnon, C. (1989) *Towards a Feminist Theory of the State*. Harvard University Press, Cambridge, MA.

Martin, P. Y. (2004) Gender as a Social Institution. *Social Forces* 82(4): 249–73.

Reinharz, S. (1992) *Feminist Methods in Social Research*. Oxford University Press, New York.

Rossi, A. (1964) Eqality Betweeen the Sexes: An Immodest Proposal. *Daedalus* 93: 607–52.

Slobin, K. An ASA Revolution 1969–1971: The Women's Caucus and SWS. Online.www.ndsu.edu/socanth/faculty/slobin/An_ASA_Revolution_1969–1970.ppt.

Smith, D. E. (1987) *The Everyday World as Problematic: A Feminist Sociology*. Northeastern University Press, Boston.

Stacey, J. & Thorne, B. (1985). The Missing Feminist Revolution in Sociology. *Social Problems* 32: 301–16.

West, C. & Zimmerman, D. (1987) Doing Gender. *Gender and Society* 2: 125–51.

feminism, first, second, and third waves

Jo Reger

The women's movement in the United States is generally broken into waves of protest, each set in different time periods with diverse tactics, ideologies, and goals. The waves are divided into a first wave, starting in the 1840s; a second wave, beginning in the late 1960s; and the third wave, emerging in the mid-1990s. Although most scholars and historians use the analytical device of waves to discuss the movement, a variety of debates have arisen around the concept, with some arguing that the wave model ignores some forms of collective action and groups.

Despite debates on the occurrence of waves within the movement, it is clear that in the United States, the women's movement shaped society, politically and culturally. As the result of campaigns addressing citizenship, suffrage, civil rights, and reproductive rights, US citizens live in a society where women are free to vote, own property, retain custody of their children, divorce and marry at will, work in traditionally male occupations, and obtain legal abortions. Beyond changes to the legislative and economic systems, feminist ideas have been incorporated into the mainstream. Ideas of feminine/female strength, independence, and free will are now a part of the cultural norms about women.

THE WAVE MODEL OF WOMEN'S MOVEMENTS

To understand why US women's activism is considered a movement, it is important to consider its characteristics. The US women's movement is enduring, having its roots in the abolition movement of the 1800s and continuing into contemporary times. It is organized, drawing on networks of activists and organizations from the first attempts at suffrage to current redefinitions of femininity and sexuality. Finally, it is dynamic, constantly changing and "spilling over" into other movements.

To describe this organized, shifting yet continuous movement, scholars break the movement into a series of waves that influence, yet differ from, each other. Each wave is characterized by a period of mass mobilization when women of different backgrounds united on common issues, followed by periods of fragmentation, when women searched for ways to acknowledge their differences and to work on a variety of issues, including those pertaining to race/ethnicity, class, and sexual identity. For example, in the first wave of feminism, women united over the goal of suffrage (among others) but experienced fragmentation when that goal was achieved and no consensus of future courses of action was identified. In addition, in the second wave of feminism, many disparate groups of feminists came together to fight for reproductive, occupational, and legal rights but experienced divisions as lesbian, working-class and women of color began to articulate how their issues and identities have been left out of feminist activism and ideology.

Studies of the first wave tend to focus on the structural and organizational aspects of the movement. Therefore scholarship on the first wave investigates the organizations that emerged, activists' and organizations' relations with the political environment, and the larger social climate (e.g., demographic shifts). While these aspects continue to define the second and third wave of the movement, scholars also incorporate more cultural analyses to capture how individuals act politically, the role of identity and community, and multiplicity of oppression.

THE FIRST WAVE

The first wave of the US women's movement emerged in a time of great social change due to industrialization, national expansion, and a public discussion on individuals' rights. As the world that they knew began to change (i.e., growing rates of urban poverty, changes in workplace and family), women were drawn to social reform with the goal of helping the "unfortunate" in society. The issue of slavery drew many women into the public sphere and in the early 1800s, women were instrumental in organizing and participating in the Abolition

Movement. In 1837, women organized the first Anti-Slavery Convention of American Women, without the assistance of men. Women were also active in the Temperance Movement struggles of the 1830s and 1840s. When denied the right to speak and visibly participate at anti-slavery and temperance conventions, women reformers organized the first women's rights convention. The Seneca Falls Women's Rights Convention, held July 14, 1848, was organized by abolitionists Lucretia Mott and Elizabeth Cady Stanton and focused on multiple issues, including education rights, property reforms, and women's restrictive roles within the family. The convention attendees drew up a Declaration of Sentiments, modeled after the Declaration of Independence, which detailed how men had denied women their rights. It was only after much deliberation that the 300 attendees decided also to address the controversial issue of women's suffrage. The Seneca Falls convention sparked women's rights activism and spawned a decade of women's rights meetings and conventions throughout small towns in Ohio, New York, Pennsylvania, Massachusetts, and Indiana in the 1850s.

In addition to this focus on the politics and the state, first wave activists and organizations also worked for cultural change. From 1851 to 1854, there was a campaign to change women's dress. Dress reform activists argued that to change women's costumes would also work to change their lives. Women who adopted the "Bloomer" outfit of a loose tunic and pantaloons found it liberating. However, the dress reform movement brought a hostile backlash and consequently, activists advocated dropping the issue, fearing it was detracting from their other points of reform.

Race/ethnicity also became a divisive issue when some activists, such as Stanton, argued that white women should be given the vote to offset the votes of African, Chinese, and "ignorant" immigrant men. Although generally a popular speaker, Sojourner Truth, a former slave and women's rights reformer, often faced hostility as she spoke at women's rights conventions. The tendency for some suffragists to place gender disadvantage over other sources of discrimination served to drive a wedge between blacks and whites who were organizing together to win the vote. It is this history of racial

divisiveness, along with the later experiences of second wave feminists, that led feminists to reconceptualize oppressions as intertwined and intersecting instead of arguing over which oppression was the most relevant.

Scholars of the first wave have focused in particular on two organizations, each pursuing different strategies for winning women the vote. The National Woman Suffrage Association (NWSA), founded in 1868 by well-known leaders Stanton and Susan B. Anthony, pursued a broad range of issues and endorsed more radical tactics. Stanton and Anthony believed that the courts were the fastest avenue to suffrage and eventually took their case to the Supreme Court. Adopting a different strategy was the American Woman Suffrage Association (AWSA), founded by Lucy Stone. Stone and her followers focused solely on suffrage issues and believed that working state by state was the most feasible strategy for winning national suffrage. The AWSA had success working with western states, and Wyoming (before it became a state) was the first to grant women suffrage.

By 1890, the focus of both groups had narrowed to suffrage so the two organizations merged, creating the National American Woman Suffrage Association (NAWSA). In 1913 the movement was again fragmented when a militant group called the Congressional Union formed. Led by Alice Paul, Congressional Union members engaged in dramatic tactics to draw public attention, such as marches, picketing, and hunger strikes. The Union, later renamed the National Woman's Party (NWP), brought new attention to suffrage and, in coalition with the NAWSA, the groups finally achieved their goal. Feminists had introduced the 19th Amendment every year since 1848 before it finally passed on August 26, 1920.

Along with the suffragist organizations, other women's groups emerged in the first wave. These organizations focused on a variety of concerns from child custody laws to lobbying for equal pay. The Women's Christian Temperance Union (WCTU) from 1874 to 1898 was one of the most visible and drew women into the public sphere as anti-alcohol reformers and activists. Other organizations, perceived as less radical and scandalous than the suffrage groups, also mobilized women at a time when educational and career opportunities were expanding for women but traditional ideas and practices constrained them. Through lobbying for suffrage and other issues and repeatedly presenting women's claims to legislators and other political actors, the first wave of the women's movement had left an important mark on American interest group politics.

In sum, the first wave of the movement has been characterized as seeking national-level policy and legislative change, populated mostly by white upper- and middle-class women within organizational contexts, and subject to factions, divisiveness, and dwindling mobilization after the suffrage victory. This focus on organizational visibility led to the common belief that the women's movement ceased to exist in the 1920s. Starting in the late 1980s, feminist scholars began to examine the ways in which the women's movement was sustained but not visible to the public. The term "abeyance" was coined by social movement scholar Verta Taylor to illustrate how the movement had not disappeared but instead continued to exist in a period of dormancy, sheltered in organizations such as the NWP. Dialogues on women's equality also continued after suffrage in networks and communities such as the Communist Party in the 1940s, 1950s, and early 1960s. By the 1950s, despite the traditional images of women, more and more middle-class white women were entering the labor force, and single motherhood and divorce rates were beginning to rise. The strain between societal expectations of domesticity and women's experiences in education and the workforce, along with other factors such as the rise of the cycle of new social movements that swept the United States and Western Europe, led to the reemergence of the movement in the 1960s and 1970s.

THE SECOND WAVE

While the structural changes that created opportunities for women to attain skills and establish networks through the workplace may have set the stage for the rise of the first wave, it was the actual lived experiences of women and the construction of a shared feminist identity among groups of women that led to the second wave. The emergence of the second

wave drew on activist networks from the first wave as well as other movements, particularly the New Left and the Civil Rights Movement. In addition, the publication of books such as Simone de Beauvoir's *The Second Sex* in 1952 and Betty Friedan's *The Feminine Mystique* in 1962 sparked primarily white middle-class women's dissatisfaction with the roles of men and women.

Two events mark the reemergence of the second wave. First was the break from the New Left and Civil Rights movements by politically educated younger women dissatisfied with these movements' failure to address gender issues. Women in the New Left and Civil Rights movements participated in a variety of protests, gaining important political organizing skills. For example, Jo Freeman and Vivian Rothstein, who later became women's liberation movement organizers, participated in the Free Speech Movement's sit-in and strike at Berkeley. However, by 1964, women were beginning to articulate their issues with the patriarchal structure and culture of the movements. In 1965, Casey Hayden and Mary King circulated a memo on sexism in the Civil Rights Movement and the "woman question" was raised at a Students for Democratic Society meeting that same year.

Second was the formation of the National Organization for Women (NOW) by a group of women enmeshed in government networks and upset at the lack of attention to workplace discrimination against women by the Equal Employment Opportunity Commission (EEOC). NOW formed October 29, 1966 during a luncheon of women at the National Conference of State Commissions in Washington, DC. NOW was created when conference participants were blocked from passing a resolution pressing the EEOC to use greater force in investigating sex discrimination cases. Founding members include Friedan, lawyer and Civil Rights activist Pauli Murray, and Kay Clarenbach, head of the Wisconsin Commission on the Status of Women. Modeled after the National Association for the Advancement of Colored People (NAACP), NOW's original goal was to expand women's economic rights and responsibilities by fighting sex discrimination in the workforce. In one of its first actions, NOW pressured the EEOC to end the practice of sex-segregated help-wanted advertisements in newspapers. Along with employment and economic issues, NOW formed task forces to deal with areas of discrimination in education and religion; family rights; women's image in the mass media; political rights and responsibilities; and problems facing poor women.

These two events, the split from contemporary movements and the formation of NOW, served as the seeds of two different branches of the movement. These branches are described in a variety of ways, including "small group sector" versus "mass movement," "collectivist" versus "bureaucratic," "younger women" versus "older women," "liberal" versus "radical," and "women's rights" versus "women's liberation." The two branches were connected through interpersonal and organizational networks, had overlapping memberships, and cooperated on some goals.

Drawing on younger, college-age students, the women's liberation branch encompassed different ideologies and organizational structures. Women's liberation groups tended to be collectivist versus hierarchical in structure, and without established leaders and organizational positions.

The women's liberation branch endorsed a more radical feminist ideology, influenced by socialist, radical, and lesbian feminist theory, and participants believed that change came through personal and systematic transformation. For example, to accomplish personal transformation, The Redstockings, a radical feminist group, began to organize consciousness-raising groups. Consciousness raising (CR) is a process by which women share personal experiences and beliefs as a means to illuminate patriarchal control and oppression. In CR groups, women discussed a variety of issues from sexuality to housework, connecting them to gender inequality. CR, as a form of a politicized personal strategy, spread into the dominant culture and into women's rights organizations, such as NOW, that recognized it for its recruitment potential.

The membership of the women's rights branch of the movement was predominantly older, middle-class professional women concerned with legislative and policy issues. The women's rights branch of feminism focused on change through legislation and placement of women in positions of power as the vehicle to equality. The ideas of liberal feminism, that men and women will become equal when they are in comparable positions in society, are reflected in the overall strategies of the women's rights branch.

Actions from both branches brought media attention and drew large numbers of women into feminism. From the years 1972 to 1982, the second wave was in what has been characterized as its heyday. Women's liberation groups continued to recruit women to feminism and caused cultural shock waves with their critiques of femininity, gender roles, and heterosexuality. During this period, the American culture was shaped by the creation of cultural institutions such as *Ms. Magazine* and Naiad Press, a lesbian book publisher, and the growth of women's music through such companies as Olivia Records. It was also during this time that women's studies programs began appearing on college campuses. In the meantime, women's rights groups won legislative victories with the 1972 passage of Title IX directed at ending sex discrimination in publicly funded education and the 1973 *Roe* v. *Wade* decision by the Supreme Court legalizing abortion. One result of this heightened activity in the United States and abroad was that in 1975 the United Nations sponsored the First International Conference on Women in Mexico City.

Although these years were times of success for feminists, it was also a period of conflict, fragmentation, and growing discord in the movement. Lesbians, working-class women, and women of color critiqued white middle-class women's control of both branches of the movement. NOW suffered from dissension over the presence of lesbians in the organization. Some lesbian feminists began to organize separately in the 1970s and, in 1973, held a national conference. NOW eventually changed its position and endorsed lesbian rights. Working-class women also struggled with the movement, believing that their work and family lives were not being addressed, and created separate organizations. For example, the Coalition of Labor Union Women was formed in 1974, when 3,000 women met to address sexism in the unions and also women's inequality in society. Women of color also worked with and separated from the second wave. Black women, along with Chicana and Asian American women, often had their racial, ethnic, and class-based experiences of discrimination ignored, so they created organizations – including the National Black Feminist Organization, the Mexican American Women's National Association, and the Pan Asian American Women – specifically designed to address their issues. Informed by the discord in the first and second waves, feminists and feminist scholars, such as the Combahee River Collective and, later, Patricia Hill Collins, conceptualized an intersectional feminist paradigm that views race/ethnicity, class, gender, and sexuality as interlocking systems of oppression, forming a "matrix of domination."

As the second wave experienced fragmentation and dissension from within, it also faced growing countermovements, particularly opposing the Equal Rights Amendment (ERA) and abortion rights. By the late 1970s, the two branches had largely united in an effort to pass the ERA, an amendment originally introduced in the 1920s by the NWP to the Constitution that would guarantee women equal rights under the law; however, the amendment was defeated in 1982. The ERA's demise and the election of conservative president Ronald Reagan instigated a period of backlash. Many of the gains of the past decade were eroded, and media pundits labeled the 1980s the "post-feminist era." Among the setbacks was a lack of compliance with Title IX, increased cases of work-related sexual harassment, increasing state restrictions on abortion and related services, escalating anti-abortion violence, and attacks on affirmative action. However, the movement survived with activists drawing on established organizations, networks, and women's communities for stability and support. In sum, the second wave of the women's movement brought about a resurgence, differentiation, and expansion of feminist activism and ideologies, along with shifting strategies and tactics from the confrontational strategy in the 1960s, to the organizational strategy in the 1970s, and the electoral strategy in the 1980s. In its two branches, movement activists influenced national policy as well as addressed personal experience and cultural norms.

Evident in these historical accounts is the continuity of feminist organizing in the United States. Influenced by structural and political shifts and maintained by organizations, networks, and communities, the movement has undergone different levels of mobilization, but it has not died. In fact, feminism continues to shape political society. For example, political sociologists have shown how feminist ideas continue to shape the polity. Women identifying as feminists account for a large portion of the gender gap on specific issues, in particular domestic issues involving social service spending. For example, in the 1992 US presidential election, feminist consciousness emerged as a significant factor in shaping women's voting behavior.

THE THIRD WAVE

The popular media and some political pundits have repeatedly declared feminism dead or in decline. Scholars and activists respond to these obituaries in different ways. Some argue that these "premature" death notices serve a larger goal, preserving the status quo by erasing women's activism. Others argue that feminism is still alive, yet suffering from a backlash and is carried on through the efforts of "older" feminists and their organizations, institutions, and policies put in place in the 1960s and 1970s. Some argue that feminism diffused into the larger culture, bringing about a "post-feminist" era where feminist goals and ideology are alive but submerged into the broader culture. Others see the movement in a state of abeyance, awaiting external impetus for remobilization. Others view the movement as fragmented, particularly because of issues of homophobia, classism, and racism, yet insist that it still remains active and vital. Related to this view, others argue that feminism has changed form and is now done in a different way by a new generation of activists.

Adopting the view that the movement has changed form and tactics, some scholars and participants refer to this phase of the women's movement as "the third wave." The idea of a third wave comes from the concept of a political generation, a period when common historical experiences form a political frame of reference for a group. Young women and men in the twenty-first century enter into feminism in a society dramatically shaped by the movement's first two waves. Through the efforts of second wave activists, a variety of feminist cultural events exist – ranging from feminist theater, cruises, and music and comedy festivals to camps, day-care programs, and workshops on feminist spirituality. Young girls and boys can read non-gendered children's books, listen to feminist music, and attend summer camps organized around gender equity. In addition, feminism is embedded in the institutions in which third wave feminists spend their lives. Their families, schools, health-care providers, and political representatives have been influenced by the beliefs and values of first and second wave feminism.

While scholars of the first and second wave trace the emergence of feminist activism to specific organizational events (i.e., the Seneca Falls Convention or the formation of NOW), the third wave's emergence is less obvious. A variety of explanations for the origin of the third wave exist. In 1991, Lynn Chancer called for a "third wave" feminism to signify a turn from the defensive posture of the 1980s feminism and its backlash. Some credit its emergence to Rebecca Walker when, in 1995, she called herself "third wave" in the introduction of her anthology, *To Be Real*. For others, the Riot Grrrl movement in the Northwest United States in the 1990s signaled the conceptualization of a new, punk-infused, generationally defined form of feminism. Finally, many credit the rise of the third wave as having its origins in the challenges made by women of color to the second wave for its lack of racial-ethnic inclusivity. In all of these origins, third wave feminism is seen as drawing on the political, cultural, and institutional accomplishments of the second wave, while finding new forms of protest and working to undo norms of racism, classism, and homophobia that marred early waves of feminism.

The third wave has organizational roots, similar to the first and second waves, along with more subcultural and submerged roots. For example, the Third Wave Foundation was formed as a social justice organization addressing a variety of gender, racial, ethnic, and sexuality related concerns in 1997 for women aged 15 to 30. The Riot Grrrl movement shifted from being musically oriented to politically oriented with a 1992 convention and saw several chapters form in the early to mid-1990s. In addition, second wave organizations such as *Ms. Magazine* also serve as a point of origin for several voices of contemporary feminism such as Jennifer Baumgardner, coauthor of *Manifesta*, and Rebecca Walker, editor of *To Be Real*. NOW has also launched several initiates to involve young feminists in the organization.

Despite these groups, many view the third wave as cultural and submerged into broader subcultures of music, social justice activism, and art. In the early 1990s, several cultural events contributed to a growing sense of a generational change from second to third wave feminism. Singer Ani DiFranco launched her record company, Righteous Babe, in 1990 and became for many young activists the voice of contemporary feminism along with other performers such as Alix Olson and the Indigo Girls. Magazines such as *Bitch* and *Bust* emerged, expanding from their do-it-yourself 'zine inceptions.

Incorporated in these cultural vehicles are familiar political issues such as sexual harassment, occupational discrimination, violence, sexual abuse, and body image that continue to concern third wave feminists. Just as the first and second wave did with protests against restrictive dress, third wave feminists attack cultural norms of femininity. However, these protests have a new twist. Using the body as a site of protest, Lesbian Avengers, a group visible in the early to mid-1990s, "ate fire" to symbolize their strength and boldness. Other young feminists engage in disparaged feminine activities such as crafting, knitting, and embracing the color pink as a way to reclaim and redefine femininity. For example, a regular column in *Bust* magazine provides readers with how-to instructions on a variety of crafts. This reclaiming of the feminine is not solely in the province of individuals. Political organizations also draw upon both traditional political strategies and inventive protests to reclaim the feminine. Code Pink, a grassroots peace and social justice movement, protested at the 2004 Republican National Convention, using the color pink as an antidote to the Bush administration state of emergency color coding system, and as a way to give President Bush the "pink slip."

Both collectively and individually, third wave feminists use the performance of identity to redefine femininity and make political statements. For example, some twenty-first-century young feminists play with gender by wearing short skirts with combat boots and masculine-looking haircuts. In this case, feminists take cultural norms and, using the body, reinvent them as a display of feminine power. Along with playing with appearance, third wave writers and activists also talk of reinventing sexuality and gender norms. Young feminist scholars argue that activists need to fight against societally defined norms of feminine sexuality as well as second wave conceptions of sexual appropriateness, reclaiming pleasure through the use of sexual play and sex toys.

The culturally focused tactics of the third wave also emerge from institutional settings, such as education. Women's studies plays an important role in the continuity and continued mobilization of feminism. Young women come to feminism through transmission from their mothers and from women's studies courses that link the theoretical with the political. Much of contemporary feminist activism by young women is being done in college or university contexts in conjunction with women's studies departments and/or women's centers.

Along with shifts in issues, contemporary feminists are also turning to new ways to mobilize and communicate. Third wave feminists are increasingly turning to the Internet as the site of protest and the source of community. Cyberfeminism, a movement started in the 1990s, uses technology to redefine femininity and address a masculinist approach to technology that can alienate women. At a 1997 international conference in Kassel, Germany, cyberfeminists refused to define themselves and instead created a list of "100 Antitheses" of what the movement is not. Those antitheses include "cyberfeminism is not a fragrance," "cyberfeminism is not an ideology," and "cyberfeminism is not a structure" (Old Boys Network 1997). The Internet is also home to a multitude of sites dedicated to feminist organizations and to communities of activists who mobilize, support, and inform each other within web pages, or through blogs (i.e., Internet diaries) or ongoing journals.

One challenge facing the third wave is the sense of generational discord that pervades both this wave and the second wave. Young feminists (i.e., third wave) often feel that older (i.e., second wave) feminists malign their more individual and performance-oriented protests and would prefer to see more traditional, organizationally focused activism. Older feminists report that their histories and efforts are often oversimplified and that the complexity of earlier feminisms is ignored. These sentiments have led to serious dissension between the two groups. For example, at the 2002 Veteran Feminists of America meeting, a group of predominantly second wave feminists bemoaned the lack of clear activism by young women, while third wave feminists reported feeling patronized and ignored. Because of this, second and third wave feminists often have difficulties in working cooperatively with each other. One area in which the generations have different views is on the issue of racial–ethnic inclusion. A major emphasis of third wave feminist ideology is acknowledging the differences between women and working to incorporate all women into feminist activism. This view is founded on the idea that first and second wave feminists failed to build inclusive organizations and networks. While many second wave feminists admit this is true, they also argue that the history presented by third wavers ignores the efforts of women who tried and sometimes successfully integrated feminist groups and worked to meet all women's needs, not just those of white middle-class women.

In sum, contemporary feminism continues to shift and change, drawing on the ideas, strategies, and institutional gains of past waves of the women's movement, at the same time as it appropriates modern technologies, the media, gender codes, and the fabric of everyday life as sources of resistance. Simply stated, feminism in the twenty-first century is the same but different. It draws on the first two waves of the women's movement, yet functions in a fundamentally different world that demands scholars' continued innovation in order to capture the complexity and dynamics of that world.

DEBATES ABOUT THE WAVE MODEL

Some scholars have argued that the wave model, although conceptually neat, ignores forms of protest activity. Scholars, such as Mary Katzenstein, argue that one reason much feminist protest in modern society goes unnoticed is because it takes place inside mainstream institutions, such as medicine, education, religion, and the workplace, rather than in the streets, in what she labels "unobtrusive mobilization." For example, the creation of submerged networks within societal institutions such as the Catholic Church and the US military has sustained the women's movement. Unobtrusive mobilization is also evident in the feminist activism inspired by cultural events such as women's movement festivals, institutionalized organizations with feminist origins, and work-oriented organizations such as unions. Within these organizations and institutions, feminism is carried out through an identity that activists use to make sense of their lives and is spread through networks promoting movement goals.

Outside of the institutional contexts, submerged networks (i.e., those not readily evident to others such as scholars, media, and politicians) may also be left out of the conceptual framework of the "wave." Scholar Nancy Naples documents the networks that emerged in neighborhood communities as a result of the 1960s War against Poverty. Activists, drawing on feminist ideologies and strategies, turned their attention from national-level policy to focus on community work. While many of the low-income urban women involved did not identify as feminists or label their work as "political," they organize in their neighborhoods drawing on the rhetoric of "activist mothering." In addition, although less visible than it was in the movement's heyday, feminism in the late 1980s and 1990s established roots in other social movements of the period. Scholars argue that the women's movement, through the creation of networks, heavily influenced the peace and anti-nuclear movements of the 1980s by spreading feminist ideological frames, tactical repertoires, and conceptions of organizational structure and leadership. In sum, scholars argue that the women's movement trained a large number of feminist activists in the 1970s who, through their networks, have participated in new social movements and integrated feminism into them. This spillover is evident in the ways in which contemporary feminists engage in a variety of global concerns. For example, the New York City Radical Cheerleaders is a grassroots organization that subverts the traditionally feminine activity of cheerleading by protesting issues such as globalization, the war in Iraq, the occupation of Palestine, and sweatshops as well as sexual harassment, homophobia, and fat bias (New York Radical Cheerleaders 2005).

Along with the criticism that the wave model leaves out some contexts of protests is the argument that the wave model excludes movements of groups marginalized in society, such as women of color, lesbians, and working-class women, and focuses more on the activities of white, middle-class, heterosexual women. Scholars adopting this view argue that the second wave was in reality one of *feminisms*, with women of color and white women working on similar issues in organizationally distinct movements. This focus on the most visible groups creates a history shaped by hegemonic (i.e., dominant) feminism and ignores a justice-based perspective toward feminism. By tracing the activism of women of color and anti-racist white women, an understanding of multiracial feminism as a movement emerges, complicating the first, second, and third wave history and the overall use of the wave metaphor.

Perhaps one of the biggest challenges to the notion of feminist waves of activism is the carryover of strategies and tactics from one wave to the next, making the waves less distinct from each other. For example, both second and third wave feminists use sexuality as an everyday political statement against hegemonic heterosexuality. Works by second wave authors such as Andrea Dworkin and Adrienne Rich are catalysts changing the way many women viewed sexual relationships and desire, along with third wave writers such as Inga Muscio, the author of *Cunt: A Declaration of Independence*. In addition, like third wave activists, first and second wave feminists challenged clothing and appearance norms, from the introduction of bloomers to the emergence of norms violating traditional femininity such as not shaving one's legs or going without a bra. In sum, instead of embracing a set of distinct historical waves, some argue that our understanding of the feminism of the day should incorporate the ambiguity and contradiction that has been present in all the "waves." Along these lines, Ednie Garrison argues that we change the conceptual model from discrete "ocean" waves to the more fluid, overlapping, and competing structure of radio waves, allowing for multiple movements and interpretation of women's activism to exist.

CONCLUSION

As we have seen, women's movement activism has flourished and receded at different times in US history and has been conceptualized as a series of waves. While first and second wave feminism were viewed through a structural and organizational lens, contemporary or third wave feminism persists in a new, more loosely structured form that seeks changes in the realms of culture, identity, and everyday life, as well as through direct engagement with the state. The overall continuity of the women's movement throughout each of these waves is sustained by distinctive feminist cultures, fostered in social networks and social movement communities, when mass political action declines. Although scholars agree that the US women's movement has a long and dynamic history, some question the viability of the wave metaphor and seek to reintroduce forms of protests and social groups left out of its history, making a more complex and richer history of women's activism.

SEE ALSO: Black Feminist Thought; Cultural Feminism; Feminism; Feminist Activism in Latin America; Gender, Social Movements and; Matrix of Domination; Riot Grrrls; Third World and Postcolonial Feminisms/Subaltern; Transnational and Global Feminisms; Women's Empowerment; Women's Movements

REFERENCES AND SUGGESTED READINGS

Alfonso, R. & Trigilio, J. (1997) Surfing the Third Wave: A Dialogue between Two Third Wave Feminists. *Hypatia* 12, online version.

Baumgardner, J. & Richards, A. (2000) *Manifesta: Young Women, Feminism and the Future*. Farrar, Straus, & Giroux, New York.

Buechler, S. M. (1990) *Women's Movements in the United States*. Rutgers University Press, New Brunswick, NJ.

Collins, P. H. (1990) *Black Feminist Thought*. Routledge, New York.

Combahee River Collective (1982) A Black Feminist Statement. In: Hull, G. T., Scott, P. B., & Smith, B. (Eds.), *But Some of Us are Brave: Black Women's Studies*. Feminist Press, Old Westbury, NY, pp. 13–22.

Costain, A. (1992) *Inviting Women's Rebellion*. Johns Hopkins University Press, Baltimore.

Echols, A. (1989) *Daring to be Bad: Radical Feminism in America, 1967–1975*. University of Minnesota Press, Minneapolis.

Evans, S. M. (1979) *Personal Politics: The Roots of Women's Liberation in the Civil Rights Movement and New Left*. Alfred A. Knopf, New York.

Evans, S. M. (2003) *Tidal Wave: How Women Changed America at Century's End*. Free Press, New York.

Flexner, E. (1971) *A Century of Struggle*. Atheneum, New York.

Freeman, J. (1975) *The Politics of Women's Liberation*. Longman, New York.

Garrison, E. (2006) Are We on a Wavelength Yet? On Feminist Oceanography, Radios and Third-Wave Feminism. In: Reger, J. (Ed.), *Different Wavelengths: Studies of the Contemporary Women's Movement*. Routledge, New York.

Hawkesworth, M. (2004) The Semiotics of Premature Burial: Feminism in a Postfeminist Age. *Signs: Journal of Women in Culture and Society* 29: 961–86.

Katzenstein, M. F. (1990) Feminism within American Institutions: Unobtrusive Mobilization in the 1980s. *Signs: Journal of Women in Culture and Society* 16: 27–54.

Mansbridge, J. (1995) What is the Feminist Movement? In: Ferree, M. M. & Martin, P. Y. (Eds.), *Feminist Organizations: Harvest of the New Women's Movement*. Temple University Press, Philadelphia, pp. 27–34.

Naples, N. (1998) *Grassroots Warriors: Activist Mothering, Community Work and the War on Poverty*. Routledge, New York.

Naples, N. (2006) Confronting the Future, Learning from the Past: Feminist Praxis in the 21st Century. In: Reger, J. (Ed.), *Different Wavelengths: Studies of the Contemporary Women's Movement*. Routledge, New York.

New York Radical Cheerleaders (2005) Who Are the NYC Radical Cheerleaders? www.nycradicalcheerleaders.org/index.php?name=about.

Old Boys Network (1997) 100 Antitheses. First Cyberfeminist International, Kassel, Germany. www.obn.org/cfundef/100antitheses.html.

Papachristou, J. (Ed.) (1976) *Women Together: A History in Documents of the Women's Movement in the United States.* Alfred A. Knopf, New York.

Reger, J. & Taylor, V. (2002) Women's Movement Research and Social Movement Theory: A Symbiotic Relationship. *Research in Political Sociology,* "Sociological Views on Political Participation in the 21st Century." 10: 85–121.

Roth, B. (2004) *Separate Roads to Feminism: Black, Chicana, and White Feminist Movements in America's Second Wave.* Cambridge University Press, New York.

Rupp, L. J. & Taylor, V. (1987) *Survival in the Doldrums: The American Women's Rights Movement, 1945 to 1960s.* Oxford University Press, New York.

Taylor, V. (1989) Sources of Continuity in Social Movements: The Women's Movement in Abeyance. *American Sociological Review* 54: 761–75.

Thompson, B. (2002) Multiracial Feminism: Recasting the Chronology of Second Wave Feminism. *Feminist Studies,* 28: 337–663.

Walker, R. (Ed.) (1995) *To Be Real: Telling the Truth and Changing the Face of Feminism.* Anchor Books, New York.

Weigand, K. (2000) *Red Feminism: American Communism and the Making of Women's Liberation.* Johns Hopkins University Press, Baltimore.

Whittier, N. (1995). *Feminist Generations.* Temple University Press, Philadelphia.

feminism and science, feminist epistemology

Anne Kerr

Feminist scholars systematically began to focus upon the gender values in the biological and medical sciences in the 1970s, drawing upon and developing a radical social constructivism where facts were treated as social products rather than objective value-free entities and knowers were seen to be part of communities rather than lone scholars. This work ran alongside other developments in social studies of science, but was shaped by political commitments to women's rights, in contrast to the intellectual agnosticism of the mainstream, predominantly male scholars of sociology of scientific knowledge.

A great deal of the focus of feminist studies of sciences has been on the ways in which gender seeps into scientific theories, and the very "discovery" of natural objects. For example, Oudshoorn (1994) showed how sex hormones were categorized during the 1920s as sexually specific: female hormones were said to make females more female and male hormones to make males more male. Scientists then went on to use these gendered molecules to explain wider biological processes such as development of gender and sexuality in embryos. However, as Oudshoorn and others have argued, sex hormones are very complex. Men and women both have so-called male and female hormones; hormones are not only produced in the ovaries or testes, but also from the adrenal glands; hormones can also be converted. Gendered categories fail to account for such complexity. Feminists have also pointed out that there is a considerable overlap between what are considered to be male and female bodies on most physiological measurements. This complexity and overlap still tends to be overlooked in popular accounts of the differences between men and women, and scientific research has traditionally perpetuated the duality. The rise of molecular biology has involved a reinterpretation of biological sex which is no less determinist. As Fausto-Sterling (2000) notes, Sry – the so-called testes-determining factor – privileges masculinity against a feminine "default" because Sry is cast as a "master switch" which makes a fetus male. The induction of testicular tissue is presented as active, while induction of ovarian tissue is presented as passive, so that male is represented as presence, female as absence. In these ways scientific studies of sex and gender often reinforce a fixed duality between male and female and overemphasize difference at the expense of an appreciation of diversity and change. Masculinity and heterosexuality are privileged, and femininity is seen as "lacking" or a "default position."

In the 1980s feminists also moved beyond criticizing the gender biases in science to advocate new ways of doing science based upon feminist epistemology. This took place against a backdrop of considerable intellectual interest, in philosophy and the social sciences, in developing a middle ground between postmodernism and empiricism, where the social construction of knowledge was recognized, but relativism did not become a barrier to better knowledge. Once again feminists' commitment to tackling social problems, including inequalities, gave their inquiries an explicit political dimension. Three main types of feminist epistemologies of science which sought to bridge the gulf between traditional feminist theories and post-modernism emerged: Harding's (1986, 1991) feminist standpoint theory developed from the work of Hartsock (1983) and Rose (1983), among others; Haraway's (1991) "situated knowledge"; and Longino (1990) and Nelson's (1990) versions of feminist empiricism.

Harding's main argument is that science would be better if scientists developed the ability to *think from women's lives*. She combines the work of Rose (1983), Hartsock (1983), Ruddick (1990) (who developed maternal thinking theory), and Gilligan (1984) (who developed theories on moral reasoning) to argue that women have a privileged standpoint because their caring labor gives them a better understanding of the world. For Harding, scientists need to learn to see the world from the perspective of the marginalized and the oppressed, with the assistance of critical social theories generated by the emancipatory movements. This type of critical reflection requires *strong* objectivity: it is essential for feminists to remain able to judge between the validity of different knowledge claims by looking to the social conditions of the knowledge production.

Haraway and others have criticized Harding's notion of a feminist standpoint, because people have a multitude of different standpoints, based on differences in class, race, and sexuality, as well as gender. This is said to undermine Harding's notion of "seeing from below" as a means of judging the validity of knowledge claims when there are so many different standpoints that one could adopt. Instead, Haraway (1991) prefers to emphasize "situated knowledge" where people do not hold one perspective on the world, but many, some of which are contradictory. This also means that people can see from other people's perspectives, the result of which is a constantly shifting set of alliances. With a sufficiently diverse group of scientists, Haraway suggests these coalitions could form the basis for

scientists' critical reflection about what influences their knowledge claims.

Longino favors a similar reinterpretation of objectivity, which she argues comes from a robust version of empiricism. This involves critical evaluation of knowledge claims based on the available evidence. She argues, as does Haraway, that it is important to focus on building a diverse community of knowers. Longino argues in favor of contextual empiricism where she says that scientists should allow their political commitments to guide their choice of particular models in science and not simply aim to uncover sexist bias. For Longino, explicit value commitments can underpin good science. Nelson advocates a similar model, drawing on the work of Quine, to argue that knowledge and values form a unified web of meaning and must therefore be explored and developed together. Both Longino and Nelson are more focused than Harding or Haraway upon change from within science.

Many scholars have engaged with these various versions of feminist epistemology of science from a range of disciplinary and political perspectives, not just feminism. Several common themes characterize their writings. The first is the issue of determinism and, more broadly, the uniqueness and value of women's perspective (and that of other marginalized groups) in guiding critical inquiry in science. The second is the precise nature of values and their relationships to scientific practice. The third is the operationalization of feminist epistemology, particularly in the physical as opposed to the social sciences.

Turning first to essentialism, despite her emphasis on women's diverse experiences and her rejection of biological determinism, Harding's feminist standpoint is often said to be problematic because of its implied gender essentialism. This is in part because she draws on Hartsock and Rose's analyses, which both incorporate a weak version of the radical feminist emphasis upon women's bodies within their broad materialism. Poststructuralist feminists' deconstruction of the sex/gender divide, and insistence on the constructedness of the biological as well as the social dimensions of womanhood, have also undermined Harding's and other feminist standpoint theorists' emphasis upon the commonality in women's experience, biologically and socially. Other critics have noted that when white, middle-class, western feminists homogenize women's experiences they perpetuate racist and imperialist erasure of black women's standpoint. Although scholars such as Hill Collins (1999) have developed feminist standpoint theory from the perspective of black women, the danger of feminist standpoint theory fracturing to represent ever smaller groups of knowers is well recognized.

Harding has defended her theory against these criticisms on the basis that her emphasis upon social location and political struggle has stimulated debate and further reflection. This, she argues, is a benefit to critical inquiry in itself, because it entails the active negotiation of modern and postmodern projects, objectivity and subjectivity, by diverse groups of knowers. Harding implies that the hostility that has been shown towards standpoint theory is a sign of resistance to the oppressed studying the oppressors and in so doing reversing the usual power relations between researchers and their subjects. Others, such as New (1998), have also defended feminist standpoint theory on the basis that it sets out a program for change – an exploration of commonality and a means of building links and shared agendas. Here the feminist standpoint is the end point rather than the starting point of critical inquiry. This means that the category of women is always open to revision and contestation rather than commonality being simply assumed.

However, many questions remain about the detailed relationships between values, knowledge, and scientific practice in feminist standpoint theory. Haraway's situated knowledge is also vague about the relationships between values, knowledge, and practice in science, stressing instead the importance of partiality and difference in perspective. Nelson's web of meaning is also difficult to unpack, given that empirical and social/political values form a "seamless web" of scientific knowledge. On an abstract level tensions between realism and constructivism can be productive. As feminist empiricists and standpoint theorists have argued, it is possible to be epistemic relativists, recognizing the social production of knowledge, without becoming judgmental relativists – all beliefs are not equally valid. Yet the problem

remains of how to adjudicate between values. In particular, the danger has been raised that values will drive inquiry so that scholars will simply find what they are looking for and use their values to insulate themselves from criticism.

The details of how values shape knowledge and how one decides between legitimate and illegitimate influences have been recently taken up by other scholars in a more rigorous fashion, more usually through the development of various types of feminist empiricism rather than standpoint theory per se. As Anderson (2004) has argued, all research design is biased in some sense because it opens some lines of inquiry while closing others. For Anderson, so long as this is acknowledged it is legitimate. However, bias in relation to hypotheses is illegitimate when it means that experiments are deliberately "rigged" so that researchers find what they are looking for. As she argues, good research involves unwelcome, surprising, and null results, for feminists as well as non-feminists. She argues there is a range of methodological tools available to researchers to guard against these types of illegitimate values, or errors. Clough (2004) makes a similar point when she distinguishes between the deadlock of global skepticism about the values and the value of all knowledge and the necessity of fallibilistic worries about the empirical accuracy of knowledge claims which are an important part of robust scholarly inquiry. Yet, for others, these types of detailed accounts of legitimacy are not very different from standard empiricism, and therefore still unable to grasp the thoroughgoing social situatedness of knowledge and inquiry. Judgments about legitimacy remain just that, and are always shaped by the convictions of the research team and the community of scholars of which they are a part. This means that gender bias might remain "legitimate" despite feminist scholars' best efforts to the contrary.

On a more general level, operationalizing feminist epistemology has also proved to be difficult, especially in the physical sciences where bodies and behaviors are not the focus of inquiry. Starting from the perspective of women's lives, feminists have successfully theorized and offered alternatives to gender biases within biomedicine. In the US in particular, in the 1980s feminists began to challenge mainstream medicine's omission of women from trials, and to put women's health on the agenda. This was taken up by the federal government and reflected in the National Institute of Health's policy on research funding. These changes were not only produced by outsiders, but also by insiders in science, and by women like Evelyn Fox Keller, who choose to locate themselves between inclusion and exclusion. Feminists have uncovered the ways in which gender structures science at the level of theory, taxonomy, research priorities, and subjects of study. They have asked questions about who stands to benefit from large-scale projects like the Human Genome Project and looked critically at the ways new genetic technologies shape women's lives, crucially, in the arena of pregnancy and reproduction.

This development of feminist epistemology has been more difficult in the so-called "hard sciences" of physics and maths. As Schiebinger (1999) has argued, questions of meaning are not typical fare for the physical sciences and are seen as matters of ethics or history. Their model of inquiry is of the individual knower rather than the collective. However, feminists have analyzed the gendered nature of the hierarchy of hard and soft science – in particular the Cartesian dualism between the practice and critical reflection about science, or objectivity and subjectivity. As such feminist epistemologies perform a valuable role in making us think more deeply about what a feminist science might mean, and of problematizing taken-for-granted paradigms and hierarchies of "soft" and "hard" sciences. Problems of essentialism are still present in the popular cultural representations of women's way of doing science, but the move towards a more grounded understanding of feminist transformations of science avoids this because it generates many different understandings of women's practice, emphasizing the local and incremental process of moving towards a feminist science, and the importance of "building bridges" between scientific and local communities.

SEE ALSO: Epistemology; Essentialism and Constructionism; Feminism; Feminism, First, Second, and Third Waves; Feminist Standpoint Theory; Gender, the Body and; Scientific Knowledge, Sociology of; Sex and Gender; Social Epistemology; Strong Objectivity; Women in Science

REFERENCES AND SUGGESTED READINGS

Anderson, E. (2004) Uses of Value Judgements in Science: A General Argument, with Lessons from a Case Study of Feminist Research on Divorce. In: Nelson, H. L. & Wylie, A. (Eds.), Feminist Science Studies Special Issue. *Hypatia* 19(1): 1–24.

Clough, S. (2004) Having It All: Naturalized Normativity in Feminist Science Studies. In: Nelson, H. L. & Wylie, A. (Eds.), Feminist Science Studies Special Issue. *Hypatia* 19(1): 102–18.

Fausto-Sterling, A. (2000) *Sexing the Body: Gender Politics and the Construction of Sexuality*. Basic Books, New York.

Fox Keller, E. (1984) *Reflections on Gender and Science*. Yale University Press, New Haven.

Gilligan, C. (1984) *In a Different Voice*. Harvard University Press, Cambridge, MA.

Haraway, D. (1991) Situated Knowledges: The Science Question in Feminism and the Privilege of Partial Perspectives. In: *Simians, Cyborgs and Women*. Routledge, New York.

Harding, S. (1986) *The Science Question in Feminism*. Cornell University Press, Ithaca, NY.

Harding, S. (1991) *Whose Science? Whose Knowledge? Thinking from Women's Lives*. Cornell University Press, Ithaca, NY.

Hartsock, N. (1983) The Feminist Standpoint: Developing the Ground for a Specifically Feminist Historical Materialism. In: Harding, S. & Hintikka, M. B. (Eds.), *Discovering Reality: Feminist Perspectives on Epistemology, Methodology, Metaphysics and Philosophy of Science*, 2nd edn. Kluwer Academic Publishers, Dordrecht.

Hill Collins, P. (1999) *Black Feminist Thought: Knowledge, Consciousness and the Politics of Empowerment*. Routledge, New York.

Longino, H. (1990) *Science as Social Knowledge*. Princeton University Press, Princeton.

Nelson, H. L. (1990) *Who Knows: From Quine to a Feminist Empiricism*. Temple University Press, Philadelphia.

Nelson, H. L. & Wylie, A. (Eds.) (2004) Feminist Science Studies Special Issue. *Hypatia* 19(1).

New, C. (1998) Realism, Deconstruction and the Feminist Standpoint. *Journal for the Theory of Social Behaviour* 28: 4.

Oudshoorn, N. (1994) *Beyond the Natural Body: An Archaeology of Sex Hormones*. Routledge, New York.

Rose, H. (1983) Hand, Brain and Heart: A Feminist Epistemology for the Natural Sciences. *Signs: Journal of Women in Culture and Society* 9(1): 73–90.

Ruddick, S. (1990) *Maternal Thinking: Towards a Politics of Peace.* Women's Press, London.

Shiebinger, L. (1999) *Has Feminism Changed Science?* Harvard University Press, Cambridge, MA.

feminist activism in Latin America

Julie Shayne

Feminism has a variety of meanings. According to Nikki Craske, despite the often-heated debates about the meaning of feminism, most would likely concur with Rosalind Delmar's assessment that feminism attempts to transform women from object to subject, specifically with respect to knowledge. In other words, feminism and by extension feminist activism is about centering the lives of women. Sonia Alvarez (1990), another leading scholar of Latin American feminisms, defines an act as feminist if it strives to transform social roles assigned to women while simultaneously challenging gender power arrangements, and advancing claims for women's rights to equality and personal autonomy.

From Julie Shayne's research about the relationship between revolutionary and feminist mobilization she argues that in Latin America feminism is most accurately defined as "revolutionary feminism." For Shayne, a revolutionary feminist movement is one born of revolutionary mobilization. Ideologically revolutionary feminists are committed to challenging sexism as inseparable from larger political institutions not explicitly perceived as patriarchal but entirely bound to the oppression of women. Or in the words of Salvadoran feminist activist Gloria Guzman, feminism is:

a political struggle for the eradication ... of women's subordination. It is a proposal for a change in the relations of power between people, men over women, and the relations of power expressed in the different realms of life. We [Salvadoran feminists] believe that it is a

political struggle that will take us specifically to new kinds of relations, economic as well as relationships of power between men and women. (Shayne 2004: 53)

HISTORY OF FEMINISM

One of the most thorough historical overviews of women, politics, and feminism in Latin America is Francesca Miller's *Latin American Women and the Search for Social Justice* (1991). Miller (and countless others) argues that, contrary to what many male leftists purport, feminism is not a western import into the region, but rather, an ideology that has emerged over the last century.

In the latter half of the nineteenth century, feminists were concerned with three specific issues: gaining women's suffrage, protective labor laws, and access to education. By the early twentieth century, the organization of International Feminist Congresses began with its first meeting in Argentina in 1910. Many of the attendees were members of women's groups and political parties, namely socialist or anarchist parties. Central to the congress was the theme of equality between men and women. A second congress then happened in Mexico in 1916, with several national ones following throughout the next 20 years addressing issues specific to women of different countries (e.g., the issue of race was quite important to Peruvian women).

Miller argues that the typical division of first and second wave feminism as applied to the US context does not entirely fit in Latin America. She suggests that the main reason for this is due to the fact that while first wave feminists in the US were successful in their campaigns to secure the right to vote (as evidenced in the passage of the 19th Amendment in 1920), parallel goals of Latin American and Caribbean women were not, thus necessitating ongoing mobilization. While women in some countries in the region earned the right to vote not long after women in the US (e.g., Ecuador in 1929), others would not obtain it until the mid-1960s (Belize 1964). In other words, if the end of first wave feminism is marked by women gaining the right to vote, then in Latin America first wave feminism did not end until the 1960s. However, even prior to the region's women gaining collective suffrage, feminist mobilization was percolating in the context of non-gendered liberation struggles.

WHAT CAUSES THE EMERGENCE OF FEMINIST MOVEMENTS?

Beyond understanding the meaning of feminism, scholars have also spent time analyzing how feminism has emerged in the region. In the 1970s and 1980s both violent and nonviolent revolutionary upheaval consumed the region. Despite many obstacles, women participated in these revolutionary movements in varying capacities (Jaquette 1973; Lobao 1990; Randall 1994; Kampwirth 2002; Shayne 2004). There is a fairly solid consensus among academics and activists that women's participation in leftist movements has been one of the central reasons for the development of Latin American feminisms. Recently, Kampwirth (2004) and Shayne (2004) have expanded the discussion through their combined analyses of Chiapas, Mexico, Chile, El Salvador, and Nicaragua.

Shayne (2004) proposes a model for the development of feminist organizations in the region. Drawing on the positive cases of El Salvador and Chile, she argues that five factors need to converge during and after a revolutionary struggle to lead to the emergence of what she calls "revolutionary feminism." First, women's experiences in revolutionary movements need to have presented permanent challenges to status-quo understandings of gendered behavior and roles, or, gender-bending. Second, women need to have acquired logistical training vis-à-vis their experiences in revolutionary movements. Third, a political opening of some sort needs to be available in the aftermath of a revolutionary struggle to provide the opportunity for feminists to organize. Fourth, women revolutionaries need to find themselves with many of their basic needs unmet by their revolutionary movements. Fifth, a collective feminist consciousness needs to emerge in order for feminists to have the will to organize.

WHAT ISSUES ARE IMPORTANT TO FEMINISTS?

Once such movements arise, upon what sorts of issues do women focus their collective attention? According to Peruvian feminist Virginia Vargas (1992), post-suffrage feminism in Latin America was organized around three streams: the feminist stream, the stream of women in political parties, and the stream of women from the popular classes. Some of the issues of greatest concern to feminist organizations are voluntary maternity/responsible paternity, divorce law reform, equal pay, personal autonomy, and challenging the consistently negative and sexist portrayal of women in the media. For some women, the primary agenda lies in the goal of increasing women's access to formal political representation, whereas women of the popular classes tend to focus their agendas on issues of economic survival and racial and ethnic justice. In other words, just as women in the region are a diverse group, so too are their feminist goals.

Though many organizations had only short lifespans, attention to the issues did not necessarily fade away with the dissolution of organizations. The Salvadoran women's *Asociación de Madres Demandantes* (Association of Mothers Seeking Child Support) and Cuban women's *Colectivo Magín* are two such examples (*Magín* means intelligence, inspiration, and imagination in Castilian). The *Madres Demandantes* was a grassroots feminist organization in El Salvador in the mid-to-late 1990s. It worked with feminists inside the Legislative Assembly to pass a series of laws, which mandated that politicians would be unable to assume office if they could not verify that they were up to date on their child support payments. Though the organization eventually disbanded, the laws themselves remain on the books and the issue of responsible paternity, voluntary motherhood, and (implicitly) legal access to safe abortion have influenced the direction of feminism in that country.

Another very challenging issue that Latin American feminists have sought to organize around is the negative portrayal of women in various media outlets, including television, school textbooks, and the like. The Cuban organization *Colectivo Magín* took as its primary goal to challenge this negative portrayal. The organization was rather short lived (1993–96), as the Cuban Communist Party eventually decided its efforts needed to be thwarted. Despite its deactivation, the conversation about the negative portrayal of women in the media as related to the subsequent negative self-image internalized by Cuban women has remained a topic of feminist conversations, isolated though they may be.

ARE ALL POLITICALLY AND SOCIALLY ACTIVE WOMEN FEMINISTS?

Related to the emergence of post-suffrage feminist activism in the region are political and social organizations of women, which have non-feminist agendas, sometimes quite explicitly. Examples include the Federation of Cuban Women (FMC), the various committees of the Mothers of the Disappeared that continue to exist throughout the region, collective soup kitchens, and women's commissions of labor unions and leftist political parties. Such organizations have focused on issues like those listed above. However, more often than not, their actions are articulated in very non-feminist terms.

Because women have played roles in various social and political organizations the tendency is to assume that all politically active women are feminists. However, in Latin America this is not always the case. Though there are many examples of this, perhaps the most illustrative are the Committees of the Mothers of the Disappeared that spread throughout the region during the dictatorships of the 1970s and 1980s. The women who organized their committees did so as mothers, wives, grandmothers, sisters, daughters, etc. of the "disappeared" men in their lives; they were in no way making a feminist statement. Rather, their efforts lay firmly in a human rights agenda which called for the end of dictatorships and their tactics of summary torture, kidnapping, and incarceration. In most cases the women demonstrated a political strength formidable enough to in part be responsible for the dissolution of the dictatorships in the region. Regardless of their strength, their goals were entirely separate from feminism. However, despite their lack of attention to feminist agendas, the women in these organizations did offer a model for women's mobilization that in some cases was mimicked by feminist organizations.

The distinction between women's activism and feminist activism is not necessarily articulated, but rather implicit. Maxine Molyneux coined this distinction "practical" (feminine) versus "strategic" (feminist) demands. Molyneux's (1985) classic article argues that a distinction exists between women organizing to meet basic needs which are the result of a patriarchal division of labor and those explicitly organizing to counter systems of patriarchy responsible for such a division. For example, a practical need would be a daycare center. The patriarchal division of labor mandates that women are the caretakers of children and thus institutionalized assistance with childcare would ease this burden. On the other hand, a strategic demand would be that of voluntary motherhood, or access to free and safe abortion. Implicit in this demand is a challenge to the patriarchal division of labor that positions women as caretakers of children and reframes it to argue that women should first be able to decide if they want to be mothers. This later political statement, from Molyneux's perspective, is feminist, whereas the former is not.

HOW HAVE WOMEN COORDINATED THEIR EFFORTS?

In addition to the national developments in Latin American countries that played a part in the evolution of feminism, regional and transnational events have also proved central to the emergence of the ideologies and movements. The most concrete example of regional and transnational influences are the Latin American and Caribbean feminist *Encuentros* (Encounters), which began in 1981 in response to the United Nations declaring 1975–85 the Decade of the Woman. The five meetings of the first decade of the *Encuentros* (1981–90) addressed questions related to the relationship between feminist movements and male leftists, and eventually between feminists and non-feminist women activists. Central to these debates was the issue of feminist autonomy. It was during this period that revolutionary upheaval was fundamental to the political backdrop in the region, as was evidenced by the debates occurring among the feminists.

As the violence in the region subsided and the transitions to democracy began, the debates that faced feminists changed significantly. Of central concern to the delegates at the 1993, 1996, and 1999 meetings were issues regarding local grassroots feminist efforts versus the increased institutionalization of feminist organizations resultant from what some have identified as hegemonic relationships between international non-governmental organizations and local feminist organizations. The final meeting in 2002 centered on feminist interpretations of globalization and its impact on the lives of women.

The meetings have varied in size, with the first and smallest one in Colombia with only 200 women in attendance, in contrast to the fifth meeting in Argentina where over 3,200 women were present. By now, nearly every country in the region has sent delegates at one point or another, but the demographic makeup still favors the wealthier, whiter, and Spanish-speaking segments of Latin America and the Caribbean.

HOW HAS THE RETURN OF CIVIL SOCIETY AFFECTED FEMINIST MOVEMENTS?

With the completion of the so-called transition to democracy in the region, feminist movements have changed significantly. Because military regimes and conflicts have more or less become a thing of the past, the place of civil society and formal politics are the social venues in which feminist battles are now played out. Furthermore, with the intensification of globalization, national and international non-governmental organizations are a permanent fixture in all aspects of politics. As a result, one manifestation of post-transition feminism is what Alvarez (1998) has dubbed the NGOization of feminist organizations.

Many feminist theorists argue that the transition to democracy in the region has virtually led to the demobilization of grassroots feminist organizations and their absorption by state-centered feminist entities (Waylen 1994; Friedman 1998). On the other hand, some scholars argue that feminist organizations have not demobilized, but taken on different forms to run parallel with the overall political and economic transformation in the region: neoliberalism.

For example, Franceschet (2003) (speaking to the case of Chile) argues that such institutionalization is not in and of itself the problem. She suggests that the National Women's Service in Chile (SERNAM), which basically functions as a ministry of women within the government, has provided an axis for the women's movement with respect to discourse and resources. She argues that the women's movement in Chile is indeed fragmented and heterogeneous, and SERNAM is fraught with problems. However, she maintains that its existence contributes to the strengthening of the movement by providing crucial resources, not the least of which is a discourse of women's rights that organizations can employ to mobilize their members. Though her research and findings speak specifically to the case of Chile, parallels certainly exist in other countries in the region, as so many had strong women's and feminist movements during the dictatorships that have since morphed with the onset of democracy.

CONCLUSIONS

The evolution of feminist mobilization in Latin America and the Caribbean is largely connected to national, regional, and global changes. When the region was consumed with militaristic regimes and civil wars, feminists and non-feminist women activists had a whole different set of issues to confront (e.g., revolutionary struggles for national liberation and the ongoing search for disappeared loved ones). As the struggles subsided (some more successful than others), women have found themselves in a variety of positions. A common trend has been the virtual dismissal of women's political contributions to their various leftist social movements that consumed the region in the 1970s and 1980s. This often-blatant ignoring of women's participation in many cases served to push women out of formal politics and to start their own autonomous feminist organizations. In other cases, women seized the opportunity provided by the emergence of civil society and new democratic structures to insert themselves into formal political structures that in many cases simply had never existed before. Some have argued that such shifts have resulted in the dissolution of previously vibrant feminist movements, while others interpret such changes in structure as inevitable and even empowering.

SEE ALSO: Collective Identity; Feminism; Gay and Lesbian Movement; Gender, Social Movements and; Materialist Feminisms; New Social Movement Theory; Political Opportunities; Radical Feminism; Sexual Cultures in Latin America; Third World and Postcolonial Feminisms/Subaltern; Transnational and Global Feminisms; Women's Movements

REFERENCES AND SUGGESTED READINGS

Alvarez, S. (1990) *Engendering Democracy in Brazil: Women's Movements in Transition Politics*. Princeton University Press, Princeton.

Alvarez, S. (1998) Latin American Feminisms "Go Global": Trends of the 1990s and Challenges for the New Millennium. In: Alvarez, S. E., Dagnino, E., & Escobar, A. (Eds.), *Cultures of Politics, Politics of Cultures: Re-visioning Latin American Social Movements*. Westview Press, Boulder, pp. 293–324.

Alvarez, S. E., Friedman, E., Beckman, E., Blackwell, M., Chinchilla, N. S., Lebon, N., Navaro, M., & and Ríos Tobar, M. (2003) Encountering Latin America and Caribbean Feminisms. *Signs: Journal of Women in Culture and Society* 28(2): 537–79.

Franceschet, S. (2003) "State Feminism" and Women's Movements: The Impact of Chile's Servicio Nacional de la Mujer on Women's Activism. *Latin American Research Review* 38(1): 9–40.

Friedman, E. J. (1998) Paradoxes of Gendered Political Opportunity in the Venezuelan Transition to Democracy. *Latin American Research Review* 33(3): 87–135.

Jaquette, J. S. (1973) Women in Revolutionary Movements in Latin America. *Journal of Marriage and the Family* 35(2): 344–54.

Kampwirth, K. (2002) *Women and Guerrilla Movements: Nicaragua, El Salvador, Chiapas, Cuba*. Pennsylvania State University Press, University Park.

Kampwirth, K. (2004) *Feminism and the Legacy of Revolution: Nicaragua, El Salvador, Chiapas*. Ohio University Press, Athens.

Lobao, L. (1990) Women in Revolutionary Movements: Changing Patterns of Latin American Guerrilla Struggle. In: West, G. & Blumberg, R. L. (Eds.), *Women and Social Protest*. Oxford University Press, Oxford, pp. 180–204.

Molyneux, M. (1985) Mobilization Without Emancipation? Women's Interests, the State, and Revolution in Nicaragua. *Feminist Studies* 11: 227–54.

Randall, M. (1994) *Sandino's Daughters Revisited: Feminism in Nicaragua*. Rutgers University Press, New Brunswick.

Shayne, J. (2004) *The Revolution Question: Feminisms in El Salvador, Chile, and Cuba*. Rutgers University Press, New Brunswick.

Sternbach, S. N., Navarro-Aranguren, M., Chuchryk, P., & Alvarez, S. E. (1992) Feminisms in Latin America: From Bogota to San Bernardo. In: Escobar, A. & Alvarez, S. E. (Eds.), *The Making of Social Movements in Latin America: Identity, Strategy, and Democracy*. Westview Press, Boulder, pp. 207–39.

Vargas, V. (1992) The Feminist Movement in Latin America: Between Hope and Disenchantment. *Development and Change* 23(3): 195–214.

Waylen, G. (1994) Women and Democratization: Conceptualizing Gender Relations in Transition Politics. *World Politics* 46(3): 327–54.

feminist anthropology

Helen Johnson

Feminism refers to the awareness of women's oppression and exploitation at work, in the home, and in society, as well as the conscious political action taken by women for progressive social and economic change toward equality and recognition of women's difference. Social anthropology has evolved from a dominant western discourse in which it explores cultural difference and uniqueness, while simultaneously seeking the similarities in human lived experiences. Feminist theoretical critiques entered social anthropology in the 1970s and are vital to ongoing theoretical and methodological developments. Feminist social anthropologists question many of the discipline's basic assumptions and have documented scholars' failure to fully explore the human experience due to the neglect of the organizing categories of "women" and "gender" as significant dimensions of social life.

The first wave of studies in the 1970s assumed universal sexual asymmetry through an assessment of the "global" subordination of women and thence tried to explain the situation from various theoretical perspectives. Critical archeologists also joined with feminist social anthropologists to charge that the role of women in human evolution had been ignored due to inherent male bias in scholarly work that privileged hunting over gathering. And, although social anthropology had included women in its empirical studies due to anthropology's traditional concern with kinship and marriage, it had not problematized the representation of women. Thus the new "anthropology of women" that began in the 1970s confronted the thorny difficulties of how women were represented in anthropological writings. The preliminary issue of male bias was seen as having three tiers: the bias imported by the anthropologist to the culture being studied; the subordination of women in most societies which is then communicated to the anthropologist, predominantly by men; and the bias in favor of men inherent in western culture (Moore 1988). Simply adding women to traditional social anthropology would not resolve the obstacle of the invisibility of women, as male bias would not simply disappear. In turn, the assumption that women could effectively study women via the "anthropology of women" was also erroneous because, while successful in making women visible and as the precursor to feminist social anthropology, "the anthropology of women" was more remedial than radical. Furthermore, female scholars could easily become marginalized within mainstream academic studies (Moore 1988). Indeed, fears of the marginalization of female scholars and of the anthropology of women were linked to the sociological category "the universal woman" that was in favor at that time. The category did not recognize that because images, attributes, activities, and appropriate behaviors are always culturally and historically specific, both the categories of "woman" and "man" need to be investigated in their given context, not assumed.

The second wave in the 1980s saw feminist social anthropologists move away from totalizing assumptions of gender asymmetry to present analyses of women's oppression from neo-Marxist perspectives. These argued that in societies prior to western invasion, gender relations were typically egalitarian because women and men participated equally in the processes of production. As a consequence, European subjugation of societies and the imposition of capitalist forms of production *created* women's inequality in formerly egalitarian societies.

Feminist social anthropology in the 1990s and onwards introduced poststructural analytical frameworks that considered how women in contemporary communities actively construct and encounter globalization through their lived experiences as consumer purchasers, users of technology, controllers of land, and negotiators of its produce. As a consequence, feminist critique in social anthropology will continue to be central to theoretical and methodological developments within the discipline. The contemporary basis for the feminist critique of social anthropology, which grew out of a specific concern with the neglect of women in the discipline, is no longer the study of "women," but the analysis of gender relations, and of gender as a structuring principle in all human societies (Moore 1988).

Hence, feminist social anthropology now studies gender, the interrelations between women and men, and the role of gender in structuring human societies, their histories, ideologies, economic systems, political structures, and development projects. It is currently accepted that it is impossible to pursue valuable social science without incorporating analyses of gender.

A key problem relating to the theoretical and political complexities of women concerns the issues of race and ethnocentric bias in favor of one's own culture. Social anthropology has a critical involvement with its colonial past and the power relationships that characterized the encounter between the researcher and the researched. While edited collections such as Buckley's (1997) presented the "voices" of Japanese feminism, the often ethnocentric bias of feminist social anthropology provided a springboard for critiques by scholars from "Asian" nation-states who questioned why they should establish further universals (re)presented through western experiences of modernity. Karim (1995) offered a critique of western concepts of power and their construction of gender hierarchies in Southeast Asian civilizations. She contended Southeast Asian civilizations derive theory and knowledge from concepts of bilateralism, that is, the need to maintain social relationships through rules of complementarity, similarity, and the application of mutual responsibility and cooperation, rather than western concepts of hierarchy, opposition, oppression, and force (Karim 1995: 16).

From a predominance of western viewpoints about women's lived experience yet anchored in subaltern social analyses, examinations of what may best encompass many Asian societies' gender relations were made, especially through their attempts to centralize the informal and private and to provide clearer insights into daily activities which concern gendered actors in culture. Karim argued that many women enact their human agency in "Asian" societies via the use of informal structures. She contends this practice is considered to be "proper" behavior. Hence, she proposes that women operate as strategic agents within socially accepted notions of custom, by non-cooperation, the strategic use of silence, leaving the household due to "overdue" visits to family, and discouraging open confrontation yet pressuring non-compliant peers and superiors through the use of "hostile harmony" (1995: 18). While similar strategies and informal structures can be found in western cultures, Karim argues that "proper" behavior in terms of discouraging open confrontation forms part of Southeast Asian people's behavior in public as well as domestic arenas and social interactions, whereas open confrontation in public arenas is more acceptable in the West and, between men, is condoned as strong-minded and/or purposive behavior (1995: 30).

Karim's (1981) early work on the belief system expressed by the Ma'Betisék of Selangor, Malaysia, in their relationship to plants and animals is concerned with the way in which ideas contained within a particular culture change from one situation to another. While drawing on Lévi-Strauss's structuralism in terms of "culture" being the product of/constituted by real and abstract phonemic differences, Karim formulates her own concept of structure by focusing on the underlying rules which guide changes in the contents of the ideology of a particular culture. Her analysis of women, culture, and the entwining of Malay

custom with Islam (Karim 1992), and her co-editing of a work that critiqued women, men, and the practice of ethnography, facilitated her work on the public social visibility of women in Southeast Asia (Karim 1995). She examined how their invisibility in formal politics or the great religions endorsed by the state has led to a questioning of the different valuations of power and prestige between women and men and the way that social intangibles such as patience, spirituality, and transference become sources of resistance and strength. She has also sought to examine the relationship between social sentiment and culture and society, and the relationship between individual emotions and social realities derived from collective sentiments, using Malay society as a basis for her research (Karim 1990). Her 1993 work is significant for its contributions to debates about how knowledge is made. She argued that it is no longer possible to separate clearly the researcher and the native into two neat categories as reflexive anthropology, generated by significant feminist social anthropology, has highlighted the ambiguous position of native scholars in anthropology and has promoted interest in western anthropologists doing research in their own societies. Further, the acquisition of knowledge about non-western cultures in a reflexive mode can help generate perspectives on humankind that are more balanced and humanitarian and can overcome generalizations that are implicitly racist. Karim, in particular, highlights the challenges of doing anthropology as a non-western anthropologist in cultures other than her own, but situated within her natal country.

Other female anthropologists have contributed to the discipline in similar yet varied ways. While Ong (1990) has examined the dynamic historical transformations of gender symbolism and gender relations wrought by massive changes in the political economy of the Southeast Asian region, Puri (1999) investigated the tensions of female bodies, desire, womanhood, and social class and the hegemonic codes that regulate the experiences and self-definitions of middle-class women's lives in the postcolonial nation-state of India. Her work links with that of Sunder Rajan (1993, 2001, 2003), who reconceptualizes the stereotyped subjectivity of "third world women" in essays that explore the representation of *sati*, wife-murder, and the gender issues surrounding the construction of the "new woman" stereotype in postcolonial India. Moreover, while appreciating Tharu and Lalitha's (1991) work as one of stupendous research, scholarship, and critical energy, Sunder Rajan notes they do not adequately theorize the category of "experience" within and across cultures, the legitimacy of the role of the subaltern/feminist historian and critic, nor the role of the "invention of tradition" in contemporary Indian society and politics.

Trinh (1989) incorporates postcolonial theory and modes of writing into her examinations of diaspora and displacement to question the normative stance of "male" as literary and theoretical producer of knowledge. Her work links to Mohanty's (Mohanty et al. 1991; Alexander & Mohanty 1997; Mohanty 2003) theories of how knowledge is made about women across cultures, particularly under the umbrella of "development," with Yoon's (1998) focus on women's potential roles in sustainable development, and Sen's (1998) critique of the stereotypic Asian working woman as a laborer on the multinational factory floor. The work of a range of feminist anthropologists in Japan also complicates debates about the diverse roles of women in the varied cultures in the region and critiques western standpoints that too simplistically categorize these as "Asian." Kondo's (1990) exceptional field research and subsequent theorizations about how Japanese women's subjectivity and identity are constructed in a work environment enduring the changes wrought by modernity are foundational to Iawo's (1994) research and to Fujimura-Fanselow and Kameda's (1995) edited collection, which analyses how the notion of "the Japanese woman" has changed across and through time.

Nagata (1984) has built on her work that analyzed the revitalization of Islam in Malaysia, its impact on the tightening of ethnic boundaries, and the definition of personal identity. She has examined the potential for ethnic, political, and institutional pluralism in Malaysia (Nagata 1975), and has lately focused on the process of nation-building in Malaysia, the role of Islam, and how it shapes the ways in which Malaysia is establishing a presence and image in the international community (Nagata 1997). In analyzing Malay women's veiling practices to explain how a symbol of dress takes on a local and global metaphor of anti-modernism among the educated classes, Nagata (1995) contends that conformity to symbols of resistance in economic, political, and ritual life does not necessarily denote powerlessness or domestication but an active reconstruction of the image of the person amidst a world where modernity is equated with progress and virtue, and government control of social change. She has criticized Karim's (1995) emphasis on the dress code of women in Malay Muslim sects as a metaphor of women's oppression in Muslim societies, which Karim has countered with her view that the imitation of "Arab" dress styles is alien to Malay culture.

The contributions of feminist anthropological scholars from a range of non-western cultures have been critical to the development of the discipline in the past decade. Throughout the 1990s feminist social anthropology confronted criticisms by indigenous and nonwestern scholars that it was defined by the concerns of white, middle-class western women who lacked understandings of race, class, and ethnicities in the constitution of social hierarchies. Contemporary feminist social anthropology acknowledged the validity of, and now works with, these challenges by paying attention to issues of international concern to women, experimenting in writing reflexive anthropology, and incorporating studies by non-western scholars into the intersections of gender and other relations of power. Nonetheless, non-western women's work is still marginalized or ignored within many western anthropological arenas, as are non-western scholars themselves. Cross-cultural research teams are potential ways forward, as the edited collections of the 1990s demonstrated in terms of bringing a range of viewpoints together from different cultural bases.

SEE ALSO: Anthropology, Cultural and Social: Early History; Culture; Culture, Gender and; Feminist Methodology; Gender Ideology and Gender Role Ideology; Knowledge; Multiracial Feminism; Social Change, Southeast Asia

REFERENCES AND SUGGESTED READINGS

Alexander, M. J. & Mohanty, C. T. (Eds.) (1997) *Feminist Genealogies, Colonial Legacies, Democratic Futures*. Routledge, New York.

Buckley, S. (1997) *Broken Silence: Voices of Japanese Feminism*. University of California Press, Berkeley.

Fujimura-Fanselow, K. & Kameda, A. (Eds.) (1995) *Japanese Women: New Feminist Perspectives on the Past, Present, and Future*. Feminist Press, New York.

Iawo, S. (1994) *The Japanese Woman: Traditional Image and Changing Reality*. Harvard University Press, Cambridge, MA.

Karim, W. J. (1981) *Ma'Betisék Concepts of Living Things*. Athlone, New Jersey.

Karim, W. J. (Ed.) (1990) *Emotions of Culture: A Malay Perspective*. New York, Oxford University Press.

Karim, W. J. (1992) *Women and Culture: Between Malay Adat and Islam*. Westview, Boulder, CO.

Karim, W. J. (1993) Epilogue: The "Nativized" Self and the "Native." In: Bell, D., Caplan, P., & Karim, W. J. (Eds.), *Gendered Fields: Women, Men, and Ethnography*. Routledge, London.

Karim, W. J. (Ed.) (1995) *"Male" and "Female" in Developing Southeast Asia*. Berg, Oxford.

Kondo, D. (1990) *Crafting Selves: Power, Gender, and Discourses of Identity in a Japanese Workplace*. University of Chicago Press, Chicago.

Mohanty, C. T. (2003) *Feminism Without Borders: Decolonizing Theory, Practicing Solidarity*. Duke University Press, Durham, NC.

Mohanty, C. T., Russo, A., & Torres, L. (Eds.) (1991) *Third World Women and the Politics of Feminism*. Indiana University Press, Bloomington.

Moore, H. (1988) *Feminism and Anthropology*. Polity Press, Cambridge.

Nagata, J. (1975) Perceptions of Social Inequality in Malaysia. *Contributions to Asian Studies – Pluralism in Malaysia: Myth and Reality* 7: 113–36.

Nagata, J. (1984) *The Reflowering of Malaysian Islam: Modern Religious Radicals and Their Roots*. University of British Columbia Press, Vancouver.

Nagata, J. (1995) Modern Malay Women and the Message of the Veil. In: Karim, W. J. (Ed.), *"Male" and "Female" in Developing Southeast Asia*. Berg, Oxford.

Nagata, J. (1997) Ethnonationalism versus Religious Transnationalism: Nation-Building and Islam in Malaysia. *Muslim World* 87(2): 129–48.

Ong, A. (1990) Japanese Factories, Malay Workers: Class and Sexual Metaphors in West Malaysia. In: *Power and Difference: Gender in Island Southeast Asia*. Stanford University Press, Stanford, pp. 385–422.

Puri, J. (1999) *Woman, Body, Desire in Post-Colonial India: Narratives of Gender and Sexuality*. Routledge, London.

Sen, K. (1998) Indonesian Women at Work: Reframing the Subject. In: Sen, K. & Stivens, M. (Eds.), *Gender and Power in Affluent Asia*. Routledge, London.

Sunder Rajan, R. (1993) *Real and Imagined Women: Gender, Culture, and Postcolonialism*. Routledge, London.

Sunder Rajan, R. (2001) *Signposts: Gender Issues in Post-Independence India*. Rutgers University Press, New Brunswick, NJ.

Sunder Rajan, R. (2003) *The Scandal of the State: Women, Law, Citizenship in Postcolonial India*. Duke University Press, Durham, NC.

Tharu, S. & Lalitha, K. (Eds.) (1991) *Women Writing in India*, Vol. 1. Oxford University Press, Delhi.

Trinh, M. (1989) *Women, Native, Other: Writing Postcoloniality and Feminism*. Indiana University Press, Bloomington and Indianapolis.

Yoon, S.-Y. (1998) Women and Sustainable Human Development: Values for a Healthy Planet. *Asian Journal of Women's Studies* 4(2).

feminist criminology

Angela M. Moe

Feminist criminology represents an effort by social scientists to center research, teaching, and activism around issues of gender and justice. Feminist criminology as a whole stands as a critique of the sexist nature of theorizing within the discipline of criminology. The history of this movement extends back to the 1960s when scholars began testing the application of traditional criminological theories and applying the philosophical tenets of the women's liberation movement (also known as the second-wave feminist movement) to female criminal offenders. Up until this time very little attention was given to women or girls in the justice system. Over the last four decades, feminist criminology has come to represent a conglomeration of conscientious efforts that focus on women and girls (and, to some extent, men and boys) in the justice system. The focus has extended beyond criminality to include the victimization of women and girls as well as women who work in criminal justice occupations. The intersections of race, ethnicity, social class, and sexual orientation with gender have also become significant to feminist criminological inquiries. A central tenet of such work, beyond theory development and empirical research, is activism (within both academe and the larger community).

The scant attention given to female offending prior to the 1960s produced distorted images premised largely on biological determinism. Genetic defects, stunted evolutionary development, chemical imbalances, particularly those arising from menstruation or menopause, and personality traits were all believed to play roles in causing women and girls to be predisposed to criminality. Such perspectives equated women's temperament and ability to control themselves strictly with their own bodily functions, excusing any need to consider social and structural components to their criminality.

Women and girls involved in the criminal justice system were necessarily deemed pathological or mentally ill, and their treatment in the justice system reflected such beliefs with heavy use of psychiatric hospitals and therapy, particularly for white women and women of middle- to upper-class standing. Because the belief was that proper social control and socialization could prevent them from yielding to their biological drives, the use of stereotypical gendered programming (e.g., sewing, cosmetology, childrearing) within correctional settings was also popular. The exception included poorer women, immigrant women, and women of color who were more often excluded from rehabilitative programming.

Even with the development of sociologically driven theories of crime during the early to mid-1900s, the social and structural components of female offending remained largely unexamined. The sociologically driven theories were predominantly created by scholars interested in the illegalities of men and boys; hence, theoretical development and empirical research were skewed toward explaining male criminality.

Beginning in the 1960s and correlating with the second-wave feminist movement as well as the influx of women in graduate education, social scientists, primarily but not exclusively women, began formally and openly critiquing the state of criminological theory, research, and

practice. Several of the individuals who led this charge came out of the critical criminological tradition, where they had critiqued the role of class and criminal justice operations. These individuals, who became known as the first feminist criminologists, recognized the gaps within the critical criminological framework when gender was excluded from analysis. Most theories at this time, while sociologically driven, still neglected women or girls. They were often assumed to apply equally to males and females despite being based almost solely on men's or male adolescents' behavior. This was especially problematic in light of the fact that gender as a variable holds enormous power to predict who is most likely to commit crime. Throughout the subsequent decades, attempts were made to apply these theories to women and girls. Overall, the findings suggested that such theories needed to be altered or disregarded as explanations of female criminality.

In the 1970s, scholars, particularly in the United States, started developing theories to explain female criminality specifically. Freda Adler's *Sisters in Crime* (1975) and Rita Simon's *Women and Crime* (1975) were not aimed explicitly at critiquing earlier individual-based theories or at applying previously developed sociologically based theories. Instead, both attempted to explain female criminality through an application of liberal feminism, arguing that greater emancipation for women would bring changes in the nature and frequency of female offending. While both works have been heavily critiqued, they did mark the first criminological studies explicitly focused on women, as well as the blending of feminism and criminology. Criminologists interested in either women's and girls' experiences in crime, or gender disparities in offending, began relying on various tenets of feminism (e.g., liberal, socialist, Marxist, radical, and later postmodernist) to understand these phenomena.

A plethora of feminist criminological research has been produced over the past four decades. Traditional criminological theories continue to be tested by feminist scholars as to their applicability to women and girls. Most of this research, termed feminist empiricism, continues to rely on the scientific (deductive) method, utilizing quantitative analyses on large datasets. A more recent trend has been the use of feminist epistemology and methodology as a foundation for research. Much of this type of work is done qualitatively within a grounded or exploratory framework. Of particular relevance is standpoint epistemology wherein the contributions to research inquiries by members of socially, historically, or economically marginalized groups are privileged above the contributions of members of more privileged groups. The study of women and girls has fit well within this framework given their marginalization in society, as well as within criminological research.

Most recently, feminist criminologists have employed postmodern perspectives in their work in order to address the essentialism that has plagued earlier research that attempted to develop succinct and generalizable explanations for all women's and girls' illegality. By questioning the ability of social research to find an absolute and objective truth, postmodernist feminist criminology has served as a reminder of the importance of producing scholarship that is mindful of the nuanced complexities of women's lives. Postmodernist feminist criminology has also informed masculinities research wherein the hegemonic notions of sexuality and gender performance have been analyzed within the context of male criminality.

Of particular relevance to both postmodernism and standpoint perspectives is the intersectionality within women's lives, without which it is assumed a researcher could only hope to understand a small aspect of an individual's decision-making and behavior. Attention to prior life experiences such as child maltreatment and intimate partner victimization, as well as to racism, ethnicity, culture, poverty, sexual orientation, age, and (dis)ability, have all become focal points in feminist theorizing about female criminality.

Feminist criminology has had an impact on victimology as well. The second-wave feminist movement is credited with focusing greater attention on female victimization, particularly rape and intimate partner assault. Feminist criminologists have addressed the power dynamics involved with (mostly male) violence against women and girls, as well as the structural components of such violence. For instance, by examining law enforcement and court responses to domestic violence, institutional inaction,

erroneous action, or complacency have been formally documented. Feminist criminologists have extended their academic work into social activism by becoming advocates for victims, serving, for example, as expert witnesses in rape cases. A focus on victimization has also helped lead to one of the current themes within feminist criminological research – that is, the link between victimization and criminal offending. Often termed pathways research, this line of inquiry has produced several new insights on the ways in which women's and girls' criminality is often linked to, if not a direct result of, prior victimization, often in the form of child abuse, sexual assault, and partner battering.

Finally, feminist criminology has addressed gender and the workplace, specifically women workers in criminal justice occupations. Studies have examined the working conditions and environment for women in criminal justice occupations within law enforcement, the court system, and the correctional system, all of which have been predominantly male occupations. Harassment, victimization, and discrimination have been documented throughout the hiring practices, training, and promotional practices of these occupations. Specific attention has focused on the enhanced discrimination and hostility encountered by women of color and lesbians within these working environments. Such work has also focused on women's positions in academe within departments of criminal justice, criminology, and sociology where women, particularly those who identify as feminists, have historically faced isolation, devaluation, and sometimes direct harassment and discrimination. Many of the first criminologists were also the first women in their departments; hence, the struggle to center criminological inquiry on women and girls has coincided with efforts to gain legitimacy within the workplace.

Feminist criminology will continue to have a significant presence within criminology. As more women and girls become involved in the criminal justice system and as greater interest abounds as to the nature of their offending, it is probable that existing and perhaps newly developed academic journals will seek feminist criminological research. Debate currently ensues as to the future of feminist criminology in relation to the discipline of criminology, however. Some scholars argue that feminist criminology ought to remain on the fringes of the discipline, where it can be given specific and concerted attention by researchers who are committed to blending academic inquiry with social justice and activism. Proponents of this perspective believe that specialized courses on gender and justice, and violence against women, are necessary in order to give the respective topics the amount of attention they deserve. They also argue that specialized journals provide critical forums for the highest-quality feminist work and that professional legitimization will come as feminist scholars and practitioners reach positions of authority. Others assert that purposely keeping feminist criminology on the fringe of the discipline only contributes to its relative isolation and devaluation within academe. Advocates of this perspective argue that legitimacy of feminist criminological work within the larger discipline of criminology will come only when it has been incorporated entirely into mainstream criminology such that all types of journals accept feminist-based work, all university and college courses include discussions of gender and feminist material, and feminist academics are as well recognized within the discipline as traditional criminologists.

SEE ALSO: Class and Crime; Criminology; Feminism; Feminism, First, Second, and Third Waves; Feminist Activism in Latin America; Feminist Methodology; Feminist Pedagogy; Gender, Deviance and; Gendered Organizations/Institutions; Inequality/Stratification, Gender; Intersectionality; Race and the Criminal Justice System; Victimization

REFERENCES AND SUGGESTED READINGS

Belknap, J. (2001) *The Invisible Woman: Gender, Crime, and Justice*, 2nd edn. Wadsworth, Belmont, CA.
Caulfield, S. & Wonders, N. (1994) Gender and Justice: Feminist Contributions to Criminology. In: Barak, G. (Ed.), *Varieties of Criminology: Readings from a Dynamic Discipline*. Praeger, Westport, CT, pp. 213–29.
Daly, K. & Chesney-Lind, M. (1988) Feminism and Criminology. *Justice Quarterly* 5: 497–538.
Edwards, A. R. (1989) Sex/Gender, Sexism and Criminal Justice: Some Theoretical Considerations. *International Journal of the Sociology of Law* 17: 165–84.
Flavin, J. (2001) Feminism for the Mainstream Criminologist: An Invitation. *Journal of Criminal Justice* 29: 271–85.
Jurik, N. C. (1999) Socialist Feminism, Criminology, and Social Justice. In: Arrigo, B. A. (Ed.), *Social Justice/Criminal Justice: The Maturation of Criminal Theory in Law, Crime, and Deviance*. West/Wadsworth, Belmont, CA, pp. 31–50.
Klein, D. (1995) The Etiology of Female Crime: A Review of the Literature. In: Price, B. R. & Sokoloff, N. J. (Eds.), *The Criminal Justice System and Women*, 2nd edn. McGraw-Hill, New York, pp. 30–53.
Leonard, E. (1995) Theoretical Criminology and Gender. In: Price, B. R. & Sokoloff, N. J. (Eds.), *The Criminal Justice System and Women*, 2nd edn. McGraw-Hill, New York, pp. 54–70.
Naffine, N. (1996) *Feminism and Criminology*. Temple University Press, Philadelphia.
Rafter, N. H. & Heidensohn, F. (Eds.) (1995) *International Feminist Perspectives in Criminology: Engendering a Discipline*. Open University Press, Buckingham.
Schram, P. J. & Koons-Witt, B. (2004) *Gendered (In)Justice: Theory and Practice in Feminist Criminology*. Waveland Press, Long Grove, IL.
Smart, C. (1995) *Law, Crime, and Sexuality: Essays in Feminism*. Sage, London.
Wonders, N. (1999) Postmodern Feminist Criminology and Social Justice. In: Arrigo, B. A. (Ed.), *Social Justice/Criminal Justice: The Maturation of Criminal Theory in Law, Crime, and Deviance*. West/Wadsworth, Belmont, CA, pp. 111–28.

feminist disability studies

Monica J. Casper and Heather Laine Talley

Feminist disability studies is an emergent interdisciplinary field of inquiry shaped by a productive yet tense dialogue between feminist studies and disability studies. It is framed as a collaborative enterprise between feminist studies, which highlights vectors through which social relations and bodies are gendered and sexed, and disability studies, which focuses on the ways socio-medico-legal discourses and practices construct impaired bodies as disabled (Thomson 2002). Both feminist studies and disability studies emerged out of twentieth-century political projects emphasizing social justice and collective action. Intellectually, both fields address questions about subject formation, power, bodies, subjugated knowledges, and normalization. Feminist disability studies is kin to and stands alongside other critical, identity-based scholarship aimed at social justice, including queer theory, critical race theory, gender studies, and ethnic studies.

Disability studies scholar Rosemarie Garland Thomson (1994) cites a 1986 essay by Nancy Mairs, "On Being a Cripple," as one possible inauguration of feminist disability studies, in that Mairs attends both to her disability and to her gender in critiquing "normal" culture and society. Yet delineating an origin story for this field is complicated, as a number of scholars studying the relationship among gender, bodies, illness, medicalization, body image, and deviance can also be read as having pursued versions of feminist disability studies without directly naming their work as such. For example, Susan Bordo's *Unbearable Weight* topic, methodology, and cultural critique, could certainly count as feminist disability studies, as could Anne Finger's *Past Due: A Story of Disability, Pregnancy, and Birth* (1990). Indeed, a current project of feminist disability studies is articulating the field's roots, theoretical concepts, methodologies, political aims, and topics (Thomson 2002; Rohrer 2005). Locating the history of the field and its intersections with other fields of inquiry is a vital component of implementing feminist disability studies as both scholarly endeavor and activist project.

Thomson (2002) criticizes disability studies scholars for either ignoring or failing to draw upon feminist studies, suggesting that there is a great deal of "wheel reinventing" going on. On the other hand, disability studies scholars, including many feminists, have criticized women's and gender studies for ignoring or excluding disability from research projects and syllabuses (DePauw 1996). Feminist disability studies attempts to bridge these gaps and elisions, bringing the insights of feminist scholarship to the study of disability and vice versa. This means that the ability/disability system

(Thomson 2002) is included among gender, race, sexuality, class, and other systems of power as a category of analysis. Like feminist theory, disability studies offers a more complex history and political analysis of bodies and embodiment than can be gained through less self-conscious sociological approaches. Feminist disability studies recognizes that disability, like gender, is a pervasive concept constructed by and embedded in all aspects of culture, including institutions, identities, practices, politics, and communities (Thomson 2002). Feminist disability studies deepens our understanding of intersectionality and the ways in which multiple systems and identities are mutually created and performed.

The fit between feminist and disability studies is a seemingly logical one, in that a gender-aware disability studies is transformed by and activates ongoing feminist conversations about body image, weight, beauty, embodiment, medicalization, illness, prenatal diagnosis, reproduction, pregnancy, sexuality, sport, mothering, and a host of other topics. Indeed, a major strategy of feminist theory and gender studies has been to frame women's bodies as "disabled," that is, as non-normative. Feminist theory has long attended to questions of normalcy and normalization and the troubling ways in which women's bodies are sculpted physically and conceptually in and through institutions and cultural practices. Gender is constructed and performed in large part through a repositioning of female bodies as the deviant opposite of the standard male. While men and male bodies are framed as normal, women are perceived always to be "throwing like a girl" (Young 1990) and subjugated accordingly. The female body, like the disabled body, never quite measures up and must be continually refashioned to fit social norms of beauty, fitness, and appropriate behavior. In its attention to normalization practices, feminist disability studies can be woven into extant theories of gender, culture, and disability.

The interjection of feminist approaches into disability studies opens up spaces for considering the uniquely gendered experiences of disability, specifically the lived experiences of disabled women and the experiences of women caregivers. This does not mean that feminist disability studies is about only disabled women.

But it does mean that if women's bodies are always framed as "monstrous," as feminist scholars have argued, then disabled women's bodies are doubly excluded from cultural conceptions of normalcy. By focusing on cultural representations and experiences of disabled women, feminist disability studies reaffirms that the normative assumptions surrounding the body are, in fact, deeply and consequentially gendered. While feminist disability studies need not erase or devalue the experiences of disabled men, it does acknowledge that disabled men are privileged in spite of their disabilities because of their status as gendered persons. Race and class further complicate hierarchies of illness and disability experiences and of informal health care.

While there are now many scholars working in the area of feminist disability studies, few have been more central to the self-conscious development of the field than Thomson (1994, 1997, 2002). As a scholar in feminist studies *and* disability studies, her integration and linkage of both fields provides a model for intersectional analysis in practice. It is widely acknowledged that we can no longer speak in monolithic terms, yet Thomson challenges scholars interested in gender and disability to consider specificity by distinguishing *feminist disability studies* from a generic feminist studies or disability studies approach. In doing so, she posits a legitimate insider's critique of each intellectual progenitor while also laying important groundwork for learning to speak across these fields.

Specifically, she argues that disability studies has failed to produce a gendered analysis of disability and that feminist studies has failed to take into account real experiences of disabled women despite a stated value of intersectional analyses. For example, Thomson contends that certain strains of feminism have posited a romantic version of the female body that emphasizes reproduction and motherhood in such a way that neglects or infantilizes disabled women. Thomson (2002) identifies four key trajectories and objects of analysis for feminist disability studies: representation, the body, identity, and activism. In outlining these disciplinary concepts for future work in feminist disability studies, Thomson's articulation of the field establishes feminist disability studies within the realm of the humanities.

Thomson's project and the work of other scholars illustrates that feminist disability studies is an emerging field. While few have explicitly identified their work as part of a feminist disability studies project, much work located in feminist studies and disability studies is compatible with the vision of feminist disability studies offered by Thomson. For example, feminist disability studies inherits from disability studies skepticism toward definitions of disability anchored in "deviant" bodies. Rather, the focus is on cultural narratives that define some bodies as non-normative, thereby subjugating and devaluing particular embodiments. Feminist disability studies is a critical enterprise in that the underlying project is to illustrate how gender and disability function to privilege certain bodies over others, resulting in differential social access and recognition by and within human communities. Scholarship that may be identified as feminist disability studies has relied largely on ethnographic methods. Yet, as an emergent field, the full range of methodological possibilities has yet to be identified.

Some examples of feminist disability studies in practice highlight both emergent contributions of the field and ongoing tensions between the field and its intellectual kin. A particularly compelling example is Gelya Frank's (2000) account of the life of Diane DeVries. The book, a cultural biography, offers Frank's personal narrative about her friend DeVries, a woman born without arms and legs. The women met at UCLA when Frank was 28 and DeVries 26, one a graduate student and the other a funny, irreverent undergraduate. *Venus on Wheels* presents DeVries as a quintessential American woman of the second half of the twentieth century, in personal language that never erases DeVries's identity at the expense of Frank's academic voice and methodological aims. De Vries, a disabled woman with guts and a sex life, is positioned as an exemplar for feminist and disability rights politics, challenging boundaries of gender and embodiment. Yet locating De Vries within both arenas – feminist studies and disability studies – highlights the ways in which neither field adequately accounts for her. She is instead an ideal model for feminist disability studies, and indeed Frank draws on her relationship with DeVries to interrogate cultural representations of women with disabilities.

Herndon (2002) builds on feminist theory and disability studies to analyze medical and social constructions of fatness as disability. She locates fatness within social, cultural, and political contexts, thereby undermining the notion that "fat" is strictly a biological category. In doing so, she shows that medicalization is not a useful tool for explaining the stigma associated with being fat – a stigma that especially affects women. While framing fatness as a disability in order to showcase the various politics animating it, Herndon also points to intense social resistance to such a construction of fatness. Herndon names this resistance as chronic reluctance to recognize fat as a social, rather than natural, category, reflecting society's aversion to according humanity, citizenship, and attendant benefits to fat people. She suggests that feminists express particular ambivalence about fatness, on the one hand wanting to politically resist "corporeal ultimatums" from the larger society and on the other hand, experiencing individual desires for a particular kind of acceptable body. Understood through a feminist disability studies perspective, fatness draws attention both to social fears of the non-normative as well as to feminism's inconsistencies, including aversion to certain body types.

Feminist disability studies broadens our understanding of reproductive technologies and politics, as well. Since the nineteenth-century platform of "voluntary motherhood" up to present ongoing struggles to preserve *Roe* v. *Wade*, the ability of women to make choices about their own bodies has been framed as central to the larger goal of securing women's liberation. Indeed, feminism has often defined reproductive choices as a litmus test of women's social and political agency. Questions of reproduction have also dominated disability studies, but disability studies has come to different conclusions. Disability studies situates the "right to choose" and related issues in a social and technological landscape wherein choice may mean deciding to abort a fetus identified as disabled. Disability studies adopts an essentially sociological perspective, asking which fetuses are mostly likely to be aborted? For disability studies, selective abortion regardless of its potential to preserve women's agency fundamentally interferes with the expression of disabled agency and embodiment.

Prenatal diagnosis, specifically, is revealed to be richly complicated when analyzed through a feminist disability studies lens. Medicalized notions of health and normalcy, along with women's fears and desires, have contributed to the ongoing expansion of diagnostic technologies and categories (Rapp 1999). The termination or birth of an affected fetus are polarized choices stemming from interpretation of the results of prenatal diagnosis. The proliferation of fetal treatments (Casper 1998) makes possible an additional, quite limited option: "fixing" an impaired fetus. Feminist disability studies draws our attention to the ways in which prenatal diagnosis is not only about expanding women's choices (a recognized feminist goal). It is also about normalcy, disability, and cultural intolerance of human variation.

Thomson (2002: 14–15) writes: "Preventing illness, suffering, and injury is a humane social objective. Eliminating the range of unacceptable and devalued bodily forms and functions the dominant order calls disability is, on the other hand, a eugenic undertaking." Feminist studies alone, in its attention to women's rights and bodily autonomy, often fails to recognize the implications of prenatal diagnosis with respect to disability and the lived experiences of people with impairments. Disability studies alone, in its attention to the eugenic implications of elimination of impaired bodies, often fails to consider the impact on women's autonomy of limitations on reproductive choice. Feminist disability studies highlights medicine's relentless focus on cure and/or elimination at the expense of collective health and well-being and also interrogates biases in feminist and disability scholarship.

As these examples illustrate, for feminist disability studies to be rooted in both feminism and disability studies and yet different from either feminism or disability studies, it must take into account the ways in which disability studies and feminist studies may be in conflict. From the perspective of feminism and disability studies, society disables and genders people in ways that yield consistent and disempowering effects. Yet, as critical intellectual enterprises with activist roots, feminism and disability studies are in tension over what each imagines as the practical implications of its theoretical perspectives. Both feminism and disability studies are interested in recovering agency lost through the hierarchical machinations of gender and disability. Each emphasizes the need for autonomy and choice for women and disabled people, respectively. A key project of feminist disability studies, then, is continually to work to disentangle conflicts and tensions between feminist agency and disabled agency, using the spaces and gaps between these productively and critically.

Feminist disability studies must also come to terms with its relationship to the academy, specifically to disciplines that may welcome feminist disability studies and simultaneously contribute to the methodological and theoretical underpinnings of the field. Feminist disability studies may find an institutional home and intellectual kinship in sociology, specifically in scholarship on the body and on differences. The project of sociology is denaturalization, in the sense that sociology is fundamentally about questioning the taken for granted. Feminist disability studies begins with the assumption that natural accounts of disability and of gender will always be inadequate for understanding people's experience. Both sociology and feminist disability studies work towards undermining or at least complicating essentialist notions of the body. Some strands of sociology, specifically symbolic interactionism and constructionism, are fundamentally concerned with how meaning is produced through social interaction, offering theoretical and analytic tools for feminist disability studies projects.

Sociology's emphasis on social structure and institutions may also contribute to feminist disability studies. As Thomson (2002) has noted, a core premise of feminist disability studies is that representation structures reality. Sociology has the tools to extend a reverse analysis revealing how social structures organize representations. In other words, a structural analysis illustrates how definitions of normalcy become embedded in social structures and thus reveals how disability is shaped on a macro level. As an activist enterprise, feminist disability studies must develop a multi-level analysis in order to address the complex processes through which oppressions emerge. Narratives of the body, bodily experience, and representation are important for developing a gendered understanding of disability, but so too are structural exclusion and institutional norms.

Feminist disability studies has employed "disability" as a catch-all to refer to bodies that are culturally identified as sick, impaired, ugly, deformed, or malfunctioning. One of the most valuable contributions of feminist disability studies is its emphasis on the importance of intersectionality. However, one question feminist disability studies must struggle with is the limitations of using "disability" in reference to widely varying bodily experiences. The deployment of disability as a universal category might be politically useful in its ability to unite large groups of people – particularly as biomedical technologies proliferate and challenge what it means to be human – and theoretically useful by highlighting the social processes underlying the identification of a variety of bodies, including those gendered female, as deviant. But there may be consequences of expanding conceptual categories of disability to include *all* non-normative bodies, for the details of a particular embodiment or impairment may be central to understanding lived experiences. For studies of difference to be fully engaged and relevant, feminist disability studies must resist generic analyses of intersectionality in favor of contextual analysis focused on specific permutations of embodied, gendered difference.

SEE ALSO: Abortion as a Social Problem; Body and Sexuality; Body and Society; Chronic Illness and Disability; Deviance; Disability as a Social Problem; Ethic of Care; Eugenics; Euthanasia; Families and Childhood Disabilities; Gender, the Body and; Genetic Engineering as a Social Problem; Illness Experience; New Reproductive Technologies; Sexual Citizenship; Stigma; Stratified Reproduction; Women's Movements

REFERENCES AND SUGGESTED READINGS

Bordo, S. (1993) *Unbearable Weight*. University of California Press, Berkeley.
Casper, M. J. (1998) *The Making of the Unborn Patient: A Social Anatomy of Fetal Surgery*. Rutgers University Press, New Brunswick, NJ.
DePauw, K. P. (1996) "Space: The Final Frontier": The Invisibility of Disability on the Landscape of Women's Studies. *Frontiers* 17(3): 19–23.

Fine, M. & Asch, A. (Eds.) (1988) *Women with Disabilities: Essays in Psychology, Culture, and Politics.* Temple University Press, Philadelphia.

Finger, A. (1990) *Past Due: A Story of Disability, Pregnancy, and Motherhood.* Seal Press, Seattle.

Frank, G. (2000) *Venus on Wheels: Two Decades of Dialogue on Disability, Biography, and Being Female in America.* University of California Press, Berkeley.

Hall, K. Q. (2002) Feminism, Disability, and Embodiment. *NWSA Journal* 14(3): vii–xiii.

Herndon, A. (2002) Disparate But Disabled: Fat Embodiment and Disability Studies. *NWSA Journal* 14(3): 120–37.

Hillyer, B. (1993) *Feminism and Disability.* University of Oklahoma Press, Norman.

Hubbard, R. (1990) *The Politics of Women's Biology.* Rutgers University Press, New Brunswick, NJ.

Mairs, N. (1986) On Being a Cripple. In: *Plaintext: Deciphering a Woman's Life.* University of Arizona Press, Tucson.

Mairs, N. (1996) *Waist High in the World: A Life Among the Nondisabled.* Beacon Press, Boston.

Prilleltensky, O. (2004) *Motherhood and Disability: Children and Choices.* Palgrave MacMillan, New York.

Rapp, R. (1999) *Testing Women, Testing the Fetus: The Social Impact of Amniocentesis.* Routledge, New York.

Rohrer, J. (2005) Toward a Full-Inclusion Feminism: A Feminist Deployment of Disability Analysis. *Feminist Studies* 31(1): 34–63.

Thomson, R. G. (1994) Redrawing the Boundaries of Feminist Disability Studies. *Feminist Studies* 20 (3): 583.

Thomson, R. G. (1997) *Extraordinary Bodies: Figuring Physical Disability in American Culture and Literature.* Columbia University Press, New York.

Thomson, R. G. (2002) Integrating Disability, Transforming Feminist Theory. *NWSA Journal* 14(3): 1–32.

Wendell, S. (1996) *The Rejected Body: Feminist Philosophical Reflections on Disability.* Routledge, London.

Young, I. M. (1990) *Throwing Like a Girl and Other Essays in Feminist Philosophy and Social Theory.* Indiana University Press, Bloomington.

feminist methodology

Nancy A. Naples

Feminist methodology is the approach to research that has been developed in response to concerns by feminist scholars about the limits of traditional methodology to capture the experiences of women and others who have been marginalized in academic research. Feminist methodology includes a wide range of methods, approaches, and research strategies. Beginning in the early 1970s, feminist scholars critiqued positivist scientific methods that reduced lived experiences to a series of disconnected variables that did not do justice to the complexities of social life. Feminists were also among the first scholars to highlight the marginalization of women of color in academic research and to offer research strategies that would counter this trend within academia (Baca Zinn 1979; Collins 1990). Feminist scholars also stress the importance of intersectional analysis, an approach that highlights the intersection of race, class, gender, and sexuality in examining women's lives (Crenshaw 1993). Some of the earliest writing on feminist methodology emphasized the connection between "feminist consciousness and feminist research," which is the subtitle of a 1983 edited collection by Stanley and Wise. Over the years, feminist methodology has developed a very broad vision of research practice that can be used to study a wide range of topics, to analyze both men's and women's lives, and to explore both local and transnational or global processes.

Feminist sociologists like Dorothy Smith (1987) pointed out that the taken-for-granted research practices associated with positivism rendered invisible or domesticated women's work as well as their everyday lives. She argued for a sociology for women that would begin in their everyday lives. Feminist philosopher Sandra Harding (1987, 1998) has also written extensively about the limits of positivism and argues for an approach to knowledge production that incorporates the point of view of feminist and postcolonial theoretical and political concerns. She stresses that traditional approaches to science fail to acknowledge how the social context and perspectives of those who generate the questions, conduct the research, and interpret the findings shape what counts as knowledge and how data is interpreted. Instead, she argues for a holistic approach that includes greater attention to the knowledge production process and to the role of the researcher. Harding and Smith both critique the androcentric nature of academic knowledge production. They argue for the importance of starting analysis from the lived experiences and activities of women and others who have been left out of the knowledge production process rather than start inquiry with the abstract categories and a priori assumptions of traditional academic disciplines or dominant social institutions.

In 1991, sociologists Mary Margaret Fonow and Judith A. Cook published a collection of essays in a book titled *Beyond Methodology: Feminist Scholarship as Lived Research*. The authors in this collection discussed how different methodological techniques could be used to capture the complexities of gender as it intersects with race, sexuality, and class. The authors also explored the ethical dilemmas faced by feminist researchers, such as: How does a researcher negotiate power imbalance between the researcher and researched? What responsibilities do researchers have to those they study? How does participatory research influence analytic choices during a research study? Feminist scholars have consistently raised such questions, suggesting that if researchers fail to explore how their personal, professional, and structural positions frame social scientific investigations, researchers inevitably reproduce dominant gender, race, and class biases (see Naples 2003).

Fonow and Cook (2005) revisited the themes that were prevalent when they wrote *Beyond Methodology* and highlighted the continuity and differences in the themes that dominate discussions of feminist methodology at the beginning of the twenty-first century. They found that the concerns about reflexivity of the researcher, transparency of the research process, and women's empowerment remained central concerns in contemporary feminist methodology. They also point out the continuity in the multiple methods that are utilized by feminist researchers, which include participatory research, ethnography, discourse analysis, comparative case study, cross-culture analysis, conversation analysis, oral history, participant observation, and personal narrative. However, they note that contemporary feminist researchers are more likely to use sophisticated quantitative methods than they were in the 1980s and 1990s.

Another important text that provides an overview of feminist methods in the social sciences is that of Reinharz (1992). Following a comprehensive review of feminist methods with illustrations from diverse feminist studies, Reinharz identifies ten features that appear in efforts by feminist scholars to distinguish how their research methods differ from traditional approaches. These include the following: (1) feminism is a point of view, not a particular method; (2) feminist methodology consists of multiple methods; (3) feminist researchers offer a self-reflective understanding of their role in the research; and (4) a central goal of feminist research is to contribute to social changes that would improve women's lives. The themes of reflexivity and research for social change are two of the most important aspects of feminist methodology that distinguishes it from other modes of research.

REFLEXIVITY

Reflective practice and reflexivity include an array of strategies that begin when one first considers conducting a research project. Reflective practices can be employed throughout the research process and implemented on different levels, ranging from remaining sensitive to the perspectives of others and how we interact with them, to a deeper recognition of the power dynamics that infuse ethnographic encounters. By adopting reflective strategies, feminist researchers work to reveal the inequalities and processes of domination that shape the research process. Wolf (1996) emphasizes that power is evident in the research process in three ways: first, the differences in power between the researcher and those she or he researches in terms of race, class, nationality, among other dimensions; second, the power to define the relationship and the potential to exploit those who are the subjects of the research; and third, the power to construct the written account and therefore shape how research subjects are represented in the text. Feminist researchers argue that dynamics of power influence how problems are defined, which knowers are identified and are given credibility, how interactions are interpreted, and how ethnographic narratives are constructed. Feminist researchers stress that if researchers fail to explore how their personal, professional, and structural positions frame social scientific investigations, researchers inevitably reproduce dominant gender, race, and class biases.

Harding (1987) argues for a self-reflexive approach to theorizing in order to foreground how relations of power may be shaping the production of knowledge in different contexts. The point of view of all those involved in the knowledge production process must be acknowledged and taken into account in order to produce what she terms "strong objectivity," an approach to objectivity that contrasts with weaker and unreflective positivist approaches. In this way, knowledge production should involve a collective process, rather than the individualistic, top-down, and distanced approach that typifies the traditional scientific method. For Harding, strong objectivity involves analysis of the relationship between both the subject and object of inquiry. This approach contrasts with traditional scientific method that either denies this relationship or seeks to achieve control over it. However, as Harding and other feminist theorists point out, an approach to research that produces a more objective approach acknowledges the partial and situated nature of all knowledge production (see Collins 1990). Although not a complete solution to challenging inequalities in the research process, feminist researchers have used reflective strategies effectively to become aware of, and diminish the ways in which, domination and repression are reproduced in the course of their research and in the products of this work. Furthermore, feminist researchers argue, sustained attention to these dynamics can enrich research accounts as well as improve the practice of social research (Naples 2003).

Feminist ethnography and feminist work with narratives are two of the methods in which feminist researchers have been the most concerned with processes of reflexivity. Examining work that utilizes both of these methods, the range of approaches that count as feminist is especially evident. For example, Chase's (1995) approach to oral narratives includes attention to the way women narrate their stories. Rather than treat the narratives as "evidence" in an unmediated sense of the term, Chase is interested in exploring the relationship between culture, experience, and narrative. Her work on women school superintendents examines how women use narrative strategies to make sense of their everyday life experiences as shaped by different cultural contexts. In contrast, Bloom (1998) adopts a "progressive-regressive method" derived from Sartre's notion of "spirals" in a life to examine how the individual can overcome her or his social and cultural conditioning, "thereby manifesting what he calls 'positive praxis.'" Drawing on Dorothy Smith's institutional ethnographic method, DeVault (1999) utilizes narratives she generates from ethnographic interviews to explore how relations of ruling are woven into women's everyday lives such that they are hidden from the view of those whose lives are organized by these processes of domination. The institutional and political knowledges that DeVault uncovers illustrate the link between institutional ethnography and feminist activism. In the context of activist research, feminist analysts using Smith's approach explore the institutional forms and procedures, informal organizational processes, as well as discursive frames used to construct the goals and targets of the work that the institution performs. This approach ensures that a commitment to the political goals of the women's movement remains central to feminist research by foregrounding how ruling relations work to organize everyday life. With a "thick" understanding of "how things are put together" it becomes possible to identify effective activist interventions.

POSTCOLONIAL AND POSTMODERN CHALLENGES

The call for reflective practice has also been informed by the critiques of third world and postcolonial feminist theorists who argue for self-reflexive understanding of the epistemological investments that shape the politics of method (Alexander & Mohanty 1997). Postmodern and postcolonial critiques of the practice of social scientific research raise a number of dilemmas that challenge feminist researchers as they attempt to conduct research that makes self-evident the assumptions and politics involved in the process of knowledge production in order to avoid exploitative research practices. Postmodern feminist scholars emphasize the ways disciplinary discourses shape how researchers see the worlds they investigate. They point out that without recognition of disciplinary metanarratives, research operates to reinsert power relations, rather than challenge them. Many feminist researchers have grappled with the challenges posed by postmodern critics. Wolf (1996) explains that for some feminist scholars postmodern theories provide opportunities for innovation in research practices, particularly in the attention they pay to representation of research participants or research subjects and to the written products that are produced from a research study. However, many other feminist scholars are concerned that too much emphasis on the linguistic and textual constructions decenters those who are the subjects of our research and renders the lives of women or others whom we study irrelevant.

Postmodern analyses of power have destabilized the practice of research, especially research that involves human subjects. If power infects every encounter and if discourse infuses all expressions of personal experience, what can the researcher do to counter such powerful forces? This dilemma is at the heart of a radical postmodern challenge to social scientific practice in general, but has been taken up most seriously in feminist research. Naples (2003) argues that one partial solution to this dilemma is to foreground praxis, namely, to generate a materialist feminist approach informed by postmodern and postcolonial analyses of knowledge, power, and language that speaks to the empirical world in which one's research takes place. For example, in her work, by foregrounding the everyday world of poor women of different racial and ethnic backgrounds in both the rural and urban US and by exploring the governing practices that shape their lives, she has worked to build a class conscious and anti-racist methodological approach (see also Alexander & Mohanty 1997).

While postmodern and postcolonial feminist scholars point to the myriad ways relations of domination infuse feminist research, they also offer some guidance for negotiating power inherent in the practice of fieldwork. For example, Mohanty (1991) calls for "focused, local

analyses" to counter the trend in feminist scholarship to distance from or misrepresent third world women's concerns. Alexander and Mohanty (1997) recommend "grounding analyses in particular, local feminist praxis" as well as understanding "the local in relation to larger, cross-national processes."

RESEARCH FOR SOCIAL CHANGE

A consistent goal expressed by those who adopt feminist methodology is to create knowledge for social-change purposes. The emphasis on social action has influenced the type of methods utilized by feminist researchers as well as the topics chosen for study. For example, feminists have utilized participatory action research to help empower subjects of research as well as to ensure that the research is responsive to the needs of specific communities or to social movements (Reinharz 1992; Naples 2003; Fonow & Cook 2005). This approach to research is also designed to diminish the power differentials between the researcher and those who are the subjects of the research. In an effort to democratize the research process, many activist researchers argue for adopting participatory strategies that involve community residents or other participants in the design, implementation, and analysis of the research. Collaborative writing also broadens the perspectives represented in the final product.

A wide array of research strategies and cultural products can serve this goal. Yet such strategies and cultural products can be of more or less immediate use for specific activist agendas. For example, activist research includes chronicling the history of activists, activist art, diverse community actions, and social movements. Such analyses are often conducted after the completion of a specific struggle or examine a wide range of different campaigns and activist organizations. This form of research on activism is extremely important for feminists working toward a broadened political vision of women's activism and can help generate new strategies for coalition-building. However, these studies may not answer specific questions activists have about the value of certain strategies for their particular political struggles. Yet these broad-based feminist historical and sociological analyses do shed new light on processes of politicization, diversity, and continuity in political struggles over time.

On the one hand, many activists could be critical of these apparently more "academic" constructions of activism, especially since the need for specific knowledges to support activist agendas frequently goes unmet. The texts in which such analyses appear are often not widely available and further create a division between feminists located within the academy and community-based activists. On the other hand, many activist scholars have developed linkages with activists and policy arenas in such a way as to effectively bridge the so-called activist/ scholar divide. Ronnie Steinberg brought her sociological research skills to campaigns for comparable worth and pay equity. She reports on the moderate success of the movement for comparable worth and the significance of careful statistical analyses for supporting changes in pay and job classifications. As one highlight, she reports that in 1991 systematic standards for assessing job equity developed with her associate Lois Haignere were translated into guidelines for gender-neutral policies incorporated by the Ontario Pay Equity Tribunal. In another example of feminist activist research, Roberta Spalter-Roth and Heidi Hartmann testified before Congress and produced policy briefs as well as more detailed academic articles to disseminate their findings about low-income women's economic survival strategies. Measures of a rigid positivism are often used to undermine feminists' credibility in legal and legislative settings. Even more problematic, research generated for specific activist goals may be misappropriated by those who do not share feminist political perspectives to support anti-feminist aims. For example, proponents of "workfare" programs for women on public assistance could also use Spalter-Roth and Hartmann's analysis of welfare recipients' income-packaging strategies to further justify coercive "welfare to work" measures.

Some feminist scholars working directly in local community actions have also brought their academic skills to bear on specific community problems or have trained community members to conduct feminist activist research. Terry Haywoode (1991) worked as an educator and community organizer alongside women in her Brooklyn community and helped establish the National Congress of Neighborhood Women's (NCNW) college program, a unique community-based program in which local residents can earn a two-year Associates degree in neighborhood studies. By promoting women's educational growth and development within an activist community organization, NCNW's college program helped enhance working-class women's political efficacy in struggles to improve their neighborhood.

CONCLUSION

Feminist methodology was developed in the context of diverse struggles against hegemonic modes of knowledge production that render women's lives, and those of other marginal groups, invisible or dispensable. Within the social sciences, feminist researchers have raised questions about the separation of theory and method, the gendered biases inherent in positivism, and the hierarchies that limit who can be considered the most appropriate producers of theoretical knowledge. Feminist reconceptualizations of knowledge production processes have contributed to a shift in research practices in many disciplines, and require more diverse methodological and self-reflective skills than traditional methodological approaches. However, some feminist scholars question whether or not it is possible to develop a reflexive practice that can fully attend to all the different manifestations of power (Stacey 1991). However, since feminist methodology is open to critique and responsive to the changing dynamics of power that shape women's lives and those of others who have been traditionally marginalized within academia, feminist researchers often act as innovators who are quick to develop new research approaches and frameworks.

SEE ALSO: Black Feminist Thought; Consciousness Raising; Feminist Standpoint Theory; Intersectionality; Matrix of Domination; Methodology; Outsider-Within; Strong Objectivity; Third World and Postcolonial Feminisms/ Subaltern

REFERENCES AND SUGGESTED READINGS

Alexander, M. J. & Mohanty, C. T. (1997) Introduction: Genealogies, Legacies, Movements. In: *Feminist Genealogies, Colonial Legacies, Democratic Futures*. Routledge, New York, pp. xiii–xlii.

Baca Zinn, M. (1979) Field Research in Minority Communities: Ethical, Methodological, and Political Observations by an Insider. *Social Problems* 27: 209–19.

Bloom, L. R. (1998) *Under the Sign of Hope: Feminist Methodology and Narrative Interpretation*. State University of New York Press, Albany.

Chase, S. E. (1995) *Ambiguous Empowerment: The Work Narratives of Women School Superintendents*. University of Massachusetts Press, Amherst.

Collins, P. H. (1990) *Black Feminist Thought: Knowledge, Consciousness, and the Politics of Empowerment*. Unwin Hyman, Boston.

Crenshaw, K. (1993) Mapping the Margins: Intersectionality, Identity Politics, and Violence against Women of Color. *Stanford Law Review* 43: 1241–99.

DeVault, M. (1999) *Liberating Method: Feminism and Social Research*. Temple University Press, Philadelphia.

Fonow, M. M. & Cook, J. A. (Eds.) (1991) *Beyond Methodology: Feminist Scholarship as Lived Research*. Indiana University Press, Bloomington.

Fonow, M. M. & Cook, J. A. (2005) Feminist Methodology: New Applications in the Academy and Public Policy. *Signs: Journal of Women in Culture and Society* 30(4): 221–36.

Harding, S. P. (Ed.) (1987) *Feminism and Methodology*. Indiana University Press, Bloomington.

Harding, S. P. (1998) *Is Science Multicultural? Postcolonialisms, Feminisms, and Epistemologies*. Indiana University Press, Bloomington.

Haywoode, T. (1991) Working Class Feminism: Creating a Politics of Community, Connection, and Concern. PhD dissertation, City University of New York.

Mohanty, C. T. (1991) Under Western Eyes: Feminist Scholarship and Colonial Discourses. In: Mohanty, C. T., Russo, A., & Torres, L. (Eds.), *Third World Women and the Politics of Feminism*. Indiana University Press, Bloomington, pp. 51–80.

Naples, N. A. (2003) *Feminism and Method: Ethnography, Discourse Analysis, and Activist Research*. Routledge, New York.

Reinharz, S. (1992) *Feminist Methods in Social Research*. Oxford University Press, New York.

Smith, D. E. (1987) *The Everyday World as Problematic: A Feminist Sociology*. University of Toronto Press, Toronto.

Spalter-Roth, R., Hartmann, H. I., & Andrews, L. (1992) *Combining Work, and Welfare: An Anti-Poverty Strategy*. Institute for Women's Policy Research, Washington, DC.

Stacey, J. (1991) Can There Be a Feminist Ethnography? In: Gluck, S. B. & Patai, D. (Eds.), *Women's Words*. Routledge, New York, pp. 111–19.

Stanley, L. & Wise, S. (Eds.) (1983) *Breaking Out: Feminist Consciousness and Feminist Research*. Routledge & Kegan Paul, London.

Wolf, D. L. (1996) Situating Feminist Dilemmas in Fieldwork. In: Wolf, D. L. (Ed.), *Feminist Dilemmas in Fieldwork*. Westview Press, Boulder, pp. 1–55.

feminist pedagogy

Vicky M. MacLean

Although many, if not most, academics and others in the public arena today assume the need for a feminist pedagogy aimed at enhancing the educational experience of women and girls globally, this has not always been the case. A growing awareness of the need for feminist pedagogy was created by the pioneering research and pedagogy of committed feminist scholars (Hall & Sandler 1982; Sandler & Hall 1986; Harding 1987, 1992; Weiler 1988; Geismar & Nicoleau 1993; Rosser 1993, 1995; Maher & Tetreault 1994). *Feminist pedagogy* begins with the premise that gender and the social inequality it represents in the wider society are often reproduced in the classroom. Existing curricula and classroom practices contain sexist biases and patriarchal assumptions as reflected in the fact that the contributions of women are often absent from textbooks; girls and women are portrayed in stereotypic ways in much of the literature of all disciplines; girls and women are often directed to certain fields of study and are directed away from others; and teaching practices typically favor the learning styles of boys and men. Teachers informed by principles of feminist pedagogy seek to express feminist values and goals in the classroom and to challenge traditional androcentric knowledge (Geismar & Nicoleau 1993). Those adopting a feminist pedagogy ultimately seek to advance the status and education of women and girls by providing them with educational experiences that encourage consciousness-raising, empowerment, and voice through active and innovative educational strategies (Naples & Bojar 2002). While there is no single definition of feminist pedagogy, basic principles include: (1) the centrality of gender as an analytical tool; (2) multiculturalism and inclusion of all students; (3) collaborative knowledge construction; (4) collaborative teaching; (5) encouraging voice through linking personal experience with learning; and (6) democratization of the teacher's authority and power. *Feminist multicultural pedagogy* is sometimes used to emphasize an awareness of the ways in which differences of race/ethnicity, class, gender, sexual orientation, age, geopolitical location, and religious diversity can potentially translate into oppressive classroom interactions that reproduce dominant hierarchies, or alternatively, can contribute to enriching cultural interactions (Weir 1991; Brady 1993).

There are at least three distinctive variants of feminist pedagogical models: psychological, liberatory, and positional (Tisdell 1995, 1998; Grace & Gouthro 2000). The *psychologically oriented model* emphasizes the importance of relational connectivity in developmental learning and seeks to create a non-combative and nurturing interaction dynamic in the classroom and between teacher and student. The psychological model is influenced by theories of women's psychology espoused by Carol Gilligan in her classic book, *In a Different Voice* (1982), and by Belenky, Clinchy, Goldberger, and Tarule's *Women's Ways of Knowing* (1986). These works provide a critique of the male-stream moral development theory of Kohlberg, arguing that women's realities are fundamentally shaped by relational contexts of connection and attachment. The feminist psychological approach to teaching is therefore based on a model that seeks to create safe and non-intimidating classroom environments for interaction, exchange, and instructor evaluation. In such environments a familial language of caring and responsibility replaces the more sterile technoscientific language of objectivity. Teachers may invest considerable energies in generating positive relationships with and among students early in the curriculum cycle, even sacrificing a measure of course content to positive experiential exercises that promote social exchange. Using experiential learning strategies, educators anticipate a long-term payoff in group dynamics and individual student development. In this context, a teacher's central authority is subtly redefined as facilitation; the teacher becomes a guide from the side as she or he facilitates the creation of a cooperative learning environment that features collaboration, mutual responsibility, and sharing. Knowledge (and sometimes evaluation) is co-created through student participation rather than being centrally located in the unilateral authority of the teacher as expert. However, connection is not limited to student–teacher and student–student relationships; it is additionally emphasized in relation to the connection of knowledge to lived experience, and of learning in the classroom to learning outside of the classroom (Baxter-Magolda 1992: 223–4; Naples & Bojar 2002). These other types of connectivity can be particularly important in the retention of women students who often fail to see the relevance of their learning to the applications of their everyday lives (Grace & Gouthro 2000). The primary strength of the psychological model lies in the importance placed on interpersonal connectivity in the developmental processes of learning. The underlying assumption of the model is that women will flourish and discover their own voices of authority in learning environments that promote connectivity, validate personal experience, and topically highlight the relevant connections of course information to everyday life outside of the classroom. Its major limitation is its tendency to universalize the generic woman, ignoring positional and subjective differences and structural relationships of power related to race or ethnicity, class, age, affectional orientation, and abilities.

The *liberatory model*, in contrast, focuses on difference in the intersections of relationships of power, not only in terms of social position such as race, ethnicity, class, and gender, but also important intersections in the personal, political, and the pedagogical. The focus is on the emancipation and empowerment of girls and women as a historically oppressed and politically disenfranchised group. Variations on the liberation model include critical approaches that take up issues of democracy, freedom, and social justice; postmodern approaches that address identity, difference, and voice; poststructural approaches that interrogate language, meaning, and multiple subjectivities; and postcolonial and black insurgent approaches. The latter address revising history and countering tradition, exploring diaspora experience, and exposing privilege, exclusion, and distorted cultural representations of race and power (Grace & Gouthro 2000: 17). Liberatory models typically address the production of knowledge, assuming that knowledge that is valued is associated with valued identities or groups in a culture. Traditional school curricula rely on bases of knowledge that are often biased and/or exclude or marginalize the contributions and experiences of oppressed groups. It is not sufficient to simply "allow" these marginalized groups to participate in discourses on traditional topics; women and other minorities must be included in the design of curricula and instruction (Hughes 1998). Recognition of differences and of exclusions also informs liberatory pedagogical practices that seek to transform social relationships through raising critical consciousness and advocating equitable policies and programs for inclusion. Finally, liberatory models of critical pedagogy also seek to address issues of authority in relationship to voice and coming to voice for women. Coming to voice involves the politics of being heard, and this often means that authority is openly debated. Liberatory models break from psychological models in that they do not work from the premise that a safe environment is a necessary prerequisite for coming to voice. In fact, the classroom environment is a contested terrain where open debate and dealing with difference is often riddled with conflict and emotion. The underlying assumption of liberatory models is that in a transformative environment some danger and risk are necessary. Because education is political, those with a stake in maintaining the status quo will resist change (Grace & Gouthro 2000: 19). Tisdell (1995: 72) notes, for instance, that liberatory pedagogies address similarities and differences among women and that the point is coming to voice in spite of discomfort.

Positional feminist pedagogy has been influenced by poststructural feminism with its emphasis on the intersecting social locations of race/ethnicity, class, and gender. Positional pedagogies seek to construct a multiperspective discourse of interrogation, disruption, and intervention in order to resist patriarchal control of knowledge, theory, and pedagogy (Luke & Gore 1992). Aware that institutional discourses as well as persons holding positions of authority coordinate knowledge, poststructural feminists value and address the multiplicity of intersections of power. Grace and Gouthro (2000: 20) note that multiple identities, subjectivities, meanings, and differences are explored with the goal of contesting the politics of patriarchal control in educational institutions as sites for the production of knowledge. Explorations of meaning and power are particularly explored from margin to center, that is, from the perspective of marginalized groups such as women and race or ethnic groups to white males as the center of power. The aim according to Luke and Gore (1992) is to develop feminist projects of *standpoint* that locate women in relation to one another and in relation to men. In the classroom this is translated to mean that pedagogical experience and texts are both politically significant and historically contingent. The feminist agenda is to confront masculinist language, theory, and cultural constructions that maintain the status quo; it seeks in the process to shift viewpoints by building a pedagogy of possibility (Ellsworth 1993). Central to this approach is the belief that knowledge is actively constructed in relationships of difference and position (Maher & Tetreault 1994; Maher 1999: 49). Maher (1999: 50) argues that in positional pedagogies, differences of authority and other variables brought to the classroom are not "fixed identities" needing bridging, but rather serve as important markers for shifting power relationships. Rather than seeking to replicate power relationships, the goal is to challenge and to change them.

Yet another example of positional pedagogy is *engaged pedagogy* promoted by bell hooks in her book *Teaching to Transgress: Education as the Practice of Freedom* (1994). Engaged pedagogy as conceptualized by hooks is not another model per se, but rather is an achievement. It is a pedagogy achieved within the intersecting locations of the personal, historical, and political spheres. It involves issues of naming and representation, agency and struggle, resistance and risk-taking. For example, a common teaching practice used by hooks is to interrogate the meanings and representations behind popular media presentations of gender and race/ethnicity within the context of contemporary "white supremacist capitalist patriarchy." She raises the important question, "whose imagery, fantasy, experience or interest is portrayed?" As critical consumers of popular culture, it is up to the individual and groups with common interests to resist distorted representations of reality. Resistance requires a choice to transform existing social relations, but this is in fact a risky undertaking that may come at considerable costs. Nonetheless, the practice of freedom requires resisting distorted representations of the self and of others. Educators drawing from an engaged pedagogy thus become holistically connected in and to their teaching and refuse to disconnect the personal from the professional. Classrooms often become "untidy spaces" as conflict and difference inform critical thinking (Grace & Gouthro 2000). In connecting private experiences to public happenings, educators and learners build knowledge bases that recognize the complexity of social relationships and the needs of individuals to be understood as whole people. Drawing from Freire's *Pedagogy of the Oppressed* (1970/1993), hooks argues that education can potentially become a practice of freedom when it is understood that knowledge is a field in which both student and teacher must labor. Hence, when the classroom becomes a place for participatory learning, personal experience and formal ideas are joined.

The models of feminist pedagogy described here are ideal constructions with many commonalities that inform teaching. Many teachers blend aspects of each of the three models described with other pedagogies that emphasize the different learning styles of different students. What sets feminist pedagogy apart is the attention given to the communal and supportive nature of learning, the recognition that social inequalities are reproduced in educational institutions, and the desire to improve the experiences and possibilities for women and girls as learners in institutions that often produce "a chilly environment" for education (Hall & Sandler 1982; Sandler & Hall 1986). The three models described are conceptualized from a common need to validate the personal experiences of students, especially women and girls, in a context that raises critical consciousness about

the masculine biases in the curriculum and in the organization of education and other social institutions. Whereas the psychologically oriented model turns on the importance of developing nurturing, non-combative developmental relationships with students, liberatory and positional pedagogies recognize that "coming to voice" can be a political and conflicted process. Liberatory and positional pedagogies make overt the relationships of power both within and outside of the classroom. Knowledge is recognized and critiqued for serving dominant group interests. Teachers utilizing such approaches recognize that experimenting with new teaching methods and bringing the experiences of excluded groups from margin to center will disrupt the traditional canon and generate oppositional standpoints. The epistemological stance underlying these two models is that truth is "political, positional and linked to the struggle for social change" (Maher & Tetreault 1994: 47). Hence, there is no safe place. Struggle for knowledge and change in this context is clearly a group undertaking, one which cannot be achieved by individuals working outside of communities of those who share similar struggles. This stance presents a more sociological and collective orientation to learning and to liberatory empowerment.

In reality, translating theories of feminist pedagogy into practice is riddled with contradictions, particularly for women and for people of diverse ethnicity, race, religion, or sexual orientations. The institution of education, with its vested interests and canonical tradition, rarely promotes or supports innovative and critical processes among its teachers. In higher education, departments of Women's and Gender Studies, African and African American Studies, and Centers for Multicultural Studies have become institutional havens for independent and radical thinkers in many respects, but they have also become "colonized" bastions for learning and political struggle. Too often teachers and academic scholars lack the community support of their home disciplines and of administrators when attempting to develop multicultural pedagogies. In higher education, feminist teachers who overvalue and/or overinvest in classroom work often pay a price when it comes to tenure and promotion. Balancing the pressures of teaching, student advising, and committee work – which too often fall unevenly on women faculty – against research and publication demands is an area of interpersonal and political struggle (Weir 1991). Hard choices are made in prioritizing workload demands. Despite these constraints, however, since the 1970s all levels of education have become infused to some degree with the principles of feminist pedagogy. A growing body of publications in the field of education has come to reflect this social transformation, although it is still a work in progress (Weiler 1988; Maher 1999; Naples & Bojar 2002).

SEE ALSO: Bilingual, Multicultural Education; Critical Pedagogy; Cultural Capital in Schools; Educational Inequality; Gender, Education and; Globalization, Education and; School Climate; Teaching and Gender; Women's Empowerment

REFERENCES AND SUGGESTED READINGS

Baxter-Magolda, M. (1992) *Knowing and Reasoning in College: Gender-Related Patterns in Students' Intellectual Development*. Jossey-Bass, San Francisco.

Brady, J. (1993) A Feminist Pedagogy of Multiculturalism. *International Journal of Educational Reform* 2(2): 119–25.

Ellsworth, E. (1993) Why Doesn't This Feel Empowering? Working Through the Repressive Myths of Critical Pedagogy. In: Geismar, K. & Nicoleau, G. (Eds.), *Teaching for Change: Addressing Issues of Difference in the College Classroom*. Reprint Series No. 25. Harvard Educational Review, Cambridge, MA.

Geismar, K. & Nicoleau, G. (Eds.) (1993) *Teaching for Change: Addressing Issues of Difference in the College Classroom*. Reprint Series No. 25. Harvard Educational Review, Cambridge, MA.

Grace, A. & Gouthro, P. (2000) Using Models of Feminist Pedagogies to Think About Issues and Directions in Graduate Education for Women Students. *Studies in Continuing Education* 22(1): 5–28.

Hall, R. & Sandler, B. (1982) *The Classroom Climate: A Chilly One for Women?* Project on the Status and Education of Women. Association of American Colleges, Washington, DC.

Harding, S. (1987) *The Science Question in Feminism*. Cornell University Press, Ithaca, NY.

Harding, S. (1992) *Whose Science, Whose Knowledge? Thinking from Women's Lives*. Cornell University Press, Ithaca, NY.

Hughes, P. (1998) Ensuring Our "Vocal Presence" in the Classroom: Considerations of a Complex Task. In: Stalker, J. & Prentice, S. (Eds.), *The Illusion of Illusion: Women in Post-Secondary Education*. Fernwood Press, Halifax, NS, pp. 134–45.

Luke, C. & Gore, J. (1992) Introduction. In: Luke, C. & Gore, J. (Eds.), *Feminisms and Critical Pedagogy*. Routledge, New York.

Maher, F. (1999) Progressive Education and Feminist Pedagogies: Issues in Gender, Power, and Authority. *Teachers College Record* 101(1): 35–59.

Maher, F. & Tetreault, M. (1994) *The Feminist Classroom*. Basic Books, New York.

Naples, N. & Bojar, K. (2002) *Teaching Feminist Activism: Strategies from the Field*. Routledge, New York.

Rosser, S. (1993) Female Friendly Science: Including Women in Curricular Content and Pedagogy in Science. *Journal of General Education* 42(3): 191–220.

Rosser, S. (1995) *Teaching the Majority: Breaking the Gender Barrier in Science, Mathematics, and Engineering*. Teachers College Press, New York.

Sandler, B. & Hall, R. (1986) *The Campus Climate Revisited: Chilly for Women Faculty, Administrators, and Graduate Students*. Association of American Colleges, Washington, DC.

Tisdell, E. (1995) Creating Inclusive Adult Learning Environments: Insights from Multicultural Education and Feminist Pedagogy. *Monograph of the ERIC Clearinghouse on Adult, Career, and Vocational Education*. Information Series No. 361.

Tisdell, E. (1998) Poststructural Feminist Pedagogies: The Possibilities and Limitations of Feminist Emancipatory Adult Learning Theory and Practice. *Adult Education Quarterly* 48(3): 139–56.

Weiler, K. (1988) *Women Teaching for Change: Gender, Class, and Power*. Critical Studies in Education Series. Bergin & Garvey, New York.

Weir, L. (1991) Anti-Racist Feminist Pedagogy, Self-Observed. *Resources for Feminist Research/ DRF* 20 (3/4): 19–26.

feminist standpoint theory

Nancy A. Naples

Standpoint theory is a broad categorization that includes somewhat diverse theories ranging from Hartsock's (1983) feminist historical materialist perspective, Haraway's (1988) analysis of situated knowledges, Collins's (1990) black feminist thought, Sandoval's (2000) explication of third world feminists' differential oppositional consciousness, and Smith's (1987, 1990) everyday world sociology for women. Many theorists whose work has been identified with standpoint theory contest this designation; for example, Smith (1992) has been particularly vocal about the limits of this classification. She explains that it was Harding (1986) who first named standpoint theory as a general approach within feminism to refer to the many different theorists who argued for the importance of situating knowledge in women's experiences. Standpoint theorists are found in a wide variety of disciplines and continue to raise important questions about the way power influences knowledge in a variety of fields. Harding (2003) has brought together the most influential essays on feminist standpoint theory to demonstrate the power and utility of standpoint theory for feminist praxis.

Feminist standpoint theory was initially developed in response to debates surrounding Marxist feminism and socialist feminism in the 1970s and early 1980s. In reworking Marx's historical materialism from a feminist perspective, standpoint theorists' stated goal is to explicate how relations of domination are gendered in particular ways. Standpoint theory also developed in the context of third world and postcolonial feminist challenges to the so-called dual systems of patriarchy and capitalism. The dual systems approach was an attempt to merge feminist analyses of patriarchy and Marxist analyses of class to create a more complex socialist feminist theory of women's oppression. Critics of the dual systems approach pointed out the lack of attention paid by socialist feminist analyses to racism, white supremacy, and colonialism. In contrast, feminist standpoint theory offers an intersectional analysis of gender, race, ethnicity, class, and other social structural aspects of social life without privileging one dimension or adopting an additive formulation (e.g., gender plus race). Standpoint theory retains elements of Marxist historical materialism for its central premise: knowledge develops in a complicated and contradictory way from lived experiences and social historical context.

SIMILARITIES ACROSS DIFFERENT APPROACHES

Despite the diverse perspectives that are identified with standpoint epistemology, all standpoint theorists emphasize the importance of experience for feminist theorizing. In this regard, many point out the significance of standpoint analysis's connection to consciousness raising, the women's movement's knowledge production method. Consciousness raising (CR) was a strategy of knowledge development designed to help support and generate women's political activism. By sharing what appeared as individual-level experiences of oppression, women recognized that the problems were shaped by social structural factors. The CR process assumed that problems associated with women's oppression needed political solutions and that women acting collectively are able to identify and analyze these processes. The consciousness-raising group process enabled women to share their experiences, identify and analyze the social and political mechanisms by which women are oppressed, and develop strategies for social change.

Standpoint theorists assert a link between the development of standpoint theory and feminist political goals of transformative social, political, and economic change. From the perspective of feminist praxis, standpoint epistemology provides a methodological resource for explicating how relations of domination contour women's everyday lives. With this knowledge, women and others whose lives are shaped by systems of inequality can act to challenge these processes and systems (Weeks 1998: 92). One example of this point is found in Pence's (1996) work to create an assessment of how safe battered women remain after they report abuse to the police. Pence specifically draws on Smith's (1987) approach to shift the standpoint on the process of law enforcement to the women who the law attempts to protect and to those who are charged with protecting them. Pence developed a safety audit to identify ways criminal justice and law enforcement policies and practices can be enhanced to ensure the safety of women and to ensure the accountability of the offender. Pence's safety audit has been used by police departments, criminal justice and probation departments, and family law clinics in diverse settings across the country. Pence asserts that her approach is not an evaluation of individual workers' performances, but an examination of how the institution or system is set up to manage domestic violence cases.

Standpoint theorists are critical of positivist scientific methods that reduce lived experiences to a series of disconnected variables such as gender, race, or class. For example, Harding has written extensively about the limits of positivism and argues for an approach to knowledge production that incorporates the point of view of feminist and postcolonial theoretical and political concerns. She argues that traditional approaches to science fail to acknowledge how the social context and perspectives of those who generate the questions, conduct the research, and interpret the findings shape what counts as knowledge and how data is interpreted. Instead, she argues for a holistic approach that includes greater attention to the knowledge production process and to the role of the researcher. Harding and Smith both critique the androcentric nature of academic knowledge production. They argue for the importance of starting analysis from the lived experiences and activities of women and others who have been left out of the knowledge production process rather than start inquiry with the abstract categories and a priori assumptions of traditional academic disciplines or dominant social institutions.

STANDPOINT DEFINED AS EMBODIED IN SPECIFIC ACTORS' EXPERIENCES

Despite the shared themes outlined above, the notion of standpoint is conceptualized differently by different standpoint theorists. Naples (2003) has identified three different approaches to the construction of standpoint: as embodied in women's social location and social experience, as constructed in community, and as a site through which to begin inquiry. Many feminist theorists understand standpoint as embodied in specific actors who are located in less privileged positions within the social order and who, because of their social locations, are engaged in activities that differ from others who are not so located. The appeal to women's embodied social experience as a privileged site

of knowledge about power and domination forms one central thread within standpoint epistemologies.

Critics of this approach to standpoint theory point out that the reliance upon a notion of women or any other marginalized group as having an identifiable and consistent standpoint leads to the trap of essentialism. For example, feminist scholars who center on the role of mothering practices in generating different gendered "ways of knowing" (e.g., Belenky et al. 1986), or who argue that there are gendered differences in moral perspective (Gilligan 1982), have been criticized for equating such gendered differences with an essentialized female identity (Spelman 1988). However, many feminist theorists who contribute to the embodied strand of standpoint theorizing argue that due to relations of domination and subordination, women, especially low-income women of color or others located in marginalized social positions, develop a perspective on social life in the US that differs markedly from that of men and middle and upper-income people (Collins 1990; Sandoval 2000). Black feminist and Chicana standpoint theorists argue that the political consciousness of women of color develops from the material reality of their lives.

However, Collins and Hartsock emphasize that there is a difference between a so-called women's standpoint and a feminist standpoint. Jaggar (1989) points out that a women's standpoint is different from women's viewpoint or women's specific experiences. In contrast, they argue, a standpoint is achieved and as a consequence of analysis from a specific social actor, social group, or social location rather than available simply because one happens to be a member of an oppressed group or share a social location (see Weeks 1998). Rather than view standpoints as individual possessions of disconnected actors, most standpoint theorists attempt to locate standpoint in specific community contexts with particular attention to the dynamics of race, class, and gender.

STANDPOINT AS A RELATIONAL ACCOMPLISHMENT

This second strand of feminist standpoint epistemology understands standpoint as relational accomplishment. Using this approach, the identity of "woman" or class or other embodied identities is viewed as constructed in community and therefore cannot be interpreted outside the shifting community context. Collins (1990) draws on the construction of community as a collective process through which individuals come to represent themselves in relation to others with whom they perceive share similar experiences and viewpoints for her analysis of black feminist thought. Collins argues that a standpoint is constructed through "historically shared, *group*-based experiences." Like the embodied approach to standpoint theorizing, group-based approaches have also been criticized for unproblematically using women's class and racial identities to define who is or is not part of a particular group. However, those who draw on a relational or community-based notion of standpoint emphasize the collective analytic process that must precede the articulation of a standpoint. Both Sandoval (2000) and Collins (1990) utilize this approach to standpoint (although Sandoval does not describe her approach as a "standpoint epistemology," it does share many of the features outlined above). Sandoval's (2000) analysis of oppositional consciousness has much in common with Hartsock and Collins's approach, in that her analysis of oppositional consciousness focuses on the development of third world feminism as a methodology by which oppressed groups can develop strategies for political resistance. Sandoval's model offers a methodological strategy that contests previously taken-for-granted categorization of women's political practice such as liberal, radical, or socialist. The oppositional methodology she presents draws on multiple political approaches such as equal rights or liberal, revolutionary, and separatist political strategies. Rather than privilege one approach, Sandoval argues that oppressed peoples typically draw on multiple strategies to form an oppositional methodology. Sandoval treats experience as simultaneously embodied and strategically created in community and concludes that this dynamic interaction affects the political practice of third world women. Although Sandoval locates her analysis in a postmodern frame and Hartsock resists such a move, the legacy of historical materialism links their work within a broadly defined feminist

standpoint epistemology. In fact, Hartsock acknowledges the power of Sandoval's analysis for challenging essentialized views of identity and identity politics.

STANDPOINT AS A SITE OF INQUIRY

The third strand of feminist standpoint epistemology provides a framework for capturing the interactive and fluid conceptualization of community and resists attaching standpoint to particular bodies, individual knowers, or specific communities or groups. Standpoint is understood as a site from which to begin a mode of inquiry, as in Smith's everyday-world institutional, ethnographic approach to epistemology. Smith (1992) explains that her approach does not privilege a subject of research whose expressions are disconnected from her social location and daily activities. Rather, she starts inquiry with an active knower who is connected with others in particular and identifiable ways. This mode of inquiry calls for explicit attention to the social relations embedded in women's everyday activities. Smith's analysis of standpoint as a mode of inquiry offers a valuable methodological strategy for exploring how power dynamics are organized and experienced in a community context.

POSTMODERN CRITIQUES OF STANDPOINT THEORY

Postmodern theorists are especially critical of standpoint theory (Clough 1994; King 1994). They argue that the notion of standpoint presumes that it is possible to identify and locate what are socially constructed and mobile social positions. While standpoint theorists emphasize that perspectives from the vantage point of the oppressed remain partial and incomplete, a central problematic of feminist standpoint analyses is to determine how partial are particular perspectives (e.g., Haraway 1988). Clough (1994) aims her criticism of Collins's approach right to the heart of standpoint analysis when she emphasizes that privileging experience in any form, even with attention to the partiality of that experience, is a problematic theoretical move.

Few postmodern critics offer alternative research strategies. Those who do offer some alternative often limit their approaches to textual or discursive modes of analysis. For example, following an assessment of the limits and possibilities of feminist standpoint epistemologies for generating what she calls a "global social analytic," literary analyst Hennessy (1993) posits "critique" as materialist feminist "reading practice" as a way to recognize how consciousness is an ideological production. She argues that, in this way, it is possible to resist effectively the charge of essentialism that has been leveled against standpoint epistemology. In revaluing feminist standpoint theory for her method, she reconceptualizes feminist standpoint as a "critical discursive practice." Hennessy's methodological alternative effectively renders other methodological strategies outside the frame of materialist feminist scholarship. However, even poststructural critics of feminist standpoint epistemology within the social sciences also conclude their analyses with calls for discursive strategies. For example, Clough (1994: 179) calls for shifting the starting point of sociological investigation from experience or social activity to a "social criticism of textuality and discursivity, mass media, communication technologies and science itself." In contrast, standpoint theory, especially Smith's (1990) approach, offers a place to begin inquiry that envisions subjects of investigation who can experience aspects of life outside discourse. Standpoint theorists like Smith tie their understanding of experience to the collective conversations of the women's movement that gave rise to understandings about women's lives which had no prior discursive existence. In this way, despite some important theoretical challenges, standpoint theory continues to offer feminist analysts a theoretical and methodological strategy that links the goals of the women's movement to the knowledge production enterprise.

CONCLUSION

In sum, standpoint theorists typically resist focusing their analyses on individual women removed from their social context. Knowledge generated from embodied standpoints of subordinates is powerful in that it can help transform traditional categories of analyses that originate from dominant groups. However, as

many feminist standpoint theorists argue, it remains only a partial perspective (Haraway 1988). Naples (2003) argues that by placing the analysis within a community context, it is possible to uncover the multiplicity of perspectives along with the dynamic structural dimensions of the social, political, and economic environment that shape the *relations of ruling* in a particular social space. Haraway (1988) explains that situated knowledges are developed collectively rather than by individuals in isolation. Hartsock (1983) and Collins (1990) both emphasize that standpoints are achieved in community, through collective conversations and dialogue among women in marginal social positions. According to Collins, standpoints are achieved by groups that struggle collectively and self-reflectively against the *matrix of domination* that circumscribes their lives. Hartsock also emphasizes that a feminist standpoint is achieved through analysis and political struggle. Given standpoint theory's emphasis on a process of dialogue, analysis, and reflexivity, the approach has proven extremely vibrant and open to reassessment and revision. As a consequence, standpoint theory remains an extremely important approach within feminist theory.

SEE ALSO: Black Feminist Thought; Consciousness Raising; Feminist Methodology; Gender Oppression; Intersectionality; Materialist Feminisms; Matrix of Domination; Outsider-Within; Strong Objectivity

REFERENCES AND SUGGESTED READINGS

Belenky, M. F., Blythe, M. C., Goldberger, N. R., & Tarule, J. M. (1986) *Women's Ways of Knowing*. Basic Books, New York.

Chodorow, N. (1978) *The Reproduction of Mothering*. University of California Press, Berkeley.

Clough, P. T. (1994) *Feminist Thought*. Blackwell, Oxford.

Collins, P. H. (1990) *Black Feminist Thought: Knowledge, Consciousness, and the Politics of Empowerment*. Unwin Hyman, Boston.

Gilligan, C. (1982) *In a Different Voice: Psychological Theory and Women's Development*. Harvard University Press, Cambridge, MA.

Haraway, D. (1988) Situated Knowledges: The Science Question in Feminism and the Privilege of Partial Perspective. *Feminist Studies* 14(3): 575–99.

Harding, S. (1986) *The Science Question in Feminism.* Cornell University Press, Ithaca, NY.

Harding, S. (2003) *The Feminist Standpoint Theory Reader: Intellectual and Political Controversies.* Routledge, New York.

Hartsock, N. (1983) *Money, Sex and Power: Toward a Feminist Historical Materialism.* Longman, New York.

Hennessy, R. (1993) *Materialist Feminism and the Politics of Discourse.* Routledge, New York.

Jaggar, A. M. (1989) Love and Knowledge: Emotion in Feminist Epistemology. In: Jaggar, A. M. & Bordo, S. R. (Eds.), *Gender/Body/Knowledge: Feminist Reconstructions of Being and Knowing.* Rutgers University Press, New Brunswick, NJ, pp. 145–71.

King, K. (1994) *Theory in its Feminist Travels: Conversations in US Women's Movements.* Indiana University Press, Bloomington.

Naples, N. A. (2003) *Feminism and Method: Ethnography, Discourse Analysis, and Activist Research.* Routledge, New York.

Pence, E. (1996) Safety for Battered Women in a Textually Mediated Legal System. PhD dissertation, Graduate Department, Sociology in Education, University of Toronto.

Sandoval, C. (2000) *Methodology of the Oppressed.* University of Minnesota Press, St. Paul.

Smith, D. E. (1987) *The Everyday World as Problematic: A Feminist Sociology.* University of Toronto Press. Toronto.

Smith, D. E. (1990) *Conceptual Practices of Power.* Northeastern University Press, Boston.

Smith, D. E. (1992) Sociology from Women's Experience: A Reaffirmation. *Sociological Theory* 10(1): 88–98.

Spelman, E. V. (1988) *Inessential Woman: Problems of Exclusion in Feminist Thought.* Beacon Press, Boston.

Weeks, K. (1998) *Constituting Feminist Subjects.* Cornell University Press, Ithaca, NY.

feminization of labor migration

Mako Yoshimura

Feminization of migration is characterized by an increase in the number of female migrants since the 1980s and by a concentration on female-specific work such as domestic helpers, nurses, entertainers, and so on in the process of globalization. While the movement of peoples, both internal and international, has been observed historically in various forms, the feminization of migration has been highlighted during the period of rapid economic globalization since the 1980s. Early research on migration noticed the differences between men and women found in immigration statistics, but paid little attention to this aspect of the subject. Gender structure only became part of the discussion after the early 1980s.

In the 1980s, gender-based academic work focused on rural–urban female labor migration in the domestic labor market in developing countries in Asia and Latin America. Many case studies focused on young women mobilized as wage labor in factories by multinational corporations in free-trade zones and industrial estates. This research was part of a discussion on theories relating to the new international division of labor (NIDL) and the way global capital was relocating labor-intensive production. There was a preference for female labor because women were considered to have "nimble fingers" that fit them for labor-intensive processes, and women were therefore exploited as lower-paid, unskilled wage labor, as had happened during the early stages of capitalist industrialization in western countries. In the late 1980s, at a second stage of internationalization of labor markets, research highlighted the fact that female migrants often worked in sweatshops and lower-skilled and lower-paid service jobs in urban areas of industrialized countries.

Research on these topics developed theoretically during the 1990s and various approaches were applied to the study of migration and gender, analyzing the topic by considering elements such as class, stratum, ethnicity, and age, along with nationality. Where traditional research on migration dealt mainly with settlement and assimilation, more recent works focus on temporary "sojourning," relations with home communities, diaspora as the migrant community, cultural gaps, conflicts, prejudice in host countries, and the like. Transnationalism is also an important subject to be analyzed.

Much of the early work on gender and migration used quantitative methods. For example, one of the earliest collections of articles on gender and migration, a special issue of

International Migration Review published in 1984, had 19 articles, and nearly all were based on quantitative analysis (Willis & Yeoh 2000: xii–xiii). Quantitative methods, such as analyzing census data and mounting large-scale questionnaire surveys, have always been popular. Interest in migrants' experiences and questions of identity have highlighted the importance of other methods. Recent trends in migrant research have led to greater use of methods such as interviews, life histories, and participant observation in order to learn about migrants' identities, networks, households, reproduction, carework, social constructions, transnationalism, gender relations, and so on. In dealing with these issues, a qualitative analysis is central to an examination of the complicated dynamics of migration and the changing gender structure at the micro-level, and to compensate for the biases and omissions of macro-level data analysis.

The International Labor Organization has estimated that there are currently 86 million migrants, half of them women. In traditional discussions, women migrants were assumed to be spouses or family members accompanying male migrants. Also, women immigrants increased as the spouses and family members of immigrants in the 1970s, when the western countries stopped new immigrants after the oil shock. However, recent works indicate that women migrate to seek economic independence and personal freedom or autonomy, as well as support for their own families.

The proportion of female migrants is high in many countries in Asia. For example, the female ratio of the total overseas migrant workers in the Philippines is 72 percent, in Indonesia it is 78 percent, and in Sri Lanka it is 84 percent. Women work primarily as domestic helpers and nurses. The female share in migration increased in the 1980s, when male migration to the Middle East (which had increased dramatically during the oil boom of the 1970s) began to fall off.

Some 7.76 million Philippine nationals work overseas (3.39 million registered, 1.51 million unregistered, and 2.87 million permanent residents) – equivalent to 10 percent of the population or 23 percent of total labor forces. While unemployment in the Philippines is nominally 10.2 percent, the estimated latent unemployment rate was above 20 percent in 2003. It is not unusual for Filipinos/Filipinas to seek overseas jobs, as Filipinos/Filipinas have worked abroad since the early twentieth century. While the early overseas workers went to plantations in Hawaii and California, the current situation is different. The sexual division of labor is clear: women work overseas as domestic helpers, nurses, entertainers, and so on, while men work overseas as construction workers, engineers, seamen, and so on. Remittances from overseas workers amounted to US $76.4 million in 2003. The Philippine government encourages overseas work and the Philippine Overseas Employment Agency (POEA), the Department of Labor and Employment (DOLE), and the Philippine Overseas Labor Office (POLO) support overseas workers by checking employers and training workers.

Domestic labor for housekeeping, childcare, or nursing care for elderly people is now engaged as paid work in the market. And it relies on migrant women and ethnic minority women. Not only in advanced industrialized or rich oil-producing countries, but also in newly industrializing economies in Asia, migrant domestic helpers are employed because of the shortage of unskilled labor in local labor markets. In developing societies such as Singapore, Taiwan, Hong Kong, and Malaysia it is a kind of status symbol for the new middle class to employ migrant domestic helpers.

In the western world in the late nineteenth century a considerable part of domestic work in middle and upper-class households was performed by servants. The nature of domestic work changed with the extension of electricity, gas, and water service and the development of home appliances. At the same time, most children ceased to be involved in economic activity and became school pupils. There was a decrease in the supply of labor from rural areas and the informal sector, along with a change in the nature of domestic work and childcare, as middle-class housewives came to bear the domestic work and the childcare.

Married women in advanced industrialized countries increasingly worked as wage labor from the 1970s onwards. The increased burden of wage labor and domestic work borne by women, together with the decline in the birth rate, a growing proportion of elderly people, labor shortages, and budget cuts for public welfare services, led to the externalization of carework, and migrant workers became an option for this sort of labor.

When women leave home to work overseas, their family members may hire women who are relatives, neighbors, or migrant women from rural areas to take their place as caregivers. A chain of carework is thus formed that transcends borders and the national framework. Hence, a discussion of migration should include transnational motherhood as well as the global chain of care work. Because of the externalization of carework, the reproduction of labor or human beings is often done outside of homes, and there are many countries that depend on migrant workers as lower-paid caregivers. The feminization of migration dissolved and transformed the national framework of reproduction, as the globalization of the economy incorporates not only production, but also reproduction.

The rights of migrant women workers are often violated. Employers or agents may keep migrants' passports and travel documents, and many migrant workers are not paid until the end of their contracts. Differences of language, culture, and religion frequently cause miscommunication and misunderstanding and are a basis for discrimination and prejudice against migrant workers. There have been many reported instances of mental and physical abuse (including verbal abuse) against migrant domestic helpers. Some employers do not allow any holidays and restrict meals, telephone calls, and occasions for going out and meeting friends. Even when employers are nice to workers, they may be forced to endure long workdays and may be on call 24 hours a day if employers have babies or small children. Migrant domestic helpers often live in employers' houses and they are not thought of as "proper" workers, since domestic work is not considered as formal work.

Moreover, many women migrants work in the sex industry. In Japan, although entertainer visas are supposed to be for performers with special skills, most female migrant workers who come as entertainers engage in the sex-related industry as bar hostesses, strippers, or prostitutes. Around 140,000 Filipino women came to Japan on entertainer visas in 2003. This is big business, partly related to the Japanese mafia and local mafias in Southeast Asia. The trafficking in persons also involves forced labor and prostitution. Mail-order brides or picture brides are sometimes used for unauthorized work or trafficking in persons in illegal sectors, including sex-related activities. It is crucial to understand how this phenomenon is a byproduct of the globalization of the economy. Research on the topic must deal not only with migrant women, but also with the host community and economies that link migration and working circumstances.

The general problem is that the protection of human rights and workers' rights is poorly developed in the case of female migrant workers because they face discrimination in the societies where they work, and also because carework is generally identified as housework or shadow work and they are not considered as skilled labor. It is important that human rights are appropriately protected, and a migrant woman should be esteemed as a worker and as a human being, regardless of her legal status.

The feminization of migration displays many aspects of the gendered structure of migration, such as the global chain of carework, gender ideology, and transnationalism. It must be examined in the context of the globalization of the economy that transformed the capitalist mechanism of utilization of female labor, and global capital's reproduction process.

SEE ALSO: Carework; Diaspora; Gender, Development and; Immigration; International Gender Division of Labor; Traffic in Women

REFERENCES AND SUGGESTED READINGS

Anderson, B. (2000) *Doing the Dirty Work? The Global Politics of Domestic Labour*. Zed Books, London.
Chant, S. (1992) *Gender and Migration in Developing Countries*. Belhaven Press, London.
International Labor Organization (2004) *Towards a Fair Deal for Migrant Workers in the Global Economy*. International Labor Organization, Geneva.
Momsen, J. H. (1999) *Gender, Migration and Domestic Service*. Routledge, London.
Nash, J. (Ed.) (1983) *Women, Men and the International Division of Labor*. State University of New York Press, Albany.
Willis, K. & Yeoh, B. (Eds.) (2000) *Gender and Migration*. Edward Elgar, Cheltenham.

feminization of poverty

Susan W. Hinze and Dawn Aliberti

Diana Pearce (1978) coined the term "feminization of poverty" in the late 1970s to describe the increasing overrepresentation of women and children among the poor in the United States. Since then the gender gap in poverty has increased, although some evidence suggests that improvements in women's earnings are beginning to close the poverty gap between women and men (McLanahan & Kelly 1999). Currently, of those in poverty, 38 percent are women, 26 percent are men, and 36 percent are children (US Census Bureau, 2004). However, the economic disadvantage of women is not a uniquely American experience, and scholarship in recent years highlights the need for a more global perspective on the feminization of poverty.

GENDER AND POVERTY IN THE UNITED STATES

The poverty line in the US is set by the Social Security Administration and calculated by multiplying the lowest cost for a nutritionally adequate food plan (as determined by the Department of Agriculture) by three. This calculation assumes a family spends one-third of its budget on food. Those falling below this set annual income are defined as poor and entitled to government assistance (for criticisms of the absolute poverty definition, see McLanahan & Kelly 1999). The official poverty rate in 2003 was 12.5 percent, or 35.9 million people, and the official poverty line for a family of four was $18,810 (US Census Bureau, 2004). The 2004 Annual Demographic Survey (a joint project between the Bureau of Labor Statistics and the Bureau of the Census) estimated that 11.2 percent of males fell below the poverty line, compared to 13.7 percent of females. Another framing is that adult women are 1.5 times more likely to be poor than are men.

McLanahan and Kelly (1999) examine trends in men's and women's absolute and relative poverty rates between 1950 and 1996. Using Census Bureau data to calculate sex poverty ratios (see Table 1), they find a dramatic increase in sex poverty ratios between 1950 and 1970. For white middle-aged adults, a "defeminization of poverty" occurred in the 1970s and 1980s. However, among the elderly, the feminization of poverty has increased significantly. Overall, poverty rates for elderly women and men have decreased since the 1950s, but men's rates fell more quickly. Hence, elderly women today are more than twice as likely to be poor as are elderly men. In summary, while women were only slightly more likely than men to be poor in the 1950s, today they are 50 percent more likely than men to be poor (US Census Bureau, 2004).

Family status matters for the feminization of poverty. In 1960, most poor families contained both men and women; by contrast, almost

Table 1 Sex poverty ratios, 1950–96

	1950 Census	*1960 Census*	*1970 Census*	*1970 CPS*	*1980 CPS*	*1996 CPS*
Whites						
Total	1.10	1.23	1.46	1.53	1.56	1.52
Young	0.83	0.99	1.00	1.33	1.48	1.47
Middle-Aged	1.16	1.24	1.51	1.50	1.43	1.33
Elderly	1.13	1.24	1.45	1.49	1.64	2.33
Blacks						
Total	1.17	1.19	1.37	1.47	1.69	1.71
Young	1.05	1.11	1.11	1.49	1.78	1.65
Middle-Aged	1.15	1.25	1.56	1.59	1.72	1.68
Elderly	1.05	1.05	1.14	1.16	1.44	2.09

Sources: Replicated from McLanahan & Kelly (1999), who used US Census data (1950–70) and Current Population Survey (CPS) (1970–96).

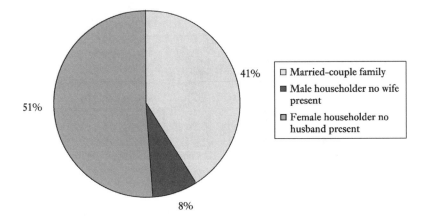

Figure 1 Poverty by household type.

51 percent of poor families today are headed by a woman with no husband present (US Census Bureau, 2004). By comparison, 41 percent of poor families are married-couple families, and 8 percent are headed by a man with no wife present. (See Fig. 1.)

A look at gender differences in median family income by household type highlights the role of family status. Median family income for all families in 2003 was $43,318. Clearly, having two parents in the home decreases the chances of poverty for families. In married-couple families, the median income is $62,405. However, even in married-couple families, the poverty rate is 5.4 percent. The median family income for family households headed by women was $29,307 for 2003 (with no husband present), compared to $41,959 for households headed by men (with no wife present). Currently, 28 percent of all female-headed households live below the official poverty line, compared to 13.5 percent headed by men. This is a significant issue since the percentage of female-headed households has grown in the past few decades (up from 10 percent in 1950) and can be accounted for by a number of factors, including high rates of divorce, later ages at first marriage, less likelihood that pregnant teens will marry, and, in some communities, the high rate of incarceration of young men.

Past analyses of poverty by gender have been criticized for overlooking or downplaying racial and ethnic inequalities. The current scholarship recognizes that the feminization of poverty can only be understood by an examination of how race/ethnicity and age intersect with economic status. Within each racial/ethnic category, women are more likely than men to be poor; however, older women and women of color have always been the most vulnerable. As Figure 2 reveals, 26.5 percent of African American women fall below the poverty line, compared to 11.5 percent of white women and 24 percent of Latino women. In short, an African American woman is almost two and a half times more likely to be poor than is a white woman and a Latino woman is twice as likely as a white woman to be poor (US Census Bureau, 2004).

Statistics also reveal that the face of poverty becomes disproportionately female with age. Figure 3 shows that 7.5 percent of men aged 75 and over are poor compared with 14.3 percent of women (US Census Bureau, 2004, March supplement). Another framing of the same data is that women 75 and over are 1.9 times as likely to be poor as men. Gender disparities are also significant for those in the 18 to 34 year category (coinciding with the childbearing years), with women 1.5 times as likely to be poor as men.

As Pearce (1978) noted in her now classic article, explanations center on work and welfare. Women are underrepresented among the beneficiaries of the more generous, work-related social insurance benefits, but overrepresented as recipients of public assistance, a far less generous, means-tested program. In short, the

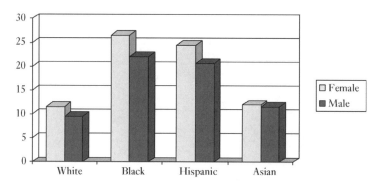

Figure 2 Percent poverty by race and gender.
Source: US Census Bureau, Current Population Survey, 2004 Annual Social and Economy Supplement.

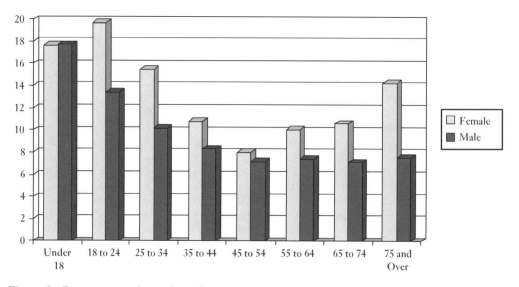

Figure 3 Percent poverty by gender and age.
Source: US Census Bureau, Current Population Survey, 2004 Annual Social and Economic Supplement.

dualistic structure of the US social welfare system works against women (Fraser 1993). The "masculine" social welfare programs are social insurance schemes (unemployment insurance, Social Security, Medicare, SSSI) primarily benefiting men as rights bearers and rewarding productive labor. The "feminine" social welfare programs (TANF, formerly AFDC, food stamps, Medicaid, public housing assistance) are less generous, have a heavy surveillance component, and devalue reproductive labor.

Following Pearce's work, McLanahan and Kelly (1999) trace how changes in the family, changes in the economy, and changes in the welfare state have contributed to the feminization of poverty. We examine each in turn, with emphasis on social policies that help or hinder women's economic progress.

First, several demographic shifts in family structure are important for understanding the feminization of poverty. Later ages at first marriage, combined with increasing divorce rates, together produce a larger proportion of adult women living independently (McLanahan & Kelly 1999). Since women tend to earn less than men, they are at greater risk for poverty. Some argue that no-fault divorce laws have contributed to the poverty of female-headed households, by changing economic outcomes for women. Spouses are treated as equals, despite evidence that in financial terms, women are rarely equal. With no-fault divorce, alimony awards are less frequent, and women are disproportionately penalized. The decline in income for women post-divorce is estimated to be between 30 and 50 percent, in part because women's salaries are lower than men's. Along with the high divorce rates, the twentieth century has witnessed increases in the proportion of children born to unmarried mothers. In 1960, approximately 6 percent of children were born to unmarried mothers, rising to 34 percent of children by 2002 (CDC Division of Vital Statistics, 2002). Birth rates for unmarried women vary widely by race/ethnicity. The proportion of births to unmarried white women is 23 percent, followed by 43.5 percent for Hispanic women and 68 percent for black women. While birth rates have been increasing slightly for unmarried white and Hispanic women, they are decreasing for unmarried black women. Since women earn less than men, and since women are more often in charge of dependants, single mothers remain at risk for poverty. The poverty of female-headed households is due, in part, to inadequate child support laws and lack of enforcement. Only about 62 percent of custodial mothers are awarded child support, and the average awards are relatively small (about $3,800 per year) (US Census Bureau, 1999). Of those who receive awards, approximately 24 percent never receive payment and another 24 percent receive only partial payment (US Census Bureau, 1997). A final demographic shift contributing to the feminization of poverty is the increase in the proportion of elderly living independently. That trend, combined with increased life expectancy, has increased poverty for women relative to men given their longer life expectancies (McLanahan & Kelly 1999).

Second, economic changes in the twentieth century have contributed to the feminization of poverty. Ehrenreich and Piven (1984) trace the feminization of poverty to the "family wage"

system, which granted men wages sufficient to support a wife and children. This achievement, an outcome of late nineteenth- and early twentieth-century labor struggles, positioned women as secondary workers, reinforced occupational sex segregation, and legitimized systematic wage discrimination against women. The legacy of this system is apparent in the persistent wage gaps between women and men that characterize today's labor market. Figure 4 shows median incomes for women and men, full-time workers only, from 1960 to 2000 (US Census Bureau, 2004).

As Table 2 shows, in 1960, women working full-time earned 61 percent of male wages. By 2003, women full-time workers earned 76.3 percent of male wages. Median earnings for women in 2003 were $31,653 compared to $41,503 for men. A robust, interdisciplinary literature exists on reasons for the wage gap; explanations include human capital differences, occupational sex segregation, wage penalties for motherhood, variation in job characteristics (e.g., industry, union membership), and discrimination. However, increases in women's labor force participation and educational levels in the past two decades have resulted in increased wages for women relative to men. Consequently, we find a "defeminization" of poverty or reduced sex poverty ratio, primarily for white, middle-aged adults. In addition, men's wages have stagnated since the 1970s, which also contributes to the declining sex gap in poverty.

Jacobs and Gerson (2004) warn that corporations benefit from a bifurcated workforce, with some workers (mostly professionals and the highly educated) working overtime, and other workers, generally those with less education, working part-time. Approximately 72 percent of part-time workers are women. Since women are disproportionately represented in the "non-standard" or contingent workforce as part-time, temporary, or home workers, their wages and earning power over the life course suffer (Presser 2003), contributing to the feminization of poverty.

Third, McLanahan and Kelly (1999) present data on the role of social security in reducing poverty among elderly women and men, and the role of welfare in reducing poverty for single mothers. After 1970, government transfers for women of childbearing age began to decline;

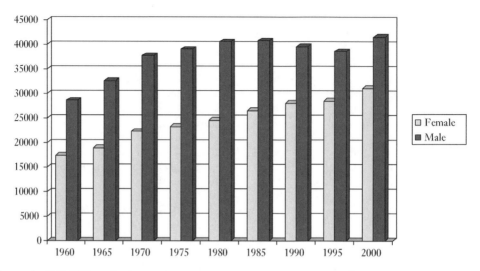

Figure 4 1960-2000 median income by gender, full-time year-round workers[a].
[a]Adjusted 2003 dollars.
Source: US Census 1960–2000.

Table 2 1960–2003 median income by gender, full-time year-round workers[a]

	1960	1965	1970	1975	1980	1985	1990	1995	2000	2003
Female	17,348	18,862	22,318	23,261	24,509	26,500	28,102	28,500	31,109	31,653
Male	28,601	32,613	37,678	38,977	40,540	40,762	39,549	38,596	41,543	41,503
%	60.7	57.8	59.2	59.7	60.5	65.0	71.1	73.8	74.9	76.3

[a]Adjusted to 2003 dollars.
% = Female income as a percentage of male income (rounded to the nearest tenth).
Source: US Census Bureau, 1960–2003.

about the same time, poverty rates for women of childbearing age stopped declining. The passage of the Personal Responsibility and Work Opportunity Act in 1996 has contributed to decreased welfare caseloads, and increased employment among recipients. However, any increased earnings from work have been offset by the loss in public assistance (Institute for Women's Policy Research, 2002). In sum, welfare reform has not helped "solve" the problem of poverty for women, and some evidence suggests it has created new problems, especially for children. Finally, during the 1950s–1970s, the rise of social security benefits for retired adults contributed to declining poverty rates for the elderly. Despite the declines, the feminization

of poverty among the elderly has persisted into the twenty-first century, for two primary reasons: (1) pensions for never-married women are lower than pensions for never-married men; (2) elderly women are more likely to live alone (given longer life expectancies), and thus more likely to live on one pension rather than two.

GENDER AND POVERTY CROSS-NATIONALLY: THE ECONOMIC NORTH

A cross-national picture of the feminization of poverty must be segmented into an examination of other Economic North (or industrialized) countries and countries of the Economic South. Cross-national comparisons with other industrialized countries prove particularly illuminating for understanding potential solutions for the US situation. In short, labor market and social welfare policies together can be significant deterrents to the feminization of poverty. As Goldberg and Kremen (1990: 36) note, "Cross-national data reinforce the conclusion that one of the world's wealthiest nations is not generous to single mothers and their children."

In their examination of five capitalist and two socialist countries from the Economic North, Goldberg and Kremen (1990) conclude that the feminization of poverty is most pronounced in the United States, where it was first identified, *and* occurs where single motherhood is widespread and where labor market or social welfare policies are insufficient to reduce poverty. In Sweden, for example, single motherhood is as prevalent as it is in the US, but a combination of labor market and social policies has together helped Sweden achieve a relatively low rate of poverty for single-parent families. Japan presents a very different case. The wage gap between women and men is much higher in Japan than in the US, and Japan has very minimal social assistance programs. However, what prevents the feminization of poverty in Japan is the low rate of single motherhood. Goldberg and Kremen (1990) argue that the prospects for single motherhood are so bleak that few mothers risk economic independence from men.

Using Luxembourg Income Study data, Christopher et al. (2000) present gender poverty ratios based upon pre-transfer, pre-tax income, and post-transfer, post-tax income (see Table 3). From row one, note that the gender poverty ratio (pre-transfer, pre-tax income) is highest for the United States (1.42) followed, in descending order, by Australia (1.37), the Netherlands (1.34), the United Kingdom (1.30), Germany (1.19), Canada (1.15), France (1.12), and Sweden (0.92). Row two reveals that the US, Australia, Canada, France, and Germany reduce the ratio of women's to men's poverty rates by 5 percent or less through tax and transfer systems, while the Netherlands and Sweden, with the most generous welfare states, do the most for women relative to men. They conclude that "the welfare states of the five other nations (the US, Australia, Canada, France and Germany) make no more than trivial redistribution that reduces the gender disparity in poverty rates" (p. 213). They also note that if Sweden is "doubly blessed" (a lower proportion of single mothers and a more generous welfare state), the United States is "doubly damned" with "high levels of single motherhood and a welfare state that is relatively stingy and redistributes little, if at all, by gender" (p. 214). Christopher et al. (2001) conclude with a warning that single motherhood is on the rise in most industrial nations, placing more women at risk for poverty in the absence of increased earnings for women or improved state subsidization of the costs of rearing children.

GENDER AND POVERTY CROSS-NATIONALLY: THE ECONOMIC SOUTH

What is the global evidence for the feminization of poverty among Economic South nations? Standardized poverty measures are difficult to obtain, but the United Nations reports issued for the Fourth World Conference on Women

Table 3 Ratio of women's to men's poverty rate in eight nations and under simulations

Ratio based on:	US 1994	Australia 1994	Canada 1994	France 1989	Germany 1994	Netherlands 1991	Sweden 1992	UK 1995
Pre-transfer, pre-tax income	1.42	1.37	1.15	1.12	1.19	1.34	0.92	1.30
Post-transfer, post-tax (disposable) income	1.38	1.30	1.13	1.11	1.18	1.14	0.73	1.20
% tax and transfer system changes ratio	−3%	−5%	−2%	−1%	−1%	−15%	−21%	−8%

Source: Replicated from Christopher et al. (2000).

(Beijing) in 1995 indicated that of the 1.3 billion people in poverty, 70 percent are women. The Platform for Action adopted at the conference called for the eradication of the persistent and increasing burden of poverty on women. However, according to a 2005 report from the Women's Environment and Development Organization, since Beijing, women's livelihoods have worsened, with increasing insecure employment and reduced access to social protection and public services. In general, women's economic contributions are undervalued (to the tune of $11 trillion per year in 1995) and women work longer hours than men, yet share less in the economic rewards.

The male/female median earnings ratios are lowest (with women earning as little as 20 percent of men's earnings) in the North African and Middle Eastern countries of Libya, Iraq, Saudi Arabia, Bahrain, United Arab Emirates, Oman, and Qatar (State of the World Atlas, 1999). While some evidence suggests the pay gap is shrinking worldwide (e.g., see UN Development Fund for Women), as in the US, other evidence from the Women's Environment and Development Organization suggests poverty is on the rise for women in Economic South nations.

Understanding women's poverty in Economic South nations requires attention to the social and legal institutions that do not guarantee women equality in basic human and legal rights, including access to and control of land or other resources, in employment and earnings, and social and political participation. In particular, the lack of land rights in Western and Central Africa keeps women in an endless cycle of poverty. According to experts at the UN women's conference sponsored by the International Fund for Agricultural Development (IFAD), rural women own 1 percent of the world's land but head at least 25 percent of all households. Internal conflicts, HIV/AIDS, male migration within and outside the country, natural disasters, and structural adjustment policies all contribute to the poverty of rural women.

What kind of reforms are necessary to reduce female poverty in Economic South nations and meet Millennium Development Goals by 2015? According to experts at the IFAD conference, discriminatory inheritance practices that disregard female ownership must be ended. Without property, women are denied credit, and without credit, women cannot generate income. Without resources, children are unable to go to school and the cycle of poverty continues. For example, in Malawi and Zambia, custom dictates that the husband's patrilineage, which includes his father, his father's sisters, his brothers, and any male descendants of the patrilineage, collects all property in event of his death. Widows, and they are increasing with the AIDS crisis, and their children are left destitute. Reforms include microfinancing programs, and greater inclusion of women in postconflict governments. While the CEDAW (Convention on the Elimination of All Forms of Discrimination against Women), adopted by the UN General Assembly in 1979, is a powerful tool for combating property discrimination, it is often trumped by traditional chiefs who dictate land ownership laws.

Since the 1970s, feminist scholars have produced an abundant literature on development and gender, highlighting the need for the use of a critical gender lens when developing measures to eradicate poverty. Development programs focused on helping southern countries convert to market economies have been criticized for being gender blind or "gender neutral," which ultimately disadvantages women (Ward 1990; Blumberg et al. 1995). For example, the introduction of high-yield rice in Asia displaced wage-earning opportunities for women through mechanization. Development projects that help local citizens grow crops for cash, rather than local food production, undercut women by diverting water from home gardens and for domestic use. Structural adjustment programs (SAPs) imposed by the International Monetary Fund resulted in cuts to wages and social services, as well as rises in the cost of basic goods and services. These cuts had a more deleterious effect on women given their greater responsibility for providing food, water, and health care for families (Blumberg et al. 1995). Furthermore, feminist scholars have argued that engendering poverty eradication measures requires close examination of gender relations and unequal distributions of resources and power, starting at the level of the household. Measures that increase women's income are more likely to positively affect family well-being than are measures to increase men's incomes because women tend to use a higher proportion of their earnings on children and household expenses. However, incorporating women into formal labor markets is not always sufficient (an "add women and stir" approach) if women end up in the informal sector of the economy, or on the lowest rungs of the labor hierarchy (Ward 1990; Blumberg et al. 1995).

In short, policies to eradicate poverty must incorporate a gender lens and close examination of the political economy of class, markets, and work processes. Beyond improving conceptual and theoretical approaches to poverty, a gender and development approach also works from the "bottom up" to empower women to transform the structures that contribute to their subordination. As women's activism in the 1980s and 1990s has demonstrated, women's agency is a powerful force for change. Sociological scholarship on the global feminization of poverty recognizes the importance of enhancing women's participation in local, national, and international decision-making and policymaking.

SEE ALSO: Culture of Poverty; Family Poverty; Gender, Development and; Gender Oppression; Income Inequality, Global; Inequality/Stratification, Gender; Inequality, Wealth; Poverty

REFERENCES AND SUGGESTED READINGS

Blumberg, R. L., Rabowski, C., Tinker, I., & Monteon, M. (Eds.) (1995) *Engendering Wealth and Well-Being: Empowerment for Global Change.* Westview Press, Boulder, CO.

Christoper, K., England, P., McLanahan, S., Ross, K., & Smeeding, T. M. (2000) Gender Inequality in Poverty in Affluent Nations: The Role of Single Motherhood and the State. In: Vleminckx, K. & Smeeding, T. M. (Eds.), *Child Well-Being, Child Poverty, and Child Policy in Modern Nations: What Do We Know?* Policy Press, Bristol, pp. 199–219.

Ehrenreich, B. & Piven, F. F. (1984) Women and the Welfare State. In: Howe, I. (Ed.), *Alternatives: Proposals for America from the Democratic Left.* Pantheon, New York, pp. 41–61.

Fraser, N. (1993) Women, Welfare, and the Politics of Need Interpretation. In: Richardson, L. & Taylor, V. (Eds.), *Feminist Frontiers III.* McGraw-Hill, New York, pp. 447–58.

Goldberg, G. S. & Kremen, E. (1990) *The Feminization of Poverty: Only in America?* Praeger, New York.

Jacobs, J. A. & Gerson, K. (2004) *The Time Divide: Work, Family, and Gender Inequality.* Harvard University Press, Cambridge, MA.

McLanahan, S. S. & Kelly, E. L. (1999) The Feminization of Poverty: Past and Future. In: Chafetz, J. S. (Ed.), *Handbook of the Sociology of Gender.* Kluwer Academic/Plenum, New York, pp. 127–45.

Pearce, D. (1978) The Feminization of Poverty: Women, Work, and Welfare. *Urban and Social Change Review* 11: 28–36.

Presser, H. (2003) *Working in a 24/7 Economy: Challenges for American Families.* Russell Sage Foundation, New York.

Ward, K. (1990) *Women Workers and Global Restructuring.* Cornell University Press, Ithaca, NY.

fertility: adolescent

Elizabeth Cooksey

Adolescent fertility refers to the childbearing of women who are less than 20 years old. Despite recent declines in adolescent fertility levels throughout the world, over 15 million babies are born to adolescent women each year. Adolescent fertility rates (defined as the annual number of live births to girls aged 15–19 per 1,000 girls aged 15–19) vary considerably by world region. The worldwide average for the period 2000–5 is estimated at approximately 50 per 1,000, but rates in Sub-Saharan Africa average 127 per 1,000 where countries such as Liberia, Niger, and Uganda have rates above 200 per 1,000. Adolescent fertility is also relatively high in Latin America and the Caribbean at 71 per 1,000. Together, the industrialized countries have an average rate of 24 per 1,000. As a region, East Asia and the Pacific has the lowest figure of only 18 per 1,000 due to rates of 5 or less in China, Japan, and Korea (UN Population Division 2002).

Regardless of the social setting within which adolescent childbearing takes place, there are potentially serious negative health implications associated with adolescent fertility, although the risks are higher in the developing world. Complications resulting from pregnancy and childbirth are the leading cause of death for female youth in less developed countries where an estimated 70,000 teenage girls die each year from causes related to pregnancy and childbirth. Maternal mortality is defined as the number of maternal deaths per 100,000 live births and is exacerbated by inadequate nutrition prior to and during pregnancy, and inadequate medical care during pregnancy, and especially during labor. Because adolescent girls have not finished growing themselves, especially in terms of their height and pelvic size, they are at greater risk of obstructed labor, which occurs when the infant cannot pass through the birth canal. Reproductive health is therefore especially worrisome when the mother is 17 or younger, as her own body is still developing and obstructed labor can lead to serious injury or death for the mother as well as for her infant. Maternal mortality ratios for girls aged 15–19 years can be more than double those of women who give birth in their twenties and early thirties, and very young mothers who are less than 14 years old when they give birth have maternal mortality rates five times higher than those of women in their early twenties.

Adolescents are also more likely than their older counterparts to suffer pregnancy-related complications that can lead to infertility and disability. Obstetric fistula is the most devastating of all pregnancy-related disabilities and is usually the result of obstructed labor. If the mother survives, she can sustain such severe tissue damage to her birth canal that she is left incontinent. Nerve damage to her legs can also make it difficult to walk. Affected women are often rejected by their husbands and shunned by their communities. They are also at risk of recurrent urinary tract infections that can eventually lead to renal failure and death.

Pregnancies may also be unwanted: an estimated 5 million girls aged 15–19 currently seek abortions every year rather than carrying their pregnancy to term. Forty percent of these abortions are performed under unsafe conditions, a factor that contributes to high rates of maternal mortality and morbidity. In Sub-Saharan Africa, for example, where abortion is either illegal or severely restricted, complications resulting from abortions are a major cause of death among adolescent women.

Infants born to teenagers also run a higher risk of low birth weight, prematurity, birth injuries, stillbirth, and dying during infancy. Low birth weight infants have a far greater risk of experiencing lifelong disabilities such as mental retardation, cerebral palsy, and autism. Worldwide, approximately 1 million children born to teenage mothers die each year. Infant mortality rates for births to teenagers are as much as 80 percent higher than those for 20- to 29-year-old women. Some of this age differential may be due to the higher level of first pregnancies among adolescents, as first pregnancies carry a higher risk of complications than do later births. However, even after the first month of life, infants born to adolescent mothers still have poorer survival prospects than those born to mothers in their twenties. Demographic and Health Surveys data from the mid- to late 1990s showed that in Sub-Saharan African countries such as Mali, Mozambique, and Niger, one of every six children born to teen mothers failed to live to age 1.

Approximately two-thirds of the world's adolescents live in Africa, Asia, the Near East, Latin America, and the Caribbean, and 80 percent of adolescent births occur in the developing countries of Asia, Africa, and Latin America where children born to teenagers account for about 13 percent of all births. Due to a legacy of past high fertility, the number of adolescents worldwide is projected to increase, and by the year 2020 about three-quarters of the world's adolescent girls will be living in the developing nations. However, this increase in numbers should be more than offset by declines in teenage birth rates as a result of ongoing urbanization, the progress being made by many nations toward providing better educational opportunities for girls, and the concomitant delay in age at first marriage.

In all developing countries, marriage constitutes the predominant context for childbearing. Teenage fertility levels are closely related to age at marriage as countries with large proportions of young women marrying in their teen years are also countries where adolescent fertility is elevated. Although the trend in many developing countries is toward a later age of first marriage, teenage marriages still prevail in many areas of the world. In Sub-Saharan Africa, for example, nearly 60 percent of women were married by age 20 in the late 1980s and early 1990s. By the late 1990s, this figure had dropped, but still about half of women married prior to age 20.

Not only is fertility closely related to the age at which women marry, but additional important related factors are urbanization and the provision of educational opportunities for girls commensurate with those available to boys. In developing countries, fewer urban than rural women begin childbearing in their teen years, in part reflecting later ages at marriage. Limited education is both a cause and effect of adolescent childbearing: girls who become pregnant are often forced to leave school, and women with more education also marry and have children later. Results from survey analyses using data from the 1990s show that, on average, the proportion of young women with primary schooling who begin childbearing as adolescents is approximately two-thirds that of women with no schooling, and for young women with secondary or higher education the proportion is less than one-third.

Education is also related to maternal and child health outcomes. In developing countries, poorly educated mothers are less likely to receive prenatal care and to be assisted by trained medical personnel at the birth of their children than are their more highly educated peers. Children of mothers with no education are also more than twice as likely to die or to be malnourished than children of mothers with at least a secondary education.

Although the negative health implications of adolescent pregnancy and childbirth exist regardless of societal structure, the extent to which adolescent fertility is viewed as problematic varies by country. In some parts of Asia and Africa where daughters are viewed as an economic liability and have the potential to bring shame on the family if they are not married at a young age, early marriage and childbearing is culturally desirable. Results from Demographic and Health Surveys data collected in the mid- to late 1990s in 11 Sub-Saharan African countries show that in nine of these countries, more than one-third of young women were married before age 18. Seventy percent of girls in Mali were married prior to age 18. In Côte d'Ivoire, Madagascar, Mali,

Mozambique, and Uganda, more than half of 18-year-olds were either already mothers or were pregnant with their first child.

In other, more industrialized areas of the world, such as the United States, adolescent childbearing is viewed with concern by society in general as it is associated with reductions in human capital, decreased labor force options, depressed earnings, and a higher likelihood of long-term poverty for both mothers and their children, increased total fertility, and a diminished likelihood of marriage. But although these associations are real enough, the question remains as to whether adolescent childbearing is the *cause* of these adolescent mothers' reduced socioeconomic well-being and the concomitant increased societal costs. Alternatively, do these adverse outcomes reflect preexisting differences in the backgrounds of teens who give birth that differentiate them from their counterparts who delay childbearing?

The task of disentangling the effect of adolescent childbearing per se from any spurious association due instead to factors that might jointly determine both adolescent fertility and the adverse consequences that occur is a difficult one. However, several studies have taken unique methodological approaches to do so. To control for the selective differences in the background and personal characteristics of teen mothers, Geronimus and Korenman (1992, 1993), for example, compared the life course of pairs of sisters raised in the same family, only one of whom became a teen mother. Hotz et al. (1997) contrasted the later educational achievements, earnings, and receipt of public assistance of teens who miscarried with those of teens who carried their pregnancies to term. Lichter and Graefe (2001) also compared teens who gave birth with those who either miscarried or aborted in order to ascertain if unwed childbearing "caused" delayed or non-marriage.

The results from these and other studies suggest that failing to account for selection bias can lead to a considerable overstating of the negative consequences that might accrue from teenage childbearing, at least with respect to achieved education and earnings, and hence to the magnitude of government subsidies expended. While teen childbearing reduces high school graduation rates, teen mothers are more likely to earn their GEDs by age 30, to work more hours, and to earn more than those who delayed – although they earned less in their teens and early twenties, the situation was reversed in their late twenties and early thirties (Hotz et al. 1997). Sometimes, however, early childbearing does appear to have permanent effects, for example to increase the total number of children born, and, by reducing the likelihood of later marriage for the vast majority of American teens who give birth outside of marriage, to increase the time spent as a single mother (Lichter & Graefe 2001). The jury is still out on how detrimental these effects might be on the children born to young mothers.

In the United States, teenage birth rates have declined more than 20 percent since 1991. While increased abstinence among teens accounts for approximately one-quarter of this fertility decline, most of the drop resulted from changes in the contraceptive behaviors of sexually experienced teens who were increasingly likely to use injectable contraceptives which have very low failure rates, and to use contraception at first intercourse, especially condoms. Abortion rates among teens also declined steeply over the same period.

Adolescent fertility rates in the United States today are less than half the level they were at the peak of the baby boom in the late 1950s: in 1957 the adolescent fertility rate was 96.3 per 1,000, whereas the comparable figure in 2001 was only 45.8 per 1,000. However, the vast majority of adolescent births during the baby boom era were to women who were married at the time of birth, and this situation is reversed today. Eighty-five percent of adolescent births were within marriage in 1957, whereas only about one-fifth of births to American teens currently occur within marriage. Most teens who give birth today continue to reside within their family of origin, and recent research has shown that adolescent childbearing can negatively impact other family members by increasing family financial hardship and stress, and by socializing younger sisters for early parenthood. Because adolescent parents have not acquired the necessary resources to parent, they need assistance from others, which also drains the resources of their extended families.

Despite quite dramatic declines in US adolescent fertility rates, US teens continue to experience substantially higher birth rates than those of teens in other industrialized countries. Data from 1998 showed that more than one-fifth of 20-year-old women in the United States had given birth while in their teens. This contrasts with 5 percent or less in Belgium, Denmark, Finland, France, Greece, Italy, Japan, Republic of Korea, Luxembourg, Netherlands, Norway, Spain, Sweden, and Switzerland (UNICEF 2001). Teenagers in the United States are also more likely than their counterparts in other developed nations to have sexual intercourse before age 15, and each year approximately 19,000 girls aged 14 and under become pregnant.

Within the United States there are significant differences in levels of adolescent fertility by various social, cultural, and demographic factors. For example, black, Hispanic, and Native American youth have traditionally had higher rates than white and Asian youth. Since 1990 the largest decline in adolescent birth rates has been among black teens, and Hispanic teens now have the highest teen birth rates among the five racial and ethnic groups. Native American youth currently have rates about one and a half times the white rate. The rate for black youth is approximately 1.7 times the white rate, and the Hispanic rate is more than twice as high. States with large rural populations, above-average poverty rates, and below-average education levels also have the highest adolescent birth rates. In some of the nation's poorest rural areas, adolescent fertility rates exceed those in many developing countries.

Adolescents are generally viewed as being too young to become parents, especially at younger ages when they may not be biologically, economically, or socially prepared for bearing and rearing children. A girl's body has yet to fully develop, making childbirth dangerous and debilitating. Parenthood can severely curtail future educational plans and it is often those adolescents who are least well prepared to successfully nurture and raise a child who are most likely to become teenage parents. Those who come from economic disadvantage tend to initiate sexual intercourse at younger ages, contracept less effectively, and have more unintended births. The cycle of poverty is a difficult one to break, but education is a key weapon in the fight as it is not only related to delayed marriage and childbearing, which pushes motherhood into developmentally safer ages, but it also prepares girls to be better mothers and have babies that are more likely to survive and thrive.

SEE ALSO: Family Planning, Abortion, and Reproductive Health; Fertility: Nonmarital; Fertility and Public Policy; Infant, Child, and Maternal Health and Mortality; Infertility; Marriage, Sex, and Childbirth; Motherhood

REFERENCES AND SUGGESTED READINGS

Geronimus, A. & Korenman, S. (1992) The Socioeconomic Consequences of Teen Childbearing Reconsidered. *Quarterly Journal of Economics* 107: 1187–1214.

Geronimus, A. & Korenman, S. (1993) The Costs of Teenage Childbearing: Evidence and Interpretation. *Demography* 30: 281–90.

Hotz, V. J., Williams, S. W., & Sanders, S. G. (1997) The Impacts of Teenage Childbearing on the Mothers and the Consequences of Those Impacts for Government. In: Maynard, R. A. (Ed.), *Kids Having Kids: Economic Costs and Social Consequences of Teen Pregnancy*. Urban Institute Press, Washington, DC, pp. 55–94.

Lichter, D. T. & Graefe, D. R. (2001) Finding a Mate? The Marital and Cohabitation Histories of Unwed Mothers. In: Wu, L. L. & Wolfe, B. (Eds.), *Out of Wedlock: Causes and Consequences of Nonmarital Fertility*. Russell Sage Foundation, New York.

UNICEF (2001) A League Table of Teenage Births in Rich Nations. *Innocenti Report Card* No. 3. UNICEF Innocenti Research Center, Florence.

United Nations Population Division (2002) *World Population Prospects: The 2000 Revision*. United Nations, New York. Online. www.un.org/esa/population/publications/wpp2000/chapter1.pdf.

fertility: low

S. Philip Morgan

Low fertility implies a "not low" referent; there are two. The first is "high fertility." High fertility can be defined as some maximal, hypothetical level for a population, i.e., one with early marriage, close birth spacing, and no attempt to control family size. Fifteen births per woman provides a reasonable estimate of mean maximal fertility. The highest observed levels of fertility are closer to ten births per woman, and even in the absence of substantial contraceptive use and abortion can be one-half this level. Regardless, low fertility implies much lower levels – levels approximating two or fewer births per woman. The fertility transition refers to the societal shift from "high" to "low" fertility (and is produced by deliberate attempts to achieve small family sizes).

A second definition, and one emphasized in most contemporary discussions of low fertility, adopts as a referent replacement-level fertility. The concept is straightforward: a birth cohort of women replaces itself if the cohort averages one female birth per woman that survives to reproductive age. After adjustment for low levels of mortality and for normal sex ratios at birth (common features of developed countries), replacement fertility is approximately 2.1 births (male and female) per woman. Given this referent, low fertility implies levels well below what is needed for replacement.

A practical weakness of this cohort fertility measure is that it cannot be calculated until the cohort reaches (or nearly reaches) the end of the childbearing years. Thus, the most commonly used measures of fertility are not cumulative measures for birth cohorts, but are measures calculated for calendar years (i.e., period measures). The most commonly used period measure, the total fertility rate (TFR), is calculated from age-specific rates for a given year and is thus unaffected by population age composition. It also has an intuitive meaning; i.e., the number of children women would have if they experienced a given year's age-specific rates throughout their childbearing years. As above, assuming low mortality levels and normal sex ratios, replacement level TFR approximates 2.1 births per woman.

Note that any fertility level below replacement, if maintained sufficiently long, would bring about dramatic population decline. But current concerns focus on very low fertility or "lowest-low" fertility, levels that imply dramatic population decline within several generations. For 2000, Paul Demeny (2003: 2) calculates the population weighted average TFR of Europe as 1.37. Given Europe's 2000 mortality rates and this fertility level, a population of 1,000 would replace itself with 645 persons and after a century the population size would be 232 persons! Of course, any designation is arbitrary, but the implications of TFRs of 1.8 and 1.3 are dramatically different. Thus, for our discussion here we define a TFR below 2.0 as low fertility and a level of 1.5 or below as very low fertility; but these two benchmarks indicate that low fertility is a matter of degree (more than kind).

THE GLOBAL SPREAD OF LOW FERTILITY AND ITS CONSEQUENCES

Low fertility is rapidly becoming a pervasive, global phenomenon. Using data for 2000, the United Nations lists only 16 (of a total of 187) countries as *not* showing clear evidence of a fertility decline. Lingering high fertility has become geographically isolated and affects fewer of the world's people. Only 3 percent of the global population lives in countries not yet in fertility transition. The UN projects that all of these countries will soon begin a transition toward replacement-level fertility. In contrast, 64 countries had replacement-level fertility or lower in 2000. Twenty-three recently made the transition to low fertility and another set of 41 countries has had several decades of low fertility punctuated by a baby boom and bust. Taking these countries together, 44 percent of the 2000 global population lived in countries with low fertility.

Between these extremes are 105 countries now experiencing fertility declines, 96 percent of which have their most recent estimate as their lowest recorded fertility. Thus, we say they are in transition because empirical evidence shows that, once begun, these declines do not stop until fertility reaches replacement or below. As of 2000, only two countries (Uruguay and Argentina) had halted their transition at a fertility level substantially above replacement levels. Others with currently high TFRs could do so, but evidence clearly suggests that arrested declines will be rare.

Given the population growth concerns of the last half-century, this evidence and UN projections of these trends portend a remarkable achievement: the diffusing of the "population explosion" and the realistic potential for an end to global population growth shortly after mid-twenty-first century. However, concerns of rapid population growth are being replaced by concerns about very low fertility. At the aggregate level, low fertility implies declines in population size and an aging population. Declines in population size, in turn, mean fewer domestic consumers, producers, and warriors. An aging society implies an increase in the ratio of older, dependent persons to working-age persons. These changes in size and composition require societal adjustments. Perhaps most crucial are labor force shortages and the provision of income maintenance and medical care for large elderly populations (compared to the working-age population). Immigration provides a partial solution but requires that immigrants are willing to come and that natives are willing to tolerate immigrant flows large enough to offset low fertility. The latter are especially challenging when large flows of immigrants are needed to compensate for very low fertility. Societies could also dramatically transform social support for the elderly. Public support could be based on need and retirement ages could be dramatically increased. The political palpability of such changes is uncertain.

DECOMPOSITION AND PROXIMATE DETERMINANTS APPROACHES TO STUDYING LOW FERTILITY

Fertility research has benefited greatly from decomposition and/or proximate determinants approaches. The former disaggregates fertility into constituent parts to assess which ones are responsible for overall change. The latter links fertility to its most important proximate causes; in turn, these proximate causes become factors to be understood. The rationale for this level of explanation is that it identifies more precisely "what needs to be explained."

Decomposition Approaches

Classic demographic approaches disaggregate fertility along two dimensions: parity (e.g., the number of prior births of the woman) and the mothers' ages at births (or the timing of fertility). If one examines fertility by parity, then one can see whether current trends are produced by changes in the birth propensity of childless women, those with one child, or those at higher parities. For example, the transition from high to low fertility has resulted from the declining incidence of higher-parity births. In contrast, fertility trends in low-fertility populations hinge on the behavior of women with no or few births. For instance, Norman Ryder (1980) shows that the fertility behavior of childless women and those with one child accounts for substantial parts of the American baby boom and bust (the 1945–80 period). John Bongaarts and Griffith Feeney's (1998) work illustrates the crucial importance of postponed first births for understanding contemporary cross-national fertility trends and differentials.

As the mention of postponed first births indicates, the age of childbearing at each parity is important. As defined above, the TFR has an intuitive meaning; i.e., the number of children women would have if they experienced current age-specific rates throughout their childbearing years. The TFR for women childless at the beginning of the year can be interpreted as the proportion that would have at least one child given current rates. This definition makes clear the hypothetical nature of the measure. No birth cohort of women necessarily experiences exactly the rates of a given period. In fact, timing shifts across cohorts are common and can be quite dramatic. For example, let us assume that 80 percent of women will always have at least one child. Now let us allow for a decline in the ages of first birth. As long as this trend toward earlier childbearing continues, the period measure will rise above 0.8. In effect, births that would have occurred in the future under the previous timing regime are being pushed earlier and are inflating the birth rate in the current year. In a parallel fashion, increases in ages at first birth push births into the future, depressing estimates of the first birth period rate in the current period. Bongaarts and Feeney (1998) show that a good estimate of this effect is the change in the mean age at childbearing at that parity. For example, if the mean age of first births increases by 0.15 a year, then the first birth TFR is reduced by a factor of 0.85 (1.0 − 0.15 = 0.85). Thus it

follows that given an underlying quantum of fertility (say 0.80 having a first birth), declines in mean age at childbearing increase the TFR, and postponement of fertility depresses TFR relative to underlying quantum.

These associations are important because changes in fertility timing can have prolonged and substantial effects on period rates. Part of the reason for low rates observed during the 1980s and 1990s was a pervasive shift upwards in the ages at childbearing (especially controlling on the woman's parity). Bongaarts and Feeney show that timing shifts can reduce period rates by 10–20 percent for up to two to three decades. Thus a country with a TFR of 1.7 may not have any birth cohort of women that averages fewer than 2.0 births (2.0/0.85 = 1.7). So shifts to later childbearing are a significant part of the contemporary story of very low fertility. But the end of postponement would still leave many countries with fertility well below replacement. Low fertility explanations thus must account for both fertility postponements (changes in timing or tempo) and for fewer births per woman (lower quantum). The causal explanation may differ for these two components and decomposition analyses push researchers to understand these twin causes: fertility postponement and fewer births.

Proximate Determinants

In settings where birth control and abortion are available and widely used, decisions to have children play a central role in models of fertility by linking more distal determinants to fertility. This framework does not suggest that intentions always play a dynamic role in contemporary fertility change. In fact, in developed countries fertility intentions have changed little in the past two decades and vary little across developed countries; there exists a remarkably persistent and pervasive desire for two children. Thus, cross-country and cross-time variation must be explained by timing changes (discussed above) and women's/couples' ability and determination to realize intentions (not changes or difference in intentions).

In this conceptualization, the level of current fertility (the TFR) equals the number of children women intend but increased or decreased by a set of factors women cannot anticipate and thus have not been incorporated into their reports of childbearing intentions. If all women realized their intended parity (IP), then the TFR = IP. Some factors inflate completed parity vis-à-vis intended fertility, e.g., unwanted fertility, replacement of children that may have died, and additional children needed to satisfy strong gender preferences. Other factors would reduce fertility relative to intentions. These factors include changes in the timing of fertility discussed above, subfecundity and infecundity associated with older ages of childbearing, and competition with other energy- and time-intensive activities that may lead persons to revise downward their intentions, especially at older ages.

The primary explanation for very low fertility codified in this model is that women (on average) fail to realize their intentions for even small and modest-sized families. This insight directs our attention to factors that influence attainment of these goals. The process producing this lower-than-intended fertility is a life course process of fertility postponement that increases the likelihood that at older ages intentions will be revised downwards or infecundity will come into play.

FUNDAMENTAL CAUSES OF LOW FERTILITY

The weakness of the decomposition and proximate determinants approaches (discussed above) is that they leave the fundamental or exogenous cause unspecified. As a result, these explanations are only partial and beg the question: why is it that childlessness is greater or intentions are more likely to be met in one country compared to another?

Few would dispute that the transition from high to low fertility results from industrialization and post-industrialization that increased "costs" (broadly conceived) of bearing and raising children. The timing of these fertility declines vis-à-vis particular aspects of socio-economic change (and the resultant changes in child cost) was variable because populations had to recognize and conceptualize changing child costs and rationalize new fertility regulation behaviors. The new fertility regime

was one of small families. No country has become economically developed without experiencing the transition to small families.

But this powerful explanation for the fertility transition is not very useful for explaining variation in low fertility or for predicting its future course. Instead, there are two competing explanations. The first focuses on the cost/difficulty of childbearing and rearing in all contemporary settings. But it views the degree of incompatibility as variable, contingent on a set of society-specific factors that decrease/increase incompatibility. For instance, all developed countries have experienced increases in female labor force participation. However, some societies experience increases in women's labor force participation with little change in fertility; for others, similar changes have accompanied sharp fertility declines. To account for these variable responses, one needs to document the institutional factors that make work and family more (or less) compatible for women in some countries than others. The most complete explanations require idiosyncratic explanations. But general patterns can be described. Peter McDonald (2000) argues that societal gender equality reduces work/family incompatibility. Specifically, when women enter the workforce but other institutions (e.g., the family, gender relations) do not make adjustments, it makes the joint roles of mother/worker very difficult. Some employed women resolve this incompatibility by having no or only one child. Greater gender equality (accompanying increases in women's non-family work) eases women's work/family burden. Such adjustments facilitate women having the moderate number of children that they intend. The state can also respond with policies that encourage gender equality and that recognize the burden of bearing and caring for children. Public provision of children's health care and day care provide important examples. Finally, the market can respond; examples include widely available flextime for employees and consumer goods and services that substitute for home production.

A second explanation (for variation in low fertility) focuses on a putative irreversible shift toward an ideology that stresses individualism and self-actualization. This ideology encourages women/couples to consider whether becoming a parent or having another child would make them happier or their life more meaningful. Dirk Van de Kaa (2001) and Ron Lesthaeghe and Paul Willems (1999) argue that this spreading ideology has fostered a second demographic transition – later union formation, greater cohabitation, frequent union dissolution, and very low fertility. Given the very high direct and indirect costs of childbearing and rearing and this ideology that makes parenthood one of a range of acceptable lifestyles, these authors are pessimistic about fertility recuperating to approximate replacement levels.

FUTURE RESEARCH AND KEY UNANSWERED QUESTIONS

A key unanswered question is whether countries now undergoing a fertility transition will experience fertility well below replacement levels in the coming decades. Current evidence and theory suggest that settings with great gender inequality may experience the most dramatic fertility declines as women in these societies undertake non-familial employment. However, the experience of developed countries may encourage more rapid adoption of strategies to reduce work/family competition for women's time and energies. The widespread adoption of effective policy responses is a second plausible scenario. Thirdly, some societies may be able to maintain fertility at/above replacement levels by embracing fundamentalist ideology or identifying motherhood/parenthood strongly with group identity. Such cultural/ideological responses gird families and women to accept the high costs of parenthood.

But equally important is the course of future fertility in countries that already have low fertility. Fertility postponement explains a significant part of contemporary very low fertility, but when postponement abates (as it eventually must), many countries will still have fertility levels well below replacement levels. One of the key questions for the twenty-first century is whether and how effectively societies will respond. Comparative research can contribute by identifying effective responses or "packages" of responses that prove effective. The challenge is fundamental because replacement of the population is required for societal survival and because the costs of childbearing and rearing in contemporary settings are huge. The changes in institutions and the redirection of resources toward parents and children that will likely be required pose a huge challenge for societies with very low fertility.

SEE ALSO: Aging and Social Policy; Demographic Techniques: Decomposition and Standardization; Demographic Transition Theory; Fertility and Public Policy; Fertility: Transitions and Measures; Gender, Work, and Family; Immigration Policy; Infertility; Migration: International; Second Demographic Transition

REFERENCES AND SUGGESTED READINGS

Bongaarts, J. (2001) Fertility and Reproductive Preferences in Post-Transitional Societies. *Population and Development Review* 27: 260–81.

Bongaarts, J. (2002) The End of Fertility Transition in the Developed World. *Population and Development Review* 28: 419–44.

Bongaarts, J. & Bulatao, R. A. (Eds.) (2000) *Beyond Six Billion: Forecasting the World's Population.* NAS Press, Washington, DC.

Bongaarts, J. & Feeney, G. (1998) On the Quantum and Tempo of Fertility. *Population and Development Review* 24: 271–91.

Demeny, P. (2003) Population Policy Dilemmas in Europe at the Dawn of the Twenty-First Century. *Population and Development Review* 29: 1–28.

Lesthaeghe, R. & Willems, P. (1999) Is Low Fertility a Temporary Phenomenon in the European Union? *Population and Development Review* 25: 211–28.

McDonald, P. (2000) Gender Equity in Theories of Fertility Transition. *Population and Development Review* 26: 427–39.

Morgan, S. P. (2003) Is Low Fertility a Twenty-First-Century Demographic Crisis? *Demography* 40: 589–603.

Ryder, N. B. (1980) Components of Temporal Variations in American Fertility. In: Hiorns, R. W. (Ed.), *Demographic Patterns in Developed Societies.* Taylor & Francis, London.

United Nations Population Division (2002) *World Population Prospects: The (2000) Revision.* United Nations, New York. Online. www.un.org/esa/population/publications/wpp2000/chapter1.pdf.

Van de Kaa, D. J. (2001) Postmodern Fertility Preferences: From Changing Value Orientation to New Behavior. *Population and Development Review* 27: 290–331.

fertility: nonmarital

Kelly Musick

Nonmarital fertility – or having a child outside of marriage – has become an increasingly important phenomenon demographically, socially, and politically. Fully one in three US births were to unmarried women in 2000, compared to just 5 percent in 1960. This change has generated a great deal of concern. Many worry because unmarried mothers tend to be younger and less advantaged socially and economically than married mothers, and their children tend not to do as well as those living with two married biological parents. Others worry that the growing number of families formed outside of marriage is weakening the institution of marriage. Policymakers have introduced measures in recent years explicitly designed to reduce the number of births to unmarried women. The 1996 welfare reform legislation, Personal Responsibility and Work Opportunity Reconciliation Act (PRWORA), for example, includes incentives for states to reduce their rates of nonmarital childbearing, and reauthorization legislation includes resources to strengthen and promote marriage through outreach and counseling.

Three indicators are used to measure the extent of nonmarital fertility: the number of births to unmarried women; the nonmarital birth rate, or the proportion of unmarried women who have a birth each year; and the nonmarital birth ratio, or the proportion of all births that occur outside of marriage. In the United States, each of these indicators shows a dramatic increase in nonmarital fertility between 1960 and 1990 and a slowing or stabilization thereafter. These trends reflect changes in marital behavior. Men and women are getting married later, they are more likely to live together before marriage, and their marriages are less likely to last. They are spending an increasing number of years unmarried and sexually active, putting them at greater risk of having a child outside of marriage.

The United States is not unique in experiencing changes in marriage and fertility. Nonmarital fertility, cohabitation, and delayed marriage are common features of family life in many western industrialized countries. The level of nonmarital childbearing in the US falls about in the middle compared to its European counterparts. Nonmarital fertility rates in the US are comparable to those in the United Kingdom and France; rates are lower than those in the Scandinavian countries and higher than those in Germany, Italy, and Spain.

The underlying causes of nonmarital fertility in the US and elsewhere must be understood in the context of changes in marriage, i.e., changes affecting the desirability, feasibility, or necessity of marriage. Four main ideas have received considerable attention in policy and academic circles. First, Gary Becker and the new home economics posit that women's growing economic independence has eroded the benefits of marriage. According to Becker and others, gains to marriage are derived from a highly specialized division of labor in which women depend on men's earnings in the labor market and men depend on women's caretaking and child-rearing at home. As men's and women's roles become more complementary, they become less dependent on marriage. Although the dramatic increase in women's labor force participation in recent decades mirrors the decline in marriage and the increase in nonmarital fertility, the bulk of the evidence does not support the economic independence hypothesis. Women with greater resources, i.e., those with more education and higher earnings potential, are in fact more likely to marry than women with poorer economic prospects.

The second commonly offered explanation for changes in marriage and fertility focuses on men's economic prospects. William Julius Wilson, Valerie Oppenheimer, and others have argued that declines in men's wages have made it more difficult for couples to establish stable family lives. In *The Truly Disadvantaged* (1987), Wilson emphasizes structural changes in the economy over the past 30 years that have drastically reduced the earning power of low-skilled men. He argues that declines in labor force participation and wages have created a lack of "marriageable men," particularly among African Americans. Research shows that men's economic prospects are an important predictor of marriage, although they cannot fully explain declines in marriage rates.

Third, welfare has been blamed for declines in marriage and increases in childbearing outside of marriage. In his 1984 book, *Losing Ground*, Charles Murray uses a fictitious couple to illustrate how the availability of government assistance makes remaining unmarried a rational choice for low-income women. He argues that because single women are eligible for more help than married women, couples are better off living together than marrying. Although welfare reform legislation in the mid-1990s attempted to change this, disincentives to marry remain. Moreover, like female employment and earnings, welfare makes women less dependent on men. Although the welfare argument continues to have considerable political currency, trends in benefit levels and family change provide little support: real welfare benefits began to erode in the 1970s and 1980s, as nonmarital childbearing continued to rise. Robert Moffitt has extensively studied the micro-level association between welfare and family formation, and concludes that welfare has affected marriage and childbearing over the years, but the magnitude of the effect is small relative to other factors.

Finally, attitudes and values have been discussed as a potentially important factor behind increasing nonmarital fertility. In recent decades, men and women have become more tolerant of nonmarital childbearing and related behaviors, including sex outside of marriage, cohabitation, and single parenthood. Greater acceptance of family life outside of marriage has reduced the social and family pressure to marry, even as young people continue to express the desire to marry. Attitudinal change has gone hand in hand with increases in nonmarital fertility and cohabitation. It is difficult, however, to determine whether changes in attitudes have fueled changes in the family or, rather, whether increasing diversity in family life has led to more tolerance of a range of family behaviors. Some see changing values as an inevitable reaction – with costs as well as benefits – to increasing individualism, secularization, and gender equality (e.g., Bumpass 1990). Others view them more skeptically as indicators of family decline with harmful consequences for children (e.g., Popenoe 1993).

A good theory of nonmarital fertility should explain not just why it has increased, but why it is more common among some groups than others. Patterns of nonmarital fertility vary considerably by socioeconomic status, race, and age. Nonmarital births tend to occur to women who are relatively disadvantaged socially and economically. In the early 1990s, for example, over half of all births to women with less than a high school degree were to unmarried women, whereas this was the case for just 5 percent of births to women with a college degree. There has been little research on education differences between married and unmarried mothers in European countries with similarly high levels of nonmarital fertility. We do know, however, that unmarried mothers are less likely to be poor in Europe than in the US. This is due in part to Europe's relatively generous public assistance programs; it may also be related to the greater likelihood of unmarried mothers in Europe to be living with their partners when their children are born. In the US, levels of nonmarital childbearing also differ significantly by race, although the gap has been closing. In 2002, 23 percent of births to white women, 44 percent of births to Hispanic women, and 68 percent of births to black women were nonmarital (data from Table 7, *National Vital Statistics Report*, Vol. 52, No. 9).

Unmarried mothers are younger on average than married mothers. Thirty percent of all nonmarital births – and most first nonmarital births – are to women in their teens. Teenage childbearing has been a public issue of great concern since the 1970s. It entered the national agenda not when it was at its peak, but as the proportion of unmarried teenage mothers grew and fewer teenagers opted into marriage following a premarital conception. Rates of teenage childbearing have reached record lows in recent years (the lowest levels since the Centers for Disease Control and Prevention began calculating them in 1976), falling substantially over the course of the 1990s, particularly among blacks. Despite declines, rates of teenage childbearing continue to be much higher (by two to ten times) in the US than in other developed countries. They remain a public issue, moreover, because the vast majority of teenage births are outside of marriage; indeed, given the delay in marriage, a much higher percent are nonmarital today than when teen births were more common.

Although age is an important dimension of nonmarital fertility, nonmarital childbearing is too often viewed as synonymous with teenage childbearing. Policy and academic discussions have focused on young first-time mothers, paying little attention to the 70 percent of nonmarital births to women in their twenties and older, many of whom already have children. Because of the focus on teenage mothers, research and debate have primarily addressed the factors leading to early sex and unintended pregnancy. The processes leading to an unmarried birth are likely very different for older women.

There is little research on the consequences of nonmarital fertility for mothers and children. Two related literatures – on single-parent families and teenage childbearing – shed light on the question but do not address it directly. Single parenthood results from nonmarital childbearing and divorce, and many studies do not distinguish between the two. Among those that do, families headed by never-married and divorced mothers seem to be related in similar ways to child well-being. Children from single-parent families tend to fare more poorly than children from biological married-parent families in terms of school achievement, occupational attainment, and income. Girls from single-parent families are also more likely to become single mothers later in life. Teenage childbearing is associated with a host of negative outcomes for mothers: teenage mothers are less likely to graduate from high school and college and more likely to live in poverty. Young unmarried mothers are less likely to marry than women without children.

While associations between well-being, single parenthood, and teen parenthood are well established, the extent to which negative outcomes are a consequence of single parenthood and teen parenthood remains unclear. Women who enter into these statuses are different from those who do not, and it is difficult to distinguish between preexisting differences and causal effects. Teenage mothers, for example, come from relatively disadvantaged families, which places them at greater risk of dropping out of high school and falling into poverty, independent of early childbearing. Analysts have carefully designed studies to minimize the preexisting differences between women who have had a teen birth and those who have not. One approach has been to compare later-life outcomes of sisters or cousins – who presumably share many

important family characteristics – with and without a teen birth. Another approach has attempted to use the "random" event of having a miscarriage to compare the outcomes of teen women who did and did not give birth but are otherwise similar. These studies find that preexisting differences account for a sizable share of the association between teenage childbearing and mothers' outcomes, but probably not all. Similarly, the relationship between single parenthood and child well-being is due at least in part to preexisting differences between women who become single mothers and those who do not. For example, children who grow up in highly conflicted two-parent families fare about as poorly on many measures as children from single-parent families, suggesting that unmeasured differences in the quality of parental relationships may account for differences between children from single-parent and two-parent families. Family background, education, and income are other dimensions on which women are differentially selected into single parenthood.

In recent years, the focus on early childbearing has given way to a more detailed examination of the romantic relationships and living arrangements of unmarried mothers. This shift has been driven by changes in the characteristics of unmarried mothers, including increases in the average age at birth and, particularly, increases in cohabitation. Since the 1970s, cohabitation outside of marriage has become a common and acceptable behavior: half of all couples now live together before marriage. As of 1995, 40 percent of all nonmarital births were to cohabiting couples, and nearly all of the increase in nonmarital fertility since the late 1980s was due to increases in births to cohabitors. Cohabitation may have very different implications for father involvement, child well-being, and welfare dependence than single motherhood. These facts are just beginning to be digested by policymakers and social commentators. Policy attention since 2000 has begun to shift from pregnancy prevention among teen women to marriage promotion among young adults.

Research is starting to address key questions about the relationship context of births to unmarried women, the stability of these relationships, and the level of father involvement typical of them. Analyses are being extended to couples' decisions to cohabit rather than marry and implications of this choice for children. The Fragile Families Study, a representative sample of nonmarital births in cities of 200,000 and over, is unique in collecting information from both parents, irrespective of their living arrangements. These data have allowed researchers to examine a range of parental relationships into which children are born, including those in which parents are uninvolved romantically, romantic visiting relationships, and cohabiting relationships. These data have shed light on the role of unmarried fathers in the lives of their children and the relationships of unmarried mothers and fathers. Recent research is also moving away from the assumption that most births to unmarried women are unintended. Kathryn Edin and Paula England are analyzing qualitative data designed to distinguish between planning a child outside of marriage, ambivalence, and contraceptive misuse and failure.

Decisions about having children, cohabiting, marrying, and ending a relationship are closely intertwined. Nonmarital fertility is difficult to study because it lies at the intersection of these family processes. In addition to conceptual difficulties, small sample sizes and truncated life histories often limit our ability to empirically examine meaningful differences in the pathways women follow through childbearing, cohabitation, and marriage. The context of nonmarital births is heterogeneous with respect to mother's age, parental relationships, and father involvement, and this heterogeneity is likely important for child outcomes. Understanding differences in the contexts of nonmarital families, while at the same time paying attention to differences in how children experience family transitions according to their sex and developmental stage, is a challenge for future research.

SEE ALSO: Family Demography; Family Diversity; Family, Men's Involvement in; Family Planning, Abortion, and Reproductive Health; Family Structure and Child Outcomes; Family Structure and Poverty; Fertility: Adolescent; Fertility and Public Policy; Intimate Union Formation and Dissolution; Second Demographic Transition; Union Formation and Dissolution

REFERENCES AND SUGGESTED READINGS

Bumpass, L. (1990) What's Happening to the Family? Interactions between Demographic and Institutional Change. *Demography* 27(4): 483–98.

Bumpass, L. & Lu, H.-H. (2000) Trends in Cohabitation and Implications for Children's Family Contexts in the United States. *Population Studies* 54: 29–41.

Carlson, M., McLanahan, S., & England, P. (2004) Union Formation in Fragile Families. *Demography* 41(2): 237–61.

Department of Health and Human Services (1995) Report to Congress on Out-of-Wedlock Childbearing. National Center for Health Statistics, Centers for Disease Control and Prevention, Hyattsville, MD.

Edin, K. & Kefalas, M. (2006) *Promises I Can Keep: Why Poor Women Put Motherhood Before Marriage.* University of California Press, Berkeley.

Hoffman, S. D., Foster, E. M., & Furstenberg, F. F., Jr. (1993) Reevaluating the Costs of Teenage Childbearing. *Demography* 30(1): 1–13.

Hotz, V. J., Williams, S. W., & Sanders, S. G. (1997) The Impacts of Teenage Childbearing on the Mothers and the Consequences of Those Impacts for Government. In: Maynard, R. A. (Ed.), *Kids Having Kids: Economic Costs and Social Consequences of Teen Pregnancy.* Urban Institute Press, Washington, DC, pp. 55–94.

McLanahan, S. & Sandefur, G. (1994) *Growing Up With a Single Parent.* Harvard University Press, Cambridge, MA.

Popenoe, D. (1993) American Family Decline, 1960–1990: A Review and Appraisal. *Journal of Marriage and the Family* 55(3): 527–42.

Wu, L. L. & Wolfe, B. (Eds.) (2001) *Out of Wedlock: Causes and Consequences of Nonmarital Fertility.* Russell Sage Foundation, New York.

fertility and public policy

John Bongaarts

Fertility levels vary widely among contemporary populations, from a high of 7.9 births per woman in Niger to a low of 0.8 in Macao (United Nations 2005). These levels are largely the result of decisions made by individual couples who are trying to maximize their families' welfare. In the least developed countries, fertility is high because children are valued for the social and economic benefits they provide to their families and the cost of childbearing and rearing is typically low. In contrast, in the most industrialized countries, couples want and have small families because the value of children is relatively low and their costs are high. The fertility that results from this individual decision-making is not necessarily optimal from a societal point of view, thus suggesting a potential role for government intervention.

Many governments regard the fertility level of their countries as unsatisfactory. A worldwide survey of population policies undertaken by the United Nations found that the proportion of countries that are not satisfied with their level of fertility has increased from 47 percent in 1976 to 63 percent in 2003 (United Nations 2004). In the developed world (Europe, North America, Japan, Australia, and New Zealand) 58 percent of countries consider fertility too low and none considers it too high. In the developing world (Africa, most of Asia and Latin America) 58 percent of countries consider fertility too high and 8 percent too low. A range of public policies have been developed in response to these concerns.

POLICY RESPONSES TO HIGH FERTILITY IN THE DEVELOPING WORLD

In the 1950s and 1960s declines in mortality caused a sharp acceleration of population growth throughout the developing world. This growth led to widespread concern about its potential adverse consequences for human welfare and the environment, particularly in the poor countries of Asia, Latin America, and Africa where growth was expected to be most rapid. As a result, in the 1960s and 1970s funding and technical assistance expanded enormously for developing country governments that were willing to take action. Efforts by these governments to curb rapid population growth focused on reducing high birth rates because other demographic changes (raising the death rate or massive emigration) were obviously not

desirable. The large majority of governments attempted to reduce high birth rates through the implementation of voluntary family planning programs. The aim of these programs was to provide information about and access to contraception to permit women and men to take control of their reproductive lives and avoid unwanted childbearing. Only in rare cases, most notably in China, has coercion been used. Newly available contraceptive methods such as the pill and IUD greatly facilitated the delivery of family planning services. Successful implementation of such programs in a few countries in the 1960s (e.g., Taiwan and Korea) encouraged other governments to follow this programmatic approach.

The choice of voluntary family planning programs as the principal policy instrument to reduce fertility is based largely on the documentation of a substantial level of unwanted childbearing and unsatisfied demand for contraception. When questioned in surveys, large proportions of married women in the developing world report that they do not want a pregnancy soon. Some of these women want no more children because they have already achieved their desired family size, while others want to wait before having the next wanted pregnancy. A substantial proportion of these women are not protected from the risk of pregnancy by practicing effective contraception (including sterilization) and, as a result, unintended pregnancies are common. In the mid-1990s, 36 percent of all pregnancies in the developing world were unplanned and 20 percent of all pregnancies ended in abortion (Alan Guttmacher Institute 1999). The existence of an unmet need for contraception, first documented in the 1960s, convinced policymakers that family planning programs were needed and would be acceptable and effective.

The effectiveness of this approach was supported by experiments such as the one conducted in the Matlab district of rural Bangladesh (Cleland et al. 1994). When this experiment began in the 1970s, Bangladesh was one of the poorest and least developed countries, and there was considerable skepticism that reproductive behavior could be changed in such a setting. Comprehensive family planning and reproductive health services were provided in the treatment area of the experiment. A wide choice of methods was offered, the quality of referral and follow-up was improved, and a new cadre of well-trained women replaced traditional birth attendants as service providers. The results of these improvements were immediate and pronounced, with contraceptive use rising sharply. No such change was observed in the comparison area. The differences between these two areas in contraceptive use and fertility have been maintained over time. The success of the Matlab experiment demonstrated that appropriately designed services can reduce unmet need for contraception even in traditional settings.

The expansion of international and national investments in family planning programs in the 1970s and 1980s coincided with a massive decline in fertility in much of the developing world. Fertility had been high and stable at about 6 births per woman until the late 1960s, when a sharp decline began. By 2000 fertility had dropped by half to about 3 births per woman on average. The largest declines occurred in Asia and Latin America, but declines are now also underway in many parts of Africa. There is little doubt that family planning programs made a substantial contribution to this decline by reducing unwanted pregnancies (Bongaarts 1997). However, it is also true that much of the decline would have happened anyway because of the rapid social and economic changes that occurred in much of the developing world in recent decades. The resulting modernization of societies has reduced desired family size which, when implemented through the rising use of birth control, has brought about lower fertility.

Family planning programs are limited in their ability to lower fertility because they aim to reduce unwanted fertility and their effect on desired family size is apparently weak or non-existent (Freedman 1997). The implication of this finding is that countries in which wanted fertility is high will need declines in preferences to complete their fertility transition. Such declines are usually achieved by improvements in socioeconomic conditions. It is widely believed that desired fertility is most responsive to improvements in human development, in particular in female education and child survival (Caldwell 1980; Sen 1999). This conclusion is strongly supported by the fact that low fertility has been achieved in some very poor societies such as Sri Lanka and the state of Kerala in India. Although poor, these populations have high levels of literacy and female empowerment and low infant and child mortality. The most effective public policies to reduce high fertility therefore pursue two general options: strengthen the family planning program and encourage human development. The former is aimed primarily at reducing unplanned pregnancy and the latter at reducing the demand for children.

POLICY RESPONSES TO LOW FERTILITY IN THE DEVELOPED WORLD

In the 1990s fertility transitions in most developing countries were well underway or even nearing completion and, as a result, these issues became less urgent. Attention of the scientific and policy communities then increasingly turned to a relatively new and unexpected development, namely the very low fertility observed in most developed societies. Until the 1990s demographers widely expected fertility to level off at or near the replacement level of about 2.1 births per woman at the end of the transition, and population projections made by international agencies such as the UN often incorporated this assumption. This view is now seen as ill-founded because fertility in virtually all modern societies has dropped below the replacement level. The average fertility of the developed world in 2000–2005 is estimated at 1.6 births per woman and in several countries fertility is less than 1.3 (United Nations 2005).

Low fertility has become of concern because further declines or even a continuation of current levels will lead to rapid population aging and to a decline in population size. These demographic developments in turn will have substantial social and economic consequences. In particular, rapid population aging threatens the sustainability of public pension and health care systems (OECD 1998; World Bank 1994). These popular programs have been successful in improving the health and welfare of the elderly. However, expenditures by widely implemented pay-as-you-go programs, which rely on transfers from younger to older generations, are becoming increasingly burdensome on the contributors and are eventually unsustainable as old-age "dependency rates" rise to high levels.

Identifying and implementing reforms of public pension and health care systems under these changing demographic conditions represent an urgent new challenge for public policy. Avoiding action is no longer a feasible option because an unprecedented and harmful accumulation of debt would then result. In the past, the rising cost of public support for the elderly has often been covered by raising taxes, but these have reached such high levels that expenditure-reducing approaches are now given highest priority. Reforms now focus on achieving reductions in future benefits even though this option is difficult politically because large proportions of pensioners receive public benefits. In addition, efforts are being considered to encourage later age at retirement by removing incentives to early retirement. Reforms adopted in recent years are generally phased in slowly, thus leaving current pensioners largely unaffected; their impact will therefore be felt mainly by future retirees.

Demographic options are generally ignored in the ongoing debate about reform. Many governments are reluctant to support pronatalist measures because of a disinclination to interfere with personal decision-making regarding family size, or because of the apparent inconsistency of advocating pronatalism at home while supporting efforts to reduce fertility in poor developing countries; in addition, they may hope that fertility will soon increase again without intervention (Caldwell et al. 2002; Demeny 2003; Gauthier 1996). Furthermore, low levels of recent fertility have not yet led to declines in population size in most developed countries, because the effects of below-replacement fertility have been offset temporarily by modest levels of immigration and population momentum. It seems likely, however, that growing concerns about the implications of population aging will stimulate more interest in efforts to encourage higher fertility directly or indirectly. For example, family support measures such as subsidized childcare, reduced taxes for families with children, and paid parental leaves are widely acceptable and could be expanded. A recent review of the impact of such measures by Caldwell et al. (2002) concludes that they do

raise fertility modestly provided the subsidies are sufficiently large. The fact that desired family size in most developed countries is still around 2 indicates that actual fertility is lower than desired and strongly suggests that birth rates can be raised by policies that reduce the cost of childbearing and help women to combine a career with childbearing.

Most governments of OECD countries are now well aware of the challenges posed by population aging caused primarily by low fertility. The modest ongoing reforms of pension and health care systems are a step in the right direction, but they are far from adequate. It is likely that further reform will include direct and indirect measures to support families to achieve their desired fertility.

SEE ALSO: Demographic Transition Theory; Family Planning, Abortion, and Reproductive Health; Fertility: Low; Fertility: Transitions and Measures; Population and Economy; Second Demographic Transition

REFERENCES AND SUGGESTED READINGS

Alan Guttmacher Institute (1999) *Sharing Responsibility: Women, Society and Abortion Worldwide.* Alan Guttmacher Institute, New York.
Bongaarts, J. (1997) The Role of Family Planning Programmes in Contemporary Fertility Transitions. In: Jones, G. W., Caldwell, J. C., Douglas, R. M., & D'Souza, R. M. (Eds.), *The Continuing Demographic Transition.* Clarendon Press, Oxford, pp. 422–44.
Caldwell, J. C. (1980) Mass Education as a Determinant of the Timing of Fertility Decline. *Population and Development Review* 6(2): 225–55.
Caldwell, J. C., Caldwell, P., & McDonald, P. (2002) Policy Responses to Low Fertility and its Consequences: A Global Survey. *Journal of Population Research* 19(1): 1–24.
Cleland, J., Phillips, J. F., Amin, S., & Kamal, G. M. (1994) *The Determinants of Reproductive Change in Bangladesh: Success in a Challenging Environment.* World Bank, Washington, DC.
Demeny, P. (2003) Population Policy. In: Demeny, P. & McNicoll, G. (Eds.), *International Encyclopedia of Population.* Macmillan Reference, New York.
Freedman, R. (1997) Do Family Planning Programs Affect Fertility Preferences? A Literature Review. *Studies in Family Planning* 29(1): 1–13.

Gauthier, A. H. (1996) *The State and the Family: A Comparative Analysis of Family Policies in Industrialized Countries*. Oxford University Press, Oxford.

OECD (1998) *Maintaining Prosperity in an Ageing Society*. OECD, Paris.

Sen, A. (1999) *Development as Freedom*. Knopf, New York.

United Nations (2004) *World Population Policies 2003*. United Nations Population Division, New York.

United Nations (2005) *World Population Prospects: The 2004 Revision*. United Nations Population Division, New York.

World Bank (1994) *Averting the Old-Age Crisis: Policies to Protect the Old and Promote Growth. A World Bank Policy Research Report*. Oxford University Press, Oxford.

fertility: transitions and measures

Sharon Kirmeyer

Childbearing, or the fertility of human populations, has changed profoundly in the last several centuries. Four aspects are basic for measuring and studying human fertility: *age*, *parity* (number of children ever born), length of *birth interval*, and *population reproductivity*. Additionally, there are cross-cutting issues of time perspective and of fertility dimensions. The variety of fertility measures at a given time is both a result of the data available and a precondition to expansions in data collection efforts.

COHORT VERSUS PERIOD ANALYSIS

Fertility measures are expressed to reflect childbearing either in the time period in which they occur, or at the end of the (reproductive) life time of a cohort.

Period fertility rates and analyses are cross-sectional and give a "snapshot" of a population for a short period of time. A major advantage of period rates is that they are immediately calculable. A second is that they provide the annual contribution to population growth through fertility.

Cohort fertility rates and analyses concern a group of persons with a common temporal experience, such as a birth or marriage date. They take into account the events occurring to women (or men) until the end of their reproductive years. More stable than period rates, they provide the means to evaluate long-term population evolution. The main disadvantage in calculating cohort measures is that they require, at minimum, 30 years of data.

The basic tool to translate period to cohort measures is through the Lexis diagram. The time of the event is on the horizontal axis, the time lapse on the vertical. A period rate employs events at given ages (or durations) for time on the horizontal axis. A cohort measure uses a diagonal span to calculate the rate for individuals entering the cohort at the stated points. More complex tools have been recently developed for period–cohort translation.

QUANTUM, TEMPO, AND DISPERSION

Fertility measures reflect three comprehensive dimensions of natality. Demographic *quantum* is the number of lifetime events per person. In fertility per se, it is the number of children ever born to a woman. Fertility *tempo* refers to the timing of births. This is most commonly expressed as the mean age of childbearing, and secondarily, the duration of intervals between births. A third dimension is that of *dispersion*. Dispersion measures variation, not central tendency, and can be based on age, parity, or birth interval.

Currently, the quantum and tempo aspects of fertility are drawing scrutiny as 20 European countries have period total fertility rates of 1.4 or below. A simple approach by Bongaarts and Feeney to remove major effects of tempo serves to approximate the fertility quantum by adjusting for changes in mean age of childbearing.

DIRECT (AGE-BASED) MEASURES OF FERTILITY

Direct measures of fertility are classically obtained from vital registration records, which provide the numerators (births), and from censuses, projections, or continuous registration systems, which provide the population denominators. Large population surveys can provide sufficient "person-years" for stable estimates of direct measures.

The *crude birth rate* (CBR) provides the number of live births per 1,000 population in a given time period. The CBR is a measure of a population's overall growth, but it can mask – or exaggerate – fertility differences between two populations which have very different age structures.

The *general fertility rate* (GFR) is the number of live births in a time period to women of reproductive age, usually expressed per 1,000 women aged 15 to 44 or 15 to 49. This measure is generally available from vital registration. It removes from the denominator most of the population not directly exposed to childbearing, and as such removes most of the age compositional differences between populations. However, it does not control for age variation within the reproductive years.

The *age-specific fertility rate* (ASFR) is the number of births to women of a certain age divided by the number of women in that age group (e.g., women aged 25 to 29). The distribution of ASFRs resembles an inverted U, conventionally starting at age 15 and ending at age 50. Birth rates are low in the teen years, rising in the twenties, and tapering off in the late thirties and forties. Many consider studying fertility changes in terms of age-specific rates the most fruitful for social and demographic comparison.

The *total fertility rate* (TFR) represents the average number of children ever born to a woman if she were to move through her reproductive years maintaining ASFRs of the current time period. Using period rates, it is a synthetic figure. As both a summary indicator and a standardized rate, the TFR is employed in health, economic, historical, and other analyses. The TFR plus coexisting mortality levels establish the "replacement-level fertility" for a population.

When women begin having children at older ages, the *mean age of childbearing* advances and the period total fertility rate falls. If childbearing moves to younger ages, the period TFR increases, at least temporarily. In recent years, the mean age of childbearing has shifted substantially to later ages in all regions but Eastern Europe. With this change in birth timing, the tempo effect depresses the TFR.

INDIRECT (AGE-BASED) METHODS AND MODELS

From the 1960s through the 1980s, a plethora of *indirect measures* was generated which estimated primarily TFRs and secondarily ASFRs in developing countries. This was due to the dual conditions of data deficiency – censuses being then the primary data source – and the national and internationally funded family planning and development programs which needed fertility measures to track outcomes. Surveys like those produced by the World Fertility Survey program were not large enough to produce reliable direct estimates. While many national surveys have become larger, indirect estimation continues to be used due to the limitations in data supply and quality.

Indirect measures of fertility are used under a variety of conditions. Indirect measures are necessary when vital statistics and large surveys are not available for calculating ASFRs and TFRs – the case when only census data are available. Also, other data are often incomplete, of dubious quality (especially in reference to age), or are based on small sample size; hence indirect measures may provide better estimates than would direct measures. Similarly, indirect measures can aid in data quality evaluation. Also, estimates are based on five-year age and time intervals; interpolation techniques provide useful single-year rates. Meaningful short- and medium-range projections of fertility are well grounded in fertility models, especially those containing alternate scenarios.

Indirect methods (i.e., indirect measures which incorporate other demographic estimates) may be classified into four groups: methods based on average number of children ever born per woman of specified ages – and often information about births in the past year; methods based on census age–sex distributions and life-table functions – which reverse-survive enumerated populations; regression-based methods yielding fertility measures from demographic variables or permitting translation among fertility measures; and methods which partially use models – the strongest employing mothers' own-children data classified by mothers' and children's ages. As surveys have increased in size, permitting statistically reliable direct estimation of age-based period measures, these indirect methods retain utility in interpreting historical data, or producing small-area (or subpopulation) estimates.

Many indirect measures are *biodemographical models*, that is, they are based on reproductive processes. Three are mentioned here, distinguished for their simplicity of expression and their ability to explain change in fertility levels and composition.

In the 1970s, the Princeton University-based European Fertility Project was established to characterize the decline of fertility that took place in Europe during the nineteenth and early twentieth centuries. A set of *indices* referring to total fertility (I_f), marital fertility, marriage, and illegitimate fertility formalized the theoretical fertility transition (Coale & Watkins 1986). Sardon provided the means to convert the I_f into the more easily interpretable TFR.

Coale and Trussell elaborated a general model consisting of marital states and fertility pertaining to those states which would closely describe age-based fertility. Their three-parameter model contains elements of natural fertility, deliberate control of childbearing (contraception and abortion), and cohabitation.

The *intermediate fertility variables* follow from the early framework of Davis and Blake and the subsequent work of many researchers who quantified elements of the reproductive process. Of the 11 variables named by Davis and Blake, Bongaarts identified four which explain the most variation between countries and are the most sensitive to change (marriage, contraception, induced abortion, and infecundability). These are often referred to as the *proximate determinants of fertility*.

Non-biodemographical models are of a statistical or mathematical nature. Through smoothing, interpolation, and projection, they generate natural ASFR curves. They have been classified as being curves expressed by parametric mathematical formulae; models based on the relational approach; non-parametric statistical models, such as those based on the principal component method; and non-parametric curves – such as the various splines and higher-degree polynomials.

PARITY-BASED MEASURES

The study of *distributions by completed parity* of either actual or synthetic (period) cohorts with emphasis on parity-progression ratios represents an evolution in perspective. As such, modern fertility is not a series of spontaneous events subject to biological factors, such as age and exposure. Rather, it is a behavioral process controlled by individual decision-making regarding whether or not to bear a subsequent child.

A *parity-progression table* parallels a conventional life table, substituting r, the number of children ever born, for the time parameter of decrement, x. The cohort is initiated with all women having yet to bear any children. The principal *parity-progression functions* and their life-table counterparts are:

$\lambda_r [\sim l_x]$, the parity attainment proportion;

$\delta_r [\sim d_x]$, the proportion at parity r at completed fertility;

$\rho_r [\sim p_x]$, the parity-progression ratio; and

$\eta_r [\sim e_x]$, the expected number of children after r;

Additional key measures derived from the basic parity-progression table include: the *maternal TFR*, which follows the observation that countries' total fertility rates vary substantially due to the proportion childless in a cohort. This rate is the mean number of children ever born to women who become mothers.

Samuel Preston transformed mothers' cohorts by parity to the number of children born to their mothers. This switches the perspective to the children's, making it possible to estimate *mean number of siblings*. Mean number of siblings is higher than a mother's average fertility rate due to overrepresentation from large families.

The *Gini mean difference*, derived directly from parity-progression functions, measures heterogeneity (or concentration) of the parity distribution. This provides a simple indicator to evaluate populations in terms of their parity dispersions.

Finally, to evaluate the impact of changing parity-progression ratios on a new (overall) fertility level, Barkalov adapted Pollard's *decomposition* technique. Applying decomposition, the percent of change in TFR may be attributed to each parity-progression ratio.

BIRTH INTERVAL-BASED MEASURES

Birth interval analysis has not been given as much attention as age-based analysis. But with the growth of large surveys containing many covariates, the study of birth intervals provides information on the dynamics of family growth, control of reproduction, health consequences for mothers and infants, as well as tempo measures for formal demographic analysis.

The extent and frequency of gathering data on birth intervals has expanded. Traditionally, limited data have come from censuses and vital registrations (primarily: last birth date). Longitudinal surveys are the most appropriate for accuracy, but are difficult to implement. An abundance of data have come from retrospective birth histories. The World Fertility Surveys of the 1970s included 60 surveys from developed and developing countries. The largest retrospective enterprise includes the multiple rounds of Demographic and Health Surveys (at least 170 surveys) and the similar Reproductive Health Surveys, both supported by the US Agency for International Development. Recently, another round of 20 surveys took place in more developed countries (Family and Fertility Surveys), including the ongoing US National Survey of Family Growth. The World Fertility Surveys spurred the development of methods to analyze birth intervals. They are based primarily on events as numerators and person-years of exposure in the denominator.

Birth intervals are ultimately bounded by age of menarche and menopause. They are classified as *first* (from time of first exposure to pregnancy) *interval, closed intervals* (between births), and the *open interval* (between the last birth and time of survey or presumed menopause). Birth interval analysis encounters several problems. Birth interval analysis is subject to expected data deficiencies: misreporting of event dates and age of mother, and underreporting of events. The first birth interval is problematic, as the date of first exposure to pregnancy is difficult to determine in almost any population. Censoring occurs when a birth interval is not complete; it biases estimates by eliminating the longer intervals characteristic of subsets of the population. Survival analysis, borrowed from mortality analysis, addresses many issues encountered in working with birth intervals.

REPRODUCTIVITY

Particular attention to measures of population replacement, or *reproductivity*, came into play during the fertility nadirs experienced by Europe and North America between the world wars and in the last decade of the twentieth century. Also, the sustained high fertility rates of many parts of the "third world" – particularly in the 1970s and 1980s – generated concern about long-run population growth. A set of measures made it possible to map where a country was in terms of replacing itself, and what that portended in the long run.

The *gross reproduction rate* (GRR) is a simple means to show, on average, the number of girls born to a woman. It is closely approximated by multiplying the total fertility rate by the concurrent proportion of babies who are female. This simple method provides a sense of the ratio of daughters who will replace their mothers. But it does not take into account the possible mortality of women prior to reaching specific childbearing ages. As such, it may greatly overstate the number of daughters replacing their mothers.

The *net reproduction rate* (NRR) is the summary measure which best represents the ratio of female births in two generations. It is calculated using life-table functions. The NRR is the average number of daughters which would be born to a woman if she passed through her lifetime conforming to the age-specific fertility *and* mortality rates of a given year. A net reproduction rate of unity signifies that a population is exactly replacing itself. Above 1, the population is more than replacing itself; conversely, an NRR of less than 1 signifies a population which is declining in size. As the NRR takes mortality into account, a rule of thumb often uses a total fertility rate between 2.1 and 2.3 as being that which equates a *replacement level of fertility*.

For many years, the *intrinsic rate of growth*, or growth rate of a closed population with constant fertility and mortality, was of heuristic interest. Dublin and Lotka's (1925) formulation was incorporated into many formal analyses and long-term projections, but had little immediate relevance. With the recent sustained low fertility and mortality of Europe, discussions concerning future national age structures and dependency ratios (vis-à-vis social security needs) are sparked by the longer generation lengths coupled with negative intrinsic rates of growth.

SEE ALSO: Age, Period, and Cohort Effects; Biodemography; Davis, Kingsley; Demographic Data: Censuses, Registers, Surveys; Demographic Techniques: Event History Methods; Demographic Techniques: Life-Table Methods; Demographic Transition Theory; Fertility: Low; Fertility: Nonmarital; Intimate Union Formation and Dissolution; Second Demographic Transition

REFERENCES AND SUGGESTED READINGS

Barkalov, N. & Dorbritz, J. (1996) Measuring Period Parity-Progression Ratios with Competing Techniques. *Zeitschrift für Bevölkerungswissenschaft* 21: 459–505.

Bogue, D., Arriaga, E., & Anderton, A. (Eds.) (1993) *Readings in Population Research Methodology*. United Nations Population Fund, Chicago.

Coale, A. & Demeny, P. (1966) *Regional Model Life Tables and Stable Populations*. Princeton University Press, Princeton.

Coale, A. & Watkins, S. (Eds.) (1986) *The Decline of Fertility in Europe*. Princeton University Press, Princeton.

Department of International and Social, Affairs (1986) *Manual X: Indirect Techniques of Demographic Estimation*. ST/ESA/SER/A/81. United Nations, New York.

Dublin, L. & Lotka, A. (1925) On the True Rate of Natural Increase. *Journal of the American Statistical Association* 20: 305–39.

Henry, L. (1954). Fertility According to Size of Family: Application to Australia. *Population Bulletin of the United Nations* 4: 8–20.

Kuczynski, R. R. (1982 [1932]) *Fertility and Reproduction: Methods of Measuring the Balance of Births and Deaths*. Akademie-Verlag, Berlin.

Lutz, W. (1989) Comparative Analysis of Completed Parity Distributions: A Global WFS Perspective. *Population Bulletin of the United Nations* 28: 25–7.

Shryock, H. & Siegal, J. (1976) *The Methods and Materials of Demography*. Condensed edition by E. Stockwell. Academic Press, San Diego.

Whelpton, P. (1954) *Cohort Fertility: Native White Women in the United States*. Princeton University Press, Princeton.

fetishism

Gert Hekma

A fetish is a more or less concrete object of sexual desire. It can be a part of the body, an object, a situation, or some abstraction. Breasts, buttocks, feet, hair, and genitals belong to the parts of the body; clothing, shoes, whips, dildos, uniforms, cars, or specific materials such as leather, silk, satin, velvet, and rubber are possible objects; situations can be cinemas, saunas, dark rooms, dinner tables, beaches, or prison cells; and more abstract examples of fetishism include youth, beauty, hospitality, power, submission, and humiliation. Ultimately, any part of the body, object, situation, or abstraction can become a fetish and, on the other hand, all sexual pleasure depends on fetishes. Naming or reading the word can be as exciting as the object to which it refers.

The term fetish comes from religion studies. The Portuguese named an object of African religious veneration a *feticao*, an object bestowed with surplus value (McClintock 1993; Nye 1993; Pettinger 1993). Karl Marx used the term in this sense for his economic theory, and in 1888 the French scholar Alfred Binet used it for the sexual theory he expounded in "Le Féti-chisme dans l'amour." In the 1880s, which saw the beginnings of sexology, Binet asked why people had obsessive desires for nightcaps or women's ponytails. According to him, the coincidental association of sexual excitement and remarking a certain object produced the concrete, contingent, and individual form of a fetish. He differentiated between small and large fetishes, the first being additional and the second being essential to sexual pleasure. Many people like large breasts, but some can only become excited when they have them in their hands or minds. Although Binet designed his view as a general theory of sexual perversion, his predominantly social theory was obscured by biological theories then current in psychiatry. The trend at that time was to explain perversion by way of physiology, not society. Several doctors wrote books in which they described concrete cases of fetishism. Only the Freudians adapted Binet's term and view for psychoanalysis, but it did not become one of their core concepts.

Since the recent postmodern turn, the erotic version of the term fetishism has been revived mostly in the humanities. It is an interesting term for the social sciences because it connects sexual pleasure to the social world where the fetish is picked up, and breaks down the dichotomy of homo- and heterosexual and of subject and object. McCallum (1999: 154) suggests that the fetish challenges "the domination of the subject over the object" and eliminates the need for other subjects. The fetish is not abstract but instrumental and stimulates agency and passion. It is beyond the genders of sexual object choice. Different from love, sexual pleasures most often have a concrete and contingent aim and the concept of fetish captures this neatly. Apter and Pietz (1993: 4) can thus assert that "feminist essentialism is resisted through fetishism's implicit challenge to a stable phallic referent." In fetishism, the sexual aim is not a gendered object but something more specific, going beyond homo-, hetero-, or bisexual choices. These characteristics make the fetish an ideal concept for post-feminist and queer theory where it has been applied profusely in the humanities (Apter & Pietz 1993), specifically in fashion studies (Steele 1996). In sociology, the concept is rarely used in its sexual meanings. It is remarkable that the grand masters of sociology, who lived in close proximity to the urban environments where sexologists and sexual subcultures are to be found, rarely paid any attention to sexual variation, and never to fetishism.

Although all people have fetishes, the term is mainly used in circles of sexual specialization such as subcultures, pornography, and Internet chat rooms and websites. The most common although still rare objects of sociological research have been leather or S/M communities. The main focus of research has been the origin of specific sexual choices or the organization of subcultures, but not specifically on fetishism. In surveys the topic of sexual choice goes rarely beyond homosexual and heterosexual, although in some cases unusual or deviant variations have been included, being an erotic interest of about 10 percent of the population. Fetishist preferences must be far more general. Most of those who are curious probably do not venture into the existing subcultures but instead play out their desires with their partner or in fantasy. The authors of the largest sex survey in the United States indicated that in most monogamous couples, sexual desires will differ. This means that the chances are minimal that partners will erotically satisfy each other's special wishes (Laumann et al. 1994). The absence of concrete physical places for the various fetishes, even in the largest cities, makes the desire highly abstract, as in most postmodern theorizing. It might be that the proliferation of websites devoted to sexual variations will favor the emergence of relevant places and organizations, as occurred in the gay world with rubber, skinheads, sports clothing, and sneakers. The variety begs the question of how to find partners. Curiosity for each other's fetishes could bridge the gap between different desires.

Given the poor state of knowledge on fetishism, the most important first step in sociological research will be qualitative research to delineate themes and contexts, for example by interviewing people about their fetishes and putting down their sexual scripts. As no studies are available, the future direction will be to demarcate the contents and contexts of fetishist interests, their organization, and their place in sexual relations. The concept has a highly theoretic quality, as it breaks down various dichotomies of gay and straight, object and subject, social and individual. It could be a central concept for a postmodern sociology of sexuality, while it reflects at the same time the realities of erotic pleasures.

SEE ALSO: Consumption, Fashion and; Cybersexualities and Virtual Sexuality; Homosexuality; Plastic Sexuality; Postmodern Sexualities; Sadomasochism; Scripting Theories; Sexual Deviance; Sexual Practices; Sexuality Research: History

REFERENCES AND SUGGESTED READINGS

Apter, E. & Pietz, W. (Eds.) (1993) *Fetishism as Cultural Discourse.* Cornell University Press, Ithaca, NY.

Binet, A. (1888) Le Fétichisme dans l'amour. In: *Études de psychologie expérimentale.* Doin, Paris.

Laumann, E., Gagnon, J., Michael, R. T., & Michaels, S. (1994) *The Social Organization of Sexuality: Sexual Practices in the USA.* University of Chicago Press, Chicago.

McCallum, E. L. (1999) *Object Lessons: How To Do Things With Fetishism.* SUNY Press, New York.

McClintock, A. (1993) The Return of Female Fetishism and the Fiction of the Phallus. In: Squires, J. (Ed.), *Perversity.* Special issue of *New Formations* 19 (Spring): 1–21.

Nye, R. A. (1993) The Medical Origins of Sexual Fetishism. In: Apter, E. & Pietz, W. (Eds.), *Fetishism as Cultural Discourse.* Cornell University Press, Ithaca, NY, pp. 13–30.

Pettinger, A. (1993) Why Fetish? In: Squires, J. (Ed.), *Perversity.* Special issue of *New Formations* 19 (Spring): 83–93.

Squires, J. (Ed.) (1993) *Perversity.* Special issue of *New Formations* 19 (Spring).

Steele, V. (1996) *Fetish: Fashion, Sex, and Power.* Oxford University Press, New York.

Feuerbach, Ludwig (1804–72)

Clifford L. Staples

Ludwig Feuerbach was born into a large, prominent, academic family in Landshut, Bavaria. His father was a distinguished professor of jurisprudence, and three of Ludwig's four brothers went on to noteworthy careers in mathematics, law, and archeology. But unwilling to heed his father's advice to steer clear of radical ideas, and unable to negotiate the repressive atmosphere of academic and political life in mid-nineteenth century Germany, Feuerbach became an important academic failure. Some social theorists and sociologists are familiar with Feuerbach's writings on religion, but most sociologists know Feuerbach primarily because of his influence on the young Karl

Marx – a central figure within the sociological tradition. Feuerbach's critique of Hegel provided Marx with the occasion to, in turn, critique Feuerbach, and in the process Marx worked his way toward a thoroughly sociological approach to such core topics as history, ideology, and social evolution – topics approached before Marx usually as theological or philosophical problems. For his time and place, Feuerbach was a radical, though not quite radical enough for Marx.

Feuerbach's life took a familiar modern trajectory from youthful religiosity toward naturalism and eventually to a materialist humanism typical, if not universal, among contemporary sociologists. Having a highly learned and opinionated father, however, made it difficult for Feuerbach to develop an independent intellectual life. As a young man he was interested in studying theology, but soon (along with many of his contemporaries) was swept up in the excitement about Hegel. Unfortunately, Feuerbach's father despised Hegel, and young Feuerbach was forced to fib his way to Berlin to hear the master by telling his father he was going off to study with the respected theologian Friedrich Schleiermacher. Eventually, and against his father's wishes, Feuerbach moved into philosophy and in 1828 successfully defended a dissertation on Hegel. But even in this early work it was already clear that he would not remain a strict Hegelian. Famously, he sent Hegel a copy of his thesis along with a suggestion that Hegel's work was not as Hegelian as it ought to be. He also pointed out that Christianity was not – as Hegel had argued – the ultimate religion. Details aside, it is Feuerbach's approach to religion, and by extension all forms of ideology, that would prove so useful to Marx and others inclined to challenge religious and political orthodoxies.

Between 1828 and 1837 Feuerbach, as a professor at the university in Erlangen, published several well-received books and articles and was on his way to a successful career as an academic. However, and once again against his father's advice, Feuerbach also published anonymously, in 1830, *Thoughts on Death and Immortality*. In this book he extended and developed his critique of Christian dogma. Specifically, he challenged accepted Christian views on the survival of the soul after death – a risky move in a near-theocracy – but, for good measure, he also poked fun at popular Christian religious beliefs. The authorities banned the book and when Feuerbach, widely suspected of being its author, refused to deny it, he found himself dismissed from his position. Thus, even before Feuerbach had written much of interest to Marx or to sociology, he had already managed to get himself fired from the only academic position he would ever hold. We might have heard nothing more from Feuerbach had he not married into a moderately wealthy family in 1837, allowing him to continue with his intellectual work without having to earn a living from it.

Up through his brief career as an academic, Feuerbach wrote in a very abstract and speculative style of metaphysics of little interest to modern sociologists. But with the publication in 1841 of *The Essence of Christianity* Feuerbach pointed the way toward a secular, materialist humanism that most sociologists, not only Marxists, now take for granted.

The Essence of Christianity made Feuerbach famous in Germany and established him as a leader, along with Bruno Bauer and eventually Karl Marx, of the "Young Hegelians" – students of Hegel who sought to realize the master's idealism by grounding it in social and political realities. What Feuerbach had to say about Christianity is less important, for the sociologist, than the paradigm shift he initiated with respect to how we might think about and understand religion and, more generally, ideology. A theologian studies religion for what it promises to tell us about God, or the nature of our relationship to God. The humanist, however – and this would include all secular sociologists from the ardent positivist to the committed interpretavist – assumes that the study of religion tells us not about God, but about human beings. Indeed, the skilled sociologist of religion is, at least heuristically, an agnostic, suspending judgment about the reality of the supernatural in order to focus on religion as a human social practice. Feuerbach, in particular, viewed religion as a projection of human needs and desires. Feuerbach, like Marx after him, wants us to see that religious striving represents an alienation of man from himself, and it is only through the proper understanding of man's relationship to himself that he will find the liberation he is seeking in God. It is

this turning away from the supernatural to the natural, material, and the human that marks Feuerbach's contribution to social thought and social analysis.

In his Paris writings of 1844 Marx laid the philosophical foundation for all his later work. Marx constructed this foundation by combining Hegel's idealism with Feuerbach's materialism. The concepts of *species being* and alienation, as well as the anthropological and materialist approach to nature, human labor, and social existence, all owe a great deal to Feuerbach.

As important as Feuerbach was to Marx's early thinking, Marx himself thought that Feuerbach's signal contribution to philosophy was his "transformative method," which Feuerbach had applied so tellingly to Hegel. Indeed, Marx himself was to use this same method to address another problem some years later. What Feuerbach found so troubling in Hegel was the master's willingness to generate abstractions (like "spirit" or "thought") which he then endowed with power and agency. Feuerbach's "method" was to reverse the equation, showing the abstractions to be the consequence or result of human thought or action. So, studying religion tells us more about people than it does about God because people created God, God did not create people.

Feuerbach's "transformative method" is nothing less than a guide to how a critical sociologist should confront the problem of reification. Reification occurs when people "forget" that ideas and institutions are created by human beings, and as a result they endow them with power and agency. This happens, for example, with the word "society," as when someone says "society turns people into consumers." At one level this is just a shorthand way of pointing to a problem that needs further analysis. However, too often, such statements are offered as an explanation or answer, and when used in this way they stunt critical sociological thinking because they treat an abstraction created by human beings, "society," as an agent.

Marx, of course, put Feuerbach's method to work on the key concepts of classical political economy, such as the commodity. *Capital* is subtitled "a critique of political economy" and by this Marx signaled that he intended to transform bourgeois abstractions into the capitalist class relations which produced them. In doing so he was doing to capitalist ideology what Feuerbach had done to Hegelian ideology.

But, of course, Marx was not entirely happy with Feuerbach. However important it was to think oneself out of the dead-ends of philosophical abstraction or the obfuscations of bougeois economics, for Marx, philosophy was always undertaken for the purpose of social transformation or revolution. It is for this reason that his final word on Feuerbach was: "The philosophers have only interpreted the world, in various ways; the point is to change it." Content with his own interpretations, Feuerbach spent his latter years reworking his earlier work and dabbling in geology. He died in 1872 at the age of 68.

SEE ALSO: Alienation; Engels, Friedrich; Hegel, G. W. F.; Humanism; Ideology; Marx, Karl; Materialism; Religion, Sociology of; Socialism; Theory

REFERENCES AND SUGGESTED READINGS

Brazill, W. J. (1970) *The Young Hegelians*. Yale University Press, New Haven.
Engels, F. (1903) *Feuerbach: The Roots of the Socialist Philosophy*. Trans. A. Lewis. Charles H. Kerr, Chicago.
Feuerbach, L. (1957 [1841]) *The Essence of Christianity (Das Wesen des Christentums)*. Trans. G. Eliot (M Evans). Harper & Row, New York.
Kamenka, E. (1970) *The Philosophy of Ludwig Feuerbach*. Routledge & Kegan Paul, London.
Wartofsky, M. (1977) *Feuerbach*. Cambridge University Press, Cambridge.

figurational sociology and the sociology of sport

Eric Dunning

The figurational tradition of sociological research and theory was pioneered by Norbert Elias (1897–1990), a German of Jewish descent who became a naturalized Englishman in 1952. His work is best seen as an attempt to synthesize the central ideas of Auguste Comte, Karl Marx, Max Weber, and Sigmund Freud. Other influences were: Georg Simmel, Kurt Lewin, Wolfgang Koehler, J. B. Watson, and W. B. Cannon. Elias studied philosophy and medicine to doctoral level in Breslau before switching to sociology in Heidelberg in 1925. There, he came under the influence of Karl Mannheim, a founder of the sociology of knowledge, and Alfred Weber, brother of the more famous Max and a leading cultural sociologist.

Three aspects of Elias's life help to explain characteristic features of his sociology. First, his experience of World War I, in which he served in the Kaiser's army on the eastern and western fronts, and the rise of the Nazis sensitized Elias to the part played by violence and war in human life. Such experiences also intensified his awareness of "decivilizing" as well as "civilizing" processes – he described the rise of the Nazis as a "breakdown of civilization" – and reinforced his view that "civilizing controls" rarely, if ever, amount to more than a relatively thin veneer. Second, the repeated interruption of his career by wider events – World War I, the German hyperinflation of 1923, the Nazi takeover ten years later, exile to France and then to Britain, internment as an "enemy alien" – helped to sensitize Elias to the interdependence and interplay of "the individual" and "the social," "the private" and "the public," "the micro" and "the macro." And third, Elias's study of medicine and philosophy helped to problematize for him aspects of philosophy, contributing to his move to sociology and his original work in what are now known as the "sociology of the body" and the "sociology of emotions." That Elias was a pioneer of the sociology of sport is perhaps best understood in that context. He opposed the "mind–body" dichotomy and did not share the common prejudice that sport is a "physical" phenomenon of lower value than phenomena connected with the realm of "mind." The theory of "civilizing processes" is generally regarded as having been Elias's major sociological contribution.

THE THEORY OF CIVILIZING PROCESSES

Contrary to a widespread misconception, Elias did not use the concept of a "civilizing process" in a morally evaluative way. He also frequently enclosed words such as "civilization," "civilized," and "civilizing" in inverted commas in order to signal this. "Civilizing process" was, for him, a technical term and he did not imply by it that people who can be shown to stand at a more advanced level than others, for example ourselves relative to people of the feudal era, are in any sense "morally superior" or "better." That, of course, is almost invariably how the people who call themselves "civilized" view themselves. But how, Elias used to ask, can people congratulate themselves when they are the chance beneficiaries of a blind process to the course of which they have personally contributed little, if anything at all? To say this, of course, is not to deny that there are victims as well as beneficiaries of "civilizing" processes.

The theory of civilizing processes is based on a substantial body of data, principally on the changing manners of the secular upper classes – knights, kings, queens, court aristocrats, politicians, and business leaders, but not, for the most part, the higher clergy – between the Middle Ages and modern times. These data indicate that, in the major countries of Western Europe, a long-term unplanned process took place involving four principal components: the elaboration and refinement of social standards; an increase in the social pressure on people to exercise stricter, more continuous, and more even self-control over their feelings and behavior; a shift in the balance between external constraints and self-constraints in favor of self-constraints; and an increase at the levels of personality and habitus in the importance of "conscience" or "superego" as a regulator of behavior. That is, social standards came to be internalized more deeply and to operate not simply consciously and with an element of choice, but also beneath the levels of rationality and conscious control.

At the risk of oversimplification, one could summarize Elias's theory by saying that he attributed these European "civilizing processes" to five interlocking part-processes, which he also studied in considerable empirical detail. They included: the formation of state monopolies on violence and taxation; internal pacification under state control; growing social differentiation and the lengthening of interdependency chains; growing equality of power-chances between social classes, men and women,

and the older and younger generations; and growing wealth.

Elias showed how, in the course of a civilizing process, overtly violent struggles tend to be transformed into more peaceful struggles for status, wealth, and power in which, in the most frequent course of events, destructive urges come to be kept for the most part beneath the threshold of consciousness and not translated into overt action. Status struggles of this kind appear to have played a part in the split between the "soccer" and the "rugby" forms of football (Dunning & Sheard 2005 [1979]).

THE "CIVILIZING" OF MODERN SPORTS

An aspect of these overall European "civilizing processes" that is crucial for understanding the development of modern sports has been the increasing control of violence and aggression within societies, though not to anything like the same extent in the relations between them. According to Elias, in "modern" societies in which the dominant groups consider themselves to be "civilized," belligerence and aggression are socially tolerated in sporting contests, including in "spectating," that is, in people's imaginary identification with the direct combatants to whom moderate and precisely regulated scope is granted for the release of such affects. In Elias's words, "this transformation of what manifested itself originally as an active, often aggressive expression of pleasure into the passive, more ordered pleasure of spectating (i.e. the mere pleasure of the eye) is already initiated in education, in the conditioning precepts for young people ... It is highly characteristic of civilized people that they are denied by socially instilled self-controls from spontaneously touching what they desire, love or hate" (Elias 2000 [1939]: 170).

A taboo on touching for all players except the goalkeeper has, of course, become the major distinguishing characteristic of the "soccer" or "Association" form of football. Data also suggest that sports themselves underwent "civilizing processes" in conjunction with these wider "civilizing" developments. That this is the case is shown by studies of: the antecedents of modern sports in the ancient and medieval

European worlds (Elias in Elias & Dunning 1986; Dunning 1999); the initial development of modern sports in eighteenth- and nineteenth-century England (Elias in Elias & Dunning 1986; Dunning 1999); the long-term development of soccer and rugby (Dunning & Sheard 2005 [1979]); and football hooliganism as an English and world phenomenon (Dunning et al. 1988; Dunning 1999; Dunning et al. 2002).

THE FIGURATIONAL/ELIASIAN SOCIOLOGY OF SPORT AND ITS CRITICS

There have so far been six generations of figurational sociologists of sport in the United Kingdom: (1) Norbert Elias; (2) Eric Dunning; (3) Patrick Murphy, Kenneth Sheard (2004), and Ivan Waddington; (4) Grant Jarvie and Joseph Maguire (Jarvie & Maguire 1994); (5) Sharon Colwell (2004), Graham Curry (2001), Dominic Malcolm (2004), Louise Mansfield, and Stuart Smith (2004); and (6) Ken Green (2004), Daniel Bloyce, Katie Liston, and Andrew Smith. To this list must be added the names of Ruud Stokvis and Martin van Bottenberg (2001) in the Netherlands and Michael Krueger (1997) and Bero Rigauer (2000) in Germany. Interestingly, Rigauer has attempted to wed a figurational perspective with a Marxist one.

Criticizing and Testing Elias

Elias insisted on the testability of his concepts and theories and called for what he described as a "constant two-way traffic" between research and theory. One consequence of this is that his concepts and theories are, like those in the natural sciences, permeated to a greater extent by factual observation, and hence are less abstract than has often been the case in sociology.

Elias's insistence on the testability of his concepts and theories is contradicted by a frequently touted judgment to the contrary. For example, Dennis Smith (1984) argued that the theory of "civilizing processes" is "irrefutable." Such an argument was echoed two years later by the anthropologist Edmund Leach when he suggested in a review of Elias and Dunning's *Quest for Excitement* (1986) that the

"theory is impervious to testing." An example from the sociology of sport is Gary Armstrong, who wrote that Elias's theory "is a fusion of untestable and descriptive generalizations" (1998: 317). Richard Giulianotti went so far as to claim that Elias introduced the concept of "decivilizing spurts" in order "to rebut ... counter evidence" (1999: 45).

These kinds of argument are wrong because they involve the false projection into Elias's work of evaluative notions such as "progress." Elias's work was about "decivilizing" as well as "civilizing processes" from the beginning. One of many examples is furnished by his discussion of feudalization (Elias 2000 [1939]: 195–236). Another is provided when he writes of "the whole many-layered fabric of historical development" as infinitely complex," and that "in each phase there are numerous fluctuations, frequent advances or recessions of the internal and external restraints" (p. 157).

Aspects of the theory have also been tested by scholars other than Elias and Dunning (see articles in Dunning et al. 2004). The sports on which these tests were carried out were: baseball, boxing, cricket, gymnastics, motor racing, rugby, and shooting. Figurational studies by Maguire and Waddington deal with sport in general, in Maguire's case with sport and "globalization" and in Waddington's with sport, health, and drugs.

SEE ALSO: Civilizing Process; Elias, Norbert; Globalization, Sport and; Sportization

REFERENCES AND SUGGESTED READINGS

Armstrong, G. (1998) *Football Hooligans: Knowing the Score*. Berg, Oxford.

Bottenberg, M. van (2001) *Global Games*. University of Illinois Press, Chicago.

Colwell, S. (2004) *The History and Sociology of Elite-Level Football Refereeing*. Unpublished PhD thesis, University of Leicester.

Curry, G. (2001) *Football: A Study in Diffusion*. Unpublished PhD thesis, University of Leicester.

Dunning, E. (1999) *Sport Matters: Sociological Studies of Sport, Violence, and Civilization*. Routledge, London.

Dunning, E. & Sheard, K. (2005 [1979]) *Barbarians, Gentlemen, and Players: A Sociological Study of the*

Development of Rugby Football. Martin Robertson, Oxford.

Dunning, E., Murphy, P., & Williams, J. (1988) *The Roots of Football Hooliganism.* Routledge & Kegan Paul, London.

Dunning, E., Murphy, P., Waddington, I., & Astrinakis, A. (Eds.) (2002) *Fighting Fans: Football Hooliganism as a World Phenomenon.* University College Dublin Press, Dublin.

Dunning, E., Malcolm, D., & Waddington, I. (Eds.) (2004) *Sport Histories: Figurational Studies in the Development of Modern Sports.* Routledge, London.

Elias, N. (1996) *The Germans: Power Struggles and the Development of Habitus in the Nineteenth and Twentieth Centuries.* Ed. M. Schroeter. Trans. with a Preface by E. Dunning & S. Mennell. Polity Press, Cambridge.

Elias, N. (2000 [1939]) *The Civilizing Process: Sociogenetic and Psychogenetic Explorations.* Blackwell, Oxford.

Elias, N. & Dunning, E. (1986) *Quest for Excitement: Sport and Leisure in the Civilizing Process.* Polity Press, Cambridge.

Giulianotti, R. (1999) *Football: A Sociology of the Global Game.* Polity Press, Cambridge.

Green, K. (2004) *Physical Education Teachers on Physical Education: A Sociological Study of Philosophies and Ideologies.* Chester Academic Press, Chester.

Jarvie, G. & Maguire, J. (1994) *Sport and Leisure in Social Thought.* Routledge, London.

Krueger, M. (1997) Zur Bedeutung der Prozess – und Figurationstheorie für Sport und Sportwissenschaft. *Sportwissenschaft* 27(2):129–42.

Leach, E. (1986) Violence. *London Review of Books* 8: 1.

Liston, K. (2005) *Playing the "Masculine–Feminine" Game: A Sociological Analysis of the Fields of Sport and Gender in the Republic of Ireland.* Unpublished PhD thesis, University College Dublin, Dublin.

Malcolm, D. (2004) Cricket: Civilizing and De-Civilizing Processes in the Imperial Game. In: Dunning, E., Malcolm, D., & Waddington, I. (Eds.), *Sport Histories: Figurational Studies in the Development of Modern Sports.* Routledge, London.

Rigauer, B. (2000) Marxist Theories. In: Coakley, J. & Dunning, E. (Eds.), *Handbook of Sports Studies.* Sage, London.

Sheard, K. (2004) Boxing in the Western Civilizing Process. In: Dunning, E., Malcolm, D., & Waddington, I. (Eds.), *Sport Histories: Figurational Studies in the Development of Modern Sports.* Routledge, London.

Smith, A. & Waddington, I. (2004) Using "Sport in the Community" Schemes to Tackle Crime and Drug Use Among Young People: Some Policy Issues and Problems. *European Physical Education Review* 10: 279–97.

Smith, D. (1984) Norbert Elias – Established or Outsider. *Sociological Review* 32(2): 367–89.

Smith, S. (2004) Clay Shooting: Civilization in the Line of Fire. In: Dunning, E., Malcolm, D., & Waddington, I. (Eds.), *Sport Histories: Figurational Studies in the Development of Modern Sports.* Routledge, London.

Twitchen, A. (2004) The Influence of State Formation Processes on the Early Development of Motor Racing. In: Dunning, E., Malcolm, D., & Waddington, I. (Eds.), *Sport Histories: Figurational Studies in the Development of Modern Sports.* Routledge, London.

film

Douglas Kellner

Film emerged as one of the first mass-produced cultural forms of the twentieth century and cinema became one of its distinctive and highly influential industries. Based on new technologies of mechanical reproduction that made possible simulations of the real and the production of fantasy worlds, cinema provided a novel mode of culture that changed patterns of leisure activity and played an important role in social life. Early films were the inventions of technicians and entrepreneurs like the Lumière brothers and Méliès in France and the Edison Corporation in the US.

The first silent films ranged from the documentaries and quasi-documentary realist fictions produced by the Lumières and Edison to the fantasy fictions of Méliès. The genres that would characterize Hollywood film began to appear during the first decades of the century with Westerns like *The Great Train Robbery* (1903), the melodramatic social dramas of D. W. Griffith, costume and historical dramas like *Ben Hur* (the first of several versions appeared in 1899), horror films, and comedies by Mack Sennett, Charlie Chaplin, Buster Keaton, and others.

From the beginning, cinema was bound up with the vicissitudes of modernity. Film was a modern, technologically mediated art form, and it captured the novelties of modern life. Cinema's motion pictures depicted the faster pace of contemporary life, showing railroads and trains, cars and buses, and airplanes changing individuals' experience of space and time in a faster, more dynamic world. Films depicted the vicissitudes of urban modernity with its styles and fashions, its class divisions, crowded streets, and surges of immigrants. Films accustomed audiences to the rhythms and forms of modernity and were, with broadcasting and other forms of media culture, an important force in integrating individuals into increasingly changing and conflicted modern societies. Early films were produced largely for working-class, immigrant, and urban audiences, and some critics of the movies thought that they had negative or subversive effects (Jowett 1976). For example, the comedies of Charlie Chaplin made fun of authority figures and romantic dramas were attacked by the Legion of Decency for promoting promiscuity. And crime dramas were frequently attacked for fostering juvenile delinquency and crime. On the other hand, films were believed to help "Americanize" immigrants, to teach their audiences how to be good Americans, and to provide escape from the cares of everyday life (Ewen & Ewen 1982).

In capitalist countries, going to the movies was an important leisure activity that helped initiate audiences into the consumer society where entertainment was paid for and commodified and the commodity of films sold the styles, goods, services, values, and spectacle of the consumer society itself. In the Soviet Union, Lenin reportedly proclaimed after the revolution of 1917 that "of all the arts, film is the most important to us" (cited in Mailer 1967). The Bolsheviks supported a highly productive film industry that in the newsreels of Dziga Vertov documented the early years of the revolution and in the films of Eisenstein, Pudovkin, Dovzhenko, and others provided powerful expressions of Bolshevik ideology and values.

Cinema was part of modern industry, organized first in the US and eventually throughout the world on the assembly-line model of production, with studios featuring houses of writers, set designers and buildings, costume and make-up crews, the sets where scenes were filmed, and the buildings where films were edited and then marketed. Films in the US and elsewhere became integrated industries combining production, distribution, and exhibition in one corporation. Its publicity apparatus helped establish the importance of advertising agencies and its star system helped to produce a new type of mass-mediated celebrity culture. Film helped to generate new public spaces where individuals congregated to consume culture, and the great movie palaces of the early era of cinema created the impression that culture was becoming increasingly democratized and accessible to the masses.

Eventually, its increasingly massified and standardized products, especially in the Hollywood studio system, but also in national cinemas elsewhere such as Mexico, Brazil, India, China, and Taiwan, helped to contribute to the rise of what sociologists saw as a mass society emerging after World War II through its standardized products and what was assumed to be a homogeneous audience watching the same mass-produced artifacts. In Europe, by contrast, the art film tradition that emerged in German Expressionism, a French poetic cinema, and individual works of auteurs like Carl Dreyer, Abel Gance, or Jean Renoir were often supported by the national state, as was the propagandistic cinema of Nazi Germany, the Soviet Union, and Italian Fascism.

Further, after World War II, many national cinema styles emerged as a reaction against Hollywood cinema, including Italian neorealism, French New Wave, Brazilian Cinema Novo, Latin American "Third Cinema," the New German Cinema, the New Taiwanese Cinema, and many other movements throughout the world that wanted to create distinctive styles and types of cinema relevant to local cultures, problems, and audiences.

Debates about relations between film and society and the social effects of film began during the silent era and the medium had both defenders and critics among major intellectuals of the era. Walter Benjamin claimed that the "mechanical reproduction" grounded in film technology and other reproducible forms of culture robbed high art of its "aura," of the aesthetic power of the work of art related to its earlier functions in magic, religious cults, and as a spiritual object in the religions of art celebrated in movements like romanticism or "art for art's sake." In these cases, the "aura" of the work derived from its supposed authenticity, its uniqueness and individuality. In an era of mechanical reproduction, however, art appeared as commodities like other mass-produced items, and lost its special power as a transcendent object – especially in mass-produced objects like photography and film, with their photo negatives and techniques of mass reproduction.

While members of the Frankfurt School like T. W. Adorno and Max Horkheimer tended to criticize precisely the most mechanically mediated works of mass culture for their standardization and loss of aesthetic quality (while celebrating those works that most steadfastly resisted commodification and mechanical reproduction), Benjamin saw progressive features in high art's loss of its auratic quality and its becoming more politicized. Such art, he claimed, assumed more of an "exhibition value" than a cultic or religious value, and thus demystified its reception. Furthermore, he believed that proliferation of mass art – especially through film – would bring images of the contemporary world to the masses and would help raise political consciousness by encouraging scrutiny of the world, as well as by bringing socially critical images to millions of spectators:

> By close-ups of the things around us, by focusing on hidden details of familiar objects, and by exploring commonplace milieus under the ingenious guidance of the camera, the film, on the one hand, extends our comprehension of the necessities which rule our lives; on the other hand, it manages to assure us of an immense and unexpected field of action. Our taverns and our metropolitan streets, our offices and furnished rooms, our railroad stations and our factories appeared to have us locked up hopelessly. Then came the film and burst this prison-world asunder by the dynamite of the tenth of a second, so that now, in the midst of its far-flung ruins and debris, we calmly and adventurously go traveling. (Benjamin 1972: 236)

Benjamin claimed that the mode of viewing film broke with the reverential mode of aesthetic perception and awe encouraged by the bourgeois cultural elite who promoted the religion of art. Montage in film, its "shock effects," the conditions of mass spectatorship, the discussion of issues which film viewing encouraged, and other features of the cinematic experience produced, in his view, a new type of social and political experience of art which eroded the private, solitary, and contemplative aesthetic experience encouraged by high culture and its priests. Against the contemplation of high art, the shock effects of film produce a mode of "distraction" which Benjamin believed makes possible a "heightened presence of mind" and cultivation of "expert" audiences able to examine and criticize film and society.

A German exile, Siegfried Kracauer, once close to Benjamin and Adorno, provided one of the first systematic studies of how films articulate social content. His book *From Caligari to Hitler* (1947) argues that German inter-war films reveal a highly authoritarian disposition to submit to social authority and a fear of emerging chaos. For Kracauer, German films reflect and foster anti-democratic and passive attitudes of the sort that paved the way for Nazism. While his assumption that "inner" psychological tendencies and conflicts are projected onto the screen opened up a fruitful area of sociocultural analysis, he frequently ignored the role of mechanisms of representation such as displacement, inversion, and condensation in the construction of cinematic images and narratives. He posits film–society analogies ("Their silent resignation foreshadows the passivity of many people under totalitarian rule," p. 218) that deny the autonomous and contradictory character and effects of film discourse and the multiple ways that audiences process cinematic material.

Sociological and psychological studies of Hollywood film proliferated in the US in the post-World War II era and developed a wide range of critiques of myth, ideology, and meaning in the American cinema. Parker Tyler's studies of *The Hollywood Hallucination* (1944) and *Myth and Magic of the Movies* (1947) applied Freudian and myth-symbol criticism to show how Walt Disney cartoons, romantic melodramas, and other popular films provided insights into social psychology and context, while providing myths suitable for contemporary audiences. In *Movies: A Psychological Study* (1950), Martha Wolfenstein and Nathan Leites applied psychoanalytical methods to film, decoding fears, dreams, and aspirations beneath the surface of 1940s Hollywood movies, arguing: "The common day dreams of a culture are in part the sources, in part the products of its popular myths, stories, plays and films" (p. 13). In her sociological study of

Hollywood: The Dream Factory (1950), Hortense Powdermaker studied an industry that manufactured dreams and fantasies, while Robert Warshow in *The Immediate Experience* (1970) related classical Hollywood genres like the Western and the gangster film to the social history and ideological problematics of US society.

Building on these traditions, Barbara Deming demonstrated in *Running Away From Myself* (1969) how 1940s Hollywood films provided insights into the social psychology and reality of the period. She argued: "It is not as mirrors reflect us but, rather, as our dreams do that movies most truly reveal the times" (p. 1). She claimed that 1940s Hollywood films provided a collective dream portrait of the era and proposed deciphering "the dream that all of us have been buying at the box office, to cut through to the real nature of the identification we have experienced there" (pp. 5–6). Her work anticipates later, more sophisticated and university-based film criticism of the post-1960s era by showing how films both reproduce dominant ideologies and also contain proto-deconstructive elements that cut across the grain of the ideology that the films promote. She also undertook a gender reading of Hollywood film that would eventually become a key part of film criticism.

Another tradition of film scholarship and criticism attempted to situate films historically and to describe the interactions between film and society in more overtly sociological and political terms. This tradition includes Lewis Jacob's (1939) pioneering history of Hollywood film, John Howard Lawson's theoretical and critical works, Ian Jarvie's (1970, 1978) sociological inquiries on the relation between film and society, D. M. White and Richard Averson's (1972) studies of the relation between film, history, and social comment in film, and the social histories written by Robert Sklar (1975), Garth Jowett (1976), and Thomas Schatz (1988). While this tradition produced useful insights into the relationships between film and society in specific historical eras, it tended to neglect the construction of film form and the ways that specific films or genres work to construct meaning and the ways that audiences themselves interact with film.

More theoretical approaches to film began emerging in the 1960s, including the ideological analyses of the work associated with the filmmakers and critics in France who published in *Cahiers du cinema*. The *Cahiers* critics called attention to the creative achievements of certain Hollywood directors and in general extolled the work of the cinematic creative artist or *auteur*. Their interest in Western and gangster films helped to generate genre theory as well.

Building on this work, in the 1970s, the extremely influential British film journal *Screen* published translations of some of the major *Cahiers* texts and other works of French film theory, including Roland Barthes, Christian Metz, and various poststructuralist critics who produced more sophisticated formal approaches to film (see Metz 1974; Heath 1981). The *Cahiers* group in turn moved from seeing film as the product of creative *auteurs* or authors (their *politique du auteurs* of the 1950s, taken up by Sarris (1968) and others), to focus on the ideological, political, and sociological content of film and how it transcoded dominant ideologies and had certain political and social effects. At the same time, French film theory and *Screen* focused on the specific cinematic mechanisms that helped to produce meaning.

During the same period of intense ferment in the field of film studies during the 1960s and 1970s, the Birmingham Centre for Contemporary Cultural Studies was discovering that gender, race, and subculture were also important elements of analyzing the relationships between culture, ideology, and society. Pushed by feminism to recognize the centrality of gender, it was argued that the construction of dominant ideologies of masculinity and femininity was a central aspect of film (Kuhn 1982; Kaplan 1983). Studies of the ways that films constructed race, ethnicity, and sexuality also became a key aspect of films studies, and various poststructuralist-influenced theories studied the role of film and media culture in the social construction of ideologies and identities (Kellner & Ryan 1988).

There are now a multiplicity of approaches competing to theorize the relations between film and society and to read and interpret film. The theory wars of the past decades have proliferated a tremendous amount of new theories that have been in turn applied to film. Consequently, structuralism and poststructuralism, psychoanalysis, deconstruction, feminism, postmodernism, and a wealth of other theoretical approaches have generated an often bewildering diversity of approaches to theorizing film which join and complexify previous film theory approaches such as the genre theory, auteur theory, and historical-sociological approaches. Within the cacophony of contemporary approaches to film, it is not a question of either/or which forces the theorist to adopt one approach, but rather a variety of approaches can be deployed to engage the relations of film to society (for elaboration of a multiperspectival model, see Kellner 1995).

In retrospect, all one-sided approaches to theorizing the relation between film and society are problematical. Although some "authors" had created distinctive and impressive bodies of work, they were often created within the constraints of a specific genre and studio system; thus to fully understand Hollywood film, for example, one needs insight into the production system, its codes and formulas, and the complex interaction of film and society, with film articulating social discourses, embedded in social struggles, and saturated with social meanings. Thus, analyzing the connection between film and society requires a multidimensional film criticism that situates its object within the context of the social milieu within which it is produced and received.

Finally, one of the most dramatic technological revolutions of all time is now unfolding with new entertainment and information technologies emerging, accompanied by unprecedented mergers of the entertainment and information industries and the transmission of increasingly globalized culture (Branston 2000). These new syntheses are producing novel forms of visual and multimedia culture in which it is anticipated that film will appear in seductive new virtual and interactive forms, accessible through computer, satellite, and new mechanisms of transmission like video recorders, DVDs, iPods, and other devices. There is feverish speculation that the Internet and its assorted technologies will create a new entertainment and information environment and currently the major corporations and players are envisaging what sort of product and delivery system will be most viable and profitable for films and other entertainment of the future. Thus, one imagines that the relationships between film and society will continue to be highly significant as we enter a new century and perhaps new cinematic era that will create novel forms of film and new perspectives on the film culture of the past.

SEE ALSO: Adorno, Theodor W.; Author/Auteur; Barthes, Roland; Birmingham School; Capitalism; Communism; Documentary; Globalization; Highbrow/Lowbrow; Ideology; Multimedia; Socialization, Agents of

REFERENCES AND SUGGESTED READINGS

Benjamin, W. (1972) The Work of Art in the Age of Mechanical Reproduction. In: *Illuminations*. Harcourt Brace Jovanovich, New York.

Bordwell, D., Staiger, J., & Thompson, K. (1985) *The Classical Hollywood Cinema*. Columbia University Press, New York.

Branston, G. (2000) *Cinema and Cultural Modernity*. Open University Press, Philadelphia.

Deming, B. (1969) *Running Away from Myself*. Grossman, New York.

Ewen, S. & Ewen, E. (1982) *Channels of Desire*. McGraw-Hill, New York.

Heath, S. (1981) *Questions of Cinema*. Indiana University Press, Bloomington.

Horkheimer, M. & Adorno, T. W. (1972 [1948]) *Dialectic of Enlightenment*. Seabury Press, New York.

Jacobs, L. (1939) *The Rise of the American Film*. Harcourt, Brace, New York.

Jarvie, I. C. (1970) *Toward a Sociology of the Cinema*. Routledge & Kegan Paul, London.

Jarvie, I. C. (1978) *Movies as Social Criticism*. Scarecrow Press, Metuchen.

Jowett, G. (1976) *Film: The Democratic Art*. William Morrow, New York.

Kaplan, E. A. (1983) *Women and Film*. Methuen, New York.

Kellner, D. (1995) *Media Culture*. Routledge, New York.

Kellner, D. & Ryan, M. (1988) *Camera Politica: The Politics and Ideology of Hollywood Film*. University of Indiana Press, Bloomington.

Kracauer, S. (1947) *From Caligari to Hitler: A Psychological History of the German Film*. Princeton University Press, Princeton.

Kuhn, A. (1982) *Women's Pictures*. Routledge & Kegan Paul, London.

Mailer, M. (1967) Success and Failure of Soviet Cinema. *Marxist* 6(1): 4.

Metz, C. (1974) *Language and Cinema*. Mouton, The Hague.

Powdermaker, H. (1950) *Hollywood: The Dream Factory*. Little, Brown, Boston.

Sarris, A. (1968) *The American Cinema: Directors and Directions, 1929–1968*. Dutton, New York.

Schatz, T. (1988) *The Genius of the System*. Pantheon, New York.

Sklar, R. (1975) *Movie-Made America: A Social History of American Film*. Random House, New York.

Tyler, P. (1944) *The Hollywood Hallucination*. Simon & Schuster, New York.

Tyler, P. (1947) *Myth and Magic of the Movies*. Simon & Schuster, New York.

Warshow, R. (1970) *The Immediate Experience*. Atheneum, New York.

White, D. M. & Averson, R. (1972) *The Celluloid Weapon: Social Comment in the American Film*. Beacon Press, Boston.

Williams, R. (1973) Base and Superstructure in Marxist Cultural Theory. *New Left Review* 82: 6–33.

Wolfenstein, M. & Leites, N. (1950) *Movies: A Psychological Study*. Free Press, Glencoe, IL.

Wright, W. (1977) *Six-Guns and Society: A Structural Study of the Western*. University of California Press, Berkeley.

finalization in science

Wolfgang Krohn

Finalization in science is a theory concerning the relationship between science and society from a historical and political perspective. It was developed in the 1970s by Gernot Böhme, Wolfgang van den Daele, and Wolfgang Krohn (Böhme et al. 1972, 1973, 1976, 1978). Its main thesis is that modern science has internal dynamics that allow it to absorb external goals of research on an increasing scale. The expression "finalization" is meant to denote this tendency (Latin *finis*; purpose, goal). This theoretical model is continuous with the paradigmatic view of Thomas Kuhn and with Imre Lakatos's methodology of scientific research programs, but adds additional features concerning the social contexts of science.

With respect to many fundamental disciplines of modern science the model assumes a typical three-phase development. The first, or explorative, phase embraces the period prior to the emergence of theories which serve to organize the field. At this point a research program internally determining the relevance and succession of problems is absent. Rather, all kinds of challenging problems can be experimentally analyzed and classified, and serve to induce competing theories. Examples can be found in mechanics previous to Newton; chemistry before the work of Lavoisier, Proust, and Dalton; electrodynamics before Maxwell; evolutionary biology before Darwin; and genetics before the double helix model. Contemporary examples are neurobiology, research on chronic diseases, and cancer research. The explorative phase allows for multiple, if contingent, couplings of external problems with scientific interests. These couplings are important because they carry the institutional and monetary support of the research fields.

The second or paradigmatic phase is determined by the emergence of an internal research program directed toward the elaboration of a fundamental and unifying theory replacing provisional middle-range theories. At this point science policy can only promote, not direct, such research, though prospects of technological returns in a more or less distant future legitimate investment of tax money.

While the formulation of these two phases roughly corresponds to other models, especially those of Kuhn and Lakatos, the original contribution of the finalization model comes from adding a third phase of theory development. Whereas Kuhnian paradigms grant researchers the unedifying business of solving puzzles and the Lakatos research program loses its capacity of progressive problemshift, the finalization model proposes a phase of finalized, or goal-oriented, theory development. Central to the argument is the fact that fundamental theories usually cannot be applied to complex empirical systems for which they are valid. Fluid mechanics is a good example of this. On the one hand, it is based on a set of equations – classical hydrodynamics – which basically cover the behavior of all fluids. On the other hand, it turned out not to be applicable to certain viscosity problems posed by aircraft technology. The development of a special "boundary layer" theory was needed – and achieved in the early twentieth century – in order to develop a theoretical model for the construction of aerofoils. These kinds of intermediary theories are called finalized theories, and make up the most important share of contemporary science. Based on a set of fundamental paradigmatic theories and conditioned by technological, ecological, and social expectations, finalized theories continuously and indefinitely fill up the stock of scientific knowledge. As compared to disciplines in phase two, paradigm formation is no longer the driving force, but rather it is the societal orientation of science that is the force. This shift from internal to external problem generation calls into question received concepts of an autonomous science or of science as an independent social system. However, the emphasis on theory development of sciences in their third phase distances the finalization model from concepts of control and steering.

The three-phase model can be taken as an ideal format of a discipline's life cycle. Additionally, finalization theory takes seriously the fact that – independent of Kuhnian revolutions – many paradigms that evolved in the disciplines' second phases remain in a stable state, which Heisenberg called "closed" theories. Classical mechanics, hydrodynamics, relativity theory, and quantum mechanics are cases in point. They serve as reliable knowledge bases for finalized research on externally induced problems. Case studies exemplify the relationships between closed and finalized theories. Contemporary science is predicted to turn to the development of finalized theories on an increasing scale. Epistemologically, such theories search for concepts that allow for the application of foundational theories to complex problems. Socially, they are guided by priorities set by institutions entitled to do so. The finalization model also accounts for normative implications. If societal issues become the guidelines of theory development, the question of interests becomes critical. Who is entitled to have a voice in setting research agendas, defining criteria of relevance, and negotiating the transformation of norms and values in theoretical knowledge? Modern ecology in its tension between including or excluding human goals from nature served as a prototype for pondering these questions.

Shortly after its first publication finalization theory caused a fierce debate among German philosophers of science that soon spilled over into the media. Their predominant point of attack in this early version of "science wars"

was the allegation that, under the cover of a new social epistemology of science, Marxian ideas of socialist planning and control were being advanced. The media resonance included accusations of seeking a "final solution" for science, of threatening science with a "1984 situation," of legitimizing "Lysenkoism." An important factor in this turmoil was the institutional setting. Finalization theory was developed in a newly founded research institute of the Max-Planck Society, with its established worldwide reputation. The institute was directed by the physicist philosopher Carl Friedrich von Weizsäcker and the sociologist Jürgen Habermas. Von Weizsäcker's public commitment for social responsibility of scientists and Habermas's writings on "knowledge and human interests" were the hidden targets of the critics. Even if they bore no responsibility for the finalization model, they were implicated to the extent to which their ideas could be traced in its content. (The controversy is documented in Böhme et al. 1983: 275–306.)

More serious criticism was raised by researchers from the emerging field of the social studies of science. For these researchers, the use of the internal–external terminology was unwarranted, the concept of "closed theories" appeared to be too rigid, the adherence to epistemic norms in theory formation was not in line with the programs of relativism, and the focus on the development of research fields was not easily compatible with the rise of laboratory studies. A new interest in finalization theory has emerged in the context of the concept of "knowledge society" and especially in the controversial discussion of the Mode II model advanced by Gibbons et al. (1994). The Mode II model claims a complete shift of the role and function of science as its context of application prevails over its basic research (Mode I). A few reservations notwithstanding, finalization can now be seen as an early attempt at understanding the new order and policy of science that seems to emerge in the contemporary development of knowledge society (Weingart 1997).

SEE ALSO: Kuhn, Thomas and Scientific Paradigms; Political Economy of Science; Science, Social Construction of; Scientific Knowledge, Sociology of; Scientific Productivity; Technology, Science, and Culture

REFERENCES AND SUGGESTED READINGS

Böhme, G., van den Daele, W., & Krohn, W. (1972) Alternativen in der Wissenschaft. *Zeitschrift für Soziologie* 4: 302–16.

Böhme, G., van den Daele, W., & Krohn, W. (1973) Die Finalisierung der Wissenschaft. *Zeitschrift für Soziologie* 2: 128–44.

Böhme, G., van den Daele, W., & Krohn, W. (1976) Finalization in Science. *Social Science Information* 2–3: 307–30.

Böhme, G., van den Daele, W., & Krohn, W. (1978) Alternatives in Science. *International Journal of Sociology* 3: 70–94.

Böhme, G., van den Daele, W., Hohlfeld, R., Krohn, W., & Schäfer, W. (1983) *Finalization in Science: The Social Orientation of Scientific Progress*. Reidel, Boston

Gibbons, M. et al. (1994) *The New Production of Knowledge: The Dynamics of Research in Contemporary Societies*. Sage, London.

Johnston, R. (1976) Finalization: A New Start for Science Policy? *Social Science Information* 15: 331–6.

Krohn, W. & van den Daele, W. (1998) Science as an Agent of Change: Finalization and Experimental Implementation. *Social Science Information* 1.

Pfetch, F. (1979) The Finalization Debate in Germany: Some Comments and Explanations. *Social Studies of Science* 115–24.

Rip, A. (1981) A Cognitive Approach to Science Policy. *Research Policy* 4: 294–311.

Weingart, P. (1997): From "Finalization" to "Mode 2": Old Wine in New Bottles? *Social Science Information* 36(4): 591–613.

financial sociology

Lois A. Vitt

Financial sociology is the study of the relationship between finance, defined as the science of money management, and human society. In addition to money management, finance includes the management of money surrogates, capital instruments and markets, organizations and institutions, households, and governments. Finance is defined, structured, and regulated within a system of national and international laws that reflect power relations within political economies and across state and global markets. In practice, finance is art (e.g., negotiation) and science (e.g., measurement). Financial measurement of the firm and of investments constitutes the major emphasis within the field of economics as a subdiscipline of finance economics. The entire field of finance may be subsumed within the larger field of economics. Likewise, topics within financial sociology can be found in publications, or taught in courses, on economic sociology.

Relevant financial laws, structures, and policies govern the circulation of money within and among nations and cover various types of money surrogates as well: (1) checks, drafts, debit cards and other plastic cards that store value, or permit deferred payment such as charge cards and credit cards; (2) marketable and unmarketable securities such as notes, stocks, bonds, and shares of other pooled interests; (3) property and the resources that derive from property such as rents, commodities, debt and equity instruments and securities; and (4) business and the resources that derive from business enterprises including skills, labor, products, and services.

Three overarching levels of analysis include *personal finance*, the financial management of individual and household income, saving, and consumption; *corporate finance*, the financial management of organizations and business; and *public finance*, the financial management of government. Areas of prospective study within (and interactions among) these three levels touch all dimensions of social life: politics, taxes, art, religion, business, housing, health care, poverty and wealth, consumption, sports, transportation, labor force participation, and education. While each has a vast accumulated sociological literature of its own, the *financing* associated with these domains of modern social life has in the past usually been subsumed under "social policy."

Yet the financial policies, institutions, structures, and practices within any given society impact well-being for every individual and social group within a society, and increasingly, global well-being. George Ritzer (1995) clearly points this out in his analysis of credit cards and society: "Money and the credit card are so centrally important in modern consumer society that they take us very quickly to the core of that world."

The idea for a "sociology of finance" was probably introduced by Randall Collins who, when reviewing Mayer's *The Bankers* (1979), wondered why sociologists were not rushing to study financial organizations. Although sociological analysis of life insurance companies and markets emerged about the same time, relatively few studies appeared until the 1990s. To date, sociological analysis that is intentionally trained upon the financial laws, policies, markets, networks, firms, transactions, costs, customs, and human interactions is still in its infancy but holds enormous promise.

Paul Hirsch, at the 1993 Annual Meetings of the American Sociological Association, suggested that sociology was still "asleep at the wheel" in tracking how the discipline examines social change and the institutions of banking and finance. At the same session, a typology of financial sociology was presented which demonstrated that relevant areas for sociological study, in fact, are so numerous that it is nearly impossible to find social reality not connected in some direct way to money and finance. Does the young but growing field of economic sociology take up the slack?

THE INTERSECTION OF ECONOMIC SOCIOLOGY AND FINANCIAL SOCIOLOGY

Auguste Comte coined the term "sociology" in 1838 and paved the way for other social thinkers to develop theories of society. As sociology became its own discipline, social problems increasingly were analyzed as if they had no economic dimension and economic problems as if they had no social dimension. Economists and sociologists seldom looked back until Richard Swedberg fostered a dialogue between the two fields. Swedberg's thought-provoking interviews in 1990 with well-known economists Gary Becker, Amartya Sen, Kenneth Arrow, and Albert O. Hirschman, and sociologists Daniel Bell, Harrison White, James Coleman, and Mark Granovetter, helped to bridge the boundary between economics and sociology.

There is a growing dialogue between these fields, as economists take on many more social topics and sociologists become interested in rational choice and other economic theories. While economic sociology begins to flourish, however, financial sociology is emerging as a subfield that would have been impossible to conceptualize during the last half of the nineteenth and much of the twentieth centuries. Although closely related, the disciplines of economics and finance are distinctive. Whereas economics makes a number of abstract assumptions for purposes of analysis, finance is a socially constructed (and manipulated) set of principles that intentionally facilitate and manage transactions between and among governments, organizations, groups, and households. Financial sociology incorporates, by definition, the painstakingly constructed theories of sociology to analyze its impact on individuals, families, and societies, and there are important purposes for such specific sociological analysis.

Human societies have taken many forms throughout history, and remarkable diversity is still evident today in the world. So are the great differences among societies that flourish and those that still struggle. These differences have been attributed to what Lenski and colleagues termed *sociocultural evolution*, the changes that occur as a society gains new technology. The more technological information a society has, the faster it evolves. However, technology alone is not all that is needed for social and economic development. New technology must be *financed*.

Hernando de Soto's (2000) analysis of capital offers sociology some insights that further explain the great differences among societies. Why, he asks, have the efforts of third world and former communist nations to organize a modern capitalist economy not been met with more success? "From Russia to Venezuela, the past half-decade has been a time of economic suffering, tumbling incomes, anxiety, and resentment." Although many of these nations have balanced budgets, cut subsidies, welcomed foreign investment, and dropped tariff barriers, according to de Soto, their efforts have been repaid with bitter disappointment. Yet the cities of the third world and the former communist countries teem with entrepreneurs who are talented, enthusiastic, and have an astonishing ability to grasp and use modern technology. In fact, the unauthorized use of communications, weapons, and consumer technology increasingly presents western nations with serious problems of patent violations and product control.

Even in the poorest countries, the poor save, according to de Soto and his team of researchers who gathered data block by block, and farm by farm, in Asia, Africa, the Middle East, and Latin America. The aggregate savings, commercial and residential buildings, businesses, and other assets of these countries are often held, however, in defective forms. There are few modern laws, working infrastructures, institutions, and markets to turn these assets into capital for investment and growth. In short, there has been little or no ability to create the financing – for individuals, businesses, or governments – that exists and is generally taken for granted in the West.

Two modern movements, however, may be transforming societies worldwide: the industrialization of developing countries through globalization and the transition of advanced societies from industrial-based into service economies. In his 1991 book *Money and the Meaning of Life*, Jacob Needleman observed: "money is the main, moving force of human life at the present stage of civilization. Our relationship to nature, to health and illness, to education, to art, to social justice, is all increasingly permeated by the money factor." More recently, Peter Marber (2003) chronicled the sociofinancial changes already in process that are impacting life expectancy, literacy, education, consumption, and growing prosperity in developing societies as a result of globalization. While industrialization in the third world has its social costs and its detractors, according to Marber, "more people in more places have access not only to goods, but also to art, ideas, and innovation," as a direct result of globalization. Radical changes are occurring globally that affect not only what people value and want, but also governance, the environment, the roles of women and families, religion, and religious conflict.

FINANCIAL SOCIOLOGY TODAY

Groundbreaking sociological research entered the literature on financial sociology during the past decade and a half. Studies of human emotions and behaviors in the context of money and finance have appeared (e.g., Millman 1991), as well as work on banking and credit at both the macro and micro levels. In *Expressing America*, George Ritzer (1995) focuses Georg Simmel's "relationist" theories (as well as the theories of Mills, Marx, and Weber) on money and credit cards to gain insight into fundamental characteristics of the social world. Ritzer finds evidence of rampant consumerism, debt, fraud and crime, and invasions of privacy, among other social problems, that go far beyond credit cards themselves. These problems are not new to sociologists, but approaching them via a financial route permits a different awareness of their causes and consequences. According to Ritzer (1995), "the credit card, as well as the industry that stands behind it and aggressively pushes its growth and expansion, is not only important in itself, but also as a window on modern society."

Robert Manning's *Credit Card Nation* (2000) chronicles the history of debt and credit since the deregulation of financial services in the US in 1980. Manning reveals the costs in human terms of Americans' growing dependence on credit cards and predicts that tomorrow's senior citizens are at risk for increasingly aging into debt. His work includes a chapter devoted to the social consequences of credit card debt on college students based on in-depth interviews and 1999 cross-sectional survey data of college students. The study, introduced by the Consumer Federation of America, was a national revelation that young lives were being ruined by credit card debt. Manning's analysis of the consequences of student debt has been noted by credit card companies as well as universities and other organizations that sponsor so-called "affinity cards" and profit by doing so.

The interactions between individuals and families and public–private interests that both enable and support the growth of financial innovations are not unique to credit cards. Such micro–macro interactions are present in many, if not all, consumer financial innovations. They positively or negatively impact the housing, health care, pension, insurance, education, retirement, and brokerage activities of modern society, depending upon the degree of oversight that exists to curb excesses. They positively or negatively affect individuals, families, and communities, and when large numbers of people are affected, they can become public issues (Ritzer 2001). For older adults, college students, low-income individuals and families, and other affected segments of society, credit card excesses and punitive practices are fast becoming public issues.

SEE ALSO: Bankruptcy; Comte, Auguste; Consumption, Mass Consumption, and Consumer Culture; Credit Cards; Economy, Culture and; Economy (Sociological Approach); Money; Taxes: Progressive, Proportional, and Regressive; Theory Construction

REFERENCES AND SUGGESTED READINGS

De Soto, H. (2000) *The Mystery of Capital: Why Capitalism Triumphs in the West and Fails Everywhere Else*. Basic Books, New York.
Hirsch, P. (1993) Notes Towards a Sociology of Banking and Finance. Unpublished paper presented at the 1993 Annual Meetings of the American Sociological Association.
Manning, R. D. (2000) *Credit Card Nation*. Basic Books, New York.
Manning, R. D. (2003) Aging into Debt. In: Vitt, L. A. (Ed.), *Encyclopedia of Retirement and Finance*. Greenwood Press, Westport, CT.
Marber, P. (2003) *Money Changes Everything: How Global Prosperity Is Reshaping Our Needs, Values, and Lifestyles*. Financial Times/Prentice-Hall, Upper Saddle River, NJ.
Millman, M. (1991) *Warm Hearts and Cold Cash: The Intimate Dynamics of Families and Money*. Free Press, New York.
Needleman, J. (1991) *Money and the Meaning of Life*. Doubleday Currency, New York.
Pahl, J. (1990) Household Spending, Personal Spending, and the Control of Money in Marriage. *Sociology* 24(1): 119–38.
Ritzer, G. (1995) *Expressing America: A Critique of the Global Credit Card Society*. Pine Forge Press, Thousand Oaks, CA.
Ritzer, G. (2001) *Explorations in the Sociology of Consumption: Fast Food, Credit Cards, and Casinos*. Sage, Thousand Oaks, CA.

flânerie

Heidi L. Reible

Flânerie, in a narrow sense, refers to the act of idle strolling in nineteenth-century Paris, while visually collecting social artifacts of metropolitan life – the human sights and material culture of the urban crowd. In a wider sense, it is immersion in an anonymous, spectatorial gaze that gives license to wandering and observing. *Flânerie* engenders reflexivity as both an action and a process of observation that perceptively elucidates social phenomena. Text and sketches of the passing moment serve as witnesses to these random readings of the crowd. *Flânerie* embodies pleasure in the form of mobile observation. It is an aesthetic action, art form, and social phenomenon that resonate in masculine public space.

The *flâneur* is a figure of modernity, a solitary man of leisure with no destination. He passionately performs the act of idle walking while furtively consuming spatial and temporal impressions. Sociologically, he stands in a contested space, as an intellectual in mass culture, as a "natural" in an artificial environment. The *flâneur* has been described as a bum, idler, artist, observer, gastronome, social commentator, literary figure, scavenger, intellectual, and poet. At the core, he possesses a way of seeing the world and being in the world that intrinsically reveals meaningful, social commentary.

Charles Baudelaire, a mid-1800s poet, and Walter Benjamin, literary critic in the early 1900s, were instrumental in creating the poetic enigma and physical entity that became the literary figure of the *flâneur*. Both described him as a man who was simultaneously a part of the crowd and yet alone on the streets of the urban landscape. They conceptualized the social type of the *flâneur* as individualized, itinerant, and dissociated from discursive group or community contact. He was a collector, an accidental detective, and a rag-picker, who possessed acuity in deriving social relevance from the fragments of everyday experience. They situated the concepts of *flâneur* and *flânerie* within visual sight of commodities and in spaces of leisure. Urban spectacle inspired Baudelaire's poetic ruminations on the subject. It was the City of Lights that became the original city of *flânerie*.

Industrialization in Paris and a subsequent increase in production of saleable commodities were instrumental events that gave rise to visually spectacular places of consumption through which the *flâneur* strolled in the early

1800s. Architectural innovations in iron-working techniques and glass manufacturing, as well as the proliferation of visual media, played an important role in developing the city. Large plate glass windows allowed strollers to view available goods. These places of consumption became spaces of leisure that privileged "visual" participation within mass culture. Buying, as well as window-shopping, became a new pastime. Advertising, architecture, technology, and the emerging presence of women shoppers drew the gaze of the *flâneur*. Mid-century, Baron Georges Eugène Haussmann developed reconstruction plans that would accommodate the economic and demographic growth that had changed the capital into a burgeoning city. More than 100,000 buildings were razed to replace old streets and disorganized districts. Several of the arcades of Paris, areas of elegant shops filled with displays of commodities, were built during implementation of the Haussmann project, and incorporated such structural innovations.

Flânerie was irrefutably a masculine pursuit. The female *flâneuse* was absent in the city, as reflected in the writings of Baudelaire and Benjamin. Gendered restrictions of movement reflecting customary societal limitations of the time excluded women from public spaces. The private space of home was a woman's approved sphere of influence. Those who chose a public presence were often looked upon as prostitutes, a corporeal commodity. Though the arcades initiated a shift in access to gendered, public sites of leisure consumption, the masculine maintained a position of privilege. Even as these newly bounded public places became acceptable spaces of leisure for respectable women, *flânerie* remained culturally intolerable. "Looking" was problematized as a gendered act of consumption; woman was object to the *flâneur*'s gaze.

This history usefully informs a culture of consumption that continues privileging the "visual." *Flânerie* maintains relevance as it raises the potential for understanding social phenomena collected as visual fragments embedded in performance of daily public life. Thorstein Veblen (1967 [1899]), in *The Theory of the Leisure Class*, was one of the first to critique leisure practices as conspicuous consumption,

and to emphasize leisure's significance to society. Television, the Internet, newspapers and magazines, billboards, movies, as well as interiors and exteriors of mass transit buses are examples of a visual culture that continues to generate opportunities for new ways of "seeing" ordinary life as it interfaces with leisure.

Recent literary discourse brings emergent interpretations of *flânerie* and its social relevancy to the present. It has been suggested that *flânerie* is allied with browsing in shopping malls, with traveling to novel places, with aural grazing of radio waves, with channel surfing television, with cooking and eating food, with wandering in Disneyland, as well as with lurking in cyberspace in chat rooms on the Internet. Future directions in research may include the use of *flânerie* as a method in the study of everyday leisure, or induce efforts to locate and observe *flânerie* as it takes place in twenty-first-century life. In addition, it is germane to continue debates that legitimate evidence to support the physical presence and perspicacity of the *flâneuse* in the urban environment, past and present. Whether these ideas are consistent with the poetic thoughts of Baudelaire, or the writings of Benjamin in the context of modernity, requires further exploration and discussion.

SEE ALSO: Benjamin, Walter; Conspicuous Consumption; Consumption, Mass Consumption, and Consumer Culture; Leisure, Popular Culture and; Veblen, Thorstein

REFERENCES AND SUGGESTED READINGS

Baudelaire, C. (1964) *The Painter of Modern Life and Other Essays*. Phaidon Press, London.
Benjamin, W. (1973) *Charles Baudelaire: A Lyric Poet in the Era of High Capitalism*. New Left Books, London.
Buck-Morss, S. (1991) *The Dialectics of Seeing*. MIT Press, Cambridge, MA.
Tester, K. (Ed.) (1994) *The Flâneur*. Routledge, New York.
Veblen, T. (1967 [1899]) *The Theory of the Leisure Class*. Viking Press, New York.

folk Hinduism

Vineeta Sinha

Accounts of Hinduism have predominantly been approached via literary and textual avenues, through which its ancient, philosophical, abstract, and transcendent features are highlighted. Even ethnographic accounts of Hinduism have been dominated by attention to the Sanskritic and Brahmanic elements derived from such a scriptural, elitist grounding. Such foci are limited because of the neglect of oral traditions and attention to Hindu practices, particularly at the local, regional levels and the role of specific household and cult deities, rituals, and festivals in sustaining a religious worldview. Writing in 1976, the late Indian social anthropologist M. N. Srinivas noted the "downgrading of folk religion" (1976: 288–90) and the scholarly neglect of the "folk" elements in Hinduism both by western and Indian social scientists, arguing that this is a viable, independent, and legitimate realm for social science theorizing.

By a "folk" variety of Hinduism is meant these specific features: the privileging of mediums and trance sessions; the intimate, familiar, unmediated approach to the deity (given the absence of a religious intermediary); the ability to sense, feel close to, and talk to deities; the importance of devotion, intuition, emotion, and religious experience; the offerings of non-vegetarian items, alcohol, and cigars to the deity; the absence of text-based, ritual procedures (*arccanai*, *abishegam*, and the chanting of *mantras*, *slokas*) for approaching the deity; a pragmatic, day-to-day orientation, valuing rituals of self-mortification and equality of all before god. The eventual turn to "folk" dimension and "little community" (Redfield 1956) has been consequential for the simple reason that it rightly draws attention to an erstwhile neglected empirical domain of study. Much is now known about the ritual universe of folk Hinduism, the mythology of specific village deities, the logic of ritual performances, the significance of festivals and other ritual events to manage the uncertainties of daily living. This description of "folk Hinduism" does not exist in isolation. This is only one half of a dichotomy that has

identified, named, and ranked two types of religious styles – captured in the more universal metaphor of the "Great" and "Little" traditions (Singer 1972). In the Hindu context, the "Sanskritic"–"non-Sanskritic" divide approximates this classification.

Despite the pervasive use of such descriptions as "folk religion" and "folk Hinduism," the category "folk" has not been sufficiently problematized (Chatterji 2001). An etymology of the English word "folk" leads to such connotations as "ordinary," "common people," and "masses." The association of "folk" with peasants and rural populations – who are further typified as being illiterate, unsophisticated, and simple-minded in contrast to the more urbane, cultured, and educated city dweller – has meant that the term is by no means neutral. Extending such logic, the folk dimension already being ranked lower, members who participate in "folk" practices are assigned specific sociological identities, and are further presumed to be carriers of specific values and mores. This awareness prompts us to ask: What is meant by "folk" varieties of religion and Hinduism? So far, there has been little debate in the literature about what these descriptions signify and the value, if any, of continuing to use them as frames of analysis. Yet, they continue to be used in a taken-for-granted manner without being adequately conceptualized. Given the history of "folk Hinduism" and the awareness that it does have a built-in comparative dimension vis-à-vis "elite" notions of Hinduism, its unreflective use is highly problematic.

Although some aspects of the folk/little/popular/non-Sanskritic Hindu (descriptions which have been used interchangeably) practice have been marginalized over time, this domain reveals a persistence (and in some places shows signs of being revived) within India, and especially amongst overseas Hindu communities in Fiji, Mauritius, South Africa, Singapore, and Malaysia. The overwhelming evidence for the preferred attachment to village-based religious practices amongst fourth and fifth Singapore and Malaysia-born Hindus is sociologically fascinating. Despite specific substantive shifts in the constitution of Hinduism in this region over time, the ritual complex surrounding the veneration of local, household, and village deities – a strong feature of folk Hinduism – is one stable element that continues. This is to be expected given the specific profile of Indian and Hindu presence in British Malaya since the nineteenth century. Large numbers of Indians were brought in from Tamilnadu to undertake infrastructure work in British Malaya. Much of this labor was drawn from the lowest rungs of the Indian class and caste hierarchy, that is, from the non-Brahmin and Adi-Dravida communities. The veneration of village deities and rituals associated with them were continued by these sectors of the migrant community in their new homes. The village deities – *gramadevata* – from Tamilnadu thereby came to Malaya and were firmly placed in the religious landscape of the Malayan Peninsula. Today, the observance of festivals such as *timiti* (fire walking) and *tai pucam*, the large numbers of temples dedicated to village deities, and the attraction to village rituals tell the story of Hindu migration to Malaya.

The Hindu communities in Malaysia and Singapore have been in the region for close to two centuries. From the outset, they have existed in a societal context that is not structured according to principles of caste and embedded in a largely non-Hindu, multiracial, multireligious environment, where Hinduism is a minority religion. The Hindu community is clearly not homogeneous in this diasporic location: caste may not be an issue as before, but new class barriers have been erected, and are felt to be in force. Agamic temples (i.e., temples adhering to the Agamas, a set of texts that outline rules and procedures for temple worship) are associated with the "well-off" crowd- Hindu elites, temple administrators, Hindu authorities, and the government, but not the Brahmin priests, who are not seen as having any real power or autonomy. This is the domain of "Official Hinduism," framed by Agamic, Saiva Siddhanta (literally, "the doctrine of Siva" and the name by which the body of literature of the Saivas – followers of Siva – is known) precepts. A preference for a different religious style sees the persistence of the "old" ways, encapsulated as the realm of "Popular Hinduism" (Vertovec 1994). Often the two Hindu spheres, which are quite different, are brought into uncomfortable proximity.

In Singapore and Malaysia, the field of "folk Hinduism" is defined by diversity. The need

for protection from, and control over, unforeseen forces in the management of concrete, day-to-day problems is cited for the continued reliance on *kaaval deivam* (guardian deities), demonstrating the prevalence of a pragmatic orientation – recognized as a typical feature of folk Hinduism. For the middle-class and upper-middle-class Hindus the realm of trances, spirit mediums, and the phenomenon of animal sacrifices are intriguing, unfamiliar, and exotic, and often deemed a superficial form of religiosity. The recognition and labeling of these as the "old" ways reveals a desire to connect with the "past." In an adherence to the ways of the ancestors, connections with "tradition" are maintained and this is seen as continuity, ideas which are collectively carried in the notion of "persistence." Yet it is precisely also in the name of tradition that new ground is being broken and boundaries transgressed. This certainly challenges the simplistic equation of modernity with change, and tradition with conservatism and backwardness. Strikingly, there is no accompanying effort to standardize the multiplicity and variation that reign here. One encounters instead a "live and let live" attitude with a desire to remain outside the purview of institutionalized religious boundaries, to practice a style of religiosity that does not need to rely on scarce and guarded resources – such as ritual procedures as dictated by religious texts, the framework of Agamic temples, Brahmin priests, and other ritual specialists and ritual paraphernalia. But their religious universe is sustained through creating and legitimating an alternative set of norms and procedures as guiding principles, but with no accompanying desire for uniformity, or the presence of a central agency trying to regulate the ritual domain. It is not without significance that these very practices which are embraced positively by proponents of the "old ways" are devalued by critics (who are supporters of "Official Hinduism") as "extreme rituals" and "superstition," and therefore rejected as "primitive and embarrassing" – in fact deemed to be "un-Hindu."

Substantively, the domain of activities and thinking defined by the phrase the "old ways" is a complex mixture of elements, drawn from diverse religious traditions. Its empirical boundaries could by no means be seen to be replicating fully the ritual style in Tamilnadu villages. In the Malaysian and Singaporean context, the world of "folk Hinduism" is defined first and foremost by a strong sense of religious syncretism. This entails a free and liberal use of deities, symbols, and ritual practices associated with "other" religious traditions, foremost amongst which is a variety of religious/folk Taoism. Almost without exception, religious structures in this domain reveal the strong presence of deities and other religious paraphernalia from the latter, together with such Taoist deities as Tua Peh Kong, Kuan Yin, and Tai Sing. Physical constructions of religious altars that would be typically recognized as part of a "Chinese temple," ritual objects such as tall joss-sticks, large and small Chinese-style urns, floating oil candles, oranges, wooden pieces for seeking permission for 4-digits (a lottery popular in Singapore and Malaysia with a combination of 4 numbers), and so on, together with deities from the vast Hindu pantheon, are also present. Thus one witnesses what the purists would consider "indiscriminate borrowing" from all strands of Hinduism, without concern for recognizing boundaries, almost to the point of being irreverent. The truly syncretic nature of "Hinduism" is evident in the co-presence under one roof of deities of the Vaisnavite, Saivite, and Sakti tradition (in the coexistence of Hanuman, Ram, Mariamman, Periyachee, Bhagvati, and Kali), the Brahmanic and non-Brahmanic styles of worship (in the veneration of village deities such as Muneeswaran, Sanggali Karuppan, Madurai Veeran with Saivite deities like Murukan, Siva, and Ganesh) and in conducting "vegetarian" and "non-vegetarian" prayers for respective deities on the same grounds, but with appropriate procedures and deference. For instance, if meat is offered to Muneeswaran, the shrine of Murukan or Ganesh is encased with a curtain or the door closed. Often the presence of a *keramat* (Malay, "grave of a Muslim saint") and "Datuk God" (literally, "Grandfather God," the name of a localized deity popularly invoked in religious Taoism, as practiced in Malaysia and Singapore) completes the mixed-up but coherent and legitimate religious scene. The prominent presence of ethnic Chinese in these spaces, as devotees, is conspicuous, and these numbers seem to be on the rise in Singapore, Penang, Ipoh, and Kuala Lumpur.

In the Indian context, the different levels of Hinduism carry a strong connotation of caste identity. The categories of "Sanskritic" and "folk" Hinduism explicitly associated the "Great Tradition" with rituals and ideas of the higher castes (if not the Brahmins), and the various instances of "Little Tradition" emanated from the ritual practices of the lower-caste groupings, if not those of the outcastes (the Harijans, untouchables). While the category "folk" carries some conceptual utility, its implicit judgmental tone and the assumed low ranking assigned to "folk" practices must be questioned. The sociopolitical, cultural, intellectual, and ideological conditions that led to the emergence of these analytical categories for making sense of Hinduism in India clearly do not exist in the vastly different spaces where migrant Hindu communities are now located. Research from the latter speaks rather of a fusion, synthesis, and reconfiguration of elements drawn from different strands of Hinduism and outside, producing a hybrid, syncretic, and innovative style of religiosity even as tradition is invoked. The continued persistence of a style of Hindu religiosity (including features that would be drawn from "folk Hinduism" but also from other sources) amongst overseas Hindu communities, such as in Singapore and Malaysia, illustrates this point well.

SEE ALSO: Hinduism; Popular Religiosity; Religion; Religion, Sociology of; Sanskritization

REFERENCES AND SUGGESTED READINGS

Bhatti, H. S. (2000) *Folk Religion: Change and Continuity*. Rawat, New Delhi.
Chatterji, R. (2001) The Category of Folk. In: Das, V. (Ed.), *The Oxford India Companion to Sociology and Anthropology*. Oxford University Press, New Delhi.
Redfield, R. (1956) *The Little Community*. University of Chicago Press, Chicago.
Singer, M. (Ed.) (1959) *Traditional India: Structure and Change*. American Folklore Society, Philadelphia.
Singer, M. (1972) *When a Great Tradition Modernizes*. Praeger, New York.
Sontheimer, G. D. (1995) The Erosion of Folk Religion in Modern India: Some Points for

Deliberation. In: Dalmia, V. & Stietencron, H. von (Eds.), *Representing Hinduism*. Sage, New York, pp. 305–24.

Srinivas, M. N. (1976) *The Remembered Village*. Oxford University Press, New Delhi.

Vertovec, S. (1994) "Official" and "Popular" Hinduism in Diaspora: Historical and Contemporary Trends in Surinam, Trinidad, and Guyana. *Contributions to Indian Sociology* 28(1): 123–47.

football hooliganism

Gary Armstrong

Combine masculinity, physicality, fantasy, and local pride, mix in sporting excitement and collective grievances, and the possible outcome, dating back to the formation of Association Football in the mid-nineteenth century, has been disorder. Since the mid-1960s, incidents in Britain involving football spectator disorder and violence have been labeled "hooliganism." Lacking a precise definition or a legal status, "football hooliganism" has for some 40 years served as a receptacle for a spectrum of prejudices and attributes. Without a precise meaning, hooliganism can have no precise causes. The research process thus needs to examine both the *concept* (and its manifestation) and the *interaction* between definer and defined (Pearson 1983). Negotiations around the criminal justice system are crucial because definitions of deviance can depend on the demands of bureaucracies and the moral entrepreneurship of police, media, and the football authorities. The resulting boundary maintenance mechanisms result in stigmatizations and degradation ceremonies offered by courtrooms and media "name and shame" projects. The establishment of police databases, increasingly via the eye of a lens, provides the ever-expanding roll call of "categorical suspicion" crucial to the construction and maintenance of a "social problem" (Armstrong & Giulianotti 1998).

Termed since the 1970s the "English disease," it is unsurprising that academics in the UK are pioneers of the hooliganism debate. Sociologists and psychologists have contributed to related social control policies, often on the basis of preconceived and, at times, bewildering arguments based on little or no empirical evidence. Early sociological explanations portrayed hooligans as a growing subculture resisting the commercial imperative pursued by many soccer clubs (Taylor 1971). In the early 1980s the hooligan problem was framed within a political crisis that threatened capitalist hegemony, and analyzed within the different conceptions of class relations in Britain (Taylor 1982). However, some scholars became disillusioned in the late 1980s as they saw their ideas enveloped in a belief that all troublemaking fans, believed to be drawn from the aspiring and residual strata of the proletariat, were morally and culturally shallow. This in turn made young working-class men fodder for racist movements and a collectivity unworthy of left-liberal sympathy (Taylor 1987, 1991).

Crowds and disorder have attracted psychologists and theories since Le Bon (1952). However, research on hooliganism has often been informed by an academic obsession with predictive profiling and "models" of disorder. Typically, avoiding contact with hooligan participants has not prevented the production of elaborate texts that bewilder the sociological imagination. Those that attempted ethnography could only retreat to the classroom and dismiss hooligan disorder as "issue-less." The fundamental problem with such an approach is this: when collective behavior occurs, which circumstance is an issue and which one is it? At the same time that politicians first debated the issue in the British Parliament, Marsh (1978; Marsh et al. 1978) attempted to produce an "ethnogenic" social psychological analysis that used observation and interviews to claim that hooliganism was ritualized conflict, common to all civilizations, and played out in particular confines by a career structure of recognizable participant "types." The work of Marsh and his colleagues provided the first attempt at qualitative understanding, but it ignored the complex sociohistorical context of rivalries.

More sophisticated applications of sociological theory appeared in the 1980s when figurationalist metatheory, organized around the idea of network interdependency as advanced by Norbert Elias, was combined with Suttles's (1968) concept of "ordered segmentation" derived in his studies of ethnicity and gang membership in Chicago. The result was a trilogy of texts from the Leicester School (at the University of Leicester) explaining that hooligans were a product of lower-working-class exclusion that produced an aggressive masculinity, uncontrolled by civilizing processes, and expressed in disruptive actions, some of which would occur at football matches (Williams et al. 1984; Dunning et al. 1988; Murphy et al. 1990). This theory has been challenged on its historical validity, questioned for its application to football hooliganism, and critically scrutinized on methodological and interpretive grounds by those who conducted qualitative research with hooligan groups. Aside from these criticisms, arguments around civilizing and decivilizing processes are impossible to test and, during a century filled with wars, seemingly inappropriate to use as explanations for fights associated with football matches. Furthermore, the transmission of social values and ideas of emulation or avoidance is complex when examining the reality of the lived experience and the fluidity of social class.

Since the early 1990s, academic research in the UK has addressed ideas about hooliganism as publicized by the police and media and favored by law-and-order politicians campaigning for support. The police and politicians, themselves coming from notoriously hierarchical occupational cultures, explained that hooligan gatherings could exist only if they had quasi-military structures. Therefore, the past 20 years have seen an obsessive search in Britain for the conspiracies of the hooligan "generals" who have a wider political and criminal agenda and whose capture and incarceration are necessary if hooliganism is to be eliminated. Subsequent high-profile arrests of suspects identified in these terms produced court cases that could not be prosecuted due to falsified evidence presented by the police. Research since the mid-1990s moved beyond Britain to study actions associated with international soccer matches. Studies by anthropologists and sociologists are generally enlightening because they present data on local sociopolitical contexts. Since the late 1990s, research on global football culture shows that disorder is endemic to the game. Whether observers label such disorder as "hooliganism" will depend on their perceptions of causes.

Research has shown that football hooliganism consists of emerging public enactments of ritualized procedures by constantly changing collections of people. It exists via inter- and intragroup negotiations which are never fully agreed upon but which give rise to future discord. Confrontations occur within normative or pragmatic confines. They involve semi-choreographed situational scenarios acted out as authorities, playing umpire, persistently try to narrow the boundaries of disorder (Giulianotti & Armstrong 2002). The young people resemble Maffesoli's (1996) "neotribes": open-ended, mainly urban groups seeking a cause to be pursued through risky actions occurring in spaces that supply them a multiplicity of meanings. Notions of "performance" and "comportment" are integral to such processes, embedded in notions of social class and habitus (Bourdieu 1984).

Unfortunately, issues of selfhood, agency, and structure have been ignored, often because research on hooliganism has been fueled by narcissistic contemplations combined with crude voyeurism. At the same time, former participants have produced popular autobiographies that often ridicule sociologists. The phenomena and epiphenomena that hooliganism generates are useful sites for exploring social performance, idealized masculinity, media imperatives, applications of commerce to public order policing, identity in urban milieus, and the construction of the status of "expert" social commentators.

SEE ALSO: Soccer; Sport; Violence Among Fans

REFERENCES AND SUGGESTED READINGS

Armstrong, G. & Giulianotti, R. (1998) From Another Angle: Police Surveillance and Football Supporters. In: Norris, C., Moran, J., & Armstrong, G. (Eds.), *Surveillance, Closed Circuit Television in Social Control*. Ashgate, Aldershot, pp. 113–35.

Bourdieu, P. (1984) *Distinction: A Social Critique of the Judgment of Taste*. Harvard University Press, Cambridge, MA.

Dunning, E., Williams, J., & Murphy, P. (1988) *The Roots of Football Hooliganism*. Routledge, London.

Giulianotti, R. & Armstrong, G. (2002) Avenues of Contestation: Football Hooligans, Running and Ruling Urban Spaces. *Social Anthropology* 10(2): 211–38.

Le Bon, G. (1952) *The Crowd*. London, Ernest Benn.

Maffesoli, M. (1996) *The Time of the Tribes*. Sage, London.

Marsh, P. (1978) Life and Careers on the Soccer Terraces. In: Ingham, R. (Ed.), *Football Hooliganism: The Wider Context*. Inter-Action Inprint, London, pp. 61–81.

Marsh, P., Rosser, E., & Harré, R. (1978) *The Rules of Disorder*. Routledge & Kegan Paul, London.

Murphy, P., Dunning, E., & Williams, J. (1990) *Football on Trial: Spectator Violence and Development in the Football World*. Routledge, London.

Pearson, G. (1983) *Hooliganism: A History of Respectable Fears*. Macmillan, London.

Suttles, G. (1968) *The Social Order of the Slum*. Chicago, Chicago University Press.

Taylor, I. (1971) Soccer Consciousness and Soccer Hooliganism. In: Cohen, S. (Ed.), *Images of Deviance*. Penguin, Harmondsworth, pp. 134–64.

Taylor, I. (1982) On the Sports Violence Question: Soccer Hooliganism Revisited. In: Hargreaves, J. (Ed.), *Sport, Culture, and Ideology*. Routledge & Kegan Paul, London, pp. 152–96.

Taylor, I. (1987) Putting the Boot into a Working-Class Sport: British Soccer After Bradford and Brussels. *Sociology of Sport Journal* 4(2): 171–91.

Taylor, I. (1991) English Football in the 1990s: Taking Hillsborough Seriously. In: Williams, J. & Wagg, S. (Eds.), *British Football and Social Change*. Leicester University Press, Leicester.

Williams, J., Dunning, E., & Murphy, P. (1984) *Hooligans Abroad: The Behaviours and Control of English Fans in Continental Europe*. Routledge, London.

Fordism/post-Fordism

Harland Prechel

Taylorism and other forms of scientific management were implemented in many industries in the late nineteenth and early twentieth centuries. However, the formalization of control over the labor process was accelerated when Henry Ford and his engineers systematically applied the principles of scientific management to the entire labor process. *Fordism* represents two critical changes in the historical process of fragmenting tasks and increasing the division of labor. First, whereas Taylorism developed work rules to standardize the production of parts, Fordism brought these standardized parts to the worker and further separated conception from execution by specifying how the assembly of parts was to be done. Second, using the assembly line to bring work to the worker made it possible to limit interruptions in the labor process and increase control over the pace of work.

By creating more precise control over the labor process and setting the pace of work, Ford discovered that he could pay high wages while maintaining high profits. His capacity to pay higher wages than other capitalists permitted Ford to be more selective when hiring workers and to impose stricter standards on those workers. The incentive of higher wages was particularly important because it allowed Ford to overcome some of the central impediments to capital accumulation during this historical period: absenteeism and labor turnover. Ford's selection of workers was done by his "sociological department," which scrutinized workers' behavior and implemented hiring practices based on his conception of a moral worker. Fordism also entailed internal labor markets by creating job classifications and hierarchies that allowed workers to be upwardly mobile within the company. These internal labor markets created competition among workers, which divided workers against one another and reduced worker solidarity. In addition to transforming the labor process, Fordism is associated with other social changes. Most notable, the mass production of inexpensive commodities contributed to a culture of mass consumption. Fordism also entails a mode of state regulation that attempted to institutionalize economic growth and stability by limiting workers' rights, creating a welfare state, and implementing Keynesian economic policies.

The limitations of Fordism became apparent in the mid-1970s when the 1973 oil crisis and the economic downturn in 1974 resulted in an abrupt halt to economic growth and stability. This capital accumulation crisis represents the transition to *post-Fordism*, which represents a new phase of capitalist development. These new institutional arrangements include an acceleration of globalization, the increased role of the state in balancing production with consumption, restructuring the production process, and the emergence of giant global corporations and financial institutions that exercise control over trade, domestic companies, and many nation-states. Despite agreement that a transition occurred, there is considerable debate among social scientists over how to characterize this form of social organization. In contrast to those who characterize post-Fordism as global corporate dominance, other scholars view this transition as creating a more flexible form of economic organization and increasing individualism and pluralistic lifestyles. There is also considerable debate over whether post-Fordism represents a historical transition or modifies previous trends. Still other scholars challenge the broad generalizations in post-Fordist theory for denying the complex and heterogeneous causal processes that operate in different places in the global economy (for more detail, see Amin 1994; Hall et al. 1995).

One dimension of this debate that has been the subject of considerable empirical research is the use of information to control the manufacturing processes. Post-Fordism maintains that access to information creates the organizational capability for instant data analysis that is essential to decisions concerning flexible manufacturing, the manufacture of specialized products, and the coordination of diverse corporate interests (Harvey 1991). Whereas some arguments suggest that information fosters decentralization and autonomy at lower levels of the organizational hierarchy (Piore & Sabel 1984), others suggest that access to information contributes to centralization (Dohse et al. 1985). These perspectives have been criticized because they represent a binary logic, conceptualize information in highly abstract terms, and fail to give explicit attention to the kind of information used, the location of information in the organizational hierarchy, who has access to it, and how it is used in the decision-making process. To determine whether decision-making is tightly controlled or subject to wide discretion, researchers have analyzed the design of information systems, and the organizational distance between the conception and execution of decisions. *Neo-Fordism* formulations suggest that contemporary forms of control have continuity with the past and share important

characteristics with Taylorism and Fordism. This line of theorizing maintains that centralization and decentralization must be treated as theoretical constructs that illuminate empirical processes rather than as empirical absolutes, and that decision-making and authority must be treated as separate variables so that the spatial location of authority apart from decision-making can be considered (Prechel 1994). This research shows that to increase product quality, corporations standardized the decision-making process by introducing more formally rational controls (Weber 1978: 224). Advanced accounting techniques and information-processing systems were established to further standardize decision-making criteria and create a unified system of control over the managerial process. These controls created the organizational flexibility to centralize authority while decentralizing the responsibility to execute production activities conceptualized by engineers and other experts in a centralized plant planning office. These formal controls made it possible to establish control over the managerial process by defining the premise of decision-making and distributing information to operating managers on a "need-to-know basis," which subjects these social actors to a higher level of discipline.

Despite agreement in some areas, there are many unsettled debates in the post-Fordist literature. Resolution of these debates will require more precise theorizing about the contingencies (e.g., geographic, historical) within which economic activity is embedded at both the societal (e.g., political-legal) and corporate levels.

SEE ALSO: Capitalism; Decision-Making; Global Economy; Information Technology; Labor Process; Taylorism; Weber, Max; Work, Sociology of

REFERENCES AND SUGGESTED READINGS

Amin, A. (Ed.) (1994) *Post-Fordism*. Blackwell, Oxford.

Dohse, K., Jurgens, U., & Malsch, T. (1985) From "Fordism" to "Toyotism"? The Social Organization of the Labor Process in the Japanese Automobile Industry. *Politics and Society* 14: 115–46.

Hall, S., Held, D., Hubert, D., & Thompson, K. (1995) *Modernity*. Polity Press, Cambridge.

Harvey, D. (1991) *The Condition of Postmodernity*. Blackwell, Oxford.

Piore, M. & Sabel, C. (1984) *The Second Industrial Divide*. Basic Books, New York.

Prechel, H. (1994) Economic Crisis and the Centralization of Control over the Managerial Process: Corporate Restructuring and Neo-Fordist Decision-Making. *American Sociological Review* 59: 723–45.

Weber, M. (1921 [1978]) *Economy and Society*. Trans. G. Roth & C. Wittich. University of California Press, Berkeley.

Foucauldian archeological analyses

James Joseph Scheurich and Kathryn Bell McKenzie

To begin to understand Foucault's archeology, it is first crucial to know that Foucault was *not* referring to archeology as an academic discipline or to any popular picture of an archeologist. Indeed, thinking of Foucault's archeology as having anything to do with digging in the earth for ancient artifacts is not useful at all. As Foucault (1972) says, *The Archaeology of Knowledge* "does not relate to geological excavation." For the most part, these allusions will only get in the way of building an understanding of his archeological method.

The archeologies are his most difficult methodologies to understand and, as a separate, second issue, his most difficult to apply. For example, Scheurich supposedly developed a "policy archeology" as a method for addressing public policy issues, but it fails as a Foucauldian archeology. The reason for this is it uses some archeological concepts, but Foucault's archeology is a complex, tightly interwoven methodology that directly depends on such concepts as *savoir*, *connaissance*, positivity, enunciations, statements, archive, discursive formation, enunciative regularities, correlative spaces, enveloping theory, level, limit, periodization, division, event, discontinuity, discursive practices, and so on. In other words, the nature of this method is

that these constructs cannot be pulled out and deployed separately without fundamentally violating the method itself. To deploy Foucault's archeology with integrity or rigor, then, requires *both* a comprehension of the meaning of each of his numerous constructs (and their relationships and connections) *and* a use of the set of constructs as an interrelated or interwoven whole.

Foucault's best synopsis or summary of his archeological methodology is available in the "introduction" to *The Archaeology of Knowledge*, which was written after he had done three book-length archeologies. He says in this introduction that this retrospective revision of his methodology is not exactly the same as he applied it in the three prior archeologies because of the problems he discovered in his three applications. Accordingly, the best suggestion for learning how to do Foucault's archeology is to read carefully and thoroughly, more than once, the three archeologies – *Madness and Civilization* (1988), *Birth of the Clinic* (1994), and *The Order of Things* (1973) – and then read in the same way his reflections on archeology as a method in *The Archaeology of Knowledge*. We suggest this course of study is suggested because virtually all social science texts, even fairly complex theoretical ones, are relatively easy to read and understand compared to reading and understanding Foucault, especially the archeologies.

Some of the difficulty with reading Foucault is typically blamed on his writing style, though this explanation is over-blown. For example, the main problem with his writing style is that he uses long sentences, and as the sentences proceed, the referents to key concepts are difficult to follow. However, once a reader has picked up the habit of carefully following the referents, Foucault's sentences are not that difficult to understand. Instead, the main problem in reading Foucault is a lack of knowledge of the French philosophical context within which he wrote and a lack of familiarity with his epistemological approach, which is poststructuralist in its assumptions and which is critical of dominant assumptions and discourses, including those of critical theory, broadly defined. Indeed, part of the difficulty in reading Foucault is that while he is inarguably "critical," his critique significantly diverges from and is critical of what we typically know as critical theory in the social sciences. Nonetheless, despite the difficulties, it is worth the effort to do the work necessary to develop an understanding of his archeologies and his archeological method. And, in doing so, a "strong" understanding of Foucault's archeological method does require the development of a solid understanding of his complex, interrelated set of concepts.

Two of the more important of these concepts illustrate the fundamental points that Foucault is making with his archeologies. These are *savoir* and *connaissance*. In a particularly useful interview, which appeared in French in 1966 and then in English in 1994 and which was done after *Madness and Civilization*, *Birth of the Clinic*, and *The Order of Things* but before *The Archaeology of Knowledge*, Foucault defined how he saw archeology at this point:

> By "archaeology" I would like to designate not exactly a discipline but a domain of research, which would be the following: in a society, different bodies of learning, philosophical ideas, everyday opinions, but also institutions, commercial practices and police activities, mores – all refer to a certain implicit knowledge [*savoir*] special to this society. This knowledge is profoundly different from the [formal] bodies of learning [*des connaissances*] that one can find in scientific books, philosophical theories, and religious justifications, but it [*savoir*] is what *makes possible* at a given moment the appearance of a theory, an opinion, a practice.

Thus, he is differentiating or contrasting these two concepts, *savoir* and *connaissance*, both of which are critical to understanding his archeological approach.

Connaissance is "formal" knowledge or bodies of knowledge that exist in "scientific books, philosophical theories, and religious justifications." That is, *connaissance* in the social sciences is the production of social scientists as part of their work; it is what academicians would know as scholarly publications or presentations in articles, books, proceedings, reports, and conferences. In sharp contrast, *savoir* includes "everyday opinions, but also institutions, commercial practices and police activities, mores," but (and this is critically important) it is *savoir* that "*makes possible* at a given moment the appearance of a theory, an opinion, a practice." Gutting (1989: 251) makes

this same contrast when he argues: "By *connaissance* [Foucault] means ... any particular body of knowledge such as nuclear physics, evolutionary biology or Freudian psychoanalysis." In contrast, *savoir*, Gutting continues, "refers to the [broad] discursive conditions that are necessary for the development of *connaissance*."

A specific example of the application of these two key archeological concepts can be drawn from *The Archaeology of Knowledge* (1972: 179):

> The lynch-pin of *Madness and Civilization* was the appearance at the beginning of the nineteenth century of a psychiatric discipline. This discipline had neither the same content, nor the same internal organization, nor the same place in medicine, nor the same practical function, nor the same methods as the traditional chapter on "diseases of the head" or "nervous diseases" to be found in eighteenth-century medical treatises.

Here, Foucault is showing that the "psychiatric discipline" that appears at the first half of the nineteenth century is qualitatively or substantively different than the "diseases of the head" and "nervous diseases" of the eighteenth century. But on examining this new discipline, we discover two things:

> what made it [i.e., the emerging discipline of psychiatry] possible at the time it appeared, what brought about this great change [i.e., changes from eighteenth-century diseases of the head to nineteenth-century psychiatry] in the economy of concepts, analyses, and demonstrations was a whole set of relations between hospitalization, internment, the conditions and procedures of social exclusion, the rules of jurisprudence, the norms of industrial labor and bourgeois morality, in short a whole group of relations that characterized for this discursive practice [i.e., psychiatry] the formation of its statements.

Thus, what created the conditions for the psychiatric discipline to appear as a formal discipline – a *connaissance* – were changes in the broader *savoir* (i.e., changes in practices, procedures, institutions, norms, etc.). For example, "this [discursive] practice is not only manifested in a discipline [i.e., psychiatry] possessing a scientific status and scientific pretensions [*connaissance* or psychiatry as a formal discipline]; it is also found in the operation in legal texts, in literature, in philosophy, in political decisions, and in the statements made and the opinions expressed in daily life [i.e., *savoir*]."

As a result, Foucault is arguing that to understand the emergence of psychiatry as a formal discipline, it is necessary to understand not only some evolution of formal knowledge (*connaissance*), but also the much less formal "hospitalization, internment, the conditions and procedures of social exclusion, the rules of jurisprudence, the norms of industrial labor and bourgeois morality" and medical texts, popular literature, political agendas, and many other, seemingly mundane, aspects of everyday life; that is, *savoir*.

It is *savoir* that is the focus of study for Foucault's archeology. He is showing that psychiatry or other formal social science disciplines do *not* simply evolve out of any prior formal disciplines. Instead, he is contending that understanding the emergence of a discipline like psychiatry requires a focus on *savoir*. Foucault's larger point, though, is that formal disciplines do *not* have a rational historical trajectory since, in fact, these disciplines emerge from the much less rational or even irrational array of practices, procedures, institutions, politics, everyday life discourses, and the like, which, as a result, undermines the rational modernist story of formal disciplines.

Thus, the larger purpose of Foucault's archeologies is to interrogate various examples – *Madness and Civilization*, *Birth of the Clinic*, and *The Order of Things* (the human sciences) – of the work of reason. And these generate one of Foucault's most important archeological contentions: the history of reason is "in *Madness and Civilization*, not wholly and entirely that of its progressive refinement, its continuously increasing rationality" (Foucault 1972: 4). In other words, when specific cases of the work of reason are examined, Foucault finds that the historical trajectory of reason is not "progressive refinement" or "continuously increasing rationality." Instead, there typically is a "discontinuity (threshold, rupture, break, mutation, transformation)" in a particular trajectory – similar, for example, to the one he found between "diseases of the head" and "nervous diseases" of the eighteenth century and a psychiatric discipline in the nineteenth century. Consequently, instead of merely critiquing the

master narrative of reason, Foucault is providing research that demonstrates that the typical characterization of this narrative of reason is not accurate, at least in his three archeological studies.

A second critical contention that emerges out of the archeologies is that disciplines or formal knowledges (*connaissance*) cannot be adequately studied in terms of only the historical trajectories of the formal knowledges themselves (*connaissance*). In contrast, Foucault argues that *connaissance* emerges out of *savoir*, which does include formal knowledge, such as academic books, but also encompasses institutions, legal decisions, mores, corporate practices, norms, and everyday discourse. Thus, in his archeologies, he shows how institutional practices, morality, and the like create the conditions or the possibility for a formal knowledge to emerge. Again, though, this contention undermines the modernist metanarrative of reason. It is no longer so pure or exalted; that is, reason is being problematized.

Problematizing reason, however, is not Foucault's last larger purpose in the archeologies. For Foucault, the other side of the coin of reason is the human subject: "Making historical analysis the discourse of the continuous [e.g., portraying formal knowledge, *connaissance*, as emerging through a rational, logical, continuous trajectory] and making human consciousness [i.e., the human subject or subjectivity] the *original* subject of *all* historical development and *all* action are the two sides of the same system of thought [i.e., modernity]" (p. 12; emphasis added). What Foucault contends here is that "man" or the human subject, especially "man" as the creator of history and reason, is an ideological assertion or assumption of modernity. However, social scientists then take this assumption as a given as they construct their theories and research. Moreover, Foucault argues that this ideologically constructed central agent – "man," the privileged subject of history and life – is simultaneously positioned as both the researcher or theorist and the object of the research or theory. However, for Foucault, this modernist ideology of humanism can be interrogated through his anti-humanist archeological methodology, especially in terms of showing that the conditions of emergence of *connaissance* occur through or within *savoir*. In other words, archeology decenters the modernist subject as the heart of history and reason. As Foucault says in the *Archaeology of Knowledge*, the purpose of his final archeological work before he turned to genealogy as a new method was "to define a method of historical analysis *freed* from the anthropological [the human subject as the center] theme" and "a method *purged* of all anthropologism" (p. 16; emphasis added). Unfortunately, Foucault's problematization of reason and the agentic subject as "two sides of the same system of thought" (Foucault 1972: 12) has largely been ignored by many of those who have appropriated his work. These theorists have used his problematization of reason, while ignoring his problematization of the subject. However, appropriating "one side" of Foucault's archeology without the other side represents a deep violation of archeology.

For those interested in Foucault and especially for those interested in his archeologies, single archeological concepts cannot just be cherry-picked and used by themselves. Foucault intended his array of archeological constructs to be deployed as an integrated set. To learn to do a Foucauldian archeology requires several readings of the three archeologies and the same for his retrospective revision of his archeological methodology in *The Archaeology of Knowledge*. In addition, there are a few books (e.g., Gutting 1989) that are useful, but there is no substantive application of Foucault's archeology available for study except his own.

SEE ALSO: Foucault, Michel; Knowledge; Knowledge, Sociology of; Poststructuralism

REFERENCES AND SUGGESTED READINGS

Foucault, M. (1972 [1969]) *The Archaeology of Knowledge and the Discourse on Language*. Trans. A. M. Sheridan-Smith. Pantheon Books, New York.

Foucault, M. (1973 [1966]) *The Order of Things: An Archaeology of the Human Sciences*. Vintage Books, New York.

Foucault, M. (1986 [1984]) *History of Sexuality, Volume III: Care of the Self*. Trans. R. Hurley. Pantheon Books, New York.

Foucault, M. (1988 [1961]) *Madness and Civilization: A History of Insanity in the Age of Reason*. Trans. R. Howard. Vintage Books, New York.

Foucault, M. (1994 [1963]) *Birth of the Clinic: An Archaeology of Medical Perception*. Trans. A. M. Sheridan-Smith. Vintage Books, New York.

Gutting, G. (1989) *Michel Foucault's Archaeology of Scientific Reason*. Cambridge University Press, Cambridge.

Foucault, Michel (1926–84)

Margaret E. Farrar

Michel Foucault was a French philosopher whose work has greatly influenced sociologists and many others, particularly in the areas of crime and deviance, gender and sexuality, health and illness, and social welfare.

Foucault was born into an upper-middle-class family in Poitiers, France, where his father was a prominent surgeon. Beginning in 1946, he attended the École Normale Supérieure, where he studied with such intellectual luminaries as Maurice Merleau-Ponty and Louis Althusser. At ENS he received his licence in philosophy in 1948, in psychology in 1949, and his *agrégation* in psychopathology in 1952. He published *Maladie mentale et personnalité* (Mental Illness and Personality) in 1954, a book that he later disavowed. After a series of jobs in Uppsala, Hamburg, and Warsaw, he returned to France in 1960 to chair the philosophy department and teach at the University of Clermont-Ferrand. He received his *Doctorat ès lettres* in 1960 for *Folie et déraison: Histoire de la folie à l'âge classique*, a history of mental illness that focused on the relationship between madness and reason (this would be abridged and published in English as *Madness and Civilization* in 1961). In 1963 Foucault published *Naissance de la clinique* (The Birth of the Clinic). Foucault's next book, *Le Mots et les choses* (published in English as *The Order of Things*), was a sweeping study of the preconditions for knowledge in the disciplines of biology, philology, and economics. It became a surprise bestseller in France when it was published in 1966, launching Foucault to international prominence.

May 1968 inaugurated what some have called Foucault's "political turn," when confrontations between students at the Sorbonne and the police ignited a general insurrection across France. Initially, groups of workers spontaneously sided with the students in the conflict; the series of strikes that ensued, however, was discouraged both by union leaders and by the French Communist Party. The rebellion was finally suppressed by the de Gaulle administration. During this time, Foucault was teaching in Tunisia, but he was profoundly affected by the events nonetheless; they confirmed Foucault's deep suspicions regarding universalist and humanist appeals to truth and history, and sparked his interest in studying the many different places that power is exercised in people's daily lives: schools, factories, hospitals, and prisons. When he returned to France, Foucault (and others of his generation, including Jacques Derrida and Gilles Deleuze) renounced the intellectual and political tradition exemplified by Jean-Paul Sartre. Speaking out against Sartre and the Marxist tradition he represented, Foucault quickly became a galvanizing figure in intellectual public life. He subsequently helped to found the *Groupe d'Information des Prisons* (the Prison Information Group, or GIP), an organization dedicated to providing a forum for addressing prisoners' concerns and needs.

In 1969 Foucault was elected to the College de France, the country's most prestigious institution of research and learning, where he became Professor and Chair of the History of Systems of Thought. Foucault published perhaps his most influential and overtly political book, *Surveiller et punir: Naissance de la prison*, in 1975 (translated into English as *Discipline and Punish* in 1977) from research that originated from his work with GIP. Soon after, he began his multi-volume history of sexuality. The first volume, *The Will to Knowledge* (previously known as *The History of Sexuality: An Introduction in English*; *Histoire de la sexualité, 1: la volonte de savoir*) was published in France in 1976. The second and third volumes (*The Use of Pleasure* and *The Care of the Self*) were translated into English shortly before Foucault's death in 1984.

THEMES IN FOUCAULT'S WORK

In an essay written near the end of his life, Foucault explained that the goal of his work over the previous two decades was not, as many thought, to elucidate the phenomenon of power. Rather, he wrote, "my objective ... has been to create a history of the different modes by which, in our culture, human beings are made subjects" (Foucault 1983: 208). According to Foucault, the human sciences (as he called them) are disciplines in both senses of that word: they are fields of expertise (i.e., in the sociological sense, they are "professions"), but they also are implicated in a particularly insidious form of power, whereby man becomes "the enslaved sovereign, the observed spectator" in the production of knowledge (see also Goldstein 1984). Heavily influenced by and indebted to Nietzsche, Foucault's work critiques the "will to knowledge" inherent in the human endeavor to understand ourselves. For Foucault, this will to knowledge operates at the intersection of knowledge and power. Foucault's studies of illness, criminality, and sexuality challenged linear narratives of progress that regard advances in knowledge as part of a clear path to emancipation (Thiele 1990; Owen 1996). For Foucault, the interplay between knowledge and freedom is never that straightforward; in fact, he argued, the modern proclivity to identify and divide the normal from the abnormal can and often does serve as a means of social control. Such categorizations always entail a normative divide between one half of the binary (healthy, sane, law-abiding, heterosexual) and the other (sick, insane, criminal, and homosexual). In his earlier work (through *The Order of Things*) Foucault called this juncture of knowledge and power an episteme, a system of thought that defines the field of possibility for the production of knowledge. With the publication of *L'Archeologie du savoir* (*The Archeology of Knowledge*) in 1969, Foucault began to write about "discursive formations" rather than epistemes, perhaps to put some distance between himself and the methods and concepts employed by theorists of structuralism (Foss et al. 1985: 194). Foucault's main concern was the way that certain kinds of language – language enmeshed in professional standards, methodological requirements, and a community of experts – are endowed with greater claims to truth than others (Dreyfus & Rabinow 1983: 48). Foucault regarded discursive formations as having a constitutive function: discursive practices make subjects by delimiting the boundaries of what it is possible to think. For Foucault, then, knowledge and power are always, and necessarily, intertwined, so that "we are subjected to the production of truth through power and we cannot exercise power except through the production of truth" (Foucault 1980: 93). For example, in *Discipline and Punish* Foucault begins with a startling juxtaposition between the gruesome public execution of Damiens the Regicide in 1757 and a blandly regimental prison timetable from 1837. How, Foucault asks, have we made the enormous transition from one form of punishment to the other in less than 80 years? Foucault's provocative answer is that it is not that we have become increasingly humane or civilized in our treatment of prisoners; rather, he contends, we have developed more efficient forms of punishment, more sophisticated technologies of power. Through observation, classification, examination, and internment, we have rationalized crime and punishment in both language and practice. The point of shifting from public executions to prisons, Foucault claims, is "not to punish less, but to punish better" (Foucault 1977: 82), and marks a sea change in how we think about crime, criminality, and society. Foucault describes this as the shift from sovereign or juridical power to disciplinary or bio-power.

In *Discipline and Punish* Foucault also describes his best-known metaphor for this new form of power: the Panopticon, Jeremy Bentham's unrealized and yet enormously influential design for prisons. The Panopticon consists of a central tower with windows on all sides that look out over a ring of cells that face the tower. Space is organized around vision, so that a maximum number of people can be observed at a minimum cost. In its ideal, most effective form, this disciplinary machine does not even need the guard in the tower in order to operate; all the prisoners require is the possibility of being watched in order to monitor their own behavior. One-way glass, for example, can take the place of an actual guard and produce the same results. As an institution that allows for

those in authority to see without being seen, the Panopticon fashions subjects that internalize the force of this authoritative gaze.

Moreover, Panopticism is not limited to prisons and prisoners. According to Foucault, the kind of power exemplified in the Panopticon has been replicated across the modern world in all kinds of institutions. "Is it surprising," he asks, "that prisons resemble factories, schools, barracks, hospitals, which all resemble prisons?" (Foucault 1977: 228). Through panopticism specifically and bio-power more generally, Foucault contends, "visibility becomes a trap." These observations lead Foucault (1977) to describe the expansion of what he calls a "carceral society" or a "society of normalization" (Foucault 1980).

In his later work, Foucault turned his attention to the production of human sexuality. In "The Will to Knowledge (An Introduction)," Foucault criticizes what he calls the "repressive hypothesis," the belief that since the nineteenth century we have "repressed" our sexuality under the influence of the Victorian bourgeoisie. Instead of repression, Foucault argues, western society "speaks verbosely of its own silence, [and] takes great pains to relate in detail the things it does not say" (Foucault 1990: 8). Foucault contends that the human sciences make sex an object of study, and serve to "discipline" and normalize various forms of sexual behavior. For Foucault, this discipline is particularly insidious because it shapes individuals' understanding of themselves. The second two volumes in the series, *The Use of Pleasure* (*Histoire de la sexualite, II: l'usage des plaisirs*) and *The Care of the Self* (*Histoire de la sexualité, III: le souci de soi*), deal with the construction of human sexuality in Greek and Roman antiquity.

It is important to note that the various transformations that Foucault documents – whether in the realm of crime and punishment, mental illness, or human sexuality – were not the result of one point of origin or a single systemic cause (Foucault 1977: 81); bio-power is not initiated by a piece of legislation, a particular group of thinkers, or even a specific economic system. Rather, it is "a multiplicity of often minor processes, of different origin and scattered location" (p. 138). What is more, Foucault contends, this form of power is never reducible to the state or to the prohibitive function of law.

Instead of focusing intellectual energy looking for the centers of power, Foucault famously claims, we need to "cut off the king's head" and examine the ways that power "induces pleasure, forms knowledge, produces discourse" (Foucault 1984: 63, 61).

INFLUENCE AND CRITIQUE

Foucault's work has had a tremendous impact in many different disciplines across the humanities and social sciences. Scholars of history, geography, religion, political theory, communications, education, and literature have had to grapple with the implications of his claims, and respond to his challenges. His *History of Sexuality* volumes are considered founding texts in queer theory, and have helped to inaugurate the field of gender studies.

Foucault's impact on sociology, then, simply cannot be overstated. Some see Foucault's work as very much an extension of, and complement to, Weber's analyses of social rationalization (O'Neill 1986; see also Owen 1996). Students of social control and deviance, particularly those influenced by labeling theory, cite *Discipline and Punish* as a revolution in the study of crime and criminality. Foucault's institutional studies also have had implications for research on organizations (Cooper & Burrell 1988).

Foucault's work has also been the subject of much debate across the social sciences. Some of the most energetic critiques have been directed at Foucault's conceptions of power and agency. Foucault rejects what he calls an "economic" model of power, whereby power is something that some "have" and others do not. Instead, Foucault sees power as "something which circulates . . . never localized here or there, never in anybody's hands, never appraised as a commodity or piece of wealth" (Foucault 1980: 98). For Foucault, power is a field in which we are all implicated. Sangren (1995) argues this conception of power reduces people and institutions to mere objects (rather than subjects) in Foucault's analyses; power thus assumes the status of an explanatory telos (see also Habermas 1987: 274–5). For this reason, Foucault and theorists influenced by Foucault (such as Judith Butler) have been taken to task for either being too deterministic (and thus incapable of providing

an account of resistance to power) or not deterministic enough (e.g., Fox 1998).

A related critique also stems from Foucault's account of power as something that is diffuse and dispersed, everywhere and nowhere at the same time. As a result, critics charge, Foucault does not adequately provide a way to differentiate between power and domination. Moreover, Foucault does not articulate a clear set of ethical standards by which to evaluate the morality of different arrangements of power. Indeed, Jürgen Habermas, one of Foucault's most persistent critics, referred to this as Foucault's cryptonormativity: his unwillingness to definitively make judgments about the justice or injustice of particular power relations. Foucault responds to this critique by rejecting what he referred to as "the blackmail of the Enlightenment," the simplistic choice of "for or against" freedom, progress, and reason put to him by his detractors (Foucault 1984: 43).

The final critique of Foucault is really a question: Is social science, as such, even possible if we take Foucault's work seriously? Foucault's work challenges the very assumptions that make social science possible. For Foucault, the difficulty with the social sciences lies in the fact that modern "man" is both the subject and the object of disciplinary knowledge; he is a being defined by his ability to observe and be observed, count and be counted, evaluate and be evaluated, rank and be ranked. Man comes to know himself both as the empirical object and the transcendental subject of knowledge (Dreyfus & Rabinow 1983: 31). Foucault calls this peculiar epistemological configuration the "empirico-transcendental doublet" that haunts the history of the human sciences, and it leads Foucault to make one of his most controversial claims: that the era of man is drawing to a close, and eventually man will disappear, "like a face drawn in sand at the edge of the sea" (Foucault 1972: 387).

If Foucault's claims have any weight, then his own analyses must also be implicated in the conditions of their own production. Foucault acknowledges this, saying that genealogies "are therefore not positivistic returns to a more careful or exact form of science. They are precisely anti-sciences" (Foucault 1980: 83). For this reason, Foucault's greatest influence may be in felt in debates about the future of the discipline itself. His supporters argue that his work helps pave the way for a post-positivist social science.

In his biography of Foucault, Didier Eribon quotes at length Pierre Bourdieu's article in *Le Monde*, written at the time of Foucault's death:

"There is nothing more dangerous," wrote Bourdieu, "than to reduce a philosophy, especially one so subtle, complex, and perverse, to a textbook formula. Nonetheless, I would say that Foucault's work is a long exploration of transgression, of going beyond social limits, always inseparably linked to knowledge and power ... I would have liked to have said this better – this thought that was so bent on conquering a self-mastery, that is, mastery of its history, the history of categories of thought, the history of the will and desires. And also this concern for rigor, this refusal of opportunism in knowledge as well as in practice, in the techniques of life as well as in the political choices that make Foucault an irreplaceable figure." (Eribon 1991: 328)

SEE ALSO: Deleuze, Gilles; Derrida Jacques; Disciplinary Society; Discourse; Femininities/ Masculinities; Foucauldian Archeological Analyses; Postmodern Sexualities; Postmodernism; Poststructuralism; Power, Theories of; Prisons; Sartre, Jean-Paul

REFERENCES AND SUGGESTED READINGS

Cooper, R. & Burrell, G. (1988) Modernism, Postmodernism, and Organizational Analysis: An Introduction. *Organizational Studies* 9: 91–112.
Dreyfus, H. & Rabinow, P. (Eds.) (1983) *Michel Foucault: Beyond Structuralism and Hermeneutics*. University of Chicago Press, Chicago.
Eribon, D. (1991) *Michel Foucault*. Harvard University Press, Cambridge, MA.
Foss, S. K., Foss, K. A., & Trapp, R. (1985) Michel Foucault. In: *Contemporary Perspectives on Rhetoric*. Waveland Press, Prospect Heights, IL.
Foucault, M. (1972) *The Archaeology of Knowledge and the Discourse on Language*. Trans. A. M. Sheridan Smith. Pantheon, New York.
Foucault, M. (1977) *Discipline and Punish: The Birth of the Prison*. Pantheon, New York.
Foucault, M. (1980) *Power/Knowledge: Selected Interviews and Other Writings 1972–1977*. Ed. C. Gordon. Pantheon, New York.
Foucault, M. (1983) The Subject and Power. In: Dreyfus, H. & Rabinow, P. (Eds.), *Michel Foucault: Beyond Structuralism and Hermeneutics*. University of Chicago Press, Chicago, pp. 208–26.
Foucault, M. (1984) *The Foucault Reader*. Ed. P. Rabinow. Pantheon, New York.
Foucault, M. (1990) *The History of Sexuality: An Introduction*. Random House, New York.
Fox, N. (1998) Foucault, Foucauldians and Sociology. *British Journal of Sociology* 49(1): 415–33.
Goldstein, J. (1984) Foucault among the Sociologists: The "Disciplines" and the History of the Professions. *History and Theory* 23(2): 170–92.
Habermas, J. (1987) *The Philosophical Discourse of Modernity*. MIT Press, Cambridge, MA.
Macey, D. (1993) *The Lives of Michel Foucault*. Hutchison, London.
O'Neill, J. (1986) The Disciplinary Society: From Weber to Foucault. *British Journal of Sociology* 37 (1): 42–60.
Owen, D. (1996) *Maturity and Modernity: Nietzsche, Weber, Foucault and the Ambivalence of Reason*. Routledge, New York.
Sangren, P. S. (1995) "Power" Against Ideology: A Critique of Foucaultian Usage. *Cultural Anthropology* 10 (February): 3–40.
Smart, B. (1982) Foucault, Sociology, and the Problem of Human Agency. *Theory and Society* 11(2): 121–41.
Thiele, L. (1990) The Agony of Politics: The Nietzschean Roots of Foucault's Thought. *American Political Science Review* 84 (September): 907–25.

frame

David A. Snow

The concept of frame designates interpretive structures that render events and occurrences subjectively meaningful, and thereby function to organize experience and guide action. Within sociology, the concept is derived primarily from the work of Erving Goffman, which is beholden in part to the earlier work of Gregory Bateson. For these scholars, as well as others who use the concept analytically, frames provide answers to such questions as: What is going on here? What is being said? What does this mean? According to Goffman, frames essentially enable individuals "to locate, perceive, identify, and label a seemingly infinite number of occurrences" within their immediate life situations or spaces.

Frames do this interpretive work by performing three core functions. First, like picture frames, they *focus attention* by punctuating or bracketing what in our sensual field is relevant and what is irrelevant, what is "in-frame" and what is "out-of-frame," in relation to the object of orientation. Second, they function as *articulation mechanisms* in the sense of tying together the various punctuated elements of the scene so that one set of meanings rather than another is conveyed, or, in the language of narrativity, one story rather than another is told. Third, frames perform a *transformative function* by reconstituting the way in which some objects of attention are seen or understood as relating to one another or to the actor. Examples of this transformative function abound, as in the de-eroticization of the sexual in the physician's office, the transformation or reconfiguration of aspects of one's biography, as commonly occurs in contexts of religious conversion, and in the transformation of routine grievances or misfortunes into injustices or mobilizing grievances in the context of social movements.

Given the focusing, articulation, and transformative functions of frames, it is arguable that they are fundamental to interpretation, so much so that few, if any, utterances, gestures, actions, or experiences could be meaningfully understood apart from the way they are framed. Indeed, one student of discourse and interaction, Deborah Tannen (1993), has claimed as much, noting that: "in order to interpret utterances in accordance with the way in which they are intended, a hearer must know what frame s/he is operating in, that is, whether the activity being engaged in is joking, imitating, chatting, lecturing, or performing a play."

In light of the relatively routine character of such activities, it is arguable that most frames are culturally embedded in the sense that they are not so much constructed or negotiated *de novo* as individuals go from one situation or activity to another, but exist, instead, as elements of the individual's or group's enveloping culture and thus contain within them situation-relevant meanings. It is also the case, however, that one can easily glean from everyday social life numerous direct and indirect ambiguities and situations calling for a more interpretive

and contextual understanding of frames. Not only is some interpretive work required when reading a new situation or encounter and deciding, however instantaneously, what extant frame should be invoked or applied, but these primary frames are themselves also subject to transformation through, in Goffman's language, various "keyings" and "fabrications." In turn, these transformations can be fleeting or enduring, thus suggesting that frames are subject to change over time rather than static cultural and/or interactional entities. Additionally, there are moments and situations in social life in which the relevance or fit of extant cultural frames is likely to be ambiguous or open to question, and thus contestable, as is often the case in the contexts in which social movements arise. Hence, frames can be understood and analyzed from both culturalist and constructivist perspectives.

The concept of frame is one of a number of concepts that are invoked to capture the interpretive and constructed nature of much of what goes on in social life. Other kindred concepts include schemas, ideology, and narrative, but it is arguable that frames are conceptually and functionally distinctive. For example, schemas (knowledge structures consisting of learned expectations about objects of orientation) and frames interact during the course of interaction between two or more individuals, with frames providing an interpretive "footing" that aligns the divergent schemas that participants may sometimes hold. Ideologies can be thought of as broad, often loosely coupled sets of values and beliefs that function as a cultural resource for the construction of frames and which, in turn, can be modified by successfully implemented frames. So frames and kindred concepts like schemas and ideology can be thought of as existing in an interactive, almost dialogic relationship.

The analysis of frames and associated processes has been conducted in relation to various activities and social categories (e.g., advertising, face-to-face interaction, gender, talk) in a variety of domains of social life (e.g., culture, organizations, politics, public policy). To date, however, the most systematic application and development of frame analysis within sociology can be found in the substantive study of collective action and social movements.

SEE ALSO: Bateson, Gregory; Collective
Action; Culture; Framing and Social Movements; Goffman, Erving; Ideology; Narrative

REFERENCES AND SUGGESTED
READINGS

Bateson, G. (1973) A Theory of Play and Phantasy.
In: *Steps to an Ecology of Mind*. Ballantine Books,
New York, pp. 177–93.
Benford, R. D. & Snow, D. A. (2000) Framing
Processes and Social Movements: An Overview
and Assessment. *Annual Review of Sociology* 26:
611–39.
Goffman, E. (1974) *Frame Analysis: An Essay on the
Organization of Experience*. Harper Colophon,
New York.
Goffman, E. (1981) *Forms of Talk*. University of
Pennsylvania Press, Philadelphia.
Snow, D. A. (2004) Framing Processes, Ideology,
and Discursive Fields. In: Snow, D. A., Soule,
S. A., & Kriesi, H. (Eds.), *The Blackwell Compa-
nion to Social Movements*. Blackwell, Oxford, pp.
380–412.
Tannen, D. (Ed.) (1993) *Framing in Discourse*.
Oxford University Press, New York.

framing and social movements

David A. Snow

Framing, within the context of social movements, refers to the signifying work or meaning
construction engaged in by movement adherents (e.g., leaders, activists, and rank-and-file
participants) and other actors (e.g., adversaries,
institutional elites, media, countermovements)
relevant to the interests of movements and the
challenges they mount in pursuit of those interests. The concept of framing is borrowed from
Erving Goffman's *Frame Analysis* (1974) and is
rooted in the symbolic interactionist and constructionist principle that meanings do not
naturally or automatically attach themselves to
the objects, events, or experiences we encounter, but arise, instead, through interpretive processes mediated by culture. Applied to social

movements, the idea of framing problematizes the meanings associated with relevant
events, activities, places, and actors, suggesting
that those meanings are typically contestable
and negotiable and thus open to debate and
differential interpretation. From this vantage
point, mobilizing grievances are seen neither
as naturally occurring sentiments nor as arising
automatically from specifiable material conditions, but as the result of interactively based
interpretation or signifying work. The verb
"framing" conceptualizes this signifying work,
which is one of the activities that social movement leaders and participants, as well as their
adversaries, do on a regular basis.

The link between framing and social movements was first noted in an experimental study
of the conditions under which authority is
defined as unjust and challenged (Gamson
et al. 1982) and then developed more fully in
a conceptualization and elaboration of "frame
alignment processes" (Snow et al. 1986). Since
then there has been an almost meteoric rise in
research on framing and social movements,
with much of the work congealing into what
is now called the framing perspective on social
movements (Benford & Snow 2000; Snow
2004). The analytic appeal and utility of this
perspective is based largely on the conjunction
of three factors. The first is the neglect of the
relationship between meaning and mobilization,
and the role of interpretive processes in mediating that relationship, by the dominant perspectives on social movements that emerged in
the 1970s – namely, the resource mobilization
and political process/opportunity perspectives;
the second is the rediscovery of culture and the
so-called discursive turn that occurred during
the 1980s; and the third is the development of a
framing conceptual architecture or scaffolding
which has facilitated more systematic theorization and empirical assessment of framing processes and effects.

Among the interconnected concepts and
processes that have surfaced as the framing
literature has expanded, there are at least six
that can be thought of as cornerstone concepts
and processes in that they provide a conceptual architecture that has stimulated much of
the research exploring the relevance of framing to mobilization, both empirically and theoretically. These key concepts or processes

include: collective action frames, master frames, core framing tasks, frame alignment processes, frame resonance, and discursive processes and fields.

Collective action frames are the resultant products of framing activity within the social movement arena. They are relatively coherent sets of action-oriented beliefs and meanings that legitimate and inspire social movement campaigns and activities. Like everyday interpretive frames, collective action frames focus attention by specifying what is "in" and "out of frame"; articulate and elaborate the punctuated elements within the frame so that a particular meaning or set of meanings is conveyed; and, as a result, often transform the meanings associated with the objects of attention, such that some situation, activity, or category of individuals is seen in a strikingly different way than before, as when everyday misfortunes are reframed as injustices or status groups like the homeless and cigarette smokers are framed as legitimate targets for social movement protest. But collective action frames differ from everyday interactional frames in terms of their primary mobilization functions: to mobilize or activate movement adherents so that they move, metaphorically, from the balcony to the barricades (action mobilization); to convert bystanders into adherents, thus broadening the movement's base (consensus mobilization); and to neutralize or demobilize adversaries (countermobilization). Much of the research on framing and social movements has focused on the empirical identification of collective action frames and specification of their functions with respect to the movements in question. In the case of the environmental movement, for example, numerous frames have been identified, such as an "environmental justice frame," a "runaway technology frame," a "conservation frame," and a "landscape frame."

Although most collective action frames are movement-specific, sometimes those that emerge early in a cycle of protest come to function like master algorithms in the sense that they color and constrain the orientations and activities of other movements within the cycle, such that subsequent collective action frames within the cycle are derivative (Snow & Benford 1992). When the ideational and interpretive scope and influence of a collective action frame expand in this way, it can be thought of as a *master frame*. Examples of master frames in recent history include the civil rights frame in relation to the resurgence of the women's movement and the flowering of movements accenting the rights of the aged, the disabled, American Indians, and other ethnic groups; the nuclear freeze frame in relation to the peace movement of the 1980s; and the environmental justice frame in relation to various environmental movements (Snow & Benford 1992; Benford & Snow 2000).

The relative success of collective action frames in performing their mobilization functions is partly contingent on the extent to which they attend to the three *core framing tasks* or challenges of "diagnostic framing," "prognostic framing," and "motivational framing" (Snow & Benford 1988). The former entails a diagnosis of some event or aspect of life as troublesome and in need of repair or change, and the attribution of blame or responsibility for the problematized state of affairs. Much research examining the substance of collective action frames suggests that diagnostic framing typically defines or redefines an event or situation as an "injustice" (Gamson 1992; Benford & Snow 2000: 615), but it is not clear that all collective action frames include an injustice component. Prognostic framing involves the articulation of a proposed solution to the problem, including a plan of attack and the frame-consistent tactics for carrying it out, and often a refutation of opponents' current or proposed solutions. Such framing, simply put, addresses the Leninesque question of "what needs to be done." Research has shown that both diagnostic and prognostic framing can generate considerable debate resulting in "frame disputes" within movements (Benford 1993). The final core framing task, motivational framing, addresses the "free-rider" problem by articulating a "call to arms" or rationale(s) for engaging in social movement activity. This has also been referred to as the "agency" component of collective action frames (Gamson 1992).

Frame alignment processes encompass the strategic efforts of social movement actors and organizations to link their interests and goals with those of prospective adherents and resource providers so that they will "buy in" and contribute in some fashion to movement campaigns and activities. Four basic alignment processes have been identified. The include "frame bridging," which involves the linkage of two or more ideologically congruent but structurally disconnected frames regarding a particular issue; "frame amplification," which entails the embellishment, crystallization, and invigoration of existing values and beliefs; "frame extension," which depicts movement interests and framings as extending beyond the movement's initial constituency to include issues thought to be of relevance to bystander groups or potential adherents; and "frame transformation," which involves changing prior understandings and perspectives, among individuals or collectivities, so that things are seen differently than before (Snow et al. 1986). Research on these alignment processes has been quite extensive and has firmly established their importance in relation to mobilization (Benford & Snow 2000; Snow 2004).

The ultimate measure of the effectiveness of proffered collective action frames and the corresponding alignment strategies is whether they resonate with targeted audiences. Those for which *frame resonance* is established facilitate mobilization; those that are non-resonant fall on deaf ears, thus failing to inspire or influence the direction of social movement activity. Two sets of interacting factors have been postulated to account for variation in frame resonance. One is the "credibility" of the proffered frame, which is affected by the consistency between claims and actions, the relative empirical credibility of claims and events, and the credibility of the frame articulators, as determined by status and knowledge considerations. The second set of factors affecting frame resonance is the "salience" of the framing to the targets of mobilization, as determined by the centrality of the beliefs and claims to the lives of the targets of mobilization, the extent to which the framing is experientially commensurable with the past or present lives of the targets, and the extent to which the framings have narrative fidelity, such that they are resonant with cultural narrations and myths (Snow & Benford 1988; Benford & Snow 2000: 619–22). Affecting both sets of factors is the failure to attend to various framing problems that can result in the commission of framing errors or mistakes that undermine the prospect of resonance. Four such problems

that appear to confront movements of all kinds include the problem of "misalignment," as when, in the case of injustice framing, attention is focused on establishing the responsible agents without first firmly establishing victimage; the problem of "scope," as when framing claims are either too broad and general or too specific and narrow; the problem of "exhaustion," as when a particular framing has been overused and perhaps taken for granted and is thus tired and spent; and the problem of "relevance," as when the frame is contradicted by the flow of events and framing efforts are insufficiently attentive to establishing one or more of the conditions of salience (Snow & Corrigall-Brown 2005). Such framing problems or vulnerabilities indicate that affecting resonance is a precarious enterprise and ongoing challenge.

The generation and modification of collective action frames occur primarily through the *discursive processes* of frame articulation and elaboration. Frame articulation involves the discursive connection and coordination of events, experiences, and strands of one or more ideologies so that they hang together in a relatively integrated and meaningful fashion. Frame elaboration involves accenting and highlighting some events, issues, and beliefs or ideas more than others, such that they become more salient in an array of movement-relevant issues (Snow 2004). Historically renowned movement leaders, such as Gandhi and Martin Luther King, Jr., were masters at frame articulation and elaboration. Gandhi's principles of *satyagraha* and *ahimsa* were based, in part, on his articulation of beliefs derived from Hinduism, Buddhism, and Christianity, and Martin Luther King's potent civil rights frame derived, in part, from his articulation and elaboration of strands of Christianity, democratic theory, and Gandhi's philosophy of non-violence.

The processes of frame articulation and elaboration occur during the course of conversations, meetings, and written communications among movement leaders and members within broader enveloping cultural and structural contexts variously called *discursive fields* (Steinberg 1999) or discursive opportunity structures (Ferree et al. 2002). Discursive fields evolve during the course of debate about contested issues and events, and encompass cultural materials (e.g., beliefs, values, ideologies, myths) of potential relevance and various sets of actors (e.g., targeted authorities, social control agents, countermovements, media) whose interests are aligned, albeit differently, with the contested issues or events, and who thus have a stake in what is done or not done about those events and issues. The discursive processes of frame articulation and elaboration draw selectively upon these cultural materials and are conducted in relation to the various sets of actors that constitute the discursive field. This suggests that the development of collective action frames is facilitated and/or constrained by the cultural and structural elements of the discursive field, further suggesting that collective action frames constitute innovative articulations and elaborations of existing ideologies or sets of beliefs and ideas, and thus function as extensions or antidotes of them. From this vantage point, social movements are viewed not as carriers of preconfigured, tightly coupled beliefs and meanings, traditionally conceptualized as ideologies, but as signifying agents actively engaged in the production and maintenance of meanings that are intended to mobilize adherents and constituents, garner bystander support, and demobilize antagonists.

Although the connection between framing and social movements has generated considerable theorization and empirical research, there are a number of issues that have not been adequately addressed. One cluster concerns issues specific to framing processes and their consequences. Much research has identified movement-specific collective action frames, but comparatively little research has examined systematically the discursive processes through which frames evolve, develop, and change. The conceptual cluster of frame articulation and elaboration and the theorized discussion of the discursive fields in which these processes are embedded provide the conceptual edifice for research on frame-discursive processes, but to date the actual occurrence of systematic research on framing processes (see Gamson 1992; Ferree et al. 2002; Snow 2004) has not kept pace with the calls for such research (Steinberg 1999; Johnston 2002; Snow 2004). A second cluster of issues that has not been sufficiently explored concerns the relationship between collective action frames and framing processes and relevant cultural and social psychological factors

such as narrative, ideology, collective identity, and emotion. Clearly, these are overlapping concepts that interact in ways not yet fully understood.

And last, our understanding of social movements will be advanced if more attention is devoted, both theoretically and empirically, to how framing intersects with the issues and processes examined via the theoretical lens of resource mobilization, political opportunity, and cultural perspectives. These perspectives should be seen not so much as competing but as shedding light on different aspects of the character and dynamics of social movements. The framing perspective emerged not as an alternative to other perspectives on social movements, but to investigate and illuminate what these other perspectives glossed over, namely, the matter of the production of mobilizing and countermobilizing meanings and ideas.

SEE ALSO: Consciousness Raising; Culture, Social Movements and; Goffman, Erving; Frame; Ideology; Political Opportunities; Resource Mobilization Theory; Social Movements

REFERENCES AND SUGGESTED READINGS

Benford, R. D. (1993) Frame Disputes Within the Nuclear Disarmament Movement. *Social Forces* 71: 677–701.

Benford, R. D. & Snow, D. A. (2000) Framing Processes and Social Movements: An Overview and Assessment. *Annual Review of Sociology* 26: 611–39.

Cress, D. M. & Snow, D. A. (2000) The Outcomes of Homeless Mobilization: The Influence of Organization, Disruption, Political Mediation, and Framing. *American Journal of Sociology* 105: 1063–104.

Ferree, M. M., Gamson, W. A., Gerhards, J., & Rucht, D. (2002) *Shaping Abortion Discourse: Democracy and the Public Sphere in Germany and the United States.* Cambridge University Press, New York.

Gamson, W. A. (1992) *Talking Politics.* Cambridge University Press, New York.

Gamson, W. A., Fireman, B., & Rytina, S. (1982) *Encounters with Unjust Authority.* Dorsey, Homewood, IL.

Goffman, E. (1974) *Frame Analysis: An Essay on the Organization of Experience.* Harper Colophon, New York.

Johnston, H. (2002) Verification and Proof in Frame and Discourse Analysis. In: Klandermans, B. & Staggenborg, S. (Eds.), *Methods of Social Movements Research*. University of Minnesota Press, Minneapolis, pp. 62–91.

Snow, D. A. (2004) Framing Processes, Ideology, and Discursive Fields. In: Snow, D. A., Soule, S. A., & Kriesi, H. (Eds.), *The Blackwell Companion to Social Movements*. Blackwell, Oxford, pp. 380–412.

Snow, D. A. & Benford, R. D. (1988) Ideology, Frame Resonance, and Participant Mobilization. *International Social Movement Research* 1: 197–217.

Snow, D. A. & Benford, R. D. (1992) Master Frames and Cycles of Protest. In: Morris, A. D. & Mueller, C. M. (Eds.), *Frontiers in Social Movement Theory*. Yale University Press, New Haven, pp. 133–55.

Snow, D. A. & Corrigall-Brown, C. (2005) Falling on Deaf Ears: Confronting the Prospect of Non-Resonant Frames. In: Croteau, D., Ryan, C., & Hoynes, W. (Eds.), *Rhyming Hope and History: Activism and Social Movement Scholarship*. University of Minnesota Press, Minneapolis.

Snow, D. A., Rochford, Jr., B., Worden, S. K., & Benford, R. D. (1986) Frame Alignment Processes, Micromobilization, and Movement Participation. *American Sociological Review* 51: 464–81.

Steinberg, M. W. (1999) The Talk and Back Talk of Collective Action: A Dialogic Analysis of Repertoires of Discourse Among Nineteenth-Century English Cotton-Spinners. *American Journal of Sociology* 105: 736–80.

franchise

David B. Bills

Franchising is a business arrangement in which a parent company contracts with one or more smaller firms to grant or sell to them the right to distribute its products, implement its processes, or use its trade name. The recent development of franchising in the US and elsewhere is characterized by steady to rapid growth in the number of franchised establishments, their increased levels of employment and sales, and their proliferation beyond the restaurant and retailing sectors in which they have been historically most prevalent into virtually all areas of post-industrial economies.

The relationship between franchisors and franchisees is based on a contract that specifies the legal responsibilities and mutual expectations of each party to the contract. Still, the fact that the franchise relationship is so nearly an exclusive one means that the franchisors and franchisees share many common interests. Franchisors acquire a generally reliable means to expand their businesses, while franchisees acquire a measure of independence, sense of ownership, and reduced risk. Franchising permits the exploitation of efficiencies from scale economies. It allows the establishments of a parent company to share the overhead costs of such factors as marketing, advertising, and monitoring. These costs are often prohibitively expensive for a free-standing establishment. About 80 percent of the time, the franchisee buys the business or a share of the business, but often the parent company retains ownership. This pattern varies a great deal across industries

There are two principal types of franchising: product franchising and business-format franchising. The US Department of Commerce defines product and trade name franchising as "an independent sales relationship between supplier and dealer in which the dealer acquired some of the identity of the supplier." It defines business format franchising as "an ongoing business relationship between franchisor and franchisee that includes not only the product, service, and trademark, but the entire business concept itself – a marketing strategy and plan, operating manuals and standards, quality control, and a continuing process of assistance and guidance." Product franchising (such as beverage bottling) is older and larger in sales value in the US than business format franchising, although the share of franchise sales in the product franchising sector is declining. Business format franchising, the most common kinds of which are quick service restaurants, lodging, retail food, and table/full service restaurants, is, however, more widespread than product distribution franchising, producing about four times as many establishments and jobs.

The roughly three-quarters of a million franchised businesses in the US generated about $1.5 trillion in sales in 2004. This figure represents about 10 percent of the national product of the US. Franchising's share of total sales is much higher in some industries. For example, franchises generate more than a third of retail sales. About 9 million Americans are directly employed in franchises, and about that many more work in jobs generated in some way by the franchise sector.

SEE ALSO: Branding and Organizational Identity; Brands and Branding; McDonaldization; Organizations and the Theory of the Firm

REFERENCES AND SUGGESTED READINGS

Birkeland, P. M. (2002) *Franchising Dreams: The Lure of Entrepreneurship in America*. University of Chicago Press, Chicago.

Dicke, T. S. (1992) *Franchising in America*. University of North Carolina Press, Chapel Hill.

Frazier, E. Franklin (1894–1962)

Mary Jo Deegan

Groundbreaking scholar on the African American family, social classes, youth, and community, Edward Franklin Frazier was born on September 24, 1894 in Baltimore, Maryland. He was the son of a former slave, Mary Clark, and James Edward Frazier. His father died when he was 10 years old, and his mother and three siblings worked together to survive this familial and financial loss.

Frazier graduated *cum laude* with an A.B. from Howard University (1916), and in 1920 he completed his master's degree in sociology from Clark University in Worcester, Massachusetts. After training at the New York School of Social Work (1920–1), he accepted a fellowship (1921–2) to study Danish folk high schools. He then taught sociology at Morehouse College in Atlanta, Georgia, and directed the Atlanta University School of Social Work. After Frazier published "The Pathology of Race Prejudice" (1927) in *Forum*, a controversy ensued and he was forced to leave Morehouse.

Frazier next received a fellowship from the University of Chicago where he earned his PhD under Ernest W. Burgess. The publication of his dissertation, *The Negro Family in Chicago* (1932), brought him to the forefront of scholarship on the black family. He taught at Fisk University from 1929 until 1934 under the supervision of Charles S. Johnson. Frazier and Johnson agreed neither politically nor personally and Frazier was relieved to move to Howard University, where he worked from 1934 to 1951. In 1948 he became the first African American elected as the president of the American Sociological Association.

In 1939, he published *The Negro Family in the United States*. It immediately generated fierce debate about the significance of illegitimate births, single parents, female-headed households, neglected children, social disorganization, family pathology, and matriarchal and patriarchal issues in black families. The book was forgotten by the general public until Daniel Patrick Moynihan, in his 1965 policy paper *The Negro Family: The Case for National Action*, used it to assert that the black family was at the root of the "tangle of pathology" in African American urban communities. This highly criticized report brought Frazier's work into contemporary debates.

He published another provocative book, *Black Bourgeoisie*, in 1955. Here he criticized the color line within the black community and its leaders' failure to take more political and courageous stances on racial issues. Many African American leaders and Marxists debated its findings. Despite these criticisms, *Black Bourgeoisie* forced many black college students of the 1950s and 1960s to reexamine their upwardly mobile goals and responsibilities to the community. Frazier trained many black students at Howard University who became leaders and civil rights activists, including Stokely Carmichael (who later became Kwame Toure).

Frazier directed the Division of Applied Social Sciences UNESCO (1951–3), where he analyzed interactions between different races and the effect of these interactions on communities.

Frazier died on May 17, 1962 in Washington, DC as the modern Civil Rights Movement was beginning to fundamentally change American life and laws.

SEE ALSO: Chicago School; Color Line; Du Bois, W. E. B.; Park, Robert E. and Burgess, Ernest W.

REFERENCES AND SUGGESTED READINGS

Deegan, M. J. (2002) *Race, Hull-House, and the University of Chicago.* Praeger, Westport, CT.
Platt, A. M. (1991) *E. Franklin Frazier Reconsidered.* Rutgers University Press, New Brunswick, NJ.

Freud, Sigmund (1856–1930)

Steve Derné

Sigmund Freud's pioneering focus on unconscious motives arising from infant experiences offers a distinctive approach to understanding human motives. His focus on how the super-ego internalizes societal demands offered a way of understanding how social norms affect individuals. His approach has had an enduring influence in sociology, shaping important research especially in gender, family, and religion.

Freud was born to a middle-class Jewish family in Moravia. Freud, who had two half-brothers from his father's previous marriage, was the favored first son of his mother, to whom he was strongly attracted. Freud recalled strong jealousies toward his younger brothers and contempt for his father, who was two decades older than his mother and whom Freud perceived to be intellectually weak and unable to confront anti-Semitism. Freud spent most of his life in Vienna, where his family moved when he was four. After studying medicine, philosophy, and science at university, he worked as a physician studying neurology. In the late nineteenth century he rejected the medical emphasis on chemical imbalances as the cause of hysteria, focusing instead on how mental processes cause physical problems. For the rest of his life, he used his psychoanalytic work with patients to develop a theory of the mind that is his lasting contribution.

Freud emphasized that the motives that impel action are unconscious. Behind every sociological theory rests some understanding of human motives. Symbolic interactionists focus on how meanings drive action; rational-choice theorists focus on individuals' conscious weighing of costs and benefits; and ethnomethodologists see action as driven by habit and taken-for-granted knowledge. Freud insisted, based on his psychoanalytic work with his patients, that unconscious motives drive human action. He discovered the unconscious through his analysis of dreams, mental illness, jokes, and slips of the tongue. His psychoanalytic work suggested that unconscious desires arise from childhood relations with parents For Freud, the self so represses infantile and childhood desires that they cannot enter the self's consciousness. Yet they nonetheless drive adults' actions.

Freud's account of psychic structure recognizes how cultural norms root themselves in the human psyche. For Freud, the "id" or "it" represents the unconscious drives that demand satisfaction. The psychic structure's "super-ego" or "over-I" represents the internalization of cultural norms espoused by parents. The super-ego is an ego-ideal in which part of the psyche (unconsciously) takes on the parents' admonishing role, punishing other parts of the self. For Freud, the "ego" is the "I" which mediates between the demands of id, super-ego, and external reality. One of Freud's fundamental contributions to sociology is the recognition that the psyche itself internalizes social demands. The super-ego, he says, is the "special agency" in which "parental influence is prolonged." (Freud 1969: 3).

Freud applied his psychoanalytic insights to understanding social phenomena. In considering religion, he argued that "in all believers ... the motives impelling them to religious practices are unknown or are replaced in consciousness by others which are advanced in their stead" (Freud 1963: 22). For Freud, it is the "infant's helplessness and the longing for the father aroused by it" that is the ultimate source of "religious needs" (p. 19). This focus on unconscious motives that derive from childhood experience is Freud's fundamental contribution to sociology, which continues to have influence in fields as diverse as the sociology of religion, the sociology of gender, and the sociology of family.

SEE ALSO: Family Theory; Marcuse, Herbert; Mental Disorder; Psychoanalysis; Religion, Sociology of

REFERENCES AND SELECTED READINGS

Brown, N. O. (1959) *Life Against Death: The Psychoanalytical Meaning of History*. Wesleyan University Press, Middletown.
Freud, S. (1961 [1930]) *Civilization and Its Discontents*. Trans. J. Strachey. Norton, New York.
Freud, S. (1963 [1907]) Obsessive Acts and Religious Practices. In: Rieff, P. (Ed.), *Character and Culture*. Collier, New York, pp. 17–26.
Freud, S. (1969 [1940]) *Outline of Psychoanalysis*. Trans. J. Strachey. Norton, New York.
Marcuse, H. (1955) *Eros and Civilization: A Philosophical Inquiry into Freud*. Random House, New York.

friendship during the later years

Rebecca G. Adams

Gerontologists were responsible for much of the early scholarship on adult friendship and continue to focus more attention on it than other researchers do. This is probably due to their historical preoccupation with theoretical questions regarding older adults' social integration, engagement, and psychological well-being. Friends are, however, important during later adulthood in many other ways as well, serving as sources of affection and social support and contributing to physical health and even to longevity.

Early studies of older adult friendship tended to focus on the effects of quantity of social contact, but more recent ones focus more on predictors of friendship patterns, including their dyadic and network processes and structural characteristics. Also in contrast to the early research on older adult friendship, more recent research focuses on its negative aspects as well as on its positive aspects.

Many of the original studies of older adult friendship were either ethnographies or surveys of small samples of older adults. Contemporary researchers now commonly compare the friendships of adults of various ages and sometimes examine friendship patterns longitudinally. Knowledge of why friendship patterns change over time is still limited, however, because researchers often use the variable "age" as a proxy measure for stage of life course and developmental maturity without distinguishing between these two aspects of aging. Furthermore, researchers have not yet conducted large longitudinal studies of the friendship patterns of multiple cohorts.

For many years, gerontologists accepted the folk wisdom that as people age, their number of friends decreases. Recent research, however, suggests that friendship circles increase or decrease depending on the characteristics of the older adults and the contexts in which they live. In some cases, the role changes that people undergo can create further constraints, and in other cases, they can be liberating. For example, men tend to have more friends than women during midlife, but older women tend to have more friends than older men and this gap continues to increase as people age. Researchers have offered various explanations for this reversal in the gender difference in size of friendship network, including men's retirement from the labor force coupled with women's reduction in domestic responsibilities. Also compelling is the argument that because of differences in the types of activities that men and women engage in with friends (i.e., women talk and men participate in physical activities together), women are more likely than men to be able to continue to meet their obligations as friends.

As during other stages of the life course, older adults tend to have friendships with people who are similar to them in terms of sex and age. Older men's friendship networks tend to be less sex-homogeneous than women's, a midlife gender difference that persists into old age and is also exacerbated by the differential survival rates of men and women. In other words, there are fewer older men available as friends due to men's shorter life spans. The studies of the age homogeneity of older adult friendships are not conclusive, but suggest that if there are gender differences, women are more likely than men to continue to have friendship networks high in age-homogeneity at older ages, possibly for the same reasons that women have more friends in old age and a higher proportion of same-sex friends.

Although research on older adult friendships continues to be more common than research on the friendships of adults at earlier stages of life, even it is becoming less common than in the past. This may be in part because of changes in federal government funding priorities (i.e., less interest in social support) or because many of the original questions that inspired researchers seem to have been adequately answered. Nonetheless, theoretical challenges still remain for gerontologists interested in the friendships of older adults. For example, most of the studies of older adult friendship have been conducted on primarily middle-class Caucasian populations residing in North America. Although a great deal is known about gender differences in older adult friendships, virtually nothing is known about class discrepancies or racial and ethnic variations, let alone about how less-commonly studied variables such as sexual orientation affect social life in old age. Furthermore, due to the lack of studies conducted outside the US and Canada, little is known about how structural and cultural context affects older adult friendship patterns. Even more broadly, scholars need to consider the implications for older adult friendship patterns of characteristics of this period of history such as the culture of individualism, the privatization of social life, and the development of communications and transportation technologies.

SEE ALSO: Aging, Longitudinal Studies; Aging, Mental Health, and Well-Being; Aging and Social Support; Aging, Sociology of; Friendship: Structure and Context; Gerontology: Key Thinkers (Hess, Beth); Leisure, Aging and

REFERENCES AND SUGGESTED READINGS

Adams, R. G. (1994) Older Men's Friendship Patterns. In: Thompson, E. H. (Ed.), *Older Men's Lives*. Sage, Newbury Park, CA.

Adams, R. G. (1997) Older Women's Friendship Patterns. In: Coyle, J. M. (Ed.), *Women and Aging: A Research Guide*. Greenwood Press, Westport.

Adams, R. G. & Blieszner, R. (Eds.) (1989) *Older Adult Friendship: Structure and Process*. Sage, Newbury Park, CA.

Blieszner, R. & Adams, R. G. (1992) *Adult Friendship*. Sage, Newbury Park, CA.

Dykstra, P. A. (1990) *Next of (Nonkin)*. Swets & Zeitlinger, Lisse.

Hess, B. B. (1972) Friendship. In: Riley, M. W., Johnson, M., & Foner, A. (Eds.), *Aging and Society*, Vol. 3. Russell Sage Foundation, New York, pp. 357–93.

Matthews, S. H. (1986) *Friendships Through the Life Course*. Sage, Newbury Park, CA.

Ueno, K. & Adams, R. G. (2006) Adult Friendship: A Decade Review. In: Noller, P. & Feeney, J. (Eds.), *Close Relationships*. Psychology Press, Abingdon.

friendship: interpersonal aspects

William K. Rawlins

Friendship refers to a broad category of positively disposed interpersonal relationships characterized by varying degrees of equality, mutual good will, affection and/or assistance. People employ the word *friend* to describe a recent acquaintance, a longtime co-worker, a family member, a romantic partner, or an irreplaceable individual they have known for years. Friendship also complements, fuses with, competes with, or substitutes for other personal and social relationships. For example, friendship can complement the professional relationship of two co-workers, but compete with the demands of a superior/subordinate relationship. Friendship can fuse so completely with spousal or sibling relationships that it is difficult to identify whether persons are acting as spouses or siblings or as friends. Finally, without close kin, friends may substitute for one's family. The range of uses of the word friendship in North American culture finds summary definitions altered according to social circumstances. Across situations, however, friendship typically invokes benign connotations and social ideals of shared good will, pleasure, assistance, and moral comportment dating back to Aristotle's treatment of the topic.

Five characteristics defining dyadic friendship – voluntary, personal, equal, mutual, and affective – occur to differing degrees in particular relationships. First, friendship is *voluntary*. While social structural factors place people in the functional proximity necessary for friendships to develop, individual persons choose to treat each other as friends. The manner and degree to which they actually act as friends is both voluntary and negotiated. This voluntary attribute of friendship contrasts with blood ties to kin that persist regardless of personal choice. Similarly, marital bonds are sanctioned legally and religiously. Persons cannot simply drift away from a spouse, as occurs with friends; legal measures like divorce and sometimes religious procedures are necessary to end a marriage. Economic contracts and external obligations regulate work relationships and partnerships instead of the volition of the parties involved. In contrast to relationships continued primarily through their connections to the social structure, persons actively communicate in mutually expected ways to sustain their friendship.

Second, friendship is *personal*. Friends are regarded as particular individuals rather than occupants of roles or members of categories. Suttles (1970) referred to the "person-qua-person" orientation of friendship. Third, friendship is *equal*. Friendship functions as a leveler despite personal attributes and social statuses that create hierarchical relationships. Friends search for ways to speak and treat each other as equals. Fourth, friendship is *mutual*. Over time it requires fairly symmetrical inputs into the relationship and to each other's welfare. Fifth, friendship is *affective*. The affections of friendship range from a positive concern for the other's well-being to a heartfelt liking and even love for friends. While friends may feel profound love for each other, the love of friendship is usually distinguished from sexual or romantic loving, with their overtones of possessiveness and exclusivity. Sexual or romantic

relationships, however, may also include or aspire to the attributes of friendship.

Through the late 1970s only scattered social scientific attention was devoted to friendship. Much work addressed friendship in the context of social attraction studies, emphasizing personality variables or residential propinquity. Friendship also appeared as a residual category of social participation in demographic and sociometric studies, contrasting friendships (often implied by the questionnaire choice, "other") with family and work relationships. Two developments expanded these conceptions. First, scholars in a variety of disciplines began examining the unique character of friendship. Moreover, various thinkers voiced the need for a more developmental perspective on the emergence, maintenance, and decline of interpersonal relationships. This view assumes that what brings people together may not keep them together. Static conceptions of relationships say little about what makes friendships "work" or why their continued interaction holds mutual significance for them. Other scholars emphasized that the dyadic development of friendships interacted with constraints and opportunities of different periods in the life course. Overall, limited findings or integrated theory existed regarding the interpersonal communication involved in forming, maintaining, and dissolving friendships across life.

Subsequent work identified four interactional tensions that shape and reflect the interpersonal challenges facing friends throughout life. The tension between the freedom to be independent and the freedom to be dependent describes the patterns of availability and obligation characterizing the voluntaristic basis of friendships. Sustaining friendships requires reconciling the autonomy and interdependence of self and other within specific relationships, as well as the demands that friends make upon each other within embracing social configurations. The tension between affection and instrumentality describes the concerns arising between caring for a friend as an end in itself or as a means to an end. All friends rely on each other for a range of emotional and practical assistance. Different meanings of friendship are implied when persons feel befriended primarily for their utilitarian assistance than in relationships where those capabilities are incidental or stem from a more fundamental mutual regard.

The tension between judgment and acceptance involves the recurring dilemmas in friendship between providing objective appraisals of a friend's activities versus unconditional support. People expect acceptance and encouragement from their friends, but also look to them for tough truths and wise counsel. A compassionately objective reaction combining evaluation and support is often viewed as constructive criticism. While reliance on a friend's opinions is a valued aspect of friendship, friends may tolerate detrimental tendencies or interpret vices as virtues. In doing so, friends may create private cultures that undermine the larger community or the common good. Criticizing or accepting friends constitutes a moral presence in social life.

Finally, the tension between expressiveness and protectiveness addresses the contrasting tendencies to speak candidly with a friend and relate private thoughts and feelings, and the simultaneous need to restrain one's disclosures to preserve privacy and avoid burdening one's friend. Throughout life people consider the ability to confide as a privilege distinguishing their closest friendships. Personal vulnerability arises from revealing sensitive information, and the responsibilities imposed on others not to misuse intimate knowledge of self make confidence and trust problematic achievements. Trust develops to the extent that friends manage the tension between expressiveness and protectiveness. Each person must limit his or her own vulnerability and strive to protect the friend's sensitivities while expressing personally crucial thoughts and feelings.

Although scholars disagree about the precise nature and extent of the differences, there are gender-linked patterns of friendship's benefits and tensions across the life course. Some argue that the emotionally involved and interdependent friendships modally associated with females are more fulfilling than the activity-based and independent ones modally associated with males. Others argue that these patterns describe qualitatively different forms of friendship that may result in equivalent satisfaction for the parties involved. Second, specific friendships involving members of either gender may deviate considerably from the norms and modal patterns discussed here. Depending on their particular friendship practices and social circumstances, women's friendships may resemble the modal patterns associated with men and vice versa. Third, the contrasts lessen in women's and men's closer friendships as friendships of both genders approach the practices and ideals of the communal friendships modally associated with females. Fourth, these patterns are based on social scientific research primarily addressing white, North American, middle-class participants. Until recently, Robert Brain's *Friends and Lovers* (1976) presented one of the few surveys of cross-cultural and ethnic variations of friendship.

Women friends tend to interweave their lives and value interdependence in confronting the tension between the freedoms to be independent and dependent. Men do not like to feel dependent upon their friends, expecting and enacting more independence in their friendships. Relatedly, women experience cross-pressures between affection and instrumentality in their friendships. Women describe themselves as more affectionate and report more emotional involvement with their friends than men do. Juggling multiple household, professional, and recreational activities, women place high demands on each other for instrumental help. The persistent requirements of caring and mutual reliance can be a source of strain in women's friendships. In contrast, men's friendships seem less emotionally charged in these areas. They do not demonstrate affection for each other in the ways and to the degree that women do. But they do offer and receive instrumental assistance with various projects, while striving to maintain their independence through reciprocity. Readiness to help without excessive sentiment is a feature of many men's friendships.

Women's friendships are energized by the potentially volatile interplay between judgment and acceptance. Because women care about and expect so much of their friends, they are more inclined to communicate their evaluations when friends disappoint them. By comparison, men seem less concerned about and more accepting of their friends' behaviors. Finally, women tend to be more expressive with their friends and to discuss and trust each other with confidences. Seemingly less willing to make themselves vulnerable or burden their friends with personal concerns and doubts, men are more reserved and protective with their friends.

Other consistent findings complement this discussion of life course patterns, gender, and friendship. Females repeatedly rate their same-sex friendships higher than their friendships with males. In contrast, males typically value their cross-sex friendships more than their same-sex friendships. Most married men report that their wife is their best friend. While many married women view their husbands as a good friend, they have a woman friend whom they consider as close or closer. Studies indicate that in later life women have more friends, a greater variety of friends, and closer friends than men. Finally, depending on their wives for close friendship in later life, many men retreat from wider participation or initiatives in making new friends.

People pursue varying degrees of closeness in their friendships. Some individuals prefer a limited number of exclusive relationships, carefully chosen, deeply validating, and precious. Others prefer easy-going but superficial connections with many people, readily making and relinquishing such friends. Still other persons pursue a combination of these involvements with others. It is unclear whether a specific style of friendship better facilitates emotional well-being. Later adults, for example, differ in their preference for multiple companions versus select, intimate friends. It may be that persons become accustomed to a style of friendship that best suits their emotional needs.

Several contemporary areas of inquiry about friendships are emerging. Returning to Aristotelian conceptions, scholars are examining the ways in which friendship facilitates moral growth and can lead persons astray during childhood and throughout life. What are friendships' contributions to the moral quality of our lives? The capacity of dyadic friendships to open outward and provide a basis for community development and meaningful political participation is being examined. How does communication function in initiating, sustaining, and ultimately leaving friendships? How voluntaristic are friendships versus their emergence primarily as byproducts of social structure? There are increasing investigations of friendships spanning and enriched by differences of religion, ethnicity, socioeconomic status, race, age, gender, and sexual orientation. Scholars are probing the value and nature of friendship in educational and work settings, and the interplay among friendship, romantic relationships, and marriage. The comparative value of intimate friends versus companions for relieving loneliness and serving life satisfaction is an important concern for gerontologists. Finally, how do narratives of friendship shape our life expectations and experiences of self, relationships, and society?

SEE ALSO: Friendship During the Later Years; Friendship: Structure and Context; Interaction; Interpersonal Relationships

REFERENCES AND SUGGESTED READINGS

Aristotle (1980) *The Nicomachean Ethics*. Trans. D. Ross. Oxford University Press, Oxford.

Friedman, M. (1993) *What Are Friends For? Feminist Perspectives on Personal Relationships and Moral Theory*. Cornell University Press, Ithaca, NY.

Hess, B. B. (1979) Sex Roles, Friendships, and the Life Course. *Research on Aging* 1: 494–515.

Matthews, S. H. (1986) *Friendships Through the Life Course: Oral Biographies in Old Age*. Sage, Beverly Hills.

Nardi, P. M. (1999) *Gay Men's Friendships: Invincible Communities*. University of Chicago Press, Chicago.

Oliker, S. J. (1989) *Best Friends and Marriage: Exchange Among Women*. University of California Press, Berkeley.

Rawlins, W. K. (1992) *Friendship Matters: Communication, Dialectics, and the Life Course*. Aldine de Gruyter, New York.

Suttles, G. D. (1970) Friendship as a Social Institution. In: McCall, G. J., McCall, M., Denzin, N. K., Suttles, G. D., & Kurth, S. (Eds.), *Social Relationships*. Aldine, Chicago, pp. 95–135.

Tillmann-Healy, L. M. (2001) *Between Gay and Straight: Understanding Friendship Across Sexual Orientation*. Altamira Press, Walnut Creek, CA.

Werking, K. J. (1997) *We're Just Good Friends: Women and Men in Nonromantic Relationships*. Guilford Press, New York.

friendship, social inequality, and social change

Graham Allan

While friendship evokes a good deal of interest in popular culture, there has until quite recently been little interest in it among social scientists. Sociologists in particular have failed to pay much heed to friendship, apparently accepting a conventional view that it represents an individual, and consequently idiosyncratic, relationship rather than one structured by social organization or having much social (as distinct from personal) consequence. Recently, though, this has begun to change, partly as a result of the rise of "the personal" in interpretations of the changes that are occurring in what has been termed late or postmodernity. In particular, changes in the demographic patterning of marriage and partnership, including the rising incidence of cohabitation, gay partnerships, and divorce, have led to sociologists showing increased interest in the ways informal ties of friendship are socially constructed and the part they play within contemporary social formations.

FRIENDSHIP AND INEQUALITY

Until the 1980s, a sociological concern with friendship was most evident in community studies. The focus of these studies on the character of local social relationships meant that often they paid heed to the extent and patterning of informal ties of sociability. While the information they contained was generally very limited, they served to highlight the social differentiations that were evident in the informal solidarities that developed. In particular, studies concerned with status divisions often drew on patterns of informal association to illustrate the boundaries constructed by and around different status groups. There was also evidence in this literature that the ways people organized their informal relationships varied depending on their material and social circumstances. This

was important because it indicated that friendships and other ties of informal sociability were not free-floating, individually ordered relationships, despite the popular ideologies surrounding them. Instead, they were relationships which built upon other aspects of people's lifestyles and consequently reflected their social and economic identities.

Middle-class friendships were found to be relatively free-ranging, with friendships being enacted in different settings. Working-class sociability, on the other hand, seemed to be more constrained, with non-kin ties often restricted to particular social contexts and understood as consequent on interaction in those settings. Allan (1998) argued that this pattern of sociability was a way of sustaining balance in relationships in circumstances of poverty and economic shortage. Other researchers emphasized other social divisions, with gender differences in friendship in particular becoming a topic of significant debate within sociology (O'Connor 1992). Numerous studies suggested that men's friendships tended to be more instrumental than women's, with women's being more expressive. This was generally related to theories of gender socialization, as well as to the idea that women acted as relationship "experts" in many settings, including the home. The friendship experiences of older people were also a significant topic of sociological interest, partly driven by social concerns over the dangers of isolation in later life. In contrast to aging and gender, the relative absence of sociological studies of ethnicity and friendship is noticeable.

Cultural understandings of friendship are generally premised on the notion that it is a relationship of equality. This has a number of dimensions. First, the organization of friendship is one in which hierarchy, in terms of authority or power, is typically understood to play no part. Within the relationship itself, friends normally perceive each other as being of equal standing, even if there is difference recognized in personality and temperament. Second, friendship is normally understood to be equal in terms of the typical exchanges that take place. It is, in other words, a reciprocal relationship. While there may be short-term imbalances, in the mid-term efforts are generally made to ensure that neither friend can be seen to be "taking advantage" of the other. Indeed, if there is an inappropriate lack of reciprocity, the friendship is liable to end, either through conflict or more gradual withdrawal. Third, friendship is generally equal in terms of the social and economic characteristics of those who are friends. While not inevitable, there is a marked tendency for friendships to be characterized by "status homophily." In other words, those who are friends are usually of a similar age, have equivalent occupations, are in the same life course position, and share other similar structural characteristics with one another.

At one level the reasons for this are obvious. Not only are those who meet in sociable arenas likely to be broadly similar to one another, but also friendship is, by definition, a tie between people who share interests and feel a degree of liking and compatibility for each other. These factors alone are likely to result in friends occupying similar social locations to one another. However, the reciprocity characteristic of friendship is equally important in these processes. In particular, reciprocity is far easier to manage when the resources and commitments of the friends are broadly similar. For example, if one of the friends has more money or more time available for leisure activities than the other, keeping the friendship balanced is likely to become that much more difficult.

Friends are also important in consolidating our identities. They do this through shared activities and conversations and by acting as a resource for helping with whatever mundane or exceptional contingencies we face. Typically, we see such talk and activity with friends as expressions of our individuality; these interactions are based on our personal rather than our social characteristics. Yet much of our talk and many of the contingencies we face emanate from the social positions we hold (i.e., our structural location). In other words, friendship interactions confirm our individuality, yet that confirmation is generally built upon, rather than distanced from, the role positions we occupy (Jerrome 1984). Consequently, through their content, friendships build on and confirm the significance of those very identities from which they appear to be independent. These processes of identity confirmation involved in friendship are themselves reciprocal. In other words, the friends each tend to confirm the identity of the other through their interactions. Thus, the more similar the friends in terms of their social location, the more likely they are to share common experiences and the more readily they can appreciate the issues, dilemmas, and contingencies the other faces. Conversely, the further apart they are structurally, the more problematic such shared, taken-for-granted understandings become.

CHANGES IN FRIENDSHIP

If existing friends do come to occupy different social locations, this often results in their friendship waning. Despite ideologies of friendship that suggest that "real" or "true" friends are lifelong, the reality of most friendships is that they do change over time. At particular periods in life, some friendships will be more active, but, as circumstances change, they are liable to become less central. Other friendships will become more active, and in this sense take their place. In general, this is an unremarkable feature of the routine organization of friendship. However, it becomes more noticeable at times of significant change in people's lives, in line with the arguments above about friendship "homophily." When, for example, people divorce, there is often a shift in their friendship networks (Terhell et al. 2004). Typically, they begin to interact less with some of their previous friends, especially those who continue to be partnered, and instead gradually spend more with others who are also separated. A major reason for this is the difficulty of sustaining reciprocity within these previous friendships, given the material and social differences that now exist. Moreover, having faced the consequences of divorce themselves, the newer friends are better able to understand and facilitate the adjustments required to being newly "single." In the process these friendships help to consolidate the new identity of "divorced" in the ways discussed above.

While individual friendships change, so too the ways in which friendships are patterned varies over time. In his important article, Silver (1990) argues that the possibility of friendship as it is now understood arose as a consequence of the development of commercial society in the eighteenth and nineteenth centuries. Unlike previous societies, this generated a legislative and normative culture in which trust could develop outside of kin ties. Other researchers have shown how the social and economic circumstances which characterize a society – or a particular segment of that society – shape the forms of friendship which develop. Oliker (1998) provides a good example of this in her discussion of nineteenth-century women's friendship patterns in the US. Recent socioeconomic changes have also had an impact on the general organization of friendship networks. In particular, the declining significance of locality in people's lives, new patterns of mobility, the growth of individualization, and shifts in the permanency of relational commitment have all fostered a greater diversity in personal networks.

This is an issue discussed at length by Pescosolido and Rubin (2000). They argue that in late modernity a "spoke" model of personal networks is tending to replace the more densely configured networks that were common previously. In other words, rather than networks in which many of those involved also know one another, now it is somewhat more common for networks to comprise relatively discrete, non-overlapping clusters of others. This is very much in line with other theorizing about late modernity, in particular Giddens's (1991) arguments about the greater freedom people have to generate different lifestyles. This pattern of network configuration is likely to facilitate the types of process discussed above through which people establish new identities as their circumstances alter. In particular, it makes it easier for them to shift the extent to which different friendships are prioritized. Equally though, it makes it possible for individuals to emphasize different elements of the self in different contexts (Allan 2001). A classic illustration of this arises when gay/lesbian identities are revealed to some people in the personal networks, but not to others (Weeks et al. 2001).

Friendship has not been a topic that has been researched widely by sociologists, though, influenced by ideas of social capital, there is an increasing recognition of its importance in influencing people's well-being. There is also a growing recognition that friendship as a form of relationship is becoming more central within social organization, partly as a consequence of contemporary changes in family solidarities and household composition. This has led to an interest in the patterning of personal networks and the different contributions friends and kin make in people's lives. However, despite this increased interest, our knowledge of friendship remains quite limited. Specifically, there is a need for more studies of friendship involvement for those in midlife, including the ways couples manage joint and individual friendships. There are studies of friendship in childhood, youth, and old age, but fewer of intermediary periods. We also need to have more longitudinal studies. As noted above, we know that friendships change over time in both content and personnel, but there is a need for far more detailed information about the ways in which this happens. Finally, there is also a need for rather more detail of the ways in which friendships are drawn upon and used. This calls for a diversification of research methods. It would be particularly useful to have more qualitative and ethnographic studies of friendship that allowed researchers to understand better the dynamics of friendship.

SEE ALSO: Cross-Sex Friendship; Friendship: Structure and Context; Friendships of Gay, Lesbian, and Bisexual People; Gender, Friendship and; Gerontology: Key Thinkers (Hess, Beth); Race/Ethnicity and Friendship

REFERENCES AND SUGGESTED READINGS

Allan, G. (1998) Friendship and the Private Sphere. In: Adams, R. & Allan, G. (Eds.), *Placing Friendship in Context*. Cambridge University Press, Cambridge, pp. 71–91.

Allan, G. (2001) Personal Relationships in Late Modernity. *Personal Relationships* 8: 325–39.

Giddens, A. (1991) *Modernity and Self-Identity*. Polity Press, Cambridge.

Jerrome, D. (1984) Good Company: The Sociological Implications of Friendship. *Sociological Review* 32: 696–718.

O'Connor, P. (1992) *Friendships Between Women*. Harvester-Wheatsheaf, Hemel Hempstead.

Oliker, S. (1998) The Modernization of Friendship. In: Adams, R. & Allan, G. (Eds.), *Placing Friendship in Context*. Cambridge University Press, Cambridge, pp. 18–42.

Pahl, R. (2000) *On Friendship*. Polity Press, Cambridge.

Pescosolido, B. & Rubin, B. (2000) The Web of Group Affiliations Revisited. *American Sociological Review* 65: 52–76.

Silver, A. (1990) Friendship in Commercial Society. *American Journal of Sociology* 95: 1474–1504.

Terhell, E., Broese van Groenou, M., & Tilburg, T. (2004) Network Dynamics in the Long-Term Period after Divorce. *Journal of Social and Personal Relationships* 21: 719–38.

Ueno, K. & Adams, R. G. (Forthcoming) Adult Friendship: A Decade Review. In: Noller, P. & Feeney, J. (Eds.), *Close Relationships*. Psychology Press, London.

Weeks, J., Heaphy, B., & Donovan, C. (2001) *Same Sex Intimacies*. Routledge, London.

friendship: structure and context

Rebecca G. Adams

Although since the days of Aristotle, Cicero, and Plato philosophers have been pondering the qualities of ideal friendship, proposing typologies of categories and functions of friendship, and analyzing the role of friendship in maintaining a stable society, very few sociologists conducted empirical research focused specifically on friendship before the late 1960s (for an exception, see Williams 1959). The friendship literature has thus developed during a scholarly period in which interdisciplinary collaboration has been more common than in the past. Nonetheless, cooperation on friendship research across disciplines has been rare, and while psychologists and communications scholars have mainly studied dyadic processes, sociologists and anthropologists have focused their research on network structure. Much of the early work in both of these traditions focused on individual variations in friendship patterns, but psychologists were concerned with how psychological disposition shaped what happened in friendship dyads, while sociologists were concerned with how social structural location affected friendship network structure. More recently there has been a general concern in the friendship literature about how context shapes relationships (Blieszner &

Adams 1992; Adams & Allan 1998). Sociologists, then, have contributed to the friendship literature by examining how friendships vary according to individuals' locations in the social structure, studying the structural characteristics of friendship networks, and theorizing about how friendships are affected by the contexts in which they are embedded.

EFFECTS OF SOCIAL STRUCTURAL LOCATION ON FRIENDSHIP

Gender is the most frequently studied antecedent of friendship patterns, though researchers do not often specify whether the effects they identify are the result of disposition or social structural location. The most robust finding reported in the literature on gender and friendship is that adult men's friendships tend to be activity-based whereas women's friendships are more likely to involve self-disclosure, reciprocity, social support, affect, and strong emotions (Adams & Ueno 2006). Given these findings, it is not surprising that compared to women, men tend to put more emphasis on having friends who are similar to themselves, and are therefore more likely to engage in the same activities with their friends and to view friendship as less important as a result of less intense involvement. Researchers have conducted very few studies comparing men's and women's friendships across the life course, so it is not clear how these gender differences change as adults age. It does appear, however, that as men age, they have less contact with their friends than women do, a finding that indicates a reversal of a midlife gender difference. During midlife men have more friends than women, but evidence suggesting that this difference also reverses in later life is not conclusive. Unlike women's friendship networks, the gender diversity of men's friendship networks increases with age and the age homogeneity of them decreases. In combination with men's emphasis on similarity and shared activities, these age shifts may explain why some researchers have reported that friendship becomes less meaningful to men as they age or at least as their health declines and constrains their types of involvement.

In contrast to the large literature on gender and friendship, very few studies focus on the effects on friendship of race or ethnicity, socio-economic status, or stage of life course (Ueno & Adams 2006). In surveys of general populations, samples include very small numbers of racial and ethnic minorities, and race or ethnicity is included as a control variable in analyses, if at all. Some studies focus on friendships within specific racial or ethnic groups or treat racial and ethnic homogeneity in friendships as an indicator of segregation. Oddly enough, given how well developed the literature is on class differences in neighboring, the literature on socioeconomic differences in friendship patterns remains undeveloped. Some studies suggest that friendship is more important to the middle class than to the working class and others show that people in different classes value different aspects of friendship (Allan 1989; Walker 1995), but there are many potential class differences in friendship patterns that remain entirely unstudied. Although studies of adult friendships within various age groups continue to be common, studies comparing friendships across stages of the life course remain rare. Even studies that do compare friendships across stages of the life course are usually cross-sectional, and thus it is not possible to distinguish life course stage, period, and cohort effects. Furthermore, these studies tend to focus on changes in friendship patterns as people move through the dating, marriage, and parenting phases of the family life course (e.g., Kalmijn 2003), rather than on other life course changes such as in the occupational realm.

STRUCTURAL CHARACTERISTICS OF FRIENDSHIP NETWORKS

Sociologists have studied the structure of friendship networks much less exhaustively than psychologists have studied their internal processes, perhaps because interviewing respondents about their networks is time consuming and therefore expensive or because the network literature tends to focus on social networks in general, without distinguishing family, neighbors, co-workers, and friends from each other and from other types of associates. Researchers have conducted fewer studies of friendship network structure during the past decade than during the previous one, though studies of dyadic friendship processes have become more common during the same time period.

Early friendship researchers often asked respondents how many friends they had (i.e., the size of their friendship network) as one variable to be scaled with other measures of social integration or engagement, but now the focus is often more on the quality of relationships than on their quantity. Many of the studies in which friendship network size is reported are of subgroups of a general population. Even in studies of general populations that include measures of friendship network size, the researchers often fail to report an average or frequencies of responses in each category. It is therefore difficult to answer questions about whether the size of friendship networks varies across subgroups or has changed over time.

Studies of friendship network density (i.e., the percentage of all possible links among friends in a network that do in fact exist) are very rare and their foci vary according to what age group is studied. Research on college student friendship network density focuses on its relationship with conformity and commitment to the larger group. For example, researchers have found that networks of college students who participate in deviant activity are relatively denser than those of students who do not, and that college students in dense networks within larger groups are not as committed to the larger groups as the members of embedded networks which are lower in density. Perhaps the two best-known studies of adult network density are Laumann's (1973) analysis of Detroit Area Study data and Fischer's (1982) report on the Northern California Study. Laumann, who only examined density among his respondents' three closest friends, found that 27 percent of them had networks that were completely interlocking (100 percent dense), 42 percent had partially interlocking networks, and the rest had radial networks (0 percent dense). Fischer reported that the average density of the network of associates was 44 percent and that the more kin and the fewer non-kin in the network, the denser it was. This suggests that friendship network density, if he had reported it, would have been lower. Research on older adult friendship network density illustrates how age homogeneity of context and physical health can influence friendship network density; studies demonstrate that nursing home residents have the highest friendship network density, residents of age-segregated apartment buildings have the next highest, and residents still living in age-integrated communities have the lowest.

Perhaps because philosophers have often defined friendship as a relationship between equals, researchers have almost completely ignored the hierarchical aspects of friend relations. Some recent studies, however, have shown that although the majority of friendships are perceived to be equal, not all of them are. For example, Neff and Harter (2003) reported that only 78 percent of college students' friendships were perceived to be equal. Similarly, Adams and Torr (1998) reported that the older adults they studied described only two-thirds of their friendships as equal in terms of power and of status. In other studies, researchers have shown that perceived equality between friends is correlated with greater relational satisfaction, emotional closeness, liking, and self-disclosure.

One of the most robust findings regarding friendship network structure is that they tend to be homogeneous (i.e., friends tend to occupy similar social structural positions). Depending on the age group studied, researchers have examined different aspects of homogeneity. They have shown for example that college students tend to have networks homogeneous in term of nationality and race, adults in terms of occupational status, ethnicity, age, marital status, social class, education, gender, and religion, and older adults in terms of gender, race, and marital status (for recent examples, see Walker 1995; Kalmijin 2003). Although sociologists generally posit a structural explanation for these findings (i.e., people have more opportunities to meet those who are similar to themselves than people who are different from them), preferences resulting from socialization may also contribute to the homogeneity of networks.

In most studies that include measures of friendship structure, the structural characteristics of friendship networks are used to predict outcome variables such as psychological well-being, occupational success, or educational achievement. Some studies, however, include examinations of the interplay between the internal structure of friendship networks and dyads and the processes that are exchanged among participants. For example, the commonly reported interaction among gender, gender homogeneity of friendships, and self-disclosure illustrates the effect of the internal structure of friendship on its interactive processes. Gender homogeneity in women's friendships facilitates self-disclosure and emotional closeness, whereas gender homogeneity in men's friendships constrains self-disclosure. Similarly, it is well documented that equality, as a structural characteristic of friendship dyads, facilitates relational satisfaction across age groups (e.g., Neff & Harter 2003). Because equality is also associated with self-disclosure, it is possible to argue that equality facilitates open communication. At the same time, however, friends in egalitarian relationships are likely to *expect* each other to share personal information. In this sense, equality may constrain the way friends communicate with each other (i.e., not being able to keep many secrets).

There are a smaller number of studies about how interactive processes in turn sustain and modify friendship structure. Many researchers seem to take for granted that ongoing friendships are sustained through regular contact, but this assumption is rarely demonstrated in empirical studies. Frequency of contact also has an impact on friendship structure beyond the dyadic level. Frequent contact with friends increases the chance that those friends know *each other*. This finding suggests that frequent contact increases the density of friendship networks over time. Similarly, studies of what interactive processes people use to sustain friendships or which ones predict friendship dissolution also illustrate ways in which friendship process affects friendship structure.

CONTEXTUAL EFFECTS ON FRIENDSHIP

During the last two decades or so, the amount of research placing friendship in context has increased. Researchers have studied friendships in a variety of specific contexts, ranging from immediate social environments to societies, and including historical and international settings. For example, Campbell's (1990) study of a 1939 neighborhood in Bloomington, Indiana, casts doubt on the presumption that past neighborhood friendship networks were significantly more sociable than contemporary ones. Similarly, Adams and Plaut's (2003) study of friendship in Ghana suggested that friendship is not a universal form, but takes different forms in different cultural worlds. These case studies are important because they challenge assumptions and raise questions about whether findings can be generalized.

In spite of an increase in the number of studies of friendships in non-North American contexts and of various subgroups within the US and other western countries, sociologists have not conducted many studies comparing friendships across cultures or across subcultures within a larger context. In lieu of such broad studies, researchers could compare findings across more narrowly focused studies and develop hypotheses about how context might affect friendship. This approach would be problematic, however, because survey researchers often neglect to include detailed discussions of contextual characteristics, and ethnographers and historians do not generally include information on individual participants in the settings they study. It is therefore important that future studies are designed to allow for comparisons of friendships across contexts (e.g., comparative international studies, historical trend analyses).

The lack of systematic evidence about how the broader social context affects friendships has not discouraged sociologists from theorizing about it. In the late nineteenth and early twentieth centuries, for example, German scholars such as Weber and Tönnies argued that the importance of friendship had declined with industrialization and urbanization. Social environments were increasingly diverse; therefore, because friendships are likely to form between people who are similar to each other, they were less conducive to friendship formation. Furthermore, because the newly developing bureaucracies hired people based on their qualifications for jobs rather than on their interpersonal connections, people relocated from their communities of origin to pursue careers, and impersonal economic incentives destroyed the love and trust that had previously existed among co-workers.

In a series of articles in the 1960s, Litwak (1985) rejected the notion that close relationships and bureaucratic organizations are incompatible and argued instead that they perform different, but complementary tasks. He pointed out that families, friends, and neighbors are better than bureaucratic employees at accomplishing simple and unpredictable tasks. Because of their personal commitment to each other, they require less supervision; because of their familiarity, they communicate more effectively. Furthermore, he argued that families are best at handling tasks that require long-term commitment, neighbors are most useful when accomplishing tasks requiring immediate or face-to-face interaction, and friends are well suited to handle tasks where similar experiences and values are important, such as helping someone cope with bereavement or make critical decisions. Therefore, he concluded, friendship has not decreased in importance; its function has merely changed.

More recently, scholars have argued that in the process of industrialization and modernization, the more communal social life of the past has been replaced with a concern for the private world of home and family. Whereas in the past, social lives centered on relationships with co-workers and neighbors, now improvements in transportation and communications technologies have reduced the importance of local ties. Some scholars have argued that this has led to increased isolation, but others have argued that people are now free to develop a wider variety of friendships (Wellman 2001).

Although sociologists have tended to study how context shapes friendships, a few have discussed how friendship affects society as well. For example, Oliker (1989) described how friendship upholds the institution of marriage. Similarly, O'Connor (1992) argued that friendship reinforces the class structure. In other words, friends teach people what is expected of them and because friends are similar to each other, the result of this process tends to be the preservation of the status quo, not changes to it. Although these authors, like the classic Greek philosophers, argue that friendship contributes to the stability of society, future research will surely also document ways in which friendship contributes to social change.

SEE ALSO: Cross-Sex Friendship; Friendship During the Later Years; Friendship: Interpersonal Aspects; Friendship, Social Inequality, and Social Change; Friendships of Adolescence; Friendships of Children; Friendships of Gay, Lesbian, and Bisexual People; Gender, Friendship and; Gerontology: Key Thinkers (Hess, Beth); Race/Ethnicity and Friendship

REFERENCES AND SUGGESTED READINGS

Adams, G. & Plaut, V. C. (2003) The Cultural Grounding of Personal Relationships: Friendship in North America and West African Worlds. *Personal Relationships* 10: 333–47.
Adams, R. G. & Allan, G. (1998) *Placing Friendship in Context*. Cambridge University Press, Cambridge.
Adams, R. G. & Torr, R. (1998) Factors Underlying the Structure of Older Adult Friendship Networks. *Social Networks* 20: 51–61.
Adams, R. G. & Ueno, K. (2006) Adult Men's Friendships. In: Bedford, V. H. & Turner, B. F. (Eds.), *Men in Relationships: Life Course and Life Span Perspectives*. Springer, New York.
Allan, G. (1989) *Friendship: Developing a Sociological Perspective*. Harvester Wheatsheaf, Brighton.
Blieszner, R. & Adams, R. G. (1992) *Adult Friendship*. Sage, Newbury Park, CA.
Campbell, K. E. (1990) Networks Past: A 1939 Bloomington Neighborhood. *Social Forces* 69: 139–55.
Fischer, C. S. (1982) *To Dwell Among Friends*. Chicago University Press, Chicago.
Kalmijn, M. (2003) Shared Friendship Networks and the Life Course: An Analysis of Survey Data on Married and Cohabiting Couples. *Social Networks* 25: 231–49.
Laumann, E. O. (1973) *Bonds of Pluralism*. John Wiley, London.
Litwak, E. (1985) *Helping the Elderly: The Complementary Roles of Informal Networks and Formal Systems*. Guilford Press, New York.
Neff, K. D. & Harter, S. (2003) Relational Styles of Self-Focused Autonomy, Other-Focused Connectedness, and Mutuality Across Multiple Relationship Contexts. *Journal of Social and Personal Relationships* 20: 81–99.
O'Connor, P. (1992) *Friendships Between Women*. Harvester-Wheatsheaf, Brighton.
Oliker, S. (1989) *Best Friends and Marriage*. California University Press, Berkeley.
Ueno, K. & Adams, R. G. (2006) Adult Friendship: A Decade Review. In: P. Noller & J. Feeney (Eds.), *Close Relationships*. Psychology Press, Abingdon.
Walker, K. (1995) "Always there for me": Friendship Patterns and Expectations Among Middle- and Working-Class Men and Women. *Sociological Forum* 10: 273–96.
Wellman, B. (2001) Physical Place and Cyber Place: The Rise of Networked Individualism. *International Journal of Urban and Regional Research* 25: 227–52.
Williams, R. (1959) Friendship and Social Values in a Suburban Community. *Pacific Sociological Review* 2: 3–10.

friendships of adolescence

Robert Crosnoe

Friendships – intimate, ongoing relationships involving shared disclosure, sustained interaction, and strong feelings of connection – play a significant role in the human life course. The significance of these interpersonal relationships is heightened during adolescence, a period of life in which young people are particularly socially oriented and in which their self-concepts are especially sensitive to the judgments of others. Consequently, friendships are a major component of adolescent life, in both positive and negative ways.

Within sociology, theory and research on adolescent friendships has traditionally had a distinctly negative tone. For the most part, it has focused on the role of friends and peers (similar others who may or may not be friends) in problem behavior and school disorder during adolescence. This tradition stands in stark contrast to the other discipline that has historically paid attention to adolescent friendships, developmental psychology, which has focused most often on the salient role of such friendships in normative social, emotional, and cognitive development during the early life course.

In fact, sociologists have virtually introduced the concept of "peer pressure," named and known in various ways, to popular culture. This concept has certainly long been central to key theoretical traditions (e.g., Sutherland's differential association theory) in criminological research on young people. In general, this criminological research has documented that association with deviant friendship groups is the strongest correlate of juvenile delinquency and substance use, through both selection and socialization mechanisms, and a major explanation for social structural and demographic differences (e.g., race, gender) in both behaviors. Likewise, this power of friends to lead adolescents off conventional developmental and social pathways has also played a prominent role in educational research on secondary school contexts and achievement processes. Two of the more prominent examples in this vein are Coleman's famous study of anti-adult peer crowds in American high schools and Ogbu's controversial oppositional culture thesis, which targeted negative anti-school messages in minority friendship groups as the foundation of race/ethnic gaps in academic achievement during adolescence. These criminological and educational literatures, disparate but related, have both articulated in convincing fashion the crucial role of adolescent friendships in many of the major social problems that have long fascinated sociologists.

Over the last three decades or so, however, the ways in which sociologists have examined adolescent friendships have slowly evolved into a more multidimensional enterprise. While the peer pressure angle is certainly still an important part of sociology, it is now coupled with other perspectives on adolescent friendships. One perspective concerns the positive developmental significance of adolescent friendships, including how they assist in the meeting and mastering of developmental tasks, influence prosocial behavior, reinforce and strengthen the influences of parents, schools, and other adult groups, and serve as resources that can buffer against hardships in other areas of life. Such research has shown that the power adolescent friends have in each other's lives can be a positive force just as often, even more often, than it is a problematic one.

A good deal of empirical and theoretical attention is now also being paid to the contexts of adolescent friendships, including the important questions of how friendships and friendship groups form and what goes on within them. For example, a wealth of qualitative work by ethnographers like the Adlers and others has generated great insight into peer cultures in childhood and adolescence. Such sociocultural research has illuminated the ways in which young people come together to construct micro-contexts of culture, often by reworking inputs from adult society, and the mechanisms by which such micro-contexts shape individual behavior in positive and negative ways. As another example, a good deal of educational research has revealed that one of the most significant influences that schools have on the developmental and behavioral outcomes of their students is their power to organize and shape the friendship associations to which young people are exposed. This phenomenon is clearly delineated in research by Hallinan and colleagues on the effects of tracking and curriculum on friendship formation as well as in investigations of the link between school racial composition and interracial friendships (see Joyner & Kao 2000; Moody 2001). Finally, the study of social networks has long been a major part of sociology and, in recent years, it has been leveraged to vastly improve our understanding of adolescent friendships with in-depth investigations of the characteristics of adolescent peer networks, the connection between these network characteristics and larger social contexts (e.g., the school, community), and the developmental significance of location and position in different types of peer networks (see Frank 1998; Haynie 2001).

In these and other forms, the study of adolescent friendships is likely to be a "growth industry" in sociology; as the size of the adolescent population continues to grow, prominent developmental theories (e.g., human ecology) emphasize the connections of friendship groups with other contexts of youth development, nationally representative samples of adolescents (e.g., National Longitudinal Study of Adolescent Health) provide data to the public for investigation of adolescent issues, and adult research increasingly recognizes the importance of adolescent experiences as foundations for the adult life course. These trends will likely spur quantitative and qualitative research that locates adolescent friendships in life course processes – as contexts of adolescent development and experience that link adolescence with other stages of life.

SEE ALSO: Friendship: Interpersonal Aspects; Friendships of Children; Friendship: Structure and Context; Gender, Friendship and; Juvenile Delinquency; Networks; Race/Ethnicity and Friendship; School Climate; Youth/Adolescence

REFERENCES AND SUGGESTED READINGS

Adler, P. & Adler, P. (1998) *Peer Power: Preadolescent Culture and Identity*. Rutgers University Press, New Brunswick, NJ.

Coleman, J. (1961) *The Adolescent Society*. Free Press, New York.

Crosnoe, R., Cavanagh, S., & Elder, G. H., Jr. (2003). Adolescent Friendships as Academic Resources: The Intersection of Friendship, Race, and School Disadvantage. *Sociological Perspectives* 46: 331–52.

Frank, K. A. (1998) The Social Context of Schooling: Quantitative Methods. *Review of Research in Education* 23: 171–216.

Haynie, D. L. (2001) Delinquent Peers Revisited: Does Network Structure Matter? *American Journal of Sociology* 106: 1013–57.

Joyner, K. & Kao, G. (2000) School Racial Composition and Adolescent Racial Homophily. *Social Science Quarterly* 81: 810–25.

Kubitschek, W. & Hallinan, M. (1998) Tracking and Students' Friendships. *Social Psychology Quarterly* 61: 1–15.

Moody, J. (2001) Race, School Integration, and Friendship Segregation in America. *American Journal of Sociology* 107: 679–716.

Ogbu, J. (1991) Low Performance as an Adaptation: The Case of Blacks in Stockton, California. In: Gibson, M. A. & Ogbu, J. (Eds.), *Minority Status and Schooling*. Grand, New York, pp. 249–85.

Sutherland, E. (1947) *Principles of Criminology*. Lippincot, Philadelphia.

friendships of children

Maureen T. Hallinan

A sociological perspective complements the conceptualization of children's friendships provided by other social science disciplines. Psychologists examine individual-level traits that affect a child's friendliness and popularity. Researchers in human development consider the role children's friendships play in the transition from early childhood to adolescence. Anthropologists identify cultural factors that influence and give meaning to children's friendships. In contrast, sociologists examine how social organization and social structure affect children's friendships.

The literature on friendship identifies five bases of interpersonal attraction: proximity, similarity, complementarity, social status, and reciprocity. Characteristics of a child's environment affect the way these factors influence friendship formation and stability. Since children spend much of their time in a school setting, most of the sociological research on children's friendships examines how school characteristics affect children's interpersonal relations.

A major influence on students' friendship choices is the organization of students for instruction. Membership in the same grade and assignment to the same class or ability group create opportunities for students to interact. Proximity enables students to recognize similarities and differences while shared activities create new similarities and complementarities. In addition, working together fosters reciprocity. The level of the ability group to which a student is assigned confers academic status on the student, with higher status associated with higher group levels (Hallinan 1979). These factors promote friendship development within ability groups. Several studies show that students assigned to the same ability group are more likely to become friends than those assigned to different groups (Hallinan & Sorensen 1985).

Membership in co-curricular and extracurricular activities similarly influences student friendship choices. Participation in the same group allows students to interact, share interests, and work toward a common goal. These shared experiences foster friendship. Ethnographic studies show that there are more friendships within these groups than among students not belonging to the same groups. The studies also show that many of these friendships dissolve when students no longer participate in the same clubs and activities (Hallinan & Williams 1987; Adler et al. 1992).

Membership in the same group has a positive effect on interracial as well as same-race friendships (Hallinan & Teixeira 1987). However, status differences complicate interpersonal attraction between students of different racial backgrounds. Research shows that when black and white students belong to the same ability group, white students are more likely than black students to make a cross-race friendship choice. While students in the same ability group have similar academic status, social status differences may act as a barrier to interracial friendship. Participation in non-academic groups is more likely to foster interracial friendships since both black and white students tend to excel in these activities. Success enhances social status, making them attractive as friends.

Male–female friendships are rare among children (Adler et al. 1992). Researchers view friendships between boys and girls as a stage in a developmental process that progresses from indifference to hostility to interest and, finally, to friendship or romantic attraction. The same organizational factors that promote same-sex and interracial friendships also influence cross-gender friendships.

In addition to organizational factors, properties of networks influence the formation and duration of children's friendships. Sociologists have identified asymmetry and intransitivity as major determinants of friendship choice. Studies show that in a dyad, asymmetric friendship choices (A chooses B but B does not choose A) are unstable and tend either to be withdrawn over time or to be reciprocated. Dyads are embedded in triads. Intransitive triads (A chooses B, B chooses C, but A does not choose C) are unstable and members are likely to add or delete a friendship tie to restore balance. Thus asymmetry and intransitivity are sources of change in friendship networks (Hallinan & McFarland 1975). A change in a single relationship has implications for relationships in the larger group. When imbalance in a dyad or triad is removed by the deletion of a friendship tie, the larger social network becomes less cohesive. Adding a friendship choice to remove imbalance increases group cohesion. Since the evolution of a group toward greater cohesion requires a period of asymmetry and intransitivity, these structural forces are critical to the development of cohesive networks.

As children grow older, they form friendship cliques. Depending on the size of the student population, a school or a grade may have one or more cliques, and a student may belong to more than one clique. A map of the social structure of a high school typically shows well-defined cliques, dyadic and triadic friendships, and social isolates. The network also may contain students who act as links or bridges between cliques or between a clique and smaller social units. More linking relationships in a social network increases the cohesion of the network. Bridging relationships also facilitate the communication of information and the development and enforcement of social norms.

A clique forms a normative and comparative reference group for a student. Peers pressure clique members to conform to the group's norms and standards and exert autocratic control over their behavior and reputation. Peer pressure plays a significant role in shaping a student's values. Coleman (1961) referred to the set of norms and values that characterize a student friendship group as a subculture. An adolescent subculture can influence a student's academic achievement, educational aspirations, extracurricular activities, leisure time activities, attitudes toward authority, and career decisions. Lack of congruence between the norms and standards defined by school personnel and those that characterize a student subculture can serve as an obstacle to student academic achievement. Efforts by adults to penetrate the friendship cliques of older youth or to utilize them for academic purposes have had little success.

Recently, sociologists began relying on life course theory to provide a more comprehensive understanding of children's friendships (Crosnoe 2000). Life course theorists view an individual's life as a series of age-related roles that a person enacts within a particular context and at a particular point in history. Children's friendships are embedded in a wider time frame than childhood. They are consequences of social, cultural, and historical factors and determinants of future relationships. By linking childhood friendships to adolescent and adult relationships, and by taking contextual and historical factors that influence friendships into account, this perspective highlights childhood friendships as the building blocks of an individual's maturation and adult social behavior.

SEE ALSO: Childhood; Cross-Sex Friendship; Friendship During the Later Years; Friendship, Social Inequality, and Social Change; Friendship: Structure and Context; Friendships of Adolescence; Friendships of Gay, Lesbian, and Bisexual People; Gender, Friendship and; Race/Ethnicity and Friendship

REFERENCES AND SUGGESTED READINGS

Adler, P. A., Kless, S. J., & Adler, P. (1992) Socialization to Gender Roles: Popularity Among Elementary School Boys and Girls. *Sociology of Education* 65(3): 169–87.

Coleman, J. S. (1961) *The Adolescent Society: The Social Life of the Teenager and its Impact on Education.* Free Press, New York.

Crosnoe, R. (2000) Friendships in Childhood and Adolescence: The Life Course and New Directions. *Social Psychology Quarterly* 63(4): 377–91.

Hallinan, M. T. (1979) Structural Effects on Children's Friendships and Cliques. *Social Psychology Quarterly* 42(1): 43–54.

Hallinan, M. T. (1980) Patterns of Cliquing Among Youth. In: Foot, H. C., Chapman, A. J., & Smith, J. R. (Eds.), *Friendship and Childhood Relationships.* Wiley, New York, pp. 321–42.

Hallinan, M. T. & McFarland, D. D. (1975) Higher-Order Stability Conditions in Mathematical Models of Sociometric or Cognitive Structure. *Journal of Mathematical Sociology* 1(4): 131–48.

Hallinan, M. T. & Sorensen, A. (1985) Ability Grouping and Student Friendships. *American Educational Research Journal* 22(4): 485–99.

Hallinan, M. T. & Teixeira, R. A. (1987) Students' Interracial Friendships: Individual Characteristics, Structural Effects, and Racial Differences. *American Journal of Education* 95(4): 563–83.

Hallinan, M. T. & Williams, R. A. (1987) The Stability of Students' Interracial Friendships. *American Sociological Review* 52(5): 653–4.

friendships of gay, lesbian, and bisexual people

Koji Ueno

Many gay, lesbian, and bisexual individuals first become aware of their orientations in adolescence and are forced to decide who should be told and who should not. Many people make their first disclosures to friends, instead of to parents or other family members (Herdt & Boxer 1993). In this sense, friendships play a critical role in the development of their sexual identities. Friends' reactions are mixed; some friendships dissolve while others increase in emotional intimacy (Herdt & Boxer 1993).

Therefore, coming out may create drastic changes in the composition of friendship networks as well as in the quality of friendship dyads.

In general, friendships tend to develop among people who share sociodemographic backgrounds (race, gender, and socioeconomic status), and this tendency already exists in adolescence. Previous studies, however, have produced mixed findings regarding whether adolescent friendships are homogeneous in terms of sexual orientation. Some studies have indicated that gay, lesbian, and bisexual adolescents are well connected with each other, but these studies tended to be based on adolescents who belong to community organizations that specifically serve the needs of these adolescents (e.g., Savin-Williams 1990; Herdt & Boxer 1993). In contrast, in the analysis of school-based data across the United States, Ueno (2005) found that a majority of gay, lesbian, and bisexual adolescents do not have school friends who share their sexual orientation and that they are no more likely than straight students to have such friends. Many gay, lesbian, and bisexual adolescents remain closeted to avoid violence and other forms of discrimination. Consequently, they are invisible to each other at school (Smith & Smith 1998). These factors may explain the sparse friendship networks among these adolescents at school.

Friendships among gay, lesbian, and bisexual people seem to be fairly common in adulthood (Ryan & Bradford 1993; Nardi & Sherrod 1994). These dense friendship networks may reflect these men's and women's desire to share unique interests and exchange support with each other, as well as their opportunities to meet each other at community organizations, bars, and social events. These existing friendship networks may also provide opportunities to meet other members of the gay, lesbian, and bisexual community.

Certain gay, lesbian, and bisexual adults are not well connected to these friendship networks, however. For example, Kirkey and Forsyth (2001) documented that gay men's friendship networks are sparse in suburban areas, where gay residents engage in social activities at home and are more integrated into the larger community than they are into the gay community. Also, gay men in prestigious occupations tend to have fewer gay friends (Weinberg & Williams 1974). The gay, lesbian, and bisexual community is sometimes portrayed as one cohesive group, but there are some subgroups within the community in which members share specific attributes and interests (e.g., leather, ethnic groups) (Peacock et al. 2001). Structural patterns of friendships most likely reflect the presence of these subgroups and indicate clusters within the community.

Behavioral processes (e.g., shared activities and conversations), affective processes (e.g., relational satisfaction), and cognitive processes (e.g., knowledge about friends) are popular topics in the general friendship literature. Although a limited number of studies focus on these processes in friendships among gay, lesbian, and bisexual people, there is some indication that their friendships are characterized by frequent contact and social support exchange as well as high degrees of emotional intimacy (Ryan & Bradford 1993; Nardi & Sherrod 1994).

Sexual activity is an important topic in the literature on straight people's cross-sex friendships. It is also a central issue for gay, lesbian, and bisexual people, whose potential pools of friends and romantic partners overlap considerably. Nardi and Sherrod (1994) documented that sexual activity is relevant to both gays and lesbians but in different ways. Gay men tend to engage in sex in the developing phase of friendships, but many discontinue sexual activities in order to create a boundary between friendships and romantic relations. On the other hand, sex with friends is not as common among lesbians, but they tend to maintain close friendships with their previous lovers.

Systematic investigations are necessary to identify unique characteristics of friendships among gay, lesbian, and bisexual people and directly compare their friendships to those of straight people. Previous studies have mostly focused on educated white gay men who are active in the gay community, but future research should include the remaining parts of this population. In addition, previous studies have focused on gay, lesbian, and bisexual people's friendships with each other, but friendships between them and straight people deserve more attention, as they are likely to be distinct from friendships within each group (Fee 2000).

SEE ALSO: Friendship: Structure and Context; Friendships of Adolescence; Gender, Friendship and; Homosexuality; Lesbianism

REFERENCES AND SUGGESTED READINGS

Fee, D. (2000) One of the Guys: Instrumentality and Intimacy in Gay Men's Friendships with Straight Men. In: Nardi, P. (Ed.), *Gay Masculinities.* Sage, Thousand Oaks, CA, pp. 44–65.
Herdt, G. & Boxer, B. (1993) *Children of Horizons: How Gay and Lesbian Teens Are Leading a New Way Out of the Closet.* Beacon Press, Boston.
Kirkey, K. & Forsyth, A. (2001) Men in the Valley: Gay Male Life on the Suburban–Rural Fringe. *Journal of Rural Studies* 17(4): 421–41.
Nardi, P. M. & Sherrod, D. (1994) Friendship in the Lives of Gay Men and Lesbians. *Journal of Social and Personal Relationships* 11: 185–99.
Peacock, B., Eyre, S. L., Quinn, S. C., & Kegeles, S. (2001) Delineating Differences: Sub-Communities in the San Francisco Gay Community. *Culture, Health, and Sexuality* 3: 183–201.
Ryan, C. & Bradford, J. (1993) The National Lesbian Health Care Survey: An Overview. In: Garnets, L. D. & Kimmel, D. (Eds.), *Psychological Perspectives on Lesbian and Gay Male Experiences.* Columbia University Press, New York, pp. 541–56.
Savin-Williams, R. C. (1990) *Gay and Lesbian Youth: Expression of Identity.* Hemisphere, Washington, DC.
Smith, G. W. & Smith, D. E. (1998) The Ideology of "Fag": The School Experience of Gay Students. *Sociological Quarterly* 39: 309–35.
Ueno, K. (2005) Sexual Orientation and Psychological Distress in Adolescence: An Examination of Interpersonal Stressors and Social Support Processes. *Social Psychology Quarterly* 68.
Weinberg, M. S. & Williams, C. J. (1974) *Male Homosexuals: Their Problems and Adaptations.* Oxford University Press, New York.

Fromm, Erich (1900–80)

Neil McLaughlin

Although best known as a Freudian revisionist, global public intellectual, and social critic, German-born scholar Erich Fromm made important and lasting contributions to twentieth-century sociology. Fromm was trained in sociology at Heidelberg University, receiving his PhD in 1922 under the direction of Alfred Weber, Max Weber's younger brother (Burston 1991). Fromm then joined the psychoanalytic profession, training and entering into therapeutic practice in Berlin and then Frankfurt. He became a core member of the early Frankfurt School network of "critical theorists" in the late 1920s and early 1930s, an influential network of neo-Marxist social theorists formed under Max Horkheimer's direction. Moving to the United States in the wake of Nazism, Fromm worked with the critical theorists, as well as the sociological methodologist Paul Lazarsfeld, at Columbia University. The Frankfurt School scholars Max Horkheimer, Theodor Adorno, Herbert Marcuse, and Leo Lowenthal, in particular, created a range of influential ideas in their time in America; they found refuge from political events in Germany with the help of a large amount of money given them by a rich German benefactor and the sponsorship of Columbia University.

After his contentious break with Horkheimer and Adorno in the late 1930s over disagreements concerning issues of psychoanalytic theory, money, intellectual style, and radical politics, Fromm went on to write a number of influential sociological works from the early 1940s until his death in 1980. Although he is not often identified as a sociologist, three major contributions Fromm made to the discipline will be discussed: his analysis of Nazism, his role as an empirical critical theorist, and his contributions as a public sociologist.

THE SOCIOLOGY OF NAZISM

If Fromm had never written another word in his life, the publication of his classic *Escape from Freedom* (1941) would still have assured him a place in the history of sociology. Written before the United States had joined the war against Hitler, *Escape from Freedom* drew on Weberian and Marxist sociological theories in order to develop an explanation of the Nazi movement. Fromm's revision of psychoanalytic theory stressed existentialist insights into the passionate and often destructive search for meaning that motivates human beings. He rejected both a Marxist determinism that suggested Nazism

was a creation of authoritarian German capitalists and a psychological reductionism that put the emphasis on Hitler's psychology and the pathology of a seemingly "mad" political movement.

Fromm's sociological explanation of Nazism was provocative (McLaughlin 1996). The modern world had created both new freedoms and increased anxieties, and the stage had been set for Nazism by both the breakdown of the security provided by feudalism and the political crisis of the 1930s. In Germany, defeat in war and economic depression had destroyed the legitimacy of democratic institutions. Hitler's "evangelism of self-annihilation had shown millions of Germans the way out of cultural and economic collapse" (Fromm 1969 [1941]: 259). The Nazi Party's racism, nationalism, militarism, and "spirit of blind obedience to a leader" were an "escape from freedom" (p. 235). The American sociological theorist Robert K. Merton introduced young scholars to *Escape from Freedom* in graduate seminars at Columbia University and the best-selling book had widespread influence throughout the social sciences.

Fromm's book was not without its flaws and limitations. The argument in *Escape from Freedom*, it is clear now, relied far too much on the questionable assumption that the Nazi movement was a lower-middle-class phenomenon. More generally, subsequent historical comparative research on genocide and far-right-wing movements has consigned *Escape from Freedom* to its status today as an inspirational if flawed early example of the sociological imagination.

The book, however, helped put the issue of totalitarianism on the scholarly agenda. *Escape from Freedom* had its origins in Fromm's research on the working class in Weimar Germany with the Frankfurt School network, work that was also instrumental in the creation of the theoretical foundation for Adorno et al.'s *The Authoritarian Personality* (1950) (Brunner 1994). This book, written by Fromm's former critical theory colleagues with the help of Berkeley social psychologists, was one of the most influential works of social psychology in the twentieth century. Developed out of an interest in explaining the psychological roots of anti-democratic political behavior and anti-Semitism, the authoritarian personality tradition helped social scientists combine theories of the psychological mechanism that explains the origins of scapegoats in political life with an empirical measure of authoritarianism called the "F" scale. Individuals whose answers to questionnaires score high on the scale developed in *The Authoritarian Personality* tend to express attitudes of reverence and blind obedience to those above them in the social hierarchy, while viewing those below them with contempt and irrational hatred. Fromm's role in developing the famous if controversial "F" scale was not well known until the publication of the manuscript *The Working Class in Weimar Germany* (1984), a piece of empirical research from the 1920s and 1930s that Fromm had worked on with Paul Lazarsfeld as his assistant (Bonss 1984).

FROMM AS AN EMPIRICAL CRITICAL THEORIST

Although Fromm's role as an early member of the Horkheimer critical theorists has often been forgotten in the "origin myths" created by the school's contemporary proponents, Fromm was the most empirical and sociological of all the major "critical theorists" including Marcuse, Adorno, and even Habermas (Jay 1973; Wiggershaus 1986; McLaughlin 1999). Fromm's *The Sane Society* (1955), in particular, laid out the basic critical theory critique of modern society and had an enormous influence on the new left generation before even Marcuse was widely known among North American activists and radical intellectuals (Bronner 1994). A key part of this story is a contentious debate between Marcuse and Fromm in the radical journal *Dissent* in 1955 and 1956 on the issue of Freudian theory and utopian possibilities within contemporary capitalism (Richert 1986). Marcuse argued that Fromm's critique of orthodox Freudian theory created a "neo-Freudian" perspective that was intellectually conformist and insufficiently radical since it suggested that some kind of psychological adjustment was possible under what Marcuse saw as the "total alienation" of modern capitalist conditions. Those sympathetic to Fromm's side of the exchange argue that Marcuse's radicalism was unrealistic and would not lead to

positive social change. This debate helped make Marcuse's name at the expense of Fromm on the eve of the publication of *Eros and Civilization* and nearly a decade before *One-Dimensional Man* (1964) made Marcuse a guru for the new left generation of the 1960s.

The Fromm–Marcuse debate helps explain why Fromm is seldom linked to the critical theory sociological tradition in our disciplinary histories and theory textbooks despite the historical facts. The orthodoxy within the Frankfurt School tradition has tended to present Fromm as a "conformist" thinker, often uncritically taking Marcuse's position on this contentious debate (Richert 1986; Bronner 1994). Fromm, however, was probably correct on the major issues at stake in his argument with Marcuse and Adorno regarding Freudian theory, as the recent work of Nancy Chodorow, Jessica Benjamin, and the larger schools of self-psychology and object relations suggests. As sociologist Neil Smelser sums up the contemporary consensus, "many elements of Freud's psychoanalytic theories have been discredited: eros and thanatos, universal dream language, the psychosexual stages of development, the primal horde." The discredited aspects of Freud's theory were, it is worth remembering, *precisely* the elements of psychoanalysis that Marcuse was defending and Fromm was criticizing based on his extensive revisionist Freudian training and writing (Roazen 1996). In addition, Fromm's critical sociology was backed up by far more empirical sociological research than anything else undertaken by the major Frankfurt School scholars, particularly in *Social Character in a Mexican Village* (1970) and the interdisciplinary *The Anatomy of Human Destructiveness* (1973). Nonetheless, by the time the social protest movements of the 1960s were in full gear, Fromm had become settled in his new home of Mexico City and did not have the direct influence on North American political events and intellectual discussions that he had during the 1940s and 1950s. While he remained active in social movements such as the anti-nuclear organization SANE (which was named after his book *The Sane Society*), the American socialist party, and American electoral politics, his association with critical theory was, over the years, lost to the collective memory of both the larger society and critical sociologists.

GLOBAL PUBLIC INTELLECTUALS AND PUBLIC SOCIOLOGIES

In addition to his scholarly contributions, Fromm was also an early example of a global public intellectual who did the kind of public sociology that former American Sociological Association president Michael Burawoy argued for in his influential address "For Public Sociology" (2004). Like the young C. Wright Mills whom he influenced through his popular new left-oriented books written in the 1940s and 1950s, Fromm wrote clearly for a general audience without the jargon-ridden prose that consigns far too much sociology to narrow professional discourse. Essential reading for young radicals for decades in North America as well as throughout Latin America and Western and Eastern Europe, Fromm was a global public intellectual who spread the sociological imagination far beyond traditional scholarly outlets. Although he had once published in the *American Sociological Review*, and a number of his books were reviewed in the leading sociology journals, Fromm was primarily a writer of commercial press books. Fromm's flair for expressing complex ideas in compelling prose flourished in such books as *The Sane Society* (1955), *The Art of Loving* (1956), and *To Have or To Be* (1976).

Fromm's influence on what we now call public sociology is also evident when one looks at the ideas and the career of American sociologist David Riesman. The author of *The Lonely Crowd* (1950), the best-selling sociology book of all time, Riesman was first a lawyer and then a sociology teacher at the University of Chicago and Harvard University. Fromm had been Riesman's analyst, and then mentor and friend; the influence of Fromm's *Escape from Freedom* and *Man for Himself* (1947) can be seen directly in the analysis of "inner-" and "other-"directed social characters outlined in Riesman's sociological classic (McLaughlin 2001).

Riesman himself is probably better remembered for his model as a public sociologist than for his professional sociology. But the Fromm–Riesman collaboration has many lessons to offer in thinking about how to combine Burawoy's professional, policy, public, and critical sociologies in ways that move the discipline forward. If Fromm provides an example of public sociology with a critical edge, alongside C. Wright Mills, Alvin Gouldner, and France Fox Piven, Riesman provides a useful political balance and a scholarly style and liberal philosophical commitment that avoids some of the excessively prophetic tone of some of Fromm's writings (Maccoby 1995). With this caveat in mind, Erich Fromm remains an important representative of twentieth-century public sociology.

FROMM'S SOCIOLOGICAL IMAGINATION

Erich Fromm was not without his critics, of course. His Frankfurt School former colleagues saw him as a simplistic popularizer, and a conformist cultural conservative. Berkeley liberal political theorist John Schaar viewed Fromm as an unrealistic utopian proponent of an "escape from authority" (Schaar 1961). Fromm was also widely attacked by neoconservatives for his opposition to the Vietnam War, American-led "modernization," and the nuclear arms race, and for his radical democratic ideas on education. Allan Bloom's best-selling book *The Closing of the American Mind* (1987) famously made Fromm a key villain in the importation of European ideas that had led to the "Nietzscheanization of the American Left." Contemporary empirical sociologists will find much in his research and theorizing that does not come up to the high standards the professionalized discipline had developed by the first decade of the twenty-first century.

Erich Fromm's place in the history of sociology, however, seems relatively secure on the creative margins of the discipline. *Escape from Freedom* is likely to be read as an exemplifier of the sociological imagination in the years to come by undergraduates and the general public alike. Critical theory also has a rich if contested future in sociology and Fromm remains an important part of the Frankfurt School tradition despite their nasty squabbles and intellectual differences. Fromm contributed to and shared the basic Frankfurt School critique of the cultural industries, the focus on alienation and subjectivity that the tradition pioneered, and the refusal to accept the normative limits of the instrumental rationality that dominates purely professional and policy-oriented social science. Erich Fromm wrote his works of the sociological imagination in accessible and clearly written prose, an example of the best kind of critical public sociology. Sociology does not "own" Erich Fromm, to be sure, given his important contributions to psychoanalysis and psychology, and his very clear interdisciplinary commitments. Nonetheless, Fromm was an important figure in the history of sociology, and his work continues to be of relevance to the discipline.

SEE ALSO: Adorno, Theodor W.; Authoritarianism; Authority and Conformity; Critical Theory/Frankfurt School; Horkheimer, Max; Lazarsfeld, Paul; Marcuse, Herbert; Mills, C. Wright; New Left; Psychoanalysis; Riesman, David; Totalitarianism

REFERENCES AND SUGGESTED READINGS

Bonss, W. (1984) Introduction. In: Fromm, E., *The Working Class in Weimar Germany*. Harvard University Press, Cambridge, MA.

Bronner, S. E. (1994) *Of Critical Theory and Its Theorists*. Blackwell, Oxford.

Brunner, J. (1994) Looking Into the Hearts of the Workers, or: How Erich Fromm Turned Critical Theory Into Empirical Research. *Political Psychology* 15(4): 631–54.

Burston, D. (1991) *The Legacy of Erich Fromm*. Harvard University Press, Cambridge, MA.

Fromm, E. (1969 [1941]) *Escape from Freedom*. Henry Holt, New York.

Jay, M. (1973) *The Dialectical Imagination: A History of the Frankfurt School and the Institute of Social Research*. Little, Brown, Boston.

Maccoby, M. (1995) The Two Voices of Erich Fromm: The Prophetic and the Analytic. *Society* 32 (July/August): 72–82.

McLaughlin, N. (1996) Nazism, Nationalism, and the Sociology of Emotions: *Escape from Freedom* Revisited. *Sociological Theory* 14(3): 241–61.

McLaughlin, N. (1998) How to Become a Forgotten Intellectual: Intellectual Movements and the Rise and Fall of Erich Fromm. *Sociological Forum* 13: 215–46.

McLaughlin, N. (1999) Origin Myths in the Social Sciences: Fromm, the Frankfurt School, and the Emergence of Critical Theory. *Canadian Journal of Sociology* 24(1): 109–39.

McLaughlin, N. (2001) Critical Theory Meets America: Riesman, Fromm, and the Lonely Crowd. *American Sociologist* 2(1): 5–26.

Richert, J. (1986) The Fromm–Marcuse Debate Revisited. *Theory and Society* 15(3): 181–214.

Roazen, P. (1996) Fromm's Courage. In: Cortina, M. & Maccoby, M. (Eds.), *A Prophetic Analyst: Erich Fromm's Contributions to Psychoanalysis*. Jason Aronson, Northvale, NJ.

Schaar, J. (1961) *Escape from Authority: The Perspectives of Erich Fromm*. Basic Books, New York.

Wiggershaus, R. (1986) *The Frankfurt School: Its History, Theories, and Political Significance*. Polity Press, Cambridge.

function

Robin Stryker

Function has been an important idea within specific sociological paradigms and in sociology more generally. Analyzing the function(s) of social practices has been central ever since Émile Durkheim, in *Division of Labor in Society* (1893), defined function as consequence, and exhorted sociologists to distinguish functions of social phenomena from their causes while examining both. Arguing that the division of labor functions to create social solidarity, Durkheim likened the "organic solidarity" associated with a complex division of labor to functional interdependence among differently specialized organs in the human body.

Examining functions of social practices need not imply viewing society as an interdependent set of differentiated structures functioning together to promote societal maintenance and well-being. However, these two ideas intertwined in the post-World War II American structural functionalist paradigm. Like Durkheim, structural functionalists examined how social order is maintained and reproduced. More recently, a metatheoretical movement called neofunctionalism tried to retain structural functionalism's core while extending it to address issues of social change and microfoundations (see Ritzer 1992).

Structural functionalism dominated American sociology in the period after World War II. Kingsley Davis, in his 1959 Presidential address to the American Sociological Association, went so far as to argue that structural functionalism was neither a special theory nor a special method, but synonymous with *all* sociology. Today, Davis's essay remains helpful for understanding structural functionalism's roots in Durkheim, its debts to anthropological functionalists including Radcliffe-Brown and Malinowski, and the intellectual and political-institutional issues that concerned its proponents and critics.

Ritzer (1992) asserts that Talcott Parsons was the most important structural functionalist theorist and Robert Merton the paradigm's most important explicator. Both proponent and constructive critic, Merton (1968) characterized functionalism as interpreting data about social practices by establishing the consequences of those practices for the larger social structures in which the practices are incorporated. A social practice is any social phenomenon that is "patterned and repetitive," including social roles, norms, structures, and institutions (p. 104). For example, in a still admired analysis, Durkheim (1893) argued that crime has positive functions for society, not because punishment deters crime, but because punishment reaffirms societal norms, reinforcing both solidarity and boundaries of acceptable behavior. For Parsons, all systems, including biological, psychological, social, and cultural, must perform four functions to meet systemic needs. These functions are adaptation (adjusting to the environment), goal attainment (defining and achieving objectives), integration (coordinating and regulating interrelationships among parts), and pattern maintenance or latency (providing or maintaining motivation or cultural patterns sustaining motivation). In social systems, adaptation is primarily associated with the economy, goal attainment with the polity, integration with law and custom, and pattern maintenance with schools, families, and churches.

Although structural functionalists dealt with social change, they were limited to doing so in a particular way. Change is a process of increasingly adaptive evolution in which distinct societal institutions such as occupations, churches, schools, families, legislatures, police, prisons, and courts proliferate and become increasingly differentiated, but also integrated into an orderly whole through common norms.

Neofunctionalists tried to expand this characteristic treatment of social dynamics.

Like Durkheim, Merton reminded sociologists that function is not equivalent to cause, motivation, intent, or purpose. He criticized assumptions of functional unity, universality, and indispensability, made explicitly or implicitly by many structural functionalists. In place of society as a consensual, unified whole, Merton noted that social practices could be functional for some organizations and groups, and dysfunctional for others. Instead of presuming that a social practice with a particular function in one setting was universally associated with that function and thus indispensable, Merton argued that there could be functional alternatives. Even if some function were required for system survival, there likely would be alternative practices that could fulfill this function. Finally, Merton highlighted unintended consequences of social practices. Intended versus unintended consequence is one dimension of Merton's (1968) famous contrast between manifest and latent functions.

Assumptions that Merton criticized figure prominently in Davis and Moore's (1945) well-known functional analysis of inequality in occupational rewards. Whereas this essay highlights pitfalls in functional analysis, Stinchcombe's (1985) functional analysis of contributory social insurance exemplifies possibilities of a functionalist approach. Notwithstanding the sensible caution against equating cause and function/consequence, Stinchcombe purposely makes the idea of function key to his causal analysis of how and why government welfare programs developed. Such a functional *causal* explanation is one in which a practice's consequences are essential elements of its cause. Key steps in considering whether it makes sense to hypothesize and test this form of explanation are: (1) finding a social practice with a consequence/function that is maintained in equilibrium notwithstanding specified tension(s) tending to upset the equilibrium; (2) finding that as these tensions rise, the social practice tends to be created or enhanced; and (3) specifying precisely *how* the function/consequence feeds back to create or enhance the social practice (Stinchcombe 1987).

Lewis Coser synthesized functionalism with conflict theory to specify the functions of social conflict. Similarly, post-war neo-Marxists from Louis Althusser to Nicos Poulantzas to James O'Connor specified how democratic governments perform accumulation, legitimation, and class organization and disorganization functions that help maintain capitalism (see, e.g., Ritzer 1992). As Stinchcombe (1987) illustrates, Marx's theory can be recast in functional terms, with the key modification that functions and dysfunctions play out in the context of unequal power relations and conflicting interests among classes. In short, even many ardent critics of structural functionalism embrace the analytic utility of the concept of function, highlighting its centrality to sociology.

SEE ALSO: Conflict Theory; Davis, Kingsley; Durkheim, Émile; Functionalism/Neofunctionalism; Marx, Karl; Merton, Robert K.; Parsons, Talcott; Structural Functional Theory

REFERENCES AND SUGGESTED READINGS

Davis, K. (1959) The Myth of Functional Analysis as a Special Method in Sociology and Anthropology. *American Sociological Review* 24: 757–73.

Davis, K. & Moore, W. (1945) Some Principles of Stratification. *American Sociological Review* 10: 242–9.

Merton, R. K. (1968) *Social Theory and Social Structure*. Free Press, New York.

Ritzer, G. (1992) *Sociological Theory*, 3rd edn. McGraw-Hill, New York.

Stinchcombe, A. (1985) The Functional Theory of Social Insurance. *Politics and Society* 14: 411–30.

Stinchcombe, A. (1987) *Constructing Social Theories*. University of Chicago Press, Chicago.

functionalism/ neofunctionalism

Donald A. Nielsen

Functionalism is a theoretical perspective in sociology, and the social sciences generally, which emphasizes the positive contributions made by any given social arrangement (e.g., institutions, cultural values, norms, rites, and so forth) to the current operation and continued reproduction of society and its cultural pattern. It has rested heavily as a theory on a broad analogy between societies and biological organisms, a tendency especially noted in the work of early functionalists such as Spencer and Durkheim. However, reliance on the organic analogy is already less evident in the work of social anthropologists such as Radcliffe-Brown and Malinowski, who drew selectively on Durkheim's work, and has become muted in more recent forms of functionalism, which draw more frequently on general systems theory and not merely on the analogy with organisms. Functionalists also regularly couple the use of analogical reasoning with a claim to the objective analysis of society through the use of scientific methods and have linked their theorizing to one or another form of positivism in philosophy.

The work of Durkheim forms the most influential predecessor of most contemporary variants of functionalism. He used a functionalist method in a variety of his studies. For example, Durkheim (1964) analyzed the division of labor in modern society and found that it functioned under normal conditions to promote the formation of a new type of social solidarity, which he called organic solidarity. His discussion of the division of labor had a strong influence on the development of Radcliffe-Brown's variant of structural functional analysis. In a similar vein, Durkheim analyzed the social functions of deviant behavior which, in his view, provided opportunities for the clarification and expression of the collective moral consciousness of society through the execution of rituals of punishment of deviant individuals. Finally, Durkheim (1995) argued that religion represented a system of beliefs and practices concerning the sacred and that its primary function was to integrate the members of society into a single moral community. This image of the integrative function of religion, and common values generally, was to have a strong influence on Parsons's functionalist theorizing.

These early functional perspectives were refined during the period after World War II and in the process often significantly modified by later thinkers such as Talcott Parsons and Robert K. Merton. Both figures created schools of thought (Parsons at Harvard and Merton at Columbia) where each trained a new generation of sociologists. Each, in differing ways, emphasized one or another form of functionalism. As a result of their work and that of their students, functionalism became the dominant theoretical perspective in the post-war period and, despite challenges from other theoretical perspectives, remained a leading trend of thought up through the mid-1960s. In such works as *The Social System* (1951), Parsons developed a grand systematic theory of society which focused on the four functional problems of all social systems: adaptation to their environment, goal attainment, integration, and cultural pattern maintenance. Parsons's systematic theory emphasized the exchanges of social performances which took place among institutions fulfilling these functions (e.g., the economy, government, law, education, religion, the family, and so forth) and the equilibrium established among them, while at the same time linking this outlook, if rather uncomfortably, to the theory of social action which he had begun to develop in his earlier work, *The Structure of Social Action* (1937). In his view, disequilibrium between and among the various institutions performing key social functions was a major way of explaining social change. Parsons also emphasized the relations between culture and society and the integrative role of common values in creating social consensus. These emphases led to a theory of social evolution which focused on increasing social differentiation and the historical development of more abstract and universalistic cultural values in modern societies. This brand of macro-functionalism was adopted by Parsons's followers such as Marion Levy, Robert N. Bellah, and Neil Smelser and its analytical schemas applied to the comparative study of societies and cultures such as China and Japan. Others, such as Kingsley Davis and Wilbert Moore, employed functionalism in the study of particular problems such as social stratification and argued that the functionalist method was largely identical with sociological analysis itself.

On the other hand, in his influential work, *Social Theory and Social Structure* (1949), Merton worked toward a more flexible "paradigm" of functional analysis with strong empirical applications. Merton argued strongly against the idea of the universal functionality of particular social arrangements, such as religion or the family. Instead, he argued for the idea of functional equivalence, in which differing concrete social arrangements could satisfy any necessary social function. In this way, he was also more successful than Parsons in uncoupling functional analysis from its potentially conservative implications. Thus, no particular way of arranging for society's needs was privileged and new social arrangements were possible. In this same spirit, Merton also emphasized both the positive functions as well as negative dysfunctions of given social arrangements. Social institutions might have both positive and negative consequences for a society or some segment of it. He also emphasized the "latent" character of many social functions and dysfunctions, that is, their largely unrecognized and unintended quality, and linked this problem to his earlier interest in the unanticipated consequences attendant upon all purposive social action. Merton's brand of functionalism was linked to a strategy of theory and research which he entitled "middle range" analysis, one which avoided both Parsons's effort to create grand theoretical systems as well as the minutiae of empirical research devoid of any theoretical orientation. Merton's more flexible emphasis on latent functions and dysfunctions allowed him and his students to engage in theoretically driven research about such topics as bureaucracy, deviance, reference groups, public opinion, propaganda, and a host of others. As a result, Merton was a less central target for those who were increasingly critical of functionalist modes of analysis.

In addition to its importance as a source of influential schools of twentieth-century social theory, especially in America, functionalism, particularly its Parsonian variety, has been a major reference point for widespread criticism by conflict theorists, symbolic interactionists, and others less persuaded by functionalists' claims. In the eyes of conflict theorists such as Ralf Dahrendorf, C. Wright Mills, Barrington Moore, and others, who often drew more heavily than Parsons on the Marxian theoretical legacy as well as Weber's theory of bureaucracy and political domination, Parsonian structural-functionalism seemed to neglect the problems of power and political conflict, as well as other forms of intergroup struggle (e.g., between social classes and racial and ethnic groups). In their view, functionalism was not only unable or unwilling to focus on or explain such persistent social realities, but also had decidedly conservative political implications. In the 1960s, movements of national liberation in the former colonies, intergenerational conflicts spearheaded by youth, the Civil Rights Movement, black nationalist currents among African Americans, the women's movement and, not least, the Vietnam War, put the problems of power, inequality, and conflict decisively back in public view. These changes made the functionalist emphases on the role of common values in integrating society and the use of the concept of disequilibrium to analyze change seem out of touch with currently explosive social realities. Parsons attempted to address anew the problems of political power from a functionalist, systems theory standpoint, by treating it (along with money) as one generalized medium of communication in society. In a related response to critiques and current changes, Neil Smelser, one of Parsons's followers, developed his *Theory of Collective Behavior* (1962), while Merton's student Lewis Coser, in his work on *The Functions of Social Conflict* (1956), had already taken up the analysis of conflict itself from a functionalist perspective by drawing on the ideas of Georg Simmel. Despite these and other efforts, after the 1960s, functionalist theorizing never fully recovered its place as the leading theoretical perspective in sociology.

Symbolic interactionists like Herbert Blumer had long been critical of functionalism for other reasons and his critique was increasingly supplemented by critical perspectives emerging from such authors as Erving Goffman, representing newer forms of analysis such as social dramaturgy and social constructionism. These microsociologists viewed the functionalist image of society, its functional problems, its emphasis on macrostructures and institutions, and its focus on common values and culture, more generally, as an egregious reification of what is essentially a complex process of social interaction among human actors whose mutually oriented actions create and sustain what the functionalists designate as "society" and "culture." Other critics of functionalism, working

from several different theoretical orientations, have generally agreed with the symbolic interactionists, even while they have also viewed the interactionist critique as insufficiently broad and systematic to meet the challenges posed by functionalist theory. For example, George Homans, in his 1964 Presidential Address to the American Sociological Association, made a plea for "bringing men back in" and in his book, *Social Behavior: Its Elementary Forms* (1961), developed an empirically based social theory rooted in a variant of social behaviorism, one which aimed at the creation of general propositions and even explanatory laws of social behavior by building the analysis of larger social structures on a foundation of individual behavioral psychology. Others, such as Peter Berger and Thomas Luckmann, sought to outflank Parsons's structural functionalism by offering, in *The Social Construction of Reality* (1966), an alternative systematic theory which combined macro and micro analyses of social action, interaction, and structures in a treatment of social reality as a socially constructed phenomenon. Their merger of ideas drawn from Marx, Durkheim, Weber, phenomenology, and symbolic interaction theory attacked functionalism on its own ground by offering what appeared to be a comprehensive theory of society and culture. In general, theorists who have emphasized the ongoing social construction of society have argued that functionalists omit any meaningful reference to the intentions of individuals and that all so-called social functions can be best understood by reducing them to the combined actions and constructions of social actors.

In the last several decades new efforts have been made to revive functionalism by a new wave of "neofunctionalists" such as Jeffrey Alexander, Niklas Luhmann, Jürgen Habermas, and several others who have injected powerful doses of conflict theory, systems theory, an evolutionary emphasis on social change, and a greater emphasis on the role of political power in society into the moribund body of functional analysis. Alexander wedded his neofunctionalism to the broader agenda of developing a multidimensional theory of society, one which would find room for both conflict and consensus, yet also retain the earlier functionalist emphasis on major historical processes such as social differentiation. Luhmann moved instead toward the merger of functionalism with systems theory and evolutionary perspectives and, in the process, emphasized the role of power as well as trust in society. While Habermas is not always grouped with the neofunctionalists, his dual emphasis on system functioning and lifeworld, as well as his evolutionary theory of social communication with its utopian intent of achieving unconstrained consensus in society, has much in common with Parsons. It represents an attempt to merge aspects of the Parsonian legacy with perspectives from linguistic analysis, phenomenological sociology, and political theory. It is of interest that all the above neofunctionalists draw on one or another element of Parsons's mature structural functional theory (e.g., social systems theory, evolutionary analysis, multidimensional grand theorizing, the role of power as generalized medium, the role of common values in society). It has provided them with decisive impetus, despite their considerable modification and supplementation of his ideas.

SEE ALSO: Conflict Theory; Durkheim, Émile; Function; Luhmann, Niklas; Merton, Robert K.; Parsons, Talcott; Spencer, Herbert; Structuralism; Symbolic Interaction; System Theories

REFERENCES AND SUGGESTED READINGS

Alexander, J. (1998) *Neo-Functionalism and After.* Blackwell, Oxford.
Coser, L. (1956) *The Functions of Social Conflict.* Free Press, Glencoe, IL.
Dahrendorf, R. (1959) *Class and Class Conflict in Industrial Society.* Stanford University Press, Stanford.
Durkheim, É. (1964 [1893]) *The Division of Labor in Society.* Trans. G. Simpson. Free Press, New York.
Durkheim, É. (1995 [1912]) *Elementary Forms of Religious Life.* Trans. K. E. Fields. Free Press, New York.
Malinowski, B. (1992) *Magic, Science and Religion and Other Essays.* Waveland Press, Prospect Heights, IL.
Merton, R. K. (1949) *Social Theory and Social Structure.* Free Press, Glencoe, IL.
Parsons, T. (1951) *The Social System.* Free Press, Glencoe, IL.
Parsons, T. (1954) *Essays in Sociological Theory*, 2nd edn. Free Press, Glencoe, IL.
Radcliffe-Brown, A. R. (1965) *Structure and Function in Primitive Society.* Free Press, New York.
Spencer, H. (1971) *Herbert Spencer: Structure, Function and Evolution.* Ed. S. Andreski. Michael Joseph, London.
Sztompka, P. (1974) *System and Function: Toward a Theory of Society.* Academic Press, New York.

fundamentalism

Enzo Pace

Roughly speaking, fundamentalism is a label that refers to the modern tendency – a habit of the heart and mind (Marty & Appleby 1991, 1993a, 1993b, 1994, 1995) – to claim the unerring nature of a sacred text and to deduce from that a rational strategy for instrumental social action. The final goal is to achieve the utopia of a regime of the truth (Pace 1998), gain political power, and rebuild organic solidarity, in jeopardy because of relativism, secularism, and weakness due to the eclipse of religion's social function of integration. This tendency has arisen in various socioreligious contexts: in Protestantism and Catholicism, Islam and the Jewish communities (both in Diaspora and in Israel after the 1967 Six Day War), in contemporary Hinduism and Buddhism, and, to some extent, even in a particular faction of Sikhism (the Khalsa, the religious order of warriors, defenders of the truth and the sacred boundaries of the Punjab). Fundamentalism made its appearance in contemporary times with such manifestations as the first march of the Moral Majority in the United States and the Iranian revolution (1979); the intensification in Sri Lanka of the tension between the Sinhalese Buddhists and the Tamil Hindu from 1977 to 1983; the appearance in Israel of many nationalist religious movements whose aim was to regain and defend the biblical boundaries of the people of Israel (*Eretz Israel*) from 1977 to 1980; and, in the Punjab, from 1984 to 1988 there was an acute crisis in relations between the Sikhs and the Indian government, culminating in an attack by the Indian army on the

Golden Temple in Amritsar and the subsequent assassination of Mrs. Indira Gandhi by a Sikh.

In light of these events, many scholars hold the view that fundamentalism is a modern global phenomenon involving the historic religions, for the most part. One of the most impressive attempts at a comparative analysis was the "Fundamentalism Project," carried out by a team of researchers coordinated by Marty and Appleby and sponsored by the American Academy, which was published in five volumes. In summing up the authors' analysis, five common features characterizing fundamentalist movements can be identified.

First, fundamentalism is characterized by the type of social action dominated by the attitude of *fighting back*. This means, on the one hand, that the social actors claim to be restoring a mythical and sacred order of the past, but, on the other hand, they act with great innovative power of mobilization. The sacred becomes the means for gaining political power. Without this close relation between religious narrative and political rhetoric, with constant mutual contamination between the two, it is impossible to distinguish between the manner of fundamentalist movements and that of traditionalist or conservative ones. The former aim to assume the absolute and unerring truth of the sacred text to legitimate a new social order, the order of an immanent god (the law), pure and integral, to affirm and preserve a pure collective identity. Retracing its collective memory, fundamentalism comes up with a sacred language that inspires the discipline of the body and the mind; through this, it implants common habits in the hearts of the people, an image of solidarity. In contrast to the modern idea of "atomized" individuals in a fragmented society, this solidarity creates a mystical community of Brothers.

The second element highlighted by the authors of the "Fundamentalist Project" – *fighting for* – is implicit in the foregoing: the ultimate goal of the movement is political, despite the furious and intense religious motivations. For instance, at the beginning of the changes in Iran in 1977–8, Islam was perceived as a set of instruments promoting liberation from dictatorship and the modernization of the country run by the Pahlavi dynasty. There was an Islamic liberation theology that later

became, when the Ayatollah Khomeini gained power, a political project to create an integral Islamic state, a process which moved away from the centralized power of the state, shifting the traditional role of the Shiite clerical institution. Up to the time of the revolution, the Shiites were the interpreters of the sacred text without any claim to impose a single model of society or political order. Yet, after coming to power, the ayatollah began to offer a sort of state hermeneutics of the sacred text. In spite of the traditional pluralism within the Shia in the matter of interpretation of canon law, the Khomeini regime imposed a uniform, and unbearable, straitjacket on a society with some degree of social differentiation, accustomed to perceiving the difference between religion and politics.

The third feature – *fight with* – refers to a specific repository of symbolic resources of use in the crusade for restoring identity and gaining political power. As a rule, fundamentalists move toward a mythical past contained in a sacred text, the shrine of the secret of the social order. Thus, they distill – drop by drop – the functional language of social action, the sociologos of the society in question. In this sense, the fundamentalist approach to both the sacred text and social action is selective: fundamentalists actually interpret the text, whilst pretending to claim its inerrancy, its ahistoricity, and generally its structural refractoriness to any rational (historical and critical) hermeneutics.

The fourth element is the *fight against*. If fundamentalism were a label that could be applied to any kind of (religious) politics of identity (in which case, for instance, the former President Milosevic of Serbia acted as a fundamentalist when he tried to combine nationalist rhetoric with a discourse on the Orthodox origins of the Serbian nation), it would be very easy to demonstrate the link between the fundamentalist mentality and the need for an enemy. Being a fundamentalist assumes the idea and feeling of being threatened by an enemy (real or imagined) as regards one's identity, territory, and survival. When he assassinated Israeli President Rabin in 1995, Yigal Amir believed he was doing what was best, since Rabin, by making peace with Arafat, was yielding to the Palestinians territories that, according to extremist movements, belonged to the promised land given by God to his people.

Finally, the fifth feature of fundamentalism – *fight under God* – represents a simple corollary of the previous assumptions. It refers to the intensity of the militants' conviction that they are "on the right path." They are certain they are called directly by a god to carry on with radical determination the struggle against the enemy. Thus, symbolic and physical violence are legitimized. Sacred violence becomes a logical consequence of the missionary function the fundamentalist feels he has received from God. The fundamentalist believes he carries out the function of defender of the rights of God and executor of his will on earth.

The term fundamentalism has given rise to heated controversy among scholars, the most significant objection being that it has been used to classify different phenomena present in very diverse socioreligious contexts. In other words, we should guard against reducing every radical conservative religious viewpoint to a manifestation of fundamentalism. Other scholars point out the difficulty of comparing different religions under the same label, fundamentalism: religions which are monotheistic with those of a non-theistic or polytheistic nature, or religions entailing the crucial importance of a sacred text (the Bible, Koran, Adi Granth) with others that do not.

Apart from these objections, those social scientists who accept the concept and assume a comparative and global approach to studying fundamentalism are divided on another issue: whether the phenomenon should be interpreted as an expression (or the quintessence) of modernity or as a simple reaction to modernity. The contrast refers to a broader debate within social theory about the classic dichotomy between tradition and modernity, postmodernity, and globalization.

To sum up, four main points of view emerge. In the first approach, fundamentalism is a clear reaction to modernity, a defensive protection against the individualization of belief and socioreligious identity (Meyer 1989). The second orientation is well represented, among others, by both Lawrence (1989) and Eisenstadt (1999); they hold that fundamentalism is a modern phenomenon, a direct consequence of modernity, characterized by the rejection of modernism. Using the advantages of modernity (the techniques of propaganda, the logic of social

mobilization, lobbying in the public and political arena, and so on), fundamentalism, according to Eisenstadt, is urged on by a modern Jacobin utopia in antithesis with modernity. Lawrence believes, on the other hand, that the disjunction between modernity and modernism enables fundamentalism to become a transnational movement claiming to give a new and absolute basis for social action and human knowledge, to the social order and the source of political power. The third approach stresses the relationship between fundamentalism and secularization (Kepel 1991), fundamentalism being a countertendency to the gradual eclipse of the sacred many scholars had predicted two decades ago.

The last point of view underlines the importance of the political objectives of the fundamentalist movements' social and religious action (Greilsammer 1991; Van der Veer 2000): their struggle tends to focus all religious energy on the public arena and consequently on political action, according to the crucial hypothesis that only through political power will it be possible to reestablish the divine law and safeguard one's identity (Hindu, Muslim, Christian, Buddhist, Sikh, Jewish, and so on). The way the fundamentalist mentality bridges the gap between religion and politics is characterized by a double abstraction used in the hermeneutics of the sacred text, as pointed out by Bhikku Parekh (1992): by abstracting from the tradition (sometimes in contrast to the traditional authority or a consolidated school of juridical thought and theological doctrine) and inventing a set of religious narratives and a political rhetoric of identity abstracted from a literal interpretation of the text itself. In this sense, fundamentalism is able to invent a tradition by reifying a sacred text and drawing from it paradigms of social action, sometimes without any substantial relation to the historical and theological context in which the sacred text was written. Even when a religious tradition does not refer to a single revealed sacred text – such as Buddhism or Hinduism – one of the most striking phenomena we have seen is the selection of one, among many other sacred texts, and the consequent construction of a sociological and cognitive map; the idea being that in the text we find the roots of our collective memory and identity, the sacred boundaries of the territory we inhabit, and the source of political authority. When such a discourse is produced by an elite of Buddhist monks in Sri Lanka during the process of nation building (which has been going on since 1955), or by a network of neo-Hindu groups and political parties (in India since 1979), which has gradually managed to gain power (with the Bharata Janata Party), there is no doubt that the habits of the heart and the attitudes of the mind are fundamentalist-oriented.

SEE ALSO: Identity Politics/Relational Politics; Islam; Judaism; Protestantism; Religion; Religion, Sociology of; Sanskritization; Secularization; Social Movements

REFERENCES AND SUGGESTED READINGS

Eisenstadt, S. (1999) *Fundamentalism, Sectarianism, and Revolution*. Cambridge, Cambridge University Press.

Greilsammer, I. (1991) *Israel: Les hommes en noir*. Presse de la Fondation Nationale des Sciences Politiques, Paris.

Kepel, G. (1991) *La Revanche de Dieu*. Seuil, Paris.

Lawrence, B. (1989) *Defenders of God*. Harper, San Francisco.

Marty, M. E. & Appleby, S. R. (Eds.) (1991) *Fundamentalism Observed*. University of Chicago Press, Chicago.

Marty, M. E. & Appleby, S. R. (Eds.) (1993a) *Fundamentalism and Society: Reclaiming the Sciences, the Family, and Education*. University of Chicago Press, Chicago.

Marty, M. E. & Appleby, S. R. (Eds.) (1993b) *Fundamentalism and the State: Remaking Politics, Economics, and Militance*. University of Chicago Press, Chicago.

Marty, M. E. & Appleby, S. R. (Eds.) (1994) *Accounting for Fundamentalism: The Dynamic Character of Movements*. University of Chicago Press, Chicago.

Marty, M. E. & Appleby, S. R. (Eds.) (1995) *Fundamentalism Comprehended*. University of Chicago Press, Chicago.

Meyer, T. (1989) *Fundamentalismus*. Rowohl Taschenbuch, Hamburg.

Pace, E. (1998) *Il regime della verità*. Il Mulino, Bologna.

Parekh, B. (1992) The Concept of Fundamentalism. University of Warwick Centre for Research in Asian Migration, Occasional Papers in Asian Migration Study, No. 1.

Van der Veer, P. (2000) *Religious Nationalism: Hindus and Muslims in India*. University of California Press, Berkeley.

gambling as a social problem

Lucia Schmidt

Gambling refers to wagering money or other belongings on chance activities or events with random or uncertain outcomes (Devereux 1979). Gambling opportunities are now widely available throughout the world and playing with and for money is socially accepted as a source of entertainment and recreation. However, a growing tendency to highlight problematic aspects is also to be noticed.

By its very nature, gambling involves a voluntary, deliberate assumption of risk, often with a negative expectable value. Traditionally, heavy gamblers who sustained repeated losses and other adverse consequences were considered derelict, immoral, or criminal. For much of the twentieth century, the prevailing view of excessive gambling continued to define that behavior as morally and legally reprehensible. Only a few decades ago, a new perspective on the problem came up in which the behavior in question is seen as a pathological one – as a form of addictive behavior in need of therapeutic treatment. The disease concept (at least partly) replaced former deviance definitions as a kind of willful norm violation, and excessive gambling increasingly is considered to be an expression of a mental disorder resembling the substance-related addictions. This change in perception has been strongly stimulated by – and reflected in – the evolving clinical classification and description of pathological gambling in the various editions (between 1980 and 2000) of the *Diagnostic and Statistical Manual of Mental Disorders* (DSM) published by the American Psychiatric Association.

The medicalization process was initiated in the US by a self-help group named Gamblers Anonymous (founded in 1957). Soon, GA formed alliances with medical experts. A small circle of problem gamblers and professional claims-makers started to bring public attention to the problem. The National Council on Compulsive Gambling (founded in 1972 and renamed the National Council on Problem Gambling in 1989) served as a model for similar organizations in other countries, all of which have become influential actors in the social construction of the new disease.

The medical conception was developed with strong references to the already established disease model of alcoholism and it highlights loss of control as a basic origin of excessive gambling. The psychiatrist Robert L. Custer was the first expert on pathological gambling who participated in one of the specialized DSM advisory committees. For the 1980 edition of DSM III, where the disease was codified for the first time, he was the *only* one. As Custer puts it in one of his classic works, "compulsive gambling is an addictive illness in which the subject is driven by an overwhelming, uncontrollable impulse to gamble. Accordingly, the afflicted gambler is controlled by his devastating disease. Rhetorical devices like this build up the image of persons as helpless, hapless victims" (Conrad & Schneider 1980).

There are remarkable regional differences in gambling opportunities that are supposed to be inherently problematic (e.g., to bear an increased addictive potential). For example, the discussion about "gambling addiction" in Germany was for years almost entirely restricted to a special kind of slot-machine, while classical forms like casino games, lotteries, and sports betting were highly uncommon. Yet this type of slot-machine was once described by Robert Custer as a harmless, not very exciting toy.

According to the National Research Council, much of the available research on all aspects of pathological gambling is of limited scientific value and reliable estimates for the national and regional prevalence of pathological gambling are hard to find (NRC 1999). However, the Research Council estimates that approximately 0.9 percent of adults in the US meet specific criteria as pathological gamblers on the basis of their gambling activities in the past year and that the current prevalence rate for pathological gambling among adolescents is considerably higher (NRC 1999: 98ff). The American Psychiatric Association states there are 1–6 percent of young people in the US and Canada who may satisfy diagnostic criteria for pathological gambling, with the rate of gambling problems rising among young people. From a sociological point of view, assertions about the extent of the problem serve as the rhetorical basis on which the discussion proceeds. Within the last few years, youth gambling has become a newly favored topic of research and political discussion. As illustrated by the title of an interdisciplinary reader on this subject – *Futures at Stake: Youth, Gambling and Society* (Shaffer et al. 2003) – rhetorical devices and drama make up an essential part of the ongoing problem-discourse on gambling.

SEE ALSO: Addiction and Dependency; Deviance; Deviance, Constructionist Perspectives; Deviance, Medicalization of; Gambling and Sport; Labeling; Labeling Theory; Medical Sociology; Mental Disorder; Social Problems, Concept and Perspectives

REFERENCES AND SUGGESTED READINGS

Conrad, P. & Schneider, J. W. (1980) *Deviance and Medicalization: From Badness to Sickness.* Mosby, St. Louis.
Devereux, E. C. (1979) Gambling. In: Sills, D. L. (Ed.), *The International Encyclopedia of the Social Sciences*, Vol. 17. Macmillan, New York.
National Research Council (1999) *Pathological Gambling: A Critical Review.* National Academy Press, Washington, DC.
Schmidt, L. (1998) *Psychische Krankheit als soziales Problem. Die Konstruktion des "Patho-logischen Glücksspiels"* (Mental Disorder as Social Problem:
The Construction of "Pathological Gambling"). Leske & Budrich, Opladen.
Shaffer, H. J., Hall, M. N., Vander Bilt, J., & George, E. M. (Eds.) (2003) *Futures at Stake: Youth, Gambling and Society.* University of Nevada Press, Reno.

gambling and sport

Ellis Cashmore

There are two likely sources for the word gambling: the Old Saxon *gamene*, which became abbreviated to the contemporary "game"; or the Italian *gambetto*, source of "gambit," a practice of sacrificing something minor in order to secure a larger advantage. Gambling now refers to playing games of luck or skill, using a stake, usually a sum of money, in anticipation of winning a larger sum.

While gambling on sports is obviously a product of the growth of organized sports from the mid-nineteenth century, playing games of chance for money or staking wagers on the outcome of events probably dates back to antiquity.

Modern forms of gambling emerged in connection with changing ideas about time and nature. As pre-Enlightenment thinkers advanced the notion that reason and rationality lay behind all earthly affairs, the roles of chance, happenstance or pure randomness were seen as increasingly problematic. In an ordered universe, ignorance of affairs was merely imperfect knowledge because everything was potentially knowable. August Comte's positivism was perhaps the epitome of this, recognizing only observable phenomena and rejecting metaphysics, theism, and anything else that lay beyond human perception. The emerging emphasis on science led to the conclusion that given greater knowledge, the seeming vagaries of nature could be comprehended and subordinated to the rational, calculating mind.

Gambling is guided by such reasoning: admittedly, the conscious thought that lies behind rolling dice or drawing lots is hardly likely to resemble any kind of calculation; these are games of chance, played with the intention of winning money. But the motive behind gambling on sports is influenced by a more rational style of thinking: that it is possible to predict the outcome of an event by the employment of a calculus of probability. No one wagers money on a sporting event without at least the suspicion that they are privy to a special knowledge about a competitive outcome. A hunch, a taste, a fancy, a "feel" – all these add to the calculus at work in the mind of even the most casual gambler when he or she stakes money on a competition.

Orientations of gamblers differ widely: some always feel a frisson whether it is in watching a horse romp home or some dice roll; others observe from a position of detachment, their interest resting on only the result. The sports gambler bets with head as well as heart; the reward is both in the winnings and in the satisfaction that he or she has divined a correct result from the unmanageable flux of a competitive event.

In his *Luck: The Brilliant Randomness of Everyday Life* (1995), Nicholas Rescher identifies a surge in popularity in wagering on contests of skill and chance during the English Civil War (1641–5) and the Thirty Years' War in continental Europe (1618–48). Starved of entertainment, soldiers and sailors killed time by wagering on virtually any activity. Returning to civilian society, the militia brought with them their habits, and the enthusiasm for gambling spread, aligning itself with the games of skill that were growing in popularity in England.

The 1665 Gaming Act was the first piece of legislation designed to outlaw gambling, principally to restrict the debts that were being incurred as a result of the growing stakes. Some activities had attracted gambling for decades, perhaps centuries. Swordplay, for example, was a pursuit that was viscerally thrilling to watch and stimulated the human passion for prediction. As the military use of swords declined, so the contests continued simply for recreation and entertainment. Dueling was perfect for gamblers. Engaging in competitive contests simply for the satisfaction they afforded the competitor and observer was exactly the kind of wasteful and sinful behavior despised by the party of English Protestants and Puritans.

Blood sports were popular in nineteenth-century England and North America. Their attraction, in part, was due to their amenability to betting. Even as the civilizing process altered the threshold of repugnance and made such grim and cruel pursuits less tolerable, cockfighting, bear baiting and other blood sports remained, principally because of gambling. Pugilism was another combat sport that attracted what was known as a "fancy" or following of ardent spectators who would pit their forecasting skills against each other. Sponsors of pugilists were often extravagant backers of their charges. The influence of gambling on prize fighting became injurious and corruption was rife.

Boxing and gambling have gone hand in hand ever since, though there were other less probable sports that attracted bettors. Cricket, for example, in the early nineteenth century, had its hardcore spectators who were prone not only to gambling but also to drinking and rowdiness. Gambling regulations remained in the laws of the game until the 1880s and betting was still very much part of the sport until at least mid-century. Lords, the home stadium of cricket's governing federation, banned gambling in the 1820s and, according to Dennis Brailsford, in his *British Sport: A Social History* one player was banned for allegedly throwing a match."

Brailsford estimates that the money staked on boxing was rivaled "and sometimes exceeded" by that involved in pedestrianism, the period's equivalent of track. Pedestrianism defined a variety of races and events, sometimes head-to-head, or against the clock, often involving both men and women. There were wheelbarrow races and hopping contests, as well as such unusual challenges as picking up potatoes. The appeal of pedestrianism was that it was possible to wager on practically anything. Opposition to working-class gambling on sports bore fruit in the form of two pieces of legislation in 1853 and 1906, which were ostensibly framed to forbid off-course betting.

In the US, where gambling was – and still is in many states – illegal, baseball nevertheless attracted gamblers. Perhaps the best-known instance of corruption had its source in gambling. The Black Sox Scandal of 1919 involved several Chicago White Sox players who were bribed by a gambling syndicate to throw a World Series against underdogs Cincinnati Reds. Money was at the root of this instance of corruption, which was chronicled by John Sayles in his movie *Eight Men Out*. The players were poorly paid and exploited by Major League Baseball long before the advent of free agency. The film and the Elliot Asinof book (of the same title) on which it is based depicts the players sympathetically, in some senses cheated by their employers.

Animal racing, from its outset, was fair game for gaming. In their modern forms, horse racing and dog racing proved the most attractive to gamblers. Dog racing has its origins in eighteenth-century coursing, and involved highly bred and trained dogs, which chased and usually killed a fleeing hare. One of the attractions of meetings was the opportunity to wager and drink convivially. Hoteliers and publicans would promote coursing meets. It became an organized sport, complete with its own organization in 1858, when a National Coursing Club was established.

As opposition to what was obviously one of a number of blood sports prevalent at the time, coursing dispensed with living hares and substituted a mechanical equivalent. The first electric hare was used in 1919 and came into popular use at the end of the 1920s. In the US, the betting norm became pari-mutuel, from the French, meaning mutual stake. (This type of betting was introduced in New Zealand as far back as 1880.) In the 1930s, this also took off in on-course British horse racing (known as the totalizer).

A new form of gambling on soccer posed threats to both greyhound and horse racing. Known as the pools, it came to life in the early 1930s and captured the British public's imagination almost immediately. Newspapers had been publishing their own versions of pools for many years, but the practice was declared illegal in 1928. Brailsford notes how the £20 million staked in the 1934/35 season doubled within two years. The outlay was usually no more than a few pence and the bets were typically collected from one's home. The aim of pools was to select a requisite number of drawn games, so it was not classified as a game of chance, but one of skill, thus escaping the regulation of gaming legislation. By the outbreak of war, there were 10 million gamblers on the pools. The popularity the pools enjoyed with working-class bettors stayed intact until the

introduction of the national lottery (modeled on the US state lotteries) in the early 1990s.

In the 1990s, betting on the spread became one of the most popular gambling forms. The bettor could wager not only on the result of a contest but on any facet of it. Spread betting was popularized in the US, then became the norm in Britain, especially in soccer.

Sports betting, while nominally illegal in most parts of the US, remains popular because gamblers typically have access to a Las Vegas bookmaker. The Internet has facilitated online betting, which effectively circumvents legal restrictions on gambling. A valid credit card and Internet access is all that is needed to gamble on practically any sports event, anywhere in the world.

Sociological research on gambling in sports has been rare because it is difficult to collect valid and reliable data. Therefore, we are left with case histories of gamblers and the athletes and teams that altered competitive outcomes or shaved points from their scores to enable gamblers, sometimes themselves, to win bets (Ginsburg 2003). Basketball presents a prime example. As Alan Wykes (1964) points out: "American basketball has been more notorious than football for its fixing scandals of the 1950s when college stars or whole teams were being bribed to throw games." Like any other competitive sport, basketball is a natural, if unwitting, ally to gambling. And history suggests that, where gambling is present, corruption is rarely far away.

Former Arizona State star Stevin Hedake Smith admitted helping a gambling ring by shaving points during his senior year as a way of relieving his own gambling debts. In one 1994 game, the Sun Devils were favored by a 14-point lead, so Smith and his accomplices had to make sure their team won by six points because the bookie wanted a cushion. Late in the game Arizona State led 40–27, but Smith began to allow more space to the shooters he was meant to be guarding and the score narrowed to finish 88–82. Smith revealed to *Sports Illustrated* (Yaeger 1998) how he could adjust his game to accommodate the various spreads, usually by easing off. By holding a victory margin to a certain number of points, players could earn $20,000. Players sometimes bet on their own games.

Gambling's association with sports continues. Some sports' enduring popularity is directly attributable to betting. In both Europe and the US, horse and dog racing thrive on a betting levy (a fixed proportion of bookmakers' revenues). Interest in jai alai revolves around betting. The movement of major boxing contests to Las Vegas is no accident: boxing's historical connection with gambling is a sturdy one and gamblers flock to Las Vegas as much to bet as to enjoy the bouts.

Any activity, whether shopping, eating chocolate or watching television, has the potential to induce dependency. Gambling also, though "compulsive gamblers" are typically drawn to games of chance rather than gambling on sports events, where elements of choice, discretion, judgment and prescience are allied to luck.

SEE ALSO: Deviance, Sport and; Gambling as a Social Problem; Media and Sport; Sport; Sport as Spectacle

REFERENCES AND SUGGESTED READINGS

Ginsburg, D. E. (2003) *The Fix Is In: A History of Baseball Gambling and Game-Fixing Scandals.* McFarland, Jefferson, NC.

Wykes, A. (1964) *Gambling.* Aldus Books, London.

Yaeger, D. (1996) *Undue Process: The NCAA's Injustice For All.* Sagamore Publishing, Champaign, IL.

Yaeger, D. (1998) Confessions of a Point Shaver. *Sports Illustrated* 89(19): November 9.

game stage

D. Angus Vail

The game stage is one of three central components of George Herbert Mead's seminal discussion of the social foundation and development of the self. According to Mead, the self has a social genesis which becomes evident if one examines the ways that people develop a sense of their own being as something separate from, but also interdependent with, other people. In essence, the self is situated in the individual's capacity to take account of themselves. By examining children's styles of play, followed by the games they play, one can see how they develop a capacity to take into account not just the role of a singular other person, but also eventually the roles of many people simultaneously. It is only once a person has reached this stage of development that she or he is said to have developed a complete self. Mead (1962: 151–4) called the second stage the game stage.

The fundamental difference between the game stage and its antecedent play stage lies in the child's ability to take the roles of multiple people at the same time. In order successfully to play an organized game or sport, the child has to be able to take account not only of his or her own actions, but also, and simultaneously, the actions of every other player involved in the game. Little league soccer makes a fine example of the distinction. At a certain age, children playing soccer stop playing swarm ball where every child on the field swarms around the ball, and they develop the capacity to play positions that require taking account of themselves, where the ball is, what their team-mates are doing, and what their opponents are doing. Thus, they learn how to play the game of soccer rather than playing at being a soccer player.

If a person is to achieve success in a game she or he has to understand the rules that govern that game. Rules organize both the players' responses to each other and the attitudes that their actions are likely to induce in others who are also playing the game. Thus, while children in the play stage will swarm around a soccer ball, children in the game stage are capable of understanding the rules that govern zone offense or defense where the team acts together.

Of course, the game is a metaphor for the ways that children and adults take account of the diverse, malleable, and emergent roles that other people play, often simultaneously, in social settings. Thus, once a person enters the game stage of development, she or he demonstrates a capacity to take account of others' actions, her or his own actions, and the often quite informal rules (collectively known as the generalized other) that govern the social situation in which they all find themselves together. Mead contends that this capacity is the true mark of development of a complete self.

SEE ALSO: Generalized Other; Mead, George Herbert; Play Stage; Preparatory Stage; Role; Self; Symbolic Interaction

REFERENCES AND SUGGESTED READINGS

Blumer, H. (2004) *George Herbert Mead and Human Conduct.* Alta Mira Press, Walnut Creek, CA.

Mead, G. H. (1962 [1934]) *Mind, Self, and Society: From the Standpoint of a Social Behaviorist.* University of Chicago Press, Chicago.

Meltzer, B. N. (1959) *The Social Psychology of George Herbert Mead.* Center for Sociological Research, Kalamazoo, MI.

Meltzer, B. N., Petras, J. W., & Reynolds, L. T. (1975) *Symbolic Interactionism: Genesis, Varieties and Criticism.* Routledge & Kegan Paul, Boston.

Weigert, A. J. & Gecas, V. (2004) Self. In: Reynolds, L. T. & Herman-Kinney, N. J. (Eds.), *Handbook of Symbolic Interactionism.* Alta Mira, New York, pp. 267–88.

game theory

Michael W. Macy and Arnout van de Rijt

Game theory is a powerful mathematical tool for modeling conflict and cooperation that originated with von Neumann and Morgenstern's (1944) seminal work. A game consists of two or more *players*, each with a set of *strategies* and a *utility function* that assigns an individual *payoff* to each combination of strategies, such that payoffs for a given strategy depend in part on the strategies of other players. This *strategic interdependence* can be represented in several ways: as a payoff matrix (the "normal form," where players act simultaneously), a decision tree (the "extensive form" for sequential moves), or as a production function (for *n*-person games). Strategic interdependence allows two types of games. In *zero-sum games*, a gain for one player is always a loss for the other, which precludes the possibility of cooperation for mutual gain. In *positive-sum* games, everyone can gain through *Pareto efficient* cooperation, where some are better off and none are worse off, compared to other outcomes.

If cooperation is Pareto efficient and both players are rational, why would cooperation ever fail? There are two reasons: the fear of being "suckered" by the partner and the temptation to cheat. These failures can be avoided through enforceable contracts that preclude "cheating" ("cooperative games") or through collusion (in "non-cooperative games").

In cooperative games, non-cooperation is contractually precluded. The problem is to negotiate the distribution of resources among a coalition of players. Sociologists use cooperative game theory to study the effects of network structure on power inequality in social exchange (Willer 1999).

Non-cooperative games have no enforceable contract. These games are generally more interesting to sociologists because they can be used to model *social dilemmas* which arise when players attempting to maximize their individual well-being arrive at a socially undesirable outcome. More precisely, a social dilemma is a game in which there is at least one Pareto deficient Nash equilibrium (NE). An NE obtains when every strategy is a "best reply" to the other strategies played; hence, no player has an incentive to unilaterally change strategy. The equilibrium is Pareto deficient when the outcome is preferred by no one while one or more individuals prefer some other outcome.

The simplest version of a social dilemma confronts two players with a binary choice: whether to "cooperate" or "defect." These two choices intersect at four possible outcomes, each with an associated payoff: R rewards mutual cooperation, S is the sucker payoff for unilateral cooperation, P punishes mutual defection and T is the temptation to unilaterally defect. In a social dilemma, mutual cooperation is Pareto efficient yet may be undermined by the temptation to cheat (if $T>R$) or by the fear of being cheated (if $P>S$) or by both. In the game of "Stag Hunt" the problem is "fear" but not "greed" ($R>T>P>S$), and in the game of "Chicken" the problem is "greed" but not "fear" ($T>R>S>P$). The problem is most challenging when both fear and greed are present, that is, when $T>R$ and $P>S$. Given the assumption that $R>P$, there is only one way this can happen, if $T>R>P>S$, the celebrated game of "Prisoner's Dilemma" (PD). In this game, defection is the dominant strategy, that is, it makes no difference whether a player knows what the partner has chosen. In other social dilemmas, the second mover should do the same as the partner (e.g., Stag Hunt) or the opposite (e.g., Chicken).

An interesting variant is called the "trust game." The first-mover chooses whether to invest resources in a "trustee" and if so, the second-mover chooses whether to betray or reward trust. More complex variations allow for N players and continuous choices, whether to "give some" or to "take some" from other players. These games are used to study the *free-rider* problem in *collective action*.

Although the games vary widely, the Nash equilibrium is a solution concept that can be universally applied. John Nash (1950) showed that every game contains at least one NE. NE predicts mutual defection in PD, unilateral defection in Chicken, and either mutual cooperation or mutual defection in Stag Hunt. NE also identifies a Pareto deficient mixed-strategy equilibrium in Chicken and Stag Hunt. (A mixed strategy cooperates with a positive probability that is less than one.)

NE in non-cooperative games is self-enforcing – no contract is necessary to guarantee compliance. This allows for the possibility that social order can self-organize, even in the absence of a Leviathan. Although this result is clearly of enormous significance across all the social sciences, there are important limitations that have spurred the search for more powerful theoretical extensions. Nash equilibrium analysis tells us if there are any strategic configurations that are stable, and if so, how they are characterized. Knowing that a configuration is an NE means that if this state should obtain, the system will remain there forever, even in the absence of an enforceable contract. However, even when there is a unique NE, this does not tell us whether this state will ever be reached, or with what probability, or what will happen if the equilibrium should be perturbed. Nor does NE explain social stability among interacting agents who are changing strategies individually, yet the population distribution remains constant, as in a homeostatic equilibrium. Put differently, NE explains social stability as the absence of individual change, not as a dynamic balance in a self-correcting distribution of evanescent individual strategies,

each of which influences others in response to the influence that it receives.

Moreover, in most games, NE cannot identify a unique solution. Both Chicken and Stag Hunt have three equilibria (including mixed-strategy). Worse yet, if these games are repeated by players who care about future payoffs in an ongoing relation, the number of NE becomes indefinitely large (even in PD, which has a unique equilibrium in one-shot play). When games have multiple equilibria, NE cannot tell us which will obtain or with what relative probability. Nor can it tell us much about the dynamics by which a population of players can move from one equilibrium to another.

Game theorists have responded to the problem of equilibrium selection by proposing procedures that can winnow the set of possible solutions. These include identifying equilibria that are risk dominant (every player follows a conservative strategy that earns the best payoff she can guarantee for herself), payoff dominant (no other equilibrium has a higher aggregate payoff over all players), Pareto dominant (every other equilibrium is less preferred by at least one player), and subgame perfect (all nodes along the equilibrium path can be reached in the extensive form). However, these equilibrium selection methods are theoretically arbitrary (e.g., there is no a priori basis for payoff dominant or risk dominant behavior) and they often disagree about which equilibrium should be selected (e.g., in Stag Hunt, payoff dominance and subgame perfection identify mutual cooperation while risk dominance points to mutual defection).

Another limitation is the analytical simplification that players have unlimited cognitive capacity with which to calculate the best response to any potential combination of strategies by other players. This allows equilibria to be identified by finding the minima of a function that describes the expected utility for any member of a homogeneous population. However, laboratory research on human behavior in experimental games reveals widespread and consistent deviations from equilibrium predictions (Kagel & Alvin 1995).

These limitations, including concerns about the cognitive demands of forward-looking rationality, have led game theorists to explore backward-looking alternatives based on evolution and learning. This development has revolutionized game theory by relaxing what had heretofore been regarded as a canonical assumption – the cognitive capacity of rational actors to accurately predict the payoffs for alternative choices. *Rational expectations* were regarded as essential for game theory because of the *consequentialist* logic by which strategic choices are explained by the associated payoffs. Consequentialist explanations defy temporal ordering by attributing the causes of past events to their future outcomes. In *analytical* game theory the calculus of rational expectations provides the necessary link to the future.

Evolution and learning provide a radically different mechanism for consequentialist explanation. Repeated experience, not rational expectations, is the link to the future. In *evolutionary* game theory, prior exposure to a recurrent decision allows strategic outcomes to explain the choices that produce them through a process of iterative search. Thus, the outcomes that matter are those that have already occurred, not those that an analytical actor might expect to obtain in the future. This relaxes the highly restrictive cognitive assumptions in analytical game theory and allows for the possibility that players rely on cognitive shortcuts such as imitation, heuristic decision, stochastic learning, Bayesian updating, best reply with finite memory, and local optimization, thereby extending applications to games played by highly routinized players, such as bureaucratic organizations or boundedly rational individuals whose behavior is based on heuristics, habits, or norms.

Evolutionary game theory models the ability of conditionally cooperative strategies to survive and reproduce in competition with predators (Maynard-Smith 1982). Biological models have also been extended to military and economic games in which losers are physically eliminated or bankrupted and to cultural games in which winners are more likely to be imitated (Axelrod 1984).

Critics charge that genetic learning may be a misleading template for models of adaptation at the cognitive level. The need for a cognitive alternative to evolutionary game theory is reflected in a growing number of formal learning-theoretic models of cooperative behavior.

In learning, positive outcomes increase the probability that the associated behavior will be repeated, while negative outcomes reduce it. The process closely parallels evolutionary selection, in which positive outcomes increase a strategy's chances for survival and reproduction, while negative outcomes reduce it. However, this isomorphism need not imply that adaptive actors will learn the strategies favored by evolutionary selection pressures. In evolution, strategies compete *between* the individuals that carry them, not *within*. That is, evolutionary models explore changes in the global frequency distribution of strategies across a population, while learning operates on the local probability distribution of strategies within the repertoire of each individual member.

Sociology has lagged behind other social sciences in embracing game theory, in part because of skepticism about the heroic behavioral assumptions in the analytical approach. However, these backward-looking alternatives show that the key assumption in game theory is not rationality; it is instead what ought to be most compelling to sociology, the *interdependence of the actors*. The game paradigm obtains its theoretical leverage by modeling the social fabric as a matrix of interconnected agents guided by outcomes of their interaction with others, where the actions of each depend on, as well as shape, the behavior of those with whom they are linked. Viewed with that lens, game theory appears most relevant to the social science that has been most reluctant to embrace it.

SEE ALSO: Coleman, James; Collective Action; Evolution; Exchange Network Theory; Norm of Reciprocity; Prosocial Behavior; Rational Choice Theories; Social Dilemmas; Social Learning Theory; Strategic Decisions

REFERENCES AND SUGGESTED READINGS

Axelrod, R. (1984) *The Evolution of Cooperation*. Basic Books, New York.

Kagel, J. H. & Alvin, E. R. (1995). *Handbook of Experimental Economics*. Princeton University Press, Princeton.

Maynard-Smith, J. (1982). *Evolution and the Theory of Games*. Cambridge University Press, Cambridge.

Nash, J. F. (1950) *Non-Cooperative Games*. Princeton University Press, Princeton.

von Neumann, J. & O. Morgenstern (1944) *Theory of Games and Economic Behavior*. Princeton University Press, Princeton.

Willer, D. (1999) *Network Exchange Theory*. Praeger, Westport, CT.

gangs, delinquent

Rod K. Brunson

Discussions of gangs in the twenty-first century stereotypically conjure up images of young minority males, outfitted in hip-hop clothing, hanging out on street corners in impoverished urban communities, and engaging in unlawful acts. Using shorthand to identify gang members may seem logical to citizens, police officers, the media, and social service workers. It fails to recognize, however, the variation that exists among gangs and gang members. This begs the question whether the focus should be on gang members or on examining the conditions and processes involved in gang formation. Both approaches require their own orientation and have specific policy implications for addressing gang membership. At the center of these issues is the lack of consistency regarding how gangs are defined.

DEFINITIONAL ISSUES

One of the most difficult tasks for social scientists interested in the study of gangs is establishing the parameters of their area of interest: in other words, what constitutes a gang. Scholars have been interested in gang definition issues for decades. One key issue is whether delinquency should be regarded as an intrinsic feature of gang involvement. Thrasher (1927) and Klein's (1971) definitions characterize two sides of the debate and have been without question among the most influential. Thrasher emphasizes the spontaneous nature of gang formation, with delinquent activities of gang members regarded as a potential outcome to be examined independently. Klein, on the other hand, maintains that the delinquent orientation of the group is a central feature of any definition of gang.

Scholars are polarized concerning whether or not delinquency should be considered an inherent trait of gang involvement. Definitions that omit delinquency are sometimes criticized or rejected because they would cause some social groups (e.g., Greek letter organizations, athletic teams, fraternal lodges) to be designated as gangs. Bursik and Grasmick (1993) urge caution, however, regarding the inclusion of the delinquent activities component because they fear it results in a tautology. Specifically, delinquency simultaneously serves as a possible outcome of gang involvement and a key component of the definition. On the other hand, several gang studies have excluded various groups *despite* their involvement in delinquency (i.e., hate groups, motorcycle clubs, prison gangs, and adolescent peer groups). These observations extend the focus beyond delinquency status and draw attention to the possible relevance of additional variables that may increase the odds of groups being labeled gangs (e.g., forms/seriousness of delinquency, characteristics of group members, and contexts where groups function).

Hagedorn (1988) has been particularly critical of gang scholars' acceptance of delinquency-based definitions and maintains that the focus on delinquency has caused much contemporary gang research to focus primarily on trying to understand gang member delinquency and its consequences, rather than examining the context in which gangs develop and how they operate within their communities. The latter approach permits analyses of the function, formation, and disbanding of gangs and thereby recognizes the fluidity of gang involvement. Hagedorn's criticism may be misplaced in that researchers who have accepted the delinquent component of gang definition have documented that gang membership is not a stable phenomenon. Specifically, youths transition in and out of gangs quite readily. Longitudinal studies have found that the typical gang member is in the gang for less than a year. Other literature does not preclude this either and acknowledges that playgroups may at times evolve into gangs and gangs may devolve into non-gang like structures.

The lack of a standard definition regarding what constitutes a gang is problematic and yet holds promise for future research in this area. Bursik and Grasmick (1993) observe that, absent such, it is not possible to put forth definitive statements about the current state of gang involvement or make inferences about purported changes that have taken place over time. Horowitz (1990) notes, nonetheless, that consensus is unlikely and discord concerning definitions may in fact serve as a catalyst for future research in previously unexamined areas. This is an important opportunity for expanding gang research to gang-like groups that might otherwise be excluded from study, or might inadvertently be classified as gangs.

GROUP STRUCTURES AND GANG TYPOLOGIES

The importance of group structure has generated interest among researchers concerned with distinguishing between particular gang types. Specifically, Maxson and Klein (1995) identified five classifications of gangs (traditional, neotraditional, compressed, collective, and specialty) characterized by age range, duration, size, the claiming of territory, the existence of subgroups, and whether offending patterns were specialized or varied. Such typologies are important beyond being extensions of gang definitions, as they clearly demonstrate the diversity of gangs. Recent scholarship on gangs demonstrates the relevance of this issue and recognizes that there is also variation among individual gang members.

Though scholars agree that gang involvement exists on a continuum rather than as an either-or status, most research on gang youth continues to sort these youths into gang versus non-gang categories. Curry et al. (2002) point out that such an approach may fail to acknowledge that there are appreciable differences regarding levels of gang involvement. For instance, scholars have found that most youth, even those who reside in distressed communities with gangs, do not report gang membership. Curry et al. (2002: 283) note that many of these youths, however, acknowledge having "some level of gang involvement," suggesting an intermediary gang status. Because of difficulties

such as this, gang scholars have recently begun to use different methods to determine whether research subjects belonged to gangs.

The variation in approaches to studying gangs has made the pursuit of a unified definition for gang membership less likely. For example, some studies rely upon self-nomination and others utilize official data to determine gang membership. This has important implications for the ability to understand the nature and extent of gang involvement as well as the characteristics of gang members, their behaviors, and where they are more likely to be geographically located.

FEMALE GANG INVOLVEMENT

For much of the history of gang research, gang involvement in most major metropolitan areas was considered a male phenomenon. In fact, scholars have been studying male involvement in gangs since the early 1900s. As recently as a decade ago, however, we had little more than cursory information about females' gang involvement, with few studies offering conclusions that were based on information from young women themselves. Historically, researchers have either stereotyped or simply dismissed as inconsequential young women's involvement in gangs. This is not the case today. The recent expanded focus concerning women's gang involvement brings to light that they are more involved in gangs than was previously thought and that their experiences within the gang are, in fact, rather varied.

Within the past two decades there has been unprecedented interest in the purported growth in the number of gangs across the nation. There has likewise been considerable attention paid to the role of females in that increase. Anne Campbell's (1984) innovative book on New York gang members, *The Girls in the Gang*, along with Joan Moore's (1991) study of Los Angeles gangs, *Going Down to the Barrio*, continue to influence gang scholars' examinations of the lives of gang-involved young women. Contemporary research has also advanced our understanding of young women's lives in the context of their gang membership. It is no mystery that gang-involved youth have garnered the attention of many criminologists who have found that these youths engage in more delinquency than their non-gang peers. In fact, research has demonstrated that gang-involved female youth have higher rates of delinquency than their non-gang peers of either gender.

FUTURE DIRECTIONS IN GANG RESEARCH

Gang members are responsible for a disproportionate amount of crime. Violent and other serious offenses, however, are more likely to come to the attention of the public and result in the misperception that these events are common in the context of gang membership. Involvement in crime accounts for a small portion of gang members' activities. In fact, the majority of their time is spent engaged in activities usually associated with adolescents (i.e., hanging out with friends, playing sports, watching television, and shopping).

It is important for social scientists to expand studies of delinquent youth groups beyond that of the standard gang/non-gang dichotomy, especially since gangs (depending upon how they are defined) account for only a small percentage of delinquent groups. Specifically, there are other delinquent peer groups that are not gangs but also have relevance even in neighborhoods with gangs. These groups also impact adolescent development and should therefore be examined as well.

It is unrealistic to expect that youth in particular types of communities will not have gang-involved family members, neighbors, or peers who they interact with at least minimally. The difficulty of discerning membership in gangs or other delinquent peer groups has implications for those who seek to intervene in the lives of youth. This is particularly important if membership in other groups is a precursor to more serious forms of delinquency or gang membership. If it is difficult for parents, school officials, and even other youth to distinguish between various peer groups and gangs, it must also be troublesome for law enforcement personnel. In fact, young people in certain neighborhood contexts comment frequently regarding their being mistaken by police as gang members.

The responses of law enforcement agents, however, have particular implications for young people. For example, external threats to non-gang peer groups by law enforcement may serve to increase cohesion among members as it has been found to do among gangs. This is important given that suppression efforts have been problematic in addressing gangs that have loose organizational structures. It is likely that this approach would also be troublesome given that other delinquent peer groups are generally less organized than gangs.

Incorrectly responding to non-gang groups of youths as though they were gangs might cause members to be increasingly socially isolated from conventional institutions that could be otherwise beneficial to them. The role of gang membership in the alienation of gang-involved youths from prosocial groups has been observed in the literature. On the other hand, simply ignoring delinquent peer groups who are not gangs is also a strategy fraught with problems.

SEE ALSO: Crime, Organized; Criminology: Research Methods; Ethnography; Feminist Criminology; Gender, Deviance and; Groups; Juvenile Delinquency; Labeling; Popular Culture; Survey Research

REFERENCES AND SUGGESTED READINGS

Bursik, R. J., Jr. & Grasmick, H. G. (1993) *Neighborhoods and Crime: The Dimensions of Effective Community Control.* Lexington Books, New York.

Curry, G. D., Decker, S. H., & Egley, A. (2002) Gang Involvement and Delinquency in a Middle School Population. *Justice Quarterly* 19: 275–92.

Decker, S. H. & Van Winkle, B. (1996) *Life in the Gang: Family, Friends, and Violence.* Cambridge University Press, Cambridge.

Esbensen, F.-A., Tibbetts, S. G., & Gaines, L. (Eds.) (2004) *American Youth Gangs at the Millennium.* Waveland Press, Long Grove, IL.

Hagedorn, J. M. (1988) *People and Folks: Gangs, Crime and the Underclass in a Rustbelt City.* Lake View Press, Chicago.

Horowitz, R. (1990) Sociological Perspectives on Gangs. In: Huff, C. R. (Ed.), *Gangs in America.* Sage, Newbury Park, CA, pp. 37–54.

Klein, M. W. (1971) *Street Gangs and Street Workers.* Prentice-Hall, Englewood Cliffs, NJ.

Miller, J. (2001) *One of the Guys: Girls, Gangs and Gender*. Oxford University Press, New York.

Miller, J. & Brunson, R. K. (2000) Gender Dynamics in Youth Gangs: A Comparison of Males' and Females' Accounts. *Justice Quarterly* 17: 421–48.

Miller, J. A., Maxson, C. L., & Klein, M. W. (Eds.) (2001) *The Modern Gang Reader*. Roxbury, Los Angeles.

Maxson, C. L. & Klein, M. W. (1995) Investigating Gang Structures. *Journal of Gang Research* 3: 33–40.

Thrasher, F. (1927 [1963]). *The Gang*. University of Chicago Press, Chicago.

gay bashing

Michael Smyth and Valerie Jenness

Often subsumed under the contemporary rubric of "hate crime," "gay bashing" denotes the perpetration of violence aimed at people identified as, or assumed to be, homosexual, including gay men, lesbians, bisexuals, and transgendered individuals. Although examples of this type of bias-motivated behavior range from acts of symbolic and rhetorical violence to physical assaults and homicide, selection of the victim based on his or her perceived non-normative sexuality is common to gay bashing in all of its manifestations. The targeting of victims based on perceived sexuality may be seen as a function of perpetrators' hatred for individuals thought to be members of a despised sexual minority. Indeed, gay bashing constitutes a form of victimization and intimidation aimed not only at a primary target, but at the entire group to which that individual is thought to belong.

Violence against people presumed to be homosexual has been documented for as long as the lives of gay men and lesbians have been documented. Boswell (1980), for example, documented violence against gay men and lesbians in Western Europe from the beginning of the Christian era to the fourteenth century. In *Gay American History*, which covers a period of over 400 years, Jack Katz (1976) documented a history of violence directed at individuals because of their sexual orientation, identity, or same-sex behavior. Although recent research indicates that young, otherwise relatively

powerless white males, acting most often in pairs or groups, are the most common perpetrators of physical violence against individuals thought to be homosexual, a variety of individuals, groups, and institutions, ranging from victims' intimates (Island & Lettellier 1991; Renzetti 1992), to strangers (Herek & Berrill 1992), to the state (Fout 1990), religion (Boswell 1980), education (Fone 2000), and medicine (Katz 1976), have been implicated in the perpetration of gay bashing.

In the twenty-first century the incidence of various types of violence against homosexuals occurs globally, across regional and national boundaries, and across cultures and ethnicities. In many countries around the world, particularly in Africa, the Middle East, and Asia, non-normative sexuality is outlawed and those suspected of not being entirely heterosexual are often arrested, imprisoned, and subjected to torture. In addition, many "homosexual" people are beaten, banished, and/or killed by non-official individuals or groups in their own communities, often by their own families or kin. Traditional Islamic law, for example, calls for those committing homosexual acts to be stoned to death or, alternatively, they may be killed by their families as a matter of honor. Commonly, even in countries where the government does not actively participate in, or openly condone, violence against "homosexuals," a climate of homophobia pervades the culture to the extent that, when incidents of gay bashing occur, police and other officials look the other way.

Due in large part to their extreme brutality and ultimately fatal consequences, certain incidents of gay bashing have received widespread public attention. The murder of Matthew Shepard in 1998, for example, garnered unprecedented media coverage in the US after the 21-year-old gay college student was pistol-whipped, tied to a fence, and left to die. His two confessed killers were convicted of murder with aggravating circumstances after separate prosecutors successfully argued that the killing had been motivated by homophobia. Six months later, in 1999, a nail bomb exploded outside the Admiral Duncan, a gay pub in central London. Three pub patrons were killed outright and approximately 80 others injured, some suffering traumatic loss of limbs. Two separate, right-wing splinter groups called the

BBC, claiming responsibility for the attack. Also in 1999, the press reported how the body of Billy Jack Gaither, a 39-year-old textile worker in the US, was burned atop two old tires doused with kerosene after he was beaten to death by two men, who alleged that the openly gay victim had made an unwanted sexual advance toward them. Two years after Gaither's killing, the press began extensive coverage of the events surrounding the murder of Eddie "Gwen" Araujo, a transgender California teenager. After the victim's biological gender was revealed to them, Araujo was initially strangled and subsequently beaten to death by a trio of young men, with whom she/he previously had sexual relations. Ironically, in April 2004, David Morley, former manager of the Admiral Duncan pub, who survived the nail bomb attack in 1999, was beaten to death in London by a group of four teenagers in the fourth fatal incident of gay bashing in that city in as many months.

Notwithstanding their notoriety, fatal examples such as these are not characteristic of the majority of gay bashings. More commonly, victims of gay bashing report being the object of verbal assaults or having objects thrown at them, as well as being chased, kicked, punched, and beaten. A number of self-report studies suggest that the perpetration of these types of non-fatal gay bashing are widespread – a majority of gay men and lesbians indicating that they have experienced either actual or threatened violence because of their sexuality – and that these types of incidents are on the rise (National Gay and Lesbian Task Force 1991; von Schulthess 1992). In addition, the entire population of gay men and lesbians has experienced the sting of rhetorical violence perpetrated by anti-homosexual politicians, religious conservatives, and others voicing a message of intolerance for sexual diversity.

In one of the first government sponsored efforts to assess the scope of anti-"homosexual" violence perpetrated by individuals or groups (as opposed to institutional or state endorsed violence), the US Department of Justice commissioned a report on bias-motivated violence in 1987. That report found that "homosexuals are probably the most frequent victims" of bias motivated violence (cited in Vaid 1995: 11). Shortly after the release of this groundbreaking report, the Federal Bureau of Investigation

(FBI) began to collect data on crimes committed because of bias against homosexuals as part of its larger effort to track bias-crime in the US. Beginning in the early 1990s, the Uniform Crime Report (UCR) documents a consistent pattern of violence directed toward both male and female homosexuals. According to the UCR, although race-based violence is the most frequently reported type of bias-crime in the US, violence based on sexual orientation is a close second. Finally, according to the UCR, reported violence against gay men is more common than violence directed toward lesbians. More recently, analyses of these official data reveal that if one adjusts for population size, homosexuals are the most frequent victims of bias-crime in the US.

In light of its historically ubiquitous and socially pervasive nature, recent research suggests that the portrayal of violence against "homosexuals" solely as a byproduct of hatred may discount the complexity of the phenomenon. Tomsen (2002), for example, found that many perpetrators view anti-homosexual violence not simply as an expression of hatred, but as a means of policing the boundaries of acceptable male sexuality and attaining heightened male status for themselves. In his study of the motives underlying anti-homosexual violence, Tomsen advances the notion that, if we are to accept homophobia as the motive for gay bashing, then our definition of the term must be more broadly conceived "to advance an understanding of the links that such acts of violence ... have to commonplace forms of male identity" as they are construed within an overwhelmingly heteronormative society. In short, to understand gay bashing requires understanding the complexities of a larger sex/gender system in which they are inspired and manifest.

SEE ALSO: Hate Crimes; Homophobia; Homophobia and Heterosexism; Homosexuality; Race (Racism); Sexuality, Masculinity and; Violence

REFERENCES AND SUGGESTED READINGS

Boswell, J. (1980) *Christianity, Social Tolerance, and Homosexuality: Gay People in Western Europe from the Beginning of the Christian Era to the Fourteenth Century*. University of Chicago Press, Chicago.

Fone, B. (2000) *Homophobia: A History.* Picador, New York.

Fout, J. C. (1990) *The Societal Impact of AIDS in the United States: A Select Bibliography of Largely Non-Medical Works.* Annandale-on-Hudson, New York.

Herek, G. M. & Berrill, K. T. (1992) *Hate Crimes: Confronting Violence Against Lesbians and Gay Men.* Sage, Newbury Park, CA.

Island, D. & Letellier, P. (Eds.) (1991). *Men Who Beat the Men Who Love Them: Battered Gay Men and Domestic Violence.* Hawthorne, New York.

Katz, J. (1976) *Gay American History: Lesbians and Gay Men in the USA: A Documentary Anthology.* Crowell, New York.

National Gay and Lesbian Task Force (1991) *Anti-Gay/Lesbian Violence, Victimization, and Defamation in 1990.* National Gay and Lesbian Task Force Policy Institute, Washington, DC.

Renzetti, C. M. (1992) *Violent Betrayal: Partner Abuse in Lesbian Relationships.* Sage, Newbury Park, CA.

Tomsen, S. (2002) *Hatred, Murder and Male Honour: Anti-homosexual Homicides in New South Wales, 1980–2000.* Australian Institute of Criminology, Canberra.

Vaid, U. (1995) *Virtual Equality: The Mainstreaming of Gay and Lesbian Liberation.* Anchor Books, New York.

von Schulthess, B. (1992) Violence in the Streets: Anti-lesbian Assault and Harassment in San Francisco. In: G. Herek and K. Berrill (Eds.), *Hate Crimes: Confronting Violence Against Lesbians and Gay Men.* Sage, Newbury Park, CA, pp. 65–75.

gay gene

Edward Stein

The idea that a gene or set of genes makes some people sexually attracted to people of the same sex has become widely accepted over the past few decades. However, scientific evidence supporting the existence of a gay gene is inconclusive and the political and legal rationale some scientists have for the "search for the gay gene" (Hamer & Copeland 1994) is dubious.

Early in the twentieth century, geneticist Richard Goldschmidt (1916) suggested that the bodies of homosexuals did not "match" their sex chromosomes. According to this hypothesis, which was accepted by many people, gay men have female-typical sex chromosomes and lesbians have male-typical sex chromosomes.

This hypothesis was shown to be false about 40 years after Goldschmidt proposed it (Pare 1956) and it is not accepted even by those who believe in the existence of a gay gene.

Today, some scientists continue to look for genes that account for differences in sexual orientations. The search for the gay gene is at least initially plausible for various reasons, in particular, in light of several recent scientific studies that purport to show that sexual orientations are biologically based and that this biological basis is inborn or determined at an early age (LeVay 1996; Stein 1999: ch. 5). The most prominent study in the search for the gay gene was done by Hamer and colleagues (1993) and it is supposed to support the conclusion that a region of the X chromosome codes for male homosexuality.

Inside of each person's cells is an elaborate chain of DNA that is like a recipe for how to make that person's body. Isolating the role that a portion of genetic material plays in the development of a human is complicated, although the Human Genome Project has recently succeeded in doing just that. Identifying the specific genetic material that leads to complex psychological traits like a person's sexual dispositions is, however, much more difficult. There are, however, less direct ways to get evidence concerning the genetic basis of a trait besides isolating specific genetic material. One way to determine whether a trait is genetic is to study different types of twins. Identical twins have the exact same genes. Fraternal twins, though like identical twins in that they are born at the same time, are only as closely related as two non-twin biological siblings are. Because identical twins are genetically identical, differences in characteristics between them must be due to differences in their pre- or post-natal environment, *not* their genes. This inference does not work in the other direction. If identical twins have the same trait, one cannot infer that this trait is genetic. If identical twins share a trait, it might be because they were raised in the same environment. For example, if both members of most pairs of identical twins know the Ten Commandments, this does not show that knowing the Ten Commandments is genetic. Applying these observations to sexual orientation, several studies suggest that sexual orientation runs in families (Pillard & Weinrich

1986; Pillard 1990). These studies indicate, for example, that the brother of a gay man is more likely to be gay than the brother of a straight man. These studies do not, however, establish that sexual orientation is genetic because most siblings, in addition to sharing about 50 percent of their genes, typically share many environmental variables.

To quantify the extent to which a trait is inherited, scientists have developed the concept of heritability, which represents the extent to which a trait was caused by genetic factors. Heritability is the ratio of genetically caused variation to the total variation among individuals with the trait. Heritability concerns the extent to which differences among people regarding a characteristic are caused by genetic differences. The heritability of a trait is importantly different from whether a trait is genetically determined; it captures some, but not all, aspects of our intuitive sense of genetic causation.

Consider one example. Having 10 fingers is a paradigmatic example of a trait that is genetically determined. The heritability of number of fingers is, however, quite low because having fewer than 10 fingers is typically due to environmental factors not correlated with genetic factors. Most cases of not having 10 fingers (though not all) are due to problems in fetal development (e.g., caused by the sleeping pill thalidomide) or to accidents (e.g., caused while cutting a bagel). The heritability of having fewer than 10 fingers is calculated by dividing the number of people who have fewer than 10 fingers due to genetic factors by the total number of people with fewer than 10 fingers. Since far more people have fewer than 10 fingers because of non-genetic causes, the heritability of this trait will be low, despite the fact that having 10 fingers seems like a paradigmatic example of a trait that is genetically determined. The heritability of a trait is contingent on features of the environment. In an environment in which no one took thalidomide or cut off a finger accidentally, the heritability of having less than 10 fingers would be much higher. This highlights the difference between showing that a trait is heritable and showing that a trait is genetically determined (Stein 1999: 140–4).

Sophisticated heritability studies have been done to assess sexual orientation in same-sex identical twins, same-sex fraternal twins,

same-sex non-twin biological siblings, and similarly-aged unrelated adopted siblings (Bailey & Pillard 1991; Bailey et al. 1993). The idea behind these studies is that if sexual orientation is genetic, then identical twins should have the same sexual orientation and the rate of homosexuality among the adopted siblings should be equal to the rate of homosexuality in the general population. If, on the other hand, identical twins are as likely to have the same sexual orientation as adopted siblings, then genetic factors make very little contribution to sexual orientation. In these studies, subjects were recruited through ads placed in gay publications that asked for gay or bisexual volunteers with twin or adoptive siblings of the same sex. Subjects were asked to rate their own sexual orientation, the sexual orientation of their relatives, and for permission to contact their siblings. In both heritability studies the concordance rates for identical twins were substantially higher than for fraternal twins. For example, 48 percent of the identical twins of lesbians were themselves lesbians, as were 16 percent of the fraternal twins, 14 percent of the non-twin biological sisters, and 6 percent of the adoptive sisters (Bailey et al. 1993).

While these results are consistent with a genetic effect, there are various problems with these studies (Byne & Parson 1993; Stein 1999: 148–53), including biases in the sample populations. For, example the twin studies would lose their significance if gay men with gay identical twins are more likely to volunteer for such studies than are gay men with gay fraternal twins (Stein 1999: 191–5).

Building on the twin studies, Hamer and colleagues (1993) endeavored to isolate the portion of the human genome responsible for sexual orientation. Starting with the idea that homosexuality runs in families and is heritable, he recruited gay men using the same methods as the twin studies. Hamer's survey of this population pointed to a distinctive distribution of male homosexuality in his subjects' families: men on the mother's side of gay men's families were more likely to also be gay than men on the father's side. This pattern among gay men's families suggested to Hamer that male homosexuality, like, for example, color blindness, is inherited from one's mother in virtue of being carried on the X chromosome.

To test the hypothesis that there is a gene for homosexuality on the X chromosome, Hamer created a pool of subjects apparently enriched for the gene he was looking for and obtained DNA samples from two gay brothers in each of these families. These samples were then analyzed using linkage analysis to determine how frequently the brothers had matching genetic material in the X chromosome. Linkage analysis is a technique for narrowing the location of a gene using DNA "markers," which act like signposts scattered throughout the human genome. This technique enables scientists to determine the likelihood that two people share genetic material in a stretch of DNA. Hamer found a higher than expected percentage of the pairs of gay brothers had matching genetic sequences in a portion of the q28 region of the X chromosome (82 percent rather than 50 percent). While Hamer did not identify a particular genetic sequence associated with homosexuality, he did find that many of the pairs of homosexual brothers had matching genetic sequences in a region of the X chromosome.

There are several problems with Hamer's study. First, two independent research teams have failed to replicate his results (Bailey et al. 1993; Rice et al. 1999). The only replication was by Hamer's own group (Hu et al. 1995). Second, Hamer's study suffers from the same sort of sampling problems as the twin studies. Third, several commentators have expressed concerns about the most significant result of Hamer's research, namely, the increased rate of homosexuality on the mother's side of the gay men's families. Some have said that the different rate of homosexuality among maternal and paternal relatives is not statistically significant (Risch et al. 1993; McGuire 1995). Further, geneticist Neil Risch has suggested that the increased rate of homosexuality on the maternal side of gay men's families could be due to the fact that gay men are less likely to have offspring than men who are not gay. To see this, suppose that there is a gene that, in certain environments, tends to cause men to be gay and suppose that it is *not* carried on the X chromosome. Even so, in such environments, people would be less likely to inherit such a gene from their fathers because the gene, by hypothesis, tends to cause men to be gay, and gay men are less likely to have offspring than

other men. Thus, a gene linked to male homosexuality would appear maternally linked even if such a gene was not on the X chromosome.

More generally, linkage analysis is best suited for discovering the genetic basis of traits controlled in a genetically simple manner rather than traits that are controlled by several genes working in concert. This technique has mistakenly indicated that a specific genetic sequence plays a role in the development of a particular trait (Bailey 1995). Such mistakes are especially likely in the case of genetically complex traits, cognitively mediated psychological/behavioral traits, or those strongly affected by environmental factors. For these general reasons linkage analysis does not seem a promising technique for the study of sexual orientation.

These concerns aside, Hamer's study simply does not justify talk about gay genes. Genes in themselves cannot directly cause a behavior or a psychological phenomenon. Genes direct RNA synthesis that in turn leads to the production of a protein that in turn may influence the development of psychological dispositions and particular behaviors. There are many intervening pathways between a gene and a behavior or a behavioral disposition, and even more intervening variables between a gene and a cognitively mediated behavior. The concept "gay gene" has no meaning unless one proposes that a particular gene, perhaps through a hormonal mechanism, organizes the brain specifically to support the desire to have sex with people of the same sex (Byne 1996). No one has presented evidence in support of such a simple and direct link between genes and sexual orientation (Allen 1997; Byne 1996; Stein 1999: ch. 7).

In light of this, why are so many people interested in finding the gay gene? For many, including some scientists, the motivation is the legal/ethical/political intuition that proof of a gay gene would establish the wrongness of discrimination against lesbians, gay men, and bisexuals and the wrongness of withholding from them legal and social benefits that heterosexuals take for granted (LeVay 1996). There are several problems with this intuition (Hamer & Copeland 1994: ch. 13; Allen 1997; Stein 1999: chs. 10–12). First, even if there is a gay gene, a person's public identity, sexual activities, romantic relationships, and involvement in childrearing are all not determined by genes even according to those who believe in a gay gene. Even if there is a gay gene, society could enforce extreme legal and social sanctions against lesbians, gay men, and bisexuals for their behaviors, identifications, and public expressions. Many human characteristics believed to be genetic – like dispositions toward disease, mental illness, or alcoholism – are highly stigmatized and people go to great lengths to avoid them. Even if there was a gay gene, homosexuality might still be deemed a disease or a socially undesirable characteristic, which might result in pressure to "cure" or prevent the birth of homosexuals. The search for the gay gene is thus not only scientifically unproven, but the legal and political motivations for this research are questionable and the social implications of this research are uncertain.

SEE ALSO: Essentialism and Constructionism; Homosexuality; Medical Sociology and Genetics; Sexuality Research: History; Sexuality Research: Methods

REFERENCES AND SUGGESTED READINGS

Allen, G. (1997) The Double-Edged Sword of Genetic Determinism: Social and Political Agendas in Genetic Studies of Homosexuality, 1940–1994. In: Rosario, V. (Ed.), *Science and Homosexualities*. Routledge, New York.

Bailey, J. M. (1995) Biological Perspectives on Sexual Orientation. In: D'Augeli, A. & Patterson, C. (Eds.), *Lesbian, Gay and Bisexual Identities over the Lifespan*. Oxford University Press, New York.

Bailey, J. M. & Pillard, R. (1991) A Genetic Study of Male Sexual Orientation. *Archives of General Psychiatry* 48:1089–96.

Bailey, J. M., Pillard, R., & Agyei, Y. (1993) Heritable Factors Influence Sexual Orientation in Woman. *Archives of General Psychiatry* 50: 217–23.

Byne, W. (1996) Biology and Sexual Orientation. In: Cabaj, R. & Stein, T. (Eds.), *Comprehensive Textbook of Homosexuality*. American Psychiatric Press, Washington, DC.

Byne, W. & Parsons, B. (1993) Human Sexual Orientation: The Biologic Theories Reappraised. *Archives of General Psychiatry* 50: 228–39.

Goldschmidt, R. (1916) Die biologischen Grundlagen der kontraren Sexualitat und des Hermaphroditismus beim Menschen (The Biological Foundation of Sexual Inversion and Hermaphroditism). *Archiv fur Rassen- und Gesellschafts-Biologie* (Archive for Racial and Social Biology) 12: 1–14.

Hamer, D. & Copeland, P. (1994) *The Science of Desire: The Search for the Gay Gene and the Biology of Behavior.* Simon & Schuster, New York.

Hamer, D., Hu, S., Magnuson, V., Hu, N., & Pattatucci, A. (1993) A Linkage Between DNA Markers on the X Chromosome and Male Sexual Orientation. *Science* 321–7.

Horgan, J. (1993) Eugenics Revisited. *Scientific American* 268: 122–31.

Hu, S. et al. (1995) Linkage Between Sexual Orientation and Chromosome Xq28 in Males But Not in Females. *Nature Genetics* 11: 248–56.

LeVay, S. (1996) *Queer Science: The Use and Abuse of Research into Homosexuality.* MIT Press, Cambridge, MA.

McGuire, T. (1995) Is Homosexuality Genetic? A Critical Review and Some Suggestions. *Journal of Homosexuality* 28: 115–45.

Pare, C. M. B. (1956) Homosexuality and Chromosomal Sex. *Journal of Psychosomatic Research* 1: 247–51.

Pillard, R. (1990) The Kinsey Scale: Is It Familial? In: McWhirter, D. P., Saunders, S. A., & Reinisch, J. M. (Eds.), *Homosexuality/Heterosexuality: Concepts of Sexual Orientation.* Oxford University Press, New York.

Pillard, R. & Weinrich, J. (1986) Evidence of Familial Nature of Male Homosexuality. *Archives of General Psychiatry* 43: 808–12.

Rice, G. et al. (1999) Male Homosexuality: Absence of Linkage in Microsatellite Markers at Xq28. *Science* 284: 665–7.

Risch, N. & Merikangas, K. R. (1993) Linkage Studies of Psychiatric Disorders. *European Archives of Psychiatry and Clinical Neuroscience* 243: 143–9.

Risch, N., Squires-Wheeler, E., & Keats, B. J. B. (1993) Male Sexual Orientation and Genetic Evidence. *Science* 262: 2063–5.

Stein, E. (1999) *The Mismeasure of Desire: The Science, Theory and Ethics of Sexual Orientation.* Oxford University Press, New York.

gay and lesbian movement

Stephen Valocchi

The gay and lesbian movement refers to the manifold collective efforts to benefit people with same-sex desire. Although an organized movement first appeared in Germany in the late nineteenth century, this effort was shortlived. The first sustained activities, organizations, and network building for the positive recognition of lesbians and gays and the improvement of their social and political conditions appeared in the United States in the 1940s and 1950s with the establishment of three organizations: the Mattachine Society, an organization for men which devoted itself mainly to social support in a climate of profound public hostility; the Daughters of Bilitis, an organization that concerned itself with the unique challenges of women with same-sex desire at a time when women were supposed to be dependent on men for economic and social support; and One Inc., which existed only as a monthly magazine and promoted the view that gay people, rather than psychiatrists or lawyers, are the most qualified to speak for themselves. With the exception of One Inc., these organizations stressed respectability and the desire to be accepted into mainstream society.

In the 1960s, the gay and lesbian movement entered a new phase as social movements created a more militant climate for disenfranchised groups in the United States and forced the movement to shift its focus, strategy, and goals. Following the Stonewall Riots of 1969 sparked by a routine police raid on a gay bar in Greenwich Village in New York City, the movement devoted itself to two somewhat conflicting goals: the pursuit of a variety of civil rights reforms, from the passage of anti-discrimination legislation to the elimination of sodomy laws, and the pursuit of fundamental social change aimed at eradicating homophobia, heterosexism, and sexual repression. The Gay Activists Alliance was most closely associated with the former pursuit, the Gay Liberation Front with the latter. By the end of the 1970s, the liberationist impulse had dissipated but the rights-based approach proved somewhat successful. At both the local and state levels, people joined organizations and promoted initiatives to combat discrimination against gays and lesbians. The strategy of "coming out of the closet," making public one's identity as gay or lesbian, contributed to this rights-based focus since it helped build a group identity, thus giving gays and lesbians access to similar language of pride and positive strategies used by other minoritized groups.

The development of the movement during this time cannot be told without reference to the tensions between men and women in the movement and to their subsequently different trajectories of community building. Post-Stonewall collaboration between men and women was sporadic as women experienced homophobia in women's liberation groups and sexism in men-led gay groups. Nonetheless, the profound influence of the women's movement led many women to build lesbian feminist organizations identified more by women's resistance to patriarchy than by women's sexual desire for other women. This tendency led in the 1980s to the development of women-identified institutions, from bookstores and cafés to sexual assault and rape crisis centers. During this same time gay men were building their own networks of community institutions, but these were of a more commercialized nature in the form of bars, nightclubs, neighborhoods, and sex clubs.

Given the association of gay men with a liberalized sexual culture and lesbians with feminism, it is not surprising that the visibility of the gay and lesbian movement in the late 1970s and 1980s led to the rise of a significant countermovement in the form of the religious right. Their many campaigns directed at state and local gay civil rights ordinances were successful not only in reversing some of these gains, but also, perhaps more importantly, in reviving the rhetoric of immorality from the earlier pre-Stonewall era. This countermovement and the election of a conservative Republican administration in 1980 left the movement vulnerable and the community without political support when AIDS starting killing thousands of gay men.

The AIDS epidemic had several consequences for the movement. First, issues of treatment, care, and funding came to dominate the agenda of the movement in the 1980s and early 1990s. Second, it led to the establishment of a dense network of AIDS service, advocacy, and treatment organizations that emerged fairly rapidly due to the already established community- and health-based resources of the gay and lesbian community. Third, its widespread impact brought many more people into the movement and propelled the movement into a period of heightened mobilization. Fourth, because of the involvement of many lesbians in this new mobilization and in those care-giving organizations, it led to a closer association between men and women in movement initiatives than had been the case since the 1970s.

The epidemic was also partly responsible for a brief but notable shift in focus for some segments of the movement in the 1990s. Dissatisfied with its narrowly rights-focused, assimilation-based goals, a new militancy invigorated the movement, first in the form of ACTUP (AIDS Coalition to Unleash Power), then with organizations such as Queer Nation and the Lesbian Avengers. These organizations rejected the standard definitions of gay, claimed the more non-normative moniker of "queer," and embraced direct action strategies that were directed both at social institutions like the government and the medical establishment and at the general culture, seen by these activists as homophobic, sexist, and anti-pleasure.

Various internal challenges also characterized the movement at this time, all of which signaled a loosening of the dominant identity categories of gay and lesbian. Women and men of color, bisexuals, and transgendered activists challenged the white middle-class nature of the movement and its notion of a fixed salient identity defined by sex of object choice and insisted the movement take their concerns seriously. Many women in the 1990s also rebelled against the rigid definitions of lesbian feminism by rejecting the androgynous styles and sex-negative attitudes of some segments of this community, embracing leather and sadomasochist sexual repertoires and reviving and re-eroticizing butch–femme modes of style and embodiment.

The most recent developments in the lesbian and gay movement can be understood against the backdrop of the somewhat more favorable political climate of the 1990s, the heightened cultural visibility of gays and lesbians in the media, and the growth of centralized advocacy organizations. Taken together, these developments led the movement to pursue several top-down policy initiatives with more resources and with a wider set of strategies than ever before. The issue of gays in the military consumed much of the movement's attention throughout this period: first in organizing to push President Clinton to make good on his

campaign promise to end discrimination against gays and lesbians; then in trying to undo the damage done by Clinton's "don't ask, don't tell" policy, which had the effect of expelling from the military men and women who expressed any statement of same-sex desire. Most recently, the movement and the nation have been captivated by the push to legalize same-sex marriages in the United States. Partly in response to court challenges in Hawaii and Massachusetts, the movement has marshaled tremendous resources to support these lawsuits, to prevent anti-same-sex marriage bills from being introduced into state legislatures and in Congress, and to push for civil unions, domestic partnerships, and bona fide marriage. Both of these policy initiatives – gays in the military and same-sex marriage – signal a decided return to a rights-based, assimilation-focused orientation to the gay and lesbian movement.

As is the case with any number of social movements, the gay and lesbian movement presents sociologists with opportunities to study the dynamics of collective action: the conditions that led to its emergence, the internal development of resources, community, and consciousness, the framing strategies the movement uses, the relationship between the collective identity and the goals the movement seeks, and the factors affecting success and failure.

Until the late 1980s, with a couple of exceptions (Adam 1978; Altman 1971), the gay and lesbian movement was not systematically studied by sociologists. Until that time homosexuality was mainly studied in the context of deviance, subcultural formations, and the formation of a homosexual identity via symbolic interaction. It was mainly the impact of the social movements of the 1960s that transformed sociology's understanding of homosexuality from a deviance perspective to the study of a minority group. It was also due to the development of theoretical frameworks that viewed collective action not as a consequence of collective alienation but as politics by other means. Resource mobilization and political process approaches called attention to the structure of opportunities in the political environment and the quantity and quality of resources of the constituency which in turn affect the emergence and success of social movements directed mainly at the state. New social movement approaches emphasize a wide array of post-scarcity movements, sometimes organized on the basis of social identities and directed not primarily to the state but to challenge "stigmatizing public discourses and representations" (Seidman 1993: 108) of different social groups. Both frameworks informed sociologists' study of the gay and lesbian movement.

Since the 1980s sociologists who have studied the movement have focused on five sets of issues. The first set involves research on the structural conditions that led to the emergence of an organized movement. This research has stressed the importance of the rise of industrial capitalism, changes in the nature of the family accompanying capitalism, the impact of bureaucracy on intimacy among men, and the rise of medical science. These factors taken together had contradictory consequences: on the one hand, they created the contexts whereby individuals with same-sex eroticism could turn that practice into an identity and find others in urban areas who did the same. On the other hand, these same factors named the identity as pathological, established a medical and regulatory apparatus to police the identity, and created the (homo)phobia regarding expressions of same-sex emotional intimacy or sexual expression. These conditions generated the political opportunities, resources, and grievances that led to mobilization on the basis of a sexual identity defined by sex of object choice.

A second set of issues involves research on the goals of the movement. The initial impulse of the movement had been the desire to change the way the culture views homosexuality: the movement emerged in a society that saw homosexuality as sin, sickness, or crime. Later, the movement shifted to working for civil rights through the state and other social institutions. This dual emphasis of the movement on changing culture and changing laws and policies makes it an interesting case study for sociologists since it allows them to engage issues of reform versus structural change, assimilation versus transformation. Work on this issue has focused on specifying the historically variable conditions that influence whether movement actors will focus on politics, culture, or some combination of the two. This research strategy brings together the concerns of political process

and resource mobilization approaches with political climate, resources, and networks and the concerns of new social movements' perspectives on changing norms and belief systems and with building a collective identity.

The third set of research issues involves the ways that the movement constructs and reconstructs collective identity. Collective identity refers to the shared definition of a group that derives from members' common interests, experiences, and solidarity. Another unique feature of the gay and lesbian movement derived from the socially constructed nature of sexuality is its concern with defining the constituency: who is the "we" that the movement represents? This feature has proven more pressing as conflicts between men and women, and battles over the inclusion of bisexual, transgendered, and intersexed persons have taken place. These battles are about the collective identity of the movement. Research on this issue seeks to explain how the boundaries are established and who gets to police them. It focuses on the material, organizational, and symbolic factors such as the class interests supporting the collective identity, the organizational structure that prevents other competing definitions from taking shape, and the symbolic messages embedded in the collective identity about "respectability" that is then communicated to the larger culture.

Related to this set of issues is a fourth focus on framing. Framing refers to "an interpretive schemata" (Snow & Benford 1992: 137) that distills the message or messages of the movement for several purposes: to recruit a constituency, create a collective identity, craft strategy, and gain outside support. Framing is fraught with dilemmas for all social movements since frames try to satisfy a number of potentially conflicting agendas. For the gay and lesbian movement, this is particularly significant given its framing as both a political and a cultural movement, the fractious nature of the collective identity, and the strength of the countermovement. Research on this issue has typically demonstrated the tensions occurring between a civil rights framing strategy – a dominant frame of many social movements – and other strategies derived from the varied nature of the movement. Frames such as sexual liberation or institutional heterosexism have competed with the civil rights frame, and these competing frames rise and fall in tandem with internal struggles around collective identity and the external opportunity structure.

A fifth focus is the impact of queer theory and politics on the study of the gay and lesbian movement. Queer theory has called attention to the instability of sex and gender categories and stresses the performative nature of identities thought to be rooted in anatomy or culture. Queer politics extends this deconstructive analysis and critiques the gay and lesbian movement for its essentialist definition of sexual identity, its construction of exclusionary boundaries, and its stabilization of the identities of gay and lesbian. According to this critique, identity-based strategies for social change deny the fluidity inherent in sexuality and invalidate the experiences of others with non-normative sexuality who may not easily fit the class and race or western-inflected definition of the identity. In addition, identity-based strategies reinforce the boundaries between gay and straight, man and woman, and thus reproduce the hierarchical relationship between the dominant and the subordinate terms of the sex/gender system. This challenge to the essentialist model of sexual identity of the traditional gay and lesbian movement was first made by ACTUP with its boundary-crossing and label-disrupting tactics and by bisexual and transgendered people who exemplify the kind of boundary crossing embraced by queer politics.

Research on the movement that has used queer insights has focused on the internal and external pressures that affect when identity-stabilizing and identity-deconstructing frames and strategies will be used, noting both the concrete gains made through interest group politics and the cultural challenges made through identity-blurring queer politics. A queer-inflected understanding of social movements has also broadened the repertoire of collective action to include strategies such as political theater, performance art, and drag. This broadening dovetails with the cultural concerns of the movement as well as with the deconstruction of sexual and gender identities that now informs some segments of the contemporary movement. The challenge for sociologists in our future work is to extend, refocus, or alter our theoretical models of emergence, development, and impact to explain collective

action repertoires as diverse as the sit-down strikes of the 1930s and the drag shows of the twenty-first century.

SEE ALSO: Collective Identity; Culture, Social Movements and; Framing and Social Movements; Homophobia; Homophobia and Heterosexism; Lesbian Feminism; New Social Movement Theory; Political Process Theory; Queer Theory; Resource Mobilization Theory; Social Movements

REFERENCES AND SUGGESTED READINGS

Adam, B. D. (1978) *The Rise of a Gay and Lesbian Movement*. Twayne, Boston.
Altman, D. (1993 [1971]) *Homosexual: Oppression and Liberation*. New York University Press, New York.
Armstrong, E. A. (2002) *Forging Gay Identities: Organizing Sexuality in San Francisco, 1950–1994*. University of Chicago Press, Chicago.
Bernstein, M. (1997) Celebration and Suppression: The Strategic Uses of Identity by the Lesbian and Gay Movement. *American Journal of Sociology* 103: 531–65.
Bernstein, M. (2002) Identities and Politics: Toward a Historical Understanding of the Lesbian and Gay Movement. *Social Science History*.
Broad, K. L. (2002) GLB+T? Gender/Sexuality Movements and Transgender Collective Identity (De)Constructions. *International Journal of Sexuality and Gender Studies* 7(4): 241–64.
Cohen, C. J. (1996) Contested Membership: Black Gay Identities and the Politics of AIDS. In: Seidman, S. (Ed.), *Queer Theory/Sociology*. Blackwell, Cambridge, MA.
D'Emilio, J. (1983) *Sexual Politics, Sexual Communities: The Making of a Homosexual Minority in the United States, 1940–1970*. University of Chicago Press, Chicago.
Epstein, S. (1999) Gay and Lesbian Movements in the United States: Dilemmas of Identity, Diversity, and Political Strategy. In: Adam, B. D., Duyvendick, J. W., & Krouvel, A. (Eds.), *The Global Emergence of Gay and Lesbian Politics: National Imprints of a Worldwide Movement*. Temple University Press, Philadelphia, pp. 30–90.
Gamson, J. (1995) Must Identity Movements Self-Destruct? A Queer Dilemma. *Social Problems* 42: 390–407.
Gamson, J. (1997) Messages of Exclusion: Gender, Movements, and Symbolic Boundaries. *Social Problems* 11(2): 178–99.

Rimmerman, C. A. (2002) *From Identity to Politics: The Lesbian and Gay Movement in the United States.* Temple University Press, Philadelphia.

Rupp, L. J. & Taylor, V. (2003) *Drag Queens at the 801 Cabaret.* University of Chicago Press, Chicago.

Seidman, S. (1993) Identity Politics in a "Postmodern" Gay Culture: Some Historical and Conceptual Notes. In: Warner, M. (Ed.), *Fear of a Queer Planet: Queer Politics and Social Theory.* University of Minnesota Press, Minneapolis, pp. 105–42.

Snow, D. A. & Benford, R. D. (1992) Master Frames and Cycles of Protest. In: Morris, A. D. & Mueller, C. M. (Eds.), *Frontiers in Social Movement Theory.* Yale University Press, New Haven, pp. 133–55.

Snow, D. A., Burke Rochford, E., Jr., Worden, S. K., & Benford, R. D. (1986) Frame Alignment Processes, Micro-Mobilization, and Movement Participation. *American Sociological Review* 51: 464–81.

Stein, A. (1997) *Sex and Sensibility: Stories of a Lesbian Generation.* University of California Press, Berkeley.

Taylor, V. & Whittier, N. E. (1992) Collective Identity in Social Movement Communities: Lesbian Feminist Mobilization. In: Morris, A. D. & McClurg Mueller, C., (Eds.), *Frontiers in Social Movement Theory.* Yale University Press, New Haven, pp. 104–29.

Valocchi, S. (1999a) The Class-Inflected Nature of Gay Identity. *Social Problems* 46(2): 207–24.

Valocchi, S. (1999b) Riding the Crest of the Protest Wave? Collective Action Frames in the Gay Liberation Movement, 1969–1973. *Mobilization* 4(1): 59–74.

Gellner, Ernst (1925–95)

Rodanthi Tzanelli

Perhaps one of the most prolific scholars of the twentieth century, Ernst Gellner remains a highly influential figure across many disciplines (sociology, history, anthropology, and philosophy). He was born in Paris, but was of Czech Jewish parentage and he grew up in Czechoslovakia. In 1939, with the resurgence of anti-Semitism in Central Europe, he moved to England, where he spent most of his life. During World War II he served in the Czechoslovakian Armored Brigade (1944–5), and later

he returned to Oxford, where he received a degree in politics, philosophy, and economics. From 1949 until 1984 he was in the department of sociology at the London School of Economics (LSE), where he completed his doctorate in social anthropology (1961) and became professor of philosophy (1962–84). He was, among other things, Visiting Fellow at Harvard (1952–3), the University of California, Berkeley (1968), and the Centre de Recherches et d'Études sur les Sociétés Méditerranéens (1978–9), member of the Social Science Research Council (1980–6), and Chairman of the International Activities Committee (1982–4). Between 1993 and 1995 he was Director of the Centre for the Study of Nationalism at the Central European University in Prague, where he died in 1995.

Gellner's initial philosophical inquiry involved a critique of linguistic philosophy as conservative, parochial, and restrictive. His *Words and Things* (1959) suggested a sociohistorical approach to theory, which contextualizes schools of thought and questions the ideological subtext of their theses. His critical approach to intellectual production and its sociopolitical origins, which was exemplified in his critique of Oxford philosophical parochialism, earned him many friends and enemies in the social sciences. The same critical spirit guided his pen later, when he reconsidered other hegemonic systems of thought, such as Islamism, psychoanalysis, relativism, and hermeneutics. An early application of this formula can be seen in *Thought and Change* (1964), where Gellner suggested that nationalism legitimates social order, especially in countries in which modernization led to social fragmentation. This Marxist conception of nationalism as a hegemonic product was reconsidered and modified by Gellner himself in his later work, but was never wholly abandoned.

Gellner's anthropological explorations began with *The Saints of Atlas* (1969), a study of Moroccan Berbers and their system of thought. In this study, Gellner defended the value of Berber conceptual frameworks of the world that contest institutional structures derived from the centralized Moroccan state model but enable an organization of social life based on indigenous beliefs. The same themes of local knowledge and hegemonic thought, particularity and fabricated universality occupied Gellner in *Patrons and Clients* (1977) and *Muslim Society* (1981). Likewise, he developed an interest in Soviet anthropology and its theoretical subtleties that were depreciated by western Marxists. His edited volume *Soviet and Western Anthropology* (1980) marks an attempt to bring together different ways of implementing Marxism in the social sciences. His interest in Soviet politics and society found renewed expression in *Conditions of Liberty: Civil Society and its Rivals* (1994), in which he offered a brilliant reassessment of Marxism through an investigation of the conditions of modernity. *Conditions of Liberty* is deemed to be one of the most scholarly contributions in the study of civil society and its future in a post-communist Russia overtaken by market values.

Gellner had a longstanding interest in the phenomenon of nationalism and its different manifestations in Western, Central, Southern European and other, non-European, societies. In *Nations and Nationalism* (1983) and *Nationalism* (1997) he examined the rise of nationalism as an ideal that advocates the dominance of a uniform culture. Revising or revisiting some of the ideas he introduced in the 1950s, he argued that nations emerge when local cultures are replaced by the culture of the "nation," which assimilates or eradicates deviating ways of living. Often, but not always, identifying the nation with the nation-state, Gellner located the emergence of national culture in the modern conditions that prevailed with the extinction of close-knit, agrarian communities and the advance of industrialization that resulted in social mobility and alienation. In this context, citizenship became the primary loyalty of the nation's participants. A homogeneous educational system that promotes common traditions, beliefs, and language is sustained by the ruling elites, so that the nation's members, equally educated, can move flexibly between places and roles without compromising the nation's solidarity. At times Gellner replaces the industrialization model with the advent of Enlightenment rationality; a modernist at heart, he located the emergence of national identity in the post-Enlightenment era. Gellner's theory was criticized by Anthony Smith, one of his students and a defender of the ethnic, historical origins of nations (an argument encapsulated in Smith's concept of *ethnie*). In October 1995 an open debate was held at the University of Warwick between Gellner and Smith, in which Gellner defended the civic model of nationalism in opposition to Smith's ethnic model. The Gellner–Smith dialogue was published in *Nations and Nationalism* (1996), the journal of the Association for the Study of Ethnicity and Nationalism based at the LSE and chaired by Smith, in 1996. Gellner was invited to continue this debate at the LSE, but he died a few months before the event.

For some, Gellner's research trajectory appears to be fragmented and lacking a coherent agenda. This is partially because his interests spanned many disciplines and subject areas. Often, Gellner changed his views on phenomena he analyzed, or developed ideas that initially appeared in the form of essays, rather than extensive monographs. His work, however, has been influential in sociology and social anthropology, and still informs the study of culture, nationalism, and modern identity.

SEE ALSO: Ethnicity; Marxism and Sociology; Modernization; Nation-State; Nationalism

REFERENCES AND SUGGESTED READINGS

Gellner, E. (1959) *Words and Things: A Critical Account of Linguistic Philosophy and a Study in Ideology*. Gollancz, London.

Gellner, E. (1964) *Thought and Change*. Weidenfeld & Nicolson, London.

Gellner, E. (1969) *The Saints of Atlas*. University of Chicago Press, Chicago.

Gellner, E. (1974) *Contemporary Thought and Politics*. Routledge & Kegan Paul, London.

Gellner, E. (Ed.) (1980) *Soviet and Western Anthropology*. Columbia University Press, New York.

Gellner, E. (1981) *Muslim Society*. Cambridge University Press, Cambridge.

Gellner, E. (1983) *Nations and Nationalism*. Blackwell, Oxford.

Gellner, E. (1994) *Conditions of Liberty: Civil Society and its Rivals*. Hamish Hamilton, London.

Gellner, E. (1997) *Nationalism*. Weidenfeld & Nicolson, London.

Gellner, E. & Waterbury, J. (Eds.) (1977) *Patrons and Clients*. Duckworth, London.

Lessnoff, M. (2002) *Ernest Gellner and Modernity*. University of Wales Press, Cardiff.

Smith, A. (1991) *National Identity*. Penguin, London.
The Warwick Debates (1996) The Nation: Imagined
or Real? Republished from *Nations and Nationalism*. Online. www.members.tripod.com.

gender, aging and

Toni Calasanti

Interest and research in gender and aging have
progressed through a variety of different phases,
each spurred by developments in both feminist
scholarship and aging studies. While each stage
has emerged from the previous, all can be found
in contemporary theory and research.

The first stage, which can be further subdi-
vided into two approaches, involved a focus
on women. Spurred by the 1970s women's
movement, in the early 1980s some scholars of
aging began to question the lack of explicit
attention paid to aging women. This was
obvious in such topic areas as retirement, where
women were routinely excluded from research.
Even national, large-scale data sets, such as the
longitudinal retirement study undertaken by
the Social Security Administration in the
1970s, only included women as primary respondents after their husbands had died. The presumed split between private and public spheres
fostered a belief that paid labor was central only
to men's identities and that, for women, retirement was either irrelevant or unimportant.

Two attempts to address the neglect of
women in aging research ensued, each representing a somewhat different approach. The
first simply added women to research. Similar
to what had occurred in other areas of sociology,
scholars began to include women in studies or
investigate them on their own. However, this
"add women and stir" tactic simply placed
women into models and theories that derived
from men's experiences. Conceptually, gender
remained an individual attribute, a demographic characteristic with no structural properties.
For example, noting differences between men
and women's labor force participation histories
led to the conclusion that women's intermittent
work histories result in lower retirement benefits. Why and how women's work histories

differed, or why policies such as Social Security
or defined-benefit plans rewarded stable labor
force participation were neither questioned nor
explored. Similarly, the equation of workforce
participation with adequate retirement finances
assumed a gender-neutral workplace in which
women and men reap similar rewards.

As important as this movement toward inclusion was, using men as the explicit or implicit
reference group ultimately rendered women
deviant. Results and subsequent theorizing
viewed women in terms of how closely they
did or did not approximate male models, but
revealed little about women themselves. In
addition, the ways in which subsequent "differences" could be interpreted and used were problematic. Gibson (1996) pointed to the bias in
the ways scholars typically discuss gender differences in old age, noting that men are used as
the implicit standard and women are described
as deviating from it. This has critical implications for future theory, research, and policies.

The realization that simply adding women
into preexisting studies and theories rendered
them as the "other" spawned a movement to
examine women on their own terms. Spurred
by developments in feminist scholarship, scholars undertook a second response to the neglect
of women, that of centering on women's experiences from their own standpoint. More common in the 1990s, research that has centered on
women has allowed for a reformulation of methods and theories that incorporate women's
experiences as well as men's.

For example, in contrast to the model
intended to discern if women were more or less
satisfied with retirement than men, research
beginning with women's experiences revealed
that, for most women, leaving the labor force
meant leaving only one job, a paid job. For
the most part, women retained their domestic
labor responsibilities. This does not necessarily
diminish their satisfaction with retirement, but
certainly shapes their experiences of this time of
life in a different way from men's. Indeed, the
notion of being "free" in retirement does not
mean the cessation of work for women, but
instead a reduced work load (for which they
may well be grateful). The heightened focus
on unpaid labor that resulted from centering
on retired women also refocused attention on
the productive activities of old people, both

men and women. While unpaid, the varieties of domestic and volunteer activities (to use just two examples) in which old people engage are vital to the economy. In particular, their unpaid labor is called upon to compensate for the increasing retraction of the state from social reproduction, and the formation of policies that continue to leave such activities as caregiving, for young and old, to "families" (i.e., women). The lack of state help and inadequate policies mean that, for instance, grandparents (particularly grandmothers) play an increasingly important role in child rearing, not only in a custodial role but also as day care providers for children who work. Without this important labor, state coffers would be strained and the economic activities of younger generations would be constrained. Thus, the focus on women in this instance has led to transformations in concepts about work, productivity, and retirement.

Continued evolution of the feminist approach in sociology and in aging studies has led to a movement away from a focus on women and aging to the second stage, with its focus on gender and aging. This implies not so much a movement away from examining women as a refinement of the theoretical lens. Centering on women's experiences leads to more explicit theories regarding power in gender relations. Further, it recognizes explicitly that both women and men have gender: "gender and aging" refers to everyone, and not just to women. From this standpoint, gender is taken to be characteristic of both social organizations and identities, embedded in social relationships at all levels, from individual interactions to institutional processes. Men and women gain identities and power in relation to one another with important ramifications for life chances (Hess 1992). As a power relation, gender describes a hierarchical system wherein men's privileges are intimately tied to women's disadvantages. This relational quality means that the situation of one gender cannot be understood without at least implicit reference to the position of the other. As a social organizing principle, then, gender shapes individual interactions as well as policy formation.

The theoretical shift toward viewing gender relations can be seen in many areas of aging research. Depicting both work and family as playing roles in both men's and women's lives

in old age is but one example. To push our example of retirement further still, a focus on gender relations over the life course sees women's and men's experiences of retirement as an outcome of the ways in which each is advantaged or disadvantaged in relation to one another in paid labor, unpaid (domestic) labor, and retirement. The presence and absence of family ties, or domestic labor, paid labor, and the like, are expressions of gender relations. It is not simply that women are constrained by families when they work for pay, or that this domestic labor shapes their retirement by lowering pensions and maintaining their burdens of housework. Both domestic and paid labor realms also influence men's *higher* retirement finances and relative freedom. That is, husbands' abilities to have successful careers rest on the unpaid work of their wives just as surely as this domestic responsibility constrains women's paid labor. Similarly, women's continued responsibility for domestic labor in later life underlies (some) men's ability to be "free" in retirement.

A newer, more sophisticated reformulation of theory results from the greater emphasis on gender relations. Attending to women and men in relation to one another also stimulates greater research interest in masculinity and men. Understanding the processes by which disadvantage occurs necessitates a similar comprehension of privileging processes and struggles. Implicit when we acknowledge that men's freedom in retirement links to women's unpaid labor, this becomes explicit in the next step when we explore the processes that privilege men in the workplace and home. Similarly, we would also investigate the relationship between privilege and widowers' risk for institutionalization or loneliness in later life. In this instance, husbands' more dominant household position also means that women are generally the ones to do the work of daily life and maintain networks. Viewing gender relations in relation to aging thus requires seeing privilege (just as we would disadvantage) as a dynamic, one that must be constantly reasserted and that this in itself has consequences for aging as well. Similarly, some of the same aspects of gender relations that are part and parcel of women's disadvantage may also emerge as sources of strength in later life.

The focus on power relations, and greater recognition of the dynamics of oppression and privilege, have led many to an emerging third stage, which emphasizes intersections of inequalities. Just as gender shapes aging, so other social hierarchies, such as those based on race, ethnicity, class, and sexuality, influence both gender and aging. From this vantage point, to speak of "gender and aging" becomes less apt. Old men and women do not exist outside their racial, sexual, and class-based locations. For example, when we look only at old men and women, we see a much higher incidence of poverty among the latter. But when we look at race, for example, we find that, as a group, black men have lower Social Security incomes than do white women. Similarly, black women who live alone have a much higher incidence of poverty than their male or white counterparts despite longer labor force histories. How then can we discuss gender and poverty in old age? As a result, scholars working in this nuanced area increasingly focus on diversity and intersecting hierarchies, and not simply on gender.

As the example of retirement shows, the focus on gender and aging – in all three phases – has led to many insights that have advanced, and often redirected, scholarship. One of the first insights was the existence of a "double standard of aging" that not only devalues women at an earlier age than men, but also leads to age discrimination in the workforce earlier in women's lives. Since then, scholars of gender and aging have continued transforming a wide array of research areas. In relation to health, for instance, researchers go beyond noting gender differences in life expectancies and health conditions to ask *why* these variations prevail, and how they relate to power relations. They point to such things as how men's attempts to achieve dominant ideals of masculinity lead them to take physical risks that women do not take; they also seek out and follow doctors' advice less frequently, actions that will adversely influence their health in later life. Similarly, scholars seek to understand how women's social location makes them more vulnerable to particular health conditions and forms a context in which such ailments will play out in old age. Thus, among other issues, analysts might point to the gender bias in Medicare that provides coverage for acute illnesses, to which men are more prone, rather than chronic conditions, which more frequently plague women, and the ramifications this might have for such things as nursing home utilization. Going further still, the diversity approach explores racial and ethnic disparities in health over the life course as this relates to occupational conditions, access to health care, and a greater reliance on Medicaid to fund nursing home placement.

Looking at other areas of research, we see that the kinds of grandparenting roles undertaken are closely related to race, ethnicity, class, and gender; those with full-time care of grandchildren are more likely to be black or Hispanic women with lower incomes. We cannot simply speak of the ways that aging influences sexuality in later life, or even women's relationships with their bodies, as it appears that old black women, for instance, are far more accepting of diverse body types and also more likely to see themselves in sexual terms than are their white counterparts. Finally, the particular historical and economic conditions under which many contemporary, working-class black men have labored means that along with dissolution of first marriages, earlier family ties often become strained as well. As a result, they are especially vulnerable to isolation and institutionalization should they become widowed or divorced in later life. The importance of these and similar findings lies in terms of the recognition that practice and policy interventions, for example, must take into account the differences among the concerns and issues of various old people.

The gender and aging scholarship has advanced tremendously, especially in recent years. However, it is still a one-way relationship, with gender scholars often influencing aging research but not vice versa. Still to come, then, is gender scholars' recognition of age relations and the ways in which they intersect and influence gender. The limited discussion of how gender might change over the life course among some aging scholars is not the same as viewing age itself as a power relation that shapes people's interactions, resources, and life chances. Recognition of age relations suggests an array of promising directions for future studies. We should ask how men, even those with the most privilege, lose status with age and struggle with younger men for power, and how this might shape their aging. Greater attention to age inequality will, in turn, allow researchers and practitioners more fully to view people in a life course context. Recognizing that ageism permeates the lives of all old people, regardless of their level of privilege in earlier life, also has tremendous emancipatory potential. The realization that ageism is the one oppression all will face could provide a bridge across many groups defined by power relations, and spur those with greater privilege to think about and understand disadvantage.

SEE ALSO: Aging, Demography of; Aging and Social Support; Cultural Diversity and Aging: Ethnicity, Minorities, and Subcultures; Gender, Health, and Mortality; Gerontology: Key Thinkers (Hess Beth); Intersectionality

REFERENCES AND SUGGESTED READINGS

Arber, S., Davidson, K., & Ginn, J. (Eds.) (2003) *Gender and Ageing: New Directions*. Open University Press, Milton Keynes.

Calasanti, T. M. (2004) Feminist Gerontology and Old Men. *Journal of Gerontology: Social Sciences* 59B(6).

Calasanti, T. M. & Slevin, K. F. (2001) *Gender, Social Inequalities, and Aging*. Alta Mira Press, Walnut Creek, CA.

Dressel, P., Minkler, M., & Yen, I. (1997) Gender, Race, Class, and Aging: Advances and Opportunities. *International Journal of Health Services* 27(4): 579–600.

Estes, C. L. & Associates (2001) *Social Policy and Aging: A Critical Perspective*. Sage, Thousand Oaks, CA.

Gibson, D. (1996) Broken Down by Age and Gender: "The Problem of Old Women" Redefined. *Gender & Society* 10(4): 433–48.

Harrington Meyer, M. (1990) Family Status and Poverty among Older Women: The Gendered Distribution of Retirement Income in the US. *Social Problems* 37(4): 551–63.

Hess, B. B. (1992) Gender and Aging: The Demographic Parameters. In: L. Glasse and J. Hendricks (Eds.), *Gender and Aging*. Baywood Publishing, New York, pp. 15–23.

McMullin, J. A. (2000) Diversity and the State of Sociological Aging Theory. *The Gerontologist* 40: 517–30.

Thompson, E. H., Jr. (1994) Older Men as Invisible in Contemporary Society. In: E. H. Thompson, Jr. (Ed.), *Older Men's Lives*. Sage, Thousand Oaks, CA, pp. 197–217.

gender bias

Jennifer Rothchild

Gender bias is behavior that shows favoritism toward one gender over another. Most often, gender bias is the act of favoring men and/or boys over women and/or girls. However, this is not always the case. In order to define gender bias completely, we first must make a distinction between the terms gender and sex. When we use the term *gender*, we mean socially constructed expectations and roles for women and men, for girls and boys. Specifically, girls and women are expected to demonstrate feminine behavior, and boys and men are expected to act masculine. By *sex*, we mean biological differences assigned to females and males in order to distinguish between the two. The biological characteristics assigned to females and males often consist of primary or secondary sex characteristics.

The term gender bias is often (wrongly) used interchangeably with the term sexism. *Sexism* is typically defined as the subordination of one sex, usually female, based on the assumed superiority of the other sex (Kendall 2005) or an ideology that defines females as different from and inferior to males (Andersen & Taylor 2005). Sex is the basis for the prejudice and presumed inferiority implicit in the term sexism. The term *gender bias* is more inclusive than the term sexism, as it includes both prejudice (attitudes) and discrimination (behavior) in its definition. Studies of gender bias also focus on gender, rather than on sex. Furthermore, the term gender bias could include instances of bias against boys and men in addition to bias against girls and women. This raises an important question: Are boys and men harmed by gender bias? While individual boys and men may suffer at the hands of gender bias, boys and men as groups benefit from gender bias embedded in our social institutions. The narrow benefits of gender bias for some are outweighed by much broader losses for all (Neubeck & Glasberg 2005). And if gender roles and expectations constrain both girls and boys and both women and men, it can be said that gender bias limits the overall development of contemporary societies.

GENDER BIAS: PERVASIVE INFLUENCE

Gender bias is part of almost every aspect of life. The most common areas of gender bias are found in the social institutions of families, education, the economy, and health.

Within the Household

At the household level, there is documented evidence of gender bias in the allocation of resources. Patriarchal households are maintained through power and control in the hands of men, particularly fathers, as the heads of households. Specifically, gendered roles assigned as "breadwinner husband" and "homemaker wife" lead to unequal distributions of power within the household. However, the numbers of dual-income families and female-headed households are growing rapidly in the US. Consequently, women's and men's attitudes towards sharing work in the household have changed over the years. Both women and men often face conflict between work and family. The juggling of work and family is complicated by the power differences between women and men in families, and these power differences often confirm gender roles, with women typically desiring more change than men (Andersen 2003). Along these lines of power differentials, gender bias within families can come in the form of violence as well. While it is certainly not the case in every family, women are significantly more likely than men to be physically abused and injured by their intimate partners (Renzetti & Curran 2003).

In Education

Gender bias is embedded in education from pre-kindergarten through graduate school. Teachers provide important messages about gender through both the formal content of their instruction and materials utilized, as well as informal interactions with students (which is commonly referred to as the hidden curriculum). Gender-related messages from teachers and other students often reinforce gender roles first taught at home (Kendall 2005).

Researchers have consistently found that teachers give more time, effort, and attention to boys than to girls (Sadker & Sadker 1994). Gender bias exists in textbooks and instructional materials as well. Women are often under-represented in course materials and/or are presented in stereotypical roles. Over time, gender bias in education undermines girls' and women's self-esteem and discourages them from taking courses such as math, science, and engineering (Raffalli 1994).

In the Economy

While it is estimated that 60 percent of all women work in the paid labor force (US Bureau of Labor Statistics 2003), women, on average, make up a weaker position in the labor market than men. Specifically, they are more likely to be unemployed, employed in temporary jobs, or employed part-time. Because of gender bias embedded in the labor market, women in the US are paid, on average, 76 cents to every dollar in wages that men are paid. Rates for women of color are even lower: 66 cents for African American women and 54 cents for Latinas. More than one million women work in jobs that pay less than the federal minimum wage (Neubeck & Glasberg 2005). Sociologists have argued that this is not a reflection of educational differences between women and men; rather, it is a product of gender bias in employment, promotion, and pay. The gender-biased economic system encourages women to go into traditional "women's jobs," and this serves employers well: they are able to pay women lower salaries for traditional "women's jobs" than for traditional "men's jobs."

In Health

The US health care system has long been dominated by men – from doctors to researchers to administrators. While more and more women are entering medical school and medical-related fields, gender bias is still embedded in the system. As discussed above, women, on average, make up a weaker position in the labor market than men. Thus, they are less likely to occupy positions that offer adequate health care insurance, even when they work full time (Neubeck & Glasberg 2005). Female-headed households are affected by this most strongly, as they are more likely to be poor than male-headed or dual-headed households.

Biases and shortcomings in the health care system's treatment of women contribute to the problems women face in getting adequate medical care (Ratcliff 2002). Specifically, gender bias embedded in the US health care system contributes to very little research done on health problems pertaining to women. For example, women have been largely excluded as research subjects in studies sponsored by the federal National Institutes of Health (NIH).

CONCLUSION

In addition to the social institutions reviewed here, gender bias is embedded in the media, sports, the state/government, and other social institutions. Gender is so pervasive in contemporary society that we often do not notice gender bias in our everyday lives. However, gender itself is not a variable that stands alone. Our race, ethnicity, social class, sexual orientation, and other social positions affect our everyday gendered experiences. Therefore, gender bias regularly intersects with other forms of bias such as ethnocentrism, racism, classism, and homophobia.

While it may appear gender bias disadvantages girls and women the most, gender bias, as well as other forms of bias, shortchanges all of us.

SEE ALSO: Gender Ideology and Gender Role Ideology; Gender Mainstreaming; Gender Oppression; Gendered Organizations/Institutions; Intersectionality; Sex and Gender

REFERENCES AND SUGGESTED READINGS

Andersen, M. (2003) *Thinking about Women: Sociological Perspectives on Sex and Gender*, 6th edn. Allyn & Bacon, Boston.

Andersen, M. & Taylor, H. (2005) *Sociology: The Essentials*. Thomson Wadsworth, Belmont, CA.

Kendall, D. (2005) *Sociology in Our Times*. Thomson Wadsworth, Belmont, CA.

Neubeck, K. J. & Glasberg, D. S. (2005) *Sociology: Diversity, Conflict, and Change*. McGraw Hill, Boston.

Raffalli, M. (1994) Why So Few Women Physicists? *New York Times Supplement* (January): Sec. 4A, 26–8.

Ratcliff, K. S. (2002) *Women and Health: Power, Technology, and Inequality in a Gendered World*. Allyn & Bacon, Boston.

Renzetti, C. M. & Curran, D. J. (2003) *Women, Men, and Society*. Allyn & Bacon, Boston.

Sadker, M. & Sadker, D. (1994) *Failing at Fairness: How America's Schools Cheat Girls*. Scribner, New York.

US Bureau of Labor Statistics (2003) Employment Status of the Civilian Population by Sex and Age. Online. www.bls.gov.

gender, the body and

Cynthia Fabrizio Pelak

Feminist thinkers have long focused on the body as an expression of power and a site of social control. As early as 1792, Mary Wollstonecraft proclaimed that "genteel women are slaves to their bodies" and that "beauty is woman's scepter" (Wollstonecraft 1988). Sixty years later, Sojourner Truth drew attention to how bodies are not only gendered but also racialized in her *Ain't I a Woman* speech of 1851. And, since the emergence of the second wave of women's movements in the US, feminists have been transforming our thinking on gender and bodies through their writings on rape, sexual assault, domestic violence, reproductive rights, beauty contests, eating disorders, sports, disabilities, cosmetic surgery, and more. Despite the recurrent focus on gender and the body, scholars have asked diverse sets of questions from various disciplinary and theoretical perspectives that have changed over time. This entry reviews some of the major questions that have been raised about gender and the body and discusses the shifting theoretical approaches that have developed in the literature.

A constant thread in contemporary feminist theory is questioning the source of sex differences. Are sex differences "naturally" produced or are they a result of social-cultural production (i.e., nurture)? If sex differences are "natural," it is thought that they cannot be altered. However, if they are socially constructed, then sex differences could be altered and possibly eliminated. The emergence of the "nature versus nurture" question within feminist theory is directly linked to dominant gender ideologies that posit gender differences as biologically determined and women's subordination and men's dominance as natural. Such gender ideologies have a long history in western societies and affect virtual every aspect of women's and men's lives in contemporary society. As discussed below, recent feminist scholarship on gender and the body critiques the terms of the nature versus nurture debate and offers a new paradigm that recognizes the inherent interaction of biological and social systems.

Perceptions and experiences of gender and the body in western societies have been grounded in dualistic thinking (Bordo 1993; Fausto-Sterling 2000). According to influential male philosophers and theologians within Greco-Christian traditions, two opposing entities constitute human existence: the mind and the body. Within this framework, the mind is understood as being superior to the body, and the body, which is associated with wanton desires, is seen as something to be overcome and controlled. Western discourses on the mind/body split developed along with other dualisms such as male/female and culture/nature. On one axis, the mind, culture, and the masculine have been located and on an opposing axis the body, nature, and the feminine are positioned. Moreover, the male body has been assumed to be the standard and the female body an inadequate deviation from the norm.

Sexist ideas about women's bodies advanced by philosophers and theologians were strengthened by medical and scientific discourses of the industrial and post-industrial eras. With the professionalization of medicine, male medical doctors became "experts" on women's bodies. Based more on ideology than empirical evidence, physicians espoused sexist beliefs about women's embodied physical fragility, intellectual inferiority, and emotional instability. In her book *The Eternally Wounded Woman* (1990), Patricia Vertinsky shows how the dominant medical discourse of the nineteenth century led to the notion that physical exercise was dangerous to women's reproductive function. Not surprisingly, the "misinformation" was meant for privileged women who were pushing for more access to the public arena and not poor, immigrant, and enslaved women who

regularly performed physically demanding labor and supposedly reproduced too much.

Since the mid-twentieth century, psychologists, sexologists, biologists, and other researchers have battled over theories of the origins of sex differences, gender identities, and gender roles (Fausto-Sterling 2000). Corresponding with the development of new technologies, the basis of "scientific" theories about bodily and behavioral differences between females and males moved from genitals to gonads to chromosomes to hormones to brains. As societal views around gender started shifting during the 1970s, feminist theories, which highlighted the importance of gender socialization and other environmental "nurture" factors, entered the debate. The infamous case of the male child who was "successfully" socialized as a girl after his penis was mutilated during a circumcision procedure was offered as proof for the social construction of gender. This evidence, however, was weakened when the socialized girl became a teenager and wanted to become a boy.

Feminist biologist Anne Fausto-Sterling (2000) argues much of this debate is deeply limited by dualistic thinking and a devotion to the notion that there are two, and only two, mutually exclusive sexes. Fausto-Sterling's work suggests that sex is more of a continuum and that the body is changeable over the life course rather than fixed at birth. She rejects the framework that views the body and the circumstances in which it reproduces as separable. Instead, she and other scholars theorize an interactive biosocial model in which internal reproductive structures and external social, historical, and environmental factors are inseparable – interacting over time and circumstance. Grosz (1994) uses the metaphor of a Möbius strip to illustrate how social meanings external to the body are incorporated into its physiological expression, as well as unconscious and conscious behavior.

Nowhere are the politics of the debate about sex and gender differences clearer than in the debates over bodies that exhibit sexual ambiguity (Kessler 1998). Although intersexuality is a fairly common phenomenon, intersexuals disappear from our view because doctors quickly "correct" them with surgery. Kessler shows how the medical management of intersexuality (repeated surgeries and hormone treatments) contributes to the construction of dichotomized, idealized genitals and normalizing beliefs about gender and sexuality. She argues that acceptance of genital and gender variability will mean the subversion of the equation that genitals equal gender.

As mentioned above, the emergence of the second wave women's movement sparked a wealth of new research on gender and the body. Much of the earlier work focused on how women's bodies were regulated, controlled, or violated. The body at this stage was viewed as a site through which masculine power operated rather than as an object of study in and of itself. The desire to counter theories of biological determinism and promote theories of social constructionism led feminists to sidestep theorizing the body. Likewise, the conceptual distinction between sex and gender, which posits sex as the biological/physiological and gender as the social/cultural, may have falsely constructed disciplinary boundaries that led feminist scholars to focus on the social (i.e., gender) and ignore the biological (i.e., sex).

The recent "discursive turn" in feminist theory and the development of poststructural challenges to binary constructs and dualistic thinking have encouraged new theorizing on gender and the body (Conboy et al. 1997). Drawing on the work of Michel Foucault, some feminist scholars are viewing bodies as texts which can be read as a statement of gender relations. Working within this framework, Judith Butler (1992) has tried to build a nondualistic account of the body and reclaim the material body for feminist thought. Butler conceptualizes the body as a system that simultaneously produces and is produced by social meaning and shows how transgressive body politics can challenge the discursive limits of "sex."

While drawing on poststructuralist thought and insights from recent scholarship on gender and the body, Bordo (1993) cautions feminist scholars not to overemphasize women's embodied resistance at the expense of examining how domination is enacted upon and through female bodies. In her analyses of eating disorders, plastic surgery, media images, and the slender body, Bordo acknowledges the possibility of women's resistance, but also draws attention to the overwhelming power of

disciplinary and normalizing processes surrounding women's bodies in our postmodern world. The emergent field of feminist disability studies also interrogates normalizing discourses and practices of gendered bodies, but draws attention to bodies that are culturally identified as sick, impaired, ugly, deformed, or malfunctioning (Thomson 2002). Feminist disability scholars critique research on bodies, embodiment, and gender that ignores how the hierarchical ability/disability system intersects with other systems of power in shaping gendered experiences of women and men.

One of the most symbolically important social institutions for the naturalization of gender differences in contemporary societies is that of competitive sports. The sociology of sport, in particular, has contributed greatly to our collective understanding of gender and the body by examining the relationships between the symbolic representations of the body and embodied experiences within concrete sociohistorical contexts. The literature on gender and sport, which includes the theoretical tensions and turns outlined above, has contributed valuable insights on femininities, masculinities, and the body (Hall 1996; McKay et al. 2000). The scholarship of Jennifer Hargreaves (1994, 2000) is exemplary in its examination of women's historical exclusion in competitive sport and the seemingly irreconcilable tension between femininity and athleticism. Her work illuminates how competitive sport, throughout history and around the world, has been a site for both maintaining and challenging dominant notions of gendered bodies.

In addressing questions about gender and the body, the history of sex testing or gender verification within the Olympic Games movement provides an ideal case study of the shifting discourses and "science" around gendered/sexed bodies. Sparked by the growing political anxieties of the Cold War, in 1968 the International Olympic Committee instituted sex testing of female athletes, first through visual examinations and then by "scientific" chromosomal testing. Over the years, it was shown that fitting bodies into two mutually exclusive categories of female and male is not so simple. The suspension of gender testing in 2000 serves as an acknowledgment of the complexities of a body's sex and a recognition, at least at some level, that labeling someone a woman or a man is a social decision (Fausto-Sterling 2000).

Recent feminist theorizing on the body and embodiment has encouraged social movement scholars to focus attention on the role of the body in collective social action. Using the body as a site of resistance has long been a strategy of collective protest against gender oppression. Suffragists in the US and England at the turn of the twentieth century adopted the tactic of hunger strikes to draw attention to their cause. Parkins (2000) argues that the daring acts of protest by suffragists challenged dominant ideas about women's bodily comportment and physical capabilities, as well as embodied notions of citizenship. The more recent history of silent vigils of the Women-in-Black movement, which first emerged in Jerusalem in 1988 to protest the Israeli occupation of Palestine, illustrates how the body still serves as an agent of social and political change (Sasson-Levy & Rapoport 2003). The recent theorizing in the social movements literature on the role of emotions and passion in political struggle has also led to new insights on gender and the body (see Goodwin & Jasper 2004). As the diverse and lengthy history of embodied social protest suggests and the various theoretical frameworks and empirical research on gender and the body illustrate, the body has been and seems will remain a central nexus to our understanding of gendered experiences, ideologies, and practices.

SEE ALSO: Body and Sexuality; Body and Society; Disability Sport; Female Genital Mutilation; Femininities/Masculinities; Feminist Disability Studies; Rape Culture; Sex and Gender; Sport and the Body

REFERENCES AND SUGGESTED READINGS

Bordo, S. R. (1993) *Unbearable Weight: Feminism, Western Culture, and the Body*. University of California Press, Berkeley.
Butler, J. (1992) *Bodies that Matter: On the Discursive Limits of "Sex."* Routledge, New York.
Conboy, K., Medina, N., & Stanbury, S. (Eds.) (1997) *Writing on the Body: Female Embodiment and Feminist Theory*. University of California Press, Berkeley.
Fausto-Sterling, A. (2000) *Sexing the Body: Gender Politics and the Construction of Sexuality*. Basic Books, New York.
Goodwin, J. & Jasper, J. (2004) *Rethinking Social Movement: Structure, Meaning, and Emotion*. Rowman & Littlefield, Lanham, MD.
Grosz, E. (1994) *Volatile Bodies: Toward a Corporal Feminism*. Indiana University Press, Bloomington.
Hall, M. A. (1996) *Feminism and Sporting Bodies: Essays on Theory and Practice*. Human Kinetics, Champaign, IL.
Hargreaves, J. (1994) *Sporting Females: Critical Issues in the History and Sociology of Women's Sports*. Routledge, London.
Hargreaves, J. (2000) *Heroines of Sport: The Politics of Difference and Identity*. Routledge, London.
Kessler, S. (1998) *Lessons for the Intersexed*. Rutgers University Press, New Brunswick, NJ.
McKay, J., Messner, M., & Sabo, D. (Eds.) (2000) *Masculinities, Gender Relations, and Sport*. Sage, Thousand Oaks, CA.
Parkins, W. (2000) Protesting Like a Girl: Embodiment, Dissent and Feminist Agency. *Feminist Theory* 1(1): 59–78.
Sasson-Levy, O. & Rapoport, T. (2003) Body, Gender, and Knowledge in Protest Movements: The Israeli Case. *Gender and Society* 17(3): 379–403.
Thomson, R. G. (2002) Integrating Disability, Transforming Feminist Theory. *NWSA Journal* 14(3): 1–32.
Vertinsky, P. (1990) *The Eternally Wounded Woman: Women, Doctors and Exercise in the Late Nineteenth Century*. Manchester University Press, Manchester.
Wollstonecraft, M. (1988) *A Vindication of the Rights of Woman*. In: Rossi, A. (Ed.), *The Feminist Papers*. Northeastern University Press, Boston, pp. 40–85.

gender, consumption and

Christine Williams and Laura Sauceda

The history of consumerism has been shaped by gender inequality. During the colonial period, when families produced most of what they consumed, a gender division of labor prevailed in which men supplied the raw materials (e.g., wheat, flax, animals) and women transformed them into commodities for consumption (e.g., bread, cloth, meals). During industrialization, the period characterized by historians as bringing about the "separation of spheres," productive activity moved outside the household and eventually became seen as an appropriately masculine endeavor. Consumption became privatized, a range of activities under the purview of women consigned to the domestic arena. Although the separation of spheres was more cultural ideal than historical practice for many marginalized social groups (African Americans, the poor, immigrants), the association of women with consumption, and men with production, prevails today and shapes research and theory on consumerism.

Four major themes characterize research on gender and consumption. The first theme analyzes women's consumer practices as an extension of their primary domestic responsibilities. Sometimes referred to in the literature as "housework" or more recently "carework," this consumer activity centers on shopping as a means to acquire the goods to sustain members of a household (e.g., to cook meals, clean the house, organize family get-togethers and other social events, and care for children and elderly parents). Marjorie DeVault's book, *Feeding the Family* (1991), was one of the first to carefully document the extensive effort involved in women's consumer activity on behalf of their families. Feminists argue that this work lacks pay and social recognition, yet it is essential for sustaining the quality of family life.

As many women have joined the paid labor force in the past decades, women's involvement in consumption has changed and in many ways increased. A current thread of research focuses on employed women who subcontract services to perform the domestic labor still expected of them as wives and mothers. Thus, we have witnessed the rise of domestic cleaning services, the proliferation of fast food restaurants, and the increase in private childcare centers. These industries cater to women forced to juggle the demands of paid work and family care. Referred to by Arlie Hochschild (2003) as the "commercialization of intimate life," these service industries are replacing the work that in previous generations women performed in their private homes without pay. The work involved in subcontracting and managing domestic labor is still mostly done by women, a vestige of the separate spheres ideology that remains deeply embedded in current gender arrangements. The subcontracted work is also performed mostly by women, typically by non-white and immigrant workers.

A second major theme in the literature on gender and consumption examines how the advertising industry has shaped cultural ideals of masculinity and femininity. Advertisers exploited the cult of domesticity in the first half of the twentieth century by encouraging women to associate the purchase of certain household products with being a good wife and mother. Although this trend continues through the twenty-first century, the focus of advertising has become more personal, centered on how commodities can enable the individual to achieve prevailing gender ideals. In other words, consumption of certain products is presented as central to femininity and masculinity.

Feminist scholars first picked up on this trend in the 1970s. Early critiques emphasized the ideological content of advertisements directed to women that seemed to undermine self-esteem while simultaneously promising relief through the purchase of their products. These products were not limited to beauty and fashion accessories, but included a full range of goods, from kitchen appliances to cars to food products, all promising to transform the body and the self to achieve ideal femininity. Early feminist studies of advertising urged resistance through consumer refusal. Thus, when *Ms. Magazine* debuted in 1972, it was free of advertisements, reflecting the feminist critique of the industry's deleterious impact on women's self-image, and its central role in perpetuating stereotypical roles for women.

In the mid-twentieth century, advertisements also began targeting men with the promise that products could enhance their masculinity. Although early ads were less focused on appearance than those targeting women, they suggested that heterosexual attractiveness could be enhanced with the purchase of expensive cars, stereo equipment, and vacations. *Playboy* magazine, which debuted in the late 1950s, is often credited with establishing the link between masculinity and consumerism, and thus challenging the conventional association of shopping with women (Ehrenreich, *Hearts of Men*, 1983). Unlike the feminist movement, political opposition from men's groups did not materialize, except from the health community, which challenged ads that equated the consumption of especially unhealthy commodities, such as alcohol and cigarettes, to expressions of masculinity.

Gender scholars have developed increasingly sophisticated understandings of how advertisements shape social ideals of masculinity and femininity. Jean Kilbourne produced an influential series of videos on gender advertisements (*Killing Us Softly*) which have been shown to generations of students in college classes all over the country. These videos demonstrate that ads on television and in magazines represent an exceptionally narrow range of acceptable appearance standards for men and women. Wealth, whiteness, and heterosexuality are taken for granted in most advertisements, suggesting that men and women who are poor, non-white, or GLBT have little chance to achieve social approval. Philosopher Susan Bordo (1993) draws on theories of postmodernism to understand the allure of advertisements that promote unrealistic weight loss and body sculpting regimens. Women are drawn to these images, however damaging and irrational, because of an internalized sense of inadequacy promoted by a sexist culture that devalues femininity. Although her scholarship recognizes the problematic depiction of both men and women, the emphasis remains on how women are especially dehumanized by their portrayal by the advertising industry and vulnerable to its messages.

Analysis of both conformity and resistance represents a third main theme in the gender and consumption scholarship. In what she calls the fashion-beauty complex, feminist scholar Sandra Bartky (1990) suggests that production, marketing, retail, and information companies work together to regulate feminine identity. Thus, pressure to conform to gender ideals goes beyond just advertisements. Department stores, for example, are spatially segregated by gender, clearly defining for customers which items should be purchased for men and for women. Genres in novels, television, and film have been gendered such that romantic stories (or so-called "chick flicks") are pitched to women while action plots are geared toward a primarily male audience.

According to Bartky, lifestyle magazines targeting teen and adult women play a critical role in the fashion-beauty complex. Teen magazines claim a significant readership among teenage girls, and these publications prime their audience to continue consuming fashion and lifestyle magazines well into adulthood. Young women are highly invested in popular culture, and research demonstrates that their peer groups tend to encourage conformity to the feminine ideal that pervades these texts. The financial success of the beauty industry suggests that women do in fact support the fashion-beauty complex. Cosmetics, dieting, and cosmetic surgery bring in billions of dollars a year, and the majority of these consumers are women. Because conformity is such big business, the industry has little impetus to diversify or alter its constructions of femininity in any way.

Despite this evidence of conformity in women's consumerism, the more micro-level question of meaning must also be considered. Cultural theorist Stuart Hall argues that dominant cultural messages may be accepted, negotiated, or even subverted. Feminist scholars, for instance, have noted that shopping represents a relatively safe and socially acceptable way for girls and women to participate in the public sphere, an experience they may find liberating. Ethnographies and interview projects have shown that women often read magazines and romance novels or watch soap operas for personal pleasure, and as a means of escape from mundane domestic responsibilities. Many take pleasure in critiquing these media, which are often considered predictable and even ridiculous in content.

An ongoing debate within feminism questions whether or not women's conformity to beauty ideals can be considered resistant. Some argue that women can use their appearance as a form of bodily capital, in a Bourdieuian sense, to exploit male weakness and gain access to resources. Others point out that such practice fails to challenge dominant expectations of idealized femininity, doing little to improve conditions for women in general. Considering the high rates of eating disorders and the dangers of cosmetic surgery, this strategy may even be harmful to women.

Sociologist Lynn Chancer emphasizes that in everyday life, oppression and resistance often occur together. In order to resolve this debate, feminists must challenge the institutional and cultural oppression of women without placing restrictions on or passing judgment about individual women's actions.

The fourth major theme of the gender and consumption literature considers the interactive dimensions of race and class. Consumer practices vary widely depending on social location. The economic realities of social class and cultural beliefs about race and gender place restrictions on what and how people consume. Education and occupation determine the amount of disposable income one possesses. Poor neighborhoods attract fewer businesses, thereby limiting the purchasing options of these areas' residents. Customers are treated differently based on employees' perceptions about one's race and/or class status.

The intersection of race, class, and gender results in a social hierarchy that privileges some while putting others at a disadvantage. The predominantly white upper class exhibits what Thorstein Veblen calls "conspicuous consumption," which is to say they purchase goods and services that overtly demonstrate their wealth and social status. In buying expensive and/or rare items, they set themselves apart from those without access to such luxuries. In this way, their consumer patterns help create and maintain class divisions.

Racial/ethnic minorities and the working class experience consumption quite differently. African American women, for example, have historically been relegated to lower socioeconomic status, in which consumption revolves around the provision of daily necessities. In the early twentieth century when beliefs about black inferiority prevailed, investing in beauty products such as hair straighteners and skin-lightening creams represented a form of resistance. These items allowed black women to more closely adhere to the dominant feminine ideal, thereby undermining negative stereotypes. These black women viewed conformity as a way to make themselves and their race more respectable to dominant society. The investment in the cosmetics industry also resulted in a significant entrepreneurial opportunity for black women, who began producing and selling products specifically for African American consumers.

Race, class, and gender shape how different groups read and interpret cultural texts as well.

African American teenage girls tend to read teen magazines with a more critical eye than their white counterparts. These girls are less likely to identify with dominant beauty standards embodied by the exceptionally thin white women who are the typical models in advertisements. As a result, they read around much of the content focused on appearance, looking instead for articles they think will give them insight into their lived experiences. Life chances associated with social class guide the consumption of cultural texts in a similar way. Privileged groups of girls are highly invested in conforming to idealized femininity, particularly in terms of appearance and behavior. In contrast, working-class racial/ethnic minority girls take interest in content addressing dating, marriage, and motherhood. Due to limited educational and career opportunities, these girls anticipate becoming wives and/or mothers earlier in life than the middle and upper-class girls. In short, these cases suggest that social location plays a significant role in determining which products, images, and messages women find relevant to their lives. Intersecting forms of privilege and oppression create different needs and interests, which translate into different consumer practices.

Topics for future research on gender and consumption include: (1) analyses of how new shopping media, such as the Internet, promote and/or undermine conventional gender ideals and practices; (2) the gender socialization of ever younger girls and boys through targeted advertisements on television; (3) the gendered features of anti-consumerist social movements; and (4) the impact of niche marketing on cultural constructions of gender, including marketing to members of GLBT communities.

SEE ALSO: Consumption and the Body; Consumption, Girls' Culture and; Consumption, Masculinities and; Sex and Gender; Sexualities and Consumption; Women's Empowerment

REFERENCES AND SUGGESTED READINGS

Bartky, S. (1990) *Femininity and Domination*. Routledge, New York.

Benson, S. P. (1986) *Counter Cultures: Saleswomen, Managers, and Customers in American Department*

Stores, 1890–1940. University of Illinois Press, Urbana.

Bordo, S. (1993) *Unbearable Weight*. University of California Press, Berkeley.

Craig, M. L. (2002). *Ain't I a Beauty Queen? Black Women, Beauty, and the Politics of Race*. Oxford University Press, Oxford.

Currie, D. H. (1999) *Girl Talk: Adolescent Magazines and Their Readers*. University of Toronto Press, Toronto.

de Grazia, V. and Furlough, E. (Eds.) (1996) *The Sex of Things: Gender and Consumption in Historical Perspective*. University of California Press, Berkeley.

Hochschild, A. (2003) *The Commercialization of Intimate Life: Notes From Home and Work*. University of California Press, Berkeley.

Scanlon, J. (Ed.) (2000) *The Gender and Consumer Culture Reader*. New York University Press, New York.

gender, development and

Christine E. Bose

Over the last half-century there have been different theoretical frameworks used to understand how women are located in global economic processes, and each has had a concomitant strategy to enhance women's position. In the middle of the twentieth century modernization approaches were common, but dependency theorists critiqued these strategies. By the 1970s these male-focused arguments were largely supplanted by women in development (WID) ones, and more recently by gender and development (GAD) approaches.

Development refers to changes in a country that are frequently measured using a country's gross domestic product (GDP), as well as its degree of industrialization, urbanization, technological sophistication, export capability, and consumer orientation. Concerns about development are most likely to be expressed by representatives of advanced capitalist core countries of the "global North" or by international agencies when they create initiatives or generate responses to a whole range of critical problems faced by what they categorize as "developing" nations or the peripheral and semi-peripheral countries of the "global South."

On the other hand, countries of the global South tend to see development as addressing survival issues like hunger and malnutrition, refugee displacement and homelessness, unemployment and underemployment, health services and disease, the destruction of the environment, and political repression and violence. Since numerous countries in the global South are former colonies of those in the global North, many survival problems result from the cumulative effects of unequal and dependent relationships that were established centuries ago and are recreated in the present using new mechanisms, especially structural adjustment programs and other economic globalization strategies promulgated by international agencies like the International Monetary Fund (IMF) and the World Bank. Indeed, it is frequently argued that development projects, promoted by core countries, have better served their own interests, in the long run, than those of their recipients.

The condition of women in developing/global South countries is integrally tied to gendered power and economic structures that were established in the colonial era. In addition, although early development programs ignored their needs, usage of women's unpaid or underpaid labor has been crucial to many development programs and policies.

Post-World War II modernization approaches assumed that developing nations needed to industrialize rapidly in order to gain economic strength, and that political democracy, gender equity, and national prosperity would follow from industrialization – consequences that were assumed to have occurred in core nations when they industrialized slowly over the course of the nineteenth century. Nonetheless, development agencies measured success only by increases in per capita income, literacy rates, life expectancy, and fertility rates, rather than by the disappearance of authoritarian regimes. Indeed, the prevalence of dictatorships in many Latin American and Caribbean countries that had achieved some degree of economic development helped to discredit the assumed connection between development and democracy. And the fact that some global South countries have greater women's political and professional participation than in the global North helps to discredit the connection between development and gender equity (Burn 2005).

The industrialization and modernization programs created by international development agencies, and formulated from the perspectives of "western" nations, relied on foreign investment and manufacturing for export rather than for local consumption and did not encourage self-sufficiency in the global South (Sen & Grown 1987). Frequently, developing nations depended on single-commodity export trade, leaving them vulnerable to the fluctuations and perils of world markets. Many developing economies were "denationalized" because foreign industrial capital often interfered with or restricted the autonomy of local governments, as well as the capacity of national industries to compete in the world market (Acosta-Belén & Bose 1995).

In the 1960s and 1970s, dependency theorists such as Gunder Frank (1969) argued that discussions of the need for "modernization" hid the fact that industrial nations were exploiting developing ones. Indeed, developing nations usually were former colonial possessions of present-day industrialized nations, and had therefore always been integrated into the capitalist system. They also noted that the modernization model was applied across the board, with little attention to specific national needs. At about the same time, other scholars underscored the problem that modernization approaches paid little attention to women's particular needs and assumed they would benefit in a "trickle-down" fashion as economies improved.

In 1975 the United Nations proclaimed the first International Women's Year and the decade 1975–85 was known as the Decade for Women. The UN's focus was intended to acknowledge that women had been active participants in the development process from the beginning, and the call to integrate women into development was more of a denunciation of the male-oriented biases in development policies and the invisibility to which development agencies had relegated women's participation:

> Indeed, the pervasive idea that men were the primary earners often led to the formulation of development policies that excluded or diminished women's productive roles and thus their status; added extra hours to their double burden when they had to replace men (now

engaged in wage labor) in the subsistence activities that were performed collectively before; and often did not even account properly for women's actual participation and contributions. (Acosta-Belén & Bose 1995: 20)

Prior to Boserup's (1970) key publication, most of the development literature ignored women's economic role and contributions. Assuming women were passive dependents, researchers and practitioners relegated them to reproductive rather than productive roles, confining them to an undervalued domestic sphere isolated from the rest of the social structure. Little attention was paid to variations in women and men's economic roles in different global South nations or to women's activities in the informal economy.

> One of Boserup's major contributions was to empirically establish the vital role of women in agricultural economies and to recognize that economic development, with its tendency to encourage labor specialization, was actually depriving women of their original productive functions and on the whole deteriorating their status. Acknowledged by many as a path breaker in the field of women and development (Benería 1982; Bolles 1988; Sen & Grown 1987), Boserup is credited with documenting the existence of a gendered division of labor across nations and showing that women's labor had not been reported in official records. (Acosta-Belén & Bose 1995: 22)

Nonetheless, there were shortcomings in Boserup's important work due to her adherence to the then-prevalent modernization approach. She paid insufficient attention to women's household labor as a basis for subordination, and to the differential outcomes of capital growth on various groups of women within colonial or former colonial settings (Benería & Sen 1981; Bolles 1988).

In spite of these problems, Boserup's research fostered an understanding of how development policies ideologically denigrate women's economic contributions, while simultaneously relying upon and exploiting women's labor. Since her initial work, numerous studies have documented the impact of development on women at the local, national, and international levels and confirmed that women's segregated labor generates their low wages and status. One result of the conceptual shift from modernization theory to the study of women in development was the increased attention paid by feminist researchers to previously ignored sectors of working women who are (or were) essential to third world economies, including African enslaved women, domestic workers, tourist-sector workers, women traders and street sellers, craft producers, and sex workers, as well as to non-husband/wife household formations, especially families headed by women, who are often landless.

With increased globalization, "development" comes in a new form, as core countries make use of "offshore production" or the transfer of assembly plants, primarily in electronics, apparel, and textiles, to global South countries. Many of the hidden aspects of offshore production occur in export processing zones (EPZs), where young women migrate from rural areas to work in their national segment of the "global assembly line" and married women take on factory "outwork," doing piecework at home. Women's transnational migration for work also has increased, and women from developing countries migrate to more developed ones, often to work (legally or undocumented) as domestics or doing other forms of carework.

Burn (2005) notes that development projects based on a WID perspective fall into three categories. The first, and most common in the 1980s, were income-generating projects, which tended to focus on traditional women's skills such as sewing and handcrafts. Burn suggests that these projects rarely were successful because of the low marketability and profit in these areas, and because women were not always included in the design of the projects. The second, but less common, type of project was to introduce labor-saving devices for women's traditional tasks – unfortunately focusing on a limited range of tools. The third approach, that has grown in international popularity since the 1980s, is to give women access to development resources, especially in the form of small loans for women micro-entrepreneurs. These quick-revolving loans with reasonable interest rates and low collateral requirements have helped finance many women's small businesses, and are believed to increase women's autonomy and improve the health status of the women's children, as more discretionary income becomes available to women (Blumberg 1995). Such

outcomes show that women are not passive victims of globalization and development processes, but see creative ways to resist subordination and become empowered.

Many development projects fomented under the WID philosophy helped women economically. However, few if any of these projects were intended to change the power relationships between women and men. In response to these limitations, a new approach, Gender and Development (GAD), was discussed by feminists and in women-focused NGOs during the 1980s, with the goal of improving women's rights and increasing gender equity. Many have called GAD an "empowerment" approach (Burn 2005; Moser 1989) because its goal is to create development projects based on the needs expressed by grassroots women and not only to provide services, but to challenge women's subordination in households and in societies. One way GAD does this is by recognizing the multiple connections between women's economic roles outside of the home and those inside the family; a second way is by encouraging women's and feminist activism.

Among the urban strategies used in the global South are organizing collective meals, health cooperatives, or neighborhood water-rights groups. Rather than privatizing their survival problems, women collectivize them and often place demands on the state for rights related to family survival. Mohanty (1991) suggests that challenging the state is not merely different, but "a crucial context" for global South women's struggles precisely because it is the state that has created laws with gender and race limitations implicit in them.

Urban organizing is not the only form of empowerment. Indigenous and peasant women in rural areas create projects around agricultural issues such as land tenure or plantation working conditions, issues that link community and labor, as well as cultural issues related to ethnic identity and survival of indigenous peoples.

Other GAD-related feminist organizing links self-determined women's development with the issues of nationality, race, class, and gender. Among examples in the Commonwealth Caribbean are the Women and Development Unit (WAND), which promotes women's activities especially through income-generating projects, local technical assistance, and government advisement; Development Alternatives with Women for a New Era (DAWN), which is a network of activist researchers and policymakers; and the Caribbean Association for Feminist Research and Action (CAFRA), whose projects have included monitoring the Caribbean Basin Initiative effects, exposing worker conditions in Jamaica's export processing zones, and aiding rural women through the Women in Caribbean Agriculture Project (Bolles 1993). A more occupationally focused group is Trinidad and Tobago's National Union of Domestic Employees (NUDE), which utilizes actions taken at UN women's conferences and other international events to mobilize for change at home (Karides 2002).

By the 1990s international development agencies had begun to adopt GAD rhetoric in their mission statements, but GAD was used more as an analytic framework than as a development strategy – possibly because it is easier to discuss empowerment than to implement it (Burn 2005). Indeed, even in supportive circumstances, when women's equality is considered an important goal of the state, as in the revolutionary experiences of Cuba or China, the changes tend to be token reforms rather than major transformations. In the case of international development agencies, they have tended to adopt the European model called "gender mainstreaming," which "requires a gender analysis to make sure that gender equality concerns are taken into account in all development activities" (Burn 2005: 151). As a result, women are actively engaged in the development process, but women's activism for gender equality is not promoted, as GAD suggests it should be.

Nonetheless, many grassroots groups are actively developing transnational linkages that promote a GAD perspective (Naples & Desai 2002) and international feminist conferences are helping to create a transnational feminism that has many commonalities across nations while retaining local forms. This combination of local creativity and the transnational sharing of ideas may well push GAD ideas forward into future tangible gender equity development programs, and/or toward creating a newer women, culture, and development (WCD) perspective of which Bhavnani et al. (2003) are proponents.

SEE ALSO: Division of Labor; Global Economy; International Gender Division of Labor; Political Economy; Women, Economy and

REFERENCES AND SUGGESTED READINGS

Acosta-Belén, E. & Bose, C. E. (1995) Colonialism, Structural Subordination, and Empowerment: Women in the Development Process in Latin America and the Caribbean. In: Bose, C. E. & Acosta-Belén, E. (Eds.), *Women in the Latin American Development Process*. Temple University Press, Philadelphia, pp. 15–36.

Benía, L. (Ed.) (1982) *Women and Development: The Sexual Division of Labor in Rural Societies*. Praeger, New York.

Benía, L. & Sen, G. (1981) Accumulation, Reproduction, and Women's Role in Economic Development: Boserup Revisited. *Signs: Journal of Women in Culture and Society* 7: 279–98.

Bhavnani, K.-K., Foran, J., & Kurian, P. A. (2003) An Introduction to Women, Culture, and Development. In: Bhavnani, K.-K., Foran, J., & Kurian, P. A. (Eds.), *Feminist Futures: Re-Imagining Women, Culture, and Development*. Zed Books, New York, pp. 1–21.

Blumberg, R. L. (1995) Gender, Microenterprise, Performance, and Power: Case Studies from the Dominican Republic, Ecuador, Guatemala, and Swaziland. In: Bose, C. E. & Acosta-Belén, E. (Eds.), *Women in the Latin American Development Process*. Temple University Press, Philadelphia, pp. 194–226.

Bolles, A. L. (1988) Theories of Women and Development in the Caribbean: The Ongoing Debate." In: Mohammed, P. & Shepherd, C. (Eds.), *Gender in Caribbean Development*. University of the West Indies, Cave Hill, Barbados, pp. 21–34

Bolles, A. L. (1993) Doing It for Themselves: Women's Research and Action in the Commonwealth Caribbean. In: Acosta-Belén, E. & Bose, C. E. (Eds.), *Researching Women in Latin America and the Caribbean*. Westview Press, Boulder, pp. 153–74.

Boserup, E. (1970) *Woman's Role in Economic Development*. St. Martin's Press, New York.

Burn, S. M. (2005) *Women Across Cultures: A Global Perspective*, 2nd edn. McGraw Hill, New York.

Gunder Frank, A. (1969) *Latin America: Underdevelopment or Revolution*. Monthly Review Press, New York.

Karides, M. (2002) Linking Local Efforts with Global Struggles: Trinidad's National Union of Domestic Employees. In: *Women's Activism and*

Globalization: Linking Local Struggles and Transnational Politics. Routledge, New York, pp. 156–71.

Mohanty, C. T. (1991) Cartographies of Struggle: Third World Women and the Politics of Feminism. In: Mohanty, C. T., Russo, A., & Torres, L. (Eds.), *Third World Women and the Politics of Feminism.* Indiana University Press, Bloomington, pp. 1–47.

Moser, C. (1989) Gender Planning in the Third World: Meeting Practical and Strategic Gender Needs. *World Development* 17: pp. 1799–825.

Naples, N. & Desai, M. (2002) *Women's Activism and Globalization: Linking Local Struggles and Transnational Politics.* Routledge, New York.

Sen, G. & Grown, C. (1987) *Development, Crises, and Alternative Visions.* Monthly Review Press, New York.

gender, deviance and

Gloria Gadsden

Missing from traditional and most contemporary discussions of deviance and crime is the notion of gender. A rather accessible definition of gender can be found in most introductory sociology textbooks. For the purposes of this entry, gender is defined as the social positions, attitudes, traits, and behaviors that a society assigns to females and males (Macionis 2004). A close examination of theories of deviance reveals an androcentric or male-oriented perspective. Early theorists and researchers in particular extrapolated from studies of boys and men when attempting to explain female deviant behavior. So, barring examinations of a few deviant behaviors, most notably shoplifting, violations of sexual norms (e.g., promiscuity, teen pregnancy, prostitution), status offenses (e.g., runaways), and infanticide, there were, and still are, few serious considerations of female deviant behavior.

Feminists, or members of society advocating equality between the sexes, have made a few strides with respect to introducing notions of gender into theories of deviance and crime. While a single comprehensive theory addressing gender and deviance is still missing from the literature, there appear to be four main schools of thought: (1) the chivalry perspective, (2) patriarchal considerations, (3) the women's liberation hypothesis, and (4) the theory of victimization.

The chivalry perspective attempts to explain why girls and women are not seen as deviants. Why do most people think of boys and men when considering deviant and criminal behavior, specifically violent deviant and criminal behavior? This theory proposes that members of society are socialized not to see girls and women as deviants. Chesney-Lind and Sheldon (1998) suggest that almost all members of society talk about delinquency, by which they generally mean male delinquency. More specifically, this argument theorizes that powerful male members of society (e.g., police officers, judges, the male-dominated media) "protect" or "save" girls/women from the label of deviance (Felson 2002). Humphries (1999) specifically postulates a chivalry approach with respect to women and cocaine use in the 1980s and 1990s. She determined that in the early media coverage of cocaine use, white middle-class women who used cocaine were presented as promiscuous and as "bad" mothers. Still, television networks showed a remarkable degree of tolerance toward these women. And with respect to domestic violence, Girschick (2002) notes that current understandings of rape and battering suggest that women are not perpetrators. More specifically, according to present-day social norms and values, women do not rape and women do not batter.

This perspective posits that members of the male-dominated criminal justice system will ignore, dismiss, and/or explain away female deviance and crime. For example, some theorists have attempted to explain away girls' accountability for their deviance by stating girls' deviant behavior commonly relates to an abusive home life, whereas boys' deviant behavior reflects their involvement in a delinquent lifestyle (Dembo et al. 1995). Girls and women, therefore, are not seen as deviant because male members of society protect them from the label. Male police officers, prosecutors, and judges have a traditionally chivalrous attitude toward women and treat them with more leniency than men. Regrettably, this theory, regardless of its potential accuracy, perpetuates the cycle of male-centered perspectives, attempting to explain female behavior by examining male attitudes and behaviors.

Patriarchal explanations posit that male-dominated social institutions, especially the family, are designed to prevent girls and women from engaging in deviance and crime. Socialization processes within the family control girls more than boys, teaching boys to be risk takers while teaching girls to avoid risk (Hagan 1989). According to Akers (2000), in patriarchal families the father's occupation places him in the "command" position (e.g., manager, supervisor, CEO) and the mother either stays at home or works in a job where she occupies the "obey" position (i.e., taking orders from supervisors). In these families, according to the theory, the behaviors of girls and women are more closely monitored and controlled (Thorne 1994). Girls are expected to adhere to stricter moral standards and face a stronger sense of guilt and disapproval when they break the rules (Chesney-Lind & Sheldon 1998).

Unfortunately, much like the previous theory, this is a male-oriented perspective. This line of reasoning argues that males control girls and women and, therefore, control female deviance and crime. These androcentric theories do not attempt to understand female deviance in and of itself, explaining female behavior by way of male behavior (Chesney-Lind & Pasko 2004). They are flawed and have been, for the most part, discredited.

The remaining two perspectives, the women's liberation hypothesis and the theory of victimization, attempt to explain the deviant behavior of girls and women apart from the attitudes/behavior of males. The women's liberation hypothesis proposes that as the gap between women's and men's social equality decreases, the gap between women's and men's deviant behavior decreases as well. This theoretical explanation suggests that the women's movement has brought about changes in traditional gender roles, greater equality for women, and an increase in the female labor force. An unintended consequence of this "liberation" for women is a greater involvement in deviance and crime. According to Adler (1975), the movement for gender equality has a darker side. Some women are insisting on equal opportunity in fields of legitimate endeavor while other women are demanding access to the world of crime.

The "liberation" hypothesis, however, has not received much empirical support. Though increasingly represented in the labor force, women continue to be concentrated in traditional "pink-collar" work – teaching, clerical and retail sales work, nursing, and other subordinate roles – that reflects a persistence of traditional gender roles (Zaplin 1998). In contrast, contemporary gender differences in quality and quantity of crime continue to parallel closely those of the thirteenth century. Additionally, Chesney-Lind and Pasko (2004) state there is no evidence to suggest that as women's labor-force participation has increased, girls' deviant behavior has also increased.

Therefore, it has not yet been compellingly demonstrated that female crime rates are significantly correlated with increasing gender equality. In fact, patterns of female deviance have remained relatively consistent over time.

One of the most persuasive theories regarding girls' and women's deviance is predicated on the reality girls and women face as victims. The theory of victimization proposes that women are deviants in part because of their status as victims of male abuse and/or violence. Chesney-Lind and Pasko (2004) recognize that girls are much more likely to be the victims of child sexual abuse than are boys. Additionally, girls are much more likely than boys to be assaulted by a family member (often a stepfather) and women offenders frequently report abuse in their life histories. About half of the women in jail (48 percent) and 57 percent of women in state prisons report experiences of sexual and/or physical abuse in their lives. Chesney-Lind and Pasko note that all of the girls in gangs interviewed hail from a more troubled background than boys in gangs. And with respect to spousal homicide, Zaplin (1998) revealed that wives are far more likely to have been victims of domestic violence and turn to murder only when in mortal fear. Husbands who murder wives, however, have rarely been in fear for their lives.

Empirical research does suggest that exposure to abuse and violence, too often a reality girls and women face, could compel girls/women to engage in various types of deviance (e.g., running away, truancy) and ultimately crime (e.g., theft, drug abuse, prostitution) (Flowers 2001). In fact, some theorists have highlighted the fact that a potential survival mechanism, running away from home, continues to be the most prevalent offense for female juvenile delinquents (Chesney-Lind & Pasko 2004). This theory, although it addresses girls' and women's relationships with boys and men, serves as a building block for theories that consider the unique status of girls and women in society and its contribution to deviant behavior.

In conclusion, contemporary research continually reflects a need to take female deviance and crime much more seriously. While there are currently four major schools of thought, two have been discredited and one has little empirical support. It is evident that studies of women and deviance are lacking, even now. There is an increasing body of research examining girls and women engaged in deviance and crime (e.g., female gang members), but most of the contemporary research continues to examine girls and women engaged in traditional deviant and criminal behaviors (e.g., status offenses, prostitution) and/or limits discussions of women and deviance to women's status as victims.

A partial explanation for this continuing trend hails from Akers (2000), who has suggested that there is little empirically to sustain the criticism that current theories are falsified or inadequate when applied to the criminal behavior of women, or to uphold the conclusion that girl/women-specific theories are needed to account for gender ratios in crime and deviance. And yet there are clear indications of differences in female and male deviant and criminal behaviors, arrest rates, and incarceration rates. What can explain these differences if no additional theoretical considerations are needed? Sociologists need to spend more time considering the unique aspects of the lives of girls and women with respect to deviance. Additionally, demographic considerations must be taken into account more systematically. Race, class, age, and many other social characteristics that are commonplace in male-oriented research on deviance and crime must be folded into theories examining girls and women. "We've come a long way baby," but we still have a long way to go.

SEE ALSO: Crime; Deviance, Crime and; Deviance, Theories of; Domestic Violence; Feminism; Feminism, First, Second, and Third Waves; Patriarchy; Rape/Sexual Assault as Crime; Sexism; Victimization; Women's Movements

REFERENCES AND SUGGESTED READINGS

Adler, F. (1975) *Sisters in Crime: The Rise of the New Female Criminal*. McGraw-Hill, New York.
Akers, R. (2000) *Criminological Theories: Introduction, Evaluation and Application*. Roxbury Press, Los Angeles.
Chesney-Lind, M. & Pasko, L. (2004) *The Female Offender: Girls, Women and Crime*. Sage, Walnut Creek, CA.
Chesney-Lind, M. & Sheldon, R. (1998) *Girls, Delinquency and Juvenile Justice*. Wadsworth, Belmont, CA.
Dembo, J. S., Sue, C. C., Borden, P., & Manning, D. (1995) Gender Differences in Service Needs Among Youths Entering a Juvenile Assessment Center: A Replication Study. Paper presented at the annual meeting of the Society of Social Problems, Washington, DC.
Felson, R. (2002) *Violence and Gender Reexamined*. American Psychological Association, Washington, DC.
Flowers, R. B. (2001) *Runaway Kids and Teenage Prostitution*. Greenwood Press, London.
Girschick, L. (2002) *Woman-to-Woman Sexual Violence: Does She Call It Rape?* Northeastern University Press, Boston.
Hagan, J. (1989) Micro- and Macro-Structures of Delinquency Causation and a Power-Control Theory of Gender and Delinquency. In: Messner, S., Krohn, M., & Liska, A. (Eds.), *Theoretical Integration in the Study of Deviance and Crime*. State University of New York Press, Albany.
Humphries, D. (1999) *Crack Mothers: Pregnancy, Drugs and the Media*. Ohio State University Press, Columbus.
Macionis, J. (2004) *Society: The Basics*. Prentice-Hall, Englewood Cliffs, NJ.
Thorne, B. (1994) *Gender Play: Girls and Boys in School*. Rutgers University Press, Piscataway, NJ.
Zaplin, R. (1998) *Female Offenders: Critical Perspectives and Effective Interventions*. Apsen Publishers, Gaithersburg, MD.

gender, education and

Jennifer Pearson and Catherine Riegle-Crumb

Social scientists and educational researchers paid relatively little attention to issues of gender in education until the 1970s, when questions emerged concerning equity in girls' and women's access to education across the world. Researchers documented a link between increasing rates of female education in developing countries and a subsequent decline in fertility rates (e.g., Boserup 1970). In the context of an emerging global economy, increasing female representation in primary and secondary education was cited as an important factor in promoting national economic development, and therefore seen as a vehicle for social change.

As the feminist movement increased awareness of widespread gender inequality within US society, researchers began to focus on the educational system as a site of and explanation for women's subordinated status. Feminist scholars documented sex discrimination in educational experiences and outcomes, and this early work led to the passage of Title IX in 1972, legislation that prohibited discrimination on the basis of sex in federally funded educational programs.

During the 1970s and 1980s, women gained access to higher education and their share of college degrees climbed steadily. Women now comprise the majority of US college students and have achieved parity with men in number of undergraduate and graduate degrees, though men are over-represented in the most prestigious colleges and universities and obtain a greater number of doctoral degrees than women (Jacobs 1996). Despite this greater equality in educational access, women remain significantly behind men in economic and social status. There remains a significant gender gap in pay, while women are also concentrated in low status, sex-stereotyped occupations and continue to bear primary responsibility for domestic tasks despite their increased labor force participation. This paradox has led researchers to shift their focus from women's educational access to their academic experiences and outcomes.

While education is seen as an important mechanism of upward mobility in US society, many sociologists of education have described the educational system as an institution of social and cultural reproduction. Existing patterns of inequality, including those related to gender, are reproduced within schools through formal and informal processes. Knowledge of how the educational system contributes to the status of women requires a look at the institution itself and the processes that occur within schools.

While women's access to education has improved, sex segregation within the educational system persists. Research following Title IX documented a wide gender gap in course-taking during high school that led to different educational and occupational paths for men and women. For example, the American Association of University Women revealed in a 1992 report titled *Shortchanging Girls, Shortchanging America* that girls took fewer advanced math and science courses during high school, and these course-taking patterns left them unprepared to pursue these fields in higher education. This contrasts with the primary school years, where girls receive better grades in math and are often over-represented in high-ability math courses, while boys are over-represented in low-ability courses. Additionally, average math test scores for boys and girls are similar, although there is more variation among boys, leaving them with the highest, but also with the lowest, scores. Girls' attitudes toward and interest in math and science begin to decline during the middle-school years (fourth through eighth grade), and gender differences in test scores in these subjects are apparent by high school.

Recent research suggests that the gaps in high school course-taking are closing, and girls and boys now take similar numbers of math and science courses. This may be the result of increased educational requirements and fewer choices in course enrollment, as girls continue to score lower on standardized tests and express less interest in these subjects. In addition, girls are now taking advanced courses such as calculus at comparable rates to boys, with the exception of physics. Furthermore, technology and computer courses remain highly gendered: though both boys and girls take computer courses, boys are more likely to take high skills classes, such as those that focus on computer programming, while girls are over-represented in courses featuring word-processing and data entry, skills associated with secretarial work (AAUW 1999). Conversely, girls are more highly concentrated in the language arts, including literature, composition, and foreign language courses, and they tend to score higher than boys on verbal skills on standardized tests. This gender gap in favor of girls does not appear to be closing, but it is given relatively little attention in discussions of gender and education.

These high school course-taking patterns foreshadow gender differences in higher education, where a high degree of sex segregation remains in terms of degrees and specializations. In the United States, women are concentrated in education, English, nursing, and some social sciences, and they are less likely than men to pursue degrees in science, math, engineering, and technology. As these male-dominated fields are highly valued and highly salaried, women's absence from them accounts for a great deal of the gender gap in pay.

Sex typing in education appears to be a worldwide phenomenon, though it varies somewhat in degree and scope between countries. In countries where educational access is limited and reserved for members of the elite, women are often as likely as men to have access to all parts of the curriculum (Bradley 2000; Hanson 1996). However, in countries with more extensive educational systems, women have lower rates of participation in science and technology (Hanson 1996), fields greatly valued because of their link to development and modernity.

Some have used a rational choice approach in explaining the persistence of educational segregation, particularly that of higher education. These scholars suggest that women choose female-dominated fields despite their lower status and pay because they will suffer smaller penalties for an absence from the workforce for child rearing; however, women in male-dominated fields not only receive higher pay but are also offered more flexibility and autonomy. Others suggest that while individual choices are at play in perpetuating sex segregation, these choices are constrained by cultural beliefs that limit what women (and men) see as possible or appropriate options (Correll 2004). Math, science, and technology are regarded as masculine subjects, especially given their emphasis on objective knowledge and rational action, and women are seen as ill-equipped for these fields. Conversely, subjects such as language arts and nursing are perceived as feminine subjects, and men are largely under-represented in these fields. In contrast to the push to include women in male-dominated fields, however, the under-representation of men in these subject areas goes largely unacknowledged and is often not regarded as problematic, probably due to the low status and low paid jobs associated with these fields.

These beliefs about appropriate interests and talents for men and women are part of a "hidden curriculum" that involves interactions and covert lessons that reinforce relations of gender, as well as those of race and social class, by teaching and preparing students for their appropriate adult roles. Several scholars have examined this hidden curriculum within schools, pointing to ways in which classroom interactions with teachers and between students impart these lessons. Observational studies by Sadker and Sadker (1994) suggest that in the same schools and in the same classes, boys receive more attention than girls. Teachers ask them more questions and offer them more feedback and constructive criticism, all of which are essential to learning. Boys monopolize classroom discussion beginning in the early school years, and girls become quieter over time, participating little in college classrooms. These classroom dynamics reinforce notions of femininity, teaching girls that they should be quiet, passive, and defer to boys, characteristics that disadvantage girls in competitive fields of math and science. Furthermore, an emphasis on social and romantic success can distract young women from their studies and make academic pursuits tangential.

Several feminist scholars have advocated single-sex schooling in order to avoid these negative consequences. They argue that girls in all girls' schools have greater achievement, higher educational and career aspirations, attend more selective colleges, take more math courses and express a greater interest in math, and hold less stereotyped notions of female roles. These benefits allegedly result from smaller classes, higher teacher quality and attention, and freedom from social pressures of romance. However, other scholars argue that single-sex education itself does not ensure any particular outcomes because these schools vary greatly in the inspirations, desired outcomes, and sociocultural environments they embody. Indeed, recent research on single-sex schools is often inconsistent, and their advantages in comparison to coeducational schools may have decreased after public schools began addressing issues of gender bias. More research is needed on school characteristics that are associated with improved outcomes for girls.

Some educational researchers suggest that concern for girls' education overshadows boys' disadvantages in education, advocating a shift in focus to boys. They argue that though the gender gap in math and science is closing, boys remain behind in language arts course-taking and verbal skills. Further, boys are over-represented in remedial and special education classes, and they are more likely to fail a course or drop out of school. Others contend that these disadvantages are short-term costs of maintaining long-term privilege: subjects in which girls outperform boys are devalued, so boys focus their energy elsewhere, such as in sports or math and science, which hold more prestige and will earn greater status and pay in the long run. Moreover, negative outcomes tend to be concentrated among working-class boys and boys of color, suggesting that these problems may reflect race and class inequality rather than disadvantages affecting all boys. Regardless, considering boys only as a contrast group to the experiences of girls, rather than examining their position within and experiences of the educational system, will not provide a complete understanding of issues of gender in education. Future research focused on the experiences and behaviors of boys in schools is needed to further this knowledge.

Research on how race and class shape gendered educational experiences and outcomes has been relatively scarce, and only in the past ten years have race and class become focal points in research on gender in education. The advantages granted boys in schools are not equal among all boys: working-class boys and boys of color do not demonstrate the same academic success as white, middle-class boys. Further, among some groups, girls surpass their male counterparts in math and science course-taking and achievement. Ferguson (2000) examines how the hidden curriculum

affects black boys, noting that many school practices disadvantage black boys, leading them to seek achievement and masculinity in ways that are detrimental to their future success. Similarly, perceived cultural differences can penalize girls who do not meet white, middle-class standards of femininity: working-class girls and girls of color are sometimes seen as troublemakers for being outspoken or assertive. Research on how the intersection of race, class, and gender shapes educational experiences and outcomes is an important direction for the future of the sociology of education.

SEE ALSO: Femininities/Masculinities; Gender, Development and; Gender Ideology and Gender Role Ideology; Hidden Curriculum; Inequality/Stratification, Gender; Math, Science, and Technology Education; Racialized Gender; Schools, Single-Sex; Standardized Educational Tests; Teaching and Gender

REFERENCES AND SUGGESTED READINGS

American Association of University Women (1999) *Gender Gaps: Where Schools Still Fail Our Children*. Marlowe, New York.
Bailey, S. M. (Ed.) (2002) *The Jossey-Bass Reader on Gender in Education*. Jossey-Bass, San Francisco.
Boserup, E. (1970) *Women's Role in Economic Development*. Allen & Unwin, New York.
Bradley, K. (2000) The Incorporation of Women into Higher Education: Paradoxical Outcomes? *Sociology of Education* 73: 1–18.
Correll, S. (2004) Constraints into Preferences: Gender, Status and Emerging Career Aspirations. *American Sociological Review* 69: 93–113.
Ferguson, A. A. (2000) *Bad Boys: Public Schools in the Making of Black Masculinity*. University of Michigan Press, Ann Arbor.
Hanson, S. L. (1996) Gender Stratification in the Science Pipeline: A Comparative Analysis of Seven Countries. *Gender and Society* 10: 271–90.
Holland, D. C. & Eisenhart, M. A. (1990) *Educated in Romance: Women, Achievement, and College Culture*. University of Chicago Press, Chicago.
Jacobs, J. A. (1996) Gender Inequality and Higher Education. *Annual Review of Sociology* 22: 153–85.
Sadker, M. & Sadker, D. (1994) *Failing at Fairness: How Our Schools Cheat Girls*. Simon & Schuster, New York.

gender, friendship and

Stacey Oliker

The subject of gender and friendship links two fields of sociological scholarship. Gender was rarely a salient theme in pioneering studies of friendship, communities, and social networks that emerged in anthropology and sociology in the 1960s. By the 1980s, though, burgeoning gender scholarship in the social sciences ignited interest in gender and friendship. For the most part, the sociology of gender and friendship has explored how differences in the meanings, expectations, experiences, and identities that are culturally associated with biological sex create patterns of difference in the friendships of men and women. A second perspective, examining friendship patterns as a force in the constitution of gender difference and inequality, is less prominent in the literature, but it is promising.

Sociologists trace the modern forms of both gender and friendship to the emergence of a market economy, the separation of work and family life, and the cultural changes that cultivated modern individualism. In the nineteenth-century public sphere that men entered as workers and citizens, men developed forms of individualism and masculine identity that emphasized autonomy, competitiveness, and the emotional toughness to suppress personal concerns that could contaminate their public roles. In the newly defined private sphere of family that became women's proper domain, women elaborated new private themes of individualism, emphasizing emotional introspection and expressiveness, which supported the new maternal role of attentive and responsive nurturer and moral exemplar. From these gender polarities in culture and experience, men and women developed distinctive versions of the warmer, more individualized friendship patterns of modern society (Oliker 1989).

In the institutions of private life, middle-class women forged new patterns of intimate friendship, while masculine intimacy developed more ambivalently – in conflict with public sphere expectations and ideals of masculinity, and in the less private sites of male camaraderie in the streets, clubs, and taverns. Contemporary patterns of gender and friendship originated in this era, where modern meanings of masculinity and femininity formed, and where institutions of work and family were reconstituted in sturdy forms that carried nineteenth-century gender ideas into the present (Oliker 1989; Oliker in Adams and Allan 1998; Walker 1994; Wellman 1992).

Since the 1980s, studies have explored gender differences in communication between friends, friendship over the life course, and network size and composition. The most frequently identified gender difference is in intimacy, that is, the exchange of self-disclosure, private experience, and emotional expression. Women talk more about themselves and show their feelings more to friends than men do. Women often bond by intimate talk, men by shared activity over time. Scholars disagree about what gender differences in intimacy mean for understanding friendship and for understanding gender. A "different but equal" position holds that we have misleadingly "feminized" our concept of intimacy: narrowly associating intimacy with expressive, self-disclosive exchange and ignoring the bonds created in the familiarities of joint activity and the exchange of instrumental help distorts our understanding of male intimacy in friendship (Wright 1998).

Those who maintain that the concept of self-disclosive intimacy is meaningful argue that conceptualizing intimacy in introspective and emotional terms illuminates the personal and social meanings of close friendship. When asked, men and women define intimacy similarly, in terms of self-disclosure and emotional warmth, and both sexes assert that this kind of intimacy is the central characteristic of close relationships. Studies of the effects of disclosive intimacy suggest that both men and women feel better off and happier in relationships when this kind of intimacy is present (Reis 1998). Though shared activities may promote emotional intimacy, the settings and tasks of shared activity may discourage the attentiveness and candor required to achieve the bonds both men and women associate with close friendship.

Intimacy, affection, trust, and commitment to friends are not the same qualities, though the literature often elides them. Plausibly, each has different meanings for and influences on individuals, relationships, and even larger institutions, such as marriage and the family. For example, through self-disclosive intimacy with best friends, women appear to actively reinforce each other's commitments to marriage and evolve strategies of marital bargaining and accommodation. Those who do not talk to close friends about problems in their marriages are unlikely to receive as much communal reinforcement of social norms of marital commitment, tailored to their particular perceptions, and do the kind of collective "marriage work" that stabilizes marriage. Gender differences in self-disclosive intimacy with friends may position men and women differently in the process of sustaining marriage commitments and stable families (Oliker 1989).

Sociologists have used depth psychology (primarily psychoanalysis), role theory, varieties of structural explanation (prominently, network concepts), and interactional approaches to explain how gender shapes friendship. With the exception of psycho-dispositional frameworks, all are deployable for an alternative approach to gender and friendship, which examines how friendship patterns shape gender. For example, studies of social networks and of foci of activity suggest how gendered divisions of labor result in men's looser-knit and more work-focused networks that give men better access to information and contacts that advance their careers, while women's denser networks (denser in kin and neighborhood ties) offer women more resources for childrearing but fewer resources for career advancement (Smith-Lovin & McPherson 1993). In these studies, structures of friendship mediate the construction of gender inequality. Interactional frameworks that examine how gender behaviors and identities are produced in friends' interactions can explain persistent gender patterns even among individuals who may not be primed by dispositions, prompted by roles, or prodded by structural constraints. Evidence that men in cross-sex friendships are more disclosive than men in same-sex friendship and that women in cross-sex friendship are less disclosive suggests an analytical move in which gender identities and inequalities emerge in friendship dynamics (Reis 1998).

Enriching the study of gender and friendship will likely involve both analytical and methodological changes. The debate about gender differences in intimacy shows the advantages of greater conceptual precision. Such precision would also make contradictory research findings easier to sort out. Two decades of qualitative research, most often studying either men or women, posits distinctive gender differences, while quantitative research finds few gender differences and small ones. Though such contradictions are entrenched, to some extent, in contrasting methods, more comparative qualitative studies and more interpretive strategies in quantitative work are likely to produce less discordant knowledge. Conceptual precision might also inspire scholarship on gender and the social, cultural, and psychological capital gains from less intimate "weak ties" of sociability and friendly acquaintance and co-participation. Finally, by shifting the analytical frame held up to gender and friendship, research exploring how friendship shapes gender could enrich the separate areas of friendship and gender, and the subject of relations between them.

SEE ALSO: Cross-Sex Friendship; Friendship During the Later Years; Friendship: Interpersonal Aspects; Friendship, Social Inequality, and Social Change; Friendship: Structure and Context; Friendships of Adolescence; Friendships of Children; Friendships of Gay, Lesbian, and Bisexual People; Intimacy

REFERENCES AND SUGGESTED READINGS

Adams, R. G. & Allan, G. A. (Eds.) (1998) *Placing Friendship in Context*. Cambridge University Press, New York.

Oliker, S. J. (1989) *Best Friends and Marriage: Exchange Among Women*. University of California Press, Berkeley.

Reis, H. T. (1998) Gender Differences in Intimacy and Related Behaviors: Context and Process. In: Canary, D. J. & Dindia, K. (Eds.), *Sex Differences in Communication*. Lawrence Erlbaum, Mahwah, NJ, pp. 203–32.

Smith-Lovin, L. & McPherson, J. M. (1993) You Are Who You Know: A Network Approach to Gender. In: England, P. (Ed.), *Theory on Gender/ Feminism on Theory*. Aldine de Gruyter, New York, pp. 311–42.

Walker, K. (1994) Men, Women, and Friendship: What They Say and What They Do. *Gender and Society* 8(2): 246–65.

Wellman, B. (1992) Men in Networks: Private Communities, Domestic Friendships. In: Nardi, P. (Ed.), *Men's Friendships*. Sage, Newbury Park, CA, pp. 74–114.

Wright, P. H. (1998) Toward an Expanded Orientation to the Study of Sex Differences in Friendship. In: Canary, D. J. & Dindia, K. (Eds.), *Sex Differences in Communication*. Lawrence Erlbaum, Mahwah, NJ, pp. 41–64.

gender, health, and mortality

Ulla Larsen

Although life expectancy at birth of women in western societies is significantly longer than that of men (e.g., 80 versus 74 years in the United States), women experience more sickness and non-fatal health problems than men (e.g., higher morbidity). Specific biological and behavioral explanations for these gender differences are largely unknown. It remains unclear whether these gender differences in health and mortality are found throughout the world. Here, the term "gender" refers to the way biological differences are socially and culturally constructed and expressed in actions and thoughts, whereas the term "sex" is used to define a biological category based on anatomical and physiological differences between males and females. "Health" is a state of complete physical, mental, and social well-being and not merely the absence of disease or infirmity, according to the World Health Organization (WHO). "Mortality" is the rate of death in a population in a specified time period.

In the year 2000, the overall life expectancy at birth ranged from a high of 81.1 years in Japan (84.7 for women and 77.5 for men) to a low of 37.5 years in Malawi (37.8 for women and 37.1 for men), as measured from the 191 Member States of the WHO. At the beginning of the twentieth century female life expectancy exceeded male life expectancy by only 2–3 years in Europe, North America, and Australia, whereas at the beginning of the twenty-first century this gender-related difference in life expectancy was more than 10 years in some countries. Fewer deaths in childbirth help women today to live longer, accounting in part for the increase in the gap between male and female longevity. Worldwide analysis reveals a few exceptions: male life expectancy is higher than that of women (by less than a year) in a few countries (including Botswana, Namibia, and Nepal). These mortality sex differences prevail at all ages, races, and social conditions.

In 2002, worldwide, the four leading causes of disease burden (premature death and disability) over age 15 included HIV/AIDS, coronary heart disease, cerebrovascular disease, and unipolar depressive disorders. More specifically, HIV/AIDS was the leading disease burden for males and the second leading one for females (7.4 percent and 7.2 percent). The number one disease burden in females was unipolar depressive disorders (8.4 percent), whereas this disease ranked fourth for males (4.8 percent). Thus, of the four major causes of disease burden, unipolar depressive disorders have the greatest gender specific difference. Coronary heart disease and cerebrovascular disease were the second and third most common cause for males (6.8 percent and 5.0 percent), and the third and fourth most common cause for females (5.3 percent and 5.2 percent). In conclusion, unipolar depressive disorders affected women relatively more than men, while coronary heart disease was somewhat more prevalent among men.

Women experience more poor health during their lives than do men. This gender difference in overall health is assessed by determining the number of days confined to bed, the frequency of sick leave from work, rates of yearly doctor and hospital visits, and the number of self-reported disease symptoms. For example, in the 1991 US National Health Interview Survey, the total proportion disabled (reporting difficulty with one or more activities of daily living) was nearly twice as high for women as men. However, the finding that women experience more health problems than men is being challenged with recent research documenting a more nuanced picture of gender differences in health, at least within developed western societies. For example, one study found no consistent gender differences in reported health symptoms for young people in England. Another study, based on men and women working full-time for an English bank, found difference by sex in symptoms of malaise (e.g., difficulty sleeping, nerves, and always feeling tired), but not in physical symptoms (e.g., hay fever, constipation, and a bad back) or in minor psychiatric morbidity (a 12-item general health questionnaire). The hypothesis that women are more willing to acknowledge and report poor health has also not been supported consistently in recent studies.

More research is needed to better understand the prevalence and causes of these general health differences between men and women. Future research will benefit from the use of health indices that have been evaluated for their validity and reliability in different research settings in order to ensure that findings between countries and across time are comparable and generalizable. In addition, the accuracy and completeness of health and mortality statistics are crucial in determining sex or gender differences. For example, measured differences might be the result of incomplete coverage of national death statistics, interviewer bias in health survey data, or because hospital and clinical data on disease include only the population attending these institutions, although women and men may be differentially admitted and treated.

Differing life span and quality of health can be due to biological factors, but medical research has not always accounted for sex differences. In 1977, in response to the adverse events following use of thalidomide and diethylstilbestrol in pregnant women, the US Food and Drug Administration (FDA) issued guidelines recommending that women in their childbearing years be excluded from phase 1 clinical trials (safety evaluations of new drugs based on healthy subjects). On scientific grounds it was justified to exclude women as clinical research participants because it was believed that men and women did not differ significantly in response to treatment in most situations, and the inclusion of women would introduce additional noise (from the hormonal variations caused by the menstrual cycle) and increase the heterogeneity of the study population. These faulty assumptions led to a period in which women were under-represented in research subject populations, a trend that may have reduced the effectiveness of new therapeutics for female patients. Thus, in 1985, the US Public Health Service Task Force on Women's Health Issues concluded that health care for women and the quality of health information available to women had been compromised by the historical lack of research on women's health. In 1993, with the National Institutes of Health Revitalization Act, the guidelines for inclusion of women became law and the FDA lifted the 1977 restrictions. In 1998 the FDA issued a rule allowing the agency to refuse new drug applications that did not appropriately analyze safety and efficacy data by sex.

In 2001 the Institute of Medicine formed a Committee on Understanding the Biology of Sex and Gender Differences, which found evidence suggesting that published research frequently did not present findings by sex, even though the data were available. It was noted that research on women's health and the inclusion of women in clinical trials would have limited value unless the actual differences between males and females were systematically studied and reported in published research. This committee noted that a number of sex-based differences in health are attributable to sexual genotype (XX in the female and XY in the male on the 23rd chromosome pair) and hormonal or genetic differences between the two sexes. Also, men and women have dissimilar exposures (e.g., work and leisure activities), susceptibilities, and responses to initiating agents. Finally, sex differences in energy storage and metabolism result in variable responses to pharmacological drugs and the development of diseases such as obesity, autoimmune disorders, and coronary heart disease.

Examining the different experience of men and women with a particular disease, such as coronary heart disease, illustrates the complex effects of sex and gender on health, as well as the need for more research. Coronary heart disease begins *in utero*, evolves through childhood and young adulthood, and becomes a serious and often fatal health problem in middle and old age. Plaques of cholesterol and other cellular materials are deposited in the coronary arteries of the heart and over time compromise the flow of blood, causing cell and organ death (myocardial infarction). In general, men manifest symptoms 10–20 years earlier than women, have higher prevalence of primary risk factors, and die at earlier ages, although women who have had a myocardial infarction are much more likely to die within a year compared to men. Female sex hormones (estrogen) reduce women's risk of coronary heart disease, in part by mitigating negative effects of serum lipids (fats in the bloodstream), while men's higher testosterone levels have unfavorable effects on serum lipids. In many non-industrial societies, sex differences in cholesterol levels are minor or absent, largely an effect of diets low in saturated fats. It might also be that sex differences in serum lipid levels are linked to body composition, men having more abdominal fat, whereas women have more hip and thigh fat.

Several longitudinal studies, such as the Framingham Heart Study (US), the Tromso Heart Study (Norway), and the National Health and Nutrition Examination Survey (US), documented that genetics, age, and environmental and lifestyle factors are associated with onset of coronary heart disease. For example, environmental agents such as smoking, diet high in calories and saturated fat, obesity, a sedentary lifestyle, and psychosocial stress are linked to high blood pressure, high cholesterol, and diabetes. These factors are risk factors for coronary heart disease in both males and females, although susceptibilities and responses vary by sex. However, these studies did not explain why such sex differences exist. Smoking is a strong risk factor for coronary heart disease and the increase in smoking among women relative to men has contributed to narrowing the gap between men and women in mortality from coronary heart disease. There is evidence suggesting that medical care reduces coronary heart disease mortality more for men than for women, at least in the US. Women's complaints about chest pains tend to get cursory attention and women are less likely to get diagnostic evaluations. The data indicate that women get treatment at more advanced disease stages and more often have emergency surgery. Finally, heart conditions often present different symptoms in men and women, but more is known about this disease in men, in part because women often were excluded from clinical trials and epidemiological studies. Results

from research on men have simply been extended and applied to women, although it is now acknowledged that men and women have different exposures to risk factors and respond differently to some of the same risk factors. This underscores the importance of designing studies that address heart disease risk factors, treatment, and prevention in women.

Men and women respond differently to stress (the perception of excessive demands with which an individual is unable to cope), which is a risk factor for coronary heart disease. Lack of control induces stress and evidence suggests that women experience less control than men. In general, women experience more stress from their work because they have relatively lower status jobs with less control, less security, and less financial reward. In addition, women usually take on a greater burden of household chores, including childcare. Women do report more stress than men, but it has been argued that women simply express their distress more than men. Recent research showed that women are not socialized to complain more than men (express more stress), although it is possible that women and men feel differently about expressing emotional problems. Thus, there is accumulating evidence from western societies that women encounter more stress than men in their daily lives. Hence, stress might be a more important risk factor for coronary heart disease for women than men, although the higher levels of estrogen somewhat protect women from the negative effects of stress.

The question is whether the effect of stress on cardiovascular health is different for women and men. Laboratory studies showed that men express greater adrenaline response to stress than women, and it is hypothesized that women are protected against elevation of adrenaline because of higher levels of circulating estrogen. Elevated levels of circulating adrenaline may be bad for cardiovascular health because adrenaline stimulates the release of metabolites that contribute to raising levels of serum cholesterol. In addition, adrenaline is involved with the regulation of blood pressure, and repeated high blood pressure may lead to sustained hypertension. Studies of men and women in a number of non-manual occupations showed significantly higher adrenaline levels in men on working days than on weekends, but no such difference for women. Furthermore, self-reported stress experienced on rest and workdays was significantly associated with adrenaline response in men, but not in women. This difference in adrenaline response was seen, even though women and men reported (by questionnaire) similar levels of stress on workdays and the weekend and both sexes reported higher stress on workdays. Men and women also reported similar mood states, with the exception that men's anxiety dropped after work, while women's did not change. Thus, differences in subjective experience could not explain differences in adrenaline response to work between men and women, suggesting the influence of biological mechanisms. In summary, sex differences in coronary heart disease and mortality appear to be due to the interaction of multiple biological and behavioral factors.

Despite the importance of understanding why women live as much as 10 years longer than men and why women experience poorer health throughout their lives, so far no behavioral or biological explanation adequately explains this paradox. It is unlikely that biological and acquired risk differences fully explain why women experience poorer health, but live longer, for psychosocial aspects of symptoms and health care seeking (illness behavior) might play an important role.

SEE ALSO: Differential Treatment of Children by Sex; Gender, Aging and; Infant, Child, and Maternal Health and Mortality; Population and Gender; Sex and Gender; Women's Health

REFERENCES AND SUGGESTED READINGS

Howson, C. P., Harrison, P. F., Hotra, D., & Law, M. (Eds.) (1996) *In Her Lifetime: Female Morbidity and Mortality in Sub-Saharan Africa*. Institute of Medicine, National Academy Press, Washington, DC.
Hunt, K. & Annandale, E. (Eds.) (1999) Special Issue: Gender and Health. *Social Science and Medicine* 48(1):1–138.
Lopez, A. D., Ahmad, O. B., Guillot, M., Ferguson, B. D., Salomon, J. A., Murray, C. J. L., & Hill, K. H. (2002) *World Mortality in 2000: Life Tables for 191 Countries*. World Health Organization, Geneva, pp. 11–14.
Pollard, T. M. & Hyatt, S. B. (Eds.) (1999) *Sex, Gender and Health*. Biosocial Society Symposium Series. Cambridge University Press, Cambridge.
Wizemann, T. M. & Pardue, M. L. (2001) *Exploring the Biological Contributions to Human Health: Does Sex Matter?* Institute of Medicine, National Academy Press, Washington, DC, pp. 21–6.
World Health Organization (2003) *World Health Report 2003: Shaping the Future*. World Health Organization, Geneva, p. 14.

gender ideology and gender role ideology

Amy Kroska

Both gender ideology and gender role ideology refer to attitudes regarding the appropriate roles, rights, and responsibilities of women and men in society. The concept can reflect these attitudes generally or in a specific domain, such as an economic, familial, legal, political, and/or social domain. Most gender ideology constructs are unidimensional and range from traditional, conservative, or anti-feminist to egalitarian, liberal, or feminist. Traditional gender ideologies emphasize the value of distinctive roles for women and men. According to a traditional gender ideology about the family, for example, men fulfill their family roles through instrumental, breadwinning activities and women fulfill their roles through nurturant, homemaker, and parenting activities. Egalitarian ideologies regarding the family, by contrast, endorse and value men's and women's equal and shared breadwinning and nurturant family roles.

Gender ideology also sometimes refers to widespread societal beliefs that legitimate gender inequality. For example, Lorber (1994: 30) defines gender ideology as "the justification of gender statuses, particularly, their differential evaluation. The dominant ideology tends to suppress criticism by making these evaluations seem natural." Used in this way, gender ideology is not a variable that ranges from conservative to liberal; instead, it refers to specific types of beliefs – those that support gender stratification. Gender ideology in the remainder of this summary refers to the first sense of the concept: attitudes that vary from conservative to liberal.

Sociologists' interest in measuring gender ideology can be traced at least as far back as the 1930s, with the development of instruments such as Kirkpatrick's 1936 Attitudes Toward Feminism scale. Interest continues today, and currently most major national surveys in the US, such as the General Social Survey (GSS) and the National Survey of Families and Households, include gender ideology scales. Two volumes by Carole Beere (1979, 1990) summarize the psychometric properties and past uses of most gender ideology instruments developed through 1988.

The most common technique for measuring gender ideology is a summated rating scale in which respondents are presented with a statement and given three to seven response options that vary from strong agreement to strong disagreement. The following statement from the GSS is illustrative: "It is much better for everyone involved if the man is the achiever outside the home and the woman takes care of the home and family." Other measurement techniques include Guttman scales, Thurstone measures, identity-vignettes in which respondents rate their similarity to fictional characters, and intensive, open-ended interviews.

Researchers have examined the correlates, causes, and consequences of individuals' gender ideology. Within the US the documented antecedents include gender and birth cohort, with males and earlier cohorts reporting more conservative attitudes than females and later cohorts. Among women, labor force participation and educational attainment decrease conservatism. More generally, conservative gender ideologies are positively related to church attendance, fundamentalism, and literal interpretations of the Bible, and negatively related to education, family income, parents' gender liberalism, and women's labor force participation (whether self, spouse, or mother).

Other correlates and consequences of gender ideological positions have also been studied. Liberalism is positively related to married men's housework and childcare contributions and negatively related to women's housework contributions. Yet gender ideology is unrelated to the affective meanings (goodness, power, activity) associated with most social roles (e.g., a husband, a wife) and self-meanings (e.g., myself as a husband) among individuals of the same sex, suggesting that gender ideology does not affect perceptions of most social roles or self-meanings within those roles.

Researchers have also investigated the way that gender ideology shapes spouses' perceptions of their marriage. Liberalism reduces women's perceived marital quality but increases men's. Women's gender ideology also moderates the relationship between housework divisions and perceptions of fairness in housework divisions: as women's gender ideology becomes more liberal, the negative relationship between housework inequities and perceptions of housework fairness becomes stronger. Women's liberalism also increases the positive relationship between perceived fairness in housework and marital stability.

Researchers have recently begun to examine discrepancies between gender ideological positions and self-identification with feminism. Schnittker, Freese, and Powell (2003) show a cohort effect in the US such that self-identification with feminism is most strongly related to liberal gender ideologies for males and females who were young adults during the second wave of feminism. In addition, Klute et al. (2002) have applied Melvin Kohn's ideas to gender ideology. They found that self-direction at work is positively related to values emphasizing self-direction rather than conformity, and that spouses who value self-direction are also more likely to hold egalitarian attitudes about marital roles. Thus, workplace experiences may have an indirect effect on gender ideologies through the values that they foster.

Cross-national research has also shown that gender ideology is also related to women's political representation. Using the *World Values Survey*, which includes individual-level information on gender attitudes in 46 countries in 1995, Paxton and Kunovich (2003) showed that a conservative gender ideology is negatively related to the percentage of female members in the national legislature of a country even when controlling for political and social structural factors.

SEE ALSO: Divisions of Household Labor; Doing Gender; Gender, Work, and Family; Ideology; Marital Quality; Role; Role Theory

REFERENCES AND SUGGESTED READINGS

Amato, P. R. & Booth, A. (1995) Changes in Gender Role Attitudes and Perceived Marital Quality. *American Sociological Review* 60: 58–66.

Beere, C. A. (1990) *Gender Roles: A Handbook of Tests and Measures.* Greenwood Press, New York.

Greenstein, T. N. (1996) Gender Ideology and Perceptions of the Fairness of the Division of Household Labor: Effects on Marital Quality. *Social Forces* 74: 1029–42.

Kane, E. (2000) Racial and Ethnic Variations in Gender-Related Attitudes. *Annual Review of Sociology* 26: 419–39.

Klute, M. M., Crouter, A. C., Sayer, A. G., & McHale, S. M. (2002) Occupational Self-Direction, Values, and Egalitarian Relationships: A Study of Dual-Earner Couples. *Journal of Marriage and Family* 64: 139–51.

Kroska, A. (2002) Does Gender Ideology Matter? Examining the Relationship between Gender Ideology and Self- and Partner-Meanings. *Social Psychology Quarterly* 65: 248–65.

Lorber, J. (1994) *Paradoxes of Gender.* Yale University Press, New Haven.

Meyers, S. M. & Booth, A. (2002) Forerunners of Change in Nontraditional Gender Ideology. *Social Psychology Quarterly* 65: 18–37.

Paxton, P. & Kunovich, S. (2003) Women's Political Representation: The Importance of Ideology. *Social Forces* 82: 87–114.

Schnittker, J., Freese, J., & Powell, B. (2003) Who are Feminists and What Do They Believe? The Role of Generations. *American Sociological Review* 68: 607–22.

gender mainstreaming

Silke Roth

Gender mainstreaming is a strategy for achieving gender equality. The approach seeks to reorganize and restructure policies, institutions, and social programs by taking women's and men's perspectives, experiences, and needs into consideration. Gender mainstreaming does not replace, but supplements, specific targeted interventions to address gender inequality such as affirmative action.

Gender mainstreaming was first introduced when UNIFEM (the women's division of the United Nations) was restructured. At the Third UN World Women's Conference in Nairobi in 1985, gender mainstreaming and empowerment were adopted in development policies due to the persistent marginalization of women with respect to access to resources, information, and decision-making, replacing the earlier "women in development" (WID) approach. The goal of gender mainstreaming is to support women and to ensure their involvement in decision-making processes and agenda setting. UNIFEM conceives gender mainstreaming as a double strategy: gender differentiation and taking into consideration the different living conditions and interests of men and women in all developmental programs and project interventions at the macro-economic and macro-political level, as well as women-specific measures in those instances where gender analyses revealed inequalities with respect to resources.

Ten years later, the systematic incorporation of gender as a factor in policymaking was formally adopted at the Fourth World Conference of Women in Beijing in 1995. Due to extensive lobbying of the European women's lobby, gender mainstreaming was included in the Amsterdam Treaty of the European Union (EU), which was signed in 1997 and ratified in 1999 (Mazey 2001). The treaty declares gender mainstreaming as a core task of the EU and thus requests that member states (and those countries which seek to join the EU) mainstream gender into policies developed in their countries. Thus, the new member states which joined the European Union in May 2004 were required to adopt gender mainstreaming. The EU enlargement process thus provided important policy instruments for increasing equality between men and women. The implementation of gender-mainstreamed regulations is monitored by the EU, but has to be carried out by the national governments.

Gender mainstreaming involves analytic tasks, taking into account inequalities in political power within households and in the domestic and unpaid sector, differences in legal status and entitlements, the gender division of labor in the economy, violence against women, and discriminatory practices. Furthermore, it encompasses policy analysis and policy development: the formulation of the policy outcome to be addressed, the definition of the information needed to assess policy options, the assessment of the implication of different options by gender, the determination of who will be consulted and how, and the formulation of recommendations for policy choices. It is based on research and informs data collection, analysis, and dissemination. Gender mainstreaming in technical assistance draws on national commitments to women's rights and gender equality, ensures that the expert team includes members with gender analysis experience, and includes the consultation of local experts on gender equality (United Nations 2002).

In addition to development, gender mainstreaming was also introduced in other institutional arenas, for example international peacekeeping, education, and medicine. In October 2000 the UN Security Council adopted Resolution 1325, recognizing the urgent need to mainstream gender perspectives into peacekeeping operations, the importance of specialized gender training, and the need to understand the impact of armed conflict on women and girls. This includes the acknowledgment of sexual violence. In local societies, in which women constitute the majority of the population, it is especially beneficial to include a significant number of women in peacekeeping since female peacekeepers more easily establish dialogue with local civilians than their male partners because women may be perceived as less threatening and cultural norms might prohibit women to interact with men who are not family members. Security procedures such as body searches of women are easier if they are carried out by female peacekeepers (Olson & Torunn 2001). Gender mainstreaming of the education sector is based on the assessment of the educational status of girls and women, boys and men and involves the review of policies, laws, regulations, plans, and programs from a gender perspective, the analysis of the impact of educational policies and programs, and recommendations for more effective mainstreaming. Gender mainstreaming in the health sector guarantees that the different needs of men and women are addressed, rather than extrapolating from male-specific findings to women. Strategies include taking full account of diseases and disabilities from which women suffer because of their sex, which are more prevalent in women, which affect women more severely than men, which have more adverse affects on women during pregnancy, and against which women are less able to protect themselves. Men have a higher death rate from acute medical conditions such as cardiovascular or cerebra-vascular episodes. Furthermore, men's workplace conditions, as well as gender stereotyping that discourages men from articulating their problems and emotions, need to be taken into consideration.

Gender mainstreaming represents a paradigm shift with respect to equality policies in as far as it declares all policy fields as relevant for women, in contrast to earlier gender policies which focused on women and developed political units (e.g., gender desks or women's ministries).This means that instead of helping women to adapt to structures which benefit men, the goal is to change the gendered structures in order to become more women friendly. Gender mainstreaming is future oriented in that it tries to anticipate gender processes in the planning and decision-making stage, while earlier strategies to achieve gender equality retroactively sought to remedy past decisions and social inequalities.

SEE ALSO: Gender and Development; Gender Inequality/Stratification; Gendered Organizations/Institutions; Transnational and Global Feminisms

REFERENCES AND SUGGESTED READINGS

Mazey, S. (2001) *Gender Mainstreaming in the EU: Principles and Practice*. Kogan Page, London.

Olson, L. & Torunn, L. T. (Eds.) (2001) *Women and International Peacekeeping*. Frank Cass, London.

Rai, S. I. (2003) *Mainstreaming Gender, Democratizing the State? Institutional Mechanisms for the Advancement of Women*. Manchester University Press, Manchester.

United Nations (2002) *Gender Mainstreaming: An Overview*. United Nations, New York.

gender oppression

Vrushali Patil

Gender oppression is defined as oppression associated with the gender norms, relations, and stratification of a given society. Modern norms of gender in western societies consist of the dichotomous, mutually exclusive categories of masculinity and femininity. Developing in tandem with industrial capitalism and the nation-state, they had particular consequences for women and men. While masculinity was to consist of rationality, autonomy, activity, aggression, and competitiveness (all qualities that made men the ideal participants in the emerging public sphere of economy and polity), femininity was defined in contrast as emotionality, dependency, passivity and nurturance – all qualities that deemed women's "place" in the private sphere. These naturalized views of gender categories were embedded in burgeoning disciplines such as biology and sociology. However, not only were they premised on a dichotomous conception of sex and gender, they were also premised on heterosexuality, middle-class status, and European ethnic origin. As such, the gender oppression embedded therein is associated not only with the category with less power in the binary (femininity), but also with subjects that somehow deviate from either category.

Mainstream sociology initially ignored gender as well as gender oppression, marginalizing feminist sociologists in the early years. The subsequent period of structural functionalism excused and even supported dichotomous gender norms and their oppression, arguing that gender roles and identities served some functions in society. Sociological recognition and theorization of gender oppression thus required the denaturalization of the concept of gender itself within the discipline. A first step occurred in the 1970s, with debates regarding the extent to which "differences between the sexes" were biological. While this exchange enabled a limited discussion of gender oppression, the next set of debates allowed a greater role for the "social" – moving from sex differences to sex roles and socialization (Ferree et al. 2000). This shift was particularly useful for elaborating the gender oppression of those who "fit" or who were able to comply with gender norms. One of the most important insights gleaned from this perspective was the relationship between the aforementioned gendering of public and private spheres and the fundamental gendering of personhood: that is, the gendering of the two spheres meant that women's primary access to personhood within society was through the uptake and performance of their roles as wives and mothers within the private sphere, while men's access to personhood was through participation in various worker and citizen roles in the public sphere (as well as through the status of head of household in the private sphere).

Studies of gender relations in societies around the world have demonstrated that almost everywhere in the modern era, though in culturally specific ways, femininity is associated with a domestic sphere while masculinity is associated with a public sphere. At the macro level, dichotomous and naturalized views of gender are evident in the gendering of economic, political, and other institutions, where especially elite men dominate every major institution in most societies around the world (see Peterson & Runyan 1999). Ultimately, this gendering shapes the experiences of different groups of women globally and is expressed in higher levels of poverty; lower levels of formal political power; trivialization and sexual objectification in media; gender-specific health issues such as eating disorders, greater risk of AIDS, inadequate food/health care, and ongoing challenges to reproductive autonomy; greater levels of fear; and greater risk of interpersonal violence, to name a few.

Presently, the sociological approach to gender is even more "socialized," and gender is now recognized as a thoroughly social entity as well as a central organizing principle in all social systems, including work, politics, family, science, etc. (Ferree et al. 2000). As such, understanding of its complexity and scope has increased as well. Hence, a central area of interest in recent years has been the intersection of gender with other dimensions of experience and oppression, including race, class, culture, sex, and sexuality. Otherwise stated, while the above perspective elaborated the gender oppression of whose who "fit" the dichotomous gender categories of masculinity and femininity, this lens is particularly useful for understanding the gender oppression of those who "do not or cannot fit" these categories. For example, the static and mutually exclusive norms of sex and gender that emerged in modernity denied the existence or personhood of the intersexed and the transgendered. Premised on heterosexuality, they denied the personhood of gays, lesbians, and bisexuals. Further premised on a masculine public sphere, working-class women who necessarily transgressed this space have also been made deviant. Moreover, these norms are fundamentally racialized in that they emerged in the context of the conflict-ridden contact between different peoples from the sixteenth century onwards. As European travelers in this period especially encountered racial and cultural "others," with their varying gender practices, European gender norms became a symbol of civilization, the deviation from which became a sign of racial and cultural inferiority. In this fashion, gender became a central vehicle for constructing racial and cultural hierarchy (Enloe 1990; McClintock 1995).

Additional emerging areas of interest in the field include gender oppression associated with varying masculinities, gender experiences and oppression in a transnational framework, and gender symbolism that may perpetuate inequalities beyond the bodies of men and women (i.e., the denigration of "feminine qualities," which denigrates not just women but any feminized entity).

SEE ALSO: Feminism; Gender Bias; Inequality/Stratification, Gender; Intersectionality; Patriarchy; Racialized Gender

REFERENCES AND SUGGESTED READINGS

Collins, P. H. (1990) *Black Feminist Thought: Knowledge, Consciousness and the Politics of Empowerment.* Routledge, Chapman, & Hall, New York.
Connell, R. W. (2000) *The Men and the Boys.* University of California Press, Berkeley.
Enloe, C. (1990) *Bananas, Beaches, Bases.* University of California Press, Berkeley.
Fausto-Sterling, A. (2000) *Sexing the Body: Gender Politics and the Construction of Sexuality.* Basic Books, New York.
Ferree, M. M., Lorber, J., & Hess, B. B. (Eds.) (2000) *Revisioning Gender.* Altamira Press, Oxford.
Katz, J. (1995) *The Invention of Heterosexuality.* Dutton, New York.
McClintock, A. (1995) *Imperial Leather: Race, Gender and Sexuality in the Colonial Conquest.* Routledge, New York.
Moghadam, V. (Ed.) (1994) *Identity Politics and Women: Cultural Reassertions and Feminisms in International Perspective.* Westview Press, Boulder.
Peterson, V. S. & Runyan, A. (1999) *Global Gender Issues.* Westview Press, Oxford.
Phillips, A. (Ed.) (1998) *Feminism and Politics.* Oxford University Press, Oxford.
Scott, J. W. (1988) *Gender and the Politics of History.* Columbia University Press, New York.

gender, social movements and

Nancy Whittier

Social movements are shaped by gender systems and they also are a source of social change in gender. Some social movements directly attempt to change gender relations; these movements, particularly women's movements, have been the focus of considerable scholarship. Increasingly, scholars also recognize the gendered nature of other social movements and the impact of systemic inequalities of gender on the opportunities, constraints, and forms of social movements in general.

Research on gender and social movements has proceeded through several stages. Initial works focused on documenting women's movements, including feminist and non-feminist movements, and explaining their emergence and development. A second phase of work began to analyze gender in social movements more broadly, including masculinity, and to analyze the intersections between gender, race, class, and nationality in social movements. Most recently, numerous scholars have begun to examine the ways that movements are gendered in their origins, collective identities, frames and discourses, organizational structures, tactics, and political and cultural opportunities. In doing so, they contribute to a rethinking of the basic concepts of the field of social movements. These phases are similar to those for scholarship on gender more broadly, which initially focused on documenting women's experiences and remedying male bias, next on gender as an institution and the intersections between gender and other major forms of social inequality, and lastly on reformulating basic sociological knowledge and theory based on a perspective that makes gender central. Sociological work on gender and social movements thus reflects the influence of the feminist movement on the academy.

Many social movements have targeted the social structures, culture, and interactional norms around gender. These include feminist movements, which in many countries focused first on gaining basic political rights such as the vote and the right to own property, and then progressed in later waves to addressing other forms of inequality between women and men ranging from responsibility for child-raising and household labor, discrimination in paid employment, sexuality, reproductive rights, health care, stereotyping in the arts and popular culture, election to public office, and so on. Parallel to these movements are anti-feminist movements, which tend to emerge in response to feminist movements and also target gender directly in an attempt to forestall or roll back changes.

Other movements have been organized around gender, without taking gender as a central or explicit target. For example, women's temperance and social reform movements in the late 1800s and early 1900s in the United States organized women based on their social responsibilities for morality, childrearing, and the promulgation of religious values. Women have organized in "mothers' movements" to challenge governmental killings and disappearances of their children (such as the Madres de la Plaza de Mayo in Argentina), or to fight against environmental degradation or for better public education. Such "maternalist politics" can uphold traditional definitions of women's place while simultaneously expanding those definitions, bringing women into the public sphere and often changing activists' own family relations and identities. Men's movements, such as the mythopoetic movement, also organize men around some traditional definitions of masculinity while simultaneously stretching those definitions by, for example, encouraging men to express emotions more freely (Schwalbe 1996).

Further, movements do not have to be oriented around gender to be shaped by it. Because gender is a central feature of social structure, culture, and daily life, all movements are gendered. The major elements of social movements are their emergence and recruitment, collective identities, frames or discourses, organizations, tactics or actions, and external contexts or political opportunities. Each of these elements is gendered.

First, movements' emergence and processes of recruitment are gendered because the status of women and men shapes their differential ability and willingness to organize on their own behalf. Gendered factors such as family structures and responsibilities, access to higher education, paid employment, and fertility rate all affect recruitment and participation in activism. These factors all vary according to race, class, and nationality as well as gender, and also change over time; such variations account for some of the differences in the level and form of women's mobilization cross-culturally and historically. Further, social movements emerge along gendered lines because they emerge from gendered preexisting organizations and networks (Taylor 1999). For example, feminist organizing during the late 1960s in the US emerged partially from the Civil Rights Movement, in which women gained organizing experience and an ideology opposing inequality, but also faced gender barriers to full participation. However, grievances and networks based on race and class cross-cut those based on gender. For African American and Latina women during the same era, their connections to mixed-sex movements around race mitigated their interest in a mixed-race movement around gender. Instead, they advocated for women's interests within mixed-sex movements (Roth 2004). Similarly, international women's conferences sponsored by the United Nations have illustrated how women in third world countries define their interests quite differently from those in the highly industrialized global North.

Second, movements' collective identities, or group definitions, are gendered. Some social movements directly try to change the definition associated with their group, as feminist movements, for example, try to change what it means to be a woman. Beyond this, movement participants bring with them a gender consciousness that affects the collective identities they construct, and they draw on ideas about gender from both dominant and oppositional cultures. For example, environmental or peace activists may define themselves as mothers concerned about the well-being of children and future generations, and participants in anti-globalization protests may draw on masculinity to define themselves as warriors standing up to the police, or they may draw on feminist and queer politics to define themselves as rejecting the dominant gender order along with capitalism.

Third, social movements construct interpretive frames to explain their grievances and issues, addressing their causes and calling for action. In doing so, they draw on mainstream discourses and also challenge and extend those discourses. Mainstream frames and discourses are built around particular definitions of the nature, roles, and responsibilities of women and men, and social movements include elements of these mainstream frames and discourses and construct alternatives. Often they may do both, as in the case of maternalist movements that draw on women's special place as mothers to argue for a greater influence by women on national affairs.

Fourth, social movements' organizational structures are gendered. For example, the American Civil Rights Movement assigned formal leadership to men while assigning women to more informal leadership roles (Robnett 1997). Recognizing these differences entails not only recognizing discrimination within the movement and bringing to light the previously unacknowledged role of women, but also redefining theories of leadership to include the ways that women exercise influence outside of official leadership positions. Beyond leadership, women and men may take on different tasks within movement organizations, with women taking more responsibility for activities such as providing food for events or monitoring the emotional climate at meetings, and men undertaking more public speaking, drafting of position papers, or providing "peacekeeping" at public demonstrations. Gendered divisions of labor within movements vary considerably across time, space, and among movements, of course. In movements that explicitly challenge the gendered status quo, such differences may be much less marked or even at times inverted;

while in movements that seek to restore traditional gender roles, they may be exaggerated.

Fifth, tactics and strategies are affected by gender. Women and men may draw on established social activities in order to work for change, as in men's use of violent intimidation compared with women's reliance on boycotts and vicious gossip in the US racist movement of the 1920s (Blee 1991). Here, too, incorporating tactics grounded in traditionally feminine activities into social movement theory suggests a broader definition of tactics and strategies that includes actions previously not seen as part of social movements.

Sixth, gendered external social structures and mainstream culture delimit the opportunities and constraints for social movements. Political opportunities are affected by gender because women and men have differential access to the state, both as elected officials and as outside activists. On a more subtle level, the state and other major social institutions operate through gendered structures, procedures, and discourses (sometimes termed gender regimes). When activists target or enter institutions, therefore, they face particular opportunities or barriers depending both on their actual gender and on the way their movement engages with or challenges existing notions of gender. For example, in working to change discourses about gender in the Catholic Church, women were able to draw on the institutional base of female religious orders but were limited by their structural subordination. As a result, they focused on *discursive* rather than structural change (Katzenstein 1998). Mainstream culture affects how movements' claims are received, as well, with activists who challenge accepted notions of gender being more likely to be marginalized. Men who openly display affection toward each other and lobby for an expansion in the definition of masculinity, for example, are the subject of considerable ridicule (Schwalbe 1996), while women who lobbied for restrictions on hunting were viewed as hysterical females treading into waters where they did not belong (Einwohner 1999).

In addition to being shaped by gender, social movements are an important force in changing gender systems. Feminist movements in the US and Western Europe have produced considerable change in cultural beliefs, the structure of paid employment, women's access to higher education, and basic rights such as the vote, credit, and property ownership. In many countries, women's activism has produced constitutional guarantees for women's minimum representation in elected office. Further, social movements have contributed to changes in the cultural codes and interactional norms that define gender. At the same time, these changes have been contested by antifeminist movements.

Several lines of research are promising. First, more analyses of the gendered dimensions of men's and mixed-sex movements will augment the extensive work on women's movements. Second, work on cases outside the US and Western Europe is examining the gender dimensions of a variety of movements. Because gender systems vary comparatively, this work promises to expand theorizing on the topic. Third, efforts to reconceptualize social movement theory based on this work have begun, and promise to produce a richer and more inclusive theoretical model.

SEE ALSO: Black Feminist Thought; Collective Identity; Culture, Gender and; Culture, Social Movements and; Emotions and Social Movements; Feminism; Feminism, First, Second, and Third Waves; Feminist Activism in Latin America; Framing and Social Movements; Gendered Organizations/Institutions; Political Opportunities; Sex and Gender; Social Movements; Women's Empowerment; Women's Movements

REFERENCES AND SUGGESTED READINGS

Banaszak, L. A. (1996) *Why Movements Succeed or Fail: Opportunity, Culture, and the Struggle for Woman Suffrage*. Princeton University Press, Princeton.

Blee, K. (1991) *Women of the Klan: Racism and Gender in the 1920s*. University of California Press, Berkeley.

Einwohner, R. (1999) Gender, Class, and Social Movement Outcomes: Identity and Effectiveness in Two Animal Rights Campaigns. *Gender and Society* 13(1): 56–76.

Katzenstein, M. F. (1998) *Faithful and Fearless: Moving Feminist Protest Inside the Church and Military*. Princeton University Press, Princeton.

Kuumba, M. B. (2001) *Gender and Social Movements*. Alta Mira, New York.

Robnett, B. (1997) *How Long, How Long? African American Women in the Struggle for Civil Rights*. Oxford University Press, New York.

Roth, B. (2004) *Separate Roads to Feminism: Black, Chicana, and White Feminist Movements in America's Second Wave*. Cambridge University Press, New York.

Schwalbe, M. (1996) *Unlocking the Iron Cage: The Men's Movement, Gender Politics, and American Culture*. Oxford University Press, New York.

Staggenborg, S. (1998) *Gender, Family, and Social Movements*. Pine Forge Press, Thousand Oaks, CA.

Taylor, V. (1999) Gender and Social Movements: Gender Processes in Women's Self-Help Movements. *Gender and Society* 13(1): 8–33.

gender, sport and

Louise Mansfield

Gender refers to the socially constructed differences between women and men, while the term "sex" is a reference to the biological and physical differences between males and females. Gender draws attention to the socially unequal distinction between femininity and masculinity. Femininity is used to describe characteristic behaviors and emotions of females and masculinity refers to the distinctive actions and feelings of the male sex. In studies of gender and sport, the concept of gender is analytically distinguished from that of sex even though the two are often used synonymously in everyday language and thought. Not all the differences between females and males are biological. But historically, ideas about the implications of biological differences between women and men have served to justify the exclusion or limited inclusion of women in sports. Such views reflect an ideology of biological determinism, where it is claimed that men, and not women, are inherently strong, aggressive, and competitive and, therefore, better suited to sports.

Since the 1970s, gender has become an important category of analysis in the sociology of sport. Research has clearly demonstrated that sports are gendered activities as well as social contexts in which boys and men are more actively and enthusiastically encouraged to participate, compared with girls and women. Evidence also shows that more males than females participate in organized competitive sports, and that male dominance characterizes the administration and coaching of sports. Sports, it is theorized, operate as a site for the inculcation, perpetuation, and celebration of a type of (heterosexual) masculine identity based on physical dominance, aggression, and competitiveness. Associated with such masculine imagery, sports serve to legitimize a perceived natural superiority of men and reinforce the inferiority of females who are defined with reference to relative weakness, passivity, and grace – the characteristics of femininity. Therefore, sports are often described as a "male preserve."

Social changes reflecting the condition of women in society have influenced the status of knowledge about the relationships between and within groups of women and men in sports. Starting in the 1970s, a consequence of the feminist movement was to raise public awareness about the need for increased opportunities for girls and women in sports. Since then there has been growing political and public recognition of the importance of health and fitness. Furthermore, emerging knowledge about the health benefits of physical activity provided a foundation for the promotion of physical activity for girls and women. Opportunities for girls and women in sports have improved and participation rates among females have increased. Scholars studying gender and sports indicate that these developments have resulted in ongoing challenges to gender stereotyping, resistance and negotiation of established gender ideology, and the initiation of important legal and political change regarding sex discrimination in sports and society. For example, Title IX of the Education Amendments of the Civil Rights Act (1972) in the US, and the Sex Discrimination Act (1975) in Great Britain were intended to counter public discrimination against women. Such legislation has been used to prevent and remove many barriers to female participation in sports.

There is now over 35 years of scholarship that theorizes gender and sport. One of the most sustained attempts at conceptualizing and theorizing about gender in the sociology of sport is found in feminist scholarship.

The first attempts to analyze women's place in sport were made in the 1960s by physical educators. The result was a corpus of largely atheoretical work on "women in sport" founded upon a liberal feminist consciousness about sport as a "male preserve" characterized by gender inequities. Between 1970 and 1980 psychological models were mainly used to explain female attitudes and motivations in sports. In the 1980s, emerging theoretical diversity and sophistication in feminist approaches led to the development of a clear sociology of women in sport. As political and theoretical feminisms have changed, so too has the focus of feminist research.

Depending on the theoretical and methodological position of the researcher, different questions about and accounts of gender and sport prevail. Debates surrounding the gendered character of sporting practices have changed with increasing awareness of feminist theories and a more sophisticated use of these theories. For example, much of the initial work on gender and sport highlighted inequities but did not explicitly deal with how the prevailing organization of sports privileged the physical experiences of boys and men. Subsequent critical analyses revealed that research focused on differences between males and females generally supported traditional claims about the biological inferiority of females and the legitimacy of efforts to control women's sports participation. Such research, it was argued, did not deal with the underlying structural and cultural sources of gender inequality. More recent scholarship has attempted to resolve the shortcomings of early research and theory by considering difference and diversity between and within groups of women, and by theoretical and methodological approaches that consider women as active agents in the construction and reconstruction of their sporting experiences.

There is no single feminist movement or theory that has informed current scholarly work on gender and sport. Liberal feminist accounts of sport are based on claims that women should have equal rights to those of men in terms of access to resources, opportunities to participate, and decision-making positions. Radical feminists are critical of the patriarchal power relations that operate to maintain the dominance of heterosexuality and construct homophobic attitudes and practices in sport. Socialist feminists have examined the connections between gender, social class, and race and ethnicity under conditions of patriarchy, capitalism, and neocolonialism. Significant theoretical influences in understanding gender and sport have also emerged in cultural studies and in work guided by the writings of Norbert Elias, Pierre Bourdieu, and poststructuralist theorists. Contemporary work in the field reflects the move toward critical analyses of the complex relationships between and within groups of women and men in sport. Current scholarship examines the ways in which gender relations are produced, reproduced, challenged, and transformed in and through sporting practices.

Three key themes have driven debates about gender and sport since the 1970s. First, leading scholars in the sociology of sport have highlighted that throughout history, sporting practices inculcated behaviors and values defined as male, manly, and masculine. Second, issues surrounding the body, physicality, and sexuality have been brought to the fore in understanding gender relations in sport. Third, it is emphasized that both women and men reinforce and challenge dominant gender ideology in sport in various ways. In this regard scholars have eschewed ideas about women and men as homogeneous categories, and have recognized and examined difference and diversity in people's gendered sporting experiences at the level of the subject and in terms of institutional politics and practice. Recent research includes work that examines the production and reproduction of gender in sport in terms of the sporting experiences of women and men from various sociocultural backgrounds.

HISTORICAL DEVELOPMENTS AND THE GENDERING OF SPORT

Sociologists of sport have illustrated that the historical development of modern sports laid the foundations for the gendered character of sporting practices. Over time, sports have been constructed and reconstructed around the assumptions, values, and ideologies of males, maleness, and masculinity. The roots of contemporary sports lie in the Victorian period in Britain, when sports began to be characterized by organized structures and standardized rules. In terms of gender, late nineteenth-century British developments in sports largely centered on the beliefs and values of white middle-class males. The prestige, status, and superiority afforded to men in society became marked at this time. In institutions such as public schools, universities, churches, and private clubs, sports came to represent a Victorian version of masculinity based on physical superiority, competitiveness, mental acumen, and a sense of fair play. Established ideals of femininity such as passivity, frailty, emotionality, gentleness, and dependence were in stark opposition to the strenuous task of playing sports. The belief that male and female traits were innate, biological, and somehow fixed prevailed. Women's participation in sports was therefore a subject of debate regarding what type and how much physical activity was appropriate for them. The marginalization of women and the dominance of men in sports is a legacy of Victorian images of female frailty that is also reflected in the making of modern sports in the US.

In both Britain and the US, changes in social life during the late nineteenth and early twentieth centuries impacted on gender relations in sport. British and American society at this time was characterized by social relations that were becoming less violent, there was a decreasing reliance on physical strength in the workplace, and home and educational environments were becoming ones in which young males spent increasing amounts of time with females. Eric Dunning (1999) and Michael Messner (1990) refer to these social transformations as the "feminization" of society. One consequence of these processes was the reconstruction of sporting opportunities and social enclaves (such as the Boy Scouts and the YMCA) for boys and men to reclaim and reassert their masculinity. While opportunities for women in sports also increased in the early part of the twentieth century, participation rates for females remained considerably smaller compared to males. Some sports were acceptable for women so long as they were not as strenuous or competitive as the male version. Women's sports were still the subject of intense debate reflecting and maintaining the Victorian myth of women's physical ineptitude.

SPORT, GENDER, POWER, AND PHYSICALITY

Many scholars have advanced an understanding about gender and sport by recognizing and examining the connections between physicality, power, and the production of gender. It is emphasized that in sport, physicality is predominantly defined in terms of bodily strength, muscularity, and athletic prowess. Connell (1995) explains such characteristics as a "culturally idealized" form of masculinity. Much has been written about the ways that contemporary sports reinforce a male model of (heterosexual) physical superiority and, at the same time, operate to oppress women through the trivialization and objectification of their physicality and sexuality. Several scholars assert that the acquisition of muscular strength and athletic skill is less empowering for women than it is for men. There is a commonsense assumption that muscularity is unfeminine, and that strong and powerful females are not "real" women. An increasing amount of work illustrates that such beliefs are reflected in the proliferation of media images emphasizing female heterosexuality at the expense of athletic prowess. The sexualization of female athletes through media representation is one way in which images of idealized female physicality are reproduced and perpetuated.

There are other mechanisms of control over female physicality in sport. Some writers explain that aerobics and bodybuilding operate to reproduce established gender ideology by feminizing the corporeal practices, rituals, and techniques in which women are involved, as well as objectifying and sexualizing women's bodies. Some consider that sexual harassment and vilification of women by male athletes provides evidence that the use of violence, aggression, and force is a defining feature of masculine identity that is constructed and legitimated in sporting contexts. There is also some scholarship that focuses on the way in which sports perpetuate the denigration of lesbians and gay men. It is argued that sports maintain a culture of homophobia in which homosexuality is feared and deemed to be unacceptable. Lesbians and gay men are discouraged from expressing their sexual identities through threatening homophobic sentiments and actions. Sports reinforce a culture of heterosexuality and effectively silence homosexual identities.

A central argument in contemporary work on gender, sport, and physicality is the idea that the empowering experience of sport for heterosexual males is not universal, fixed, or unchallenged. Robert Connell illustrates the inherent contradictions in hegemonic masculinity. Strength, power, skill, and mental and physical toughness are not the only defining characteristics of masculinity. Not all sports privilege the values of aggression and physical domination associated with culturally established ideals of masculinity. It is also the case that the dominant image of masculinity, most often represented in sport, is one that can be limiting and restrictive for some men as well as most women. There are fewer opportunities for boys and men to participate, without prejudice, in sports that are not based on strength, power, and domination. There is work that shows that boys and men who are not good at sport, or who do not participate, have their heterosexual masculinity called into question. The sports experience is a negative and disappointing one for such males.

SPORT, GENDER, AND CONTESTED IDEOLOGY

It is increasingly emphasized in studies of sport and gender that dominant ideals of masculinity and femininity exist at the same time as emergent and residual ones. Such work is concerned with the relational character of gender. Michael Messner explains that in terms of gender, sport is a "contested terrain." This means that at any moment in history and in specific sporting contexts, there are competing masculinities and femininities. There are many scholars who now recognize that in sport, as well as in other social settings, some women are more powerful and influential than other women and men, and some women are empowered at the expense of other women and men.

Scholars in the sociology of sport have illustrated that many people are empowered by being involved in sport in spite of traditional gender ideology. Examples show how sport is a site where established values about gender have been resisted, negotiated, and sometimes transformed. The assumption that homosexuality does not exist in sport is challenged in research about the many gay men competing in sports at recreational and elite levels. There are events such as the Gay Games that allow athletes to compete in a relatively unprejudiced environment where they have less to fear about derogatory and violent responses to their publicized sexual orientation. Several scholars question the assumption that sport is a site for the oppression of women by exploring the ways in which women gain from their sporting achievements. Such research shows that it is possible for women to experience feelings of independence, confidence, and increased self-esteem from their involvement in a variety of sporting practices. Female participation in physical activity can also contribute to broadening and alternative definitions of physicality that are not simply based on traditional ideals about feminine appearance. In the case of professional sports, some women are able to gain considerable financial wealth and worldwide recognition from their sporting achievements.

The extent to which sports are oppressive and liberating for women and men is culturally specific and related to the political and economic conditions in which they live their lives. There is increasing interest in the relationships between sport, gender, race, and ethnicity, and work on this topic emphasizes that questions of femininity and masculinity are inseparable from questions of race and ethnicity. In the main, research on sport, race, and ethnicity has examined issues connected with black sportsmen. Recent research takes a closer look at the complex relationships between masculinity, blackness, and sport. Critical examinations of the historical development of sport emphasize that sports were constructed in the image of particular ideals about white masculinity. Analyses of the racial significance of sport illustrate that sporting practices can provide black males with (symbolic) opportunities for resistance to racism through the assertion of manly qualities such as athleticism, aggression, and toughness. These writings also illustrate that sport reflects the historically constructed (subordinate) place of black males in (Western) societies. Dominant images of black male athleticism tend to

reinforce stereotypes of black men as powerful, aggressive, and hypersexual.

Scholars concerned with the relationship between sport, ethnicity, and femininity emphasize that sportswomen are not a homogeneous group. Increasingly, there is literature that presents a challenge to dominant universalistic conceptions of women in sport that serve to construct white, western, middle-class, able-bodied women's experiences as representative of all sportswomen. Sociologists of sport have argued that the dominant assumption about female sports operates to marginalize or even silence the sporting triumphs and struggles of women who live outside the West and those who represent minority groups of females. A central feature of scholarship in this area is the recognition of difference between and within groups of women in relation to ethnicity, religious affiliation, social class, age, and physical (dis)ability. Jennifer Hargreaves (2000) explains that a sense of difference is characterized by power relations operating simultaneously at the personal and institutional level. In many ways, sport can be empowering for black women, Muslim women, Aboriginal women, lesbians, and disabled women. At the same time, these women are incorporated into the wider social networks of power in which they live out their lives.

SEE ALSO: Body and Cultural Sociology; Gender, the Body and; Identity, Sport and; Ideology; Leisure; Media and Sport; Race/Ethnicity, Health, and Mortality; Sexuality and Sport; Sport

REFERENCES AND SUGGESTED READINGS

Birrell, S. (1988) Discourses on the Gender/Sport Relationship: From Women in Sport to Gender Relations. *Exercise and Sport Sciences Review* 16: 459–502.

Coakley, J. (2004) *Sports in Society: Issues and Controversies*, 8th edn. McGraw-Hill, New York, pp. 202–41.

Connell, R. (1995) *Masculinities*. University of California Press, Berkeley.

Dunning, E. (1999) *Sport Matters: Sociological Studies of Sport, Violence and Civilization*. Routledge, London, pp. 219–40.

Hall, A. (1996) *Feminism and Sporting Bodies*. Human Kinetics Publishers, Leeds.

Hargreaves, J. (1994) *Sporting Females*. Routledge, London.

Hargreaves, J. (2000) *Heroines of Sport: The Politics of Difference and Diversity*. Routledge, London.

Messner, M. (1990) *Sport, Men and the Gender Order: Critical Feminist Perspectives*. Human Kinetics Publishers, Leeds.

Scraton, S. & Flintoff, A. (2002) Sport Feminism: The Contribution of Feminist Thought to Our Understandings of Gender and Sport. In: Scraton, S. & Flintoff, A. (Eds.), *Gender and Sport: A Reader*. Routledge, London, pp. 30–46.

Theberge, N. (2002) Gender and Sport. In: Coakley, J. & Dunning, E. (Eds.), *Handbook of Sport Studies*. Sage, London, pp. 322–33.

gender, work, and family

Elizabeth Thorn

Gender, work, and family is the study of the intersection of work and family, with a focus on how those intersections vary by gender. This research is motivated in large part by the tremendous growth in labor force participation among women in their childbearing years during the second half of the twentieth century. This influx of wives and mothers into the workforce has raised questions about the division of labor in the family and whether state and corporate policies are sufficient to support new family types. Researchers also examine the causes of the divergent outcomes men and women experience in the workplace, as well as the effects labor force participation has on family formation, dissolution, and carework. These questions are most frequently researched quantitatively, but qualitative and theoretical work also contributes to the understanding of gender, work, and family.

THE MYTH OF SEPARATE WORLDS

Rosabeth Moss Kanter's pivotal book *Work and Family in the United States* (1977) laid much of the groundwork for the study of gender, work, and family. Kanter made the case that changing family structures and increasing labor force participation among women were creating a new and complex set of interactions that were not being sufficiently studied in the traditional domains of the sociology of the family and the sociology of the labor force. Social scientists, Kanter claimed, subscribed to the "myth of separate worlds," a belief that work and family are separate and non-overlapping spheres, each of which operates free from the influence of the other and can be studied independently. She locates the origins of this myth in antinepotism policies and employer claims on worker loyalty, in the increasing geographical separation of home and work, and in American individualism.

Kanter's counterargument is that the structures of work are actually quite crucial in shaping personal lives. Occupations have different levels of absorptiveness; some occupations may require little of the worker outside of the workplace, but workers in other occupations, such as foreign service and military officers, clergy, and high-level executives, must behave in certain ways even when officially off duty. The time and timing of work is another important consideration. Time that workers spend at work and commuting is time they do not spend with their families, and business travel and nonstandard work schedules may make spending time with family difficult even when the number of hours in itself is not onerous. Work is associated with rewards and resources, meaning that different workers have very different levels of compensation available to share with their families. Occupational cultures may become part of workers' worldview, shaping their values and especially the way they raise their children. Finally, the emotional climate of the workplace can produce feelings of self-confidence or tension in the worker, affecting relationships within the family.

Similarly, family can influence workers' behavior in the workplace. Cultural traditions held by the family may shape workers' decisions about work. Family firms may offer employment to family members, and family connections may open doors to job opportunities. Families of workers in highly absorptive occupations have an impact on the worker's performance in that role; an executive, for example, might be hampered in his career mobility without the expected "corporate wife."

Finally, the emotional climate of the home may affect family members in their roles as workers.

The myth of separate worlds was so strongly gendered that the ways in which men's and women's work and family roles were studied were quite different prior to Kanter's book. Research often lumped all working women together without acknowledgment of the specificities of their work. At the beginning of the twenty-first century, societal norms are still such that gender is an important consideration in the study of work and family.

TIME USE

One of the intersections of work and family Kanter identified is the time and timing of work, an area which has been extensively studied by subsequent scholars. Work and family responsibilities are both quite time consuming. As more and more women joined the labor force, researchers became increasingly curious about how families manage to find the time for paid employment, unpaid work in the home, and leisure. Most research has found striking and persistent differences in time allocation by gender.

Arlie Hochschild's (Hochschild with Machung 2003) ethnographic study of dual-earner households with children living at home found that mothers were working what amounted to a "second shift" of housework and childcare when they got home from their paid jobs. Their husbands, by comparison, shouldered a much lighter load. There were some variations in the division of labor associated with different gender ideologies, with couples who shared an egalitarian ideology sharing the work of the second shift most equally, but the effects of those ideologies were mediated by the constraints of employment and actual feelings about work and family responsibilities. Hochschild attributed the uneven workload of the second shift to a stalled revolution, in which women had begun participating in the traditionally male domain of the labor force to a much greater extent than men had begun participating in the traditionally female activities of childcare and housework.

Other researchers have found that the imbalance might not be as extreme as the second shift suggests (Bianchi et al. forthcoming). Time diaries show that across broader samples of American adults, there is less difference in the amount of work – both paid and unpaid – that men and women do. Although women as a group do more of the unpaid work in the home, they also tend to work fewer hours for pay than do men. Historical trends indicate that as women increased their hours in the labor force, they decreased the amount of time they spent on housework. Men have decreased the amount of time they spend in the labor force to some extent, generally by entering at later ages and by retiring earlier, and have increased the amount of housework they do, but not by as much as women have decreased their hours of housework.

An important related question is how much time fathers and mothers spend with their children, and how that has changed since more mothers began participating in the labor force. After all, it is one thing to spend less time on housework than was done in the 1960s and another to spend less time with one's children. However, in the United States, mothers' time with children has remained remarkably constant between 1965 and 1998, and if anything has grown slightly. Married fathers spend much more time with their children than did their counterparts in 1965, and this time is not just in playing with and teaching their children, but also in childcare activities such as dressing, bathing, and putting children to bed.

Another approach is to look at the time use of families, rather than that of men and women as individuals. Family structures have changed considerably since the middle of the twentieth century. Whereas most families with children in the 1950s and 1960s had a dedicated homemaker, today's families are much more likely to have two employed parents or be single-parent families. It is in these families in which all adults are employed that work–family conflict – in this case a "time crunch" – is most likely to be felt (Jacobs & Gerson 2004). Dual-earner families with children find it particularly difficult to balance the requirements of work and family. At the same time, however, there are also many families whose members are not able to find enough hours of paid work.

In addition to looking at the numbers of hours worked by men and women and different family types, it is also important to consider *when* those hours are worked (Presser 2003). It is often assumed that paid employment takes place from nine to five, Monday through Friday. However, as of 1997, in a quarter of dual-earner married couples, at least one spouse worked something other than that standard schedule. Looking only at married dual-earner couples with children, that fraction increases to a third. Those non-standard schedules have a number of consequences for the family. Non-standard schedules are associated with lower marital quality and marital instability, especially when there are children in the home. Non-standard work schedules make childcare arrangements more complex and difficult to manage, particularly in families with young children. One interesting consequence of non-standard work schedules is greater participation by men in what are generally considered female household tasks and childcare.

FAMILY ROLES AND THE LABOR FORCE

Family roles and statuses are associated with different outcomes in the labor market. Some roles are linked to increased productivity and income, while others are related to decreased wages. Gender, work, and family researchers examine the relationships between various family positions and labor market outcomes and try to establish the causes of differences. Different positions within the family may actually cause different labor market outcomes through the family's effect on productivity. Alternatively, employers may discriminate based on family roles. A third possibility is one of selection; perhaps the same sort of person is likely to be found in both certain family roles and in certain labor market positions. Conversely, labor force positions may affect family functions, such as propensity towards marriage or divorce.

Much research has demonstrated that married or cohabiting men earn more than their single counterparts. Data from longitudinal studies (Korenman & Neumark 1991) suggest that this is not merely a selection effect – that is, it is not just that men who are likely to do well in the labor force are also likely to get

married. Rather, wage growth is faster for married men than single men, and married men receive higher performance ratings. This lends support to the idea that married men are either more productive or are more desirable to employers than are single men. Men may become more productive in the labor market because their new partner takes on more of the responsibilities in the home, which allows men to develop those skills that are most marketable. Research indicates that although men's earnings go up when they form an intimate union, their overall financial position may not change much, largely because their spouse's labor market activity may be reduced, causing a reduction in family income. For women, on the other hand, marriage does not seem to be associated with significant changes in wages.

Like union formation, the transition to parenthood is another large shift in family roles, and the labor market outcomes associated with becoming a parent vary by gender. Fathers are more likely to be employed and to work more hours than childless men, but the opposite is true for women. Wages are affected as well. Budig and England (2001) found a motherhood wage penalty of 7 percent per child. That is, each child a woman has is associated with an additional 7 percent decrease in wage rate. This wage penalty may be explained in part by new mothers exiting the labor force or reducing their hours, but even after controlling for work experience, Budig and England still find a penalty of 5 percent per child. They attribute this penalty to either a reduction in productivity or discrimination on the part of employers.

Lundberg and Rose (2000) also found that motherhood is associated with reduction in wages – 5 percent in their calculations. Fatherhood, in contrast, is associated with a 9 percent increase in wages. However, they attribute much of this difference to increased specialization on the part of the new parents; mothers' salaries decrease because their new roles divert their attentions and energies from the labor force, which lowers their productivity. When the analysis is restricted to couples in which the new mother is continuously employed, a different pattern emerges. These mothers work fewer hours, but at the same wage. The new fathers, on the other hand, work slightly fewer hours, but at a *higher* wage rate. Women may avoid a wage penalty if they remain continuously employed upon the transition to parenthood, but men generally see a boost in wages upon becoming fathers, whether they reduce or expand their work time.

Family roles influence labor force outcomes. The reverse is also true: labor force positions can influence family roles. To take one example, the historical changes in women's labor force participation are associated with the increasing importance of women's earnings for marriage formation. Among younger cohorts, women with higher earnings are more likely to marry than women who earn less. Women now contribute significantly to their families' incomes, so women with high incomes are more desirable marriage partners. Men's earnings have long been associated with their chances of marrying. Labor force position can influence union dissolution as well as formation. Because women's labor force participation increased at the same time as divorce rates, it has often been supposed that women's employment leads to divorce. However, as indicators of marital dissatisfaction are much more accurate predictors of divorce than a wife's employment, it is more likely that employment allows women to leave bad marriages than women's employment causes marital disharmony. Occupation may also influence the likelihood of a woman remaining childless. Highly educated women in high-level positions in the labor force are much more likely than other women to not have children, either because they always planned to pursue only a career, or because the tradeoffs associated with child rearing were too great.

PUBLIC POLICY AND GENDER, WORK, AND FAMILY

Public policy in the United States and Europe has historically assumed that most families fit the breadwinner/homemaker model. However, as fewer and fewer families match the breadwinner/homemaker model and gender roles in work and family change, policymakers have had to adapt many policies. Examples of changing policy include family leave, welfare reform, and dependent care policy. In some cases, these new policies play a role in shaping gender norms in work and family.

One of the most striking examples of policy change is in the growth of family leave. In the US, family leave was first enacted at the federal level in 1993 as the Family and Medical Leave Act (FMLA). The FMLA provides certain workers with 12 weeks of job-protected, unpaid leave to care for a new child or a sick family member, or in the case of the worker's own serious illness. The implementation of this right displays a recognition that workers are often also responsible for care-taking in the home and cannot rely upon the efforts of a non-employed family member. However, use of FMLA leave is gendered along traditional lines; women are more likely to use it than men, and they are more likely than men to use it to care for others. While leave is unpaid under the federal law, in 2004 the state of California began offering leave-takers a wage replacement rate of 55 percent, up to a maximum of $728 per week.

European countries typically offer longer leave, plus wage replacement. Norway and Sweden, exceptional even in Europe, offer new parents a choice between 42 weeks of leave at 100 percent of pay and 52 weeks of leave at 80 percent of pay. The time can be split between the parents as they decide, but a minimum of four weeks is reserved for the father. The "father quota" was established in these countries in the hopes that it would both improve father–child relationships and balance gender roles within the family. There is some evidence that this policy does affect gender roles; men report that the father quota makes it easier to approach employers about taking leave, and researchers have found that new fathers who take leave are more likely to share in housework and childcare tasks. At a minimum, the policy has encouraged more men to use parental leave. Before it was established, only 4 percent of fathers took any leave in Norway, but in 1996, after the father quota went into effect, 80 percent of eligible fathers took leave (Boje & Leira 2000).

The availability of family leave does not necessarily support new gender norms and roles. Some countries in Europe, such as France, Germany, and Finland, have long leaves of two or three years. Leave of this length has a deleterious effect on experience, training, and opportunity for promotion, and is overwhelmingly used by women, weakening women's labor force attachment. As a result, women's labor force participation rates decline, and the traditional breadwinner/homemaker family model becomes more common again.

Welfare reform in the United States is another example of policy changing to reflect new gender norms in work and family. Aid to Families with Dependent Children (AFDC), the original welfare program, was established to provide for the rare family that lost its breadwinner – usually through death or abandonment – and assumed that women with young children would not be in the labor force. This became increasingly untenable politically as single-parent families were more frequently formed through non-marital childbirth and as it became normative for married mothers to be employed. State-level reforms were initiated during the first half of the 1990s, and on the federal level, AFDC was replaced in 1996 by Temporary Aid for Needy Families (TANF). TANF revised welfare policy by creating work requirements for aid recipients and by imposing lifetime limits on receipt of aid. These measures are in line with new gender norms that support women's participation in breadwinning. It is not only accepted but also expected that single women will provide economic support for their families.

Welfare reform has apparently had an impact. The 1990s saw a dramatic increase in the employment rates of single mothers, and welfare caseloads shrank dramatically. However, welfare reform also had other objectives, including encouraging marriage and discouraging non-marital fertility. The most prominent provision to address these concerns was the broadening of eligibility to include two-parent families. Theoretically, this would remove the disincentive to marriage that existed under AFDC. Researchers have found that welfare reform has instead led to *fewer* new marriages, but also fewer new divorces (Bitler et al. 2004). Nor has welfare reform led to reduced rates of single-mother families (Fitzgerald & Ribar 2004). It is hypothesized that the economic independence fostered by TANF weakens the attractiveness of marriage.

Child and elder care policy in the United States has yet to catch up with new gender norms in work and family, perhaps reflecting ambivalence about these changes, particularly when young children are involved. While the US has a patchwork of relevant policies – tax deductions for a portion of dependent care expenses, dependent care savings accounts, Head Start and Early Head Start, and childcare assistance to families receiving benefits through TANF – child and elder care costs are high and quality is highly variable. Childcare remains gendered in the family, with mothers reducing paid employment to care for children to a much greater extent than fathers. Similarly, women are much more likely to provide elder care than men. Childcare policy will continue to be an important issue, and with the aging of the population, elder care will become increasingly important.

SEE ALSO: Divisions of Household Labor; Doing Gender; Earner–Carer Model; Family, Men's Involvement in; Family Structure and Poverty; Feminization of Poverty; Fertility and Public Policy

REFERENCES AND RECOMMENDED READINGS

Bianchi, S. M., Robinson, J. P., & Milkie, M. A. (forthcoming) *Changing Rhythms of American Family Life*. ASA Rose Series. Russell Sage, New York.

Bitler, M., Gelbach, J., Hoynes, H. W., & Zavodny, M. (2004) The Impact of Welfare Reform on Marriage and Divorce. *Demography* 41(2): 213–36.

Boje, T. P. & Leira, A. (Eds.) (2000) *Gender, Welfare State, and the Market: Towards a New Division of Labor*. Routledge, London.

Budig, M. & England, P. (2001) The Wage Penalty for Motherhood. *American Sociological Review* 66: 204–25.

Fitzgerald, J. M. & Ribar, D. C. (2004) Welfare Reform and Female Headship. *Demography* 41(2): 189–212.

Goldin, C. (2004) The Long Road to the Fast Track: Career and Family. *Annals of the American Academy of Political and Social Science* 596: 20–35.

Gornick, J. C. & Meyers, M. K. (2003) *Families that Work: Policies for Reconciling Parenthood and Employment*. Russell Sage, New York.

Hochschild, A. R. with Machung, A. (2003) *The Second Shift*. Penguin Books, New York.

Jacobs, J. A. & Gerson, K. (2004) *The Time Divide: Work, Family, and Gender Inequality*. Harvard University Press, Cambridge, MA.

Kanter, R. M. (1977) *Work and Family in the United States: A Critical Review and Agenda for Research and Policy*. Russell Sage, New York.

Korenman, S. D. & Neumark, D. (1991) Does Marriage Really Make Men More Productive? *Journal of Human Resources* 26: 282–307.

Lundberg, S. & Rose, E. (2000) Parenthood and the Earnings of Married Men and Women. *Labour Economics* 689–710.

Presser, H. B. (2003) *Working in a 24/7 Economy: Challenges for American Families*. Russell Sage, New York.

Smolensky, E. & Gootman, J. A. (2003) *Working Families and Growing Kids*. National Academies Press, Washington, DC.

gendered aspects of war and international violence

Shahin Gerami and Melodye Lehnerer

Research has shown that gender is an integral element of violence (Tiger & Fox 1971; Elshtain & Tobias 1987; Goldstein 2001). Most cases of violence are committed by men against men. While women can be combatants in armed conflicts (Enloe 2000; Goldstein 2001), they are more likely to be victims than organizers and perpetrators of international violence. The intersection of social categories of gender, class, and nationality informs the effects of international violence for groups and individuals. Working-class and peasant women pay higher prices, both directly and indirectly, for international violence. In violence between states, women of the South are victimized more often, more harshly, and pay higher costs during and after wartime. In fact, the benefits of peace reach them later and in smaller amounts.

International violence is collectively planned and systematically implemented by a group against another for political and economic goal(s). Four types of international violence are identified here. First, there are empire-building, multinational wars. Second, there are bilateral wars between two nation-states most often over territorial disputes. A third type of international violence results from liberation movements when the colonized fight the colonizers for their sovereignty. Revolutions against a tyrannical government fall under this category because they frequently involve foreign players and interests. Lastly, there are civil wars that occur within a nation-state. International forces often influence civil wars.

With regard to international violence, World War I marks a point in military history in which systematic and deliberate attacks on civilians became a pronounced strategy of war (Barstow 2000). Moving from the trench campaigns of World War I to the massive aerial bombings of World War II to more contemporary international conflicts of varying sizes, the ratio of combatant to civilian casualties has changed from 8:1 to 1:1 to 1:8 (Barstow 2000: 3). The great majority of these civilian casualties are women and those whom they care for – children and the elderly. This time period is also significant because, beginning with World War I, the "home front and the war front became intimately connected" (Goldstein 2001: 9).

The reach of new technology allowed targeting goals beyond the front line. Large-scale street battles in urban areas became possible and a strategy of the war itself, not just for control of cities after the conquest. Unlike earlier periods, in which mass killing of civilians was more a consequence of the war, the reach of new technology allowed civilian targets to be integrated into war planning. Most importantly, the social distinction of public and private that had kept women away from the battlefront and its effects was obscured. Women, children, and the elderly, along with able-bodied men, were constructed as the enemy and subject to annihilation. The violent consequences of this change for women were twofold: bodily injury and social role disruption.

VIOLENT ASSAULT: BODILY INJURY AND SOCIAL ROLE DISRUPTION

"Mass rape has long been a deliberate strategy of military leaders. By marking the raped women as 'polluted,' mass rapes destroy families and weaken communal life" (Barstow 2000: 45). The violence of bodily assault includes physical injury from a weapon, torture, malnourishment, disease, and, most noteworthy, sexual assault. Sexual assaults on women can be an offensive or a defensive strategy. Sexual assaults as offensive strategy are planned and executed to destroy the enemy, his house, and his future offspring. Mass rape as a defensive tactic is carried out with the hope of increasing the invaders' descendants. Murder and maiming of women destroys the home base, demolishes the soldiers' morale, and often cripples the backbone of the war machinery.

When the Germans invaded Belgium in August of 1914, and as they marched through, reports of rape are documented along with villages burned and civilians bayoneted (Brownmiller 1975: 41). A clear-cut pattern emerged: rape of women in war is not for sexual pleasure but for control and therefore has propaganda purposes to humiliate and demoralize the enemy. Similarly, the victimized community may exaggerate the atrocities to mobilize the combatants to avenge the dishonoring of women.

What did not get public attention was the huge price that women paid indirectly through social role disruption. It is well documented that French and Belgian families – men, women, and children – lost homes and lives in the first three months of the war. Less well documented are the experiences of Russian women. The Russian women served at the front in Women's Death Battalions, worked the field, served as caretakers at the back of the lines, and lived in destitute conditions during the war, the 1917 Revolution, and the aftermath of these events (Clements et al. 1991). It is this aspect of international violence, disruption of women's roles, which contributes to communal disruption.

Socially, disruption of women's roles as caregivers and network organizers destroys the social fabric of the enemy's home base. Planned scarcity, economic blockades, and disruption of basic services harm women physically and mentally, making their tasks harder to perform. Shortage of basic medicine or water sanitation means sick and starving children for distraught women to mind. The social disruption of women's roles has far-reaching consequences

for women's and girls' lives. Not only is the impact in the moment, it is also for generations to come.

SEXUAL AND PHYSICAL ASSAULT: THE PRIMARY CONSEQUENCE OF INTERNATIONAL VIOLENCE

In 1993, the UN Commission on Human Rights recognized the systematic rape, forced slavery, forced pregnancy, and forced prostitution of women as war crimes (Barstow 2000: 237). In 1996, this recognition led to the indictment of eight Bosnian Serb military and police officers solely on the charges of raping Bosnian Muslim women (Enloe 2000: 135). Over time, five patterns of sexual assault have been identified, regardless of the ethnicity of the perpetrators or the victims. These patterns were officially identified in the Final Report of the UN Commission of Experts on Serbia (1994). Nevertheless, they hold true for any time period and any type of international conflict. Not all patterns of sexual violence may be used in any one conflict, but often a combination of patterns does apply.

In the first pattern, looting and intimidation accompany sexual assault prior to widespread fighting. Assaults take place in women's homes and in front of family members. In addition, rape may occur in public. The intent is to terrorize local residents in hopes they will flee or passively submit (Final Report 1994). The second pattern of sexual violence occurs during fighting. Once attacking forces have secured a town or village, those men, women, and children who remain are rounded up and then divided by sex and age. Women and girls are raped in their homes or in public. Those who survive are transported to detention facilities. The intent of this practice is to traumatize those detained as well as those who escape. Victims and witnesses are unlikely to return to the scene of such events (Final Report 1994). The third pattern of sexual violence occurs in detention facilities or other sites where refugees are kept. Again, the detainees in these "collection centers" are divided by sex and age. Men of fighting age are tortured, executed, or sent to work camps. The women who remain are raped or sexually assaulted by soldiers, camp guards, paramilitaries, and civilians. There are two variations to this pattern of assault dependent upon location and visibility. In the first scenario, women are selected and raped at a separate location from the "camp" in which they are housed. Sometimes they are returned; other times they are killed. Alternately, women are raped at the location where they are detained in front of other detainees. On occasion, detainees, both women and men, are forced to assault each other. The obvious goals are multiple: humiliation, demoralization, and/or ultimately death.

A fourth pattern of sexual assault occurs in camps that are specifically identified as rape/death camps. These camps are set up for the purpose of punishing women through sexual assault and other forms of torture (Salzman 2000). In the case of Serbia, these camps were specifically set up to impregnate women with the "conqueror's seed" (Salzman 2000). The intent of this practice is to achieve ethnic cleansing through women's reproductive capabilities. The fifth and last pattern of sexual assault is the establishment of camps as sites of prostitution. Women are held in these camps to "service" soldiers returning from the front lines. In most instances, the women in these camps are eventually killed (Final Report 1994). This is a common practice wherever there are military bases in occupied territories.

SOCIAL ROLE DISRUPTION: A SECONDARY CONSEQUENCE OF INTERNATIONAL VIOLENCE

While the sexual abuse of women by the enemy has received some attention by international tribunals and can possibly be compensated for, the many other categories of harm that are more widespread, more intense, and have more long-term effects are rarely documented, defined as war crimes, or accounted for in war reparations. International violence impoverishes masses, and among these masses women carry greater responsibilities and receive fewer opportunities. Such practices as the bombing of residential areas, home invasions, and economic blockades prevent women from carrying out their roles as wives and mothers. When homes are destroyed to disperse men, women's domain

is destroyed and families displaced. When economic blockades lead to planned scarcity of food, water, medicine, or population movements, women refugees, as caregivers, face more hardships than male combatants whose task it is to fight and to survive.

Women's injuries in the war from bombing, landmine explosion, street combat, unexploded ordinance (ammunition), and chemical exposure are of lower priority in the scarcity of health care and rehabilitation of the wounded. The secondary physical and psychological sufferings due to stress and scarcity of the war are not considered in war casualties, while men's shell shocks are documented. As in any period of stress, a side-effect of post-war trauma is domestic abuse (Amnesty International 2005). Women are told, and they believe, that their suffering is part of their role, and complaining makes them selfish at best and traitors at worst.

CONCLUSION

While the focus here has been on immediate and long-term physical and social harms of international violence for women, international violence goes beyond harms to women. Men are forced to fight and, when they refuse, are drafted, kidnapped, and killed more frequently than women. Furthermore, the duality of soldier-prostitute, soldier-wife, or soldier-mother overlooks the multifaceted roles that women perform in international violence. For example, Cynthia Enloe discusses "militarized women" in her book *Maneuvers* (2000). These militarized women include prostitutes, rape victims, mothers, and wives of military personnel, nurses, women in the military, and feminist activists. Simplistic dualities also overlook women's agency as individuals or collectivities (Gerami & Lehnerer 2001). Women suffer, but also gain in international violence in terms of economic independence, individual freedom of actions and mobility, and feminist consciousness. International violence puts social mores in a flux, allowing women to engage in activities not permitted before, expand their public role, and acquire greater responsibility and, with it, greater decision-making ability and empowerment.

This deconstruction of the binary mode of gender and international violence also applies to any analytical evaluation of gender and peace. Gender narratives of men/soldiers and women/peacemakers on the one hand ignores the role of men in peace movements, and on the other hand implies gender determinism of violence and peace. As Ruddick (1989) reminds us, even anti-militaristic feminism can fall prey to this binary interpretation of war and peace.

SEE ALSO: Gender, Development and; Gender Ideology and Gender Role Ideology; Gender Oppression; International Gender Division of Labor; Rape Culture; Third World and Postcolonial Feminisms/Subaltern; Traffic in Women; War

REFERENCES AND SUGGESTED READINGS

Amnesty International (2005) Iraq: Iraqi Women – The Need For Protective Measures. Online. web.amnesty.org/library/index/engmde140042005.

Barstow, A. L. (Ed.) (2000) *War's Dirty Secret: Rape, Prostitution, and Other Crimes Against Women*. Pilgrim Press, Ohio.

Brownmiller, S. (1975) *Against Our Will: Men, Women, and Rape*. Simon & Schuster, New York.

Clements, E., Engel, B., & Worobec, C. (1991) *Russia's Women: Accommodation, Resistance, Transformation*. University of California Press, Berkeley.

Elshtain, J. B. & Tobias, S. (1987) *Women, Militarism, and War*. Rowman & Littlefield, Lanham, MD.

Enloe, C. (2000) *Maneuvers: The International Politics of Militarizing Women's Lives*. University of California Press, Berkeley.

Gerami, S. & Lehnerer, M. (2001) Women's Agency and Household Diplomacy: Negotiating Fundamentalism. *Gender and Society* 15: 556–73.

Goldstein, J. (2001) *War and Gender: How Gender Shapes the War System and Vice Versa*. Cambridge University Press, New York.

Ruddick, S. (1989) *Maternal Thinking: Toward a Politics of Peace*. Beacon Press, Cambridge.

Salzman, T. (2000) Rape Camps, Forced Impregnation, and Ethnic Cleansing. In: Barstow, A. L. (Ed.), *War's Dirty Secret: Rape, Prostitution, and Other Crimes Against Women*. Pilgrim Press, Ohio, pp. 63–92.

Tiger, L. & Fox, R. (1971) *The Imperial Animal*. Holt, Rinehart, & Winston, New York.

UN Security Council (1994) *Final Report of the Commission of Experts*. United Nations, New York.

gendered enterprise

Gill Kirton

What do we mean when we say that enterprise or organization is gendered? As Acker (2003) argues, "to say that an organization, or any other analytic unit, is gendered means that advantage and disadvantage, exploitation and control, action and emotion, meaning and identity, are patterned through and in terms of a distinction between male and female, masculine and feminine." However, the traditional approach to organizational analysis is criticized by a number of contemporary authors, including Acker, for its neglect, up until the 1980s at least, of women and gender. This neglect occurred firstly because organizational research often focused on senior levels of the hierarchy where men predominate. Secondly, men dominated the academic research process and generally showed little interest in female employees or gender as a unit of analysis. Critics argued that within traditional organizational analysis men's experiences and interpretations of organizational life were taken as universal, producing gender-neutral knowledge, which failed to recognize gender as a significant dynamic of organizations and rendered women invisible. Although some of the criticisms remain valid in regard to mainstream organization and management studies, there is now a significant and growing body of gender and organization literature, largely produced by women and often with women as the analytic focus, which sees organizations as important sites in which gendered meanings, identities, practices, and power relations are produced, enacted, and reproduced.

Much of the gender and organization literature is influenced by liberal, socialist, and postmodernist/poststructuralist feminist theories. Generally, the literature can be characterized according to one main feminist orientation, while perhaps reflecting insights from others. To summarize, liberal feminism conceives of people as autonomous individuals aspiring to fulfil themselves through a system of individual rights. Women's inequality is rooted in attitudes, customs, and legal constraints standing in the way of their entry to and success in public life. Socialist feminism conceives of women as an oppressed social group facing a common struggle against male domination and exploitation. Women's inequality is rooted in the capitalist and patriarchal systems of production and reproduction. Postmodernist/poststructuralist feminism conceives of gender as a discursive practice through which femininities and masculinities are produced, sustained, and reproduced. There is less a concern with women's material inequality than with demonstrating the ambiguous, unstable, complex nature of social categories and the subjectivity of identity. Influenced by feminist theories, the gender and organization literature has over time taken various turns producing a number of strands, although the themes and foci often overlap. However, no precise chronology of the emergence of the strands can be proffered, and indeed different strands continue to coexist in the contemporary literature.

One dominant strand of this literature, most strongly influenced by liberal feminism, focuses on women managers and vertical gender segregation. Here it is assumed that individuals aspire to climb the organizational hierarchy and that the fair organization will allow both men and women to realize their capabilities within a merit system. The research concerns include gender differences in leadership, work commitment, motivation and satisfaction, sex stereotypes, and gender biases in recruitment and selection. The conclusion often drawn is that if women became or behaved more like men (i.e., if gender difference were eliminated) then they would defy sex stereotypes and succeed in organizations. Therefore, there is a focus on women's "deficiencies" rather than on any in-built unfairness within organizations, with policy recommendations such as assertiveness training courses, or "dressing for success" with the general aim for the fair organization conceived as needing to "fix the women" (Kolb et al. 2003). More recently the perceived existence of gender difference is seen less as something in need of correcting than as a potential organizational resource to be celebrated. Critical authors generally regard this strand of the literature as an inadequate and one-dimensional way of analyzing gender and organizations.

Kanter's *Men and Women of the Corporation* (1977) is an example of an important turn in the literature in that it set out to show that gender differences in organizational behavior are due to structure rather than to the characteristics of men and women as individuals. Hence, from this perspective, it is organizations that need to change, rather than women, in order to encourage more women to join the race to the top. This perspective remains influential and policy-oriented studies examining the gender structure of organizations continue to investigate the ways organizations might accommodate gender difference. For example, the contemporary "women in management" literature explores the problem of the invisible barriers to women's advancement (often referred to as the glass ceiling). These include the lack of senior female role models in organizations, the culture of presenteeism, and the evaluation of individuals according to their ability to separate home and work. Policy recommendations, which are compensatory in nature, are postulated, including the establishment of mentoring for women, women's business/professional networks, and schemes to enable women to reconcile work and family. However, the literature influenced by liberal feminism is uncritical of organizations fundamentally, for example the gendered processes of organizational decision-making (e.g., why is it necessary to work excessively long hours?) or the dominant ideal of meritocracy (e.g., how is merit measured and judged?) are rarely questioned.

Another strand of the gender and organization literature is influenced more strongly by socialist feminist theory. This posits that paid work cannot be the sole unit of analysis and that the intersection between the public and private spheres (or work and the home) must be explored in order to understand women's position in the labor market. Analytically, research is often concerned with the macro level of the labor market and the temporally and spatially persistent pattern of vertical *and horizontal* gender segregation, which is seen to disadvantage women. However, empirical studies are often situated at micro level, although seeking to raise questions and offer arguments and illustrations that are applicable to the wider labor market. Research tries to uncover the social processes and relations involved in sustaining and reproducing women's inequality and calls for transformation of organization structures and cultures. Generally, organization researchers influenced by this theoretical orientation favor qualitative case-study methods that make visible informal gendered processes, relations, and practices.

For example, Collinson et al. (1990), through their detailed case studies of recruitment practices in the banking, mail order, insurance, hi-tech, and food manufacturing industries, show that gender divisions of labor at home and in employment are both a routine condition and consequence of organizational recruitment and a common means of legitimizing sex-discriminatory practices. Collinson et al. also show how sex discrimination is reproduced in recruitment practices through the agency of management, labor, men, and women to highlight how the perpetuation of job segregation is characterized by a self-fulfilling vicious circle incorporating three key recruitment practices of reproduction, rationalization, and resistance. They argue that taken-for-granted beliefs about the male "breadwinner" and female "homemaker" inform the preference for either men or women in particular jobs so that preconceptions about the domestic responsibilities of both sexes are often perceived to be of central relevance to selection decision-making.

The themes of reproduction, rationalization, and resistance are also evident in Cockburn's (1991) case-study research situated in retail, local, and central government and trade unions. For example, Cockburn explores the way that powerful men in organizations use cultural means to deter women from aspiring to senior jobs by striving to retain women's loyalty to men and to the status quo. This then discourages women who are successful from identifying with women at the bottom of the organization. Cockburn is also concerned with horizontal segregation, what she calls the "ghetto walls," which keep the majority of women, especially mothers and other women with domestic ties, in low-paid, part-time work. To bring down the ghetto walls, she argues, it is necessary to institute structural change in organizations by redesigning jobs or retraining staff; reevaluating occupations and restructuring grade systems to reduce differentials

between people at the bottom and people at the top. Cockburn's work is important in that it integrates class analysis with the study of gender in organizations, shifting the focus simply from managerial and professional women to consider the majority of women in low-level employment.

Similarly, Bradley's *Gender and Power in the Workplace* (1999) argues for a theoretical integration of gender and class in order to understand change and continuity in the gendered nature of organizations. She also draws attention to the polarization between younger and older women, whereby younger women are grasping the opportunities provided by the feminization of work and organizations and by "woman friendly" policy developments. However, Bradley finds marked patterns of gender segregation in her case-study organizations, which are maintained in part, she argues, by a powerful set of gendered images about masculine and feminine attributes and their association with particular jobs and forms of employment. For example, as Cockburn (1991) and Collinson et al. (1990) assert, the jobs of trade union official and insurance sales person are permeated with masculine meaning, while the lower-status, less well-paid jobs of retail sales assistant and clerical support worker are permeated with feminine meaning. This powerful gender symbolism means that individual women or men who transcend traditional gendered occupational boundaries (e.g., women fire fighters, male nurses) often find themselves in a precarious and isolated position such that both sexes more typically keep to "gender appropriate" jobs. An interest in the gendered rhetorical devices, discourses, and imagery that sustain gender segregation is now a prominent theme in the gender and organization literature.

Arguably, this interest is influenced by postmodernist ideas within the social sciences, although authors take these ideas in different directions. For example, Bradley retains an interest in "real" differences "out there" between men and women and their experiences of organizations, while perceiving discursive constructs as significant in constituting the gendered social relations that contribute to producing the differential "real" experiences. Other authors influenced by postmodernism have less of an interest in material gender inequalities or setting out policy implications and more in the "performance" and "accomplishment" of gender by individual men and women in organizational contexts.

Another research focus in the strand of gender and organization literature influenced by postmodernist/poststructuralist feminist theories is on "femininities" and "masculinities." These terms point beyond categorized, biological sex differences, treating them more as forms of subjectivities and using them to describe cultural beliefs without any close connection to men and women. In terms of what this means for the study of gender and organization, it is argued that men and masculinity remain taken for granted, hidden, and unexamined in much of the literature, which more typically equates gender with women. In contrast, studying masculinities is regarded as central to understanding the process and structuring of gender relations and discriminatory experiences. In this vein Collinson and Hearn (1994) call for men to be "named as men" in order to expose men's power, discourses, and practices which underpin the asymmetrical gender relations found in organizations. They identify five discourses and practices of masculinity that remain pervasive and dominant in organizations: authoritarianism, paternalism, entrepreneurialism, informalism, and careerism. The consequence of their reproduction is a perpetuation of women's inequality arrived at through the exercise and development, particularly by managers, of coercive power, protective practices, competitive approaches to business and performance, informal relationships between men, and aggressive concern with hierarchical advancement.

Some authors note the class differences in masculinities, arguing that although paid work as a source of masculine identity and power transcends class boundaries, class is a variable in terms of how masculinities are practiced in organizations. For example, a number of studies show how male manual workers seek to maintain masculine identities through discourses and practices of identification and differentiation, including heterosexualized humor and sexual harassment. Sexual humor, it is argued, constructs an image of men as assertive,

independent, and powerful and one of women as passive and dependent.

Having evolved over time, the gender and organization literature is now at a crossroads, with some authors arguing for the integration of gender into mainstream organization analysis and others foreseeing dangers in integration, namely the neglect of gender as a unit of analysis once again. It is clear, though, that studying gender will no longer mean studying just women.

SEE ALSO: Femininities/Masculinities; Feminist Methodology; Gender Ideology and Gender Role Ideology; Gender Mainstreaming; Gendered Organizations/Institutions

REFERENCES AND SUGGESTED READINGS

Acker, J. (2003) Hierarchies, Jobs, Bodies: A Theory of Gendered Organizations. In: Ely, R., Foldy, E., & Scully, M. (Eds.), *The Blackwell Reader in Gender, Work and Organization*. Blackwell, Oxford, pp. 49–61.

Alvesson, M. & Billing, Y. (1997) *Understanding Gender and Organizations*. Sage, London.

Calas, M. & Smircich, L. (1996) From "The Woman's" Point of View: Feminist Approaches to Organization Studies. In: Clegg, S., Hardy, C., & Nord, W. (Eds.), *Handbook of Organization Studies*. Sage, London, pp. 218–57.

Cockburn, C. (1991) *In the Way of Women*. Macmillan, London.

Collinson, D. & Hearn, J. (1994) Naming Men as Men: Implications for Work, Organization and Management. *Gender, Work and Organization* 1(1): 2–22.

Collinson, D., Knights, D., & Collinson, M. (1990) *Managing to Discriminate*. Routledge, London.

Ely, R., Foldy, E., & Scully, M. (Eds.) (2003) *The Blackwell Reader in Gender, Work and Organization*. Blackwell, Oxford.

Kanter, R. M. (1977) *Men and Women of the Corporation*. Basic Books, New York.

Kolb, D., Fletcher, J., Meyerson, D., Merrill-Sands, D., & Ely, R. (2003) Making Change: A Framework for Promoting Gender Equity in Organizations. In: Ely, R., Foldy, E., & Scully, M. (Eds.), *The Blackwell Reader in Gender, Work and Organization*. Blackwell, Oxford, pp. 10–15.

gendered organizations/ institutions

Lauren Rauscher

CONCEPTUAL BEGINNINGS

Understanding organizational practices and processes is central to explaining gender inequality. While women remain clustered in secondary labor markets marked by lower wages, uncertainty, short career ladders, and few if any benefits, most men find employment in primary labor markets characterized by greater economic rewards. Occupational and job segregation continue to be an enduring feature within most firms. Additionally, gender differences in income, power, authority, autonomy, and status translate into men, particularly white men, enjoying systematic advantages over women. Despite changing social and economic conditions and legislation prohibiting sex discrimination, these inequalities persist and subsequently inform an impressive body of labor market and workplace analyses.

The study of "gendered organizations" as a distinct area of scholarly inquiry has developed over the last 15 years in an effort to explain such inequality. The concept, coined by Joan Acker, means that "advantage and disadvantage, exploitation and control, action and emotion, meaning and identity, are patterned through and in terms of a distinction between male and female, masculine and feminine" (Acker 1990: 146). Although relatively new, this field has roots in second wave and radical feminist scholarship dating back at least to the 1960s. Scholars began merging gender studies with organizational literature in an effort to render visible women's experiences, place men's experiences in a gendered context (rather than a universal experience shared by all), and identify the ways in which gender inequality is (re)created and maintained over time.

Early work by Heidi Hartmann, Rosabeth Moss Kanter, Catharine MacKinnon, and Kathy Ferguson revealed organizational dynamics that produce gender-specific outcomes, which disadvantage women and advantage men. For example, Kanter's classic study, *Men and Women of the Corporation* (1977), demonstrates how one's structural position within a firm (e.g., the job one holds in the hierarchy) determines one's "success," defined in terms of career mobility, authority, and power. One's job also affects one's personality, behavior, and aspirations, such as women acting timid. Thus, women's disadvantaged location stems from being disproportionately concentrated and "stuck" in positions with limited power and short to nonexistent career ladders. One of the primary strengths of Kanter's work lies in the shift from individual-level behavior of men and women to a structural explanation of gender inequality. Although Kanter provides mechanisms for how, once in place, gender inequality is maintained through occupational sex segregation, she neglects to explain the *origins* of segregation that leads to an array of unequal work rewards.

Turning to Marxist feminist scholars such as Heidi Hartmann helps find an explication of the origins of gender segregation and its consequences. According to Hartmann, capitalism and patriarchy are separate but interlocking systems that work in concert to structure social organization. (Hartmann defines patriarchy as a set of social relations with a material base, where hierarchical relations between men and solidarity among them enable men to control women.) Specifically, she contends that capitalism and patriarchy operate to subordinate women as individuals and as a collective group through various modes of production, the gendered division of labor, and subsequent sex segregation. Therefore, according to this perspective, patriarchy proceeds yet interacts with capitalism so that women enter the wage labor market at a disadvantage, and men's actions maintain women's subordinate position while protecting their own privileges. Hartmann's theory acknowledges the interconnections between gender and other institutions. She also shows that men's actions matter in maintaining gender inequality in addition to men and women's structural positions, thereby making the link between structure and agency explicit. Since Hartmann's account, feminist scholars have demonstrated the ways in which gender infuses our lives through all institutions. Because institutions are intertwined and interdependent, we can use gender as a lens through which to describe and understand people's experiences within them.

Joan Acker argues that despite such advances in gender theorizing, conceptions of institutions (other than "the family") remain gender free or gender neutral, when, in fact, gender permeates their ideologies, practices, and symbols. Indeed, many argue that gender constitutes an institution in and of itself, in addition to shaping other forms of social organization. That is, gender is not only an individual attribute but also a major organizing system that structures patterns of interactions and expectations across other major social institutions (Lorber 1994). Thus, gender fundamentally structures family and kinship, the economy, language, education, culture, interpersonal relationships, sexuality, ideology, and personality. Conceiving institutions as genderless, separate entities is problematic because this obscures the fundamental processes of creating and maintaining power inequities between men and women.

According to Acker, the gendering of institutions and organizations occurs through the following processes. First, there is the division of men and women into distinctly different realms, in terms of the type of labor performed, physical work locations, and acceptable behaviors and emotions. Second, symbols and images, such as language and culture, are constructed that reinforce these divisions. Third, gendering processes occur in interpersonal interactions between and among women and men. Individual identities also promote and reinforce gendered outcomes to the extent that people enact and internalize gender-specific scripts for behavior. Fourth, gender constitutes one of the fundamental organizing elements of creating organizational structures.

In a pathbreaking article, Acker (1990) uses complex, bureaucratic organizations as an example to detail how organizations reflect specific gendered expectations and relations. More specifically, she shows that jobs, work rules, contracts, evaluation systems, and firm cultures (e.g., organizational logics) are not gender neutral. Rather, she draws on feminists such as Dorothy Smith, Joan Scott, and Sandra

Hardin, who advocate that gender constitutes a meaningful analytic category to argue that a gendered substructure undergirds the entire bureaucratic organizational system. Notably, this substructure is gendered masculine, with the interests of men at its center. Therefore, gender inequality stems from the very organization of bureaucracies rather than being produced solely by the actions of particular gendered individuals enacting gendered scripts for behavior within them.

To illustrate, in organizational terms "jobs" constitute an abstract category, filled by an abstract worker, one with no gender. In this conception, the successful performance of a job requires a worker to focus on a set of tasks commensurate with a certain level of skills, credentials, and remuneration. Also, we expect a worker to be unencumbered by competing obligations that would interfere with job demands. Acker makes clear, however, that real people fill jobs; that is, jobs are embodied. And by examining jobs this way, we can see that the abstraction best reflects men's lives, since men stereotypically assume the majority work in the public sphere while having few competing demands in the private sphere. Instead, women perform reproductive, childrearing, domestic, and care work in the private sphere, which enables men to work outside the home. Thus, Acker shows that a gendered division of labor provides the foundation for the conception of a job.

Procreation, childrearing, and stereotypically feminine emotions upset the successful functioning of jobs within bureaucratic organizations, again making clear that jobs are based on men's lives, men's bodies, and masculinity, while relegating women to the margins. Thus, despite the inroads women have made into traditionally male-dominated occupations and the greater number who have entered the ranks of management, gender inequalities between men and women remain remarkably stable. Although Kanter's theory would have predicted more equality as more women changed structural positions within organizations, Acker suggests that such mobility offers a futile attempt at disrupting gender differentials due to the gendered substructure privileging men that operates as a fundamental structuring element of the organization itself.

EMPIRICAL EVIDENCE

Empirical projects examining Acker's theoretical claims can be found in a burgeoning literature bridging multiple academic disciplines. For instance, significant work is devoted to the ways in which *occupations and jobs* are gendered. In her book *Gender Trials* (1995), Jennifer Pierce demonstrates how norms and expectations for lawyers and paralegals in corporate law firms are culturally constructed, symbolized, and reinforced through masculinity and femininity, respectively. For instance, successful lawyers are characterized by their "Rambo"-litigating techniques where they obliterate their enemies in fierce competition. Token women lawyers (tokens because they represent a numerical minority in the occupation) must also conform to these ultra-masculine behaviors in order to achieve success and not be considered weak and incompetent (or impotent). In contrast, women paralegals must nurture and mother their bosses or suffer consequences of criticism from them. Yet men paralegals do not experience the same set of constraints and experiences.

This work is similar to Williams's (1992) account of how men as librarians, elementary school teachers, and nurses face different experiences than women in the same occupations. Although these occupations are gendered feminine, men are promoted at exceptional speeds, "riding the glass escalator" rather than facing barriers to advancement. Such scholarship varies significantly from Kanter's findings of how women experience tokenism as having little power, needing to prove themselves, and exclusionary. These findings illustrate how a masculine gendered substructure operates to benefit men even where men constitute the numerical minority of workers in a given occupation or firm.

Other scholars have studied *gendered organizational practices and policies* across a broad spectrum of settings ranging from restaurants and prisons to an Anglican parish, Malawi NGOs, and a Latino health organization in Los Angeles. For example, Britton (1997) shows how training materials and examples for prison officers are presented as generic, but in actuality are constructed as though all of the trainees are men. The material neglects issues and information germane to women's prisons (only men's), and completely ignores sexual harassment of officers from inmates.

The journal *Gender, Work and Organization* was created to advance interdisciplinary theoretical and empirical work on the process and outcomes of gendered organizational structures. Additionally, one can now find scholarship in this area in business journals, which historically have neither published extensively on women's experiences nor analyzed men's positions as gendered beings. *Gender and Society* also devotes considerable space to analyses on gendered processes and outcomes across a variety of institutions and organizations. Although challenges to integrating literature on gender, work, and organizations remain along theoretical, gender, and geographic lines, there is excitement about both the possibilities of "striking out" into new territories and problematizing current work in an effort to enrich this field.

FUTURE DIRECTIONS

Several scholars have responded to Acker's original treatment of gendered organizations, including Acker herself. Consensus exists on at least two of the future directions for work in this field.

First, scholars must seriously consider the specific context in which gendering processes occur to avoid criticisms that arguments of a gender substructure are essentialist and ahistorical. That is, instead of conceiving organizations as stable and rigid structures, Acker and others emphasize the process-oriented and contextual nature of gendering. For instance, in "The Epistemology of the Gendered Organization" (2000) Dana Britton notes that one of the major themes in this field claims that bureaucratic organizations are *inherently* gendered masculine. Britton argues that turning a testable proposition into an underlying assumption stifles potential for changing the ways that workplaces (re)produce gender inequality, short of eradicating complex bureaucracies and replacing them with collectivist organizations. Moreover, such a static conceptualization does not account for the ways in which some formal bureaucratic practices benefit women (see Cook

& Waters 1998) and protect women from sexual harassment.

Additionally, Britton cautions scholars examining the ways in which occupations and jobs are gendered, most of whom rely on the extent to which occupations are male or female dominated. According to Britton, this approach presents the tendency to conflate sex with gender while simultaneously neglecting the complex historical process that leads to occupations being gender typed as feminine or masculine.

Context also remains important as organizational boundaries and contemporary work configurations change, partially fueled by globalization. Patricia Yancey Martin and others call for more systematic analyses of how contemporary practices, such as flattened hierarchies, team-based approaches, telecommuting, and e-commerce, affect gendered occupations and practices and subsequent inequalities.

Second, a substantial body of literature demonstrates that inequality is patterned along gender, race, and class lines. Moreover, the intersections of these stratification systems translate into white men enjoying systematic advantages over other men as well as all women. In some instances, white women experience privileges that men and women of color do not, depending on the context. Thus, patterns of inequality are far more complex than simply noting gender inequities between all men and all women.

In response, scholars argue to move beyond solely examining the gendering of organizations to account for other axes of inequality, namely race. In *What a Woman Should Be and Do* (1996) Stephanie Shaw provides an exemplary study of how teaching as an occupation is both gendered and raced. Moreover, Collins (2000) draws on work by Barbara Omolade to argue that organizations maintain (white, masculine) power by having professional black women in supervisory positions who "serve white superiors while quieting the natives" (e.g., other women of color).

In addition to her suggestions noted above, Britton calls for greater theoretical clarification and refinement in an effort to create meaningful strategies for social change. Patricia Yancy Martin, Jeffrey Hearn, and colleagues contest this call for synthesis, finding strength in the "ambiguity, contradiction, paradox, and multiplicity" that accompanies the diverse literature in this field (Martin & Collinson 2002).

SEE ALSO: Femininities/Masculinities; Gender Mainstreaming; Gendered Enterprises; Hegemonic Masculinity; Institution; Occupational Segregation; Patriarchy; Women, Economy and

REFERENCES AND SUGGESTED READINGS

Acker, J. (1990) Hierarchies, Jobs, and Bodies: A Theory of Gendered Organizations. *Gender and Society* 4: 139–58.

Britton, D. (1997) Gendered Organizational Logic: Policy and Practice in Men's and Women's Prisons. *Gender and Society* 11(6): 796–818.

Collins, P. H. (2000) *Black Feminist Thought: Knowledge, Consciousness, and the Politics of Empowerment*, 2nd edn. Routledge, New York.

Cook, C. & Waters, M. (1998) The Impact of Organizational Form on Gendered Labor Markets in Engineering and Law. *Sociological Review* 46(2): 313–39.

Ferguson, K. (1984) *The Feminist Case Against Bureaucracy*. Temple University Press, Philadelphia.

Hartmann, H. (1976) Capitalism, Patriarchy, and Job Segregation by Sex. *Signs: Journal of Women in Culture and Society* 1(3): 137–69.

Hearn, J., Sheppard, D. L., Tancred-Sheriff, P., & Burrell, G. (Eds.) (1989) *The Sexuality of Organizations*. Sage, London.

Kanter, R. M. (1977) *Men and Women of the Corporation*. Basic Books, New York.

Leidner, R. (1993) *Fast Food, Fast Talk: Service Work and the Routinization of Everyday Life*. University of California Press, Berkeley.

Lorber, J. (1994) *Paradoxes of Gender*. Yale University Press, New Haven.

MacKinnon, C. (1979) *Sexual Harassment of Working Women*. Yale University Press, New Haven.

Martin, P. Y. & Collinson, D. (2002) "Over the Pond and Across the Water": Developing the Field of "Gendered Organizations." *Gender, Work, and Organizations* 9(3): 244–65.

Reskin, B. & Roos, P. (1990) *Job Queues, Gender Queues: Explaining Women's Inroads into Male Occupations*. Temple University Press, Philadelphia.

Williams, C. (1992) The Glass Escalator: Hidden Advantages for Men in the "Female" Professions. *Social Problems* 39: 253–68.

genealogy

Steve Fuller

The appeal to genealogy as a general historical method is usually attributed to Michel Foucault, who contrasted it with both teleology and his own preferred "archeology," which suspends the search for causation altogether in favor of treating socio-epistemic structures (or epistèmes) as superimposed space-time strata, each of roughly coexistent events. (The palimpsest was thus Foucault's model for historiography.) Foucault's foil was Friedrich Nietzsche, whose *Genealogy of Morals* resurrected worries of legitimate lineage that had dominated the reproduction of social life prior to the constitution of the modern nation-state. Replacing traditional legal concerns that political succession might be based on fraudulent documents, Nietzsche argued that contemporary morality might rest on forgotten etymologies, whereby "obligations" turn out to be strategies for the weak to inflict a sense of guilt on the strong, simply for being stronger. Here Nietzsche was explicitly siding with the survivalist ethic of Social Darwinists against socialists who argued that the rich "owed" their success to the collaboration of the poor.

A natural question to ask is what led Nietzsche to think that a defunct method for establishing right to rule should provide the basis for a deep understanding of society. Here the appeal to biology is crucial. Ernst Haeckel, Darwin's staunchest German defender, famously declared "Ontogeny recapitulates phylogeny," by which he meant the biological development of the individual organism (i.e., the gestation period) repeats the stages undergone in the evolution of all organisms. Nietzsche cleverly reworded Haeckel's slogan for his own purposes: "Ontology recapitulates philology." Nietzsche, a prodigy in the study of classical languages, unsurprisingly found Haeckel's slogan appealing.

Darwin had depicted – and Haeckel popularized – evolution as a "tree of life" founded on a principle of common ancestry of morphologically similar species, ultimately deriving from a unitary "origin of life." The imagery remains powerful today as both a principle of biological taxonomy and an account of migration patterns within species or closely related species (e.g., the idea that all humans emerged out of Africa). Both uses are indebted to Darwin's own inspiration, the comparative linguist August Schleicher, who drew the first "tree of life" (or "cladogram") to show the interrelatedness of Indo-European languages, which together implicated an ultimate ancestor, a pure "Aryan" language probably spoken in Western India. Many of Schleicher's fellow philologists were inclined to think of this inferred source as the medium in which the biblical deity originally communicated with Adam. However, Darwin and Nietzsche were prepared to take at least one aspect of the tree of life metaphor literally, namely, that language – and life – began arbitrarily at a particular place and time.

The contingency of origins is crucial for the genealogical method. To see this point, consider that history may be considered from two general perspectives: from the past looking forward into the future, and from the present looking back at the past. The former standpoint focuses on "turning points" when the future is open to multiple alternate futures, with the decisions taken at those times generating what economists call "path-dependent" outcomes. In contrast to such "underdeterminism," the latter standpoint tends to presume "overdeterminism," whereby when and where the origin actually occurs is irrelevant because eventually the outcome will turn out the same. Overdeterminism produces teleology, underdeterminism genealogy. In the latter, the perceived sense of "necessity" in current ways of knowing and being merely reflects the reinforcement of an original moment of decision.

It is worth observing that Nietzsche wrote at a time – the final quarter of the nineteenth century – when the inexorability of human progress was a default position among intellectuals. Thus, the shock value of the genealogical method was stronger then than now, when, under the influence of postmodernism, relatively few intellectuals take seriously Nietzsche's teleological foil. In Nietzsche's day, genealogy's potential to scandalize was perhaps best presented in Henrik Ibsen's "bourgeois dramas," whereby some apparently ordinary situation turns out to betray the traces of a sordid past that persists, albeit in some hidden form that veers between sanctification and mystification. The moral dilemma that repeatedly arises in Ibsen's plays is whether knowledge of that past should be allowed to influence contemporary judgments.

Darwin, Nietzsche, and Ibsen all lived before the incorporation of Mendelian genetics into modern evolutionary theory, which occurred in earnest only in the 1930s. Thus, they operated with a semi-coherent sense of hereditary transmission, in which an older Lamarckian view of the inheritance of acquired traits was grafted onto a much less teleological view of offspring simply manifesting a blended version of their parents' family traits. Yet, despite its semi-coherence, it was precisely this view that fueled the imagination of Freud, who saw his psychoanalytic practice as a micro-application of Nietzsche's genealogical method. Freud replaced the rogue ancestor, whose identity is revealed in the course of the bourgeois drama, with the rogue incident in the patient's past – say, the source of the Oedipus or Electra Complex – that anchored his or her subsequent conduct.

In terms of earlier theories of genealogy and inheritance, Mendelian genetics constitutes a turn toward essentialism that undermines the need for extensive historical investigation. According to Mendel, the traits expressed in an individual's life (i.e., its phenotype) reflect a limited range of possibilities circumscribed by its genetic program (i.e., its genotype). In other words, an individual's inheritance can be ascertained simply through an intensive examination of that individual. A case in point is the increasing use of genetic profile, whereby "susceptibility" to, say, crime or disease is determined by genetic sequences that an individual shares with others who bear no obvious family relation. In this context, Gilles Deleuze's views about the "virtualization" of identity have considerable purchase.

SEE ALSO: Biosociological Theories; Deleuze, Gilles; Foucauldian Archeological Analyses; Foucault, Michel; Historical and Comparative Methods; Nietzsche, Friedrich; Social Darwinism

REFERENCES AND SUGGESTED READINGS

Cavalli-Sforza, L. (2000) *Genes, Peoples, and Languages*. Farrar, Straus & Giroux, New York.
Deleuze, G. (1994) *Difference and Repetition*. Columbia University Press, New York.
Foucault, M. (1970). *The Order of Things: An Archaeology of the Human Sciences*. Random House, New York.
Foucault, M. (1975). *The Archaeology of Knowledge*. Harper & Row, New York.
Fuller, S. (2006) *The New Sociological Imagination*. Sage, London.
Richards, R. (1987). *Darwin and the Emergence of Evolutionary Theories of Mind and Behavior*. University of Chicago Press, Chicago.

general linear model

Xitao Fan

The social science researcher's repertoire of statistical tools ranges from simple techniques (e.g., *t*-test) to sophisticated multivariate analytic techniques (e.g., structural equation modeling). Many of these statistical techniques appear to be different analytic systems designed for different research situations. The distinctions, however, are often superficial. Fundamentally, many techniques are related to each other to such a degree that they can be considered as variations of a more general statistical model. For quantitative researchers in social sciences, understanding the relationship among the seemingly different analytic techniques is important, because such understanding helps researchers make judicious choices of analytic techniques in research.

In the social and behavioral sciences, traditionally, techniques involving categorical independent variables (e.g., *t*-test, ANOVA) and those involving continuous variables (e.g., correlation, regression) used to be treated as distinctly different data analysis systems "intended for types of research that differed fundamentally in design, goals, and types of variables" (Cohen et al. 2003: xxv). Despite the superficial differences, these and many other statistical techniques share one thing in common: they are designed to analyze linear relationships among variables. Cohen (1968) demonstrated that ANOVA-type techniques and regression-type techniques were statistically equivalent. Because of this, many techniques can be conceptualized as belonging to a general statistical model called the general linear model (GLM).

The GLM underlies most of the statistical techniques used in social science research. In the conventional (and narrower) sense, GLM may be conceptualized as a regression-based model. In regression analysis, the independent variable is assumed to be a continuous variable. In ANOVA-type methods, the independent variable is a categorical variable representing group membership (either naturally occurring groups such as gender or ethnic groups, or groups based on manipulated variables such as treatment vs. control groups in an experimental design). However, it is easy to extend the regression technique to subsume ANOVA-type methods (e.g., *t*-test, ANOVA, ANCOVA, MANOVA) by converting the group membership categories to some form of "pseudo" quantitative coding. "Dummy coding" and "effect coding" are the two most popular coding schemes for this purpose, and both are illustrated in a typical regression analysis textbook (e.g., Cohen et al. 2003). This conceptualization of GLM is currently implemented in the major statistical software packages (e.g., SPSS, SAS).

Broadly speaking, the concept of GLM goes beyond the regression model. As discussed more than 30 years ago (Kshirsagar 1972: 281), "most of the practical problems arising in statistics can be translated, in some form or the other, as the problem of measurement of association between two vector variates x and y." (Here, x and y are vectors each containing multiple variables.) This extension allows for linear combinations of *multiple* dependent variables, thus extending the GLM concept to such multivariate techniques as discriminant function analysis and canonical correlation analysis (Thompson 1991; Fan 1996). The more recent development of the structural equation modeling (SEM) technique further suggests that SEM should be conceptualized as the most general of the general linear models, because it is the most general analytic technique for analyzing linear relationships among variables,

and it subsumes most parametric analytic techniques widely used in social and behavioral sciences (Bagozzi et al. 1981; Bentler 1992; Fan 1996; Jöreskog & Sörbom 2001). So GLM should not only be understood as an analytic model, such as that implemented in statistical software packages like SPSS and SAS, but more importantly, GLM should be viewed as a conceptual framework that subsumes a variety of analytic techniques as its variations or special cases.

The concept of GLM has some important implications for social science researchers. First, the concept of GLM makes it clear that the choice of an analytical technique does not contribute to the validity of any causal inferences that a researcher may make. Some researchers often have the misconception that ANOVA-type methods are closely related to experimental design, thus are more suitable for research studies intended for making causal inferences. Even some textbooks on research methods (e.g., Gall et al. 1996) unintentionally contribute to this misconception by linking analysis techniques to research designs (e.g., ANOVA-type methods for experimental designs, and correlation/regression for correlation/observation research designs). The GLM concept informs us that the choice of statistical technique has no bearing on the validity of causal inference, and only the research design does.

Another issue is related to the often observed research practice of categorizing an independent continuous variable (e.g., categorizing family income originally measured in dollars into three income levels: high, medium, and low) so that ANOVA-type methods can be applied. This is often done because a researcher wants to know if families at different income levels (high, medium, low) differ on the outcome variable of interest. This research practice is ill-advised because analytic precision is reduced in the categorization process, and the same question can be more precisely answered by preserving the original measurement scale and applying correlation/regression type analysis.

SEE ALSO: ANOVA (Analysis of Variance); Multivariate Analysis; Regression and Regression Analysis; Statistics; Structural Equation Modeling

REFERENCES AND SUGGESTED
READINGS

Bagozzi, R. P., Fornell, C., & Larcker, D. F. (1981) Canonical Correlation Analysis as a Special Case of Structural Relations Model. *Multivariate Behavioral Research* 16: 437–54.
Bentler, P. M. (1992) *EQS Structural Equations Program Manual.* BMDP Statistical Software, Los Angeles.
Cohen, J. (1968) Multiple Regression as a General Data-Analytic System. *Psychological Bulletin* 70: 426–43.
Cohen, J., Cohen, P., West, S. G., & Aiken, L. S. (2003) *Applied Multiple Regression/Correlation Analysis for the Behavioral Sciences,* 3rd edn. Lawrence Erlbaum, Mahwah, NJ.
Fan, X. (1996) Canonical Correlation Analysis as a General Analytical Model. In: Thompson, B. (Ed.), *Advances in Social Science Methodology: A Research Annual,* Vol. 4. JAI Press, Greenwich, CT, pp. 71–94.
Gall, M. D., Borg, W. R., & Gall, J. P. (1996) *Educational Research: An Introduction,* 6th edn. Longman, White Plains, NY.
Jöreskog, K. G. & Sörbom, D. (2001) *LISREL 8: User's Reference Guide.* SSI Scientific Software International, Lincolnwood, IL.
Kshirsagar, A. M. (1972) *Multivariate Analysis.* Marcel Dekker, New York.
Thompson, B. (1991) A Primer on the Logic and Use of Canonical Correlation Analysis. *Measurement and Evaluation in Counseling and Development* 24: 80–95.

generalized other

D. Angus Vail

The generalized other is one of George Herbert Mead's central concepts in his seminal discussion of the social genesis of the self. According to Mead, the self resides in the individual's ability to take account of himself or herself as a social being. It thus requires the individual to take the role of the other as well as taking account of how his or her actions might affect the group. *Generalized other* is Mead's (1962: 154–8) term for the collection of roles and attitudes that people use as a reference point for figuring out how to behave in a given situation. This term is often used in discussions of the play and game stages of development.

According to Mead, selves develop in social contexts as people learn to take the roles of their consociates such that they can with a fair degree of accuracy predict how one set of actions is likely to generate fairly predictable responses. People develop these capacities in the process of interacting with one another, sharing meaningful symbols, and developing and using language to create, refine, and assign meanings to social objects (including themselves). In order for complex social processes such as these to work, people have to develop a sense for the rules, norms, roles, understandings, and so on that make responses predictable. While they learn these sets of rules from concrete others, their aggregate constitutes a generalized other.

Since different social settings are governed by different sets of rules, competent social actors have to be able to take account of different sets of rules as they move from one social setting to another. Each setting, then, is governed by its own generalized other. If one were to invoke Mead's preferred sports metaphor, the athlete has to be able to take account of different sets of rules as she or he moves from sport to sport.

As people develop more complete selves, then, they learn to internalize and recognize a greater diversity of perspectives operating among different communities. As they move among settings and/or communities, they have to take into account the aggregate expectations of the people they are likely to encounter in that setting, the culture that is likely to make that aggregate make sense, and the reasons that aggregate is different from other aggregates. Thus, while children in the play stage take the role of a single other, and children in the game stage learn to take the roles of several others, a person who has developed a sense of a *generalized* other can take the role of abstract sets of attitudes, beliefs, and norms she or he expects *concrete* others to embody.

In a sense, then, the generalized other is the process through which the individual internalizes and takes account of society's expectations. As society is processual, emergent, and contextual, so must be the person's ability to take account of different generalized others that are likely to govern people's behaviors from setting to setting.

SEE ALSO: Game Stage; Mead, George Herbert; Play Stage; Preparatory Stage; Role; Self

REFERENCES AND SUGGESTED READINGS

Blumer, H. (2004) *George Herbert Mead and Human Conduct*. Alta Mira Press, Walnut Creek, CA.
Mead, G. H. (1962 [1934]) *Mind, Self, and Society: From the Standpoint of a Social Behaviorist*. University of Chicago Press, Chicago.
Meltzer, B. N. (1959) *The Social Psychology of George Herbert Mead*. Center for Sociological Research, Kalamazoo, MI.
Meltzer, B. N., Petras, J. W., & Reynolds, L. T. (1975) *Symbolic Interactionism: Genesis, Varieties and Criticism*. Routledge & Kegan Paul, Boston.
Weigert, A. J. & Gecas, V. (2004) Self. In: Reynolds, L. T. & Herman-Kinney, N. J. (Eds.), *Handbook of Symbolic Interactionism*. Alta Mira Press, New York, pp. 267–88.

generational change

Martin Kohli

In its most obvious sense, generational change means change occurring along succeeding generations, showing up in differences between them. In a more fundamental sense, it expresses the idea that social change needs to be understood in terms of the sequence of generations, and is to a considerable extent driven by their dynamics.

The concept of generation can be defined with regard to society or to family – two levels which are usually analyzed separately but should be treated in a unified framework (Kohli & Szydlik 2000). At the level of the family, generation refers to position in the lineage. At the societal level, it refers to the aggregate of persons born in a limited period (i.e., a birth cohort according to demographic parlance) who therefore experience historical events at similar ages and move up through the life course in unison.

At both levels, the concept of generation is a key to the analysis of movement across time. In the sequence of generations, families and societies create continuity and change with regard to parents and children, economic resources, political power, and cultural hegemony. In all of these spheres generations are a basic unit of social reproduction *and* social change – in other words, of stability over time as well as renewal (or sometimes revolution).

SOCIAL AND INTELLECTUAL CONTEXT

In some "simple" traditional societies without centralized political power and class-based social stratification, age and gender are the basic criteria for social organization. The most obvious type are the societies – to be found mostly in East Africa – based on formal age classes (or age-sets, as they are sometimes called). A subtype of particular relevance are those societies in which the basis is not age but generation – that is, position in the family lineage. Here, the sequence of generations in the family directly conditions the position of the individual in the economic, political, and cultural sphere. Family filiation is linked with material security, power, and social status.

In modern societies these features of social organization have been differentiated and are now institutionalized in separate spheres. But they need to be linked at least conceptually, so that shifts in the relative importance of these spheres may be detected. There are indications, for instance, that in the West the main arena of intergenerational conflict has shifted from the political and cultural to the economic sphere. The political and cultural cleavage between generations, so highly visible and outspoken in the "silent revolution" of the 1960s and 1970s (Inglehart 1977), has turned into a distributive cleavage played out around the institutions of the labor market and the welfare state.

Generational dynamics have always been a major engine of social change. In structural as well as symbolic terms, generations define themselves (or are defined) against each other; new generations come into being by setting themselves apart from and competing with existing older ones (Attias-Donfut 1988).

Under conditions of modernity, this has taken on a special twist. Each new generation – both at the level of society and of family – is socially expected to come into its own and acquire some measure of autonomy. Adolescence and youth have thus become a period of particular unrest.

This was the situation faced by Mannheim (1928) when he put the problem of generations on the agenda of modern sociology. Mannheim did not invent the concept as such; when he wrote his seminal paper he identified two distinct traditions of thought on the subject that he labeled the French and the German:

> The first, born of the spirit of positivism (Auguste Comte), was the search for an objective (external) historical rhythm and thus for a general law of social change. Comte and his followers thought that they had found this rhythm in the regular sequence of human generations.
>
> The second, born of the spirit of hermeneutics (Wilhelm Dilthey), was the search for the inner totality (*Gestalt*) of an historical epoch and thus for what sets it apart from all others. Dilthey and his followers believed that this totality could be found in the specific historical experience of a generation. (Mannheim 1928)

Mannheim took up the "German" tradition, but gave it a sociological turn by combining it with some of the formal analysis characteristic of the "French" one. The problem that Mannheim defined was how experiential generations (as in the hermeneutic tradition) became political generations that created social dynamics (as in the positivist tradition).

Following Comte, Mannheim proposed a simple thought experiment: What would happen to a society if its members lived on indefinitely and no new members were born? In his view the likely consequence would be that change would be stifled. Social innovation – for Comte and Mannheim – is brought about by the onset of new generations. The young are the natural carriers of the new. On the other hand, people have to die in order to allow social renewal to take place. Generations must make room for the next ones at regular intervals. "Creative destruction" – to use Schumpeter's famous term – depends on the disappearance of the old. It follows that – all things being equal – societies with shorter lives are more dynamic. We should note that modern societies have

institutionalized a functional equivalent for physical death: retirement.

This conception is based on a very strong presupposition: that people acquire their basic worldview and dispositions early in life and then more or less stick (or are stuck) with them. For Mannheim, the formative experiences are those of adolescence when the mind awakens to a reflexive conscience of itself. This argument is in line with his sociology of knowledge (later elaborated upon by phenomenological sociology). The first worldview or structure of knowledge that an individual acquires colors all later additions and corrections, positively or negatively.

A great deal of work has been devoted to assessing the validity of this presupposition; that is, whether there is stability of basic orientations and dispositions over the life course, and as a corollary, whether the elderly are less able and willing to innovate than the young. In developmental psychology there is broad evidence for learning and development throughout the life course; the potential for change thus remains until late in life, but in many dimensions the prevailing empirical pattern is one of continuity, with a possible trend towards less controlling and more accommodating action styles. The evidence in terms of political psychology is discussed by Braungart and Braungart (1993). From a sociological perspective, it can be argued that personal continuity may be less a product of "innate" tendencies or developmental path-dependency than of the institutional commitment to stability (or the lack of institutional incentives for change) during adulthood. But as with other "big questions," the overall answers have so far been rather unsatisfactory in terms of elegance and simplicity. At the most general level what can be asserted on the basis of this large body of research is that stability (or lack of innovation) is the general rule in *some* domains, under *some* conditions, and in *some* periods. In recent years, research activity seems to have slackened even though the basic issues have not really been resolved.

The three basic domains are those of political, economic, and family generations. There have also been studies on cultural generations, such as those in the world of art or of science, but given the close links between, for example, literary and political intellectuals (Wohl 1979), this will now be discussed as part of the political field.

POLITICAL GENERATIONS

There are additional reasons why generational cleavages have deepened over the course of modernization. The first is the increasing age-grading of social organization brought about by the institutionalization of the life course (Kohli 1986). The second is that other cleavages which organized early industrial societies have lost some of their salience, especially those of class.

In the history of most western welfare states, the key "social question" to be solved was the integration of the industrial workers – in other words, the pacification of the class conflict. This was achieved by giving workers some assurance of a stable life course, including retirement as a normal life phase funded to a large extent through public pay-as-you-go contribution systems or general taxes. In the twenty-first century, class conflict seems to be defunct and its place taken over by the generational conflict. The new prominence of the latter is due both to the evolved patterns of social security, predicated upon the institutionalized tri-partition of the life course (which has turned the elderly into the main clients of the welfare state), and to the demographic challenge of low fertility and increasing longevity. Demographic discontinuity creates unequal life chances among generations (Easterlin 1980).

It remains essential, however, to assess the extent of generational cleavages per se and the extent to which they mask the continued existence of the received cleavages between rich and poor (or capitalists and workers); in other words, the extent to which new *intergenerational* conflicts have really crowded out traditional *intragenerational* ones. There are moreover other intragenerational cleavages that are usually categorized as "new" dimensions of inequality (in distinction to the "old" ones of class), such as those of gender and ethnicity.

There is thus a problem of internal differentiation. An individual does not live in a specific generational space only, but also belongs to a specific class, gender, ethnic group, and so on. By assuming the homogeneity of all those living together in the same stratum of historical time,

and neglecting the dimensions of conflict within this generation, the concept can even become ideologically tainted.

In political survey research, there has been a series of attempts to identify political generations as aggregates with specific orientations and dispositions. The broadest and best-known comparative research program in this respect is that of Inglehart, who has made a strong case for a basic generational shift starting in the 1960s from materialism to post-materialism. Smith (2005) analyzes the extent of the "generation gap" – the difference between the young and the old – in a wide range of attitudes, values, and behaviors and its change over the 25 years from 1973 to 1997 based on the US General Social Survey. He finds a wide generation gap at the beginning of this period with a narrowing thereafter, in line with the notion that the main cultural transformation occurred in the 1960s and that people who grew up during or after this time can be expected to have more in common with each other than those who were raised before. We may expect that in Eastern Europe the early 1990s would again be a transition with the potential of widening the generation gap.

But this is only the first level in the formation of a political generation. What is at issue here can be expressed analytically as a progression from (1) a common social location and experience to (2) consciousness of this shared reality to (3) getting organized together to form a unified political actor. This framework has obvious parallels to Marx's distinction between *Klasse an sich* and *Klasse für sich*, which has been put to good use in studies of the historical formation of labor movements and labor organizations, and is now also being applied to gender and ethnicity. Studies of political generations can be set up in similar ways – Mannheim developed his framework as an explicit analogy to Marx's terms – but appear to face a more difficult task.

In fact, the formation of a generation as a unified political actor seems rather unlikely because it is not based on a membership characteristic that is clearly visible in social life and so cannot be easily shed (such as gender or ethnicity), or refers to well-defined resource positions and ways of life (such as class).

Many authors have concluded that, while there may be groups that share certain social locations, experiences, and dispositions, there are no generations in the sense of population groups that are conscious of sharing them, and even act on this consciousness. Against this skepticism, historical reality has time and again tended to reaffirm the existence of such political generations, and to put forth phenomena which can be understood only within a generational framework. These phenomena have manifested themselves as (often revolutionary) movements at various points in the course of modernization (Roseman 1995). They are often youth movements, and they often occur at major historical watersheds, such as 1914, 1945, 1968, and 1989. They may be focused on literary and intellectual groups (Wohl 1979) or on political groups and elites as such. There may be competing movements within a generation – "generational units" in Mannheim's terms – such as left-wing and right-wing ones. An example of the latter was the German National Socialist takeover in 1933 which brought to power a large group of young adults, including a number of top-level political functionaries who were about as old as the century – that is, in their early thirties – and after the demise of the Thousand Year Reich, in their mid-forties. That social movements tend to be generational in spite of the presumed unlikeliness of generation-based mobilization may again be explained by the age-graded structure of the modern life course (Kohli 1986). People are typically processed by the institutions of schooling, army, labor market, and welfare in groups of age peers. Such groups have the opportunities to organize as well as the moral resources – because they know each other, they more easily develop the necessary closeness and trust.

ECONOMIC GENERATIONS

In the study of political generations economic opportunities have traditionally entered the picture as a key component of social location, although interest has always focused on their consequences in terms of political action. This is now changing. As mentioned above, the main arena of conflict in western societies has shifted from the political to the economic sphere. The issues of politics (power, hegemony) have given way to the issues of welfare (economic security,

resource allocation). The political conflict between generations has turned into a (potential) distributional conflict.

These issues are often framed as a conflict between young and old, or younger and older generations, and discussed under the label of "generational equity" (Kohli 2005). It refers to the argument that the elderly have got more than their fair share of public resources, and that this comes at the expense of the non-aged population, especially children. In generational terms, this means that today's older generations have profited from the expansion of public old age security without having had to pay full contributions, while the younger generations who now have to bear an increasing contribution load will not get the corresponding benefits any more. The growth of this argument into a full-blown political discourse can be dated to the mid-1980s. From the US the discourse has been imported to the UK and to the European continent, where institutionalization has been slower but with more current weight (Attias-Donfut & Arber 2000).

The discourse of generational equity has clearly been one of the more effective ones in shaping the public agenda of welfare retrenchment over the last two decades, even though its impact in changing popular attitudes and beliefs has so far been less impressive. The political consequences drawn by the proponents of generational equity go in the direction of reducing public spending for the elderly (e.g., by privatizing parts of old age security, reducing benefits, and increasing the retirement age). Other demands include age-based rationing for some types of medical care, and age tests for a range of issues such as driving or even voting. In Europe, the demands are often grouped under the term *sustainability*, which links the long-term survival of social security schemes to issues in the domain of ecology.

Against these claims it has been pointed out that the expansion of old-age security should be seen as a success that – far from unduly privileging the elderly – has only given them their due share by finally bringing them up to par with the active population. Moreover, improving their well-being does not necessarily come at the expense of other population groups; the distribution of resources between young and old is not a zero-sum game.

One line of research examines the input side: welfare state spending targeted to different population groups (among them, the young and the old) and how it is brought about by welfare state institutions. This concerns not only the large redistributive programs such as old age income security or health insurance, but also arrangements only partially organized or subsidized by the state, such as long-term care. An important extension is that of generational accounting which includes contributions as well as spending, and tries to establish full life-time balances of contributions and benefits for each successive cohort.

The result is usually that the older generations, through the expansion of pension and health care programs over the past decades, benefit at the cost of the young and future generations. A direct comparison between spending on the elderly and on children and youth is misleading, however. In modern welfare states, incomes and services for the elderly are to a large extent publicly financed, while those for the young are still mostly borne by their families. The one exception is the educational system, but even this is often not fully accounted for. As Bommier et al. (2005) show, the usual intergenerational picture is turned upside down when public education is included in generational accounts along with pensions and health care. They estimate that in terms of benefits received minus taxes paid, all US generations born 1950 to 2050 will be net gainers, while many of today's old people are net losers. Windfall gains for early generations when Social Security and Medicare started up only partially offset windfall losses through the expansion of public education.

The more straightforward way of validating the claims of the generational equity discourse is to assess the output side: the outcome of market distribution and state redistribution in terms of the economic well-being of the young and the old (Kohli 2005). Comparative OECD data show that from the mid-1980s to the mid-1990s children have indeed lost ground, and that their income position is considerably below that of the active population. The income position of the elderly has improved in most countries, but also remains below that of the active population, particularly so in the UK with its "residual" welfare state. Moreover, the position

of those above age 75 is clearly less favorable than that of the "young old." It is obvious from these results that in terms of generational equity families with young children should indeed be the target of supplementary welfare efforts. But the results give no reason to strip the elderly of (part of) their current benefits.

Thus, the potential for distributional conflicts among generations certainly exists and is fueled by the current challenges of public finances and demography. However, the discourse of generational equity overstates the extent and inevitability of such conflicts, and sharpens them at the expense of conflicts along the more traditional cleavages of class. Survey data regularly show that the public generational contract still enjoys high legitimacy among all ages and segments of the population. There are some age and generation effects, but they are much less pronounced than the public discourse would lead us to believe. A critical factor is the institutions – such as parties or unions – that mediate generational conflicts by favoring or disfavoring age integration in the political arena.

FAMILY GENERATIONS

The family is the institution where the concept of generation has its most basic meaning: the creation of offspring. While the generational process within a specific family lineage is highly discontinuous, at the population level it is continuous: births occur more or less regularly. There is thus no immediately available "translation" of family generations into political or economic generations. But there is a link relating the generational succession in the family to that in the polity. It is the claim that political innovation or rebellion is favored by generational conflict between parents and children. This claim has already been put forth as an attempt at explaining the movements of 1968. The shift away from authoritarian towards more egalitarian socialization styles in western families would then be another reason for the weakening of the generational conflict in the political arena.

Another link pertains to the reasons why age and generation effects in attitudes towards redistribution through the welfare state even today are so relatively modest. For the young, the institutionalization of income-maintaining retirement pensions means that they are freed from any expectation of income support towards their parents. They can moreover count on services such as grandparenting, and in many cases they can also expect material support. The public resource flow to the elderly has enabled the latter to transfer resources to their offspring in turn (Kohli 1999).

Recent research on *inter vivos* family transfers demonstrates that such transfers are considerable, that they occur mostly in the generational lineage, and that they flow mostly downwards, from the older to the younger generations. There may be expectations of reciprocity, or other strings attached, but by and large parents are motivated by altruism or feelings of unconditional obligation, and direct their gifts to situations of need. For Germany, our survey in 1996 showed that 32 percent of those above age 60 made a transfer to their children or grandchildren during the 12 months prior to the interview, with a mean net value of about 3,700 euros. Thus, part of the public transfers from the active population to the elderly was handed back by the latter to their family descendants. The aggregate net *inter vivos* transfers by the elderly population amounted to about 9 percent of the total yearly public pension sum. This link needs to be qualified, but the overall pattern is clear: the public generational contract is partly balanced by a private one in the opposite direction. These family transfers function to some extent as an informal insurance system for periods of special needs. Even more important in monetary terms are bequests. They are more frequent and much higher in the upper economic strata, but now also increasingly extend into the middle and lower ranks.

A similar picture emerges for other forms of support among adult family generations, as well as for their geographical proximity and emotional closeness. In all of these domains, the widespread idea of the nuclearization of the modern family and the corresponding structural isolation of the older generations – made popular not least by sociological theories of modernization such as those by Durkheim and Parsons – has proven to be highly exaggerated. Conflicts or isolation between family generations do exist to some extent, but not nearly as pervasively as the conventional story of modernization has made us believe.

THE FUTURE OF GENERATIONAL CONFLICTS

There are still many issues where our current knowledge is severely limited. Due in part to the difficulties mentioned above, the generational framework has not yet been put to full use in accounting for political mobilization and cultural and economic innovation. The links between political, economic, and family generations need to be drawn out more clearly. The limitations are also partly due to the lack of appropriate data. Most studies so far have been limited to cross-sectional evidence, or repeated cross-sections at best. For a field in such rapid evolution this is especially regrettable.

Given these limitations, what can we say about the likely future? Much will depend on the opportunities and constraints created by institutions. The age-grading of the life course, and thus the age-based structure of benefits and obligations, may be expected to weaken somewhat, but it will not whither away. The discontinuities produced by the demography and the economy may even deepen, so that the potential for generational conflicts over issues of (re-)distribution will remain strong. The bonds between the generations in the family and in the polity have so far been effective in defusing this potential, but whether this will remain so depends on whether there will be enough welfare state support for the family, and age-integrating organizations in the political arena.

A crucial issue will be that of innovation. For aging societies, it is critical that the capacity to innovate should extend beyond adolescence and early adulthood into the later life phases. To some extent this would also lower the potential for generational conflict. Whether this will be the case obviously depends on the institutional incentives for continuing education and social participation.

SEE ALSO: Age, Period, and Cohort Effects; Aging and the Life Course, Theories of; Family Structure; Intergenerational Conflict; Intergenerational Relationships and Exchanges;

Life Course Perspective; Mannheim, Karl; Socialization, Adult; Welfare State

REFERENCES AND SUGGESTED READINGS

Attias-Donfut, C. (1988) *Sociologie des générations. L'empreinte du temps.* Presses Universitaires de France, Paris.

Attias-Donfut, C. & Arber, S. (2000) Equity and Solidarity Across the Generations. In: Arber, S. & Attias-Donfut, C. (Eds.), *The Myth of Generational Conflict: The Family and State in Ageing Societies.* Routledge, London, pp. 1–21.

Bommier, A., Lee, R., Miller, T., & Zuber, S. (2005) Who Wins and Who Loses? Public Transfer Accounts for US Generations Born 1850 to 2090. Paper presented at the 25th International Population Conference, Tours.

Braungart, R. G. & Braungart, M. M. (Eds.) (1993) *Life Course and Generational Politics.* University Press of America, Lanham, MD.

Easterlin, R. A. (1980) *Birth and Fortune: The Impact of Numbers on Personal Welfare.* Basic Books, New York.

Inglehart, R. (1977) *The Silent Revolution.* Princeton University Press, Princeton.

Kohli, M. (1986) The World We Forgot: A Historical Review of the Life Course. In: Marshall, V. W. (Ed.), *Later Life: The Social Psychology of Ageing.* Sage, Beverly Hills, pp. 271–303.

Kohli, M. (1999) Private and Public Transfers Between Generations: Linking the Family and the State. *European Societies* 1: 81–104.

Kohli, M. (2005) Aging and Justice. In: Binstock, R. H. & George, L. K. (Eds.), *Handbook of Aging and the Social Sciences,* 6th edn. Elsevier, San Diego.

Kohli, M. & Szydlik, M. (Eds.) (2000) *Generationen in Familie und Gesellschaft.* Leske & Budrich, Opladen.

Mannheim, K. (1928) Das Problem der Generationen. *Kölner Vierjahrshefte für Soziologie* 7: 157–85, 309–30.

Roseman, M. (Ed.) (1995) *Generations in Conflict: Youth Revolt and Generation Formation in Germany 1770–1968.* Cambridge University Press, Cambridge.

Smith, T. W. (2005) Generation Gaps in Attitudes and Values from the 1970s to the 1990s. In: Settersten, R. A., Furstenberg, F. F. J., & Rumbaut, R. G. (Eds.), *On the Frontier of Adulthood: Theory, Research, and Public Policy.* University of Chicago Press, Chicago, pp. 177–221.

Wohl, R. (1979) *The Generation of 1914.* Harvard University Press, Cambridge, MA.

genetic engineering as a social problem

Gabriele Abels

Genetic engineering (GE) is the technique and science of intervention into the genetic mechanisms of an organism, whether it be microorganism, plant, animal, or human. GE is one of the most socially contested of technologies. In the public debate, the terms GE and biotechnology are often used synonymously; yet, in a narrower sense, GE is only one important technique in the field of biotechnology.

The first successful gene-splicing experiment integrating genes from a different species into an organism was undertaken in 1973. Immediately a debate started – and is still going on today – about whether or not GE should be regulated, and in what way. Different regulatory approaches were developed (e.g., product versus process regulation), and (legal) regulations on GE and its various applications were adopted. Based on environmental, safety, and health concerns, GE was perceived as a risk technology from the beginning (Krimsky 1982). Sociologists of risk often refer to GE; for example, for Ulrich Beck, GE is a paradigmatic case for the risk society.

There are two main fields of application of GE: agriculture and food production and medical genetics. Both fields are socially contested, yet the latter is more complex with regard to the social problems involved. The medical field has been revolutionized by the Human Genome Project. Started in 1990 and led by US scientists, it was an outstanding international and multidisciplinary endeavor to map and sequence the human genome (Kevles & Hood 1992). The project was completed in 2004 and is now followed by a functional analysis of the genome (genomics, proteomics, and pharmacogenomics). The project led to an immense growth in knowledge on human genetics, contributing to the development of diagnostics and (pharmaceutical and genetic) therapies as well as population genetics. The project also fostered a trend toward "geneticization": genetics is increasingly referred to as an explanation not only for medical conditions, but also for social behavior (e.g., homosexuality, criminality, alcoholism). This shift is reflected in everyday culture where the gene has become a "cultural icon." The study of ethical, legal, and social impacts (ELSI) became an integral part of the Human Genome Project and numerous sociological studies were conducted on issues such as changing patient–physician relationships, the concept of autonomy, or the impact of the media on public perception.

For some time, GE has increasingly been combined with infertility treatment and embryo research ("reprogenetics"). Artificial reproductive technologies such as different techniques for prenatal testing (e.g., amniocentesis or chorionic villi biopsy), artificial insemination, and in vitro fertilization, first developed in the 1970s and today routine procedures, employ GE (e.g., pre-implantation genetic diagnosis).

GE gives rise to a number of questions that relate to issues of social (in)equality, especially with regard to human genetics. Any kind of biological – including genetic – information can be socially powerful and used to stigmatize social and ethnic groups as well as individuals and to discriminate against them (Wilkie 1993; Nelkin & Tancredi 1994). There is ongoing debate about the specific status of genetic information: unlike other medical data, genetic information is permanent, cannot be altered, and has a prognostic power. It affects not only the individual, but also his or her relatives. Proponents of "genetic exceptionalism" argue for special legal regulation of genetic information, for example with regard to its use in the insurance sector or by employers. Others claim that a similar condition applies for a lot of non-genetic biological information (e.g., use of blood samples in medical employment tests) and that there is no need for special regulation, but instead existing rules should be extended to genetic information and strengthened in order to protect individuals as well as the interests of third parties. Both positions share the concern that genetic information may create a new social cleavage between "genetically affected persons" and those deemed healthy, this cleavage potentially leading to genetic discrimination. The question of an individual's (or even a group's) control over the use of his or her genetic data and access to this information by third parties thus becomes a prominent social and legal issue, that of genetic privacy.

Cultural perceptions about health, sickness, and disability are a further issue. Especially with regard to the use of GE in reproductive medicine, cultural meaning and social effects of disability are under debate. Radical disability rights activists raise the question of whether the (although until today imperfect) technical option to prevent babies being born with disabilities, so far usually by late-term abortion, might lead to a negative cultural perception of disability as being avoidable and to discrimination against people with disability. Others object that only a few disabilities can be detected early on and most are acquired during one's lifetime, and, second, they emphasize the burden on parents and their reproductive rights. In this way, GE revives the old debate about reproductive rights and adds some new topics. Because of women's and men's different share in the reproductive process, GE affects women and men differently.

A third dimension of discrimination concerns race and ethnicity. Many genetic conditions are related to racial and ethnic origin, for example beta thalassemia is most common in the Mediterranean, African, and Southeast Asian populations, sickle-cell anemia in the African population, or aggressive forms of breast cancer among African American women. This could give rise to a specific combination of racial/ethnic and genetic discrimination, above all if economically disadvantaged groups are affected.

Besides discrimination, GE in the human field has fostered safety, ethical, and philosophical debates about the future of humankind with regard to techniques such as different forms of gene therapy, enhancement, and human cloning. Gene therapy can be conducted on affected cells (somatic cell GE); the objective is to correct defective genes in individuals by inserting non-defective ones. Conducted for the first time in 1990, it is still an experimental therapy and safety concerns dominate the debate. A more fundamental gene therapy would directly alter the genetic structure of the germ line, and thereby also change the genetic structure of future generations. This could be done for therapeutic reasons in order to ultimately correct defective genes. However, germ line therapy also opens the way for enhancement of human beings for non-medical reasons. This technical option is socially highly contested (cf. Bernard 2001; Fukuyama 2002; Habermas 2003). Critics argue that any form of enhancement is eugenics and leads to a slippery slope; they often recount Nazi "racial hygiene" as the historically most extreme case of eugenics. The major philosophical basis is Kant's reasoning that a human should not be instrumentalized by anybody for personal interests but has a value of his or her own. Proponents argue that there is no strong theoretical argument against enhancement. The selective choice of a fetus in order to later use the baby, for example as a bone marrow donor for an affected sibling, as well as human cloning have become contested issues for much the same ethical reasons as germ line therapy and enhancement.

The early debate over GE was dominated by a risk discourse. Increasingly, ethics has gained prominence and often even takes center stage in scholarly as well as political debates, especially with regard to the medical field. Yet, ethics is today also more prominent with regard to the agricultural and food sector. Along with this change in the framing of the debate went a shift from the narrow issue of legal regulation of GE to the broader one of social regulation. Legal regulation in the medical field pertains to issues of research (e.g., informed consent, use of embryos or stem cells) to application in (medical) practice (e.g., informed consent, access to data, safety standards) as well as to commercialization (e.g., coverage by health insurance providers). Most legal regulation is in the form of national laws or self-regulation by professional groups such as physicians. In the last decade, there has been a growing trend for more international legal regulation of some issues, such as research and cloning, by organizations such as the United Nations, the Council of Europe, or the European Union.

Social regulation pertains to broader questions of science (genetics) and society including who should participate in decision-making and policy deliberation on these contested issues, and what counts as relevant knowledge. This

is reflected in institutional change in policy deliberation. Since the 1990s, special bodies have been set up in many countries in order to advise policymakers on ethical, social, and legal policy issues concerning GE and its application to humans (e.g., national ethics committees). Along with this professionalization of the debate has been democratization, insofar as many social experiments with enhanced citizen participation in science policy have been conducted (e.g., consensus conferences or citizens' juries).

GE is a prominent topic in interdisciplinary social studies of science and technology (STS). A first strand in sociological research focuses on the social history of GE and conflicts within science as well as between science, politics, and the public. One strand of research addresses issues of public risk perception and media representation as well as different cultures of risk regulation, including the precautionary principle. Yet most of this research deals with regulation in the field of agricultural biotechnology, while the application to humans still requires scholarly attention. A third strand is concerned with social changes, for example geneticization effects on reproductive choice, disability rights, or the general topic of the social reinvention of nature, often including a gender perspective. While early research sometimes argued along the lines of technological determinism, today research is taking into account the complexity of how GE and society shape each other. Social justice and equality or, more specifically, Foucault's concepts of biopolitics and governmentality are prominent theoretical approaches.

The ongoing social conflicts over GE have recently been analyzed from a perspective of the changing relation between science and society and build on changes in political culture and "civic epistemologies" (Jasanoff 2005). "Science governance" is a keyword. This concept criticizes the older approach of "public understanding of science" as insufficient. It identifies public ignorance as the key factor in conflicts over technologies and holds that technology assessment is best conducted by experts. According to the science governance perspective, new methods for technology assessment have to be developed that include a variety of social actors. New "participatory" or democratic models criticize the epistemological deficiencies of expert-oriented policy deliberation and attend to the decreasing authority of scientific knowledge (expert dilemma). Proponents of participatory models argue for the need to integrate a plurality of knowledges and aim to democratize expertise. This governance perspective allows us to link conflicts over GE to broader social transformations. It requires above all a theoretical embedding of technology assessment as well as the broader concept of science governance in social theory. This is one of the major tasks for future research.

SEE ALSO: Cloning; (Constructive) Technology Assessment; Eugenics; Expertise, "Scientification," and the Authority of Science; Gay Gene; Human Genome and the Science of Life; Medical Sociology and Genetics; Risk, Risk Society, Risk Behavior, and Social Problems; Science and the Precautionary Principle; Science and Public Participation: The Democratization of Science

REFERENCES AND SUGGESTED READINGS

Bernard, G. (2001) Genetic Engineering. In: Becker, L. & Becker, C. (Eds.), *Encyclopedia of Ethics*, 2nd edn. Vol. 1. Routledge, London, pp. 602–6.

Fukuyama, F. (2002) *Our Posthuman Future: Consequences of the Biotechnology Revolution*. Picador, New York.

Habermas, J. (2003) *The Future of Human Nature*. Polity Press, Cambridge.

Jasanoff, S. (2005) *Designs on Nature: Science and Democracy in Europe and the United States*. Princeton University Press, Princeton and Oxford.

Kevles, D. J. & Hood, L. (Eds.) (1992) *The Code of Codes: Scientific and Social Issues in the Human Genome Project*. Harvard University Press, Cambridge, MA, and London.

Krimsky, S. (1982) *Genetic Alchemy: The Social History of the Recombinant DNA Controversy*. MIT Press, Cambridge, MA.

Nelkin, D. & Tancredi, L. (1994) *Dangerous Diagnostics: The Social Power of Biological Information*. University of Chicago Press, Chicago.

Wilkie, T. (1993) *Perilous Knowledge: The Human Genome Project and Its Implications*. University of California Press, Berkeley.

genocide

Susanne Karstedt

Genocide has been termed the crime of the twentieth century and in many ways it epitomizes this "age of extremes" (Hobsbawm 1994). It was in this century that the word genocide was first coined, and it was legally defined and criminalized. The international community committed itself to the protection of threatened populations and to the prosecution and punishment of those who were responsible for mass killings, and was successful in a number of high and low-ranking cases; at the end of the century, international intervention in cases of genocide started. Most importantly, it was the century of the archetypical example of genocide in modern times, the Nazi Holocaust of the European Jews and other groups, the most horrible single crime in human history. On most accounts, it is the century if not with the highest numbers of incidents, then the highest numbers of victims of genocide in the known history of humankind.

The word genocide was coined by Raphael Lemkin, a lawyer of Polish-Jewish origin, in 1944. It was legally defined in the United Nations Convention on the Prevention and Punishment of the Crime of Genocide in 1948, preceded by a resolution of the General Assembly proclaiming that "genocide was the deprivation of the right to existence of a group in the same fashion that homicide was the denial of the right to exist of an individual" (Rubinstein 2004: 308). The UN Convention's definition was drafted in response to the Nazis' extermination of the Jews, and was based on the experience of the Nuremberg Trials 1945–6, which became a landmark in the legal prosecution of perpetrators of genocide. However, it did not start to play a role in international law and politics until the 1970s, and in particular after the end of the Cold War, when the mass killings in Cambodia, and later in Latin America, the former Yugoslavia, and in Rwanda alerted the international community to the continuous and global threat of genocidal practices.

The Convention states that "genocide means ... acts committed with intent to destroy, in whole or in part, a national, ethnic, racial or religious group." Such acts as detailed in the Convention include: killing members of the group; causing serious bodily or mental harm to them; deliberately inflicting conditions of life calculated to bring about their physical destruction in whole or in part; imposing measures intended to prevent births within a group; and forcibly transferring children of the group to another one. The Convention's definition is remarkable in two respects. First, it did not imply that genocide is the total destruction of a whole group; second, it included a range of acts besides mass killings, and thus took into account the *process character* of genocide. However, the definition limited genocide to these groups, and specific actions, and excluded groups defined by class and political affiliation. As such, the Convention's definition was untenable in the light of the Universal Declaration of Human Rights adopted in the same year. In fact, the mass killings of peasants in the Soviet Union under Stalin, or the genocide of its own people by the Khmer Rouge in Cambodia, are currently counted as genocide by most authors.

The Convention's limitations started an ongoing debate about the definition of genocide, and currently, the terms "mass killings" (Valentino 2004), "mass atrocities" (Osiel 1997), "democide" or "deaths by government" (Rummel 1994, 1998), and "murderous ethnic cleansing" (Mann 2005) are all in use. Most of these extend the scope of genocide beyond the groups to which the Convention still gives a special status. Though genocide is clearly set apart from war, in particular by its illegitimacy, which is enshrined in the Convention, national criminal laws, and evidenced by the secrecy and complicity in the conduct of genocide (Shaw 2003), a number of authors include specific types of acts of war as genocide (e.g., Kuper 1981; Rubinstein 2004). The scope of the definition is decisive in two respects: first for the estimates of victims and perpetrators, and second for the history of genocide.

Estimates for the victims of genocide and mass killings as distinguished from war deaths range from 60–150 million for the twentieth century alone (Valentino 2004), with most estimates at about 80 million, and some considerably higher (Rummel 1998). For the second half of the twentieth century since 1945, estimates range from 9–20 million in more than

40 episodes of genocide (Valentino 2004; Gurr 1993). These horrifying figures testify to the "discriminate targeting" of groups in mass killings and their finally "indiscriminate" victimization (Shaw 2003). The perpetrators in contrast are comparably small in numbers. A very conservative estimate gives the figure of Germans who directly participated in mass slaughters of Jews as 100,000, to which a considerable number of members of police and other forces should be added. An estimate of immediate involvement in the Rwandan genocide suggests 200,000 direct participants; however, the regular and irregular military forces who did most of the killing number about 10,000. A similar estimate is given for the perpetrators in former Yugoslavia (Osiel 2005). Genocide is the crime in which victims massively outnumber perpetrators, but the group of perpetrators is large enough to include a considerable proportion of the population. Bystanders, those who tacitly or openly approve of or witness all measures leading up to the killings and finally the mass killings themselves, can comprise large parts of the population, depending on the type of action taken against the targeted group. Historical accounts and counts of episodes of genocide put the twentieth century into perspective, depending on the scope of the definition used. Both Rummel (1998) and Rubinstein (2004) estimate high numbers of victims of genocidal practices before the twentieth century. Rubinstein (2004) identifies five distinct types and periods in the history of genocide: in pre-literate societies, in the age of empires and religions (from 500 BCE to 1492), colonial genocides from 1492–1914, in the age of totalitarianism (1914–79), and contemporary ethnic cleansing and genocide since 1945. He concludes that pre-literal societies were probably more murderous than modern ones, thus contesting the assumed link between modernity and genocide.

Genocide involves three distinct elements, which provide the basis for all attempts to explain why and how genocides happen, and why apparently "ordinary men" (Browning 1992) – and very rarely women – engage in the indiscriminate killing of men, women, and children, who might have been their neighbors. These elements are (1) the "identification of a social group as an enemy ... against which it is justified to use physical violence in a systematic way"; (2) "the intention to destroy the real or imputed power" of this group; and (3) "the actual deployment of violence . . . through killing . . . and other measures" (Shaw 2003: 37). Genocides are more often than not related to wars, mounting social crises, and threatening social change, including the total breakdown of social order (Staub 1989). Though genocide and mass killings at least in the twentieth century take place in comparably short time periods, and most of the victims are killed within a few months (Valentino 2004), the development of the three decisive elements and the process character of genocide can be clearly identified.

Three explanatory approaches have been most influential: genocide as the product of *modernity*, with Bauman (1989) as the most prominent proponent; the *structural and psychosocial perspective*, which focuses on broad social, cultural, and political factors; and finally the *strategic perspective*, according to which specific goals and strategies of high political and military leaders are decisive for the precipitation of genocide (Valentino 2004), and which links genocide to "degenerate wars" (Shaw 2003). The link between modernity and genocide is established by modernity's defining features, such as new technologies of warfare, new administrative techniques that enhance the power of state surveillance, and new and "excluding" ideologies that categorize people. It is the development of the power of the modern state that finally facilitates genocide and makes it a defining characteristic of modernity. In contrast, the structural and psychosocial approach focuses on a number of preexisting structural and cultural factors, which are however neither sufficient nor universally necessary causes of genocide. Among these factors the most important are deep cleavages between social and ethnic groups, with a clear structure of domination and "superimposition of inequalities" (Kuper 1981). These are exacerbated in social crises and in difficult living conditions, which increase the competition between groups for power and economic gains. Even if genocide generally involves "irrational and fantastical beliefs" (Shaw 2003), it is also a "rational" strategy for the perpetrators to enrich themselves and firmly establish power. Cultural factors include dehumanizing attitudes towards targeted groups, scape-goating in times of social crises, justifications of violence and exclusion, moral disengagement such as the erosion of norms of social responsibility and solidarity, and a cultural pattern of authoritarian and obedient attitudes. The concentration of unchecked power in undemocratic and authoritarian regimes has been identified as a causal factor by a number of authors (e.g., Rummel 1998). The twentieth century provides ample evidence for the role of dictatorships and authoritarian states in conducting mass killings; however, the role of democracies as bystanders and facilitators should not be underrated. Mann (2005) makes the failure of democracy and democratization responsible for murderous ethnic cleansing and explains it as the "dark side of democracy."

The strategic perspective (Valentino 2004) differs from both the above approaches in its focus on situational and process factors, as well as political-ideological conditions. From this perspective genocide is a powerful political and military tool for leaders, elites, and their imminent followers to achieve strategic goals. Valentino argues that the impetus usually originates from a relatively small group of political and military leaders, for whom mass killings are part of an instrumental policy, and strong incentives exist to instigate these as a "final solution" to real or imputed threats. He identifies six types of mass killings which can be grouped into two general categories. "Dispossessive" mass killing results from policies that strip large groups of the population of their possessions, their homes, their way of life, and finally their lives. Collectivization and political terror, ethnic cleansing, colonial enlargement, and expansionist wars are in this category. "Coercive mass killings" occur in major armed conflicts, when political and military leaders use massive violence to coerce large numbers of civilians and their leaders into submission, and when this escalates into genocide. Counterguerrilla, terrorist, and imperialist mass killings are in this category.

While the structural perspective identifies long-term social and *collective* processes that contribute to the ultimate precipitation of genocide, the strategic perspective focuses on the short-term *strategic* process of genocide, which involves only a small elite group and their

followers. Both provide widely differing explanations for the *individual* processes that turn
mostly ordinary men into mass murderers.
From the structural perspective, social and cultural preconditions create a large pool of potential perpetrators, so that finally everyone can
become actively involved in mass killings
should the situation arise. The Milgram experiments were mostly designed to confirm this
assumption. In contrast, the strategic perspective (Valentino 2004: 6) implies that the "pre-
ferential selection of sadistic or ideologically
fanatic individuals and the influence of situational and group pressures and elite manipulation," including incentives for perpetrators,
explains the behavior of most rank-and-file perpetrators of mass killings. Historical evidence
and case studies do not give unequivocal support to either of these perspectives, but it is
obvious that perpetrators go through a process
of stepwise preparations and different stages of
moral disengagement and justification of their
actions, during which group pressures and
incentives, as well as imputed threats, play an
important role (Browning 1992; Waller 2002;
Mann 2005).

The UN Convention obliges the international community to prevent genocide, which includes intervention into ongoing mass killings.
Both require the observation of critical situations and the identification of warning signs.
Prevention and intervention include international military intervention, economic sanctions,
the deployment of international peace forces
and the disarmament of groups involved, and
the provision of humanitarian assistance. From
the structural perspective of "root causes,"
long-term measures are preferable. These include the promotion of minority rights, democratic values that protect individuals, the rule of
law, and democratic regimes. Democratization,
however, appears to be a double-edged sword,
since genocide episodes often followed on
the heels of failed democratization efforts
(Valentino 2004; Mann 2005). With its focus
on small groups, situational and precipitating
factors, on the shorter time frame of the actual
road to genocide, and the identification of steps
towards the "final solution," the strategic approach appears to be more suitable to design
and implement interventions and preventive

measures, and to identify premonitions of
potential genocides (Osiel 2005).

The UN Convention committed the international community to the prosecution and punishment of perpetrators, and made individuals
accountable under international law. The acts
punishable under the Convention comprise conspiracy, public incitement, and complicity, and
thus allow for the indictment of "constitutionally responsible rulers, public officials or
private individuals" (Article IV), for which the
International Military Tribunal at Nuremberg
had been a promising start. In addition, the
Convention committed the ratifying nations to
prosecuting perpetrators in their own territory.
It was not until the last decade of the twentieth
century that the international community developed the requisite institutional framework,
first with the International Tribunals for the
Former Yugoslavia (Hagan 2003) and Rwanda,
and finally with the adoption of the Rome
Statute of the International Criminal Court in
1998, and its establishment in 2002 (Schabas
2004). The tribunals and the court are confronted with numerous legal and procedural problems in the prosecution and punishment of
mass atrocities. The sheer numbers of perpetrators and victims in particular pose problems to
less developed systems of criminal justice as in
Rwanda, or might exacerbate group conflicts in
a situation of political and social crisis. Truth
commissions, truth and reconciliation commissions, the combination of legal procedures with
amnesties, or other frameworks of restorative justice are currently seen as promising solutions to
the problems of making perpetrators accountable and doing justice to the victims of genocide.

SEE ALSO: Arendt, Hannah; Authoritarian Per-
sonality; Burundi and Rwanda (Hutu, Tutsi);
Ethnic Cleansing; Ethnonationalism; Fascism;
Holocaust; Milgram, Stanley (Experiments);
Truth and Reconciliation Commissions; Vio-
lence; War

REFERENCES AND SUGGESTED READINGS

Bauman, Z. (1989) *Modernity and the Holocaust.*
Cornell University Press, Ithaca, NY.

Browning, C. R. (1992) *Ordinary Men: Reserve Police Battalion 101 and the Final Solution in Poland.* Harper Collins, New York.

Gurr, T. R. (1993) *Minorities at Risk: A Global View of Ethnopolitical Conflicts.* United States Institute of Peace Press, Washington, DC.

Hagan, J. (2003) *Justice in the Balkans: Prosecuting War Crimes in the Hague Tribunal.* University of Chicago Press, Chicago.

Hobsbawm, E. (1994) *The Age of Extremes: A History of the World 1914–1991.* Michael Joseph, New York.

Kuper, L. (1981) *Genocide.* Yale University Press, New Haven.

Mann, M. (2005) *The Dark Side of Democracy: Explaining Ethnic Cleansing.* Cambridge University Press, Cambridge.

Osiel, M. (1997) *Mass Atrocities: Collective Memory and the Law.* Transaction Publishers, New Brunswick.

Osiel, M. (2005) The Banality of Good: Aligning Incentives Against Mass Atrocities. *Columbia Law Review* 105(6): 1751–862.

Rubinstein, W. D. (2004) *Genocide.* Pearson Longman, London.

Rummel, R. J. (1994) *Death by Government.* Transaction Publishers, New Brunswick.

Rummel, R. J. (1998) *Statistics of Democide.* Lit, Muenster.

Schabas, W. A. (2004) *An Introduction to the International Criminal Court,* 2nd edn. Cambridge University Press, Cambridge.

Shaw, M. (2003) *War and Genocide: Organized Killing in Modern Society.* Polity Press, Cambridge.

Staub, E. (1989) *The Roots of Evil: The Origins of Genocide and Other Group Violence.* Cambridge University Press, Cambridge.

Valentino, B. A. (2004) *Final Solutions: Mass Killing and Genocide in the Twentieth Century.* Cornell University Press, Ithaca, NY.

Waller, J. (2002) *Becoming Evil: How Ordinary People Commit Genocide and Mass Killing.* Oxford University Press, Oxford.

genre

Roger Horrocks

A genre is any group of texts identified as sharing a cluster of characteristics (such as structure, theme, style, mood, spatial or temporal setting, or function). The term may imply a precise list of characteristics or be used more flexibly as a way of exploring "family resemblances" (in Wittgenstein's sense of that phrase). New genres are constantly being identified, but use-value determines whether a proposed grouping gains long-term acceptance. The most useful tend to be highly specific groupings of examples which are closely related in space and time as well as form, regarded as "subgenres" of traditional genres. The idea of genre is not only a conceptual tool of scholars, but is also employed constantly in everyday life in the production, distribution, and reception of media products. In that sense it calls for investigation as an important social and industrial (as well as creative) phenomenon. Indeed, it has been studied for so many centuries that sophisticated traditions of theory and criticism have developed around it, reflecting changing conceptions of the text and its relationship with social contexts. Those traditions have sometimes remained specialized and separate (within the arts, linguistics, and media industries), but in recent years there has been an increased emphasis on interdisciplinary approaches that seek to articulate the semiotic with the social.

The identification of a genre is the beginning rather than the end of analysis. Because of the breadth of the term it is important to specify the particular methods of construction or analysis linked with it, but basic to all is the activity of sorting or classification. Like "generalization" and "gender," the English word "genre" looks back to *genus*, the Latin word for type or kind. The organization of textual study by genre is analogous to the biological classification of living organisms in terms of species and genus; and historical research on the development of genres may be likened to the study of evolution. Since genre analysis sees value in a researcher's knowledge of many examples, it has potentially a quantitative as well as qualitative dimension. This aspect became increasingly important as the mass production of media products and their availability expanded. At the same time the term genre came to be associated with debates about the vulgarity of "mass culture" and the ideological conformity it was seen as promoting. Most scholars today would insist on a value-free use of the term genre, but until recently genre criticism has tended to combine formal analysis with aesthetic or moral value judgments.

The idea of distinguishing genres and subgenres was already present (under various terms) in the work of ancient thinkers such as Aristotle, who wrote in his *Poetics*: "Our subject being Poetry, I propose to speak not only of the art in general but also of its species and their respective capacities." Such criticism became a common activity in all the arts. It was often based on the aesthetic appreciation of ideal rather than typical examples, and social aspects such as the relationship with audiences tended to be analyzed by a process of deduction. In relation to artistic production and distribution, the idea functioned in very complex ways, since it not only described what had already been made, but reinforced the natural tendency for artists to learn and borrow from one another. Genres developed distinctive traditions and strict conventions, with specialist producers and connoisseurs. This tendency also assisted marketing. Shakespeare parodied its uncritical use in Polonius's remarks to Hamlet about a troupe of actors he regarded as the best in the world for all the main theatrical genres – "tragedy, comedy, history, pastoral, pastoral-comical, historical-pastoral, tragical-historical, tragical-comical-historical-pastoral . . . [etc.]."

In European art criticism, lists of genres (such as the list established by the *Académie Française*) tended to carry hierarchical implications. In the twentieth century a new approach to status was proposed by social theorists such as the Frankfurt School, who associated "genre" with the commercial products of mass culture, contrasting them with individualized examples of art that were too complex to be adequately discussed in generic terms. This tradition of genre analysis focused on standardization and gave rise to many Marxist studies of the ideology said to be embedded in particular genres. As an adjective, the term genre came to be widely used as a critical shortcut, with "genre films" (for example) contrasted with "art films." Later researchers have tended to reject the value assumptions implied by this tradition and its neglect of some of the complexities of reception. (They also see no reason why "art films" should not be analyzed in generic terms.) Nevertheless, the Frankfurt tradition retains relevance for any critique focusing on cultural mass production and the centralized control of media industries.

Less polemical forms of genre analysis developed in linguistics. Bakhtin's (1986) essay proposed a taxonomy of types of "utterance" associated with various social activities. Literary readings or scientific lectures might be more complex than speeches of greeting or farewell, but all were part of the same spectrum of human communication, involving "relatively stable and normative forms." Artistic (or "secondary") speech genres such as the play or the novel drew upon everyday ("primary") speech genres and transformed them for their own purposes. Applied to both written and spoken communication, this type of generic analysis has come to be used not only in linguistics but also in general education, with students acquiring both social and linguistic competence as they develop a repertoire of "text types." In some respects this tradition looks back to the Renaissance study of rhetoric in its emphasis on generic conventions and social effectiveness. Many forms of social analysis – including organizational and business studies – have found it important to acknowledge the generic aspects of human communication. Each change in media technology has provided the linguist with new types of text to classify, such as Internet communication with its expanding genres of email, website, chatroom, and blog.

There have also been cognitive studies of the process of genre recognition at work in all forms of sorting, from Internet searching to library classification. Many American libraries use a standard system of generic classification known as GSAFD (Guidelines on Subject Access to Individual Works of Fiction, Drama, Etc.). Generic approaches compete or are combined with alphabetical, chronological, and geographical systems of ordering. Classification systems have become an important object of study in themselves, with changes in genre categories cited as historical evidence. Skeptical writers have sought to question the adequacy and social influence of all such systems. Jorge Luis Borges, once Director of the National Library of Argentina, created a witty cautionary tale in his story "The Analytical Language of John Wilkins," which imagined an encyclopedia based on a taxonomy that defied all conventional logic.

The concept of genre, in both judgmental and non-judgmental forms, continues to pervade daily life. Faced with a proliferation of media products, consumers struggle to locate texts of the types that interest them. Advertising and packaging for books and recordings, films and television programs (or channels) make use of generic terms as a marketing shorthand. Stores are divided generically to assist both the customer and the store assistant to locate a particular item or group of related items. Categories vary from country to country and from one retailer to another, but customers adapt quickly because they are familiar with the process. The discovery of a genre and evidence of public interest in it imply the existence of a particular audience or market niche, thus encouraging the creation of similar products to satisfy a known taste. This is important for expensive, high-risk media such as film and television. As a genre attains stability, specialist producers emerge (publishers, film companies, writers, technicians, record labels, etc.), along with distribution and exhibition networks (such as specialized stores, film distributors, radio stations, television channels, cinemas, etc.).

There have been a number of studies in recent years of reading communities associated with particular genres of popular culture, seeking (in a non-judgmental way) to analyze the uses and gratifications involved. Janet Radway's *Reading the Romance* (1984) was an influential study of women reading "romance" novels, combining textual analysis of the genre with an ethnographic study of reception. Such studies have made us more aware of the complex nature of the transaction with formulaic material. The genre enthusiast derives convenience and pleasure from the mix of old and new ingredients, developing a comfortable sense of familiarity and insider knowledge as well as the opportunity to attempt to predict and to be surprised. Recent reception and industrial studies have revealed an unexpected complexity in popular culture and popular genres, despite the calculated simplicity of their surface features.

Popular music offers some particularly striking examples both of these cultural phenomena and of the scholarly work that analyzes them. The increased size, energy, and diversity of popular music have undercut sweeping criticisms of its mass-produced nature. Change is extremely rapid, with each genre generating a rapid succession of subgenres, reflected in the changing organization of any large music store. (The genre of Electronic Dance Music, for example, rapidly diversified as House, Jungle, Drum and Bass, Techno, Gabber, Trance, Acid House, Trip Hop, Ambient, Breakbeat, and a myriad of other subgenres, sometimes mating with larger genres such as Hiphop, Reggae, or Heavy Metal.) These changes have been particularly interesting for those involved in cultural studies because forms of popular music are often associated with distinctive subcultures (an area of study developed by Dick Hebdige). Such a subculture involves particular kinds of venue, slang, styles of dance, types of dress, iconic heroes, etc. These social and cultural conjunctions have been the subject of recent studies by Simon Frith, Steve Redhead, and Nabeel Zuberi.

Various forms of industrial analysis have been applied to the commercial contexts of genre. Many studies of the media have focused on texts and their production, or in recent years on reception. Distribution and retailing remain relatively neglected topics, despite the importance of those activities in limiting access to cultural products. Artists are highly aware of them because of the difficulty of gaining distribution or visibility for work that cannot be marketed in terms of current categories. Some academics have expressed a similar suspicion of the conservative functioning of genre in the marketplace. This is one area in which the concerns of Frankfurt School critics such as Adorno are still compelling. At the same time, there are many complexities to be taken into account, for the idea of genre has many stakeholders – including fans, production companies, distributors, retailers, censors, and critics, as well as creative people. While some groups are able to exercise greater power, each group has its own perspective and priorities, and all are to some extent interdependent.

In contrast to early genre criticism which tended to focus on a few ideal, permanent, uncontested types, the modern approach tends to be empirical and inductive, aware of diversity and rapid change, and fascinated by social context. But how to interpret the links between a genre and its audience? Psychoanalytical approaches have often been applied to genres such as the horror film. There are strong connections with the social sciences in the industrial, ideological, subcultural, and ethnographic methods of analysis discussed above. How a genre develops in textual terms can sometimes be linked to technological changes – for example, the evolution of film musicals as sound equipment became more flexible, or the new wave of films based on fantasy and comic-book characters made possible by computer special effects. Yet single-factor explanations are seldom adequate in this complex field and researchers need to consider audience responses and commercial trends as well as production possibilities. Major social changes can have an obvious impact on established genres, for example in the more prominent roles played by women in western popular culture since the 1960s, or the more explicit treatment of sexuality. Such changes have had an impact on many genres, from the thriller to the romance novel. Yet cultural and media studies writers remind us that such trends within a stylized genre still involve a sophisticated process of mediation, for example by fulfilling escapist desires.

The subject of film studies has provided a particularly important site for the analysis of genre. The concept of the auteur (or director with a unique style and vision) has sometimes been opposed to the concept of genre, but French critics such as André Bazin valued the genre as a context in which auteurs could display their individuality – as John Ford reshaped the western and Alfred Hitchcock experimented with the thriller. Both auteur and genre forms of criticism are based on groupings of related texts. Artists in all fields have been attracted to genres, as rich concentrations of cultural activity and as useful frameworks. Some innovators, such as composer Igor Stravinsky, have found their very constraints creatively stimulating.

From the 1960s, however, structuralist criticism shifted attention from auteurs to the collective structures of language and culture. It also helped to move criticism away from value judgments, including its tendency to privilege realism. It applied Saussure's relational approach to language to the relationship between texts, and its genre studies drew upon Propp's analysis of folktales and Lévi-Strauss's studies of myths – their variant versions, their "bricolage" (or recombination of existing elements), and their problem-solving functions. Structuralist critics saw genres as mechanisms for mediating fundamental tensions – for example, oppositions in the western between law and disorder, civilization and wilderness, nature and culture, male and female, East and West, etc. But structuralism

tended to move beyond genre to a broader understanding of discourse. Gerard Genette saw genre as only one of a range of types of "transtextuality." Poststructuralism went still further in announcing the "death of the author" and rejecting any notion of the unitary text – or genre – as an illusion. Although the concept of genre was discussed by Barthes, Kristeva, and Derrida, their basic aim was to destabilize it. Though coming from a different angle, ethnographic studies of reception have also tended to shift attention away from genres as patterns of regularity towards the freedom and diversity of reading practices.

Despite these challenges to traditional criticism, the basic concept of genre has survived strongly – in everyday life, as a linguistic tool, and as a subject of industrial and cultural analysis. It has emerged from the debates of the last thirty years in a more flexible form, shedding any residual tendency to essentialism, reification, or moralism. It is expected today that anyone doing genre criticism will at least consider the complexities of reception and production (though other industrial aspects such as distribution may still be skimmed over). While continuing to value skills of textual analysis, genre criticism has moved to a complex awareness of social contexts – such as readers, subcultures, institutions, and commercial networks – combined with an interest in historical change. This eclectic and sometimes provocative approach provides new perspectives on texts of every kind, regardless of their milieu or status. Genre-building has itself been studied as a form of social construction and this has encouraged the activity to become more self-critical and reflexive. The conventions, styles, and social contexts of text production associated with any academic field – such as genre criticism, or sociology – can be usefully subjected to genre analysis.

Such articulation of the semiotic with the social has so far mainly benefited the fields of cultural and media studies, but some sociologists have taken an interest. As an example of this fruitful exchange, Thomas Luckmann, one of the authors (with Peter Berger) of *The Social Construction of Reality*, has contributed to the study of communicative genres. Many aspects of sociological investigation can benefit from a more than perfunctory appreciation of their linguistic, semiotic, or rhetorical aspects, and genre analysis offers a valuable set of tools.

SEE ALSO: Discourse; Film; Hegemony and the Media; Mass Culture and Mass Society; Media; Media and Consumer Culture; Popular Culture Forms (Soap Operas); Television

REFERENCES AND SUGGESTED READINGS

Aristotle (1995) *Poetics.* In: *The Complete Works of Aristotle: The Revised Oxford Translation,* Vol. 2. Princeton University Press, Princeton.
Bakhtin, M. M. (1986) *Speech Genres and Other Late Essays.* University of Texas Press, Austin.
Bergmann, J. R. & Luckmann, T. (1994) Reconstructive Genres of Everyday Communication. In: Quasthoff, U. (Ed.), *Aspects of Oral Communication.* DeGruyter, Breling.
Berkenkotter, C. & Huckin, T. (1995) *Genre Knowledge in Disciplinary Communication.* Erlbaum, Hillsdale, NJ.
Duff, D. (2000) *Modern Genre Theory.* Pearson Education, London.
Freedman, A. & Medway, P. (Eds.) (1994) *Genre and the New Rhetoric.* Taylor & Francis, London.
Geertz, C. (1983) Blurred Genres: The Refiguration of Social Thought. In: *Local Knowledge.* Basic Books, New York.
Grant, B. K. (Ed.) (1995) *Film Genre Reader III.* University of Texas Press, Austin.
Radway, J. (1984) *Reading the Romance: Women, Patriarchy and Popular Literature.* University of North Carolina, Chapel Hill.
Todorov, T. (1990) *Genres in Discourse.* Cambridge University Press, Cambridge.

gentrification

Jason Patch and Neil Brenner

Gentrification entails the reinvestment of real estate capital into declining, inner-city neighborhoods to create a new residential infrastructure for middle and high-income inhabitants. In coining the term "gentrification" in 1964, Ruth Glass emphasized that class relations lie at the core of the process, which has generally involved the displacement of working-class residents from inner-city zones and the gradual influx of a new "gentry" of well-off professionals.

Equally relevant, but often less noted, is the role of gentrification in accelerating the displacement of blue-collar jobs from the urban core. Since the 1960s and 1970s, most manufacturing cities in the United States, Great Britain, and continental Europe have seen a steady decline in industrial production. As capitalists relocated manufacturing activities from the inner cities to the suburbs and abroad, disinvested property remained, and was often left in a derelict, decaying condition. Subsequently, as of the 1980s, information-based financial and producer services industries gradually superseded the traditional manufacturing-based urban economies of the Fordist epoch. Within the new, post-Fordist configuration of urban development, professionals and white-collar workers generated a new demand for upscale housing in closer proximity to revitalizing downtowns. Under these conditions, devalued inner-city property was increasingly seen by large real estate capital as a basis for reinvestment and profiteering. As Neil Smith indicates, one crucial precondition for the process of gentrification is the existence of a "rent gap" enabling real estate capitalists to exploit the difference between the potential value of a property under some future "highest and best use" and its actual value under the inherited land-use regime. While considerable debate persists among urban scholars regarding the degree to which the existence of rent gaps can effectively explain the timing and location of gentrification, there is today widespread agreement that this process has been facilitated in crucial ways through the speculative inner-city investments of real estate capitalists.

As gentrification proceeds apace, inner-city neighborhoods and other marginalized urban enclaves undergo significant sociospatial changes. Most significantly, there is a transformation of the built environment. New buildings are constructed; extant buildings are converted into luxury housing; industrial space is converted to mixed live-work or residential space; and new commercial establishments (such as upscale restaurants, coffee shops, boutiques, art galleries, and high-end clothing shops) are introduced. The New York City neighborhoods of SoHo in the 1960s and 1970s and Williamsburg,

Brooklyn in the 1990s represent classic instances in which the shift from small-scale manufacturing factories to artist lofts, gallery spaces, and new retail activities has occurred. In addition, there is also a significant rearticulation of the social fabric. Established class-based and ethnic milieux are destabilized or dissolved as new economic and cultural elites – often, but not always, composed of whites – move into the area. Philadelphia's Society Hill, with its predominantly African American community, was an early site of this wholesale change in a neighborhood's class and racial composition.

The first signs of gentrification became evident, albeit in highly localized forms, during the 1960s in the older inner cities of North America, Western Europe, and Australia. During this early phase, gentrification was guided by national and local governments concerned to counteract economic decline in inner-city neighborhoods by encouraging private investment. Processes of gentrification became far more widespread throughout the older industrialized world following the global economic recession of the 1970s, as capitalists sought new opportunities for profitable investment in the real estate sector. Thus, between the late 1970s and the early 1990s, a second phase of gentrification unfolded. During this period, inner-city reinvestment articulated with deeply rooted economic changes such as deindustrialization, the globalization of urban production systems, the enhanced urban concentration of corporate command and control capacities, and the rise of the so-called FIRE (finance, insurance, and real estate) industrial cluster as an important engine of urban economic growth. During this period, moreover, the spatial frontiers of gentrification were expanded significantly as formerly marginalized neighborhoods, such as New York City's Lower East Side, were now targeted for extensive, high-end real estate development. In the early 1990s, with the recession in the United States, some scholars predicted an "end to gentrification" as investor capital evaporated. Instead, following the recession of the early 1990s, a third wave of gentrification has begun to crystallize, as additional neighborhoods, located ever further from the city core, have experienced significant capital-led redevelopment. In the US context, according to Smith & Hackworth (2001), this third wave of

gentrification has been supported, and in many cases directly financed, by local and national government agencies.

One major geographic consequence of gentrification in the US has been to unsettle the socioeconomic geographies that were inherited from earlier rounds of capitalist development, generating an urban sociospatial configuration that appears to be gradually inverting Ernest Burgess's famous concentric circle model. In the new model, the wealthy and middle classes have come to dominate the central zones of the city, whereas the working class and ethnic minorities are increasingly relegated to distant commuter zones. However, even as the process of gentrification spirals outwards from inner-city zones to colonize new neighborhoods, it must also be viewed as a cyclical phenomenon in which individual neighborhoods often experience multiple rounds of reinvestment.

In addition to these structural, political-economic, and geographical aspects, urbanists have also devoted detailed attention, on a microsociological level, to the *agents* of gentrification processes. In the earliest stages of gentrification, marginalized social groups – such as artists, gays, and middle-class blacks – have played key roles. These "early" gentrifiers renovated dilapidated housing using their own sweat equity. These new residents have helped restore buildings, thus increasing their property value. Artists have often converted warehouses into mixed live-work space; and they have aided in transforming formerly industrial areas into residential areas. City governments and local landlords have generally favored such small-scale conversions, which are viewed as a means to increase property taxes and rents. In deference to these new residential patterns, city governments have often retroactively rezoned industrial areas to permit mixed uses. Ultimately, however, these gentrifying segments of the middle class have tended to colonize working-class or ethnic minority neighborhoods and to price out long-term and low-income tenants. Furthermore, many early gentrifiers eventually become the victims of their own renewal efforts. By improving local property and lobbying for more city services, early gentrifiers increase property values and rental prices, thus creating the conditions for later, intensive rounds of gentrification and their own displacement.

As a subject for study, gentrification has generated multidisciplinary attention, especially among urban geographers and urban sociologists. While gentrification always unfolds in place-specific forms, urbanists have debated extensively regarding its overarching features and consequences. In particular, Smith's rent gap theory, mentioned above, has provoked considerable debate. Smith's work emphasizes the essential role of real estate capital in animating the process of gentrification. In this manner, Smith's influential writings supersede earlier explanations that attributed neighborhood reinvestment to the renewed desire of middle-class populations to live in the inner city. Concurrent with and subsequent to Smith's supply-side analysis, however, other scholars have reexplored the demand-side aspects of gentrification through a materialist lens. David Ley (1996), for instance, suggests that the new middle classes created a broad aesthetic appreciation for urban life in conjunction with the countercultural movements of the 1960s and 1970s and the subsequent round of urban restructuring. Similarly, Damaris Rose (1984) and Liz Bondi (1994) emphasized the distinctive gender patterns related to gentrification, in part due to the changing life conditions of middle-class women. Indeed, the question of how to reconcile the demand-side and supply-side elements of gentrification remains an enduring, but productive, intellectual tension in this research field. Loretta Lees (2000), among others, has sought to pinpoint lacunae in gentrification research, and on this basis, to direct attention towards crossnational comparisons and ethnographic forms of spatial analysis. Additionally, art historians have taken an interest in gentrified neighborhoods as venues for new forms of art production, as sites for artistic creativity, and as a source of political conflict within the art world itself. And finally, city planners and architects have approached gentrification less as a theoretical issue than as an opportunity to rethink key aspects of urban design and urban development strategy.

Multiple ethnographic and demographic case studies examine particular types of gentrifiers, such as artists, gays, college graduates, single women, and young professionals. Such studies create typologies between "early" or "marginal" gentrifiers (low-income newcomers who invest sweat equity into their residences) and "late", "super," or "yuppie" gentrifiers (those with the financial resources to purchase property outright). Gentrification may thus enable members of socially marginalized groups to secure their own property as well as community resources. Gays and lesbians, for instance, are often key players in the gentrification process as they seek to avoid areas of overt discrimination and to find locations in which they can be "out" in their own commercial enterprises and public social activities. Similarly, artists looking for large open studio spaces frequently agglomerate in former industrial zones and engage in extensive renovations of space. Zukin's (1989) study of SoHo in New York City discusses the archetypical case of artists appropriating manufacturing warehouses, with city government and landlord encouragement, leading in turn to subsequent waves of high-end gentrification.

Many scholars use the case of gentrification as a basis for conceptualizing both the hopes and the horrors of urban living. In contrast to most of mainstream urban sociology, many writers on gentrification are influenced by radical or Marxist scholarly traditions, and thus tend to view middle-class forms of urban reinvestment as expressions of growth machine politics and narrowly private accumulation strategies. Indeed, the struggle over neighborhood space, aesthetics, and resources is often thought to exemplify contemporary class and racial tensions within major metropolitan regions. However, many case studies show a more complicated picture. Often, the most fervent resisters to gentrification are themselves early gentrifiers who fear being priced out of neighborhoods to which they have grown attached. Many long-term residents are able to partake in new services, and those who own property are often able to realize profits on long-undervalued holdings. Also, the key concern about gentrification, the displacement of low-income residents, is complicated by countervailing policy initiatives that sustain the location of minority residents in neighborhoods that are undergoing intense redevelopment. Still, many landlords, especially absentee and corporate ones, aggressively seek to remove low-income tenants in order to realize higher rents. In this sense, as Neil Smith (1996) has argued in an influential intervention, gentrification can be viewed as a medium and expression of the new forms of urban exclusion and "revan-chism" that have been consolidated during the last two decades.

In the past decade gentrification studies have moved well beyond their original geographic homes in New York and London. Gentrification is now found throughout North America, Australia, Eastern Europe, and also in rural, industrial towns on the outskirts of major cities in the US and the UK. Its expansion may be expected to continue for the foreseeable future, and so too may scholarly attempts to decipher its origins, dynamics, and consequences.

Several other forms of urban restructuring – such as mass suburbanization – continue to surpass gentrification in terms of the number of people involved, the amount of capital invested, and political significance. However, gentrification's prominence in contemporary urban scholarship rests in some measure upon its role as a metaphor for the urban condition under modern capitalism. As in previous rounds of urban restructuring, city life is still perceived as being precariously balanced between the worst manifestations of capitalism – the breakdown of traditional family, social, and cultural structures, alienation, and intensifying racial and class polarization – and initiatives oriented towards urban renewal, preservation, creativity, and the "right to the city."

SEE ALSO: Built Environment; Growth Machine; Invasion-Succession; Public Housing; Uneven Development; Urban Community Studies; Urban Political Economy; Urban Renewal and Redevelopment; Urban Space

REFERENCES AND SUGGESTED READINGS

Atkinson, R. (2003) Introduction: Misunderstood Saviour or Vengeful Wrecker? The Many Meanings and Problems of Gentrification. *Urban Studies* 40: 2343–50.

Bondi, L. (1994) Gentrification, Work, and Gender Identity. In: Kobayashi, A. L. (Ed.), *Women, Work, and Place*. McGill-Queens University Press, Buffalo, pp. 182–200.

Hamnett, C. (2000) Gentrification, Postindustrialism, and Industrial and Occupational Restructuring in Global Cities. In: Bridge, G. and Watson, S. (Eds.), *A Companion to the City*. Blackwell, Oxford, pp. 331–41.

Lees, L. (2000) A Reappraisal of Gentrification: Towards a "Geography of Gentrification." *Progress in Human Geography* 24: 389–408.

Ley, D. (1996) *The New Middle Class and the Remaking of the Central City*. Oxford University Press, New York.

Rose, D. (1984) Rethinking Gentrification: Beyond the Uneven Development of Marxist Urban Theory. *Environment and Planning D – Society and Space* 2: 47–74.

Smith, N. (1996) *The New Urban Frontier: Gentrification and the Revanchist City*. Routledge, New York.

Smith, N. (2002) New Globalism, New Urbanism: Gentrification as a Global Urban Strategy. In: Brenner, N. & Theodore, N. (Eds.), *Spaces of Neoliberalism*, Blackwell, Oxford, pp. 58–79.

Smith, N. & Hackworth, J. (2001) The Changing State of Gentrification. *Tijdschrift voor Economische en Sociale Geografie* 92(4): 464–77.

Zukin, S. (1989) *Loft Living: Culture and Capital in Urban Change*. Rutgers University Press, New Brunswick, NJ.

Germani, Gino (1911–79)

Arturo Grunstein and Louise Barner

Gino Germani legitimately stands as one of the founding fathers of academic sociology in Latin America. From the start of his academic career, Germani affirmed the need to overcome the two "anti-positivist" dominant traditions in Latin American social analysis: abstract philosophical speculation and conceptually poor empiricism.

To many scholars, Germani was the pioneer and leading representative of structural functionalism and modernization theory in the region. Nevertheless, scholars have often missed the complexity of Germani's work, particularly its rich theoretical eclecticism (including, among other influences, those of Max Weber, Durkheim, Parsons, Merton, Freud, Mannheim, and José Medina Echavarría) as well as its innovative empirical studies and comparative historical sociological analyses of Latin American development. In the context of an ideologically polarized Argentina of the 1960s and 1970s, many of his contemporaries, particularly a younger generation of critical Marxian and *dependentista* scholars, singled him out as a stalwart defender of the capitalist status quo and a reactionary sociologist. However, from an early twenty-first-century post-Cold War perspective, Germani emerges as an advocate of liberal democratic development.

Throughout most of his personal and professional life, Germani struggled against what he conceived as the retrograde forces of tradition and irrationalism including religious dogma, totalitarian fascism, authoritarian peronism, and left-wing revolutionary extremism. He firmly believed that the promotion of a scientific study of society was part and parcel of the advancement of liberal democratic modernization, which he closely associated with the twin processes of secularization and rationalization.

Born in Rome in 1911, as a young man Germani participated in the opposition against Mussolini. As a result, he was jailed for almost a year. The experience of repression and incarceration was critical in the formation of his political and sociological ideas. One of his central concerns became the changing meaning of freedom in complex societies.

Shortly after being released from prison, Germani began taking classes at the University of Rome, studying economics and accounting. In addition to enrolling in courses, he read many of the great classic and then contemporary authors including Kant, Hegel, Marx, Pareto, Spencer, and Durkheim.

In 1934 Germani and his mother migrated to Argentina. While working as a mid-level federal bureaucrat, he registered for classes at the University of Buenos Aires (UBA). In 1943, he concluded undergraduate studies in philosophy. By that time, he was already a researcher at the UBA's Institute of Sociology. However, his professional career was temporarily derailed with the rise to power of Juan Domingo Perón in 1946. Once established, the peronista fascist-inspired regime embarked upon the persecution of opposition politicians and intellectuals. As part of this repressive campaign, Germani, along with other liberal and antiperonista professors, was purged from the UBA. In response, Germani joined a group of other opposition scholars in establishing a private independent college, Colegio Libre de Estudios Superiores.

In 1955, Germani published his first book, *Estructura social de la Argentina*. This work constituted a landmark and a model of empirical research in Argentina and the rest of Latin America. In researching and writing *Estructura social*, Germani mainly utilized the national census of 1947. Arguing that the book could threaten "national security," peronista censors impeded its publication. Shortly after a coup d'état overthrew Perón, Germani returned to the University of Buenos Aires. In 1957, the Institute was complemented with the foundation of a sociology department. The late 1950s were a truly golden age for Germani as he became the nation's leading sociologist. With the sympathetic support of the Frondizi government and various US foundations, Germani garnered financial resources that enabled the Institute and department to recruit professors, train students, and bring prestigious guest lecturers from Europe and the US. He was also able to travel and enjoy short academic residences at Harvard, the University of Chicago, and the University of California at Berkeley, where he met and established solid links with several leading US sociologists, including Robert Merton, Seymour Martin Lipset, and Reinhard Bendix.

By the early 1960s, Germani's department and Institute came under heavy criticism from both the right and the left. The Catholic Right charged that sociology would undermine traditional beliefs about God, nation, and the family; the extreme left wing attacked Germani for accepting grants from "imperialistic" US foundations and adopting a "reactionary" structural functionalist perspective.

This irrational ideological polarization convinced Germani of the fragility of liberal democracy in Argentina and the inevitability of another military coup. He was quite prescient about his adopted country's debacle. Shortly after his arrival in the United States, another military coup ousted the constitutional government in June 1966. Germani spent most of the last years teaching at Harvard University. He died in his native Italy in 1979.

UNDERSTANDING THE "TRANSITION": THE MODERNIZATION PROCESS IN LATIN AMERICA

A review of Germani's publications immediately reveals that he held multiple sociological interests and had a diverse research agenda. Nonetheless, it also clearly evinces a central intellectual concern: Latin America's modernization process. He was particularly interested in identifying the social, political, cultural, and psychological factors intervening in the transition from "traditional" to "industrial" society. Thus, in his principal studies, Germani consistently pursued two fundamental and closely interrelated objectives: (1) the elaboration of a general or ideal-typical model of the transition process from traditional to modern society and (2) the historical-sociological and empirical analysis of this process in Latin America, paying central attention to the case of Argentina.

Germani's definition of *social structure* is akin to Parsons's: "a conjunction of different interrelated parts in which people act and interact in accordance with shared sociocultural codes and environmental conditions." From the outset, Germani acknowledged the diversity of traditional and industrial societies and, more importantly, the existence of "various forms of transition from the former to the latter." Still, he singled out three basic types of social change: (1) changes in the normative structure that regulate social action and their corresponding psychosocial or "internalized" attitudes; more specifically, he refers here to the dwindling of prescriptive forms of action and the gradual rise, extension, and prevalence of elective action; (2) increasing specialization of values and institutions; and (3) the institutionalization of change. Thus, Germani explained that modern industrial society is characterized by the secularization of knowledge, an increasingly complex division of labor based on efficiency criteria, and the transformation of family from extended to isolated nuclear units.

Nevertheless these changes take place in an *asynchronic* fashion. In other works there are lags and disequilibria between sectors and spheres. In his analysis of Latin American political development, Germani underlined one fundamental form of asynchronism – the imbalance between social mobilization and integration. These two sociopolitical notions, mobilization and integration, are essential to understanding the transition and particularly the dynamics of intergroup conflict in the context of long-term processes of social change.

Germani defined an integrated society as one in which reciprocal congruence prevails in the normative, psychosocial, and environmental spheres. In an integrated society the system and subsystems of norms, statuses, and roles correspond sufficiently to allow a relatively stable functioning of society. Individuals have also adequately internalized compatible sets of values, roles, and attitudes. Finally, the environmental context (including material and non-material conditions) is well matched with actions based on predictions and expectations stemming from the dominant normative and psychosocial structures. Conversely, social "disintegration" takes place when norms, values, their internalization, and the context in which actions evolve lack adjustment.

In some cases this lack of adjustment produces a state of anomie, affecting group behavior and the functioning of formally established legal spheres. According to Germani, under conditions of unsuccessful integration, anomie may lead to irrational social action on behalf of both elite and popular groups. Anomic tendencies initially emerge only in limited spheres of the social structure but frequently spread to others in a domino effect. Therefore, anomic forces commonly threaten the stability of systems and subsystems and impede or delay the modernization of normative spheres and adequate civic behavior. Specifically regarding the political system, a state of anomie can be catastrophic, as social discontent may result in unmanageable conflicts and the rise of opportunistic authoritarian leaders.

For Germani "integrated society" was only an ideal type. Virtually all societies manifest varying degrees of "disintegration." Since social change is almost always asynchronic it entails a certain measure of disintegration, or the loss of adjustment within and/or between the three – normative, psychosocial, and environmental – spheres.

Germani then focused on participation as one particular, albeit fundamental, aspect of social integration. In traditional societies participation is spatially limited to small areas, economic activities take place in isolation, most community members do not partake in political decision-making, and a majority are excluded from enjoying the material and non-material fruits of general culture. In contrast, in industrial society, mass participation is found in most or all of these social activities.

Subsequently, Germani further distinguished between "integrated participation," that is, under conditions of normative, psychosocial, and environmental congruence, and "disintegrated participation," that is, without correspondence to what is normatively and psychosocially expected and what is possible, given the existing environmental context.

Disintegration in one of the three basic dimensions mentioned leads to what Germani denominated "disposability," indicating that "the groups affected must notice the change and perceive it as an alteration which makes former prescriptions inapplicable."

Based on these concepts, Germani elaborated a transition model for Latin America. The following discussion focuses on the sphere of political development, which Germani privileged in his analysis. In specific reference to sociopolitical changes, he identified several fundamental stages:

- Wars of liberation.
- Civil wars, *caudillismo*, anarchy.
- Unifying autocracy.
- Representative democracies of limited participation.
- Representative democracies of extended participation.
- Representative democracies of full participation.
- National-popular revolutions (as an alternative to the three previous stages).

Germani was perfectly aware of the important limitations inherent in such a scheme. First and foremost, considerable national and even regional or subnational variations could be found. He explained, however, that his scheme was merely a starting ground that would necessarily undergo corrections and modifications on the evidence of individual cases. The three phenomena – mobilization, integration, and disposability – are central in his sociohistorical analysis.

The first generation of creole political elites attempted to build modern democratic nation-states disregarding their societies' deep-seated traditional structures. The Latin American bourgeoisie were in an embryonic phase and the remaining groups and classes – a large majority of the population – were deeply enmeshed in traditional normative and psychological structures. In addition, the power vacuum following the collapse of the colonial authorities led to severe cultural and territorial isolation of most of the population.

Consequently, independence was followed by a second phase of territorial disarticulation, political anarchy, and civil wars between *caudillo*-led factions. As charismatic authorities, *caudillos* enjoyed broad popular support, but they seldom altered the existing traditional social structures. In many nations, this period of chaos and violence concluded when one *caudillo* was able to defeat his rivals and emerge as a dominant political figure nationwide.

During the third stage, "unifying autocracy," the basic sociocultural traditional structures persisted, but some dictators forcefully promoted economic modernization by opening up their nations to international markets as producers of primary goods, foreign capital investments especially for infrastructural development such as railroads and ports, and, in some countries, the influx of massive immigration.

During the fourth stage, democracy with limited participation, personal dictatorship was replaced with oligarchic rule. Even though only a minority of the population were allowed to participate, the rules of the political game were being gradually institutionalized. Economic modernization led to a dual structure: the rapid growth of modern infrastructure and export enterprises in central zones accelerated urbanization and the emergence of new middle and working classes. Meanwhile, most of the nation's inhabitants remained trapped in traditional patterns characterized by subsistence agriculture, small isolated communities, and local authoritarian forms of domination. In most instances, these social sectors remained politically passive. This was partly as a result of oligarchic authoritarian exclusion, but, as Germani pointed out, it was mainly due to enduring traditional psychosocial factors. In some nations, the process of mobilization, especially of the urban middle sectors, gradually led to an awakening of some sectors and the widening of the sphere of political participation.

The next stage, which Germani termed "extended participation," dawned with the formation of an alliance between the strengthened middle classes and recently mobilized segments of the mostly urban working class, also undergoing rising expectations regarding their incorporation into the national political arena. In the most advanced countries of the region, these previously marginal groups were successfully integrated and their participation was institutionalized. While intergroup conflicts frequently erupted, these new legitimate popular members of the national polity increasingly accepted the existing rules of the game. Still, during this phase, broad sectors of the population, particularly those living in rural areas, remained excluded.

"Total participation," the sixth and final phase, takes place when these residual groups are finally integrated. Germani devoted considerable attention to this last period. By the mid-twentieth century, no Latin American country had successfully institutionalized mass political participation. Most nations, including the most developed ones, experienced knotty transition processes marked by unrelenting cycles of progressive democratization and authoritarian retrogression. Not even Argentina, which had moved dynamically from extended to total participation, had managed to build stable integrative mechanisms.

Why had Latin America been unable to complete the transition to fully participatory modern democracy? Why couldn't Latin America match the transition patterns and eventually catch up with advanced western nations? Based on his theoretical and historical-sociological scheme, Germani identified three principal causes.

The first factor was that significant structural differences – in norms, values, etc. – were found between Latin America and western societies. In effect, one could refer to the existence of both traditional and modern aspects in general, ideal-typical terms. Still distinctive, deep-seated historical specificities led to a "relative inapplicability (of a higher or lower degree depending on individual cases) of the western model" to analyze the transition in Latin America.

Although asynchronisms were, indeed, present in every transition process, they were more acute and widespread in late modernizing societies such as Latin America's. The fact that modernization was late and often triggered by external forces generated intense demonstration and fusion effects. Consequently, the pattern of social change diverged significantly from the western experience. Not only were the rhythm and speed different, but also the sequence of the transition was altered. Thus, for instance, social mobilization leading to popular consumption demands and unionization often exceeded the development of the national economy's productive capacity and a fluent internalization of socio-structural change. In many western nations, the equilibrium of the social system at different stages "was assured by the fact that the population not yet included does not exert pressure (or, at least, not a dangerous degree of pressure) because it remains passive, and the sequence is such that when it later becomes active there should be existing mechanisms capable of channeling participation without catastrophic disturbances for the system (although obviously not without relatively sharp conflicts)." In contrast to the European experience, the extension of political rights in Latin America was taking place in a swift if not explosive fashion, giving almost no leeway to building effective institutional channels of participation and the internalizing of adequate civic values and attitudes by mobilized groups.

Compared to the US and most of Europe, the historical-ideological "climate" was overall adverse to the assumption of liberal democratic institutions as mechanisms for mass integration. In most Latin American nations, extensive mobilization took off in the age of the "welfare state." In advanced nations, the "welfare state" was the culmination of a protracted developmental process, including the evolution from proprietary to corporate capitalism. However, by the mid-twentieth century, the ideal of social citizenship was universalized. Consequently, mobilized popular groups in economically and politically laggard nations, among those many Latin American nations, demanded the extension of social rights within a compressed point in time. Just as this occurred, World War I led to a prolonged crisis of liberal democracy and it was challenged by both right- and left-wing authoritarian and totalitarian alternatives, offering new forms of sociopolitical integration. Although fascism was defeated in World War II, during the Cold War soviet communism became an increasingly powerful modernization model for many late-developing countries, including Latin America's. Thus, "ideologies of industrialization" in Latin America often assumed a mix of authoritarian conservative nationalism and socialism. These movements and regimes, which Germani classified as national-popular, were difficult to classify on conventional right–left criteria.

Germani emphasized that the appearance of national-popular movements is what made Latin America's transition to extended and total participation distinct from the classical western liberal democratic path. Elites usually elaborated these doctrinal hybrids in order to manipulate and contain the pressures stemming from mass popular mobilization. These elites allowed lower-strata participation only to the extent that it did not effectively threaten existing social structures. In the process of social integration, nationalist symbols, a powerful means to integrate widely diverse mobilized popular groups, replaced liberal democratic values and institutions. The traumatic process of transition from traditional to industrial society in most of Latin America explained, according to Germani, the tendency of certain popular sectors to support authoritarian (both left- and right-wing) movements and regimes. However, sooner or later, participation for broad sectors of the population revealed itself as "ersatz" or illusory, and not as a genuine process of politically institutionalized integration. Such was the case of peronism, which, for obvious reasons, Germani studied at great length.

From its origins, peronism had a close ideological affinity with fascism. However, in sociological terms, the peronista version differed markedly from its European counterpart. In Argentina's sociopolitical context, Perón could not find and recruit large-scale support from a mobilized petty bourgeois sector seeking to shut off proletarian participation. Instead, Perón maneuvered to build a strong popular basis of support for himself, consisting mostly of the recently mobilized working classes that migrated to Buenos Aires and other large urban centers from the interior provinces. These previously marginalized groups had experienced radical and sudden social changes within the span of approximately a decade. While General Perón ostensibly opened up the gates of the national public arena for these social groups, once incorporated he rigorously conditioned and limited their participation. Unionization was encouraged, important wage increases were granted, and working conditions improved. Labor enhanced its bargaining position vis-à-vis employers. Still, the authoritarian regime managed to keep a tight lid on popular organizations and their political activities and demands. In other words, Perón conceded to the workers, so long as it could be done without compromising his regime's statist authoritarian project. Most importantly, reforms were never geared toward real long-term structural changes such as the establishment of steady channels of participation. On the contrary, they were often aimed at preventing them. Under Perón, the working masses had been partially integrated but not on the basis of modern, liberal democratic institutions.

Why, then, did the masses stubbornly support peronism? Herein lies what Germani referred to as the "irrationalism" of Argentinean popular political behavior.

A central factor was the swiftness of the transition, including the spatial movement from relatively stagnant rural zones to rapidly modernizing urban centers. Mobilized groups surpassed the capacity of available integration mechanisms, thus becoming "disposable." Moreover, these mobilized and disposable masses had only partially internalized modern values, norms, and attitudes. About 57 percent of these migrants arrived in Buenos Aires after 1938, and by 1947 a majority had come from the most backward provinces, measured in terms of literacy, employment, and poverty levels. Partially stuck to traditional normative and psychosocial structures and lacking a sophisticated political culture, they were susceptible to Perón's charismatic leadership and national-popular blandishments.

Germani acknowledged that the new working classes certainly had important reasons to back Perón. It was undeniable that they had enjoyed both the material and psychic benefits of "peronista freedoms" (to organize in unions, to gain public recognition and even respect as laborers, to improve their working conditions and consumption levels). Nevertheless, the historic costs of these concessions were high and consequential: in exchange for short-term gains, the workers lost political and organizational independence, thus blocking the possibility of attaining durable channels of effective participation.

As events following Perón's downfall revealed, Argentina persistently faced insurmountable difficulties in attaining adequate integration of the mobilized masses. Consequently, conflicts often culminated in extensive violence. Building and maintaining a stable participatory political and social structure based on liberal democratic institutions became virtually hopeless.

It would be erroneous to underestimate Germani's scholarship. Despite serious adversities, he was the principal force behind the foundation of academic sociology in Argentina. His theses concerning the asynchronic mode of late modernization, the dynamics of social mobilization and structural change, and the sociological meaning of different manifestations of authoritarianism are now considered as fundamental points of analytical departure in Latin American studies.

His principal works should also have inspired a more ambitious research agenda in macro-comparative Latin American historical sociology. Thus, for instance, Germani's critics often overlook his comments on our lack of sufficient empirical and historical knowledge regarding working-class ideologies and political culture, and his enthusiastic calls for such investigations. Only then, he contended, will we be able to elaborate firmer arguments on changing popular attitudes toward authoritarian and populist leaders, movements, and regimes. Using one of Germani's own concepts, the "historical climate" of his times may have been unfavorable not only for liberal democratic modernization, but also for a more balanced and productive evaluation of his theoretical and empirical findings. As the twenty-first century dawns, his intellectual and political concerns have gained tremendous pertinence for contemporary debates on the region's future. This is particularly so regarding the structural obstacles to liberal democracy in Latin America based on both morally and intellectually compelling questions about the societal underpinnings of freedom and oppression.

SEE ALSO: Authoritarianism; *Caudillismo*; Fascism; Fromm, Erich; Mannheim, Karl; Merton, Robert K.; Nation-State and Nationalism; Parsons, Talcott; Populism; Stuctural Functional Theory

REFERENCES AND SUGGESTED READINGS

Germani, G. (1955) *Estructura social de la Argentina.* Editorial Raigal, Buenos Aires.

Germani, G. (1962 [1956]) *La sociologia científica: apuntes para su fundamentación*, 2nd edn. Instituto de Investigaciones Sociales, Universidad Nacional, Autónoma de Léxico.

Germani, G. (1971) *Sociología de la modernización.* Ed. Paidós, Buenos Aires.

Germani, G. (1977) *Política y sociedad en una época de transición.* Ed. Paidós, Buenos Aires.

Germani, G. (1978) *Authoritarianism, Fascism, and National Populism.* Transaction, New Brunswick, NJ.

Germani, G. et al. (1977) *Populismo y contradicciones de clase en Latinoamérica.* Ed. ERA, Mexico City.

Germani, A. (2004) *Gino Germani: del antifascismo a la sociología.* Taurus, Buenos Aires.

Kahl, J. (1976) *Modernization, Exploitation, and Dependency in Latin America.* Transaction, New Brunswick, NJ.

Mannheim, K. (1940) *Man and Society in an Age of Reconstruction.* Harcourt, Brace, New York.

Parsons, T. (1967) *The Social System.* Routledge, New York.

Skidmore, T. & Smith, P. (2001) *Modern Latin America.* Oxford University Press, Oxford.

gerontology

Jason L. Powell

Gerontology can be defined as the scientific and social analysis of aging. The discipline of gerontology is concerned with understanding age and aging from a variety of perspectives and integrating information from different social science and human science disciplines such as psychology and sociology. The concern of gerontology is in the definition and theorization of age. In western societies a person's age is counted on a chronological or numerical foundation, beginning from birth to the current point of age, or when an individual has died. Chronological aging is a habit we all engage in: birthdays and wedding anniversaries, for example. Counting age is a social construction because it is a practice underpinned by the development of industrial capitalism.

Age has three main focal points of interest to gerontology. First, the aging of an individual takes place within a particular period of time and space. By virtue of this, individual experiences of age are enabled or constrained by their location in time, space, and cultural uniformity. Second, society has a number of culturally and socially defined expectations of how individuals of certain ages are supposed to behave and how aging impacts upon how they are compartmentalized into the "stages of life." Historically, the stages of life were presented as a religious discourse which formed the basis for the cultural expectations about behavior and appearance. The life stage model is still used in taken-for-granted popular usage in society, which impinges on how our lives are structured. Third, age and aging have a biological and physiological dimension, so that over time and space the appearance of physical bodies changes. This latter definition has been illustrated by "biomedical gerontology," advocating scientific explanations of aging.

Gerontology as a *scientific discipline* has been dominated with a preoccupation with biomedical sciences and its constituent elements of "decline" models of biology and psychology. Gerontology based on *social* explanatory models sees aging as a socially constructed category with differential epistemological prisms (e.g., functionalism and feminist gerontology). However, while both definitions are fundamental to the complexities of aging in the social world, the theoretical interpretations of aging are in their infancy when compared to the analysis and attention afforded to class, "race," and gender in sociological theorizing.

If we take the scientific and social dimensions of gerontology, we can illuminate both the relevance and importance they have for understanding constructions of aging. We can suggest that gerontology has two focal points in its broad conceptualization.

Psychological aging processes include changes in personality and mental functioning. According to Kunkel and Morgan (1999: 5), "changes

are considered a 'normal' part of adult development, some are the result of physiological changes in the way the brain functions." What is meant by "normal" development? The "decline" aspect of aging is something which was picked up by the historical rise of scientific discourse and Enlightenment discourses of truth and rationality. Indeed, age and aging have a biological and physiological dimension, so that over time and space the appearance of physical bodies changes. Physical aging, for the biomedical gerontology, is related to changing characteristics on the body: the graying of hair, wrinkling of the skin, decrease in reproductive capacity and cardiovascular functioning, etc. An interesting question is whether these physical changes are inevitable, "natural" consequences of aging.

Biological aging is related to changes of growth and decline within the human body. For example, Bytheway (1995) suggests that the notion of "growth" is a central scientific discourse relating to the true changes associated with human aging to the biological body. Growth is seen as a positive development by biologists in that a "baby" grows into a "child" who grows into an "adult," but then instead of growing into "old age" the person declines. This scientifically sanctioned perception is that growth "slows" when a person reaches "old age" and is subsequently interpreted as "decline" rather than as "change" that is taken for granted with earlier life-course transitions.

The effects of the decline analogy can be seen in the dominance of biomedical arguments about the physiological "problems" of the "aging body." The "master narrative" of biological decline hides the location of a complex web of intersections of social ideas comprising an aging culture. Indeed, a distinctive contribution of sociology as a discipline has been to highlight how individual lives and behavior which were thought to be determined solely by biology (Powell 2005) are, in fact, heavily influenced by social environments in which people live and hence are heavily *socially constructed*.

The broad pedigree of sociological perspectives of aging can be located to the early post-war years with the concern about the consequences of demographic change and the potential shortage of "younger" workers in the US and UK. Social gerontology emerged as a field of study which attempted to respond to the social policy implications of demographic change (Phillipson 1982). Such disciplines were shaped by significant external forces: first, by state intervention to achieve specific outcomes in health and social policy; second, by a political and economic environment which viewed an aging population as creating a "social problem" for society.

This impinged mainly upon the creation of functionalist accounts of age and aging primarily in US academies. Functionalist sociology dominated the sociological landscape in the US from the 1930s up until the 1960s. Talcott Parsons was a key exponent of general functionalist thought and argued that society needed certain functions in order to maintain its well-being: the stability of the family; circulation of elites in education drawing from a "pool of talent" (Powell 2005). Society was seen as akin to a biological organism: all the parts (education/family/religion/government) in the system working together in order for society to function with equilibrium.

A key point to note is that theories often mirror the norms and values of their creators and their social times, reflecting culturally dominant views of what should be the appropriate way to analyze social phenomena. The two functionalist theories contrasted here follow this normative pattern; *disengagement* and *activity* theories suggest not only how individual behavior changes with aging, but also imply *how* it should change. Disengagement theory is associated with Cumming and Henry (1961), who propose that gradual withdrawal of older people from work roles and social relationships is both an inevitable and natural process: "withdrawal may be accompanied from the outset by an increased preoccupation with himself: certain institutions may make it easy for him" (p. 14). Such withdrawal prepares society, the individual older person, and those with whom they had personal relationships for the ultimate disengagement: death. For this variant of functionalism, this process benefits society, since it means that the death of individual society members does not prevent the ongoing functioning of the social system. Cumming and Henry further propose that the process of disengagement as an inevitable, rewarding, and universal process of mutual withdrawal of the individual and society from each other with advancing age was normal and

to be expected. This theory argued that it was beneficial for both the aging individual and society that such disengagement takes place, in order to minimize the social disruption caused at an aging person's eventual death.

Retirement is a good illustration of the disengagement process, enabling the aging person to be freed of the responsibilities of an occupation and to pursue other roles not necessarily aligned to full-pay economic generation. Through disengagement, Cumming and Henry argued, society anticipated the loss of aging people through death and brought "new blood" into full participation within the social world.

A number of critiques exist: first, this theory condones indifference toward "old age" and social problems. Second, disengagement theory underplays the role cultural and economic structures have in creating, with intentional consequences, withdrawal. In order to legitimize its generalizations, disengagement theory accepted the objective and value-free rigor of research methods: survey and questionnaire methods of gerontological inquiry. In a sense, arguing for "disengagement" from work roles under the guise of objectivity is a very powerful argument for governments to legitimize boundaries of who can work and who cannot based on age.

The second functionalist perspective in gerontology is called activity theory and is a counterpoint to disengagement theory, since it claims a successful "old age" can be achieved by maintaining roles and relationships. Activity theory actually predates disengagement theory and suggests that aging can be a lively and creative experience. Any loss of roles, activities, or relationships within old age should be replaced by new roles or activities to ensure happiness, value consensus, and well-being. For activity theorists, disengagement is not a natural process as advocated by Cumming and Henry. For activity theorists, disengagement theory is inherently agist and does not promote in any shape or form "positive aging." Thus, "activity" was seen as an ethical and academic response to the disengagement thesis and recast retirement as joyous and mobile.

Despite this, activity theory neglects issues of power, inequality, and conflict between age groups. An apparent "value consensus" may reflect the interests of powerful and dominant groups within society who find it advantageous to have age power relations organized in such a way (Powell 2005). Such functionalist schools in gerontology are important in shaping social theory responses to them; such functionalist theories "impose" a sense of causality on aging by implying you will either disengage or will be active.

Marxist gerontology or the *political economy of old age* was coined as a critical response to the theoretical dominance of functionalism. This critical branch of Marxist gerontology grew as a direct response to the hegemonic dominance of structural functionalism in the form of disengagement theory, the biomedical paradigm, and world economic crises of the 1970s. As Phillipson (1982) pointed out in the UK, huge forms of social expenditure were allocated to older people. Consequently, not only were older people viewed by governments in medical terms, but also in resource terms. This brought a new perception to attitudes to age and aging. For example, in the US, political economy theory was pioneered via the work of Estes (1979). Similarly, in the UK, the work of Phillipson (1982) added a critical sociological dimension to understanding age and aging in advanced capitalist societies. For Estes (1979) in the US, the class structure is targeted as the key determinant of the position of older people in capitalist society. Estes's political economy challenges the ideology of older people as belonging to a homogeneous group unaffected by dominant structures in society.

A critical evaluation of the political economy of old age is that it over-concentrates analysis on the treatment of older people in terms of class relations within capitalist societies and neglects differences between capitalist societies in the treatment of older people. The approach homogenizes and reifies older age by discounting potential for improvements in the social situation of older people. Hence, the complexity of social life is more of a continuous, never-ending project with variable outcomes than the political economy theory allows.

Another emerging perspective is *feminist* gerontology. In recent years there has been a small but growing body of evidence that in mainstream sociological theory the interconnection of age and gender has been under-theorized and overlooked. "Mainstream" refers to dominant theories in the gerontological field such as functionalist and Marxist theory that could be accused of being "gender blind." In their

pioneering work, Arber and Ginn (1995) point out there exists a tiny handful of feminist writers who take the topic of age seriously in understanding gender. They suggest that the general failure to incorporate women into mainstream theoretical perspectives on aging is a reflection of our resistance to incorporate women into society and hence into sociological and psychological research. They further suggest that because older women tend to occupy a position of lower-class status (especially economic status) than men of all ages and younger women, they are given less theoretical attention.

In all known societies the relations of distribution and production are influenced by gender and thus take on a gendered meaning. Gender relations of distribution in capitalist society are historically rooted and are transformed as the means of production change. Similarly, age relations are linked to the capitalist mode of production and relations of distribution. "Wages" take on a specific meaning depending on age. For example, teenagers work for less money than adults, who in turn work for less money than middle-aged adults. Further, young children rely on personal relations with family figures such as parents. Many older people rely on resources distributed by the state.

There is a "double standard of aging," with age in women having particularly strong negative connotations. Older women are viewed as unworthy of respect or consideration (Arber & Ginn 1995). The double standard is seen as arising from the sets of conventional expectations as to age-pertinent attitudes and roles for each sex which apply in patriarchal society. These roles are defined as a male and a female "chronology," socially defined and sanctioned so that the experience of prescribed functions is sanctioned by disapproval. For example, male chronology hinges on employment, but a woman's age status is defined in terms of events in the reproductive cycle.

Unfortunately, feminist theories that focus upon the social problems of older people may have promoted the agism that many are arguing against. Old age as a term can no longer be used to describe and homogenize the experiences of people spanning an age range of 30 to 40 years. The pace of cohort differentiation has speeded up, with different age groups reflecting cohort differences in life chances that are created by period-specific conditions, policies, and economic transformations. Hence, there is differentiation of *subjective* experiences of aging in the lifestyles of older people.

As a reaction against macro theories of gerontology such as functionalism, political economy of old age, and feminist theorizing, postmodern gerontology has emerged as a school of thought. The work of Featherstone and Hepworth (1993) and Featherstone and Wernick (1995) is important in this respect, and has fed into wider debates on postmodernism in Canada and the US. They expose and deconstruct both the scientific gerontology and macro stances about old age, particularly claims of objectivity and truth about bodies. Featherstone and Hepworth (1993) maintain that old age is a mask that conceals the essential identity of the person beneath. That is, while the external appearance is changing with age, the essential identity is not, so that one may be surprised that one looks different than the unchanging image in one's head. Furthermore, Gilleard and Higgs (2001) claim that life-course models that propose universal stages of life are fundamentally flawed. To exemplify the fluid and blurred nature of aging identity, Featherstone and Hepworth (1993) argue that in western society "children" are becoming more like adults and adults more childlike. There is an increasing similarity in modes of presentation of self – gestures and postures, fashions and leisure-time pursuits – adopted by both parents and children. If correct, this can be seen as a move towards a uni-age style. The "private sphere" of family life is becoming less private, as children are granted access to adult media such as television where previously concealed aspects of adult life (such as sex, death, money, and problems besetting adults who are anxious about the roles and selves they present to children) are no longer so easy to keep secret. A uni-age behavioral style is also influenced by the advent of media imagery that, as a powerful form of communication, bypasses the controls that adults had previously established over the kinds of information believed to be suitable for children. Coupled with this, Katz (1996) and Powell (2005) have developed *Foucauldian* gerontology in analyzing power relations, surveillance, and governmentality in their applicability to understanding aging.

As a critique of postmodern gerontology and its emphasis on deconstructing universal narratives of aging, Phillipson (1998) suggests that in a restructuring of social gerontology we should acknowledge how the "global" and the "local" articulate and recognize that globalization is unevenly distributed and is also a western phenomenon indicative of the unequal power relations between the "west and the rest." Phillipson suggests that occidental globalization impinges on the poverty status of older people universally.

Gerontology is then multidisciplinary and is the principal instrument of orthodox theorizing about human aging. It provides a space for the search for meaning about what it is to be "old" in modern society, not for issuing prescriptions but for alternative interpretations about aging.

SEE ALSO: Aging and the Life Course, Theories of Aging and Social Policy; Aging, Sociology of; Childhood; Demography of Aging; Gender; Gerontology: Key Thinkers; Marxism and Sociology; Postmodernism

REFERENCES AND SUGGESTED READINGS

Arber, S. & Ginn, J. (Eds.) (1995) *Connecting Gender and Ageing: A Sociological Approach.* Open University Press, Milton Keynes.

Bytheway, W. (1995) *Ageism.* Open University Press, Milton Keynes.

Cumming, E. & Henry, W. (1961) *Growing Old: The Process of Disengagement.* Basic Books, New York.

Estes, C. (1979) *The Aging Enterprise.* Jossey Bass, San Francisco.

Featherstone, M. & Hepworth, M. (1993) Images in Ageing. In: Bond, J. & Coleman, P. (Eds.), *Ageing in Society.* Sage, London.

Featherstone, M. & Wernick, A. (1995) *Images of Ageing.* Routledge, London.

Gilleard, C. & Higgs, P. (2001) *Cultures of Ageing.* Prentice-Hall, London.

Katz, S. (1996) *Disciplining Old Age.* University Press of Virginia, Charlottesville.

Kunkel, S. & Morgan, L. (1999) *Aging: The Social Context.* Pine Forge Press, New York.

Phillipson, C. (1982) *Capitalism and the Construction of Old Age.* Macmillan, London.

Phillipson, C. (1998) *Reconstructing Old Age.* Sage, London.

Powell, J. L. (2005) *Social Theory and Aging.* Rowman & Littlefield, Lanham, MD.

gerontology: key thinkers

All subfields in sociology have their own key figures beyond the more generally influential people discussed throughout this Encyclopedia. In this entry, several of the key figures (Beth Hess, Donald Kent, Mathilda White Riley, Ethel Shanas, and Donald Spence) in the history of the study of issues relating to gerontology are discussed. – *GR*

Hess, Beth (1928–2003)

Elizabeth W. Markson

The many scholarly contributions of Beth (Bowman) Hess to the field of sociology include those to the subfields of aging and the life course, gender studies, and friendship and its relationship to age cohort. Hess brought to her work intellectual curiosity, breadth of knowledge, analytic powers, impeccable editing and writing ability, and lack of pretentiousness.

The only child of upper-middle-class parents, Hess attended private elementary and high schools in Buffalo, New York and received her BA degree in 1950 from Radcliffe College *magna cum laude*, where she majored in government. After a brief interlude as a file clerk in a New York City advertising agency, she and her new husband, Dick Hess, moved to Paris. Returning in the mid-1950s to New Jersey where she lived for the rest of her life, she became, as she later described it (Hess 1995), temporarily enveloped in the *zeitgeist* of suburban motherhood. When her younger child entered kindergarten in 1962, Hess entered the graduate sociology program at Rutgers University. While a doctoral candidate working with Matilda White Riley, she began research on the sociology of aging, age stratification, and friendship, compiling the massive inventory of research findings in the first volume (1968) and editing each chapter of all three volumes of *Aging and Society*.

Her doctoral dissertation (1971) laid the basis for her seminal article, "Friendship" (1972). Hess examines how age influences friendship types developing between friends at various ages, whom one has as a friend, conditions in which friendships form, dissolve, or persist, and how friendships contribute both directly and indirectly to socialization throughout the life course. Age, a cohort attribute as well as indicator of life stage, signifies a common history that adds to friendship homophily as members of a friendship pair age

together, sharing the same sequence of life stages and historical events.

When Hess published her formulations on friendship, little research attention had been given to the topic and it was regarded more as a residual category rather than a major role. Indeed, Hess herself initially contrasted friendship with "major" social roles, and wrote her last full explication on friendship studies in 1979. Her work, however, prepared the way for a spate of interest on the import of social support, especially in later life. Subsequently, gerontologists have examined size of social networks, structure and process of friendships, and relationship to well-being. The importance of gender for friendship roles – a theme highlighted by Hess in her later work both on aging and gender – has also become salient.

In 1969 Hess joined the full-time faculty of the County College of Morris, where she was a professor until her retirement in 1997. Her decision to accept a position in a community college, largely governed by compatibility with family obligations and geographical convenience, could have been the entry into safe obscurity had she not had a strong commitment to advancement of the discipline. Drawing attention to race, class, gender, and social inequities before it was sociologically fashionable to do so, her contributions include textbooks such as *Aging and Old Age* (Hess & Markson 1980), the five editions of *Sociology* (Hess et al. 1996), and *The Essential Sociologist* (Hess et al. 2001). The first two editions of her reader *Growing Old in America* (1976, 1980) were published when courses in social gerontology were relatively new in college and university curricula and, like later editions (1985, 1991), carefully examined the current state of knowledge about later life. As a social gerontologist, Hess urged readers, whether colleagues or students, toward the essence of the sociological imagination: connections between personal problems and public issues and the interplay of race, class, and gender with the life course.

With a firm grounding in theory – encompassing both often-forgotten early feminist sociologists such as Harriet Martineau and Charlotte Stetson Perkins Gilman and the more usual male pantheon of Durkheim, Marx, Simmel, Weber, and others – Hess was remarkably up to date on the latest findings and events. Whether scholarly books or journal articles, popular news articles, the most recent census data, or other government reports, she had not only read them, but also synthesized complex and often contradictory materials into a meaningful, sophisticated sociological argument, expressed with semantic precision. As a feminist scholar, she emphasized how gender organizes social arrangements, personality, and cognition. *Controversy and Coalition: Three Decades of the Feminist Movement* (three editions, Ferree & Hess 2000), *Analyzing Gender* (Hess & Ferree 1987), and *Revisioning Gender* (1998) illuminate the many ways in which feminist scholarship has transformed the social sciences.

Central to the governance and organization of many scholarly associations, Hess was executive officer of the Eastern Sociological Society, president of the Association for Humanist Sociology, Sociologists for Women in Society, the Eastern Sociological Society, and the Society for the Study of Social Problems (1994–5), secretary of the American Sociological Association (1989–92), and chair of the Behavioral and Social Science Section of the Gerontological Society of America. Listed in *Who's Who of American Women*, her scholarly contributions were recognized by the Lee Founders Award presented by the Society for the Study of Social Problems and as a Fellow of the Gerontological Society of America.

The many honors she received and offices held in sociological organizations are but a small token of her readiness to give her time and energy to advance the field. Amid her ability to balance the mastery of material, to write rapidly, coherently, and eloquently, to be active in the profession, and to mentor others, was her passion for integrity and justice reaching beyond the academy. As a feminist, she was dedicated not only to equality for women, but also a political activist and fierce defender of *all* human rights. Above all, Beth Hess was a passionate sociologist – passionate about clear and elegant writing, passionate about intellectual integrity, and passionate about the human condition. Her work, cross-cutting many venues from general sociology to the sociology of aging and feminist theory, reflects these passions.

SEE ALSO: Aging and Social Support; Gender, Aging and; Gender, Friendship and

REFERENCES AND SUGGESTED READINGS

Ferree, M. M. & Hess, B. B. (Eds.) (2000) *Controversy and Coalition: The New Feminist Movement through Three Decades of Change*. Twayne, New York.

Hess, B. (1972) Friendship. In: Riley, M. W., Johnson, M., & Foner, A. (Eds.), *Aging and Society*, Vol. 3: *A Sociology of Age Stratification*. Russell Sage Foundation, New York.

Hess, B. B. (1989) Foreword. In: Adams, R. G. & Blieszner, R. (Eds.), *Older Adult Friendship: Structure and Process*. Sage, Newbury Park, CA.

Hess, B. B. (1995) An Accidental Sociologist. In: Goetting, A. & Fenstermaker, S. (Eds.), *Individual Voices, Collective Visions: Fifty Years of Women in Sociology*. Temple University Press, Philadelphia.

Hess, B. B. & Ferree, M. M. (Eds.) (1987) *Analyzing Gender: A Handbook of Social Science Research*. Sage, Newbury Park, CA.

Hess, B. B. & Markson, E. W. (1980) *Aging and Old Age: An Introduction to Social Gerontology*. Macmillan, New York.

Hess, B. B. & Markson, E. W. (Eds.) (1991) *Growing Old in America*. Transaction Books, New Brunswick, NJ.

Hess, B. B., Markson, E. W., & Stein, P. J. (1996) *Sociology*. Allyn & Bacon, New York.

Hess, B. B., Stein, P. J., & Farrell, S. A. (2001) *The Essential Sociologist*. Roxbury Publishing, Los Angeles.

Kent, Donald P. (1916–72)

Jon Hendricks

Donald P. Kent, a key figure in social gerontology, was both a sociologist and government official who helped ensure passage of the Older Americans Act and was instrumental in establishing the Administration on Aging. Born in Philadelphia, Kent received degrees from Pennsylvania State

University (1940) and Temple (1945), and his PhD from the University of Pennsylvania (1950). Following his undergraduate degree, Kent taught high school and declared himself a conscientious objector during World War II. While working on his dissertation, published as *The Refugee Intellectual* (1953), Kent served as an instructor at Penn and subsequently joined the sociology faculty (1950–7) at the University of Connecticut before becoming director of its Gerontology Center (1957–61).

While in the latter role Kent also chaired the Connecticut Commission on Services for Older Persons and in that capacity was not only a vocal advocate but also acceded to high-profile involvements in the federal government's emerging concern with aging issues. Kent was instrumental in planning the first White House Conference on Aging (1961) and led the Connecticut delegation. Nominated by Senator Abraham Ribicoff, patron and sponsor, to become director of what was to become the Administration on Aging, Kent ran into a maelstrom over his status as a conscientious objector. Subjected to ringing personal derision, Kent was on the verge of withdrawing until Ribicoff convinced him to stay the course. In 1961 he became special assistant to the US Secretary of Health, Education, and Welfare and vice-chairman of President John F. Kennedy's Council on Aging. As director of the US Office on Aging (1961–5), later renamed Administration on Aging, Kent worked tirelessly behind the scenes and on the hill to ensure passage of the Older Americans Act. Present at the Rose Garden signing of the OAA by President Lyndon Johnson, Kent's direct involvement in pressing the federal government's aging agenda was also drawing to a close. As he had previously, he continued to provide briefings for federal, state, and local governments on aging issues, and remained involved in study sections for NICHD, but longed to return to academia. In 1965 he was named chair, department of sociology and anthropology, at Pennsylvania State University, a position he occupied until his death. Kent's verve, statesmanship, and craft were invaluable during the arduous process leading to the implementation of the Older Americans Act and were characteristics that served him well throughout his governmental and academic service.

A firm believer in what would later be termed "action research," Kent was intent on bridging the gulf between social research and policy formulation. He personified Cicero's admonition that "virtue without action is meaningless" and in research project after research project his agenda was to train and utilize indigenous staff, use them as a kind of "kitchen cabinet," and set them up for further employment. As part of a major study of inner-city minority elderly in Philadelphia, Kent and colleagues implemented a volunteer referral service suggested by field staff not content to walk away from interviewees once unmet needs had been identified. Without cost to the funding agency an intervention network was implemented, as disembodied research was an anathema. Kent, Kastenbaum, and Sherwood's *Research, Planning and Action for the Elderly: The Power and Potential of Social Science* (1972) provides a comprehensive summary and prescription for action research on behalf of older persons and stands as a how-to guide for generations of gerontologists.

Once back in academia Kent assumed editorship of the *Gerontologist* (1967–70) and took as his personal missions the mentoring of would-be authors and the premise that outcomes of social research need to include practical and pragmatic implications. He utilized the occasion of his last publication to digest recommendations of the 1971 White House Conference on Aging in terms of whether they would directly benefit older persons or simply fuel the bureaucracy. He also stressed the need for robust and appropriate research methodologies to buttress policy recommendations and cautioned researchers about looking at real-world experiences through a lens ground to their own specifications.

In recognition of Kent's many contributions, the Gerontological Society of America implemented the prestigious Donald P. Kent Award to recognize gerontologists embodying the highest standards of the field through teaching, service, and interpretation of gerontology to the larger society. The Kent Award remains one of the most prestigious recognitions a gerontologist may receive.

SEE ALSO: Action Research; Gerontology

REFERENCES AND SUGGESTED READINGS

Kent, D. P. (1965) Aging: Fact and Fancy. *Gerontologist* 5: 51–6, 111.

Kent, D. P. (1969) From N to Ego. *Social Casework* 50: 117–21.

Kent, D. P. (1972) Planning-Facilities, Programs, and Services: Government and Non-Government. *Gerontologist* 12: 36–48.

Riley, Matilda White (1911–2004)

Anne Foner

In her long and productive career Matilda White Riley devoted much of her scholarly work to setting forth and elaborating a sociology of age. This work followed her achievement as an innovative methodologist and her research on mass communications (with her husband, John Riley, Jr.), adolescent values, and family relations. The methodological sophistication and the interconnections between methods and theory that characterized this early work served to underpin her study of age as a social phenomenon. Her analysis of aging and society gave new understandings to a "taken-for-granted" phenomenon and helped establish the sociology of age as a key substantive field in the discipline.

Riley embarked on an academic career in sociology at New York University and Rutgers in 1950. Before that she had had a top position in market research, where she honed her skills in all aspects of survey research. When she started teaching research methods to sociology students she went beyond a narrow conception of methodology to demonstrate the interplay of theory and research and to explore the full range of quantitative and qualitative methods. This broad approach was elaborated in her 2-volume *Sociological Research* (1963), which examined how the conceptual framework of key classical studies was translated into empirical operations. In the process, she gave students a sweeping overview of some of the most significant sociology then available.

Riley turned her attention to the study of aging and society in the 1960s when she was commissioned to codify social science knowledge about the middle and later years. The project resulted in the monumental 3-volume *Aging and Society* (1968–72.) It provided a synthesis of the considerable body of relevant research and in the process

identified methodological fallacies that had contributed to myths about old age and aging. In volume 3 it set forth an overarching analytical framework for understanding age as an element in the social structure and aging over the life course as influenced by and in turn influencing changes in the society.

In Riley's view human aging is a lifelong, complex, mutable process, shaped by social, psychological, and biological interdependencies. People in successive cohorts grow up and grow older in different ways as societies and their social structures undergo change. While the aging of individuals over the life course and historical changes in society are intertwined, these two dynamic processes have different rhythms, leading to pressures for structural changes, including changes in age criteria for filling roles, for access to social goods, and for social relationships.

These fundamental ideas of the *Aging and Society* paradigm became widely influential as Riley developed them in numerous publications and lectureships, in her roles as university professor, as president of the American Sociological Association and the Eastern Sociological Society, and as first associate director for Behavioral Sciences Research at the National Institute on Aging, where she initiated funded research on social and behavioral aspects of the aging process. As an exemplar and mentor she helped launch new scholars in the study of age and aging. Her contributions to the biosocial sciences have been recognized by many awards, including honorary degrees from Radcliffe, Rutgers, and the State University of New York, and election to the National Academy of Sciences. She continued to make contributions to and receive accolades from the discipline in her ninth decade.

SEE ALSO: Aging, Demography of; Aging and the Life Course, Theories of; Aging, Sociology of; Life Course Perspective

REFERENCES AND SUGGESTED READINGS

Riley, M. W. (1973) Aging and Cohort Succession: Interpretations and Misinterpretations. *Public Opinion Quarterly* 37: 35–49.

Riley, M. W. (1987) On the Significance of Age in Sociology. *American Sociological Review* 52: 1–14.

Riley, M. W. (1994) Aging and Society: Past, Present, and Future. *Gerontologist* 34: 436–46.

Riley, M. W. & Foner, A. (1968) *Aging and Society*, Vol. 1: *An Inventory of Research Findings*. Russell Sage, New York.

Riley, M. W., Johnson, M., & Foner, A. (1972) *Aging and Society*, Vol. 3: *A Sociology of Age Stratification*. Russell Sage, New York.

Shanas, Ethel (b. 1914)

Gloria D. Heinemann

Born in Chicago, Ethel Shanas received her education from the University of Chicago. After receiving her doctorate in sociology, she remained at the University of Chicago as Research Associate/Instructor, Committee on Human Development (1947–52) and as Senior Study Director, National Opinion Research Center and Research Associate, Department of Sociology (1956–61). From 1965 to 1982, when she retired, she was Professor, Department of Sociology, University of Illinois at Chicago (UIC) and, beginning in 1973, Professor, School of Public Health, UIC Medical Center. Throughout her career, Shanas, who was a wife and mother, successfully combined a meaningful career and family life during a period when women had few supports for career development and advancement.

The courses Shanas taught at UIC exemplify her major areas of interest and contribution to sociology: medical sociology and sociology of aging, which included considerable material about aging, health, and long-term care. She used the social survey to inquire about older persons, their families and intergenerational relationships, family help patterns, living arrangements, health status and incapacity, financial status, and work and retirement. These studies provided baseline data that debunked myths about and presented accurate portrayals of older persons living in the community. One of the major contributions from her research was the development of the Index of Incapacity.

Shanas also was a consultant to numerous international, governmental, and local university and community agencies and committees. Major contributions resulted from her consultations, such as the Long-Term Care Minimum Data Set and the National Institute on Aging. Other major contributions of Shanas include her service to professional organizations and her service on the editorial boards of professional journals. Much of her work was multidisciplinary and multicultural. This collaborative effort is evident in the research project and resulting book, *Old People in Three Industrial Societies* (Shanas et al. 1968) and in the two editions of the *Handbook of Aging and the Social Sciences* (Binstock & Shanas 1976, 1985), which presents perspectives from a broad array of social sciences.

Shanas was elected a Fellow of the American Sociological Association and the Gerontological Society of America. She was the Keston Memorial Lecturer at the University of Southern California (1972) and received GSA's Kleemeier Award (1977), the National Council on Family Relations' Burgess Award (1978), the GSA's Brookdale Award (1981), the American Sociological Association, Section on Aging's Distinguished Scholar Award (1987), and an honorary doctor of letters degree from Hunter College (1985). In 1979 she was elected to membership in the Institute of Medicine, National Academy of Sciences.

SEE ALSO: Aging, Sociology of; Aging and Health Policy; Aging and Social Policy; Aging and Social Support; Elder Care; Family Theory; Intergenerational Relationships and Exchanges; Kinship; Medical Sociology; Survey Research

REFERENCES AND SUGGESTED READINGS

Shanas, E. (1979) The Family as a Social Support System in Old Age. *Gerontologist* 19: 169–74.

Shanas, E. (1979) The Robert W. Kleemeier Award Lecture. Social Myth as Hypothesis: The Case of the Family Relations of Old People. *Gerontologist* 19: 3–9.

Shanas, E. & Maddox, G. L. (1985) Health, Health Resources, and the Utilization of Care. In: Binstock, R. & Shanas, E. (Eds.), *Handbook of Aging and the Social Sciences*, 2nd edn. Van Nostrand Reinhold, New York.

Shanas, E., Townsend, P., Wedderburn, D., Friis, H., Milhøj, P., & Stehouwer, J. (1968) *Old People in Three Industrial Societies*. Routledge & Kegan Paul, New York.

Spence, Donald L. (1930–89)

Victor W. Marshall

Donald L. Spence stands as a major influence in the sociology of aging and in the area of gerontology education. His 1965 doctoral dissertation at the University of Oregon, under Robert Dubin, was on retirement, and aging remained his lifelong passion. A member of the American Sociological Association continuously from 1959 and of the Society for the Study of Symbolic Interaction from 1977 until his death, he contributed effectively to an interdisciplinary field while maintaining a strong theoretical position as a sociologist and influencing many sociologists in the aging field.

Spence had a lasting impact on many sociologists working in the substantive area of aging. This was more as a mentor and role model than through his specific substantive research. He brought intellectual rigor and a commitment to theory to his own research, most of which was quite applied in nature, but mostly he is remembered for his commitment to theory and his mentorship of young investigators.

While "ABD," Spence began teaching in 1962 in a new sociology department at the University of Alberta, Calgary, but he returned to his native California in 1965 to conduct aging research at the Langley Porter Neuropsychiatric Institute. There, he directed the Human Development Training Program in the department of psychiatry at the University of California, San Francisco. In 1973 he moved to the University of Rhode Island as associate professor, department of child development and family relations and coordinator of that university's Program in Gerontology. He became director of the Program in Gerontology at the University of Rhode Island in 1976, professor of gerontology in 1982, and professor emeritus in 1989. During his period at URI he was also adjunct associate professor in community health at Brown University, where he served as founder and first director of the Southeastern New England Long-Term Care Gerontology Center.

Spence left a multifaceted legacy. He was a dedicated and enthusiastic teacher, with a passionate and rigorous commitment to sociological theory. Initially, he could be characterized as a functionalist, and he also took pains to ensure that his students were well grounded in the philosophy of the social sciences. While at University of California- San Francisco he became a close friend of Anselm Strauss and formed a strong commitment to symbolic interactionism. His shift in perspective led to vigorous theoretical disagreements and his departure from the "Four Stages of Life" project, on which he was a project coordinator for several years. His commitment to theory inspired a small, informal grouping of sociologists who wanted to see a more theorized approach to gerontology and led to an increased appreciation of theory among gerontologists.

Spence's later publications and papers focused on interdisciplinary health care teams and other aspects of care of the elderly, as well as on gerontological education. He was a founding member of the Association for Gerontology in Higher Education in 1974, served on every committee of that association and was its president (1982–3). He thus played an important role in the shaping of gerontology education during its major era of expansion. He was also a Fellow of the Gerontological Society of America.

SEE ALSO: Aging, Sociology of; Aging and the Life Course, Theories of; Symbolic Interaction

REFERENCES AND SUGGESTED READINGS

Spence, D. L. (1986) Some Contributions of Symbolic Interaction to the Study of Growing Older. In: Marshall, V. (Ed.), *Later Life: The Social Psychology of Aging*. Sage, Beverly Hills.

ghetto

Joanna Michlic

The term ghetto is a concept with many meanings. It is frequently used to describe any dense areas of Jewish residence, even if no compulsory policies of residential segregation were imposed. It is also employed as a description of the geographical and social isolation of minorities other than Jews; for example, it is applied to African Americans and other ethnic communities in the US and to minorities in Japan such as ethnic Koreans. Scholars recognize that the term has assumed a life of its own since its first application and have called for systematic examination of the history of its changing meaning from the time it was first used in connection with Jews until the present (Ravid 1992).

Originally, the term referred to the establishment of a compulsory segregated Jewish quarter, ghetto or *ghetti* in pre-Enlightenment Europe. Although compulsory, segregated, and enclosed Jewish quarters had existed prior to 1516 in a few cities in Europe such as Frankfurt, the first involuntarily segregated quarter called a ghetto was established in Venice in that year. The Venetian government, motivated by utilitarian economic considerations of *raison d'état*, granted Jews charters, which allowed them to live in Venice. However, it required that as infidels Jews be kept in their place, both to demonstrate their inferiority for Christian theological reasons, and more practically, to restrict as much as possible social contacts, including sexual interaction, between them and the local Christian population. To ensure the complete segregation of Jews, the area allocated for their residence was walled up and the Christian owners of the dwellings within it were required by the Venetian government to evict their local Christian tenants. This was the first instance of a segregated compulsory quarter for Jews in a walled-up form. The Venice ghetto existed for the next 281 years and was abolished in the early summer of 1797 in the aftermath of the dissolution of the Venetian government.

The term ghetto derives from the Italian word *gettare* (to pour or cast metal). The word was originally used to describe the old ghetto (*Ghetto vecchio*) and the new ghetto (*Ghetto nuovo*) for Jews in Venice. Both these quarters were located in the area where the municipal copper foundry was previously based. Subsequently, the term has been used loosely and imprecisely in Jewish history and sociology. The varied usages in different senses have created a certain blurring of the historical reality, especially when the term is used in phrases such as "age of the ghetto," "out of the ghetto," and "ghetto mentality," which are often applied to the Jewish experience in Central and Eastern Europe in the seventeenth, eighteenth, and nineteenth centuries (Ravid 1992). The term in the original Italian sense of a compulsory, segregated, and walled-up Jewish quarter cannot be used to describe the Jewish experience in Eastern Europe because the history of Jewish residence there lacks the main characteristic of the Italian ghetto. If the word ghetto is to be applied in its original literal sense in connection with Eastern Europe, then it must be asserted that the ghetto arrived there only during the German occupation of the region in World War II. However, unlike those Italian ghettos of the Counter-Reformation era, which were designed to provide Jews with a clearly defined, permanent position in Christian society, the ghettos established in German-occupied Eastern Europe constituted a stage in the Nazi anti-Jewish policies, which culminated in the genocide of European Jewry.

The concept of the ghetto as a closed premodern environment that isolated Jews from the rest of society also had a major impact on early scholarly attempts to understand the forces that held together ethnic neighborhoods of European immigrants in American society in the early twentieth century. In 1928 the Chicago sociologist Louis Wirth published *The Ghetto*, in which he compared the Chicago ghetto – the voluntarily established Jewish immigrant neighborhood on Chicago's Westside – to the medieval Frankfurt Jewish quarter. Wirth assumed that Jewish immigrants in Chicago moved into a certain ethnocultural space because the centuries of separate settlement in Europe had imprinted the "ghetto experience" on the Jewish mind. Drawing on his mentor Robert Park, Wirth saw a correlation between the assimilation of immigrants and their residential mobility. For him, the Chicago ghetto was a passageway in time and space from premodern European ghettos into mainstream American society. Jeffrey Gurock (1979) dismisses Wirth's thesis about the ghetto-like pattern of settlement of Jewish immigrants in the US.

The idea of the ghetto has also often been applied to describe the African American experience in different geographical localities of the US between 1900 and the 1960s. The African American ghetto is a creation of the early twentieth century and its historical origins are linked to the large-scale black migration to cities such as Chicago and Detroit. The African American ghetto is the result of the forces of racial segregation. Although the US Supreme Court banned explicit zoning by race in 1917, by 1920 the color line in Northeastern cities had been fully established. The reinforcement of ethnic and racial barriers was not limited only to anti-black initiatives in Northern US cities. The South had created its vast array of Jim Crow laws at the end of the nineteenth century. In the West, whites also used restrictive covenants against Asians. African American segregation in ghettos – inner-city communities such as Harlem in New York – continued to rise until it reached its peak in the 1960s. The abolition of legal restrictions in the 1960s meant that barriers that were needed to keep areas white were gone. However, this process has not resulted in the end of the African American ghetto. African American ghettos have not become any less black. The persistence of subtle forms of barriers and economic factors are cited in scholarly and public discussions about the persistence of the African American ghettos in contemporary North American cities (Glasser 1997).

In recent scholarly literature the concept of the ghetto has been linked to the ideal of multiculturalism. Kymlicka (2001), for example, argues that the ideal of multiculturalism in Canada encouraged the idea that immigrants should form "self-contained ghettos" alienated from the mainstream. He calls this process ghettoization, which may mark the latest manifestation of the concept in the social sciences.

SEE ALSO: Diaspora; Genocide; Holocaust; Multiculturalism; Urban Community Studies; Urbanism, Subcultural Theory of

REFERENCES AND SUGGESTED READINGS

Glasser, E. (1997) Ghettos: The Changing Consequences of Ethnic Isolation. *Regional Review* (spring): 2–9.

Gurock, J. (1979) *When Harlem was Jewish 1870–1930.* Columbia University Press, New York.

Kymlicka, W. (2001) *Politics in the Vernacular.* Oxford University Press, Oxford.

Ravid, B. (1992) From Geographical Realia to Historiographical Symbol: The Odyssey of the Word Ghetto. In: Ruderman, D. B. (Ed.), *Essential Papers on Jewish Culture in Renaissance and Baroque Italy.* New York University Press, New York, pp. 372–85.

Ravid, B. (2003) *Studies on the Jews of Venice, 1382–1797.* Ashgate Variorum, Aldershot.

Pullan, B. (1983) *The Jews of Europe and the Inquisition of Venice.* Blackwell, Oxford.

Wirth, L. (1928) *The Ghetto.* University of Chicago Press, Chicago.

gift

Rodanthi Tzanelli

The concept of the gift has been explored by anthropologists, philosophers, sociologists, and social theorists, who recognized in it a heuristic tool for the study of kinship relations, exchange and reciprocity, and interconnections of power, economics, and morality. In all these cases the gift can assume the form of tangibles (material items such as artifacts or human beings) and intangibles (ideas, religious rituals, or titles).

Marcel Mauss's *The Gift* (1954) is considered the seminal work in this area, both because of its theoretical coherence and its plethora of ethnographic material. Mauss identified the practice of gift exchange as a universal phenomenon that exemplifies the pervasivess of a sense of obligation in all societies, archaic and modern. He claimed that the nature of gift exchange is reciprocal; such exchange involves both individuals and groups (clans, families) that establish social relations and reproduce themselves through the act of giving and receiving. Controversially, Mauss claimed that the gift itself compels and ensures reciprocation, simply because the gift owner and the gift cannot be separated: the object received as a gift binds the giver and the recipient with a moral force. Therefore, to reciprocate becomes for the recipient obligatory insofar as the violation of reciprocation can lead to magical repercussions. The obligation of giving gifts and reciprocating them forms the basis of the archaic "system of total services" that aims to establish alliances (e.g., marrying one's daughter into another clan to secure friendly relations, offering military titles to an ally) or to seal rival relations. The latter is encapsulated in the potlatch (meaning "to consume") tradition of Nootka Indians, in which competitors for social titles organize festivities and waste or distribute possessions to claim superiority. For Mauss, therefore, the practice of gift giving has an inherently ambiguous nature that encompasses both self-interest and selflessness, calculation and moral obligation.

These two types of gift giving have been reconceptualized by Marshal Sahlins and Karl Polanyi as reciprocity (gift giving for alliance) and redistribution (potlatch). Following Mauss's idea of "total services," they purported that reciprocal and redistributive exchange relations between two groups are continuous rather than separate in societies characterized by social differentiation. Whereas reciprocity regulates exchange between parties with different interests, redistribution is applied to the collective as a whole, as it is regulated by a central authority (e.g., the chief of a tribe) (Sahlins 1972). This argument presents redistribution as a more advanced, politicized form of gift giving that ensures social bonding in centralized communities, whereas reciprocity is viewed as a rationalized system of exchange that functionalizes gift giving. Bataille (1988) criticizes this dominant economic assumption as much as he rejects the idea that humans have a natural inclination to produce and save. His starting point is that human nature is inherently greedy and favors destruction and consumption. Social solidarity is thus secured through rituals that celebrate waste and go against the logic of social differentiation through wealth. To consolidate his thesis Bataille used as an example Aztec sacrificial offers and the potlatch ceremonies of American Indians, which are characterized by excessive waste of resources that could, according to the economic logic, be appropriated. For Bataille, this uncontrolled expenditure secures the situational power of the giver, which can, in turn, be challenged by reciprocal expenditure by the initial recipient. Generosity here is not inseparable from strategic calculation, but they form a continuum inherent in the "general economy" of giving (as opposed to the "restricted economy" of saving).

An empirically grounded approach to the gift in contemporary welfare provision was pioneered by Titmuss. Titmuss (1970) conducted a comparative study of the British and the American blood supply system, attempting to answer a fundamentally moral question: How is it possible for people to donate blood to strangers? Highlighting the difference between the British system, in which donation is a voluntary act, and the American system, in which giving blood is formally remunerated, he argued for the superiority of morally bound forms of giving that stem from altruism, as opposed to those subjected to the laws of the market. Although situated in social and administration studies, Titmuss's research did not deviate from former anthropological studies that examined gift giving as a moral obligation. In a similar vein, Zelizer (1978) explored changing perceptions of life insurance in the American context. The initial commercialization of this service, and its presentation in monetary terms ("buying" life insurance for someone, subjecting life to the laws of economic transaction), was not welcomed by Americans. It was only when life insurance was presented as a way in which one can express care for one's family or spouse (by continuing to provide for the loved ones even after one's death) that hostile American attitudes towards this service subsided. According to Zelizer, the shift was enabled by the dissociation of life insurance from market exchange, and its presentation as a gift, a sacred offer that cannot be reciprocated by the living ones.

A thorough exploration of the gift's potential to restore collective bonding was offered by Berking (1999). Berking reconsidered the meaning of the gift and the messages of power, duty, and status that it communicates through an extensive excursus in anthropological and sociological theory. By exploring historical conceptions of the sacrifice, sharing, and giving as the basic institutions on which archaic societies were based, he attempts to reconcile modern self-interest with the archaic ideal of communal good. Operating within the confines of the longstanding Durkheimian tradition, Berking argues for a moral economy that surpasses the market rationale and promotes the altruistic ideal.

SEE ALSO: Bataille, Georges; Durkheim, Émile; Gift Relations; Kinship; Moral Economy; Recognition

REFERENCES AND SUGGESTED READINGS

Bataille, G. (1988 [1967]) *The Accursed Share: An Essay on General Economy*. Zone Books, New York.

Berking, H. (1999) *Sociology of Giving*. Trans. P. Camiller. Sage, Thousand Oaks, CA.

Mauss, M. (1954 [1925]) *The Gift: The Form and Reason of Exchange in Archaic Societies*. Free Press, London.

Polanyi, K. (1957 [1944]) *The Great Transformation: The Political and Economic Origins of Our Time*. Beacon Press, Boston.

Sahlins, M. (1972) *Stone Age Economics*. Aldine, Chicago.

Titmuss, R. M. (1970) *The Gift Relationship: From Human Blood to Social Policy*. Allen & Unwin, London.

Zelizer, V. (1978) Human Values and the Market: The Case of Life Insurance and Death in 19th-Century America. *American Journal of Sociology* 84(3): 591–610.

gift relations

Craig D. Lair

Though the study of gift relations spans a range of intellectual disciplines (e.g., anthropology, ethnology, and sociology), one general theme has tended to unite the diverse works in these areas: more than being simply matters of economic transactions, gifts and gift giving are fundamentally *social* activities. That is, gifts are not exchanges of mere material objects, but rather objects and actions imbued with social meanings. Thus, to engage in a gift relationship is to engage in a *social relationship*.

The social nature of gift relations is a central theme found in the work that is often considered as being seminal in the study of gifts and gift exchange: Marcel Mauss's *The Gift* (2000). Mauss, drawing upon ethnographic data from Oceanic and Native American societies, as well as "ancient" legal and economic systems (e.g., Roman law), sees gift exchanges as a force that both engenders and sustains social solidarity. As Mary Douglas says in her introduction to *The Gift*: "A gift that does nothing to enhance solidarity is a contradiction" (p. vii). In part this is because, though gift giving appears as a voluntary action, it is in fact socially obligatory and socially regulated. In the study of gift exchanges in "archaic" societies, Mauss finds three obligations inherent in the gift-giving process: to give gifts, to receive gifts, and to reciprocate gifts given, often with "interest" (i.e., to give more than one has received). To refuse to engage in this process (i.e., to not give or receive) is "tantamount to declaring war" because gift exchanges are not simple economic transactions between individuals, but rather a "total service" – an activity that is a mixture of moral, juridical, economic, spiritual, religious, and social structural elements that is collectively carried out. To not engage in gift-giving activities is to reject the whole of a society – its thoughts, beliefs, and entire worldview. However, to participate in this cycle of gifts and counter-gifts, a cycle that once established is seemingly self-perpetuating, and thus one that acts to bind social groupings together over time, is to be engaged with, and intertwined in, the whole of a society. As such, the obligatory nature of gift giving acts to bind individuals and groups together in social relationships that are sustained over time and in this way they are mechanisms of social solidarity.

The social nature of gift exchanges has been a theme that has been picked up by most of those who have studied gift relations after Mauss. For Bataille (1989), gift exchange, in the form of the potlatch or competitive gift giving, was a means to obtain honor. That is, it was a means by which one could secure *social* status. Baudrillard (1993), before making his postmodern turn, saw in "symbolic exchanges" a non-acquisitive cycle of gifts and counter-gifts, a radical alternative to both capitalism and socialism (both, in Baudrillard's mind, rested upon the same logic of production and utility, the only difference being how the fruits of this labor were distributed). Thus, for a time, Baudrillard saw in the gift relations of past and non-western societies a means by which modern *social* relations could be reordered in a fundamentally different manner. Helmut Berking, in his *Sociology of Giving* (1999), argues that modern individualism encourages not only self-centered views but also, and paradoxically so, altruistic values. Thus, for Berking, a "solidarity of individualism" is not incompatible with notions of charity and giving. Rather, individualism is a means by which these values can be given greater prevalence in social life.

From the early studies by Mauss, to more contemporary works exploring gift giving in modern times, one general theme has remained the same: gifts, above and beyond any economic value they may have, are elements of a social exchange. Thus, to engage in a gift relationship is, at the same time, to engage in a social one as well.

SEE ALSO: Bataille, Georges; Gift

REFERENCES AND SUGGESTED READINGS

Bataille, G. (1989 [1967]) *Accursed Share*, Vol. 1: *Consumption*. Trans. R. Hurley. Zone Books, New York.
Baudrillard, J. (1993 [1976]) *Symbolic Exchange and Death*. Trans. H. Grant. Sage, Thousand Oaks, CA.
Mauss, M. (2000 [1924]) *The Gift: The Form and Reason for Exchange in Archaic Societies*. W. W. Norton, New York.
Weiner, A. (1992) *Inalienable Possessions: The Paradox of Keeping-While-Giving*. University of California Press, Berkeley.

Gilman, Charlotte Perkins (1860–1935)

Michael R. Hill

Charlotte Perkins Gilman was an influential and sometimes controversial contributor to early American sociology. Her *Women and Economics* (1898) launched a searching feminist sociological critique of the economic position of women in patriarchal societies. The primary site for Gilman's continuing sociological work was the *Forerunner* (1909–16), a monthly journal that Gilman wrote and self-published. The socially problematic issues that Gilman explored in her works echo theoretical proposals of Lester F. Ward (1841–1913), a founding American sociologist who admired Gilman and vice versa. Ward's concept of gynecocentric (i.e., woman-centered) social theory reinforced Gilman's strong belief in the fundamental rationality of women's values and social contributions. Gilman developed this perspective at length in her non-fiction works. Gilman was an early member of the American Sociological Society, published in the *American Journal of Sociology*, was respected by contemporary sociologists, and was widely known by lay readers in the public generally.

Gilman shared the feminist pragmatist tenet, that women's values make for better societies, in common with American sociologist Jane Addams (1860–1935). Antecedent to Gilman's sprightly *Herland* saga is Addams's witty and biting essay, "If Men Were Seeking the Franchise" (1913). Addams, a friend and colleague of Gilman, described a hypothetical society of men and women in which women dominate the populace and have the political power to deny men the right to vote. Addams whimsically concluded that men cannot be allowed to share in government until they abandon their selfish and destructive ideas.

Gilman's *Herland* (1915), set in a fictional utopia populated only by women, is the first half of an accessible sociological critique of American life. *Ourland* (1916) continues and completes the *Herland* saga. In *Ourland*, Ellador (a native of Herland) and Vandyke Jennings (an American sociologist who discovered the remote Herland and subsequently married Ellador) leave the all-woman paradise so that Ellador can tour and see the "real world" for herself. Suffice it to say, Ellador is appalled and aghast at the waste, wars, and patriarchal injustices that men have perpetrated around the globe.

In addition to *Woman and Economics*, Gilman's major non-fiction sociological treatises, some serially published in the *Forerunner*, include: *Concerning Children* (1900), *Human Work* (1904), *The Dress of Women* (1915), and *Social Ethics* (1916), among others. In sum, wrote Gilman in *Social Ethics*, we have failed to teach even "a simple, child-convincing ethics based on social interactions, because we have not understood sociology."

SEE ALSO: Addams, Jane; American Sociological Association; Ward, Lester Frank

REFERENCES AND SUGGESTED READINGS

Deegan, M. J. (1997) Gilman's Sociological Journey from Herland to Ourland. In: Gilman, C. P., *With*

Her in Ourland: Sequel to Herland. Greenwood, Westport, CT, pp. 1–57.

Gilman, C. P. (1935) *The Living of Charlotte Perkins Gilman: An Autobiography*. D. Appleton-Century, New York.

Hill, M. R. (1996) Herland. In: Magill, F. N. (Ed.), *Masterpieces of Women's Literature*. HarperCollins, New York, pp. 252–4.

Hill, M. R. & Deegan, M. J. (2002) Charlotte Perkins Gilman on the Sociology of Dress. In: Gilman, C. P., *The Dress of Women*. Greenwood, Westport, CT, pp. ix–xxvii.

Hill, M. R. & Deegan, M. J. (2004) Charlotte Perkins Gilman's Sociological Perspective on Ethics and Society. In: Gilman, C. P., *Social Ethics*. Greenwood, Westport, CT, pp. ix–xxvii.

Gini coefficient

Ivan Y. Sun

The Gini coefficient is the most commonly used measure of inequality. The coefficient is named after the Italian statistician and demographer Corrado Gini (1884–1965), who invented the measure in 1912. While the Gini coefficient is often used to measure income and wealth inequality, it is also widely employed to indicate uneven distribution in other social issues, such as industrial location and development, health care, and racial segregation. The coefficient ranges from 0 to 1, with 0 representing perfect equality (i.e., everyone has the same income) and 1 perfect inequality (i.e., a single person has all the income). An extension of the Gini coefficient is the Gini index, which equals the Gini coefficient multiplied by 100.

The Gini coefficient is calculated based on the Lorenz curve (Lorenz 1905) of income distribution. The graphical depiction of the Gini coefficient is shown in Figure 1. The Lorenz curve is plotted showing the relationship between the cumulative percentage of population and the cumulative percentage of income. The diagonal or 45 degree line indicates a perfect distribution of population and income (e.g., 30 percent of the population earns 30 percent of the income and 80 percent of the population earns 80 percent of the income).

The Gini coefficient is the ratio of the area between the Lorenz curve of income distribution and the diagonal line of perfect equality (the shaded area or area A in Fig. 1) to the total

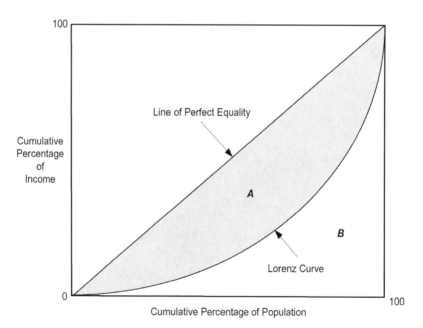

Figure 1   Graphical depiction of the Gini coefficient (A/A + B).

area underneath the line of perfect equality. Putting it into an equation: the Gini coefficient = area A/(area A + area B). The further the Lorenz curve is below the line of perfect equality, the greater the inequality in the distribution of income.

Countries with Gini coefficients between 0.2 and 0.35 are generally viewed as having equitable distribution of income, whereas countries with Gini coefficients from 0.5 to 0.7 are considered to have high inequality in income distribution. Most European countries and Canada have Gini coefficients varying from 0.2 to 0.36, while many African and Latin American countries have high values of Gini coefficients exceeding 0.45. Most Asian nations have Gini coefficients between 0.25 and 0.45 (United Nations 2005). Income inequality in the United States showed an upward trend over the past three decades, increasing from a Gini of 0.39 in 1970 to 0.46 in 2000.

One needs to be cautious about the national measures of Gini coefficients for they may obscure great variations in income inequality across sectors of the population within a country. In the United States, for example, minorities (African Americans and Latinos) have higher levels of income inequality than non-Hispanic whites (US Census Bureau 2005). The Gini coefficient is also useful in understanding the impact of economic development. For example, a nation may experience rapid economic growth and an increasing Gini coefficient simultaneously, indicating that income becomes less evenly distributed and thus inequality and poverty are not necessarily improving.

SEE ALSO: Income Inequality, Global; Income Inequality and Income Mobility; Inequality and the City; Inequality, Wealth

REFERENCES AND SUGGESTED READINGS

Allison, P. D. (1978) Measuring Inequality. *American Sociological Review* 43: 865–80.

Lorenz, M. C. (1905) Methods of Measuring the Concentration of Wealth. *Journal of the American Statistical Association* 9: 209–19.

Ryscavage, P. (1999) *Income Inequality in America: An Analysis of Trends.* M. E. Sharpe, Armonk, NY.

Sen, A. (1973) *On Economic Inequality.* Clarendon Press, Oxford.

United Nations (2005) *Human Development Reports.* Online. hdr.undp.org/reports/global/2005/.

United States Census Bureau (2005) Historical Income Inequality Tables. Online. www.census. gov/hhes/income/histinc/ineqtoc.html.

global economy

Leslie Sklair

While they are often used interchangeably, the idea of the *global* economy should be clearly distinguished from the idea of the *international* economy. The international economy refers to the sum of all the relations between the national economies of all the countries in the world, particularly binational and multinational exchanges, whereas the global economy refers to the sum of all the relations between economic agents whether they are state or private or of other mixed forms. In practice, this distinction boils down to the analytic choice between a state-centrist analysis of economic relations and regulation, and a transnational analysis of economic actors, practices, and institutions. This distinctive concept of the global economy comes from globalization theorists and researchers who have identified globalizing corporations and their local affiliates, those who own and control them, and those in influential positions who serve their interests as the dominant economic forces in the world today (Dicken 1998; Sklair 2001).

Theory and research on the global economy has focused on several interrelated phenomena, increasingly significant since the 1960s. The transnational corporations (TNCs) have attracted an unprecedented level of attention in this period, not only from academic researchers but also from activists in the fields of human rights in general and child labor, sweatshops, and environmental justice in particular. The ways in which and the consequences of how transnational corporations have facilitated the globalization of capital and the production of goods and services, the rise of new global forms of organization of the capitalist class based on ownership and control of TNCs, and transformations in the global scope of the corporations that own and control the mass media, are no longer the sole province of international economists and trade specialists, but are now commonplace in many textbooks in the social sciences (Sklair 2002) and bestsellers read by students and concerned citizens alike (Klein 2000). In this respect, at least, the global economy has become popularized.

Interest in the connections between an increasingly globalizing capitalism and the rise of a global economy dominated by transnational corporations grew perceptibly from the 1960s. The context of theoretical and empirical interest in competing national capitalisms in the international economy was (and for many still is) the history of colonialism and imperialism. This is overlaid with several versions of the theory that capitalist states could more or less successfully plan their own economic futures. As direct imperialism and colonialism came to an end and as more and more very large TNCs began to emerge in the 1960s, attention began to shift decisively from the international to the global economy.

This manifested itself at first in the sociology of development, where the dependency approach to development and underdevelopment of Gunder Frank and the related world-systems approach of Wallerstein, highlighted the systemic nature of capitalism as a worldwide phenomenon over several centuries. While both of these theoretical innovations can be said to have prepared the ground for it, neither entirely succeeded in establishing a coherent concept of the global economy. Wallerstein's analysis of core, semi-periphery, and periphery in the world-systems approach is based on national economies (Wallerstein 1979), though to some extent the theoretically more ambitious concept of commodity chains has been elaborated in more globalizing terms (Gereffi & Korzeniewicz 1994).

The novelty of theories of the global economy, in the sense used here, originates in the proposition that capitalism entered a new, global phase in the second half of the twentieth century. By the new millennium, the largest TNCs had assets and annual sales far in excess of the gross national products of most of the countries in the world. The *World Development Report* (published annually by the World Bank) for 2000 shows that only about 70 countries had GNPs of more than US$10 billion. By contrast, the 2000 *Fortune* Global 500 list of the biggest corporations by turnover reported that about 450 of them had annual sales greater than US $10 billion. This comparison, however, underestimates the economic scale of major corporations compared with sovereign states, as TNC revenues are usually counted as part of GNP.

The global scope of TNCs has also expanded dramatically. Many major corporations earn more than half of their revenues outside the countries in which they are legally domiciled. This is true for TNCs from countries with relatively small domestic markets (for example, Switzerland, Sweden, Canada, Australia), as well as for those legally domiciled in the USA and Japan. Most of the biggest corporations are still headquartered in the First World, though several dozen companies originating in what is conventionally called the Third World – mainly the newly industrializing countries (NICs) – have been numbered in the *Fortune* Global 500. This group has included the state-owned oil companies of Brazil, India, Mexico, Taiwan, and Venezuela (owned by the state, but increasingly run like private corporations), banks in Brazil and China, and Korean manufacturing and trading conglomerates like Hyundai and Samsung (Sklair & Robbins 2002).

Some scholars argue that the global economy is a myth because most major TNCs are legally domiciled in the US, Japan, and Europe, and because they trade and invest mainly between themselves. Against this conclusion, proponents of the global economy argue that an increasing number of corporations operating outside their countries of origin see themselves as developing global strategies of various types, as is obvious from the contents of their annual reports and other corporate publications (Sklair 2001). While all parts of all economies are clearly not globalizing equally, an increasing volume of empirical research indicates that the production and marketing processes of most major industries are being deterritorialized from their countries of origin and that these processes are being driven by the TNCs (Dicken 1998). The central issue for debates around the global economy is the extent to which TNCs domiciled in the US, Japan, and European and other countries can be more fruitfully conceptualized as expressing the national interests of their countries of origin (sometimes termed the globo-skeptic argument) or what can be conceptualized as the private interests of those who own and control them. Even if historical patterns of TNC development have differed from country to country and region to region, it does not logically follow that TNCs and those who own and control them express any type of national interest or national character.

The formal ownership of capital and the corporations has been transformed since the 1960s. The ownership of share capital has increased throughout the world by means of greater participation (though still a tiny minority in most communities) of the general population in stock markets and the indirect investments that hundreds of millions of people, mainly in rich countries, have through their pension funds and other forms of savings. However, formal ownership rarely means effective control over the capital, resources, and decisions of TNCs.

The globalization of cross-border finance and trading can be fruitfully analyzed in terms of the progressive weakening of the nation-state and the growing recognition that major institutions in the global economy, notably transnational financial and trading organizations, are setting the agenda for these weakened nation-states. Theory and research on this issue has, not surprisingly, led to an increased interest in the politics of the global economy.

The politics of the global economy is debated intensely inside and outside the social sciences. Since the disintegration of the Soviet empire from the late 1980s, the struggle between capitalism and communism has been largely replaced by the struggle between the advocates of capitalist triumphalism and the opponents of capitalist globalization. Many theorists have discussed these issues within the triadic framework of states, TNCs, and international economic institutions. From this perspective, the global economy is dominated by the relations between the major states and state systems (US, EU, and Japan), the major corporations, and the international financial institutions (World Bank, IMF, WTO, supplemented in some versions by other international bodies, major regional institutions, and so on). Such considerations draw attention to the management of the global economy as an ideological-political project, closely related to the rise of neoliberalism in the 1980s associated with the policies and practices of the Thatcher government in Britain and the Reagan administration in the US. This was theorized by some as the so-called Washington Consensus, which sought to bring together a new orthodoxy of economic theory, a new theory of minimizing government intervention in the economy, and new strategies for development by the major international financial institutions. While controversy still rages over the effectiveness of neoliberalism (the Washington Consensus has not been much discussed since the 1990s), many policies promoted by their proponents have been adopted by governments all over the world. This has stimulated interest in who runs the global economy.

One explicit approach to this large question focuses on the concept of the transnational capitalist class (TCC). The TCC may be analytically divided into four main fractions: (1) TNC executives and their local affiliates; (2) globalizing politicians and bureaucrats; (3) globalizing professionals; (4) consumerist elites of merchants, media, and advertising (Sklair 2001). It is transnational in several senses: its members have outward-oriented global rather than inward-oriented national perspectives on a variety of issues (e.g., support for free trade and neoliberal economic and social policies); they are people from many countries, more and more of whom begin to consider themselves as citizens of the world as well as of their places of birth and residence (these might differ); and they share similar lifestyles, particularly patterns of higher education (in cosmopolitan universities and business schools) and consumption of luxury goods and services. The sociological analysis of the economic base, the political structure, and the culture-ideology of the transnational capitalist class provides a fruitful research program for understanding the global economy and explaining its dynamics.

The dominant culture-ideology of the global economy is widely agreed to revolve around consumerism, and many researchers argue that a globalizing effect due to the mass media is taking place all over the world. Ownership and control of television, including satellite and cable systems, and associated media like newspaper, magazine, and book publishing, films, video, records/tapes/compact discs, and a wide variety of other marketing media (notably, the Internet), are concentrated in relatively few very large TNCs. The predominance of corporations from the US is being challenged by corporations from Japan and Europe in the global arena, and even by media empires from elsewhere (Herman & McChesney 1997).

While Marxist and Marx-inspired theories of the inevitability of a fatal economic crisis of the capitalist global economy appear to have lost most of their adherents, at least two related but logically distinct crises have been identified. The first is the simultaneous creation of increasing poverty and increasing wealth within and between societies (the class polarization crisis), not to be confused with Marx's emiseration thesis, which failed to predict significant increases in wealth for rapidly expanding minorities all over the world. The second is the unsustainability of the global economy as it is presently organized (the ecological crisis). In most communities around the world the absolute numbers of people who are becoming global consumers have been increasing rapidly over recent decades. At the same time, in some communities the absolute numbers of the destitute and near-destitute are also increasing, often alongside the new rich consumers. The best available empirical evidence (for which see the United Nations Development Program *Human Development Report*, published annually since 1990) suggests that the gaps between rich and poor have widened since the 1980s in many parts of the world. The very poor cannot usually buy the goods and services that the global economy offers in such abundance. While there is a long way to go before consumer demand inside the rich first world is satisfied, the gap between the rich and the poor all over the world is not welcome news for TNCs. In addition to the profits lost when poor people who want to buy goods and services do not have the money or even the credit to do so, the increasing visibility of the new rich and the new poor in an age of constant global media exposure directly challenges capitalist claims that everyone eventually benefits from the global economy.

The ecological crisis is also directly connected with consumerism, illustrated in the struggles over the concept of sustainable development. In recent decades most major TNCs have formulated policies in response to the challenges of environmental harm and declining stocks of resources essential for the maintenance of the global economy. However, the persistence of problems of pollution, health risks, environmental degradation, and waste management intrinsic to the system suggests that ecological crisis will be difficult to avoid. In this context, the attempt by transnational corporations and their supporters in governments, international bureaucracies, and the professions (globalizing politicians, bureaucrats, and professionals) and the mass media to capture the idea of sustainable development and to reconcile it with the progress of the global economy is worth further study.

SEE ALSO: Capitalism; Global Justice as a Social Movement; Globalization; Globalization, Consumption and; Globalization and Global Justice; Globalization, Values and; Glocalization; Grobalization

REFERENCES AND SUGGESTED READINGS

Dicken, P. (1998) *Global Shift: Transforming the World Economy*, 3rd edn. Paul Chapman, London.
Gereffi, G. and Korzeniewicz, M. (Eds.) (1994) *Commodity Chains and Global Capitalism*. Praeger, Westport, CT.
Herman, E. and McChesney, R. (1997) *The Global Media: The New Missionaries of Corporate Capitalism*. Cassell, London.
Klein, N. (2000) *No Logo*. Flamingo, London.
Sklair, L. (2001) *The Transnational Capitalist Class*. Blackwell, Oxford.
Sklair, L. (2002) *Globalization: Capitalism and Its Alternatives*, 3rd edn. Oxford University Press, Oxford.
Sklair, L. & Robbins, P. (2002) Global Capitalism and Major Corporations from the Third World. *Third World Quarterly* 23(1): 81–100.
Strange, S. (1996) *The Retreat of the State: The Diffusion of Power in the World Economy*. Cambridge University Press, Cambridge.
Taylor, P. J. (2004) *World City Network: A Global Urban Analysis*. Routledge, New York.
United Nations Development Program (1990 to date) *Human Development Report*. Oxford University Press, New York.
van der Pijl, K. (1998) *Transnational Classes and International Relations*. Routledge, New York.
Wallerstein, I. (1979) *The Capitalist World Economy*. Cambridge University Press, Cambridge.

global justice as a social movement

Matthew Williams

The global justice movement is a transnational social movement, rooted in the confluence of the human rights, labor, environmental, indigenous, peasant, and feminist movements' shared opposition to neoliberal globalization and vision of a more democratic, equitable, ecologically sustainable world. Neoliberal globalization refers to those structural changes in the global economy being carried out under a discourse of free markets that weaken or eliminate policies that favor grassroots social actors, such as labor unionists, environmental activists, and indigenous peoples, while creating a regulatory apparatus that favors transnational corporations (TNCs). The global justice movement is truly global in scope, with strong constituent movements in western countries, Latin America, South and Southeast Asia, and parts of Africa; it is weakest in the Middle East, East Asia, and the former Soviet bloc. Constituent organizations range from traditional nonprofits and volunteer groups in the global North (first world), to large grassroots labor, peasant, and indigenous organizations in the global South (third world). The global justice movement is a relatively young movement, coalescing in the 1990s and only becoming highly visible with the massive 1999 protests against the World Trade Organization (WTO) in Seattle, Washington.

Given the movement's newness, sociologists have only recently begun to study it. Most research has focused on case studies of particular campaigns, coalitions, or social movement organizations using a combination of ethnography and in-depth interviews, although surveys of global justice activists at various protests and conferences have been done as well. Some researchers have taken advantage of the heavy use of the Internet to communicate by global justice activists, mining online archives of email lists and websites as an additional source of data. It is as yet unclear how well traditional theories of social movements, which were developed based on analyses of movements in western democracies, apply to the global justice movement, given its global scope and strong Southern character. Indeed, most research remains focused either on transnational coalitions or on the movement in the North, with relatively little work done by sociologists looking at constituent movements in Southern countries.

Often referred to, somewhat inaccurately, as the anti-globalization movement, global justice activists oppose only the current form of economic globalization – neoliberalism – and favor what they sometimes call globalization from below. They critique neoliberalism for taking critical economic decisions out of the democratic, public sphere and placing them in the hands of either TNCs or intergovernmental organizations with little democratic accountability, particularly the International Monetary Fund (IMF), World Bank, and WTO. Critics charge that, under neoliberalism, decisions are made primarily on the basis of short-term profit maximization, resulting in growing poverty and ecological degradation.

Global justice activists generally believe that democratic, public oversight of corporations and markets is needed to ensure an equitable, ecologically sustainable economy. In the more radical wing of the movement, this suspicion of markets takes the form of full-blown anti-capitalism. Global justice activists also stress the importance of political democracy; their vision of democracy is a participatory and deliberative one, moving beyond notions of democracy that are limited to elections and lobbying. Although most global justice activists would agree with the principle of subsidiarity – that decisions should be made at the most local level possible – there is much disagreement about what this would mean in practice, with some emphasizing the importance of a global regulatory apparatus, others stressing the empowerment of local communities. Although many global justice activists seek to strengthen nation-states' capacity to regulate markets, many others are as suspicious of states as they are of markets. In its moderate form, this manifests as an emphasis on the need for a vigorous, global civil society to serve as a watchdog on both business and government. Among radicals, this often takes the form of emphasizing the need to create democratic spaces, autonomous from both markets and states. In the North, this radicalism primarily takes the form of anarchism; while a minority in numbers, anarchists have been influential, playing an important role in organizing many major protests, thereby disseminating ideas about participatory democratic organization and the tactics of direct action. In the South, this radicalism is increasingly embraced by many large grassroots organizations of peasants, indigenous peoples, and the urban poor; these Southern groups generally do not share Northern anarchists' absolute rejection of nation-states, but there is nonetheless an emphasis on fundamentally reshaping political relations to empower grassroots social actors over political and economic elites.

The global justice movement emerged as a response to the neoliberal transformations of the global economy that began in the 1970s. These changes resulted in social movements facing a new, more complex system of political opportunities and constraints, operating at multiple levels, both national and transnational, which led to the formation of transnational coalitions and changes in movements' tactical repertoires.

As Southern governments, in debt to and under pressure from the IMF and World Bank, began to reform their economies along neoliberal lines in the 1970s, they increasingly faced large anti-austerity protests. Although these governments would often reverse the reforms to quell the protests, they would later reimplement them in a piecemeal fashion that did not arouse public opposition but satisfied the IMF and World Bank. But just as neoliberalism closed many political opportunities at the national level, it created new, powerful targets at the transnational level, albeit targets that are far more difficult to pressure effectively. A number of campaigns evolved in the 1980s to challenge these organizations. Activists targeted the World Bank using traditional advocacy methods such as lobbying by environmental and indigenous rights activists, who charged that many of the development projects funded by the Bank, such as large dams and oil pipelines, were environmentally destructive and displaced indigenous people without adequate compensation. As TNCs increasingly moved production (and therefore jobs) between countries in an effort to cut labor costs, labor unions began to create transnational organizing campaigns targeting particular TNCs. In addition

to these adaptations of traditional tactics, activists developed a new, innovative repertoire of consumerist tactics such as economic boycotts to pressure TNCs guilty of particularly egregious actions into changing their environmental, labor, and other policies. Many of these campaigns depended on the ability of Northern allies to use their political or economic clout to pressure the World Bank or TNCs on behalf of Southern constituencies, who in turn provided the testimonies to legitimate the Northern activists' campaigns. Campaigns at this point in time focused primarily on changing individual TNC and World Bank policies, not the fundamental structures of the global economy.

The late 1990s and early twenty-first century saw a dramatic expansion of activists' tactical repertoires – alongside advocacy, labor organizing, and consumerist repertoires, global justice activists began to employ mass-based direct action. In the North, this has primarily taken the form of protests, starting with those against the WTO in Seattle, in which activists attempt to shut down or disrupt high-level meetings of international political and business leaders, such as the annual conferences of the IMF and World Bank and negotiations to create free trade agreements. These protests mark a dramatic shift away from the highly routinized, contained legal protests of the 1970s and 1980s. Police have, however, grown relatively adept at containing these protests through a number of countertactics, including mass, preemptive arrests. There has also been a wave of direct action in the South as well, particularly Latin America, where mass protests, road blockades, and other such actions have forced governments to reverse neoliberal initiatives and driven presidents from office. This also marks a noteworthy tactical shift, away from the armed struggles of the 1960s, 1970s, and 1980s. Even the indigenous Zapatista guerrilla army of Chiapas, Mexico has focused more on mass protest and creating a parallel system of participatory democratic government than on armed struggle. Paralleling this shift to direct action, activists have expanded their demands from individual policy changes to dismantling the entire neoliberal system.

The results of this can be seen in the outcomes of the WTO talks in Cancun, Mexico and in the Free Trade Area of the Americas

(FTAA) talks in Miami, Florida, both in 2003. Although the protests outside these summits were relatively small, the WTO talks collapsed when Southern delegates walked out and the US was forced to compromise with Southern delegates in the FTAA talks to avoid a similar walkout. In part, this was the result of increasing discontent on the part of Southern elites, who often wish for more autonomy than neoliberalism grants them; but it was also in part a reaction to the growing unrest they face in their home countries. While some political opportunities closed as economic policymaking was moved from the national and public forums to transnational and closed ones, other opportunities opened at both the national and transnational level, in part because of the actions of social movements themselves.

The organizational networks of the global justice movement began to take shape during the initial campaigns of the 1980s, which usually involved partnerships between grassroots groups in the South and large development or environmental non-profits in the North. As these networks thickened in the 1990s, the scope of the groups involved grew to include smaller, more confrontational and radical groups in the North. Many have stressed the importance of the Internet and other advances in telecommunications in the formation of the movement; more important, however, have been face-to-face meetings among activists, allowing people from very different backgrounds to build ties of trust between them, ties that were then maintained through the Internet. While in the 1980s, activists met primarily to work on specific campaigns, in the 1990s and early twenty-first century, regular international conferences focusing on confronting neoliberalism as a whole began to take place, including the Zapatista *encuentros* (encounters) and the World Social Forum. Those activists who formed relationships at such meetings then served as brokers between their respective constituencies. They were able to bridge their differences and work together, forming a "movement of movements," by framing their particular issues in shared terms of global justice and opposition to neoliberalism. The 1990s also saw the development of several permanent transnational coalitions with broader goals, including Fifty Years is Enough, dedicated to either dramatically reforming or abolishing the IMF and World Bank; Jubilee 2000, a network founded to abolish third world debt; and People's Global Action, an explicitly anti-capitalist alliance of small Northern radical groups and some of the large Southern grassroots organizations.

The networks that have evolved, at both the national and international levels, have striven for democratic relationships between groups working together. The global justice movement has developed a flexible, inclusive collective identity, with most activists being willing to put aside ideological and other differences to work on concrete projects, emphasizing dialogue over conformity.

There are, however, also a number of tensions around issues of organization and democracy in practice. The participatory democratic character of the new wave of global justice activists does not mesh well with the bureaucratic organization of the older advocacy-oriented non-profits and labor unions, both North and South, leading to difficulties in working across these divides. Differences in power, resulting from both access to resources and location in the world-system, have also produced tensions. Many Southern grassroots groups are dependent on Northern non-profits for part of their funding; these tensions also exist between non-profits and grassroots groups within Northern countries. In some cases, these power differences have resulted in Northern activists launching campaigns without consulting their Southern "beneficiaries," sometimes producing results Southerners find not in their best interests. There have also been issues because of Northerners conveying a different message than their Southern allies would like to TNCs, the IMF, and World Bank, to which the former have more access than the latter. Over time, activists have grown more conscious of the need to take into account these power differences. While they cannot be erased short of a radical transformation of the world economy, more dialogue between Northern and Southern groups has gone some way to addressing these problems, though tensions certainly remain.

It should be noted that despite the growing importance of transnational networks and campaigns, most groups remain locally rooted. They may address domestic issues, framing them in terms of global justice, or they may address international issues by pressuring their national governments to either change their policies or press for reforms in intergovernmental organizations of which they are a part.

SEE ALSO: Anarchism; Direct Action; Environmental Movements; Global Economy; Globalization and Global Justice; Indigenous Movements; Labor Movement; Neoliberalism; Political Opportunities; Social Movements, Participatory Democracy in; Transnational Movements

REFERENCES AND SUGGESTED READINGS

Bandy, J. & Smith, J. (Eds.) (2005) *Coalitions Across Borders*. Rowman & Littlefield, Lanham, MD.

Della Porta, D. & Tarrow, S. (Eds.) (2005) *Transnational Protest and Global Activism*. Rowman & Littlefield, Lanham, MD.

Keck, M. & Sikkink, K. (1998) *Activists Beyond Borders*. Cornell University Press, Ithaca, NY.

Mertes, T. (Ed.) (2004) *A Movement of Movements*. Verso, New York.

Smith, J. (2002) Globalizing Resistance. In: Smith, J. & Johnston, H. (Eds.), *Globalization and Resistance*. Rowman & Littlefield, Lanham, MD, pp. 207–27.

global politics

Lloyd Cox

Global politics refers to patterns of political relations and activities that stretch across state borders, and whose consequences are, potentially and/or actually, worldwide in scope. As such, global politics includes but is not limited to interstate relations, and is not explicable in terms of those approaches conventionally deployed by realist scholars of international relations (IR). The latter have routinely assumed the primacy of sovereign, bounded territorial states, which act in their own national interest in a sharply demarcated "external" political environment defined by zero-sum power equations. Many theorists argue that such views do not accurately reflect the new realities of what some have

referred to as a post-Westphalian or post-international world. In this world, states allegedly have had their capacities eroded, the boundaries separating domestic and foreign policy are increasingly blurred, and the sources of political authority, legitimacy, and governance have multiplied beyond the territorial state. This has created a "democratic deficit" between the nominal sites of political participation (national states) and more remote global sources of political power and decision-making, in turn raising questions about contemporary forms of political community and citizenship. These shifting realities have been prompted by a number of developments encompassed by the term globalization.

While the definition of globalization has been fiercely contested, it can be reasonably understood as the sum of those processes involved in the growth of worldwide interconnectedness and interdependence, where social relations are stretched across existing boundaries and time and space are compressed to an extent that the whole planet becomes an object of human consciousness and action. Although "globe-talk" only really takes off in the 1980s, it is traceable by numerous intellectual threads to earlier intimations of a global political awareness. In 1774, Herder rhetorically asked: "When has the entire earth ever been so closely joined together ...? Who has ever had more power and more machines, such that with a single impulse, with a single movement of a finger, entire nations are shaken?" (cited in Hopkins 2002: 12). Similarly, in the nineteenth century, Marx argued that capitalism is predisposed to expand beyond its geographical point of origin, to "nestle everywhere, settle everywhere, establish connexions everywhere" across the entire planet. For Marx, such globalizing processes are inherently political, and would be further elaborated by the next generation of Marxists in various theories of imperialism (Hilferding, Bukharin; Lenin, Kautsky, and Luxemburg), and later still by dependency and world-systems theorists (Frank, Amin, Wallerstein).

In non-Marxist social science, theories of globalization and global politics were anticipated from the 1960s in both sociology and political science. In a seminal article, Moore (1966) advocated the development of a "global sociology," while Roland Robertson and his various co-authors raised the specter of a global comparative sociology of different paths to and through modernity (Nettle & Robertson 1968). In political science and IR there were similar trends among scholars dissatisfied with the dominant realist paradigm. Modelski's (1972) treatise on world politics was particularly significant in this respect, as it was one of the first works in the social sciences actually to deploy the concept of globalization. This was followed by Falk's (1975) appeal for mainstream political science and IR to take a more "global approach," and Keohane and Nye's (1977) important contribution on "complex interdependence." These and associated analyses were premised on the view that world politics could no longer (if indeed it ever could) be understood exclusively with reference to the interests of competing states within a largely anarchic interstate order, the central claim of realism. This resonated in subsequent analyses of "global governance," "transnational politics," "international regimes," and "global interdependence," which grew in stature in the 1980s and 1990s.

The periodization of political globalization has also been widely debated. Globalization has been variously described as being coterminous with European global expansion from the late fifteenth century, with European imperialism in the late nineteenth century, and with US-led globally integrating economic and technological developments in the post-World War II era. Regardless, most would agree that globalization has accelerated since the early 1970s. The breakdown of the Bretton Woods system of international financial regulation, the global resurgence of economic liberalism, the revolution in communications, the later emergence of global terrorism, and the collapse of the Eastern Bloc and its (and China's) incorporation into the circuits of global capitalism, are all viewed as important manifestations and constituents of globalization. These are trends that have frequently been analyzed through the lens of economic, technological, and cultural convergence, but they also clearly have important political dimensions that lend some substance to the notion of global politics.

One key element of global politics is the growth of "international regimes." An international regime can be defined as "implicit or explicit principles, norms, rules, and decision-making procedures around which actor

expectations converge in a given issue area of international relations" (Krasner 1983: 2). Such regimes find an institutional embodiment in the proliferation of international non-governmental organizations (INGOs) and intergovernmental organizations (IGOs) over the past century. The former increased from around 200 in 1900 to over 5,000 in 1996, while the latter increased from 27 to 260 over the same period (Held et al. 1999: 53). In both cases the largest absolute increases have occurred after 1960, in response to economic, technological, environmental, and security challenges that transcend the capacities of individual states, thus demanding new forms of transnational regulation and cooperation.

These increases have been paralleled by the consolidation and extension of military and trading blocs and other supranational institutions that are widely viewed as being more than the sum of their national parts. The European Union (EU), for example, is now much more than just a trading bloc of member states, but also encompasses a number of suprastate political functions and institutions to which member states agree to cede some hitherto taken-for-granted prerogatives and capacities. While the EU is a "regional" rather than a "global" institution, many would view it as an aspect of the broader globalization of politics, which has the potential to become a bulwark against US global dominance and which also portends similar suprastate arrangements in other parts of the world.

For many globalization theorists these developments signify the extent to which states have become more deeply enmeshed in webs of global political connections and multi-layered governance, based on structures of overlapping authority. This implies a degree of "governance without government." Many of the functions of political coordination and regulation once the preserve of formal governments are now accomplished through more informal mechanisms, and with the participation of NGOs, IGOs (e.g., the IMF and WTO), transnational corporations (TNCs), and global media, which are allegedly beyond the jurisdiction of individual governments. If this is true, it clearly places serious limits on the exercise of democracy, which is still largely organized within the limited horizons of individual national states whose governments are increasingly beholden to informal governance emanating from beyond their borders. This in no way entails the emergence of "world government" – a concept that suggests something far more unitary and directed than the realities of multi-layered governance – though it has had implications for the United Nations (UN) system. In particular, since the early 1990s the UN has played a more interventionist role in policing a liberal democratic model of democracy on the one hand, and asserting a human rights discourse and practice on the other; albeit one that has been very unevenly applied. The former has been accomplished through the UN's involvement in and monitoring of electoral processes in countries as diverse as Nicaragua and Angola, South Africa and Ukraine. The latter has been manifested in a multiplication of UN humanitarian interventions and peacekeeping missions across Africa, Asia, and the Balkans.

The idea of universal human rights that trump the sovereign rights of states to non-interference by other states, and the realization of this idea in practices of humanitarian intervention, is a relatively recent one. Although universal human rights have been encoded in various covenants and protocols of international law since the late 1940s (including the UN Charter and Universal Declaration of Human Rights in 1948, the Convention against Genocide in 1948, the Covenant on Civil and Political Rights in 1966, and the Covenant on Economic, Social, and Cultural Rights in 1966), it has only been since the end of the Cold War that states and coalitions of states have been actively prepared to enforce these principles. Enforcement through armed intervention has only been applied, however, in faltering steps and in very selective cases, with geopolitical calculation and domestic political considerations still being very important in determining when human rights do and do not get defended. This has led many scholars to question the assumption that humanitarian intervention represents the opening up of a post-Westphalian global political order where states are answerable to powers and principles beyond their borders. This draws into sharp relief what is perhaps the key debate surrounding global politics; namely, whether or not states are still the central actors of global politics and, therefore, whether or not a

post-Westphalian, post-international political universe has in fact emerged.

Scholars who argue that such a new global political universe now exists typically emphasize four related points: (1) that state capacities and *de facto* sovereignty have been compromised in various ways by the globalization of economic, political, and cultural processes; (2) that national borders are increasingly porous with respect to the movement of information, commodities, and people, which contributes to point (1) above and problematizes the clear demarcation of domestic and foreign politics; (3) that politics has been partially "deterritorialized" as a result of points (1) and (2); and (4) that taken together, (1), (2), and (3) represent a qualitative break from the state-centric, international world order that is assumed to have characterized world politics for the 300 or so years following the Peace of Westphalia (1648). The latter concluded the Thirty Years War in Europe and is often taken to have initiated the modern era of state sovereignty, with its presumptions of absolute and indivisible territorial authority, and rights to non-interference by external actors. Mutual recognition of these sovereignty rights is said to have regulated conduct between states and been the central ordering principle of the Westphalian system, which has now been transcended by the globalization of politics.

Many critics dispute these claims, and reject the whole idea of a post-international, global political environment. They point out that so-called Westphalian sovereignty was always more of a normative ideal than it was a political reality, with states throughout the "Westphalian period" frequently having their claims to absolute authority constrained and subverted by other states and non-state actors. Furthermore, the suggestion that state capacities have been uniformly eroded neglects the massive power discrepancies between different states, and glosses over the strengthening of some state capacities (the policing of immigration) even as others are eroded (the capacity to determine some aspects of economic policy autonomously). The US's recent shift to political unilateralism is held up as proof of the fundamental era of deprecating state powers. Finally, the idea that there has been a deterritorialization of politics is said to be out of step with both the past (where clearly not all political phenomena could be explained with reference to relations between territorial states) and with the present (where politics still has a demonstrable territorial dimension, as reflected in the continued salience of territorialized nationalist conflicts). In this view, global politics is, and will always remain, filtered through the prism of national institutions.

More recently, synthetic contributions to the globalization debate have emerged that try to transcend the stark dichotomies outlined above. These scholars focus on the contradictions inherent in global politics, between simultaneous tendencies towards integration and fragmentation, universalism and particularism, which exhibit both continuities and discontinuities with the past. In this view, states and interstate politics remain crucial, but are now overdetermined by other global actors and processes.

SEE ALSO: Citizenship; Empire; Globalization; Nation-State and Nationalism; Political Sociology; Politics; Postnationalism; Sovereignty

REFERENCES AND SUGGESTED READINGS

Falk, R. (1975) *A Global Approach to National Policy*. Harvard University Press, Cambridge, MA.

Ferguson, Y. H. & Mansbach, R. W. (2004) *Remapping Global Politics: History's Revenge and Future Shock*. Cambridge University Press, Cambridge.

Held, D., McGrew, A., Goldblatt, D., & Perraton, J. (1999) *Global Transformations: Politics, Economics and Culture*. Polity Press, Cambridge.

Hopkins, A. G. (Ed.) (2002) *Globalization in World History*. Pimlico, London.

Keohane, R. O. & Nye, J. (1977) *Power and Interdependence*. Little Brown, Boston.

Krasner, S. (1983) *International Regimes*. Cornell University Press, Ithaca, NY.

Modelski, G. (1972) *Principles of World Politics*. Free Press, New York.

Moore, W. (1966) Global Sociology: The World as a Singular System. *American Journal of Sociology* 71(5): 475–82.

Nederveen Pieterse, J. (2004) *Globalization or Empire?* Routledge, New York.

Nettle, J. & Robertson, R. (1968) *International Systems and the Modernization of Societies*. Faber, London.

Rosenau, J. (1997) *Along the Domestic–Foreign Frontier*. Cambridge University Press, Cambridge.

Rosenberg, J. (2000) *The Follies of Globalization Theory*. Verso, London.

global/world cities

Jamie Paquin

"Global city" discourse posits and investigates the emergence of a small number of cities occupying commanding roles in a globalizing economic system. The emergence of global cities signals the shift in the organization of capital accumulation and economic production since the late 1970s and a corresponding shift in the nodal functions of some cities away from local, regional, or national contexts to more varied and uneven connections to other cities and regions in the world. Specifically, the designation "global city" is applied to those urban areas consisting of a disproportionate number of major economic headquarters and services, including corporate management, banking, finance, legal services, accounting, technical consulting, telecommunications, computing, international transportation, research, and higher education (Friedmann & Wolff 1982: 320). To the extent to which the hypotheses of this literature withstand scrutiny, numerous questions arise regarding the social implications of a greater disjuncture between proximity and connectedness in urban life.

Though the concept of world cities in the recent and distant past is not entirely new (Geddes 1924; Hall 1966), it was Friedmann (1986; see also Friedmann & Wolff 1982) who first made a direct link between contemporary "global forces" and "urban processes" in his "world city hypothesis" essay. Elsewhere, Sassen (1994, 2001) provides key empirical data corroborating some of the assertions made about an emergent system of global cities as sites of concentrated global economic activity. This conceptualization of a global city problematic is essentially economic, as the designation of "world" or "global" city is applied to those cities which become central to the accumulation, control, and deployment of international capital and whose morphologies are transformed by the needs of global capital. Yet, as we can see, this perspective leads to the view that despite their "command and control" functions, global cities are not really "in control" as they are themselves shaped and produced in relation to the interests and demands of external economic forces.

The result of the emergent urban order is then greater difference not only between cities but within them as well, meaning that a world of global cities is both hierarchical and polarized, for even within the "truly" global cities there is a growing divergence in incomes and rights to the city (Friedmann 1986; Knox & Taylor 1995; Marcuse & van Kempen 2001; Sassen 1994, 2001). This polarization stems directly from their articulating role in the global economy, for by serving as the base for global industries and institutions, an "elite" professional class who are "well-educated, socially mobile, footloose and cosmopolitan in origin and outlook" (Clark 1996: 139) become a key driving force in the formation of a corresponding economy of low-waged and low-skilled employment. Sassen's work (1994, 1996, 2001; see also Mellenkopf & Castells 1991) investigates in great depth this polarization, finding that in the cases of London, Tokyo, and New York the growth in elite professions and services creates the need "for a vast army of low-skilled workers" (Sassen 1996), embodied by legal and non-legal immigration flows and those displaced by the decline of manufacturing employment resulting from global restructuring.

Novel forms of concentration and dispersal also bring forth new uses and functions of urban space. For those cities capable of attracting the premier command and control functions, high-tech business districts, convention centers, international airports, and other transportation linkages become crucial components of their infrastructures, while for lower-tier cities – places hollowed out by the migration of manufacturing with little chance of becoming preeminent global cities – the strategy of economic survival is often to cultivate spaces and economies geared toward "culture" and consumption. Some cities like Manchester have been relatively successful in their efforts to rebound from the loss of traditional industries through such initiatives, while other large-scale

revitalization schemes have failed to attract the desired capital, consumers, and jobs. Moreover, with the shift toward consumption activities, which often occur in older urban areas, already marginalized populations have sometimes been negatively affected, either because they are pushed from "revitalized" areas through gentrification, or more directly because they become subject to increased surveillance and policing aimed at making these spaces "safe" and desirable. Thus, to the extent to which spaces such as business and trade centers, airports, high-tech zones, and even revitalized historical districts of contemporary cities exist as the result of responses to changes in the relationship between proximity and connectedness in an age of globalization, they signal a novel development in the history of urban spaces and the meaning of place.

The global cities literature enriches the globalization debates by perusing and interpreting its spatial causes, manifestations, and requirements. In placing emphasis on urban dynamics and spaces as both the bearers and generators of economic globalization it also brings important scrutiny to the longstanding state-centrism of social science, which typically assumes and constitutes national entities with little consideration to the greater specificity of cultural, economic, and political activities and connections. Finally, the global cities literature raises crucial questions regarding the implications of these transformations both between and within cities, drawing attention to the potential for increased social and economic polarization and eroded political capacities associated with transnational economic restructuring. Such changes leave observers such as Sassen (1996) rightly asking, "whose city is it?"

However, global cities discourse and research suffers from significant evidentiary and conceptual limitations. Many critics have called attention to the empirical weakness – or what Short et al. (1999) call the "dirty little secret" of world cities research, since both the criteria for assessment and measurement are inconsistent and questionable (Taylor 2004). Additionally, some studies have found that for some cities, polarization is not necessarily accompanying globalization, and even where it has occurred, local and national policies may be as significant as global forces in intensifying income and other inequalities. The biggest weakness of this literature, however, is the economic reductionism and determinism underlying the conceptualization and investigation of the global city. Finding certain cities to be disproportionately central in the articulation of global economic activity may provide important insight into some global processes and their implications, but given that concentration is not that new – think of London, Paris, or New York as colonial centers – what stands to be gained by this approach to investigating the relationship between globalization and the city? Secondly, what contribution can such a literature make to the broader sociological problematic of the life-world of cities in an age of globalization?

One way to address these shortcomings is to expand inquiry into the global city beyond economic questions through more culturally attuned research which investigates the multiple ways in which global flows are affecting the composition and texture of everyday urban life and subjectivity (cf. Appadurai 1996). Smith's (2001) reconceptualization of the global city problematic as a matter of transnational urbanism is an important contribution in this regard, as it highlights the fact that the designation of global (with its connotation of homogeneity) is less accurate than a language of transnationality or translocality when dealing with the extra-local forces shaping contemporary urban life. In transnational urbanism we have then a more particular yet expanded conceptualization of the city in a context of globalization which emphasizes the numerous and diverse networks and flows of people, objects, information, capital, remittances, and media which are major dimensions of place and cultural formation of a global character, regardless of their status in the world cities hierarchy. From this approach, then, many cities will appear uniquely and deeply "global(izing)" despite their peripheral significance to the articulation of global capital. For example, despite Tokyo's global economic preeminence, it lacks the ethnic diversity of a city like Toronto, which although much lower in the "world city" hierarchy, is one of the most demographically diverse cities in world history, and a place where the collective cultural imaginary is heavily attuned to this diversity as a part of living in a global age. Cities like Toronto are thus places where "globalized" cultural forms are being worked out, and as such, they can be viewed as thoroughly "worldly," if not "global" – a designation just as sociologically significant as the emergence of a small number of "global" cities responsible for the command and control of global economic activity. By adopting an expanded conceptual framework then, we will discover that cities globalize in a variety of ways related to the particular forms of linkages and flows they are both constituted by and generate.

Despite the conceptual and empirical limits of global cities research, the attention it brings to the spatial dimensions of globalization constitutes a fundamental contribution to the study of both globalization and contemporary urbanism, as it enables the apprehension of actual global processes as they operate through and produce spaces and places in conjunction with actual social actors and institutions. And by expanding the conceptualization of the global city to include cultural and political questions in the context of everyday urban life, the global cities perspective can become an especially powerful approach to the study and delineation of globalization as a complex, variable, and spatially manifest phenomenon.

SEE ALSO: Chicago School; Ethnic Enclaves; Inequality and the City; Mumford, Lewis; Primate Cities; Spatial Relationships; Transnationalism; Urban; Urban Space; Urbanism/ Urban Culture

REFERENCES AND SUGGESTED READINGS

Appadurai, A. (1996) *Modernity at Large*. University of Minnesota Press, Minneapolis.

Clark, D. (1996) *Urban World/Global City*. Routledge, London.

Friedmann, J. (1986) The World City Hypothesis. *Development and Change* 17: 69–83.

Friedmann, J. & Wolff, G. (1982) World City Formation: An Agenda for Research and Action. *International Journal of Urban and Regional Research* 3: 309–44.

Geddes, P. (1924) A World League of Cities. *Sociological Review* 26: 166–7.

Hall, P. G. (1966) *The World Cities*. Heinemann, London.

Knox, P. L. & Taylor, P. J. (Eds.) (1995) *World Cities in a World-System*. Cambridge University Press, Cambridge.

Marcuse, P. & van Kempen, R. (Eds.) (2001) *Globalizing Cities: A New Spatial Order?* Blackwell, Oxford.

Mellenkopf, J. & Castells, M. (Eds.) (1991) *Dual City: The Restructuring of New York*. Sage, London.

Sassen, S. (1994) *Cities in a World Economy*. Pine Forge Press, Thousand Oaks, CA.

Sassen, S. (1996) Whose City Is It? Globalization and the Formation of New Claims. *Public Culture* 8: 205–23.

Sassen, S. (2001) *The Global City*, 2nd edn. Princeton University Press, Princeton.

Short, et al. (1999) The Dirty Little Secret of World Cities Research. *International Journal of Urban and Regional Research* 20: 697–717.

Smith, M. P. (2001) *Transnational Urbanism: Locating Globalization*. Blackwell, Oxford.

Taylor, P. J. (2004) *World City Network: A Global Urban Analysis*. Routledge, London.

globalization

Larry Ray

Globalization has become one of the central but contested concepts of contemporary social science. The term has further entered everyday commentary and analysis and features in many political, cultural, and economic debates. The globalized world order originates in the international organizations and regulatory systems set up after World War II – including the United Nations, General Agreement on Tariffs and Trade (now the World Trade Organization), the International Monetary Fund, and the World Bank. However, the end of the Cold War was the prelude to the maturity of the concept of globalization, since after 1989, it was possible at least to imagine a "borderless" world in which people, goods, ideas, and images would flow with relative ease and *the* major global division between East and West had gone. A world divided by competing ideologies of capitalism and state socialism gave way to a more uncertain world in which capitalism became the dominant economic and social system. Coinciding with these changes, a major impetus to globalization was the development and availability of digital communication technologies from the late 1980s with dramatic consequences for the way economic and personal behavior were conducted. The collapse of communism and growth of digital technologies further coincided with a global restructuring of the state, finance, production, and consumption associated with neoliberalism.

There are many views on the nature and impact of globalization, which is not a single process. Economic globalization refers to such things as the global dominance of transnational corporations, global finance, flexible production and assembly, and the rise of information and service economies. Political globalization can be understood in terms of the growth of international organizations, subnational regional autonomy, the spread of post-welfare public policies, and global social movements. Further, globalization possibly weakens the effectiveness and cohesion of the nation-state as its traditional functions are "hollowed out" – transferred "upwards" to international organizations and "downwards" to regional bodies. Again globalization is a cultural process, indicated by the growth of global consumption cultures, tourism, media and information flows, and transnational migration and identities. The latter half of the twentieth century saw the growth of global brands and media that carry both cultural and economic significance. A globalized world is one of increasing instantaneity, where events are experienced instantly even by people in spatially distant locations through access to digital communicative technologies. This creates a complex range of social interconnections governed by the speed of communications, thereby creating a partial collapse of boundaries within national, cultural, and political space. However, the meaning and significance of globalization remains far from clear. Some are optimistic (e.g., Friedman 2000), but some are more pessimistic and critical about globalization's consequences (e.g., Falk 1999). Urry (2003) and Giddens (1999) regard globalization as an emergent process with effects in its own right, although this view is rejected by Rosenberg (2000), for whom it is the *effect* of a complex combination of social, economic, cultural, and political changes such as internationalization, imperialism, the "weightless economy," post-Fordism, and neoliberalism. It might appear as though global western media create a homogeneous world culture dominated by global brands and TV networks. But at the same time they create increased heterogeneity between globalization winners and losers, global cities and surrounding locales, and eclectic hybrids of local and global cultures.

Globalization is a spatial process that has facilitated the emergence of a new kind of global city based on highly specialized service economies that serve specific, particularized functions in the global economic system at the expense of former logics of organization tied to manufacturing-based economies. To enable global markets to function effectively, they need to be underpinned by specialized managerial work that is concentrated in cities. Further, privatization and deregulation during the 1980s and 1990s shifted various governance functions to the corporate world, again centralizing these activities in urban centers. In post-industrial cities there is a concentration of command functions that serve as production sites for finance and the other leading industries, and provide marketplaces where firms and governments can buy financial instruments and services. Global cities become strategic sites for the acceleration of capital and information flows, and at the same time spaces of increasing socioeconomic polarization. One effect of this has been that such cities have gained in importance and power relative to nation-states. There have emerged new "corridors" and zones around nodal cities with increasingly relative independence from surrounding areas. Networks of global cities densely connected by air have also emerged (Sassen 1996).

There is a wide range of social theories of globalization. Robertson was one of the first sociologists to theorize globalization and central to his approach is the concept of "global consciousness," which refers to "the compression of the world and the intensification of consciousness of the world as a whole" (1992: 8). Through thought and action, global consciousness makes the world a single place. What it means to live in this place, and how it must be ordered, become universal questions. These questions receive different answers from individuals and societies that define their position in relation to both a system of societies and the

shared properties of humankind from very different perspectives. This confrontation of worldviews means that globalization involves "comparative interaction of different forms of life" (1992: 27). Unlike theorists who identify globalization with late (capitalist) modernity, Robertson sees global interdependence and consciousness preceding the advent of capitalist modernity. However, European expansion and state formation have boosted globalization since the seventeenth century and the contemporary shape of the world owes most to the "takeoff" decades after about 1875, when international communications, transportation, and conflict dramatically intensified relationships across societal boundaries. In that period, the main reference points of fully globalized order took shape: nation-state, individual self, world-system, societies, and one humanity. These elements of the global situation became "relativized" since national societies and individuals, in particular, must interpret their very existence as parts of a larger whole. To some extent, a common framework has guided that interpretive work; for example, states can appeal to a universal doctrine of nationalism to legitimate their particularizing claims to sovereignty and cultural distinction. But such limited common principles do not provide a basis for world order.

By the end of the twentieth century, if not before, globalization had transformed the way people saw themselves in the world. Everyone must now reflexively respond to the common predicament of living in one world. This provokes the formulation of contending worldviews. For example, some portray the world as an assembly of distinct communities, highlighting the virtues of particularism, while others view it as developing toward a single overarching organization, representing the presumed interests of humanity as a whole. In a compressed world, the comparison and confrontation of worldviews are bound to produce new cultural conflict. In such conflict, religious traditions play a special role, since they can be mobilized to provide an ultimate justification for one's view of the world – a case in point being the resurgence of "fundamentalist" groups that combine traditionalism with a global agenda. A globalized world is thus integrated but not harmonious, a single place but also diverse, a construct of shared consciousness but prone to fragmentation.

For Anthony Giddens the concept of time-space distantiation is central. This is a process in which locales are shaped by events far away and vice versa, while social relations are disembedded, or "lifted out" from locales. For example, peasant households in traditional societies largely produced their own means of subsistence, a tithe was often paid in kind (goods, animals, or labor), money was of limited value, and economic exchange was local and particularistic. Modernization replaced local exchange with universal exchange of money, which simplifies otherwise impossibly complex transitions and enables the circulation of highly complex forms of information and value in increasingly abstract and symbolic forms. The exchange of money establishes social relations across time and space, which under globalization is speeded up. Similarly, expert cultures arise as a result of the scientific revolutions, which bring an increase in technical knowledge and specialization. Specialists claim "universal" and scientific forms of knowledge, which enable the establishment of social relations across vast expanses of time and space. Social distance is created between professionals and their clients as in the modern medical model, which is based upon the universal claims of science. As expert knowledge dominates across the globe, local perspectives become devalued and modern societies are reliant on expert systems. Trust is increasingly the key to the relationship between the individual and expert systems and is the "glue" that holds modern societies together. But where trust is undermined, individuals experience ontological insecurity and a sense of insecurity with regard to their social reality.

Ohmae's (2005) concept of a "borderless world" epitomizes enthusiasm and the belief that globalization brings improvement in human conditions. Ohmae describes an "invisible continent" – a moving, unbounded world in which the primary linkages are now less between nations than between regions that are able to operate effectively in a global economy without being closely networked with host regions. The invisible continent can be dated to 1985 when Microsoft released Windows 1.0, CNN was launched, Cisco Systems began, the

first Gateway 2000 computers were shipped, and companies like Sun Microsystems and Dell were in their infancies. Back then, the economic outlook was gloomy and few saw this embryonic continent forming. Now, of course, it affects virtually every business. Transnational corporations increasingly do not treat countries as single entities and region states make effective points of entry into the global economy. For example, when Nestlé moved into Japan, it chose the Kansai region round Osaka and Kobe rather than Tokyo as a regional doorway. This fluidity of capital is creating a borderless world in which capital moves around, chasing the best products and the highest investment returns regardless of national origin. The cyberworld has changed not only the way business works but also the way we interact on a personal level – from buying and selling online to planning for retirement, managing investment and bank accounts. Decisions made on the invisible continent (the "platforms" that are created by businesses rather than governments) determine how money moves around the globe.

Giddens (1999) is less unambiguously enthusiastic about globalization than Ohmae and describes it as a "runaway world" which "is not – at least at the moment – a global order driven by collective human will. Instead, it is emerging in an anarchic, haphazard fashion, carried along by a mixture of economic, technological and cultural imperatives." The global order is the result of an intersection of four processes – capitalism (economic logic), the interstate system (world order), militarism (world security and threats), and industrialism (the division of labor and lifestyles). However, Giddens does not say what the weight of each of these factors is and whether they change historically.

Similarly, David Harvey emphasizes the ways in which globalization revolutionizes the qualities of space and time. As space appears to shrink to a "global village" of telecommunications and ecological interdependencies and as time horizons shorten to the point where the present is all there is, so we have to learn how to cope with an overwhelming sense of *compression* of our spatial and temporal worlds (1990: 240–2). Time-space compression that "annihilates" space and creates "timeless time" is driven by flexible accumulation and new technologies, the production of signs and images, just-in-time delivery, reduced turnover times and speeding up, and both de- and reskilling. Harvey points for support to the ephemerality of fashions, products, production techniques, speedup and vertical disintegration, financial markets and computerized trading, instantaneity and disposability, regional competitiveness. For Harvey, flexibilized computer-based production in Silicon Valley or the "Third Italy" epitomizes these changes.

John Urry argues that the changes associated with globalization are so far-reaching that we should now talk of a "sociology beyond societies." This position is informed by the alleged decline of the nation-state in a globalized world, which has led to wider questioning of the idea of "society" as a territorially bounded entity. This in turn prepares the ground for claims to the effect that since "society" was a core sociological concept, the very foundations of the discipline have likewise been undermined. The central concepts of the new socialities are space (social topologies), regions (interregional competition), networks (new social morphology), and fluids (global enterprises). Mobility is central to this thesis since globalization is the complex movement of people, images, goods, finances, and so on that constitutes a process across regions in faster and unpredictable shapes, all with no clear point of arrival or departure.

Despite the contrasting theoretical understandings of globalization, there is some measure of agreement that it creates new opportunities or threats. For example, globalization offers new forms of cosmopolitanism and economic growth but also new threats and global risks such as ecological crisis, global pandemics, and international crime and terrorism. Globalization may be seen as encroachment and colonization as global corporations and technologies erode local customs and ways of life, which in turn engenders new forms of protest and assertion of local cultural identity. Enthusiasts argue that the effects are positive and that integration into the global economy increases economic activity and raises living standards. Legrain, for example, claims that in 2000 the per capita income of citizens was four times greater than that in 1950. Between 1870 and 1979, production per worker became 26 times greater in Japan and 22 times greater in Sweden. In the whole world in 2000 it was double what it was in 1962. Even more significantly, he argues that those countries isolated from the global capitalist economy have done less well than those that have engaged with it. Poor countries that are open to international trade grew over six times faster in the 1970s and 1980s than those that shut themselves off from it: 4.5 percent a year, rather than 0.7 percent. He claims that cross-national data indicate how openness to international trade helps the poor by a magnitude roughly equal to each percentage increase in GDP (Legrain 2002: 49–52). By contrast, it can be argued that global patterns of inequality have become increasingly polarized. According to UN data, the richest 20 percent in the world "own" 80 percent of the wealth; the second 20 percent own 10 percent; the third 20 percent own 6 percent; the fourth 20 percent own 3 percent; and the poorest 20 percent own only 1 percent. Throughout the world, 2.7 billion people live on less than $2 per day. These global inequalities predate globalization, of course, but there are global processes that are maintaining a highly unequal social system (Akyuz et al. 2002).

Contradictions in the global economy are illustrated in other ways too. Liberalization and globalization of capital may not have driven costs down in developed countries where few workers are prepared to tolerate the conditions this new model creates. Flexible global ordering systems need not just produce flexible labor, but flexible labor in excess, because to manage the supply of labor it is necessary to have a surplus. Migrants, many of whom are drawn into the North by collapsing agricultural prices at home, have met this need. But in the wake of hostility manifest in many developed countries, especially following threats of terrorist attack, migrants face tightening border controls and deportation of those who are not in areas where there is a shortage of skills.

Globalization has been the focus of extensive social movement activism and resistance, especially to neoliberal globalism represented by bodies such as the WTO. Glasius et al. (2002) identify the emergence of a "global civil society" in, for example, the growth of "parallel summits" such as the 2001 Porto Alegre meeting in Brazil attended by 11,000 people to protest against the Davos (Switzerland) World Economic Forum. These are organized through multiple networks of social actors and NGOs operating on local and international levels. There may appear to be an irony that many of the internationally organized or linked movements use globalized forms of communication (notably the Internet) and operate transnationally, mobilizing a global consciousness and solidarities. However, many activists are not necessarily opposed to globalization as such but to economic neoliberal globalization and a corporatist agenda that is intent on constricting individual freedom and local lifestyles in the name of profit. Some further claim that globalization is a new form of imperialism imposing western (especially US) political and economic dominance over the rest of the world. For anti-globalization critics, international bodies such as the World Bank and IMF are not accountable to the populations on whom their actions have most effects – for example, when loans are made conditional on structural adjustment and privatization of public facilities such as health, water, and education. Activists also point out that globalization creates a "borderless" world for capital and finance but not for labor, since strict and increasingly severe immigration controls exist in most developed countries while labor lacks basic rights in many developing countries. The movement (if something so diverse can be called a "movement") is very broad, including church groups, nationalist parties, leftist parties, environmentalists, peasant unions, anti-racism groups, anarchists, some charities, and others. If we take a broad view of globalization, though, these movements are themselves part of the process by which global solidarities (albeit rather weak and transitory ones) come to be formed.

SEE ALSO: Global Economy; Global Justice as a Social Movement; Global Politics; Global/World Cities; Globalization, Consumption and; Globalization, Culture and; Globalization, Education and; Globalization and Global Justice; Globalization, Religion and; Globalization, Sexuality and; Globalization, Sport and; Glocalization; Grobalization; Neoliberalism

REFERENCES AND SUGGESTED READINGS

Akyuz, Y., Flassbeck, H., & Kozul-Wright, R. (2002) *Globalization, Inequality, and the Labour Market.* UNCTAD, Geneva. Online. www.flassbeck.de/pdf/GLOBALIZ.PDF.

Falk, R. (1999) *Predatory Globalization: A Critique.* Polity Press, Cambridge.

Friedman, T. (2000) *The Lexus and the Olive Tree.* Anchor Books, New York.

Giddens, A. (1999) *Runaway World.* Polity Press, Cambridge.

Glasius, M., Kaldor, M., & Anheier, H. (Eds.) (2002) *Global Civil Society 2002.* Oxford University Press, Oxford.

Harvey, D. (1990) *The Condition of Postmodernity.* Blackwell, Oxford.

Legrain, P. (2002) *Open World: The Truth About Globalization.* Abacus, London.

Ohmae, K. (2005) *The Next Global Stage: Challenges and Opportunities in our Borderless World.* Warton School Publishing, Philadelphia.

Robertson, R. (1992) *Globalization.* Sage, London.

Rosenberg, R. (2000) *Follies of Globalization Theory.* Verso, London.

Sassen, S. (1996) Cities and Communities in the Global Economy: Rethinking Our Concepts. *American Behavioral Scientist* 39(5): 629–39.

Urry, J. (2003) *Global Complexity.* Polity Press, Cambridge.

globalization, consumption and

Beryl Langer

The terms globalization and consumption combine with reference to the emergence of a global consumer culture: the same products, services, and entertainment sold in the same kinds of retail and leisure spaces (malls, plazas, theme parks, cineplexes) to consumers around the world. From luxury cars and designer clothes to jeans, t-shirts, toys, snack food, and bottled water, markets are global rather than national. The same electronic equipment, cosmetics, children's toys, and grocery lines are consumed in cities as remote from each other as Sydney and Stockholm, Bahrain and Birmingham. Product availability is less tied to specific places, first because the same global brands are on sale at the same time throughout the world and second because traders catering to deterritorialized immigrants recreate the retail environment of their homeland by importing familiar products. Starbucks, McDonald's, Pizza Hut, and Kentucky Fried Chicken are everywhere – as are family-run restaurants selling "ethnic" food to customers in search of either the taste of "home" or the exotic. It is no longer necessary to go to Paris and Milan to buy Dior and Armani, the US to get a baseball cap, India to get a sari, or the Middle East and Southeast Asia for hijabs and burkhas. All are on sale in cities around the world, although the different circumstances of their circulation serve to remind us that globalization is not one process, but many.

Globalization and consumption emerged as key concepts in social theory in the last decades of the twentieth century. Developments in electronics and information communication technology took what the geographer David Harvey calls "time-space compression" to new levels, accelerating the flow of information, money, people, and goods across national borders to create a world market with a global division of labor and global consumers. Relocation of production in "newly industrializing countries" where labor was cheaper and less regulated turned subsistence farmers into urban workers (a process begun in England 200 years earlier), bringing new cohorts of consumers into the market and the global cultural economy. Human societies no longer can be understood in terms of bounded cultures within nation-states. Social identities are increasingly defined and expressed through consumption and lifestyle rather than work and class position.

Both terms are subject to conceptual, substantive, and evaluative debate. Globalization has been problematized in relation to its history, the extent to which its processes are separable from the activities of nation-states, and whether its consequences are positive or negative. Debate on consumption has centered on a number of key issues: the continuing relevance of class as a basis for understanding social relations, whether consumer capitalism as a social

form represents an advance in freedom or a shift in the locus of exploitation, and whether the collective rights and responsibilities of citizenship have been replaced by diminished notions of consumer sovereignty based on individual choice and capacity to pay. At the intersection of these contested areas, questions focus on the implications of the global cultural economy for the survival of local cultures and national identities, the political economy of the global division of labor involved in its production, and its social and environmental consequences.

The question of what, if anything, distinguishes "global consumption" from the consumption of goods and culture distributed across borders by traders and invaders throughout human history is part of a broader debate about the status of globalization as a concept. Critics like Hirst and Thompson (1996) argue that neither the flows of trade, capital investment, and labor migration, nor the impact of new technology between 1950 and 2000, are remarkable when compared to the period between 1850 and 1914. On the other hand, proponents of the globalization thesis such as Castells (1994), Giddens (1999), and Held (1999) argue that the intensification of patterns of interconnectedness mediated by new information technology justifies the conceptualization of the contemporary global system as distinctive – a "global economy" that "works as a unit in real time on a planetary scale" (Castells 1994: 21).

From a Marxist perspective, the globalization of consumption is part of the systemic logic of capitalism, which can only sustain profits through continuous growth. While Marx's predictions of intensifying class struggle did not anticipate the capacity of capitalist mass production to offer workers consumer durables instead of "immiseration," his observation that "the need of a constantly expanding market for its products chases the bourgeoisie over the whole surface of the globe" proved remarkably prescient. Marx's view that the globalization of consumer markets was a logical outcome of capitalism finds contemporary expression in the work of Immanuel Wallerstein and his followers in "world-systems theory," who argue that the processes to which the term globalization refers are not new, but have existed for the

500-year "life cycle of the capitalist world-economy" (Wallerstein 1974).

From the "figurational perspective" of Norbert Elias and his followers, globalization and consumption are understood in terms of an even longer trajectory of human development involving population growth and geographic expansion from the earliest "survival units" of human society. According to this view, the economic processes of production and consumption theorized by Marx tell only one half of the story, in that the movement of goods and people across geographical space is also dependent on physical security – protection from pirates and brigands. Expansion of networks linking producers to consumers therefore required both faster transport and the monopolization of violence by states to secure trade routes. Norbert Elias's early work on "the civilizing process" in Western Europe is thus seen as documenting "the middle part of the long-term story of globalization and its antecedents in one region of the world" (Mennell 1990: 360), and his later work as extending this story back to the role of "survival units" in human prehistory and forwards to the dynamics of nuclear power between global superpowers in the second half of the twentieth century. The interdependence of global consumption and the monopolization of the means of violence can be demonstrated in relation to both "legal" and "illegal" commodities. Global consumption, whether of oil or heroin, depends on securing the sites of production and networks of distribution through the exercise of violence, whether by states or drug cartels.

Globalization of consumption is often equated with Americanization, an argument reinforced by the number of prominent global brands with corporate headquarters in the US, including Coca-Cola, Disney, Levi's, McDonald's, Nike, Microsoft, and Starbucks. Coca-Cola is in that sense iconic, with the term "Coca-Colanization" used to signify economic and cultural domination by the US (Wagnleitner 1994). So, too, McDonald's, its golden arches metonyms of American culture and its restaurants regular targets for anti-American protest (Ritzer 2004a). From this perspective, "global culture" is in fact "American culture" and its consumers are "Coca-colonials." Critics of this view point out

that the sources of global culture are not all American, arguing that Ikea furniture, Indian ("Bollywood") movies and food, Japanese animation, electronics, and sushi – not to mention the global audience for soccer, a sport in which the US is an inconsequential player – all point to more complex processes of global cultural flow.

Equating the globalization of consumption with Americanization is a variant of the claim that globalization of consumption eliminates cultural diversity, leading inexorably to a homogeneous world in which everyone everywhere is the same. Against this, however, are two kinds of arguments. The first focuses on the culturally specific ways in which global products are consumed, and the different meanings attached to global products in different cultural contexts. Ethnographic studies of McDonald's restaurants in East Asia, for example, suggest that while the popularity of McDonald's has had an impact on local eating habits, particularly among the young, local customs have equally affected McDonald's by rejecting the "fast food" ethos and using McDonald's restaurants as places to "hang out," effectively turning them into leisure centers and youth clubs (Watson 1997).

The fact that people consume global products does not tell us what this consumption means to them. For example, Daniel Miller's account of what drinking Coca-Cola means in Trinidad suggests that the global product is appropriated into local culture and meaning, becoming "Trinidadian" rather than American – hence the title of his essay, "Coca-Cola: A Black Sweet Drink from Trinidad" (Miller 1998). According to Hannerz (1996; Hannerz & Lofgren 1994), global culture is always consumed locally, resulting not in homogenization but in what he calls a "global ecumene" produced through the intersection of global and local in four social and organizational settings: the state, the market, social movements, and the form of life. What is available for consumption in the market is just one factor in a complex cultural process involving the appropriation of global products into different "habitats of meaning" – as, for example, when anti-American activists drink Coca-Cola or wear Levi's while expressing hostility towards "US imperialism."

The assumption that globalization of consumption leads to homogenization is also called into question by Arjun Appadurai's (1990) conceptualization of the global cultural economy as a "complex, overlapping, disjunctive order" that can no longer be understood in terms of center–periphery models. Globalization is not one process but many, not just the circulation of global products and media but of people who recreate "deterritorialized" versions of diverse homeland cultures in countries of immigration. "Global consumption" is as much a matter of buying a sari from an Indian shop in Chicago or Birmingham as of buying Levi's in Mumbai or Delhi, watching "Filipino television" in Los Angeles as watching Disney-Asia in Manila.

Globalization has contradictory implications for consumption. On the one hand, the global flow of commodities undermines the viability of "local" products and contributes to the sense that cultural difference is being submerged beneath a global uniform of jeans, t-shirts, sneakers, and baseball caps, a nutritional regime of American fast-food, and a cultural diet of CNN, MTV, and Disney. On the other hand, the global flow of people circulates cultural difference; diasporic groups create deterritorialized versions of "homeland" culture in restaurants and stores that serve two markets – one hungering for the familiar, the other for the exotic. Global tourism is similarly contradictory – packaged holidays and hotel chains that insulate travelers from different cultures, Lonely Planet Guides for those in search of authentic alterity. Global consumption is the spread of McDonald's and Disney to Asia, but it is also the availability of Thai curry paste and Hong Kong action movies in Sydney and Seattle. Such examples suggest *interplay* between the world market and cultural identity, between consumption and cultural strategies, rather than a one-way process of cultural homogenization, which inevitably and inexorably renders us all the same (Appadurai 1990; Friedman 1990, 1995; Kahn 1995).

The idea that consuming global products involves interplay between global and local rather than cultural homogenization gives rise to the terms "glocal" and "glocalization" (Robertson 1995) to describe what happens when consumers incorporate global culture into local practice and meaning to produce culture that is neither fully global nor strictly local. By implication, globalization of consumption increases cultural diversity, adding "glocal" hybrids to the existing pool of local cultures. A less optimistic view would see "glocal" cultures as replacing rather than coexisting with "local" cultures, with the balance between global and local shifting inexorably in favor of the global as what's left of the local in "glocal" decreases over time. Ritzer (2004b) has coined the term "grobalization" for this process – an interplay between "grobal" and "glocal" which leaches hybrid forms of locally specific content ("something") and offers global consumers an ever-expanding universe of centrally conceived and controlled products that lack distinctive content or character ("nothing").

Global consumption raises questions of social justice and environmental sustainability that might be seen as more important than those of cultural diversity, although the three are inextricably linked. "Consumer culture" is not just hamburgers and Hollywood, but what Raymond Williams called "a whole way of life." To what extent is this way of life sustainable, and what are the consequences of extending its consumption patterns and expectations to all corners of the globe? Can the desire of people in newly industrializing countries for the comforts and conveniences taken for granted in the North – cars, air conditioners, refrigerators, and washing machines – be met without rendering the planet even less habitable? Writing in 1905, in *The Protestant Ethic and the Spirit of Capitalism*, Max Weber observed that the "tremendous cosmos of the modern economic order" in which material goods had "inexorable power" over people's lives had an inescapable logic, which would continue to determine the lives of all within it "until the last ton of fossilized coal" was burnt. A hundred years later, the "iron cage" of this logic circles the globe.

SEE ALSO: Consumption, Green/Sustainable; Consumption, Mass Consumption, and Consumer Culture; Consumption, Tourism and; Globalization; Grobalization; McDonaldization; Media and Consumer Culture

REFERENCES AND SUGGESTED READINGS

Appadurai, A. (1990) Disjuncture and Difference in the Global Cultural Economy. *Theory, Culture and Society* 7: 295–310.

Castells, M. (1994) European Cities, the Informational Society, and the Global Economy. *New Left Review* 204: 18–32.

Featherstone, M. (1993) Global and Local Cultures. In: Bird, J. et al. (Eds.), *Mapping the Futures: Local Cultures, Global Change*. Routledge, London, pp. 169–87.

Friedman, J. (1990) Being in the World: Globalization and Localization. *Theory, Culture and Society* 7: 311–28.

Friedman, J. (1995) *Cultural Identity and Global Process*. Sage, London.

Giddens, A. (1999) *Runaway World: How Globalization is Reshaping Our Lives*. Profile, London.

Hannerz, U. (1996) *Transnational Connections: Culture, People, Places*. Routledge, London.

Hannerz, U. & Lofgren, O. (1994) The Nation in the Global Village. *Cultural Studies* 8: 198–207.

Held, D. et al. (1999) *Global Transformations: Politics, Economics and Culture*. Polity Press, Cambridge.

Hirst, P. & Thompson, G. (1996) *Globalization in Question: The International Economy and the Possibilities of Governance*. Polity Press, Cambridge.

Kahn, J. (1995) *Culture, Multiculture, Postculture*. Sage, London.

Mennell, S. (1990) The Globalization of Human Society as a Very Long-term Social Process: Elias's Theory. *Theory, Culture and Society* 7: 359–71.

Miller, D. (1998) Coca-Cola: A Black Sweet Drink from Trinidad. In: Miller, D. (Ed.), *Material Cultures: Why Some Things Matter*. University College of London Press, London.

Ritzer, G. (2004a) *The McDonaldization of Society*, revd. edn. Pine Forge Press, Thousand Oaks, CA.

Ritzer, G. (2004b) *The Globalization of Nothing*. Pine Forge Press, Thousand Oaks, CA.

Robertson, R. (1995) Glocalization: Time-Space and Homogeneity-Heterogeneity. In: Featherstone, M. et al. (Eds.), *Global Modernities*. Sage, London.

Wagnleitner, R. (1994) *Coca-Colonization and the Cold War: The Cultural Mission of the United States in Austria after the Second World War*. University of North Carolina Press, Chapel Hill.

Wallerstein, I. (1974) *Capitalist Agriculture and the Origins of the European World-Economy in the Sixteenth Century*. Academic Press, New York.

Watson, J. (Ed.) (1997) *Golden Arches East: McDonald's in East Asia*. Stanford University Press, Stanford.

Weber, M. (1930) *The Protestant Ethic and the Spirit of Capitalism*, trans. Talcott Parsons. George Allen & Unwin, London.

globalization, culture and

Roland Robertson

As the debate about globalization has rapidly expanded and become more, rather than less, contentious, there has emerged what might be called a "negative consensus" concerning the idea of global culture. While there is most definitely no widespread agreement, either "globally" or "locally," about what we might mean by the term global culture(s), there is – for many, a seemingly reluctant – confirmation of the proposition that the issue of global culture is of paramount significance.

In this regard we are witnesses of and participants in the continuation of an older debate as to whether national societies function primarily within the parameters of a societal culture, variously called the dominant ideology, the hegemonic discourse, the central value system, the common culture, or whatever. The key point here is that social scientists and students of culture have at least converged on the thesis that the question of which particular modes of contested cultural expression and discourse are predominant at any given time and/or place is a matter of importance. This much has been conceded by even the most committed of those of a materialistic persuasion. Indeed, there are few serious analysts of the global-human condition who would now claim that ideational perspectives and commitments are mechanical products of autonomous material processes.

The conventional treatment of culture in mainstream sociology, greatly influenced by social and cultural anthropology, was for long that of a binding agent, a phenomenon that provided ideational cohesion and normative guidelines to the members of a society. Over time this perspective has undergone increasingly strong challenges and in this regard the recognition that societies are not insulated monads has played a crucial role. And it might well be said that it is strange to consider now that until recently in the social sciences – with the problematic exception of international relations – analysis hinged upon such a viewpoint.

Consideration of culture in global or at least transnational terms has led to much rethinking of the concept of culture and its part in social life, not least because practitioners of the meta-discipline of cultural studies have made major interventions in the discussion of globalization, globality, transnationality, global modernities, and so on. Thus, the oft-called cultural turn has had a major part in elevating culture to a position of significance in the globalization debate (Robertson 1992: 32–48; Inglis 2005: 110–36). This is not to say, however, that the cultural factor is totally accepted as central to the thinking of those working on matters global.

Almost certainly, the most controversial question in the general, non-reductionist discussion of globalization concerns whether the world as a whole is being swept by homogenizing cultural forces, at one extreme, or whether the world is, on the other hand, becoming increasingly marked by variety and difference. The middle-ground position between total homogeneity and total heterogeneity of global culture as involving sameness-within-difference (or, perhaps, difference-within-sameness) is somewhat analogous to Durkheim's ideas of a century or more ago concerning national societies. Durkheim argued that at the societal level the form of social solidarity had shifted over evolutionary time from a condition of mechanical solidarity, involving sameness, to one of organic solidarity, involving the "coordination" of difference. (While Durkheim saw this issue mainly in relational terms, the concern here is with the problem in cultural terms.) Total homogeneity entails such a lack of vitality in human life that there would be a very strong entropic tendency across the world as a whole, while total heterogeneity suggests a world so completely marked by difference that there would be little or no sharing of worldviews or lifestyles, no solidarity at all. Thus, put in these hypothetical but actually realistically impossible terms, the two extreme positions are really

descriptions of, or recipes for, the collapse of the global-human condition. This is actually an interesting, if apocalyptic, line of deliberation, one worth pursuing, particularly in light of the global trauma of recent years, but which cannot be taken up here.

Insofar as the globalization-equals-homogenization thesis has been so much in evidence in recent years, often in tandem with the conceptually unacceptable claim that Americanization is the same as globalization (Beck et al. 2003), the emphasis here is more on heterogeneity than homogeneity. Nonetheless, the motif of sameness is not relegated to the background. For the relationship between universal (or universals) and the particulars is a crucial, indeed *the* pivotal issue in the study of globalization, considered as a long-term, multidimensional process. Globalization – conceived, of necessity, as *glocalization* (Robertson 1992: 173–4; 1995) – is a self-limiting process. In the light of the idea of glocality, globalization can only take hold unless globalizing forces can find or produce a niche in relation to the local and the particular. This is to be seen in the maxim that it is the particular which makes the universal work.

Put simply, globalization is defined as involving a move in the direction of unicity or oneness, with (1) a deepening and extending of reflexive global consciousness and (2) an increase in global connectivity and density. Both those phenomena are intimately related (Tomlinson 1999). One major manifestation of this relationship may be clearly seen in the current intimacy of economy and culture. They are complicitous in the specific sense that the worldwide production, promotion, distribution, and sale of goods and services has led to an increasing sensitivity to actual or constructed/cultural difference. In fact, cultural difference is a major selling point, in that the exotic alterity of a product is much used as a suggested rationale for consumption. On the other hand, the commodification of culture – in the form of cultural goods (Cowan 2002; Brown 2003) – makes them increasingly open to economic considerations and analysis.

PERSPECTIVES ON GLOBAL CULTURE

The idea of reflexive global consciousness is a critical aspect of any intervention in the debate about global culture. It can usefully be approached via Marx's distinction between a class-in-itself and a class-for-itself. Clearly, global humanity has existed for millennia, but without possessing anything like the degree of widespread, but contested, sense of the fate of the concrete world as a whole in which we are participants in these early years of the twenty-first century. In other words, the *problem* of the world-for-itself is increasingly constitutive of the Durkheimien conscience collective of our time. This can be seen in various manifestations, most notably since the near-global trauma of September 11, 2001. For in this very recent – and still ongoing – case, many, many people around the globe have been drawn in one way or another to consider the future and nature of our planet and its inhabitants, although increasingly in recent decades a way was prepared for this in millennialistic movies and books.

Notwithstanding the significance of access to the oil of the southern republics of the former Soviet Union, as well as the issues of Realpolitik, there can be no denying that the September 2001 attacks on the World Trade Center and the Pentagon, and the airplane that crashed near Pittsburgh, Pennsylvania, have brought cultural issues to the forefront of the global arena. This is to be seen in the way in which the theme of civilized versus uncivilized and the clash between different values and beliefs has been a conspicuous aspect of the post-September 11 world situation (Barkawi 2006). In addition, the theme of anti-Americanism is clearly a cultural phenomenon, even though much of the anti-Americanism refers to the exercise of the economic and political strength of the US.

But the significance of September 11, 2001 should not be exaggerated. Or, conversely, there have been many events and circumstances recently, as well as in past centuries, that have extended and intensified the sense of a world-for-itself. One crucial factor in this respect is the extent to which consciousness of such events and circumstances is widespread and no longer confined to relatively small and/or isolated elites. Leaving any truly careful consideration of the latter reservation largely on one side, in relatively modern times the voyages of "discovery" of the fifteenth and sixteenth centuries; the Napoleonic wars; rapid improvements in means of travel and communication

during the nineteenth century; plus a large number of global events; natural catastrophes; and the inauguration of supranational or global institutions during the twentieth century (Robertson 1992) – all of these have heightened the sense of globality, as experienced now. On the other hand, much has been done of late to show that the sense of oneness of the world has been closed to modern scholarship. Only relatively recently have we come to recognize that consciousness of globality is much, much older than we have been led to believe, this being due in large part to the blinkering effect of disciplinarity.

Quotations from two recently published books can illustrate these themes. In their study of the Renaissance entitled *Global Interests: Renaissance Art between East and West*, Jardine and Brotton (2000: 8) write of their recognition that "for purposes of artistic and other material transaction, the boundaries between ... East and West were thoroughly permeable in the Renaissance." They go on to say that along with recognizing cross-fertilization and a two-way traffic in influence "comes the inevitable recognition that cultural histories kept utterly distinct and kept traditionally separate, are ripe to be written as shared East/West undertakings." Accentuating the elitist nature of global consciousness more fully, Wills (2001: 3) writes in his *1688: A Global History* that "even today, with all our opportunities for world travel and our instantaneous communications, the number of people who have a steady sense of the world as one world or even among several major parts of it is not as great as we would like to think." Wills adds that "in 1688 a full sense of the variety of the world's places and peoples, of their separations and their connections, was confined to a few Europeans," such as philosophers, Jesuit missionaries, travelers, and literate urbanites, although elite Chinese, for example, "were aware of the Europeans as a new element on the far margins of their 'All under Heaven,' but hardly at all of Africa and the Americas."

Now, of course, we live at a time when via numerous world events and worldwide trauma – not to speak of worldwide ecological problems and pandemics, as well as space travel – our global consciousness continues to grow in reflexivity in both senses of the latter term. On the one hand, we think and act in unreflective reaction to global events. On the other hand, we are also constrained to think and act reflectively in relation to these, this being the most important conception of reflexivity involved here.

Although not unconnected with the theme of global consciousness, the issue of *a* global culture raises rather different considerations. The study of culture in global terms is not merely somewhat different from the study of culture in societal terms, but that the concern with globalization has led to a rethinking of the study of societal cultures. However, without relinquishing this thesis, it must be said that this argument can be taken too far. Whether there is *a* global culture can be considered by invoking the work of Boli and Thomas (1999:17): "Culture lies at the heart of world development. Technical progress, bureaucratization, capitalist organization, states, and markets are embedded in cultural models, often not explicitly recognized as such, that specify 'the nature of things' and the 'purposes of action.' These cultural conceptions do more than orient action; they also constitute actors." The same authors go on to argue that it is worldwide "cultural principles" that define actors in certain ways – as having needs, emotions, and capacities and by providing templates for identities, roles, and selves. In the same way, cultural models also "define" collective identities and interests of such entities as firms, states, and nations. Moreover, actors do not act so much as they *enact* (Jepperson 1991). Boli and Thomas (1999: 18) go further and maintain that "the enactment of cultural models … thus represents broad homologies, with actors everywhere defining themselves in similar ways and pursuing similar purposes by similar means, *but specific actions in specific contexts vary almost without limit*" (emphasis added). The end of this sentence is highlighted because it draws attention to *glocal* issues and also because it inhibits any temptation to consider the propositions of Boli and Thomas as presenting a classical dominant culture model. Nonetheless, these writers do clearly insist on there being a definite world or global culture. And in this regard they are posing an extremely important question: Why do we find so much similarity with respect to "actors" and institutions across more-or-less the entire world? This query is discussed with much sophistication by Lechner and Boli (2005).

While Boli, Thomas, and Lechner are keen to recognize that individual and collective actors "actively draw on, select from, and modify shared cultural models, principles, and identities" (Swidler 1986), they show much more interest in world-cultural models than processes of selection and rejection of such. Moreover, such processes appear in their work as more or less confined to selection from (or rejection of) *world-cultural* models rather than models presented by other actors. These authors (Boli and Thomas in particular) might well respond that since *all* "actors" are subject to the constraints of world-cultural models, then ostensible emulation of other societies means that such emulation is in effect still enactment of such models.

In any case, the key consideration is that we find here a persuasive argument for the idea of a single global culture, one which derives in large part from the perception that there is a remarkable similarity in general terms among institutions across the world, as well as in the cognitive construction of "definitions, principles, and purposes" (Boli & Thomas 1999: 19) Thus, in a sense, the existence of a single global culture is largely derived from the observation of such homologies and isomorphisms. This is very different from Wallerstein's "metaphysical presuppositions" that are sometimes invoked as a way of accounting for the continuity of his world capitalistic system. In fact, indirectly, the stance of Boli and Thomas derives its significance partly from a cogent rejection of Wallerstein's general approach (Robertson 1992: 65–8).

The contested nature of world-cultural models is by no means denied in the Boli–Thomas perspective, but nonetheless they maintain that conflicting models and discourse "share fundamental conceptions regarding actors, agency, technique, societal purposes, and much more" (Boli & Thomas 1999: 19). Moreover, universal cultural principles may in themselves produce conflict in that, if actors have identical goals, they are likely to compete for the same resources. However, this concession – if such it may be called – concerning competing cultural models tends to underestimate discontinuities, discontinuities that can and do lead to conflict and contestation. This is clearly the case with respect to the current "war on terror." That having been said, the program of Boli and

Thomas, as well as other members of the so-called Stanford School who have been much influenced by John Meyer (Boli & Thomas 1999: v), has been undeservedly neglected.

In summary, it can be said that the approach to global or world culture of Meyer, Boli, and Thomas et al. is in a number of respects very cogent. For, working mainly from the observation of homologies and isomorphic connections, it comes to the almost inevitable conclusion that there must be "something" upon which these are based. On the other hand, there is a kind of disconcerting neatness about this overall argument, leading to a neglect of what might be called the messiness of world culture. Indeed, this is precisely why there is a need to present *other* ways of considering the latter. (It is worth stating here that the work of Lechner with Robertson has led to an important convergence with respect to the discussion of world or global culture.)

Perhaps the most neglected of all the ingredients of global culture is that which is involved in interactions – better, interpenetrations and comparisons – between nation-states, indeed of international blocs and of entire civilizations. To put this somewhat abstractly, we can envisage the contemporary world as being made up of a large series of dyadic relations between nation-states. Thus – to take a few salient cases – we could consider the following as exemplars: France–Germany; the US–UK; China–Japan; Greece–Turkey; France–US; Argentina–the UK; Israel–the US; Russia–China, and so on and so forth. Each of these cultures of nation-state interaction has unique features although, of course, no dyad stands alone. Each is embedded in a vast complex of networks. Probably the most crucial point that should be made here, without going into the specifics of any particular dyadic case, is that to some large extent national identities are formed with respect to the interpenetration of sociocultural features of each society, or one nation-state internalizes the image that the other nation is perceived to hold of "self." A very interesting case of national-identity interpenetration is provided by the Japan–US relationship in historical perspectives.

Quite closely related to this is the way in which externally generated characterizations of

a nation-state become central to a nation-state's identity. The classic example is how de Tocqueville's *Democracy in America* – written over 150 years ago – has been continuously reproduced in order to declare the central tenets of US American identity within the American context. Parallel examples abound of other societies' reliance on the interpretations of external observers. And it should be said that the general – not to say highly problematic – notion of national "identity" illustrates the sameness/difference question very well. For while the very mention of identity summons up ideas concerning uniqueness and difference, the fact is that there is something like a global recipe or template for the production and presentation of national identities, this having much to do with models of and for the well-worn theme of the invention of tradition that blossomed globally at the beginning of the twentieth century (Robertson 1992: 146–63).

Westney (1987) has well described the growth of selective emulation (in tandem with national identity formation) in Meiji Japan. In so doing she has emphasized that Meiji emulation of selected features of western nation-states was greatly facilitated by the fact that it was also occurring among European nation-states themselves. This late-nineteenth-century scenario may usefully be generalized to relations among all nation-states in more recent times. In this regard there has been institutionalized, at the international level, an ongoing series of processes of comparison, with the academic observer becoming increasingly interested in what could be called the comparison of comparison. As has already been implied, this has much bearing on the issue of homologous and isomorphic relationships between and among the "appearance" of similar phenomena in a variety of societies. This emulation, as well as the rejection, process, provides a dynamic addition to the Meyer–Boli–Thomas position described previously.

At the same time, the circulation of practices, ideas, and institutional forms around the world is a central aspect of global culture. This has in the past often been indicated by the term cultural diffusion. But the latter term in itself lacks explicit sensitivity to the glocalizing character of the circulation of sociocultural phenomena. The same is true of what are frequently cast as flows from one context to others. In recent times non-governmental organizations (NGOs) have played a big part in this as they have in the promotion and sustaining of diasporic relations with the "homeland." In this case the multiplication of loyalties via population movements has become a crucial element of global culture. In particular, the assimilation of immigrants in the fully fledged sense is rapidly declining, so much so that the vast question of national societal membership and citizenship is a central and increasingly controversial problem of our time, particularly since 9/11 and, in the UK, 7/7. Thus, the increasing significance of transnational communities with their own cultures (Portes 2000), the prominence of these being greatly facilitated by the new and still expanding forms of electronic communication, the relative cheapness of air travel, and the growth of the illicit traffic in human beings.

The culture of images of the constitution of the world as a whole is a perspective on culture that pivots upon the different forms in terms of which the world as a whole is envisaged (Robertson 1992: 61–84). In addition, however, there is a need to indicate the ways in which what have been called global futures also constitute a significant element of contemporary global culture. While there have been for many centuries both utopian and dystopian prognoses of the future of the world, the current concern with the processes of globalization (however defined) has led increasingly to speculation about and programs for its future. What were for the most part conceived as "anti-globalization" movements have become transformed inexorably into movements advocating alternatives to the currently perceived views of the state of the world.

These two aspects of images of the world – rather simplistically divided into normatively diagnostic and normatively prognostic – are closely linked. The "global futures" trend has meant that serious theoretical and empirical typifications of "really existing" images of the world have been neglected, to the detriment of the "realism" of projected utopias. For example, the much-flourished phrase "globalization from below" entails virtually no attention as to how the structure of the world in its most general contours is or can be envisaged.

So we must turn to "really existing" images of the world. In the present frame of reference images of how the world is constituted may be cast in terms of four fundamental components of the world arena: nation-states; individual selves; international relations (or the system of modern societies); and humankind. Images of the world, whether upheld by individuals or by small or large collectivities, revolve around these tendencies. In one sense, this is a purely hypothetical perspective. On the other hand, it reflects closely the form that globalization has taken in recent centuries (Robertson 1992: 25–31, 58–9, 75–83). Holton (1998) sketches four main images of world order: (1) a single worldwide community with strong bonds; (2) a world of bounded communities with weaker bonds at the global level; (3) a world government in federal form, with relatively strong bonds; and (4) a world composed of bounded nation-states that are not strongly bonded but are relatively open and guided primarily by conceptions of national interest. As Holton (1998: 41) remarks, this kind of work on world images "assists in opening up excessively economic or political accounts of globalization to wider issues of cultural representation and evaluation." He goes on to say that in this perspective globalization is as much about ideals and values as economic development, about ideals of what the world should be as well as what it currently is or is thought to be. This nicely captures the significance of images of world order, thinking that is as much empirically rooted as it is about ideals for the future.

Nonetheless, the advocacy of globalization from below, to repeat, must surely entail a realistic form of utopianism. Otherwise globalization from below simply becomes a kind of culture of resistance, something which is true of much of so-called postcolonial and subaltern theory.

CONCLUSION

Four major, non-exclusive aspects of the theme of global culture have been explored in the foregoing. The conclusion may be drawn that the inexhaustive list of themes that have been indicated shows that what can be reasonably included under the rubric of global culture is considerable. In fact it would be perfectly plausible to insist that global culture is much richer and "thicker" than the culture of any given nation-state. It is indeed more than a pity that so much intellectual energy has been expended in debating the homogenization-cum-Americanization thesis, as well as in arguing about the degree to which global (or any other) culture should, if at all, be considered epiphenomenally, when there is so much to address with respect to the diversity of global culture or cultures.

A return to the events of September 11, 2001 and their aftermath is more than appropriate. Presciently, Bamyeh (2000: 84–5) suggested well before that day that Huntington's (1996) prognosis of a "clash of civilizations" could in fact become a self-fulfilling prophecy; although Bamyeh surely errs in attributing "the shift to the cultural" as "the victory of capitalism," for while capitalism has indeed been a major vehicle in recent times for the resurrection of the cultural factor (Robotham 2005), the latter's significance had been hidden previously by capitalism itself. We should not be tempted by or pushed into averting our attention to the cultural factor simply because Huntington "wrote the script" for September 11. For surely on that very day culture sprang back, perversely, into its rightful place in the analysis of processes of globalization. All the millions of words that have been uttered about it so far, as well as visual representations of it and its aftermath are, it should be heavily emphasized, *cultural* by definition.

SEE ALSO: Civilizations; Culture; Discourse; Diversity; Durkheim, Émile; Globalization; Glocalization; Grobalization; Ideological Hegemony; Ideology; McDonaldization; Nation-State and Nationalism; NGO/INGO; Religion

REFERENCES AND SUGGESTED READINGS

Bamyeh, M. A. (2000) *The Ends of Globalization*. University of Minnesota Press, Minneapolis.

Barkawi, T. (2006) *Globalization and War*. Rowman & Littlefield, Lanham, MD.

Beck, U., Sznaider, N., & Winter, R. (Eds.) (2003) *Global America? The Cultural Consequences of Globalization*. Liverpool University Press, Liverpool.

Boli, J. & Thomas, G. M. (1999) INGOs and the Organization of World Culture. In: Boli, J. & Thomas, G. M. (Eds.), *Constructing World Culture: International Nongovernmental Organizations since 1875*. Stanford University Press, Stanford, pp. 13–49.

Brown, M. F. (2003) *Who Owns Native Culture?* Harvard University Press, Cambridge, MA.

Cowan, T. (2002) *Creative Destruction: How Globalization is Changing the World's Cultures*. Princeton University Press, Princeton.

Holton, R. J. (1998) *Globalization and the Nation-State*. St. Martin's Press, New York.

Huntington, S. (1996) *The Clash of Civilizations and the Remaking of World Order*. Simon & Schuster, New York.

Inglis, D. (2005) *Culture and Everyday Life*. Routledge, London.

Jardine, L. & Brotton, J. (2000) *Global Interests: Renaissance Art between East and West*. Reaktion Books, London.

Jepperson, R. L. (1991) Institutions, Institutional Effects, and Institutionalization. In: Powell, W. W. & DiMaggio, P. J. (Eds.), *The New Institutionalism in Organizational Analysis*. University of Chicago Press, Chicago, pp. 143–63.

Juergensmeyer, M. (Ed.) (2003) *Global Religions: An Introduction*. Oxford University Press, New York.

King, A. D. (2004) *Spaces of Global Cultures: Architecture, Urbanism, Identity*. Routledge, London.

Lechner, F. J. & Boli, J. (2005) *World Culture: Origins and Consequences*. Blackwell, Oxford.

Portes, A. (2000) Globalization From Below: The Rise of Transnational Communities. In: Kalb, D. et al. (Eds.), *The Ends of Globalization: Bringing Society Back In*. Rowman & Littlefield, Lanham, MD, pp. 253–70.

Robertson, R. (1992) *Globalization: Social Theory and Global Culture*. Sage, London.

Robertson, R. (1995) Glocalization: Time-Space and Homogeneity-Heterogeneity. In: Featherstone, M., Lash, S., & Robertson, R. (Eds.), *Global Modernities*. Sage, London, pp. 25–45.

Robotham, D. (2005) *Culture, Society and Economy: Bringing Culture Back In*. Sage, London

Swidler, A. (1986) Culture in Action. *American Sociological Review* 51 (April): 273–86.

Tomlinson, J. (1999) *Globalization and Culture*. University of Chicago Press, Chicago.

Westney, F. E. (1987) *Imitation and Innovation: The Transfer of Western Organizational Patterns to Meiji Japan*. Harvard University Press, Cambridge, MA.

Wills, J. E. (2001) *1668: A Global History*. Granta Books, London.

globalization, education and

Keiko Inoue and Francisco O. Ramirez

The globalization of education refers to the expansion and increased interconnectedness of education-related activity throughout the world. Much of the sociological research on this broad subject has focused on the following dimensions of the globalization of education: expansion of educational enrollments at all levels, nationalization of schooling, standardization of education, and the rise of an international educational sector. These studies are guided by functionalist, conflict, and institutional theories of education.

EXPANSION

Access to education has become a primary concern for states, societies, and transnational organizations. Education as human capital and education as a human right are widely held principles that fuel this concern. Earlier fears of the "overeducated" or "diploma diseases" have given way to efforts to identify and correct enrollment deficiencies. The achievement of universal primary education by 2015 is a United Nations Millennium Development Goal that commands great consensus. And indeed, primary, secondary, and tertiary enrollments relative to the appropriate age cohorts have sharply increased since World War II. The world primary enrollment ratio increased from about 80 percent in 1970 to nearly universal (99 percent) in 2000. Similar expansionary trends are found for both secondary and tertiary enrollment ratios. The corresponding change for secondary schooling is also impressive, with the secondary enrollment ratio more than doubling, from 32 percent in 1970 to 75 percent in 2000. Yet the most striking growth is found at the level of tertiary education, which more than quadruples in this period, from 7 percent in the earlier period to nearly 30 percent by the end of the century. While secondary and tertiary enrollments were concentrated in developed countries in the earlier periods, much of the current observable growth is due to

expansionary trends in less developed countries. What started as a "world educational crisis" (Coombs 1968) in primary schooling has now dramatically transformed education worldwide, with more optimistic world education agendas prevailing (Meyer et al. 1992).

To explain this phenomenon functionalists tout the role of education in development, often using human capital theory to argue that investments in education produce a well-trained labor force spurring economic growth (Schultz 1961). Increased exposure to schooling, and especially to quality schooling (Hanushek & Kimko 2000), enhances individual productivity, and subsequently, economic growth. Modernization theories emphasize broader skills and capacities, but they too suggest that education grows because it contributes to the well-being of individuals and of society (Inkeles & Smith 1974). These arguments are often restricted to lower levels of schooling, since the link of higher education to economic growth is more questionable. The crucial assumption underlying these theories is that education is primarily a process of socialization.

Conflict theories view educational expansion as the outcome of competition between different social classes and ethnic groups seeking to monopolize or to acquire certificational advantages (Collins 1979). Within this perspective education is primarily a process of allocation to differentially valued positions within society. To the degree that allocation via education rules triumph worldwide, one should expect to find worldwide educational expansion. In a world of unequal economic and political relations, the preference for education allocation rules in core states should result in their adoption in peripheral ones, leading to educational growth but also undercutting local educational autonomy (Altbach 1977).

Institutional theories share some of the skepticism of conflict theories regarding the functions of education. These theories emphasize the widespread belief in education as the driving source of economic growth and social progress. This belief in turn reflects the degree to which education is a process of legitimation, defining what constitutes proper knowledge and reasonable personnel in society (Meyer 1977). From this perspective the worldwide growth of education is shaped by world models

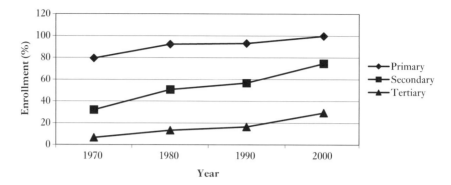

Figure 1   Mean educational enrollment ratio by level, 1970–2000.
Source: All data are from the *World Development Indicators 2004* database (available online at www.worldbank. org/data/wdi2004/index.htm).

of progress and justice and the degree to which an increasing number of countries are linked to these models.

Whether driven by processes of socialization, allocation, or legitimation, or a combination of these processes, the phenomenal expansion of education is the first and perhaps most significant manifestation of the globalization of education.

NATIONALIZATION

There are several indicators of the degree to which education has been nationalized over time. One measure is the extent to which a national compulsory rule has been adopted. Earlier debates about the reasonableness of such a rule or the right of the state to compel schooling (see Mangan 1994) have disappeared. The proportion of countries which adopted such a rule increased to over 80 percent by the late 1980s (Ramirez & Ventresca 1992). Failure to fully comply with this law is widely regarded as a problem, as evidenced by current debates about attendance rates in some countries. A similar measure of nationalization involves the establishment of national ministries of education, that is, state agencies with direct or indirect authority over schooling. For instance, data from the *Stateman's Year-Book* series from 1814 to 2003 show that the founding of ministries of education has been fairly constant over the past two centuries. Almost a third of the national ministries of education

were established during the nineteenth century, mostly in Western Europe but also in Latin America as well as in Japan and Ethiopia. With decolonization after World War II, many more countries nationalized their expanding school systems.

From a functionalist perspective, states take over schooling because states assume managerial controls over all societal activities deemed important. Conflict theories have emphasized the degree to which the nationalization of schooling is a reaction to multi-ethnic conflicts (Collins 1979) or class-based contestations (Spring 1972). Instead of social fragmentation, national integration is maintained via state controls over education. Lastly, from an institutional perspective the issue is one of identity. The proper nation-state commits itself to schooling and to a school system linked to transnationally validated national goals and purposes. In other words, the nationalization of education is driven by the need to affirm proper nation-state identity. There is little evidence that nationalization is more likely to occur under the conditions of expanded education or increased conflict imagined by functionalist and conflict theories (Ramirez & Rubinson 1979). However, recent developments in the direction of educational decentralization, privatization, and marketization were unanticipated within the institutional perspective. Addressing these new developments, functionalists assume that considerations of efficiencies constitute the underlying dynamic, while conflict theorists contend that transnational capitalist elites are

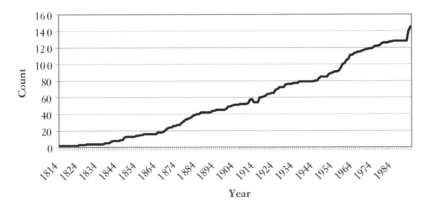

Figure 2 Cumulative number of education ministries by founding year (1814–1993).
Source: Data are from the *Stateman's Year-Book*, 1814–2003.

undermining national states, and thus, the nationalization of education.

Further studies are needed to ascertain which features of the nationalization of education are withering and which continue to thrive. National goals and purposes may continue to be affirmed, even as schooling increasingly relies on subnational sources of funding. These studies need to take into account the multidimensional character of the nationalization of education, as well as the multiple and at times inconsistent sources of influence that impinge on national educational decision-making bodies.

STANDARDIZATION

Broad and common principles of education as human capital and education as a human right inform national educational goals, structure, curricula, and reform discourse. National education goals are remarkably similar, with economic growth and social progress at the top of the list. Human development, of course, is the key to both economic growth and social progress. Additionally, human development is to unfold within classrooms, within schools. De-schooling society proposals linger but are weak, while informal education is almost always coopted and becomes part of formal schooling. In practice, education has become schooling and the structure of schooling has become standardized.

Curricular content has also become more similar across countries (Meyer et al. 1992). What is to be taught and how much of it commands overall curricular time varies less than one would expect if national school curricula were truly distinctive. History and geography subjects, for example, tend to be bundled around a more child-centric social studies curriculum (Wong 1991). Even the study of science undergoes change to become more socially and personally relevant (McEneaney & Meyer 2000). Standardization is more evident with respect to primary and secondary schooling, but increasingly more and more universities converge on the principle that universities should be more broadly accessible, socially useful, and organizationally flexible. In Europe the driving force is the Bologna Declaration, but elsewhere standardization is conditioned by more associational processes reflecting the influence of educational professionals and organizations worldwide.

Does standardization take place because there are optimal forms of structure and curricula that trump everywhere? Do within-nation and between-nation conflicts lead to common compromises in the form of common educational structures and curricula? What is it about some structural forms and curricular emphases that make them more likely to be associated with a more legitimate nation-state identity? These are the research questions that the different theoretical perspectives need to tackle in the face of growing educational standardization. More broadly, a robust sociological inquiry into the globalization of education needs to engage educational reform discourse to make more explicit its taken-for-granted assumptions. Does not the search for "best practices" in education presuppose a high degree of transnational portability? And does not this assumption fly in the face of calls for a nationally distinctive and relevant curriculum? Is "lifelong learning" an extraordinarily optimistic assessment of human malleability and capacity? Or does the retreat of the state and welfare safety nets give rise to the lifelong learning mantra? Similar sociological probes needs to be undertaken with respect to "teaching for understanding" and "developing higher order skills."

INTERNATIONALIZATION

The globalization of education has also involved the formation of an international educational sector. The latter consists of the organizations and professionals that articulate educational standards, setting forth appropriate educational goals and targets that foster the expansion and standardization of education discussed earlier. The school systems and universities of the more developed or more dominant countries have influenced educational developments throughout the world for over a century (Epstein 1994). This influence may be due to the greater attractiveness of the educational system of economically or politically successful countries. Alternatively, coercive processes reflecting power dependency ties between countries may shape educational outcomes in the more dependent ones (Altbach 1977).

In addition to mimetic and coercive mechanism, normative ones stemming from professional influence may also be at work. With the founding of the United Nations Educational, Scientific, and Cultural Organization (Unesco) in 1946, a series of international educational conferences have been the sites for much educational standard setting and international cooperation in education discourse (Chabbott 2003; Mundy 1998). These conferences have given greater visibility to shared or privileged educational goals and to portable school and university curricula, pedagogy, and structures. They have thus fostered globalization of education via internationalization and international influences as well as globalized international interrelated educational activities.

To illustrate internationalization, consider the case of the Education For All (EFA) initiative, with world conferences held in Jomtien in 1990 and Dakar in 2000. The EFA movement created a space for governments of developed and developing countries, as well as their non-governmental counterparts, to embrace the task of achieving universal primary education by 2015. The movement is orchestrated by Unesco, the World Bank, the United Nations Children's Fund (Unicef), and the United Nations Development Program (UNDP), but non-governmental organizations have become increasingly active in the promotion of universal primary education. Global Campaign for Education, for instance, has brought together NGOs and teachers' unions in over 150 countries, creating a transnational web of organizations behind the EFA movement. Such networks of international organizations in turn act as "teachers of norms" (Finnemore 1996), resulting in increased standardization in goals and structures of educational systems around the world.

Addressing inequalities of access to schooling by gender and other social characteristics has also been a special focus of EFA and related international initiatives. For instance, the United Nations Girls' Education Initiative addresses the gender gap in primary education enrollment. Though gender disparities are evident, the worldwide trend has been in the direction of greater equality at all educational levels. In fact, the growth rate for women's share of educational enrollment was greater than the increase in overall rate of educational expansion between 1970 and 2000. With respect to higher education, for instance, women's share of higher education has increased from 5 percent in 1970 to 32 percent in 2000. Even in fields traditionally regarded as male dominated, such as science and engineering, women's enrollment has increased (Ramirez & Wotipka 2001).

In light of this discussion, the argument commonly held by conflict theorists involving the hegemonic influence of powerful donor countries or multilateral organizations is worth revisiting. The active participation of southern NGOs at the World Education Forum in Dakar in 2000 is a testament to the extensive

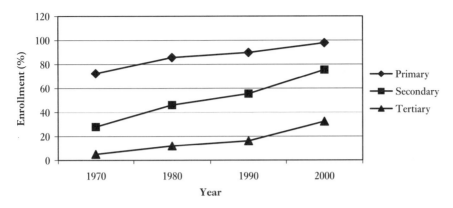

Figure 3 Mean female share of educational enrollment by level, 1970–2000.
Source: All data are from the *World Development Indicators 2004* database (available online at www.worldbank. org/data/wdi2004/index.htm).

grassroots engagement fueling the movement. In fact, non-governmental contribution produced the *NGO Declaration on Education for All* in Dakar, reflecting civil society's long-term commitment to the movement. NGOs have also been crucial to the formation of other education-related initiatives, including active promotion of the United Nations Decade for Human Rights Education (1995–2004).

Why have governmental and non-governmental organizations unvaryingly embraced the global initiative to promote education, particularly universal primary schooling? A closer examination of EFA and other education-related initiatives highlights the great faith placed on education in eradicating obstacles to development and overcoming other social ills. The proclamation in the Millennium Development Goals is straightforward in linking EFA with economic growth: education is development. The Global Campaign for Education not only correlates EFA with poverty alleviation, but it also bases its work on the belief that education is a universal human right that can produce "sustainable human development." Education is a means to national economic growth and stability, as well as a source of individual empowerment. The penetration of the EFA movement at the global and local levels demonstrates the extent to which education has become the most legitimate mechanism for pursuing common goals of economic productivity, political democracy, and social justice.

SYNTHESIS

To better understand the nature of educational globalization, further research should focus on three areas. First, given the interconnected relationship between the global and the local, a multilevel analysis that takes into account international activity and its link to grassroots work is pertinent. Currently, researchers tend to focus solely on broad trends at the global level or the impact of globalization in a particular context at the local level. Second, researchers should take advantage of newly available education-related variables and further explore the persistent gender, income level, and regional gaps. Third, more research is needed to problematize the assumed link between education and economic productivity and individual empowerment. The commonly held belief that education is the key ingredient to progress and justice should also be questioned and revisited.

More direct tests of the implications of alternative theories of the globalization of education would further our understanding of this worldwide dynamic with multiple repercussions. The possible coercive and hegemonic nature of educational expansion also needs to be reconsidered. And finally, a further examination of the taken-for-granted character of educational globalization would allow for a broader understanding of the political and cultural dimensions of the massification of education. Functionalist, conflict, and institutional theories continue to frame sociological research questions about the mechanisms underlying the globalization of education.

SEE ALSO: Colleges and Universities; Conflict Theory; Education; Globalization; Schooling and Economic Success; Stratification and Inequality, Theories of; Structural Functional Theory

REFERENCES AND SUGGESTED READINGS

Altbach, P. G. (1977) Servitude of the Mind? Education, Dependency and Neo-Colonialism. *Teachers College Record* 79(2): 187–203.
Chabbott, C. (2003) *Constructing Education for Development: International Organizations and Education for All*. Routledge Falmer, New York.
Collins, R. (1979) *The Credential Society: A Historical Sociology of Education and Stratification*. Academic Press, New York.
Coombs, P. H. (1968) *The World Educational Crisis: A Systems Analysis*. Oxford University Press, New York.
Epstein, E. H. (1994) Comparative and International Education: Overview and Historical Development. In: Husén, T. & Postlethwaite, T. N. (Eds.), *The International Encyclopedia of Education*, 2nd edn. Pergamon, New York, pp. 918–23.
Finnemore, M. (1996) Norms, Culture, and World Politics: Insights from Sociology's Institutionalism. *International Organization* 50(2): 325–47.
Hanushek, E. & Kimko, D. (2000) Schooling, Labor Force Quality, and the Growth of Nations. *American Economic Review* 90(5): 1184–208.
Inkeles, A. & Smith, D. H. (1974) *Becoming Modern: Individual Change in Six Developing Countries*. Harvard University Press, Cambridge, MA.
McEneaney, E. H. & Meyer, J. W. (2000) The Content of the Curriculum: An Institutionalist Perspective. In: *Handbook of Sociology of Education*. University of Notre Dame Press, Notre Dame, IN, pp. 189–212.
Mangan, J. A. (Ed.) (1994) *A Significant Social Revolution: Cross-Cultural Aspects of the Evolution of Compulsory Education*. Woburn Press, Portland.
Meyer, J. W. (1977) The Effects of Education as an Institution. *American Journal of Sociology* 83(1): 55–77.
Meyer, J. W., Kamens, D. H., & Benavot, A. (1992) *School Knowledge for the Masses: World Culture and National Curricula, 1920–1986*. Falmer Press, London.
Meyer, J. W., Ramirez, F. O., & Soysal, Y. N. (1992) World Expansion of Mass Education, 1870–1980. *Sociology of Education* 65(2): 128–49.
Mundy, K. (1998) Educational Multilateralism and Word (Dis)order. *Comparative Education Review* 42(4): 448–78.
Ramirez, F. O. & Rubinson, R. (1979) Creating Members: The Political Incorporation and Expansion of Public Education. In: Meyer, J. & Hannan, M. (Eds.), *National Development and World Systems*. University of Chicago Press, Chicago, pp. 72–84.
Ramirez, F. O. & Ventresca, M. J. (1992) Building the Institution of Mass Schooling: Isomorphism in the Modern World. In: Fuller, B. & Rubinson, R. (Eds.), *The Political Construction of Education: The State, School Expansion, and Economic Change*. Praeger, New York.
Ramirez, F. O. & Wotipka, C. M. (2001) Slowly But Surely? The Global Expansion of Women's Participation in Science and Engineering Fields of Study, 1972–92. *Sociology of Education* 74(3): 231–51.
Schultz, T. (1961) Investment in Human Capital. *American Economic Review* 51: 1–17.
Spring, J. (1972) *Education and the Rise of the Corporate State*. Beacon Press, Boston.
Wong, S.-Y. (1991) The Evolution of Social Science Instruction, 1980–86. *Sociology of Education* 64: 33–47.

globalization and global justice

Dieter Rucht

Global justice movements (GJMs) are a loose alliance of contemporary leftist movements whose common denominator is their resistance to globalizing neoliberalism that promotes free trade, deregulation, and privatization as keys to universal progress. In the eyes of its critics, neoliberalism serves the interests of economic and political elites at the cost of the large majority of the population within, but especially beyond, the most developed countries (Rucht 2003). GJMs identify the driving force of neoliberalism in relentless profit-seeking that causes a plethora of evils, such as violation of human and civil rights, destruction of indigenous cultures, growing unemployment and increasingly precarious jobs, environmental degradation, and the widening gap between the affluent and the poor.

According to most mass media, the birth of what they dub the "anti-globalization movement" was marked by the protests of a broad transnational coalition, ranging from left-wing radicals to trade unionists to Catholic associations, against the 1999 summit of the World Trade Organization (WTO) in Seattle. While many groups initially accepted their designation as the anti-globalization movement, they now widely reject it. Rather, they refer to themselves as global justice movements (or global solidarity movements) because, first, they deliberately create transnational networks and organize transnational, if not global, campaigns; and second, they oppose only some forms and aspects of (economic) globalization while promoting globalization of democracy, justice, and solidarity. Hence, they are anti-global in some respects and pro-global in others.

Contrary to common perception, GJMs had already emerged before the Seattle protests. The creation of loose alliances relating different issues and mobilizing transnationally to some degree can be traced to the nineteenth century (Boli & Thomas 1999). Also, challenging official summits is not a new tactic. As early as 1972, a counter-summit took place at the UN Conference on the Human Environment in Stockholm. In 1985 dozens of groups protested against the G7 summit in Cologne and in Bonn (though most of these groups came from the summit's host country). The Berlin meeting of the World Bank and the International Monetary Fund in 1988 was accompanied by a "week of action" that culminated in a protest rally attended by some 80,000 people (Gerhards & Rucht 1992). More recent protests, such as the one against the G8 meeting in Genoa in 2001, attracted more than 200,000 participants. Some of these protests were marked by severe clashes between a minority of mostly young demonstrators and police.

Most GJMs can be seen as an outgrowth or second generation of the so-called "new social movements" that have flourished since the 1960s, focusing on issues such as human and citizen rights, participatory democracy, peace and disarmament, environmental protection, urban renewal, and third world problems. Compared to this older family of "new" movements, GJMs focus more on transnational and even global issues, they target international governmental bodies and multinational corporations, and they create transnational movement infrastructures (della Porta & Tarrow 2005; Tarrow 2005). Because they identify the globalizing market economy as a source of a number of acute problems, many trade unions that tended to keep the new social movements at arm's length have also become allies or even integral parts of the GJMs.

Groups associated with the contemporary GJMs differ widely regarding their social, cultural, and organizational background. Among them are well-known scientists, impoverished farmers, professional trade union organizers, and unemployed, gray-haired activists from the Old Left, in addition to politically inexperienced students, delegates from Northern religious congregations, and representatives of Southern indigenous people. The organizational forms include local and informal grassroots groups, firmly structured national and transnational non-governmental organizations (NGOs), scientifically oriented think-tanks, loose alliances and campaigns, leftist parties and sects, trade unions, farmer associations, student bodies, etc.

Unlike many earlier left movements that were often preoccupied with internal cleavages (if not bitter fights), the GJMs, in general, tend to exhibit a more tolerant attitude in terms of internal differences. This has caused many GJM groups to praise their overarching unity and identity as a new "movement of movements." However, some observers rather stress the differences and cleavages among and within these movements. Apart from anti-neoliberalism as the negative common denominator of almost all GJMs, numerous gaps exist that make it difficult to speak of one unified movement. Some currents pursue a reformist course aimed at mitigating the negative side effects of economic globalization, while other groups promote a strictly anti-capitalist course and maintain the need for a revolutionary change. Accordingly, there is disunity about the questions of whether to cooperate with or instead fight against national and international governmental bodies, whether a free market has to be applied in a restricted manner or whether it should be rejected altogether, and whether disruptive actions or even violence on the part of the movements is a legitimate means of pursuing the movements' goals. These differences are not only verbally expressed, but sometimes also have led to the physical separation of different ideological currents. This separation can be observed in the various parallel protest marches that occasionally take place at one single event, as well as at various Social Forums that have been split into a mainstream component and a – normally smaller – radical counterpart.

Thus far, the GJMs have been visible to the larger public mainly through three kinds of activities. First, they have organized counter-summits and protests at official meetings of the World Bank and the International Monetary Fund, the WTO, G8, and EU summits, thematically oriented UN conferences, and the like (Pianta 2001). Second, they have launched several major campaigns on issues such as land-mines, the Multilateral Agreement on Investments, the trading of toxic waste, debt relief (or debt cancellation) for the poorest countries, and precarious working conditions in Europe, etc. Some of the more regionally focused movements, such as those addressing the struggles of the Mexican Zapatistas, landless farmers in Brazil, and the people against the Narmada dam system in India, received worldwide attention and support. Third, GJMs have created their own infrastructures. Some of the most significant examples are the Social Forums, which today exist from the local to the global level. A starting point was the World Social Forum (WSF) in Porto Alegre (Brazil) in 2001. This WSF, with some 20,000 participants, was conceived as a critical counterpart to the elitist World Economic Forum that has been held in the Swiss mountain resort of Davos annually since 1970. In the past few years the WSF has become a major event in its own right (Sen et al. 2004). The fifth WSF in 2005, again taking place in Porto Alegre, was attended by 155,000 participants from 135 countries. In the past few years, continental and national forums have also been held in Asia, Africa, Latin America, and Europe. The European Social Forums that took place in Florence, Paris, and London were each attended by tens of thousands of participants. Yet the forum idea spread very disproportionately. For example, social forums are marginal in the USA – a country that otherwise has an active community of global justice groups. In Germany the forum idea only gained momentum in 2003. By the end of 2005 around 60 local forums had come into existence. In Italy, where the concept of forums emerged in the wake of the protests against the G8 summit in Genoa in 2001, perhaps as many as 150 local forums already exist.

Thus far, the social forums at the continental and global levels have mainly been a market-place of ideas for how to expose domestic and cross-national problems, exchange experiences, make contacts, and create new networks. The WSF, in particular, has been defined as an open platform for a heterogeneous mix of groups which excludes only leftist guerrilla fighters, right-wing extremists, and political parties. The platform concept, however, does not remain unchallenged. Some leftist groups have criticized the forum as being a kind of "talk shop," unwilling and unable to engage in political activity that has any visible impact. These radicals would like to turn the WSF into a more unified actor that takes binding decisions and engages in joint action. While these radical groups have occasionally organized separate marches or camps within the WSF framework in previous years (most notably in Mumbai in 2004), it seems that fewer of these groups participated in the 2005 event, which was not marked by an identifiable split. Another point of internal criticism against the WSF is the somewhat opaque recruitment procedure for the International Council, which decides the location and structure of the WSF.

An additional significant infrastructural component are those groups and networks that are not coalitions of preexisting groups focusing on women's rights, climate change, rainforests, etc., but which have been genuinely created to promote the overarching ideas of the GJMs. One example of these new creations is "Fifty Years is Enough," a group that was established to deliberately challenge the uncritical celebration of the 50th anniversary of the International Monetary Fund and the World Bank in 1994. Another such group is Attac, which was first established in France in early 1998 and then spread to dozens of other countries. Although initially created to promote a tax designed to reduce the cross-border flow of speculative capital (the Tobin Tax), Attac soon broadened its agenda, becoming a multi-issue group that incorporated the majority of relevant themes and claims of the GJMs. Attac exerts a strong influence on the WSF process. Even though the group is nonexistent in several large countries such as the US, Attac has become a central player of the GJMs in many other countries. In Germany, media tend to equate Attac with the movements at large. Attac Germany was successful in building an alliance with major trade unions; one of these, representing approximately 2.5 million members, has even joined the much smaller Attac group (16,000 individual members).

A third significant infrastructural component is the creation of Indymedia, a network of alternative media groups that basically utilize the Internet for their purposes. The first local group was set up during the Seattle protests in late 1999. In its mission statement, which clearly mirrors the essential creed of the GJMs as a whole, the group defined itself as "a grassroots organization committed to using media production and distribution as a tool for promoting social and economic justice . . . We seek to generate alternatives to the biases inherent in the corporate media controlled by profit and to identify and create positive models for a sustainable and equitable society." By summer 2005 the Indymedia network was comprised of 153 groups, most of which are located in the US and Europe.

In sum, these growing infrastructures contribute to creating a backbone of the GJMs, which otherwise would hardly be more than a conglomerate of disparate groups who occasionally join forces.

Within a relatively short time period GJMs have become known to a worldwide public. They can no longer be ignored as a critic of established (international) politics. Not surprisingly, media, political and economic elites, movement activists, and even scientific observers differ widely in their evaluations of these movements. While conservative media and established elites tend to view the movements' positions and claims as unfounded, naïve, or even dangerous, liberal and left media react in a more differentiated, if not supportive, way. Even some representatives of international and national governmental bodies, without embracing the GJMs per se,

perceive these as legitimate political actors who point to undeniable problems and, for the most part, ask the right questions. Some proposals of these movements, such as the Tobin tax, have been seriously considered by both political leaders like French President Jacques Chirac and by economic experts. The moderate wing of the movements, and knowledge-based NGOs in particular, are accepted as discussion partners and occasionally become part of official delegations. These developments are met with suspicion by more radical groups, who fear that parts of the GJMs are in the process of being coopted and thus compromised.

GJMs were successful both in building an agenda and in undermining the neoliberal creed (often dubbed the "Washington Consensus"), which had previously largely gone unchallenged. Their critique has triggered self-reflection and moderate procedural as well as institutional changes in some international governmental bodies, but it has not been able to influence the overall direction of these institutions thus far. Only in some areas and regarding some issues can a substantial impact be observed. The Multilateral Agreement on Investment, for example, was cancelled, landmines have largely been banned, and a partial debt relief of the poorest countries has been announced.

SEE ALSO: Civil Society; Collective Action; Global Justice as a Social Movement; Globalization; Neoliberalism; New Social Movement Theory; Social Movements; Transnational Movements

REFERENCES AND SUGGESTED READINGS

Boli, J. & Thomas, G. (Eds.) (1999) *Constructing World Culture: International Governmental Organizations since 1875*. University of California Press, Stanford.

della Porta, D. & Tarrow, S. (Eds.) (2005) *Transnational Protest and Global Activism*. Rowman & Littelfield, Lanham, MD.

Gerhards, J. & Rucht, D. (1992) Mesomobilization: Organizing and Framing in Two Protest Campaigns in West Germany. *American Journal of Sociology* 98(3): 555–95.

Pianta, M. (2001) Parallel Summits of Global Civil Society. In: Anheier, H., Glasius, M., & Kaldor, M.

(Eds.), *Global Civil Society 2001*. Oxford University Press, Oxford, pp. 169–94.

Rucht, D. (2003) Social Movements Challenging Neoliberal Globalization. In: Ibarra, P. (Ed.), *Social Movements and Democracy*. Palgrave Macmillan, New York, pp. 211–28.

Sen, J., Anand, A., Escobar, A., & Waterman, P. (Eds.) (2004) *World Social Forum: Callenging Empires*. Viveka Foundation, New Delhi.

Tarrow, S. (2005) *The New Transnational Activism*. Cambridge University Press, Cambridge.

globalization, religion and

Peter Beyer

Globalization describes the historical process by which all the world's people come to live in a single social unit. Religion constitutes an important dimension of globalization through its worldwide institutional presence, its importance in structuring individual and collective cultural difference, and as an effective resource for local and global social mobilization for various goals. Religion is a highly contested, occasionally powerful, and often conflictual domain of some consequence in the global social system.

GLOBALIZATION AND RELIGION AS CONTESTED CATEGORIES

Various scholars in the social sciences started using the neologism "globalization" in the 1980s. The first sociologist to do so consistently was Roland Robertson. Since that time, it has become a highly charged and popular word with diverse meanings. The most widespread of these refers primarily to recent or modern developments in global capitalism, through which this world economic system comes to have a determinative influence in all people's lives, for good or for ill.

Other, often connected, meanings emphasize the international political system of states, the recent intensification of the worldwide network of communications and mass media, or

other transnational structures and phenomena ranging from non-governmental organizations and crime syndicates, to global migration, tourism, and sport. Some observers, in subsuming the latter, argue for the existence of a transnational civil society that parallels economy and the state system. Many of these perspectives also understand globalization in terms of a sometimes contradictory, sometimes complementary relation between local and global forces. The world is not just becoming a more homogeneous place; resistance to these processes or their heterogeneous particularization in diverse regions is as constitutive of globalization as capitalism and international relations. In comparatively little of the vast literature on globalization, however, has there thus far been much discussion of the role of religion, the only real exception being analyses of Islamicist and other religious militancy under such headings as fundamentalism. That situation may be changing.

Although there is currently no general agreement on what religion means and what should count under this heading, a limited set of institutionalized religions is accorded broad legitimacy in virtually every corner of the globe, most consistently Christianity, Islam, Buddhism, and Hinduism. To these, different people and different regions add a variable list of other religions, such as Judaism, Sikhism, Daoism, Shinto, Candomblé, and African Traditional Religion (ATR), as well as other less institutional phenomena ranging from morality and fundamental worldviews to ecstatic experiences and anything that is deemed to offer access to transcendence of the everyday. Moreover, like globalization, religion is often a highly contested category, especially with respect to what does or does not belong to a particular religion and what role religion should play in social life. If nothing else, such conflict over religion shows that it maintains its importance as a field of human endeavor and understanding under conditions of globalization.

RELIGION AS GLOBAL INSTITUTION

Sociological discussion about the relation of religion and globalization has for the most part focused on institutional religion, although certain perspectives argue that highly indivi-dualistic and non-institutional forms under headings like spirituality are becoming increas-ingly dominant. Three aspects of the institu-tional variety have received the most attention: the importance of religion in the context of transnational migration, the global extension of a great variety of religious organizations and movements, and the role of religion in social and political movements that respond specifically to the globalized context.

Literature on human migration, whether from rural to urban areas, into neighboring countries, or to other parts of the world, often focuses on the various problems migrants face when adapting to a new environment. These problems include issues of integration into the host society, questions of personal and cultural identity, differences among first generation migrants and their locally born children, rela-tions between migrant communities and the countries of origin, and links among diverse diaspora locations of the same cultural group. Although the majority of studies in this area pay scant attention to religion in these matters, a substantial and growing number center spe-cifically on the role of religious institutions. Churches, temples, or mosques are frequently the first collective institutions that migrant communities will found. These are established for centrally religious purposes, but they most often also serve a host of other functions including as places of cultural familiarity, social service providers, educational and recreational centers, and resources for community and poli-tical mobilization. At least as critical, these religious institutions facilitate important trans-national links with the countries of origin and other diaspora communities, thus contributing to the communicative networks and flows across the world that are such an important feature of the globalized context. Although much of the literature on such subjects focuses on migrants that have come from non-western to western countries, a sizable portion of it looks at different situations, such as Japanese communities in Latin America and Southeast Asians in Middle Eastern countries.

The religious establishments founded by migrant communities are far from the only way that religious institutions have created a worldwide presence. In fact, the spread of religious ideologies, institutions, and specialists has been a major factor in the historical esta-blishment of the contemporary globalized situ-ation, as well as in the creation of different sub-global but still vast civilizations of the past. The part that the Christian church played in medieval European civilization after the fall of the Roman Empire is one instance; but even more impressive is the role of Islam in the creation of empires from North Africa to Cen-tral and South Asia after the sixth century. At its height, Islamic civilization extended from Southeast Asia to Central Africa, structuring the most global of all social systems before the modern era. The trading links created by Mus-lim merchants, the networks of Sufi brother-hoods, the system of Islamic centers of learning, Muslim pilgrimage, and Islamic political empi-res informed by Islamic legal systems, were all vital social structures in this regard.

In the development of modern globalization, however, Christian missionary movements have played a critical role up until at least the middle of the twentieth century, with the result that Christian churches, including but by no means limited to the Roman Catholic Church, today make up a complex and worldwide network of non-governmental organizations and transna-tional social movements. The linkages that these institutions establish have long since ceased to be unidirectional, from the dominant western core to the rest of the world. Christian Pentecostalism during the twentieth century grew in a highly multi-centered way to become the second largest Christian identification in the world, with hundreds of millions of adher-ents distributed across virtually every region of the globe. Its highly diverse and localized forms maintain a wide variety of links with one an-other through publications, conferences, electro-nic media, and travel. Like many of the more tightly organized denominations such as the Anglican and Seventh-day Adventist churches, Pentecostalism's demographic center of grav-ity is not in western countries but rather in Africa, Latin America, and parts of Asia. In-deed, one of the general peculiarities of global religious organizations and movements in com-parison with other institutional domains is that the bulk of religious action occurs away from the economic, political, media, and scientific core of the global social system. While this fact is perhaps more obvious in the case of religions such as Hinduism, Islam, and Buddhism, it is only somewhat less the case for Christianity. This different distribution manifests itself in a variety of ways. Missionary activity, for example, such a critical element in the initial global expansion of western influence, now takes a number of different directions, with South Korean and Latin American Christian missionaries in Africa, and African Christians seeking to "return the favor" by reevangelizing Western Europe and North America.

Buddhist and Muslim movements, organizations, and leaders have likewise established and expanded their presence in various global regions beyond their historical heartlands, such as, for instance, the Chinese Buddhist Fo Guang Shan, the Japanese Buddhist Soka Gakkai, the West African Murid Sufi order, or the South Asian Islamic Tablighi Jamaat. To these selected examples one could add the international organizations and movements that represent a great many other religions, from Rastafarianism and Judaism to Baha'i and Sikhism.

Although these explicitly religious institutions are the foundation of religion's global social presence, it is the implication of religion in other social, but especially political, movements that has thus far received the most attention in social scientific literature. It is no mere coincidence that the political impact of religion in developments ranging from the Islamic revolution in Iran and the New Christian Right in the United States to the Hindu nationalism of the Bharatiya Janata Party in India and the religiously defined cleavages of Orthodox, Catholic, and Muslim in the former Yugoslavia, appeared on the global scene at roughly the same time as the notion of globalization. The often invidious term fundamentalism has gained a corresponding popularity, referring to religious movements like these, ones that advocate the public enforcement of religious precepts or the exclusive religious identification of state collectivities. Characteristic of such movements is that they seek to enforce highly particular and frequently absolutist visions of the world in their countries, but with explicit reference to the globalizing context which they deem to be the prime threat under such epithets as "global arrogance" (Iran) or "one-worldism" (US). The religious visions that inform them are the basis for this combination of a claim to universal validity with being centered in a particular part of the world among a particular people. Thus does religion serve as a globally present way of making cultural difference a prime structural feature of a globalized world that also relativizes all such differences by incorporating everyone in a single social system.

RELIGION AND RELIGIONS AS GLOBAL SYSTEM

A further approach to the relation of religion and globalization focuses on the degree to which both modern institutional forms and modern understandings of religion are themselves outcomes of globalization. During the long historical development of today's global society, religion came to inform a global religious system consisting primarily of mutually identified and broadly recognized religions, especially the ones indicated above. These religions, as noted, have an institutional presence and broad legitimacy in virtually every region of the globe. While the idea that religion manifests itself through a series of distinct religions may seem self-evident, that notion is historically of quite recent provenance. In Europe, where this understanding first gained purchase, it dates back at the earliest to the seventeenth century. Elsewhere, such as in most regions of Asia, one must wait until at least the nineteenth century. The development and spread of this understanding of religion is entirely coterminous with the period most theories identify as the prime centuries of globalization.

The emergence of this religious system is not only recent. It is also quite selective; not every possible religion, not everything possibly religious, counts. Symptomatic of both aspects are ongoing and recent debates among scholars of religion concerning the meaning of the concept and its supposed Eurocentrism. One perspective insists that religion is at best an abstract term, but not something "real" that is actually out there in the world. A prime argument in support of this position is how the ideas of religion as a separate domain of life and of the distinct religions are so demonstrably products of relatively recent history and so clearly implicated in the concomitant spread of Christian and European influence around the world. Another is that "the religions" is empirically too narrow, that what is meant by them does not cover enough of what is manifestly religious using slightly different notions of religion. These criticisms, however, do not exclude the conclusion that a peculiar way of understanding religion and institutionally embodying religion has nonetheless developed in conjunction with and as an expression of the process of globalization. Similar to global capitalism and the global system of sovereign states, the institutionalization of this idea excludes as well as includes. It also involves power and imposition, as do all human institutions. And just as anti-globalization movements are themselves important manifestations of that which they oppose, so too is controversy around the idea of religion and the religions symptomatic of the social and cultural reality which it contests.

FUTURE DIRECTIONS FOR RESEARCH

The explicit study of religion in the context of globalization is only in its beginnings. The sociological neglect of this topic may be due to the fact that religions usually ground themselves in tradition as opposed to contemporary developments, to the close relation between religion and local and regional culture, and perhaps to the lingering effect of secularization perspectives which have led many social scientists to expect religion to be irrelevant in the modern world. Be that as it may, a now rapidly growing literature that sees religion as an important player in today's global context heralds a much needed new direction in this regard.

SEE ALSO: Buddhism; Christianity; Fundamentalism; Globalization, Culture and; Islam; Migration: International; Multiculturalism; Religion; Religion, Sociology of; System Theories

REFERENCES AND RECOMMENDED READINGS

Beyer, P. (1994) *Religion and Globalization*. Sage, London.
Beyer, P. (Ed.) (2001) *Religion in the Process of Globalization* (Religion im Prozess der Globalisierung). Ergon Verlag, Wurzburg.
Coleman, S. (2000) *The Globalization of Charismatic Christianity: Spreading the Gospel of Prosperity*. Cambridge University Press, Cambridge.
Ebaugh, H. R. & Chafetz, J. S. (Eds.) (2002) *Religion Across Borders: Transnational Migrant Networks*. Altamira Press, Walnut Creek, CA.
Esposito, J. L. & Watson, M. (Eds.) (2000) *Religion and Global Order*. University of Wales Press, Cardiff.
Haynes, J. (1998) *Religion in Global Politics*. Longman, London.
Hopkins, D. N., Lorentzen, L. A., Mendieta, E., and Batstone, D. (Eds.) (2001) *Religions/Globalizations: Theories and Cases*. Duke University Press, Durham, NC.
Martin, D. (2002) *Pentecostalism: The World Their Parish*. Blackwell, Oxford.
Marty, M. E. & Appleby, R. S. (Eds.) (1991–5) *The Fundamentalism Project*, 5 vols. University of Chicago Press, Chicago.
Meyer, B. & Geschiere, P. (Eds.) (1999) *Globalization and Identity: Dialectics of Flow and Closure*. Blackwell, Oxford.
Peterson, D. & Walhof, D. (Eds.) (2002) *The Invention of Religion: Rethinking Belief in Politics and History*. Rutgers University Press, New Brunswick, NJ.
Robertson, R. (1992) *Globalization: Social Theory and Global Culture*. Sage, London.
Rothstein, M. (Ed.) (2001) *New Age Religion and Globalization*. Aarhus University Press, Aarhus.
Roudometof, V. (2001) *Nationalism, Globalization, and Orthodoxy: The Social Origins of Ethnic Conflict in the Balkans*. Contributions to the Study of World History. Greenwood Press, Westport, CT.
Rudolph, S. H. & Piscatori, J. (Eds.) (1997) *Transnational Religion and Fading States*. Westview Press, Boulder.
Van der Veer, P. (Ed.) (1996) *Conversion to Modernities: The Globalization of Christianity*. Routledge, London.
Vasquez, M. A. & Marquardt, M. F. (2003) *Globalizing the Sacred: Religion across the Americas*. Rutgers University Press, New Brunswick, NJ.
Woodhead, L. & Heelas, P. (Eds.) (2002) *Religions in the Modern World*. Routledge, London.

globalization, sexuality and

Jon Binnie

The globalization of sexuality refers to the sexualized and embodied nature of processes associated with the movement of people, capital, and goods across national boundaries. It also refers to how the consciousness of the world as a single place is sexualized. The globalization of sexuality is manifest in a range of processes and phenomena that are often couched and approached in highly emotive terms (e.g., the trafficking of women into prostitution, mail-order brides, the development of the sex indus- try and sex tourism). It is also characterized by the AIDS pandemic, mass international tour- ism, and the development of cyberspace. Each of these has in turn intensified consciousness of the status of sexual minorities and the uneven- ness of their treatment across the globe. Key to our understandings of the globalization of sexu- ality is the relationship between sexuality and economics. While debates on the globalization of gay identity have been marked by an ambiva- lence over the development of gay identities and politicized communities outside of the West, work on the globalization of sexuality more generally has tended to have been marked by concerns with the worse excesses of what Smith (1997) has termed the "satanic geogra- phies of globalization." Here we are concerned with the trafficking of women forced into pros- titution. Contemporary moral panics on the scale and extent of the trafficking of women for prostitution across national borders mask the extent to which sex work has been intimately connected to the development of the global capitalist system. The transnational migration of sex workers has taken place for centuries. However, there is a perception we are seeing an acceleration in the scale of the phenomenon resulting from increased mobility across na- tional borders – as witnessed by the increasing numbers from Eastern Europe working in the sex industry in Western Europe.

One dominant discourse on the global sex trade within western feminism is that third world women working in prostitution need res- cuing from their plight and need to receive moral guidance, as they are incapable of making decisions about their sexual practice. They are passive victims who are uneducated and have no choice but to be forced into prostitution. Kempadoo and Doezema (1998) argue that this way of conceptualizing the global sex trade is redolent of neocolonialism, as it takes no account of the agency of women involved in sex work. The conditions of work for sex workers in developing areas may be poor, but so it is argued are conditions for other workers. It is claimed that some anti-trafficking campaigns may also cause harm to the very women they are designed to assist. For instance, Murray (1998) argues that in Australia anti-trafficking campaigns targeting Asian sex workers may cause harm in reinforcing racist stereotypes of Asian women as weak victims, which may mark them out as easier targets for abuse. She argues that feminists who seek the abolition of prostitution speak for all women and do not listen to working-class women who work in the sex industry. Murray suggests that there is complicity between feminists involved in groups such as the Global Alliance Against Traffic in Women (GAATW) and homophobic right-wing religious fundamentalists who seek to control and regulate all forms of non-procrea- tive sexual practices.

Buss and Herman (2003) argue that academic discussions of transnational social movements tend to stress their progress, radical nature, and agency in contrast to conservative global orga- nizations such as the World Bank. In their discussion of the transnational organization of the Christian Right they note a forging of alli- ances across religious boundaries on the basis of a common moral agenda around the protection of the sanctity of the family. These alliances lobby the United Nations to promote anti- abortion agendas. Buss and Herman note that Christian Right groups are increasingly target- ing homosexuality despite the fact that lesbian and gay rights activist groups have had little success at the global level – reflected in the failure of the International Lesbian and Gay Association to regain its consultative NGO sta- tus at the UN since this status was withdrawn in 1994.

One of the main vectors of the globalization of sexuality is the global AIDS pandemic. Indeed, AIDS has often been seen as a meta- phor for globalization itself, as it has brought into sharp relief how lives on the planet are interconnected with the impotence of nation- states to control flows of people with HIV across national borders. While helping to shape our consciousness of the world as a single place, the AIDS pandemic has impacted disproportio- nately on specific localities – the impact of the pandemic is experienced unevenly. Policy responses to the AIDS pandemic have been held responsible for the promotion of modern western models of gay identity as opposed to indigenous or folk models of sexual identity in developing countries. The globalization of sexuality is often assumed to mean the export of a western model of sexuality (Wright 2000). However, can we simply see the West as the original starting point from which other models of sexuality are considered or studied? Folk or indigenous models of sexuality are often set in opposition to western models of sexuality; however, to what extent can we generalize about an egalitarian model of same-sex relationships within the West? For instance, men who have sex with men in western countries may not identify with a gay identity or community.

A considerable body of work has been produced on the globalization of gay identity (Altman 1996, 2001; Philips 2000; Stychin 2003). We have witnessed the growth of a global gay consciousness and an associated activism and politics. For instance, the International Lesbian and Gay Association founded in 1978 now represents 370 organizations in 90 countries. The Internet is also playing a major role in facilitating the intensification of transnational activism around the rights of sexual dissidents. At the same time, global gay tourism has become visible through the development of global mega-events such as the Gay Games and pride events such as Sydney's Mardi Gras.

Debates on the globalization of gay identity have focused on whether the export of a western model of gay identity reflects the imposition of cultural imperialism, or whether the development of a global gay consciousness is a positive and empowering example of a cosmopolitan cultural politics which is forging transnational solidarities against homophobic policies and regimes. At the same time, it should be noted that groups and organizations such as the Christian Right that are hostile towards sexual dissidents also operate on a global scale. Postcolonial writers have challenged the ethnocentricity of the notion of a global gay identity and the ethnocentricity of lesbian and gay studies more generally (e.g., Puar's (2002) study of gay tourism in the Caribbean). Research on the globalization of sexuality is now drawing critical attention to the sexualized nature of the politics of nationalism, as this has often been overlooked

in debates on sex tourism and the politics of global gay identity.

Technological change is driving the acceleration of the globalization of sexuality. The development of the Internet in particular is significant in facilitating globalizing processes at a mundane level – for instance in aiding men's search for mail-order brides, but also enabling those involved in campaigning against the trafficking in women to maintain and develop transnational activist networks. However, the Internet also plays a powerful role in shaping sexualized identities and desires in late capitalism. The Internet therefore encourages the development of what Schein (1999) terms an "imagined cosmopolitanism" – the commodification of desires for worldliness reflected in global media and advertising. This is the desire for foreign products that reflect a sophistication and yearning to transgress the boundaries of the nation-state through, for instance, window-shopping and gazing on displays of imported foreign consumer goods. Schein's work on cosmopolitan commodity culture in contemporary China is an example of work on the more mundane ways in which global capital and desire intersect.

Future work on the globalization of sexuality will need to examine critically the everyday ways in which economic, political, and cultural components of globalization are sexualized and resist the moralizing tendencies of those who would seek to police sexual practices and sexual dissident communities.

SEE ALSO: Gendered Aspects of War and International Violence; HIV/AIDS and Population; Sex Tourism; Sexual Citizenship; Sexual Cultures in Africa; Sexual Cultures in Asia; Sexual Cultures in Latin America; Sexual Cultures in Russia; Sexual Cultures in Scandinavia; Third World and Postcolonial Feminisms/Subaltern; Traffic in Women; Transnational and Global Feminisms

REFERENCES AND SUGGESTED READINGS

Altman, D. (1996) Rupture or Continuity: The Internationalization of Gay Identities. *Social Text* 14(3): 77–94.

Altman, D. (2001) *Global Sex*. Chicago University Press, Chicago.

Binnie, J. (2004) *The Globalization of Sexuality*. Sage, London.

Buss, D. & Herman, D. (Eds.) (2003) *Globalizing Family Values: The Christian Right in International Politics*. University of Minnesota Press, Minneapolis.

Desai, J. (2002) Homo on the Range: Mobile and Global Sexualities. *Social Text* 20(4): 65–89.

Kempadoo, K. & Doezema, K. (Eds.) (1998) *Global Sex Workers: Rights, Resistance, and Redefinition*. Routledge, London.

Murray, A. (1998) Debt-Bondage and Trafficking: Don't Believe the Hype. In: Kempadoo, K. & Doezema, K. (Eds.), *Global Sex Workers: Rights, Resistance, and Redefinition*. Routledge, London, pp. 51–64.

Patton, C. (2002) *Globalizing AIDS*. University of Minnesota Press, Minneapolis.

Phillips, O. (2000) Constituting the Global Gay. In: Stychin, C. & Herman, D. (Eds.), *Sexuality in the Legal Arena*. Athlone Press, London, pp. 17–34.

Puar, J. (2002) Circuits of Queer Mobility: Tourism, Travel, and Globalization. *GLQ: A Journal of Lesbian and Gay Studies* 8(1–2): 101–37.

Schein, L. (1999) Of Cargo and Satellites: Imagined Cosmopolitanism. *Postcolonial Studies* 2: 345–75.

Smith, N. (1997) The Satanic Geographies of Globalization: Uneven Development in the 1990s. *Public Culture* 10: 169–89.

Stychin, C. (2003) *Governing Sexuality: The Changing Politics of Citizenship and Law Reform*. Hart Publishing, Oxford.

Wright, T. (2000) Gay Organizations, NGOs, and the Globalization of Sexual Identity: The Case of Bolivia. *Journal of Latin American Anthropology* 5(2): 89–111.

globalization, sport and

Joseph Maguire

Modern sport is bound up in a global network of interdependency chains that are marked by uneven power relations. Consider the consumption of sports events and leisure clothing. People across the globe regularly view satellite broadcasts of English Premier League and European Champions League matches. In these games the best players drawn from Europe, South America, and Africa perform. The players use equipment – boots, balls, clothing, etc. – that are designed in the West, financed by multinational corporations such as Adidas and Nike and hand-stitched, in the case of soccer balls, in Asia using, in part, child labor. This equipment is then sold, at significant profit, to a mass market in North America and Europe. Several transnational corporations are involved in the production and consumption phases of global soccer – some of whom own the media companies and have, as in the case of Sky TV, shareholdings in the soccer clubs they screen as part of what sociologists term the "global media-sport complex."

The sport/leisure-wear industry is an example of how people's consumption of cultural goods is bound up with global processes. As a fashion item, the wearing of sports footwear has become an integral feature of urban lifestyles and consumer culture. One premier brand is Nike. The purchase and display of Nike footwear by soccer players are but the final stages in a "dynamic network" involving designers, producers, suppliers, distributors, and the parent or broker company. Though Nike's headquarters are located in Oregon, US, the range of subcontractors involved straddles the globe. Its suppliers and production companies are located in a host of Southeast Asian countries, including Thailand, Singapore, Korea, and China. Its designers provide soccer boots with a worldwide demand that will also appeal to local tastes. Local franchise operations ensure appropriate distribution backed by global marketing strategies. Here again, Nike uses the media-sport production complex by endorsing sports stars such as the Brazilian soccer player Ronaldo and/or sports–leisure festivals such as soccer's World Cup. In addition, Nike uses advertising within the television schedules that carry these sports and other consumer-targeted programs. In the 2000–1 Premier League season it was reported that Nike was to become the official sponsor of Manchester United with a deal brokered at some £300 million over 15 years. In brief, elite sport now occurs on a worldwide scale and is patterned in connection with "global flows" of capital, culture, and people.

Global flows involve several dimensions: the international movement of people such as tourists, migrants, exiles, and guest workers; the technology dimension is created by the flow between countries of the machinery and equipment produced by corporations and government agencies; the economic dimension centers on the rapid flow of money and its equivalents around the world; the media dimension entails the flow of images and information between countries that is produced and distributed by newspapers, magazines, radio, film, television, video, satellite, cable, and the worldwide web; and finally, the ideological dimension is linked to the flow of values centrally associated with state or counter-state ideologies and movements. All five dimensions can be detected in late twentieth-century sports development. Thus the global migration of sports personnel has been a pronounced feature of recent decades. This appears likely to continue. The flow across the globe of goods, equipment, and "landscapes" such as sports complexes and golf courses has developed into a multi-billion dollar business in recent years and represents a transnational development in the sports sphere. In economic terms, the flow of finance in the global sports arena has come to center not only on the international trade in personnel, prize money, and endorsements, but also on the marketing of sport along specific lines. The transformation of sports such as American football, basketball, golf, and soccer into global sports is part of this process.

Closely connected to these flows have been media-led developments. The media-sport production complex projects images of individual sports labor migrants, leisure forms, and specific cultural messages to large global audiences. Consider the worldwide audience for the 2004 Olympic Games: over 300 television channels provided 35,000 hours of Olympic coverage delivering images of Athens 2004 to an unduplicated audience of 3.9 billion in 200 countries and territories. The power of this media-sport complex has forced a range of sports to align themselves to this global model that emphasizes spectacle, personality, and excitement. At the level of ideology, global sports festivals such as the Olympics have come to serve as vehicles for the expression of ideologies that are transnational in character. Note, for example, how the opening and closing ceremonies of the Athens Games were designed to project traditional images and "modern" messages about Greece to both its own people and to a global audience.

Three additional points need to be grasped in linking sport and globalization. First, studies of sport that are not studies of the societies in which sports are located are studies out of context. Here, emphasis is being placed on the need to examine the interconnected political, economic, cultural, and social patterns that contour and shape modern sport. Attention has also to be given to how these patterns contain both enabling and constraining dimensions on people's actions – there are "winners" and "losers" in this global game. Societies are no longer and (except in very rare cases) were never sealed off from other societies. Ties of trade, warfare, migration, and culture have existed through human history. Witness, for instance, the connections made throughout Renaissance Europe. More recent globalization processes have unleashed new sets of "interdependency chains," the networks that have (inter) connected people from distant parts of the globe. It is in this context of global power networks that the practice and consumption of elite modern sport is best understood. Secondly, in order to trace, describe, and analyze the global sports process it is wise to adopt a long-term perspective. A historical and comparative approach enables us to explain how the present pattern of global sport has emerged out of the past and is connected with a range of what Maguire (1999, 2005) has termed "civilizational struggles."

The third point of significance concerns the concept of globalization itself. What does the concept refer to? This is a matter subject to intense debate. Here is not the place to examine the merits of these arguments. It is sufficient to note that the concept refers to the growing network of interdependencies – political, economic, cultural, and social – which bind human beings together, for better and for worse. Globalization processes are not of recent origin, nor do they occur evenly across all areas of the globe. These processes involve an increasing intensification of global interconnectedness, are long term in nature, and gathered momentum during the twentieth century. Despite the "unevenness" of these processes, it is more difficult to understand local or national experiences without reference to these global flows. In fact, our living conditions, beliefs, knowledge, and actions are intertwined with unfolding globalization processes. These processes include the emergence of a global economy, a transnational cosmopolitan culture, and a range of international social movements. A multitude of transnational or global economic and technological exchanges, communication networks, and migratory patterns characterize this interconnected world pattern. As a result, people experience spatial and temporal dimensions differently. There is a "speeding up" of time and a "shrinking" of space. Modern technologies enable people, images, ideas, and money to cross the globe with great rapidity. These processes lead to a greater degree of interdependence, and to an increased awareness of a sense of the world as a whole. People become more attuned to the notion that their lives and place of living are part of a single social space: the globe.

Globalization processes, then, involve multidirectional movements of people, practices, customs, and ideas that involve a series of power balances, yet have neither the hidden hand of progress nor some all-pervasive, overarching conspiracy guiding them. Although the globe can be understood as an interdependent whole, in different areas of social life there is a constant vying for dominant positions among established (core) and outsider (peripheral) groups and nation-states. Given this growth in the multiplicity of linkages and networks that transcend nation-states, it is not surprising that we may be at the earliest stages of the development of a "transnational culture" or "global culture," of which sport is a part. This process entails a shift from ethnic or national cultures to "supranational" forms based upon either the culture of a "superpower" or of "cosmopolitan" communication and migrant networks. In this connection there is considerable debate as to whether global sport is leading to a form of homogenized body culture – specifically, along western or American lines. There is some evidence to support this. Yet global flows are simultaneously increasing the varieties of body cultures and identities available to people in local cultures. Global sport, then, seems to be leading to the reduction in contrasts between societies, but also to the emergence of new varieties of body cultures and identities.

In making connections between globalization and modern sport several findings stand out. Globalization processes have no "zero starting point." It is clear that they gathered momentum between the fifteenth and eighteenth centuries. These processes have continued apace since the turn of the nineteenth century. Research has identified several recent features of these processes, including an increase in the number of international agencies, the growth of global forms of communication, the development of global competitions and prizes, and the development of standard notions of "rights" and citizenship that are increasingly standardized internationally. The emergence and diffusion of sport in the nineteenth century is clearly interwoven with this overall process. The development of national and international sports organizations, the growth of competition between national teams, the worldwide acceptance of rules governing specific (that is, "western") "sport" forms, and the establishment of global competitions such as the Olympic Games and the men's and women's soccer World Cups, are all indicative of the occurrence of globalization in the sports world.

It would also appear that global sport processes are not solely the direct outcome of nation-state activities (e.g., the International Olympic Committee (IOC) operates independently of any specific nation-state). Rather, these processes need to be accounted for in relation to how they operate relatively independently of conventionally designated societal and sociocultural processes. In addition, while the globalization of sport is connected to the intended ideological practices of specific groups of people from particular countries, its pattern and development cannot be reduced solely to these ideological practices. Although elite sports migrants, officials, and consumers are caught up in globalization processes, they do have the capacity to reinterpret cultural products and experiences into something distinct, as the local acts back on the global. Furthermore, the receptivity of national popular cultures to nonindigenous cultural products can be active and heterogeneous; that is, local lives make sense of global events. That is not to overlook, however, that there is a political economy at work in the production and consumption of global sport products. Globalization then is best understood as a balance and blend between diminishing contrasts and increasing varieties, a commingling of cultures and attempts by more established groups to control and regulate access to global flows.

The emergence and diffusion of modern sport is therefore bound up in complex networks and interdependency chains marked by unequal power relations. Political, economic, cultural, and social processes contoured and shaped the development of sport over the past three centuries. This global development has undoubtedly led to a degree of homogenization – in common with broader globalization processes. In addition, the spread of British/European/western sports has had elements of cultural imperialism infused with it. Further, while there was no "master plan" in the early phases of this process, more recently transnational corporations have sought to strategically market their products to consumers across the globe. Westeners have been the global winners at their own games both on and off the field. The male members of "western" societies were acting as a form of established group on a world level. Their tastes and conduct, including their sports, were part of this, and these practices had similar effects to those of elite cultural activities within "western" societies themselves. They acted and act as signs of distinction, prestige, and power. Yet, this is not the whole story.

The rise of the "West" was contested and its "triumph" was not inevitable. Furthermore, "western" culture had long been permeated by non-western cultural forms, people, technologies, and knowledge. In sum, these cultural interchanges stretch back to long before the "west" momentarily achieved relative dominance in cultural interchange. It also needs to be recognized that both the intended and unintended aspects of global sport development need inspection. That is, while the intended acts of representatives of transnational agencies or the transnational capitalist class are potentially more significant in the short term, over the longer term unintended, relatively autonomous transnational practices predominate. These practices "structure" the subsequent plans and actions of the personnel of transnational agencies and the transnational capitalist class.

In addition, global sport has not led to complete homogenization: the consumption of non-indigenous cultural wares by different national groups is both active and heterogeneous. Resistance to global sportization processes has also been evident. Yet there is a political economy at work in the production and consumption of global sport/leisure products that can lead to the relative ascendancy of a narrow selection of capitalist and western sport cultures. Global sport processes can therefore be understood in terms of the attempts by more established white, male groups to control and regulate access to global flows and also in terms of how indigenous peoples both resist these processes and recycle their own cultural products. We are currently witnessing the homogenization of specific body cultures – through achievement sports, the Olympic movement, and sports science programs – and simultaneously the increase in the diversity of "sports"/body cultures.

It is possible, however, to overstate the extent to which the West has triumphed in terms of global sports structures, organizations, ideologies, and performances. Non-western cultures resist and reinterpret western sports and maintain, foster, and promote, on a global scale, their own indigenous recreational pursuits (e.g., Kabbadi, a traditional game/sport reputedly developed in India and now played in many parts of South Asia). Clearly, the speed, scale, and volume of sports development is interwoven with the broader global flows of people, technology, finance, images, and ideologies that are controlled by the West, and by western men. In the longer term, however, it is possible to detect signs that the disjunctures and non-isomorphic patterns that characterize global processes are also leading to the diminution of western power in a variety of contexts. Sport may be no exception. Sport may become increasingly contested, with different civilizational blocs challenging both nineteenth and twentieth-century hegemonic masculine notions regarding the content, meaning, control, organization, and ideology of sport. By adopting a multi-causal, multi-directional analysis that examines the production of both homogeneity and heterogeneity, we are better placed to probe the global cultural commingling that is taking place.

SEE ALSO: Figurational Sociology and the Sociology of Sport; Postcolonialism and Sport; Sport and Culture; Sportization

REFERENCES AND SUGGESTED
READINGS

Guttmann, A. (1994) *Games and Empires: Modern Sports and Cultural Imperialism.* Columbia University Press, New York.

Maguire, J. (1999) *Global Sport: Identities, Societies, Civilizations.* Polity Press, Cambridge.

Maguire, J. (2005) *Power and Global Sport: Zones of Prestige, Emulation and Resistance.* Routledge, London.

Maguire, J., Jarvie, G., Mansfield, L., & Bradley, J. (2002) *Sport Worlds: A Sociological Perspective.* Human Kinetics, Champaign, IL.

Miller, T., Lawrence, G., McKay, J., & Rowe, D. (2001) *Globalization and Sport.* Sage, London.

Van Bottenburg, M. (2001) *Global Games.* University of Chicago Press, Chicago.

globalization, values and

Christine Monnier

Global values refer to the moral and normative conceptions shared by individuals and social actors (such as international governmental and non-governmental organizations, transnational corporations, and global institutions) across national boundaries and that pertain to the future cultural shape of globalizing society. Global values have to be understood in the larger framework of cultural globalization and the globalization of culture. Far from being the product of a harmonious consensus, the delineation of global values is a contentious work-in-progress that reflects the complexities and ambiguities of the whole globalization process.

As defined by Roland Robertson (1992), globalization refers "both to the compression of the world and the intensification of consciousness of the world as a whole ... both concrete global interdependence and consciousness of the global whole." As a process of social change, globalization involves deterritorialization – the lifting off of social relations from territorial boundaries as well as the transformation of local relations. And as Robertson's definition indicates, globalization is also a reflexive process that involves a greater awareness of the

impact of global phenomena on people's lives as well as of the potential impact of local matters at the global level. Globalization is therefore a process marked by unevenness (it produces winners and losers and integrates different regions at variable speeds and intensity), complexity (different global processes, economic, political, cultural, are not synchronized), and contention.

Cultural globalization refers to the global expansion of cultural flows – transmission of symbols, ideas, artistic and consumption products – on a global scale. Technologies of transportation and communication have facilitated such cultural diffusion and the corresponding emergent global consciousness. Arjun Appadurai (1996) delineates these flows (or "scapes") as part of the process of cultural globalization. They comprise mediascapes (flow of information through the mass media, television, the Internet), financescapes (flow of capital through the global financial system), technoscapes (flow of technology or flows made easier thanks to technology), ethnoscapes (flow of people, immigration, refugees, tourists), and ideoscapes (flow of ideas such as consumerism, market, democracy or human rights). The arena of cultural globalization is where the future moral contours of global society and conflicting value systems are debated.

The globalization of culture refers to the ways in which different cultures are shaped by, and respond to, culturally globalizing flows. It points to the emergence of a global culture, or, as Frank Lechner and John Boli (2005) conceptualize it, a world culture. World culture is the "culture of world society, comprising norms and knowledge shared across state boundaries, rooted in nineteenth-century western culture but since globalized, promoted by non-governmental organizations as well as for-profit corporations, intimately tied to the rationalization of institutions, enacted on particular occasions that generate global awareness, carried by the infrastructure of world society, spurred by market forces, riven by tension and contradiction, and expressed in the multiple ways particular groups relate to universal ideals." As this definition shows, if people and social actors share a global consciousness, they do not share consistent views of what the global order should look like. These different imagined global futures display contrasting value systems and are promoted by different groups.

Jan Nederveen Pieterse (2004) delineates three major global value systems: cultural differentialism, cultural convergence, and hybridization. The cultural differentialist paradigm postulates the preeminence of the local. If there is to be a global culture, it is a global mosaic, composed of discrete territorial, cultural entities anchored in different regions of the world. This is the view popularized as "clash of civilizations" or the "West vs. the Rest": different regional blocs have radically different values that can only generate conflicts between civilizational blocs. As Samuel Huntington postulates, the value system of a global society should be based on the universalization of western values, founded on the Enlightenment, democracy, and free markets. Whereas Huntington argues for the universalization of a particular value system (the West), other cultural differentialists argue for a strong version of cultural relativism. A global culture should be based on the preeminence of local values, free from outside interferences necessarily perceived as threat of cultural destruction. Such a view is popular among the anti-globalization movements, especially in groups focused on the preservation of indigenous societies and the assertion of their cultural rights. In such a view, the core global value is preservation of cultural diversity. Both the clash of civilizations and cultural relativism views are based on an essentialist view of culture based on territory and boundaries. They reify cultural systems and promote open-air museums in the guise of local empowerment. They ignore historical traditions of cultural exchanges as well as contemporary global flows and global deterritorialization.

The main fear articulated by cultural relativists is the fear of cultural convergence or cultural synchronization: the spread of American or western values, especially values related to the sphere of consumption, akin to cultural imperialism. In this view, the spread of global capitalism and western imperialism creates a world society based on a consumerist universalism. Borders and locales no longer matter as individuals all become part of a homogeneous world culture guided by principles of McDonaldization (Ritzer 2004) and Disneyization

(Bryman 2004) whereby most social relationships become commodified, including locales, in the case of international tourism. Mass consumption becomes the one and only significant universal value at the expense of all the local value systems that constitute the human mosaic. This dystopic view of world culture is also endorsed by world-system analysts who view it as the ideology of the world capitalist system generated in order to sustain it. The homogeneity created within nations, at the expense of local culture and particularist values, produces a form of hegemony: global culture is the culture of capitalism. The universalist values it promotes are those of individualism and satisfaction through material comfort alongside the predominance of rationalized modes of production (McDonaldization) and consumption (Disneyization). In this view, a global ideology is being created that is spread worldwide through the western-controlled mass media to sustain the consuming needs of the world-economy. However, there is a utopian side to the view of the global spread of western capitalism, popularized as "creative destruction." In this view, global mass consumption expands the menu of choice offered to individuals no matter what particular society they live in. There may be more cultural homogeneity between societies, but the expansion of the market provides more consuming diversity within societies as more objects of consumption become globally available. Cultural convergence produces greater individual choice irrespective of territorial base. In the utopian version of this view, the spread of western values can only be conducive to more democracy and choice where individuals are liberated from the tyranny of place – a view convincingly debunked by Amy Chua's analysis of the rise of market-dominant minorities in the face of politically dominant majorities. Chua shows that globalization as the double process of democratization (popular access to political institutions) and increased wealth concentrated in the hands of a few minority groups (such as Chinese in the Philippines) creates the conditions not for utopian combination of democracy and mass consumption but rather for brutal ethnically based conflict.

Such a cultural imperialist view is simplistic as it assumes that globalization is unilateral, from the core to the periphery: wherever western values and institutions spread, they automatically become dominant and the cultural forms they encounter cannot resist. In other words, both cultural differentialist and cultural convergence analyses assume that global cultural processes flow one way, with no obstacles in their path: from imperialist core areas (western consumption patterns) to a passive recipient periphery powerless to stop such flows.

Both the cultural differentialist and the cultural convergence views assume that global values are part of a process of universalization of the particular (Robertson 1992), that is, the universal application of values specific to certain cultural systems. The reality of global culture and values is more complex, contentious (as the previous two paradigms indicate), and multidirectional. As much as there is determination of local circumstances through global structures, this does not eliminate the possibility of local impact in global processes, such as the Zapatistas' rebellion in Mexico in reaction to NAFTA. What does get threatened is the functionalist emphasis on coherence and boundaries that create social integration as transcultural flows shape both the local and the global. Global values may involve universalization of the particular, but they also involve the reverse process of particularization of the universal. This process has been variously called hybridization (Nederveen Pieterse 2004), creolization (Tomlinson 1999), or glocalization (Robertson 1992). All these designations involve the complex dynamics through which global processes and values are integrated into local contexts to produce cultural hybrid practices, such as world music.

In this context, western values may not so much be imperialistically delivered to peripheral areas as much as they are glocalized. Western values such as individual freedom, democracy, human rights, gender equality, and sexual autonomy as well as scientific and technological rationality are undeniably spreading globally, supported by the development of global movements, institutions, and infrastructures. However, how these values are integrated into local contexts, that is, glocalized, involves a complex interplay of local and global factors. For instance, feminist social movements are different in Japan than in western countries as they adapt the general concept to their local circumstances.

At the same time, cultural and institutional globalization has seen the emergence of global values that have originated not in western countries but either in peripheral areas or in global institutions. For instance, cultural diversity and sustainable development, as global moral imperatives, have generated resistance both in core and peripheral areas. In core areas, cultural diversity is perceived as a threat to rather homogeneous populations and long-established nations. For instance, the veil controversy in France illustrates how any encroachment on secular institutions can generate nationalist reactions in the face of multiculturalist demands. Similarly, sustainable development demands serious economic and moral reconsideration of western consumption practices that are perceived as impediments to the "freedom to consume," so to speak. On the other hand, peripheral countries have sometimes perceived intimations to sustainable development as normative impositions that impede sovereignty and development choices. Similarly, Muslim countries have consistently insisted on opt-out options regarding human and women's rights out of respect for local traditions. It is precisely in the process of glocalization that areas of contention emerge regarding how global values are to be integrated or assimilated into local contexts.

As Lechner and Boli (2005) show, although world culture is riddled with conflict regarding what value system should prevail and shape the future of world society, the different United Nations world conferences on global topics (such as population, environment, or women's rights) reveal a global consensus on certain basic premises (the value of global negotiation and a common definition of global problems to be addressed in a global forum where all voices can be heard, even if confrontation arises), processes, and structures. In spite of such contentious debates, global responsibility is a value whose legitimacy is implicitly agreed upon although who/what is responsible for whom/what is precisely what is vigorously debated. Similarly, global responsibility becomes a moral imperative that displaces the perceived outdated morality of proximity (Tomlinson 1999) where one is only responsible for one's own limited and localized circle of territorial relationships. Instead, the appeals to the global community are multiplied to intervene to stop genocides, provide relief against famines and natural disasters, and unite against the threat of global terrorism. Conversely, the intimation to "think global, act local" injects global responsibilities into personal actions.

Similarly, the anti-globalization movement does not stand outside of globalization but asserts a value system with global claims, another instance of universalization of the particular in the constantly contentious debate regarding the value foundation of global society. In this case, anti-globalization activists assert the global relevance of their value system even if what they demand is de-globalization, that is, a return to the local. The claim may be for the preeminence of the particular, but it is asserted globally as having global relevance and legitimacy. In this sense, as much as they advocate for a return to the local and traditional values and social organizations, such groups as religious fundamentalists and indigenous populations' rights activists are promoting their own version of global society based on local values understood as the only source of legitimacy.

Indigenous populations present an interesting case of how global cultural values, far from being a reflection of western imperialism, promote emancipation. The visible struggle for respect for indigenous traditions and rights obscures that the cultural and political form most responsible for the silencing of minority voices has historically been the nation-state. As Anderson (1983) has shown, the creation of nations as imaginary communities involved a deep imperialist process of nationalization, that is, elimination (cultural or physical) of marginal populations and their cultural practices, traditions, and values. The very possibility for indigenous populations to have their struggle recognized as legitimate on the global stage and their rights included in global documents, such as the Earth Charter, reflects a value shift in favor of cultural diversity and multiculturalism as opposed to national homogeneity. When the Zapatistas appeal to the global community to support their struggle, they recognize the legitimacy of the global stage as proper institutional context. They also promote an ethical glocalization: the integration of the global when liberating (global networks of support), but its rejection when oppressive (World Trade Organization).

There is no set of neatly defined global values. Rather, because global society is connected and integrated (through flows) but neither unified nor centralized or harmonious, the sources of value systems are multiple, contradictory, and contentious. Such value conflicts reflect the often underestimated cultural nature of globalization and its complexity as traditional or popular explanations, clash of civilizations or cultural imperialism, fail to account for the hybrid nature of globalizing culture and values.

SEE ALSO: Consumption; Creolization; Cultural Imperialism; Culture; Dependency and World-Systems Theories; Disneyization; Distanciation and Disembedding; Global Justice as a Social Movement; Globalization; Globalization, Consumption and; Globalization, Culture and; Globalization and Global Justice; Glocalization; Grobalization; Hybridity; Indigenous Movements; McDonaldization; Values; Values: Global

REFERENCES AND SUGGESTED READINGS

Anderson, B. (1983) *Imagined Communities: Reflections on the Origin and Spread of Nationalism.* Verso, London.
Appadurai, A. (1996) *Modernity at Large.* University of Minnesota Press, Minneapolis.
Bryman, A. (2004) *The Disneyization of Society.* Sage, Thousand Oaks, CA.
Lechner, F. J. & Boli, J. (2005) *World Culture.* Blackwell, Oxford.
Nederveen Pieterse, J. (2004) *Globalization and Culture.* Rowman & Littlefield, Lanham, MD.
Ritzer, G. (2004) *The McDonaldization of Society: Revised New Century Edition.* Pine Forge Press, Thousand Oaks, CA.
Robertson, R. (1992) *Globalization.* Sage, Thousand Oaks, CA.
Tomlinson, J. (1999) *Globalization and Culture.* University of Chicago Press, Chicago.
Wallerstein, I. (1990) Culture as the Ideological Battleground of the Modern World-System. In: Featherstone, M. (Ed.), *Global Culture.* Sage, Thousand Oaks, CA, pp. 31–55.
Waters, M. (2001) *Globalization.* Routledge, London.

glocalization

Melanie Smith

The neologism "glocalization" has emerged in recent years in economic, sociological, and cultural theories in response to the proliferation of writings about globalization and its local implications. It might best be described as the relationship between global and local processes, which are increasingly viewed as two sides to the same coin rather than being diametrically opposed (e.g., Robertson, 1992). The age of global mobility has created more fluid and seamless relationships. For example, the work of Castells (1996) on the network society and Appadurai's (2001) discussion of flows gives some indication of how global mobility has affected local environments and their inhabitants.

Giddens (1998) suggests that globalization was originally a political and economic term. It could be argued that glocalization, on the other hand, represents the intersection of political economics and sociocultural concerns, with its emphasis on the local and community impacts of global structures and processes. Ritzer (2004: 73) defines glocalization as "the integration of the global and the local resulting in unique outcomes in different geographic areas." Glocalization can thus represent the consequences (both tangible and intangible) of globalization, e.g., the creation of heterogeneous or hybridized cultures, communities, and identities. In business terms, it might represent the local orientation of global product marketing, taking into consideration local social and cultural characteristics and traditions. In postmodern architecture, it may include "organic" approaches to the construction of new buildings (i.e., taking into account local environmental and historic features). In the context of global tourism, international visitors are brought into contact with local environments and their communities, thus influencing cross-cultural exchange. Tourism can also sometimes help to strengthen the importance of retaining place identities and local character.

Nevertheless, glocalization could also be viewed somewhat negatively. For example, Bauman (1998) suggests that the term glocalization is best thought of as a restratification of society based on the free mobility of some and the place-bound existence of others. Tourist flows, for example, are mainly unidirectional (e.g., West to East, or developed to less developed countries). For this reason, tourism has sometimes been described as a new form of imperialism, which causes acculturation and radical social change rather than hybridization (the inevitable consequence of sustained foreign influence over time). Similarly, global economic and business developments are often deemed "imperialistic," even where they have a local orientation.

Ritzer (2004) suggests that this dominance of capitalist nations and organizations might be termed "grobalization" rather than "glocalization." He argues, like Robertson (1994), that the key characteristics of glocalization are sensitivity to differences, the embracing of cosmopolitanism, and respect for the autonomy and creativity of individuals and groups. The notion that the local is largely passive in the face of globalization is therefore a misrepresentation. For example, Barber (1995) sees "Jihad" as being the local response to the homogenizing influence of "McWorld." Friedman (1999) sees "healthy glocalization" as a process by which local communities incorporate aspects of foreign cultures that enrich them, but reject others that would negatively affect their traditions or identity. The accessibility of new communications and technology also allows many societies to propagate local cultures globally.

Overall, therefore, glocalization could be seen as a positive interpretation of the local impacts of globalization, that is, a process by which communities represent and assert their unique cultures globally, often through new media.

SEE ALSO: Cultural Imperialism; Globalization; Globalization, Culture and; Grobalization

REFERENCES AND SUGGESTED READINGS

Appadurai, A. (2001) *Globalization*. Duke University Press, Durham, NC.

Barber, B. (1995) *Jihad vs. McWorld*. Times Books, New York.

Bauman, Z. (1998) *Globalization: The Human Consequences*. Polity Press, Cambridge.

Castells, M. (1996) *The Rise of the Network Society*. Blackwell, Oxford.

Friedman, T. (1999) *The Lexus and the Olive Tree: Understanding Globalization*. Anchor Books, New York.

Giddens, A. (1998) *The Third Way*. Polity Press, Cambridge.

Ritzer, G. (2004) *The Globalization of Nothing*. Sage, London.

Robertson, R. (1992) *Globalization: Social Theory and Global Culture*. Sage, London.

Robertson, R. (1994) Globalization or Glocalization? *Journal of International Communication* 1: 33–52.

Goffman, Erving (1922–82)

Gregory W. H. Smith

The work of Erving Goffman centered on explicating the structures and processes of the "interaction order," the domain of social life brought about and facilitated by the physical co-presence of persons. In a series of extraordinary writings published from the early 1950s through the early 1980s, Goffman developed an utterly singular vision of social life, expressed in a highly distinctive language that reflected his extraordinary observational acuity and his unmatched sociological grasp of metaphor and irony.

Born in Mannville, Alberta, Canada to Jewish migrants from the Ukraine, Erving Manual Goffman was educated at the universities of Manitoba (1939–42), Toronto (BA 1945) and Chicago (MA 1949; PhD 1953). His doctoral studies included a spell at Edinburgh University's department of social anthropology, which sponsored and funded 12 months of fieldwork on the remote Shetland island of Unst. Following research posts at Chicago and with the National Institute of Mental Health (where he conducted fieldwork at St. Elizabeth's Hospital, Washington, DC for *Asylums*), he was appointed to the faculty of the University of California, Berkeley's sociology department in 1958, becoming a full professor in 1962. While teaching at Berkeley he influenced a number of graduate students, including John Lofland, Dorothy Smith, David Sudnow, and Harvey Sacks. He also used his proximity to Nevada to undertake participant observation of casino life, first as a gambler, then as a croupier. Goffman relocated to the University of Pennsylvania in 1968, where his work became increasingly sensitized to sociolinguistic and gender issues. He remained there until his death in 1982 from stomach cancer.

Goffman's primary contribution to sociology was to show how social interaction was fundamentally organized in social terms and amenable to close sociological investigation. He demonstrated how the building blocks of social encounters – the talk, gestures, expressions, and postures that humans constantly produce and readily recognize – were responsive not to individual psychology or social structural constraints but to the locally specific demands of the face-to-face social situation. This central analytic aim was pursued through a score of papers and eleven widely read books, including *The Presentation of Self in Everyday Life* (1959), *Asylums* (1961), *Stigma* (1963), and *Frame Analysis* (1974). In opening the interaction order as a distinct sub-area of sociology Goffman brought a novel analytic attitude, a spirit of inquiry, and a persistent skepticism that connected narrow disciplinary concerns to wider social currents.

INTELLECTUAL AND SOCIAL CONTEXTS

While Goffman's sociological project was unprecedented, his development of the sociology of the interaction order bore the imprint of the early social and intellectual contexts he encountered. Often characterized as a leading exponent of symbolic interactionism, Goffman brought a modulated determinism and critical edge to this perspective that owed something to the cultural influence of his Canadianism. At Toronto important influences were anthropologist C. W. M Hart, who introduced students to then-untranslated portions of Durkheim, and the founder of kinesics, Ray Birdwhistell, whose class exercises involved close observation of ordinary behavior in natural settings.

These initial interests were firmed up after 1945 when Goffman moved south to join the talented cohort of students and faculty sometimes referred to as the second Chicago School of Sociology. Chicago proved to be the crucible in which a number of critical influences were condensed into the distinctive approach now immediately identifiable as "Goffman's sociology." Social psychological, sociological, anthropological, and literary lines of influence shaped the emergent Goffman. First, there was the legacy of G. H. Mead's social psychology, codified as "symbolic interactionism" by Mead's student Herbert Blumer in 1937. While Goffman absorbed Mead's teachings about the formation of self through social interaction, he did so critically, acknowledging that in complex contemporary societies where the sources of moral consensus were increasingly differentiated, role-taking was often more problematic than Mead envisaged. Cooley and Dewey were also major influences. A leading sociological influence was Simmel's formal sociology, mediated via the Chicago School's founding figure, Robert E. Park, who attended Simmel's lectures at Berlin. One of Park's students, Everett C. Hughes (whom Goffman considered his most important teacher at Chicago), passed the Simmel torch to the postwar generation. Simmel's pioneering "sociational" conception of society that prioritized interactions between persons over large-scale structures and institutions was congenial to Goffman, as was his proposal that sociology's core method was to extract the "formal" features of sociation. As a formal sociologist, Goffman sought to elucidate and analyze a variety of forms of the interaction order, such as the basic kinds of face-work, the forms of alienation from interaction, the arts of impression management, or the stages of remedial interchange. The anthropological influence on Goffman's thought derives from the late "symbolic" Durkheim of *The Elementary Forms of the Religious Life*. This line of influence passed from Durkheim to British social anthropologist A. R. Radcliffe-Brown – whom Goffman almost met in 1950 – through to W. Lloyd Warner (another significant Chicago teacher, and adviser for the research element of Goffman's two graduate degrees). The literary influence was represented by Kenneth Burke's writings, especially from *Permanence and Change*

(1935), from which Goffman extracted Burke's method of perspective by incongruity, evident in the many irreverent comparisons and unexpected contrasts that became a Goffman trademark. Burke himself apparently approved of *Presentation of Self* as a sociological application of his own dramatistic approach.

These lineage lines contextualize the formation of Goffman's sociology, but do not explain its unique shape and preoccupations. Goffman grew exasperated by critics who sought to label – and thus assimilate – his ideas to sociology's major paradigms. In his view, sociological traditions were there to be creatively applied and modified, not slavishly followed. Throughout his career Goffman showed a remarkable facility to respond to and incorporate into his analyses ideas drawn from other theoretical approaches (game theory, ethology, phenomenology, feminism, conversation and discourse analysis). While his writings displayed clear systematic intent, the drive to build a single system was absent. Goffman was much more at home with the essay mode, never providing a final cumulative statement of his sociology. His judgment was that interaction analysis was too undeveloped to aspire to anything more than some robust conceptual distinctions. More than many significant twentieth-century sociologists, Goffman's oeuvre demands to be reconstructed by the reader; Goffman did not provide any obvious interpretive key to his work.

MAJOR SUBSTANTIVE CONTRIBUTIONS

Goffman burst onto the scene with the 1959 US publication of *The Presentation of Self in Everyday Life*, a book that breathed new life into the ancient "all the world's a stage" metaphor. Embarking from a psychobiology that emphasized the immediate symbolic functions of the expressions humans constantly "give" (through the content of their talk) and "give off" or exude (through tone, posture, gesture, facial expression, and the like) when in the presence of others, Goffman brilliantly analyzed the "dramaturgical" aspects of this conduct. Using a wide range of illustrative materials – ranging from respectable treatises, ethnographies, and social histories through memoirs, popular journalism, and novelistic accounts to his own acute observations of human conduct – Goffman showed how interactional details could be cogently understood in sociological terms as "performances" fostered by an "audience" requiring cooperative "teamwork" among performers to bring off a desired definition of the situation. Performances may be presented in "front" regions (such as workplaces or formal ceremonial settings) that are usually differentiated by "barriers to perception" from "back regions," the back-stage areas (bathrooms, restaurant kitchens, private offices) where performers prepare themselves. Goffman went on to examine how "discrepant roles" and "communication out of character" can threaten the fostered reality. A recurrent theme in his writings was that successful interaction needs not Parsonsian role-players enacting the institutionalized obligations and expectations of a status, but rather "interactants" skilled in "the arts of impression management."

In Goffman's subsequent writings a range of figures – notably game, ritual, and ethological metaphors – were used as methodological devices to highlight otherwise taken-for-granted features of social encounters. Face-to-face interaction was a species of social order, which he named "the interaction order" (a term coined in his 1953 PhD dissertation, then seemingly forgotten, and only revived for his posthumously published, valedictory American Sociological Association Presidential Address; see Goffman 1983). Confining his analytical attention to this face-to-face realm of embodied expression, Goffman produced both systematic examinations of the general forms of the interaction order (including *Behavior in Public Places*, 1963; *Relations in Public*, 1971; and *Forms of Talk*, 1981) and dissections of certain of its problematic aspects (notably *Asylums*, 1961; *Stigma*, 1963; and *Gender Advertisements*, 1979). Though Goffman always sought to maintain his own distinct position, his later work was increasingly preoccupied with issues that ethnomethodology had brought to the fore of sociological analysis, and his longest book, *Frame Analysis* (1974), can be read as a sustained response to Garfinkel's *Studies in Ethnomethodology* (1967). One major point of difference was the social self, which was for Goffman an abiding sociological referent.

Most generally, Goffman's interaction analysis acknowledged the centrality of informational (or "communicative" or "system") and ritual demands on interaction. The former concerned the communication and control of information given and exuded by the interactant (mood, intention, competence, trustworthiness, etc.) and was ultimately constrained by the physical limits of the human body's vision, voice, hearing capacities, and so forth. Goffman mobilized dramaturgy and game theory to analyze the levels of mutual awareness that can emerge in inference making in ordinary encounters. It was these emphases that yielded complaints about Goffman's "cynical" or "Machiavellian" view of human nature. The ritual model offered very different imagery. Ritual elements concern the expression and control of the interactant's feelings towards both self and others. Here Goffman creatively adapted Durkheim's theory of religion, applying it to the secular world of social encounters. In his work on face-work, deference and demeanor, and supportive and remedial interchanges, Goffman showed how greetings and farewells, apologies and avoidance practices illustrated the need for persons to monitor their interactional conduct when in the presence of that sacred deity, the self of the other. From first to last, Goffman was a Durkheim revisionist.

Goffman's analyses constantly distinguish out-of-awareness features of encounters that, once identified, become instantly recognizable. His pivotal distinction between focused and unfocused interaction is a case in point. Focused interaction, with its single joint focus of attention (e.g., a card game, a conversation, a physical task jointly carried out), is straightforward enough to grasp. But unfocused interaction, when persons orient their conduct simply by virtue of the co-presence of others (e.g., walking down a busy street), opens up for sociology hitherto unenvisaged sources of social orderliness. A rule of "civil inattention" constrains the conduct of unacquainted others on the street, persons walking past each other silently being likened to passing cars dipping their lights. Civil inattention is one of a special class of social rules that regulate interaction known as "situational proprieties," departures from which Goffman found especially instructive. Situational *im*proprieties were less a matter of psychopathology as they were an expression of alienation from the community, social establishments, social relationships, and encounters.

Goffman arrived at this conclusion after his monumental study of the plight of mental patients in *Asylums*, and his psychologically astute analysis of the identity implications of departures from normality in *Stigma*. Like his dissertation, in *Asylums* Goffman strove to overcome the limitations of his case study by generating an analytic ethnography that pursued selected conceptual themes. The mental hospital was seen as part of the larger class of "total institutions" that also included prisons, concentration camps, and monasteries. Social processes of "mortification" were common to them all. Mental patients underwent shared changes in self-conception – a shared "moral career" that was at once cause and consequence of their current predicament as they were sucked into a "betrayal funnel." Patients developed an underlife, rich in "secondary adjustments," which created space for conceptions of self at odds with officially prescribed conceptions. The practice of psychiatry was described as a form of service work, a "tinkering trade" that offered precious little real service to the mental patient. *Asylums*, however, was not simply an influential critique of mental hospitals that brought Goffman to the attention of non-sociological audiences: it remains a vivid exploration of resistance to authority and the social sources of selfhood under extreme conditions.

Stigma also drew acclaim from outside academic sociology. It provided a careful analysis of normality and those temporarily or more extensively excluded from full social acceptance. Although Goffman defined a stigma as a "deeply discrediting attribute" and was much concerned with the situation of groups such as the disfigured, the differently abled, and ethnic minorities, his emphasis was once again on acts and relationships, not personal attributes. *Stigma* also anticipated identity politics. Later, and in part in response to his feminist-oriented students, Goffman presented an "institutional reflexivity" theory that saw gender difference as a thoroughly social construction. He illustrated his approach to gender difference through an analysis of some 500 advertising images in *Gender Advertisements*, a book that still stands as an unrivalled piece of visual sociology. While Goffman's thinking on gender difference did not attract the acclaim of his earlier ideas, it anticipated many of the key points of Judith Butler's celebrated performative theory by more than a decade, and showed Goffman's continuing sensitivity to social currents beyond the academy.

Goffman deepened his perspective with his longest book, *Frame Analysis*, which provided a modulated phenomenological dimension to his sociology. Frames are perceptual principles that order events, sustained in both mind and activity. For Goffman, frames were constantly shifting features of situational social life, analyzeable into primary frameworks and two kinds of transformed frame, the keying and the fabrication. We can make sense of two persons quarreling in terms of a primary framework, a "domestic argument," but can also come to see it as keyed if the couple are rehearsing a scene in a play, or as fabricated if one party is being set up for a reality TV program. Frames structure events, but our understandings can also be altered if participants seek to shift from a literal frame to a joking one. Goffman emphasized both the determinative characteristic of frames and the capacity of interactants to change the currently prevailing frame. This theme is refined in his last book, *Forms of Talk* concept of "footing" is designed to capture the shifting alignments of persons to their own and others' talk. Goffman's later work focuses more consistently on the syntactical relations between the acts of co-present persons, but the self does not disappear from view. Goffman's earlier two-selves viewpoint (where an unsocialized self seems to lie behind the presented self, directing it) gives way to a more sociologically consistent view of the self as a "changeable formula" with no more depth than is encoded in interactional conduct.

RELEVANCE TO HISTORY OF CONTEMPORARY SOCIOLOGY

One of the more readable (and certainly one of the most quotable) of twentieth-century sociologists, Goffman's deceptively accessible writings can be understood at many levels and in a range of different ways. This is evident in the proliferation of a range of readings of his ideas: interactionist, structuralist, existentialist, ethogenic, modernist, and postmodernist. His sociology has attracted extremes of assessment from extravagant commendation to outright dismissal – the latter evaluations tending to originate from within sociology. The core of these objections concerns his cavalier approach to questions of method. Goffman was master of his own craft and did not have a method in the conventional sense of a set of procedures that can be taught to graduate students. His principled indifference stemmed from a conviction that actual research practice was always going to be at variance with proclaimed methodological procedures. Alternative valuations have concentrated on Goffman's artful use of a range of rhetorical devices. Goffman's texts adopt a distinct format made up of several components: the essay mode; conceptual framework development as a preferred discursive structure; pressing the deployment of metaphor to the point of exhaustion; and use of a range of sociological tropes, including perspective by incongruity, parataxis, irony, and humor. But the deconstruction of Goffman's texts in this way does not explain the ongoing fertility of his ideas. The brilliance and idiosyncrasy of his writings have so far proved a tough act to follow.

In the image originally applied to Simmel, Goffman left a cash legacy to be spent as successors consider fit. The primarily conceptual character of Goffman's legacy has proved to be adaptable to a variety of analytic enterprises. Theoretically, Goffman's ideas play an important role in the grand syntheses of Giddens and Habermas. Practically, *Asylums* impacted the deinstitutionalization movements of the 1960s and 1970s. *Stigma* remains a pivotal text for groups advancing the interests of the differently abled. In empirical terms, researchers have developed more fully explanatory theory from Goffman's initial conceptions. Examples include theories of politeness, interaction ritual chains, the centrality of frame analysis to social movements theory, and social psychological versions of impression management theory. Ethnographers of various hues have been equipped with an extensive and powerful analytic vocabulary. As might be expected from the cash legacy notion, the influence of Goffman's sociology, both direct and diffuse, continues to be far-reaching.

SEE ALSO: Blumer, Herbert George; Dramaturgy; Facework; Frame; Interaction; Interaction Order; Public Realm; Self; Simmel, Georg; Stigma; Symbolic Interaction

REFERENCES AND SUGGESTED READINGS

Branaman, A. & Lemert, C. (Eds.) (1997) *The Goffman Reader*. Blackwell, Oxford.

Burns, T. (1992) *Erving Goffman*. Routledge, London.

Ditton, J. (Ed.) (1980) *The View from Goffman*. Macmillan, London.

Drew, P. & Wootton, A. (Eds.) (1988) *Erving Goffman: Exploring the Interaction Order*. Polity Press, Cambridge.

Fine, G. A. & Smith, G. W. H. (Eds.) (2000) *Erving Goffman*. Sage Masters of Modern Social Thought, 4 vols. Sage, London.

Goffman, E. (1983) The Interaction Order. *American Sociological Review* 48(1): 1–17.

Manning, P. (1992) *Erving Goffman and Modern Sociology*. Polity Press, Cambridge.

Riggins, S. H. (Ed.) (1990) *Beyond Goffman: Studies on Communication, Institution and Social Interaction*. Mouton de Gruyter, Berlin.

Smith, G. W. H. (Ed.) (1999) *Goffman and Social Organization*. Routledge, London.

Smith, G. W. H. (2005) *Erving Goffman*. Routledge, London.

Treviño, A. J. (Ed.) *Goffman's Legacy*. Rowman & Littlefield, Lanham, MD.

Waksler, F. (Ed.) (1989) Special Issue: Erving Goffman's Sociology. *Human Studies* 12(1–2).

Gökalp, Ziya (1876–1924)

Serif Mardin

Turkish sociologist Ziya Gökalp was the first to use western sociological theory as a foundation of his thought. He is known as the originator of a systematic theory of Turkish nationalism. This theory was elaborated in the confluence of three problematic issues in the Ottoman Empire at the end of the nineteenth century.

One was the policy of "Ottomanism," an attempt by the reformist Ottoman bureaucracy to modernize the empire. Ottomanism attempted to present Ottoman reform to the Concert of Europe (composed of Russia, Prussia, Austria, and Great Britain) as having modernized the structure of the empire and granted a new status to non-Muslim communities. It was hoped this would make Turkey worthy of acceptance in the Concert. This strategy was successful (1856), but met with much criticism from various groups inside the empire. The second Ottoman problem was the question of the viability of a union of all Muslims under Ottoman leadership. This issue was known as Islamism or *İslamcılık*. The third issue was an option increasingly discussed among Ottoman intellectuals in the 1890s, i.e., the ideology of rallying all Ottomans around "Turkishness."

In Cairo in 1904, an article appeared in the Young Turk periodical *Turk* entitled "Three Types of Policies" that weighed all three alternatives, condemning Ottomanism and "pan-Islamism" but expressing a hope for the promotion of a Turkish national culture. The author was Yusuf Akçura, a Turkic émigré from Russia. Exactly the same issue was later to be discussed in a set of articles by Gökalp with the title "Underscoring One's Turkishness, Islamicness and Modernity" (*Türkleşmek, İslamlaşmak, Muasırlaşmak*), with *modernity* as an added option in the list of alternatives.

Gökalp's birthplace, Diyarbakır, was a provincial center distant from the Ottoman capital. However, it had profited from more of an input of the western-oriented reform movement, the *Tanzimat*, than might be imagined. Diyarbakır had an official gazette published by Gökalp's father, and it had a lycée (*idadi-i mülki*), a product of reform that Ziya attended. Ziya came from a prominent local family and his father's house had a large library, presumably containing nineteenth-century geographical atlases and other reference works.

There was a sufficient number of secular intellectuals around to alert Gökalp to the ideas of materialism that came out of the West. He appears to have been introduced in his youth to Dr. Abdullah Cevdet, an intellectual who was to become a key representative of nineteenth-century western secular materialism in Turkey. One of Gökalp's mentors, a Greek physician who was his teacher of biology in school, had a permanent influence on his intellectual development. His uncle, Hasip Efendi, introduced him to Islamic mysticism. These crosscurrents resulted in a depression that led to an attempted suicide (1895).

Gökalp was involved in a number of subversive activities encouraged by the Young Turk presence in Diyarbakır for which he was imprisoned in 1898. He thereafter went to Istanbul to study at the Veterinary School, from which he graduated. In 1903–7 Gökalp occupied a bureaucratic position in Diyarbakır. In 1907, leading a group of protestors, he occupied the Diyarbakır telegraphic office and sent a collective telegram to the sultan asking him to stop the depredation of a local tribal sheikh who was taking advantage of his position as a quasi-gendarme to fleece the local population. Following the Young Turk Revolution and their accession to power on July 23, 1908, Gökalp was once again in Diyarbakır filling the position his father had occupied as the editor of the province's official journal.

Gökalp was a local delegate to the Young Turk Congress of Salonika in 1909 and impressed the leaders of the party. Traveling back and forth between Salonika and Diyarbakır, he found time to increase his knowledge of western philosophy and sociology in Salonika where he read books ordered from Europe. He also taught sociology in the Salonika lycée in 1910 and established relations with a literary group and its publication, *Genç Kalemler*. *Genç Kalemler* paid special attention to linguistic issues and the elaboration of a literature expressed in the vernacular Turkish.

In the election of 1912 to the reestablished Ottoman parliament, Gökalp was elected as representative from Ergani. During World War I he took up the role of ideological mouthpiece for the Young Turks, following in his writings their various shifts of interest from Pan-Turkism to Islam. He may be considered to have adumbrated some of their emerging secularism in articles he wrote before the war.

In 1911 Akçura had started a new review, *Türk Yurdu* (*The Turkish Hearth*). It was here that Gökalp published his article "Underscoring One's Turkishness, Islamicness and Modernity" in 1912. According to Akçura, *Türk Yurdu* itself was a continuation of the

Tercüman, edited by Gaspıralı İsmail (Ismail Gasprinski) in the Caucasus since 1883. Akçura therefore underlined the much earlier interest of the Turkic population of Russia in the questions he reviewed in "Three Types of Policies." This emphasis on the greater experience and sophistication of the Tatar as compared to the Ottomans was to remain a sticking point between the two men and led to a break in their relation after 1912. At the time, Ziya Gökalp was immersed in a much wider intellectual Ottoman debate about the three options detailed by Akçura. In this debate figured Süleyman Nazif (1869–1927), an "Ottomanist," Ahmet Ağaoğlu (1869–1934), a "Turkish nationalist," Babanzâde Ahmet Naim (1872–1934), an "Islamist," Ali Kemal (1867–1922), an "Ottomanist," and Yusuf Akçura, a "Turkist."

During World War I, Ziya Gökalp was increasingly enmeshed in the ideological themes promoted by the Young Turks. With the financial help of the Party of Union and Progress, he founded in 1914 the bi-monthly *İslam Mecmuası*, which continued publication until 1917. The review went along with a new interest of the Young Turks for the reform of the Ottoman Islamic institutions. This interest concentrated on the ways in which religion could be integrated with the state the Young Turks were constructing. Gökalp wrote a report for the 1916 Convention of the Union and Progress Party where he explored the same issue.

Following the defeat of the Ottoman Empire, the Young Turks abolished the Party of Union and Progress on November 5, 1918. On December 21, the Young Turk leaders fled, the Ottoman parliament was dissolved, and Gökalp was interrogated over his involvement in the Armenian deportations. On January 30, 1919, allied occupational forces landed in Istanbul, picked up a number of prominent Young Turks, and sent them into exile or prison in Malta. As a member of the Central Committee of the Young Turks, Gökalp was among their number. After returning from Malta in 1921, he went to Ankara where the new (later republican) regime was being organized. His return to Diyarbakır in 1922 probably reveals the suspicion Ankara still felt toward a former Young Turk responsible for the ruin of the empire.

In Diyarbakır Gökalp published a new review, *Küçük Mecmua*. This phase of his life shows he was somewhat insensitive to the acceleration of the new regime's secularist policies. On November 1, 1922, the sultanate was abolished and on November 18 an Ottoman prince was nominated as caliph without the title of sultan. Following the abolition of the sultanate, Gökalp discussed the issue of the caliphate, maintaining that it was a religious institution that should only be concerned with matters of faith (see Gökalp 1959: 223–7). Unfortunately, this view, which tacitly accepted the role of a purely religious caliph in Turkey, was diametrically opposed to the position taken by the minister of justice Seyyid Bey in the Turkish parliament on March 3, 1924. Seyyid Bey argued that the caliphate was a purely political position and therefore had no role to play in a republic that did not allow devolution of power. Seyyid Bey's speech led to the abolition of the caliphate on the same day. The coolness that developed at the time between Gökalp and Ankara is therefore understandable. However, this difference seems to have been patched up when Gökalp was asked to direct the bureau in charge of publication and translation. He thereafter applied himself to promoting the ideology of the government in a brochure *Doğru Yol* (*The Right Way*).

GÖKALP'S INNOVATIONS

Gökalp's key concepts of the *umma*, the nation, and the international community show an evolutionist view of society. Although he outlined the stages of the process, it was difficult for him to specify the specific stage at which the Ottoman Empire found itself in the early twentieth century. Many of his statements should therefore be seen as part of a general program to be implemented in relation to "social facts" and their change over time.

Up to the time of Gökalp's writings, the critique of the policies implemented in the empire was focused on their capability and efficacy in confronting western ideologies promoting "progress" and "civilization." Gökalp turned the defensive attitude around. He stated that one should build a response to these pressures by observing social facts as components of Ottoman society. In his view, these had been approached by the *Tanzimat* with a somewhat superficial understanding of the processes involved both in western influences and in the internal social changes the empire was undergoing. For instance, a structuring element of modernity the reformers had not taken into account was the division of labor that produced a general differentiation in social, economic, and political functions of society. A more general process could be observed that furnished the dynamic element of modernization and stood behind the division of labor, namely "new life ... an ideal which is in the process of emerging from the [sic] social consciousness. Today this ideal has to remain somewhat ambiguous. This ambiguity will be cleared by time and by the guidance of social convention" (Gökalp 1959: 315)

The central point of departure for Gökalp's sociology was the *umma*, the Islamic community at large. The *umma* could not be kept intact in the changing social structure of the Ottoman Empire, but, nevertheless, it had to remain in a modified form as a receptacle of faith. The remaining element of the *umma* was to be given a new foundation by retaining the Arab alphabet (a common feature of Muslim culture), by working on a common terminology for all Muslims, by promoting *umma*-wide congresses taking up common educational policies to establish communication links between Muslims of all nations, and by keeping the crescent as a common symbol.

Even in the Ottoman Empire the social division of labor had expanded and had given rise to a society of occupational groups. Consequently, the collective consciousness of Muslim and Christian communities had begun to weaken. The ground was thus set for the emergence of a new type of society, the nation. This process was propelled by three types of forward motion: first, the social density that would create the effervescence necessary for change (something that Gökalp probably picked up from Durkheim's view on religion). This effervescence, in turn, brought to the surface of society the component of its specific "ethos." The integration of the component of the ethos produced a "culture" (*hars*) and its expression in a language. People of the same language tended to embrace the same faith. This somewhat confusing aspect of Gökalp's ideas has had a prolongation in contemporary Turkish

nationalism, and can only be fully understood in the following quotation from Gökalp: "As language plays a part in decoding religious affiliation, so religion plays a part in determining membership in a nationality. The Protestant French became Germanized when they were expelled from France and settled in Germany. The Turkish aristocracy of the old Bulgars became Slavicized following their conversion to Christianity" (1959: 81).

The society to emerge from this process was the nation. The forces that propelled the nation ahead, however, were not simply those of a social structure. They also depended on changes in communication patterns that accompanied the division of labor. According to Gökalp, Gabriel Tarde discerned two levels in this innovation. The first was the newspaper. The newspaper, using the vernacular version of a language, created a sense of shared identity among its readers, uniting them into a public. The second element was the book, which worked to promote a further associational bond in the sense that it addressed itself to persons who shared abstract ideas, e.g., the scholar and the scientist. This was the foundation of the international community, the next stage of social evolution with which the Ottomans had to integrate.

The nation is thus seen by Gökalp "as that ethnic group which, as it emerges after a long period of fusion in an empire, strives to regain and revive its identity." The emergence and maintenance of this identity, however, can only be understood in relation to Gökalp's belief in a "social mind" of a transcendental character in relation to organic social phenomena.

Although many of Gökalp's speculations on Turkism show the use of the concept of race (1959: 75), in 1917 he was clear in preferring the new use by the French geographer Vacher de Lapouge of the concept of *ethnie*. He stated his preference for the term "ethnic family" instead of race when speaking of groups of smaller units, *kavm*, a group of individuals who have a common language and usage (Gökalp 1959: 127).

The name Turk was both a repository of *mores* and the name of a vernacular folk language that had been overlaid by a hybrid court culture. The nation, having once emerged, would be supported by systematic research concerned with retrieving Turkic folk motifs, symbols, and usages. The emergence of the nation did not mean that the function of the *umma* disappeared. What had to happen was the creation of an "up-to-date Turkism" (1959: 76). The Turks would still consider themselves to be of the *umma* of Islam, the Qur'an to be their sacred book, and Muhammad their sacred prophet. However, many of the items that the *ulema* saw as part of the *şeriat*, such as the approval of polygamy, had no relation whatsoever to religious commands.

For Gökalp, the map of a future Turkey was Turkism, which included the search for authentic culture still buried in the culture of the people, doing away with the Ottoman written language and reforming language to fit the vernacular of folk literature. Like many of his contemporaries, Gökalp promoted populism and probably received these ideas from Turkic Russian émigrés. He contributed to a periodical entitled *Towards the People*, in which the Russian populist ideology was echoed. His populism, however, shows the element of authoritarianism that appears in many of his ideas.

Gökalp's idea of solidarity rests on Durkheimian foundations and on Durkheim's use of solidarity. However, Gökalp's solidarity is to be distinguished from French solidarism. It had an authoritarian content that is evident in his views on property: "Individual ownership is legitimate only insofar as it serves social solidarity. The attempts of the socialist and communist to abolish private property are not justified. However, private wealth which does not serve social solidarity cannot be regarded as legitimate" (1959: 312).

Influences on Gökalp included Durkheim's concepts of the division of labor as well as the social bond of solidarity. The contrast of *Gemeinschaft* and *Gesellschaft* appears without a clear reference to Tönnies, and Fichte is mentioned in relation to the "Germanic ideal." The ideas of Gabriel Tarde and Fouille's *idées force* are part of Gökalp's theoretical foundations. He thought Bergson the most original thinker of his time. Gökalp took from him the idea of an *élan vital* and that of creative evolution. But even in their cumulation, these vitalist foundations can only be understood in relation to Gökalp's less often expressed view of an active social mind that was transcendental in

character. He may have been predisposed to this view by his conviction of the profundity of Islamic Sufism.

Conscience collective and collective representation were both concepts Gökalp received from Durkheim, but he used them somewhat differently. In Durkheim, collective conscience is the source of control of moral transgressions. In Gökalp, it is the cement of nationality. This is an illegitimate extension of the term that may have links with his admiration of Ibn Arabi and Arabi's theory of eternal essences. Gökalp's use of "collective representations" as mental patterns common to members of a society expressed through symbolism as part of the culture of that society is closer to the Durkheimian use.

Ziya Gökalp's *Türkleşmek, İslamlaşmak, Muasırlaşmak*, later transformed into his *The Principles of Turkism* (*Türkçülüğün Esasları*) (1921), was used as an ideological frame for nationalists of the republican era. Intransigent Kemalists nevertheless neglected the central role that Gökalp still gave to Islam. It appears that this role had already disappeared in his *Principles of Turkism*. The extreme nationalist right has also found a source of inspiration in his ideas. The poem *Turan*, with its references to a Central Asian Turkic "hearth" as an ideal to be followed by all Turks, has kept its force as an inspiration for Turkish nationalists. Although Gökalp had investigated the status of Kurdish tribes in his birthplace and published the result of his investigation, there is no mention of Kurds in the *Principles of Turkism*.

SEE ALSO: Collective Consciousness; Culture; Developmental Stages; Durkheim, Émile; Ethnic Groups; Ideology; Islam; Mass Media and Socialization; Modernization; Nationalism; Popular Culture; Positivism; Progress, Idea of; Science and Culture; Solidarity; Tönnies, Ferdinand

REFERENCES AND SUGGESTED READINGS

Binark, İ. & Sefercioğlu, M. N. (1971) *Doğumunun 95. Yıldönümü Münasebetiyle Ziya Gökalp Bibliyografyası*. Türk Kültürünü Araştırma Enstitüsü, Ankara.

Bolay, S. H. & Anar, S. (1996) Gökalp, Ziya. In: *Türkiye Diyanet Vakfı İslam Ansiklopedisi*, Vol. 14. TDV İSAM, Istanbul, pp. 124–37.

Gökalp, Z. (1918) *Türkleşmek İslamlaşmak Muasırlaşmak*. Yeni Mecmua, Istanbul.

Gökalp, Z. (1921) *Türkçülüğün Esasları*. Matbuat ve İstihbarat Matbaası, Ankara.

Gökalp, Z. (1923) *Türk Töresi*. Matbaa-i Amire, Istanbul.

Gökalp, Z. (1925) *Türk Medeniyeti Tarihi*. Matbaa-i Amire, Istanbul.

Gökalp, Z. (1950) *Foundations of Turkish Nationalism: The Life and Teachings of Ziya Goekalp*. Luzac, Harvill, London.

Gökalp, Z. (1959) *Turkish Nationalism and Western Civilization*. Trans. and Ed. N. Berkes. George Allen & Unwin, London.

Gökalp, Z. (1968) *The Principles of Turkism*. Trans. and annotated by R. Devereux. E. J. Brill, Leiden.

Gökalp, Z. (1995) *Hars ve Medeniyet*. Ed. Y. Toker. Toker Yayınları, Istanbul.

Kadri, H. K. (1989) *Ziya Gökalp'in Tenkidi*. Dergah Yayınları, Istanbul.

Parla, T. (1989) *Ziya Gökalp, Kemalizm ve Türkiye'de Korporatizm*. İletişim Yayınları, Istanbul.

Goldman, Emma (1869–1940)

Melissa Sandefur

Emma Goldman was a social and political writer, revolutionary activist, and one of the most accomplished speakers in American history. Goldman was a proponent of individualistic anarchism, which she described as the philosophy and theory that government and man-made laws are intrinsically coercive and harmful to individual liberty (Goldman 1969). Her commitment to anarchism and to the ideal of freedom led her to champion the causes of labor, anti-militarism, freedom of religion, prison reform, and sexual and reproductive freedom. Her most important contributions to political and social thought include the incorporation of sexual politics into anarchism and her many essays on contemporary issues such as education, birth control, women's emancipation, modern drama, national chauvinism, and crime. A passionate feminist, Goldman believed that a purely political solution was not the answer to inequality between the sexes, but that equality would come only from a massive transformation of values and from women themselves.

Emma Goldman was born on June 27, 1869 in the Jewish quarter of Kovno, Russia (now Lithuania) to innkeeper-parents Taube Bienowitch Goldman and Abraham Goldman. Goldman spent a harsh and sometimes violent childhood (at the hand of her father) in Kovno, Popelan, and Königsberg. In 1881 when Emma was 13, the Goldman family moved to St. Petersburg, just after Tsar Alexander II's assassination. It was there that she was influenced by the radical student circle of St. Petersburg (Wexler 1984). Goldman attended school for 6 months, but because of family economic hardships she dropped out to work in a glove factory. Goldman's father attempted to arrange a marriage, but Emma, then only 15, refused with threats of suicide. She escaped the harsh conditions of Russia by moving to the US with her half-sister Helena; they joined another sister, Lena, in Rochester, New York. Her 2-volume, 56-chapter autobiography *Living My Life* (1931) begins with her arrival in the US. Goldman worked at a clothing factory where working conditions were hazardous and where she was subjected to anti-Semitism, low pay, and 15-hour workdays. Goldman discovered that for a Jewish/Eastern European immigrant, America was not the Promised Land. These early experiences and her readings on communist anarchy, socialism, and Marxism influenced Goldman's belief that many problems of individual freedom stemmed from the social conditions resulting from capitalism.

Goldman was first drawn to anarchism following the Haymarket Square Strike and the subsequent Riot of 1886 in Chicago. This tragedy began as a confrontation between police attempting to disperse marchers protesting police violence, and striking workers in Haymarket Square. A riot ensued when an unidentified person threw a bomb, triggering a gun battle. Eight anarchists were arrested, charged, and tried for crimes and deaths associated with the riot; seven were found guilty, sentenced to death, and eventually four were hanged. Goldman followed the events intensely and on the day of the hangings resolved to become a revolutionary. As an anarchist Goldman adopted syndicalist leanings, rejecting private property ownership and promoting free worker cooperatives in place of capitalism (Wexler 1984).

In 1887 Goldman married fellow factory worker Jacob A. Kersner, thus gaining US citizenship. Ten months later, she divorced Kersner and moved to New Haven, Connecticut, where she worked at a factory and met other Russian socialists and anarchists (Wexler 1984). Goldman then relocated to New York City, where she met her mentor, German anarchist Johann Most, editor of *Die Freiheit*, and her closest friend and lifelong comrade, Alexander Berkman. As a writer and prominent orator, Most encouraged Goldman to become a public speaker and deepened her interest in anarchist philosophy. Goldman's initial lectures were delivered in Yiddish or German, but in time she gained confidence and considerable skill as a speaker in English. Most also stimulated her interest in the social revolutionary potential of the arts. However, Goldman became dissatisfied with Most's attitude toward her as a woman, believing that he viewed her as his subordinate and mistress more than an equal comrade. She gravitated toward Berkman, who became her lover and closest comrade in the anarchist movement. Of the many men in her life, Goldman felt that only Berkman treated her as an equal, never pressuring her to fill the traditional roles of wife and mother (Solomon 1987).

Early in her anarchist career, Goldman advocated violence as an acceptable means to an end. She helped Berkman plot to assassinate industrialist Henry Clay Frick in 1892 after Frick used force to suppress strikers, leaving 9 dead. Goldman and Berkman hoped that the assassination of Frick would ignite a revolution. The assassination attempt was a failure, however, as Frick was only slightly injured, and the workers were not incited to revolt. Berkman received a 22-year prison sentence for the attempted assassination, but Goldman's involvement was never proven (Wexler 1984). In her autobiography, Goldman unburdened herself of her clandestine involvement with Berkman in the Frick debacle. She wrote: "my connection with Berkman's act and our relationship is the leitmotif of my 40 years of life" (Falk 2003: 3). As her thinking evolved, Goldman rejected violence in favor of political organizing. For the next 30 years she lectured, studied nursing, edited and wrote for the radical anarchist magazine *Mother Earth*, and mobilized political protests advocating anarchism, free speech, and civil liberties.

Though Goldman did not support the women's suffrage cause, she criticized the social and economic subordination of women and was an early advocate of the right of women to practice birth control. She was arrested several times for violating the 1873 Comstock Law prohibiting the distribution of birth control literature. She saw birth control as a social issue and argued that the choice to have sexual relations without fear of unwanted pregnancy was critical to the human spirit and liberty as well as necessary to the empowerment of women (Wexler 1984). In her writings on women, Goldman argued that pursuing the vote would not bring women true emancipation. Instead, she advocated for institutional changes, particularly related to women's sexual freedom, economic independence, and marriage. Goldman discussed marriage as an impediment to love and to the ideal relationship between the sexes. Because of her belief in absolute freedom and her own disappointing experience of marriage, Goldman believed individuals should enter into and leave personal relationships without constriction. "If I ever love a man again," she said in 1889, "I will give myself to him without being bound by the rabbi or the law, and when that love dies, I will leave without permission" (Goldman 1931: 36). Marriage, in her opinion, was a legalized form of prostitution, in which women traded sex for economic and social standing (Solomon 1987). Building on her critique of women's suffrage, Goldman claimed that no political solution would free women from the internal constraints of public oppression. Goldman argued that if women are to be emancipated they must stand on their own ground and insist on unrestricted freedom (Goldman 1969).

During the depression of 1893, Goldman was arrested in New York's Union Square and convicted for "inciting to riot" (Wexler 1984). She was sentenced to a year at Blackwell's Island Penitentiary where she served as a nurse to the inmates, studied, and read freely. She became more fluent in English while working with prisoners and resolved to address

English-speaking audiences in promoting "real social changes" (Goldman 1931: 155). Her experience with prison, both from her own internment and from the writings of Berkman, led her to address the deplorable conditions of prisons and the failure of the criminal justice system. Her 1917 publication *Anarchism and Other Essays* included an essay on "Prison: A Social Crime and Failure." Pointing out that the methods used by society to deter crime were unsuccessful, Goldman promoted understanding of the social conditions leading to criminal behavior and called for a radical restructuring of political and economic institutions. She further advocated for the importance of providing prisoners with meaningful work and adequate pay as the primary mode of rehabilitation (Solomon 1987). "My Year in Stripes," published in the *New York World* the day after Goldman's release, told the story of her arrest and of the humiliating living conditions in prison. Goldman later declared before a crowd of supporters that if the representatives of government intended to prosecute women for talking, they would have to "begin with their own mothers, wives, sisters and sweethearts" (Falk 2003).

On September 6, 1901, self-proclaimed anarchist Leon Czolgosz shot President William McKinley in Buffalo, New York, at the Pan-American Exposition and later stated that a lecture by Goldman motivated his attack. Authorities arrested and interrogated Goldman but found no evidence linking her to the assassination (Wexler 1984). Goldman continued her public tours and gained much public favor among the middle class and liberal organizations that supported progressive causes and opposed 1903 legislation banning anarchists from entering the country (Solomon 1987). Goldman also began a new series of lectures on the Russian Revolution as tensions in Tsarist Russia mounted. In 1903 the Jewish community suffered a wave of pogroms: planned campaigns of persecution or extermination sanctioned by the government. Hundreds of Jews were killed in Kishinev and the final blow came in 1905 during "Bloody Sunday" when political dissidents demonstrating at the Winter Palace were slaughtered by Russian troops. For 2 years, Goldman toured and drummed up support for the Russian Revolution (Wexler 1984).

In the years between 1908 and 1916, Goldman's lecture tours throughout the US and Canada took on a new level of intensity after she met and became the lover of Dr. Ben L. Reitman, a gynecologist who began to manage her engagements. Her prominence as a speaker is evident in the expansiveness of her audience. According to Solomon (1987: 26), in a 6-month tour in 1910 Goldman spoke in 25 states to an audience of 40,000 and she sold 10,000 articles of literature. Another boost to Goldman's popularity came in 1906 when Berkman was freed from prison after serving out 14 years of his 22-year sentence. Together, Goldman and Berkman resumed their advocacy for political education. Berkman wanted to achieve anarchism through the labor movement, while Goldman's ideology cut across class lines and attracted followers from the middle class. They founded *Mother Earth*, a radical periodical edited by Goldman until it was censored by the US government in 1917 (Wexler 1984). Many of Goldman's lectures and writings were devoted to drama, a venue that allowed her to promote radical ideas through the arts. *Anarchism and Other Essays* contained writings on anarchism, social criticism, women's emancipation, prison reform, and modern drama; it received widespread publicity and reviews. In 1914 Goldman published a series of lectures (*The Social Significance of the Modern Drama*) critiquing social morality as represented by modern playwrights. Goldman addressed plays such as *A Doll's House*, a critique of women's roles and marriage, Shaw's *Major Barbara*, and Ibsen's *Ghosts*. Through her use of drama Goldman brought her social critique to a new audience (Solomon 1987).

"Red Emma," a prime target of the US government, was arrested 16 times and jailed on several occasions. In 1917 Goldman and Berkman were imprisoned for protesting military conscription. Then in 1919, during the post–World War I anti-Bolshevik fervor, the government revoked Goldman's citizenship and both Goldman and Berkman were deported to Russia (Wexler 1984). After 2 years Goldman fled the new Soviet Union, profoundly disillusioned with the authoritarian state and its disregard for civil liberties. Goldman subsequently wrote *My Disillusionment in Russia* (1923) and attempted to discredit Bolshevism and to defend her own revolutionary principles. She wrote of her experiences in Soviet Russia from 1920 to 1921 and what she saw as the Bolsheviks' betrayal of the Revolution. Goldman argued true communism was never present in the Soviet Union, as the class system there was never abolished – just reformatted. In addition, Goldman noted that the Bolsheviks wielded even more power than the tsars they overthrew, and party officers spent most of their time seeking greater influence and prestige.

Emma Goldman spent the last two decades of her life traveling between France, England, and Canada, still actively promoting her humanist brand of anarchism. In June 1925, still exiled from the US, Goldman married a British friend and anarchist, James Colton, in order to secure British citizenship. She then moved to a small cottage, purchased by friends, near St. Tropez, France, where she wrote her autobiography with Berkman's editorial assistance. Goldman maintained her friendship with Berkman, who lived in exile in Nice, and helped to support him financially. However, as Berkman's health and financial situation deteriorated he became depressed and in June 1936 he shot himself, leaving Goldman feeling devastated and hopeless. Goldman was reenergized, however, when she was invited by Augustine Souchy, head of a Spanish anarcho-syndicalist group, to support the Spanish workers' rebellion. While fundraising for the Spanish revolutionaries in Canada, Goldman suffered a paralyzing stroke and died 3 months later, on May 14, 1940. At the request of friends, she was buried at Waldheim Cemetery in Chicago, near the graves of the Haymarket strikers (Solomon 1987).

Emma Goldman's contributions to sociology are most evident in her political critiques of major social institutions: the family and marriage, religion, industrial capital, education, and most importantly, the state. Mentored by the most prominent anarchists of her time, she incorporated various strains of anarchy into a social movement reflective of a historical period of American radicalism often lost to historians. Rather than simply advocating anarchism as an intellectual exercise, she tested and expressed her theory through public speaking and her published works in the tradition of sociological "praxis." Goldman was concerned both with

educating the public about anarchism as well as providing a critique of social problems that stemmed from society as it was structured. Although Goldman was interested in political and social issues, she gave theoretical primacy to the individual and to the principle of self-determination. Despite what was sometimes an absence of logic in her orational rhetoric, Goldman's emphasis on freedom was always at the center of her activism and of her revolutionary thinking. Goldman's lasting influence on American history is evident in the fact that many of her historical proclamations continue to ring true today.

SEE ALSO: Anarchism; Communism; Family Conflict; Gender, Work, and Family; Inequality/Stratification, Gender; Radical Feminism; Sex and Gender

REFERENCES AND SUGGESTED READINGS

Drinnon, R. (1961) *Rebel in Paradise: A Biography of Emma Goldman*. University of Chicago Press, Chicago.

Drinnon, R. & Drinnon, A. M. (1975) *Nowhere at Home: Letters from Exile of Emma Goldman and Alexander Berkman*. Schocken Books, New York.

Falk, C. (1990) *Love, Anarchy, and Emma Goldman*. Rutgers University Press, New York.

Falk, C. (2003) *Emma Goldman: A Documentary History of the American Years*. Vol. 1: *Made for America, 1890–1901*. University of California Press, Berkeley.

Goldman, E. (1914) *The Social Significance of the Modern Drama*. Richard C. Badger, Boston.

Goldman, E. (1923) *My Disillusionment in Russia*. Doubleday, Page, Garden City, NY.

Goldman, E. (1924) *My Further Disillusionment in Russia*. Doubleday, Page, Garden City, NY.

Goldman, E. (1931) *Living My Life*. Alfred A. Knopf, New York. (Reprinted 1970 Dover, New York.)

Goldman, E. (1969 [1917]) *Anarchism and Other Essays*. Dover Publications, New York.

Potter, D. (1983) *Vision on Fire: Emma Goldman on the Spanish Revolution*. Commonground Press, New Paltz.

Schulman, A. K. (1971) *To the Barricades: The Anarchist Life of Emma Goldman*. Thomas Y. Crowell, New York.

Solomon, M. (1987) *Emma Goldman*. Twayne Publishers, Boston.

Wexler, A. (1984) *Emma Goldman: An Intimate Life*. Pantheon Books, New York.

governmentality and control

Susanne Krasmann

In his lectures at the Collège de France at the end of the 1970s, the French philosopher Michel Foucault developed a new analytics of power, making the concept of governmentality the focus of his interest. This concept first of all refers to the historical emergence of an "art of government": governing becomes an object of problematizing the best possible mode of exercising power. "Art," therefore, alludes to an artificiality of government, something fabricated by humans and implying certain techniques and forms of knowledge, and to a capacity of producing effectiveness. The rationality of government, then, does not consist in a substantial reason, as what seems to be rational results from a relation between the object operated on, the objective pursued, the application of suitable means, techniques, and so forth. In short, rationality is itself a reflection of the conditions of government. It is by no means timelessly valid; rather, the historical context and the perspectives of a society or a local culture give the structure that facilitates its emergence, and here especially the knowledge itself that comes into use. *Governmentality studies* examines rationalities of government that form the techniques, procedures and ways of action, and the economy of power that these technologies create.

In this sense, the concept also refers to a type of power that, according to Foucault, has become preeminent throughout the West: the art of "governing people," which makes the individual become an active subject of its own government. Accordingly, the notion of government does not just refer to state and politics in its common-use sense today, but also means the education of children, the organization of household and family, management strategies, the government of communities, and the control of social problems. The term already implies this wide range of meanings in modernity, and Foucault reconstructs the genealogy of the art of government as a history of problematizations. These in the first place concentrate on the inquiry into the reason of state: what is the

convenient way to go about fostering and defending the power of the state independently of the person of the ruler? Later on, the population will be discovered as an object of government in itself. Demographic developments and problems, like diseases and poverty arising from the growing industrial work and developing urban structures, were being made operational – and thus controllable – using statistical methods. Finally, the economy is becoming an independent science, posing the question of how the functioning of the economy can be reconciled with social welfare. Consequently, the economy, the social, and the political came out of these kinds of rationalizations as objects of knowledge and government. Their separation in different spheres therefore is on no account timeless, but the product of historical processes.

The exploration of governmentalities departed in the 1990s from the Anglo-Saxon reception of Foucault's lectures (cf. Burchell et al. 1991). Studies on the history and the effects of contemporary technologies of government made the most diverse social fields objects of investigation, ranging from genetics via philosophies of management to crime control. Yet, it is no accident that the "history of the present" was first written in the Anglo-Saxon countries, in particular in Great Britain under Thatcherism (cf. Barry et al. 1996), as the concept is especially suitable for critically dealing with the political rationality of neoliberalism. Liberalism in this perspective is conceived of not as a theory or a philosophy defending freedom as a civil right only, but as an art of government recognizing liberty as an indispensable element for effective government. Freedom therefore is not a naturally preexisting entity, not something we own. Rather, it is presupposed artificially and thus becomes a resource of government, the use of which at the same time has to be organized.

Historically, liberalism initially expressed itself as a critique of too much interference and dissociated itself from the police science of the seventeenth and eighteenth centuries that was constantly concerned with the social order and its regulation. Nevertheless, Foucault above all regards a liberal government as a specific type of power which has to be dissolved from this historically specific constellation, a mode of governing people operating on the basis of possibilities that are being created, structured, and restricted. According to liberal reason, in order to conduct the behavior of people it is not necessarily indispensable to exercise force; rather, it is more effective to grant and structure the practice of freedom. Thus, freedom might take the effect of a promise mobilizing the capacities of individuals. They will learn to conceive of themselves as free subjects, as entrepreneurs that invest, citizens claiming their rights, creative persons on their way to self-realization – and thus governing themselves. To be governed and to govern oneself is, according to Foucault (1993), inextricably linked together.

But liberalism also threatens the liberty that it itself founded, and this too can be deciphered as a kind of strategy: the free play of the market forces that it presupposes, the freedom of personal development, or the safety of the citizens it claims to guarantee, all these rights have to be secured. Insecurity, then, is a complement of liberty taking the effect of a negative promise – the threat of dangers, risks, and insecurities demands the implementation of security mechanisms that themselves constrain freedom. Security and liberty represent not only two main cornerstones of the liberal constitutional state, but also basic elements of technologies of government. By playing them off against each other and at the same time interweaving them, individuals are being convinced that they have had to subordinate their personal concerns in favor of the safety of all, or that in their own interests they have had to undertake endeavors to secure their own existence. Also insecurity is a precondition that allows for regulating the proper use of freedom politically (cf. Hindess 1996; Lemke 1997).

There are at least four aspects under which the concept of governmentality is opening up a new perspective for the analysis of power and domination, whereas the term "government" has to be posed in between these two poles. It refers neither to a spontaneous, ephemeral form of exercising power restricted to situations nor to conditions of domination already consolidated. Focusing on an intermediate level of rationalities and technologies of government, the concept firstly allows for scrutinizing the manners in which political tactics and strategies mold the subjectivities of people, how political programs first of all produce imaginations, necessities, and endeavors and thus indirectly steer the behavior of people and their lifestyles. Forms of subjectivation are the effect of technologies of power but at the same time their vanishing point: we cannot presume a subject capable of creating itself in an act of free will any more than that this is determined socially. Rather, it can be deciphered as a point of resistance, making the forms of exercising power visible at the same time as they are being bent, refracted, varied. Therefore, a category like that of homosexuality might equally reflect a social strategy of stigmatization and an emancipating countermovement. Differently from the term "social control," the concept of governmentality does not focus on individuals as mere objects of control ambitions but is interested in scrutinizing how the exercise of power on the one hand results in producing subjects and the activation of people, and how on the other hand it brings about counterpower, which is what the term of the subject implies.

Secondly, government is a practice, and the knowledge it requires is always also a practical knowledge, a *knowhow*. Technologies of government therefore cannot merely be deciphered as systems of meaning or ideology but as techniques and procedures that themselves are capable of bringing really new objects and subjects of government into being. Technological inventions thus made it possible to gather, copy, and retrieve data according to respective requirements, seemingly resulting in more efficient procedures of administration and control. Persons, therefore, find themselves sorted according to the most different criteria into a variety of risk groups. Computer programs may identify them as recipients of social benefits or, depending on their habitual drug consumption, as prospective patients or, as a result of a dragnet investigation, as suspects. Each time, the control technology focuses only on certain aspects of a person recorded into technically codified samples of data. The individual thus becomes a "dividual" (Gilles Deleuze).

Being concerned with the analysis of how historical forms of knowledge tie together with practices of government and how political rationalities form the view of people, of society and its problems, governmentality studies thirdly focuses on the power of political programs to produce reality. Programs, in stating problems and aspiring to appropriate strategies of dealing with them, not only describe reality but also shape it. They create the preconditions of their own acceptance, singling out certain aspects of reality and problematizing them according to their own rules. They not only indicate the direction of the change to be performed, but also offer the criteria for the evaluation that seems proper according to the respective rationality. They fabricate reality, telling what one could and should do, and at the same time presuming what kind of person one is and could be. They prescribe while seeming to describe. Sure enough, this does not predicate the conditions under which problematizations will prevail. But this is precisely the question to which governmentality studies applies. It does not refer to a general theory of society, but rather maps out society along the lines of its practices. It examines how these practices are being implemented and rationalized, whether they come up against resistance or acceptance, and thus shape society.

Fourthly, rather than conceiving the state as a singular actor, pursuing its own interests, the state has to be analyzed as an effect of heterogeneous technologies of government. This means not searching for functional logics and ultimately postulating the state as a historically continuous figure. This normative perspective finds itself too easily approved, attesting, for instance, to a loss of sovereignty in the face of dominating interests of the economy or of processes of transnationalization. The examination of technologies of government, in contrast, allows processes of constant readjustment to be traced: spheres deemed to pertain to the state and to be subjected to its competence vary historically, as does the meaning of "public" and "private." Foucault in this sense alludes to a "governmentalization of the state": it is less instructive to apply the analysis to the state, understood as a unifying principle of power, in order to trace the *étatisation* of society in history than to the technologies of government shaping state and society (cf. Foucault 2004).

Governmentality studies has repeatedly been accused of playing down the power of the state or the economy, and of fancying liberalism, putting freedom at the center of its analysis. Indeed, it has concentrated particularly on making visible forms of "governing through

freedom" that guide the conduct of people through incentives and options rather than through enforcement or direct interventions. Moreover, in this perspective the neoliberal restructuring of the state and society, noticeable in the West since the 1970s, does not appear as an "unleashing of capitalism" rolling back the state, and in the face of which politics feels itself powerless and at its mercy; finally, nor do the most recent ambitions of providing security appear as a reemergence of a surveillance state.

Government studies, in contrast, has been able to stress that relations of power cannot adequately be described by dichotomies such as consensus or violence, manipulation or free will; rather, power is effective just at that point at which individuals display their own subjectivity. It has also stressed that forms of political participation and civil commitment originate beyond common divisions such as public versus private, state versus citizen. Thus "the retreat of the state" appears not as a political necessity but as a strategy rearranging social realms and privatizing, for example, fields of responsibility once genuinely run by the state: security is commercially provided, community crime prevention programs demand civil commitment.

Analyzing political rationalities allows for conceiving an orientation on the market not only as a particularity of "the economy" but also as a mode of thinking that might prevail in society and that also affects politics itself, enhancing the "economization of the social" (cf. Bröckling et al. 2000). This might result in measuring the success of social work, for example, less in terms of quality and outcome than in terms of quantity and output, not according to the intensity of the support of "clients" but according to the number of "customers" showing up; this might result in the (neo)liberal ideal of economic government taking shape in strategies of crime control that no longer aim at changing, medicating, or amending people but shift to preventing crime by design, by architectural arrangements, and at the same time locking up the incorrigible for life. This might also finally result in a rearrangement of the relation between the state and citizen itself, so that, for instance, social benefits can no longer be claimed as a social right but derive from contractually defined accomplishments. The activity of those receiving benefits becomes a social duty, while responsibility for their conditions of life will be delegated to themselves.

In view of new security laws and strategies, a new formation of a state of surveillance and security is currently being discussed. However, this is misleading insofar as security has not to be taken as the singular concern of a unilateral power of the state but involves both the participation and the provision of commercial security. To conceive of the state as a varying entity means to grasp that the designation of public or private, and of state concern and legitimate interference, is not only a question of jurisdiction but also changes with the techniques of government.

Liberal modes of government are not limited to liberalism; even despotic regimes rely on cooperation. Conversely, liberal modes must not be equated either with more freedom or with soft forms of control; rather, they are about *powers of freedom* (Rose 1999) that are inextricably linked to other forms of exercising power: to violence, force, and exclusion.

If governmentality studies has recently centered on "insecurity" as a systematic component of technologies of government and programs of mobilization (cf. O'Malley 2000), this also demonstrates the challenge the Foucauldian concept poses to our present: forms of violence and of threat are not extrinsic to technologies of freedom but are generated systematically by them (cf. Dean 2002).

The combat against social insecurities (unemployment, the precariousness of a safe existence) or against threats to one's physical integrity (from disease, crime, or war) is carried out as a combat against external threats and in the name of freedom, while not refraining from violence and force, and with the result that the freedom of the individual is restricted.

SEE ALSO: Disciplinary Society; Discourse; Foucault, Michel; Knowledge; Social Control

REFERENCES AND SUGGESTED READINGS

Barry, A., Osborne, T., & Rose, N. (Eds.) (1996) *Foucault and Political Reason: Liberalism, Neo-Liberalism, and Rationalities of Government*. University of Chicago Press, Chicago.
Bröckling, U., Krasmann, S., & Lemke, T. (Eds.) (2000) *Gouvernementalität der Gegenwart: Studien zur Ökonomisierung des Sozialen*. Suhrkamp, Frankfurt am Main.
Burchell, G., Gordon, C., & Miller, P. (Eds.) (1991) *The Foucault Effect: Studies in Governmentality*. Harvester Wheatsheaf, Hemel Hempstead.
Dean, M. (2002) Powers of Life and Death Beyond Governmentality. *Cultural Values* 6(1/2): 119–38.
Foucault, M. (1993) About the Beginnings of the Hermeneutics of the Self. *Political Theory* 21: 198–227.
Foucault, M. (2004) *Sécurité, territoire, population: Cours au Collège de France (1977–1978)*. Gallimard, Paris.
Hindess, B. (1996) *Discourses of Power: From Hobbes to Foucault*. Blackwell, Oxford.
Lemke, T. (1997) *Eine Kritik der politischen Vernunft. Foucaults Analyse der modernen Gouvernementalität*. Argument, Berlin and Hamburg.
O'Malley, P. (2000) Uncertain Subjects: Risks, Liberalism, and Contract. *Economy and Society* 29: 460–84.
Rose, N. (1999) *Powers of Freedom: Reframing Political Thought*. Cambridge University Press, Cambridge.

graduate study

Baranda J. Fermin

Graduate study, including the master's degree but more specifically the pursuit of a PhD, is an extremely focused educational experience that is designed to produce a professional trained in the research, creation, and critique of knowledge within a given field. Graduate study is an essential part of the modern knowledge economy. The processes of graduate study create scholars, research, and academic criticism through an increasingly technological, yet staunchly traditional study, apprenticeship, and sponsorship model.

The nineteenth-century ideal of uniting advanced study and research training with the work of individual scholars engaged in scientific research was heavily based on the German model popular at that time. Over time and across national systems graduate education has shifted away from this model. Today, the form and content of graduate education are heavily influenced by the US model of prescribed curriculum, coupled with more formalized research training, culminating in a largely independent research project and the thesis or dissertation that demonstrates an original empirical or theoretical contribution to one's field. Due to the particular constraints of national systems and cultures, the extent to which this model is observed in its purest form varies considerably from country to country.

The idea and development of the research university first began in Germany with what is known as the Humboldtian model of study. Central to this model was the pursuit of new knowledge through academic research. In the nineteenth century, research, teaching, and study were brought together in academic settings where skilled veteran professors worked closely with students to focus on the creation and development of particular areas of knowledge. As the nineteenth century was drawing toward an end, German universities were by far considered the most advanced in the world and attracted students and scholars from many other countries. However, as a result of political and social tension, within the first four decades of the twentieth century this shifted. Thus, after World War II, the US emerged as the preeminent force in graduate education.

Graduate education in the US is historically a rather young endeavor. The first formal graduate program was at Yale University, where in 1861 three doctoral degrees were awarded to students of its Scientific School. Previous attempts to establish graduate education in the US had failed, despite outspoken proponents from among social and political leaders. When the Association of American Universities (AAU) was first organized in 1900, a central concern was the opinion of US graduate programs by institutions overseas. Today, this opinion can be measured not only by the quantity and quality of social networks and collaborations between US institutions and those abroad, but also by the high volume of doctorate degrees granted to students from other countries by US graduate programs.

In general, across national models, master's programs are larger and more diverse, and doctoral programs are smaller and more concentrated. However, prominent in the organization and practice of graduate education is the structural requirement for a sequence of prescribed courses and for research training experiences. A master's degree (Master of Philosophy, Master of Education, Master of Arts, Master of Science) typically involves a combination of comprehensive coursework and a culminating project or examination. The project may be a thesis, a lengthy theoretical or empirical research project, or some other capstone activity showcasing the skills gained through study. The completion of a master's program for a student enrolled in full-time study is typically anywhere from one to two academic years.

Even within the same national system, master's programs are tremendously varied in terms of their type, purpose, and expectations. The primary function of many programs is the preparation for doctoral study. Others function solely to advance the student's stock of knowledge in a particular field. Still others provide the student with a marketable skill or vocational qualification. This variation in part contributes to the fact that there is more debate surrounding the consistency of standards of master's degrees than either the baccalaureate or doctorate.

When students begin doctoral studies, coursework and research tasks are often similar to those involved in the master's degree. Earning a doctorate, however, involves the completion of a dissertation: an in-depth, extensive, independent, and original research and writing project. The undertaking of independent and original research for the dissertation is the culminating experience of doctoral study. A graduate committee, advisor, and/or chair provide guidance and approval of the coursework and research activities of a PhD student. The primary advisor or chair closely guides, advises, and supports the student through the arduous process, including aspects of professional development and professionalism in the academy in addition to academic and research expectations.

Although the financing of graduate education is costly across all national systems, the US has the most diverse base of funding for graduate study. Unstable as it is, the organizational arrangement for the finance of graduate education in the US is the least tenuous in comparison to Japan, Germany, the UK, and

France. Institutions in the US and the students who pursue graduate study at these institutions must tenaciously seek funds from a variety of sources. This is an arduous but feasible task, as institutional endowments, philanthropic foundations, and (since World War II) the national government are major sources of loans, grants, and fellowships to defer, totally or in part, the costs of graduate education.

In the other countries the source of funding is also unstable, but concomitantly more focused, as the French, Japanese, German, and British national ministries of education are responsible for managing the financing of graduate education in their respective national systems. In these countries the central location of funding constraints illuminates two primordial problems within the systems. The first is the extreme dependence of higher education institutions on their respective national governments. The second is the increasingly lucrative and organized research units that exist outside academia. As an extension of these two issues a paramount concern, especially in the UK, is the quality of graduate education.

Due to the particular constraints of national systems and cultures, the extent to which the model present in the US is observed in its purest form varies considerably. The US model is by far the largest and most complex system for graduate-level training. The German, British, French, and Japanese systems have smaller enrollments, more homogeneous institutions, and less elaborate structural arrangements for student progression through their graduate programs in comparison with the US model.

The systems of both the UK and Japan have struggled with an insufficient critical mass. The highly selective nature of the systems results in relatively small populations of advanced graduate students and the nature of research study and training results in even smaller numbers of earned doctoral degrees. Intense fiscal constraints on the advanced educational sector, particularly in comparison to industry research development and training, exacerbates the problem.

The German and French systems have had difficulty providing opportunities for hands-on research training to the advanced students in their systems. Particularly in the case of Germany, there has been, since the closing of the twentieth century, an issue with preserving the unity of research, teaching, and study. Segments of the national system have abandoned this Humboldtian ideal, while others struggle to maintain it. At the center of this struggle is finding the organizational and funding patterns that will keep the commitments of this model intact.

In the UK, although there has been increased enrollment in graduate programs, on the whole, graduate studies remain a small and marginalized sector of education within the nation's system. In the Japanese system, large enrollment numbers in the overall university sector mask the challenges the graduate sector faces regarding size. Although 60 percent of Japanese universities have graduate programs, only 7 percent of university graduates advance to master's programs and the total graduate student population – including doctoral students – accounts for a mere 4 percent of the total university population (United States Library of Congress 1995). The German system suffers from unevenness across fields in its graduate sector. Although overall enrollment may appear sufficient and stable, the disproportionate distribution of enrollments across sectors in graduate education is problematic for the entire system of advanced study in Germany due to the effects this has on faculty and fiscal capacity.

Due to its social and historical context, the US has virtually eluded contemporary issues concerning sufficient size and critical mass. However, in part due to huge demand and in part as a result of historical structural discrimination, the noteworthy issues facing the US graduate education sector have centered on educational equity in relation to race and gender. Over the last 20 years the number of US racial–ethnic minority doctorate recipients has grown as a result of the social movements impacting higher education access during the 1960s and 1970s. Overall, the gains in doctorates awarded to Asian Americans and Latinos have been far greater than the gains experienced for Native Americans and African Americans. In the last 25 years the number of women doctorate recipients has increased in the social sciences, humanities, physical sciences, and life sciences. Women were the recipients of 45 percent of all the doctorates granted in 2003; 25 years previously they represented only 27 percent of the doctorate recipients in the US (Hoffer et al. 2004).

Despite advances in technology in engineering, physics, and medicine, and the advent of new methods of data analysis in the social sciences, the process of earning graduate degrees mirrors a quaint form of apprenticeship and sponsorship in most national systems. This is true despite differing social, political, and fiscal contexts. The significance placed on the various aspects of graduate education – research, study, and teaching – varies across contexts. Differences across systems are strongly influenced by the diffusion or centrality of fiscal contributors to the nation's education sector. As all systems experience fiscal constraints, the research arena in Germany, Japan, France, the UK, and the US is becoming increasingly segmented as private and industry sector actors involve themselves in research more intensely.

SEE ALSO: Colleges and Universities; Education, Adult; Professions; Professors

REFERENCES AND SUGGESTED READINGS

Clark, B. R. (Ed.) (1993) *The Research Foundations of Graduate Education: Germany, Britain, France, United States, Japan.* University of California Press: Berkley.

Glazer, J. (1986) *The Master's Degree: Tradition, Diversity, Innovation.* ASHE-ERIC monograph no. 6. Association for the Study of Higher Education, Washington, DC.

Goodchild, L. F. & Wechsler, H. S. (Eds.) (1997) *ASHE Reader on the History of Higher Education,* 2nd edn. Ginn Press, Needham, MA.

Hoffer, T. B. et al. (2004) *Doctorate Recipients from United States Universities: Summary Report 2003.* National Opinion Research Center, Chicago.

Thelin, J. R. (2004) *A History of American Higher Education.* Johns Hopkins University Press, Baltimore.

United States Library of Congress (1995) Country Studies: Japan. Federal Research Division of the US Library of Congress, US Department of the Army, Washington, DC.

Gramsci, Antonio (1891–1937)

Alastair Davidson

Antonio Gramsci was born in Ales, Sardinia, on January 22, 1891, and died in Rome on April 27, 1937. Gramsci's father was a petty-bourgeois notable employed in the Land Registry and his mother was from a local landowning family. At 4 years old Antonio was left a hunchback after a fall. His father was imprisoned for malpractice in 1898 and the family lived in straitened economic circumstances. Antonio took a job. Then sent by his mother to middle and high school, in 1912 he won a scholarship to Turin University to study arts. Quickly involved in socialist politics, he discontinued his study and renounced a future career in linguistics. In 1913–16 he was a journalist for the socialist press. In 1917 he started to formulate his novel views in the single number of *La Città futura* and became a firm supporter of the Russian Revolution, which he typified as a "revolution against Marx," understanding it to have reversed all determinist understandings of Marxism as a messianic creed by refocusing socialist attention on the force of willful mass proletarian action to change the world. Together with Palmiro Togliatti, Angelo Tasca, and Umberto Terracini, in 1919 he established the newspaper *Ordine Nuovo* whose object was to promote an Italian version of "soviets" or workers' councils in the factories of Turin. The *ordinovisti* established close links with the workers' organizations in 1919–20, becoming their voice during a mass occupation of factories in Northern Italy. This action was endorsed by Lenin. Gramsci became a founder of the Italian Communist Party in 1921 when it split from the Socialist Party, which was blamed for "missing out" on the Revolution. He went to work in the Communist International in Moscow.

The rise to power of the Fascists in Italy in 1922 put both the communists and socialists on the defensive. Internal disputes over reunification led to Gramsci returning to Italy and emerging as party leader in 1924. He was elected to parliament and created the newspaper *l'Unità*.

In 1926 the Communist Party was made illegal by the Fascist regime and in 1928 Gramsci, with much of the leadership, was imprisoned, in his case for over 20 years. His incarceration started as Stalinism imposed itself. Gramsci's relations with the CPSU and Communist International, already tense because of his opposition to the cult of the leader, took on harsher forms. The Party almost disappeared under Fascist oppression until his death.

While in prison he made the notes for a contribution *für ewig* on the nature of the "popular creative mind" and how it was produced. By 1937 he had filled 29 notebooks on that subject and supporting themes. They constitute a major contribution to Marxist theory, whose "red thread" is the concept of hegemony (in 2003 the subject of 650 titles). Today, his work is the most translated of any Italian. While fragmentary, as he never wrote a synthesis of his work and died of prison-exacerbated illnesses, it is in these works that we find his main reflections on sociology.

GRAMSCI AND THE MASTERS OF SOCIOLOGY

The social Darwinism of Cesare Lombroso and Alfredo Niceforo and the determinism of Achille Loria dominated Italian social sciences in Gramsci's childhood and youth. The first two applied a social determinism (using even phrenology) to show that Southern Italians like Gramsci were naturally primitive. Gramsci detested both authors and their widely shared belief in deterministic social laws. His first published article was on Achille Loria, professor of sociology in Turin – who influenced Weber. Gramsci wrote, scathingly, that Loria had established that the most perfect human type, the ideal of eugenics, was the university professor. To their elitism and determinism he preferred the liberal idealism of Benedetto Croce, with its emphasis on individual endeavor in creating freedom.

Gramsci was at Turin University when Robert Michels (Weber's protégé) and Gaetano Mosca were professors there. Vilfredo Pareto also maintained links with the university. There is no evidence that any of these people influenced him at the time, but their elitist political sociology and (in the case of Michels and Pareto) early institutional links with Fascism could have predisposed him to further associate sociology with anti-humanism and elitism.

After 1917, his growing knowledge of Marxism and Leninism and their view that sociology was expressly anti-Marxist meant that there was little reference in his writings to the great masters of social science. His first real interest was provoked by Nicolai Bukharin's *Historical Materialism: A Popular Textbook of Marxist Sociology* (1921). This book stated that historical materialism was a sociology. It thus departed from the Marxist and Leninist orthodoxy that sociology was simply a bourgeois science and it relied heavily on the sociological masters, particularly on the equilibrium theory in Pareto's *Trattato di sociologia generale*. Gramsci made a critique of this book and the converse views of Henri de Man a central theme of his Prison Notebooks. In it he develops his understanding of sociology and its limits, denies that historical materialism is a sociology and yet intimates that it might contain a sociology.

GRAMSCI'S THEORY OF SOCIOLOGY

Gramsci (2001: 1432–3) asks "What is sociology?" and replies: "Is it not an attempt at a so-called exact science [that is, positivist] of social facts … that is philosophy in embryo." He proceeds to state that it had been an attempt to create a scientific method based on evolutionary positivism for explaining history and politics. As a "philosophy of non-philosophers" it tried to classify historical facts systematically using the natural sciences as a method. Its object was thus to establish laws of evolution of society so that it could foresee the future with "the same certainty as an acorn grows into an oak." It could not therefore grasp any social transformation that was qualitative. He thus identifies as its limits (1) that it applies natural scientific laws to social facts and (2) it sees causes in what is merely nominal classification. "One describes a series … of facts by the mechanical process of abstract generalization and derives a statement of similarities; this is called a law and assumed to have a causal function" (p. 1433).

It followed that he had great reservations about the "laws of large numbers" and statistical series. This did not mean he dismissed them outright, admitting that when social groups and structures were relatively unchanging and "passive," statistical inquiry might have some limited validity. On the other hand, its application could have disastrous consequences if used to guide political action. It encouraged laziness and superficiality in a domain where the object was action, which destroyed the validity of statistical laws.

Objective historico-social reality was merely the "historically subjective." Reality, including the "laws" of natural science themselves, was no more than historically valid. Historical facts had to be studied scientifically and non-scientifically. The propositions made in the first realm had no force until taken up by great masses and made "practical." This meant that any foresight was made true only because great masses of humans acted as if it were (Gramsci 2001: 1403–5). He regarded technological determinism as nonsense. Necessity was linked to "regularity" as revealed by series only when there was a premise to which human beings had been driven which could be formulated along the lines of the Ricardian "given that . . ." So to the calculable material presence there had to be added that complex of passions and imperious sentiment that led to action (p. 1480).

It was the essential "premise" of "popular belief" that Gramsci wished to study and this brought him closest to the traditional concerns of some Italian and European sociology. It bore resemblance to Pareto's concern with residues and to Mosca's theory of sentiments and to de Man's desire to establish how groups felt and thought. Gramsci's theory of common sense might be described as a study of the "passive" group. But what concerned him as a believer in the *Theses on Feuerbach* was how such common sense could become "good sense." He therefore regarded de Man as inferior to both Proudhon and Sorel (Gramsci 2001: 1501). For him, de Man took the position of a determinist scientist, a zoologist studying a world of insects, who studied popular feelings, and did not feel *with* them to guide and lead them to catharsis. He argued that de Man's book *Il superamento di Marx* stimulated us to inform ourselves about the real feelings of groups and individuals and not the feelings that sociological laws suggest exist. So de Man raised an empirical criterion to a scientific principle without knowing how to limit the criterion sufficiently. He thus ended up creating a new statistical law and (unconsciously) a new method of social mathematics and external classification, a new abstract sociology (Gramsci 2001: 1430–1). To accept what was thought by the mass as eternal would be the worst form of fatalism (pp. 1501, 1506). De Man's work resulted in a commonplace based on the error that theory and practice can be separate and not act on each other constantly. For Gramsci, the only way to understand was to work "with."

There are few secondary comments on Gramsci and sociology. They started at the Gramsci studies conferences in 1958 and 1967. Subject to limitations, they confirm the above account. Where the implicit relation with later Parsonian and "social action" theory has been touched on, the commentary adds nothing to challenge the overall thesis advanced above (Calello 1986: 209ff.). There has been an interesting attempt to suggest a Gramscian sociology or post-sociological method (Misurata et al. 1977: 485–505).

SEE ALSO: Communism; Fascism; Ideological Hegemony; Lombroso, Cesare; Marx, Karl; Marxism and Sociology; Michels, Robert; Pareto, Vilfredo

REFERENCES AND SUGGESTED READINGS

Buttigieg, J. (Ed.) (1992) *Antonio Gramsci: Prison Notebooks*. Columbia University Press, New York.

Calello, H. (1986) *Perfiles del marxismo. La filosofia della praxis de Labriola a Gramsci*. Caracas, Alfadel Ediciones.

Gramsci, A. (1971) *Lettere dal carcere*. Einaudi, Turin.

Gramsci, A. (2001) *Quaderni del carcere*, 4 vols. Einaudi, Turin.

Hoare, Q. & Nowell-Smith, G. (Eds.) (1973) *Selections from the Prison Notebooks of Antonio Gramsci*. International Publishers, New York.

Misurata, P. et al. (1977) Razionalità teorico-scientifica e razionalità storico-politica. In: *Politica e storia in Gramsci II*. Riuniti/Istituto Gramsci, Rome.

grandparenthood

Maximiliane E. Szinovacz

Grandparenthood can be considered at three distinct levels: the societal level (referring to societal norms, functions, and esteem of grandparents), the family level (referring to interactions and supports among grandparents, parents, and grandchildren), and the individual level (referring to the meaning and significance of grandparenthood to the grandparents). The meaning and significance of grandparenthood often derive from societal and familial contexts that are beyond grandparents' own control. On the societal level, the prevalence and duration of grandparenthood as well as the normative underpinnings of the grandparent role reflect cultural and demographic change. On the familial level, grandparents' functions within the family context are often shaped by special needs of the children or grandchildren rather than by grandparents' own aspirations. On the personal level, individuals experience the transition to grandparenthood as a countertransition, contingent on the fertility decisions of their children, and access to grandchildren is often mediated by the parent generation.

GRANDPARENTHOOD IN SOCIETAL CONTEXT

Grandparents' Status and Esteem

At the societal level, grandparenthood reflects norms about kinship and kin responsibilities. The definition of grandparenthood itself depends on kinship norms. Some societies may acknowledge grandparents only on the paternal or maternal side, while bilateral kinship rules in modern western societies assign grandparent status equally to paternal and maternal grandparents. However, increases in the divorce rate, adoptions, and artificial fertility methods can render assignment of grandparenthood status problematic in western societies. Grandparents of adopted grandchildren or of stepgrandchildren sometimes express ambiguity about their grandparent status.

Societal contexts further influence grandparents' functions and their interactions with grandchildren. Recent anthropological research suggests that increases in longevity during the Upper Paleolithic (about 30,000 years ago) provided the foundation for grandparents' functions as childcarers and culture transmitters, both functions contributing to population expansion and increased creativity. In more recent times, the drug and AIDS epidemics have been partially responsible for the growing number of grandparents raising grandchildren, while the high divorce rates since the latter part of the twentieth century promoted the development of legal statutes regulating grandparents' visitation with their grandchildren. Grandparents also play a significant economic role, both as consumers (e.g., of children's toys) and as service providers (e.g., care of grandchildren by grandparents can enable mothers to remain in the labor force).

Grandparents' social esteem and image are often tied to the status of elders in societies. Although modernization sometimes undermines elders' status and implicitly that of grandparents by reducing their economic control and their importance as transmitters of knowledge, it can also enhance their status through elders' access to old-age security entitlements. Furthermore, lack of familial authority on the grandparents' part may promote more congenial grandparent–grandchild relationships. In the US, Grandparents' Day or the proclamation of 1995 as Year of the Grandparent speak to the social significance of grandparenthood. The image of grandparents in the media has tended to lag behind times, providing stereotyped images that depict grandparents as old, passive, and powerless, although more recent research suggests a shift toward positive grandparent portrayals in children's books.

Demographics of Grandparenthood

In contrast to many other family transitions, the demographics of grandparenthood are defined by events in two generations, that of the grandparent and that of the grandchild's parent (referred to as the "middle generation" below). To become a grandparent requires that both oneself and one's children bear children. Contingent on medical advancements both in the treatment of infertility and in birth control as well as on economic conditions, rates of childlessness varied considerably during the twentieth century. Childlessness peaked during the Depression era, then declined sharply until the last quarter of the twentieth century, and is now again on the rise (Uhlenberg & Kirby 1998).

Similarly, grandparents experienced a significant decline in the number of grandchildren born during the last century – from an average of over 12 to about 5–6 currently (Uhlenberg & Kirby 1998) – although the relatively high prevalence of early deaths among children at the beginning of the twentieth century curtailed the supply of older grandchildren. This trend is likely to continue well into the twenty-first century. Between 1976 and 2002 the average number of children born to US women declined from 3.09 to 1.93 (Downs 2003), and even more dramatic declines in fertility are evident in many European countries. Within the US, this trend applies across racial and ethnic groups, but fertility remains somewhat higher for African Americans and especially Hispanics. Thus, by the middle of the twenty-first century, many grandparents will have only 3 or 4 grandchildren. Both trends imply a significant decline in the supply of grandchildren well into the twenty-first century.

In contrast, trends in longevity have altered the significance of grandparents in grandchildren's lives. Uhlenberg and Kirby (1998) estimate that in 1900 fewer than a quarter of grandchildren had all four grandparents alive at the time of birth, and fewer than 1 percent had all four grandparents alive at age 20, compared to 68 percent and 10 percent, respectively, in 2000. However, survival of grandparents is also contingent on the timing of births. Early childbearing especially during the baby boom period meant a relatively early transition to and a long duration of grandparenthood at the end of the twentieth century. Delays in childbearing since this time period will reverse this trend. Because increases in the delay of childbearing will probably be more pronounced than increases in longevity, the supply of grandparents to grandchildren (both in terms of number of living grandparents and duration of grandparenthood) may well have peaked at the end of the twentieth century. By the middle of the twenty-first century, exposure to grandparents'

deaths will again occur at earlier ages of the grandchildren, the transition to grandparenthood will be moved to later ages, and fewer grandchildren will be able to enjoy contacts with grandparents into their adulthood. Once again this trend will vary considerably by race and ethnicity. Delayed childbearing predominates among non-Hispanic whites and Asians and Pacific Islanders and is less common among Hispanics and African Americans (Downs 2003). Thus, by the mid-twenty-first century we can expect considerable racial and ethnic variations in the supply of grandparents to grandchildren and in grandparents' roles and relationships with their grandchildren.

GRANDPARENTS IN FAMILY SYSTEMS

Grandparents' interactions with their grandchildren and grandparents' roles are intricately linked to dynamics of the family system as a whole and especially to circumstances surrounding the children's parents. These linkages are most evident in research referring to parents' mediation of grandparent–grandchild contacts and to grandparents' roles as caregivers and care recipients.

The mediation of grandparent–grandchild relationships through the middle generation is both direct and indirect. Indirectly, asymmetry in maternal and paternal kinship ties leads to a matrilineal advantage that furthers stronger bonds to maternal grandparents in general and maternal grandmothers in particular. Because proximity exerts a strong influence on grandparent–grandchild relations, grandparent–grandchild contacts are also affected by mobility decisions of the parents at least as long as grandchildren are young or reside with their parents. More direct mediation is evident from the strong associations between closeness between grandparents and the middle generation and closeness of grandparent–grandchild ties, although it is not clear whether grandparents' attachment to their own children or to their children-in-law is more significant.

Grandparents are often described as family stabilizers or family watchdogs, signifying that their role is augmented during times of family crisis. Research has focused on two such crises, namely, parents' divorce and parental inability to raise their children. Divorce in the middle generation can both enhance and undermine grandparent–grandchild relationships. On the one hand, grandparents often step in to help their divorced children through supports that include grandchild care or help grandchildren in adjusting to the parents' divorce. On the other hand, tensions among divorcing parents are often transferred to the grandparent generation, leading to disruption of grandparent–grandchild ties, especially for non-custodial parents. In extreme cases, grandparents have attempted to overcome such barriers through court-ordered visitation rights.

During the past two decades, grandparents' role as surrogate parents has been the dominant research theme in grandparent research in the US. The number of grandchildren raised in grandparent-headed households increased dramatically during the last decades of the twentieth century, from 2.2 million or 3.2 percent of children under 18 in 1970, to 3.9 million or 5.5 percent in 1997, but has since leveled off (3.8 million or 5.2 percent) in 2003 (US Bureau of the Census 2003). Among children in grandparent-headed households, over one third lived in skip-generation households (neither parent in the household) and close to one half with single parents and grandparents. According to the 2000 Census, 5.8 million grandparents co-resided with grandchildren. However, a sizable number of grandparents who co-reside with their adult children and grandchildren either play a secondary caregiver role or are themselves dependent on their adult children (Simmons & Dye 2003). Surrogate parenting can put considerable strain on grandparents. They not only have to deal with the adverse circumstances resulting in the surrogate parenting arrangement (e.g., children's drug addiction, AIDS, incarceration) and the demands of grandchild care, but also complain about problems with custody, finances, and grandchildren's behaviors, as well as conflicts with the grandchildren's parents. Such problems manifest themselves in lowered well-being of the grandparents themselves, such as increased depressive symptoms (Minkler et al. 1997; Hayslip & Goldberg-Glen 2000).

Less attention has been paid to situations where grandparents are physically or economically dependent on adult children, and grandchildren participate in grandparents' care. Grandchildren in this situation lament lacking attention by their parents, reduction in leisure due to the demands of "grandma" sitting, and household upheaval caused by demented grandparents.

GRANDPARENT ROLE: SIGNIFICANCE AND FUNCTIONS

Despite concerns that grandparents have "opted out" of the grandparent role (Kornhaber 1996), research in the US and other western countries indicates that most grandparents maintain close contacts with grandchildren on a regular basis, fulfill various functions in their grandchildren's lives, and derive satisfaction from the grandparent role (Attias-Donfut & Segalen 1998). For example, a nationally representative US study of grandparents conducted in 1997/98 revealed that over one half of grandparents had contacts with grandchildren on a weekly basis and only 16 percent had fewer than monthly contacts. Furthermore, over three quarters of these grandparents reported talking with their grandchildren about personal concerns or sharing activities with them, and 80 percent attributed extremely high salience to the grandparent role (Silverstein & Marenco 2001). The frequency of grandparents' contacts with grandchildren depends on multiple factors, including geographical proximity, urban versus rural background, kin relationship (matrilineal advantage), age and number of grandchildren, family structure, and closeness to the grandchildren's parents.

The occurrence and relative prevalence of specific functions and activities in a grandparent's role repertory has led to diverse typologies of grandparents' roles. Such classifications refer to such dimensions as comfort, significance, style, role meaning and salience, frequency of contacts, instrumental assistance, relationship quality, type of activities with grandchildren, or influence of grandparents in their grandchildren's lives. The major functions performed by grandparents are socializing, support, and information. Grandparents' engagement in social activities with grandchildren has led to labels such as funseekers, buddies, or companions. Grandparents also provide various supports either to the grandchild's parents in the form of babysitting and childcare or to the grandchildren themselves through emotional comfort, gifts, or help with transportation and school work. In addition, grandparents function as socialization agents, as transmitters of values and culture, and as family historians. However, grandparents' role as socialization agents remains ambiguous and is constrained by norms of noninterference into the parents' domain, although this norm seems weaker among African American families. Native American grandparents have been instrumental in the transmittal of tribal traditions, while Hispanic and Asian grandparents serve as cultural conservators.

FUTURE RESEARCH

Grandparent research has bloomed during the past two decades. This research demonstrated that grandparenthood remains a significant role in modern societies, and that grandparents fulfill important support functions, especially in times of family crisis.

Despite the multitude of recent studies devoted to grandparenthood, most research was limited to a few themes (extent and predictors of involvement, grandparents as caregivers, satisfaction with the grandparent role). Given ongoing and expected demographic changes, other themes may deserve more attention in the future. Declines in fertility and thus in the supply of grandchildren may increase competition between paternal and maternal grandparents, while delays in childbearing will increase relatively young grandchildren's exposure to frail grandparents and to grandparents' deaths. There is also a need for expansion of old themes. We need to know more about grandparents' roles in cases of parental divorce and about the long-term influences of grandparents' care on the grandchildren. Diversity among grandparents from different racial/ethnic, rural/urban, and socioeconomic backgrounds also deserves increased attention in future research.

SEE ALSO: Aging, Demography of; Elder Care; Family Structure; Gender, Aging and; Intergenerational Conflict; Kinship; Life Course and Family

REFERENCES AND SUGGESTED READINGS

Attias-Donfut, C. & Segalen, M. (1998) *Grandparents. La Famille à travers les générations.* Éditions Odile Jacob, Paris.

Bryson, K. & Casper, L. M. (1999) *Coresident Grandparents and Grandchildren.* US Bureau of the Census, Washington, DC.

Cherlin, A. J. & Furstenberg, F. F. (1986) *The New American Grandparent.* Basic Books, New York.

Downs, B. (2003) *Fertility of American Women: June 2002.* US Bureau of the Census, Washington, DC.

Hayslip, B., Jr. & Goldberg-Glen, R. (Eds.) (2000) *Grandparents Raising Grandchildren: Theoretical, Empirical, and Clinical Perspectives.* Springer, New York.

Kornhaber, A. (1996) *Contemporary Grandparenting.* Sage, Thousand Oaks, CA.

Minkler, M., Fuller-Thomson, E., Miller, D., & Driver, D. (1997) Depression in Grandparents Raising Grandchildren: Results of a National Longitudinal Study. *Archives of Family Medicine* 6: 445–52.

Silverstein, M. & Marenco, A. (2001) How Americans Enact the Grandparent Role Across the Family Life Course. *Journal of Family Issues* 22: 493–522.

Simmons, T. & Dye, J. L. (2003) *Grandparents Living with Grandchildren: 2000.* US Bureau of the Census, Washington, DC.

Szinovacz, M. E. (Ed.) (1998) *Handbook on Grandparenthood.* Greenwood Press, Westport, CT.

Uhlenberg, P. & Kirby, J. B. (1998) Grandparenthood Over Time: Historical and Demographic Trends. In: Szinovacz, M. E. (Ed.), *Handbook on Grandparenthood.* Greenwood Press, Westport, CT, pp. 23–39.

US Bureau of the Census (2003) Children with Grandparents by Presence of Parents, Gender, Race, and Hispanic Origin for Selected Characteristics: 2003 (Table C4). Online. www.census.gov/population/www/socdemo/hh-fam/cps2003.html.

Great Depression

A. Allan Schmid

On "Black Thursday," October 24, 1929, the New York stock market dropped precipitously and then recovered. On Monday, it dropped again but did not recover. Tuesday was the most devastating day in the history of the exchange as everyone wanted to sell, but there were no buyers. After nearly a decade of extraordinary growth, business leaders insisted business was still sound. Yet, a year later factories were shuttered, production fell, and upwards of 30 percent of the workforce were to be unemployed. The depression lasted for 10 years and spread around the world. Industry did not suddenly rust and become inoperative. Resources and knowledge did not evaporate. This was an institutional failure, not a technological one. It was a function of cognition, human organization, and relationships, not one of physics. Years of rising expectations, greed, and a sense that it was possible to be rich without working turned into hopelessness and despair.

The spectacular rise in stock prices between 1922 and 1928 was built on borrowed money, innovations such as investment trusts and holding companies, and deliberate manipulation. Speculators could borrow as much as 90 percent of the cost of a stock from their brokers, who in turn borrowed from the banks, who in turn borrowed from Federal Reserve Banks. All is well until prices drop and margin calls occur. Investment trusts were early versions of today's mutual funds allowing even small investors to diversify. People speculated in the stock of the trust, and supertrusts borrowed money to buy other trusts. Pyramid schemes and Ponzi finance using new investors' money to give dividends to previous investors were common. There were no conflict of interest laws to prevent banks organizing a trust to buy its own stock. Pools of large investors aggressively bought a block of stock, driving up its price, spread rumors of some mysterious factor that would further increase its value, and then sold out to the unsuspecting general public.

Investment in plant and equipment or in financial instruments is a function of expectations. Expectations are a social artifact – reinforced and spread similar to a social movement. Shared expectations are learned images of what might be as much as civil rights or feminist movements. The investment of others increases the chance of success of the ideas of an entrepreneur or speculator. In a climate of optimism, banks are eager to make loans. The rising expectations are self-fulfilling prophecies, but eventually the returns to investment do not

meet expectations and investors withdraw. The lowered expectations and investment reduce aggregate demand and actual profits. Firms cut employment to remain solvent. This makes sense for the individual firm, but as many firms follow suit the layoffs reduce incomes and aggregate demand falls again. Again the firm has excess inventory and again reduces the number of employees (circular and cumulative causation). This new equilibrium at less than full employment lasts until investors are convinced there is no way but up or until governments use fiscal policy to stimulate aggregate demand. In the case of the Great Depression, the US government became the employer of last resort and hired the unemployed to build public infrastructure. Still, massive unemployment lasted until the outbreak of World War II when government military procurement put people back to work.

Economists are divided on the causes of the Great Depression. Friedman blamed it on too little money supply, while others said it was too much. Kindleberger blamed it on the decline in foreign trade. The US had loaned large sums to Western Europe to finance their imports of American goods after World War I that could not be repaid when faltering banks called loans. Galbraith (1979: 169) argued that "Far more important than rate of interest and the supply of credit is the mood." Since no definitive experiment is possible, it remains a matter of what one finds persuasive. If you like numbers and assume the underlying rationality of market participants, then you prefer explanations in terms of money, gold, and mistaken public policy. There are no comparable data series on mood and attitude. Still, some are persuaded by the written expressions of participants.

The popular, and even academic, literature on crashes often uses language suggestive of sin to describe booms and busts. After the fact, an unsupported runup in investment and stock prices is regarded as excessive greed, or in the words of Alan Greenspan, Federal Reserve chief, "irrational exuberance." Keynes referred to the phenomenon as "animal spirits." Nevertheless, while many know all bubbles burst, it is hard to resist the sirens and find a Ulyssian solution. For example, a trust manager who goes liquid too soon and misses a big runup will have no customers long before the crash proves itself. Even those responsible for the health of the financial system, such as the Federal Reserve bankers, found it hard to act to burst the bubble, even though some recognized that an earlier bursting would wreak less havoc than later. No one wanted to be recognized as the one who had destroyed the promise of ever-growing riches that many began to believe was their birthright. Whether president or banker, it is better to let the system destroy itself and blame it on impersonal forces than to be seen as the one who "sabotaged prosperity."

Bubbles and their bursting are not new phenomena. Tulip Mania, the South Sea Company, John Laws's Banque Générale, and the Mississippi Bubble have entered into folklore. The only economic system to avoid booms and crashes was that of the Soviet Union, but the price was rather constant doldrums.

In the context of the global economy it is becoming even harder for a nation to insulate itself from other faltering economies. For example, South Korea's collapse in 1997 caused financial organizations to call loans all around the world. The chain reaction threatened the solvency of international banks, which was only contained by extraordinary coordination led by the US central bank. The latest cycle of boom and bust was the information technology referred to as the dot.com business. In the 1990s, few proposals went without enthusiastic backers. Then when profits were not realized, investors wanted out and the stock of the new (and old) IT firms collapsed. In contrast, after a period of rapid growth, Japan suffered a prolonged recession throughout the 1990s. History has not yet written the conclusion on these episodes.

SEE ALSO: Capitalism; Culture, Economy and; Emotions and Economy; Global Economy; Self-Fulfilling Prophecy; Unemployment

REFERENCES AND SUGGESTED READINGS

Clavin, P. (2000) *The Great Depression in Europe, 1929–1939*. St. Martin's Press, New York.
Galbraith, J. K. (1979) *The Great Crash, 1929*. Houghton Mifflin, Boston.
Kahn, H. A. (2004) *Global Markets and Financial Crises in Asia*. Palgrave Macmillan, New York.
Kindleberger, C. (1989) *Manias, Panics, and Crashes: A History of Financial Crises*. Basic Books, New York.
Klein, M. (2001) *Rainbow's End: The Crash of 1929*. Oxford University Press, New York.
Stiglitz, J. E. (2003) *The Roaring Nineties*. W. W. Norton, New York.

grobalization

J. Michael Ryan

Grobalization is a term coined by sociologist George Ritzer (2004) in his book *The Globalization of Nothing*. It is meant to serve as a companion to the widely employed concept of glocalization. While glocalization represents the unique combinations resulting from the interpenetration of the global and the local, grobalization represents "the imperialistic ambitions of nations, corporations, organizations, and the like and their desire, indeed need, to impose themselves on various geographic areas" (p. 73). Thus, glocalization would be most closely associated with postmodern, pluralistic ideas of heterogeneity, whereas grobalization represents a more modern, imperialistic, and homogenizing perspective.

It is important to note that no value judgments are intended for either glocalization or grobalization. Many things which are glocal (as well as local) can be "bad" (e.g., discrimination) while many things which are grobal can be "good" (e.g., the spread of medical technology).

Grobalization theorists would generally argue that the world is becoming increasingly less diverse as transnational economic, cultural, political, and social entities seek to impose their influence throughout the world. The agent in this perspective has relatively little power to maneuver within, between, or around structures. Their ability to construct their own identity and world is seriously impinged on by the growing forces of grobal powers, particularly commodities and the media. Social processes are deterministic and overwhelm the local, limiting its ability to interact with, much less act back against, the global.

Although grobalization encompasses a number of subprocesses, the main three are Americanization, McDonaldization, and capitalism (Ritzer & Ryan 2003). The quest for profits under capitalism, the most powerful of the subprocesses, has led corporations to seek ever-expanding global markets. The process of McDonaldization has facilitated the expansion of corporate entities and cultural patterns. Americanization can be closely tied to the dominant influence of the US in the world today. Taken together, these three subprocesses constitute some of the main drivers of grobalization.

SEE ALSO: Globalization; Globalization, consumption of; Glocalization; McDonaldization

REFERENCES AND SUGGESTED READINGS

Ritzer, G. (2004) *The Globalization of Nothing*. Pine Forge Press, Thousand Oaks, CA.
Ritzer, G. & Ryan, J. M. (2003) Toward a Richer Understanding of Global Commodification: Glocalization and Grobalization. *Hedgehog Review* 5(2): 66–76.
Robertson, R. (1994) Globalization or Glocalization? *Journal of International Communication* 1: 33–52.
Robertson, R. (2001) Globalization Theory 2000+: Major Problematics. In: Ritzer, G. & Smart, B. (Eds.), *Handbook of Social Theory*. Sage, London, pp. 458–71.

grounded theory

Kathy Charmaz

The term grounded theory refers to a set of methods for conducting the research process and the product of this process, the resulting theoretical analysis of an empirical problem. The name grounded theory mirrors its fundamental premise that researchers can and should develop theory from rigorous analyses of empirical data. As a specific methodological approach, grounded theory refers to a set of systematic guidelines for data gathering, coding, synthesizing, categorizing, and integrating concepts to generate middle-range theory. Grounded theory methods are distinctive in that

data collection and analysis proceed simultaneously and each informs the other. From the beginning of the research process, the researcher analyzes the data and identifies analytic leads and tentative categories to develop through further data collection. A grounded theory of a studied topic starts with concrete data and ends with rendering them in an explanatory theory.

Barney G. Glaser and Anselm L. Strauss developed grounded theory methods when they studied the social organization of dying in hospitals. They articulated their methodological strategies in their cutting-edge book, *The Discovery of Grounded Theory* (1967). Prior to its publication, field researchers had learned qualitative methods through an oral tradition combined with lengthy immersions in fieldwork. Glaser and Strauss revitalized qualitative research in sociology and brought new impetus to pursuing it through explicating systematic methods for analyzing qualitative data. They called for reestablishing the qualitative tradition in sociology at a time when quantification had achieved disciplinary dominance. Quantitative researchers had embraced a logico–deductive model and derived hypotheses from grand macrosociological theories. A sharp division of labor between theorists and methodologists had deepened, while the gap between grand theories and empirical realities had widened. Glaser and Strauss argued that qualitative research could generate theory and qualitative methodologists could close the gap between theory and the empirical world. Thus, they proposed that (1) qualitative inquiry could make significant theoretical and empirical contributions it its own right, rather than merely serve as a precursor to quantitative research; (2) qualitative analysis could be codified in analogous ways as quantitative analysis had been; (3) inductive methods could be used to develop middle-range theory; and (4) the divide between theory and methods was artificial.

Glaser and Strauss introduced grounded theory as a comparative method for analyzing basic social and social psychological processes. Glaser built on his quantitative training at Columbia University and aimed to codify qualitative methods as his mentor Paul Lazarsfeld had successfully codified quantitative methods. Glaser developed the language of grounded theory from his quantitative background and imported certain positivist objectives and assumptions into the method. Hence, the logic of grounded theory relied on discovery, externality, neutrality, and parsimony. Strauss brought Chicago School traditions of ethnographic fieldwork, pragmatist philosophy, and symbolic interactionism to grounded theory. Thus, he emphasized first-hand data, assumed an agentic actor, viewed social life as emergent and open-ended, and acknowledged the crucial role of language, symbols, and culture in shaping individual and collective meanings and actions.

These early grounded theorists searched for discoveries in an external empirical world – and in theory construction. For Glaser and Strauss, and particularly Glaser (1978, 1992, 1998, 2001), theory construction was and is an emergent process accomplished through systematic engagement with data. They advocated that grounded theorists delay the literature review to avoid relying on extant ideas.

Glaser and Strauss and a number of their followers adopted roles as neutral scientists who subjected data to dispassionate, systematic analysis. Although grounded theory methods inform the entire research process, both Glaser (1978, 1992, 1998) and Strauss (1987) emphasized the analytic phases. They assumed that thorough analyses remedied researchers' possible biases and made grounded theory a self-correcting method.

The originators of grounded theory shared commitments to analyzing social processes, using comparative methods, accepting a provisional view of truth, fostering the emergence of new ideas, and providing tools for constructing substantive and formal middle-range theories. Glaser's (1978) emphasis on the fit, relevance, modifiability, and usefulness of a grounded theory remained congruent with Strauss's pragmatist conceptions of inquiry and truth. Nonetheless, the marriage of positivism and pragmatism in grounded theory produces tensions in the method. Glaser (1978, 1998) stresses objectivist analyses based on variables, a concept-indicator approach, and context-free theoretical statements. Strauss emphasizes rich contextual analyses of meaning and action and the development of substantive and formal theories of action.

Since its publication, *The Discovery of Grounded Theory* has struck a resonant chord among aspiring qualitative researchers, many of whom have cited it to legitimize their studies. However, many researchers still misunderstand grounded theory and relatively few adopt all of its guidelines. Divisions between Glaser and Strauss, their separate revisions of grounded theory, and new variants of it complicate these misunderstandings. Now what grounded theory is, which and whose innovations and revisions are acceptable, and which version should hold sway are contested issues.

Despite epistemological and practice differences, grounded theorists of various persuasions assume that (1) theory construction is a major objective of grounded theory, (2) the logic of grounded theory differs from quantitative research, and (3) the grounded theory emerges from rigorous data analysis, not from adopting preconceived theories. What stands as preconception, however, differs among grounded theorists. Glaser (1998) remains adamant about delaying the literature review to avoid forcing data into preconceived categories. He implies that researchers can come to their studies without prior influences shaping their views. In contrast, Dey (1999), Charmaz (2000, 2006), Bryant (2002), and Clarke (2003, 2005) contend that researchers' interpretive frameworks, situations, and interests influence what they see and how they render it. Charmaz emphasizes using sensitizing concepts to open the research process. Henwood and Pidgeon (2003) enter the fray with the sound advice that grounded theorists adopt the critical stance of "theoretical agnosticism."

When involved in conducting their studies, diverse grounded theorists do agree on the following strategies: (1) collecting and analyzing data simultaneously; (2) using comparative methods during each analytic stage; (3) devising analytic categories early in the research process; (4) engaging in analytic writing throughout; and (5) sampling for the purpose of developing ideas. How researchers interpret and enact these strategies may reveal sharp differences. Yet researchers' rigorous analytic scrutiny of data can inform their further data collection and spur developing successively more abstract interpretations that explicate what is happening in the field setting.

Currently, most qualitative researchers engage in early analytic work, but it seldom takes the systematic form of the grounded theory method. Coding in grounded theory is at least a two-phased process: *initial* and *focused*. During initial coding, researchers ask: "What category does this incident indicate? What is actually happening in the data?" (Glaser 1978: 57). Grounded theorists attempt to be open to all possible answers. Then they define what is happening by assigning brief categories to each line or incident in the data. Coding for actions furthers the grounded theory goal of studying process. As grounded theorists do initial coding, they compare lines of data or incidents to define the properties of what is happening, learn how it developed, and what it means. Even during this early phase of analysis, grounded theorists move beyond concrete description and take their data apart. Close examination of data combined with comparisons between data prompts researchers to see their data in new ways. Initial coding also alerts the researcher to potential *in vivo* codes given in the setting or participants' direct statements.

Focused coding increases a researcher's analytic control and precision. As researchers engage in comparing and coding data, certain codes assume greater analytic power than others and often appear more frequently. They select these codes as focused codes to sift large batches of data. Through focused coding, researchers can reassess tacit meanings and actions in earlier data and generate preliminary categories for the emerging theory. This coding also provides the grist to interrogate the data and to contemplate what's missing in it.

Memowriting is the pivotal intermediate strategy that bridges coding and report writing. Memos are analytic notes covering all the researcher's ideas and questions about the codes that occur at the moment. From the beginning of the research, grounded theorists see through the lens of their codes. Memos commit to writing what they see. Such writing helps to avoid meandering data collection and losing flashes of insight. Early memos record and discuss hunches and begin taking the data apart to explore meanings and actions. Rather than follow recipes for writing memos, researchers draw on their analytic sensibilities and follow the analytic leads they define in their memos. In early memos, grounded theorists raise certain codes to preliminary categories and then explore them.

In later memos, they develop specific categories through making more incisive comparisons and begin to integrate their categories. Hence, they compare category with category, as well as compare data with the relevant category.

After establishing analytic categories, researchers typically find gaps in their data, if not gaping holes. They seek more data through theoretical sampling, a selective, systematic, and strategic way of gathering specific additional data to develop the emerging theory. Theoretical sampling has been poorly understood and applied. Many researchers mistake theoretical sampling with purposive or representative sampling. In contrast, grounded theorists use theoretical sampling to elaborate the properties of a category, to make the category more precise, and to discover variation in it or between theoretical categories and make them more precise. Theoretical sampling may lead to returning to earlier research participants and settings. It often means seeking new research participants and settings that answer researchers' *analytic* questions – and reveal the relative generality of their theoretical categories. Hence, grounded theorists may move between types of people and across settings to conduct theoretical sampling. Although many researchers stop short of theoretical sampling, it can increase the definitiveness, generality, and usefulness of their work.

The first major division among grounded theorists occurred after Strauss and Corbin published *Basics of Qualitative Research* (1990). They introduced new techniques, treated grounded theory as a set of procedures, and advocated verification. The flexible guidelines and comparative methods of earlier texts are less apparent, although Strauss and Corbin show how to study contextual relationships and to specify causes, conditions, and consequences of social processes. Glaser (1992) rejected Strauss and Corbin's innovations because he saw them as preconceived procedures that forced data into categories. For Glaser, their approach resulted in conceptual descriptions, not grounded theories.

Charmaz (2000, 2006) articulated the second major division by distinguishing between constructivist and objectivist grounded theory. Constructivist grounded theory (1) places priority on the studied phenomenon rather than techniques of studying it; (2) takes reflexivity and research relationships into account; (3) assumes that both data and analyses are social constructions; (4) studies how participants create meanings and actions; (5) seeks an insider's view to the extent possible; and (6) acknowledges that analyses are contextually situated in time, place, culture, and situation. In this view, researchers and their participants *produce* data through interaction and therefore construct the meanings, actions, and situations that researchers observe and define. Constructivsts realize that grounded theorists can import preconceived ideas into their work when they remain unaware of their starting assumptions. Thus, constructivism fosters researchers' reflexivity about *their* interpretations as well as those of their research participants. In short, constructivism moves grounded theory further into interpretive social science.

In contrast, objectivist grounded theory (1) seeks discoveries in an external, knowable world; (2) assumes a neutral, passive observer but active analyst; (3) studies the phenomenon from the outside as an objective external authority; (4) treats representation of research participants as unproblematic; (5) distinguishes between facts and values; and (6) regards completed analyses as objective reports. Objectivist grounded theorists learn the parameters of the worlds they study and analyze processes within them, but they do not become immersed in these worlds. They often aim for thoroughness and accuracy, although Glaser (1998) takes a laissez-faire stance toward data collection and rejects quests for accuracy and detail as derailing the analytic process. Despite some differences, the objectivist approach contains inherent positivist assumptions and practices.

Although Charmaz (2006) states that most grounded-theory works contain elements of both constructivism and objectivism, Charmaz (2000) views both Glaser's and Strauss and Corbin's methodological statements as different forms of objectivist grounded theory. Corbin and Strauss's (1988) empirical work, however, assumes an interpretive approach and demonstrates its constructivist antecedents.

Glaser (1992, 1998, 2001) remains in the objectivist camp. Nonetheless, he has somewhat altered his earlier grounded theory guidelines

sufficiently to constitute a third revision of the method. Although his revision leaves the pragmatist underpinnings behind, Glaser claims his version represents classic grounded theory. Glaser still argues for a direct and often narrow empiricism consistent with mid-century positivism, but he has grown more insistent about opposing a quest for accurate data. He aims to develop emergent theoretical categories and advocates using comparative methods and constructing abstract theoretical analyses, all of which have fundamentally defined the grounded theory method. In a major departure from earlier statements, however, Glaser (1998) has abandoned the objective of studying a basic social process because he views it as forcing inquiry. Instead, he favors analyzing a core category, although criteria for such a category remain vague. For him, the goal of grounded theory should be a theoretical analysis of how people resolve a major concern. Glaser has also revised his earlier endorsement of line-by-coding because he now views it as generating a hodge-podge of unintegrated codes that clutter and encumber the analytic process.

Charmaz (2000, 2006), Bryant (2002), and Clarke (2003, 2005) aim to use grounded theory methods without allegiance to its positivistic presuppositions. They acknowledge the contextual positioning of data and theory and encourage a reflexive stance on the research process. Moreover, they each see building on symbolic interactionism as a way to undermine what Bryant (2002) views as "any inclination toward object-centered, mechanistic, and technicist thinking." Clarke (2005) and Charmaz (2006) call for extending the direction of grounded theory inquiry to include theorizing difference, controversy, and injustice. Clarke (2003, 2005) argues that grounded theory has always contained properties now attributed to postmodernism, such as the provisional, multiple views grounded theorists routinely take toward their data. She explicitly aims to integrate postmodern concerns into grounded theory and to go beyond them to reposition grounded theory in a reflexive pragmatism that addresses all kinds of differences explicitly and maps them in fluid, abstract forms of theorizing. In short, releasing grounded theory from positivism and reconstructing it from pragmatism holds enormous potential for revitalizing the practice of theorizing.

SEE ALSO: Induction and Observation in Science; Methods, Mixed; Naturalistic Inquiry; Qualitative Computing

REFERENCES AND SUGGESTED READINGS

Bryant, A. (2002) Re-Grounding Grounded Theory. *Journal of Information Technology Theory and Application* 4(1): 25–42.

Charmaz, K. (2000) Constructivist and Objectivist Grounded Theory. In: Denzin, N. K. & Lincoln, Y. (Eds.), *Handbook of Qualitative Research*, 2nd edn. Sage, Thousand Oaks, CA.

Charmaz, K. (2006) *Constructing Grounded Theory: A Practical Guide Through Qualitative Analysis.* Sage, London.

Clarke, A. E. (2003) Situational Analyses: Grounded Theory Mapping After the Postmodern Turn. *Symbolic Interaction* 26: 553–76.

Clarke, A. E. (2005) *Situational Analysis: Grounded Theory After the Postmodern Turn.* Sage, Thousand Oaks, CA.

Corbin, J. M. & Strauss, A. (1988) *Unending Care and Work.* Jossey-Bass, San Francisco.

Dey, I. (1999) *Grounding Grounded Theory.* Academic Press, San Diego.

Glaser, B. G. (1978) *Theoretical Sensitivity.* Sociology Press, Mill Valley, CA.

Glaser, B. G. (1992) *Basics of Grounded Theory Analysis.* Sociology Press, Mill Valley, CA.

Glaser, B. G. (1998) *Doing Grounded Theory: Issues and Discussions.* Sociology Press, Mill Valley, CA.

Glaser, B. G. (2001) *The Grounded Theory Perspective: Conceptualization Contrasted with Description.* Sociology Press, Mill Valley, CA.

Henwood, K. & Pidgeon, N. (2003) Grounded Theory in Psychological Research. In: Camic, P. M., Rhodes, J. E., & Yardley, L. (Eds.), *Qualitative Research in Psychology : Expanding Perspectives in Methodology and Design.* American Psychological Association, Washington, DC, pp. 131–55.

Strauss, A. L. (1987) *Qualitative Analysis for Social Scientists.* Cambridge University Press, Cambridge.

Strauss, A. L. & Corbin, J. (1990) *Basics of Qualitative Research: Grounded Theory Procedures and Techniques.* Sage, Newbury Park, CA.

Strauss, A. L. & Corbin, J. (1998) *Basics of Qualitative Research: Grounded Theory Procedures and Techniques*, 2nd edn. Sage, Thousand Oaks, CA.

group processes

Jeffrey W. Lucas

Sociology's group processes perspective is one of the three "faces" of sociological social psychology (Smith-Lovin & Molm 2000). The perspective is characterized by theoretical development and basic research on fundamental social processes that occur in group contexts. Work in the group processes tradition dates to scholars who were interested in the interactions of individuals in small groups. As the perspective has developed, its focus has largely evolved to an interest in the processes that occur in group contexts rather than in groups themselves.

Much of the work in sociology's group processes tradition has its roots in the work of Bales and colleagues in the 1950s (see, e.g., Bales 1950). Bales developed a procedure called interaction process analysis (IPA) to code interactions in groups. The procedure treated each behavior in a group as an "act" and involved classifying acts into various categories. Bales's approach allowed investigators to objectively study interactions in groups and spurred researchers to develop new ways to classify group behavior.

A focus on group processes, of course, implies an interest in two things – groups and processes. As the group processes perspective has developed, the focus of the area has shifted to a greater interest in processes than in the groups in which the processes occur. In large part because of the perspective's roots in the classification of behavior in small groups, however, sociologists not in the group processes perspective will frequently treat studying "small groups" and studying "group processes" as interchangeable.

What interests those in the group processes perspective is how various social processes operate in groups. The groups in which the processes operate need not be small. Two of the processes that dominate work in the perspective are power and status. These processes occur in groups both large and small, and they provide examples of the perspective's major focus on processes that occur in groups rather than on the groups in which processes occur.

Power, in simple terms, is the ability to control resources that people value. Your boss, for example, has the ability to fire you from your job. If you value your job, this ability gives your boss power. Early treatments of power generally focused on the characteristics of powerful people that made them powerful. This research was limited by the fact that almost anyone put in the right position can be powerful. In other words, nothing about your boss herself gives her power over you. Your boss's power comes not from individual traits but instead from a position in a structure. Group processes scholars focus their efforts on discovering the conditions of groups rather than of people that give rise to power differences (see Markovsky et al. 1988 for an excellent example). Note that the groups in which these conditions arise need not be small. The president of a university, for example, has power (the ability to control resources) over a group (the university's employees and students) because of her structural position.

Status is a position in a group based on esteem or respect. Perhaps the most well-developed group processes theory is a theory of status named *status characteristics theory* (Berger et al. 1977). Status, like power, is relative; in other words, people do not have status or power in and of themselves, but instead only in relation to other people. It is meaningless to say that medical doctors are high in status, for example, except in the context of other, lower-status occupations.

Status characteristics theory specifies the processes that lead some people to have more status in groups than others. According to the theory, status orders in groups develop out of the characteristics held by group members. Examples of status characteristics include gender, age, appearance, race, and education. Status characteristics theory proposes that individuals act as though they develop performance expectations consistent with larger cultural beliefs about the characteristics held by themselves and other group members. Members with characteristics accorded higher expectations have higher-status positions in the group and are likely to be evaluated more highly than others and to have more influence.

A few of the other processes studied in the group processes perspective are justice, legitimacy, identity, and bargaining. Although they do not necessarily follow from an interest in group processes, most work in sociology's group processes tradition shares two additional features: formal theoretical procedures and experimental investigations.

Investigators adopting formal theoretical procedures construct theories with explicitly defined concepts, general propositions that logically follow from theoretical assumptions, and well-specified scope conditions that lay out the domains of their theories. Tests of the theories then operationalize theoretical concepts in empirical settings and formulate hypotheses that provide tests of the theory's propositions (see Cohen 1989 for a discussion of formal theoretical procedures).

In experiments, investigators test hypotheses in carefully controlled environments in which different groups of participants are randomly assigned to different experiences. In that experiments usually involve the study of small groups of participants, the fact that most group processes research is carried out in experimental laboratories might seem to contradict the assertion that group processes scholars are not tyically interested in small groups. The use of experimental methodology in group processes studies, however, follows not from an interest in small groups but rather from an interest in testing formal theories of basic social processes. The use of experiments, in fact, results from an interest in social processes. Group processes scholars attempt to understand the fundamental nature of the processes they study, independent of any particular group context. Experiments have the advantage of allowing researchers to simplify natural environments, eliminating aspects of the environments not germane to an understanding of the basic process under study.

Although experimental investigations in the group processes tradition follow from an interest in understanding the fundamental nature of basic social processes, their use nevertheless contributes to the misconception that the concepts "group processes" and "small groups" can be used interchangeably. The group processes perspective is young, however, and as knowledge from the area is applied to ever larger and more diverse groups it will likely shed its association with small groups, with a greater recognition of the primary emphasis on the "processes" in "group processes."

SEE ALSO: Exchange Network Theory; Experiment; Groups; Power; Social Psychology; Status

REFERENCES AND SUGGESTED READINGS

Bales, R. F. (1950) *Interaction Process Analysis: A Method for the Study of Small Groups.* Addison-Wesley, Reading, MA.

Berger, J., Hamit Fisek, M., Norman, R. Z., & Zelditch, M., Jr. (1977) *Status Characteristics and Social Interaction: An Expectation States Approach.* Elsevier, New York.

Cohen, B. P. (1989) *Developing Sociological Knowledge: Theory and Methods*, 2nd edn. Chicago, Nelson-Hall.

Markovsky, B., Willer, D., & Patton, T. (1988) Power Relations in Exchange Networks. *American Sociological Review* 53: 220–36.

Smith-Lovin, L. & Molm, L. (2000) Introduction to the Millennium Special Issue on the State of Sociological Social Psychology. *Social Psychology Quarterly* 63: 281–3.

groups

William Bezdek

The term "group" refers to at least two distinct forms of social cooperation. On the one hand, it refers to small groups where local patterns of order emerge from the abilities, needs, and interests of the members. On the other hand, it refers to formal organizations where order is imposed by formal rules and sanctions imposed by appointed authorities. Groups structured according to attributes of the group members are generally informal, face-to-face groups. Groups structured by rules and authorities are generally large-scale business, service, and governmental organizations.

Associations are a type of organization in which a small core of specialists performs all the work of the association on behalf of a large membership. Associations do not structure the daily work life of their members; associations advise their members, act as advocates for them, and plan activities for them. As Alexis de Tocqueville noted in the 1830s, Americans were distinguished from their European ancestors by forming an enormous number of associations to promote a varied assortment of special interests. Today, the number of special interest groups in the US ranges from the Association of American Alumni Associations to the American Zoological Association, from the Pagan Web Crafters' Association to the Association for the Freedom of Association.

In addition to small groups and large-scale organizations and associations, there is another category of groups referred to as aggregates or collectivities. Membership in a collectivity is defined by a common attribute (such as race, gender, or age) or a common interest (such as hunting or farming). Members of collectivities are generally dispersed, unknown to one another, and have no intrinsic form of organization. Collectivities, however, provide a constant source for the development of small groups, associations, and organizations, particularly as selected members of a collectivity organize to publicly advocate for, serve the interests of, or protest the treatment of an entire collectivity. Members of dispersed collectivities share no obligatory social relations with one another, still their natural affinities enable them to mobilize for social action. Collectivities have an increasing effect in the modern world because modern technologies of mass communication make possible the mobilization of collectivity members into virtual associations that can coordinate the actions of dispersed and anonymous individuals who share the same interest or attribute. Many small groups working for the benefit of the same collectivity can unite in a social movement. The many phases of the women's movement provide an example of the ebb and flow of social movements that depend on grassroots support from small groups that promote the interests of a collectivity.

Crowds are a special type of collectivity distinguished by their being together in the same general location at the same time. Crowds can share a focus of attention such as a football game or a military parade, focal points that provide the crowd with a shared experience that creates a temporary sense of social solidarity that can be mobilized for collective action under certain circumstances. Not all crowds, however, share a central focus of attention. Workers, shoppers, and tourists who overflow the sidewalks at closing time in the downtown areas of large cities constitute a crowd whose members display a rudimentary form of social organization in which individuals will generally keep both bodily and eye contact to a respectful minimum as they maneuver along crowded sidewalks. This minimal social orientation creates orderly patterns of movement in the crowd. When individuals in a crowd shove, push and trample on others during life-threatening catastrophes such as a fire, the social order of a crowd degenerates into a social disorder.

All individuals are assumed to have two personal attributes critical for the study of all types of group life. First, it is assumed that all individuals have the capacity to act as self-directed agents who optimize their self-interest. Second, it is assumed that all individuals have the capacity to engage in symbolic communication. Taken together, these characteristics form a foundation for all life in human groups. G. H. Mead proposed that symbolic interaction provides the ability to "take the role of the other" during any interaction, thus making it possible for individuals to anticipate the reaction of others at the same time as they plan their own actions. This ability, according to Mead, provides the foundation for the development of both self and society. Jürgen Habermas emphasizes communicative action as the backbone of all human social formations. Because those with a vested interest in a particular issue tend to distort their persuasive communications, he was forced to construct an ideal pattern of communication to demonstrate that departures from it were in fact distortions in communication that impeded the development of effective communication. An ideal pattern of communication requires truthfulness, normative sensitivity, and personal authenticity, orientations that he took to be necessary prerequisites for the rational formation of a just society. Symbolic communication plays a secondary role for rational choice theorists, who are more likely to begin their study of group life by examining how individuals adapt their self-interest to the self-interest of others in order to develop the cooperation required for many forms of human group formation.

Because groups can be studied as the intersection between individuals and society, and because they constitute a readily accessible site for gathering information, they have served different research and theoretical agendas in different eras of sociology's history. During the first two decades of the twentieth century, sociologists were preoccupied with defining the subject matter and the methods appropriate to their field. Georg Simmel (1858–1918), an influential German theorist who began publishing articles in American sociology journals in the 1890s, called attention to the unsuspected significance between a group comprised of two persons, and a group comprised of three (or more) persons. In a group of two persons, if one person leaves, the group ceases to exist; in a three-person group, one person may leave, and the group can continue to exist. In principle, a three-person group can last indefinitely if the following condition is met: when one current member leaves, she or he is replaced with one new member. This potential for a group to persist, even with a total change in membership, has been used to investigate the way group norms and practices maintain themselves or change over time. The ability of groups to replace their membership, with minor changes in the group's goals, practices, and organization, highlights the concept of a group as a relatively enduring set of relationships and social practices as distinct from the specific individuals that constitute a group at any given time. Because any group can be recognized as the "same group" in spite of changes in its membership, they have been, and will continue to be, a prime site for studying social development, social control, and social change.

Georg Simmel, among others, was also important in distinguishing two major types of groups: those in which personal attributes dominate the relationship (as in friendship and family groups) and those in which an individual's official position or role dominates the relationship (Simmel gives the example of the way in which the official role of a Catholic priest dominates his relationship with his parishioners). This distinction between groups constituted by personal relationships and groups constituted by impersonal duties toward one another is now known mainly as the difference between primary group functions (more typical of small groups) and secondary group functions (more typical of organizations and associations). Emphasizing primary and secondary functions instead of primary and secondary groups suggests that individuals in all groups will have some relationships that are more personal and some that are more impersonal, although it is still possible to distinguish primary groups from secondary groups in terms of the dominant mode by which individuals relate to one another within the group. Ferdinand Tonnies (1855–1936), perhaps the original sociological source for the primary/secondary group distinction, used the German terms *Gemeinschaft* (roughly corresponding to primary groups) and *Gesellschaft* (roughly corresponding to the forms of association found in impersonal groups, but more specifically he sought to identify the principles of social formation in modern, urban societies as opposed to social formation in premodern societies). In the 1920s, Robert Park (1864–1944) insisted "all social problems turn out upon analysis to be problems of the social group." In differentiating sociology from psychology, he emphasized that collective action precedes individual action: since all individuals are born into preexisting group cultures, they must learn the ways of the groups before they can take part in the group's activities and through these activities find ways to give social expression to their individual interests. John Searle (1995) gives collective interests equal philosophical footing with an individual's self-interest. Collective interest, as analytically distinct from self-interest and symbolic communication, provides a third dimension for theorizing group formation and maintenance, adding to self-interest and communicative action to form the foundations of group life.

In the 1930s and 1940s there were several innovations in the study of groups. Lewin, Lippit, and White, for instance, invigorated the field of social psychology in an experimental study with obvious references to the threat posed by Hitler to democratic regimes. The importance of this study lies as much in its methodology, a sophisticated experimental design, as in its findings that group members in the long run, though not in the short run, are more productive and more satisfied with democratic leaders than with authoritarian leaders. At the same time, W. W. Whyte (1914–2000) published his pathbreaking study of a small, street-corner gang exposing the gang's internal structure as it was related to the larger

community. The success of Whyte's book *Street Corner Society* (1943) succeeded in spreading participant observation methods in sociology as an alternative to both experimental methods and detached observational methods. In this same period, J. L. Moreno asked members of small groups simple questions, such as "Who are the persons in this group who are your three best friends and who are your three favored co-workers?" He plotted the results in a sociogram, where each individual was represented by a dot on a piece of paper, and lines connecting the dots displayed a visual pattern of friendship and work relations within the group. This technique was the predecessor of network analysis, one of the major tools for mathematical modeling of subjective preferences that exist between individuals in groups. Subjective preferences (such as friendship and work preferences) help social investigators understand the stability or instability of a group, and network analysis, which depends on the individual's subjective preferences, has become a major empirical method for sociologists who favor rational choice and self-interest as the preferred foundation for the study of group life.

Beginning in the second half of the twentieth century, the major thrust of sociological theory and research in small groups was possibly the work of R. F. Bales, particularly in his collaboration with the dominant American theorist of the time, Talcott Parsons. Using a sophisticated observation technique, Interaction Process Analysis (IPA), Bales developed instructions for a detailed analysis of group conversations. Sitting behind one-way windows, research assistants observed groups of five or six individuals, often assembled together for the first time, as they tried to reach agreement on a hypothetical problem presented by an academic investigator. Each group's conversation was recorded and the words divided into small units, which were then coded into one of 12 preestablished categories. Studies using this method demonstrated the relation between task-oriented phases of group problem solving and socio-emotional phases in group problem solving, a finding that constituted an empirical demonstration of Parsons's theoretical analysis of societies as organized around the division of task functions (i.e., the functions generally associated with secondary groups) and socio-emotional functions (i.e., the functions generally associated with primary groups). Some have criticized these findings as a tautological restatement of the 12 categories used to code the behavior of the group members. George Homans provided a major alternative to Parson-Bales's structural-functional orientation when he explained the interpersonal dynamics of a professional work group in terms of "social behavior as exchange." Homans observed that the less competent workers in the group continually asked for help from a more accomplished co-worker. To help them, the more competent member was forced to reduce the time spent on his own work. In return, he received expressions of respect from his colleagues. The tradeoff was peer deference in exchange for expert help and advice. This study enlarged the theoretical boundaries of economic exchanges to encompass theoretical accounts of social exchanges.

George Herbert Mead (1863–1931) shifted the emphasis from groups as foundational social units to the process of interaction that leads to the formation of groups. For Mead, it is the communicative action between individuals that establishes the social reality of groups. Later, in the 1960s, theorists would embrace the perspective of "interaction" and "communication," without paying particular attention to the structure of the concrete groups in which interactions take place. Near the end of the 1950s, for instance, Erving Goffman began his series of publications on what he was later to call the "interaction order." Initially inspired by Emile Durkheim (1858–1917), who had theorized the importance of sacred rituals in the maintenance of social order, and following the lead of the philosopher John Locke (1632–1704), who had substituted the term "self" for Descartes's sacred "soul," Goffman made the leap from sacred rituals to rituals in everyday life. Individuals in everyday interactions, he concluded, would consider the self as possessing some of the mystery and authority associated with the soul, and would thus feel a deep impulse to show respect for the sacred-like expressions of self displayed by their companions. When individuals are denied the respect they believe is their due as persons possessing a sacred self, Goffman saw the simple rituals of everyday life as a means to restore an

individual's lost self-respect, drawing attention away from the emotional disturbances caused by threats to the self, and restoring the group's attention to the predominant functions of the group. More recently, Randall Collins (2004) has expanded the rituals of everyday life to examine a wide variety of social relationships.

Emmanuel Schegloff, a student of Goffman, collaborated with Harvey Sacks and others to develop Conversation Analysis (CA) as a method for recording and analyzing face-to-face interactions. Schegloff and Sacks conceptualize social interactions by examining written transcripts of conversations recorded during everyday interactions. The transcripts are enhanced by a notational system for capturing many of the verbal intonations, pauses, and overlapping speech patterns that are important for mutual understanding in face-to-face interactions. As with the previous attempt by Bales in constructing Interaction Process Analysis, CA analysts also exclude interior, private experience (such as the experience of the self as directing one's actions). CA differs radically from Bales's analysis, however, in that it rejects the idea of using preestablished categories to code social meanings in conversation. Instead, CA relies on a close examination of the structure of the conversation to construct its meanings. This method of sociological analysis even challenges what seems to be a necessary and reasonable assumption in sociology – that all symbolic communication is built around shared, intersubjective meanings. Schegloff's (1992) criticism of intersubjectivity as the basis for social formation presents a serious alternative to the concept of norms as shared, intersubjective understandings as the underpinning of orderliness in everyday social life.

CA was one way to address Howard Garfinkel's program of ethnomethodology, an ontological position in sociology opposed to the dominance of grand theorizing, as exemplified in the work of Talcott Parsons. Garfinkel, a student and admirer of Parsons, proposed that social organization does not exist independent of everyday social practices. For Garfinkel, social order is recreated in the living, ongoing achievements of everyday life. He believed that abstract conceptual and cognitive approaches to human relations only get in the way of the proper study of sociology, and that CA provides a way to demonstrate this. In his famous phrase, individuals in everyday life "are not cultural dopes." Feminist sociologist Dorothy Smith finds ethnomethodology congenial to the problems faced by women who live in a world of concepts developed by men who had conceptually marginalized women in everyday life, relegating them to care of children and home. She sees ethnomethodology and allied viewpoints as counteracting the one-sided view of society that comes from male-dominated conceptualizations and by logical extension from abstract conceptualizations in general. More recently, Garfinkel's emphasis on everyday social practices has influenced organizational studies as well as small group studies.

At the beginning of the twenty-first century, the study of communicative interaction (read communication in groups) was spread among several disciplines. In addition to sociology and anthropology, communicative interaction is studied in linguistics, social psychology, hermeneutics, cognitivist psychology, communication theory, computational neuroscience, and computer mediated interaction studies (see Grant 2003). The linguistic turn in both the humanities and the social sciences has emphasized the study of social interaction as social communication, and the techniques of CA have become its preeminent methodology. The shift from the study of groups to the study of the communicative interaction within groups makes it possible, in principle, to track styles of discourse and persuasion as they travel back and forth between the centers of social power and the interactions of everyday life. This project, if rigorously pursued, could form an important bridge between the particularities of social interaction and the abstractions that allow us to conceptualize groups and total societies.

One may clarify the relations between groups and interaction as the relation between a social process and a social outcome: social interaction is the process; the group is the outcome. Both the concept of group and the concept of interaction are at least one step removed from the everyday practices of social life. Theorists like Howard Garfinkel and Dorothy Smith have suggested ways to balance the simplifications inherent in the use of conceptual terms in the study of human associations.

SEE ALSO: Dyad/Triad; Ethnomethodology; Group Processes; In-Groups and Out Groups; Interaction; Interaction Order; Mediated Interaction; Mesostructure; Networks; Public Realm

REFERENCES AND SUGGESTED READINGS

Collins, R. (2004) *Interaction Ritual Chains*. Princeton University Press, Princeton.

Goffman, E. (1967) *Interaction Ritual: Essays on Face-To-Face Interaction*. Doubleday-Anchor, Garden City, NY.

Grant, C. (Ed.) (2003) *Rethinking Communicative Interaction: New Disciplinary Horizons*. John Benjamins, Philadelphia.

Olmsted, M. & Hare, A. P. (1978) *The Small Group*, 2nd edn. Random House, New York.

Schegloff, E. (1992) Repair After Next Turn: The Last Structurally Provided Defense of Intersubjectivity in Conversation. *American Journal of Sociology* 97(5): 1295–345.

Searle, J. (1995) *The Construction of Social Reality*. Free Press, New York.

Whyte, W. W. (1943) *Street Corner Society*. University of Chicago Press, Chicago.

growth machine

Andrew E. G. Jonas

The growth machine concept first appeared in 1976 in an article published in the *American Journal of Sociology* (Molotch 1976). It describes how in America city politics is generally a politics of growth. Although the concept in fact explains the systemic properties of cities, it has also been interpreted as referring to the presence in almost every American city of property-dependent business interests actively engaged in local politics and civic affairs. This is so much so that the city itself can be seen, in its very essence, to be an instrument of profit for land-based interests. Moreover, those involved frequently form coalitions with other players likewise dependent on local development, and mobilize to shape the policies and institutions of local government in a fashion such that future urban growth patterns and land use policies profit all participants; in this way, the city building process operates like a growth machine. Growth machine actors promulgate an ideology of growth, which often proves a potent force to such an extent that all other interests either become incorporated within the essential logic of the machine or face defeat.

The growth machine thesis arose as a critical reaction against the sterility of extant social science approaches to the city: social ecology, the rank size rule, community power, and the like. Conventional social science was preoccupied with matters of urban social, spatial, and political form. In comparison, the growth machine concept gets to the substance of urban economic power, the structures and agents of urban development, and those day-to-day actions of urban-growth dependent economic elites, which are so decisive in shaping land use and the distribution of resources and jobs within localities and through the urban system (Molotch 1999). The concept materialized during a time of growing skepticism about the role of government, increased public awareness of the limits to growth, and the brute materiality of the urban fiscal crisis, notably New York City's in 1975. Already in the 1970s, there were signs that the American growth machine system was facing new challenges and an emergent counter-coalition appeared to be redirecting the focus of local government away from growth and towards stronger environmental regulation (Molotch 1976). Although the US federal government had not yet abandoned urban policy, the New Federalism and anti-tax revolts pointed to the neo-conservative, anti-urban, and devolutionary trend that was to follow. The growth machine focused attention on how powerful economic interests tied to particular places (such as developers) depend on the power, resources, and authority of local and state government in order to create conditions conducive to their profit-making activities.

The growth machine concept injected fresh ideas into a corpus of empirical urban research generally lacking in concepts linking urban form to broader political and economic trends. If community power studies had taught social scientists about who wields influence in the city, the growth machine thesis demonstrates what they do with their power. It makes an argument about how cities, suburbs, and metropolitan areas are constructed, who constructs them, their role in the national political economy, and what the fiscal, social, and environmental consequences of untrammeled growth are likely to be for people who live in these urban places (i.e., the majority of the national population).

After teaming up with John Logan, Molotch coined the term "rentiers" to describe collectively the growth machine players and their various auxiliaries, such as the media, universities, utilities, professional sports franchises, chambers of commerce, and the like (Logan & Molotch 1987). More than a case of instrumental manipulation of local government, rentiers strive to ensure that the local citizenry are receptive to growth by engineering a sense of community around which locals can unite. Here the growth machine toils to connect the social standing of a place, village, township, city, or urban region to its economic fortunes. However, the growth-promotion activities of rentiers are shot through with conflict, actual and latent. The main source of conflict around growth is that of the use of land versus its exchange. Use values are rooted in the neighborhood or community as a living place inhabited by residents with deep psychological attachments to their homes and communities, or as a place to trade or produce goods. Threats to such attachments might arise from land use and demographic changes which satisfy the objective interests of growth machine players in maximizing exchange value, but represent serious disruptions to the livelihoods and personal psyche of residents. Conflicts result when factions compete to harness the legislative, fiscal, and legitimating powers of local government. Local government is not a value-free interest in this process because, dominated by growth profiteers, it strives to influence land use outcomes and the distribution of resources within and between cities, often rationalizing desired outcomes as a source of fiscal betterment. It, too, is a participant in the growth machine system (Logan & Molotch 1987).

Unlike urban regime theory (Stone 1989), growth machine analysis is not primarily concerned with the detailed division of labor between state and market actors in urban politics and institutions. Nevertheless, the state – its organization and geography – is important because neighborhoods, cities, metropolitan regions, and states form a hierarchy of territories possessing different powers and resources potentially of use to the growth coalition. Growth-oriented coalitions will tend to coalesce around that level of government seen as having capacity to bestow the relevant fiscal and infrastructural capacities (Molotch 1976). Interest groups sometimes in competition for federal, state, or local resources within a city or region may well collude for the growth of the city-region as a whole. In this way, the formation and activities of growth machines are scalar dependent and their organizational scope is contingent upon how they access the geography of the state apparatus.

Economic globalization has contributed to a rethinking of the spatial context in which economic growth-oriented urban regimes exist and operate (Horan 1991). Localities, cities, and regions are inserted into a global economic development system. In some cases, international capital works in partnership with local property interests to circumvent local resistance to inward investment (Molotch & Logan 1984). By the same token, land development interests and activities are much more globalized. This implies a weaker link between local property dependence and a propensity to be involved in local growth coalitions (Cox & Mair 1989). Yet the growth machine concept remains durable in part because of the extent to which in many countries land use planning and the urban land market have been deregulated. Moreover, the state continues to be important if perhaps for different reasons than an earlier emphasis on local government manipulation by growth coalitions. National states have sought to activate local business–local state partnerships along the lines of the public-private redevelopment partnerships found in many US cities. In this way, the growth machine may have been retooled in a neoliberal age remarkable for its fiscal austerity and hyper-mobile capital (Jessop, Peck, & Tickell 1999).

Close engagement with the growth machine concept has prompted critique and further elaboration of the theory. Research has tried to prove empirically the presence or absence of a growth coalition and of the distributional and land use effects of its activities. In a comprehensive survey, Logan, Whaley, & Crowder (1997) demonstrate the concept's resilience, but conclude that the changing nature of regional economic development and matters of social distribution pose questions for empirical research. Others have questioned its theoretical assumptions. A lack of understanding of the causal properties of geographically immobile versus mobile businesses, workers, residents, and local states in a capitalist mode of production is viewed by some to be a particular weakness in the thesis; the overriding emphasis on land use dynamics overlooks a variety of alternative forms of, and participants in, local and regional development (Cox & Mair 1989). Further research is required into the activities and interests of the poor, working women, racialized groups, unions, non-profits, and so forth as these engage with development agendas and interests in cities. Additionally, business elites, chambers of commerce, and booster clubs have cultural and organizational logics, which can defy a straightforward political economy interpretation. Extensions of the growth machine concept emphasize at least three general issues: the generative and receptive contexts for discourses and ideologies of growth; the role of incentives, participants, and wider policy networks in growth machine-like economic development coalitions; and the internationalization of the growth machine concept (Jonas & Wilson 1999).

First, the growth machine thesis is essentially all about local boosterism: the conscious attempt to (re)present a city or region in a positive light to a wider constituency such that it becomes more attractive to inward investment, outside visitors, government expenditures, etc. The growth machine thrives, not only by creating the material preconditions for urban development, but also by convincing people of the importance of growth to their well-being. The emphasis on ideologies of community in the original thesis arguably fails to delve more deeply into the metaphorical power of "other" discourses (e.g., those of "race" or class) often associated with, for instance, the redevelopment and gentrification of central-city neighborhoods (Wilson 1996). Growth coalitions are especially adept at shaping public values about the necessity for growth and identifying the locality's potential civic and moral saviors, the local heroes whose influence transcends the local yet somehow captures the essential moral virtues of the place (Cox & Mair 1988). As Molotch himself recognized, this takes politics into realms far beyond the formal conventions of programs, policies, and regulations, which nonetheless continue to preoccupy urban political theorists.

The second concern sees the growth machine thesis as a place-based model of urban governance, yet these days more of a process-oriented and global approach is required. This is not an argument for studying the city *qua* the local as determined by global trends; globalization is itself a deeply misunderstood process. Not only is there an uplink from the growth machine to wider state structures and the global economy (Gotham 2000), but there are also cross-links between all sorts of urban places connected by growth networks and entrepreneurial modes of governance (Molotch 1999). Moreover, urbanists now realize that cities and regions are locked into international flows of commodities, which serve to undermine the essential causal integrity of the urban, the fundamental spatial field of play for the growth machine. Yet, in its defense, the growth machine thesis is not so much an argument for an urban-scale theory as laying out a general approach to the political economy of place. For example, cities, it seems, are making a comeback as sites of creativity, innovation, and drivers of national economic recovery. A growth machine perspective on the idea of the "resurgent city" would perhaps attempt to identify a necessary condition for resurgency in a collective place-dependent agency, a redistribution of government resources, interventions in land development, and/or a class of property interests.

Third, the jury is still out regarding the transferability of the growth machine thesis outside the US. Comparative growth machine analysis has enabled us to identify the range of conditions essential to rentier-like activities, emphasizing the diverse ways in which urban land is commodified and regulated, how inward investment is managed, and the scope of state intervention in urban development in different national settings (Molotch 1990; Molotch & Vicari 1988). Given differences between states in terms of functions and geography, it is

difficult to determine *a priori* whether the growth machine exists or operates the same way in other countries, especially those that have very different institutions, ideologies, and cultural traditions governing land use, urban development, or territorial integration than the US (Kirby & Abu-Rass 1999). Extra-territoriality is a significant factor in understanding the geography of urban growth networks at the international scale (Leitner & Sheppard 2002). Claims about the hollowing out of the nation-state and the changing geography of economic development indicate the value of looking at cross-national and interregional differences in the organization of growth coalitions and attendant activities.

The attraction of the growth machine thesis is its ability to articulate an essential feature of the political economy of place development in capitalism: the political role of various locality-dependent economic interests and their capacity to shape institutional structures and spatial patterns of land development in ways that can be socially and environmentally detrimental for the vast number of people who live in cities and their immediate surrounding regions.

SEE ALSO: Black Urban Regime; Gentrification; Uneven Development; Urban Renewal and Redevelopment

REFERENCES AND SUGGESTED READINGS

Cox, K. R. & Mair, A. J. (1988) Locality and Community in the Politics of Local Economic Development. *Annals of the Association of American Geographers* 72: 307–25.

Cox, K. R. & Mair, A. J. (1989) Urban Growth Machines and the Politics of Local Economic Development. *International Journal of Urban and Regional Research* 13: 137–46.

Gotham, K. F. (2000) Growth Machine Up-Links: Urban Renewal and the Rise and Fall of a Pro-Growth Coalition in a US City. *Critical Sociology* 26: 268–300.

Horan, C. (1991) Beyond Governing Coalitions: Analyzing Urban Regimes in the 1990s. *Journal of Urban Affairs* 13: 119–35.

Jessop, B., Peck, J., & Tickell, A. (1999) Retooling the Machine: Economic Crisis, State Restructuring and Urban Politics. In: Jonas, A. E. G. &

Wilson, D. (Eds.), *The Urban Growth Machine: Critical Perspectives Two Decades Later.* State University of New York Press, Albany, pp. 141–59.

Jonas, A. E. G. & Wilson, D. (Eds.) (1999) *The Urban Growth Machine: Critical Perspectives Two Decades Later.* State University of New York Press, Albany.

Kirby, A. & Abu-Rass, T. (1999) Employing the Growth Machine Heuristic in a Different Political and Economic Context: The Case of Israel. In: Jonas, A. E. G. & Wilson, D. (Eds.), *The Urban Growth Machine: Critical Perspectives Two Decades Later.* State University of New York Press, Albany, pp. 213–26.

Leitner, H. & Sheppard, E. (2002) "The City is Dead, Long Live the Net": Harnessing European Interurban Networks for a Neoliberal Agenda. *Antipode* 34: 495–518.

Logan, J. R. & Molotch, H. L. (1987) *Urban Fortunes: The Political Economy of Place.* University of California Press, Berkeley.

Logan, J. R., Whaley, R. B., & Crowder, K. (1997) The Character and Consequences of Growth Machines: An Assessment of Twenty Years of Research. *Urban Affairs Review* 32(5): 603–30. (Reprinted in Jonas, A. E. G. & Wilson, D. (Eds.), *The Urban Growth Machine: Critical Perspectives Two Decades Later.* State University of New York Press, Albany.)

Molotch, H. L. (1976) The City as a Growth Machine: Toward a Political Economy of Place. *American Journal of Sociology* 82: 309–30.

Molotch, H. L. (1990) Urban Deals in Comparative Perspective. In: Logan, J. R. & Swanstrom, T. (Eds.), *Beyond the City Limits: Urban Policy and Economic Restructuring in Comparative Perspective.* Temple University Press, Philadelphia, pp. 175–98.

Molotch, H. L. (1999) Growth Machine Links: Up, Down and Across. In: Jonas, A. E. G. & Wilson, D. (Eds.), *The Urban Growth Machine: Critical Perspectives Two Decades Later.* State University of New York Press, Albany, pp. 247–66.

Molotch, H. L. & Logan, J. R. (1984) Tensions in the Growth Machine: Overcoming Resistance to Value-Free Development. *Social Problems* 31: 127–43.

Molotch, H. L. & Vicari, S. (1988) Three Ways to Build: The Development Process in the US, Japan and Italy. *Urban Affairs Quarterly* 24: 48–69.

Stone, C. N. (1989) *Regime Politics: Governing Atlanta, 1946–1988.* University Press of Kansas, Lawrence.

Wilson, D. (1996) Metaphors, Growth Coalition Discourses, and Black Poverty Neighborhoods in a US City. *Antipode* 28: 72–96.

Guattari, Félix (1930–92)

Gary Genosko

French activist-intellectual Pierre-Félix Guattari was inspired by Jean-Paul Sartre's political sociology and trained as a psychoanalyst by Jacques Lacan. Guattari was internationally recognized for his collaborations with Gilles Deleuze on the capitalism and schizophrenia volumes *Anti-Oedipus* (1977), *A Thousand Plateaus* (1987), and *What is Philosophy?* (1994).

In *Transversality and Psychoanalysis* (1972), Guattari developed his key concept of transversality that became the cornerstone of a new kind of analytic practice he called schizoanalysis. Beginning in 1953, Guattari and his colleague Jean Oury organized the Clinique de la Borde (his workplace for almost 40 years) around a complex, rotating system of tasks and responsibilities that scrambled power relations among staff and patients by having them change roles and take on unfamiliar duties. Called "the grid," this made possible detailed analyses of relations of power by providing a context in which the institution itself could be exposed, and if necessary modified in a way that encouraged patients to accept new responsibilities and answer new demands within innovative universes of reference.

Guattari developed a Sartrean-inflected theory of groups by distinguishing non-absolutely between subject groups that actively explored self-defined projects and subjugated groups that passively received directions; each affected in divergent ways the relations of its members to social processes and potential for maintaining an irreducibly polyphonic subjectivity.

Guattari described schizoanalysis as a non-neutral, politically progressive, and provisional transformation of situational power relations in a little-known book, *The Machinic Unconscious* (1979). Eschewing neutrality, the schizoanalyst's micropolitical task is to discern among expressive assemblages of components those with mutational potential, explore the textures of their matters, and produce and extract singularities from them for the sake of the subject's self-invention.

Guattari rejected sociological definitions of groups. Rather, subjectivity is a group phenomenon, but defined as an assemblage of heterogeneous types of components with varying existential consistencies undergoing certain kinds of transformations in self-generated fields with describable semiotic features and observable pragmatic consequences. Guattari introduced the machinic as a principle of productive connectivity irreducible to specific technologies; machines form assemblages of component parts whose molecular becomings the schizoanalyst then helps to facilitate.

In *Schizoanalytic Cartographies* (1989) and *Chaosmosis* (1995), Guattari elaborated four ontological functions of the unconscious – material Fluxes, existential Territories, machinic Phyla, and incorporeal Universes – and explained how the schizoanalyst tries to bridge virtuality and actuality by discerning how virtual universes become real by gaining existential consistency, balancing manifestation and surplus potentiality as subjectivity emerges and pursues dissident vectors of singularization sitting astride abstract Phyla and material Fluxes.

As a political testament, Guattari called for ethico-aesthetic responsibility of subject formation that resists Integrated World Capitalism (globalization) at the intersection of art and ecology in *The Three Ecologies* (2000).

SEE ALSO: Deleuze, Gilles; Lacan, Jacques; Sartre, Jean-Paul

REFERENCES AND SUGGESTED READINGS

Genosko, G. (2002) *Félix Guattari: An Aberrant Introduction*. Continuum, London and New York.

Guattari, F. (1972) *Psychanalyse et transversalité* (*Transversality and Psychoanalysis*). Maspero, Paris.

Guattari, F. (1979) *L'Inconscient machinique* (*The Machinic Unconscious*). Recherches, Fontenay-sous-Bois.

Guattari, F. (1989) *Cartographies schizoanalytiques* (*Schizoanalytic Cartographies*). Galilée, Paris.

Guattari, F. (1995) *Chaosmosis*. Trans. P. Bains & J. Pefanis. Indiana University Press, Bloomington.

Guattari, F. (1998) La grille (The Grid). *Chimères* 34: 7–20.

Guattari, F. (2000) *The Three Ecologies*. Trans. I. Pindar & P. Sutton. Athlone Press, London.

Guattari, F. & Deleuze, G. (1977) *Anti-Oedipus*. Viking, New York.

Guattari, F. & Deleuze, G. (1987) *A Thousand Plateaus*. University of Minnesota Press, Minneapolis.

Guattari, F. & Deleuze, G. (1994) *What is Philosophy?* Columbia University Press, New York.

Gumplowicz, Ludwig (1838–1909)

Bernd Weiler

Around 1900, Ludwig Gumplowicz was internationally regarded as one of the most influential sociological theorists and, together with his fellow countryman Gustav Ratzenhofer (1842–1904), as the leading representative of the so-called Austrian Struggle or Conflict School. Born into an assimilated Jewish family in the quarter of Kazimierz in the Free State of Cracow, which was incorporated into the Austro-Hungarian Monarchy in 1846, the young Gumplowicz strongly identified with Polish culture and fervently supported the movement for greater autonomy of Galicia. After graduating in law from the Jagiellonian University in 1861, Gumplowicz joined the liberal democratic and positivist circles of his deeply conservative hometown and, as a lawyer, journalist, political activist, and chief editor of the progressive newspaper *Kraj* ("The Country"), took an active part in the educational, social, and political affairs of Cracow. Disappointed at his failure to bring about the desired reforms, he left Cracow in 1875 and moved to Graz, where he became a lecturer and in 1893 a full professor of law. Throughout his life, however, he maintained a strong interest in the politics of his native Galicia. Apart from numerous works on Austrian administrative and constitutional law, the prolific writer Gumplowicz dedicated his scientific work to the newly emerging discipline of sociology. After the publication of his booklet *Rasse und Staat: Eine Untersuchung über das Gesetz der Staatenbildung* (1875), in which he first sketched his sociological principles, Gumplowicz wrote *Der Rassenkampf: Sociologische Untersuchungen* (1883), followed shortly thereafter by his most famous work, *Grundriss der Sociologie* (1885), *Die sociologische Staatsidee* (1892), *Sociologie und Politik* (1892), and the posthumously published *Socialphilosophie im Umriss* (1910). Already during his lifetime his main sociological works were translated into several languages, including English, French, Italian, Spanish, Polish, Russian, and Japanese. His theories were especially influential in Italy and the US. In 1909, two years after his retirement, Gumplowicz, who suffered from an incurable cancer of the tongue, and his half-blind wife committed suicide.

Impressed by the rise of the natural sciences in the second half of the nineteenth century and entrenched in the tradition of positivism, Gumplowicz forcefully argued that it was sociology's prime function to prove that social phenomena were governed by universal laws. Several years before, Émile Durkheim, the Polish-born scholar, who sought to establish the autonomy of sociology, claimed that the laws of social life were not reducible to biological, psychological, or environmental factors, but constituted a field of investigation sui generis. As Gumplowicz is often classified as a social Darwinist, it is worth mentioning that he was highly critical of the applicability of Darwinian principles to social life and that he developed his sociological theories in explicit reaction to biologistic understandings of society.

Differing from most of his predecessors, Gumplowicz rejected not only the organicist-holistic conception of society as a biological organism (Comte, Spencer, Schäffle, etc.), but also the atomistic viewpoint according to which social phenomena had to be explained in terms of the purposeful actions of independent individuals (Smith, etc.). Gumplowicz claimed that sociology was essentially the study of groups (hordes, tribes, races, social elements, etc.) and their interrelations. Society was nothing but an aggregate of groups which, in turn, completely determined the individual's thoughts, actions, and emotions.

Gumplowicz saw no need to undertake empirical investigations as he believed that sufficient data had already been collected in order to deduce the laws governing social life and to establish a grand and final sociological system. Drawing primarily upon ethnographic and prehistoric material but also upon his personal observations of the national struggles in the Habsburg Empire, he argued for the polygenetic origin of humanity, the presence of diverse groups in all societies, the high degree of intragroup solidarity – "syngenism" in Gumplowicz's terminology – and the inherently hostile nature of intergroup relationships. Whereas this emphasis on the inherently hostile character of intergroup relations led him to deny the optimistic view, held for example by L. F. Ward and many of his contemporaries, that humanity was steadily moving upward, his emphasis on the inevitability of the laws governing social life and of the impotence of the individual to influence those laws in turn led him to criticize reformist attempts to interfere with the course of society and history. On the practical side, sociology could prove the futility of any human intervention.

In Gumplowicz's sweeping, conjectural, and at times contradictory interpretation of the history of humanity, the time of the formation of the state assumed particular importance. In prestate societies the encounters of ethnically different groups had usually ended with one group exterminating the other. States came into existence when one group conquered and subjugated another group, thereby institutionalizing slavery or other forms of economic exploitation. In this so-called "conquest hypothesis," it was always the minority that ruled over the majority. Over time new groups might emerge by differentiation, "amalgamation," or further subjugation. Rejecting the ideas of the inalienability of human rights and of the impartiality of law in general, Gumplowicz argued that the legal system at all times reflected the actual power relations between the various groups within the state. Despite its more complex structure, modern political life was still characterized by the incessant struggle of groups. Similar to the elite theorists Mosca and Michels, who were both well acquainted with his work, Gumplowicz argued that the essential character of social life had remained unchanged throughout history. Because of this emphasis on social constants, he also saw no need, in contrast to Weber, Simmel, or Durkheim, to develop a sociological theory of modernity. Despite the fact that he offered no analysis of modernity, and despite the conjectural and highly deductive nature of many of his historical interpretations, his radical anti-individualism, and his nineteenth-century positivist outlook, Gumplowicz's almost obsessive focus on the differential power relations within society and his thorough attempt to replace the study of society at large by the study of intergroup relations still deserve attention.

SEE ALSO: Comte, Auguste; Conflict (Racial/Ethnic); Conflict Theory; Durkheim, Émile; Positivism; Ratzenhofer, Gustav; Simmel, Georg; Small, Albion W.; Social Darwinism; Spencer, Herbert; State; Ward, Lester Frank

REFERENCES AND SUGGESTED READINGS

Barnes, H. E. (1948) The Social Philosophy of Ludwig Gumplowicz: The Struggles of Races and Social Groups. In: Barnes, H. E. (Ed.), *An Introduction to the History of Sociology*. University of Chicago Press, Chicago, pp. 191–206.

Gella, A. (Ed.) (1971) *The Ward–Gumplowicz Correspondence: 1897–1909*. Trans. and with an Introduction by A. Gella. Essay Press, New York.

Gumplowicz, L. (1883) *Der Rassenkampf: Sociologische Untersuchungen*. Wagner, Innsbruck.

Gumplowicz, L. (1885) *Grundriss der Sociologie*. Manz, Vienna.

Gumplowicz, L. (1980) *Outlines of Sociology*, rpt. of the 2nd edn, 1963. Transaction, New Brunswick, NJ.

Mozetic, G. (1985) Ein unzeitgemäßer Soziologe: Ludwig Gumplowicz. *Kölner Zeitschrift für Soziologie und Sozialpsychologie* 3: 621–47.

Zebrowski, B. (1926) *Ludwig Gumplowicz – Eine Bio-Bibliographie*. Prager, Berlin. [Includes the most comprehensive bibliography of L. Gumplowicz.]

Gurvitch, Georges: social change

Phillip Bosserman

On June 22, 1962, Georges Gurvitch and his wife Dolly were victims of a terrorist attack aimed at assassinating this deeply dedicated Sorbonne professor of sociology. He had enormous intellectual gifts and possessed a dazzling legal mind with a wonderfully creative sociological imagination. The distinguished social historian Fernand Braudel proclaimed him the brightest person he had ever known.

Gurvitch found himself opposed to French groups such as the OAS (Organisation de l'Armée Secrète) seeking to keep Algeria a French colony. Students poured into Gurvitch's sociology classes from North and Sub-Saharan Africa longing for independence from their French occupiers. Freedom was in the air and Gurvitch favored decolonization. In all likelihood, then, it was OAS terrorists armed with plastic bombs who destroyed the Gurvitchs' Paris apartment on that summer night in 1962, bringing paralyzing fear into their lives. They took refuge in the home of the celebrated painter Marc Chagall.

The moral facts, those principles upon which Gurvitch acted, were centered in a commitment to liberate Algeria from French colonialism. Gurvitch headed an academic activist group at the University of Paris that viewed the brutal and bloody Algerian war as unjust. His leadership tells much about the sociology he taught and lived. The roots of this spontaneous act of creative freedom came from living through the turbulent revolutionary years in Russia, experiencing the vast cataclysmic social changes that reverberated throughout his native land.

Georges Gurvitch was born October 20, 1894, in the Black Sea port of Novorossisk, Russia. About 1910, the family moved to Dorpat, Estonia, where the young Gurvitch's intellectual journey began. The first years of his university training (1912–14) were divided between summer sessions in Germany and winter classes in Russia. During these years he visited scholars in Germany and Central Europe who awakened in him a growing interest in the rising popularity of phenomenology as taught by Scheler and Husserl. Through them, Gurvitch gained a fundamental appreciation of the emotional, intuitive, and affective side of social reality. He absorbed the writings of Bergson and Fichte, who expanded on these approaches. Frederic Rauh provided Gurvitch with the basis for his sociology of moral life.

Just prior to the outbreak of World War I, Gurvitch studied with Emil Lask, who introduced him to Max Weber's thought. Later Gurvitch would make Weber's typological approach a prominent feature of his social change theory. Lask's rigorous dialectic, mostly indebted to Fichte, eventually led Gurvitch to see *we-ness* as ontologically prior to the individual, thus making the social real.

The defining experience that deeply affected Gurvitch's whole being was the Russian Revolution that erupted during February and March 1917. He joined a group of students on the margins of that chaotic political storm. Gurvitch saw creative freedom break forth spontaneously "in the faults or interstices of the determinisms [then in place]" (Choi 1978: i; see also pp. xiii–xiv). His group of students would ask a withering barrage of questions about the changes being made by Lenin's Bolshevik party.

Gurvitch became increasingly displeased with what he was seeing and experiencing. In the spring of 1920, after a memorable walk and talk with his wife Dolly along the banks of the Karpovka River in St. Petersburg, they agreed to leave Russia for Czechoslovakia. Gurvitch taught in the Russian Institute of the University of Prague for four years before moving to Paris. During World War II he accepted an invitation from the New School of Social Research in New York City, returning to France in 1945, eventually occupying Durkheim's chair at the Sorbonne.

Gurvitch's lived experiences of societies in crises and revolution led him to ponder the causes of social change. Mirroring the current challenging work of Michael Burawoy, Gurvitch in the 1950s and 1960s called for sociology to be a *vocation*, not a job, a calling that would make a positive contribution to the group or global society of which sociologists are a part. Gurvitch personally felt motivated to do something about the colonial wars in Algeria and elsewhere. As described above, his actions invited the 1962 terrorist attack against his home.

Central to Gurvitch's sociological thought on social change is the freedom or liberty to act. He went so far as to say sociology's underlying principle is this freedom to question the status quo, to dissent, to go against and change what is. Such freedom gives every human being the possibility of creative, positive activity. Gurvitch identified six degrees or stages of freedom:

1 *Arbitrary liberty* relies on subjective preferences which are driven by unconscious, repetitious patterns similar to the movements of a mobile; such liberty takes precedence over needs or desires; contingency remains strongly present; it is a lazy kind of liberty.

2 *Innovative freedom* rests on a stronger, more determined will resulting in a more concrete application of rules and directives that constitute a moderated, patient, and attentive choice of action.

3 *Liberty choice* employs a more intense, clairvoyant will to guide actors in overcoming closed minds and total negativism by choosing the multiplying alternatives.

4 *Innovative liberty* is a means by which to escape those alternatives that are too cumbersome, present, and too menacing by inventing some possibilities for reorienting the will. Inventive freedom is an invitation to consider new strategies and new maneuvers for overcoming obstacles staring one in the face. This inventive liberty can rely on cunning, or can discover new models, signs, symbols, values, ideas, and the like.

5 *Decisive liberty* intends to overturn the present order, break down, destroy, and eliminate every obstacle that voluntary actions find in their path (Gurvitch 1963: 101). It seeks to confront the purest obstacle, i.e., a committed heroic role, prepared to risk everything.

6 *Creative liberty* is the profoundest level of human freedom. From this degree of human freedom change agents emerge who consciously strive to produce art, religion, and knowledge. They possess god-like skills whose creative impulses are renewed by the other degrees of freedom (Balandier 1974: 17).

The vast capacity of all the degrees of liberty is often called *agency*; the collective acts of agents create social change. Individual and collective efforts to change the status quo are nearly always vigorously opposed by other actors who do not want any tinkering with what is. For Gurvitch, all of these actions make history.

Freedom plays off of determinism. Human actors function within groups, and groups possess a dynamic oneness resulting from the constant motion within what Gurvitch and Mauss called the *total social phenomenon*. Constantly in motion, these total social phenomena are evidenced in ever-present structuration and destructuration.

Gurvitch's discussion of sociability, what he calls microsociology, contrasts mass, community, and communion in terms of the intensity of *we-ness*. What becomes apparent is that change is as critical to Gurvitch's sociological program as freedom or liberty. By employing radical (hyper)empiricism, he can observe the dialectical dance of freedom (free will) and determinism (the centripetal forces of each group's unity).

Gurvitch saw the struggle for change as a primary characteristic of human social life. The human actor, both individual and collective, possesses the freedom to act. "[This] liberty attempts not only to modify obstacles external to the action, but also to modify its own agents . . . [This freedom] aims to consider all the data, all the fluctuations of collective experience, *and* to take . . . account of the fact that in perceiving them it modifies them" (Balandier 1974: 17). Gurvitch's hyperempiricism requires fidelity in examining every type of experience, whatever it takes.

The dialectic illuminates social change. Gurvitch saw three primary aspects to its character. First, it is a concrete, constant movement to find unity (totality) while struggling with instability. Second, the dialectic is a method for grasping and understanding this real, changing human totality. Third, all the while this dialectical character underlines the engaged aspect of the human being who is wholly involved (Gurvitch 1962: 36–7).

In short, the dialectic rejects the pat answer, the hardened system, the simple explanation. Social reality's nature is a fluid, dynamic, ever-changing, explosive, paradoxical, affective domain, the opposite of stable, static, and rigidly functional. Gurvitch proposed five dialectical processes:

1   *Complementarity*: No social whole is reducible to any one factor.
2   *Mutual implication*: What seems to be heterogeneous such as psychological and sociological phenomena overlap and combine, each implying the other.
3   *Ambiguity*: Thanks to Freud, social wholes are moving toward a tentative equilibrium or go in the opposite direction of destructuration.
4   *Polarization*: Conflict, extreme tension, the tearing apart of the structures and subjacent levels are good examples.
5   *Reciprocity of perspectives*: The opposite of polarization in which the immanence or presence of the other is nearly total.

These operative processes immensely help one grasp Marcel Mauss's ingenious admonition "to reconstruct the whole." Gurvitch agreed with Mauss that social scientists have divided and abstracted social phenomena too severely. In fact, he would make Mauss's conception of the total social phenomenon (TSP) his own. Furthermore, the TSP is horizontally arranged on a continuum of varied social frameworks from simple social bonds to friendship circles, family groups, neighborhoods, sports teams, social classes, and full-blown global societies. The TSP is also vertically anchored, occupying different levels varying in terms of accessibility. The surface level of ecology is easiest to view and describe. Gurvitch identified ten levels but always left the exact number open. As one plunges into the depth levels of social organization, roles, creative collective behavior, and to the collective mind itself, the task of discovering how each contributes to the whole of social reality becomes increasingly difficult to discern. Dialectical analysis becomes indispensable. These intersecting relationships are dynamic and moving. "All of these depth levels interpenetrate; more than this, they are in perpetual conflict, tension, and threatened by estrangement or antinomy. The degree of their discontinuity and continuity, their mutual implication, or their polarization is a question of fact, and fact only" (Gurvitch 1963: 103).

Dialectics particularly aid in developing social change theory as it relates to the types of global, historical societies. Gurvitch called them Promethean for they possess "the elements of collective and individual consciousness concerning the capacity of human liberty to be an active and effective intervention in social life" (Gurvitch 1963: 221). Gurvitch rejects Weber's ideal types. These contemporary historical societies are *real*, and committed (engaged) sociologists will be using the dialectical processes to study them.

Because their field of labor is human social reality, sociologists cannot be enclosed in an ivory tower or a laboratory. There is no escaping the human condition. Moreover, if it is human, it is social. Again, *we-ness* is ontologically prior to the *I*. Those whom sociologists examine are thinking, willing, conscious persons – they are also a part of the same global humanity.

As noted above, a striking contemporary voice to Gurvitch's view of practicing sociology is that of Michael Burawoy, president of the American Sociological Association (2004). "A critical, engaged sociology ought to be a sociology about the public, for the public," as Burawoy puts it. "The vocation of science cannot survive without the vocation of politics." Burawoy sees four types: professional politics, the politics surrounding policy issues, the politics stimulating public discussion, and the engagement with the students we teach, calling for critical deliberation. In short, sociologists are *engagés*. There is no alternative.

Gurvitch's dialectic allows the sociologist to acknowledge the implicit relationship between values and method, between the subject and object, the observer and the observed. Social reality is dialectical by nature, requiring each program of research to be dialectical as well. A researcher or teacher cannot avoid taking a position based on certain values. Howard Zinn asserts this in the title of his autobiography, *You Can't Be Neutral On a Moving Train* (2002). He explains why by asking this question: "Does not the very fact of concealment (failure to reveal to your students who you are and where you come from) teach something terrible – that you can separate the study of literature, history, philosophy, politics, and the arts, from your own life, your deepest convictions about right and wrong?" (2002: 7). Gurvitch would have approved of Zinn's stance. Indeed, Gurvitch made it clear which type of global society he favored by self-disclosing his preferences. He was deeply committed to realizing a society that rests on democratic principles of justice and fair play, where all citizens are participants, and decisions move from local grassroots councils upward so the rights of all are kept in balance. Ownership is federalized, i.e., property is jointly owned by individuals embedded in community. To this end, while still in New York, Gurvitch wrote an ambitious blueprint entitled *La Déclaration des droits sociaux* (1944) for post-World War II France that could guide those who had oversight of the vast job of reconstruction. The project was an example of planned social change.

SEE ALSO: Braudel, Fernand; Collective Action; Colonialism (Neocolonialism); Decolonization; Phenomenology; Revolutions; Social Change; Weber, Max

REFERENCES AND SUGGESTED READINGS

Balandier, G. (1974) *Georges Gurvitch*. Trans. M. A. Thompson, with K. A. Thompson. Harper & Row, New York.

Bosserman, P. (1968) *Dialectical Sociology: An Analysis of the Sociology of Georges Gurvitch*. Porter Sargent, Boston.

Choi, C. (1978) *Freedom and Determinism: The Promethean Sociology of Georges Gurvitch*. PhD. New School of Social Research, New York.

Gurvitch, G. (1946 [1944]) *The Bill of Social Rights*. International Universities Press, New York.

Gurvitch, G. (1957 [1950]) *La Vocation actuelle de la sociologie*, 2nd edn. Presses Universitaires de France, Paris.

Gurvitch, G. (1958, 1960) *Traité de sociologie*, 2 vols. Presses Universitaires de France, Paris.

Gurvitch, G. (1962) *Dialectique et sociologie*. Flammarion, Paris.

Gurvitch, G. (1963) *Déterminismes sociaux et liberté humaine*. Presses Universitaires de France, Paris.

Gurvitch, G. (1964) *The Spectrum of Social Time*. Trans. M. Korenbaum, with P. Bosserman. Reidel, Dordrecht.

Zinn, H. (2002) *You Can't Be Neutral On a Moving Train*. Beacon, Boston.

habitus/field

Anne F. Eisenberg

European sociology serves as an interesting contrast to American sociology in terms of theory and theoretical development, as exemplified by Pierre Bourdieu's writings and particularly with his ideas of habitus and field. On the one hand, most typical of theoretical development in American sociology is to build on an existing body of theoretical work rather than seeking to create something novel, and secondly to attempt to find ways to link theory to empirical research by operationalizing the theory. Examples of such programs include theories addressing justice, balance, and identity (micro-level theories) as well as institutionalism, social change, and revolutions (macro-level theories). European, particularly continental, sociology has tended to take a somewhat different approach by focusing on integrating key theoretical ideas across different perspectives, as well as creating new language with which to express such integrative ideas. Additionally, another key distinction between American and European sociology is that American sociology highlights what some writers consider to be false distinctions and dichotomies in a range of areas – such as theory versus research methods, objective versus subjective, qualitative or interpretive methods versus quantitative or positivistic methods, macro versus micro, and structure versus agency. European sociologists argue against creating and maintaining such arbitrary boundaries in describing and explaining the social world. Bourdieu's ideas of habitus and field provide a new way of explaining key aspects of the social world that integrates key ideas from different sociological perspectives.

In the first chapter of *Outline of a Theory of Practice* (1977) Bourdieu explicitly addresses the problems inherent in limiting our understanding of human society to the false distinctions that represent typical sociological explanations – particularly, the distinctions between objective versus subjective and structure versus agency. He argues that the structure of society (as represented by social institutions and macrostructures) is far more dynamic than as normally portrayed, and that human agency has far more input in shaping social structures and social institutions than is normally discussed by sociologists. This discussion provides a natural segue to his discussion of habitus in the second chapter. Habitus epitomizes Bourdieu's interest in linking phenomenological and symbolic interactionist perspectives (sometimes equated with the subjectivist view) with the more structuralist approach (sometimes equated with the objectivist view) of American and some European sociologists. Additionally, habitus also illustrates the intimate connection between structure and agency as represented in the social actor, where the social actor can be an individual, a group, or any large collectivity.

Bourdieu defines habitus as the way in which actors calculate and determine future actions based on existing norms, rules, and values representing existing conditions. It is important to understand key aspects of habitus. One key element of this definition is that Bourdieu argues that existing norms, rules, and values have been mentally and cognitively integrated into the actor's frame of reference, and that they represent general social standards as well as specific situational and personal experiences. This illustrates his way of integrating the macro elements of a structured social world that imposes its will on actors with the dynamic agency that enables actors to engage in individually determined actions. Additionally, this illustrates the integration of an objective reality created by existing structural elements in society with the subjective reality of the social actor. A second key element of habitus is that "future" actions refer to a range of possible actions, from what you do immediately upon reading this entry to what you might plan to do on your next vacation. Bourdieu states that social actors engage in a continuously dynamic interaction with their environment and other actors such that they are aware of negotiating from a range of possible actions to take. A third key element associated with his definition of habitus is that, in identifying actors' agency in calculating actions, Bourdieu explains that this process is rational in that it takes into account potential outcomes for any specific action as well as something other than rational in that it also takes into account subjective motivations. In other words, habitus reflects actors' emotional and spontaneous reactions to particular situations and the other actors involved. The final key element of the idea of habitus is that it represents a fluid set of guiding principles for the social actor. While actors in similar positions in society may share similar habitus, as their environment and the other actors in the environment change, so does the habitus. It is consistent across actors, which allows us to understand particular settings and cultures as well as what is unique to each individual.

Bourdieu's idea of field also serves to demonstrate the intimate connection between objective and subjective realities as well as between structure and agency. His discussion of fields also integrates a Marxist focus on conflictual relations with a Weberian focus on formal hierarchies. Fields represent the network of relations between and among positions actors hold within particular structural or organizational systems. For example, Bourdieu examines artistic or literary fields and he describes them in terms of the positions actors hold relative to one another. Additionally, he argues that there are several hierarchies of fields as well as hierarchies within each field. The specific positions held by actors linked in terms of similar structural or organizational systems are embedded in fields of power, which are then embedded in fields of class relations. The connection to Marxist and Weberian ideas is immediately evident when you view the

field as a set of interconnecting positions that occur on several different levels – similar to 3-D chess, where the players must be aware of not only the first board, but also how the chess pieces on two other levels of boards are interacting with, and affecting, the primary or first board. There are several ways that Bourdieu's idea of fields overcomes the dichotomies of American sociology. First, in his discussion of the network of relations among positions, Bourdieu allows the actors to be individuals as well as corporate actors. Along with the interlocking levels of fields, he bridges the perceived gap between micro and macro levels of social phenomena. Second, Bourdieu argues that while the positions reflect objective reality through their organizational or structural existence, they also reflect the subjective reality of individual actors who occupy such positions. Third, in the tradition of the early French anthropologists, Marx, Weber, and Durkheim, Bourdieu uses empirical research to develop this theoretical concept.

SEE ALSO: Agency (and Intention); Bourdieu, Pierre; Networks; Phenomenology; Structure and Agency; Structuralism; Symbolic Interaction

REFERENCES AND SUGGESTED READINGS

Bourdieu, P. (1977) *Outline of a Theory of Practice*. Cambridge University Press, New York.

Bourdieu, P. (1990) *Reproduction in Education, Society and Culture*, 2nd edn. Sage, London.

Bourdieu, P. (2002) The Field of Cultural Production, or: The Economic World Reversed. In: Calhoun, C., Gerteis, J., Moody, J., Pfaff, S., & Vick, I. (Eds.), *Contemporary Sociological Theory*. Blackwell, Oxford, pp. 289–304.

Erickson, B. (1996) Culture, Class, and Connections. *American Journal of Sociology* 102(1): 217–51.

Guiffre, K. (1999) Sandpiles of Opportunity: Success in the Art World. *Social Forces* 77(3): 815–32.

Ritzer, G. (2003) *Contemporary Sociological Theory and Its Classical Roots: The Basics*. McGraw-Hill, New York.

Turner, J. H. (2003) *The Structure of Sociological Theory*, 7th edn. Thomson/Wadsworth, Australia.

Wacquant, L. J. D. (1998) Pierre Bourdieu. In: Stone, R. (Ed.), *Key Sociological Thinkers*. New York University Press, New York, pp. 215–29.

Halbwachs, Maurice (1877–1945)

Suzanne Vromen

The French sociologist Maurice Halbwachs was a prominent representative of Durkheimian sociology during the interwar years, and an important contributor to the *Annales sociologiques*. He was also a statistician, a demographer, an expert at analyzing working-class budgets, and an urban sociologist. His pathbreaking contribution to sociology, however, consists in the way he conceptualized how memory is socially constructed.

Maurice Halbwachs was born in Reims, France, in a Catholic family of Alsatian origin that opted to remain French when Alsace was annexed by Germany in 1871. Liberal in political ideas, the family moved to Paris in 1879. Influenced by Henri Bergson, his teacher at the Lycée Henri IV, Halbwachs studied philosophy at the Ecole Normale Supérieure, the elite school where most great French teachers are educated, and in 1901 he obtained his *agrégation*, the competitive diploma required to teach in the French secondary system.

Halbwachs soon became attracted to the social sciences, acquired two doctorates and sharpened his mathematical skills. He joined the Durkheim group, and from 1905 he contributed extensively to the *Année sociologique*. Bergson's influence on him, however, remained undeniable. Halbwachs's central program, the analysis of memory, was a lifelong attempt to reconcile some Bergsonian insights into consciousness, time, and remembering with Durkheimian perspectives.

With the end of World War I, higher education opened up for Halbwachs. From 1919 to 1935 he taught at the University of Strasbourg, first as professor of sociology and pedagogy, and from 1922 as France's first professor of sociology. Thanks to his reputation and the university's interdisciplinary climate, Halbwachs was invited to serve on the editorial committee of the *Annales d'histoire économique et sociale* launched by his historian colleagues Lucien Febvre and Marc Bloch, and he became a valued contributor. During the Strasbourg years he produced major works, among them *Les Cadres sociaux de la mémoire* (*The Social Frameworks of Memory*) (1925), *Les Causes du suicide* (*The Causes of Suicide*) (1930), and *L'Évolution des besoins dans les classes ouvrières* (*The Evolution of Needs in the Working Classes*) (1933).

In 1935 he moved to the Sorbonne, where he occupied positions in the history of social economics (1935–7), the methodology and logic of the sciences (1937–9), and sociology (1939–44). At the same time, official honors were showered upon him, including membership of the Academy of Moral and Political Sciences (1932) and in the International Institute of Statistics (1935), and presidency of the French Institute of Sociology (1938).

In May 1944 he was appointed to the Chair of Collective Psychology at the Collège de France. But in July, detained by the Gestapo following his son's arrest for resistance activities, father and son were deported together to Buchenwald, where Halbwachs died in March 1945.

In the interwar years Halbwachs was a major promoter of Durkheimian sociology in France, broadening its development in dialogue with other disciplines such as psychology and history. A prolific worker and sophisticated statistician, with an expansive intellectual curiosity, he engaged critically with Durkeim's theories of suicide and of social morphology (*Morphologie sociale/Social Morphology*, 1938), and he also analyzed empirically aspects of urban and working-class life in contemporary societies, subjects neglected by other Durkheimians.

With his theory of collective memory Halbwachs opened for sociological analysis a subject formerly left to literature and psychology. He intended to sociologize consciousness and to bring out the dependence on the social context of faculties traditionally considered uniquely and totally individual. For him, individual memory was shaped by the very fact of social existence. He postulated temporality and spatiality as intrinsic parts of consciousness, and considered memory as the convergence of multiple solidarities and as the ordering of experience. To remember, one needed others. He redefined time from a homogeneous and uniform category to coordinator of social experiences. By pointing the way to an analysis of the concrete situations of everyday life in their temporality and spatiality with the meanings attached to them, Halbwachs adopted a phenomenological position. On the collective level, his analysis of memory was functional: group memories ensured cohesion and social continuity. They were didactic and effective because they included both concrete and abstract elements, images, and concepts. Space was to be understood in terms of a group's attitudes and intentions toward it, and localizations served as means of legitimation. Besides *Les Cadres sociaux de la mémoire*, Halbwachs developed his theory of collective memory in *La Topographie légendaire des Evangiles en Terre Sainte* (*Legendary Topography of the Gospels in the Holy Land*) (1941) and in *La Mémoire collective The Collective Memory*) (1950), a collection consisting of an article on the collective memory of musicians and of extensive notes found in his papers after his untimely death, indicative of his intention to write another book on the subject of memory. The volume on the legendary topography of the Holy Land illustrates his concern with empirical data through a detailed and systematic examination of the localizations of holy places. Revered by Christians in Palestine, these holy places shifted according to historically significant doctrinal and political changes, thus the spatial framework of memory was continually reshaped by the varying concerns of the living people who did the remembering. Here Halbwachs offered a concrete reinterpretation of the sociology of knowledge, and questioned what images and concepts in a group's past best fulfilled didactic or legitimation purposes. A large collection of Halbwachs's notes and personal letters have recently been archived, and French sociologists are mining them to acquire a more complete sense of his work so tragically interrupted.

Halbwachs's constant focus on concrete facts of everyday life is apparent in his examination of family budgets, of expropriations, of working-class budgets, and of memory. This emphasis on the concrete and the familiar differentiates him fundamentally from Durkheim, for he had no general evolutionary social philosophy.

For our postmodern age, Halbwachs's sociological theory of memory with its redefinition of time offers original lines of inquiry and feeds into modern analyses of ideological forgetting and remembering, while his insights into how values are embodied in material forms provide contributions both to urban sociology and to the sociology of knowledge.

SEE ALSO: Annales School; Collective Memory; Durkheim, Émile; Knowledge, Sociology of

REFERENCES AND SUGGESTED READINGS

Becker, A. (2003) *Maurice Halbwachs un intellectuel en guerres mondiales 1914–1945* (*Maurice Halbwachs: An intellectual in World Wars 1914–1945*). Agnès Viénot Editions, Paris.

Besnard, P. (Ed.) (1983) *The Sociological Domain: The Durkheimians and the Founding of French Sociology*. Cambridge University Press, Cambridge.

Halbwachs, M. (1950/1980) *The Collective Memory*, intro. Mary Douglas. Harper & Row, New York.

Halbwachs, M. (1992) *On Collective Memory*, ed. and trans. Lewis Coser. University of Chicago Press, Chicago.

Vromen, S. (1975) *The Sociology of Maurice Halbwachs*. Doctoral dissertation. New York University, New York.

hate crimes

Jack Levin

The term hate crimes has been employed since the mid-1980s to identify criminal acts motivated either entirely or in part by the fact or perception that a victim is different from the perpetrator. The term first appeared in newspaper accounts of a 1986 racial incident in the Howard Beach section of New York City, in which a black man was killed while attempting to flee a violent mob of white teenagers, shouting racial slurs. By the early 1990s the hate crime designation was being applied not only to attacks based on race and religion, but also on sexual orientation, national origin, disability status, and gender.

In legal terms, the groups protected by hate crime laws differ from state to state. By 2003,

45 states had some form of hate crime statute that covered individuals targeted because of race, religion, or ethnicity; 30 also included disability status or sexual orientation; only 27 protected gender (Anti-Defamation League 2003).

In some states a separate statute exists which prohibits hate crime behavior, while in other states the hate crime statute is a "penalty enhancement." This means that if an existing crime is committed and it is motivated by bias, the penalty on the existing crime may be increased. Finally, a federal hate crimes statute exists, allowing federal prosecution of crimes based on race, color, religion, or national origin for certain constitutionally protected activities such as voting.

In a sense, the term hate crimes is somewhat misleading in its emphasis on hate as a defining basis for choosing and attacking a particular victim. The level of brutality in certain hate attacks suggests the presence of intense hostility or anger (i.e., hatred) in the motivation of the assailants. In the more typical hate crime, however, perpetrators may be motivated more by a desire for belonging or profit than by hatred for a particular victim. In addition, extreme dislike toward the victim may be present in many hate crimes, even if the primary motivation for the offense turns out to be something other than bias; such crimes can confound efforts to apply a consistent definition of hate crimes.

In terms of offender motivation, hate crimes can be categorized as four major types: thrill, defensive, retaliatory, and mission (Levin & McDevitt 2001). The majority seem to be thrill hate crimes: recreational offenses committed by youngsters – usually males operating in groups – who seek excitement at someone else's expense. Such young offenders get from their attack on a victim "bragging rights" with their friends. Though many of the hate crimes directed against property – acts of desecration and vandalism – can be included in the thrill-seeking category, there are also numerous thrill hate offenses that involve intimidations, threats, and brutal assaults.

A second type of hate crime is defensive. That is, the attack is designed to protect an individual's neighborhood, workplace, school, or women from those who are considered to be outsiders. Defensive hate crimes have often occurred when a family from a different racial group – especially black or Asian – moves into a previously all-white neighborhood. Wherever it occurs, a defensive attack is often an act of domestic terrorism because it is designed to send a message to every member of the victim's group.

Retaliatory hate crimes are motivated by an individual's need for revenge as a result of a hate attack directed against his or her own group members. The targets of a retaliatory crime are not necessarily the particular individuals who had perpetrated the initial offense. More than any other type of hate crimes, a series of retaliatory offenses may contain the basis for escalating from individual criminal acts into large-scale group conflict.

A final type of hate crime is a mission offense, usually committed by the members of an organized hate group. Actually, no more than 5 percent of all hate crimes nationally are committed by the members of organizations like the Ku Klux Klan or the White Aryan Resistance. Yet organized hate groups continue behind the scenes to support much larger numbers of violent offenses committed by non-members who may be unsophisticated with respect to the ideology of hate – racist skinheads, alienated teenagers, or hate-filled young men.

Organized hate groups are found not only in our communities, but in our penitentiaries. Established in many states around the country, for example, the Aryan Brotherhood introduces inmates to the theology of the Identity Church, according to which Jews are the children of Satan and blacks are sub-human "mud people."

Like other aspects of the Uniform Crime Reports (FBI 2003), hate crime incidents, offenders, and victims are voluntarily reported by local jurisdictions to the FBI. Some 86 percent of the population of the US is now covered in nationally reported hate crime statistics. Of course, there is still reason to believe that hate crimes are vastly underestimated. Whether from ignorance, fear of retaliation, or distrust of the police, many victims of hate attacks simply do not report their victimization to the police.

In 2002 there were only 17 hate-motivated murders reported to the FBI. On the other hand, there were 8,832 hate crimes reported, 68 percent of which were directed against persons. The location of hate crime incidents varied, but they seemed to be concentrated in homes, on the streets, and in schools and colleges. Race was the most common basis for committing a hate offense, with anti-black attacks most likely to occur and anti-white attacks in second place. Anti-gay, anti-Jewish, anti-Latino, and anti-Muslim offenses were also quite prevalent. A wide range of groups were represented among the victims of hate crimes, including people with physical and mental disabilities, Asians, Protestants, Catholics, and American Indians.

SEE ALSO: Gangs, Delinquent; Gay Bashing; Homicide; Violent Crime

REFERENCES AND SUGGESTED READINGS

Anti-Defamation League (2003) Online. www.adl.org/adl.asp.
Federal Bureau of Investigation (2003) *Crime in the United States: 2002*. US Government Printing Office, Washington, DC.
Levin, J. & McDevitt, J. (2001) *Hate Crimes Revisited*. Westview Press, Boulder.
Potok, M. (2003) The Year in Hate. *Intelligent Report*. Online. www.splcenter.org/intel/intelreport/article.jsp?aid=374.

Hawthorne Effect

William H. Swatos, Jr.

The Hawthorne Effect is the name that has been given to the possibility that a subject in a research project may change his or her behavior in a positive manner simply as a result of being aware of being studied. This concept takes its name from research studies conducted from 1924 to 1933 at the Western Electric Company's Hawthorne plant near Chicago, Illinois, that ultimately came under the direction of Elton Mayo of Harvard University. The specific research associated with the Hawthorne Effect was the first step among several and was conducted by engineers at the plant from 1924

to 1927, prior to Mayo's entry. This experiment involved increasing the lighting within a work area, using both experimental and control groups. Measuring worker output before and after the change in lighting showed an increase in productivity in *both* the experimental and control groups. Additional experiments with results along these lines led the researchers to conclude that the increased worker output occurred simply because of the increased attention directed toward the workers. It was at this point that Mayo entered the research, and the focus moved from simple variation in illumination to a variety of alterations in actual worker activity. As a whole, the research provided the initial grounding for Mayo to create the human relations movement, particularly in complex organizations.

With respect to research strategies themselves, later research has raised considerable doubts about whether the conclusions drawn across the studies as a whole are supported from the data. Subsequent studies show that the Hawthorne Effect has a variety of limits and may also have been influenced by its novelty at the time. Limits include the relative reasonableness of the alterations, the conduct of the researchers, and the nature of the work and workplace. At the same time, however, the implications associated with the Hawthorne Effect have been extended beyond classical experimental designs, which are relatively rare in sociology, to issues within survey research. Persons who are told that their opinions are valuable may quickly form opinions on topics about which they know very little, or they may modify their actual opinions in ways that they believe will be socially acceptable – either to the interviewer or to members of a group in a group interview setting. These various possibilities underscore the unique character of humans as subjects of research: the ability of humans to construct meaning within research contexts independent of the intentions of the researchers.

At the level of applied sociology in management, however, the Hawthorne studies have been incorporated into consultative approaches to labor management and productivity. That is, designing approaches to output that involve management–labor contact and worker opinion in the manufacturing process can be used as a strategy to improve productivity regardless of the process itself. Although this tactic is subject to the same limits as occur with respect to research subjects, it nevertheless has become a fairly standard component of worker-friendly management styles.

SEE ALSO: Experimental Design; Management Theory; Work, Sociology of

REFERENCES AND SUGGESTED READINGS

Franke, R. H. & Kaul, J. D. (1978) The Hawthorne Experiments. *American Sociological Review* 43: 623–43.
Roethlisberger, F. J. & Dickson, W. J. (1939) *Management and the Worker*. Harvard University Press, Cambridge, MA.

health behavior

William C. Cockerham

Health behavior is defined as the activity undertaken by people for the purpose of maintaining or enhancing their health, preventing health problems, or achieving a positive body image (Cockerham 2000: 159). This definition goes beyond the one provided by Kasel and Cobb (1966), who depicted health behavior solely as the activity of healthy people to prevent illness. This latter definition is too limiting because health behavior does not just consist of healthy people trying to stay that way. While the health behavior of many people is intended to prevent sickness and injury, or to prolong their lives, other people may have other objectives. People with chronic diseases like heart disease and diabetes, for example, also engage in health behavior when they seek to control their disease through diet, exercise, and other forms of health-related activity. Some people who are primarily motivated to enhance their bodily appearance and physical fitness through health-promoting activities like diet and exercise likewise are engaging in health behavior even if the desire to look and feel good is more important to them than being healthy.

For most people, health behavior consists of actions to maintain, restore, or improve their health, prevent health problems, increase their life span, or achieve a healthy appearance. These actions include a wide range of activities, including eating healthy foods, not smoking, exercising, brushing one's teeth, taking medication to control blood pressure or reduce cholesterol, getting 7 to 8 hours of sleep a night, and so on. What has brought health behavior t the attention of sociologists is that considerations of health outcomes are increasingly important influences on the daily routines of social life. In past historical periods, a person was either healthy or unhealthy and tended to take this situation more or less for granted. Today, however, this view has changed. In developed societies, good health has become a condition to be achieved and maintained through personal effort. In order to be healthy, people are expected to "work" at it, and believed to risk disease and premature death if they do not. This circumstance has its origins in the public's recognition that medicine cannot cure chronic diseases and the close association of such diseases with unhealthy lifestyles (Crawford 1984). The realization that responsibility for one's own health ultimately falls on one's self, not the medical profession, is viewed as a major reason for the renewed interest in health behavior that originated in the physical fitness movements (e.g., jogging, aerobic exercise) of the 1960s.

One of the first major accounts of health behavior in sociology was provided by the French sociologist Claudine Herzlich (1973; Herzlich & Pierret 1987). Health was described by people in her study as a necessity for both the individual and society, and the means by which a person achieves self-realization. Herzlich identified a shift in thinking in French society away from taking health for granted toward a norm of a "duty to be healthy." This norm was strongest in the middle class, but appeared to be spreading, as many lower-class people expressed the same orientation. "The right to health," stated Herzlich and Pierret (1987: 231), "implies that every individual must be made responsible for his or her health and must adopt rational behavior in dealing with the pathogenic effects of modern life."

The standard approach to the study of health behavior in public health views such behavior as largely a matter of individual choice and targets the individual to change his or her harmful health practices largely through education (Gochman 1997). The theoretical models used in such research, like the Health Belief Model and the Stages of Change Model, are typically based on individual psychology. While this research is useful in certain contexts, it neglects the social situations and conditions that may ultimately be responsible for causing the health problem. A sociological perspective allows the researcher to analyze health behavior as a social phenomenon that goes beyond the psychology of the individual. The source of the behavior may be located in the norms, practices, and values of groups, social classes, and society at large that influence the individual. A sociological approach also helps the researcher address macro-level conditions like poverty, the stress of economic recessions, and environmental pollution, over which the individual has little or no control but must cope with because of his or her social circumstances. These conditions not only cause unhealthy living situations, but also promote unhealthy behavior when heavy alcohol use, smoking, inattention to diet, and the like are the response.

The focus of research in sociology is not on the health behavior of the individual; rather, it is on the transformation of this behavior into its aggregate or collective form: health lifestyles. Health lifestyles are collective patterns of health-related behavior based on choices from options available to people according to their life chances (Cockerham 2000: 160). Invariably, the better a person's life chances, as typically indicated by his or her class position, the healthier the lifestyle and, conversely, the worse the person's chances in life, the less healthy the person's lifestyle and the higher the probability for a shorter life.

SEE ALSO: Health and Culture; Health Lifestyles; Health Locus of Control; Health and Medicine; Health Risk Behavior; Health, Self-Rated; Health and Social Class; Illness Behavior; Life Chances and Resources

REFERENCES AND SUGGESTED READINGS

Cockerham, W. C. (2000) The Sociology of Health Behavior and Health Lifestyles. In: Bird, C. E.,
Conrad, P., & Fremont, A. M. (Eds.), *Handbook of Medical Sociology*, 5th edn. Prentice-Hall, Upper Saddle River, NJ, pp. 159–72.

Crawford, R. (1984) A Cultural Account of Health: Control, Release, and the Social Body. In: McKinlay, J. (Ed.), *Issues in the Political Economy of Health*. Tavistock, New York, pp. 60–103.

Gochman, D. S. (Ed.) (1997) *Handbook of Health Behavior Research*, Vols. 1–4. Plenum Press, New York.

Herzlich, C. (1973) *Health and Illness: A Social Psychological Analysis*. Academic Press, New York.

Herzlich, C. & Pierret, J. (1987) *Illness and Self in Society*. Johns Hopkins University Press, Baltimore.

Kasel, S. & Cobb, S. (1966) Health Behavior, Illness Behavior, and Sick Role Behavior. *Archives of Environmental Health* 12: 246–66.

health care delivery systems

Fred Stevens and Jouke van der Zee

A health care delivery system is the organized response of a society to the health problems of its inhabitants. Societies choose from alternative health care delivery models and, in doing so, they organize and set goals and priorities in such a way that the actions of different actors are effective, meaningful, and socially accepted. From a sociological point of view, the analysis of health care delivery systems implies recognition of their distinct history over time, their specific values and value patterns that go beyond technological requirements, and their commitment to a set of normative standards (Parsons 1951; Selznick 1957). The term "system" is used here in a sociological sense (Parsons 1951; Philipsen 1980). Typical system features are functional specificity (operational goals), structural differentiation (the division of labor), goal-setting (including effectiveness, efficiency), coordination (of activities, occupations, and facilities by mutual agreement, standards, or hierarchy), and boundary maintaining autonomy (in relation to political, economic, or normative structures). Some health care delivery systems comply more with these system characteristics than others. Where health care delivery systems vary, it is mainly due to long-term cultural and structural developments.

Consequently, a health care delivery system is typified by its structure, its relationships between actors and organizations, and its specific pattern of underlying norms, values, and value orientations.

Three factors are significant in understanding the origins of modern health care delivery systems: (1) the socioeconomic level of development of a society, (2) its demographic situation, and (3) the epidemiological state of affairs. As shown in Table 1, modern societies developed from agricultural economies through industrialization to service economies in a *societal transition*. They initially focused on survival and self-sustenance of the small landholder and his or her (extended) family, but evolved toward economies creating surpluses (wealth) and added value to products that could be traded. Surpluses were commonly used to institute new roles and occupations that were important but not necessarily productive, such as priests, soldiers, tax collectors, and healers. Surpluses accumulated during long periods, in which stages of prosperity alternated with times of recession, due to war, famine, and pandemics. As societies further developed and modernized, more structures and institutions came into existence that reduced the risks of daily life.

Table 1 shows that widespread kinship-based arrangements to cope with these risks were gradually supplemented and replaced by collective arrangements. This culminated in a *demographic transition* consisting of the reduction of a population's fertility. In modern societies it was no longer imperative to have many children as a provision against old-age poverty. At the end of the nineteenth century, at first in Germany, social security systems against loss of income due to accidents and disabilities came into existence. These further developed to include public pension schemes several decades later. In addition to these collective arrangements, financial surpluses were the foundation of economic growth, by extending educational facilities, also creating more services and typical professions, like teachers, health care providers, lawyers, and engineers. In Europe, taxes or fee collection were the primary mechanisms and financial resources for these

Table 1 Societal transitions and the development of health care delivery systems.

Societal transition	AGRICULTURE (rural) ⟶		INDUSTRY (urban) ⟶			SERVICES (suburban)
	Multi-generation family		Nuclear family			Individual households
Social tensions, revolutions, war ⟶						
Main health issues	Demographic transition					
	Infectious diseases ⟶		Declining fertility	Aging population ⟶		Chronic diseases, diseases of civilization
	Declining mortality			Epidemiological transition		
Focus of care	Hygiene, public health, informal care ⟶		Emerging curative care, social security, welfare state ⟶			High tech care, professional home care

collective arrangements. In the course of this modernization process, the *epidemiological transition* took place that reflected a gradual shift from the sheer necessity to overcome infectious diseases (mainly affecting infants) toward dealing with chronic diseases (primarily affecting the late middle aged and elderly). Nowadays, health care delivery systems in modern societies are largely focused on the changing needs and demands of an aging population.

Health care organizations usually lag behind changing patterns of population needs. The reason is that modern, more sophisticated health care delivery systems, characterized by an advanced division of labor, high levels of complexity, and structural means for coordination and planning, require extensive financial resources. Yet only advanced economies are able to put aside sufficient resources for health care. Consequently, the extent to which resources can be generated for health care signifies a nation's stage of economic development. Evidently, on both micro (individual) as well on macro (societal) levels, there is a strong association between health and wealth.

Several conclusions can be drawn. First, the wealth of a society is a major determinant of health. Second, it is more difficult to improve health in affluent societies than in poor ones. Third, in countries with low levels of income (usually typified as developing societies), hygiene, sanitation, vaccination, nutrition, and immunization are the important objectives for health care. Modern societies, with higher average levels of income, largely have to cope with rising costs due to the increasing demand for chronic care, as a consequence of an aging population.

TYPES OF HEALTH CARE DELIVERY SYSTEMS

A simple, traditional market structure consists of bilateral relations between buyers and suppliers. The health care sector differs essentially from such a market structure, as interactions between actors are not organized in bidirectional relations of pairs of producers and consumers and the price of a health care procedure is not the balancing mechanism. Instead, health care delivery systems consist

of five principal actors. These are the consumers (patients), first-line providers (usually general practitioners), second-line providers (hospitals, institutional facilities), the state, and insurers (Evans 1981). They are organized multi-directionally, as an interacting system. Dependent on organization and system features, consumers (1) have direct access to hospital services; (2) may need a referral from a GP; (3) get their health care expenses reimbursed from an insurer; (4) have total or partial health care insurance coverage and pay taxes or insurance premiums for that reason; or (5) have to pay their bill directly to the provider (like the simple market structure).

Yet in typifying a nation's health system the role of the state in funding is decisive (Evans 1981; Hurst 1992; Marrée & Groenewegen 1997). Ideal typical ways of state funding involvement are:

- *Largely absent*: the state propagates non-interventionism, leaving room primarily for private insurance to fill this role. The organization and provision of health care in the US and Switzerland are typical examples.
- *In-between*: the state harmonizes the arrangements that developed between groups of citizens (e.g., employers, employees). This is the case in many European countries.
- *Central*: the state controls funding, *with* or *without* the provision of health care. The former is/was typical of Eastern Europe and Russia; the latter is typical for the National Health Services (NHS) model as found in the UK.

The *free market* model applies when the state conducts a policy of non-interventionism and restricts its interference in health care matters to the bare essentials, leaving all other expenses to private funding and corporate provision (HMOs). This is the typical situation in the US, except for Medicaid (indigent) and Medicare (elderly) state interventions. Private insurance fills the gap to some degree, however, leaving about 16 percent of the US population uninsured for health care costs or loss of income due to illness and disability.

The second model is the *social insurance system*, founded in the late nineteenth century in

Germany. Typical for the social insurance system is that patients pay an insurance premium to a sickness fund which has a contract with first-line (GP) and second-line (hospital and specialist) providers. The role of the state is limited and confined to setting the overall terms of contracts between patients, providers, and insurers. The social insurance system is funded by premiums paid and controlled by employers and labor unions. These, however, have little control over the provision of services. This is left to the professions, specifically to the medical profession and to professionalized care organizations (e.g., home nursing, home help). For people with lower and middle-class salaried incomes, collective arrangements are available (sick funds). Founded in Germany, the social security model was almost immediately adopted by Czechoslovakia during Austrian-Hungarian rule, Austria, Hungary, and Poland. During World War II it was imposed on the Netherlands (1941) and later adopted by Belgium and France. The social insurance system survived two world wars and National Socialism, and in essence still exists in Germany, the Netherlands, Belgium, France, Austria, Switzerland, Luxembourg, and Japan (Saltman & Figueras 1997).

The third model, typically found in the UK, is the taxed-based *National Health Services (NHS) model*. It was first introduced in 1948, is also centralized and is funded by means of taxation, while the state is responsible for the provision of institution-based care (hospitals). The medical profession has a rather independent position. Self-employed GPs are the gatekeepers in primary health care. Before visiting a hospital or a medical specialist one needs a referral from a GP. The NHS model leaves some room for private medicine. Through processes of diffusion and adaptation, the NHS model was first adopted in Sweden, and then by the other Nordic countries: Denmark, Norway, and Finland. At present, the NHS model applies to the United Kingdom, Ireland, Denmark, Norway, Sweden, Finland, Iceland, and outside Europe by Australia and New Zealand. Four Southern European countries have adopted, or are in the process of adopting, this tax-based model. These are Spain, Italy, Portugal, and Greece (Saltman & Figueras 1997).

The fourth, most centralized health care delivery systems model, the *Soviet model*, dates from 1920. It is characterized by a strong position of the state, guaranteeing full and free access to health care for everyone. This is realized by state ownership of health care facilities, by funding from the state budget (taxes), and by geographical distribution and provision of services throughout the country. Health services are fully hierarchically organized. They are provided by state employees, planned by hierarchical provision, and organized as a hierarchy of hospitals, with outpatient clinics (polyclinics) as lowest levels of entrance. Among the nations that, until recently, had a health care system based on the Soviet model were Russia, Belarus, the Central Asian republics of the former USSR, and some countries in Central and Eastern Europe. Many former Soviet Republics, however, are in a process of transition toward a social insurance-based system.

The four models make up a continuum in terms of their "system" character, with state interventionism and centralized health care at one end, and non-interventionism at the other. Centralized systems provide best mechanisms for cost control, while absence of state intervention does not appear to be fruitful, as soaring costs in the US evidently show. The four health delivery systems models are to be seen as pure types which can be found in many combinations and varieties. They also reflect stages and outcomes of a historical process. Consequently, system models that came into existence in highly developed economies in the first half of the twentieth century can now still provide useful options to choose from in developing countries or transitional economies like in Eastern European societies.

HEALTH CARE DELIVERY SYSTEMS REFORM

While the models presented reflect the major types that can be found in industrialized countries in Europe, the US, and Asia, none of these countries fully complies with the characteristics of one particular model. In a Weberian sense, they should be seen as ideal types. Through processes of adaptation and diffusion, national health care delivery systems deviate from these models. For example, social insurance-based health care delivery systems and the enterpreneurial system of the US were faced with problems of rising costs in the 1960s and 1970s. The NHS delivery systems and Soviet-like delivery systems of Eastern Europe had problems of neglect, underfunding, and extensive bureaucracy in the 1970 and 1980s. In some countries, specifically those with social security based health care systems, this has led to more state regulation to curb the costs of health care. In other countries it resulted in less state intervention, and in the introduction of different forms of managed competition. For example, in Eastern Europe, after the fall of the Berlin Wall, we see the demise of state funding and state provision due to economic deficits. In the countries that have adopted the social insurance model we see more state regulation in order to introduce more planning and to curb the rising costs of health care. One of the consequences has been a stronger position of hospitals. In the UK we have seen a movement towards more decentralization, which was realized by a separation between purchasers (the government) and providers (Saltman & Figueras 1997; Tuohy 1999).

CULTURAL ROOTS AND VALUE ORIENTATIONS

Health care organization is also influenced by cultural circumstances. For example, nations with collective arrangements have more state intervention, a small private sector, a preference for tax rather than insurance funding, and comprehensive coverage with universal entitlement based on the notion of common rights. In contrast, societies steeped in individualism prefer private enterprise and insurance funding with selective coverage and high responsiveness to consumer demand. In societies which have equity as an important root we see explicit attempts to avoid discrimination and to facilitate public participation. In other words, values and value orientations play a role in the structuring of health care delivery systems.

Anthropologists have argued that differences between health care delivery systems are embedded in the values and social structure of the societies involved (Helman 1996). Based on specific histories, traditions, customs, and so on, differences in health care organization reflect the way in which societies define and deal with issues

of health and illness. Health and health care are embedded in value systems which give explanations why and how in specific cultures health problems are dealt with. For example, in some societies health care is considered a collective good for the benefit of all citizens. In other ones, health care is seen more as a "commodity" that can be bought or sold on a free market, or as an individual investment in human capital. As Gallagher (1988) notes: "The concept of health care as a calculable resource is an essential feature in its role as a carrier of modernity." The notion of health care as a commodity, however, has not been accepted everywhere. It seems to be more established in the essentially market-oriented organization of health care in the US than it is in Europe or Asia. Nowhere in Europe has it become part of health policy objectives. This is notwithstanding a wide range of health care reforms in recent years introducing market oriented approaches with incentives to introduce more competition between providers and to use resources more economically (Saltman & Figueras 1997). Health care as a collective good for the benefit of all prevails in European health policy and in systems typified as national, social insurance, and so on. Health care as a commodity dominates in the US, although several European countries are moving in a similar direction.

Cultures or nations can vary in value orientations to a considerable degree. For example, values of equity, solidarity, and autonomy may have different health care implications in different societies (Hofstede 1984). Emphasis on hospital care versus home care or care for the elderly, on individual responsibilities versus solidarity between people, reflect a society's general value orientations that have an impact on its health delivery systems model (Stevens & Diederiks 1995; Saltman & Figueras 1997; Philipsen 1980; Hofstede 1984). Or to put this differently, the free market, insurance, and tax-based health care delivery models to be found in the US, Germany, and the UK, respectively, are to a certain degree reflections of central values in their societies.

CONVERGENCE AND DIVERGENCE

There is ample evidence that contingencies like increasing health care costs, an aging population, changing disease patterns, technological developments, growing public demand, and so forth impose a common logic in terms of institutional performance and the structuring of modern health care. In the literature a wide range of convergencies in health policy and health care organization have been listed (Field 1989; Mechanic and Rochefort 1996; Raffel 1997; Saltman & Figueras 1997). These include (1) the concern of governments to control health care costs while at the same time improving the effectiveness and efficiency of the system; (2) the increasing attention for health promotion and healthy lifestyles such as abstinence from substance use (alcohol, smoking, drugs), and healthy behavior; (3) reduction of health care inequalities and differences in access; (4) the stimulation of primary health care while cutting back extensive medical specialization; (5) the promotion of patient involvement in care and treatment and improving patient satisfaction; and (6) the reduction of fragmentation of services and the promotion of continuity of care.

Yet the convergence of modern health care delivery systems is not undisputed. Even if societies are faced with similar contingencies, their societal structures have to be consonant with culturally derived expectations (Lammers & Hickson 1979). Consequently, while there is substantial evidence that modern societies are evolving into the same direction with efficiency equity and utilitarian individualism as core value orientations, differences exist in degree and similarity of these developments. Modern societies still vary considerably in their dealing with issues of health and illness (Anderson et al. 1995). Moreover, while nations may have similar goals, alternative options are available to reach these. National health delivery systems are the outcome of a dialectical tension between universal aspects of technology and medicine on the one hand, and particularistic cultural characteristics of each nation on the other (Field 1989). These particularistic cultural characteristics refer to the historical foundations of health care delivery systems, to the societal and national context, and to specific values and value orientations of societies and health care delivery systems under consideration. Health care institutions are still largely country specific (Pomey & Poullier 1997). Such country specific elements would include social, economic, institutional, and ideological structures, the dominant belief system, the role of the state versus the market, patterns of health care coverage, and centralization or decentralization of political authority (Saltman & Figueras 1997, 1998).

SEE ALSO: Health and Culture; Health Maintenance Organization; Health Professions and Occupations; Health and Social Class; Hospitals; Socialist Medicine; Socialized Medicine

REFERENCES AND SUGGESTED READINGS

Anderson, J. G., Oscarson, R., & Yu, Y. (1995) Japan's Health Care System: Western and East Asian Influences. In: Gallagher, E. & Subedi, J. (Eds.), *Global Perspectives on Health Care*. Prentice-Hall, Englewood Cliffs, NJ, pp. 32–44.

Evans, R. G. (1981) Incomplete Vertical Integration: The Distinctive Structure of the Health-Care Industry. In: Van der Gaag, J. & Perlman, M. (Eds.), *Health, Economics, and Health Economics: Proceedings of the World Congress on Health Economics, Leiden, The Netherlands, September 1980*. North-Holland, Amsterdam, pp. 329–54.

Field, M. (1989) The Comparative Evolution of Health Systems: Convergence, Diversity and Cross-Cutting Issues. In: Lüschen, G., Cockerham, W., & Kunz, G. (Eds.), *Health and Illness in America and Germany*. Oldenbourg, Munich, pp. 15–30.

Gallagher, E. B. (1988) Modernization and Medical Care. *Sociological Perspectives* 31: 59–87.

Helman, C. G. (1996) *Culture, Health and Illness*. Wright, London.

Hofstede, G. (1984) *Culture's Consequences: International Differences in Work-Related Values*. Sage, London.

Hurst, J. (1992) *The Reform of Health Care: A Comparative Analysis of Seven OECD Countries*. Organization for Economic Cooperation and Development, Paris.

Lammers, C. J. & Hickson, D. J. (1979) *Organizations Alike and Unlike: International and Inter-Institutional Studies in the Sociology of Organizations*. Routledge & Kegan Paul, London.

Lüschen, G., Cockerham, W., Van der Zee, J., et al. (1995) *Health Systems in the European Union*. Oldenbourg, Munich.

Marrée, J. & Groenewegen, P. P. (1997) *Back to Bismarck: Eastern European Health Care in Transition*. Avebury, Aldershot.

Mechanic, D. & Rochefort, D. A. (1996) Comparative Medical Systems. *Annual Review of Sociology* 22: 239–70.

Parsons, T. (1951) *The Social System*. Free Press, New York.

Philipsen, H. (1980) Internationale vergelijking van welvaart, gezondheidszorg en levensduur: het probleem van Galton. *Gezondheid en Samenleving* 1: 5–17.

Philipsen, H. (1995) Gezondheid en gezondheidszorg in België en Nederland. Gezondheid en Samenleving 5: 223–31

Pomey, M. & Poullier, J. (1997) France. In: Raffel, M. (Ed.), *Health Care and Reform in Industrialized Countries*. Pennsylvania State University Press, University Park.

Raffel, M. W. (1997) Dominant Issues: Convergence, Decentralization, Competition, Health Services. In: Raffel, M. (Ed.), *Health Care and Reform in Industrialized Countries*. Pennsylvania State University Press, University Park, pp. 291–303.

Saltman, R. B. & Figueras, J. (1997) European Health Care Reform. *WHO Regional Publications, European Series*. World Health Organization, Regional Office for Europe, Copenhagen.

Saltman, R. B. & Figueras, J. (1998) Analyzing the Evidence on European Health Care Reforms. *Health Affairs* 17: 85–105.

Selznick, P. (1957) *Leadership in Administration*. Harper & Row, New York.

Stevens, F. C. J. & Diederiks, J. P. M. (1995) Health Culture: An Exploration of National and Social Differences in Health-Related Values. In: Lüschen, G., Cockerham, W., Van der Zee, J., et al. (Eds.), *Health Systems in the European Union*. Oldenbourg, Munich, pp. 75–88.

Tuohy, C. H. (1999) Dynamics of a Changing Health Sphere: The United States, Britain, and Canada. *Health Affairs* 18: 114–31.

health and culture

Stella Quah

The cumulative knowledge from nearly a century's worth of studies confirms that the sociological analysis of health and illness would be grossly incomplete without the consideration of culture. Culture is both the context and an important determinant of the behavior, beliefs, and norms of individuals affected by illness and who are making decisions on help-seeking, as well as of people and organizations whose role it is to help and to heal.

Many definitions of culture have been offered by scholars over the past century. Those definitions range from Parsons's "patterned system of symbols" to one or more characteristics of a group's or community's way of life, such as philosophical, linguistic, and artistic expressions; their collective norms of behavior; and their ethnic and/or religious customs and beliefs, among other features. Of these components of culture, the most commonly included in sociological studies of health and health-related behavior are ethnicity and religion. As Stanley King aptly summarized it in 1962, ethnicity is understood as the combination of a common "language, customs, beliefs, habits and traditions," "racial stock or country of origin," and "a consciousness of kind" in Weber's sense. A group's religion or cosmology – that is, its interpretation of life, birth, and death, of right and wrong – gives shape to a consistent body of health beliefs and practices that are endorsed and implemented by individuals, typically with the tacit or active support and scrutiny of their social networks.

The intellectual context of the study of health and culture has been characterized by multidisciplinarity and the presence of a wide range of conceptual frameworks. The early anthropological studies of primitive cultures in the late nineteenth and early twentieth centuries paved the way for the analysis of ethnic differences in illness and health-related behavior by sociologists already schooled in the seminal ideas of Durkheim, Weber, Simmel, and Parsons. Parsons himself was influenced by anthropological and psychoanalytical perspectives. By the mid-twentieth century, sociologists, social psychologists, and psychologists began collaborating in the analysis of the influence of beliefs and personality upon health-related attitudes and behavior. The Health Belief Model was one of the first among several conceptual frameworks generated out of such collaboration. The incorporation of cultural variables in medical sociology research until then was modest and did not follow directly these conceptual developments.

Nearly all theoretical perspectives in sociology concur that ethnicity is socially constructed, is negotiable, and thus has permeable boundaries. However, medical sociology studies (predominantly research on traditional healing beliefs and practices) confirm Kevin Avruch's crucial reminder (in Stone and Dennis 2003: 72) that while ethnicity is permeable from the perspective of the sociologist-observer, from the subjects' perspective their culture is immutable because it "stretches back in an unbroken chain to some primordial antiquity." Indeed, studies of traditional healing systems indicate that people typically cite the perceived ancient authority of their culture as prescribing and sanctioning their traditional healing beliefs and practices (Quah 2003).

Different conceptual perspectives in sociology consider health generally as a state of well-being (physical and/or psychological), but theories differ in their interpretation of the social meaning of illness. Some examples will suffice (Gerhardt 1989). Structural-functionalism regards illness as "loss of role capacity" and assigns responsibility for one's health to the individual. The symbolic interactionalist perspective sees illness in terms of stigmatization and proposes that societal and cultural influences impinge upon individuals' perception of health, self-determination, and ability to negotiate their situation. Phenomenology sees the situation as "trouble-trust dialectics" (following Garfinkel's approach to trust), where illness as "physical, psychological and role incompetence and incapacities" that break everyday life "trouble-trust cycles" may be remedied by "reestablishing trust" in the form of medical treatment. Conflict theory addresses the questions of power and domination and associates illness with a surfacing of the everyday conflict that results from social, "political, and economic inequity" (Gerhardt 1989), an argument also pursued by Marxist and neo-Marxist approaches. Of these theoretical frameworks, symbolic interactionism incorporates culture most directly, mainly in the form of socially constructed and subjectively perceived meanings of illness, definitions of illness severity, and labeling.

The two main perspectives that Gerhardt identified in 1989 as representing the major theoretical contention in medical sociology were the illness-as-deviance perspective and the power-domination perspective. These two perspectives have been in confrontation throughout most of the past six decades. Against this backdrop, it is worth pointing out that the inclusion of culture (subjects' values, beliefs, and customs) in research designs based on either of these main perspectives helps to elucidate their explanatory power. The incorporation of culture in a research design means addressing important questions such as how culture impinges upon people's subjective perception of health, illness, power, and stigma; upon the meaning they attach to illness and health; upon their sense of trust, normality, and deviance; and upon their health behavior. In fact, in the large and rapidly expanding body of biomedical and social science research on health and illness, the serious analysis of culture is a distinguishing feature of medical sociology and medical anthropology.

Increased interest in the cultural dimension of health has been prompted over the past six decades by major sociohistorical events and global upheavals, such as World War II, that motivated the examination of the idea of a sick society (Gerhardt 1989: 353); major movements of populations as the result of forced and free migration (leading to higher rates of ethnic minorities in Europe, North America, Australia, and New Zealand); and epidemics affecting a multitude of culturally diverse communities. The growing attention to the cultural or ethnic dimension of health and illness and the necessity to elucidate the complex web of attitudes, perceptions, and decisions on health risks and health options leading to the spread of epidemics such as HIV/AIDS and outbreaks of infectious diseases like SARS (severe acute respiratory syndrome) have led to a wealth of cross-cultural and comparative research involving ethnic communities within countries and across different countries. This research trend has also been propelled by some slow-pace but substantial changes in people's lifestyle (e.g., diet, rate of physical activity, leisure activities, long-distance travel, exposure to environmental hazards, and high stress levels) and demographic trends, particularly longer life expectancy and the resultant increase in the proportion of older age cohorts and in the incidence of chronic diseases (e.g., cardiovascular diseases).

The wealth of studies of culture and health may be roughly classified into two main dimensions based on the principal unit of inquiry: some studies focus on the subjects affected by illness, while others concentrate on the expected or actual sources of healing. Research on individuals, small groups, and communities affected by illness includes the sources of illness as well as people's health-related behavior, attitudes, and beliefs at all the three main stages of the health–illness trajectory: preventive health behavior, illness behavior, and sick-role behavior. Studies dealing with the expected and actual sources of help and healing concentrate on individuals as healers as well as on groups, networks, and organizations whose main objective is healing, or helping the sick, or safeguarding the health of others.

Concerning changes over time, one of the most important developments in the past two decades has been the noticeable increase in cross-national and comparative research on cultural determinants of health-related behavior involving different ethnic and religious communities. Illustrations of this type of research are studies on attitudes and behavior regarding prevention of and response to HIV/AIDS (e.g., condom use, sexual habits, and stigmatization) and other infectious diseases; and smoking, alcohol drinking, and dietary patterns in connection with cancer and cardiovascular diseases.

Some main trends may be identified in the wide array of current studies on health and culture. As indicated earlier, a continuing feature of medical sociology research on culture and health since the mid-twentieth century is the concurrent advancement of theorizing and empirical research. Some critics have argued that theorizing has not moved significantly beyond middle-range theories. Although this is true, the slow progress in grand theorizing and the presence of contending conceptual perspectives are common trends across sociology subfields of inquiry and general sociology. Another current trend is the continued interest in the study of the body, especially within the phenomenological, feminist, and postmodern perspectives. A third trend is that health behavior studies guided by one or more social psychology theories (such as the health belief model, protection motivation theory, self-efficacy theory, and the theory of reasoned action) are now paying more attention to cultural variables. The fourth and perhaps one of the most robust and faster-growing research areas with the potential to highlight the relevance of culture is the study of the impact of social networks and modes of help-seeking on health behavior (Thoits 1995; Levy & Pescosolido 2002). The link between

health and illness and people's ethnic identity, their sense of belonging to a family, network of friends, and community, and the concomitant trust people place in their care and advice in times of distress and illness, are all social phenomena that can be analyzed fruitfully by research on social networks and help-seeking.

The methodological challenges confronting medical sociology are found in all other subfields of the discipline. One of the most difficult challenges in studies of health and culture is the refining of methods to ascertain sociocultural and illness-related phenomena. For example, while Weber's idea of "a consciousness of kind" has been elegantly discussed as part of the concept "ethnicity," it is difficult to devise a valid method to ascertain a person's consciousness of kind through observation, interaction, or interviews. The same challenge is posed by many other concepts, such as the permeability of a group's culture, stress levels, trust in others, meaning of social support, and a social network's level of cohesiveness and reliability as help provider. The second main challenge is establishing causality. The study of culture and health confront us with the problem of ascertaining causality in many aspects, such as the link between everyday stress and illness. But the question of causality is particularly difficult when trying to establish whether culture is part of the social structure (i.e., the context of agency) within which health attitudes and behavior evolve, or a determinant of health attitudes and behavior, or both.

Future advances in research, theory, and methodology of studies on health and culture need to give serious consideration to three aspects. First, the emphasis on the construction, verification, and improvement of conceptual frameworks is a very valuable feature of this field and must continue to mark the development of medical sociology research on health and culture. Second, the impact of culture as norms shaping attitudes toward health illness and guiding health behavior is an area that requires active consideration by sociologists engaged in social networks and social support research; social networks and help-seeking have become very productive research areas in the past decade and will continue to expand. Third, the dearth of authentic cross-cultural research needs to be resolved. The bulk of research on health and culture up to the end of the 1990s was addressed to the majority versus minority contrast (or immigrant versus non-immigrant comparisons) within the same country, mostly in the US and in some European countries. This serious limitation needs to be overcome by comparative or cross-national studies. Comparative research can provide the basis for more effective understanding of the relative permeability or resilience of cultural boundaries and its effect on health; of the permanent or temporary transformation in belief systems; and of the way cultural beliefs and norms influence accounts of disease incidence and prevalence across communities and countries.

SEE ALSO: Conflict Theory; Ethnicity; Health Behavior; Health Lifestyles; Health and Medicine; Health, Neighborhood Disadvantage; Health and Race; Health and Social Class; Phenomenology; Structural Functional Theory; Symbolic Interaction

REFERENCES AND SUGGESTED READINGS

Albrecht, G., Fitzpatrick, R., & Scrimshaw, S. (Eds.) (2000) *Handbook of Social Studies in Health and Medicine*. Sage, London.

Blaxter, M. (1990) *Health and Lifestyles*. Routledge, London.

Cockerham, W. (2001) *The Blackwell Companion to Medical Sociology*. Blackwell, Oxford.

Cockerham, W. (2004) *Medical Sociology*, 9th edn. Prentice-Hall, Upper Saddle River, NJ.

Gerhardt, U. (1989) *Ideas about Illness: An Intellectual and Political History of Medical Sociology*. New York University Press, New York.

Levy, J. & Pescosolido, B. (Eds.) (2002) *Social Networks and Health*. JAI Press, New York.

Norman, P., Abraham, C., & Conner, M. (Eds.) (2000) *Understanding and Changing Health Behaviour*. Hardwood Academic Publishers, Amsterdam.

Quah, S. (2003) Traditional Healing Systems and the Ethos of Science. *Social Science and Medicine* 57: 1997–2012.

Ritzer, G. (2001) *Explorations in Social Theory: From Metatheorizing to Rationalization*. Sage, London.

Stone, J. & Dennis, R. (2003) *Race and Ethnicity: Comparative and Theoretical Approaches*. Blackwell, Oxford.

Thoits, P. (1995) Stress, Coping and Social Support Processes: Where Are We? What Next? *Journal of Health and Social Behavior* extra issue: 53–79.

Turner, B. (1995) *Medical Power and Social Knowledge*, 2nd edn. Sage, London.

health lifestyles

William C. Cockerham

Health lifestyles are collective patterns of health-related behavior based on choices from options available to people according to their life chances (Cockerham 2000). The behaviors that are generated from these choices can have either positive or negative consequences for a person's health status, but nonetheless form an overall pattern of health practices that constitute a health-oriented lifestyle. Health lifestyles are becoming an increasingly common form of social behavior given the limits of medicine in treating chronic illnesses like heart disease, cancer, and diabetes and the association of such diseases with unhealthy lifestyles. The recognition that the individual is ultimately responsible for his or her own health often promotes a healthy lifestyle.

The most common health lifestyle practices investigated by researchers are alcohol use, smoking, dietary habits, and exercise. Other practices include drug abuse, personal hygiene, rest and relaxation, automobile seatbelt use, and similar behaviors related to health. Health lifestyle practices also include contact with the medical profession for preventive care and routine checkups, but the majority of activities take place outside the health-care delivery system.

Sociological theorizing about health lifestyles generally begins with Max Weber (1978). Weber did not address health practices, but focused on the relationship between lifestyles in general and social status. He found that status groups originate through a sharing of similar lifestyles. The lifestyles of status groups are based not so much on what they and the people within them produce, but on what they consume. This is because the consumption of goods and services conveys a social meaning that displays the status and social identity of the consumer. Weber's work helps us understand that health lifestyles are also a form of consumption in that the health produced is used for something, such as a longer life, work, or enhanced enjoyment of one's physical being (Cockerham 2000). Health lifestyles are also supported by an extensive consumer products industry of goods and services (e.g, running shoes, sports clothing, diet plans, health foods, club and spa member-ships) promoting consumption as an inherent feature of participation.

Weber shows that lifestyles have two major components: life choices (self-direction) and life chances (the structural probabilities of realizing one's choices). Weber does not consider life chances to be a matter of pure chance; rather, they are the chances people have in life because of their social circumstances. His overall thesis is that chance is socially determined and social structures are an arrangement of chances. Therefore, lifestyles are not random behaviors unrelated to structure, but typically are deliber-ate choices influenced by life chances.

Weber's most important contribution to con-ceptualizing lifestyles is identification of the dialectical interplay of choice and chance in life-style determination (Cockerham et al. 1997). Choices and the constraints of life chances work off one another to determine a distinctive life-style for individuals and groups. It can be said that individuals have a range of freedom, yet not complete freedom, in choosing a lifestyle; that is, they have the freedom to choose within the social constraints that apply to their situation in life. As Zygmunt Bauman (1999) points out, individual choices in all circumstances are con-fined by two sets of constraints: (1) choosing from among what is available and (2) social rules or codes telling the individual the rank order and appropriateness of preferences.

Two other theorists, Anthony Giddens and Pierre Bourdieu, are also important in concep-tualizing health lifestyles. Through his notion of the duality of structure, Giddens (1991) helps us understand that social structural resources in lifestyle selection can empower choices, not just constrain them. Furthermore, he observes that social situations tend to push people into choos-ing a particular lifestyle that connects to an orderly pattern of behavior shared with other people. His basic message is that lifestyles not only fulfill utilitarian needs, but also provide a material form to a person's self-identity.

Bourdieu (1984) introduces the concept of habitus to lifestyle research that can be described as an individual's organized reper-toire of perceptions that guide and evaluate behavioral choices and options. It is a mindset that produces a relatively enduring framework of dispositions to act in particular ways and originates through socialization and experience consistent with the reality of the person's class circumstances. These dispositions gener-ate stable and consistent lifestyle practices that typically reflect the normative structure of the prevailing social order and/or some group or class in which the individual has been socia-lized. The habitus produces enduring disposi-tions toward a lifestyle that becomes routine and when acted out regularly over time, repro-duces itself. This suggests that health lifestyle practices are usually habitual modes of behavior strongly influenced by class and other social structural variables, such as age and gender.

The research literature on health lifestyles in sociology began to develop only in the 1980s. The focus in most studies is on determining differences between social classes in health life-style participation. Among the earliest and most influential lifestyle studies considering health practices is that of Bourdieu (1984). He constructed a model of stratified lifestyles based on differing cultural tastes in food, art, music, dress, and the like. He found that distinct class differences existed in relation to food and sports preferences and detailed how a class-oriented habitus shaped these health lifestyle practices. Another early study was that of Wil-liam Cockerham and his colleagues (1988), who examined similarities in health lifestyles in the US and Germany and determined how such lifestyles could spread in varying degrees across class boundaries. In Great Britain, however, Mildred Blaxter (1990) found that important differences in health lifestyles persisted between social classes and that living conditions played an important role in determining health prac-tices. A universal finding is that people in the upper and upper-middle classes tend to take better care of their health than those in the working class and lower class. Females invari-ably live healthier lifestyles than males. More recent research in Russia and other former socialist countries in Europe shows that unhealthy lifestyle practices (heavy drinking and smoking, high-fat diets, and little or no exercise) are the primary social determinant of the significant increase in male heart disease mortality in the region (Cockerham 1999; Cockerham et al. 2002).

SEE ALSO: Bourdieu, Pierre; Health Behavior; Health Risk Behavior; Health and Social Class; Health, Self-Rated; Health and Sport; Life Chances and Resources; Lifestyle; Lifestyle Consumption; Weber, Max

REFERENCES AND SUGGESTED READINGS

Bauman, Z. (1999) *In Search of Politics*. Stanford University Press, Stanford.

Blaxter, M. (1990) *Health and Lifestyles*. Routledge, London.

Bourdieu, P. (1984) *Distinction*. Harvard University Press, Cambridge, MA.

Cockerham, W. (1999) *Health and Social Change in Russia and Eastern Europe*. Routledge, London.

Cockerham, W. (2000) The Sociology of Health Behavior and Health Lifestyles. In: Bird, C., Conrad, P., & Fremont, A. (Eds.), *Handbook of Medical Sociology*, 5th edn. Prentice-Hall, Upper Saddle River, NJ, pp. 159–72.

Cockerham, W., Kunz, G., Lueschen, G., & Spaeth, J. (1988) Social Stratification and Health Lifestyles in Two Systems of Health Care Delivery: A Comparison of the United States and West Germany. *Journal of Health and Social Behavior* 29: 113–26.

Cockerham, W., Rutten, A., & Abel, T. (1997) Conceptualizing Contemporary Health Lifestyles: Moving Beyond Weber. *Sociological Quarterly* 38: 321–42.

Cockerham, W., Snead, C., & De Waal, D. (2002) Health Lifestyles in Russia and the Socialist Heritage. *Journal of Health and Social Behavior* 43: 42–55.

Giddens, A. (1991) *Modernity and Self-Identity*. Stanford University Press, Stanford.

Weber, M. (1978) *Economy and Society*, 2 Vols. University of California Press, Berkeley.

health locus of control

Brian P. Hinote

Health locus of control refers to the degree of control that people believe they possess over their personal health. More generally, locus of control measures indicate the degree of control (internal or external) an individual has over a particular life situation. People reflecting an internal locus of control believe that they can exert control over their environment to bring about desirable consequences. Consequently, those possessing an internal health locus of control believe that their personal health-related outcomes are for the most part determined by their own choices and behaviors. Conversely, people with an external locus of control believe that larger social forces, powerful persons or groups, or plain luck will determine their fate. Those displaying an external health locus of control consider their personal health-related outcomes largely a matter of influences extending beyond their own control (Cockerham & Ritchey 1997; McGuigan 1999).

While interest in the notion of health locus of control is seen in medical sociology, the concept was initially derived from Julian Rotter's (1996) social learning theory in psychology. Most early studies investigating this topic used the scale developed by Rotter, the internal-external (I-E) scale, to assess locus of control, but researchers have more recently utilized instruments like the Health Locus of Control (HLC) scale, which distinguishes between an internal or external health locus of control. However, behavioral scientists have employed a large number of locus of control scales in research spanning over the past 40–50 years (Wallston & Wallston 1978; Lefcourt 1982; Seeman & Seeman 1983; Cockerham & Ritchey 1997).

Early studies suggesting a significant correlation between locus of control and health first appeared about 40 years ago. More attention, and thus more studies, followed, and over the years investigators uncovered a number of characteristics, behaviors, and outcomes exhibiting correlations with the health locus of control measure. These findings have helped underscore the fact that the widely accepted medical model may not adequately consider the role that one's personal sense of control plays in health and illness behaviors (Seeman & Evans 1962; Seeman & Seeman 1983).

For example, social class often shows a significant correlation with this variable, with persons in lower socioeconomic strata exhibiting the strongest external health locus of control. On the other hand, individuals occupying relatively higher socioeconomic positions tend to show more signs of internal health locus of control. Indeed, such differences in health locus of control manifest themselves in the perception of illness symptoms and the use of physicians, with the least advantaged seeing physicians more regularly for illness symptoms and the more affluent exercising more control over health and illness (Cockerham et al. 1986). In addition, persons showing higher degrees of internal control tend to express increased mastery of information in their immediate social environment, so much so that patients characterized as "internals" more actively seek out relevant information to learn more about their particular disease or diagnosis (Seeman & Evans 1962).

With regard to mental health, depression is associated with feeling as if outcomes (good, bad, or both) are beyond one's control (external locus of control), and one's sense of control, whether internal or external, reflects the circumstances of a person's social and economic status (Mirowsky & Ross 1990). More destructive health behaviors like smoking also exhibit correlations with this concept. Research suggests that young people who display characteristics consistent with an external health locus of control represent those at greatest risk to start smoking and to become chronic, long-term smokers (Clarke et al. 1982). In addition, studies show that demographic characteristics like age can also correlate with health locus of control. Research indicates that between the ages of 18–50 individuals generally tend to show overall high, stable levels of perceived control, but within increasingly older age groups control appears to gradually decrease (Mirowsky 1995).

While findings may show some degree of inconsistency at times, perhaps due to differences in measurement and to interaction effects, the significance of health locus of control within medical sociology appears well established. However, this measure represents only one in a potentially complex constellation of sociological factors influencing health behavior, illness behavior, and outcomes. Regardless, the concept likely possesses a number of implications for both researchers and policymakers. For example, health locus of control measures may be utilized in evaluating health promotion campaigns. That is, developing and fostering attributes of internal control could help such programs become increasingly successful. Perhaps programs aimed at behavioral deterrence should specifically target personality characteristics consistent with externality in order to increase their overall efficacy in real-world applications (Wallston & Wallston 1978; Clarke et al. 1982).

SEE ALSO: Aging, Mental Health, and Well-Being; Health Behavior; Health Lifestyles; Health Risk Behavior; Health and Social Class; Illness Behavior; Medical Sociology; Mental Disorder; Social Learning Theory; Smoking

REFERENCES AND SUGGESTED READINGS

Clarke, J. H., MacPherson, B. V., & Holmes, D. R. (1982) Cigarette Smoking and External Locus of Control Among Young Adolescents. *Journal of Health and Social Behavior* 23: 253–9.

Cockerham, W. C. (2004) *Medical Sociology*, 9th edn. Prentice-Hall, Upper Saddle River, NJ.

Cockerham, W. C. & Ritchey, F. J. (1997) *Dictionary of Medical Sociology*. Greenwood Press, Westport.

Cockerham, W. C., Lueschen, G., Kunz, G., & Spaeth, J. L. (1986) Social Stratification and Self-Management of Health. *Journal of Health and Social Behavior* 27: 1–14.

Lefcourt, H. M. (1982) *Locus of Control: Current Trends in Theory and Research*. Lawrence Erlbaum, Hillsdale, NJ.

McGuigan, F. J. (1999) *Encyclopedia of Stress*. Allyn & Bacon, Boston.

Mirowsky, J. (1995) Age and the Sense of Control. *Social Psychology Quarterly* 58: 31–43.

Mirowsky, J. & Ross, C. (1990) Control or Defense? Depression and the Sense of Control Over Good and Bad Outcomes. *Journal of Health and Social Behavior* 31: 71–86.

Rotter, J. B. (1966) Generalized Expectancies for Internal versus External Control of Reinforcement. *Psychological Monographs* 80: 1–28.

Rotter, J. B. (1990) Internal versus External Control of Reinforcement: A Case History of a Variable. *American Psychologist* 45: 489–93.

Seeman, M. & Evans, J. W. (1962) Alienation and Learning in a Hospital Setting. *American Sociological Review* 27: 772–83.

Seeman, M. & Seeman, T. A. (1983) Health Behavior and Personal Autonomy: A Longitudinal Study of the Sense of Control in Illness. *Journal of Health and Social Behavior* 24: 144–60.

Wallston, B. S. & Wallston, K. A. (1978) Locus of Control and Health: A Review of the Literature. *Health Education Monographs* 6: 107–17.

Wallston, K. A., Maides, S., & Wallston, B. S. (1976) Health-Related Information Seeking as a Function of Health-Related Locus-of-Control and Health Values. *Journal of Research in Personality* 10: 215–22.

health maintenance organization

Douglas R. Wholey and Lawton R. Burns

A health maintenance organization (HMO) is a managed care organization that integrates health insurance and delivery functions in an effort to contain costs and maximize quality. HMOs differ from indemnity health insurance, where the insurer compensates the consumer for the cost of specified services. On the continuum between indemnity health insurance and HMOs lie organizations such as preferred provider organizations (PPOs) that manage care delivery more than indemnity health insurance yet do not integrate health insurance and services.

There are five HMO types: independent practice associations (IPAs), network, group, staff, and mixed. IPAs contract with physicians in solo or small single-specialty group practice. Network and group HMOs are based on physicians in multi-specialty group practice: a network HMO contracts with several multi-specialty groups, while a group HMO contracts with a primary multi-specialty group. Staff HMOs contract with physicians as salaried employees in a multi-specialty group. Mixed HMOs include physicians in both solo and multi-specialty group practices. In contrast to IPAs, physicians in HMOs based on multi-specialty organizations are more integrated, communicate more regularly with medical directors, and are more likely to have a joint governance structure for personnel and practice decisions (Wholey & Burns 1993).

HMOs initially developed in the 1910s and 1920s as prepaid group practices (PGPs) to provide health care services to lumber mill owners and rural farmers' cooperatives in exchange for a monthly premium. Early PGPs encountered active opposition from organized medicine, particularly the AMA. The late 1930s and 1940s saw the formation of HMOs by construction firms (e.g., Kaiser) and consumer cooperatives (Group Health Care) who sought to provide access to care for their members. HMO development at the national level began to accelerate with the passage of the HMO Act of 1973 (amended 1976) which overrode restrictive state laws that blocked HMOs, provided some funding for start-up HMOs, and allowed HMOs to require employers to offer federally qualified HMOs. The late 1980s saw rapid growth of HMOs, with growth continuing at a slower rate through the mid-1990s, and a slight contraction and industry consolidation in the late 1990s. HMO census data show 68 HMOs with 4.5 million enrollees in 1973 (Schlenker et al. 1974), 393 and 18.9 million in 1985, 582 and 53.9 million in 1995, and 424 and 70 million in 2003 (Inter Study 2004). The industry structure also changed, moving from a dominance of non-profit network, group and staff HMOs to for-profit IPAs.

Two factors driving the growth in HMOs were health care costs and small area variations. Escalating costs, due in part to the Medicare program, led to strong federal interest in cost containment using HMOs. Small area variations (i.e., the large variation in utilization rates between geographic regions) appeared to be due to provider practice style (Wennberg & Gittelsohn 1973). If medicine is indeed evidence based, the magnitude of these variations suggested that health care could be improved while reducing costs.

HMOs manage care by managing either enrollee or physician behavior. Enrollee behavior is managed through panel closure, benefit design, and demand management. Panel closure requires that HMO enrollees obtain services only from physicians contracting with the HMO. By channeling patients to contracted physicians, HMOs increase the dependence of the physician on the HMO, which supports the use of provider management tools. Some HMOs do offer an open-ended option (typically for a higher premium and co-payment) that allows enrollees to see specialists outside the HMO panel. Benefit design refers to premiums, co-payments, deductibles, and covered health services (e.g., medically necessary services covered, experimental services not covered). A key point about benefit design is that the employers purchasing the HMO product, and not the HMO, typically determine what services are covered. Demand management includes activities such as consumer education to promote healthier lifestyles. In the earlier phases of their development, HMOs provided greater coverage than indemnity for well-care visits, such as physicals and immunizations, which enhance preventive care.

Physician behavior is managed in three broad ways: staffing, incentives, and health care management. Staffing refers to the decision on which providers to include on the HMOs panel. HMOs can manage costs and quality by selecting and retaining only providers who meet particular cost and quality standards. Incentives are the methods for compensating providers for providing care. Indemnity insurance pays providers on a fee-for-service (FFS) basis. HMOs modify this by paying a discounted FFS. Staff HMOs pay physicians on a salary basis. Capitation, perhaps the most controversial method of compensating providers, pays physicians a fixed payment per unit of time to provide a set of services (e.g., all primary care, all primary and specialty care, all primary, specialty, and hospital care) to an enrollee. Capitation shifts risk of utilization to the provider, but allows the provider to substitute nurses or physician assistants for physicians. There is inconclusive evidence whether capitation causes providers to skimp on health care provision to maximize their income.

Health care management refers to tools such as utilization review, profiling, case management, disease management, and education. Utilization review includes prospective review, such as pre-certifying hospital admissions, concurrent review, such as monitoring the progress and length-of-stay of patients in the hospital, and retrospective review, where patterns of health care use are monitored and profiled. Case management uses a care coordinator for patients with severe, expensive conditions. Disease management identifies patients with a particular condition, such as diabetes or congestive heart failure, and integrates services for that patient based on the evidence-based guidelines. A typical goal is to reduce the use of costly services such as hospital admissions by using aggressive preventive care and patient education. Provider education is a key component of profiling and disease management.

Because HMOs seek to contain costs and improve the quality and management of care, they have the potential for adversely affecting health care delivery. A series of reviews show that HMOs and FFS do not differ significantly in quality of care and that HMOs reduce costs by reducing use of hospitals and expensive resources (Hellinger 1998; Miller & Luft 1994, 2002) and by obtaining discounts from providers (Cutler et al. 2000). Competition among HMOs results in these savings being passed along to consumers as lower premiums (Wholey et al. 1995). However, consumer satisfaction surveys show that HMO enrollees are less satisfied than those not in HMOs with provider access and care delivery processes. Finally, although there is some research that suggests that individuals with chronic conditions may not do worse in HMOs than in other settings, the research results are heterogeneous and inconclusive.

SEE ALSO: Health Care Delivery Systems; Health and Medicine; Hospitals; Managed Care; Patient–Physician Relationship; Professional Dominance in Medicine

REFERENCES AND SUGGESTED READINGS

Cutler, D. M., McClellan, M., & Newhouse, J. P. (2000) How Does Managed Care Do It? *Rand Journal of Economics* 31: 526–48.

Hellinger, F. J. (1998) The Effect of Managed Care on Quality: A Review of Recent Evidence. *Archives of Internal Medicine* 158: 833–41.

Inter Study (2004) *The Interstudy Competitive Edge, Part II: HMO Industry Report as of July 1, 2003.* Inter Study, St. Paul, MN.

Miller, R. H. & Luft, H. S. (1994) Managed Care Plan Performance since 1980: A Literature Analysis. *JAMA* 271: 1512–19.

Miller, R. H. & Luft, H. S. (2002) HMO Plan Performance Update: An Analysis of the Literature, 1997–2001. *Health Affairs* 21: 63–86.

Schlenker, R. E., Quale, J. N., Wetherille, R. L., & McNeil, R. J. (1974) *HMOs in 1973: A National Survey.* Inter Study, Minneapolis.

Wennberg, J. & Gittelsohn, A. (1973) Small Area Variations in Health Care Delivery. *Science* 182: 1102–8.

Wholey, D. R. & Burns, L. R. (1993) Organizational Transitions: Form Changes by Health Maintenance Organizations. In: Bacharach, S. (Ed.), *Research in the Sociology of Organizations*, Vol. 11. JAI Press, Greenwich, CT, pp. 257–93.

Wholey, D., Feldman, R., & Christianson, J. B. (1995) The Effect of Market Structure on HMO Premiums. *Journal of Health Economics* 14: 81–105.